MANAGEMENT
CONTROL SYSTEMS

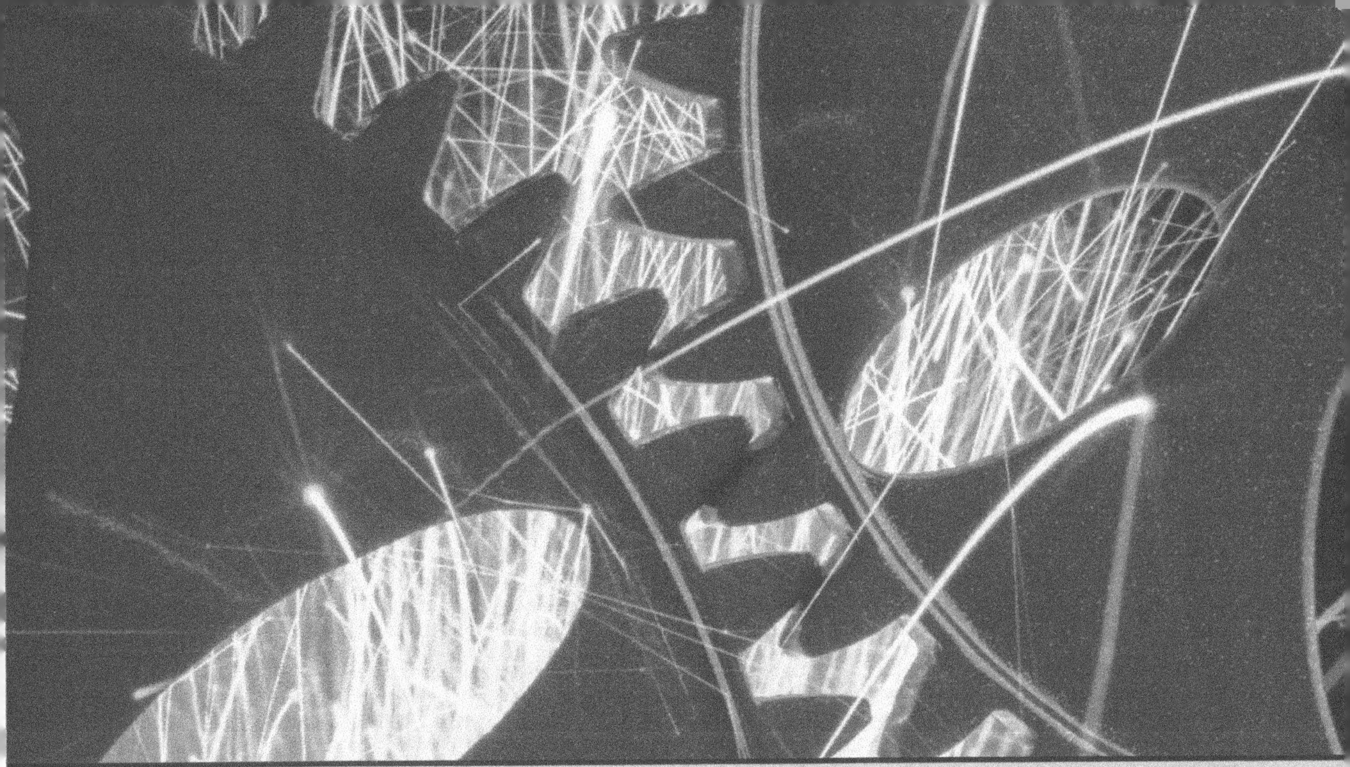

MANAGEMENT CONTROL SYSTEMS

Performance Measurement, Evaluation, and Incentives

Kenneth A. Merchant
University of Southern California

Wim A. Van der Stede
London School of Economics

Fourth edition

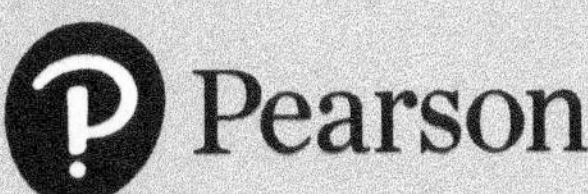

Harlow, England • London • New York • Boston • San Francisco • Toronto • Sydney • Dubai • Singapore • Hong Kong
Tokyo • Seoul • Taipei • New Delhi • Cape Town • Sao Paulo • Mexico City • Madrid • Amsterdam • Munich • Paris • Milan

PEARSON EDUCATION LIMITED
Edinburgh Gate
Harlow CM20 2JE
United Kingdom
Tel: +44 (0)1279 623623
Web: www.pearson.com/uk

First published 2003 (print)
Second edition published 2007 (print)
Third edition published 2012 (print and electronic)
Fourth edition published 2017 (print and electronic)

ISBN: 978-1-292-11055-4 (print)
978-1-292-11058-5 (PDF)
978-1-292-18187-5 (ePub)

British Library Cataloguing-in-Publication Data
A catalogue record for the print edition is available from the British Library

Library of Congress Cataloging-in-Publication Data
Names: Merchant, Kenneth A., author. | Van der Stede, Wim A., author.
Title: Management control systems: performance measurement, evaluation and incentives / Kenneth A. Merchant, University of Southern California, Wim A. Van der Stede, London School of Economics.
Description: Fourth Edition. | New York: Pearson, [2017] | Revised edition of the authors' Management control systems, 2012.
Identifiers: LCCN 2016053625| ISBN 9781292110554 (print) | ISBN 9781292110585 (pdf) | ISBN 9781292181875 (epub)
Subjects: LCSH: Industrial management. | Cost control. | Managerial accounting. | Performance—Measurement. | Industrial management—Case studies. | Cost control—Case studies. | Managerial accounting—Case studies.
Classification: LCC HD31 .M3972 2017 | DDC 658—dc23
LC record available at https://lccn.loc.gov/2016053625

10 9 8 7 6 5 4 3 2 1
21 20 19 18 17

Print edition typeset in 9/12, Charter ITC Std Regular by iEnergizer Aptara® Ltd.

NOTE THAT ANY PAGE CROSS REFERENCES REFER TO THE PRINT EDITION

To our families

Gail, Abbidee, Madelyn (KM)

Ashley, Emma, Erin (WVDS)

BRIEF CONTENTS

CONTENTS

PREFACE

This text provides materials for a comprehensive course on management control systems (MCSs). MCSs are defined broadly to include everything managers do to help ensure that their organization's strategies and plans are carried out or, if conditions warrant, are modified. Thus, the text could also be used in any course that focuses on topics related to the back end of the management process, such as strategy implementation or execution.

Because management control is a core function of management, all students interested in business or management can benefit from this text. However, courses based on the materials presented here should be particularly useful for those who are, or aspire to be, managers, management consultants, financial specialists (e.g. controllers, budget analysts, auditors), or human resource specialists (e.g. personnel directors, compensation consultants).

This edition includes 70 cases for classroom use. Case studies that stimulate learning through the analysis of complex situations such as those often faced in the "real world" are generally recognized to be perhaps the best pedagogical conduit for teaching a MCSs course. Because MCSs, the contexts in which they operate, and the outcomes they produce, are complex and multidimensional, simple problems and exercises cannot capture the essence of the issues managers face in designing and using MCSs. Students must develop the thinking processes that will guide them successfully through decision tasks with multiple embedded issues, incomplete information, and large amounts of relatively unstructured information. They must learn to develop problem-finding skills as well as critical thinking and problem-solving skills, and they must learn how to articulate and defend their ideas. Case analyses, discussions, and presentations provide an effective method for simulating these tasks in a classroom.

Although the text was designed primarily for use with graduate students and practicing professionals, it can be, and has been, used successfully with undergraduate students who have had a prior management accounting course. All that should be recognized when using this material with pre-work experience students is that some of the cases might be too challenging. That said, there are several suitable candidates to select from among the set of cases at the end of each chapter to tailor to various audiences and/or to achieve various course objectives (see also below).

This text is different from other MCS texts in a number of important ways. First, the basic organizing framework is different. The first major module discusses management controls based on the object of control: results, actions, or personnel/culture. The object-of-control framework has considerable advantages over other possible organizing frameworks. It has clean, clearly distinguishable categories. It is also relatively all-inclusive in the sense that the reader can relate many management controls and other control classifications and theories (for example, proactive vs. reactive controls, prevention vs. detection controls, and agency theory concepts such as adverse selection and monitoring vs. incentives) to it. It is also intuitive; that is, students can easily see that managers must make choices from among these categories of management control. Thus, using the object-of-control focus, the text is structured around a framework that describes the core management control problems that need to be addressed, the MCSs that can be used to address those problems, and the outcomes that can be produced, both positive (intended) and negative (unintended).

Second, the treatment of management control is broad. Like all MCS textbooks, this text focuses intensively on the use and effects of financial performance measures and associated *results controls*, which are in common use at managerial levels in many organizations. However, it also provides a broader treatment of management controls (organized around the object-of-control framework) to put the financial results controls in proper perspective. For example, the text describes many situations where financial results controls are not effective and discusses the alternatives that managers can use in those situations (such as nonfinancial performance indicators or greater reliance on stronger cultures).

Third, the text provides considerable discussion on the causes and remedies of the most common and serious management control-related problems, including the implications of issues of uncontrollability on manager's behaviors; the tendency of managers to adopt a short-term horizon in their decision-making; and managers' and employees' propensities to engage in distortive "gameplaying" evidencing misalignment with organizational objectives.

Fourth, the text provides a whole chapter of ethics coverage. There are many management control-related ethical issues, and both erstwhile and recent scandals across industries, including the automobile and banking sectors, but also the public and not-for-profit sectors, clearly suggest the need to develop managers' and prospective managers' ethical reasoning skills more fully. Related to this is coverage of corporate governance, to which we also devote a chapter.

Fifth, the important concepts, theories, and issues are not discussed just in abstract terms. They are illustrated with a large number of real-world examples, far more than typically included in any other MCS textbook. The examples make the textual discussion more concrete and bring the subject to life.

Finally, the mix of cases provided here is different from those included in other MCS textbooks in four important ways:

- Nearly all of the cases are real (that is, they describe the facts of an actual situation) although some of them are disguised (that is, they do not use the company's real name and/or use scaled figures/data to avoid identification or to protect data confidentiality). The relatively small number of cases that do not describe the (disguised) facts of an actual situation are "vignettes" that are, even so, almost always based on an observed situation but do not describe all of it. Instead, they focus on a particular (narrower) issue. Reality (and lack of disguise where possible) enhance student interest and learning about, for example, types of industries, companies, and organizational roles.
- Most of the cases (except the vignettes) include rich descriptions of the context within which the MCSs are operating. The descriptions give students opportunities to try to identify and address management control problems and issues within the multidimensional situations within which practicing managers cope with them.
- Most of the cases are of relatively recent vintage, and the set of cases has been chosen to ensure coverage of the latest MCS topics and issues, such as related to stress testing of budgets; mitigating management myopia; balancing sustainable value creation; motivating ethical behaviors; and using the EVA™ or Balanced Scorecard measurement systems or alternative budgeting approaches, just to name a few.
- The cases are descriptive of the operations and issues faced by companies located in many different countries and regions around the world, including Asia, Europe, Latin America, Oceania, as well as North America.

The cases permit the exploration of the management control issues in a broad range of settings. Included are cases on both large and small firms, manufacturing and service firms, domestic-focused and multinational firms, and for-profit and not-for-profit organizations. The cases present issues faced by personnel in both line and staff roles at corporate, divisional, and functional levels of the organization, as well as by members of boards of directors. Instructors can use this set of cases to teach a management control course that is broad in scope or one that is more narrowly focused (for example, MCSs in service organizations by focusing on the cases from the retail, financial, healthcare, education and other service sectors).

The cases provide considerable scheduling flexibility. Most of the cases cut across multiple topic areas because MCSs are inherently multidimensional. For example, the classroom focus for the Statoil case in Chapter 11 might be on performance measurement, as Statoil uses a key-performance-indicator (KPI) structure that is "balanced scorecard"-like. Or it could be on Statoil's planning and budgeting system, which separates the functions of target setting, forecasting and resource allocation using the principles of "Beyond Budgeting." To illustrate the latter further or in more depth, Statoil could be followed (or preceded) by the Mainfreight case, which offers ample opportunity for students to discuss and critically challenge the idea of beyond budgeting. In that context, both cases could be taught related to the subject matter in Chapter 8 on planning and budgeting instead of with Chapter 11. Yet, there are still sufficient cases listed with Chapter 11 to focus on remedies to the myopia problem, such as the new Johansen's case that describes a retail company that has adopted a balanced scorecard-based performance evaluation system. Students also have to consider the industry characteristics, the organization structure, the characteristics of the people in key positions, and the company's history (e.g. a recent merger), so instructors can choose to use the Statoil case, say, when they wish to focus on the effects of one or more of these factors on the design of MCSs. As a consequence, the ordering of the cases is not intended to be rigid. Many alternatives are possible. A case overview sheet in the accompanying Instructors Manual to this text provides a matrix that helps instructors disentangle the various relevant topics for which each case could be fruitfully used.

In this fourth edition, we made various updates, most obviously in those areas where the world has been moving fast during the past few years, particularly since the 2008–2009 financial crisis and subsequent economic recession. This includes changes in incentive systems (Chapter 9), corporate governance (Chapter 13), and also ethics-related concerns (Chapter 15). Throughout the text, we incorporated recent research findings and updated the survey statistics and examples provided. We also added some new, exciting cases. Twenty-one of the 70 cases included in this edition are new, and an additional 12 were revised or brought up to date. Some of the new cases cover relatively recent and/or perennially pivotal topics, such as "mobile monitoring" of employees (Witsky and Associates, Inc.); planning and budgeting flexibility (Wessanen N.V.); alternatives to traditional budgeting (Mainfreight); project management (The Stimson Company); comprehensive multi-criteria performance evaluations (Johansen's); "hands-on" relative performance evaluations using real-world data (Fine Harvest Restaurant Group); as well as crucial ethical considerations (Ethics@Cisco). Others were intended to address the topics in new and different settings, such as King Engineering Group (an ESOP, or "employee stock ownership plan," company), or in relevant control-related roles, such as corporate risk officers (Andrew G. Scavell, CRO).

In developing the materials for this fourth edition, we have benefited from the insightful comments, helpful suggestions, and cases of many people. Ken owes special thanks to the two professors who served as his mentors at the Harvard Business School: William Bruns and Richard Vancil. Ken also appreciates the valuable research assistance from Michelle Spaulding. And Wim is especially grateful to Olivia Hanyue Luo for her capable research assistance. At Pearson Education, we are indebted to Commissioning Editors Caitlin Lisle and Rebecca Pedley for their support of this revision project from start to finish. Finally, Abhishek Agarwal of Aptara and Matthew Van Atta made very detailed and helpful suggestions in copyediting the manuscript.

We thank the Asia Case Research Center at the University of Hong Kong for granting permission to use two of their Poon Kam Kai Series cases (PCL and Sunshine Fashion). We appreciate Darden Business Publishing's help with their permission for use of the Johansen's case, and we also thank Winnie O'Grady for letting us use the Mainfreight case. Finally, we thank our co-authors on several cases included in this text, the names of whom are listed with the cases.

In closing, we wish to acknowledge that there is certainly no one best way to convey the rich subjects related to MCSs. We have presented one useful framework in the best way we know how, but we welcome comments about the content or organization of the text, or regarding any errors or omissions. Please direct them to us.

Kenneth A. Merchant
Deloitte & Touche LLP Chair of Accountancy
Leventhal School of Accounting
Marshall School of Business
University of Southern California
Los Angeles, CA 90089-0441
U.S.A.

Phone: (213) 821-5920
Fax: (213) 747-2815
E-mail: kmerchant@marshall.usc.edu

Wim A. Van der Stede
CIMA Professor of Accounting and Financial Management
London School of Economics
Department of Accounting
Houghton Street
London WC2A 2AE
U.K.

Phone: (020) 7955-6695
Fax: (020) 7955-7420
E-mail: w.van-der-stede@lse.ac.uk

ACKNOWLEDGEMENTS

We are grateful to the following for permission to reproduce copyright material:

Figures

Figures 7.1, 7.2, 8.1, 8.2, 8.3, 14.1, and 14.2: from *Modern Management Control Systems: Text and Cases*, Prentice Hall (Merchant, K. A. 1998), pp. 308, 309, 388, 390, 391, 640, and 642, respectively; MERCHANT, KENNETH A., MODERN MANAGEMENT CONTROL SYSTEMS: TEXT & CASES, 1st Ed., © 1998. Reprinted and electronically reproduced by permission of Pearson Education, Inc., New York, NY.

Tables

Tables 3.1, 3.2, 3.3, 4.1, 5.1, 6.1, 7.1, 7.2, 9.1, 10.1, 10.2, 10.3, 10.4, and 10.5: from *Modern Management Control Systems: Text and Cases*, Prentice Hall (Merchant, K. A. 1998), pp. 30, 31, 130, 166, 224, 253, 303, 306, 427, 545, 546, 547, p. 547, and 548, respectively; MERCHANT, KENNETH A., MODERN MANAGEMENT CONTROL SYSTEMS: TEXT & CASES, 1st Ed., © 1998. Reprinted and electronically reproduced by permission of Pearson Education, Inc., New York, NY.

Text

Extracts on pages 4 and 6: from 'Bankers Not Only Ones Pushing Ethical Boundaries', *The Financial Times* (September 25, 2015), © The Financial Times Limited, All Rights Reserved. Extracts on pages 5 and 6: from 'Atlanta's Schools – the Reckoning', *The Economist* (April 6, 2013), online at www.economist.com. Extract on page 5: from 'Accounting Scandal Set to Shake Up Toshiba', *The Financial Times* (July 16, 2015), © The Financial Times Limited, All Rights Reserved. Extract on page 6: from 'Scathing Report Says Toshiba CEOs Had Role in Accounting Scandal', *The Financial Times* (July 20, 2015), © The Financial Times Limited, All Rights Reserved. Extract on page 6: from 'Deutsche Bank in $6bn "Fat Finger" Slip-Up', *The Financial Times* (October 19, 2015), © The Financial Times Limited, All Rights Reserved. Extract on page 7: from 'Two Accused of INS Shredding Spree', *The Los Angeles Times* (January 31, 2003), p. B5 (Morin, M.). Extract on page 16 from 'German Regulator Warns Deutsche Bank on Commodity Trading', The Financial Times (June 19, 2014), © The Financial Times Limited, All Rights Reserved. Extract on page 17: from 'Rio Tinto Shifts to Driverless Trucks in Australia', *The Financial Times* (October 19, 2015), © The Financial Times Limited, All Rights Reserved. Extract on page 87: from 'Manage Like a Spymaster', *The Economist* (August 29, 2015), online at econ.st/1U8j8KK, The Economist by ECONOMIST NEWSPAPER LTD.; reproduced with permission of ECONOMIST NEWSPAPER LTD. in the format Educational/Instructional Program via Copyright Clearance Center. Extract on page 88: from Association of Certified Fraud Examiners, 2014, online at www.acfe.com. Extract on page 91: from 'Digital Taylorism', *The Economist* (September 12, 2015), The Economist by ECONOMIST NEWSPAPER LTD.; reproduced with permission of ECONOMIST NEWSPAPER LTD. in the format Educational/Instructional Program via Copyright Clearance Center. Extract on page 100: from 'Method in the Madness of the Alibaba Cult', *The Financial Times* (September 7, 2014). Extract on page 131: from 'Tesco Monitors Employees with Motorola Armbands', *Business Week* (February 13, 2013), online at www.bloomberg.com/bw/articles/2013-02-13/tesco-monitors-employees-with-motorola-arm-bands. Extract on page 132: from *Report to the Nations on Occupational Fraud and Abuse 2014 Global Fraud Study*, Association of Certified Fraud Examiners, 2014, online at www.acfe.com/rttn/docs/2014-report-to-nations.pdf. Extract on page 135: from 'Struggling with Employee Complacency? Kill Your Stupid Rules', *Forbes* (October 30, 2013) with the permission of Lisa Bodell, CEO futurethink, author of *Why Simple Wins*. Case Study on page 183: This case was prepared by Grace Loo (Lao) under the supervision of Professor Neale O'Connor, Copyright © by The Asia Case Research Centre, The University of Hong Kong. Extract on page 188: from 'CFO Insights: Can Internal Audit Be a Command Center for Risk?' *Deloitte* (2014), online at deloi.tt/1OidCMB. Extract on page 189: from 'Banks Increase

Efforts to Stay on Right Side of Law', *The Financial Times* (September 28, 2014), online at on.ft.com/1FmAXiS. Extract on page 194: from 'Tesco's Accounting Problems Not So Funny', *The Economist* (October 27, 2014), The Economist by ECONOMIST NEWSPAPER LTD., reproduced with permission of ECONOMIST NEWSPAPER LTD. in the format Educational/Instructional Program via Copyright Clearance Center. Extract on page 200: from 'Insiders and Outsiders', *The Economist* (November 18, 2010), pp. 7–9, The Economist by ECONOMIST NEWSPAPER LTD., reproduced with permission of ECONOMIST NEWSPAPER LTD. in the format Educational/Instructional Program via Copyright Clearance Center. Case Study on page 205: prepared by Grace Loo under the supervision of Professor Neale O'Connor, Copyright © by The Asia Case Research Centre, The University of Hong Kong. Extract on page 238: from 'How Corporate Culture Affects the Bottom Line', *Duke's Fuqua School of Business News Release* (November 12, 2015), online at www.fuqua.duke.edu/news_events/news-releases/corporate-culture; and *Corporate Culture: Evidence from the Field*, online at https://papers.ssrn.com/sol3/papers.cfm?abstract_id=2805602. Extract on page 238: from 'VW Needs More Therapy to Change Its Flawed Mindset', *The Financial Times* (December 14, 2015), online at on.ft.com/1FmAXiS, © The Financial Times Limited, All Rights Reserved. Extract on page 240: from 'Will the Affordable Care Act Affect Doctors? Yes', The Heritage Foundation (June 26, 2013), online at www.heritage.org (Moffit, R. E., PhD). Extract on page 326: from 'The Quantified Serf', *The Economist* (March 7, 2015), The Economist by ECONOMIST NEWSPAPER LTD., reproduced with permission of ECONOMIST NEWSPAPER LTD. in the format Educational/Instructional Program via Copyright Clearance Center. Extract on page 340: from 'Integrated Performance Management: Plan. Budget. Forecast', *Deloitte* (2014), online at www.planbudgetforecast.com. Extract on page 392: from 'Executives Ask: How and Why Should Firms and Their Employees Set Goals', *Academy of Management Executive*, 18, no. 4 (November 2004), pp. 122–3 (Kerr, S. 2004). Extract on page 406: from 'Bonuses and the Illusion of Banking Performance', *The Financial Times* (November 25, 2015), online at on.ft.com/1FmAXiS, © The Financial Times Limited, All Rights Reserved. Extract on page 408: from 'Small Chinese Cities Steer Away from GDP as Measure of Success', *The Financial Times* (August 13, 2014), online at on.ft.com/1FmAXiS. Extract on page 408: from 'Bonuses Are Bad for Bankers and Even Worse for Banks', *The Financial Times* (January 25, 2016), online at on.ft.com/1FmAXiS, © The Financial Times Limited, All Rights Reserved. Extracts on page 439 and 497: from 'Top Managers' Pay Reveals Weak Link to Value', *The Financial Times* (December 28, 2014), online at on.ft.com/1FmAXiS. Extract on page 487: from 'The Accounting Wizardry behind Banks' Strong Earnings', *Bloomberg* (January 14, 2014), online at bloom.bg/1mc0IcA. Extract on page 488: from 'Unicorns Beware: Markets Get It Wrong on Tech Valuations', *The Financial Times* (November 13, 2015), online at on.ft.com/1FmAXiS, © The Financial Times Limited, All Rights Reserved. Extract on page 489: from 'China Seeks End to Gold Medal Fixation', *The Financial Times* (January 27, 2015), online at on.ft.com/1FmAXiS, © The Financial Times Limited, All Rights Reserved. Extract on page 489: from 'HSBC Suffers 20% Fall in Profits', *The Financial Times* (May 7, 2014), online at on.ft.com/1FmAXiS, © The Financial Times Limited, All Rights Reserved. Extracts on page 491 and 712: from 'Christine Lagarde Calls for Shake-up of Bankers' Pay', *The Financial Times* (May 6, 2015), online at on.ft.com/1FmAXiS, © The Financial Times Limited, All Rights Reserved. Extract on page 491: from 'Fidelity Challenges Companies on Long-term Incentives', *The Financial Times* (September 22, 2013), online on.ft.com/1FmAXiS, © The Financial Times Limited, All Rights Reserved. Case Study on page 516: Copyright 2016 by the University of Virginia Darden School Foundation, Charlottesville, VA; All Rights Reserved. Case Study on page 526: Copyright © Winnie O'Grady; All Rights Reserved. Extract on page 669: from 'New Code of Conduct for Internal Auditors', *The Financial Times* (September 9, 2012), online at on.ft.com/1FmAXiS, © The Financial Times Limited, All Rights Reserved. Extract on page 712: from 'A Bigger Stick', *The Economist* (June 13, 2015), online at econ.st/1MsDNRB, The Economist by ECONOMIST NEWSPAPER LTD., reproduced with permission of ECONOMIST NEWSPAPER LTD. in the format Educational/Instructional Program via Copyright Clearance Center. Extract on page 722: from 'Credit Suisse Spooked by What Lurks Within', *The Financial Times* (March 25, 2016), online at on.ft.com/1FmAXiS, © The Financial Times Limited, All Rights Reserved. Extract on page 738: adapted from 'Tech Firm's Korean Growth Raises Eyebrows', *The Wall Street Journal* (August 8, 2000), p. C1 (Maremont, M., Eisinger, J. and Song, M.), reprinted with permission of The Wall Street Journal, Copyright © 2000 Dow Jones & Company, Inc., All Rights

Reserved Worldwide, License numbers 4032150712139 and 4032150524598. Extract on page 755: from 'Sustainability Matters, but What Does It Mean for Your Company?' *NACD Directorship* (July 30, 2015), online at www.nacdonline.org/Magazine/Article.cfm?ItemNumber=17504. Extract on page 760: from 'Debate Heightens over Measuring Health Care Quality', *The Wall Street Journal* (January 30, 2015), online at on.wsj.com/1EvciGo, reprinted with permission of The Wall Street Journal, Copyright © 2015 Dow Jones & Company, Inc., All Rights Reserved Worldwide, License numbers 4032140775190 and 4032140995347. Case Study on page 769: from Bendle, N., copyright 2014, Richard Ivey School of Business Foundation; Ivey Publishing, Ivey Business School, Western University, London, Ontario, Canada, N6G 0N1, cases@ivey.ca, www.iveycases.com; one-time permission to reproduce granted by Richard Ivey School of Business Foundation on January 11, 2017.

SECTION I
The Control Function of Management

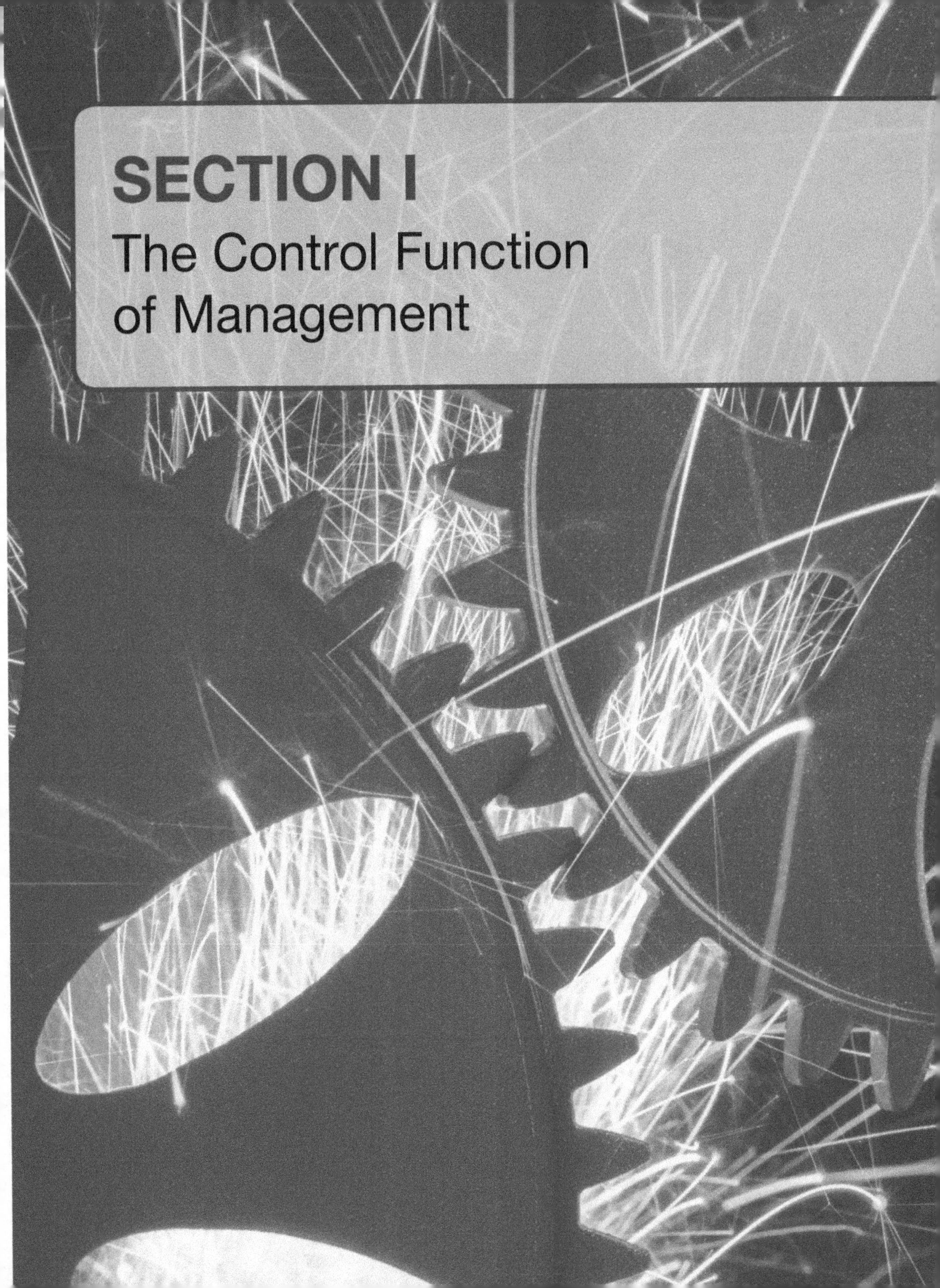

CHAPTER 1
Management and Control

Management control is a critical function in organizations. Management control failures can lead to large financial losses, reputation damage, and possibly even organizational failure. To illustrate this, let us start with some examples in the financial services sector that, since the financial crisis have been beset by a raft of control failures related to rusty information systems;[1] misconduct related to misselling financial services such as pay-protection insurance stemming from aggressive sales-based tactics;[2] allegations that financial services companies helped their clients evade taxes;[3] manipulation of interest rates, such as the venerable LIBOR (the benchmark inter-bank rate that is used to calculate interest rates on major financial transactions throughout the world);[4] faults in internal controls surrounding the reporting of commodity prices by banks' trading desks; more isolated but crippling unauthorized "rogue trades";[5] and anti-money-laundering violations,[6] just to name the most striking ones.

To provide some more detail about one particular case to demonstrate its relevance to management control systems (MCSs) and the significant risks when they fail, the Financial Services Authority (FSA) fined UBS, a Swiss-based global bank, £29.7 million (discounted from £42.4 million for early settlement) for systems and controls failings that allowed an employee (Kweku Adoboli) to cause substantial losses totaling US$2.3 billion as a result of unauthorized trading. In particular, UBS' failings included the following:[7]

- The computerized system operated by UBS to assist in risk management was not effective in controlling the risk of unauthorized trading.
- The trade capture and processing system had significant deficiencies, which Adoboli exploited in order to conceal his unauthorized trading. The system allowed trades to be booked to an internal counterparty without sufficient details, there were no effective methods in place to detect trades at material off-market prices, and there was a lack of integration between systems.
- There was an understanding amongst personnel supporting the trading desk that the operations division's main role was that of facilitation. They focused mainly on efficiency as opposed to risk control, and they did not adequately challenge the front office.
- There was inadequate front office supervision. The supervision arrangements were poorly executed and ineffective.
- The trading desk breached the risk limits set for their desk without being disciplined for doing so. These limits represented a key control and defined the maximum level of risk that the desk could enter into at a given time. This created a situation in which risk taking was not actively discouraged or penalized by those with supervisory responsibility.

- Failing to investigate the underlying reasons for the substantial increase in profitability of the desk despite the fact that this could not be explained by reference to the end-of-day risk positions.
- Profit and loss suspensions to the value of $1.6 billion were requested by Adoboli, and these were accepted without challenge or escalation. The combined factors of unexplained profitability and loss suspensions should have indicated the need for greater scrutiny.

The FSA report concluded that these failings were particularly serious because:[8]

- Market confidence was put at risk, given the sudden announcement to the market and size of the losses announced. Negative announcements, such as this, put at risk the confidence which investors have in financial markets.
- The systems and controls failings revealed serious weaknesses in the firm's procedures, management systems and internal controls.
- The failings enabled Adoboli to commit financial crime.

Global regulators have similarly exposed flaws in banks' internal control systems that allowed traders to manipulate interest rates, such as LIBOR, around the world.[9] To add, Stuart Gulliver, the chief executive of HSBC, the largest financial institution in Europe, admitted that "our anti-money-laundering controls should have been stronger and more effective, and we failed to spot and deal with unacceptable behavior."[10]

The press headlines to which these examples are selectively referenced speak for themselves. Of course, not all banks have been entangled in each and every issue. However, that the list of those being caught in these nets has been so long, sparing few, is surprising for organizations whose reputations are among their most valuable assets. Failures of this type and magnitude also damage the integrity of the wider market and financial system on a global scale. But these failures have also been costly money-wise, where the wave of fines and lawsuits that has swept through the financial sector since the financial crisis has cost big banks a whopping $260 billion, according to research from Morgan Stanley. The report also suggests that "actions taken by banks to prevent future litigation issues include everything from changing remuneration [compensation] policies [which we discuss under the rubric of *results controls* in Chapter 2 and *incentive systems* in Chapter 9] to a greater focus on 'non-financial metrics' [Chapter 11], adding compliance staff [Chapters 3 and 14], to elevating chief risk officers to boards [Chapter 13] and using 'robo-surveillance' in trading rooms [a form of *action controls* which we discuss in Chapter 3]" (brackets added).[11] Clearly, the issues illustrated here touch on, and cut across, many of the issues we discuss in this text.

To add, though, here is a quote from a *Financial Times* columnist that builds nicely on the above but extends it to other sectors:

> It turns out that bankers may not be alone. The traders who rigged Libor and foreign exchange rates cheated clients out of money. Volkswagen, we now know, deliberately polluted our air. The carmaker had a choice: install additional emissions cleaning equipment; admit that its diesel cars were not very fuel efficient; or spew out illegal amounts of nitrogen oxide. It chose the last of these options, and covered it up by designing software to deceive the US regulators. [...] This round-the-world tour of fraud also takes in Toshiba. The nuclear-to-semiconductor conglomerate was hit by a record fine from Japan's stock exchange and ordered to improve its governance and internal controls, in the wake of a $2bn accounting scandal. [...] Not even the tech industry has proved immune. European researchers revealed this week that Google has been charging advertisers for having their ads seen on YouTube, even when fraud-detection systems discover that the 'viewer' is a robot. That practice is clearly not in the same league as rate-rigging,

> years of accounting fraud or emission test deceit. But the disclosure reinforces a growing sense that companies around the world are pushing ethical boundaries [which we discuss in Chapter 15].[12]

Another article commented that the issues at VW were predictable because of VW's lax boardroom controls (which we discuss in Chapter 13) and its peculiar corporate culture (Chapter 3): "The scandal clearly also has to do with structural issues at VW ... There have been warnings about VW's corporate governance for years, but they didn't take it to heart and now you see the result," says Alexander Juschus, director at IVOX, the German proxy adviser.[13]

Effective cultures, structures, and controls are quintessential as the above examples suggest, but not only in the for-profit sector, as the next example illustrates (we discuss non-profit organizations in Chapter 16). Consider the case of an award-winning teacher who at the time headed Atlanta's public schools, and who had been praised by the American Association of School Administrators for the significant gains in student achievement she had overseen, where Atlanta's schoolchildren made sizable gains on the standardized tests used to determine yearly progress. At one school, for instance, the share of 13-year-olds who passed the test's maths section rose from 24% to 86%, and the share of those who "exceeded expectations" rose from 1% to 46% – both in a single year. However,

> [...] the state of Georgia alleges that those remarkable leaps rested on neither pedagogy nor determined study, but something far more invidious: cheating. A report by a special investigative team [...] found widespread evidence of cheating [...]. Sometimes teachers gave pupils the correct answers. Sometimes they erased pupils' answers after the test and filled in the correct ones themselves. The investigative team ferreted out cheating by analyzing erasure marks on test sheets. They flagged classrooms with an average number of wrong-to-right erasures more than three standard deviations above the state average. The chance of that occurring randomly is one in 370. More than half of Atlanta's elementary and middle schools had such classrooms, and many had erasures more than 20 to 50 standard deviations above the norm. Of the 178 teachers accused of having taken part in the cheating, 82 confessed. [The head], said the report, either knew or should have known what was going on. [...] Prosecutors did not charge [the head] with taking part in the cheating, but with *putting "unreasonable pressure" on principals and teachers to do well, and for creating "an environment where achieving the desired end result was more important than the students' education."*[14]

This is an example of results controls (Chapter 2) and, clearly, not only the functional but also the behavioral displacements that they can create (Chapters 5 and 11), in part due to target pressure (Chapter 8), but also employees' and organizations' moral failures (Chapters 3 and 15).

Excessive target pressure was also identified as a culprit in the accounting scandal at Toshiba that was mentioned in passing earlier:

> In April 2015, an improper accounting scandal came to light that inflated profits by well over $1bn at Toshiba, the Japanese industrial conglomerate, which makes laptops, memory chips and nuclear reactors. A panel of external lawyers and accountants that was appointed to investigate was said to have uncovered emails showing that Hisao Tanaka, chief executive, and Norio Sasaki, former chief executive and then vice-chairman, "instructed employees to delay the booking of costs to make the financial figures look better" [...] and that "the problems were worsened by reporting procedures for projects that were time-consuming and old-fashioned. Some of the paperwork was being done by junior employees in their first few years at the company." Experts further commented that "the accounting issues at Toshiba also exposed concerns around Japanese corporate governance practices [which we discuss in Chapter 13], including the weak role of external

directors and the extensive power that many former chief executives continue to exercise."[15] The scathing panel report also detailed what it said "were 'institutional' accounting malpractices [Chapter 5] and a corporate culture [Chapter 3] in which employees were afraid to speak out against bosses' push for increasingly unachievable profits [Chapter 8]. [...] Pressures to meet aggressive, short-term profit targets [Chapter 11] – known as 'the challenge' – existed from the presidency of Atsutoshi Nishida, who headed the company from 2005 to 2009 and remained an adviser. Those pressures escalated as the company's earnings deteriorated in the wake of the global financial crisis and [...] the Fukushima nuclear accident. The panel declared that Mr. Tanaka and Mr. Sasaki were aware that profits were being inflated and did not take any action to end the improper accounting. In some instances, the report added, top executives pressured employees to achieve their targets with suggestions that the company may withdraw from underperforming businesses if they were not met. But the panel found no evidence any of the three current and former chief executives had given specific instructions to division chiefs to inflate profit figures."[16] They described a corporate culture – one of exerting pressure on employees to meet aggressive, short-term profit targets spanning three generations of chief executives – in which employees were afraid to speak out against bosses when they pushed for unrealistic earnings targets.[17]

The consequences of failures of organizational control (which we define more precisely in the later sections of this chapter) can reach far and wide beyond the organizations in which they take place. As mentioned above, the banking failures have undermined the integrity of the wider market and financial system on a global scale. But there are other major impacts:

> Shareholders and customers are obvious victims of the current flood of bad news. They are seeing their investments shrink, having their cars recalled and paying too much for goods and services. But there is another set of losers: the employees and shareholders of the companies that try to play fair. Back in the early 2000s, a company called WorldCom upended the telecommunications industry by repeatedly posting profit margins that its rivals simply could not match. Five big groups, including AT&T, responded by slashing about 5 per cent of their combined workforces – more than 20,000 jobs. In 2002, WorldCom was exposed as the US's largest accounting fraud and its chief executive sentenced to jail. However, the employees who were laid off at rival companies did not get their jobs back.[18]

And in the case of Atlanta's schools:

> [...] the scandal's real casualties are Atlanta's schoolchildren. Schools that cheated their way to false improvements lost federal funds which could have been used to make actual improvements. Because of their apparently high test scores, struggling pupils were denied the help they needed and deserved. A generation of Atlanta's students have, in fact, been left behind.[19]

We discuss these impacts in the light of organizations' *corporate social responsibility* and their concerns about *sustainability* and the wider stakeholder communities in Chapter 16.

Not all control failures are as consequential, or of similar magnitude, as the examples listed above; yet they can, and do, inflict costs and/or embarrassment. For example,

> [...] this happened when Deutsche Bank paid $6 billion to a hedge fund client by mistake in a 'fat finger' trade, where a junior member of the bank's forex sales team, while his boss was on holiday, processed a gross value instead of a net value, meaning that the trade had 'too many zeroes'. Whereas the bank recovered the money from the U.S. hedge fund the next day, the incident was "an embarrassing blow to the bank" and it also "raised fresh questions about Deutsche's operational controls and risk management." The $6bn error

> also raised questions about why it was not spotted under the bank's 'four eyes principle' [an *action control* discussed in Chapter 3], requiring every trade to be reviewed by another person before being processed.[20]

Other examples of this type also occur in the public sector and do not always involve money being inadvertently wired. This happened at the Bank of England (BoE), where its head of press mistakenly sent an email to the media revealing that officials were quietly researching the impact of Britain's exit from the European Union, a major blunder given the secrecy of this study. What had caused this mistake? The "auto-complete" tool in BoE's internal email service. The BoE confirmed that following this incident, it had switched off auto-complete from its email system – that is, staff now have to write the full name of the recipient of their email messages rather than being automatically proposed through the Outlook auto-complete functionality – "to preserve the security of its data."[21]

Employees do not always have to steal or engage in fraudulent activities to cause harm. Sometimes it suffices to just "fall asleep." This happened when a bank teller was making a payment of €64.20, but as he fell asleep, he left his finger on the number 2 key, accidentally putting through a payment of €22,222,222.22. The payment almost went through when the supervisor who was supposed to be looking out for such mistakes allegedly failed to notice and approved the transaction. The mistake was spotted only by another colleague who managed to correct it before it was too late.[22] As we will see, this is an example of a rather simple *internal control* procedure. We discuss internal controls as one type of what we call *action controls* in Chapter 3, and we discuss how tightly they should be applied in Chapter 4. The example further illustrates that not every control problem involves fraud, yet adequate control systems must also be able to prevent mistakes. Furthermore, when there are irregularities or control breaches, money or *incentives* like bonuses are not always the motive for the wrongdoing. For example,

> [...] two clerical workers at the Laguna Niguel, California-based service center of the U.S. Immigration and Naturalization Service (INS) were accused of destroying thousands of immigration documents, including visa applications, passports, and other papers. According to the probe, the clerks started shredding unprocessed paperwork after an inventory revealed a processing backlog of about 90,000 documents. A month later, the backlog was reported to be zero. The shredding allegedly went on for about another month to keep the backlog at zero, until INS officials discovered the shredding spree during an evening shift.[23]

Although it is not entirely clear what the clerks' motives were, there were no bonuses involved here, and maybe they were concerned about keeping their job and/or also not doing their job well or being lazy and cutting corners. Nonetheless, their actions were completely inappropriate, and thus proper control systems are needed to mitigate such undesirable behaviors.

However, *more* controls should not always be equated with *better* controls. When copious MCSs are stifling, they can exacerbate rather than mitigate control problems. We discuss this further in Chapters 4 and 5, where we consider not only direct, explicit, more easily quantifiable, out-of-pocket costs, but also various types of *indirect, implicit* costs of tightening the controls. For example, when financial irregularities were discovered at Eurostat, the European Commission's statistical service, it was not immediately clear whether these had occurred for the personal enrichment of those involved; instead, some argued that the "secret accounts" may at least initially have been set up to give Eurostat a way to pay for research quickly without going through the Commission's cumbersome procedures. Ironically, then, while the Commission had elaborate procedures to prevent financial fraud, these procedures may not only have proved insufficient (because they clearly could be circumvented), they may actually have made the problem worse. Because tortuous form-filling was required to request funds, requesters had to jump through a number of bureaucratic hoops to get anything approved, and funds delivery was notoriously slow, commission officials and staff may have taken to cutting corners and finding "creative" ways to expedite the process. Of course, these "work-arounds" should be a red flag for possible exploitation and potential improprieties, too.[24]

By this point, it should be no surprise that we are claiming, but also that it is widely accepted, that good MCSs are important. Comparing the books and articles written on management control is difficult, however, because much of the MCS language is imprecise. The term "control" as it applies to a management function does not have a universally accepted definition. An old, narrow view of a MCS is that of a simple *cybernetic* or *regulating* system involving a single feedback loop analogous to a thermostat that measures the temperature, compares the measurement with the desired standard, and, if necessary, takes a corrective action (turn on, or off, a furnace or air conditioner). In a MCS feedback loop, managers measure performance, compare that measurement with a pre-set performance standard, and, if necessary, take corrective actions.[25]

In this text, however, we take a broader view. Many management controls in common use, such as direct supervision, employee selection and retention, and codes of conduct, do not focus on measured performance. They focus instead on encouraging, enabling, or sometimes forcing employees to act in the organization's best interest. This is consistent with the observation that all the above examples have one key question in common: how can organizations of all types ensure that their employees up and down the hierarchy carry out their jobs and responsibilities properly? Moreover, some management controls are *proactive* rather than *reactive*. Proactive means that the controls are designed to *prevent* problems before the organization suffers any adverse effects on performance. Examples of proactive controls include planning processes, required expenditure approvals, segregation of duties, and restricted access. Management control, then, includes all the devices or systems that managers use to ensure the behaviors and decisions of their employees are consistent with the organization's objectives and strategies. The systems themselves are commonly referred to as *management control systems* (MCSs).

Designed properly, MCSs influence employees' behaviors in desirable ways and, consequently, increase the probability that the organization will achieve its goals. Thus, the primary *function* of management control is to influence behaviors in desirable ways. The *benefit* of management control is the increased probability that the organization's objectives will be achieved.

Management and control

Management control is the back end of the management process. This can be seen from the various ways in which the broad topic of management is disaggregated.

Management

The literature includes many definitions of management. All relate to the processes of organizing resources and directing activities for the purpose of achieving organizational objectives. Inevitably, those who study and teach management have broken the broad subject into smaller, more discernable elements. Table 1.1 shows the most prominent classification schemes. The first column identifies the primary management functions of the value chain: product or service development, operations (manufacturing products or performing/delivering services), marketing/sales (finding buyers and making sure the products and services fulfill customer needs), and finance (raising money). Virtually every management school offers courses focused on only one, or only part of one, of these primary management functions.

Table 1.1 Different ways of categorizing the broad area of management

Functions	Resources	Processes
Product (or service) development	People	Objective setting
Operations	Money	Strategy formulation
Marketing/sales	Machines	Management control
Finance	Information	

Source: K. A. Merchant, *Modern Management Control Systems: Text and Cases* (Upper Saddle River, NJ: Prentice Hall, 1998), p. 3.

The second column of Table 1.1 identifies the major types of resources with which managers must work: people, money, machines, and information. Management schools also offer courses organized using this classification. These courses are often called human resource management, accounting and finance, production and operations management, and information systems, respectively. These are sometimes also referred to as the support management functions.[26]

The term *management control* appears in the third column of Table 1.1, which separates the management functions along a *process* involving objective setting, strategy formulation, and management control. Control, then, is the back end of the management process. The way we use the term management control in this text has the same meaning as the terms *execution* and *strategy implementation*. In most organizations, focusing on improving MCSs will provide higher payoffs than will focusing on improving strategy. A *Fortune* study showed that 7 out of 10 CEOs who fail do so not because of bad strategy, but because of bad execution.[27] The above examples reinforce this, too.

Many management courses, including business policy, strategic management, and management control systems, focus on elements of the management process. To focus on the control function of management, we must distinguish it from objective setting and strategy formulation.

Objective setting

Knowledge of *objectives* is a prerequisite for the design of any MCS and, indeed, for any purposeful activities. Objectives do not have to be quantified and do not have to be financial, although that is how they are commonly thought of in for-profit organizations. A not-for-profit organization's primary objective might be to provide shelter for homeless people, for example; but even in these organizations, there have been calls to express the achievement of these objectives in financial or *quasi*-financial terms, such as social return on investment.[28] However, many for-profit organizations also have nonfinancial objectives, such as related to sustainability or personnel development and well-being (see Chapter 16). In any organization, however, employees must have a basic understanding of what the organization is trying to accomplish. Otherwise, no one could claim that any of the employees' actions are purposive, and no one could ever support a claim that the organization was successful.

In most organizations, the objectives are known. That is not to say that all employees always agree unanimously as to how to balance their organizations' responsibilities to all of their stakeholders, including owners (equity holders), debtholders, employees, suppliers, customers, and the society at large. They rarely do.[29] That said, organizations develop explicit or implicit compromise mechanisms to resolve conflicts among stakeholders and reach some level of agreement about the objectives they will pursue. As Jason Luckhurst, managing director of Practicus, a UK-based project-management recruitment firm, argues:

> [To achieve organizational success], it takes a clear vision around which the entire business [can] be designed, [and I] think it is something you should be able to communicate

> **simply to everyone, whether a client or [an employee]. Having a simple and easily understood statement of intent is vital for setting clear objectives and targets.[30]**

Strategy formulation

Having set the firm's strategic intentions or objectives, *strategies* then define how organizations should use their resources to meet these objectives. A well-conceived strategy guides employees in successfully pursuing their organization's objectives; it conveys to employees what they are supposed to be doing. Or, as Mr. Luckhurst at Practicus states:

> **All the planning in areas as diverse as marketing, branding, financing and training, is designed around [our] objective – as are [our] incentive [systems]. We have a detailed road map, but it starts with a simple vision that everyone can understand and buy into. Everything else we do comes on the back of those goals. In effect, we can reverse-engineer the business to those objectives.[31]**

Many organizations develop formal strategies through systematic, often elaborate, planning processes (which we discuss further in Chapter 8). Put differently, they have what can be called an *intended strategy*. However, strategies can sometimes be left largely unspecified. As such, some organizations do not have formal, written strategies; instead they try to respond to opportunities that present themselves. Major elements of these organizations' strategies *emerge* from a series of interactions between management, employees, and the environment; from decisions made spontaneously; and from local experimentation designed to learn what works well. Nonetheless, if some decision-making consistency exists, a strategy can be said to have been formed, regardless of whether managers planned or even intended that particular consistency. In that sense, strategic visions sometimes come about through dynamic organizational processes rather than through formalized strategic planning.[32]

Not even the most elaborate strategic visions and statements are complete to the point where they detail every desired action and contemplate every possible contingency. However, for purposes of designing MCSs, it is useful to have strategies that are as specific and detailed as possible, if those strategies can be kept current. The formal strategic statements make it easier for management both to identify the feasible management control alternatives and to implement them effectively. The management controls can be targeted to the organization's critical success factors, such as developing new products, keeping costs down, or growing market share, rather than aiming more generally at improving profitability in otherwise largely unspecified ways.

Formal strategic statements are not a sufficient condition for success, however. As Adrian Grace, managing director of Bank of Scotland – Corporate, states:

> **I have seen businesses with 400-page documents outlining their strategy and it's clear they should have spent less time outlining the vision and more time thinking about how they will deliver on it. You can have the best vision in the world but if you can't put it into effect, you are wasting your time.[33]**

It is on the execution side of the management process that MCSs play a critical role. Jason Luckhurst explained:

> **The difference between merely having a strategic vision and achieving strategic success is having a detailed understanding of what that vision means for every level of the business – how much funding you need, the branding and marketing strategy, which channels you will develop, how many people you need in which areas and when and what the organizational structure will be. It is also important to revisit the vision often and be aware of how close you are to achieving it at any given stage. This helps everyone in the company to stay focused.[34]**

Management control

Management control focuses on execution, and it involves addressing the general question: Are our employees likely to behave appropriately? This question can be decomposed into several parts:

- First, do our employees understand what we expect of them?
- Second, will they work consistently hard and try to do what is expected of them – that is, will they pursue the organization's objectives in line with the strategy?
- Third, are they capable of doing a good job?

Finally, if the answer to any of these questions is negative, what can be done to solve the management control problems? All organizations who must rely on their employees to accomplish organizational objectives must deal with these basic management control issues. Addressing management control issues, therefore, involves reflecting on how to influence, direct, or align employees' behaviors toward the achievement of organizational objectives consistent with the espoused strategy.

From a management control perspective, strategies should be viewed as useful but not absolutely necessary to the proper design of MCSs. When strategies are formulated more clearly, more control alternatives become feasible, and it becomes easier to implement each form of management control effectively. Managers can, however, design and operate some types of MCSs without having a clear strategy in mind. As Adrian Grace, managing director of Bank of Scotland – Corporate, proffers: "If you don't have [a strategy] but you know how to deliver, you might still make it. Success in business is 25% strategy but 75% execution."[35] Or, the other way around, to devise a strategy and write it down is one thing; it is another thing entirely to make the plan work in practice. That said, there is some evidence that organizations with formal systems for managing the execution of strategy outperform those that do not.[36]

Behavioral emphasis

Management control involves managers taking steps to help ensure that the employees do what is best for the organization. This is an important purpose because it is people in the organization who make things happen. Management controls are necessary to guard against the possibilities that people will do something the organization does not want them to do, or fail to do something they should do. For example, aiming to achieve greater cost control is open to question without reference to people because costs do not control themselves; people control them. As many examples throughout the text will illustrate, employees can work against or around systems, thereby leaving many objectives unmet or producing unintended consequences.

This behavioral orientation has long been recognized by practitioners. For example, Roman Stanek, chief executive of GoodData in San Francisco, a business analytics company, acknowledged that:

> **Having a vision and having confidence doesn't mean anything unless you're able to communicate it to your team [...]. The ability to communicate well didn't come easily for me. I always assumed that everybody would see things the same way I see them, and now I understand it takes a lot of time *to get people aligned*.**[37]

If all employees could always be relied on to do what is best for the organization, there would be no need for a MCS. But employees are sometimes unable or unwilling to act in the organization's best interest, so managers must take steps to guard against the occurrence of undesirable behaviors and encourage desirable behaviors.

Causes of management control problems

Given the behavioral focus of controls, the next logical question to ask is: What is it about the employees on whom the organization must rely that creates the need to implement MCSs? The causes of the needs for control can be classified into three main categories: lack of direction, motivational problems, and personal limitations.

Lack of direction

Some employees perform inadequately simply because they do not know what the organization wants from them. When this *lack of direction* occurs, the likelihood of the desired behaviors occurring will be haphazard or random. Thus, one function of management control involves informing employees as to how they can direct their contributions to the fulfillment of organizational objectives. Indeed, this is also the key point that came through in the quote from Stanek above.

Lack of direction is not a trivial issue in many organizations, although it is often taken for granted (as the quote from Stanek also suggests). For example, survey evidence collected by KPMG, a big-four professional services company providing audit, tax, and advisory services, from approximately 4,000 US employees spanning all levels of job responsibility across a wide range of industries and organizational sizes revealed that 55% of the sample respondents had a lack of understanding of the standards that apply to their jobs.[38] Moreover, a study of 414 World-at-Work members in mostly managerial positions at large North-American companies suggested that 81% of the respondents believe that senior managers in their organizations understand the value drivers of their business strategy; 46% say that middle management understands these drivers; but just 13% believe non-management employees understand them. This indicates that organizational goals are not cascading down to all levels in the organization. And while 79% of the respondents in this study believed that their employees' goals are aligned with organizational goals, 44% also stated that employees set goals based on their own views rather than direction from leadership.[39]

Another survey from KPMG asked what factors might cause managers and employees to engage in misconduct, which, as we will see across several chapters in this text, is an important management control problem. The answer, in fifth place and mentioned by 59% of the respondents, was "a lack of understanding of the standards that apply to their jobs."[40] Another survey of 5,000 respondents, including "techies" (e.g. software developers or engineers), indicated that only 28% of the techies said they understood their companies' vision compared with (also only) 43% of non-techies.[41] And, in a university one of the authors of this text is familiar with, a staff survey revealed that only half of the employees responded affirmatively to the question whether "they had a clear understanding of the purpose and objectives of [the university]," whereas (also only) 68% said this to be the case for the objectives of their department.[42] All told, then, it should not be taken for granted that employees have a clear understanding of direction. To the contrary, the survey evidence suggests that a lack of direction may be quite a common occurrence.

Motivational problems

Even if employees understand what is expected of them, some do not perform as the organization expects because of *motivational problems*. Motivational problems are common because individual and organizational objectives do not naturally coincide – individuals are self-interested.

Employees sometimes act in their own personal interest at the expense of their organization's interest. Frederick Taylor, one of the major figures in the *scientific management* movement that took place in the early twentieth century, wrote: "Hardly a competent worker can be found who does not devote a considerable amount of time to studying just how slowly he can work and still convince his employer that he is going at a good pace."[43] Such *effort aversion* and *other self-interested behaviors* are still a problem today. Gary Gill, the author of KPMG's Fraud Barometer for Australia, believes that broad economic conditions have a significant effect on fraud levels: "It goes up following a boom period. People want to maintain their standard of living, even if it means criminal activity."[44] Another survey suggests that fraud is on the increase in the United Kingdom's public sector as austerity programs imply personnel reductions and fewer resources being spent on internal controls, according to a report from PwC, a big-four competitor of KPMG.[45]

Overall, survey evidence suggests that wasting, mismanaging, and misappropriating organizational resources, among other types of employee misconduct, are prevalent in most organizations.[46] Even ostensibly inconsequential forms of wasting time on the job can have high costs. Surfing the Internet while on the job, for example, has been estimated to have cost US employers in the billions of dollars per year.[47] All told, survey participants in the most recent report by the Association of Certified Fraud Examiners estimated that the typical organization loses 5% of its annual revenue to fraud. Applied to the estimated 2014 Gross World Product, this figure translates to a potential global fraud loss of more than $3.7 trillion.[48] Staggering as these statistics may be, they suggest that it should not be taken for granted that employees will always reliably act with the best interest of their organizations in mind. Because of this, the costs to organizations are nontrivial, to say the least.

Indeed, the most serious forms of employees' misdirected behaviors, such as fraud, can have severe impacts, including deteriorated employee morale, impaired business relations, lost revenues from damaged reputations, investments in improving control procedures, legal fees and settlements of litigation, fines and penalties to regulatory agencies, and losses from plummeting stock prices. Many of the examples that we included at the start of this chapter illustrate this,[49] and various fraud or integrity surveys, some of which have been conducted over many years by major organizations, reinforce this with statistics.[50]

These huge fraud costs can be traced back to human weaknesses but also, and importantly, as we will see later in this text, to the lack of effective MCSs. Anecdotal assertions abound. For example, one manager claimed, rather brashly, that "every single person in your [business] is trying to steal from you."[51] Another manager's estimate, while more measured, still suggests that:

> **Between 10 and 20% of a company's employees will steal anything that isn't nailed down. Another 20% will never steal; they would say it is morally wrong. The vast majority of people are situationally honest; they won't steal if there are proper controls.**[52]

Regardless of these opinions, one might argue that "stealing" is a rather literal, peculiar, and perhaps too extreme or negative type of behavior to illustrate self-interest. Taking "stealing" less literally, many other forms of misaligned behaviors occur when employees, for example, manipulate their performance reports, either by falsifying the data or by taking decisions that artificially boost performance, with the intention of earning higher, but undeserved, incentive pay (see also Chapter 15). The most common cause of this is reported to be pressure to do "whatever it takes" to meet business targets.[53] This goes to the heart of *results controls* (which we discuss in Chapter 2) and related performance targets (Chapter 8) and incentives (Chapter 9). Well-designed MCSs are needed to protect organizations against these behaviors.

However, in addition to focusing on how MCSs can be used to prevent or mitigate these *negative* or *dysfunctional* behaviors, this text's emphasis is also, even primarily, on how MCSs can be employed to motivate *positive* or *productive* behaviors; that is, how they encourage employees to work consistently hard to accomplish organizational objectives. As we will discuss further below, whenever feasible, *motivation* should be the primary focus of effective MCSs, most commonly brought about through *results controls* (Chapter 2) while also providing any necessary behavioral constraints and/or mitigating any behavioral displacements through a well-designed combination or "configuration" of *action* and *personnel/cultural controls* (Chapter 3).[54]

Personal limitations

The final behavioral problem that MCSs must address occurs when employees who know what is expected of them, and may be highly motivated to perform well, are simply unable to perform well because of any number of other limitations. Some of these limitations are person-specific. They may be caused by a lack of aptitude, training, experience, stamina, or knowledge for the tasks at hand. An example is the too-common situation where employees are promoted above their level of competence; that is, when employees are "over their heads." Sometimes jobs are just not designed properly, causing even the most physically fit and apt employees to become tired or stressed, leading to on-the-job accidents and decision errors.

Regarding lack of training, for example, Illinois-based Ace Hardware was forced to restate its earnings for four fiscal years because of a $152 million accounting error made by a poorly trained employee, who incorrectly entered accounts in ledgers in the Finance department at the company's headquarters. Ace CEO Ray Griffith stated: "We are embarrassed by it. We did not provide the training, oversight or checks and balances to help that person do (the) job."[55] Errors such as these are not uncommon. For example, when Bank of America, a global US-based bank, disclosed that it had made a significant error in the way it calculates a crucial measure of its financial health, which led the bank to report that it had $4 billion more capital than it actually had, the error raised serious questions about the "quality of its accounting employees."[56] Similarly, at Tesco, the largest UK supermarket chain, when it announced to have overstated its expected profits by £250 million, one commentator observed that "even if there was no fraudulent intent and the problems stem from a misunderstanding of the rules [...], the apparent scale of the error suggests that, at the very least, Tesco's internal controls need a thorough overhaul."[57]

Moreover, research in psychology and behavioral economics suggests that all individuals, even intelligent, well-trained, and experienced ones, face limitations in their abilities to perceive new problems, to remember important facts, and to process information properly (or rationally). In looking at the future, it has been shown, for example, that people tend to overestimate the likelihood of common events and events that have occurred relatively recently (both of which are easier to remember) as compared with relatively rare events and those that have not occurred recently. Such biases may, for example, affect employees' propensities to assess risks by biasing their estimates of either the likelihood or impact, or both, of certain risk events. Sometimes training can be used to reduce the severity of these limitations. Nonetheless, these limitations are a problem because they reduce the probability that employees will make the correct decisions or that they will correctly assess the problems about which decisions should be made.[58]

These three management control problems – lack of direction, motivational problems, and personal limitations – can obviously occur simultaneously and in any combination. However, all that is required to call for the necessity of effective MCSs is that at least one of these problems occurs, which will almost inevitably be the case in complex organizations as the above arguments and examples have suggested.

Characteristics of good management control

To have a high probability of success, organizations must therefore maintain good management control. *Good* control means that management can be reasonably confident that no major unpleasant surprises will occur. The label *out of control* is used to describe a situation where there is a high probability of poor performance, either overall or in a specific performance area, despite having a sound strategy in place.

However, even *good* management control still allows for some probability of failure because *perfect* control does not exist except perhaps in very unusual circumstances. Perfect control would require complete assurance that all control systems are foolproof and all individuals on whom the organization must rely always act in the best way possible. Perfect control is obviously not a realistic expectation because it is virtually impossible to install MCSs so well designed that they guarantee good behaviors. Furthermore, because MCSs are costly, it is rarely, if ever, cost effective to try and implement *enough* controls even to approach the idealized perfect control.

The cost of not having a perfect control system can be called a *control loss*. It is the difference between the performance that is theoretically possible given the strategy selected and the performance that can be reasonably expected with the MCSs in place. More or better MCSs should be implemented only if the benefits by which they would reduce the control loss exceed the costs. Except in cases where the consequences of failure are incalculable, *optimal control* can be said to have been achieved if the control losses are expected to be smaller than the cost of implementing more controls. Because of control costs, perfect control is rarely the optimal outcome (or even conceivable). The benchmark, therefore, is adequate control rather than perfect control, except again in cases where failure is not an option and where control must be uncompromisingly focused on avoiding failure at any cost (such as in nuclear plants).

Assessing whether good control has been achieved must be future-oriented and objectives-driven. It must be *future-oriented* because the goal is to have no unpleasant surprises in the future; the past is not relevant except as a guide to the future, such as in terms of experiences or lessons learned from control failures. It must be *objectives-driven* because the objectives represent what the organization seeks to attain. Nonetheless, assessing whether good control has been achieved is difficult and subjective. It is difficult because the adequacy of management control must be measured against a future that is inevitably difficult to predict, as are predictions of possible unintended consequences of the controls. Good control also is not established over an activity or entity with multiple objectives unless performance on *all* significant dimensions has been considered. As difficult as this assessment of management control is, however, it should be done because organizational success depends on good MCSs.

As the examples at the beginning of this chapter illustrate, organizations that fail to implement adequate MCSs can suffer loss or impairment of assets, deficient revenues, excessive costs, inaccurate records, or reports that can lead to poor decisions, legal sanctions, or business disruptions. At the extreme, organizations that do not control performance on one or more critical dimensions can fail.

Control problem avoidance

Implementing some combination of the behavior-influencing devices commonly known as MCSs is not always the best way to achieve good control; sometimes the problems can be avoided. *Avoidance* means eliminating the possibility that the control problems will occur.

Organizations can never avoid all their control problems, but they can often avoid some of them by limiting exposure to certain types of problems and problem sources, or by reducing the maximum potential loss if the problems occur. Four prominent avoidance strategies are activity elimination, automation, centralization, and risk sharing.

Activity elimination

Managers can sometimes avoid the control problems associated with a particular entity or activity by turning over the potential risks, and the associated profits, to a third party through such mechanisms as subcontracting, licensing agreements, or divestment. This form of avoidance is called *activity elimination.*

Managers who are not able to control certain activities, perhaps because they do not have the required resources, because they do not have a good understanding of the required processes, or because they face legal or structural limitations, are those most likely to eliminate activities. Here is an example:

> When the German financial regulator ordered Deutsche Bank "to do more to ensure that commodity prices cannot be manipulated by its traders," the bank responded that it "has since shut trading desks dedicated to energy, agriculture, dry bulk and freight and base metals. Other commodity businesses have been transferred to Deutsche's non-core bank where they will be wound down or sold, while some parts remain active," adding that "we significantly scaled back our commodities business and exited entirely non-precious metals trading. As we have previously said, we continue to cooperate with authorities in their industrywide review of certain benchmarks and are investing to further improve our control environment."[59]

When managers do not wish to avoid completely an area that they cannot control well, they are wise at least to limit their investments, and hence (some of) their risks, in that area. An example is cloud computing, which means that companies obtain computing resources (processing, storage, messaging, databases, and so on) from outside, and pay only for what they use, rather than develop their own computing infrastructure and run their own systems. With the increase in demand for servers to store and process data, many companies would need to multiply their server capacity manyfold, for which they sometimes have neither the money nor the skills, nor the interest, because doing so falls outside of most companies' core competencies. By using cloud computing services, firms can leave all that to be managed by those who have the competencies and, hence, can provide essential control over the process. Whereas this does not eliminate all risks, it partially avoids some control problems related to data management and all that it entails.

Indeed, many companies have been expanding their use of cloud services, with growing numbers running systems such as email services, human resources, and administrative processes via the cloud, as well as data storage and backup. James Petter, UK managing director of EMC, the data storage and software group, said: "Organizations move to the cloud for a number of reasons, but they most often relate to agility, *control* and efficiency" (italics added). "More than just hosting services, the cloud is ensuring availability and performance, protecting data and helping businesses with change management by deploying functions and lessening disruption," Joe King, senior vice-president at JDA, the supply chain software group, added.[60]

The economics-based literature that focuses on whether specific activities (transactions) can be controlled more effectively through *markets* (external) or through organizational *hierarchies* (internal) is known as *transaction cost economics.* A detailed examination of the theories and evidence in this field of study is outside the scope of this text.[61] We just note that the cost/benefit tradeoffs of dealing with management control issues internally do not always favor arms-length, market-based transactions or inter-organizational arrangements, and thus a careful balance has to be struck.[62] Referring back to the cloud services, for example, one issue that sometimes holds companies back is a concern about security. As such, organizations will always have to rely on MCSs internally, which have been found to be effective in a broad range of settings. The prevalence of large diversified organizations has depended to a large extent on good MCSs.

Automation

Automation is a second avoidance possibility. Managers can sometimes use computers, robots, expert systems, and other means of automation to reduce their organization's exposure to some control problems. These automated devices can be set to behave as required, and when they are operating properly, they perform more consistently than do humans. Computers eliminate the human problems of inaccuracy, inconsistency, and lack of motivation. Once programmed, computers are consistent in their treatments of transactions, and they never have dishonest or disloyal motivations. Here is a representative quote from the mining industry:

> **Rio Tinto has rolled out fully automated driverless truck fleets at two of its iron ore mines in the Pilbara in Western Australia. [...] "Our autonomous fleet outperforms the named fleet by an average of 12 per cent, primarily by eliminating required breaks, absenteeism and shift changes," said Andrew Harding, Rio's iron ore chief executive. "Innovation and technology is critical in our efforts to improve safety." [...] The world's biggest miners are turning to technology to cut costs. [...] This follows a similar trend across a wide range of industries, from car manufacturing to computing, whereby robots or artificial intelligence are increasingly taking roles traditionally performed by humans. [...] "Removing people from the mine environment is safer," said Dr. Carla Boehl, a lecturer at Curtin University – "It has cost advantages too. It can be very costly for companies if employees are hurt onsite." [...] "We have also seen a 13 per cent reduction in load and haul costs due to the greater efficiency," Mr. Harding said. Dr. Boehl said embracing technology could create more interesting jobs while making lower skilled positions obsolete. "You will tend to lose the boring, repetitive jobs performed in the 50 degrees centigrade heat in the Pilbara but you can also create new innovative roles in analyzing data and developing technology," she said.[63]**

As technology has advanced, organizations have substituted machines and expert systems for people who have been performing quite complex actions and making sophisticated judgments and decisions. In hospitals, for example, artificial intelligence systems are able to perform many of the tasks doctors and nurses used to perform. These systems monitor the patients' conditions and trends and alert the medical staff of possible problems; they assist in making diagnoses; they order the needed drugs; and they check for potential drug interactions and allergic reactions. Computer-aided insertions of central venous catheters are more accurate and reduce complications (such as punctured arteries that can lead to infections).[64] And so on. Importantly, these systems allow hospitals to avoid one of the behavioral problems – the personal limitations of the medical staff. In the vast majority of situations, these systems are more likely than are medical personnel to recall all the details of every condition, medication, and possible complications to initiate the proper response. Needle injection robots use tracking algorithms to keep the blood vessel aligned, and thus, are more accurate. Hence, these systems make it more likely that no major, unpleasant surprises will occur; in this case, avoidable medical errors and complications.

Similarly, many legal tasks, although sometimes quite complex, are variations on a theme, where the production of certain types of legal documents does not differ vastly from one instance to another. Legal firms are therefore increasingly using what is called *document assembly software*, allowing them to reduce the time needed to put together a certain type of legal document (such as a trademark registration or a real estate lease) to a fraction of the time it takes an employee to do the same and, possibly, more consistently and accurately with fewer errors. Moreover, automating these onerous processes reduces costs and allows lawyers to spend more time dealing with their clients.[65]

Another example is where banks (when they have not exited parts of the trading business as Deutsche Bank did in the example above) have sped up digital trading to settle trades via automated processes to minimize human intervention because traditional trading over the phone has come under intense regulatory scrutiny due to alleged manipulation of benchmarks such as currency fixes and interbank lending rates. Automation leads to a better client experience at lower cost with stronger control, thereby reshaping a once opaque but lucrative business to become less risky.[66]

In most managerial situations, however, automation can provide only a partial control solution at best. One limitation is *feasibility*. Humans have many talents – particularly those involving complex, intuitive judgments – that no machines or decision models have been able to duplicate. There are often also regulatory constraints, where the regulators may be understandably wary of fully autonomous systems in some settings, such as in health care. In other settings, such as automated trading in banks, they may welcome them. Regulators may find fully autonomous or "self-driving" cars not yet feasible, but they are likely to welcome semi-autonomous systems that help "take the human error out of driving".[67]

A further limitation is *cost*. Automation often requires major investments that may be justifiable only if improvements in productivity, as well as in control, are forthcoming. Finally, automation may just replace some control problems with others, or introduce different control issues. The elimination of source documents can obscure the audit trail; the concentration of information in one location can increase security risks; and placing greater reliance on computer programs can expose the company to the risks of programmer errors or fraud.

Centralization

Centralization of decision-making is a third avoidance possibility, which is a key element of almost all organizations' MCSs. High degrees of centralization, where all the key decisions are made at top management levels, are common in small businesses, particularly when they are run by the founder or owner. High degrees of centralization also exist in some large businesses whose top managers sometimes have reputations for being "detail oriented" or "control freaks." When that is the case, top management reserves the important, and sometimes the not-so-important, decisions for themselves, and in so doing, they avoid having the lower-level employees make poor judgments.

Centralization inevitably exists to some extent in all organizations, as well as at all levels of management within organizations, as managers tend to reserve for themselves many of the most crucial decisions that fall within their authority. Common candidates for centralization are decisions regarding major acquisitions and divestments, major capital expenditures, negotiation of pivotal sales contracts, organization changes, and hiring and firing of key personnel. However, in most organizations of even minimal size, it is not possible to centralize all critical decisions, and other control solutions are necessary. As we will see in Chapters 2 and 7, results controls play a critical role when decisions are decentralized. When decisions are decentralized, results controls need to be in place to hold the managers who enjoy the decision authority accountable for the results of their decisions. Accountability for results is what makes delegated authority legitimate.

Risk sharing

A final, partial avoidance possibility is risk sharing. Sharing risks with outside entities can bound the losses that could be incurred by inappropriate employee behaviors. Risk sharing can involve buying *insurance* to protect against certain types of potentially large losses the organization might not be able to afford. Many companies purchase fidelity bonds on employees in sensitive positions (such as bank tellers) to reduce the firm's exposure. These insurance contracts pass at least a portion of the risk of large losses and errors to the insurance providers. Another way to share risks with an outside party is to enter into a *joint venture* agreement. This shares the risk with the joint venture partner.

These avoidance alternatives are often an effective partial solution to, or bounding of, many of the control problems managers face. It is rarely possible to avoid all risks because firms are rewarded for bearing risk, but most firms use some forms of elimination, automation, centralization, and risk sharing in order to limit their exposure to the management control problems.

Control alternatives

For the control problems that cannot be avoided, and those for which decisions have been made not to avoid, managers must implement one or more control mechanisms that are generally called *management controls*. The collection of control mechanisms that are used is generally referred to as a *management control system* (MCS).

MCSs vary considerably among organizations and among entities or decision areas of any single organization. That said, they commonly include a *combination* of action, results, and personnel/cultural controls, which we discuss in depth in the next two chapters. The MCSs of some organizations consist primarily of trying to hire people who can be relied upon to serve the organization well. Other organizations provide modest performance-based incentives, and still others offer incentives that are highly leveraged. Some organizations base incentives on the accomplishment of targets defined in terms of accounting numbers, others use nonfinancial measures of performance, and still others evaluate performance subjectively. Some organizations have elaborate sets of policies and procedures that they expect employees to follow, whereas others have no such procedures, or they allow the procedures that were once in place to get out of date. Some organizations make extensive use of a large professional internal audit staff, while others only ensure to be in minimal compliance with regulatory requirements in this regard. These are just examples. The distinctions that can be made among the MCSs in use are numerous.

Management control choices are not random, however. They are based on many factors. Some controls are not effective, or are not cost-effective, in certain situations. Some types of controls are better at addressing particular types of problems, and different organizations and different areas within each organization often face quite different mixes of control problems. Some types of controls have some undesirable side effects that can be particularly damaging in some settings. And some controls merely suit particular management styles better than others. A major purpose of this text is to describe the factors affecting management control choice decisions and the effects on the employees and the organization when different choices are made.

Outline of this text

The text discusses MCSs from several different angles, each the focus of one major section. Section II distinguishes controls based on the *object of control*, which can focus on the results produced (*results control*), the actions taken (*action control*), or the types of people employed and their shared norms and values (*personnel and cultural control*). Chapters 2–6 in Section II discuss each of these forms of control, the outcomes they produce (which can be both positive and negative), and the factors that lead managers to choose one object of control over another.

Section III focuses on the major elements of *financial results-control systems*, an important type of results control in which results are defined in financial terms. This section includes discussions of financial responsibility structures (Chapter 7), planning and budgeting systems (Chapter 8), and incentive systems (Chapter 9).

Section IV discusses some major problems managers face when they use financial results-control systems and, particularly, the performance measurements that drive them. These problems include the tendency of accounting measures to cause managers to be excessively short-term oriented (myopic), the tendency for return-on-investment measures of performance to cause poor investment and performance evaluation decisions, and the likelihood of negative behavioral reactions from managers who are held accountable for factors over which they have less than complete control. Throughout Chapters 10–12, we also discuss several approaches organizations can rely on to mitigate these problems.

Section V discusses some key organizational control roles, including those of controllers, auditors, and audit committees of the board of directors. It also discusses recent developments in corporate governance (Chapters 13 and 14) as well as common control-related ethical issues and how to analyze them (Chapter 15).

Given the focus on financial results controls in primarily Sections III and IV, in the final section (Chapter 16), we come back to broaden this focus by discussing the pertinence of MCSs even when financial results are not the primary *raison d'être* of the organization, such as in non-profit organizations, or where there are broader missions or concerns beyond the financial realm, such as regarding sustainability and corporate social responsibility.

Notes

1 See, for example, and selectively only, "Royal Bank of Scotland Fined £56m for IT Meltdown," *Financial Times* (November 20, 2014), online at on.ft.com/14PBtV9.

2 See, for example, and selectively only, "Banks Braced for Additional £22bn in PPI Claim Payout," *Financial Times* (April 4, 2016), online at on.ft.com/1VoDSwj.

3 See, for example, and selectively only, "BNP Paribas Made Ethical and Legal Mistakes, Says Chairman," *Financial Times* (February 15, 2015), online at on.ft.com/1ITIql4.

4 Too many articles on the LIBOR scandal have appeared in the press to make a sensible selection. For a taste, and indicatively only, type "Libor Investigation" in the search box on next.ft.com.

5 See, for example, and selectively only, "Hong Kong Market Regulator Fines RBS for Trading Control Failure," *Bloomberg* (April 22, 2014), online at bloom.bg/1VKR9l2; "London Whale Complains of Unfair Blame for $6.2bn JPMorgan Losses," *Financial Times* (February 23, 2016), online at on.ft.com/1SR98Ek.

6 See, for example, and selectively, "BNP Paribas Made Ethical and Legal Mistakes, Says Chairman," op. cit.; "HSBC Monitor Says Bank's Compliance Progress Too Slow – Bank Needs to Do More to Fix Corporate Culture, Update Technology, Compliance Monitor Says," *The Wall Street Journal* (April 1, 2015), online at on.wsj.com/1ajxzqz.

7 "FSA Fines UBS £29.7 Million for Significant Failings in Not Preventing Large Scale Unauthorized Trading," *Financial Services Authority* (November 26, 2012), online at www.fsa.gov.uk/library/communication/pr/2012/105.shtml or at www.fsa.gov.uk.

8 Ibid.

9 "Libor Probe Said to Expose Collusion, Lack of Internal Controls," *Bloomberg* (February 15, 2012), online at www.bloomberg.com.

10 "HSBC Reveals Problems with Internal Controls," *The New York Times* (July 12, 2012), online at nyti.ms/NO7PkC.

11 "Bank Litigation Costs Hit $260bn – with $65bn More to Come," *Financial Times* (August 23, 2015), online at on.ft.com/1JHtT1P.

12 "Bankers Not Only Ones Pushing Ethical Boundaries," *Financial Times* (September 25, 2015), online at on.ft.com/1FmAXiS.

13 "Boardroom Politics at Heart of VW Scandal," *Financial Times* (October 4, 2015), online at on.ft.com/1hiU1CQ.

14 "Atlanta's Schools – the Reckoning," *The Economist* (April 6, 2013), online at www.economist.com.

15 "Accounting Scandal Set to Shake Up Toshiba," *Financial Times* (July 16, 2015), online at on.ft.com/1fMNz7h.

16 "Scathing Report Says Toshiba CEOs Had Role in Accounting Scandal," *Financial Times* (July 20, 2015), online at on.ft.com/1KgFnZB.

17 "Toshiba Chief Hisao Tanaka Resigns over $1.2bn Accounting Scandal," *Financial Times* (July 21, 2015), online at on.ft.com/1edzVbE.

18 "Bankers Not Only Ones Pushing Ethical Boundaries," op. cit.

19 "Atlanta's Schools – the Reckoning," op. cit.

20 "Deutsche Bank in $6bn 'Fat Finger' Slip-Up," *Financial Times* (October 19, 2015), online at on.ft.com/1QMFz2q.

21 "Bank of England Moves to Stamp Out 'Fat Finger' Errors," *Financial Times* (June 14, 2015), online at on.ft.com/1JNEF5M.

22 "Bank Clerk Nods Off with Finger on Keyboard and Gives Away £189m," *Evening Standard* (June 11, 2013), p. 3.

23 "Two Accused of INS Shredding Spree," *The Los Angeles Times* (January 31, 2003), p. B5.

24 "The Road to Perdition: Are the EU's Financial Controls so Exasperating that They Force Its Own Staff to Evade Them?," *The Economist* (July 24, 2003), p. 39.

25 For an academic article on the various concepts of management control, see T. Malmi and D. A. Brown, "Management Control Systems as a Package – Opportunities, Challenges and Research Directions," *Management Accounting Research*, 19, no. 4 (December 2008), pp. 287–300. For a lighter reading, see also "How Not to Lose Control," *Finance & Management*, 242 (April 2016), pp. 14–15, online at www.icaew.com.

26 For a classic text, see, for example, M. E. Porter, *Competitive Advantage: Creating and Sustaining Superior Performance* (New York: The Free Press, 1985), Chapter 2.

27 "Why CEOs Fail," *Fortune* (June 21, 1999), online at www.businessbuilders.bz/why-ceos-fail.pdf. See also "How to Execute a New Business Strategy Successfully," *Financial Post* (August 8, 2013), online at natpo.st/21Klsrs.

28 M. Hall, Y. Millo, and E. Barman, "Who and What Really Counts? Stakeholder Prioritization and Accounting for Social Value," *Journal of Management Studies*, 52, no. 7 (November 2015), pp. 907–34.

29 See R. E. Freeman, *Strategic Management: A Stakeholder Approach* (Cambridge: Cambridge University Press, 2010). See also "Shareholders vs. Stakeholders: A New Idolatry," *The Economist* (April 24, 2010), online at econ.st/KA1p7h; "Analyse This," *The Economist* (April 2, 2016), online at econ.st/1V9hSFB.

30 "Keep Sight of Your Vision," *The Sunday Times* (March 23, 2008), online at www.business.timesonline.co.uk.

31 Ibid.

32 A seminal framework for "strategy analysis" is that by M. E. Porter, *Competitive Strategy: Techniques for Analyzing Industries and Competitors* (New York: The Free Press, 1980). A seminal contributor to the "emergent strategy" view is H. Mintzberg, "Crafting Strategy," *Harvard Business Review*, 65, no. 4 (July–August 1987), pp. 66–75. For a recent edition of a textbook on strategic management, see R. M. Grant, *Contemporary Strategy Analysis*, 9th ed. (Chichester, UK: Wiley, 2016). For a recent empirical study on the "ongoing riddle" of formal and/or emergent planning practices, see R. B. Bouncken, V. Fredrich, and R. Pesch, "Configurational Answer to the Ongoing Riddle of Formal and/or Emergent Planning Practices," *Journal of Business Research*, 69, no. 9 (September 2016), pp. 3609–3615.

33 "Keep Sight of Your Vision," op. cit.

34 Ibid.

35 Ibid.

36 R. S. Kaplan and D. P. Norton, *Execution Premium* (Boston, MA: Harvard Business School Press, 2008); see also D. C. Hambrick and J. W. Fredericksen, "Are You Sure You Have a Strategy?," *Academy of Management Executive*, 15, no. 4 (November 2001), pp. 48–59.

37 "A Good Manager Must Be More Than a Messenger," *The New York Times* (May 30, 2013), online at nyti.ms/12Skw5l.

38 *KPMG 2005/2006 Integrity Survey* (KPMG LLP, 2005).

39 World-at-Work, Sibson, and Synygy, *The State of Performance Management* (Survey Report, August 2004); and J. Kochanski and A. Sorensen, "Managing Performance Management," *Workspan* (September 2005), pp. 21–6.

40 *KPMG 2013 Integrity Survey* (KPMG LLP, 2013), p. 16, online at www.kpmg.com/CN/en/IssuesAndInsights/ArticlesPublications/Documents/Integrity-Survey-2013-O-201307.pdf.

41 "The Other Side of Paradise," *The Economist* (January 16, 2016), online at econ.st/1URPB3P.

42 A [university] staff survey (2016); source withheld for confidentiality reasons.

43 F. Taylor, *The Principles of Scientific Management* (New York: Harper, 1929).

44 "Employee Fraud Is a Growing Problem, Survey Shows," *The Australian* (June 25, 2010), online at www.adelaidenow.com.au.

45 "PWC Survey Shows Rise in Fraud by Public-Sector Staff," *The Independent* (July 4, 2010), online at www.independent.co.uk.

46 *KPMG 2013 Integrity Survey*, op. cit.

47 "Are Employees Wasting Time Online?" PCWorld.com (August 2, 2001); see also "These Charts Show What We're Not Doing because We're Online All the Time," *Business Insider* (October 21, 2013), online at read.bi/16qZVGz.

48 *Association of Certified Fraud Examiners – 2016 Report to the Nations* (ACFE, 2016), online at www.acfe.com/rttn2016.aspx (hereafter *ACFE 2016 Report*).

49 See, for example, "Bank Litigation Costs Hit $260bn – with $65bn More to Come," op. cit.

50 *KPMG 2013 Integrity Survey*, op. cit.; *ACFE 2016 Report*, op. cit.

51 "Thou Better Not Steal," *Forbes* (November 7, 1994), p. 170.

52 "Crime Is Headed Up – and So Is Business," *Boston Globe* (February 15, 1983), p. 47.

53 *KPMG 2013 Integrity Survey*, op. cit.

54 For a recent study of "configurations" of the various types of MCSs that organizations employ, see, for example, D. S. Bedford and T. Malmi, "Configurations of Control: An Exploratory Analysis," *Management Accounting Research*, 27, no. 2 (June 2015), pp. 2–26. For another recent study in a non-profit setting that pertinently illustrates the "inter-relatedness" of pay-for-performance, autonomy (related to *incentives* or *results controls*), and mission congruence (related to *personnel/cultural control*), see M. A. Barrenechea-Méndez and A. Ben-Ner, "Mission Congruence, Incentives and Autonomy: An Empirical Analysis of Child-Care Facilities in Minnesota, the U.S.," *Working Paper* (2016), online at papers.sioe.org/paper/848.html.

55 "Poorly Trained Finance Worker Makes $152m Flub," *CFO.com* (January 14, 2008), online at ww2.cfo.com.

56 "Bank of America Finds a Mistake: $4 Billion Less Capital," *The New York Times* (January 14, 2008), online at nyti.ms/1mR3FLb.

57 "Not So Funny: Booking Revenues, Like Comedy, Is All about Timing," *The Economist* (September 27, 2014), online at econ.st/1qxwvPw.

58 For a flavor of research in this area of behavioral economics, see, for example, R. Thaler, *Misbehaving: The Making of Behavioral Economics* (London: Allen Lane, 2015).

59 "German Regulator Warns Deutsche Bank on Commodity Trading," *Financial Times* (June 19, 2014), online at on.ft.com/T9Xacd.

60 "Companies Take to The Cloud for Flexible Solutions," *Financial Times* (January 28, 2014), online at on.ft.com/1evKHmS.

61 Oliver Williamson is generally recognized as the most prominent theoretical contributor in the area of transaction cost economics, and went on to win the Nobel Prize in Economics for it in 2009. For a layman's overview of some of the key ideas behind his seminal contributions, see "Reality Bites," *The Economist* (October 15, 2009), p. 92.

62 For a more detailed discussion and overview of the issues related to inter-organizational controls, see S. W. Anderson and H. C. Dekker, "The Role of Management Controls in Transforming Firm Boundaries and Sustaining Hybrid Organizational Forms," *Foundations and Trends in Accounting*, 8, no. 2 (November 2014), pp. 75–141.

63 "Rio Tinto Shifts to Driverless Trucks in Australia," *Financial Times* (October 19, 2015), online at on.ft.com/1W1IJGh.

64 See, for example, "Medical Robotics: To the Point," *The Economist* (April 11, 2015), online at econ.st/1JpkkjU.

65 "Curbing Those Long, Lucrative Hours," *The Economist* (July 22, 2010), p. 66.

66 "Banks Speed Up Shift to Forex Automation," *Financial Times* (June 22, 2014), online at on.ft.com/1lhky2N.

67 "Google's Self-Driving Cars Get Boost from U.S. Agency," *Bloomberg* (May 30, 2013), online at www.bloomberg.com.

CASE STUDY
Leo's Four-Plex Theater

Leo's Four-Plex Theater was a single-location, four-screen theater located in a small town in west Texas. Leo Antonelli bought the theater a year ago and hired Bill Reilly, his nephew, to manage it. Leo was concerned, however, because the theater was not as profitable as he had thought it would be. He suspected the theater had some control problems and asked Park Cockerill, an accounting professor at a college in the adjacent town, to study the situation and provide suggestions.

Park found the following:

1. Customers purchased their tickets at one of two ticket booths located at the front of the theater. The theater used general admission (not assigned) seating. The tickets were color coded to indicate which movie the customer wanted to see. The tickets were also dated and stamped "good on day of sale only." The tickets at each price (adult, child, matinee, evening) were prenumbered serially, so that the number of tickets sold each day at each price for each movie could be determined by subtracting the number of the first ticket sold from the ending number.
2. The amounts of cash collected were counted daily and compared with the total value of tickets sold. The cash counts revealed, almost invariably, less cash than the amounts that should have been collected. The discrepancies were usually small, less than $10 per cashier. However, on one day two weeks before Park's study, one cashier was short by almost $100.
3. Just inside the theater's front doors was a lobby with a refreshment stand. Park observed the refreshment stand's operations for a while. He noted that most of the stand's attendants were young, probably of high school or college age. They seemed to know many of the customers, a majority of whom were of similar ages, which was not surprising given the theater's small-town location. But the familiarity concerned Park because he had also observed several occasions where the stand's attendants either failed to collect cash from the customers or failed to ring up the sale on the cash register.

4. Customers entered the screening rooms by passing through a turnstile manned by an attendant who separated the ticket and placed part of it in a locked 'stub box.' Test counts of customers entering and leaving the theater did not reconcile either with the number of ticket sales or the stub counts.

Park found evidence of two specific problems. First, he found a few tickets of the wrong color or with the wrong dates in the ticket stub boxes. And second, he found a sometimes significant number of free theater passes with Bill Reilly's signature on them. These problems did not account for all of the customer test count discrepancies, however. Park suspected that the ticket collectors might also be admitting friends who had not purchased tickets, although his observations provided no direct evidence of this.

When his study was complete, Park sat down and wondered whether he could give Leo suggestions that would address all the actual and potential problems, yet not be too costly.

This case was prepared by Professor Kenneth A. Merchant.

CASE STUDY
Wong's Pharmacy

Thomas Wong was the owner/manager of Wong's Pharmacy, a small, single-location drugstore. The store was founded by Thomas's father, and it had operated in the same location for 30 years. All of the employees who worked in the store were family members. All were hard workers, and Thomas had the utmost trust in all of them.

Although the store thrived in its early years, performance in the last few years had not been good. Sales and profits were declining, and the problem was getting worse. The performance problems seemed to have begun approximately at the time when a large drugstore chain opened a branch two blocks away.

This case was prepared by Professor Kenneth A. Merchant.

CASE STUDY
Private Fitness, Inc.

"I don't know how much money I might have lost because of Kate. She is a long-time friend whom I thought I could trust, but I guess that trust was misplaced. Now I've got to decide whether or not to fire her. And then I've got to figure out a way to make my business work effectively without my having to step in and do everything myself."

Rosemary Worth was talking about the consequences of a theft that had recently occurred at the business she owned, Private Fitness, Inc. Private Fitness was a small health club located in Rancho Palos Verdes, California, an upscale community located in the Los Angeles area. The club offered personal fitness training and fitness classes of various types, including aerobics, spinning, body sculpting, air boxing, kickboxing, hip hop, step and pump, dynamic stretch, Pilates, and yoga. Personal training clients paid $50 per hour for their instructor and use of the club during prime time. During slower times (between 9:00 a.m. and 4:00 p.m.) the price was $35 per hour. The price per student for each hour-long fitness class was $12. Some quantity discounts were offered to clients who prepaid. Unlike the large health clubs, Private Fitness did not offer memberships for open access to fitness equipment and classes.

Prior to starting Private Fitness, Rosemary had been working as an aerobics instructor and fitness model. She had won many local fitness competitions and was a former finalist in the Ms. Fitness USA competition. She wanted to go into business for herself to increase her standard of living by capitalizing on her reputation and knowledge in the growing fitness field and to have more time to spend with her two young children. Private Fitness had been operating for six months.

To open the club, Rosemary had to use almost all of her personal savings, plus she had to take out a bank loan. The building Rosemary rented, located in a convenient strip mall with ample parking, had formerly been operated as a fresh food market. Rosemary spent about $150,000 to renovate the facility and to buy the necessary fitness equipment. The club was comprised of five areas: an exercise room, a room containing aerobic equipment (e.g. treadmills, stair climbers, stationary bicycles, cross-country ski machines), a room containing weight machines and free weights, men's and ladies' locker rooms, and an office.

Rosemary contracted with five instructors she knew to run the classes and training sessions. The instructors were all capable of running personal training sessions, but they each tended to specialize in teaching one or two types of fitness classes. Rosemary herself ran most of the spinning classes and some of the aerobics classes. The instructors were paid on commission. The commission, which ranged between 20% and 50% of revenue, varied depending on the instructor's experience and on whether the instructor brought the particular client to Private Fitness.

As manager of the business, Rosemary hired Kate Hoffman, one of the instructors and a long-time friend. Kate's primary tasks included marketing, facility upkeep, scheduling of appointments, and record keeping. Kate was paid a salary plus a commission based on gross revenues. During normal business hours when Kate was teaching a class, one of the other instructors, or sometimes a part-time clerical employee, was asked to staff the front desk in return for an hourly wage. Private Fitness was open from 5:30 a.m. to 9:00 p.m., Monday through Friday. It was also open from 6:00 a.m. to noon on Saturday and noon to 3:00 p.m. on Sunday.

Rosemary was still in the process of building the volume necessary to operate at a profit. Typically, one or two private fitness clients were in the facility during the prime early morning and early evening hours. A few clients came in at other times. Classes were scheduled throughout the times the club was open. Some of these classes were quite popular, but many of them had only one or two students, and some classes were cancelled for lack of any clients. However, Kate's marketing efforts were proving effective. The number of clients was growing, and Rosemary hoped that by the end of the year the business would be earning a profit.

As the quote cited above indicates, however, Rosemary gradually realized that Kate Hoffman was stealing from the club. On one occasion when Rosemary came to the club she noticed $60 in the cash drawer, but she noticed when she was leaving that the drawer contained only $20. She asked Kate about it, and Kate denied that there had been $60 in the drawer. Rosemary wondered if other cash amounts had disappeared before they had been deposited at the bank. While some clients paid by credit card or check, others, particularly those attending fitness classes, often paid cash.

Rosemary became very alarmed when, during a casual conversation with one of the other instructors, the instructor happened to mention to Rosemary some surprising "good news." The good news was that Kate had brought in a new private fitness client who was working out in the 1:00–2:00 p.m. time period on Monday, Wednesday, and Friday. Kate was doing the training herself. However, Rosemary checked the records and found no new revenues recorded because of this new client. She decided to come to the club during the period to see if this client was indeed working out. Since the client was there and no revenue entry had been made, she confronted Kate. After first explaining that she had not yet gotten around to making the bookkeeping entry, Kate finally admitted that this client had been writing her checks out to Kate directly, in exchange for a discount. Kate said that she was very sorry and that she would never be dishonest again.

Rosemary realized she had two major problems. First, she had to decide what to do with Kate. Kate was a valuable instructor and a longtime friend, but her honesty was now in question. Should she forgive Kate or fire her? Second, Rosemary also realized that she had an operating problem. She did not want to step in and assume the managerial role herself because she had significant family responsibilities to which she wanted to be able to continue to attend. But how could she ensure that her business received all the revenues to which it was entitled without being on site at all times herself? Should she leave Kate, who promised not to steal again, in the manager position? Or should she hire one of the other instructors, or perhaps a non-instructor, to become the manager? And in either case, were there some procedures or controls that she could use to protect her business's assets?

This case was prepared by Professor Kenneth A. Merchant.

CASE STUDY
Atlanta Home Loan

In late 2002, Albert (Al) Fiorini was becoming more and more frustrated and depressed. In September 2002, he had taken a leave of absence to return to school to earn his MBA, and he had trusted some employees to run the mortgage lending business he had founded. Now it was clear to Al that those employees had schemed to wrest control of the business away from him. And amazingly, they seemed to have been successful. Al lamented, "They didn't just steal some of my assets. They stole my whole business!" Being 2,500 miles away and busy with his studies, Al felt nearly powerless to stop them. He had spent many sleepless nights wondering what he could and should do to get his business back. He also thought about where he went wrong – what he should have done to prevent this problem from happening in the first place.

The company

Atlanta Home Loan (hereafter AHL) was a mortgage lending and financing company based in Atlanta, Georgia. Al Fiorini founded the company in April 2002, with an initial investment of about $40,000. He started operating the company from his home.

Al had many years of experience in the mortgage banking industry. He had worked for several different companies and had also served a year as president of the Orange County Chapter of the California Association of Mortgage Brokers. Under his direction, AHL's business grew rapidly in its first quarter of operation. By the summer of 2002, the company consisted of four telemarketers and eight loan officers, all of whom worked from their homes. "Telecommuting" was convenient for the employees because Atlanta was a large city with heavy traffic.

Al established banking relationships that allowed AHL clients to borrow money at wholesale rates. The actual loan terms varied depending on the clients' FICO scores.[1] In summer 2003, banks might offer an AHL client with a very high FICO score (over 620) a rate of 6.25–6.75% on a fixed 30-year mortgage. This rate provided the bank with an operating margin of 1.5% to 2.0%. AHL earned a fee of 1.50% of the loan amount for every loan funded. This provided AHL with an average revenue per loan of $3,200.

[1] FICO® scores provide a numeric representation of an individual's financial responsibility, based on his or her credit history. FICO scores are based on a scale from 300 to 900. Most individuals actually have three FICO scores, one from each national credit bureau (Equifax, Experian, TransUnion). These three FICO scores are the measure that most lenders look at when evaluating credit or loan applications. FICO is an acronym for Fair Isaac Credit Organization, the developer of the credit-rating analytics.

AHL bought leads from list brokers for $0.20 per name. These lists provided information as to whether the individuals owned their homes; if so, when they bought their homes; and when, if ever, they had refinanced their mortgages.

The telemarketers called people on the lead lists to assess their interest in refinancing. Al knew from industry experience that telemarketers should generate a minimum of one lead per hour. They were paid a combination of an hourly wage plus a performance bonus ($10.00) for each lead produced. Since most of them worked part-time, AHL's telemarketers generated, on average, about four new leads per person per day.[2] They gave the leads, the potential clients' names, to Al Fiorini. Al distributed the names to AHL's loan officers.[3]

The loan officers helped the prospective clients to fill out their loan applications and to assemble the needed backup documents, such as W-2s, pay stubs, and bank statements. After the clients' information had been collected, office support personnel, called "loan processors," would order an appraisal and a credit report, open escrow, and independently verify the financial information. After all the information was collected and verified, the completed file would then be submitted to the prospective lenders either electronically or in paper form.

AHL did not yet have electronic links to the processors' files that would allow monitoring of the progress of the applications before they were submitted. Capabilities for those links were being put into place. However, each application required a credit inquiry, so Al monitored the activities of his loan officers by tracking the number of credit inquiries each requested. This provided him with an early indication of how many applications were being submitted. The loan application/lead ratios varied from 5% to 20% depending on the skill of the loan officer. Al also closely monitored these ratios and their trends.

In the mortgage lending industry, a 30% "fallout ratio" (the proportion of loans submitted to processing that were not funded) was typical. AHL's fallout ratio was slightly less than 30%.

Once approved, the legal loan documents were prepared. At that time, Al knew the revenue due to his company and the fees due to the loan officer involved. AHL paid the loan officers 40% of this total loan revenue on loans that AHL originated, and 60% on loans they originated (by generating their own leads). At closing, AHL received its funds directly from the proceeds. A broker's check would be overnight mailed to AHL's office, or the money would be wired directly into AHL's general account.

Back to school

For years Al had been thinking about earning an MBA degree. In June 2002, he was admitted to the executive MBA (EMBA) program at the University of Southern California in Los Angeles, and he decided to enroll. While in California, he planned to start another mortgage lending company.

Al had several options for AHL. He could find someone to run it; he could try to sell it; or he could shut it down. If he chose to shut it down, he would turn the unfunded applications over to a contract processing firm. The contract processing firm would be responsible for ordering credit reports and appraisals and for interfacing with the escrow companies and attorneys until the loans were funded. For its services, this firm would charge AHL $300–$400 per contract.

But Al decided that he did not want to close AHL. It was a profitable business with considerable growth potential. In September 2002 alone, AHL loan officers were preparing to submit 30–40 new applications to banks for funding, and the volume of business was continuing to grow. Al enlisted the services of a business broker who placed a value of $600,000 on the company. However, Al doubted that he had enough time to find a buyer before he left for California. He decided to find someone to operate the company in his absence.

A partner

Joe Anastasia[4] was one of AHL's loan officers. He had 20 years' experience in the mortgage lending business. Although Al had known him for only about two months, his initial judgments about Joe were quite favorable. Joe seemed to have excellent sales ability; he was people-oriented; and he was knowledgeable about all areas of mortgage lending and financing. On his resume, he described himself as "dependable and honest." Before joining AHL, Joe had worked for 10 years as vice president of operations for a sizable financial corporation

[2] AHL also developed leads from the Internet, as it operated the website www.lowerrate.com.

[3] In Georgia, unlike in some other states, loan officers are not licensed.

and had previously operated his own mortgage service company for three years. Since Joe joined AHL, he had closed a higher loan volume than any of the other loan officers.

Impressed by Joe's background and performance, Al decided to make Joe a deal to be his partner. In July 2002, Al and Joe reached a verbal partnership agreement. Joe would invest $8,400, which was used to rent an office and to purchase some office equipment, and Joe and Al would share AHL's profits equally.

Curiously, however, on the day when the two partners were to meet their new landlord, Joe did not show up for the meeting. Al could not find him for two days.[5] In the first 10 working days after becoming Al's partner, Joe showed up in the office only three times.

Al did not feel comfortable letting Joe continue to run the company. Two weeks after their partnership agreement had been struck, he made Joe a deal. In exchange for terminating their agreement, Al agreed to pay Joe 100% of the fees earned on loans that Joe closed. Al then brought in an acquaintance, one with banking experience, to run AHL in his absence, but this manager lasted only three days before quitting. Faced with limited options and desperate to find someone to run the company before he left for Los Angeles the next day, Al turned again to his first option – Joe. Joe apologized for his absences with the admittedly weak excuse that "he had been partying, but it wouldn't happen again." So Al and Joe reinstated the previous agreement. When Al left for Los Angeles in August 2002, AHL had 90 loan applications in the pipeline, constituting nearly $300,000 in potential revenue.

Al started monitoring AHL from afar. He learned that in the following two weeks, Joe went to the office only four times. One day he took a large batch of loan files home and did not return to the office for three days.

A new partner and licensing agreement

In September 2002, Al made a final decision that he could not trust Joe. He turned to Wilbur Washington, to whom Al had been introduced by Joe several months earlier. Like Al and Joe, Wilbur had considerable experience in mortgage banking. Al judged quickly that Wilbur would be quite good at sales. He had the requisite knowledge, and "he was smooth." On the basis of these quick judgments, on September 1, 2002, Al signed a written partnership and licensing agreement with Wilbur. This agreement stated that Al would offer Wilbur the use and privileges of AHL as an ongoing business until he returned, and Wilbur would provide AHL with his management services. AHL would make commission payments to Wilbur at 100% on all loans closed less a monthly licensing fee of $5,000 or 10% of all revenue, whichever was greater. Wilbur would also be responsible for interviewing and hiring all new loan officers, paying the expenses of running the office, and managing the entire staff.

Wilbur asked for authority to sign checks written against AHL's main bank account, but Al refused. Instead, as a gesture of good faith, Al left with Letitia Johnson (the office manager) four signed, blank checks written against the main account. Al's instructions to Letitia were that the checks were not to be used without Al's permission.

Letitia had been with Al since May 2002. She had effectively managed the telemarketers and had demonstrated her loyalty to Al. In August 2002, because of slow funding loans, Al was unable to pay Letitia her full salary. He asked her whether she would like to find employment elsewhere or go through the hardship with AHL. Letitia responded that she would like to stay with AHL. Al promised to pay Letitia the deferred part of her salary as soon as some loans got funded, which they did in September. Al trusted Letitia.

Later that month, when Joe found out what was happening, he became quite upset. Not only was he no longer the managing partner of AHL, he thought Al owed him a lot of money. He wanted his $8,400 investment back. But Al refused to pay him until he returned all of AHL's leads and loan files in his possession. Not only had his dereliction of duty caused AHL great harm, but none of Joe's loans had closed since August, which Al found suspicious.[6] In response, Joe filed a civil lawsuit demanding payment.[7]

[4] All names, with the exception of Al Fiorini's, are disguised.

[5] Al found out later that Joe had a problem with alcoholism.

[6] Al later also found out that Joe had used a friend to close his loans, which violated legal regulations for the mortgage business. Another reason for Al's suspicion was that one of AHL's loan officers had originated a loan and asked Joe to bring it to the office, but Joe never brought it in.

[7] The court dismissed this lawsuit on December 5, 2002.

Monitoring from California

While he was no longer managing the day-to-day operations of the company, Al continued to monitor AHL's operations closely. Daily, or as soon as the information was available, he tracked the employee head count, the number of leads produced, credit inquiries requested, loan applications funded, office expenses, and bank activity. Al was also on the phone three to four hours per day talking with employees and, particularly, loan officers. He thought that this would allow him to monitor the employees' emotional states, an important leading indicator of forthcoming company performance. Al also had all of AHL's corporate mail forwarded to his California address. Al was particularly concerned about Wilbur keeping overhead expenses in line with production levels so that he would be able to pay the employees, to whom Al continued to feel a responsibility, as well as Al himself.

In late September, Wilbur hired a new loan processor. Al knew from experience that every loan officer believes that there is never enough processor time available to get "his" particular loan documents completed on a timely basis. But Al's experience also told him that each processor should be able to fund 20 loans per month, so the company needed only one processor for every four loan officers. Al thought that Wilbur was now employing one, or maybe even two, too many processors and/or salaried, overhead personnel. He sent Wilbur a note telling him that his processor-to-loan-officer ratio was too high. But Wilbur reacted angrily. He told Al "not to tell him what to do," that he was managing the company in the best way he saw fit.

Subsequent events

At the time Wilbur took over the operation of AHL, four loans, which would generate total revenues of $11,700, were about to be funded. This amount was supposed to be wired into AHL's main corporate checking account at Bank of America (BofA). When the loans funded, however, on October 1, 2002, without Al's permission, Wilbur personally collected the four checks himself from the closing attorneys, pooled them together, and deposited them into BofA. After depositing the checks, Wilbur immediately wrote checks to himself and Letitia for the entire amount of $11,700 using the four pre-signed checks Al had left.[8] However, since Wilbur wrote the checks against uncleared funds, the checks bounced.

Al had been monitoring the activity in the BofA account on the Internet from Los Angeles. He noticed that the four checks had been written without his knowledge and that they had all bounced. He immediately called Wilbur for an explanation. Wilbur told Al that he had withdrawn money from the account to pay the employees. Al did not believe this explanation, in part because the checks were made out to Wilbur and not run through the payroll account where payroll taxes would be withheld if the checks were meant for employees. On October 7, 2002, Al sent a fax and certified letter to Wilbur and Letitia and also spoke directly to them, ordering them not to write any more checks without his permission and to make sure that there were sufficient funds in the account to cover the checks they wrote. With the returned check charges, the main AHL account was already $1,533.09 overdrawn.

Al also called BofA to stop payments on the four checks and asked the bank to transfer the funds from the general checking account to a side payroll account to which Wilbur would not have access. However, Wilbur managed to release the stop payments on the checks. He transferred the money from the payroll account back into the general account and cashed the checks. Bank personnel apparently assumed that Wilbur had authority over the account since he had deposited the funds in the first place.

Angry and frustrated, Al decided that he could no longer trust Wilbur and could not do business with him. On October 9, 2002, Al asked a friend of his who used to be a sales manager in the mortgage company that Al had worked for previously to act as his agent. The friend was to go to AHL's office and fire all the employees. Among other things, Al was particularly concerned that AHL had over 100 client files with sensitive personal information that might be misused. However, when Al's agent went to the AHL premises to fire the employees, they all refused to go. Al called in the police to support the firing action, but when they arrived, Wilbur told the police that he was the owner, not Al. Not knowing who was telling the truth, the police just left.

On October 14, 2002, Al sent a letter to all 100+ AHL clients whose loans were in process that the company had to drop their applications. The key phrase in the letter was, "We are no longer going to be able to service your application."

[8] Al found out later that Wilbur and Letitia were actively dating.

On October 15, Wilbur opened a new account at Citizens Bank & Trust (CBT) in Atlanta, a bank where he did his personal business and where he knew the manager personally. Wilbur wired the funds being held in AHL's corporate name at the offices of the closing attorneys into this new bank account. He now had signing authority over the checks.

Al discovered the second bank account when a "Welcome" letter from CBT arrived to his California address. Al was outraged that personnel at CBT did not ask Wilbur for any corporate documents:

> Wilbur showed no documentation whatsoever . . . You would expect highly regulated institutions like banks to provide better protection for the public, but . . .

Al immediately called bank personnel and informed the manager that Wilbur had opened a fraudulent account with CBT. But CBT refused to freeze the account or return the money. As a last resort, Al informed the Atlanta police and the FBI, thinking that they might be interested in this identity theft case. However, possibly due to the relatively small amount of money involved, neither the police nor the FBI gave the case any attention.

To make things worse, the day Wilbur opened the fraudulent bank account at CBT, he also filed two applications for warrants for Al's arrest. Wilbur claimed that Al was the one who had taken the proceeds received from the closing attorneys out of the company's accounts. Al had to return twice to Atlanta to defend himself. Both cases were dismissed, but Al incurred over $7,500 in legal fees and travel costs, and he wasted substantial time and energy dealing with these frivolous lawsuits.

During all this time, the AHL personnel were maintaining their daily routines. Wilbur renegotiated a lease with the landlord and established AHL as his own company. Al suspected that Wilbur had used all of his means of persuasion to mislead the employees in order to break their bonds with Al. Al received his $5,000 licensing fee in September, but that was the last money he received. By December, Al realized that he had already lost at least $15,000 in licensing fees, and possibly more that might have been realized from the funding of the loans in the pipeline. Moreover, he had lost his company. Al said, sadly, "I have no idea how much revenue ended up being taken in my name."

Sensing defeat, Al finally asked the Georgia Department of Banking and Finance to withdraw AHL's mortgage banking license. Not only had he lost his business and his income, he had also lost his credit rating since he had incurred bills that he was unable to pay. And in February 2003, Al was forced to sell his home.

In the summer of 2003, Al had still not decided what he should do. Should he fight to regain control over AHL? But what was left of it? Perhaps only about $25,000 worth of equipment. Or should he give up, let these crooks get away with it, and try to rebuild somewhere else?

Al also pondered how he had gotten into this mess. What might he have done to prevent this disaster from happening?

This case was prepared by Professors Kenneth A. Merchant and Wim A. Van der Stede, and research assistant Clara (Xiaoling) Chen.

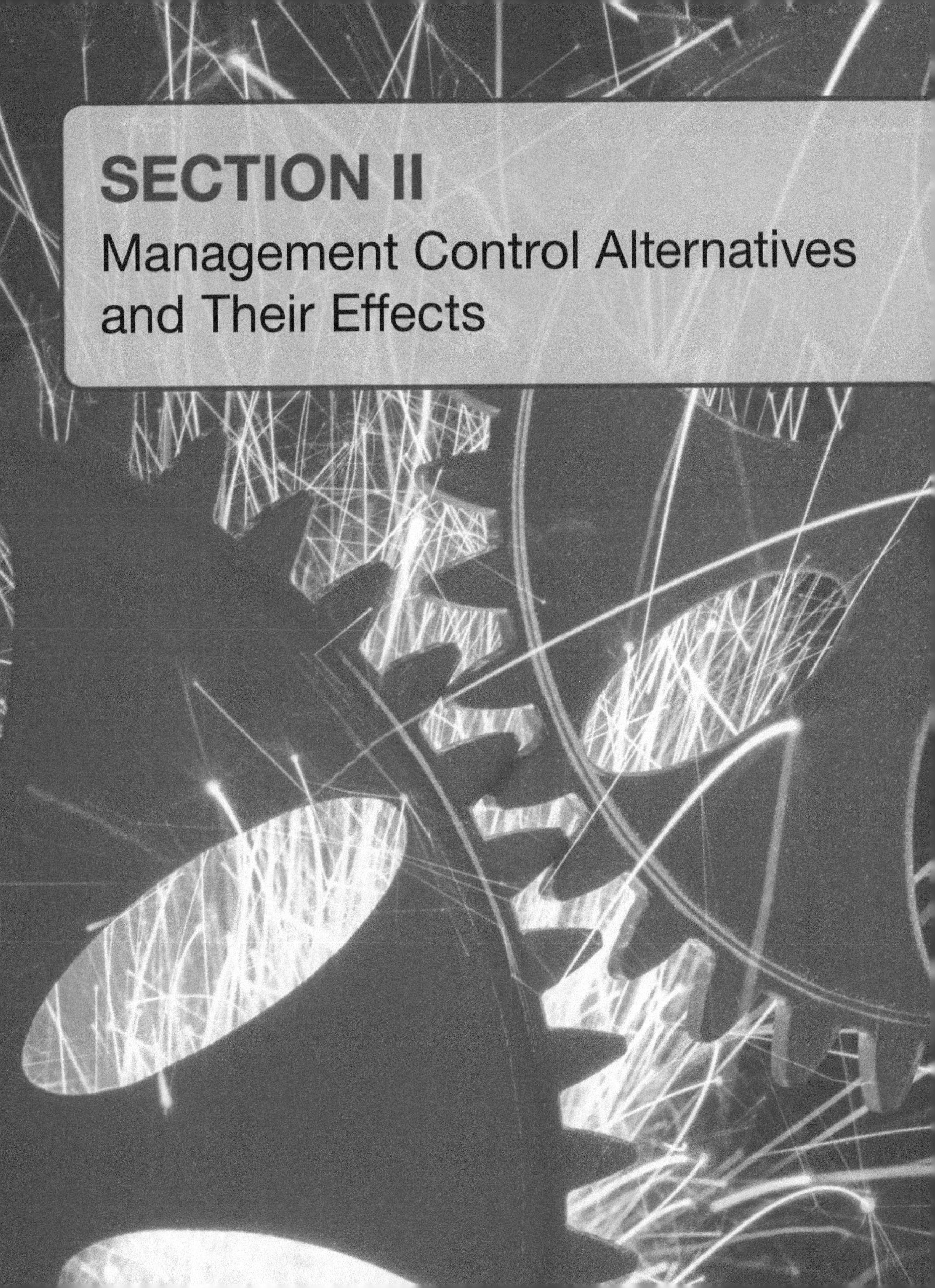

SECTION II

Management Control Alternatives and Their Effects

CHAPTER 2
Results Controls

If asked to think about powerful ways to influence behavior in organizations, most people would probably think first about pay-for-performance, which is no doubt an effective motivator. For example, at Thor Industries, a large recreational vehicle manufacturer, CEO Wade Thompson attributes much of the company's success to its incentive compensation system. Among other things, the company shares 15% of each division's pretax profits with the division managers, because, Mr. Thompson explained, "I want every one of our company heads to feel like it is their business, in their control. If they don't perform, they don't get paid very much. If they do, there is no cap to what they can make."[1] Indeed, Vicky Wright, managing director at Hay Group, a compensation consultancy firm, argues:

> [Many] companies on the Most Admired list [a list of companies produced annually by *Fortune*] have chief executives who understand what performance measurement is all about. It's about learning how to motivate people – how to link those performance measures to rewards.[2]

Pay-for-performance is a prominent example of a type of control that can be called *results control* because it involves rewarding employees for generating good results. Identifying what are *good* results, as we will see, is crucial. Indeed, following the financial crisis through to today, pay-for-performance systems, especially in banks, have received a hard look, in part because, rather than producing "good" results, they have been bashed for having bred "bonus cultures" of *greed* and *short-termism*. Even the chief executives of such major banks as Barclays admitted that their bonus systems were overly "geared," created temptations for employees to "cut corners," and may have backfired through "ethical lapses," while the chief executive of Deutsche Bank touched on the basic underlying motivational effect of bonuses by contemplating that "[he] ha[d] no idea why [he] was offered a contract with a bonus in it because [he couldn't imagine he would] work any harder or any less hard in any year, in any day because someone is going to pay [him] more or less."[3]

Nonetheless, even in the aftermath of the financial crisis, investors, regulators, and politicians did not indiscriminately call to do away with pay-for-performance; rather, their calls for reform were typically directed at making compensation *more closely* tied to *sound* performance, particularly long-term value creation.[4]

Setting aside possible idiosyncrasies of the financial sector, where one could argue that good employees work hard every day in other organizations without monster bonuses, results controls of the pay-for-performance variety are widely used, even increasingly so in the non-profit sector. For example, the National Health and Hospitals Reform Commission in Australia argued that the fee-for-service system of healthcare rebates often fails to promote the most effective treatments because doctors get paid for each consultation or clinical activity regardless of whether the patient recovers well or not. In considering how to reform this system, the Commission recommended to link the pay of doctors and nurses to measures of how well they treat their patients or how quickly they are seen.[5] Similar initiatives to create "accountable care organizations" by providing extra rewards for efficiency and quality performance have also been considered elsewhere, particularly in the United States.[6] "The idea is to see whether shifting financial incentives for hospitals can make people healthier and save the U.S. money before Medicare's hospital trust fund becomes depleted, which could happen by 2024."[7]

Clearly, designers of results controls of the pay-for-performance variety have "good" results (e.g. long-term value creation) – even perhaps lofty results (e.g. making people healthier and saving a country's healthcare system from ruin) – in mind when implementing them, brought about through the motivational, results-driven effects such systems purportedly can have. Anecdotal as well as research evidence, however, have repeatedly thrown the potency of these systems into sharp relief by suggesting that either they have weak or no effects or, where they do, they can produce the wrong results or have severe unintended consequences.

Even so, and despite, perhaps, a prevalent emphasis on *pay*-for-performance in many contexts, the rewards that can be linked to results go far beyond monetary compensation. Other rewards that can be usefully tied to measured performance include job security, promotions, autonomy, plum assignments, and recognition. (We discuss the vast array of rewards that can be given more fully in Chapter 9.)

Furthermore, results controls create *meritocracies.* In meritocracies, the rewards are given to the most talented and hardest-working employees, rather than to those with the longest tenure or the right social connections. At Koch Industries, a conglomerate, results controls are seen as the "secret sauce" with two main ingredients – meritocracy and operational efficiency. Charles Koch, its boss, is proud to proclaim that "workers can earn more than their bosses [and] high-school-educated farm boys from Kansas can rise faster than Ivy League MBAs" based on their performance.[8]

The combinations of rewards linked to results inform or remind employees as to what result areas are important and motivate them to produce the results the organization rewards. Results controls influence actions or decisions because they cause employees to be concerned about the *consequences* of their actions or decisions. The organization does not dictate to employees what actions or decisions they should take; instead, employees are *empowered* to take those actions or decisions they believe will best produce the desired results. Results controls also encourage employees to discover and develop their talents and to get placed into jobs in which they can perform well.

For all these reasons, well-designed results control systems can help produce the results desired. A review of studies on the use of incentives to motivate performance found an average gain in performance of about 22% stemming from the use of incentive programs.[9] Like all other forms of controls, however, results controls do not operate in isolation[10] and, equally, cannot be used in every situation. They are effective only where the desired results can be clearly defined and adequately measured by the organization, and where the measured results can be sufficiently controlled by the employee.[11] We discuss the conditions for the effective use of results controls in greater depth in this chapter.

Prevalence of results controls

Results controls are commonly used for controlling the behaviors of employees at many organizational levels. They are a necessary element in the employee *empowerment* approach to management, which became a major management trend starting in the 1990s.[12] Results controls are particularly dominant as a means of controlling the behaviors of *professional employees*; those with *decision authority*, like managers. Reengineering guru Michael Hammer even defines a professional as "someone who is responsible for achieving a result rather than [for] performing a task."[13]

Results controls are consistent with, and even necessary for, the implementation of decentralized forms of organization with largely autonomous entities or responsibility centers (which we discuss in more detail in Chapter 7). For example, business pioneer Alfred Sloan observed that he sought a way to exercise effective control over the whole corporation yet maintain a philosophy of decentralization.[14] At General Motors (and numerous other companies that followed), the results controls under Sloan's leadership were built on a return-on-investment (ROI) performance measure (which we discuss in more detail in Chapter 10). By using this type of control system, corporate management could review and judge the effectiveness of the various organizational entities while leaving the actual execution of operations to those responsible for the performance of the decentralized entities – the entity managers.

Many large corporations have gone through the process of instituting decentralized forms of organization with a concurrent increased emphasis on results control. For example, DuPont replaced a complex management hierarchy by splitting the company into 21 *strategic business units* (SBUs), each of which operates as a free-standing unit. The SBU managers were given greater responsibility and asked to be more entrepreneurial and more customer-focused. They were also asked to bear more risk, because a large portion of SBU managers' compensation was based on SBU performance (sales and profitability). The managers noticed the change. One SBU manager said, "When I joined DuPont [21 years ago], if you kept your nose clean and worked hard, you could work as long as you wanted. [But today] job security depends on results."[15] The change was perceived as being successful: A *Business Week* article noted that, "The image of DuPont has morphed from giant sloth to gazelle."[16]

In 2010, Sanofi-Aventis, a large pharmaceutical company, divided its vast resources into decentralized disease-based units, each with its own departments for research and development, regulatory affairs, marketing, and sales – a plan designed to identify promising drugs more quickly and weed out failures before spending large amounts of money on unsuccessful drugs. One industry expert noted that "the [model of] fully independent units, operating under the parent company's umbrella, [constitutes] a break from the traditional big pharma business model, and represents companies' interest in duplicating the flexibility and cost-efficiencies of small biotech and biotech-like companies."[17] By establishing accountability for a fully integrated entity's results, where the entity manager closest to the business makes the tradeoffs and takes responsibility over the entity's budget, the company aims to instill a "performance culture" that encourages both operating discipline (efficiency) and greater responsiveness to local business needs (flexibility).

In other words, decentralization attempts to replicate an "entrepreneurial model" within typically large corporations, where entity managers are given decision authority but then held responsible for the results that their decisions produce. Accountability for results was exactly the driving motive behind a recent reorganization into "reporting segments" at Air Products Chemicals Inc., a large industrial gases producer, which Seifi Ghasemi, Air Products' chief executive, claimed would retain Air Products' leadership position through "a decentralized, simpler, and more efficient structure which creates true profit and loss (P&L) accountability at many levels of the organization."[18]

Similarly, when Nick Reilly became CEO in late 2009 of troubled Opel, the German car manufacturer owned by General Motors, he announced that he wanted to encourage an entrepreneurial spirit at Opel by delegating most decisions to country heads and dismantling GM's bureaucratic style of centralized management that fostered a "debilitating culture of passing the buck." "It might seem obvious, but it isn't the way GM was managed and there was definitely some confusion about who was accountable," he said. "From the top line of revenue to the bottom line of profit, this is now the responsibility of the managing directors of the major entities," Reilly added.[19]

However, managers will act in an entrepreneurial manner necessary to thrive in competitive environments not only if they are subjected to the same market forces and pressures that drive independent entrepreneurs, but also if they are promised commensurate rewards for the risks they bear from doing so. As such, Richard Chandler, founder of Sunrise Medical, a medical products company, defended his company's decentralized organization and lucrative incentives by stating that "people want to be rewarded based on their own efforts. [Without divisional accountability] you end up with a system like the U.S. Post Office. There's no incentive [for workers to excel]."[20]

Results controls need not be limited to management levels only; they can also be driven down to lower levels in the organization, as many companies have done with good effects. Lincoln Electric, a worldwide leader in the production of welding products, serves as the poster child of companies that use results controls down to the lowest organizational level. Lincoln Electric provides wages based solely on piecework for most factory jobs and lucrative performance-based bonuses that can more than double an employee's pay.[21] This incentive system has created such high productivity that some of the industry giants (General Electric, Westinghouse) found it difficult to compete in Lincoln Electric's line of business (arc welding) and exited the market. A *Business Week* article observed that "in its reclusive, iconoclastic way, Lincoln Electric remains one of the best-managed companies in the United States and is probably as good as anything across the Pacific."[22] And even though Lincoln's legendary *Incentive Performance System* has essentially remained the same since it was installed in 1934, the company is still acclaimed for its systems and performance today, such as in the book *The Modern Firm*.[23]

Whereas decentralization is an effective way to empower employees in a results-control context, there can, and even should, be limits to empowerment in certain circumstances. One problem is infighting, as exemplified at Sears, a struggling US retailer. Edward Lampert, the investor who had tried for eight years to turn around the company, "divided Sears into more than 30 units, each with their own presidents, chief marketing officers, boards of directors and profit-and-loss statements, which former executives say has caused infighting."[24]

Other issues stem from loss of economies of scale or increased costs and inefficiencies, or even inconsistencies, and complexity. This is reflected in the situation that Alex Gorsky, a 21-year Johnson & Johnson veteran who was named CEO in April 2012, inherited:

> **The J&J that Gorsky inherited was superficially easy to understand: 40% of sales came from drugs, another 40% from medical devices, and the rest from consumer products. Dig deeper and it was unimaginably complex: 275 operating companies, 450 distribution centers, more than 120 manufacturing sites, 500 outside manufacturers, and 60 enterprise resource-planning systems. It was more a flotilla of speedboats than a single ship. In the past, that famous decentralization inspired entrepreneurial thinking. Lately, it caused quality-control problems that bedeviled the company.[25]**

Gorsky said: "We have to be more decisive and disciplined, and more efficient. Otherwise, it is too complex, and it costs too much." Part of that was addressing decentralization: Gorsky introduced a program to centralize procurement, which would enhance J&J's buying power. He also ordered up new quality and compliance controls to ensure consistent standards.[26]

Decentralization may also increase overlap, and curiously, it "may also create more opportunities for corruption by increasing the number of decision makers with the power to exploit the decision-making process for personal gain."[27] For example, when pursuing rapid growth in China, French hypermarket Carrefour faced systemic corruption among its management ranks at the local levels. Unlike the centralized approach to management that Wal-Mart employed in China, Carrefour empowered local managers to take charge of virtually all aspects of running their stores, including product pricing and promotions, supplier selection, and store design. Whereas this high degree of flexibility gave ample leeway for managers to expand fast in the early stages of building the chain, it also encouraged widespread bribe-taking at the local level and, over time, led to higher operating costs and reputation risk than would a centralized system.[28]

But decentralization puts decision making closest to where the detailed knowledge and understanding of the business resides, allowing greater responsiveness. "A decentralized structure provides better information over time, which helps decision-making and accountability," said Lambert of Sears,[29] and echoed by Airbus chief Fabrice Bregier:

> Now is the time to give a little bit more power to local teams in our countries, in our programs, in our plants [as] we need to take decisions faster. This is a weakness of Airbus. It takes much too long to make decisions, I want to speed it up and simplify it.[30]

The chief executive at China's Huawei, Ren Zhengfei, put it as follows:

> The future model is to give the biggest say to our local teams who are closest to our customers and empower them so they have flexibility in interaction with customers. The headquarters or corporate functions will change into a more supporting and service function.[31]

And at Samsonite, the luggage maker, chief executive Tim Parker said:

> I think we were trying to run a very centralized business in a marketplace where our consumers differed enormously. We had to decentralize our decision-making. So we created an Asian business, a Europe business and an American business, and that allowed each management team to concentrate on local customers.[32]

The multitude of examples above also illustrate that firms can decentralize by geographical regions, business groups or segments, product lines, or a variety of other lines of delegation in their organization structure. One critical point, however, is that *decentralization* or "delegation of decision rights" to managers, and the design of *incentive systems* to motivate these managers to generate the desired results, are two critical organizational design choices in a results-control context; they are part of what organizational theorists call the *organizational architecture*. This literature maintains that organizational choices about decentralization and incentive systems should be made *jointly*, and that concentrating on one element to the exclusion of the other will lead to poorly designed organizations.[33]

Results controls and the control problems

Results controls provide several preventive-type benefits. Well-defined results inform employees as to what is expected of them and encourage them to do what they can to produce the desired results. In this way, the results controls alleviate a potential lack of direction. Results controls also can be particularly effective in addressing motivational problems. Even without direct supervision or interference from higher up, the results controls induce employees to behave so as to maximize their chances of producing the results the organization desires. This motivational effect arises particularly when incentives for producing the desired results also further the employees' own personal rewards. Finally, results controls also can mitigate personal limitations. Because results controls typically promise rewards for good performers, they can help organizations to attract and retain employees who are confident about their abilities.

Results controls also encourage employees to develop their talents to position themselves to earn the results-dependent rewards.[34]

The performance measures that are a part of the results controls also provide some non-motivational, detection-type control benefits of a cybernetic (feedback) nature, as was mentioned in Chapter 1. The results measures help managers answer questions about how various strategies, organizational entities, and/or employees are performing. If performance fails to meet expectations, managers can consider changing the strategies, the processes, or the managers.[35] Investigating and intervening when performance deviates from expectations is the essence of a *management-by-exception* approach to management, which large organizations commonly use.

Elements of results controls

The implementation of results controls involves four steps: (1) defining the dimension(s) on which results are desired; (2) measuring performance in the chosen dimensions; (3) setting performance targets for employees to attain for each of the measures; and (4) providing rewards for target attainment to encourage the behaviors that will lead to the desired results. While these steps are easy to list, executing them effectively can be challenging.

Defining performance dimensions

Defining the right performance dimensions involves balancing an organizations' responsibilities to all of their stakeholders, including owners (equity holders), debtholders, employees, suppliers, customers, and the society at large. Should a firm's sole aim be to maximize shareholder returns, or should it also, or even primarily, be customer- or employee-focused? Are these performance foci mutually exclusive, or are they rather mutually reinforcing?[36] Where do performance dimensions such as innovation and sustainability belong? And so on.

As challenging as defining the desired performance dimensions may be, it is equally critical to choose performance measures that are *congruent* or *aligned* with the chosen performance dimensions because the goals that are set and the measurements that are made will shape employees' views of what is important. Phrased differently, *what you measure is what you get*. For example, firms may define one of their desired performance dimensions to be shareholder value creation, and yet measure performance in terms of accounting profits. This implies that employees are likely to try to improve the *measured performance* (in this example, accounting profits) regardless of whether or not it contributes to the *desired performance* (in this example, shareholder value). We discuss this problem, and the difficulties related to this particular example, further in Chapters 5, 10, and 11.

Similarly, firms may aim to pursue innovation, yet they end up measuring patents filed. Anxious to promote innovation, many companies offer incentives to their employees to develop patentable ideas, and such incentives are likely to produce results in the form of an increase in the number of patents filed. But as Tony Chen, a patent attorney with Jones Day in Shanghai, notes, "patents are easy to file, but gems [can be] hard to find in a mountain of junk."[37]

Citibank's chief executive, Michael Corbat, slightly rephrased this adage by proclaiming that "*you are what you measure*."[38] He felt he needed to measure performance in five categories to try to alleviate the singular focus of managers on one measure, exactly because *you get what your measure*. His plan was welcomed by an analyst who commented that "the most important job of a CEO is to make sure that the right incentives are in place [because] improper measures lead to improper behavior."[39] We discuss the use of multiple measures of performance, such as by way of so-called scorecards, which Mr. Corbat advocated at Citibank, in Chapter 11.

The problem of misalignment has also been at the heart of some of the work by Jean Tirole, the 2014 Nobel Prize winner in economics. Tirole examines the undesirable consequences that performance-dependent incentives in the measured areas can have, either by skewing how employees approach their jobs, shifting effort away from less-easily measured (and hence unrewarded) tasks such as long-term investments, employee development, and within-firm cooperation; or by undermining work ethic by encouraging excessive risk-taking, inducing "managed" performance or producing "fudged" performance metrics.[40] The first part of this problem – the skewing part – is known in the literature as the *multitasking* problem, and we discuss it in more detail in Chapter 5.

Even though *Bloomberg* concluded that "there's a role for Tirole to advise on how to structure compensation without inciting the kind of disastrous risk-chasing that sparked the financial crisis,"[41] this important congruence problem also surfaces in many other sectors, including the non-profit sector. For example, a study by the Home Office in the United Kingdom found that organized trafficking was a "thriving industry" that "makes a killing," amassing healthy profits with little risk of detection. The study suggested that one of the reasons for this was the ill-defined performance targets that the police had to meet. Solving high volumes of simple crimes such as petty thefts and home burglaries is easier and cheaper than the long-drawn-out and expensive police work that is needed to crack down on trafficking rings. Even though the goal was to reduce crime, the result may have been that hardened criminals were let off.[42]

Hence, not only do firms need to decide what is desired, but they also must ensure that their measurements of the desired performance dimensions are aligned with what is desired. If they are not, the results controls are likely to encourage employees to produce *undesired* results. The results controls can then be said to have *unintended consequences.*

Measuring performance

As per the above, then, measurement is a critical element of a results-control system. The object of the measurement is typically the performance of an organizational entity or an employee during a specific time period. Many *objective* financial measures, such as net income, earnings per share, and return on assets, are in common use. So, too, are many objective nonfinancial measures, such as market share, customer satisfaction, and the timely accomplishment of certain tasks. Some other measurements involve *subjective* judgments involving assessments of qualities; for example, "being a team player" or "developing employees effectively."

Performance measures typically vary across organizational levels. At higher organizational levels, most of the key results are defined in either stock market terms (such as share price) and/or financial or accounting terms (such as a return on equity). Lower-level managers, on the other hand, are typically evaluated in terms of operational measures that are more controllable at the local level. The key result areas for a manager in charge of a manufacturing site, for example, might be a combination of measures focused on production efficiency, inventory control, product quality, and delivery time. The variation in the use of financial and operational performance measures between higher- and lower-level management creates a *hinge* in the management hierarchy. That is, at some critical middle organizational level, often a profit center level (see Chapter 7), managers must translate financial goals into operational goals. These managers' goals are defined primarily by financial measures, so their communications with their superiors are primarily in financial terms. But because their subordinates' measures are primarily operational, their downward communications are primarily in operational terms.

If managers identify more than one result measure for a given employee, they must attach *weightings* to each measure so that the judgments about performance in each result area can be aggregated into an overall evaluation. The weightings can be additive. For example, 60% of the overall evaluation is based on return on assets and 40% is based on sales growth. The weightings can also be multiplicative. For example, achievement of profit and revenue goals might be multiplied by a score assessed on the basis of environmental responsibility. If the environmental responsibility score is less than 70%, say, the multiplier is zero, yielding no bonus. Sometimes, organizations make the weightings of performance measures *explicit* to the employees, as in the example just presented. Often, however, the weightings are partially or totally *implicit*, such as when the performance evaluations are done subjectively. Leaving the weighting implicit blurs the communication to employees about what results are important. Employees are left to infer what results will most affect their overall evaluations. That said, evidence suggests that implicit weights can generate improvements in performance and, thus, can be effective as an alternative, or at least complement, to the explicit weighting of performance measures in incentive contracts.[43]

Setting performance targets

Performance targets are another important results-control element because they affect behavior in two ways. First, they improve motivation by providing clear goals for employees to strive for. Most people prefer to be given a specific target to shoot for, rather than merely being given vague statements like "do your best" or "work at a reasonable pace."[44] Second, performance targets allow employees to assess their performance. People do not respond to feedback unless they are able to interpret it, and a key part of interpretation involves comparing actual performance relative to target. The targets distinguish strong from poor performance. Failure to achieve the target signals a need for improvement. (We discuss performance targets and target setting processes in more detail in Chapter 8.)

The following example illustrates both points. Maria Giraldo, a nurse in the intensive care unit at Long Island Jewish Medical Center, used to be evaluated on such criteria as leadership, respectfulness, and how well she worked with others. A few years ago, her hospital implemented a new computer-based performance system that broke down her job description into quantifiable goals, such as to keep infection rates for her unit low and patient satisfaction scores high, all relative to specific target levels. Ever since this new system was implemented, at review time, the discussion does not linger on about how Ms. Giraldo had performed. Either she hit the targets, or she did not. The clarity about measures and goals, and the reviews "by the numbers" that they allow, changed Ms. Giraldo's views about success and what she needs to do to get ahead in her career – all for the better, she believed.[45] (In Chapter 9, we discuss the drawbacks of relying exclusively on objective, formulaic performance evaluations in more detail.)

Providing rewards

Rewards or *incentives* are the final element of a results-control system. The rewards included in incentive contracts can come in the form of anything employees value, such as salary increases, bonuses, promotions,[46] job security, job assignments, training opportunities, freedom, recognition, and power. Punishments are the opposite of rewards. They are things employees dislike, such as demotions, supervisor disapproval, failure to earn rewards that colleagues earn, or, at worst, dismissal.

Organizations can elicit motivational effects from linking the prospect of rewards (or punishment) to results that employees can influence. For example, organizations can use any of a number of *extrinsic rewards*. They can grant additional monetary rewards, such as in the form of cash or stock. They can use non-monetary rewards, such as by granting high-performing employees public recognition and more decision authority. Alternatively, in entities where performance is mediocre or poor, they can threaten to reduce the decision authority and power that managers derive from managing their entities or decline to fund proposed projects.

Results measures can provide a positive motivational impact even if no rewards are explicitly linked to results measures. People often derive their own internally generated *intrinsic rewards* through a sense of accomplishment for achieving the desired results. For example, when William J. Bratton became the New York City police commissioner, he gave his police force one clear, simple goal: cut crime.[47] (Previously the thinking had been that crime was due to societal factors beyond the department's control, so the police were measured largely by how quickly they responded to emergency calls.) He also implemented a results-control system. He decentralized the department by giving the 76 precinct commanders the authority to make most of the key decisions in their police units, including the right to set personnel schedules, and he started collecting and reporting crime data daily. Even though Commissioner Bratton legally could not award good performers with pay raises or merit bonuses, the system was deemed effective. In the subsequent two years, major felonies in New York fell first by 12% and then a further 18%, respectively. This clearly could not have been attributable to pay-for-performance in the strictest sense; it was instead due, at least in part, to providing officers with clear goals and empowering them to go about fighting crime. Seeing the results of their initiatives may have given police officers a sense of accomplishment and a greater intrinsic motivation to perform well.

The motivational strength of any of the extrinsic or intrinsic rewards can be understood in terms of several motivation theories that have been developed and studied for over 50 years, such as *expectancy theory*. Expectancy theory postulates that individuals' motivational force, or effort, is a function of (1) their *expectancies*, or their belief that certain outcomes will result from their behavior (e.g. a bonus for increased effort); and (2) their *valences*, or the strength of their preference for those outcomes. The valence of a bonus, however, is not always restricted to its monetary value; it also may have valence in securing other valued items, such as status and prestige.[48]

Organizations should promise their employees the rewards that provide the most powerful motivational effects in the most cost-effective way possible. But the motivational effects of the various forms of reward can vary widely depending on an individual's personal tastes and circumstances. Some people are greatly interested in immediate cash awards, whereas others are more interested in increasing their retirement benefits, increasing their autonomy, or improving their promotion prospects. Reward tastes also vary across countries for a number of reasons, including differences in cultures and income tax laws.[49] However, if organizations can tailor their reward packages to their employees' individual preferences, they can provide meaningful rewards in a cost-efficient manner. But tailoring rewards to individuals or small groups within a large organization is not easy to accomplish and is sometimes even seen as possibly, or even legally, inequitable. A tailored system will likely be complex and costly to administer. When poorly implemented, it can easily lead to employee perceptions of unfairness and potentially have the opposite effects of those intended: demotivation and poor employee morale. We discuss the choice of different forms of incentives and incentive system design in more detail in Chapter 9.

Conditions determining the effectiveness of results controls

Although they are an important form of control in many organizations, results controls cannot always be used effectively. They work best only when *all* of the following conditions are present:

1. Organizations can determine what results are desired in the areas being controlled;
2. The employees whose behaviors are being controlled have significant influence on the results for which they are being held accountable; and,
3. Organizations can measure the results effectively.

Knowledge of desired results

For results controls to work, organizations must know what results are desired in the areas they wish to control, and they must communicate the desired results effectively to the employees working in those areas. *Results desirability* means that more of the quality represented by the results measure is preferred to less, everything else being equal.

As we alluded to earlier, even if one might agree that (one of) the primary objective(s) of for-profit firms or corporates is to maximize shareholder value, this does not imply that the desired results, even if the overall objective is understood, will be unequivocally known or have unambiguous meaning at all intermediate and lower levels in the organization. The disaggregation of overall organizational objectives into specific expectations for all employees lower in the hierarchy is often difficult. Different parts of the organization face different tradeoffs.

For example, purchasing managers create value by procuring good-quality, low-cost materials on time. These three result areas (quality, cost, and schedule) can often be traded off against each other, and the overall organizational objective to maximize profit provides little guidance in making these tradeoffs. The importance of each of these results areas may vary over time and among parts of the organization depending on differing needs and strategies. For example, a company (or entity) short of cash may want to minimize the amount of inventory on hand, which may make scheduling the dominant consideration. A company (or entity) with a cost leadership strategy may want to emphasize the cost considerations. A company (or entity) pursuing a unique product quality image or differentiation strategy may emphasize meeting or exceeding the specifications of the materials being purchased. Thus, to ensure proper purchasing manager behaviors, the importance orderings or weightings of these three results areas must be made clear and aligned with the strategy.

If the wrong results areas are chosen, or if the right areas are chosen but given the wrong weightings, the combination of results measures will not be *congruent* with the organization's intended objectives. Using an incongruent set of results measures may then result in motivating employees to take the wrong actions. In the above setting, for example, ill-guided cost considerations may damage the company's pursued product-quality reputation.

Ability to influence desired results (controllability)

A second condition that is necessary for results controls to be effective is that the employees whose behaviors are being controlled must be able to affect the results in a material way in a given time period. This *controllability principle* is one of the central tenets of responsibility accounting (which we discuss in more detail in Chapters 7 and 12). Here are some representative expressions that have stood the test of time of this perennial principle:

> **It is almost a self-evident proposition that, in appraising the performance of divisional management, no account should be taken of matters outside the division's control.[50]**

> **A manager is not normally held accountable for unfavorable outcomes or credited with favorable ones if they are clearly due to causes not under his control.[51]**

The main rationale behind the controllability principle is that results measures are useful only to the extent that they provide information about the desirability of the actions or decisions that were taken. If a results area is totally uncontrollable, the results measures reveal nothing about what actions or decisions were taken. Partial controllability makes it difficult to infer from the results measures whether or not good actions or decisions were taken.

In most organizational situations, of course, numerous uncontrollable or partially uncontrollable factors inevitably affect the measures used to evaluate performance. These uncontrollable influences hinder efforts to use results measures for control purposes. As a consequence, it becomes difficult to determine whether the results achieved are due to the actions or decisions taken or, rather, to uncontrollable factors or *noise*. Good actions and decisions will not necessarily produce good results. Bad actions or decisions may similarly be obscured.

In situations where many significant, uncontrollable influences affect the available results measures, results control is not effective. Managers cannot be relieved of their responsibility to respond to some uncontrollable factors or be exempted from dealing with reasonable or normal uncertainty in their environment; but if these factors, or the uncertainty, are difficult to separate from the results measures, results controls do not provide good information for either evaluating performance or motivating good behaviors. We discuss the methods that organizations use to cope with uncontrollable factors in results-control systems in more detail in Chapter 12.

Ability to measure controllable results effectively

Ability to measure the controllable results effectively is the final constraint limiting the feasibility of results controls. Often the controllable results that the organization desires, and that the employees involved can affect, cannot be measured effectively. In virtually all situations, *something* can be measured; but often, however, the key results areas cannot be measured *effectively*.

The key criterion that should be used to judge the effectiveness of results measures is the ability to evoke the desired behaviors. If a measure evokes the right behaviors in a given situation – that is, if the measure can be said to be *congruent* with the desired results area – then it is a good control measure. If it does not, it is a bad one, even if the measure accurately reflects the quantity it purports to represent; that is, even if the measurement has little measurement error.

To evoke the right behaviors, in addition to being *congruent* and *controllable*, results measures should be *precise*, *objective*, *timely*, and *understandable*. Even when a measure has all of the above qualities, it should also be *cost efficient*; that is, the costs of developing and using the measure should be considered.

Precision

Measurements inevitably contain error, some random, some systematic. Error makes the measurement inaccurate. Measurement *accuracy* refers to the degree of closeness of measurements of a quantity to its actual (true) value. *Precision* is the degree to which repeated measurements under similar conditions show the same result; if they do, the measurements can be said to be *reliable*. Using a bull's-eye analogy, *accuracy* describes the closeness of arrows (measurement) to the target (true value). When all arrows are grouped tightly together, the cluster of arrows (measurement) is considered *precise* since they all struck close to the same spot, even if not necessarily near the bull's-eye.

Reducing systematic error (or *bias*) improves accuracy but does not change precision. However, it is not possible to achieve accuracy in measurement without precision; that is, when the measures contain mostly random error or, thus, when they are unreliable. In other words, and in the bull's-eye analogy, if the arrows are not grouped close to one another, they cannot all be close to the bull's-eye. Therefore, lack of precision is an undesirable quality for a results measure to have. But even precise measures that are biased (i.e. that contain systematic error) may not be of great use for control purposes. If the degree of the systematic error is not known; then the measurement will be systematically *biased* by either showing greater or lesser values than the actual value (see the next section on *objectivity*).

It is obvious that some aspects of performance (such as social responsibility, leadership acumen, and personnel development) are difficult, or even impossible, to measure precisely, either because the measurements contain random error or are systematically biased (such as may be the case when subjective performance evaluations are used). Precision, therefore, is important because without it, the measure loses much of its information value. Imprecise measures increase the risk of misevaluating performance. Employees will react negatively to the inequities that inevitably arise when equally good performances are rated differently.

Objectivity

An *objective* measure here means that it is not influenced by personal feelings, mental states, emotions, tastes, or interpretations – hence, that it is *unbiased*. Measurement objectivity will be inevitably suspect where either the choice of measurement rules or the actual measuring is done by the persons whose performances are being evaluated. Low objectivity is likely, for example, where performance is self-reported or where evaluatees are allowed considerable discretion in the choice of measurement methods. Indeed, and referring to the earlier definition related to measurement precision, low objectivity is likely to introduce systematic error due to, for example, selectivity, leniency, or lack of self-criticalness. If that is the case, the measurement may be precise, but it will not be accurate. Good measures for control purposes therefore should be both precise (reliable) and objective (unbiased).

There are two main ways to increase measurement objectivity. The first is to have the measuring done by people independent of the processes that generate the results, such as by personnel in the controller's department. The second is to have the measurements verified by independent parties, such as auditors.

Timeliness

Timeliness refers to the lag between the employee's performance and the measurement of results (and the provision of rewards based on these results). Timeliness is an important measurement quality for two reasons. The first is motivational. Employees need repeated performance pressure to perform at their best. The pressure helps ensure that the employees do not become complacent, inattentive, sloppy, or wasteful. Measures, and thus rewards, that are delayed for significant periods of time lose most of their motivational impact. The sustained pressure can also encourage creativity by increasing the likelihood that employees will be stimulated to repeatedly search for new and better ways to improve results.

As *The Financial Times* noted about deferred bonuses in banks, "beloved by the regulators because they allow the payout to be adjusted if conditions change, [they do, however,] reduce the motivational value of bonuses – by the time the employees receive the money they may not remember what was being rewarded,"[52] making it also unlikely that the rewards will affect or adjust the behaviors that led to those results.

A second advantage is that timeliness increases the value of interventions that might be necessary. If significant problems exist but the performance measures are not timely, it might not be possible to intervene to fix the problems before they cause (more) harm.

Understandability

Two aspects of *understandability* are important. First, the employees whose behaviors are being controlled must understand what they are being held accountable for. This requires communication. Training, which is a form of communication, may also be necessary if, for example, employees are to be held accountable for achieving goals expressed in new and different terms, such as when an organization shifts its measurement focus from accounting income to, say, economic value added (more on this in Chapter 11).

Second, employees must understand what they must do to influence the measure, at least in broad terms. For example, purchasing managers who are held accountable for lowering the costs of purchased materials will not be successful until they develop strategies for accomplishing this goal, such as improving negotiations with vendors, increasing competition among vendors, or working with engineering personnel to redesign certain parts. Similarly, employees who are held accountable for customer satisfaction must understand what their customers value and what they can do to affect it. The same holds for teachers in universities who often do not understand what specific teaching skills or approaches result in better (or worse) teaching evaluations by their students at the end of the term.

When employees understand what a measure represents, they are empowered to work out what they can do to influence it. In fact, this is one of the advantages of results controls: good control can be achieved without knowing exactly how employees will produce the results.

Cost efficiency

Finally, measures should be *cost efficient*. A measure might have all of the above qualities and yet be too expensive to develop or use (e.g. when it involves third-party surveys of customers, say, to collect the data), meaning that the costs exceed the benefits. When that is the case, the firm may need to settle for an alternative, more cost-efficient measure. Advances in technology and data analysis, such as related to "big data," have made data that had hitherto been hard to obtain or analyze more readily available. But data are not information, and these data do not uniformly have good properties, where much of it is unstructured. For example, understandability in terms of the claimed relationships with specific actions and decisions often is particularly problematic. And even objectivity can be an issue, perhaps surprisingly, because, as it has been said, "torture the data long enough and they will confess to anything."[53]

For example, California's MemorialCare Health System is part of a movement by hospitals around the United States to change how doctors practice by monitoring their progress toward goals. What is different this time, some hospital executives argue, is that "new technology enables closer, faster tracking of individual doctors," where MemorialCare is keeping detailed data on how the doctors perform on many measures, including adolescent immunizations, mammograms, and keeping down the blood-sugar levels of diabetes patients. The results are compiled, number-crunched, and eventually used to help determine how much money doctors will earn, where the new insurance payments also factor in quality goals. An assessment of this "doctor-data" system indicates that it has helped reduce the average stay for adult patients, trimmed the average cost per admitted adult patient, and led to improvements in indicators of quality, including patient re-admissions, mortality, and complications. This has not been uncontentious, however. Cardiologist Venkat Warren said that he worried that "some bean-counter will decide what performance is" and wondered whether doctors would be pushed to avoid older and sicker patients who might drag down their numbers.[54]

Overall, many measures cannot be classified as either clearly good (effective) or poor (ineffective). Different tradeoffs among the measurement qualities create some advantages and disadvantages. For example, measures can often be made more congruent, controllable, precise and objective if timeliness is compromised. Thus, in assessing the effectiveness of results measures, many difficult judgments are often necessary. These judgments are discussed in more detail throughout several chapters of this text.

Conclusion

This chapter described an important form of control, results control, which is used at many levels in most organizations. Results controls are an indirect form of control because they do not focus explicitly on the employees' actions or decisions. However, this indirectness provides some important advantages. Results controls can often be effective when it is not clear what behaviors are most desirable. In addition, results controls can yield good control while allowing the employees whose behaviors are being controlled high autonomy. Many people, particularly those higher in the organizational hierarchy but also so-called *knowledge workers*, value high autonomy and respond well to it, although they may not always respond well to the measures used, particularly when these suffer from significant weaknesses in terms of the various measurement properties we discussed.

Results controls are therefore clearly not effective in every situation. Failure to satisfy all three effectiveness conditions – knowledge of the desired results, ability to affect the desired results, and ability to measure controllable results effectively – will impair the results controls' effectiveness, if not render them impotent. Worse, it could produce dysfunctional side effects, various forms of which we discuss in later chapters.

That said, results controls usually are the major element of the management control system (MCS) used in all but the smallest organizations. However, results controls often are supplemented by action and personnel/cultural controls, which we discuss in the next chapter.

Notes

1 "Lord of the Rigs," *Forbes* (March 29, 2004), p. 68.

2 "Measuring People Power," *Fortune* (October 2, 2000), p. 186.

3 "Bank Bonuses: Bashing Ignores the Benefits for Investors," *Financial Times* (November 27, 2015), online at on.ft.com/1kXpBJ9.

4 Ibid. See also "Geithner: Link Executive Pay to Performance," *The Washington Times* (June 10, 2009), online at washingtontimes.com.

5 "Performance Pay Likely for Doctors," *The Australian* (May 6, 2009), online at www.theaustralian.com.au.

6 "Hospitals Prescribe Big Data to Track Doctors at Work," *The Wall Street Journal* (July 11, 2013), online at www.wsj.com.

7 "Medicare's $963 Million Experiment," *Business Week* (September 6, 2012), online at www.bloomberg.com.

8 "From Alpha to Omega," *The Economist* (August 15, 2015), online at econ.st/1J5S3AE.

9 S. J. Condly, R. E. Clark, and H. D. Stolovitch, "The Effects of Incentives on Workplace Performance: A Meta-Analytic Review of Research Studies," *Performance Improvement Quarterly*, 16, no. 3 (2003), pp. 46–63.

10 I. Friis, A. Hansen, and T Vamosi, "On the Effectiveness of Incentive Pay: Exploring Complementarities and Substitution between Management Control System Elements in a Manufacturing Firm," *European Accounting Review*, 24, no. 2 (2015), pp. 241–76.

11 As an example of several results-control issues that can arise when these conditions are not met, see S. Kerr, "The Best-Laid Incentive Plans," *Harvard Business Review*, 81, no. 1 (January 2003), pp. 27–40.

12 See, for example, K. H. Blanchard, J. P. Carlos, and W. A. Randolph, *The Three Keys to Empowerment* (San Francisco, CA: Berrett-Koehler Publishers, 1999). Also see "C. Oswick, "Engaging with Employee Engagement in HRD Theory and Practice," *Human Resource Development Review* (2015), pp. 1–9, particularly Figure 1, p. 2.

13 M. Hammer, *Beyond Reengineering: How the Process-Centered Organization is Changing Our Work and Our Lives* (New York: Harper Business, 1996).

14 A. P. Sloan, *My Years with General Motors* (New York: Doubleday, 1964).

15 "For DuPont, Christmas in April," *Business Week* (April 24, 1995), p. 130.

16 Ibid., p. 129.

17 "Sanofi Seeks Efficiencies with New Model," *The Boston Globe* (August 16, 2010), online at www.boston.com.

18 "Air Products Unveils Widespread Reorganization," *The Wall Street Journal* (September 18, 2014), online at on.wsj.com/1w5yrGy.

19 "In Break with Past, No More Passing the Buck at Opel," *Reuters* (December 6, 2009), online at www.reuters.com.
20 R. H. Chandler, quoted in "Sunrise Scam Throws Light on Incentive Pay Programs," *The Los Angeles Times* (January 15, 1996), p. D3.
21 The details of Lincoln Electric's legendary *Incentive Performance System* are described in the case bearing the company's name at the end of Chapter 4. See also "Ohio Firm Relies on Incentive-Pay System to Motivate Workers and Maintain Products," *The Wall Street Journal* (August 12, 1983), p. 23; and "Lincoln Electric: Where People Are Never Let Go," *Time* (June 18, 2001), p. 40. Today, the company's website states that "Every year since 1934, eligible employees have received a profit sharing bonus in December. Lincoln's pay-for-performance culture, rewards employees for their contributions to the success and profitability of the Company. The average bonus award over the last 10 years is 40% of an employee's year to date, base earnings" (www.lincolnelectric.com/en-us/company/careers/Pages/lincoln-tradition.aspx; accessed December 2015).
22 "This Is the Answer," *Business Week* (July 5, 1982), pp. 50–2.
23 J. Roberts, *The Modern Firm: Organizational Design for Performance and Growth* (New York: Oxford University Press, 2004).
24 "Lampert Cuts Sears Below 50% to Meet Redemptions," *Bloomberg* (December 4, 2013), online at bloom.bg/1RodSO2.
25 "Embracing the J&J Credo," *Barron's* (December 14, 2013), online at www.barrons.com.
26 Ibid.
27 "OECD Casts Doubt on Indonesia Growth View," *The Wall Street Journal* (September 27, 2012), online at on.wsj.com/1Oao9zG.
28 "Carrefour Contends with Bribes in China," *Forbes* (August 27, 2007), online at www.forbes.com.
29 "Lampert Cuts Sears Below 50% to Meet Redemptions," op. cit.
30 "Airbus Chief Bregier to Empower Local Sites in Company Overhaul," *Bloomberg* (September 10, 2012), online at www.bloomberg.com.
31 "Huawei's Chief Breaks His Silence," *Business Week* (May 9, 2013), online at www.bloomberg.com.
32 "Samsonite Sees Rapid Growth in Asia," *The Wall Street Journal* (December 29, 2013), online at on.wsj.com/1zDPRcr.
33 See, for example, J. Brickley, C. Smith, and J. Zimmerman, *Managerial Economics and Organizational Architecture* (Boston, MA: McGraw-Hill Irwin, 2001).
34 For the so-called "selection effect" benefits of (results) controls, see, for example, D. Campbell, "Employee Selection as a Control System," *Journal of Accounting Research*, 50, no. 4 (September 2012), pp. 931–66.
35 See, for example, D. Campbell, S. Datar, S. L. Kulp, and V. G. Narayanan, "Testing Strategy with Multiple Performance Measures: Evidence from a Balanced Scorecard at Store 24," *Journal of Management Accounting Research*, 27, no. 2 (Fall 2015), pp. 39–65.
36 "Shareholders vs. Stakeholders: A New Idolatry," *The Economist* (April 24, 2010), pp. 65–6.
37 "Patents, Yes; Ideas, Maybe," *The Economist* (October 14, 2010), pp. 78–9.
38 "Citi's CEO Is Keeping Score," *The Wall Street Journal* (March 4, 2013), online at www.wsj.com.
39 Ibid.
40 See, for example, R. Benabou and J. Tirole, "Bonus Culture: Competitive Pay, Screening and Multitasking," *Working Paper 18963* (Cambridge, MA: National Bureau of Economic Research, 2013).
41 "Banker Bonuses Get a Nobel Dis," *Bloomberg View* (October 13, 2014), online at bv.ms/1toxQQN.
42 "Making a Killing," *The Economist* (July 16, 2009), p. 36.
43 D. Campbell, "Nonfinancial Performance Measures and Promotion-Based Incentives," *Journal of Accounting Research*, 46, no. 2 (2008), 297–332.
44 G. P. Latham, "The Motivational Benefits of Goal-Setting," *Academy of Management Executive*, 18, no. 4 (November 2004), pp. 126–9.
45 "Performance Reviews by the Numbers," *The Wall Street Journal* (June 29, 2010), online at online.wsj.com.
46 See, for example, D. Campbell, "Nonfinancial Performance Measures and Promotion-Based Incentives," *Journal of Accounting Research*, 46, no. 2 (2008), 297–332.
47 "A Safer New York City," *Business Week* (December 11, 1995), p. 81.
48 V. H. Vroom, *Work and Motivation* (New York: Wiley, 1964).
49 E. P. Jansen, K. A. Merchant, and W. A. Van der Stede, "National Differences in Incentive Compensation Practices: The Differing Roles of Financial Performance Measurement in the United States and the Netherlands, *Accounting, Organizations and Society*, 34, no. 1 (January 2009), pp. 58–84.
50 D. Solomons, *Divisional Performance: Measurement and Control* (Homewood, IL: Richard D. Irwin, 1965), p. 83.
51 K. J. Arrow, "Control in Large Organizations," in M. Schiff and A. Y. Lewin (eds.), *Behavioral Aspects of Accounting* (Englewood Cliffs, NJ: Prentice Hall, 1974), p. 284.
52 "Bank Bonuses: Bashing Ignores the Benefits for Investors," op. cit.
53 "A Different Game: Information Is Transforming Traditional Businesses," *The Economist* (February 25, 2010), online at http://econ.st/KA1qb8.
54 "Hospitals Prescribe Big Data to Track Doctors at Work," op. cit.

CASE STUDY
Office Solutions, Inc.

In December 2014, Bob Mairena, president of Office Solutions, Inc., an office supply distributor based in Southern California, was considering making a significant change in the compensation plan for his sales personnel. The company's current compensation plan for all sales personnel was based on sales commissions, plus the potential for an incentive of 2–4% for achievement of some specific sales goals.

However, Bob had come to believe that a commission-based compensation system was appropriate only for the few individuals bringing in significant amounts of new business, those whom he called "hunters." Most of the company's salespeople were not hunters; they were not generating significant amounts of *new* business. They were more like account managers who, Bob thought, should be compensated with a lower-risk plan based on a relatively high proportion of guaranteed salary, supplemented with a performance-dependent bonus. Because of lower job pressure and more stable compensation, the account managers should be paid less than sales reps. Office Solutions could use the cost savings to funnel more money to the relatively few salespeople who were generating growth opportunities for the company. But Bob was not yet totally sure how the new system should be designed and what kind of transition would be required to get the salespeople comfortable with the change.

The company

Office Solutions, Inc., headquartered in Yorba Linda, California, sold and distributed a full range of office supplies to customers in Southern California, from San Diego in the south to Santa Barbara in the north. The company was founded in 1984 by a husband-and-wife team, Bob and Cindy Mairena.

Prior to starting Office Solutions, Bob worked for UPS and Cindy worked for an office supply company. Both Bob and Cindy had an entrepreneurial spirit and were looking for an opportunity to start their own business. They saw an opportunity in the early 1980s. Personal computers were just coming into prominence, creating a new need for computer supplies. Traditional office supply companies did not have the technical expertise to sell computer supplies effectively. Bob and Cindy prepared themselves by taking computer classes at night. By 1984, they had gained enough expertise to start a company called Data Extras, the predecessor to Office Solutions.

For several years, Data Extras successfully provided supplies to companies with computers. Eventually, however, computer supplies became a commodity, and the expertise and consulting services that Data Extras offered were no longer as valuable and the business was not scalable. Bob and Cindy made a strategic decision to expand the business to carry a full line of office supplies. In 1989, the Data Extras name was changed to Office Solutions to reflect the change in service scope.

Over the years, Office Solutions grew both organically and by acquisition. In 2014, it was generating approximately $36 million in annual revenue. The company had 110 employees, including 40 salespeople who sold four product lines: office supplies, office furniture, facility supplies, and print services. (Exhibit 1 shows an organization chart.) Office Solutions used 23 company-owned trucks to deliver its products to customers.

Office Solutions used sophisticated management techniques. Its distribution system was very efficient. The company carried only the most basic supplies in its own warehouse. Most of the products sold were delivered to them on the following morning and delivered to the customer with a 98.5% fill ratio. The company was also metrics-driven. A vital-factor spreadsheet, which tracked sales, sales leads, and multiple other measures, was produced regularly. An electronic ticker on the wall tracked call-service statistics in real time.

Office Solutions had many long-tenured employees and a fun working atmosphere. For example, Bob was a proponent of fitness. He encouraged employees to wear exercise gear at work, and most of them participated in a company exercise break twice a day.

Office Solutions offered every employee, excluding those included in any other incentive plan, a quarterly incentive of 1% of salary if the company made its quarterly profit numbers. This incentive was designed both to enhance unity of purpose and to share profits and risks with the employees.

Industry environment

Until the mid-1980s, the office supply industry was dominated by small, independently owned dealers, some owned by the same families for generations. Then three large big-box retailers – Staples, Office Max, and Office Depot – as well as consolidators – such as Corporate Express, USOP, and BT, who were more focused in the commercial contract space – entered the market. These office supply giants built nationwide distribution networks and retail presence. They enjoyed economies of scale, and they shaved margins. Among other things, they offered "loss leaders," selling some popular products at or below cost to attract new customers. In 2013, Staples, the largest office supply retailer, had annual revenues of $23 billion. Office Depot and Office Max merged in November 2013 and had combined 2013 revenue of $17 billion. The success of the big-box stores drove thousands of independent dealers out of business. But in 2014, the office supply industry still included the two remaining big-box companies, thousands of independent retailers, and, increasingly, online retailers such as Amazon that had moved into the office supply space. By early 2015, an additional merger between Staples and Office Depot had been negotiated and was awaiting FTC approval.

The independent dealers that survived consolidation and the onslaught of the retailers were strong dealers that were competitive. Independents still owned about 35–45% of the market, and they were especially strong in the small and medium business space. Two major wholesalers served this market. They both provided depth and breadth of product offerings and published the two major marketing catalogs that were customized by the individual dealers to provide branding consistency in their specific markets.

Adding to the management challenges in the industry, sales of office supplies were shrinking. As customers moved toward digital information sharing, they needed fewer supplies such as paper, toner, files, and binders. Some privately owned distributors posted small positive, single-digit sales growth in 2013,[1] but the big-box companies in the industry were reporting continuing sales declines. Sales at Office Depot fell 4% in 2013, excluding effects of the merger with Office Max. Staples' sales declined 5% in 2013, and the company announced plans to close more than 225 of 2,000 stores.[2]

The Office Solutions strategy

Office Solutions managers' understanding of the competitive landscape allowed it to carve out a successful competitive niche. They categorized industry customers using a pyramid paradigm (see Figure 1). At the bottom of the pyramid were small customers, defined as businesses with 1–15 employees. These customers typically bought office supplies directly from retail outlets or online.

Figure 1 Customer pyramid

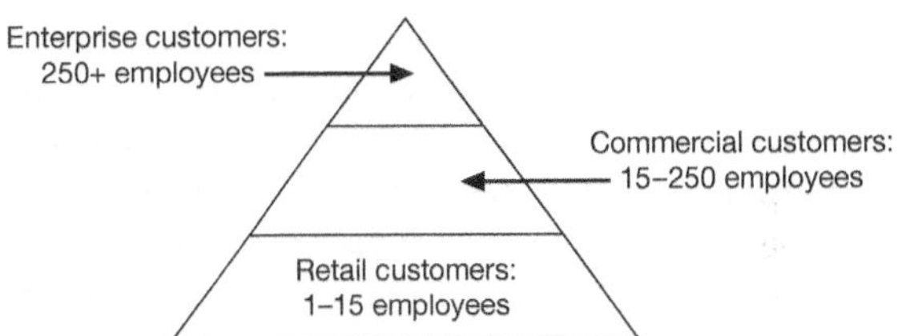

At the top of the pyramid were enterprise customers, defined as businesses with 250+ employees. These businesses typically had multiple employees purchasing office supplies, but prices and product choices were controlled with a contract between the company and the dealer that was negotiated at the corporate level. Staples and Office Depot served most of the enterprise customers. Pricing strategy was the key to winning enterprise business. Dealers in this market segment offered popular products at low prices to win contracts; margins for some products could be as low as 5%. These dealers had to bid carefully and have an excellent understanding of product mix so that they could win contracts and still earn a reasonable profit.

[1] M. E. Biery (2014). Office Supply Stores Seeing Profit Margins Erased, Forbes.com, April 13.

[2] SEC filings.

Office Solutions' primary market included those companies in the middle of the pyramid, commercial customers with 15–250 employees. These businesses typically worked with dealers and had a single decision maker responsible for all of the office supply purchases. Commercial customers were the most likely to value strong relationships and excellent customer service.

Office Solutions had recently started moving up the customer pyramid, competing for enterprise-level contracts. Bob recognized the mergers of the big-box suppliers as an opportunity. Enterprise customers usually considered three bids. With only two, or maybe only one, big box distributors remaining, Bob reasoned that Office Solutions could be a viable second or third option.

The role of the sales representatives was different at the enterprise level. They were responsible for initially requesting participation in the RFP and for building enough of a relationship to understand the expectations and priorities of the customer. The formal bid response and margin management was wholly provided by corporate. Once the contract was established, the role of the representative became less important as customer service provided more direct and immediate contact and problem resolution.

Bob also recognized the move towards e-commerce. He committed a growing share of company resources towards the company website and online marketing.

A major growth engine for Office Solutions was the acquisition of other office supply dealers. Over the years, Office Solutions had acquired quite a few smaller companies. The purchase of an office supply company was, in essence, the purchase of the target's salespeople and their customer relationships. Every effort was made to retain the target's salespeople for at least a year, at which point their customer relationships were transferred to Office Solutions.

The sales role

The role of the sales personnel at Office Solutions was threefold:

1. Retention: Sales reps were responsible for keeping their current customers happy. Customer service responsibilities included consultative services, ensuring that customer orders were handled correctly and on time, handling rush orders and other special requests, and general relationship building.
2. Penetration: Sales reps were responsible for increasing sales to their existing customers. They could increase product penetration by introducing, marketing, and selling additional products and services to existing customers.
3. Acquisition: Sales reps were expected to open doors for the acquisition of new customer accounts. After the door was opened, Office Solutions supported the reps as needed with specialists in the areas of furniture, printing, and janitorial supplies. At the enterprise level, sales reps were expected to identify when current contracts expired and to register Office Solutions for the contract bid process. Once in the bid process, Office Solutions management became involved with the contract negotiations (e.g. pricing) and responded directly to customer queries without the input of the sales rep.

Sales personnel were also charged with maintaining the accuracy of the information in Office Solutions' sales-related systems.

The reps were not responsible for pricing because they did not understand the business well enough to consider all the relevant factors and all of the dynamics affecting pricing.

The office supply market in Southern California was huge, estimated at $1.2 billion per year, so plenty of opportunities existed for Office Solutions sales personnel. The sales people were free to develop new business wherever they thought their potentials were highest; they were not assigned to sales territories. They could use Office Solutions' customer-relationship-management (CRM) system and identify potential customers that were not already buying from Office Solutions. The salespeople lived all over Southern California, and they tended to call on customers near where they lived.

The existing sales compensation program

Sales personnel were included in a commission-plus-bonus program.[3] They earned a commission of 25% of the gross profit generated by sales to their customers. A commission-based compensation structure had the obvious benefit of making the sales compensation costs

[3] In 2014, a few sales personnel were in different compensation programs. They had joined Office Solutions as part of an acquisition, and they remained on the compensation structure provided by their former employer.

Table 1 Calculation of base bonus

Achievement of gross profit goal	Bonus earned (% gross profit)
100.00–104.99%	0.4%
105.00–109.99%	0.5
110.00–114.99%	0.6
115.00–119.99%	0.7
> 120%	0.8

variable. If sales declined, costs declined with them, thus reducing profit risk.

Bonuses were paid only if the sales personnel met or exceeded their gross profit goal. The goal was set by top management based on a targeted growth rate. Sales managers met with their sales reps to explain the goal and to secure commitment to the goal. They spent time breaking down the goal by month, category, and customer and discussing how it could realistically be achieved.

The base bonuses ranged in value from 0.4% to 0.8% of the gross profit earned by the sales rep's accounts according to the step function shown in Table 1. The sales reps could earn an additional bonus of 0.15% of gross profit for each of three smaller product categories (furniture, facility supplies, printing) if they exceeded a category revenue goal. These sales categories were smaller and more volatile than the office supply category, but they were also more profitable.

Under this system, bonuses amounted to a relatively small part of the overall compensation package, maxing out at less than 4.8%[4] of a sales rep's total compensation.

Additional accountability

Office Solutions tracked several measures in addition to the official gross profit goal in a report called the vital factor spreadsheet (VFSS). (Exhibit 2 shows an excerpt from a VFSS.) This report tracked sales leads all the way from initial contact to a yes-or-no decision, as reported by the sales reps. The sales reps did not like reporting their leads in such detail, but the information was vital for management to correct slumps before they materialized into low sales numbers.

Managers and sales reps met together as a group every month to discuss their performance against their official goals and the other measures on the VFSS. The meetings could be unpleasant for those who did not meet their goals. Performance against goals was also discussed during annual performance reviews.

Finally, Office Solutions held annual sales meetings where the top sales reps were recognized. Bob found that the recognitions were surprisingly motivating. He explained:

> **I can think of some sales reps who were perfectly content with their compensation, but became very unhappy when they were no longer recognized as one of the top sales reps at the sales meeting.**

Concerns

Bob recognized some shortcomings in the current compensation structure. First, it did not seem to provide adequate motivation to generate new business. Bob noted that while there were some exceptions,

> **Most people don't enjoy hunting. Hunting only happens when you have to and that happens when you are building your book of business.**

Bob wanted the sales reps to generate more new business. He had ambitious growth goals for the company. But many, perhaps even most, of the sales personnel could seemingly earn enough money to satisfy their lifestyle needs just by retaining the customers that they were already serving.

Second, the compensation structure was perhaps too lucrative. Office Solutions was competing with the big-box stores that had lower costs of sales. Bob wanted to reduce his company's overall cost of sales so that they were more in line with the competition.

Finally, the commission structure attempted to motivate the reps with "carrots." The reps acted too much like independent contractors. Bob thought that he needed a better way to express dissatisfaction with job performance, and he needed objective criteria for terminating underperforming employees. He explained:

> **In addition to setting the pay structure, you need to manage the activity. You have to monitor what they are doing and motivate them to sell more. People slack off when they have met their own needs. For**

[4] Maximum bonus is 1.25% of GP. Maximum total compensation is 25% of GP (commission) + 1.25% of GP (bonus). Max percent of incentive compensation in the form of bonus is 1.25%/26.25% =4.76%.

> example, one of our reps—I'll call him Tom—seems perfectly happy earning $40,000 a year. I suspect that he spends as much time as a tennis instructor as he does as a sales rep. We reprimand Tom privately after every monthly sales meeting, but that seems to be of no consequence to him.
>
> By age 50, most of the reps are cruising. They are not out generating new accounts. I need to grow the business. Should I fire all of my established reps who are not willing to hunt?

A proposal for change

In determining what changes to make, Bob decided that he should divide the sales personnel into two groups – sales reps and account managers – and differentiate their compensation programs. Those designated as sales reps would be just those personnel who were bringing in significant amounts of new business. The sales reps' compensation structure would continue to be based almost exclusively on commission.

To illustrate the characteristics of a near-ideal sales rep, Bob thought immediately of Marsha:

> Marsha is in her late 40s. She will do about $3 million in sales this year. She is a pure hunter, and she loves competing. She lost a $600,000 account last year because her client was acquired, but she has replaced it already. Her weakness is that she deals with too much minutiae. When she is ready, I will give her an assistant to do computer set-ups and the like. I want her focused on new business.

The non-hunter sales reps would be placed into the account manager category. Many of these personnel were excellent at customer relations and retention of accounts, but, for whatever reason, they did not bring in significant amounts of new clients. Bob explained:

> If a sales rep is only retaining existing customers, his or her job description should be changed to an account manager with a pay structure that makes sense for those job responsibilities. Theoretically I would love to have a company full of sales reps who are aggressively pursuing new business, but I don't want to use a sales rep compensation model to pay someone who is actually functioning as an account manager or really working as an outside customer service representative.
>
> William is a good example of someone who should be an account manager. He has been with us for many years and is our #2 salesperson, responsible for $2.5 million in sales. He works 24/7. He is up all the time checking backorder reports. The customers love him. He micro-manages their accounts to make sure that nothing goes wrong. He does a great job of customer retention and selling more categories of products to his accounts. But he hasn't generated even two new accounts each year. I have had a sales manager go with him to help him develop new leads, but that is just not what he is good at.

Bob's instinct was to leave the compensation plan for those in the sales rep category just as it was. The compensation mix for the account managers would change dramatically to a targeted 70% base salary and 30% variable compensation, which included both commission and bonus. The expected total compensation of the account managers would be set to be slightly lower than the current compensation levels, reflecting the reduced compensation risk.

Transition

Through some early, casual discussions, Bob had gotten some indications that the transition to a new compensation structure for the account managers would not be easy. Bob raised the subject first with William, someone who was important to the company but also the perfect candidate for the switch to account manager. Bob offered William what he thought was a generous package: a base salary that was 90% of William's current commission level, with the potential to earn an additional 10–15% as a bonus. (Exhibit 3 shows William's compensation calculations.) But William resisted. He insisted that he wanted to continue as a sales rep despite Bob's warnings that there would be a lot more pressure to win new accounts should he choose to remain in that role.

Bob suspected that the conversations would be even more difficult if the change in structure was combined with the reduction in expected compensation, as Bob thought it should. For the reps who wished to stay on the commission structure, should he add a negative consequence if they failed to acquire new accounts?

Bob knew that he still had some details to work out.

Exhibit 1 Office Solutions Organization Chart, December 2014

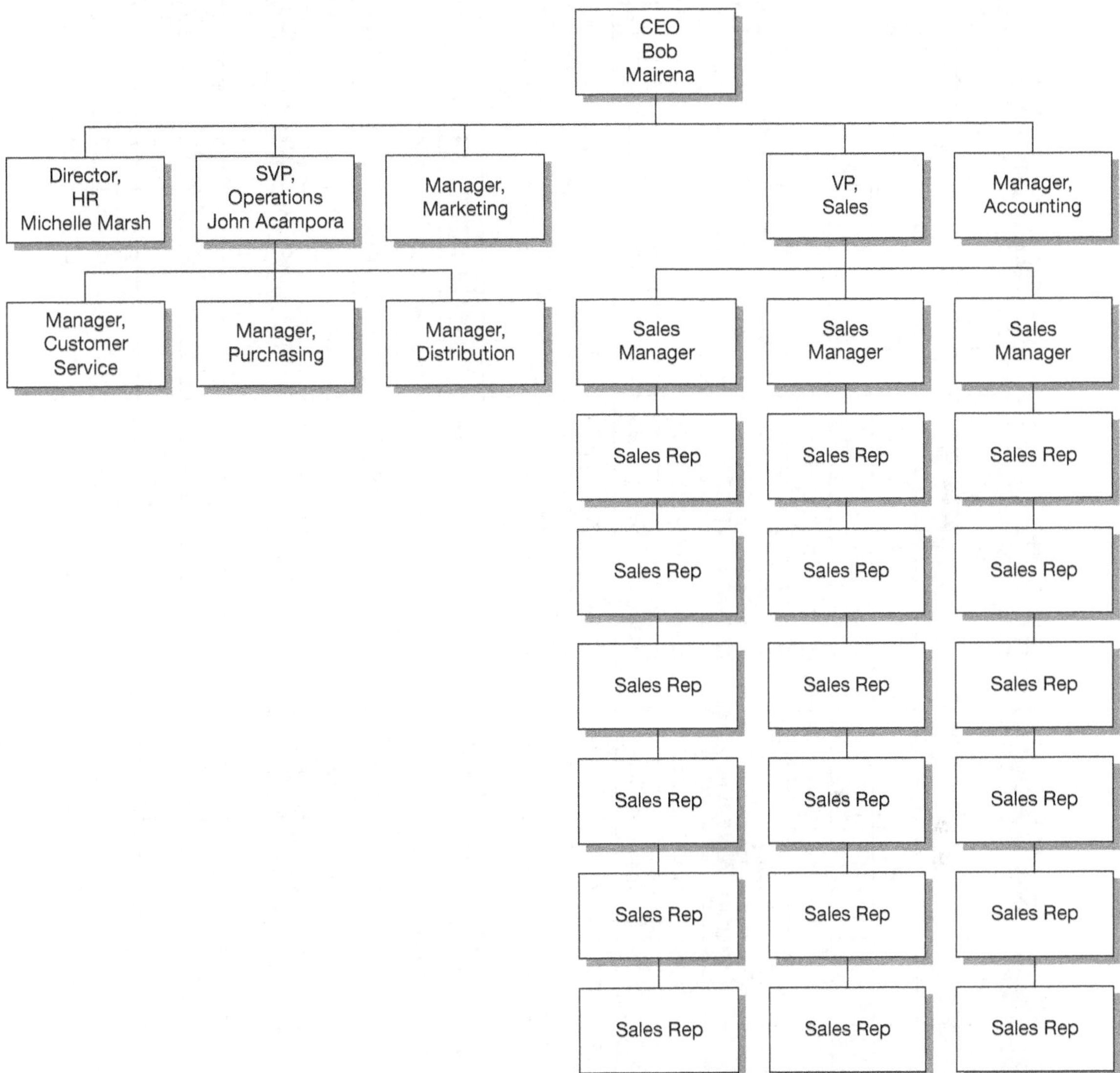

Exhibit 2 Excerpt from the VFSS

New Accounts	Jan-14	Feb-14	Mar-14	Apr-14	May-14	Jun-14	Jul-14	Aug-14	Sep-14	Oct-14	Nov-14	Dec-14	Total
Manager 1	8	9	14	13	7	6	8	16	6	10	4	8	109
Manager 2	10	4	12	9	4	5	3	9	9	6	2	7	80
Manager 3	9	7	10	12	20	10	9	8	6	17	6	5	119
Manager 4	1	1	7	1	3	2	2	4	0	4	1	4	30
Manager 5	3	1	0	2	1	3	0	0	1	2	2	0	15
Total	**31**	**22**	**43**	**37**	**35**	**26**	**22**	**37**	**22**	**39**	**15**	**24**	**353**
Cumulative Revenue for New Customers in 2013													
Manager 1	13,448	21,730	23,271	18,861	52,671	26,750	28,146	59,864	67,255	67,957	45,639	47,417	473,008
Manager 2	9,559	9,278	13,053	18,043	20,620	22,450	21,629	27,317	32,833	41,019	31,279	32,591	279,672
Manager 3	3,949	3,542	13,771	17,779	29,084	40,260	43,052	42,337	82,297	84,185	54,250	70,911	485,418
Manager 4	-	19,583	37,788	18,107	1,125	16,267	5,159	5,779	8,290	1,747	64,215	106,122	284,182
Manager 5	-	-	-	-	-	847	8,479	301	1,266	5,874	7,974	17,879	42,620
Total	**26,956**	**54,133**	**87,882**	**72,790**	**103,500**	**106,574**	**106,465**	**135,598**	**191,941**	**200,782**	**203,358**	**274,921**	**1,564,899**
Total Goal	**37,750**	**69,000**	**100,750**	**132,400**	**169,750**	**206,500**	**238,750**	**264,500**	**296,250**	**333,250**	**353,000**	**364,500**	**2,566,400**
Variance	(10,794)	(14,867)	(12,868)	(59,610)	(66,250)	(99,926)	(132,285)	(128,902)	(104,309)	(132,468)	(149,642)	(89,579)	(1,001,501)
Var %	−28.6%	−21.5%	−12.8%	−45.0%	−39.0%	−48.4%	−55.4%	−48.7%	−35.2%	−39.8%	−42.4%	−24.6%	−39.0%
Bids:	Jan-14	Feb-14	Mar-14	Apr-14	May-14	Jun-14	Jul-14	Aug-14	Sep-14	Oct-14	Nov-14	Dec-14	Total
Manager 1	5	27	35	21	17	18	19	14	11	10	11	4	192
Manager 2	16	13	17	12	11	9	17	6	11	6	3	10	131
Manager 3	5	12	13	13	10	9	14	7	12	8	4	4	111
Other	2	4	5	4	5	4	4	6	5	2	2	2	45
Total	**28**	**56**	**70**	**50**	**43**	**40**	**54**	**33**	**39**	**26**	**20**	**20**	**479**

Exhibit 2 *Continued*

Opportunities	Jan-14	Feb-14	Mar-14	Apr-14	May-14	Jun-14	Jul-14	Aug-14	Sep-14	Oct-14	Nov-14	Dec-14	Total
Stage 1 - Qualifying	430	484	507	544	545	541	520	577	552	566	576	394	
Stage 2 - Initial Meeting	351	379	426	425	440	416	340	366	368	357	367	289	
Stage 3 - Developing Proposal	163	167	193	216	219	200	174	166	164	155	157	134	
Stage 4 - Presentation	118	114	113	114	121	108	146	149	157	169	162	127	
Stage 5 - Commitment to Buy	51	70	98	58	57	51	45	47	51	53	56	50	
Total Current Opportunities	**1,113**	**1,214**	**1,337**	**1,357**	**1,382**	**1,316**	**1,225**	**1,305**	**1,292**	**1,300**	**1,318**	**994**	
Stage 6 - Won	255	272	284	293	304	318	319	348	387	418	436	321	
Stage 7 - Lost	180	192	226	244	270	268	299	318	413	440	468	333	
Total All Opportunities	**1,548**	**1,678**	**1,847**	**1,894**	**1,956**	**1,902**	**1,843**	**1,971**	**2,092**	**2,158**	**2,222**	**1,648**	

(*Continued*)

Exhibit 2 *Continued*

2013 Web Analytics	Jan-14	Feb-14	Mar-14	Apr-14	May-14	Jun-14	Jul-14	Aug-14	Sep-14	Oct-14	Nov-14	Dec-14
Sessions	20,812	17,825	18,806	18,780	18,182	34,969	37,566	35,964	37,869	39,959	31,827	28,523
Users	8,851	7,813	8,297	8,045	7,974	14,681	15,957	15,895	16,603	16,805	14,381	13,634
Pageviews	35,903	30,877	33,137	33,426	34,216	304,010	325,674	309,291	318,452	345,600	275,187	238,281
Pages/Visit	1.73	1.73	1.76	1.84	1.88	8.69	8.67	8.6	8.41	8.65	8.65	8.35
Visit Time	2:46	2:48	2:41	2:42	2:44	7:33	7:25	7:05	6:56	7:14	7:06	6:52
Bounce Rate	66.02%	66.55%	67.09%	66.57%	67.10%	42.62%	43.87%	44.11%	44.29%	43.22%	43.76%	45.86%
% New Visits	31.16%	30.63%	31.61%	30.11%	31.44%	35.92%	30.98%	31.52%	31.13%	29.45%	30.77%	31.69%

Session: A session is a period time where the user is actively engaged with your website.
User: Users have had at least one session within the selected date range. Includes both new and returning users.
Pageviews: The total number of pages viewed. Repeated views of a single page are counted.

Exhibit 3 William's Compensation Calculator

William's 2014 performance

	2014 Goal	2014 Actual	Variance	Variance %
Total Revenue	$ 2,104,350	$ 2,254,393	$ 150,043	7.1%
Office Supply Rev.	$ 1,411,512	$ 1,403,717	$ (7,795)	–0.6%
Furniture Rev.	$ 313,899	$505,495	$ 191,596	61.0%
Facility Supply Rev.	$ 228,071	$239,152	$ 11,081	4.9%
Printing Rev.	$ 150,868	$106,029	$ (44,839)	–29.7%
Gross Profit	$ 502,939	**$538,799**	$ 35,860	**7.1%**
Revenue from New Accounts	$ 39,000	$1,200	$ (37,800)	–96.9%

William's 2014 compensation under commission structure

	Percentage	Gross Profit Base	Compensation
Commission	25.00%	$538,799	$134,700
Base Bonus	.50%	$538,799	$2,694
Furniture Bonus	.15%	$538,799	$808
Facility Bonus	.15%	$538,799	$808
Printing Bonus	0		0
Total Compensation			$139,010

William's compensation under new proposal

	AS OFFERED TO WILLIAM	
	90% base/10% bonus	If 70% base/30% bonus
Base Salary	$121,230	$94,290
Bonus Potential	$ 13,470	$40,410
Total Compensation	**$134,700**	**$134,700**

This case was prepared by Professor Kenneth A. Merchant and Research Assistants Michelle Spaulding and Seung Hwan (Peter) Oh.

CASE STUDY
Puente Hills Toyota

In December 2003, Howard Hakes, vice president of Hitchcock Automotive Services, reflected on some of the challenges his team faced in managing his company's stable of automobile dealerships. He illustrated his points by discussing the challenges faced at Puente Hills Toyota, Hitchcock's largest dealership, although all of the Hitchcock dealerships faced essentially the same problems.

> **This is very much a people business. It's people who give us our biggest successes as well as our biggest challenges. At our Toyota store, in sales, I would say that about 20% of our people are loyal to the company and really want to do a good job. The other 80% are just in this for the money . . . and they can make more money here than anywhere else. Our compensation attracts some very talented people. But some of these people are sharks who try to get away with whatever they can. Others have personal problems. They live from paycheck to paycheck; that is their mentality. Still others are cancers whose bad habits can spread. We coach and counsel; we give written notices; and for most of the employees, once they get the message that is the end of the problems. But for some others . . .**
>
> **I think the key to management in this business is all about managing attitude. How can we keep the team moving in the same direction, to get everybody to be part of the team, and prevent the cancers from spreading?**

The company and industry

Hitchcock Automotive Services was a privately held corporation comprised of seven automobile dealerships – three Toyota dealerships and one each for Volkswagen, Ford, Hyundai, and BMW – and a large body shop. All of the entities were located in southern California. Four of the dealerships, including Puente Hills Toyota, were situated adjacent to each other in City of Industry, California, about 25 miles east of Los Angeles. The others were located in Anaheim, Hermosa Beach, and Northridge.

It was important for the dealerships to keep two important constituencies – manufacturers and customers – happy. The manufacturers allocated larger numbers of their best-selling models to their better performing dealers. The manufacturers evaluated their dealers in terms of their abilities to fulfill their market potential: to meet sales targets the manufacturers set for each geographical trading area, known as the *primary market area*. The dealerships also had to satisfy the manufacturers' licensing and certification standards. The manufacturers regularly performed compliance audits to evaluate dealership practices in comparison with the established standards. However, Howard Hakes believed that short of flagrant violations of standards (e.g. selling competing brands under the same roof), fulfilling market potentials was the primary factor affecting the dealers' relationships with the manufacturers.

Customer satisfaction was obviously important in obtaining repeat sales and, hence, future profits. Customer satisfaction surveys were given to every customer who bought or leased a vehicle or had one serviced at a dealership. A copy of the survey given to all Toyota customers who purchased or leased a vehicle is shown in Exhibit 1.[1] The responses to these survey questions were mailed directly to the manufacturer and aggregated into a *customer satisfaction index* (CSI), to which considerable attention was paid by both the manufacturer and dealership managers. Manufacturers sometimes changed dealership vehicle allocations when CSI ratings fell below acceptable levels in three consecutive years.

Puente Hills Toyota

Puente Hills Toyota (PHT) was a large Toyota dealership. Annual sales were about $85 million, including

[1] Toyota also required the use of a *service* survey, which asked service customers a comparable set of questions focused on satisfaction with (1) making the service appointment, (2) writing up the service order, (3) work quality, (4) work timeliness, (5) price, and (6) the facilities.

approximately $10 million from the body shop, which provided services to all of the Hitchcock dealerships in City of Industry. PHT had a total of 145 employees, and annual profits totaled about $1.8 million.

PHT had won many awards for excellent performance. For example, the dealership had been awarded Toyota's President's Award for overall excellence in each of the prior 13 years.

In 2003, PHT moved into a new, state-of-the-art, $13 million facility with 119,000 square feet of space. The new building provided the latest in customer amenities, including a children's play area, a movie theatre, efficient work layout areas, and room for growth.

PHT's organization structure was fairly typical in the industry. Reporting to the dealership general manager were a general sales manager whose organization included both new and used vehicle sales, a service manager, a body shop manager, a parts manager, and a director of finance and insurance (F&I) (see Exhibit 2). The one unique feature of the organization was the combined new and used vehicle sales department. Only about one in five auto dealerships, typically the smaller ones, had such a combined vehicle sales department. More typically, the managers of the new and used vehicle sales departments reported directly to the dealership general manager. But PHT managers liked the flexibility of having their sales personnel sell whatever vehicle customers wanted, new or used, and some customers wanted to look at both new and used vehicles.

Each of PHT's departments was managed as a profit center. Many indirect or overhead expenses, such as dealership administrative salaries and dealership advertising expenditures, were assigned or allocated to the departments. Only some infrastructure-related expenditures (e.g. rent and equivalent) and some other expenditures over which the department managers had little or no control (e.g. insurance, taxes, legal, and auditing) were not allocated to them.

Exhibit 3 shows one page of the financial statement report that PHT was required to submit monthly to Toyota Sales Corporation. The other pages in this report called for an extensive array of information, including the profitability of the other departments, balance sheet data, unit sales by model, personnel counts by department and category, and a variety of performance ratios (e.g. total bonuses as a percentage of sales, gross profit average per unit of each model sold).

The profitability of PHT's departments varied widely. As in most dealerships, new vehicle sales at PHT were only marginally profitable. Used vehicles provided a better profit source, as Howard Hakes explained:

> **This is one of the last barter businesses left. For some new vehicles, there is only an $800 difference between the window sticker price and dealer cost, so there is not much margin and not much room for bargaining. In used vehicles, we have a little more profit opportunity. We can sometimes take a trade-in for $2,000, put $1,500 worth of work in it, and sell it for $6,000.**

The service department was consistently PHT's most profitable department, with margins typically in the range of 15–20%. (See comparison statistics from an industry consulting report shown in Appendix A.)

As required by Toyota, PHT managers kept separate records for new and used vehicle sales, as if they were separate departments, even though all PHT salespeople could sell both new and used vehicles. The separation of new and used vehicle profits required some allocations of expenses. With rare exceptions, all items of expense were split 70% to new vehicles and 30% to used vehicles, an allocation formula that was typical in the industry. Howard Hakes knew that this formula was somewhat arbitrary. For example, he knew that some forms of advertising, such as half-hour television shows or "infomercials" on Spanish language television stations, were solely aimed at selling used vehicles. But, he explained, "I'll bet we aren't off by more than 5% with the 70–30 split. Maybe it's 65–35, one way or the other, but we won't be further off than that."[2]

All interdepartmental transfers were done at market prices. Thus, for example, when PHT's used vehicles were serviced in the PHT shop, the sales department paid full retail price for parts and labor. This policy gave the used vehicle manager some negotiating power in the service area. Paying full retail price ensured that internal used vehicle service jobs would not be given lower priority.

Valuations of used vehicle trade-ins sometimes created disagreements. These valuations were important primarily because the sales personnel earned commissions based on the profits of the "deals" they closed. Such disagreements were common in dealerships

[2] The industry consulting report showed that for FY 2002, the average overhead expenses (equivalent to line 57 in Exhibit 3) in the industry were $2.6 million for new vehicle departments, or 7.22% of sales (equivalent to line 1 in Exhibit 3) or 94.48% of new vehicle department profit (equivalent to line 33 in Exhibit 3). For used vehicle departments, average overhead expenses in the industry amounted to $1.4 million, or 8.12% of sales or 85.78% of used vehicle department profit.

because new car salesmen were often motivated to *over* pay the customer for trade-ins to secure the new car sale. And at PHT, and indeed all dealerships, needed repairs on trade-ins were sometimes not spotted at the time of the sales deal. This could happen anytime, but at PHT it was most likely to happen on Sundays when the service department was closed and no service advisor could be called in for a second opinion on estimated trade-in repair costs. As Howard explained:

> On Mondays, we often have animated discussions between sales and service about the repairs that the service department claims are required on trade-ins. But we stick to the market price rule! If the costs of repair are higher than what the salesmen had anticipated on Sunday, it eats into their deal profit. If they don't agree with the service repair cost estimate, they are free to sell the trade-in "as-is" on the wholesale market. Sometimes they even get lucky when the repair problem isn't spotted there either. That's why some used vehicles come to be called "lemons."

Performance measures and incentives

Compensation of line personnel at PHT was high, particularly given the employees' generally relatively modest education levels. Even young salespeople, those still in their early 20s, could earn $6,000–$7,000 per month if they hustled and followed up effectively with customers. Top sales personnel could earn $20,000 per month, or even more. Some service technicians earned over $10,000 per month. Performance-based incentives were a significant part of the compensation of all line personnel.

A. Incentives in the sales department

All personnel in the sales department were paid a relatively modest base salary plus incentive pay. The *salesmen* and *assistant sales managers* earned commissions on the deals they closed. The average commission rate was 20% and 7% of deal gross profit for salesmen and assistant sales managers, respectively. The *general sales manager, used vehicle sales manager,* and *sales desk managers*' bonuses were based on a proportion of departmental profit after overhead expenses but before taxes (line 59 in Exhibit 3). The general sales manager and desk sales managers were paid 2.25% and 1.2–1.5% of this amount for the total sales department, respectively. The *used vehicle sales manager* was paid 5% of this amount for the used vehicle department only.

The bonuses, which were typically 250 –300% of the sales employees' base salaries, provided a significant proportion of total compensation. The salaries were paid semi-monthly, and commissions and bonuses were paid monthly.

Howard Hakes explained that one side benefit of having a combined new and used vehicle sales department was that, combined, the department was generally profitable, whereas new vehicle sales departments alone often were not.[3] Howard wondered how managers provided "profit-based" incentives in sales departments that were losing money.

All of the sales managers' bonus plan contracts also included the following wording:

> *Adjustments.* "Any cancelled sales or subsequent changes to the account as a result of a returned product will be calculated into the commissionable gross profit and will be used to calculate your commissions earned for each month. Adjustments may also be made to correct errors, or for rewrites to the deal; unwinds, null and voided deals; customer receivables not collected (including, but not limited to down payments, drive-off fees, insurance coverage, or penalties on trade-in), or policy adjustments."
>
> *Other Factors.* "Other factors such as the Customer Satisfaction Index (CSI)[4] and Employee Satisfaction Index (ESI)[5] score may be taken into account in determining bonuses."

How these nonfinancial performance indices were taken into account for bonus determination was left vague. They could be used in a positive sense, to provide "discretionary" bonus awards, or they could be used to limit the formula bonuses. However, no one at PHT could remember any situations where they had made a substantive difference in the bonuses awarded, perhaps because at PHT, the indices had never fallen below acceptable levels.

For comparison purposes, Appendix B provides

[3] The consulting report showed that about one in three new vehicle sales departments incurred a loss (see note (2) in Appendix A).

[4] CSI was explained earlier in the case. The sales customer survey form is shown in Exhibit 1.

[5] ESI was calculated from the results of a survey designed by a consulting firm given annually to all PHT employees. Each employee was asked to indicate the level of agreement, on a scale from 1 (strongly disagree) to 5 (strongly agree), with 26 statements, such as "I feel my work is valued by the dealership" and "Overall the managers are honest and fair in their treatment of employees."

excerpts from a consulting report showing vehicle dealership department manager compensation data. In this appendix, Schedule 1 shows data about the amounts and forms of monetary compensation given to department managers. Schedule 2 shows the measures used in allocating formula bonuses. Schedule 3 shows the incidence and size of discretionary (nonformula) bonuses.

B. Incentives in the service department

The *service technicians* were paid from $10 to $23 per "flag hour" of work completed. The actual hourly rate depended on each individual's technical specialty and their certifications (e.g. master technician). Flag hours were standards set by the manufacturer for the accomplishment of specific tasks. The standards were set so that an average qualified technician could achieve them. However, it took technicians at PHT, who were generally very experienced, about 45 minutes on average to do one flag hour of work. For some technicians the disparity between flag and actual hours was much higher. Jesus Barragan, PHT's service manager, said "Our top guy, who is a 'natural,' beats the flag time by 600%." The disparity also varied by area.

The *service advisors* earned a base salary of approximately $2,000 per month. They also earned bonuses as follows:

8% commission on customer-paid labor and parts;

6% commission on manufacturer-paid labor under warranty;

6% commission on labor and parts paid for internally at PHT.

The PHT *service* manager was paid a base salary of $3,000 per month plus a bonus based on a percentage of the service department gross profit (before overhead expenses). The percentage was 3.75% if the gross profit figure was $195,000 or less in any given month; the percentage rose to 4% if gross profit exceeded $195,000. The $195,000 was the total annual budgeted amount divided by 12.

C. Gameplaying temptations in the service area

Because they were paid by the job, service technicians had temptations to cut corners. For instance, for a typical Electronic Engine Control (EEC) repair, the technician might be required to diagnose the problem, replace the defective electronic module, hook up a test recorder, and test-drive the vehicle. The flag rate for this job might be 48 minutes. A technician who wanted to cut corners might skip the test drive. Knowing that a supervisor would check the vehicle's mileage-in and mileage-out, he would have to put the vehicle up on a hoist and run it for, perhaps, three minutes to increase the odometer mileage. But by cutting corners, he might be able to complete the entire job in less than 15 minutes.

PHT managers had two types of controls over these gaming behaviors. First, if the time spent on a job was very low, service managers asked the technician for an explanation of the anomaly. Second, management monitored the number of "re-checks," instances where the problem was "not fixed right the first time." In the industry, a 1% re-check rate was considered good. The re-check rate usually could not go to zero because some of the re-checks were not the technician's fault. The cause might be simply that a needed part was unavailable.

Technicians who cut corners were "written up," that is, given notice, and their ticket was deducted. "Bad habits can be corrected; bad mechanics can't," Jesus Barragan observed.

Howard Hakes had some confidence that this gaming problem was under control because the service area at PHT was averaging only about four re-checks per month for approximately 700 completed service jobs. If service technicians were cutting corners in a significant way, he estimated that the re-check rate would be significantly higher.

The service technicians at PHT were very loyal to the company, because "we treat them as people, not mechanics," Jesus said. "We also train and pay them well." Turnover was virtually zero.[6] But the mechanics had to buy their own tools. Jesus Barragan noted that "one of our guys has bought well over $535,000 worth of tools during his 36-year career with us, but then, he makes $130,000 per year too."

Management Issues

Howard Hakes knew that his PHT management team had not solved all their problems. He lamented about the fact that, in general, sales personnel were not effective at following up with customers. Follow-up means that

[6] This is in stark contrast with turnover in the sales department, which Howard described as "horrid" (about 60% per year, as opposed to only about 5% in service).

the sales staff keeps in touch with potential customers with whom there has been an initial contact. Follow-up includes outreaches (e.g. phone calls, thank you cards) to customers who visited the sales department but have not yet decided to purchase a vehicle, as well as sales approaches to customers who are driving an older vehicle that has recently been serviced at PHT. PHT had established regular processes for both types of follow-up. For example, service advisors were encouraged to explain to customers which service costs were likely to occur on their older vehicle in the coming years and to invite the client to visit the sales department. However, these activities consumed time, and the service advisors regularly ignored them. Could incentives be provided to encourage follow-up and referral behaviors?

Howard also worried that the CSI measure, which could provide useful information, sometimes had questionable validity. Howard had heard that some dealerships regularly "gamed" the measures because they had become so important. The CSI ratings were important inputs for the influential ratings of automobile reliability published by the firm J.D. Power & Associates and, as mentioned above, the manufacturers used those ratings to allocate their vehicles. As a consequence, in the quest for "perfect" ratings, customers were regularly "coached" on how to complete the questionnaire at the time they purchased a new vehicle. And, sometimes, dealerships asked customers to drive to the dealership when they received the questionnaire from the manufacturer. When they arrived, the customer would give the questionnaire to a dealership employee and receive a present, such as a full tank of gas. The employee would complete the questionnaire and send it to the manufacturer. Howard was not sure whether some of his "shark" salesmen also engaged in such practices, and if they did, what he should do about it.

Despite these issues, Howard was confident that PHT was one of the best-managed dealerships in the country.

Exhibit 1 Puente Hills Toyota: Customer satisfaction survey

TOYOTA ***Purchase/Lease Survey***

- *To respect your privacy, we will not share individual survey results with dealerships without your permission.*
- *Please use pencil or blue or black ink to fill in the box with an X.* Example: ☒

Our records show you purchased/leased your 2002 SIENNA VIN# 1A2BC34D56E00000
at Anytown Toyota on March 18, 2002

Do you own/lease this vehicle? ☐ Yes (Continue) ☐ No ☐ Never owned *(if you marked no or never owned, please return survey in envelope provided)*

Did you purchase/lease at this dealership? ☐ Yes (Continue) ☐ No *(Please return survey in envelope provided)* 0203271015547

Product presentation

1 Please rate your **SALESPERSON** on each of the following:

	Excellent	Good	Average	Fair	Poor	Not Applicable
Prompt initial greeting	☐	☐	☐	☐	☐	
Courtesy/friendliness	☐	☐	☐	☐	☐	
Integrity	☐	☐	☐	☐	☐	
Matched vehicle to your needs	☐	☐	☐	☐	☐	
Considerate of your time	☐	☐	☐	☐	☐	
Ability to answer your questions	☐	☐	☐	☐	☐	☐
Test drive	☐	☐	☐	☐	☐	
Knowledge of models/features						

Comments on question 1:

Negotiation

2 During your price/payment **NEGOTIATION** experience, how would you rate the following?

	Excellent	Good	Average	Fair	Poor
Simple and straightforward	☐	☐	☐	☐	☐
Honesty	☐	☐	☐	☐	☐
Your comfort with the process	☐	☐	☐	☐	☐
Consideration for your time	☐	☐	☐	☐	☐
Knowledge of purchase/finance options	☐	☐	☐	☐	☐

Comments on question 2:

Final paperwork

3 Thinking about the **PERSON WHO COMPLETED YOUR FINAL PAPERWORK** (financing/leasing, registration, insurance, service contracts) how would you rate the following?

	Excellent	Good	Average	Fair	Poor
Concern for your needs	☐	☐	☐	☐	☐
Courtesy/friendliness	☐	☐	☐	☐	☐
Integrity	☐	☐	☐	☐	☐
Knowledge of products/services offered	☐	☐	☐	☐	☐
Explanation of documents/paperwork	☐	☐	☐	☐	☐
Ability to answer your questions	☐	☐	☐	☐	☐
Consideration for your time	☐	☐	☐	☐	☐
Accurately completed your paperwork	☐	☐	☐	☐	☐
Fulfilled negotiated commitments	☐	☐	☐	☐	☐

Comments on question 3:

Receiving your vehicle

4 When you picked up your new Toyota **(VEHICLE DELIVERY)**, how would you rate the following?

	Excellent	Good	Average	Fair	Poor	Not Applicable
Provided all accessories as promised	☐	☐	☐	☐	☐	☐
Explanation of features/controls	☐	☐	☐	☐	☐	
Explanation of maintenance schedule and warranty	☐	☐	☐	☐	☐	
Ability to answer your questions	☐	☐	☐	☐	☐	
Consideration for your time	☐	☐	☐	☐	☐	
Expressed appreciation for your business	☐	☐	☐	☐	☐	

Comments on question 4:

Elite-View™ forms by NCS Pearson MM243702-4 654321 Printed in U.S.A. ⟨2⟩ 373232

(Continued)

Exhibit 1 *Continued*

5 When you picked up your new Toyota **(VEHICLE DELIVERY)**, did the following occur...

	Yes	No	Not Applicable
Offered a scheduled time for delivery	☐	☐	☐
If yes, kept to scheduled time	☐	☐	
Received a full tank of gas or a gas voucher	☐	☐	
Vehicle delivered clean	☐	☐	
Introduced to service area/personnel (if department was open)	☐	☐	☐

6 Did you have any concerns with your vehicle **WHEN YOU PICKED IT UP** from the dealership?
☐ No *(Skip to Question 7)*
☐ Yes
➥ 6b If yes, please check the appropriate box and describe the concern in the blank: *(Check all that apply)*
☐ Noise/rattle: ______ ☐ Wheel alignment/steering: ______
☐ Malfunction: ______ ☐ Missing item: ______
☐ Not clean: ______ ☐ Other: ______
☐ Chip/scratch/dent: ______

6c Has the dealership resolved the concern? ☐ Yes ☐ No

Dealership communications

7 After your purchase/lease, did the dealership phone, mail or e-mail you to determine your satisfaction with your purchase/lease experience?
☐ No *(Skip to Question 8)*
☐ Yes → 7b

If yes, how would you rate the follow-up contact?	Excellent	Good	Average	Fair	Poor
	☐	☐	☐	☐	☐

Please explain: ______

8 At any point during or after the purchase/lease process, did you ask the dealership to resolve any concerns?
☐ No *(Skip to Question 9)*
☐ Yes → 8b

If yes, how would you rate the following?

	Excellent	Good	Average	Fair	Poor
Efforts of dealership personnel to resolve the concern	☐	☐	☐	☐	☐
Outcome of the contact	☐	☐	☐	☐	☐

Please explain: ______

Facilities

9 Please rate the following:

	Excellent	Good	Average	Fair	Poor
Cleanliness of dealership facilities	☐	☐	☐	☐	☐
Ease/convenience of parking at the dealership	☐	☐	☐	☐	☐

Overall

10 How would you rate your **OVERALL PURCHASE/LEASE EXPERIENCE** at this dealership?
☐ Excellent ☐ Good ☐ Average ☐ Fair ☐ Poor

11 Would you:

	Yes	No	Undecided
RETURN to this dealership to purchase/lease another Toyota?	☐	☐	☐
RECOMMEND this dealership to a friend or relative as a place to purchase/lease a Toyota?	☐	☐	☐
SERVICE your new Toyota at this dealership?	☐	☐	☐

Please explain why or why not: ______

12 What aspects of your purchase/lease experience did you **LIKE MOST**? ______

13 What aspects of your purchase/lease experience **COULD HAVE BEEN IMPROVED**? ______

14 Although we do not identify you with your individual check box results to the dealership, may we associate your name with your written comments?
☐ Yes, you can identify me when sharing my comments with the dealer
☐ No, I do not wish to share any information on this survey with the dealership

3

373233

Exhibit 2 Puente Hills Toyota: Organization structure

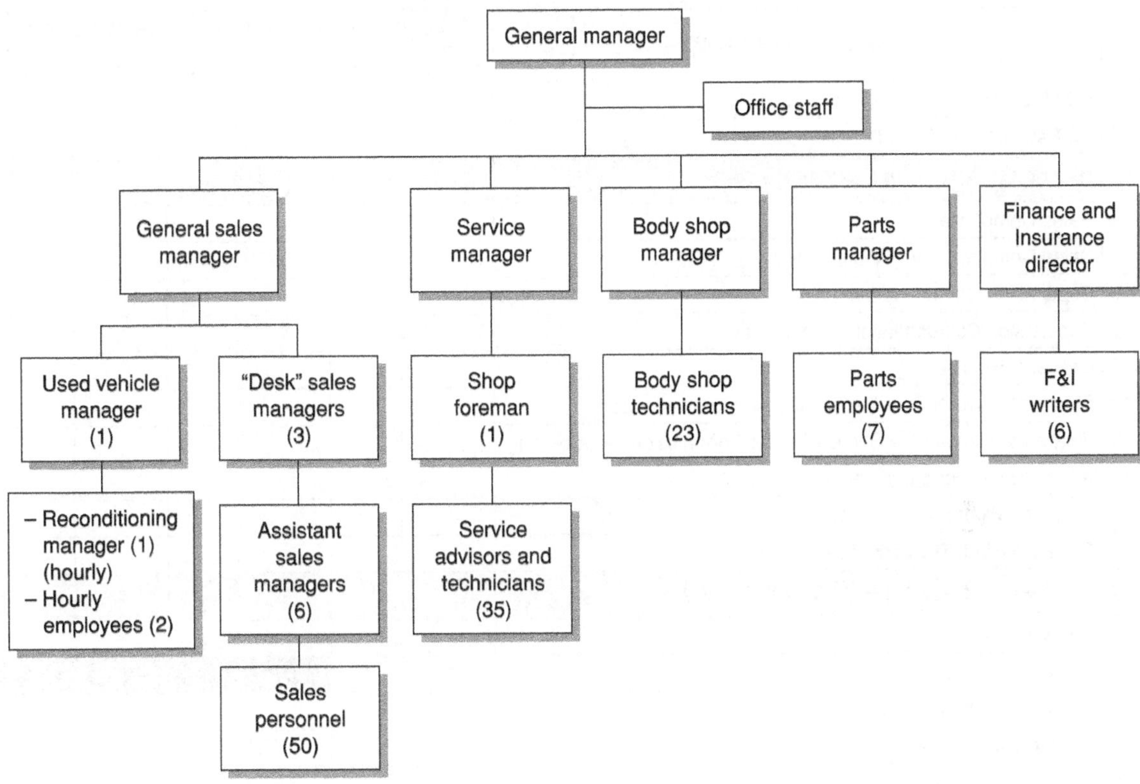

Exhibit 3 Puente Hills Toyota: Sample page of financial reporting package

	NAME OF ACCOUNT	DEALERSHIP		NEW CAR DEPT		USED CAR DEPT	
		MONTH	YTD	MONTH	YTD	MONTH	YTD
1	**TOTAL SALES**						
2	**TOTAL GROSS PROFIT**						
3	**DEPARTMENTAL SELLING EXPENSES**						
4	Sales Compensation						
5	Sales Compensation – Scion only						
6	Supervision Compensation						
7	Supervision Compensation – Scion only						
8	Delivery Expenses						
9	Financing, Insurance & Service Center Commissions						
10	Financing, Insurance & Service Center Commissions – Scion only						
11	Advertising – Departmental						
12	Interest – Floor Plan						
13	**TOTAL SELLING EXPENSES** (Lines 4 to 12 incl.)						
14	**DEPARTMENTAL OPERATING EXPENSES**						
15	Policy Adjustments						
16	Claims Adjustments						
17	Demos & Company Vehicles – Departmental						
18	Inventory Maintenance						
19	Personnel Training						
20	Outside Services – Departmental						
21	Freight						
22	Supplies & Small Tools						
23	Laundry & Uniforms						
24	Equipment & Vehicles – Departmental						
25	Equipment Maintenance, Repair & Rental – Departmental						
26	Miscellaneous Expenses						
27	Salaries & Wages						
28	Clerical Salaries						
29	Vacation & Time Off Pay						
30	**TOTAL OPERATING EXPENSES** (Lines 15 to 29 incl.)						
31	**TOTAL SELLING & OPER. EXPS.** (Lines 13 & 30)						
32	**TOTAL SELL. & OPER. EXPS. % OF GROSS PROFIT**						
33	**DEPT. PROFIT (LOSS)** (Line 2 Less Line 31)						

Exhibit 3 *Continued*

	NAME OF ACCOUNT	DEALERSHIP		NEW CAR DEPT		USED CAR DEPT	
		MONTH	YTD	MONTH	YTD	MONTH	YTD
34	**OVERHEAD EXPENSES**			PRORATION OPTIONAL			
35	Rent & Equivalent						
36	Salaries & Wages – Administrative & General						
37	Owners Salaries						
38	Payroll Taxes						
39	Employee Benefits						
40	Pension Fund/Profit Sharing						
41	Advertising – General & Institutional						
42	Stationery & Office Supplies						
43	Data Processing Services						
44	Outside Services – General & Institutional						
45	Company Vehicles – Administration						
46	Contributions						
47	Dues & Subscriptions						
48	Telephone						
49	Legal & Auditing						
50	Postage						
51	Travel & Entertainment						
52	Heat, Light, Power & Water						
53	Furniture, Signs & Equip.-Depreciation, Maint., Repair & Rental						
54	Insurance – Other than Buildings & Improvements						
55	Taxes – Other than Real Estate Payments & Income Taxes						
56	Interest – Other than Floor Plan & Real Estate Mortgage						
57	**TOTAL OVERHEAD EXPENSES** (Lines 35 to 56 incl.)						
58	**TOTAL EXPENSES** (Lines 31 & 57)						
59	**ADJUSTED DEPT. PROFIT (LOSS)** (Line 2 Less 58)						
60	**OPERATING PROFIT (LOSS)** (Line 2 Less 58)						
61	**NET ADDITIONS OR DEDUCTIONS** (Pg. 2 Line 77)						
62	**NET PROFIT (LOSS) BEFORE BONUS** (Line 60 Less 61)						
63	Bonuses – Employees						
64	Bonuses – Owners						
65	**NET PROFIT (LOSS) BEFORE TAXES** (Line 62 Less 63, 64)						
66	Estimated Income Taxes						
67	**NET PROFIT (LOSS) AFTER TAXES** (Line 65 Less 66)						

Appendix A Puente Hills Toyota: Excerpts from Consulting Report showing automobile dealership and department data (FY 2002)[1]

	1st Quartile	Median	3rd Quartile	Average	St. Dev.
1. NEW VEHICLE DEPARTMENT					
Sales ($000)	17,217	27,134	42,470	36,479	34,585
Net profit ($000)[2]	−49.7	197.2	706.7	530.0	1,195.7
Return on sales	−0.002	0.008	0.021	0.009	0.020
2. USED VEHICLE DEPARTMENT					
Sales ($000)	10,000	14,533	21,016	17,240	11,601
Net profit ($000)[2]	− 22.7	20.0	451.4	258.6	470.4
Return on sales	− 0.003	0.014	0.026	0.013	0.025
3. SERVICE DEPARTMENT					
Sales ($000)	1,560	2,257	3,594	32,846	1,926
Net profit ($000)[2]	54.8	180.8	346.3	246.6	324.1
Return on sales	0.028	0.081	0.130	0.072	0.093
4. TOTAL DEALERSHIP					
Sales ($000)	34,326	49,933	73,502	62,236	47,286
Net profit ($000)[2]	43.4	100.2	1772.0	1,443.9	1,742.8
Return on sales	0.015	0.020	0.022	0.031	0.015

[1]Data obtained from 256 dealerships. The sum of the sales and profits of the service and the new and used vehicle departments do not add up to the dealership totals because sales and profits associated with body and parts are not included.

[2]Note that 30.2% of the new vehicle departments, 27.8% of the used vehicle departments, 16.9% of the service departments, and 5.1% of the dealerships incurred a loss.

Appendix B Puente Hills Toyota: Excerpts from Consulting Report showing department manager compensation data (FY 2002)

Schedule 1: Department Manager Compensation: Total and Breakdown into Components – Base Salary, Formula Bonuses, and Discretionary Bonuses (overall averages)

	Base salary	Formula bonus	Discretionary bonus
NEW VEHICLE DEPARTMENT MANAGERS			
(Average total compensation = $78,428)[1]			
Average ($)	$31,901	$44,829	$5,104
Percent receiving	79.23%	64.48%	23.50%
Average % of total compensation	44.89%	36.77%	4.26%
USED VEHICLE DEPARTMENT MANAGERS			
(Average total compensation = $72,195)[1]			
Average ($)	$31,672	$40,376	$4,046
Percent receiving	85.04%	66.14%	27.56%
Average % of total compensation	47.12%	38.32%	5.03%
SERVICE DEPARTMENT MANAGERS			
(Average total compensation = $61,422)[1]			
Average ($)	$33,278	$30,575	$2,302
Percent receiving	90.00%	68.00%	20.00%
Average % of total compensation	56.00%	34.26%	3.53%
ALL DEPARTMENT MANAGERS COMBINED			
(Average total compensation = $70,189)[1]			
Average ($)	$32,379	$37,993	$3,739
Percent receiving	84.90%	66.27%	23.14%
Average % of total compensation	49.80%	36.17%	4.17%

[1] TOTAL COMPENSATION consists of any or all of the following components: BASE SALARY, FORMULA BONUSES (maximum of three), DISCRETIONARY BONUS, and SPIFFS.

Definitions:

*FORMULA BONUSES are based on quantitative performance measures (e.g. department profit). Some contracts have up to three formula bonuses, although the majority of the managers (60%) receive one formula bonus only. Across departments, the first formula bonus is on average 85% of the total formula bonus. Also, the first formula bonus is on average more than seven times larger than the second formula bonus.

*DISCRETIONARY BONUSES are based on the supervisor's subjective judgments of the managers' performances.

*SPIFFS are miscellaneous rewards (not reported above), which are difficult to characterize in a standard way. Common examples are the use of promotional vehicles and certain incentives provided by the vehicle manufacturers (e.g. vacation trips). Although receipt of spiffs is common (about 63% of the managers receive them), their economic significance is relatively low (about $4,593 for those who receive spiffs, compared at $15,000 to $20,000 for those who receive a discretionary bonus).

(Continued)

Appendix B *(Continued)*

Schedule 2: Dealership Performance Measure Used in Department Manager Formula Bonuses (as a percentage of all formula contracts)

		Formula bonus	#1	#2	#3
Dealership	Gross profit		1.8	1.7	0.0
	Net profit		27.0	10.9	20.0
	Gross profit		6.4	6.9	0.0
New vehicle sales	Net profit		5.8	1.7	2.9
	Inventory		0.0	1.1	0.0
	Unit sales		0.0	6.3	2.9
	Gross profit		5.9	4.6	14.3
Used vehicle sales	Net profit		2.2	5.2	8.6
	Inventory		0.2	2.9	14.3
	Unit sales		0.5	7.5	2.9
	Gross profit		14.5	4.6	2.9
New = used	Net profit		8.6	6.9	11.4
	Inventory		0.0	0.0	5.7
	Unit sales		0.3	8.6	2.9
	Gross profit		2.7	1.1	0.0
Parts	Net profit		1.9	2.3	0.0
	Revenue		0.2	0.0	0.0
	Gross profit		9.4	4.0	0.0
Service	Net profit		8.6	6.9	5.7
	Revenue		0.8	0.0	0.0
Body, parts, & service	Gross profit		2.6	5.7	2.9
	Net profit		0.6	10.9	2.9
	% Gross profit		43.3	28.7	20.0
	% Net profit		54.8	44.8	51.4

Schedule 3: Average Discretionary Bonus for Managers Who Receive a Discretionary Bonus (dollars and percentage of total compensation)

		Average discretionary bonus	
	Pct. receiving	Dollars	% tot. comp.
New vehicle department managers	23.5%	$21,958	18.1%
Used vehicle department managers	27.6%	$15,719	18.3%
Service department managers	20.0%	$11,801	17.7%
All department managers	23.1%	$16,664	18.0%

This case was prepared by Professors Kenneth A. Merchant and Wim A. Van der Stede of the University of Southern California and Pieter Jansen of the University of Groningen (the Netherlands).

CASE STUDY
Kooistra Autogroep

When he took over as CEO of the Kooistra Autogroep in 2002, Tom Kooistra made significant changes to his company's management control system. Most significantly, he decentralized decision-making authority, developed a performance reporting system that included both financial and nonfinancial information, and introduced a pay-for-performance system for the company's dealership and department managers. Tom explained:

> **My father had been running this company like a family, but we've become too big to operate like this. Besides, we need to be more competitive to survive. That's why I am so keen on implementing the new pay-for-performance plan. With decentralization comes accountability for performance. If our people are willing to accept that accountability, then I am quite willing to share with them a fair proportion of the company's success.**

But while the company's managers seemed to value the increased authority and performance-related information, their feelings regarding the pay-for-performance system were mixed. In 2007, Tom was considering whether he should try to reinforce the system by telling the managers that the system was here to stay and that they needed to learn how to make it work, or whether he should revise, or possibly even abandon, the system.

The company

Kooistra Autogroep was a family-owned automobile retailing company founded in 1953. Over the years, Kooistra grew from a small company that sold and serviced cars of only one or two brands from a single location to a top-20 player in the Dutch car dealership market. In early 2007, it owned and operated 13 dealership locations selling 10 brands of automobiles and employed approximately 325 people.

The Kooistra dealerships were located in the city of Tilburg and in smaller surrounding towns in the southern part of the Netherlands. Kooistra owned five Opel dealerships, three Toyota dealerships, one Citroën dealership, one Suzuki dealership, one Saab dealership, one Alfa Romeo dealership, and one combined Chevrolet, Cadillac, Corvette, and Hummer dealership. Opel (a brand of General Motors) had been the market leader in the Netherlands since the 1970s, with a market share of almost 10% in 2006. Toyota was the sixth-largest brand, with a 7% market share. Citroën had a market share of 4%, and Suzuki and Chevrolet had market shares of about 2–3%. The other brands sold by Kooistra – Saab, Alfa Romeo, Cadillac, Corvette, and Hummer – all had market shares of less than 1%. For these smaller brands, the nearest competing dealership was typically located far away. In addition to the car dealerships, the Kooistra Autogroep also owned a body repair shop and a car lease company.

In the context of Dutch automobile retailers, Kooistra was large. Even in 2007, the typical Dutch car dealership sold and serviced cars of only one brand from a single location. Most dealerships were family-owned, with about 20 employees on average.

In the early 2000s, as a consequence of the weak economic conditions and increased competition, the financial performance of most Dutch car dealers deteriorated. This performance deterioration gave rise to many changes in the industry. One important change was industry consolidation. Many larger car dealerships expanded through acquiring several formerly family-owned dealerships. Kooistra Autogroep was among the first to expand the number of brands sold, standardize operating procedures, and exploit economies of scale.

In 2002, Tom Kooistra's father retired, and Tom took over as the company's CEO. Tom chaired the company's top-management team (see Exhibit 1). Also on the top-management team were Anna Lubbers, CFO, and eight managers. Five of the managers were dealership managers, each responsible for several dealership locations selling between one and five brands. Each dealership location employed a sales manager, a service manager, a workshop manager,[1] and a parts manager. The other three top-level managers were responsible for the body repair shop,[2] the car lease company, and the group's central after-sales department.[3] These managers supervised receptionists, salesmen, technicians, and warehousemen. Also in the company was a central corporate staff responsible for finance and accounting, marketing, quality management, personnel and organization, used car auctions,[4] and fleet sales.[5]

Although some of its dealerships had been performing quite well, recent overall performance of the Kooistra Autogroep was subpar, but still in line with industry averages. To ensure adequate resources necessary for business continuity, a rule of thumb in the Dutch car dealership business was that the return on sales (net profit over sales) should be at least 2%. However, due primarily to generally poor economic conditions, the average returns of Dutch car dealerships had not been near this level since the late 1990s (see Table 1).

Table 1 Average return on sales in the Dutch car dealership sector (2001–2005)

	2001	2002	2003	2004	2005
Average Netherlands	1.02%	1.35%	1.19%	1.05%	0.31%

Source: BOVAG Autodealers 2006. Reproduced with permission.

The new management control system

As Kooistra Autogroep became a larger and more complex organization, Tom Kooistra concluded that the company's management control system needed to change. Tom's father used to make most of the significant decisions across all the company's operations. Tom, however, believed that he needed to decentralize decision-making. Tom thought that the dealership managers should have substantial authority for the critical decisions in their business, including the hiring, firing, and supervising of their dealership personnel; advertising investments; sales promotions in their local markets; and price reductions that might be needed to move excess inventory or to meet the competition.

But Tom also believed that with decentralization came results accountability. To make this accountability possible, Tom implemented three new systems when he took over as the CEO in 2002: performance reporting, budgeting, and pay-for-performance. These new systems were to be implemented by fiscal year 2003.

1. Performance reporting

The new performance reporting system included both financial and nonfinancial information. It was used as an instrument to communicate the company's most important objectives to the dealership and department managers; to provide these managers with the information they needed to do their jobs; and to provide feedback to top management so that they could monitor the lower-level managers' performances. Tom explained:

> **My father needed to inform the dealership managers and the department managers only about the most important performance indicators because he made most of the operational decisions. I decentralized an important part of his decision-making authority. But when I made the operating managers responsible for achieving the required performance, I also had to communicate much more detailed performance information to them.**

One type of performance report, which was referred to as the "Balanced Scorecard" within the Kooistra organization, was distributed to the managers on a weekly

---

[1] Some of the dealerships were located in close proximity. For these dealerships, Kooistra Autogroep maintained one central workshop managed by the after-sales department (see Exhibit 1), which serviced several brands. The dealerships in the other locations had their own workshop. The workshops essentially serviced both the sales and service departments. For service jobs, customers went through the service department, which determined the work that needed done as well as the (estimated) cost and time for completion of the work. In addition, the workshop performed get-ready work for new cars sold by the sales department, installation of accessories on new cars, and service and reconditioning work on used cars for resale by the dealership.

[2] Like the service workshop, the body repair shop obtained business internally through the service department and from used car sales for reconditioning body work. The body repair shop, however, also had its own reception for walk-in customers, as not all Dutch car dealerships provided car body repair work. Another significant source of business consisted of contracts with insurance companies for repairs related to car accidents.

[3] Because the centralized service workshop was quite large, the role of after-sales manager was created to oversee several workshop supervisors who, in turn, supervised the mechanics (see Exhibit 1).

[4] Customers who bought a car often expected the dealership to purchase their old car. Like most dealerships, Kooistra Autogroep classified these used cars into two categories. Cars that were in good enough condition were offered for sale by the dealership to used car customers. Cars in poor condition, however, considering the reputation of the dealership, were auctioned off in batches by the auction sales department to other companies that specialized in selling these (cheaper) cars outside of a brand name dealership network.

[5] The fleet sales department was responsible for establishing and maintaining relationships with, and selling cars to, companies that bought cars in large numbers.

basis. It reported year-to-date summary performance on key metrics for each individual manager's operations (e.g. a dealership) with an indication of progress towards budget target accomplishment. Exhibit 2 shows this so-called Balanced Scorecard for the Toyota dealership. In addition to the weekly balanced scorecards, the managers also received far more detailed monthly reports, with sometimes up to hundreds of line items pertaining to their areas of operation.

The dealership and department managers apparently used the performance reports actively. Tom explained:

> **Every Thursday at 2 o'clock, the dealership and department managers receive their Balanced Scorecards by email. When I walk through the company on Thursday afternoon and the reports have not yet been emailed, department managers ask me what's up. The department managers are interested in their performance and, particularly, in comparing their performance *vis-à-vis* target.**

2. Budgeting

At the same time, Tom introduced a formal annual budgeting process. Although various types of financial and nonfinancial information were considered during the budgeting process, the main focus was on determining net profit targets for the forthcoming year.

Net profit was defined as revenues minus controllable expenses, which in practice meant that most corporate overhead allocations were "below the line" on which the operating managers focused. However, Tom felt that continued decentralization would eventually lead the company to improve its methods of allocating shared service costs to obtain more inclusive net profit numbers and, thus, to allow even better accountability at lower organizational levels.

The budgeting process was intended to be bottom-up. The responsible managers prepared their own budget proposals. The budget proposals were then reviewed by Tom and the CFO, Anna Lubbers, followed by what they both described as "rather tough, sometimes vociferous, discussions" with each manager. Tom and Anna decided the final budgets.

The budget discussions served several useful purposes. Most managers were inexperienced with budgeting and only few of them had had any formal business education. Anna noted that,

> **For these and other reasons we can't always trust the initial budget proposals, so we have to have a very hard look at them. In the end, however, I believe that we find the proverbial happy medium for targets that we feel the manager should be willing to commit to.**

But not only did the budgeting discussions serve a training role, they also were a valuable communication tool to focus discussions about the business, which allowed Tom and Anna to solicit information from those who were closest to the day-to-day operations from which they themselves had become farther removed.

Tom and Anna monitored performance through weekly reviews of the Balanced Scorecards. When they saw performance patterns that were of concern to them because they were not consistent with the budget targets and/or the performance of other company entities, they had conversations with the managers. The entire top-management team also held monthly meetings to review performance issues and discuss other company-wide business matters.

The net profit budget targets were believed to be achievable with considerable effort. As Exhibit 2 shows, the Toyota dealership had almost achieved its 2006 net profit target even though there were still five weeks to go in the budget year. When asked, the Toyota dealership manager estimated that at the time his budget was approved, his likelihood of achieving the net profit target was around 90%. He also pointed out that "Although I've made my budget in each of the past three years, it was rather close. But not all of my department managers met their budget each year. My workshop department had some cost control issues and did not always achieve its net profit targets." The Toyota dealership was among the best-performing entities in the Kooistra Autogroep.

Some of the other dealership managers, however, complained that they had trouble meeting their budget targets due to factors outside of their control. For example, the combined Chevrolet, Cadillac, Corvette, and Hummer dealership complained that recent hikes in fuel prices had negatively impacted car sales beyond what could have been foreseen at budget time. He wasn't sure, however, that Tom would be sympathetic if he failed to meet his budget, which he likely would this year.

But Tom also could sometimes "help" the dealerships make their target. Kooistra Autogroep had a sizable contract with a big rental car company that specified the number and type of cars (e.g. small cars, medium-sized family cars, vans), but not the brand, that the rental car company purchased. Thus, when the Opel dealership was close to making its target but needed "a little help," Tom could offer the Opel Astra model to the rental car company. Alternatively, if the Toyota dealership needed some help, he could propose the Toyota Corolla instead. Tom noted that, because of this leverage, he faced considerable lobbying from the dealership managers to go with their brand. He said, "I never hear any complaints when good fortune comes their way. It's only when they miss their targets that I hear them grumbling."

3. Pay-for-performance

A third major change was the expansion of a pay-for-performance system for salespeople and the implementation of a pay-for-performance system for dealership and department managers. Some salespeople already received a bonus. But now Tom introduced a pay-for-performance bonus plan for the managers.

Traditionally, compensation for nearly all personnel in the Netherlands was not performance-dependent. It was based on a job rating, an assessment of the training and experience needed for executing a job, rather than on the individual performance of the employee. The job ratings were linked to pre-established salary increases. Hence, the relationship between levels of compensation and actual employee performance was usually weak.

To bypass the limits of salary increases for a certain job grade, top-performing individuals often were promoted to jobs with a higher job rating when those positions became available. For example, sometimes, excellent car salespeople were promoted to sales manager positions. These promotions sometimes happened even when the dealership would have benefited more from the individual's continued selling efforts than it would from their management skills.

For years at Kooistra, salespeople had had monthly sales targets, defined in terms of the number of (new and used) cars sold. Some of the salespeople were eligible for bonus payouts. In 2007, these bonus-eligible salespeople earned €18.50 per car sold. In addition, when the salesperson met his or her monthly sales target, the bonus amount was doubled to €37.00 per car for the month. On average, bonus payments were about 25% of salary for salespeople who met their targets.

However, not all salespeople were yet eligible for bonuses. Of the 45 salespeople at Kooistra Autogroep, only 25 were bonus-eligible because some of them had negotiated a compensation package without a bonus contingency when they were hired, sometimes at a dealership that had been acquired. These contracts could not easily be renegotiated. Considering these factors, Kooistra's top managers admitted that the sales bonus plan was limited in scope. It also was still subject to change. Anna Lubbers, CFO, explained that management was considering fine-tuning the sales bonus plan by incorporating other performance criteria – perhaps gross, or even net, profit per car.

Tom's new pay-for-performance system for managers added a bonus element to the managers' compensation package. The bonuses were added on top of the managers' salaries. Target bonuses for dealership managers were set between 10% and 20% of annual salary. Target bonuses for department managers were set at 8% of annual salary. For dealership and department managers, the bonuses were based on the extent to which the managers met their annual net profit targets as set during the budgeting process. Only managers who met their net profit target earned their target bonus. No bonuses were paid for below- or above-target performance.

Both Tom and Anna believed that the bonus plan specifically, and the idea of pay-for-performance more generally, was putting the company on the right track. Tom explained:

> I introduced bonuses primarily to make managers conscious of the fact that something had changed [...] that department managers were not only given more decision-making authority but that their responsibilities to meet expected performance also had changed. I think the plan had that desired effect.

Management also had the authority to reduce any or all bonus awards. However, in the first three years since implementation of the system, such discretion had never been applied. Moreover, the criteria that might justify a bonus reduction were not yet clear, as Tom explained:

> Theoretically we might reduce bonuses because, for example, administrative procedures were not followed or customer satisfaction ratings were too low. But a bonus reduction would be a very subjective decision. We need to articulate the criteria for such decisions more clearly. This is a priority for the coming year.

Issues

Pay-for-performance was a relatively unknown phenomenon in Dutch companies. For example, one study showed that in 2001, only 10% of the department managers in Dutch car dealerships received a formula bonus, and only 7% received a "discretionary" (subjectively assigned) bonus (see Exhibit 3). For sales managers, these percentages were somewhat higher: 20% and 7%, respectively (not tabulated in Exhibit 3).

However, several studies had shown that Dutch companies (not just car dealerships) were increasingly relying on pay-for-performance practices, which was commonly attributed to increased international competition. One study concluded that although only a minority of Dutch companies applied some form of pay-for-performance, the trend towards doing so was upward, with 33%, 36%, and 40% of a sample of Dutch firms using some form of pay-for-performance in 1997, 1999, and 2001, respectively.[6]

Because such systems were rare in Dutch dealerships, perhaps not surprisingly, Kooistra Autogroep faced considerable skepticism from its employees when it first introduced its pay-for-performance system. A survey conducted by a consultant showed that the vast majority of Kooistra employees preferred a salary raise over a bonus, even if the raise was significantly lower than the expected bonus. To illustrate this point, Edwin Vliering, a dealership manager, recounted the following conversation he had had with one of his salesmen:

> In terms of profit and sales volume, the last three–four years were generally bad years for Dutch car dealerships. At the beginning of 2006, one of my top salesmen asked for a salary raise. I offered her a bonus instead. In her situation the bonus would have resulted in more money than the raise she had asked for, even in the poor last couple of years. Nevertheless, she was unhappy. She clearly valued the security of a fixed income. I'd say that she is quite representative of the vast majority of employees around here.

Did the pay-for-performance system provide a significant motivational boost? Edwin thought the answer to this question was *no*:

> Due to the economic situation, the last couple of years were not good years. Consequently, my dealership and some of my department managers did not make their targets and did not receive their bonus. In my opinion, however, this has not affected the motivation of any of us. We are all still working hard. On the other hand, even in good years the level of the bonuses is, I think, too low to motivate, particularly for the department managers. In all truth, I wouldn't mind if we abolished the bonuses for department managers.

On the other hand, Tom Kooistra and Anna Lubbers were convinced that the bonuses could, and did, affect motivation. Tom explained:

> Our managers are certainly highly motivated. This was true in recent years even though, due to the poor economic situation, some of them were unable to realize their performance targets. But I am convinced that they make considerable extra effort when they have a chance to meet their targets. For example, they organize extra sales activities when realization of the target is possible. I also know that they feel good when they achieve their targets. That is part of the motivation. But the money is obviously important as well.

Anna Lubbers agreed that the bonuses could provide strong motivational effects, although she believed that that depended strongly on the likelihood that the managers can meet their targets:

> It is important to set realistic targets. Only bonuses that are based on realistic targets have a motivating effect. Setting realistic targets is particularly important in years of an economic slump, like in recent years. When the target is a *pie in the sky*, the bonus will not work.

[6] For example, see S. Bekker, D. Fouarge, M. Kerkhofs, A. Román, M. de Voogd-Hamelink, T. Wilthagen, and C. de Wolff, *Trend-rapport: Vraag naar Arbeid 2002* (Tilburg, August 2003, ISBN 906566 0623).

Exhibit 1 Kooistra Autogroep: Organization structure

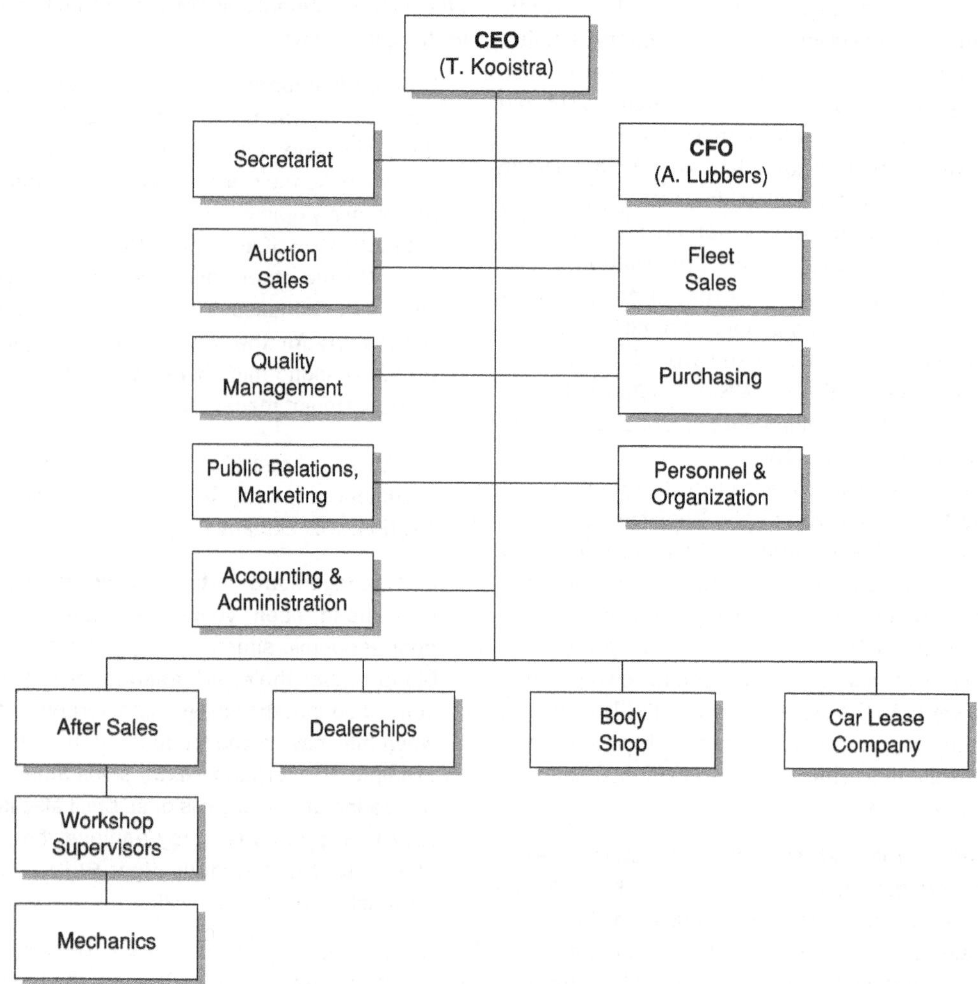

Exhibit 2 Kooistra Autogroep: Sample summary performance report for a dealership (2006)

Eindhoven Toyota 1 Jan–17 Nov 2006 (47 wks)		2006 Target	2006 Actual	2006 Percent	2005 Actual
				47/52 wks = 90%	
Sales Department					
New car units		250	229	92	221
Used cars units		225	231	103	225
New car revenues		5,900,000	5,467,522	93	5,298,521
Used car revenues		3,100,000	2,978,644	96	2,906,335
Sales revenues		9,000,000	8,446,166	94	8,204,856
New car net		125,000	112,135	90	107,154
Used car net		5,000	3,504	70	982
Sales net [1]		130,000	115,639	89	106,172
Sales net margin		1.44%	1.37%		1.29%
New car net /unit		500	490		485
Used car net /unit		22	15		–4
Used car warranty expenses		84,275	82,364	98	90,264
Warranty expense/used car		375	357		401
Manufacturer incentives		150,000	122,687	82	165,922
Service Workshop					
Service revenues		860,000	815,367	95	845,648
Service net [2]		215,000	191,819	89	201,087
Service net margin		25.00%	23.53%		23.78%
Number of orders		1,650	1,621	98	1,648
Number of cars handled		1,050	1,002	95	1,010
Capacity (number of hours)	a	8,800	8,745	99	8,800
Productive hours	b	8,350	8,328	100	8,319
Invoiced hours	c	7,400	7,149	97	7,380
Productivity	b/a	95%	95%		95%
Invoiced hours percentage	c/a	84%	82%		84%
Parts Department					
Parts revenues		1,325,000	1,318,879	100	1,291,820
Parts net [3]		275,000	276,312	100	256,562
Parts net margin		20.75%	20.95%		19.86%
Parts rev./invoiced hrs workshop		179	184		175
Interest Expenses [4]		245,000	216,560	88	232,487
Total revenues		11,185,000	10,580,412	95	10,342,324
Total net [1] + [2] + [3] – [4]		375,000	367,210	98	331,334
Total net margin		3.35%	3.47%		3.20%
Inventory					
New cars in stock		50	47		58
New cars average days in stock		45	40		51
New cars in stock >90 days		10	8		14
Number of backorders		50	62		49
Used cars in stock		60	55		60
Used cars average days in stock		50	45		60
New cars in stock >90 days		0	1		12
Used cars stock (euros)		475,000	424,954		287,469
Parts in stock (euros)		135,000	133,659		136,953

(Numbers are disguised.)

Exhibit 3 United States vs. Netherlands comparison of compensation plans used in car dealerships

	US sample (1998)				Netherlands sample (2001)			
	Base salary	Formula bonus	Discretionary bonus	Spiffs	Base salary	Formula bonus	Discretionary bonus	Spiffs
General Managers	[N = 250] Avg. Tot. Comp. = $190,658 (n = 240)				[N = 61] Avg. Tot. Comp. = €58,303 (n = 61)			
Comp. package breakdown	56.8%	36.5%	3.9%	2.9%	96.9%	2.6%	0.4%	0.1%
Number receiving	n = 238	n = 170	n = 49	n = 110	n = 61	n = 9	n = 3	n = 1
Percent receiving	95.2%	68.0%	19.6%	44.0%	100%	14.8%	4.9%	1.6%
Average amount	$82,262	$136,724	$36,449	$10,458	€56,029	€13,079	€6,000	€3,000
Avg. pct. of total comp.	58.2%	51.5%	18.9%	6.3%	96.9%	17.5%	8.1%	5.1%
Department Managers	[N = 526] Avg. Tot. Comp. = $72,390 (n = 510)				[N = 145] Avg. Tot. Comp. = €36,318 (n = 145)			
Comp. package breakdown	49.8%	36.2%	4.2%	9.9%	98.7%	0.9%	0.2%	0.3%
Number receiving	n = 433	n = 338	n = 118	n = 323	n = 145	n = 15	n = 10	n = 30
Percent receiving	82.3%	64.3%	22.4%	61.4%	100%	10.3%	6.9%	20.7%
Average amount	$35,757	$53,751	$15,149	$4,585	€35,745	€3,992	€940	€457
Avg. pct. of total comp.	58.7%	54.6%	18.0%	15.6%	98.7%	8.6%	2.7%	1.2%

Capital "N" indicates the total number of managers in each sample; small "n" indicates those managers in each sample receiving the particular compensation element. Averages are computed for those that receive the respective compensation element (n), as opposed to being computed on the total sample (N). TOTAL COMPENSATION is the sum of BASE SALARY, FORMULA BONUS, DISCRETIONARY BONUS, and SPIFFS. SPIFFS are miscellaneous rewards, such as the use of promotional vehicles and certain incentives provided by the car manufacturers (e.g. vacation trips). All numbers are annualized.

Source: Jansen, E. P., K. A. Merchant, and W. A. Van der Stede (2009), "National Differences in Performance Dependent Compensation Practices: The Differing Roles of Financial Performance Measurement in the United States and The Netherlands." Accounting, Organizations and Society, 34(1): 58–84.

This case was prepared by Professors Pieter Jansen, Kenneth A. Merchant, and Wim A. Van der Stede.

CASE STUDY
Houston Fearless 76, Inc.

In late 2000, M.S. Lee, president/CEO of Houston Fearless 76, Inc. (HF76), was considering making a major change in the company's sales incentive system:

> **We need revenue growth and consistent profitability, and right now we don't have them. I think our primary problem relates to sales, which have slowed. Some of this is due to market conditions, but I also think that our sales effort and sales support can be improved. I want to take care of our people and give them opportunities to be successful, but I also want the company to get to the next level of performance. Are our structures set up to motivate them to do that?**
>
> **I think we have a range of problems. We're clearly not doing enough to develop new markets, to expand our existing markets, or to develop synergies among our markets. We have an obvious mismatch between our company objectives and our**

sales force incentives because our commissions are based on sales, not product profitability. We use different compensation structures for different products, and I have heard some grumbling among the sales people about equality. And our sales forecasts are inconsistent. Forecast accountability is not strong since there is no downside for salespersons for overstating forecasts. This sometimes causes production planning problems.

So we need to make some changes to improve performance. We need better systems now more than ever because we are entering some new markets that are more competitive than those to which we have been accustomed.

With these concerns in mind, Mr. Lee asked his son, James (who joined HF76 in 1998 and later became head of corporate development and operations, and who was attending the University of Southern California Executive MBA Program), to critically evaluate HF76's sales function and to revamp the sales incentive plan. M.S. and James Lee planned to present a proposal for change at the annual sales meeting to be held in mid-December 2000.

Company history

Houston Fearless 76, Inc. was a privately held company headquartered in Compton, California. Annual company sales were approximately $15 million. The company had 120 employees. HF76 was a worldwide leader in the design, manufacturing, marketing, and service of high-quality micrographic products, photographic film and paper processors, photographic chemical handling equipment, and photographic quality control accessories.

HF76's roots dated back to 1939 when H.W. Houston, one of Howard Hughes's movie-making business partners, founded a company around the development of the first automatic roll film processor. Most of the H.W. Houston Co.'s early customers were closely connected to the motion-picture industry. Later in the 1940s, the company went public and expanded into a manufacturing company that produced a wide range of products, including film processors, hair-clips, turbine blades, and radar. At one time it was one of the largest manufacturing companies in the Los Angeles area. In 1950, the company merged with Fearless Camera Corporation of Culver City and became known as the Houston Fearless Corporation. Later, however, the company faced many problems, and it was forced to file for bankruptcy and to liquidate its assets.

In 1976, M.S. Lee, a former Houston Fearless employee, and two partners bought the Houston Fearless Photo Division. They named their company Houston Fearless 76, Inc., both to take advantage of the excellent reputation the company had developed, especially in film-processing circles, and to commemorate the year of their acquisition. Mr. Lee later acquired all of his partners' shares.

HF76 prospered in the 1970s and 1980s. In the 1990s, however, film-based product markets experienced a dramatic decline. Many corporate customers, including those in the banking, healthcare, and movie industries, were moving toward digital production and record-retention technologies. Facing the declining market demand, several of HF76's competitors had exited the film-product market. Mr. Lee believed, however, that "the demise of film was greatly exaggerated." He wanted the company to continue serving its traditional film-based market, particularly in good niche markets, as it repositioned itself in faster-growing markets.

In the 1990s, Mr. Lee aggressively expanded in both the traditional film market and growing digital market through a series of acquisitions. In 1990, HF76 acquired Extek Microsystems, an innovator of film-duplicating technology that served a customer base similar to that of HF76's in the micrographics marketplace. Extek's operations were integrated into HF76's Compton facility. In 1997, HF76 acquired Houston International, Inc. which manufactured large-volume, specialized (e.g. long roll) film processors. This division was renamed HF International, but its operations were not moved from its Yuma, Arizona, location. In 1999, HF76 acquired 80% of Mekel Engineering, located in Brea, California, which produced scanners that converted microfilm and microfiche to digital format, lightweight film and video cameras, heads-up display units for fighter aircraft, and traffic photo-citation analyzers.

For over 30 years, HF76 also had a government division, called HF North, that supported the US Air Force through a variety of special projects that involved film processers, power distribution systems, mobile shelters, climate control units, and pollution control systems. This division was located at Beale Air Force Base, near Sacramento.

HF76 was also attempting to diversify its product line by capitalizing on potentially sizable commercial applications of the pollution control systems developed by HF North originally for the US Air Force. These innovative pollution control systems separated practically all kinds of water contaminants, from heavy metals to toxic biohazardous waste. A production facility for these systems had just been started in the Compton location.

The company in 2000

After the 1999 Mekel acquisition, HF76 was organized into four product divisions (see Exhibit 1). Each division operated as a profit center. Corporate staff provided support and coordination of activities. The pollution control business was being developed at the corporate level under the purview of James Lee.

The HF76 culture was close-knit, family-like, and casual. M.S. Lee, the president/CEO, was a former local "entrepreneur of the year." He was a strong central figure, but he was also perceived as being highly caring, honest, and nurturing. Staff were given recognition and periodic awards (e.g. parties, logo merchandise).

M.S. Lee described the company's strategy as follows:

> **We now have products at different market stages. We have some emerging products, particularly pollution control systems and traffic photo-citation analyzers. We have some potentially high growth markets for some of our scanner products. And we have a lot of mature products, such as our processors and duplicators.**
>
> **Each market requires a different strategy. For example, for products in the emerging and growing markets, we need our sales force to identify new customers and new markets. For products in the mature markets, our sales force should capitalize on our brand name and maintain as much volume as possible in the niche market, probably through targeting local government and accounting firms and through special trade-in programs to stimulate the replacement of old machines.**

The HF76 divisions each did their own manufacturing. Most product lines had some standard products, or at least subassemblies. In these cases, HF76 would build to inventory, based on demand forecasts. In the microfilm and motion-picture film processing markets, customers typically waited about 30 days for delivery of machines that required some customization. Largely custom products were built after the order was booked, and the wait in such cases could be several months.

HF76 suffered from the sales/operations frictions common to many companies. Operation managers often complained that salespeople were not aware of the required lead times and that some of their rush orders imposed significant overtime labor costs. Sales, on the other hand, complained that they sometimes lost orders because their operations department could not meet the required delivery schedule.

HF76 product gross margins averaged approximately 28%, but they varied significantly across product lines and models. Relatively low profit margins (10–15%) were earned on processors and pollution control systems. Duplicator sales were relatively profitable (30–35% margins). However, HF76's managers were selling some specific models of their older product lines at minimal, or even negative, gross margins. They did so because they wanted to retain their customer base in order to earn profits on forthcoming replacement part sales, the margins on which were usually in excess of 40%.

Industry performance benchmarks were difficult to establish accurately because HF76's smaller competitors were all privately held and their larger competitors (e.g. Eastman Kodak, Bell & Howell) were so large that they could bury their HF76-relevant financial results in aggregated financial statements. However, HF76's managers believed that their company's performance was lagging behind that of its major competitors on all dimensions. For example, in 1999, HF76's profit margin (as a percentage of sales) was only 0.04%, while the industry benchmark, as given to HF76 management by a management consulting firm, was 5.7%. HF76's inventory turnover was 2.6 compared to the industry benchmark of 4.9. The HF International division, which was operating at a loss, was creating concern.

Marketing and sales efforts

All of the HF76 products, with the exception of replacement parts, sold for significant prices, so they were capital equipment for the buyers. For example, a typical new photo processing machine, one of HF76's low-end products, sold for approximately $60,000, and some of the high-end products sold for several hundred thousand dollars. Thus, the sales process usually involved more than just taking an order. For many of the products, the sales cycle was lengthy, a year or more. In many cases, particularly for the more advanced products, the salespeople had to serve as consultants, helping their customers to solve problems.

Until the last few years, most of HF76's sales were made through a network of dealers (sometimes referred to as "strategic partners") and independent sales representatives. The dealers and reps provided HF76 with a professional sales effort, local customer knowledge, and, in the case of the dealers, sales of complementary products and a service capability, with little or no fixed costs. However, most of the dealers and reps did no proactive marketing; they merely responded to inquiries.

Further, having the dealers and reps do the selling was expensive because HF76 had to offer them significant price concessions (typically 40% off list price) or high commission rates (typically 7–10%). One active independent rep was also paid a fixed retainer fee. She was somewhat like an employee, but with a lower salary and no benefits, and a higher commission rate. She also had no obligation to serve HF76's interests (e.g. market development) if she did not believe that those efforts would lead to her own commissions.

To provide a more effective and more company-focused selling effort and, secondarily, to cut costs, HF76 managers were trying to build up the company's own internal sales force. All of HF76's competitors sold all their products direct to customers. For internal sales, HF76's goal was to keep the sales costs (compensation and expenses) to less than 10% of total sales, but they did not always achieve that goal.

The tasks required to sell the various HF76 products varied significantly depending on a number of factors, including the product characteristics, the market conditions, and the company's customer relationships. Despite some redundancy (e.g. some of HF76's salespeople for different equipment lines called on the same customers), HF76 managers did not think that they could organize the company's sales effort entirely geographically. Selling the HF76 products required considerable technical knowledge, for example, about optics, micrographics, and software. Little of that knowledge was consistent across product lines.

The **photo processing** business (HF International) was mature. Most sales in this market involved replacement of existing equipment and replacement parts, so the potential customer base was quite well known. The US photo processing market had 1,000–1,500 potential customers, mostly those who did wholesale photo finishing (e.g. school portraits, weddings). One HF76 salesperson, Brett Hutchins, covered the eastern half of the country. Sales in the western half were made through independent sales reps.

The **micrographics** and **motion-picture processing** markets (Extek) were also mature. Most of the microfilm customers were local government entities. (Most corporations had moved to digital storage of documents.) The vast majority of sales in this market were made through a network of approximately 125 dealers, only some of which were active. HF76 had one salesman, Matt Petilla, working in the micrographics and motion-picture markets. Matt was also given the task of culling the dealer list to a smaller number. HF76 managers wanted their dealers to be more aggressive. They were planning to require the dealers to do some significant selling in order to remain on the dealer list. In return, they were going to promise some exclusive territory protection.

The **scanner** business (Mekel), which had more high-tech products with higher growth potential, used all the sales channels. The company had two in-house salespeople. Jim Mancini sold throughout the United States. Ryan Chase was responsible for Asia and Latin America. And some sales were made through dealers and independent reps. One rep, Stephanie Eller, described earlier as being on retainer, generated almost one-sixth of Mekel's total scanner sales in 2000. HF76 managers estimated that its customer base for scanner products numbered about 300–400, but it did not know the names of all its customers because some distributors did not share their lists.

One HF76 salesman, Mark Fogarty, was responsible for selling **pollution control** systems. Mark was a technical person with little sales experience. By late 2000, HF76 had just gotten to the point that it could build the pollution control systems in any volume, and only one system had been sold.

One constant across all the divisions was that the salespeople were not, by themselves, actively developing new customers. They generally relied on a list of regular customers to contact and on company advertising to interest customers. They then responded to telephone and email inquiries.

The in-house salespeople reported to Bob Smith (VP Marketing), although in reality they worked relatively independently. The salespeople were geographically spread across the country. For example, Brett Hutchins (Houston International) lived in Maryland; Matt Petilla (micrographics) lived in St. Louis; Bob Smith lived in Atlanta. All of the salespeople traveled extensively to meet with their customers. The salespeople had the authority to discount up to 5% off list price. Larger discounts had to be proposed to and approved by Mr. Lee.

Assistants at both corporate and division levels provided support to the sales force. Among other things, they made some follow-up telephone calls to customers, maintained the databases, delivered the sales contracts to production, designed the company's advertisements, and set up the marketing shows. They also helped alleviate some of the salespeople's weaknesses. For example, one salesperson had no typing or computer skills. Thus, he needed more support in preparing sales contracts.

Bob Smith managed the sales function primarily by monitoring the weekly sales reports. He also periodically observed salespersons' behaviors on sales trips and trade shows. About the evaluation process, Bob noted: "I can distinguish good performers from poor ones through the ways they deal with clients. But more directly, their performances are reflected automatically in the reports of items shipped to their territory." Bob also noted that HF76 had not had formal performance evaluations in two years. He said, "We can't afford raises, so why bother evaluating people?"

HF76 had gradually been computerizing its sales tracking systems. Previously, all tracking had been manual.

Sales forecasts

The sales personnel were asked to provide an annual sales forecast at the beginning of each year. Then they were asked to update their forecasts on 30-, 60-, and 90-day rolling bases. The forecasts were important for production planning purposes; for example, for decisions about which parts to buy and what subassemblies to produce to inventory.

However, according to Mr. Lee, the sales forecasts were inconsistent:

> Forecast accountability does not really exist in our current compensation structure. There is no mechanism to prevent salespersons from overstating forecasts or sandbagging. Thus, the salespeople tend to be optimistic, and efficient production planning sometimes becomes very difficult.

Bob Smith, on the other hand, thought that the sales forecasts were reasonably accurate. He noted:

> Last year our sales goals were too tough. We worked hard, but the market was soft. This year's targets are more realistic, so I think we'll do better. But we can't control all of the results. Things happen. For example, some sales get held up past the period end. This year one of our big customers, Olin Mills, cut their budget at the last minute, and we did not get a large order that we expected. On the other hand, we sometimes get a "bluebird" [a large order that was not forecast]. We surely have to be out there working with our customers to know what is going to happen, but even so we can't control everything.

Ryan Chase (Scanner Product Sales – Pacific Rim) explained the forecasts from his perspective:

> I don't have an annual forecast because I'm relatively new on the job. I have no basis for a forecast. I guess if they forced me, I would forecast 10 scanners per year. I got lucky last year with sales of 14, but my big sale took me two years of effort. The year before last I sold only two scanners . . . In my forecasts, I wouldn't mention the name of a company if the probability of the sale is less than 80% or 90%. You often don't get a solid answer from international customers until the last minute.

The old sales incentive plan

Up through 2000, all of the salespeople, except Mark Fogarty,[1] were paid a base salary plus commission. The salespersons' base salaries looked relatively low, typically \$40,000–\$60,000, but the total compensation packages and their structure were industry competitive. Commissions were set at a defined percentage of sales, measured as revenue from items shipped within the salesperson's assigned territory. The commission rate differed across salespeople on a negotiated basis with specific attention paid to product characteristics and market situation. Two salesmen, Brett Hutchins and Matt Petilla, earned a 4% commission. Ryan Chase earned a 2% commission because he was relatively new in his job. Bob Smith earned 1% on all company sales within the United States, Canada, and Mexico. The actual commissions the salespeople earned were typically in the range of 50% of base salary, but they could be substantially more.

The sales assistants shared a small bonus pool if HF76 met its overall sales goals. In 1999, each assistant was given approximately \$1,000. One assistant, Eva Colton (Mekel), described her reaction to the bonus.

> I had forgotten about the bonus. The \$1,000 came as a total shock . . . If we make this year's goal, and right now we're behind, it'll be great. But there is not much I can do to help us get there.

A new incentive plan being contemplated

M.S. Lee wondered what could be done to improve the company's marketing and sales efforts. He explained:

> Some causes of our low profits and cash flows are obvious, such as a declining film-based product market and our decision to invest strategically for

[1] Mark Fogarty had been assigned to the job of marketing and sales of pollution control systems only recently, and he had not yet been included in the current incentive plan. However, he was lobbying for inclusion, and a decision on that had to be made soon.

future gains. However, I believe that we are not fully exploiting market and profit opportunities for either our traditional products or our new products. In particular, our sales force has not done what I want them to do. I want them to open new markets, to sell in more profitable markets, and to give us more lead time for better operational planning.

After a series of discussions, M.S. and James Lee concluded that they needed to make a major change in the company's sales incentive plan to attempt to alter behaviors in the desired ways. James observed:

It was pretty clear that the old incentive plan was not working. The commissions were exclusively based on sales volume. While we tried to tell the sales force which products were most profitable, they seemed to be willing to push sales at any cost or price. They also were paying little attention to other strategic goals, such as the opening of new markets or accounts or improving the accuracy of their forecasts. This is perhaps natural because they were not evaluated on those factors. In addition, the linkage between efforts and rewards was unclear. Sales people received compensation for items shipped within their territory regardless of whether they were instrumental in making the sales or not. So, overall, the old incentive plan created distorted incentives.

To overcome the problems in the old system, M.S. and James were considering a quite different incentive plan that they thought would translate HF76 missions and strategies into sales actions. They planned to leave base salaries at current levels but were planning to implement a new incentive plan consisting of three elements: (1) a commission based on product gross margins, but with no commissions paid until gross margins exceeded 70% of forecast; (2) a bonus based on forecast accuracy; and (3) a bonus based on achievement of individual management-by-objectives targets.

The objective of basing **commissions on product gross margins** was to encourage salespeople to focus their effort where company profit potentials were greatest. M.S. and James hoped that the salespeople's knowledge of product gross margins, combined with the incentive reinforcements, would affect their sales behaviors beneficially.

One unsolved issue: M.S. and James had not yet decided what commissions they should pay on negative and low-gross-margin products. They thought that it was sometimes in the company's strategic interest to make some of these sales. Should they report "phony" gross margins to the salespeople to motivate them to sell these low margin products? Or should they weight the commission payouts according to the "strategic importance" of the sale? If the latter, how should strategic importance be defined, and how should it be explained to the salespeople?

The actual commission slopes would be set for each individual so that at 100% of plan, each salesperson could expect to earn in commission slightly more under the new plan than they would have earned under the old plan. This feature was considered essential for securing the salespersons' easy acceptance of the change. However, the **commission structure** (see Exhibit 2) would be quite different. No commissions would be paid for sales up to a minimum performance standard, defined as 70% of the annual gross margin forecast. This feature was intended to allow for greater payout leverage at high performance levels. Between 70% and 100% of the planned annual gross margin, commissions would be paid at rates that were much higher than would be the case if commissions were paid on all sales. That is, if commissions were paid on all sales, the commission rate (as a percentage of gross margin) would be in the range of 10 –12% on high margin sales and 30–35% on low margin sales. Because of the leverage provided by the minimum performance standard, the actual commission rate paid on gross margins earned above the 70% threshold could be raised to 30–100%. For sales above 100% of the annual gross margin plan, the slope on the commission curve would be 25% higher than in the 70 –100% range, to encourage the higher performers to develop new markets and customers effectively. No cap was placed on the maximum commissions that could be earned. Salespeople were to be paid commissions on an annual basis, but monthly cash advances would be paid at a rate of 80% of annual plan to allow the salespeople to smooth out their cash flow.

To encourage the salespeople to take their sales forecasts seriously, a second element of the plan promised an extra bonus based on the **accuracy of the sales forecasts.** The salespeople would earn an extra 5% of base salary if their total gross margins were within 10% (plus or minus) of the annual gross margin forecasts. M.S. and James Lee hoped that this "truth-inducing" feature of the plan would motivate the salespeople to reveal their best estimates of their market prospects rather than be optimistic, as had been typical in the past, or conservative, as might be expected with the new 70%-of-forecast minimum performance standard.

The third element of the contemplated new plan, the **MBO targets**, was designed to facilitate communication and reinforcement of management desires and expectations in any of a variety of areas. The target areas and specific targets would be negotiated between each individual and management. Typical MBO targets might include items such as the following:

- adding a significant number of new customers;
- coordinating well with production;
- keeping annual travel expenses below travel expense forecasts;
- strengthening ties with professional associations;
- improving communications through effective use of email;
- learning and utilizing Microsoft Office and other software.

Assessment was subjective and intended to lean in favor of the employee. If top management deemed the salesperson's performance in all of the defined areas as satisfactory, the salesperson would be given an extra 5% of base salary.

No changes were planned to the bonus system for the sales assistants.

Concerns

M.S. and James were preparing to present their proposal for the new sales incentive plan at the company's annual sales meeting, to be held on December 13, 2000. However, both of them were concerned. They knew that changes of this magnitude could be made only rarely, so it was important that this change be made correctly. They were offering to pay their salesmen significantly more money. Would they be getting at least equivalent value in return? And even more importantly, was this plan what the company needed to push itself to a higher level of performance?

Exhibit 1 Houston Fearless 76, Inc., corporate organization chart, 2000

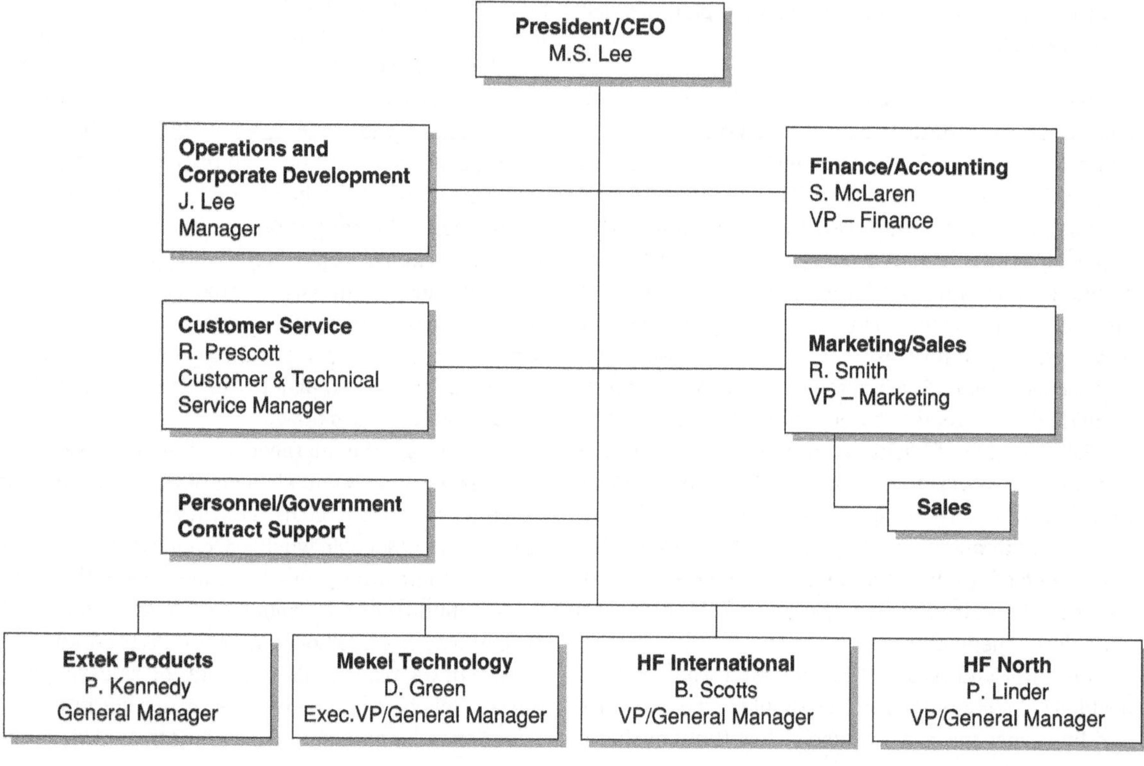

Exhibit 2 Comparison of old and new commission structure

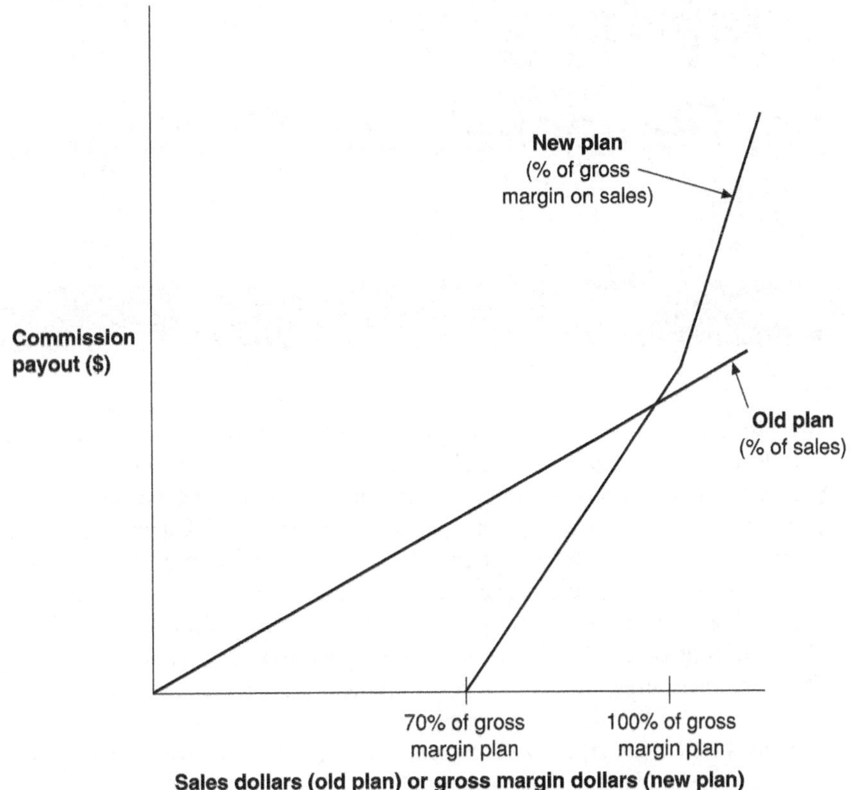

This case was prepared by Professors Kenneth A. Merchant and Wim A. Van der Stede and Research Assistant Liu Zheng.

CHAPTER 3
Action, Personnel, and Cultural Controls

Results controls are not the only form of control. Organizations can supplement or replace results controls with other forms of control that aim to make it more likely that employees will act in the organization's best interest.[1] One such type of control, *action controls*, involves ensuring that employees perform (do not perform) certain actions known to be beneficial (harmful) to the organization. Although action controls are commonly used in organizations, they are not effective in every situation. They are feasible only when managers know what actions are (un)desirable and have the ability to ensure that the (un)desirable actions (do not) occur. Other forms of control, *personnel controls*, are designed to make it more likely that employees will perform the desired tasks satisfactorily *on their own* because the employees are experienced, honest, and hard-working and derive a sense of self-realization and satisfaction from performing tasks well. Related, *cultural controls* exist to shape organizational behavioral norms and to encourage employees to monitor and influence *each other*'s behaviors. Action, personnel, and cultural controls are part of virtually every management control system (MCS). In some organizations, they are so important they can be said to be the dominant form of control.

Action controls

Action controls are the most direct form of management control because they involve taking steps to ensure that employees act in the organization's best interest by making their actions themselves the focus of control. Action controls take any of four basic forms: behavioral constraints, preaction reviews, action accountability, and redundancy.

Behavioral constraints

Behavioral constraints are a "negative" or, as the word suggests, a "constraining" form of action control. They make it impossible, or at least more difficult, for employees to do things that they should not do. The constraints can be applied physically or administratively.

Most companies use multiple forms of *physical constraints*, including locks on desks, computer passwords, and limits on access to areas where valuable inventories and sensitive information are kept. Some behavioral constraint devices are technically sophisticated and often expensive, such as magnetic identification card readers and fingerprint or retina readers. In situations where a high degree of control is desired, such as in facilities where radioactive materials are processed, secret service agencies where classified information is gathered, or casino count rooms where cash is handled, the benefits of such sophisticated controls outweigh their costs. But physical constraints are important in more everyday settings, too, such as retailing. For example, a study by the Center for Retail Research indicated that theft by employees is the second-largest source of "inventory shrinkage" – that is, losses stemming from shoplifting, theft by employees, supplier/vendor fraud, or accounting errors. According to this study, in the year to June 2010, retailers spent $26.8 billion (or 0.34% of sales) on preventing theft.[2] Or, as another report suggested:

> "To put retail shrinkage in perspective, total dollars lost to shrinkage is almost the same amount as the total investment made each year by the entire Canadian retail industry in their Information Technology (IT) departments and more than what retailers invested in their Finance departments. Unlike IT and Finance spending however, shrinkage provides no benefits to retailers and requires significant time and expense to identify, manage and prevent," said Paul Beaumont, Director of PwC's Canadian Retail Consulting Services practice.[3]

To control losses in both store and warehouse environments, retailers use closed circuit TV/DVR recording systems, observation mirrors, and "tip lines" to report incidents.

Effective physical constraints are also increasingly crucial in the context of data protection and privacy concerns faced by virtually all organizations, both private and public, that electronically store information about their clients, customers, patients, or citizens. In a survey focused on the issue of data theft, the vast majority of respondents (84%) perceived data theft as a significant risk to their business, while more than half of the respondents (52%) thought that the risk of data theft would only increase and become an even more serious threat. Furthermore, even though most data theft coverage focuses on the risks presented by external attackers, nearly two-thirds of the respondents (64%) suggest that employees, who inevitably have access to company data in the normal course of business, are the most likely perpetrators of data theft.[4]

For example, venerable HSBC's Swiss private bank arm had to apologize embarrassingly to its clients, whose data were stolen by a former employee who should not have had, but did retain, access to client information.[5] Similarly, a US Internal Revenue Service (IRS) employee took home a computer thumb drive containing unencrypted data on 20,000 fellow workers, where "the Social Security numbers, names and addresses of employees and contract workers were potentially accessible online because the thumb drive was plugged into the employee's unsecure home network," IRS commissioner John Koskinen said, adding that, "this incident is a powerful reminder to all of us that we must do everything we can to protect sensitive data – whether it involves our fellow employees or taxpayers." This IRS breach, significant as it was in terms of poor controls, nonetheless was much narrower in scope than the security incident at Target, the US retailer, where hackers stole credit-card information used by millions of shoppers; or at Barclays, the large UK bank, where confidential data of 27,000 of its customers (including their earnings, savings, mortgages, health issues, insurance policies, passports, and national insurance numbers) were allegedly stolen and offered for sale by the hackers.[6]

The growing importance of such data systems risks cannot be overstated, as suggested by a correspondent at *The Economist*:

> Until recently, for most businesses security was a question of buying decent locks, doors and windows, installing CCTV, making sure that reception staff sign visitors in and out, and trying not to leave confidential papers in the photocopier. But attacks on their computer systems, be they by business rivals, political activists, criminals or foreign governments, are much harder to defend against – and can have far worse consequences than a physical break-in. A company can suffer a devastating blow to its reputation, its intellectual property, or its ability to serve customers – not to mention its bank balances. It may never learn

who has attacked it or why, or how much information has been taken; so it may never be sure if it has done enough to plug the leak.[7]

Of course, the controls evolve, too. For example, companies can hire *penetration testers* to check their data defenses. They also set traps, called *honeypots,* which are bogus but convincing computers, networks, or files to lure hackers while revealing their presence and tactics. And organizations keep sensitive information in separate chunks with no single person in possession of them all, which is a variation of the physical world's *segregation of information* principle.

In addition to, or in lieu of, physical constraints, *administrative constraints* can be used to place limits on an employee's ability to perform all or a portion of specific tasks or actions. One common form of administrative control involves the restriction of decision-making authority. Managers at a low organizational level may be allowed to approve expenditures of up to, say, $1,000 only, those at a higher level up to $5,000, and so on. Above those limits, the purchasing department is instructed not to place the order. The senior managers who restrict the decision-making authority in this way are trying to minimize the risk that resources are being disbursed by employees without proper approvals. However, this process of supervisory checks critically assumes that managers higher in the hierarchy are doing their job of checking and approving well and/or can be trusted. Survey evidence suggests that this, perhaps, should not be taken for granted and, thus, that the checkers also require checking. This is in evidence from the penultimate bullet point below taken from a recent occupational fraud survey:[8]

- Survey participants estimated that the typical organization loses 5% of revenues each year to fraud.
- Occupational frauds can be classified into three primary categories: asset misappropriations, corruption and financial statement fraud. Of these, *asset misappropriations* are the most common, occurring in 85% of the cases in our study, as well as the least costly, causing a median loss of $130,000. In contrast, only 9% of cases involved *financial statement fraud*, but those cases had the greatest financial impact, with a median loss of $1 million. *Corruption schemes* fell in the middle in terms of both frequency (37% of cases) and median loss ($200,000).
- Tips are consistently and by far the most common detection method. Over 40% of all cases were detected by a tip—more than twice the rate of any other detection method. Employees accounted for nearly half of all tips that led to the discovery of fraud.
- Organizations with hotlines were much more likely to catch fraud by a tip, which our data shows is the most effective way to detect fraud. These organizations also experienced frauds that were 41% less costly, and they detected frauds 50% more quickly.
- The higher the perpetrator's level of authority, the greater fraud losses tend to be. Owners/executives only accounted for 19% of all cases, but they caused a median loss of $500,000. Employees, conversely, committed 42% of occupational frauds but only caused a median loss of $75,000. Managers ranked in the middle, committing 36% of frauds with a median loss of $130,000.
- Collusion helps employees evade independent checks and other anti-fraud controls, enabling them to steal larger amounts. The median loss in a fraud committed by a single person was $80,000, but as the number of perpetrators increased, losses rose dramatically. In cases with two perpetrators the median loss was $200,000, for three perpetrators it was $355,000 and when four or more perpetrators were involved the median loss exceeded $500,000.

Another common form of administrative control is generally referred to as *separation of duties.* This involves breaking up the tasks necessary to accomplish certain sensitive duties, thus making it impossible, or at least difficult, for one person to complete the entire task on their own. There are many examples of separation of duties. One common example involves making sure that the employee who makes the payment entries in the accounts receivable ledger is not the employee who receives the checks. If an employee who is diverting company checks to a personal account has only the payment-entry duties – that is, opening the mail and listing, endorsing, and totaling incoming checks – customers will eventually complain about being dunned for amounts they had already paid. But a person with both check-receiving and payment-entry duties could divert the checks and cover the action by making fictitious entries of returns of goods or, perhaps, price adjustments.

Separation of duties is one of the basic requirements of what is known as *internal control*, which is the control-oriented term used by the auditing profession. The effectiveness of separation of duties is limited, however, as it cannot completely eradicate possible *collusion*, such as between those with the check-receiving and payment-entry duties. Although collusion requires employees with malign intent to reveal their intentions to other employees whom they seek to engage in the scheme as their accomplice, survey evidence (such as in the last bullet point of the list above) suggests that it does occur, and that it can pay off. Regardless, inadequate internal controls heighten the risks of fraud and misconduct. Two-thirds of executives surveyed by KPMG admitted that when fraud and misconduct go unchecked in their organizations, it is likely due to *inadequate internal controls*.[9]

Sometimes physical and administrative constraints can be combined into so-called *poka-yokes* that are designed to make a process or system *foolproof*.[10] A poka-yoke is a step built into a process to prevent deviation from the correct order of steps; that is, where a certain action must be completed before the next step can be performed. A simple mechanical poka-yoke example is the inclusion of a switch in the door of a microwave oven so that the oven cannot be operated with the door open. Similar mistake-preventing poka-yokes can also be built into some production and administrative processes. For example, airlines make their pilots use *idiot-proof* software on laptops or handheld devices in the cockpit instead of letting them make manual preflight calculations that are error-prone. The software does not slip up on the math and flashes a warning if an out-of-range number is entered, such as a 10-ton mistake in the weight of the plane or fuel load.[11] In hospitals, greater use of computerized provider order entry can substantially reduce costly and potentially harmful drug errors; a study of the Institute for Healthcare Improvement in Cambridge, Massachusetts, found that processing a prescription drug order through a computerized system led to a 48% reduction in the likelihood of an error.[12] Similarly, signature-verifying software can be used to authorize cash disbursements. Only after all the required signatures have been recognized by the software will the order be released or the transaction be approved.

It is often difficult to make behavioral constraints foolproof, especially when the organization is dealing with disloyal, deceitful employees. For example, despite reasonable safeguards, a former secretary at Bear Stearns, a now-defunct global investment firm, used disappearing ink to write checks that her boss requested. After the manager signed the checks, she would erase the name of the payee and rewrite the checks for cash. In her eight months with the firm, she made more than $800,000 vanish from her boss's bank accounts.[13] Or at Tiffany's, the jeweler, a manager allegedly stole, very slowly and systematically it seems, $1.3 million worth of jewelry by checking out the jewelry for professional reasons – marketing purposes, showing potential buyers, and so on – and then not returning them, and by being careful to keep only items that were valued under $10,000 because Tiffany's has a policy of investigating only missing inventory valued over $25,000.

Chris McGoey, a security advisor, believes that other employees at Tiffany's may have had suspicions long before the investigation, but were afraid to speak up. "I guarantee you that a company like Tiffany's has checks and balances," he says. "But it didn't apply to her. People

reported to her, and they had to relinquish their inventory to her, based on her say-so." Even if they had concerns about why the jewelry she was checking out wasn't being returned, they might've been reluctant to raise any red flags – "nobody wants to rat out their boss," he said.[14]

Preaction reviews

Preaction reviews involve the scrutiny of action plans. Reviewers can approve or disapprove the proposed actions, request modifications, or ask for a more carefully considered plan before granting final approval. A common form of preaction review takes place during planning and budgeting processes, characterized by multiple levels of reviews of planned actions and budgets at consecutively higher organizational levels (see Chapter 8).

Action accountability

Action accountability involves holding employees accountable for the actions they take. The implementation of action accountability controls requires: (1) defining what actions are acceptable or unacceptable, (2) communicating those defined actions to employees, (3) observing or otherwise tracking what happens, and (4) rewarding good actions or punishing actions that deviate from the acceptable.

The actions for which employees are to be held accountable once properly defined are typically communicated through work rules, policies and procedures, contract provisions, and/or company codes of conduct. It is common in fast-food franchises to prescribe and communicate through procedures and clarify and reinforce through training how virtually everything should be done, including how to handle cash, how to hire personnel, where to buy supplies, and what temperature to keep the oil to fry chips. At McDonald's, for example, a memo from the vice chairman stated:

> While we don't want to limit your creativity, from an operations standpoint there are three must-dos:
>
> 1. Staff your fry station all day long.
> 2. Check times and temperatures three times a day.
> 3. Remember to salt your fries properly.[15]

Similarly, nurses use preoperative checklists to help ensure that they prepare patients thoroughly for surgery. These checklists remind them to check on the patient's allergies, drug-taking history, and time of last meal. Train operators are provided with detailed sets of procedures communicated through safety rules and procedures handbooks that they must know and follow. The importance of the procedures is reinforced through training and examinations.

Sometimes the actions desired cannot be communicated in detail. In many operational audits, post audits of capital investment decisions, and peer reviews of auditors, lawyers, doctors, and managers, individuals are held accountable for their actions that involve *professional judgment*. The desirability of the actions of professionals generally cannot be clearly prescribed in advance. Nonetheless, these individuals are held accountable for their actions under the premise that they are expected to 'act professionally.'

Although action accountability controls are most effective if the desired actions are well communicated, communication is not sufficient by itself to make these controls effective. The affected individuals must understand what is required and be confident that their actions will be noticed and rewarded or punished. Actions can be tracked in several ways. Employee actions can be observed directly and nearly continuously, as is done by direct supervisors on production lines. This is called *direct supervision* or *monitoring*. They can be tracked periodically, such as retail stores' use of undercover *mystery shoppers* to evaluate the service provided by store clerks. They can also be tracked by examining evidence of actions taken, such as activity reports or expense documentation. Examining evidence about compliance with pre-established action standards is a key function of *internal audit* (which we discuss in more detail in Chapter 14). Technological advances have allowed greater monitoring in terms of both scope and frequency:

> Technology allows time-and-motion studies to be carried to new levels. Several firms, including Workday and Salesforce, produce peer-review software that turns performance assessments from an annual ritual into a never-ending trial. Alex Pentland of MIT has invented a "sociometric" badge worn around the neck that measures such things as your tone of voice, gestures and propensity to talk or listen. Turner Construction is using drones to monitor progress on a sports stadium it is building in California. Motorola makes terminals that strap to warehouse workers' arms to help them do their jobs more efficiently—but also to keep tabs on them.[16]

Action accountability is usually implemented with negative reinforcements; that is, with punishments instead of with rewards. For example, employees late for their shift might lose a day's bonus, and those who miss their shift may lose their bonus for the week. Truck drivers whose every move is tracked with a GPS device can be disciplined for driving unsafely or for taking extra time on their lunch breaks.[17]

Redundancy

Redundancy, which involves assigning more employees (or equipment) to a task than is strictly necessary, or at least having backup employees (or equipment) available, also can be considered an action control because it increases the probability that a task will be reliably completed. Redundancy is common in computer facilities, security functions, and other critical operations. However, it is rarely used in other areas because it is expensive. Further, assigning more than one employee to the same task usually results in conflict, frustration, and/or boredom.

Action controls and the control problems

Action controls work because, like the other types of controls, they address one or more of the three basic control problems. Table 3.1 shows the types of problems addressed by each of the action controls.

Behavioral constraints are primarily effective in eliminating motivational problems. Employees who might be tempted to engage in undesirable behaviors can be prevented from doing so. Preaction reviews can address all three of the control problems. Because they often involve communications to the employees about what is desired, they can help alleviate a lack of direction. They can also provide motivation because the review of an employee's actions usually prompts

Table 3.1 Control problems addressed by each of the action control types

Type of action control	Control problem		
	Lack of direction	Motivational problems	Personal limitations
Behavioral constraints		x	
Preaction reviews	x	x	x
Action accountability	x	x	x
Redundancy		x	x

Source: K. A. Merchant, *Modern Management Control Systems: Text and Cases* (Upper Saddle River, NJ: Prentice Hall, 1998), p. 30.

extra care in the preparation of the expenditure proposal, budget, or action plan. Preaction reviews also mitigate the potentially costly effects of the personal limitations, since a good reviewer can add expertise if it is needed. The reviews can prevent mistakes or other harmful actions from happening. Action accountability controls can also address all of the control problems. The prescriptions of desired actions can help provide direction and alleviate the types of personal limitations due to inadequate skills or experience. The rewards or punishments help provide motivation. Finally, redundancy is more limited in its application. It is primarily effective in helping to accomplish a particular task if there is some doubt as to whether the employee assigned to the task is either motivated to perform the task satisfactorily or capable of doing so.

Prevention vs. Detection

Action controls can also be usefully classified according to whether they serve to *prevent* or *detect* undesirable behaviors. This distinction is important. Prevention controls are, when they are effective, the most powerful form of control because the costs and harm stemming from the undesirable behaviors will be avoided. Detection controls differ from prevention controls in that the former are applied *after* the occurrence of the behavior. Still, they can be effective if the detection is made in a timely manner and if it results in a cessation of the behavior and a correction of the effects of the harmful actions. Also, the promise of prompt detection of harmful actions is itself preventative; it discourages individuals from purposefully engaging in such behaviors.

Most action controls are aimed at preventing undesirable behaviors. The exception is action accountability controls. Although action accountability controls are designed to motivate employees to behave properly, one cannot verify whether proper actions were taken until evidence of the actions is gathered. However, if the evidence-gathering is concurrent with the activity, as it is with direct supervision and real-time monitoring, then action accountability control can approach the desired state of prevention of undesired actions. For example, truck drivers are monitored by way of so-called "critical event reports" generated by a truck's computers, recording things such as hard braking, activation of the vehicle's stability control system, or other events that might indicate unsafe driving; and traders in banks are monitored by "transactions reports," which use aggregated data to spot insider trading and market manipulation.[18]

Table 3.2 shows examples of common forms of action controls classified according to whether their purpose is to prevent or detect problems.

Table 3.2 Examples of action controls classified by purpose

	Control purpose	
Type of action control	Prevention	Detection
Behavioral constraints	Locks on valuable assets Separation of duties	N/A
Preaction reviews	Expenditure approvals Budget reviews	N/A
Action accountability	Pre-specified policies linked to expectations of rewards and punishments	Compliance-oriented internal audits Cash reconciliations Peer reviews
Redundancy	Assigning multiple people to an important task	N/A

Source: K. A. Merchant, *Modern Management Control Systems: Text and Cases* (Upper Saddle River, NJ: Prentice Hall, 1998), p. 31.

Conditions determining the effectiveness of action controls

Action controls cannot be used effectively in every situation. They are effective only when both of the following conditions exist, at least to some extent:

1. Organizations can determine what actions are (un)desirable; and,
2. Organizations are able to ensure that the (un)desirable actions (do not) occur.

Knowledge of desired actions

Lack of knowledge as to what actions are desirable is the constraint that most severely limits the use of action controls. This knowledge is often difficult to obtain. Although the actions required of employees on a production line may be straightforward to define relatively completely, the definitions of preferred actions in highly complex and uncertain task environments, such as those of salespeople, research engineers, or managers, often are incomplete and imprecise. Most organizations do not have a good idea as to how employees in these roles *should* best spend their time.

Knowledge of the desired actions in feasible roles often can be established by analyzing the action patterns in a specific situation or similar situations over time to learn what actions produce the best results. For example, loan approval decisions in banks tend to be quite structured. Over time, lenders observe which borrowers are likely to fail their loan payments. In so doing, banks can develop a loan approval protocol, delegate loan approval decisions, and monitor or audit the decisions in accordance with their adherence to the decision protocol.

It is important that the actions for which employees are to be held accountable are, in fact, the actions that will lead to the highest probability of accomplishment of one or more of the organization's goals, or at least the proper implementation of the strategy being pursued. In the same respect as with results controls, which we discussed in Chapter 2, many organizations have actually found themselves encouraging employees to take the *wrong* actions. This happens, for example, when policies and procedures are not kept up to date or are applied too tightly (see Chapter 4), causing the action controls to produce unintended side effects, which we discuss in Chapter 5.

Ability to ensure that desired actions are taken

Knowing what actions are desirable is not sufficient by itself to ensure good control; organizations must have some ability to ensure or observe that the desired actions are taken. This ability varies widely among the different action controls.

The effectiveness of the behavioral constraints and preaction reviews varies directly with the reliability of the physical devices or administrative procedures the organization has in place to ensure that the (un)desired actions are (not) taken. Clearly, these devices and procedures are not always effective. For example, a rogue currency trader at Allfirst Financial, who had lost about $700 million in foreign exchange trading, was said to have "targeted every control point in the system and systematically found a way around them." When called aside by managers for going over his trading limits, the trader complained that the computerized risk-monitoring system he used to check his risk exposure during the day was too cumbersome. He got away with it.[19] To cover up his losses, the trader allegedly started selling bogus option contracts. This practice was not detected in a timely manner, either, in part, because the responsibility for the monitoring and reporting of the trader's foreign-exchange risks was given to a junior, relatively inexperienced staff member.[20]

Examples such as these are consistent with the findings of numerous fraud surveys that suggest that misconduct occurs and goes undetected not only because of poor internal controls (many of which fall into the category of what we call *behavioral constraints*) but also due to *management override* of the controls. According to the occupational fraud survey cited above, one-third of the reported cases could have been prevented if there had been better internal controls; but one-fifth could have been prevented if managers had done a sufficient job of reviewing transactions, accounts, or processes; and yet another one-fifth could have been prevented had there not been an override of existing internal controls.[21] Or, to quote another report, "companies find that one of the greatest challenges in countering fraud is that unscrupulous management may override otherwise effective internal controls."[22]

Action tracking also provides a significant challenge that must be faced in making *action accountability* controls effective. Usually some actions can be tracked even where employees' actions cannot be observed directly. But this tracking is not always effective. The criteria that should be used to judge whether the action tracking is effective are precision, objectivity, timeliness and understandability (as we also discussed in Chapter 2 in a results-control context). If any of these measurement qualities cannot be achieved, action accountability control will not be effective in evoking the desired behaviors.

Precision refers to the amount of error in the indicators used to tell what actions have taken place. If action tracking involves direct supervision, can the supervisors accurately distinguish good actions from bad actions? If action tracking involves scrutinizing transaction records, do those records reliably tell whether the proper actions were taken? For example, an initiative aimed at tracking whether salespeople spend enough time on market development activities, as opposed to direct sales activities, is doomed to fail until precise definitions can be developed as to which actions fall into each of these two areas. Here is an example of this:

> **Elaine Murszewski worked in customer service for more than 30 years. The job she found two years after getting laid off was in customer service too, but her new employer monitored her closely, *taking the personal touch out of the job*, she said. The new employer, kept track of the length of her phone calls, the amount of time she took between calls, and the times she wasn't at her desk. *If a caller was particularly difficult, she said, the numbers didn't reflect that.* "Metrics are an employee's worst enemy," she said.[23]**

A similar precision failure of an action control exists within the context of the US Foreign Corrupt Practices Act. This act was intended to make 'bribes' to foreign officials illegal, but it allowed 'facilitating payments' to lower-level officials. The distinction between bribes and facilitating payments is not precise, however, causing concern for company officers who cannot be sure that their interpretations of the actions by company personnel in foreign countries will match those made by independent observers (such as a jury) at a later date in lawsuits of bribe allegations.

Objectivity, or absence of bias, is a concern because reports of actions prepared by those whose actions are being controlled cannot necessarily be relied upon. Project- and sales-oriented personnel are frequently asked to prepare self-reports of how they spend their time. In most cases, these reports are precise, as the allocations may be in units of time as small as by the minute. But the reports are not objective. If the personnel involved want to obscure the true time patterns, perhaps to cover a bad performance or to allow some personal time, it is relatively easy for them to report that most of their time was spent on productive activities. Most companies use direct supervisors and internal auditors to provide objectivity checks on such reports, as well as, increasingly, advanced monitoring technologies as mentioned above. Without objectivity, management cannot be sure whether the action reports reflect the actual actions taken, and the reports lose their value for control purposes.

Timeliness in tracking actions is important as well. If the tracking is not timely, interventions are not possible before harm is done. Further, much of the motivational effect of the feedback is lost when the tracking is significantly delayed. Again, technology has allowed timeliness to be sometimes real time, which is often decried by those being monitored as oppressing.

Finally, it is important that the actions for which individuals are to be held accountable are *understandable*. Although employees presumably can easily understand prescriptions to arrive at work on time or to not steal, understanding and consistently acting in full compliance with the detailed rules and regulations contained in procedures handbooks is obviously much more challenging. Forensic investigations often suggest that incidents and accidents are often due to a lack of employees' understanding of (and, hence, inevitably curtailed compliance with) all of the necessary procedures.

Implementing action controls where one of these action-tracking qualities cannot be achieved will lead to undesirable effects. (These are discussed further in Chapter 5.) However, like results controls, action controls usually cannot be made near-perfect, or at least it would be prohibitively expensive to make them near-perfect. As a consequence, organizations use personnel and cultural controls to help fill some gaps. These controls motivate employees to control their own behaviors (*personnel controls*) or to control each other's behaviors (*cultural controls*).

Personnel controls

Personnel controls build on employees' natural tendencies to control or motivate themselves. Personnel controls serve three purposes. First, some personnel controls help clarify expectations. They help ensure that each employee understands what the organization wants. Second, some personnel controls help ensure that each employee is able to do a good job; that they have all the capabilities (e.g. experience, intelligence) and resources (e.g. information and time) needed to do the job. Third, some personnel controls increase the likelihood that each employee will engage in self-monitoring. *Self-monitoring* is an innate force that pushes most employees to want to do a good job, to be naturally committed. Self-monitoring is effective because most people have a conscience that leads them to do what is right, and they are able to derive positive feelings of self-respect and satisfaction when they do a good job and see their organization succeed. Self-monitoring has been discussed in the management literature under a variety of labels, including *intrinsic motivation* and *loyalty*.

Personnel controls can be implemented through (1) selection and placement, (2) training, and (3) job design and resourcing. In other words, finding the right people to do a particular job, training them, and giving them both a good work environment and the necessary resources is likely to increase the probability that the job will be done properly.

Selection and placement

Organizations devote considerable time and effort to employee selection and placement. A large literature studies and describes how that should best be accomplished. Much of this literature describes possible predictors of success, such as education, experience, past successes, personality, and social skills.

Employee selection often involves reference checks on new employees, which many organizations have stepped up in response to heightened worries over workplace security while ensuring fair, inclusive and equitable recruiting practices.[24] But beyond screening new employees to mitigate security issues, organizations primarily focus on matching job requirements with job applicants' skills. For example, Home Depot, the large American retailer of home improvement and construction products and services, has an in-house computer system that contains the names of pre-screened candidates who have the right skills and experience. This allows managers to find qualified candidates quickly when the need arises. But the automated system also provides cues about what interview questions to ask, what answers to listen for, and even what advice to give the interviewees.[25]

Social media also has emerged as a major background-check tool for employers, where one survey indicates that over two-thirds of them decide against hiring after finding negative details about the candidates. Meanwhile, though, many employers surveyed said they are likely to hire a person if they find on social media that the candidate's personality is a good fit within the company culture, has strong communication skills, is creative, and possesses a wide range of interests, among other presumably desirable traits.[26]

Employee selection can be expensive, but the benefit is to help find the best talent and to avoid hiring someone who is a "poor fit" with the company. One estimate for the United States is that the cost per hire averages about $4,500, and the average time to fill ranges anywhere from 25 days (production positions) to 88 days (executive positions).[27]

Training

Training is another common way to increase the likelihood that employees do a good job. Training can provide useful information about what actions or results are expected and how the assigned tasks can be best performed. Training can also have positive motivational effects because employees can be given a greater sense of professionalism, and they are often more interested in performing well in jobs they understand better.

Many organizations use formal training programs, both through in-company training and by supporting in-classroom continued education, to improve the skills of their personnel. This is important in all sectors because, for example, a global study of hospitals in developed countries found that competition, hospital size and independence, and professional management and decision autonomy were among the most important factors that explain hospital performance.[28] Factors such as professional management and decision autonomy, however, require training to help develop the skills for managers to perform well. But training is also important at the worker level, where some companies see "a mismatch in the labor market between what businesses need and the kind of education young people are getting," said Nader Imani, chief executive of Festo Didactic, the stand-alone education division of Germany's robotics company Festo AG.[29]

Much training takes place informally, such as through employee mentoring. For example, every month, new *and* some existing franchisees for The Pita Pit, a quick-service sandwich chain with more than 240 locations across the United States and over 580 worldwide, assemble in Coeur d'Alene, Idaho, for several days of training. However, Peter Riggs, vice president of The Pita Pit, wants to make sure that the franchisees also share their experiences after the formal training is completed. "Anyone can learn systems," he said; but then he hinted at the need to continually transfer knowledge among employees, which he saw as perhaps the most important aspect of the training and the way it was provided.[30] At Jaburg Wilk, a law firm in Phoenix, Arizona, junior colleagues have two monthly mentoring meetings for 30 minutes to an hour each with a senior colleague, which is seen as an effective way to help the junior colleagues improve their marketing and networking efforts to attract more sophisticated clients. Scott Allen, a consultant, notes that through mentoring, "you will get insights [from the] one-on-one face time that no market research report could ever give you; and if the mentor is lucky, [that person] may even learn a thing or two [too]."[31] A similar approach is followed in other professional services firms. At Moneta Group, an investment adviser, its training program spans five years and includes extensive coaching on business development because "if we weren't intentional about replacing our top people who will be retiring in the next decade, our company's ability to stay independent would be in jeopardy," said Gene Diederich, the firm's chief executive.[32]

Firms also make growing use of social media for their training and coaching needs. "Social learning platforms" are redefining the learning experience by providing employees with a virtual community to interact, engage, share, and learn; and social media are used to establish a dialogue with colleagues and instructors before, during, and after training sessions. These approaches expand the traditional classroom, creating a culture of collaboration and learning across multiple offices, job families, and teams.[33]

Job design and provision of necessary resources

Another way to help employees act aptly is simply to make sure that the job is designed to allow motivated and qualified employees a high probability of success. Some organizations do not give all their employees a chance to succeed. Some jobs are too complex. Salespeople may be assigned too many accounts to handle effectively. Employees also need a particular set of resources available to them in order to do a good job. Resource needs are highly job-specific, but they can include such items as information, equipment, supplies, staff support, decision aids, or freedom from interruption. In larger organizations, particularly, there is a strong need for transfer of information among organizational entities so as to maintain the coordination of well-timed, efficient actions and decisions. This latter point was illustrated pertinently in the example of The Pita Pit above, where the purpose of training, and the way in which it was delivered, also included and facilitated ways to allow transfer of knowledge, experiences, and best practices. But there are circumstances where the situation is less conducive:

> Matt Taibi routinely works 12-hour days as a driver for UPS, the U.S. parcel company. The company would rather pay him and other drivers overtime instead of hiring more workers. Taibi has no complaints about his pay. He makes $32.35 an hour, plus benefits, and has job security as a teamster [union member]. But he wonders how much longer he can keep up the breakneck pace. "There's more and more push towards doing more with less workers," said Taibi. "There are more stops, more packages, more pickups. What's happening is that we're stretched to our limits and beyond."[34]

Cultural controls

Cultural controls are designed to encourage mutual monitoring; a powerful form of group pressure on individuals who deviate from group norms and values. In some collectivist cultures, such as Japan, incentives to avoid anything that would disgrace oneself and one's family are paramount. Similarly, in some countries, notably those in Southeast Asia, business deals sometimes are sealed by verbal agreement only. In those instances, the dominant social and moral obligations are stronger than legal contracts. But strong cultural controls produced by mutual-monitoring processes also exist within single organizations.

Cultures are built on shared traditions, norms, beliefs, values, ideologies, attitudes, and ways of behaving. The cultural norms are embodied in written and unwritten rules that govern employees' behaviors. Organizational cultures remain relatively fixed over time, even while goals and strategies necessarily adapt to changing business conditions. To understand an organization's culture, ask long-time employees questions like: What are you proud of around here? What do you stand for? What does it take to get ahead? If a strong organizational culture exists, the seasoned employees will have consistent answers to these questions even when the answers are not otherwise codified. When that is the case, strong organizational cultures can prompt employees to work together and be aligned. It also implies, however, that despite the benefits of direction and cohesiveness, strong cultures sometimes can become a source of inertia or create blind spots, which can get in the way of needed change and adaptation in rapidly changing environments.

Organizational cultures can be shaped in many ways, both in words and by example, including by way of codes of conduct, group rewards, intra-organizational transfers, physical and social arrangements, and tone at the top.

Codes of conduct

Most organizations above minimal size attempt to shape their organizational culture through what are known, variously, as codes of conduct, codes of ethics, organizational credos, or statements of mission, vision, or management philosophy. These formal, written documents provide broad, general statements of organizational values, commitments to stakeholders, and the ways in which management would like the organization to function. The codes are designed to help employees understand what behaviors are expected even in the absence of a specific rule; that is, they are to some extent principle-based rather than merely rule-based. They may include important messages about dedication to quality or customer satisfaction, fair treatment of employees and customers, employee safety, innovation, risk taking, adherence to ethical principles, open communications and willingness to change. To be effective, the messages included in these statements should be reinforced through both formal training sessions and informal discussions or mentoring meetings among employees and their superiors.

A recent study from the Institute of Business Ethics (IBE) estimated that four-fifths of FTSE 100 companies had an explicit code of conduct or equivalent in 2010, increasing from only an estimated one-third in 1993.[35] But codes of conduct can vary considerably in form across firms. There are an increasing number of defensive, compliance-oriented, or legitimizing reasons to establish or review a code, but a more meaningful motive proactively and regularly communicates the organization's distinctive culture and shared sense of purpose. The latter may involve developing the code to properly calibrate the organization's rules-based policies with a more values-based approach to drive ethical decision-making. As such, other than to comply with legal requirements, effective codes aim to shape a shared company culture and to protect or improve the organization's reputation. The most commonly cited values embedded in the codes are integrity, teamwork, respect, innovation, and client focus. In addition to general policy statements, which almost all codes of conduct necessarily elaborate, some codes provide guidance on specific issues, such as regarding confidential information, accuracy of reporting (fraud), protection of corporate property, and dealing with gifts and entertainment. If such guidance is included, then the detailed behavioral prescriptions provide a form of action accountability control because employees who violate the prescriptions can be reprimanded. Many companies use e-learning modules to implement their code and have an ethics hotline and whistle-blower mechanisms to report violations and misconduct.[36]

Do codes of conduct work? The evidence is equivocal. One study in the financial services sector found that:[37]

- Over two-thirds of the firms in the survey had raised awareness of the importance of ethical conduct over the last three years, and roughly the same number had strengthened their formal code of conduct and the system for evaluating employee behavior, but only two-fifths said their firms had introduced career or financial incentives to encourage adherence to ethical standards.
- While respondents admitted that an improvement in employees' ethical conduct would improve their firm's resilience to unexpected and dramatic risk, half think that career

> progression at their firm would be difficult without being flexible on ethical standards; the same proportion thinks their firm would be less competitive as a consequence of being too rigid in this area; and less than two-fifths think their firm's financials would improve as a result of an improvement in the ethical conduct of employees at their firm.

All told, even though two-thirds of FTSE 350 respondents stated that ethics plays a part in their company's recruitment process, and over four-fifths stated that conformity to the company's code of ethics is included in contracts of employment,[38] the weakness remains that three-fifths also believe that, when push comes to shove, the code of conduct is not taken seriously.[39]

Overall, the latter survey suggests that the most commonly cited factors that contribute to misconduct in the workplace were not only cynicism toward the organization's code of conduct, but also pressure to meet targets; fear of job loss if targets are not met; systems that rewarded results over means; lack of understanding of standards that apply to the job; lack of resources to get the job done without cutting corners, and a belief that policies or procedures are easy to bypass or override. The sum of these issues underlines the importance of the types of controls we have discussed throughout this chapter.

Group rewards

Providing rewards or incentives based on collective achievement also encourages cultural control. Such incentive plans based on collective achievement can come in many forms. Common examples are bonus, profit-sharing, or gain-sharing plans that provide compensation based on overall company or entity (rather than individual) performance in terms of accounting returns, profits, or cost reductions. Encouraging broad employee ownership of company stock, with effective corporate communications to keep employees informed and enthusiastic, encourages all employees to think like owners. According to Sarah McCartney-Fry, member of Parliament and the All Party Parliamentary Group on Employee Ownership, there is a "growing interest in [...] businesses [that] are substantially or majority owned by its employees, [because] co-owned firms appear adept at managing innovation and change and are underpinned by very high levels of productive employee engagement."[40]

Indeed, evidence suggests that group-based incentive plans create a culture of "ownership" and "engagement" to the mutual benefit of organizations and their employees.[41] Specifically, a review of 70 studies over a 25-year period found that both employee ownership and profit-sharing programs improved employee productivity, company performance, and company survivor rates.[42] According to an employee engagement study by the Corporate Executive Board's Corporate Leadership Council, employees most committed to their organizations put forth 57% more effort and are 87% less likely to leave their company than employees who consider themselves disengaged. The study concluded that "it should be no surprise then that employee engagement, or lack thereof, is a critical factor in an organization's overall financial success."[43]

Group rewards are discussed here as a type of cultural control rather than as a results control (as we do in Chapter 9) because they are quite different in character from rewards given for individual performance. With group rewards, the link between individual efforts and the results being rewarded is weak, or at least weakened. Thus, motivation to achieve the rewards is not among the primary forces affected by group rewards; instead, communication of expectations and mutual monitoring are. That is not to suggest that group rewards cannot have positive effects on motivation, even if only indirectly. Group rewards can encourage teamwork, on-the-job training of new employees (when assigned to teams that include experienced colleagues), and the creation of peer pressure on individual employees to exert themselves for the good of the group. All told,

> [...] for many organizations, teamwork is a fundamental building block in their culture, and is a feature the CIPD [Chartered Institute of Personnel and Development] research showed

> they wanted to keep. Although personal achievement was rewarded, it was also seen as important to develop a way of acknowledging and promoting teamwork since good company results are not achieved by a single person. [...] At UKFast, a business-to-business hosting company, reward is a device to reinforce team culture. Rather than giving high-performing people individual cash rewards, the money is pooled to fund a team event. [...] These rewards create shared memories, help team bonding, increase appreciation of people's different personalities and reinforce the company's values of being supportive, caring and fun.[44]

Other approaches to shape organizational culture

As mentioned earlier, other common approaches to shape organizational culture include intra-organizational transfers, physical and social arrangements, and tone at the top.

Intra-organizational transfers or *employee rotation* help transmit culture by improving the socialization of employees throughout the organization, giving them a better appreciation of the problems faced by different parts of the organization, and inhibiting the formation of incompatible goals and perspectives.

Physical arrangements (such as office plans, architecture, and interior decor) and *social arrangements* (such as dress codes, institutionalized habits, behaviors, and vocabulary), can also help shape organizational culture. Some organizations, such as technology firms in Silicon Valley, have created informal cultures, with open office arrangements and casual dress codes that deliver messages about the importance of innovation and employee equality. For example, Alibaba – not a Silicon Valley company, but one that accounts for more than three-quarters of China's retail ecommerce – "credits its awesome growth over the past 15 years to a uniquely corporate culture and the visionary leadership of founder Jack Ma," replete with distinctive, cult-like features:

> Both admirers and detractors alike credit the creativity and drive that got the company this far to Alibaba's somewhat cult-like *esprit de corps* – and the quirky Mr. Ma. [...] Investors [must] decide what stomach they have for Alibaba's quirks – its governance structure gives virtually all power to 27 board members, and very little to ordinary shareholders. They will also have to have a high tolerance for sometimes bizarre antics by senior managers, and a corporate culture that is more colorful than its world-spanning peers like Google and Facebook. [...] The Chinese company's 22,000 employees, known as *Aliren*, appear to be fuelled by adrenalin and inspired by Kung Fu novels. [...] "Corporate culture is still Chinese, [the] appraisal system is that of a Chinese company," said Jasper Chan, formerly Alibaba's senior corporate communications manager, who worked for the company from 2007–12. Employees are constantly evaluated by managers on their commitment to six core values: *teamwork*, *integrity*, *customer first*, *embrace change*, *commitment* and *passion*. "An employee could have great sales, they could bring in a ton of revenues, but if they don't score well in core values, they could still lose their job," she said.[45]

But many other "old-economy" companies also possess, and are reputed for, their unique cultures. At Disneyland, employees are called *cast members*; being on the job is being *onstage* (off the job is *offstage*); a work shift is a *performance*; and a job description is a *script*. This vocabulary, which is imparted on joining the company and is reinforced through training, separates Disney employees from the rest, brings them closer together, and reminds them that they are performers whose job is to help fulfill the company's mission—that is, that "every product tells a story" and that "entertainment is about hope, aspiration and positive resolutions."[46]

Finally, management can shape culture by setting the proper *tone at the top*. Their statements should be consistent with the type of culture they are trying to create, and, importantly, their actions and behaviors should be consistent with their statements. Managers serve as role models and, as the various surveys quoted earlier in this chapter suggest, are a determining factor in creating a culture of integrity in their organizations. Management cannot say one thing and do another. That said, management sometimes sets the *wrong* tone by not responding appropriately to matters brought to their attention, such as ethics concerns or reports of misconduct.[47] All too common, *whistle-blowers* (employees who draw attention to suspected malpractice) are ignored, and so forth. Several studies, indeed, paint a rather gloomy picture of tone at the top. For example, a survey commissioned by PwC suggests that while tone from the top is vital in developing and maintaining the ethical integrity of the business, nearly half of the respondents reported that leaders do not always act as role models in setting the right tone.[48]

Personnel/cultural controls and the control problems

Taken together, personnel/cultural controls are capable of addressing all of the control problems although, as shown in Table 3.3, not each type of control in this category is effective at addressing each type of problem. The lack-of-direction problem can be minimized, for example, by hiring experienced personnel, by providing training programs, or by assigning new personnel to work groups that will provide good direction. The motivational problems, which may be minimal in organizations with strong cultures, can be minimized in other organizations by hiring highly motivated people or by assigning people to work groups that will tend to make them adjust to group norms. Personal limitations can also be reduced through one or more types of personnel controls, particularly selection, training, and provision of necessary resources.

Table 3.3 Control problems addressed by the various ways of effecting personnel and cultural controls

	Lack of direction	Motivational problems	Personal limitations
Ways of effecting personnel controls			
Selection and placement	X	X	X
Training	X		X
Job design and provision of necessary resources			X
Ways of effecting cultural controls			
Codes of conduct	X		X
Group-based rewards	X	X	X
Intra-organizational transfers	X		X
Physical arrangements			X
Tone at the top	X		

Source: K. A. Merchant, *Modern Management Control Systems: Text and Cases* (Upper Saddle River, NJ: Prentice Hall, 1998), p. 130.

Effectiveness of personnel/cultural controls

All organizations rely to some extent on their employees to guide and motivate themselves. Some corporate control systems are dominated by personnel controls. William F. Cronk, now-retired president of Dreyer's Grand Ice Cream (since acquired by Nestlé), said at the time that, "We consider hiring the most important decision we can make. We hire the smartest, most inspired people we can find, give them the resources they need, then get out of their way."[49] Cultural controls can also, by themselves, dominate a control system.[50] The best chance to create a strong culture, however, seems to be early in an organization's life when a founder can imbue the organization with a distinctive culture. Examples are the "cult-like" cultures created by the late Steve Jobs at Apple, Jack Ma at Alibaba, Jeff Bezos at Amazon, and Herb Kelleher at Southwest Airlines, just to name a few notorious ones.[51] Cultural controls often have the advantage of being relatively unobtrusive. Employees may not even think of the shared norms or "the way we do things around here" as being part of the "control" system. As such, organizational cultures can substitute for other formal types of controls. In other words:

> A company's culture is likely to affect every aspect of how the organization operates and how people work. Research from the Chartered Institute of Personnel and Development (CIPD) has consistently found that culture will affect a business's success because, unlike strategy, *it is hard to imitate and can differentiate organizations from their competitors*. In the words of management guru Peter Drucker, "culture eats strategy for breakfast."[52]

As such, personnel/cultural controls can have distinctive advantages over results and action controls. They are usable to some extent in almost every setting, their cost is often lower than more obtrusive forms of controls, and they might produce fewer harmful side effects. Moreover, "soft" personnel/cultural controls have also been shown to make "economic sense" as surveys and evidence suggest that "it *pays* to be nice to employees."[53] At the SAS Institute, the large, privately held software and business intelligence systems company, employee loyalty is instilled with an unusual array of perks for its roughly 3,000 headquarter employees. These include a profit-sharing plan; a free health clinic; daycare centers; private offices for everyone; flexible 35-hour weeks; free sodas, fresh fruit, and pastries in the coffee-break rooms; and even a pianist in the subsidized lunch and recreation room. SAS's turnover rate has been about 4% for years, compared to an industry average of about 20%. Stanford University professor Jeffrey Pfeffer concluded, "The roughly $50 million per year that SAS saves with its low turnover pays for all the family-friendly stuff. And, while the free company clinic costs $1 million per year to operate, that is $500,000 less than what it would cost the company if employees were treated elsewhere."[54]

However, the degree to which personnel/cultural controls are effective can vary significantly across individuals, groups, communities, and societies. Some people are more honest than others, and some communities and societies have stronger ties among their members. Cultures that are "too strong" can also be a disadvantage, especially when they need changing.[55] Culture change requires strong "culture carriers" – role models who embody the new values – and strong reinforcements, such as changes in emphasis in the reward systems:

> "Take somebody who's produced millions of revenues but is sometimes a bit disruptive: how do you judge them against somebody who has lower financial performance but is a great culture carrier?" Colin Fan, the co-head of investment banking at Deutsche Bank, asks. "We used to have those debates. Today, it's not even a debate. The first group gets knocked out of that year's promotion process."[56]

And sometimes it requires a change at the top, such as at Toshiba, the Japanese electronics-to-nuclear conglomerate, where top executives played a role in a company-wide accounting scandal involving at least Y152 billion ($1.2 billion) in inflated profits over a seven-year period:

> In an 82-page summary of its findings, a panel of external lawyers and accountants detailed what it said were "institutional" accounting malpractices and a corporate culture in which

employees were afraid to speak out against bosses' push for increasingly unachievable profits. "There existed a corporate culture at Toshiba where it was impossible to go against the boss' will," the report said. Pressures to meet aggressive, short-term profit targets – known as "the challenge" – existed from the presidency of Atsutoshi Nishida, who headed the company from 2005 to 2009. Those pressures escalated as the company's earnings deteriorated in the wake of the global financial crisis and the March 2011 earthquake and the Fukushima nuclear accident. Top executives pressured employees to achieve their targets with suggestions that the company may withdraw from underperforming businesses such as television if they were not met. [...] Hisao Tanaka, chief executive, stepped down after making a 15-second bow of contrition at a packed news conference in Tokyo, saying that "Toshiba had suffered what could be the biggest erosion of its brand image in its 140-year history."[57]

Conclusion

In this chapter, we provided an overview of the most direct type of controls, *action controls*, which take any of several different forms: behavioral constraints, preaction reviews, action accountability, and redundancy. Action controls are the most direct type of management control because they ensure the proper behaviors of the people on whom the organization must rely by focusing directly on their actions.

We also described *personnel* and *cultural controls*, which managers implement to encourage either or both of two positive forces that are normally present in organizations: self- and mutual-monitoring. These forces can be encouraged in a number of ways, including effective personnel selection and placement, training, job design and provision of necessary resources, codes of conduct, group rewards, intra-organizational transfers, physical and social arrangements, and tone at the top.

Personnel and cultural controls, sometimes referred to as *soft* controls, have become more important in recent years. Organizations have become flatter and leaner. Managers have wider spans of control, and elaborate hierarchies and systems of action controls (bureaucracies) have been dismantled and replaced with empowered employees. In this environment, shared organizational values have become a more important tool for ensuring that everyone is acting in the organization's best interest.[58]

Notes

1 See, for example, M. A. Abernethy, H. C. Dekker, and A. K. Schulz, "Are Employee Selection and Incentive Contracts Complements or Substitutes," *Journal of Accounting Research*, 53, no. 4 (September 2015), pp. 633–68.

2 "Five-Fingered Discounts," *The Economist* (October 23, 2010), p. 80.

3 "Stealing Retailer's Thunder: PwC Estimates Canadian Retailers Are Losing over $10 Million a Day to Shrinkage," *PwC* (October 31, 2012), online at www.pwc.com/ca/en/media/release/2012-10-31-canadian-retailers-losing-ten-million-a-day-shrinkage.html.

4 *European Data Theft Survey 2012* (KPMG, 2012), online at www.kpmg.de/docs/central-and-eastern-european-data-theft-survey-2012.pdf. See also "Business Warned of Enemy Within on Fraud and Cyber Crime," *The Financial Times* (November 23, 2015), online at on.ft.com/1lDkSwe.

5 "Mass Leak of Client Data Rattles Swiss Banking," *The Wall Street Journal* (July 8, 2010), online at on.wsj.com/1mnN0U0.

6 "IRS Employee Took Home Data on 20,000 Workers at Agency," *Bloomberg* (March 18, 2014), online at bloom.bg/1MjMWKM; see also "Barclays Launches Investigation after Reported Customer Data Leak," *The Financial Times* (February 9, 2014), online at on.ft.com/1J9wSdF.

7 "Manage Like a Spymaster," *The Economist* (August 29, 2015), online at econ.st/1U8j8KK.

8 *Report to the Nations on Occupational Fraud and Abuse 2014 Global Fraud Study* (Association of Certified Fraud Examiners, 2014), online at www.acfe.com/rttn/docs/2014-report-to-nations.pdf (hereafter *2014 Global Fraud Survey*).

9 *Effectiveness of Fraud Risk Management Efforts* (KPMG LLP, 2009).

10 D. Stewart and R. Chase, *Mistake-Proofing: Designing Errors Out* (Portland, OR: Productivity Press, 1995). *Poka-yoke* is the Japanese term for *foolproof*. It was introduced to the management literature by the Japanese quality guru Sigeo Shingo.

11 "At Some Airlines, Laptops Replace Pilots' 'Brain Bags,'" *The Wall Street Journal* (March 26, 2002), p. B1.

12 "Computer Systems Cut Hospital Drug Errors," *Medpage Today* (February 22, 2013), online at www.medpagetoday.com/HospitalBasedMedicine/GeneralHospitalPractice/37496.

13 "Bear Stearns Ex-Staffer Pleads Guilty to Taking Funds in Check Scheme," *The Wall Street Journal*, (February 26, 2002), p. C14.

14 "How a Tiffany's Employee Stole $1.3 Million in Jewelry," *Business Week* (July 8, 2013), online at www.bloomberg.com/bw/articles/2013-07-08/how-a-tiffanys-employee-stole-1-dot-3-million-in-jewelry.

15 "Memorable Memo: McDonald's Sends Operations to War on Fries," *The Wall Street Journal* (December 18, 1997), online at on.wsj.com/1xjJzSy.

16 "Digital Taylorism," *The Economist* (September 12, 2015), online at econ.st/1QqLUAM.

17 "Tracking Workers' Every Move Can Boost Productivity – and Stress," *The Los Angeles Times* (April 8, 2013), online at www.latimes.com/la-fi-harsh-work-tech-20130408,0,6413037.story.

18 "Driver Fatigue Cited as Cause of Crash that Injured Comedian," *AP* (August 11, 2015), online at bigstory.ap.org/urn:publicid:ap.org:d1bab7054636428c81e75ea540a3c619; "Deutsche Bank Fined £4.7m by FCA over Reporting Blunders," *The Financial Times* (2014), online at on.ft.com/1fylDCW.

19 "Allfirst Officials Raised Concern about Trader in a 1999 Memo," *The Wall Street Journal* (February 25, 2002), p. C16.

20 "Controls at Allied Irish's Allfirst Likely Failed in Important Ways," *The Wall Street Journal* (February 20, 2002), p. C1.

21 *2014 Global Fraud Study*, op. cit.

22 *Driving Ethical Growth: New Markets, New Challenges* (Ernst & Young 11th Global Fraud Survey, 2010); see also *Integrity Survey 2013* (KPMG Forensic, 2013) – where 57% of the respondents reported that they "believe that policies or procedures are easy to override" as a root cause for managers and employees to engage in misconduct – online at www.kpmg.com/CN/en/IssuesAndInsights/ArticlesPublications/Documents/Integrity-Survey-2013-O-201307.pdf.

23 "Tracking Workers' Every Move Can Boost Productivity – and Stress," op. cit.

24 "New Background Check Survey Reveals Security Issues in the Screening Process," *Security Info Watch* (July 3, 2014), online at www.securityinfowatch.com/article/11545613/new-hireright-survey-highlights-potential-security-gaps-in-the-screening-process. See also "Are Workplace Personality Tests Fair?," *The Wall Street Journal* (September 29, 2014), online at on.wsj.com/1KHI7cY.

25 "To Hire a Lumber Expert, Click Here," *Fortune* (April 3, 2000), pp. 267–70.

26 "Social Media Emerges as Major Tool for Background Check of Employees: Survey," *DNA* (September 14, 2014), online at dnai.in/cn4m; "Survey: Social Media Background Checks, Policy Enforcement," *HR Daily Advisor* (September 4, 2014), online at shar.es/1GNk1e.

27 "Three Approaches to Pre-Screening Job Candidates," *ERC* (July 14, 2013), online at www.yourerc.com/blog/post/3-Approaches-to-Pre-Screening-Job-Candidates.aspx.

28 "How to Save Lives," *The Economist* (October 23, 2010), p. 72.

29 See, for example, "German-Style Training for American Factory Workers," *The Wall Street Journal* (September 9, 2014), online at on.wsj.com/1lU4XsG.

30 "Improve Your Employee Training Sessions," *Business Week* (February 2, 2010), online at www.businessweek.com.

31 "Mentors Make a Business Better," *Business Week* (March 20, 2008), online at www.businessweek.com.

32 "Firm Shares Tips for Succession Planning," *The Wall Street Journal* (January 24, 2014), online at on.wsj.com/1caDnQH.

33 "Skillsoft Selected as Gold Winner in Excellence in Social Learning by Chief Learning Officer Magazine," *Business Wire* (September 26, 2012), online at www.businesswire.com/news/home/20120926005748/en/Skillsoft-Selected-Gold-Winner-Excellence-Social-Learning.

34 "As Employers Push Efficiency, The Daily Grind Wears Down Workers," *The Los Angeles Times* (April 7, 2013), online at fw.to/yxImz0M.

35 *Codes of Conduct: A Barrier or Breakthrough for Corporate Behaviour?* (PwC, 2013), online at www.ibe.org.uk/userassets/surveys/pwccodesofconductreport2013.pdf.

36 "Business Codes of the Global 200: Their Prevalence, Content and Embedding," *KPMG* (June 16, 2008); *2013 UK and Continental European Survey* (Institute of Business Ethics, 2013), online at www.ibe.org.uk/userfiles/codes_survey_2013_interactive.pdf.

37 *A Crisis of Culture* (The Economist Intelligence Unit, 2013), online at https://www.cfatoronto.ca/cfast/Content/Site_Navigation/Publications/EIU_Crisis_of_Culture.pdf.

38 *2013 UK and Continental European Survey*, op. cit.

39 *Integrity Survey 2013*, op. cit.

40 "Employee Benefits: Share Ownership Schemes – Should You CoCo?," *HR Magazine* (September 1, 2008), online at www.hrmagazine.co.uk. See also "Could the John Lewis Model Work in Any Industry," *The Telegraph* (November 14, 2014), online at www.telegraph.co.uk/finance/festival-of-business/11229674/Could-the-John-Lewis-model-work-in-any-industry.html; and "TSB Bank to Move Towards John Lewis Model," *The Financial Times* (June 5, 2014), online at on.ft.com/1kN8dhN.

41 C. Rosen, J. Case, and M. Staubus, *Equity: Why Employee Ownership Is Good for Business* (Boston, MA: Harvard Business School Press, 2005).

42 J. Blasi, D. Kruse, and A. Bernstein, *In the Company of Owners: The Trust about Stock Options (and Why Every Employee Should Have Them)* (New York: Basic Books, 2003).

43 "The Role of Employee Engagement in the Return to Growth," *Business Week* (August 13, 2010), online at www.bloomberg.com/news/articles/2010-08-13/the-role-of-

employee-engagement-in-the-return-to-growth. See also "Organizations in Central and Eastern Europe with High Employee Engagement Are Achieving Better Business Results, Says Aon Hewitt," *PR Newswire* (December 3, 2012), online at www.prnewswire.co.uk; and *State of the American Workplace* (Gallup, 2013), online at www.gallup.com/services/178514/state-american-workplace.aspx.

44 "Reward Culture: Strong Foundations," *Pay & Benefits* (August 27, 2014), online at www.payandbenefitsmagazine.co.uk/article/reward-culture-strong-foundations.

45 "Method in the Madness of the Alibaba Cult," *The Financial Times* (September 7, 2014), online at on.ft.com/WAoqTa.

46 See the company's website, online at corporate.disney.go.com/careers/culture.

47 See, for example, "Tone at the Top: Why Investors Should Care," *Strategic Finance* (March 2013), online at www.imanet.org/docs/default-source/sf/03_2013_king-pdf.pdf?sfvrsn=0.

48 *Tone from the Top – Transforming Words into Action* (PwC, 2013), online at www.ibe.org.uk/userimages/pwc_tone_from_the_top_2013.pdf.

49 Quoted in D. Ferguson, "Do Entrepreneurial Companies Lose Their Innovative Spark as They Grow Larger?" *Cal Business* (Fall 1995), p. 12.

50 In addition to the brief description of the Alibaba culture earlier in this chapter, Southwest Airlines is another poster child of a firm with an acclaimed corporate culture. See, for example, G. Smith, "An Evaluation of the Corporate Culture of Southwest Airlines," *Measuring Business Excellence*, 8, no. 4 (2004), pp. 26–33; and M. Thomas, "Strategic Principles at Southwest Airlines," *Strategic Direction*, 31, no. 8 (2015), pp. 10–12.

51 Many articles have been written about these and other leaders, but to mention one as an illustration, see "Jeff Bezos Reveals His No. 1 Leadership Secret," *Forbes* (April 4, 2012), online at www.forbes.com/forbes/2012/0423/ceo-compensation-12-amazon-technology-jeff-bezos-gets-it.html.

52 "Reward Culture: Strong Foundations," op. cit.

53 See, for example, "People Work Harder When They're Happy, Study Finds," *The Telegraph* (March 21, 2014), online at www.telegraph.co.uk/news/health/10713606/People-work-harder-when-theyre-happy-study-finds.html; "Virgin Pulse Named One of *Boston Business Journal*'s Healthiest Employers," *Business Wire* (March 27, 2014), online at www.businesswire.com.

54 "An Idyllic Workplace under a Tycoon's Thumb," *The Wall Street Journal* (November 23, 1998), online at on.wsj.com/1sMFu7O.

55 See, for example, "Satya Nadella: This Is How I'm Really Going to Change Microsoft's Culture," *Business Insider* (July 15, 2014), online at read.bi/1wpztta.

56 "Colin Fan, Deutsche Bank: 'OMG, Colin's Video Has Gone Viral," *The Financial Times* (October 12, 2014), online at on.ft.com/1tlRYDc; "Deutsche Bank Warns Traders in Video over Boasting and Vulgarity," *The Financial Times* (May 16, 2014), online at on.ft.com/1jl1ocj.

57 "Scathing Report Says Toshiba CEOs Had Role in Accounting Scandal," *The Financial Times* (July 20, 2015), online at on.ft.com/1KgFnZB; "Toshiba Chief Hisao Tanaka Resigns over $1.2bn Accounting Scandal," *The Financial Times* (July 21, 2015), online at on.ft.com/1edzVbE.

58 For further study and a recent academic perspective and overview of the control literature in the area of what we call personnel/cultural controls, see M. Loughry, "Peer Control in Organizations," in S. Sitkin, L. Cardinal, and K. Bijlsma-Frankema, *Organizational Control* (New York: Cambridge University Press, 2010), chap. 11.

CASE STUDY
Witsky and Associates, Inc.

Brayton McLaughlin was a young associate at Witsky and Associates, Inc., a management consulting firm that helped small and family businesses with a variety of issues, including strategy, operations, logistics, and corporate governance. Brayton had joined Witsky two years ago immediately after completing his MBA degree.

In early June, Brayton was assigned to do time-and-motion studies at an office supply warehouse and distribution center located in Riverside, California. Management needed accurate cost data to be able to negotiate profitable contract terms in the forthcoming year. They were also concerned that some of the warehouse personnel were not performing all of their activities efficiently.

It was expected that Brayton would have to be on site for approximately 30 hours, at various times since the center operated 24/7, to observe the proper mix of activities with enough detail. Then Brayton would have to prepare and submit his report. As Brayton was also working on other projects, the due date for his report was the end of June.

Brayton reported to Pete Mahlendorf, Witsky's managing partner and the lead consultant on the job, that he visited the warehouse and distribution center on several days in June, both during the day and night shifts. He submitted his report on time and on budget.

On July 1, Pete got a phone call from Jeremiah Jones, operations manager at the Riverside distribution center. Jeremiah wanted to know when he could see Brayton's report. Pete said that he had just received it, and he would send it right over. But Jeremiah expressed surprise that the report was finished. He told Pete that:

> **As far as I know, Brayton only visited the warehouse once, and that was for a quite brief time. How could he have finished his report? Maybe he was here when I was out, but I have not heard others mention his presence either.**

Pete checked again with Brayton, and Brayton assured him that he had completed all the needed work.

A few days later, rather by chance, Pete mentioned Jeremiah's surprise reaction to Priscilla Musso, Witsky's chief financial officer. After some reflection, Priscilla suggested that they perhaps should check the location-tracking data provided by Brayton's cell phone. Witsky paid the cell phone bills for the firm's staff, and location tracking was one of the applications that the staff was required to keep turned on.[1] The firm had never had an occasion to use these data, but Priscilla thought that it might be useful to look at it in this instance. Pete and Priscilla checked the computer records and found, indeed, that Brayton had been near Riverside only once in the month of June.

Pete called Brayton into his office and asked him to explain the discrepancy. Brayton immediately broke down in tears. He explained that because of some personal problems he was way behind in his work. To try to cope, he took the shortcut of creating a report based mostly on data he had found on the Internet. He admitted that he had not spent the requisite time at the Riverside warehouse and distribution center.

[1] The firm's legal advisors were of the opinion that use of these data did not violate any laws.

This case was prepared by Professor Kenneth A. Merchant.

CASE STUDY
The Platinum Pointe Land Deal

In early December 2006, Harry Hepburn, president of the Southern California Division of Robinson Brothers Homes, was faced with a significant challenge. The markets his division served had slowed considerably. To sell its homes, the division often had to make significant price concessions. But construction costs were continuing to rise, so margins were getting squeezed. It was clear that the division was not going to achieve its 2006 sales and profit plan. But what was worse, corporate executives were recommending a significant downsizing of the division in 2007 to wait until the housing market rebounded. Harry resisted this idea. He thought he had assembled a great employee team. The division's performance had been outstanding during the good years in the early 2000s. He wanted to keep his team intact. But that required finding a continuing stream of good projects for them to work on.

One promising project on the horizon was called Platinum Pointe. It was a large project that promised to provide over $100 million in revenue and nearly $14 million in profits in the 2008–11 time period. It would keep a lot of employees productively busy. Harry really wanted to do the project. However, the financial projections suggested that the project would not quite earn the returns that the corporation required for projects with this level of risk. He contemplated preparing projections that were a "little more optimistic" to ensure that the project would be approved.

The company

Robinson Brothers Homes (RBH) was a medium-sized homebuilder. The company built single-family and higher-density homes, such as townhouses and condominiums. By 2006, RBH built almost 2,000 homes per year. Because it was much smaller than the largest homebuilders who had economies-of-scale advantages,[1] RBH focused on building higher quality/higher price homes for first and second move-up buyers. In 2006, the average closing sales price for an RBH home was slightly more than $400,000.

RBH's stock had been traded publicly since 1995. The company had been highly profitable throughout the past decade, but finances were expected to be much tighter in 2007 because of the homebuilding slowdown that had started in early 2006. The stock price had declined almost 50% from the all-time peak in 2005.

RBH's organization was comprised of a headquarters staff located in Denver, Colorado, and 15 divisions located in most of the metropolitan areas of the Central, Mountain, and Southwest areas of the United States. The headquarters staff was small, comprised mainly of specialists in the areas of finance, accounting, legal, information systems, sales and marketing, and customer service, and their staffs.

Each division was largely self-contained, with its own construction supervision, customer care, purchasing, sales and marketing, land development, land acquisition, and accounting staffs. The only major function that was outsourced was construction. RBH's construction superintendents supervised the general contractors who built the homes to RBH's specifications.

Exhibit 1 shows the organization chart for the Southern California division. This division, one of RBH's largest, employed approximately 120 people. In 2006, it was projected to sell 637 homes, generating $235 million in revenue and $40 million in net income.

Land acquisition

Land acquisition was a key function in the homebuilding business. RBH's land acquisition personnel had to find land on which the company could build homes that could be sold at a good profit. The lag between acquisition of the land and sale of the final house built was typically three to five years. Sometimes the permit-acquisition process itself dragged on for years, with the company fighting lengthy, emotional battles with city councils and other permit-granting organizations. On the other hand, sometimes land was acquired at "retail price," with all the permits already having been granted.

As a standard part of the land acquisition process, RBH's land acquisition personnel were required to prepare a detailed land acquisition proposal. These proposals provided detailed information on:

- the nature of the request;
- the location;
- entitlements;
- infrastructure;
- product design;
- market overview;
- environmental considerations;
- development fees and costs;
- special assessments and homeowner association dues (if any);
- school information;
- project milestones;
- risk evaluations; and,
- financial projections.

Many of the detailed proposals were 100 or more pages in length and often included detailed maps, product sketches, and excerpts from consultants' reports.

An important part of the proposal-writing process was a detailed evaluation of the project's risk in four areas: political, development, market, and financial. The risk in each area was evaluated subjectively into three categories: low, moderate, or high. The risk

[1] For example, D. R. Horton, Inc., the largest homebuilder in the United States, was building over 50,000 homes per year.

assessments in these areas were translated into a minimum internal rate of return (IRR) requirements for the project, according to the procedure shown in Exhibit 2.

Many land acquisition ideas failed to progress to the approval stage for any of a number of reasons, including inadequate financial returns, excess risk in the permit-granting process, or a mismatch between the needs of the market and the company's capabilities. If the proposals were approved by the division president and RBH's CEO and CFO, the division president then presented them to the Executive Land Committee of the Board of Directors for final approval. Only then could the monies be released.

The Platinum Pointe site

The Platinum Pointe site was identified by Michael Borland, the vice president of land acquisition for the Southern California Division. The Platinum Pointe site was located in the Emerald Estates master planned community being developed by Jackson Development Company.

Jackson Development was recently formed by Tom Jackson, who had formerly worked as division president of one of RBH's competitors. Michael Borland and Tom Jackson were long-time friends, back to their time together as fraternity brothers at San Diego State University. Michael called Tom soon after he learned of the formation of Jackson Development. He looked forward to developing some projects jointly with Tom.

Michael discussed with Tom several sites in the planned Emerald Estates community. They finally settled on a 21-acre site on the northeast corner of the master planned community. The proposed purchase price was $22,500,000 plus a profit participation by Jackson Development in the amount of 50% above 9% net profit, with a soft cost allowance of 20%.[2]

[2] Soft costs are costs related to items in a project that are necessary to complete the nonconstruction needs of the project, which typically include such items as architecture, design, engineering, permits, inspections, consultants, environmental studies, and regulatory demands needing approval before construction begins.

Michael's experience suggested to him that higher-density housing, rather than single-family detached homes, would provide the best use of this site. Over the forthcoming several months, he fleshed out the idea with the division and corporate specialists, particularly in the areas of sales and marketing and construction. He also contracted for special studies from two outside consulting firms. One consulting firm prepared a report detailing projections of the costs needed to develop the site. The other prepared a marketing study that provided pricing and absorption rate estimates based on analyses of competitive offerings and forecasts of market trends in the geographical area.

Michael wrote a detailed proposal for building 195 homes in two formats: a triplex townhome and a six-plex cluster home. Other RBH divisions had produced similar homes, but the format had not been previously offered in Southern California, and some modifications were made to appeal to southern California buyers. The homes would range from 1,628 to 2,673 square feet and be priced from $445,000 to $705,000. The executive summary of the detailed proposal, with the required risk assessments and financial projections, is shown in Exhibit 3.

Michael was disappointed when he saw the projected IRR for the project. It was only 21%, which was below the minimum required for a project with this level of risk – 24.5%. He decided to discuss the problem with Harry Hepburn to see what, if anything, could be done.

What to do?

Harry, too, was disappointed. He had hoped that the Platinum Pointe project would provide a significant proportion of the revenues and profits that the division would need over the next four-year period. He still wanted to do the project. So he and Michael sat down to take another look at the detailed proposal. What modifications could they make to lower the required IRR or to raise the projected IRR to ensure that the project would be approved?

Exhibit 1 Robinson Brothers Homes, Southern California Division, organization chart

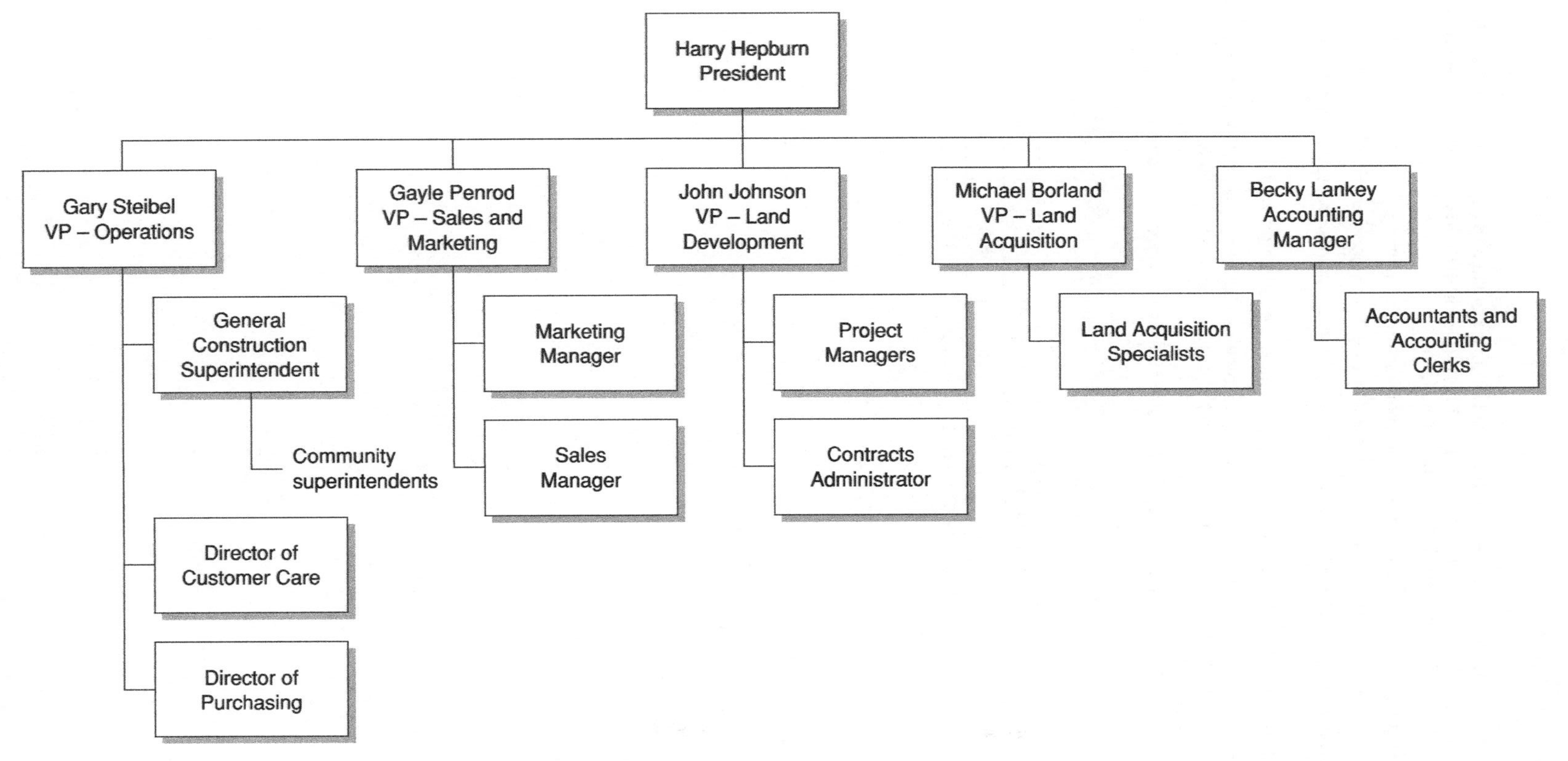

Exhibit 2 IRR requirements

Land acquisition opportunities and the related product choices continue to expand for Robinson Brothers Homes. Given that risks can vary greatly from opportunity to opportunity, guidelines to assess risk and the required minimum returns have been established. The risks to be assessed are as follows:

1. Political/Entitlement – ability to achieve expected entitlements and timing;
2. Development – site conditions and ability to accurately project development costs;
3. Market – experience with proposed product type, product price points, buyer types, current market conditions both current and future;
4. Financial/Financing – ability to achieve projected results and obtain proposed financing.

Based on these factors, a minimum unleveraged IRR is to be established. Risk ratings are to be assessed based on the projects' specific characteristics. Each area is to be rated as *Low*, *Moderate*, or *High*. A numerical value is to be attached to assessment as follows:

The minimum IRR for the project is assessed as the sum of the ratings assigned in each of the four assessment areas.

	Low	Moderate	High
Political	5.0	6.5	8.0
Development	5.0	6.5	8.0
Market	5.0	6.0	7.0
Financial/Financing	4.0	5.0	6.0

Exhibit 3 Platinum Pointe investment proposal – executive summary (initial draft)

The Southern California Division is requesting approval to acquire the 21-acre site known as Platinum Pointe in Carlsbad, CA. The site will yield 198 detached and attached homes. The purchase price is $22,500,000. The projected IRR is currently 21%, and the required IRR is 24.5%. Close of escrow is projected to occur in June 2007.

LOCATION

The site is located on the east side of Interstate 5 in the City of Carlsbad, located 30 miles north of San Diego. The site is in the Emerald Estates community being master planned by Jackson Development Company, Inc. The master planned community is comprised of just over 200 acres to yield approximately 1,000 units. The community will have a range of product from townhomes to duplexes, as well as single-family homes on lots ranging in size from 4,500 to 7,500 s.f.

PURCHASE

The Seller is Jackson Development Company, Inc. The purchase price of the property is $22,500,000 for 21 net acres. The purchase price is not tied to unit count. We are currently projecting construction of 123 townhome units and 72 cluster units. The Master Development Plan approval is a closing contingency. Should the Master Development Plan not be approved, we have the option to waive the condition or terminate the Agreement. The close of escrow is targeted for June 1, 2007. We have the option to purchase two non-refundable nonapplicable 30-day extensions should our tentative tract map not yet be approved. Should the Seller cause a delay that would prevent us from processing our entitlements in a timely manner, we will be granted the right to have the extensions without payment of the extension fee. This project includes profit participation by the Seller for the amount of 50% above 9% net profit, with a soft cost allowance of 20%. We have run multiple scenarios to include interest rate increases, financing options, construction delays, and a slow down in absorption. We are comfortable that we will stay below the 20% threshold.

We have explored the option of negotiating this deal with no profit participation. Jackson was open to negotiations where we would increase the land price and move forward with no profit participation on the back end of the deal. But the increase in land price would decrease the projected IRR on the project.

RISK EVALUATION

► Political

The property is located within the Emerald Estates Master Plan area. It is zoned PCD (Planned Community Development). The Seller is preparing a detailed Master Development Plan (MDP) that will be submitted to the City of Carlsbad in early January 2007. Our proposed project will be part of that submission. The Seller has been working with the City throughout the creation of the MDP and has gained support of the project. If one contingency – preservation of habitat for the Western Speckled Toad possibly located in the area – can be solved, the Seller projects that the guidelines will be approved by the City in March 2007. A neighbor claims that the site is habitat for the Toad, but the Environmental Impact report has not yet been completed. If the Toad issue is real, we will have to place a permanent habitat on the property. We think we can do this without losing any buildable lots.

With the approval of the MDP, our review by the Design Review Committee will be expedited. Our proposed project will be designated R-M (Medium Residential, 8 –10 duplexes/acre). Our current site plan shows a total of 195 units, which is approximately 9.29 duplexes/acre. We have met with the Director of Development Services three separate times. We believe that our latest site plan incorporates the City's requests. We will need to process a tentative map and to obtain approval from the Design Review Board for the site plan and architecture. The tentative map is expected to be received by May 2007, and all appeal periods are expected to expire before we close in June 2007.

- Overall political risk is moderate.

► Development

Site Development

The site is currently raw land, but it will be delivered as a mass-graded pad. The Seller received the grading permit on November 7, 2006, and has started grading. Grading will be completed in January 2007. The Seller will construct all offsite backbone sewer, water, storm drain, dry utility, street improvements, and perimeter landscaping. The street and storm drain plans are approved, as well as the sewer and water plans. Backbone utility plans are currently being designed. The Seller will provide utility stubs to the site if we are able to give them fixed entry locations prior to their installing the improvements. Otherwise, we will have to connect to the systems. The Emerald Estates master development infrastructure will not be completed prior to our close, but the Seller will soon begin the improvements. The improvements are being funded by the CFD [Community Facilities District]. Should the Seller fail to make the improvements in the timeline presented in the agreement and their failure to complete the improvements affects our site specifically, we have the right to

(Continued)

Exhibit 3 *Continued*

assume responsibility for completion of the remaining Seller work, and Seller shall reimburse Buyer at 110% of the third party direct costs. In addition to cooperating with Buyer without limitation, Seller shall insure that Buyer is able to draw against or obtain reimbursement from the CFD for completing the remaining improvements.

As mentioned above, the CFD will be funding the entire infrastructure for the site. The CFD has an approved Resolution of Intent. The Resolution of Formation went to City Council and was continued to January 12, 2007. The CFD is confident that the formation will be heard at the January 13th meeting. The bonds will be sold in two issues. The first bond sale, expected to be $30–35 million will cover backbone infrastructure, including sewer, water, streets, and storm drain. This is expected to occur in March 2007. The second bond sale will occur approximately six months later and will include dry utilities and landscaping. The CFD has told us that the appraisal is underway and should be completed shortly. They do not see any issues with the appraisal meeting the 3:1 coverage requirement. The bid package for the first bond sale is complete and will be submitted for City review in January/February 2006. Furthermore, the City of Carlsbad is the lead agency and is pushing to get the backbone infrastructure constructed. The improvement plans have been through multiple plan checks and the tax rate will be approximately 1.8%.

In addition to the infrastructure, the CFD will be funding certain impact fees. We are expecting to receive a $8,500 plus credit per unit from the CFD to cover a portion of the fees. The fees that will be covered by the CFD include webbed toed lizard, drainage fees, signalization fees, sewer and water connection fees, supplemental water fees, and Art in Public Places fee. Our in-tract development costs are derived from a cost estimate based on our current site plan, which was prepared for us by the Evensen Group. These costs, including fees and net of the planned CFD reimbursement, come to $63,088 per unit. This total includes a 15% contingency on construction items and a 10% contingency on fees.

A site visit was performed by an environmental consultant and previous Phase I report were also reviewed. Other than the possible Western Speckled Toad issue, there are no potential environmental concerns and no additional assessment appears to be necessary. A geotechnical investigation concluded that the site was suitable for the intended use.

The Seller will also be establishing a Master Homeowners Association to maintain the perimeter and median landscaping. We will create our own sub-association to maintain our on-site landscaping detention basin and recreation facilities.

The Seller will be mass grading the well and park sites and designing the park. We will be responsible for constructing the well site improvements, excluding the well itself, and construction of the park. We have included $1.0 million for the park and well site. The well site improvements consist of a block perimeter wall, some landscaping iron drive gates and drive approach. The park improvements are in the preliminary planning stages and are expected to include landscaping, a tot lot, picnic tables, shade structures, walkways and lighting, and possible restroom facilities. The costs of the park and well site will be initially funded from equity in the short term but will be reimbursed through the CFD. The well site will be deeded to the Carlsbad Water District (CWD), and the park will be deeded to the City of Carlsbad. Both the well site and the park will be maintained by each entity respectively.

Direct Construction

The townhome product consists of new plans that we have not built before and direct construction costs continue to rise. However, the cluster product is a modification of product our Phoenix Division has built before. The direct construction estimates we have used are derived from our actual costs in building the 10-plex product in El Cajon, which is coming in at about $80 psf. There we added an additional $10 psf to account for the increased specs we are including in these new townhomes.

Overall we conclude that the risks associated with both site development and direct construction are moderate.

- Overall development risk is moderate.

▶ Competitive Analysis/Market Risk

We will be building two product types, a triplex townhome and a six-plex cluster product. The triplex townhome ranges in square footage from 1,753 square feet to 2,442 square feet and will be priced from $445,000 to $595,000. We feel this product will appeal to buyers who work in north San Diego County and second home owners (weekend or seasonal) who are attracted to a low maintenance home with a larger yard. The cluster will range in square footage from 1,628 square feet to 2,673 square feet and be priced from $450,000 to $705,000. These pricing projections are the exact prices recommended from our marketing consultant, the Blackfield Group. This is an upgrade version of a product that was very successful in Phoenix. It will be highly amenitized. The master baths have been revised to meet the new "wow" factor that is pervasive in this submarket. There is currently very little competition for attached or mid-density product in the Carlsbad area. We are currently unaware of any other 8 –10 units/acre development projected within the City of Carlsbad at this time, but we continue to monitor new development projects within the City. We have a completed marketing study by the Blackfield Group that supports our product type and pricing. We are comfortable with the absorption recommendation from Blackfield given the two very separate product lines. The models in our estimates are currently slated to open in July 2008. Our absorption would maintain 15 homes per month average as recommended by the Blackfield Group. But there

Exhibit 3 *Continued*

is risk. The north San Diego County market has experienced a noticeable downturn in the last 12–18 months. If interest rates continue to increase and if prices in markets throughout north San Diego County continue to moderate, we may not be able to maintain our absorption rate, or we will have to shave our margins.

- The risk associated with the market is moderate to high.

▶ Financial/Financing Risk

All indications are that interest rates will continue to rise. In the event that interest rates increase substantially during the life of this project, our product will still be positioned in a more affordable segment of the market. Given the size of the transaction ($48 million at March 2009), some form of outside capital will be used. Lot option and or joint venture will be considered and leads to the moderate financial risk.

- The financial/financing risk is moderate given the previously discussed political and development risks.

IRR REQUIREMENTS

Based on the above analysis and assessed risk, the IRR requirements are as follows:

Political	Moderate	6.5
Development	Moderate	6.5
Market	Moderate/High	6.5
Financial	Moderate	5.0
	Required IRR	24.5%

FINANCIAL SUMMARY

Total Sales Revenue:	$112,050,000
Profit ($):	$13,707,000
Profit (%):	12.2%
Equity Required:	$8,722,000
Home Size Triplex:	2,151 sf weighted average
Home Size Cluster:	2,126 sf weighted average
Direct Costs Triplex:	$93/sf weighted average
Direct Costs Cluster:	$82/sf weighted average
Base Sales Price Triplex:	$531,667/unit weighted average
Base Sales Price Cluster:	$571,667/unit weighted average
Base Sales Price Triplex: ($/sf)	$247.17/sf weighted average
Base Sales Price Cluster: ($/sf)	$268.89/sf weighted average
IRR Leveraged:	41.4%
IRR Unleveraged:	21.0% (Required 24.5%)
TOTAL PEAK EQUITY	$11,809,000

This case was prepared by Professor Kenneth A. Merchant.

CASE STUDY
EyeOn Pharmaceuticals, Inc.

In early 2016, Frank DeMartino, senior vice president of Science and Technology at EyeOn Pharmaceuticals, Inc., reflected on his concerns about the challenges his company faced in controlling its research and development (R&D) activities:

> **R&D is the most critical part of EyeOn's business. The company will thrive only if we are effective at developing new breakthrough products. In managing the research function, we have to address three difficult but important issues. First, we have to decide how much to spend on R&D. Then we have to decide how to allocate the resources among the various programs and projects. And, finally, we have to ensure that the resources are used effectively. How we address these issues determines how productive our research activity will be.**
>
> **I am especially concerned about the third issue – how to control the use of our resources. I don't think we do a very good job of measuring our productivity. At the time we are spending our resources, both money and time, and even for some time after they have been spent, it is very difficult to tell how productive we are being and have been. We could be missing some important information about problems we might be having. I feel we should do some thinking about this issue and what we can do to improve the tracking of our R&D productivity.**

The company and its products

EyeOn Pharmaceuticals, Inc. (EyeOn) focused on the ophthalmology segment of the pharmaceutical market. It developed, manufactured, and sold a wide range of products for the diagnosis and treatment of ophthalmic disorders; that is, those used in the treatment of defects and diseases of the eye. The company marketed both prescription and nonprescription drugs, a wide variety of products for use in ophthalmic surgery and for the care of hard, soft, and gas-permeable lenses, and a few dermatological products. Despite continuing price pressure from the cheaper generic drugs entering the market, EyeOn revenues and profits nearly tripled over the period between 2005 and 2015. In 2016, EyeOn sold products in over 80 countries, and worldwide sales totaled almost $1 billion.

EyeOn used a traditional product-line organization structure. Reporting to EyeOn's CEO were the managers of each of the product lines, and the managers of Science and Technology (Mr. DeMartino), Finance and Administration, International, and Legal.

The R&D organization

R&D was critical to the maintenance of EyeOn's rate of growth. Over 25% of 2016 sales were from products released in just the past five years.

The company's R&D department was headed by Dr. Prakash Kumar, who reported to Mr. DeMartino. The department included 350 people – 290 scientists (80 of whom had PhD degrees) and 60 support staff. The purpose of the R&D organization was to develop new, marketable eye-care products that would fuel the company's growth. EyeOn's board of directors established broad research policies based on the long-term strategies of the marketing divisions, but the board depended heavily on Mr. DeMartino and Dr. Kumar to provide the guidance and direction necessary to ensure effective research activities.

Mr. DeMartino and Dr. Kumar complemented each other well in terms of knowledge and experience. Mr. DeMartino had an in-depth knowledge of EyeOn's products and markets because he had advanced through the sales organization. Dr. Kumar was a chemist.

The R&D department was organized in matrix form, with eight key senior directors (plus staff support) reporting to Dr. Kumar. On one dimension of the matrix were four medical specialty groups: ophthalmology, optical, dermatology, and basic research. Personnel in these groups specialized in particular types of diseases. The basic research group was distinguished from the other three medical specialty groups in that its work took place early in the drug development cycle (described below). On the other dimension of the matrix were four preclinical science departments: microbiology, chemistry, toxicology, and pharmaceutical sciences. Personnel in these departments were experts in one of these scientific fields. Each research program and project was managed by a medical specialty expert. The preclinical science personnel were assigned to programs and projects when needed. They often had more than one assignment at any particular time.

The personnel on the research staff had needs and characteristics that were different from those of employees in other parts of the EyeOn organization. Managers in the R&D department had to be sensitive to those differences. The senior director of the basic research group explained:

> We're not an organization comprised of conformists, and we don't want to be. The other companies can have those people. Good researchers are unique. They are creative and intelligent, and although they can be aloof and seemingly disengaged, they will work their tails off when they get on a project they like. But their feelings are easily hurt. It's very easy to kill ideas. We have to be careful because if we use punishment, discouragement or penalties for failure, we may never get another idea.

Product development cycle

The product development cycle in pharmaceutical companies such as EyeOn was long, typically totaling up to 15 years for a totally new drug and from 3 to 5 years for a simple product. Often the cycle started with some basic research designed to provide a better understanding of the underlying biochemistry of the disease processes at the molecular level. In 2016, EyeOn had five basic research programs underway, all in the area of ophthalmology: inflammation, immunology, glaucoma, diabetic retinopathy/cataracts, and drug delivery.

When a new product concept was formed, the product development cycle was said to begin. Development consisted of a number of relatively distinct steps. First was the discovery phase of development, the purpose of which was to identify compounds with potential commercial applications. Scientists designed and tested new drug compounds against the characteristics of the diseases they were studying both in test tubes and later in live animal subjects. For most new drug concepts, these screening and testing activities would last from two to five years.

When the compounds moved into the discovery phase of development, EyeOn management assigned the effort a development program number. This number identified the effort until the product entered the clinical phase of testing. In 2016, EyeOn had a total of 11 development programs underway, 4 each in ophthalmology and optical, and 3 in dermatology.

A successful culmination of the discovery phase of development was marked by the identification of a compound that showed promise. Such compounds were moved into the optimization phase of development. This phase usually involved one to two years of studies of how the compound might act in the body. Scientists would study how the compound was absorbed, distributed, metabolized and excreted in animal subjects. They would do some exploratory testing of toxicity (i.e. harmful side effects) and stability (i.e. length of time the drug retains its effectiveness when stored). By the end of this phase of development, the scientists would prescribe a preliminary chemical formulation and make a preliminary packaging decision (i.e. mode of delivery and size of dosage).

Drugs continuing to show promise were moved into the preclinical phase of development. This phase involved better controlled laboratory experiments to validate the results of the exploratory tests conducted in the optimization phase of development. The preclinical phase of development usually lasted about 6–12 months. The drugs that continued to show promise were filed as IND (Investigation of a New Drug) candidates with the US Food and Drug Administration (FDA). At this point, a reasonably complete composition and specification existed, and a manufacturing procedure suitable for the preparation of clinical supplies was in place.

Once the IND was filed, the project moved into the clinical phase of development. This phase involved toxicity and stability testing of a longer-term nature than had been done previously. The testing was performed on live subjects: first normal human subjects and then diseased human subjects. During this testing, the scientists would make judgments of the safety and efficacy of the drug candidates and make final decisions about the dosages and modes of delivery to be used.

The clinical phase of development generally lasted between five and eight years. When a product entered the clinical phase of development, a project number was assigned. This number would stay with the effort until the product received FDA approval or the effort was abandoned. In 2016, EyeOn had a total of 30 active projects.

A drug that passed clinical testing was filed as an NDA (New Drug Application) with the FDA. The FDA approval process took from one to three years. Approval was needed before the drug could be marketed in the United States. However, the product could be sold in many other countries after it had passed clinical testing.

Exhibit 1 shows an overview of the product development cycle. The times shown in the exhibit for completion of each of the phases in the cycle are for development of major drugs. For fairly simple drugs and optical devices, the times were considerably shorter where INDs were often filed within 12 months, and clinical testing took between 12 and 18 months.

A shift in emphasis

Through most of its history, EyeOn had relied heavily on other pharmaceutical companies not involved in ophthalmic markets as sources of new product ideas. EyeOn scientists would screen compounds developed from these companies, and if they showed promise, EyeOn would license the compounds and introduce tailored forms of them into ophthalmic markets. Compounds screened in such a manner were entered into the product development process in the preclinical phase of development because the properties of the compounds were already understood.

In recent years, however, EyeOn management had been shifting their R&D efforts to emphasize more basic research. As the ophthalmic markets had grown, other pharmaceutical companies had entered some of EyeOn's market segments. These companies were less prone to offer EyeOn their newest compounds. Thus, the research focus had been evolving toward larger-scale, longer-term studies of more complex and sophisticated diseases of the eye. This is because EyeOn already had a broad product line covering most niches in the eye-care market, and to meet the company's aggressive growth targets, new breakthrough products were needed. The inevitable shift toward more basic research made management even more concerned about having measures of research productivity available for control purposes because the investments in basic research were longer-term and riskier. As Mr. DeMartino explained:

> **What's important in conducting research is to keep achieving progress on a daily basis. When it takes ten years to develop a product, you can't wait until tomorrow to get the work done. The important questions are: Are we doing everything we can to ensure that we are being productive every day? And how can I tell if we're being productive?**

Drug investments and payoffs

New product development involved high-risk investments for potentially lucrative payoffs. Across the industry, only about 1 of every 10,000 compounds investigated in the early exploratory research stages eventually proved to be commercially successful. The probabilities of failure of a typical compound in each of the phases of the product development cycle were approximately as follows:

Phase	Probability of Failure
Discovery	90%
Optimization	50%
Preclinical	25%
Clinical	70%
FDA & Patent	Negligible

The payoffs from the research were highly dependent on the magnitude and duration of the competitive advantage that EyeOn enjoyed when the new products were developed. Some drugs were breakthrough products that provided significant advantages over the competition in large market segments. Others were either minor modifications of already-existing EyeOn products or were aimed at small market segments. Sometimes competing firms developed alternatives to commercially successful new drugs in periods as short as two to three years, while on other occasions EyeOn products were sold for 20 years or more with little or no competition. As Mr. DeMartino noted:

> **From my perspective, it's not very important whether a product costs $30 million or $60 million to develop. When we are working on a drug that will give us several billion dollars in sales over 15 years**

> **and a 75 percent gross margin, overspending a little on research doesn't matter much as long as the drug gets created.**

The timing of the development efforts was critical. If the development of a particular drug was pursued too early, the company could be subject to a high probability of failure and/or significant extra development expenses and, if problems were found after introduction, possible legal liability expenses. If the development was pursued too late, the result would be a "me-too" product.

Planning and budgeting

EyeOn used a well-developed set of management systems to help manage its R&D effort. Planning and budgeting was done on an annual cycle, which took place from mid-July to mid-September. Planning was an iterative process. Mr. DeMartino and Dr. Kumar began the process by setting program and project objectives and priorities and by outlining an overall budget for the R&D department. In establishing these guidelines, they met with EyeOn directors and top-level managers to ensure that they had a good understanding of market trends and the amount of resources the company was willing to spend on R&D. Then directors and managers in each medical specialties group and each preclinical science department determined the labor hours and resources required to satisfy project and program objectives. This process was accomplished through a series of meetings between directors and managers.

As compared to plans for the development projects, plans for the basic research programs were easier to prepare because they used few resources from the preclinical science departments. Thus, very little cross-organizational coordination was required. Most development projects required the assistance of all, or at least most, of the preclinical science groups, so many meetings between the managers of the medical specialty groups and the director of Pre-Clinical Sciences were required to ensure that resources were allocated appropriately and, if necessary, that steps were taken to procure additional resources.

After the plans were prepared, Dr. Kumar reviewed them and made suggestions and adjustments as necessary. Then the plans were consolidated and compared with the overall targets. Sometimes further adjustments were necessary.

By February, all EyeOn employees were required to develop, in consultation with their immediate supervisor, personal objectives for the year. The company did not require the use of a standardized form or format for documenting these objectives, but the objectives had to be written down, and this document had to be signed by both the employee and the supervisor.

During the year, budget updates were prepared on a quarterly basis consistent with the planning schedule. The budget analysis process, like the annual planning processes, was very informal because, as Dr. Kumar explained:

> **We do not expect the scientists to act like businessmen when they plan new product activity. We want to encourage them to develop new ideas without many constraints, and they don't like a lot of paperwork.**

Indeed, one research program manager explained his dislike for paperwork requirements:

> **We work only on programs with payoffs so potentially large that a monkey can run the figures showing that the investment is worthwhile. The trick is to make the new product work, not to try to figure out that a new breakthrough therapy for glaucoma will pay off. It will!**

Mr. DeMartino had two main concerns about the planning process. First, he wondered if too much detail was still being required. Second, he wondered if requiring numbers about the research activities made the managers and scientists conservative in presenting their ideas. Given the company's need for good ideas, he thought it was important that no administrative barriers to ideas be erected.

Measurement and reporting

Accounting in the R&D department was done on a full absorption cost basis. Direct expenses, both labor and materials, were charged to specific programs and projects. Labor was charged on the basis of time sheets completed weekly by R&D personnel. Costs not specifically identifiable with a particular project or program were allocated monthly on the basis of direct labor hours.

EyeOn produced an extensive set of cost reports. Many of the reports were on a project, program, or medical specialty basis. They showed costs by line item compared to budget. These reports were available on a monthly basis. Another set of reports showed expenses aggregated by cost center. The R&D department was divided into 75 cost centers. The cost reports were summarized by type of medical specialty and by type of project or program. The program/project cost accounting system provided the information necessary to monitor the flow of resources to medical specialty areas, research versus development, and long term versus short term.

The project/program and cost center reports were sent to the managers responsible for the costs. The managers reviewed the reports, but they were not required to explain variances. This was because most of the variances were caused by changes in the scope or timing of the project/program, and such changes were almost always preapproved by Mr. DeMartino and/or Dr. Kumar.

EyeOn management recognized that the cost reports were useful for measuring the *inputs* to the R&D processes, but they were not useful for measuring the productivity of the R&D activity because they did not reflect any *outputs*. The outputs, which might be measured in terms of profits generated or value created, would not be known for years. The significant lag between the investments in R&D and the returns generated ensured that traditional accounting measures, such as return on investment, were not very meaningful except in very long measurement windows.

To date, Mr. DeMartino and Dr. Kumar had focused their attention on the department's consolidated financial summary (actual versus plan) and on the major R&D achievements of the year. In the last few years, these achievements were as follows:

	2013	2014	2015
INDs filed	3	4	3
NDAs filed	6	5	3
Research publications	25	19	17
Patent applications filed	15	9	8
Patents indicated allowable	7	8	5
Patents issued	5	6	4

They realized, however, that none of these indicators was a totally reliable indicator of forthcoming commercial success.

Incentive plans

EyeOn used two formal incentive plans offering cash awards for good performance, one for scientists and one for senior-level managers. The *scientist incentive plan* was introduced in the R&D department in 2013. Four cash awards of $25,000 each were made annually for technical excellence. The awards were split between scientists doing basic research and those involved in development activities.

Candidates for the scientist award were nominated by senior directors in the R&D department. The candidates' accomplishments were judged by a seven-person committee which included four working-level scientists, two director-level managers, and one person from outside R&D (e.g. from corporate marketing). The committee assigned the awards based on "perceptible contributions or unusual problem-solving capabilities which are perceptible to fellow workers."

The *management incentives* were provided through a company-wide program which provided stock options and bonuses to managers down to the director level of the firm. Each year an incentive award pool was assigned to the R&D department based on a predetermined percentage of EyeOn profits. This pool was allocated by R&D management to R&D employees included in the plan in conjunction with the annual performance review.

For purposes of assigning the awards in the R&D department, R&D employees were classified into three categories of achievement: (1) distinguished performance (DP), (2) superior performance (SP), and (3) good solid performance (GSP). (A fourth category called "Needs Improvement" was also used on occasion, but, as Dr. Kumar observed, "these colleagues don't get to stay very long.") Table 1 shows the approximate percentage of people who were classified in each category of achievement and the bonuses that could be expected in an average year in each of the categories.

Table 1

Category of Achievement	Percent So Evaluated	Average Award (% of salary)
DP	< 1%	30–35%
SP	50–60%	15–20%
GSP	40–50%	10%

The evaluations were based on a weighted average of three factors: (1) meeting the technical milestones in the annual plan; (2) discovering new product candidates; and (3) getting new products with commercial potential through FDA approvals. The factors used for weighting accomplishments in each of these areas were pre-established at the beginning of the year. In general, the highest weightings were given to the accomplishments that could be measured in a tangible fashion in the next 12 months.

The weighting factors varied significantly among the various areas of the department. For example, managers in development areas (as opposed to those in basic research) were expected to have products progress through the FDA approvals, but they were not expected to generate many new product leads.

The standards used to assess performance also varied significantly among the areas, reflecting the probability of payoffs of the various activities. For example, to be evaluated as SP (superior performance), managers of basic research activities might be expected to achieve 40% of their objectives in a given year. For managers of ophthalmology drug development activities, however, the achievement of 50% of their objectives might qualify only as GSP; SP might require the achievement of 70%. For product development managers in optical, GSP might require achievement of 60% of their objectives, and SP might require achievement of 80%.

Management concerns

EyeOn managers felt they had an excellent research team that had produced an ever-increasing set of new products that had fueled the company's growth. Mr. DeMartino highlighted a critical success factor – hiring:

> Eighty percent of the really good ideas – those that lead to breakthrough products – come from 20 percent of our colleagues. It is important for us to hire as many of those good people as we can, and perhaps even more important not to lose any we've already employed. But it is very difficult to tell who the really good people are until their accomplishments are apparent, and that might not be for some years after they were hired.

Mr. DeMartino's continuing concern was that EyeOn did not have a good early warning system in place to signal potential problems on a timely basis because of the difficulty in measuring R&D productivity, and this might be particularly costly as the emphasis shifted toward more basic research.

Mr. Kumar had two related concerns. One was the challenge he faced in demonstrating the productivity of his department to his boss and the board of directors.

> In defining what we mean by productivity, we have to be careful in how we define our terms and the measures that we rely on. For example, we rarely terminate projects, but we do adjust priorities and let some of them sit in an inactive state until a solution to a particular problem surfaces. Should the inactive projects reflect negatively on our productivity? . . . It's important that whatever measures we use be simple enough to assemble and use without devoting too much time away from the job at hand – doing promising, leading research.

His second major concern was about the growing complexity in his department:

> We now have 11 programs and 30 projects underway, and the growth has made coordination of the groups more difficult. It is increasingly difficult to keep up with the status of each program and project well enough to be able to decide priority issues. In the last six months, we have started an effort to try and identify a set of standard product development milestones and decision points around which a computerized information system could be built and used for control purposes. Because of the great variance among projects, however, not everybody is convinced how much use there is to organize an information system around a standardized process that doesn't really match any real project.

Exhibit 1 Product development cycle

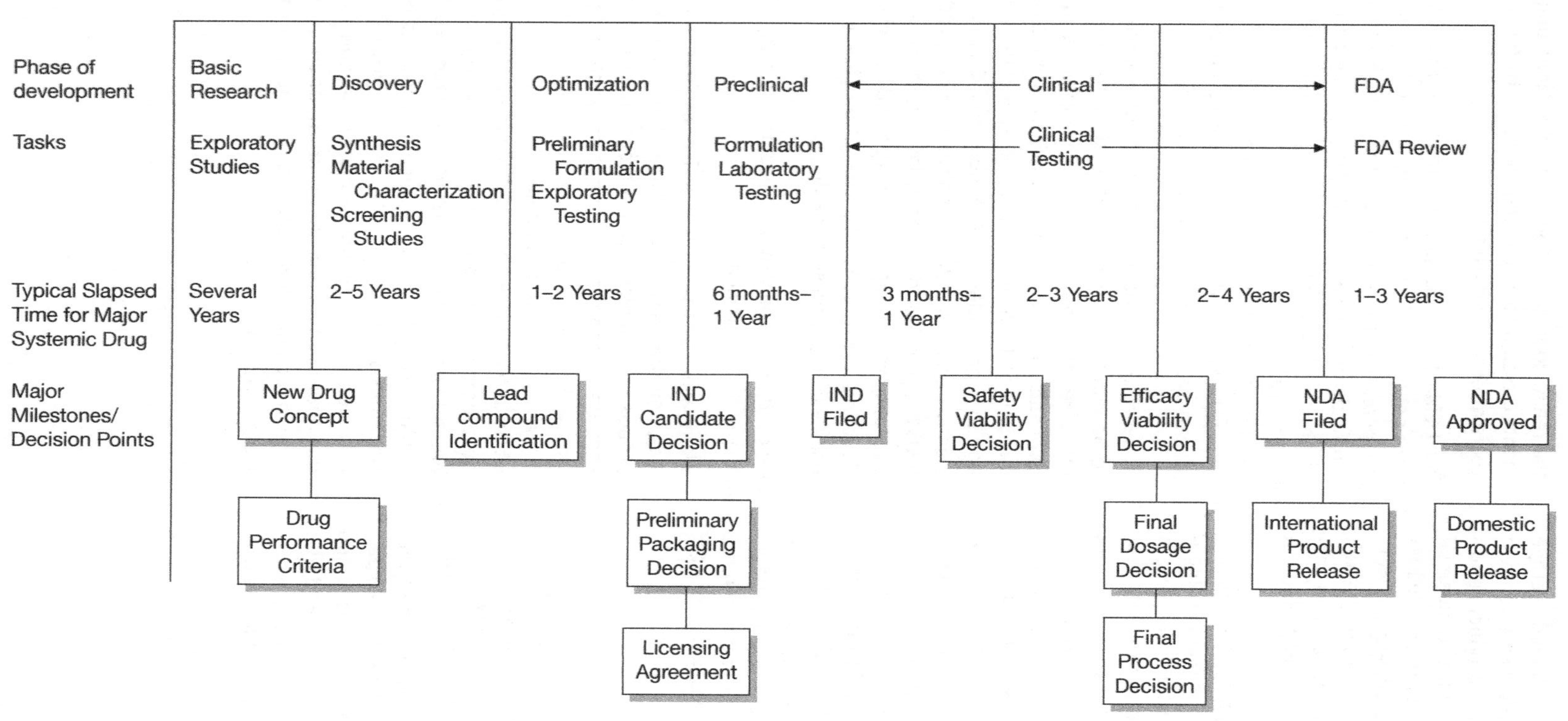

This case was prepared by Professor Kenneth A. Merchant.

CASE STUDY
Axeon N.V.

In October 2016, Anton van Leuven, managing director of Axeon N.V., a large Dutch chemical company, was faced with a difficult decision. Ian Wallingford, managing director of Axeon's British subsidiary, Hollandsworth, Ltd., and Jeremy Noble, a member of Hollandsworth's board of directors, were frustrated that an investment proposal that had been presented some time ago had not yet been approved. The board member had even threatened to resign his post. But Mr. van Leuven had received advice from some of his other managers to reject the Hollandsworth proposal.

The company

Axeon N.V. was headquartered in Heerlen, in the southern part of the Netherlands. Axeon produced an extensive product line of industrial chemicals in 24 factories.

Early in its history, Axeon had a simple functional organization structure, with just one manufacturing division and a sales division. Over the years, however, Axeon acquired some foreign companies. These included Saraceno, S.p.A., in Milan; Hollandsworth, Ltd., in London; and KAG Chemicals, AB, in Gothenburg, Sweden. To take advantage of the geographical expertise in these acquired companies, each of these subsidiaries was asked to assume responsibility for sales of all Axeon products in their assigned territory: Southern Europe for Saraceno; the United Kingdom for Hollandsworth; and Scandinavia for KAG. Southern Europe, the United Kingdom, and Scandinavia, respectively, accounted for 8%, 14%, and 6% of Axeon's total sales. All other sales were handled by Axeon's organization in the Netherlands (see Exhibit 1).

The style of Axeon's top-level managers was to emphasize a high degree of decentralization. Hence, the subsidiary managers had considerable autonomy to decide what to sell in their territories. For products produced in the Netherlands, the Axeon Dutch sales organization would quote the subsidiaries the same prices as they quoted agents in all countries. The subsidiaries could bargain, but if, in the end, they did not like the price, they did not have to sell the product.

In some cases, the foreign subsidiaries produced products that competed with those produced by Axeon factories in the Netherlands. To date, little attempt had been made to rationalize the company's production. The subsidiaries were allowed to continue to produce whatever mix of products they deemed appropriate. The subsidiary managers were also encouraged to propose the development of new products, and they were allowed to build their own manufacturing plants if they could justify the investment in their own markets.

Management personnel were included in a bonus plan that provided rewards based on achievement of divisional revenue growth and "economic profit" targets set as part of the company's annual planning and budgeting process. Economic profit was defined as operating profits less a capital charge on the division's average assets, computed monthly. The capital charge was adjusted annually based on Axeon's weighted average cost of capital. In 2016, the annual charge was set at 10%. In prior years, it had been as high as 14%. Achievement of the annual targets could earn divisional managers bonuses of 50% or more of base salary. If they exceeded their targets, they could more than double their base salaries.

Hollandsworth, Ltd.

Hollandsworth was purchased by Axeon in 2009. During the first three years of Axeon's ownership, Hollandsworth's sales were in slow decline. In 2012, they totaled £111 million. Hollandsworth's board of directors[1] decided that the company needed a new management team and a major overhaul. Mr. Ian Wallingford, a 39 year old with university degrees in

[1] The outsiders on the Hollandsworth board included Anton van Leuven from Axeon; Jeremy Noble, a prominent London banker; and James Bedingfield, the managing director of a large industrial company located outside of Manchester, England.

engineering and commerce, was hired. Ian had experience as a manufacturing engineer, a marketing manager for a British subsidiary of an American company, and a profit center manager in a large UK industrial company.

In the first four years of Ian's presidency, Hollandsworth's sales increased to £160 million, and profits improved markedly, to levels that Axeon's management deemed acceptable. The board concluded that a number of factors contributed to Hollandsworth's turnaround. An important part was Ian's ambition, hard work, and management skill. Ian made some good personnel hires and implemented a number of effective changes in production methods, marketing strategy, market research, financial planning, and organization structure. In addition, industrial activity in the United Kingdom increased significantly during this period.

In an article in a local English business publication, Ian was quoted as saying:

> This has been an enjoyable challenge. When I took the job, I had several offers from other companies, and I am still getting calls from executive recruiters, but I thought that Hollandsworth had potential. The Axeon management team promised me considerable freedom to make the changes that I thought were necessary. And I was able to put into practice many of the modern management practices that I learned in my previous jobs. I know that if I do a good job here, I will have the confidence of the executives in Heerlen, and succeeding here will make me an even better manager.

The proposal

In late 2015, Ian informed the Hollandsworth board that he proposed to study the feasibility of constructing a factory in England to manufacture a protective coating chemical known as AR-42. He explained that Hollandsworth's product engineers had developed a new way of helping users to store and apply this coating. In his judgment, Hollandsworth could develop a market in the United Kingdom that would be almost as large as Axeon's present worldwide market for AR-42. Approximately 600 tons of AR-42 was then being produced annually in an Axeon plant in the Netherlands, but none of this output was being sold in the United Kingdom. Ian observed that the board seemed enthusiastic at this initial meeting, but they wanted to see the detailed plan.

Hollandsworth managers developed the proposal over the following six months. They interviewed potential customers and conducted trials in the factories of three of them and proved that the large cost savings would indeed materialize. In the end, they estimated the total UK market potential for AR-42-like coatings at 800 tons per year. If they could sell the product for £3,700 per ton, they would capture half of the total market, or 400 tons per year, within a three-year period.

Ian asked the head of the Corporate Engineering Division in Heerlen for help in designing a plant to produce 400 tons of AR-42 per year and in estimating the cost of the investment. A team comprised of engineers from both Corporate Engineering and Hollandsworth estimated that the plant could be built for £1,400,000.

In July 2016, Ian presented the results of the analysis, the net-present-value calculations and supporting explanations (Exhibits 2–5) at a Hollandsworth board meeting. With Ian were his directors of manufacturing, sales, and finance. Here are some excerpts from Ian's presentation:

- "You can see from the summary chart [Exhibit 2] that this is a profitable project. We will obtain a rate of return of 20% and a present value of £916,000 for an initial investment of £1,400,000 for equipment and £160,000 for working capital. I used an 8% discount rate because I can borrow money in England at that rate to fund this project ..."
- "The second chart [Exhibit 3] shows the operating cash flows that we expect from the AR-42 project in each of the seven years. The sales forecast for the first seven years is shown in row (2). We did not extend the forecast beyond seven years because our engineers estimate that production technologies will continue to improve, so major plant renovations will be called for around the end of the seventh year. Actually, we see no reason why demand for this particular product, AR-42, will decline after seven years ..."
- "The estimated variable cost of £2,000 per ton, shown in row (3), is our estimate of the full operating cost of manufacturing AR-42 in England. This figure takes into account out-of-pocket fixed costs such as plant supervision, but excludes depreciation. These fixed costs must, of course, be included because they are incremental to the decision ..."
- "As row (4) shows, we are confident that we can enter the market initially with a selling price of £4,000 per ton, but in order to gain market share and achieve full market penetration, we will reduce the selling price to £3,700 at the beginning of the second year ..."
- "These figures result in variable profits shown in rows (5) and (6). Row (7) presents the marketing

expenditures that are needed to promote the product and achieve the forecasted sales levels. Row (8) shows the net operating cash flows before tax, based on figures in the preceding columns ..."

- "The cost of the plant can be written off for tax purposes over a five-year period. As shown in row (9), the taxable income figures are computed by subtracting this amount from the before-tax cash flow. The tax in row (10) is then subtracted from the before-tax cash flow to yield the after-tax cash flow in row (11) ..."
- "My third chart [Exhibit 4] summarizes our estimates of the requisite investment in working capital. We'll need about £160,000 to start with. We'll need small additional amounts of working capital in the next two years. These amounts are shown in row (4). Altogether, our working capital requirements will add up to £190,000 by the end of our second full year of operations ..."
- "The last chart [Exhibit 5] shows some asset recovery values. At the end of seven years, the plant should be worth £1,400,000, at the very worst. We'd have to pay tax on that because the plant would be fully depreciated, but this would still leave us with a positive cash flow of £840,000. The working capital should also be fully recoverable. So the total value at the end of seven years would thus be £1,030,000 ..."
- "Gentlemen, it seems clear from these figures that we can justify this investment in England on the basis of sales to the UK market. It meets your policy of having all new investments yield at least 12%. This particular proposal promises to return 20%. My management team and I strongly recommend this project."

Ian and his managers answered the few questions raised by the board members.

At the end of the meeting, Ian and his team went to a neighborhood pub to celebrate. They all felt that the meeting went extremely well. Soon thereafter, they were pleased to learn that the proposal was placed on the agenda for the next meeting of the Axeon board of directors, which was scheduled in three weeks' time.

The board meeting

The presentation to the Axeon board also went well. Ian explained:

> It took only an hour. Mr. van Leuven said in the meeting that the decision seemed to be clear.
>
> Some board members asked some interesting questions, mainly about the likelihood that we would eventually be able to sell more than 400 tons of AR-42 per year and about how we would finance the project. I explained that we in the UK believed strongly that we would reach 400 tons per year even in the first year, but we felt constrained to show a conservative estimate and a conservative transition period. We also showed how we could finance further expansions through borrowings in the UK. If our 400 tons were reached quickly, banks would easily lend any further expansion. The UK member of the board supported our conclusion.

At the end of the hour, the Axeon board voted unanimously to allow construction of the plant.

Dispute between parent and subsidiary

About a week later, Mr. van Leuven called Ian and said,

> "Since the board meeting, I have been through some additional discussions with the product and marketing people here in the Heerlen. They agree with your engineering design and plan cost projections, but they think you are too optimistic on your sales forecast. I must ask you to justify this more."

Ian pushed for an immediate meeting, which was scheduled for the following week. The meeting was attended by Ian and his key functional directors and four Axeon managers based in Heerlen: Anton van Leuven, Willem Backer (senior VP-Dutch operations), Marc Oosterling (director of manufacturing), and Geert De Rijcke (director of sales).

Ian described the meeting from his perspective:

> It was one of the most frustrating meetings of my life. It lasted all day. Mr. De Rijcke said that from their sales experience in other countries our estimates of the UK market potential and our share were too optimistic. I explained to him several times how we arrived at our figures, but he wouldn't change his over-optimism argument. He said that Axeon's current total worldwide market for AR-42 for Axeon was only 600 tons a year, that it was being produced in the Netherlands at this level, and that it was inconceivable that the UK alone could take 400 tons.
>
> Then Mr. Oosterling started preaching that AR-42 production is complicated and that he had had difficulties producing it in the Netherlands, even with trained workers who have long experience. I told him I only needed five trained workers and that he could send me two men for two months to train

our people to do the job. I told him that, "If you can manufacture it in the Netherlands, you can manufacture it for us in England until we learn, if you don't have confidence in English technology." But he kept saying over and over that the difficulties in manufacturing were great. I stressed to him that we were prepared to learn and to take the risk, but for some reason I just couldn't get him to understand.

At 6 p.m., everybody was exhausted. Mr. Backer had backed up his two functional directors all day, repeating their arguments. Mr. van Leuven seemed just to sit there and listen, occasionally asking questions. I can't understand why he did not back me up. He had seemed so agreeable in the previous meetings, and he had seemed so decisive. Not so at this meeting. He seemed distant and indecisive. He stopped the meeting without a solution and said that he hoped all concerned would do more investigation of this subject. He vaguely referred to the fact that he would think about it himself and let us know when another meeting would be held.

Ian returned home to London and reported the meeting to his own staff and to the two English members of his board. They were all extremely disappointed. One of the Hollandsworth staff members said, "Axeon's management seem to talk decentralization, but at the same time they act like emperors."

Mr. Noble, the English banker on the Hollandsworth board, expressed surprise:

I studied this proposal very carefully. It is sound business for Hollandsworth, and AR-42 will help to build one more growth company in the English economy. Somehow the management in Heerlen has failed to study this, or they don't wish the English subsidiary to produce it. I have today dictated a letter to Mr. van Leuven telling him that I recognize that the Dutch managers have the right to their own thoughts, but I don't understand why the proposal is being delayed and possibly rejected. I am prepared to resign as a Hollandsworth director. It is not that I am angry or that I believe I have a right to dictate decisions for the whole worldwide Axeon. It is simply that if I spend my time studying policy decisions and my judgments do not serve the right function for the business, then it is a waste of my time to continue.

In the meeting with Mr. Noble, Ian said:

While I certainly wouldn't say this in a broader meeting, I think that those Dutch production and sales people simply want to build their own empire and make the money in Axeon Netherlands. They don't care about Hollandsworth and the UK. Theirs is a slippery way to operate. We have the ideas and initiative, and they are trying to take them and get the payoff.

After Mr. van Leuven received Mr. Noble's letter, he contacted Messrs. Backer, Oosterling, and De Rijcke and Arnold Koonts (Axeon's VP-finance). He told them that the English AR-42 project had become a matter of key importance for the whole company because of its implications for company profits and for the autonomy and morale of subsidiary management. He asked them to study the matter and report their recommendations in one month. Meanwhile, he sent Ian the following e-mail message: "Various members of the division and corporate headquarters are studying the proposal. You will hear from me within about six weeks regarding my final decision."

Report of the director of manufacturing

A month later, Marc Oosterling (director of manufacturing) sent Mr. van Leuven a memorandum explaining his reasons for opposing the UK AR-42 proposal, as follows:

At your request, I have reexamined thoroughly all of the cost figures that bear on the AR-42 proposal. I find it highly uneconomical to manufacture this product in England for two reasons: overhead costs and variable costs would both be higher than projected.

As to the former, we can produce AR-42 in the Netherlands with less overhead cost. Suppose that Hollandsworth does sell 400 tons per year so that our total worldwide sales increase to 1,000 tons. We can produce the whole 1,000 tons in the Netherlands with basically the same capital investment as we have now. If we produce 1,000 tons, our fixed costs will decrease by £240 per ton.[2] That means £144,000 in savings on production for domestic and export to countries other than the UK and £240,000 for worldwide production including the UK (1,000 tons).

[2] The total fixed cost in the Netherlands is the equivalent of £360,000 per year. Divided by 600, this equals £600 per ton. If the cost were spread over 1,000 tons, the average fixed cost would be £360 per ton.

Regarding the variable costs, if we were to produce the extra 400 tons in the Netherlands, the total production of 1,000 tons per year would allow us to have longer production runs, lower set-up costs, and larger raw material purchases, which lead to mass purchasing and material handling and lower purchase prices. My accounting department has studied this and concludes that our average variable costs will decrease from £1,900 to £1,860 per ton (Exhibit 6). This £40-per-ton difference would save us £24,000 on Dutch domestic production and £40,000 on total worldwide production, assuming that the UK takes 400 tons per year. There would be some additional shipping and duty costs, but these would be negligible. Taxes on these added profits are about the same in the Netherlands as in the UK.

So I conclude that that UK plant should not be built. Ian is a bright young man, but he does not know the coatings business. He would be over his head with costly production mistakes from the very beginning. I recommend that you inform Hollandsworth management that it is in Axeon's interest to buy their AR-42 product from the Netherlands.

Report of the Vice President-Finance

The same day, Mr. van Leuven received the following memorandum from Arnold Koonts (VP-Finance):

I am sending you herewith estimates of the working capital requirements if Axeon increases its production of AR-42 in our Dutch plant from 600 to 1,000 tons per year (Exhibit 7). Initially we will need £120,000, mostly for additional inventories. By the end of the second year, this will have increased to £160,000. I have also looked at Marc's calculations for the fixed and variable manufacturing costs, and I am in full agreement with them.

Ian's thoughts at the time

In an interview about this same time, Ian expressed impatience.

I have other projects that need developing for Hollandsworth, and this kind of long-range planning takes a lot of time and energy. It's not like this is all I have to do. I also have to keep on top of a lot of normal operating problems. Sometimes I feel like giving up, telling them just to go and sell AR-42 themselves.

Exhibit 1 Axeon N.V. organization chart

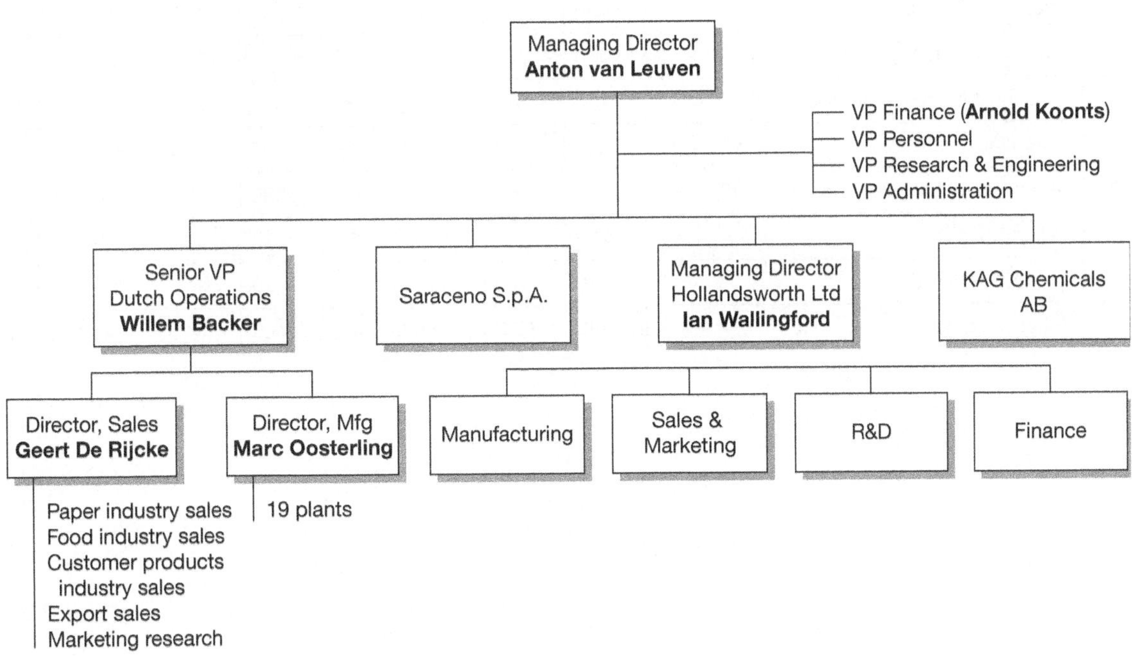

Exhibit 2 Axeon N.V. proposal for manufacture of AR-42 in England – Financial Summary (£000)

Year	0	1	2	3	4	5	6	7	Total
Equipment	(1,400)								
Working capital	(160)	(10)	(20)						
Cash operating profit		196	328	460	460	460	348	348	
Recovery value of equipment and working capital								1,030	
Total	(1,560)	186	308	460	460	460	348	1,378	2,040

Net present value (@ 8%)	£ 916,000
Payback period	4½ years
Internal rate of return	20%

Exhibit 3 Axeon N.V. estimated operating cash flows from manufacture and sale of AR-42 in England

(Figures in rows (3) – (5) in £; rows (6) – (11) in £000)

(1)	Year	1	2	3	4	5	6	7	Total
(2)	Sales (in tons)	200	300	400	400	400	400	400	2,500
(3)	Variable costs per ton	2,000	2,000	2,000	2,000	2,000	2,000	2,000	
(4)	Sales price per ton	4,000	3,700	3,700	3,700	3,700	3,700	3,700	
(5)	Variable profit margin per ton (4) – (3)	2,000	1,700	1,700	1,700	1,700	1,700	1,700	
(6)	Total variable profit margin (2) x (5)	400	510	680	680	680	680	680	4,310
(7)	Promotion costs	260	150	100	100	100	100	100	910
(8)	Net operating cash flows before tax (6) – (7)	140	360	580	580	580	580	580	3,400
(9)	Depreciation	280	280	280	280	280	-	-	1,400
(10)	Tax 40% of (8) – (9)	–56	32	120	120	120	232	232	800
(11)	Net cash flow after tax (8) – (10)	196	328	460	460	460	348	348	2,600

Exhibit 4 Axeon N.V. estimated working capital required for manufacture and sale of AR-42 in England (£000)

	Year	0	1	2	3 and later	Total
(1)	Inventory at cost	160	180	200	200	
(2)	Other current assets less current liabilities	0	–10	–10	–10	
(3)	Working capital (1) + (2)	160	170	190	190	
(4)	Change from previous year	160	10	20	0	190

Exhibit 5 Axeon N.V. estimated end-of-life value of UK assets

Plant	£1,400,000	
Less: tax on gain if sold at this price	560,000	
Net value of plant		840,000
Working capital recapture		190,000
Net value of UK assets after 7 years		£1,030,000

Exhibit 6 Axeon N.V. estimated variable cost of manufacturing AR-42 in the Netherlands for shipment to the United Kingdom

Variable costs per ton:	
Manufacturing	£1,860
Shipping from Netherlands to United Kingdom	100
UK import duty	100
Total variable cost per ton	£2,060
Total variable cost, 400 tons to United Kingdom	£824,000

Exhibit 7 Axeon N.V. estimated working capital required for manufacture of AR-42 in the Netherlands for sale in the United Kingdom (£000)

	Year	0	1	2	3 and later	Total
(1)	Inventory at cost	100	110	120	120	
(2)	Other current assets less current liabilities	20	30	40	40	
(3)	Working capital (1) + (2)	120	140	160	160	
(4)	Change from previous year	120	20	20	0	160

This case was prepared by Professors Kenneth A. Merchant and Wim A. Van der Stede, with the research assistance of Xiaoling (Clara) Chen.

CHAPTER 4
Control System Tightness

The benefit of any management control system (MCS) is derived from the increase in the likelihood that the organizational objectives will be achieved relative to what could be expected if the MCS were not in place. This benefit can be described in terms of MCS *tightness* (or *looseness*). Tighter MCSs should provide greater assurance that employees will act in the organization's best interest.

How tightly to apply management controls is a major management decision that has received relatively little attention in the literature, and when it has, it has been primarily discussed in a results-control context. The concept of tight control can certainly be applied to results controls. Tight results controls might involve detailed (often line-by-line) and frequent (monthly or even weekly) budget reviews of performance as well as appropriately geared incentives.[1] But there are many other ways to effect tight management control, both with the other forms of control and with reinforcing combinations of control types.

Conceptually, effective implementation of tight control requires that management has a good understanding of how one or more of the control objects – results, actions, and personnel/culture – relate and contribute to the overall organizational objectives. The following sections describe how each of the management control types can be used to generate tight control.

Tight results control

The achievement of tight results control depends on characteristics of the definitions of the desired result areas, the performance measures, and the reinforcements or incentives provided.

Definitions of desired results

For management control to be considered tight in a results-control system, the results dimensions must be congruent with the "true" organizational objectives; the performance targets must be specific; the desired results must be effectively communicated and internalized by those whose behaviors are being controlled; and, if results controls are used exclusively in a given performance area, the measures must be complete.

Congruence

Chapter 2 discussed congruence as one of the main determinants of the effectiveness of results controls. Results-control systems may suffer congruence problems either because managers do not understand the organization's true objectives well or because the performance dimensions on which the managers choose to measure results do not reflect the true objectives well.

For many types of organizations and many specific areas within organizations, it is a reasonable assumption that the true objectives are well understood. For example, it is clearly desirable for production workers to be more efficient and for sales personnel to sell more, all else being equal. In many other organizations, however, a good understanding of the true objectives and/or how they should be prioritized is not a reasonable assumption.[2] In many types of government agencies and non-profit organizations, key constituents often disagree as to the organization's objectives. Is the primary objective of a government agency to provide more services or to reduce its costs (and tax burden)? Clarity of objectives is a necessary precursor for congruity.

Moreover, choosing measurable performance dimensions that reflect an organization's true objectives is also often challenging. For example, are annual profits a good indicator of the success of a company with significant growth prospects? Is the number of patents granted a good indicator of a research and development entity's contribution to its company's performance, which depends critically on developing commercially successful ideas for new products?[3] Is the number of visitors a good indicator of the success of a museum? If the chosen measurable performance dimensions are not good indicators of the organization's true objectives, then the results-control system cannot be tight, regardless of any of the other systems characteristics.

Specificity

The degree of tightness of results control also depends on having performance expectations described in specific terms. Specificity of performance expectations, or targets, requires disaggregation and quantification, such as a 15% return on assets per year; less than 1% customer complaints; or $2.29 in labor costs per unit of production. Organizations usually can, and do, set such specific, quantified targets in financial terms. But in many performance areas, such as with respect to sustainability and environmental performance, control is loose(r) because organizations do not set specific, quantified targets and merely evaluate the global performance area subjectively. "Profits are easy to measure; the many and often conflicting demands [arising from corporate social responsibility] are not."[4] Control in the difficult-to-measure areas can be tightened by disaggregating the global performance area into its various components, such as energy usage, volume and type of waste generated, and extent of recycling. In some performance areas, however, detailed and specific targets and measures are not feasible. It is difficult to be specific about how many cases a lawyer should handle in a year or about what is meant by ethical behavior or social justice. Nonetheless, specificity of expectations is one of the elements necessary for the implementation of tight results controls.

Communication and internalization

For results controls to be tight, performance targets must also be communicated effectively and internalized by those charged with their accomplishment. Only then can the results controls influence performance. The degree to which goals are understood and internalized is affected by many factors, including the qualifications of the employees involved, the perceived degree of controllability over the measured results areas, the reasonableness of the goals, and the amount of participation allowed in the goal-setting processes. Internalization is likely to be low when employees perceive they lack the ability to perform well in the expected performance area, when they consider the desired results to be unduly affected by factors outside of their control, when they believe the goals are unachievable, or when they were not allowed to participate in setting the goals. We discuss the conditions for effective target setting further in Chapter 8.

Completeness

Completeness is the final requirement for tight results controls. Completeness means that the result areas defined in the MCS include all the areas in which the organization desires good performance and over which the employees involved can have some impact. What is not measured becomes less visible, or perhaps even invisible. Thus, when the defined result areas are incomplete, employees often allow performance in the unmeasured areas to slip. For example, purchasing personnel evaluated solely on meeting cost standards might allow quality to slip. Similarly, salespeople who are asked to meet sales volume quota are likely to strive for volume, possibly at the expense of smaller but more profitable sales.

Thus, results-control systems should capture, as completely as possible, all information about employees' effects on firm value, weighted properly, so that employees' efforts are appropriately balanced across the multiple dimensions of their jobs. At managerial levels, however, where jobs are complex, results controls are almost inevitably incomplete. Commonly, then, managers direct their efforts only to measured tasks and may ignore other important-but-unmeasured tasks (such as by focusing on improving short-term profits at the expense of long-term customer relations).[5] This is a typical example of *managerial myopia* due to incomplete results controls, which we discuss further in Chapters 10 and 11.

When the results controls are incomplete, other types of control, including action and personnel/cultural controls, should be designed to try to fill the void left by the incomplete results controls. Examples of *complementary* control mechanisms are action controls that include quality controls, or cultural controls that aim to instill a mind-set toward sustainable performance or innovation to counter myopic results-driven behaviors.

Performance measurement

Tight results control also depends on the adequacy of the performance measures that are used. As discussed in Chapter 2, results controls rely on measures that are precise, objective, timely, and understandable. A results-control system that is used to apply tight control requires that all of these measurement qualities are met to a high degree. If the measurements fail in any of these areas, the control system cannot be characterized as tight because behavioral problems are likely. Chapters 10–12 deal with the complex nature of designing effective performance measurement systems.

Incentives

Results controls are likely to be tighter if meaningful rewards are directly and definitely linked to the accomplishment of the desired results. A *direct* link means that the accomplishment of results translates explicitly and unambiguously into rewards. A *definite* link between results and rewards means that no excuses are tolerated. Both elements are pertinently illustrated in a quote from a former president at Bausch & Lomb: "Once you sign up for your target number, you are expected to reach it." Managers who failed to achieve annual profit targets by even a small amount received "paltry" bonuses, while those who exceeded them earned "hefty" payouts.[6] Equally, in the public sector, the head of the Philippines' Bureau of Internal Revenue, the tax authority which brings in most of the government's revenues, resigned over the agency's "failure to meet its targets." Upon announcing the resignation, the president's office stated: "He has not performed well and he said he takes responsibility for it."[7] And, in the United Kingdom, the gas and electricity markets regulator Ofgem slapped an £11.1 million fine on British Gas because the firm failed to meet deadlines to insulate homes under two energy-efficiency schemes that ran until the end of 2012. Although British Gas did ultimately reach its targets, the delay meant that thousands missed out on the measures during the winter of 2012–13. Sarah Harrison, an Ofgem senior partner, said: "British Gas's failure to deliver two environmental obligations on time is unacceptable." The sector riposted, saying that they were "deeply disappointed" with the penalty and that they "believe the design of the CESP [Community Energy Saving Program] was flawed and significant problems were encountered with scheme delivery." However, these arguments – perhaps *excuses* – did not sway the regulator in deeming the targets to be *definitively* missed, thus warranting the fine.[8]

Although most organizations, including non-profit and public sector organizations, appear to make the link between incentive compensation and performance more direct and more definite, there is much debate and controversy about this important topic. We discuss the key factors that determine the effectiveness of, and issues arising from, performance-linked incentives in more depth in Chapter 9.

To end this section with an example, there also is a fine line between tight results control and results control that is *too* tight or "too controlling." Put another way, "there is a fine line between micromanaging and house arrest," as the *Irish Independent* says when commenting on Tesco's use of Motorola armbands to monitor employees at the large grocer's Dublin distribution center. Each armband "measures employee productivity so closely that the company even knows when they take a bathroom break":

> The armbands, officially known as Motorola arm-mounted terminals, look like something between a Game Boy and Garmin GPS device. The terminals keep track of how quickly and competently employees unload and scan goods in the warehouse and gives them a grade. It also sets benchmarks for loading and unloading speed, which workers are expected to meet. The monitors can be turned off during workers' lunch breaks, but anything else – bathroom trips, visits to a water fountain – reportedly lowers their productivity score. Tesco did not respond to requests for comment, so it's hard to know if the arm bands have been a success.[9]

Analytically, however, Tesco's system provides a good example of tight results control. It pushes its workers hard, but Tesco claims that workers are also well paid and that worker conditions are good. Tesco compares each worker's performance every day with a computerized projection of what performance should have been – the so-called *benchmarks*. Workers who cannot meet the standards are given suggestions for improvement. Hence, this control system meets every characteristic of tight results control. The results measures seem to be congruent with the company's goal of efficiency, as its "*every little helps*" corporate tagline suggests. The measures seem to be complete at the worker level. Distribution center workers have no other significant responsibilities beyond handling merchandise with care and efficiency. The performance targets are specific; measurement is thorough and done on a frequent basis (in real time, actually); and the rewards, which include job security, are important to the employees involved, where the company states that the goal is to improve productivity while improving conditions.[10]

America's Wal-Mart, the giant retailer, has similar systems in place to "have better control over operating expenses" through "improving supply chain efficiency" and "tight control over its distribution and transportation expenses":

> The retailer's work assignment projects such as MyGuide and OneTouch have helped it in effective handling and movement of merchandise. MyGuide is designed to keep track of Wal-Mart's employees' time spent on each task. As a result of these initiatives, cases handled per hour increased by 3% in the quarter.[11]

Tight action controls

Since the action-control types are quite different from each other, we discuss the ways in which each action-control type might be used to achieve tight control separately. Overall, action-control systems should be considered tight only if it is highly likely that employees will engage consistently in all actions critical to the operation's success and will not engage in harmful actions.

Behavioral Constraints

Behavioral constraints, either physical or administrative, can produce tight control in some areas of an organization. Physical constraints come in many forms, ranging from simple locks on desks to elaborate software and electronic security systems. No simple rules can be provided as to the degree of control they provide except, perhaps, that extra protection usually costs more.

Administrative constraints also provide widely varying degrees of control. *Restricting decision authority* to higher organizational levels provides tighter control if it can be assumed that higher-level personnel will make more reliable decisions than lower-level personnel. At Super Micro Computer, a California-based computer maker, co-founder and CEO Charles Liang "obsesses over every detail of the business, from approving the custom orders that are the company's specialty to dictating the environmentally themed, green neckties that executives wear to customer meetings." Despite its peculiarities, Super Micro has been a thriving, publicly traded business, beating its competitors to market by three to six months and offering the fastest, most compact, energy-efficient computers to demanding corporate customers such as eBay and Yahoo. "[Mr. Liang] is the person who approves and looks at everything the company is doing – every new product, marketing effort, sales effort, anything you want to do or promote," said Scott Barlow, a former sales manager at Super Micro. "If [Mr. Liang] says a product will be on schedule, it will be on schedule," added Don Clegg, a vice president. However, despite the seemingly effective control arising from centralized decision-making, Mr. Liang "is considered so vital to the operation that the company warns investors in regulatory filings that his loss could derail the company's business, culture and strategic direction."[12]

Separating duties between two (or more) employees, another type of administrative constraint, makes the occurrence of a harmful activity less likely because one person cannot complete the entire task without involving another person. Good separations of duties make the control system tighter.

Netflix, the global provider of on-demand internet streaming media, sued Mike Kail, its former vice president of information technology (IT) operations, for fraud, breach of fiduciary duties, and other improper actions, alleging that Mr. Kail accepted commissions of 12–15% from the $3.7 million the company paid to IT service companies, which he then funneled into his personal consulting company, according to the complaint:

> Experts seized on one line from the suit, filed in California Superior Court, Santa Clara County, that suggests Netflix may have granted Mr. Kail too much freedom: "Kail was a trusted, senior-level employee, with authority to enter into appropriate contracts and approve appropriate invoices. *This is a classic segregation of duties violation*," said Christopher McClean, a corporate governance analyst at Forrester Research Inc., adding that "*individuals should not have the authority to both choose and approve payment to a vendor because it opens the door for corporate malfeasance.*"[13]

For administrative constraints to be effective, however, those who do not have authority for certain actions or decisions cannot violate the constraints that have been established. Evidence suggests, however, that both *overrides* of internal controls and *collusion* among employees contribute significantly to fraud in organizations:

> [There is a] strong correlation between a fraudster's level of authority and the financial impact of the fraud. In our 2014 data, owners/executives accounted for less than one-fifth of all frauds, but the median loss in owner/executive cases was $500,000, approximately

> four times higher than the median loss caused by managers and nearly seven times that of employees. *Authority tends to be strongly correlated with loss because high-level fraudsters generally have greater access to organizational assets and are better able to evade or override controls than lower-level employees.* [. . .] *Additionally, because higher-level fraudsters are typically in a better position to circumvent controls, it generally takes longer for victim organizations to detect these schemes.*[14]

This is echoed by Richard Powell, a partner at KPMG Forensic in the United Kingdom: "Companies clearly have a challenge on their hands [when] the perpetrators [of fraud] are members of senior management, whose status in the company makes it easier for them to bypass internal controls and inflict greater damage on the company."[15]

Preaction reviews

Preaction reviews can make MCSs tight if the reviews are frequent, detailed, and performed by diligent, knowledgeable reviewers. Preaction reviews are invariably tight in areas involving large resource allocations because many investments are not easily reversible and can, by themselves, affect the success or failure of an organization. Tight preaction reviews of this kind involve formal scrutiny of business plans and requests for capital by experts in staff positions, such as in the Finance Division, and multiple levels of management, including top management.

But some organizations also use tight preaction reviews before employees can spend even small amounts of money. For example, at Amazon, the retailing giant, founder and CEO Jeff Bezos:

> [. . .] keeps an eerily tight rein on expenses, eschewing color printers in favor of trusty old black-and-white models. No one flies first class (though Bezos sometimes rents private jets at his own expense). Experiments are hatched and managed by the smallest teams possible; if it takes more than two pizzas to feed a work group, Bezos once observed, then the team is too big. Offices still get cheap desks made of particleboard door planks, a 1990s holdover that Bezos refuses to change.[16]

But Bezos's approach is tight not only just in terms of control for control's sake, but also in the sense of being consistent with strategy, thus providing "good control" as defined above:

> Lots of retailers talk about holding down costs and passing the savings to the consumer. Few do so as intently as Amazon, where "frugality" is one of eight official company values. The reward for putting up with cheap office furniture: a $90 billion stock market valuation and 35% revenue growth.[17]

Tight preaction controls can also be exercised at the level of the board of directors. For example, Ted Turner, while chair of Turner Broadcasting, had made decisions that several times pushed the company close to insolvency. As a consequence, his board of directors would not let him spend more than $2 million, a tiny amount for such a large company, without the board's approval.[18]

The extent to which organizations tighten their controls also often varies with their fortunes. For example, as Citigroup sought to recover from its crippling losses following the 2008 financial crisis, it tried many fixes, some involving major restructurings and consequent layoffs. But the banking giant apparently was not satisfied. A memo by John Havens, head of Citigroup's Institutional Clients Group (ICG), urged employees to be much more frugal in their expenses. "Managing our expenses is not only a critical aspect of our strategy, it is also an important part of our jobs," Mr. Havens wrote. "Each of us must do our part to manage our expenses by challenging every dollar we spend to ensure that it is truly necessary and in compliance with our policies." Many of the policy changes include stricter controls on how much bankers can spend on client meetings and how often executives can call upon management consultants. "Our current usage of management consultants is too high," Mr. Havens declared. "Management consultants should only be engaged for those limited instances where a specific expertise which does not reside within our organization is absolutely required." He also noted that "color presentations are unnecessary for internal purposes, therefore [. . .] color copying and printing should only be used for client presentations. Also whenever possible, presentations should be printed double sided to reduce unnecessary paper usage." He emphasized that these "expense policies and pre-approval procedures will take effect immediately [and that] these policies and procedures apply to all ICG employees and the functional support areas dedicated to ICG, in all regions."[19]

The requirement of reviews by top-level officers or committees or even the board of directors does not, however, automatically signify that the preaction control is tight. Many busy top managers and even capital committees do not take the time to examine carefully all expenditure proposals, particularly smaller ones. They merely *rubber stamp* them. Or, when cajoled into signing off on exceptions such as to allow an "exceptional" expense claim for a "special" client, the authorizing manager caves and the tight policy loses its bite.

Action accountability

Action-accountability controls produce tight control in a manner quite similar to tight results controls. The amount of control generated by action-accountability controls depends on characteristics of the definitions of desirable (and undesirable) actions, the effectiveness of the action-tracking system, and the reinforcements (rewards or punishments) provided.

Definitions of Actions

To achieve tight action-accountability control, the definitions of actions must be congruent, specific, well communicated, and complete. *Congruence* means that the performance of the actions defined in the control system will indeed lead to the achievement of the intended organizational objectives.

Tighter control can also be achieved by making the definitions of actions *specific* in the form of work rules (such as prohibiting alcohol during work) or policies (such as the requirement to obtain three competing bids before releasing a purchase order), as opposed to relying solely on less specific guidance (such as to exercise good judgment or to treat colleagues and customers with respect).

Tight action control depends on the *understanding* and *acceptance* of the work rules, policies, or guidance by those whose behaviors are being controlled. If the employees involved do not understand the rules, policies, or guidance, they will be inconsequential. If the employees do not accept the rules, they may try to find ways to avoid them. Understanding and acceptance can be improved through communication and training and by allowing employees to participate in the development of the rules, policies, or guidance.

If the MCS relies extensively on action accountability, the definitions of (un)desired actions must be *complete*. Completeness means that all the important, acceptable (and unacceptable) actions are well defined. "We have procedures for everything" is an indicative comment from someone who is working in a tight action-accountability environment. Indeed, in the words of a manager at a care home for the elderly:

> **We have procedures for everything . . . including a policy on confidentiality; a staff complaint procedure; a comprehensive job description; a record of training in care; and company rules. [The company rules] include a variety of policies from health and safety to smoking, and a section on gross misconduct.[20]**

The co-owner at another care home for young people stated:

> A disciplined environment underpins everything that we do; adherence to regulations and procedures is part and parcel of everyone's work. Government regulations on care home and child protection require documentary evidence on most aspects of our day to day operations. I can tell you what a child resident ate on a particular day six years ago, what mood he got up in, what social worker s/he was with . . . The social workers have to write all this down; it all gets typed up. We keep the records for 10 years.[21]

Although tight action controls can be relied on extensively for the proper functioning of organizations in certain environments, such as banks, nuclear power facilities, hospitals, and critical healthcare homes, they are not effective in all circumstances. In some situations, the desired actions cannot be defined nearly completely because the tasks are complex and require considerable discretion or creativity. When the desired actions cannot be properly defined, action-accountability controls will not produce tight control; they may even be counterproductive, as they are likely to limit professional judgment, stifle creativity, erode morale, and cause decision delays and slow strategic responses to changing market conditions. At SAP America, a division of the world's largest provider of Enterprise Resource Planning (ERP) software, the tight control exercised by SAP's headquarters in Germany was seen as utterly *irritating*.[22] As an example of improving strategic responsiveness,

> [. . .] even at companies known for their engaging cultures, rule killing can improve business – or even shift business models. In the early days of Zappos, the company focused simply on providing the best online selection of shoes. But after receiving tons of customer feedback, they learned that surprise shipping upgrades and positive customer communication had a tremendous impact on loyalty. So they got rid of approvals for free shipping and VIP perks so call-center employees had access to the same tools as managers. Nowadays, Zappos' customer service is as renowned as its product selection.[23]

But "there is a fine line between restoring trust and strangling opportunity through high compliance costs; [. . .] worse, the environment for bankers has been made so suffocating that the best leave, desperate to breathe again in a lighter-regulated landscape."[24] Apply the reins too tightly, and the controls become stifling; leave the reins looser, and face the risk of improprieties.

Action Tracking

Control in an action-accountability control system can also be made tighter by improving the effectiveness of the action-tracking system. Employees who are certain that their actions will be noticed, and noticed relatively promptly, will be affected more strongly by an action-accountability control system than those who feel that the chance of getting "caught" is small. Constant direct supervision is one tight action-tracking method. Detailed audits of action reports are another (e.g. detailed reviews of expense reports). For example, banks or the regulator can employ so-called *analytics* – sophisticated technological tools for analyzing millions of trades for patterns that suggest suspicious activity by comparing a broker's or investment advisor's trades against significant events such as merger announcements to flag possible insider trading, say.[25]

> A new generation of workplace technology is allowing white-collar jobs to be tracked, tweaked and managed in ways that were difficult even a few years ago. Employers of all types – old-line manufacturers, nonprofits, universities, digital start-ups and retailers – are using an increasingly wide range of tools to monitor workers' efforts, help them focus, cheer them on and just make sure they show up on time.[26]

But there is a catch:

> **"People in sales are continually measured and always know where they stand. Now this is happening in the rest of the white-collar work force," said Paul Hamerman, a workplace technology analyst with Forrester Research. "Done properly, it will increase engagement. Done in the wrong way, employees will feel pressured or micro-managed."[27]**

Action Reinforcement

Finally, control can be made tighter by making the rewards or punishments more significant to the employees affected. In general, significance varies directly with the size of the reinforcement. Whereas rewards (incentives) are the most common form of reinforcement that organizations provide in results-control settings, punishments (disciplinary actions) are common in action-control settings because they often involve employee violations of rules and procedures. Although, as with rewards, different individuals react differently to identical punishments, one type of significant disciplinary action – the threat of dismissal – is likely universally understood.

The way commercial airlines control the actions of their pilots provides a good example of a tight action-accountability control system. The pilots are given detailed checklists specifying nearly all required actions, not only for normal operations but also for all conceivable contingencies, such as engine failure, fire on board, wind shear, and hijacking. Intensive training helps ensure that the procedures are understood, and frequent checking and updating help ensure that they remain in the pilot's active memory. The tracking of irregular actions is precise and timely, as all potential violations are thoroughly screened by objective investigators. Finally, reinforcement is significant because pilots are threatened with severe penalties, including loss of profession, not to mention the fear for loss of life when accidents do happen.

Even the most detailed action specifications can be undercut by the lack of action tracking and reinforcement. For example, rules and procedures will not be followed if top management does not show interest in having them followed. Thus, for action accountability to be tight, *all* of the elements of the action-control system – definitions of actions, action tracking, *and* reinforcement – must be properly designed. Moreover, action controls are sometimes seen as hindering efficiency. As such, reengineering efforts focused on improving efficiency sometimes imprudently downgrade preaction reviews, segregation of duties, paper trails, and reconciliations as *non-value-added*. While these controls might seemingly not add value, they can help prevent losses that might arise from accidents or misconduct.

Surveys of practice, however, suggest that sophisticated frauds have been on the rise, in part explained by an increase in computer-based transactions as part of complex IT systems that handle virtually all company transactions including sales accounts, cost accounts, personnel administration, and general ledger. Although computer-based transactions are now commonplace in most organizations, control of such transactions is sometimes loose (compared to control of "old-economy" paper-based transactions). There is no reason why control of computer-based transactions cannot be tight, even tighter than paper-based transactions; but due to system complexity, companies do not always fully understand the control risks involved.

Moreover, and as a recent study by KPMG pointed out, "although IT systems form a core part of [most business], many organizations suffer from not having people in the business clearly identified to be responsible and accountable for their usage." The study showed that more than two-thirds of the executives surveyed believe that effective control is hampered because they put too much focus on technology and fail to address the organizational and procedural changes that are required. Moreover, although more than three-quarters of the sampled organizations cite that they lack the skills or capabilities in the area of internal audit of information technology, only one-third bring in external support.[28] These weaknesses, due to lack of attention and/or resources, can lead to major security weaknesses, even in organizations where one would not expect it. For example, the US Government Accountability Office (GAO) said that the US Securities and Exchange Commission (SEC), the stock market watchdog, failed to consistently protect against possible cyber intrusions or encrypt sensitive data on a key financial system, among several information security weaknesses:

> **"Cumulatively, these weaknesses decreased assurance regarding the reliability of the data processed by the key financial system and increased the risk that unauthorized individuals could gain access to critical hardware or software and intentionally or inadvertently access, alter, or delete sensitive data or computer programs," the GAO said. Moreover, the GAO report stated that "while the SEC generally protected physical access to its facilities, the SEC didn't sufficiently control access to one sensitive computing area at its headquarters. It also didn't update and test its contingency and disaster recovery plans or consistently require tough user passwords.[29]**

Several GAO audits have raised concerns about the SEC's internal controls over the years. The latest report quoted above says the information security weaknesses collectively led the GAO to conclude that "the SEC had a *significant deficiency in its internal controls over financial reporting*."[30] Top financial institutions face similar vulnerabilities in their IT systems, making them susceptible to cyber attacks and crime either for financial gain or to disrupt services.[31]

But the spotlight has been put back on the importance of internal controls also following major corporate scandals in the early 2000s, such as at Enron and WorldCom. For example, Section 404 of the Sarbanes-Oxley Act of 2002 (see also Chapter 13) requires that publicly traded companies in the United States provide in their annual reports a statement by management on the effectiveness of the company's system of *internal controls*, many of which are of the action-control type. Section 404 further stipulates the responsibilities of the company's independent auditor in performing an audit of the internal controls in conjunction with an audit of financial statements.[32] As a consequence of the required compliance with Section 404 of the act, many public companies in the United States have both improved the documentation of their internal controls and made them significantly tighter.

Tight personnel/cultural controls

In some situations, MCSs dominated by personnel/cultural controls also can be considered tight. In charitable and voluntary organizations, personnel controls usually provide a significant amount of control, as most volunteers derive a keen sense of satisfaction just from doing a good job, and thus are motivated to do well. Tight personnel/cultural controls can also exist in for-profit businesses. They are common in small, family-run companies where personnel/cultural controls may be effective because of the overlap or congruence between the organizational interests and those of the individuals on whom it must rely for pursuing them.

Some organizations use multiple forms of personnel/cultural controls that, in combination, produce tight control. For example, among the controls used in production areas of Wabash National Corporation, a truck-trailer manufacturer located in Lafayette, Indiana, are:

- *Walk and talk* interviews in which job applicants get to observe the *frenetic factory pace*.
- Group incentive plans, including a profit-sharing plan that gives employees 10% of after-tax earnings and a retirement plan that bases contributions on profit margins.
- Required training. New employees are strongly encouraged to take two specified Wabash improvement classes on their own time and are rewarded with pay raises for doing so. Supervisors are promoted only after they take special classes and pass a test.

Visitors to Wabash often remark that they have "never seen a work force that motivated," which the company's attributes to its focus on "a strong emphasis on maintaining good employee relations and development through competitive compensation and related benefits, a safe work environment and promoting educational programs and quality improvement teams."[33]

In a different context – in the wake of the 2008 financial crisis and a series of scandals and reputational blows – all employees of Deutsche Bank and Barclay's, and all senior bankers at Goldman Sachs, were taken through programs aimed at reinforcing codes, values, behavior, and a strong, positive corporate culture.

> Given the recent record of the banks, such programs invite skepticism. Even assuming the companies can cement good behavior, it is hard to guarantee their managers will successfully monitor, measure and maintain adherence to the values, particularly when competitive pressure mounts as markets revive. Dan Ostergaard, Managing Partner of Integrity-By-Design, a Swiss-based group that advises on culture change and ethical training, is cautiously optimistic, pointing out that if banks do not address organizational structure, including the whole process of recruitment, promotion, remuneration and how they take day-to-day business decisions, it could be "an expensive dog-and-pony show."[34]

In many instances, indeed, the degree of control provided by personnel/cultural controls alone is less than tight. In most firms, the natural overlap between individual and organizational objectives is smaller than that in family firms or tight-knit organizations. Moreover, a divergence between individual and organizational objectives often comes unexpectedly, although, as studies suggest, it is not a rare occurrence. For example, a survey by KPMG Forensic suggests that "the typical company fraudster is a trusted male executive who gets away with over 20 fraudulent acts over a period of up to five years or more." More generally, "61 percent of fraudsters are employed by the victim organization; of these, 41 percent were employed there for more than 6 years; in 70 percent of frauds, the perpetrator colluded with others."[35] The steps that might be taken to increase the strength of personnel controls are difficult to assess and potentially unreliable. Factors such as education, experience, rank, and tenure are not unequivocally reliable predictors of misconduct. Or, to combine the prior section with this one by way of a quote from the KPMG report (p. 6): "Having good internal controls is important, but with any control you are ultimately relying on the human element."

Cultural controls can help make people more reliable and affect an organization's ability to sustainably generate value.[36]

> A strong ethical culture at a company is widely seen as a bulwark against compliance failures, because it makes employees more prone to question what they see as unethical behavior. At the same time, it's hard to go about establishing such a culture. Enron famously had a high-sounding code of ethics that failed to deter its executives from an accounting fraud that brought down the company.[37]

For example, Kellogg, the cereal maker, decided they needed to embed its code of ethics more effectively within the businesses. In so doing, they wanted to make the code less a series of rules and more a means to promote and incorporate its so-called *K-values* of integrity, accountability, passion, humility, simplicity, and results through targeted training. The company went through each section of its ethics code and picked out what was relevant in terms of each K-value. It then structured the revised code so employees could refer to it daily as they worked through ethical issues, and it included real-life examples of situations in which employees could recognize themselves. In addition to a main training for all employees, there is also a targeted training for specific roles depending on the level and the audience with which employees in these roles interact. The idea is that, "together, this should guide employees' decisions, which should lead to better outcomes," Vice President of Internal Audit and Compliance Jim Sholl said.[38]

Dell, the PC maker, also overhauled its ethics code with the aim to get employees to be "believers" rather than "obeyers":

> While both believers and obeyers need to follow the rules, having believers makes them ambassadors for the company's ethics and values and gets them to inspire others to do the right thing. "They feel a sense of pride," Dell Chief Ethics and Compliance Officer Mike McLaughlin said. "I think if they're infused with that kind of pride it helps with their interactions with customers and others. It shows externally and internally."[39]

To accomplish that, the company made its code more aspirational in tone. To get more employee buy-in, Dell asked employees worldwide for input; so when the code was released, it would "truly feel to them what we believe in, as opposed to being told what you should believe in," Mr. McLaughlin said. The message was spread through various channels, including blogs, social media, and even a game called the *Honesty Project*. The game was designed to reinforce the lessons of why ethics and compliance are important by allowing employees to describe the damage that corruption and bribery can cause, recognize red flags that may indicate corruption or bribery, and identify who to contact if they are asked to pay a bribe or witness a bribe being paid. In the first six days after the game was introduced, more than 5,200 employees completed it – some taking it more than once. Is all this effective?

> To measure how effective the effort has been, Dell sent out a voluntary survey to its employees, and received back more than 33,000 responses, Mr. McLaughlin said. "In that data we've seen employees with increased engagement and awareness of these topics," he said.[40]

All told, however, tight control probably cannot be achieved with the use of personnel/cultural controls *alone*, and tight control will inevitably involve relying on a *combination* of action, results, and personnel/cultural controls.

Conclusion

This chapter focused on an important characteristic of MCSs: their degree of tightness. We defined tight control in terms of a high degree of assurance that employees will behave in the organization's best interests. All of the control types discussed in Chapters 2 and 3 can be used to provide tighter control, but none of them in isolation is likely to be sufficient to provide fully tight control. Table 4.1 presents a summary of the characteristics of each of the control types that can be varied to affect tight control.

In some organizations, a particular type of control can be replaced or supplemented with another type that provides a better fit with the situation for the purpose of tighter controls.[41] Some organizations, perhaps because they have suffered major losses due to breaches of authority and weak internal controls, tighten controls by recalibrating their results controls toward using additional detailed, procedures-based action controls. Others, often as they grow and become more decentralized, go the other direction by placing increasingly more emphasis on results controls.

But managers are not limited to tinkering with the characteristics of just one form of control or to replace one for another. To tighten controls, organizations must inevitably rely on multiple forms of controls and align them with one another. For example, large, decentralized organizations can develop strong, supporting ethics codes to guide their largely results-control-driven delegated decision-making. The controls then either reinforce each other or overlap, thus filling in gaps so that they, in combination, provide tight control over all of the factors critical to the organization's success. Lincoln Electric, whose case study appears at the end of this chapter, is a

Table 4.1 A summary of the characteristics that make a control "tight"

Type of control	What makes it tight
Results or action accountability	Definition of desired results or actions: • Congruent with true organizational skills • Specific • Effectively communicated and internalized • Complete (if accountability emphasized) Measurement of results or tracking of actions: • Congruent • Precise • Objective • Timely • Understandable Rewards or punishments: • Significant to person(s) involved • Direct and definite link to results or actions
Behavioral constraints	Reliable Restrictive
Preaction reviews	Frequent Detailed Performed by informed person(s)
Personnel/cultural controls	Certainty and stability of knowledge linking personnel/cultural characteristics with desired actions

Source: K. A. Merchant, *Modern Management Control Systems: Text and Cases* (Upper Saddle River, NJ: Prentice Hall, 1998), p. 166.

good example of a company that effectively uses *multiple-overlapping* and *mutually reinforcing* results, action, and personnel/cultural controls.

It should also be recognized that organizations sometimes deliberately choose to *loosen* their controls. They do so because an inappropriate use of controls causes harmful side effects, such as operating delays or employee frustration and demotivation. These side effects cause many to have negative feelings when they hear the mere mention of tight control. In the next chapter, we discuss more fully the costs and negative side effects associated with some control types and, particularly, with imperfect, overly tight, or inappropriate uses of controls.

Notes

1 See, for example, W. A. Van der Stede, "Measuring Tight Budgetary Control," *Management Accounting Research*, 12, no. 1 (March 2001), pp. 119–37.

2 For a general discussion on priorities among "stakeholders," see, for example, "Shareholders vs. Stakeholders: A New Idolatry," *The Economist* (April 24, 2010), pp. 65–6.

3 "Patents, Yes; Ideas, Maybe," *The Economist* (October 14, 2010), pp. 78–9; "Ford Applies for Record Number of Patents as CEO Eyes Innovation," *Bloomberg Business* (December 22, 2015), online at bloom.bg/1MtesVD.

4 "Companies Aren't Charities," *The Economist* (October 21, 2010), p. 82.

5 See, *inter alia*, W. A. Van der Stede, "The Pitfalls of Pay-for-Performance," *Finance & Management* (December 2007), pp. 10–13; W. A. Van der Stede, "Designing Effective Reward Systems," *Finance & Management* (October 2009), pp. 6–9. See also J. Roberts, *The Modern Firm* (New York: Oxford University Press, 2004), and other work by John Roberts and colleagues, as well as R. Benabou and J. Tirole, "Bonus Culture: Competitive Pay, Screening and Multitasking," *Working Paper 18963* (Cambridge, MA: National Bureau of Economic Research, 2013).

6 "Blind Ambition: How the Pursuit of Results Got Out of Hand at Bausch & Lomb," *Business Week* (October 23, 1995), p. 81.

7 "Manila's Tax Chief Resigns for Not Meeting Targets," *Forbes* (November 2, 2009), online (www.forbes.com).

8 "British Gas Told to Pay £11.1m Penalty by Ofgem," *BBC News* (December 4, 2014), online at www.bbc.co.uk/news/business-30324764.

9 "Tesco Monitors Employees with Motorola Armbands," *Business Week* (February 13, 2013), online at www.bloomberg.com/bw/articles/2013-02-13/tesco-monitors-employees-with-motorola-arm-bands.

10 Ibid. See also "Wearables at Work: The New Frontier of Employee Surveillance," *The Financial Times* (June 8, 2015), online at on.ft.com/1IB7dz1.

11 "Wal-Mart's Worth $80 Despite Soft Quarter," *Forbes* (May 22, 2013), online at onforb.es/10lPJMF.

12 "Super Micro Computer: A One-Man, or at Least One-Family, Powerhouse," *The New York Times* (November 23, 2008), online at nytimes.com. See also *Super Micro 2014 Annual Report*, particularly p. 18, in respect of the company's dependence on Charles Liang, the company president, CEO, and chair.

13 "Netflix Complaint against Mike Kail Suggests Governance Problems, Experts Say," *The Wall Street Journal* (November 26, 2014), online at blogs.wsj.com/cio/2014/11/26/netflix-complaint-against-mike-kail-suggests-governance-problems-experts-say.

14 *Report to the Nations on Occupational Fraud and Abuse 2014 Global Fraud Study* (Association of Certified Fraud Examiners, 2014), online at www.acfe.com/rttn/docs/2014-report-to-nations.pdf.

15 "Adequate Procedures Report – Blessing in Disguise," *KPMG* (July 10, 2010), online at http://rd.kpmg.co.uk.

16 "Jeff Bezos Reveals His No. 1 Leadership Secret," *Forbes* (April 4, 2012), online at www.forbes.com/forbes/2012/0423/ceo-compensation-12-amazon-technology-jeff-bezos-gets-it.html.

17 Ibid.

18 R. Goldberg and G. Goldberg, *Citizen Turner: The Wild Rise of an American Tycoon* (New York: Harcourt Brace, 1995).

19 "Trimming Expenses, Citi Holds Back on Color Copying," *The New York Times* (August 26, 2008), online at nytimes.com.

20 Quoted in P. Edwards, M. Ram, and J. Black, *The Impact of Employment Legislation on Small Firms: A Case Study Analysis*, Employment Research Series No. 20 (London: Department of Trade and Industry, September 2003), p. 52.

21 Ibid., p. 128.

22 "SAP's U.S. Chief Plans Reorganization of Unit," *The Wall Street Journal* (May 26, 2000), p. B7.

23 "Struggling with Employee Complacency? Kill Your Stupid Rules," *Forbes* (October 30, 2013), online at onforb.es/17wUbzd.

24 "Strict Rules Are Changing How Financial Institutions Do Business," *The Financial Times* (October 18, 2015), online at on.ft.com/1kfJvOR.

25 "SEC Deploying New Tool to Spot Insider Trading, White Says," *Bloomberg* (January 27, 2014), online at bloom.bg/1hkljZn.

26 "Data-Crunching Is Coming to Help Your Boss Manage Your Time," *The New York Times* (August 17, 2015), online at http://nyti.ms/1IXM5yx.

27 Ibid.

28 "Too Much Faith in Technology Leads to Lapses," *KPMG* (June 16, 2008), online at rd.kpmg.co.uk; *KPMG's 2013 IT Internal Audit Survey* (KPMG, 2013), online at www.iia.nl/SiteFiles/ITA_Survey_ok_web.pdf.

29 "GAO Faults SEC for Lax Cybersecurity," *The Wall Street Journal* (April 17, 2014), online at on.wsj.com/1eF2HkW.

30 Ibid.

31 "Bank of England to Oversee 'Ethical Hacking' of Financial Groups," *The Financial Times* (April 21, 2014), online at on.ft.com/1nDfO6f.

32 Sarbanes-Oxley Act of 2002 (107th Congress of the United States of America, January 23, 2002).

33 This example is taken from "Hard Driving: A Productivity Push at Wabash National Puts Firm on a Roll," *The Wall Street Journal* (September 7, 1995), p. A1. See also Wabash National Corp. 10-K *SEC Filing* (February 27, 2015), p. 15.

34 "Bankers Back in the Classroom," *The Financial Times* (October 16, 2013), online at http://on.ft.com/19OvxpC.

35 "Profile of a Fraudster: Trusted Male Manager – and Getting Away with It for Years," *KPMG* (April 17, 2007), online at rd.kpmg.co.uk; "Global Profiles of the Fraudster: White-Collar Crime – Present and Future" (KPMG, 2013), online at assets.kpmg.com/content/dam/kpmg/pdf/2013/11/global-profiles-of-the-fraudster-v2.pdf.

36 "UK Boards Urged to Take Control of Ethical Values," *The Financial Times* (July 21, 2014), online at on.ft.com/1zVgono. See also "The Top Companies for Culture and Values," *Forbes* (August 22, 2014), online at onforb.es/1lm7hIv.

37 "Turning Employees into Ethics Believers," *The Wall Street Journal* (September 26, 2014), online at blogs.wsj.com/riskandcompliance/2014/09/26/turning-employees-into-ethics-and-compliance-believers.

38 Ibid.

39 Ibid.

40 Ibid.

41 "Siemens CFO: Our Internal Control System Works Like a Charm," *The Wall Street Journal* (January 15, 2013), online at blogs.wsj.com/corruption-currents/2013/01/15/siemens-cfo-our-internal-control-system-works-like-a-charm.

CASE STUDY
Controls at the Bellagio Casino Resort

In our world, good controls mean good business. A lot of our controls are dictated to us by the Nevada Gaming Control Board, but we would institute most of the same controls they require anyway. The State wants its share of the revenue. We want to earn profits.

Trent Walker, Bellagio Casino Controller

MGM MIRAGE and its properties

The Bellagio was one of 23 properties of MGM MIRAGE (NYSE: MGM), one of the world's leading hotel and gaming companies. In addition to the 23 properties shown in Exhibit 1, MGM MIRAGE was also developing a major resort in Macau (with a joint-venture partner) and a new multibillion dollar "urban metropolis" on 66 acres of land on the Las Vegas strip. At the end of 2005, the company had over 66,000 employees and total assets of over $20 billion (see Exhibits 2 and 3).[1]

MGM MIRAGE operated primarily in one industry segment, the operation of casino resorts, which included gaming, hotel, dining, entertainment, retail, and other resort amenities. All the MGM MIRAGE casino resorts operated 24 hours a day, every day of the year. Over half of the company's net revenue was derived from nongaming activities, a higher percentage than many of MGM MIRAGE's competitors.

Primary casino operations were owned and managed by the company. Other resort amenities sometimes were owned and operated by the company, owned by the company but managed by third parties for a fee, or leased to third parties. The company, however, generally had an operating philosophy that preferred ownership of amenities, since guests had direct contact with staff in these areas and the company preferred to control all aspects of the guest experience. However, the company did lease space to retail and food and beverage operators in certain situations, particularly for branding opportunities.

As a resort-based company, MGM MIRAGE's operating philosophy was to provide a complete resort experience for guests, including nongaming amenities that commanded a premium price based on quality. The company's operating results depended highly on the volume of customers at its resorts, which in turn impacted the price it could charge for hotel rooms and other amenities. MGM MIRAGE also generated a significant portion of its operating income from the high-end gaming segment, which also caused variability in operating results. Results of operations tended not to be highly seasonal in nature, but a variety of factors could affect the results of any interim period, including the timing of major Las Vegas conventions, the amount and timing of marketing and special events for high-end customers, and the level of play during major holidays, including New Year's Day and the Chinese New Year. However, the company's significant convention and meeting facilities allowed it to maximize hotel occupancy and customer volumes during off-peak times such as midweek or during traditionally slower leisure travel periods, which also allowed for better labor utilization.

MGM MIRAGE's casino resorts generally operated in highly competitive environments. They competed against other gaming companies as well as other hospitality and leisure and business travel companies. At the end of 2005, Las Vegas, for example, had approximately 133,200 guestrooms.

The principal segments of the Las Vegas gaming market were leisure travel; premium gaming customers; conventions, including small meetings and corporate incentive programs; and tour and travel. The company's high-end properties, which included Bellagio, MGM Grand Las Vegas, Mandalay Bay, and the Mirage, appealed to the upper end of each market segment, balancing their business by using the convention and tour

[1] In April 2005, MGM MIRAGE acquired Mandalay Resort Group at a total acquisition cost of approximately $7.3 billion. As a result of the acquisition, MGM MIRAGE became a much larger company with, for example, over 66,000 employees versus 40,000 and total assets of over $20 billion versus $11 billion (see Exhibit 3).

and travel segments to fill the midweek and off-peak periods.[2] The company's primary methods of competing successfully in the high-end segment consisted of:

- locating resorts in desirable leisure and business travel markets, and operating at superior sites within those markets;
- constructing and maintaining high-quality resorts and facilities, including luxurious guestrooms along with premier dining, entertainment, and retail amenities;
- recruiting, training, and retaining well-qualified and motivated employees to provide superior and friendly customer service;
- providing unique, "must-see" entertainment attractions; and
- developing distinctive and memorable marketing and promotional programs.

A key element of marketing to premium gaming customers was personal contact by marketing personnel. Direct marketing was also important in the convention segment. MGM MIRAGE maintained Internet websites that informed customers about its resorts and allowed customers to book hotel rooms and make restaurant and show reservations. The company also operated call centers to service customers by phone to make hotel, restaurant, and show reservations. Finally, MGM MIRAGE utilized its world-class golf courses in marketing programs. The company's major Las Vegas resorts offered luxury suite packages that included golf privileges, such as golf packages at special rates or on a complimentary basis for premium gaming customers.

In this environment, the company's key revenue-related performance indicators were:

- ***Gaming revenue indicators***, such as table games *drop* and slot machines *handle* (volume indicators) and *win* or *hold* percentages (profitability indicators). These performance indicators are discussed in detail in the later sections of the case.
- ***Hotel revenue indicators***, such as hotel occupancy (volume indicator), average daily rate (ADR – a price indicator), and revenue per available room (REVPAR – a summary measure of hotel results that combined ADR and occupancy rate).

Most of MGM MIRAGE's revenue was cash-based. Customers typically wagered with cash or paid for non-gaming services with either cash or credit cards. The business, however, was capital intensive, and the company relied heavily on the ability of its resorts to generate operating cash flow to repay debt financing, fund maintenance capital expenditures, and provide excess cash for future developments.

MGM MIRAGE was making increasing use of advanced technologies to help maximize revenue and operational efficiency. For example, the company was in the process of combining its player-affinity programs, the Players Club and Mandalay's One Club, into a single program. This integration would link all MGM MIRAGE's major resorts and consolidate all slots and table-games activity for customers with a Players Club account. Under the combined program, customers qualified for benefits ("comps") across all of the company's resorts, regardless of where they played. This program enabled the company to get to know its better customers and to market to them more effectively.

A significant portion of the slot machines at the MGM MIRAGE resorts operated with the EZ-Pay™ cashless gaming system, including the Mandalay resorts that had recently converted their slot machines. This system enhanced both the customer experience and increased the revenue potential of the slot machines.

Technology was a critical part of MGM MIRAGE's strategy in nongaming operations and administrative areas as well. For example, the hotel systems included yield management modules that allowed maximizing occupancy and room rates. Additionally, these systems captured most charges made by customers during their stay, including allowing customers of any of the company's resorts to charge meals and services at other MGM MIRAGE resorts to their hotel accounts. In short, this system enhanced guest service and improved yield management across the company's portfolio of resorts.

The Bellagio

The Bellagio, located in the heart of the Las Vegas strip, was widely recognized as one of the premier casino resorts in the world. Inside the richly decorated resort was a conservatory filled with unique botanical displays that changed with the season. In front was an

[2] MGM MIRAGE's marketing strategy for Treasure Island, New York-New York, Luxor, and Monte Carlo was aimed at attracting middle- to upper-middle-income guests, largely from the leisure travel and, to a lesser extent, the tour and travel segments. Excalibur and Circus Circus Las Vegas generally catered to the value-oriented and middle-income leisure travel and tour and travel segments.

eight-acre lake featuring over 1,000 fountains that performed a choreographed ballet of water, music, and lights. Amenities and entertainment options at the Bellagio included an expansive pool, a world-class spa, exquisite restaurants, a luxuriant nightclub and several bars and lounges, and shows by Cirque du Soleil, as well as a gallery of fine arts. The Bellagio also featured 200,000 square feet of convention space.

In the casino operations area, the Bellagio operated 2,409 coin-operated gaming devices (slot machines) and 143 game tables (see Exhibit 1), slightly over half of which were blackjack tables. The other table games included primarily baccarat, craps, and roulette. The casino also operated a keno and poker area. The games operated on a 24/7 basis in three shifts per day: day (8 a.m.– 4 p.m.), swing (4 p.m.–midnight), and graveyard (midnight–8 a.m.) shifts. Approximately 1,000 people were employed in casino operations.

As in most companies in this industry, the gaming (casino) and nongaming operations in each of the MGM MIRAGE properties such as the Bellagio were run as separate profit centers. Exhibit 4 shows the Table Games Division organization chart. Bill Bingham, vice president of table games, reported directly to Bill McBeath, Bellagio's president/CEO. The vice president of the separate Slot Machines Division of the casino also reported directly to Bill McBeath.

The unique feature of a casino resort organization, as compared to that in most corporations, was the relatively large size of the finance staff. In the Bellagio, about 1,000 of the total of approximately 4,000 employees were in the finance organization, reporting in a direct line to Jon Corchis, executive vice president/CFO (Exhibit 5). Strict separation was maintained between operations and recordkeeping. The finance organization was large because it had responsibility for cash control and recordkeeping, both important functions in the casino and food and beverage parts of the business, particularly. Thus, the finance organization included credit operations personnel, casino change personnel (cage operations), pit clerk personnel, and count room personnel, in addition to people who were normally part of a finance organization, such as accounting clerks and financial analysts.

Laws and regulations over gaming activities

This case is focused on the controls used in the casino, especially in the difficult-to-control table games areas such as the blackjack pits. Many of these controls were legally mandated because the gaming industry was highly regulated. Each company had to maintain its licenses and pay gaming taxes to be allowed to continue operations. Each casino was subject to extensive regulation under the laws, rules, and regulations of the jurisdiction where it was located. These laws, rules, and regulations generally concerned the responsibility, financial stability, and character of the owners, managers, and persons with financial interest in the gaming operations. Violations of laws in one jurisdiction could result in disciplinary action in other jurisdictions. Exhibit 6 shows a more detailed description of some of these regulations as applied in the State of Nevada.

In connection with the supervision of gaming activities at the company's casinos, specifically, MGM MIRAGE maintained stringent controls on the recording of all receipts and disbursements. These controls included:

- locked cash boxes on the casino floor;
- daily cash and coin counts performed by employees who were independent of casino operations;
- constant observation and supervision of the gaming area;
- observation and recording of gaming and other areas by closed-circuit television;
- timely analysis of deviations from expected performance; and
- constant computer monitoring of slot machines.

Used in the casino, these controls were intended to ensure that the casino and the various governmental entities each kept their fair share of the money that was wagered.

Some of the regulations required extensive training of casino personnel to ensure compliance. For example, the last paragraph of the regulations shown in Exhibit 6 dealt with the reporting of so-called *suspicious activities* related to money laundering and/or the structuring of transactions by customers to avoid reporting to the US Internal Revenue Service (IRS) tax authority. This regulation, particularly, had regained importance subsequent to the signing into law of the US Patriot Act of 2001 following the terrorist attacks on the United States. Because a casino is not a bank, where every transaction can be more easily traced, and because the law required the reporting of any cash transaction in excess of $10,000 *as a result of one or a combination of transactions over a 24-hour period*, the company provided extensive training to standardize the handling, aggregation, and reporting of same type or dissimilar cash transactions by single customers on a single or multiple visits within a 24-hour period.

The company's businesses were also subject to various other federal, state, and local laws and regulations in addition to gaming regulations. These laws and regulations included, but were not limited to, restrictions and conditions concerning alcoholic beverages, environmental matters, employees, currency transactions, taxation, zoning and building codes, and marketing and advertising.

The game of blackjack and the roles of dealers

In a short case, it is not possible to describe all of the many controls that were employed in the casino. To simplify the discussion, all references will be to the table game of blackjack.[3] The following section provides a brief description of blackjack and the personnel involved in running it.

Blackjack is a very popular card game where up to seven patrons play against the house. The players' object is to draw cards whose total is higher than the dealer's total without exceeding 21.

Each blackjack table was run by a dealer whose job was to sell chips to customers, deal the cards, take losing wagers, and pay winning wagers. Dealing was a skilled profession that required some training and considerable practice. Experience was valuable, as the dealer's value to the casino increased with the number of games that could be dealt within a given time period, and speed usually increased with experience. Experience was also valuable in identifying players who might be cheating.

Dealers assigned to a table worked for one hour and then were replaced by a *relief dealer* during their 20-minute break. Relief dealers worked at three different tables. The frequent breaks were required because the job was mentally and physically taxing – dealers were required to be standing up while they dealt; they had to maintain intense concentration, as errors in paying off bets were not tolerated; and they had to maintain good humor under sometimes difficult conditions (e.g. dealing to players who became irritable because they were losing).

Bill Bingham, vice president of table games, described a good dealer as follows:

> A good dealer makes a minimum number of mistakes and is productive in terms of hands per hour. But we don't clock our dealers. We believe that customers gravitate towards a dealer they are comfortable with, and that means different things for every customer. Some players prefer a slower pace.
>
> We only hire experienced dealers, and so we assume that they have mastered the technical aspect of dealing. For us, *customer satisfaction* is key, meaning that dealers have to be welcoming and engaging. They smile; they make eye contact and conversation with the players; and they wish them well. We also value attendance. Dealers with perfect attendance over a six-month period earn an extra vacation day.
>
> Regarding speed, you may have noticed as you walked through the casino that some tables have only one or two customers. You might ask why I don't close these tables. As a matter of fact, a low number of customers at a table doesn't worry me at all. If a good dealer can do 60 hands per hour on a table with, say, five customers, then that same dealer probably can do nearly 300 hands with just one customer! And, as I said, some customers don't like to join a busy table, and so it all works out in the end.

Bellagio dealers were paid well. While they earned a base wage of only \$6.15 per hour, their total compensation was usually in the range of \$85,000–\$100,000 per year, including *tokes* (tips), which were shared equally among all dealers. Because the total compensation was high, perhaps among the top two or three casinos in Las Vegas, the Bellagio was seen a desirable place to work. The company hired only dealers with a minimum of two years' experience. Dealer turnover was low – less than 3%.

The blackjack tables at Bellagio were spread across six *pits* containing 16–30 blackjack tables each. *Floor supervisors* (also called *floor persons*) supervised three to six blackjack tables, depending on the so-called *table minimum* (i.e. the minimum dollar amount to be wagered at the table). Each shift was also staffed by

[3] This is done with little loss of generality. Control over all the table games in the Bellagio was nearly identical. The one major exception was that one extra level of supervision (*box person*) was used at the crap tables (see Exhibit 4). In the slot machines area, control was simpler because machines eliminated the human element (dealers). The machines did, however, have to be inspected regularly for evidence of tampering.

three to five *pit managers* (also called *pit bosses*), as well as a *shift manager* and an *assistant shift manager*. Hence, for example, when fully operating during a busy day shift, pit number 4, which contained 30 blackjack tables, employed about 30 dealers (depending on the number of tables that were open in the pit), 10 relief dealers, up to 10 floor persons, and one pit manager (plus relief).[4] In total, the Bellagio employed about 775 dealers, 225 floor (and box) supervisors, and 16 pit managers. Because they did not share in tokes, floor persons and pit managers earned less than dealers; on average about $62,000 and $85,000 per year, respectively.

Controls over cash and credit

Because most of the casino business was conducted in terms of cash or cash equivalents (i.e. chips), having good control over the many stocks of cash and chips located within the casino and over movements of these stocks without loss was essential. Moreover, because *marker play* (play on credit) represented a significant portion of the table games volume at Bellagio, the company also maintained strict controls over issuing credit. Overall, then, Bellagio's cash and credit control system can be described in terms of four main elements: (1) individual accountability for cash and (cash equivalent) stocks; (2) formal procedures for transfers of cash; (3) strict controls over credit issuance; and (4) tight control in the count rooms.

A. Individual accountability for cash stocks

All cash stocks – with the exception of those kept at a game table or those taken from a game or slot machine for counting – were maintained on an *imprest* basis. This meant that most personnel who dealt directly with cash, such as change personnel, coin redemption personnel, cashiers, and chip fill bank personnel, were held individually accountable for a specific sum of money that was charged out to them. These personnel were required to turn in the exact amount of money for which they were given responsibility, and any large shortages or persistent patterns of shortages were grounds for dismissal.

B. Formal procedures for transfers

Strict procedures had to be followed when transferring cash or chips to or from *nonimprest* funds (e.g. a game table). All transfers required the creation of formal transactions signifying the transfer of accountability for the money involved. These procedures can be illustrated by describing the so-called *drop standards* and what was required to move cash or chips to and from a blackjack table.

When the Bellagio casino opened in 1998, the *drop box* affixed to each table was removed and its contents were counted at the end of each shift. But little or no use was made of the shift-by-shift information, so in 2004, the practice was changed to just one drop per day, a so-called *24-hour drop*.

The drop for each table had to be reconciled with other recorded transactions that occurred during the day. First, at the close of each shift, the incoming and outgoing pit managers proceeded through their pits and counted the chips (for blackjack) on each table, and recorded them on a *table inventory sheet* (see Exhibit 7). Table inventory sheets indicated the date, shift, game table number, and count by denomination and in total. Both the incoming and outgoing pit managers were required to sign the table inventory sheet verifying the accuracy of the count. When completed, one copy of the table inventory sheet was dropped in the pit drop box and the duplicate copy was delivered to the casino cage,[5] where the cage cashier or cage supervisor entered the table inventory amount (by denomination and in total) for each table into the computer system. Pit managers did not have access to the computer system that would allow them to add, change, or delete table inventory amounts.

As the game was played, several transactions could take place. One involved players buying chips from the dealer for cash or credit. Cash was deposited immediately in the drop box. Players could not make reverse exchanges (chips for cash) at the tables. They had to take their chips to the casino cage where this type of exchange was made. Credit had to be approved by checking the customer's credit authorization limit through the use of a computer terminal located in the pit. If the credit was approved, a so-called *marker* was prepared. This process is described in the next section.

Transfers of chips to and from a gaming table were also common. Chip transfers to a table took place each time a table was opened for play or when additional chips were needed at an already open table. When the pit boss decided to open a blackjack table, or a floor

[4] This pit also contained a few other table games, such as roulette wheels.

[5] This was a secure work area within the casino where the casino bankroll was kept.

person noticed that additional chips were needed at a table, a request for a particular mix of chips was input into the computer terminal in the pit (using a so-called *input form*) and relayed to the fill bank cashier in the casino cage, where a four-part, serially numbered *fill slip* was printed (see Exhibit 8). The fill bank cashier then summoned a security guard and filled the order in the guard's presence. Both the chip bank cashier and the security guard then signed copies 1, 2, and 3 of the fill slip. Copy 4 of the fill slip was retained by the cage to forward to casino accounting daily. The security guard then transported copies 1 and 2 of the fill slip and the fill to the table where the fill was required. The chip bank cashier retained copy 3 of the fill slip. The guard then gave copies 1 and 2 of the fill slip to the pit manager and placed the fill on the table. The dealer counted the fill by breaking down the chips in public view, agreed the count to the fill slip, and signed copies 1 and 2 of the fill slip. The pit manager also signed copies 1 and 2 of the fill slip. The dealer then placed the fill in the table tray and inserted copy 2 of the fill slip and copy 2 of the input form into the drop box. Copy 1 of the fill slip was given to the security guard who returned it to the chip bank cashier in the cage. Copies 1 and 3 of the fill slip were later forwarded to the casino accounting department.

A similar process was followed when a table was closed or an overabundance of chips had to be transferred to the cage, in which instance the transaction was traced through the use of an *input form* and *credit slip* (instead of a *fill slip*).

The so-called *drop* procedure, the process through which the table drop box was removed at the end of each gaming day, operated as follows. At least two security guards first obtained the soft count room key, locked storage carts with empty drop boxes, and the drop box release keys from the cage. They then proceeded to the table game pits where they unlocked the cart padlocks utilizing the drop box storage cart keys, removed the empty drop boxes, and placed them on their respective table. Pit managers and security guards observed the empty drop boxes from the time they were removed from the carts until placed on their respective gaming table. After setting out the empty drop boxes, the security guards removed the full drop boxes from the table using the drop box release keys. Empty drop boxes were then locked on the tables and the full drop boxes were immediately stored in carts. When the drop was complete but prior to transport, the carts were secured with a different padlock designated for carts with full drop boxes. Neither security guards nor pit managers had access to the keys for this padlock. At a minimum, two security guards and one pit manager transported the full drop boxes in the locked carts to the soft count room where they were secured until the count took place. Multiple drop teams were utilized such that each made only one trip to and from the casino floor for the placement and collection of drop boxes. The security guards completed the drop cycle by returning the keys to the cage.

C. Strict controls over credit issuance

When players wanted to gamble with money borrowed from the casino, as was common, they were issued what was called a *marker* (or *counter check*). Players' credit limits had to be preapproved.

Strict controls were applied over the issuance of markers. Marker paperwork contained multiple parts; (1) the original, which was maintained in the pit until the marker was settled, after which it was transferred to the cage; (2) an *issuance stub*, signed by the dealer and floor supervisor and inserted into the table drop box when the marker was issued; and (3) a *payment stub*. If the marker was paid in the pit, the payment stub was signed by the dealer and floor supervisor and inserted in the table game drop box. If paid at the table, there were strict rules for the dealer to follow when advancing the chips in the amount of the marker to the customer (e.g. the dealer had to break down the chips in full public view – and, obviously, in full view of the surveillance camera overhead – prior to advancing the chips). If the marker was not paid, the payment stub was transferred to the cage with the original marker. All these documents contained a check number, customer number, shift, pit number, type of table game, table number, date and time, and the approved dollar amount, in addition to the required employee signatures and ID numbers. There was also a time limit (30 minutes) within which the marker issuance process had to be completed, as well as strict rules for voiding markers.

Because marker play represented a significant portion of the table games volume at Bellagio, the company also aggressively pursued collection from those customers who failed to pay their marker balances timely. These collection efforts were similar to those used by most large corporations when dealing with overdue customer accounts, including the mailing of statements and delinquency notices, personal contacts, the use of outside collection agencies, and civil litigation. A significant portion of the company's accounts receivable, for amounts unpaid resulting from markers which were not collectible through banking channels, was owed by major casino customers from Asia. In this instance, the collectability of unpaid markers was affected by a number of factors, including changes in currency exchange rates and economic conditions in the customers' home countries.

D. Tight security in count rooms

Wins (or losses) on a particular game table could not be determined until the funds in the drop box were counted. All counting from table games was done in the soft count room,[6] a highly secure room located adjacent to the casino cage. Tight security and supervision was necessary in the count rooms to ensure that the winnings were tallied accurately and that all the money to which the casino was entitled was added to stores in the casino cage.

All cash and chips inventory storied in the soft count room was secured from unauthorized access at all times. Access to the count room during the count was restricted to members of the drop and count teams, authorized observers, supervisors for resolution of problems, authorized maintenance personnel, and personnel performing currency transfers. Access to stored table game drop boxes, full or empty, was restricted to authorized members of the drop and count teams. When counts from various revenue centers occurred simultaneously in the soft count room with the table game count, each count table could contain funds from only one revenue center and the tables had to be adequately spaced to prevent commingling of funds. During the count, a minimum of three persons had to be in the count room until the monies were transferred and accepted into cage accountability. Full-time count personnel independent of the pit department and the subsequent accountability of count proceeds had to be maintained by the casino to ensure the staffing of a count team with at least three members each day.

The count began with the opening of the first table game drop box and ended when a member of the cage signed the *master games worksheet* and assumed accountability of the drop proceeds. During the actual counting process, very strict procedures were followed, as described in Exhibit 9. The counting process was filmed by the cameras located in the room. After the money was counted, it was transferred to the casino cage.

Only after the cash and markers in the drop box had been counted was it possible to calculate the winnings for each table. Specifically, the win for a particular gaming table was calculated by determining the total drop (= cash + markers in the drop box) adjusted for table inventory (= beginning table inventory + fills − credits − ending table inventory), as illustrated in the following (simplified) example taken from the Bellagio master games worksheet for January 17, 2006:[7]

GAME: BJ	
SHIFT: ALL	
PIT: ALL	
DATE: 01/17/06	
TOTAL BEGINNING INVENTORY	29,497,800.00
TOTAL FILLS	3,923,960.00
TOTAL CREDITS	21,500.00
TOTAL ENDING INVENTORY	32,548,000.00
TOTAL CASH DROP	583,008.00
TOTAL COUNTER CHECKS	626,500.00
WIN (LOSS)	357,248.00

As illustrated in this example for the blackjack game, the results for all games for each shift were reported on the *master games worksheet*, which was produced daily and summarized by type of game. The uses of this document as a control report are described further in a later section of the case.

[6] This money was mostly bills and markers; hence the name *soft count* room. Coins taken from the slot machines were counted in the *hard count* room, which was about to disappear due to the use of slot machine tickets, rather than coins.

[7] Numbers in this example were disguised to safeguard company restrictions on the release of internal operating data.

Control of games

As discussed, the table games and the slot machines provided the only ways by which the casino made money. The table games were particularly difficult to control because of the need to rely on people who might be tempted by the extremely large amounts of money that could exchange hands very quickly.

In response to this difficult control problem, multiple forms of control were required by the Nevada Gaming Control Board (GCB) and used in the Bellagio to help ensure that the casino kept the cash to which it was entitled. These included: (1) licensing of casino personnel; (2) standardization of actions of personnel running the games; (3) careful supervision and surveillance of the actions taking place at the table; (4) monitoring of results; and (5) strict auditing procedures. These are discussed in the following sections.

A. Licensing

All employees of the casino (referred to by the GCB as *gaming employees*)[8] had to be registered with the GCB. The casino was required to submit a report to the GCB containing the name, social security number, position held, and date of hire of each gaming employee hired during the previous month. In addition, a registration packet had to be submitted for each employee. The key contents of the registration packet were the *gaming employee registration application* (which contained all the basic information about the employee [name, address, social security number] and employer), the *gaming employee questionnaire* (which contained additional information relating to the background of the applicant), and the *fingerprint form*. The registration process itself essentially involved a background check of gaming employees against police department records. When applicants did not pass the registration process, they could not be kept in employ by the casino. Successful registration, on the other hand, resulted in the issuing of a *gaming card* (essentially a gaming work permit), which expired after five years, at which time a new application had to be filed.

Similarly, on or before the 15th of the month after a calendar quarter, the casino was required to submit a report to the GCB containing the name, social security number, position held, and date of termination of each gaming employee terminated or separated from service within the previous quarter.

The Bellagio, however, performed its own employee screenings independent of the required registration process. The intent of these background checks was to avoid hiring people who had been involved in crimes or violations of casino rules, or those who might be attracted because of a need for quick cash. In the words of Bill Bingham, vice president of table games, "We know from experience that dealers with addiction issues, either alcohol, drugs, or gambling, are the ones to watch out for; they need cash to satisfy their addiction, and there is plenty of cash around here."

Moreover, Robert Rudloff, vice president of internal audit, noted that, "Dealers who, say, steal at one casino could still get in under the radar screen at another casino if the stealing was not reported to the police, which is basically what the GCB checks against. Our own preemployment screening hopefully can catch this." Trent Walker, casino controller, added: "What we really need though is a casino-wide system, kind of like an alert system, that links the whole city."

While the required background checking for gaming employees was relatively simple, checks on so-called *key employees* were more elaborate. Key employees included any executive, employee, or agent of a gaming establishment having the power to exercise a significant influence over decisions concerning any part of the gaming operation. The GCB required key employees to be licensed, a process that involved comprehensive background checks and extensive information, including the scrutiny of employment history, personal financial statements, and tax returns.

B. Standardization of actions at the tables

At the gaming tables, most of the dealers' physical motions were standardized in order to make supervision and surveillance easier. For example:

1. All cash and chip exchanges were to be made in the middle of the gaming table in full public view to make them easier to see by supervisory personnel and the surveillance camera overhead.
2. Tips were to be accepted by tapping the cash or chips on the table and placing them in a clear, locked *toke*

[8] Simply put, *gaming employees* essentially included all casino personnel except bartenders, cocktail waitresses, or other persons engaged exclusively in preparing or serving food or beverages.

box attached to the gaming tables. This was done to distinguish these exchanges from wagers.

3. Before dealers left their tables, they were required to place their hands in the middle of the table and to show both the palm and back of their hands. This was done to prevent them from *palming* money or chips in order to take it from the table as they left. Dealers were also required to wear attire that was designed to make it more difficult for them to pocket cash or chips.

C. Supervision and surveillance

Front-line gaming personnel (e.g. dealers) were subjected to multiple forms of supervision and surveillance. Direct supervision was provided by the floor persons and pit bosses. One of their primary functions was to watch the gaming activity and spot events that were out of the ordinary. As highly experienced gaming people, they had a keen sense of the activity going on around them and, thus, were generally good at spotting nonroutine events, such as dealers paying losing bets in blackjack or customers marking cards in blackjack or switching dice in craps.

Extra surveillance of the table games was provided through a system of closed-circuit cameras, one fixed above each gaming table. In total, the Bellagio employed 2,000 cameras located throughout the property. The cameras had lenses powerful enough to zoom in to view objects as small as the date on a dime on the table. The pictures were viewed in a security room located on the mezzanine level of the casino. The system provided the capability to record the activities shown on videotape for later viewing, or, if necessary, as evidence (e.g. if malfeasance was suspected). The tapes from each camera were retained for a minimum of seven days. But in some cases where problems were identified, the tapes were retained indefinitely. To ensure that the surveillance was done objectively, strict separation was maintained between the personnel working on the casino floor and those working in the surveillance areas.

The Bellagio also used *mystery shoppers* to evaluate the dealers. A mystery shopper evaluated each dealer at least once every 1.5 years. The mystery shoppers evaluated only customer service, not speed. Each dealer was rated as *superior*, *expected*, *needs improvement*, or *unsatisfactory*. Eighty-five percent of the dealers were rated superior or expected. The mystery shoppers revisited the other 15% at a later time. No dealer was ever fired based on the mystery shopper ratings. If the poor performance persisted, supervisors worked with the dealer to improve. Dealers that consistently performed poorly usually did not need to be told; they usually did not get as many customers at their table. Bill Bingham explained, "The mystery shopper program is geared more towards keeping our customer orientation in check rather than being a performance evaluation tool of dealers *per se*."

The levels of casino management above the pit bosses, such as shift managers and the vice president of table games, did little direct supervision of the gaming activity. They were mainly involved in trouble shooting (e.g. resolving cases of malfeasance), keeping good customers happy, resolving special problems that arose (e.g. staffing issues), and improving the casino operations.

D. Monitoring of results

The *master games worksheet* provided three key indicators of the results of the gaming activity: drop, win, and hold percentage.

1. The *drop*, which was essentially the sum of *cash drop* and credit amounts (*markers*), was interpreted as the total amount of money the customers were willing to bet against the casino. However, the drop number had some limitations as an activity indicator of some table games (e.g. blackjack) as it was biased upward when table game players exchanged money for chips at the table but did not bet, thereby creating what was called *false drop*; and it was biased downward when players gambled with chips bought at another table, perhaps even on another shift or day. A better indicator of activity would have been the *handle*, the total value of wagers made, but there was no way to determine this number for blackjack and some other table games.
2. The *win* was the casino's gross profit number. It was calculated as shown in the example in the previous section of the case.
3. The *hold* percentage was the primary measure of casino profitability. It was defined as the win divided by the drop.

An example of a *master games worksheet* summary report is shown in Exhibit 10. However, a comprehensive set of reports also was produced that provided these performance measures in various levels of detail, by table, shift, and time period. One such report is shown in Exhibit 11.

Bellagio's management watched the total drop and hold numbers carefully. The drop number was the best available measure of the volume of betting activity, and as such, it was useful as an indicator of the success of the company's marketing strategies and credit policies.

The hold percentage was the best available measure of casino profitability. Using these numbers, Bellagio's management looked for patterns. They knew that each table game should maintain a certain hold percentage; for example, Bellagio's normal table games win percentages were in the range of 18–22% of the table games drop.[9] If the hold percentage was low across the casino table games operation, on all shifts and all tables, and that pattern persisted for a period of, say, several days, the managers in casino operations, including the vice president of table games, had a hard look at the operations and control system to try to tie down the root cause of the unfavorable trend in the hold percentage. Moreover, the drop, win, and hold percentage measures were standard throughout the gaming industry, and competitive analyses were facilitated because summaries were prepared and distributed through several industry sources and trade associations.

The managers in casino operations also looked at the hold generated on each shift in each pit and at each table, but dealers and floor people were not always assigned to the same tables, so management did not have information to tie them to hold percentages. Also, because of the 24-hour drop procedure described above, at least six dealers were at a given table during that time period (that is, at least one dealer and one relief dealer during each shift, times three shifts), and sometimes personnel did not work exact shifts. Thus, Bellagio management did no analysis of results – hold percentage – at the table level. Bill Bingham explained, "We used to monitor the reports on a table-by-table basis, but we never caught anybody doing anything. We did use surveillance on one dealer whom we suspected, but to no avail."

Pit bosses had to make independent estimates of the drop by shift for each table in their pit, which were reconciled with the actual count. This was done on a so-called *cash drop variance report*, as shown in Exhibit 12. When unusual deviations were observed, game table supervisory personnel, such as the shift manager or even the vice president of table games, could go back and ask the pit personnel to explain why the deviation occurred. Sometimes, the reason for the deviation was just due to a high roller on a hot streak, but if there were any doubts about the explanation, or if the deviation could not be pinpointed easily, extra surveillance was called in. Estimated versus actual data were also aggregated on a daily basis for the Table Games Division as shown in Exhibit 13. This report, as mandated by the GCB, required that a deviation between the actual and estimated drop exceeding +/−10% had to be investigated and explained.

Finally, the GCB required the casino controller to investigate on a monthly basis all statistical fluctuations by game type in excess of +/−5% resulting from the comparison of the previous calendar year to that of the current month. Reasons for the deviations could include the activity of customers whose play materially affected the results of the month (the so-called *high-roller-on-a-hot-streak* explanation); the effects of any changes to the rules, types of wagers, or game play procedures; the effect of any errors or mistakes made during the operation of the game during the month; the effect of any thefts or other improper acts by employees or patrons; or any other unusual occurrences during the month being reviewed.

E. Auditing procedures

As a final control mechanism, personnel independent of the transactions and the accounting thereof were assigned to perform stringent and frequent auditing procedures. There were audits of all types of transactions and their accompanying documentation, such as of transfers and their accompanying fill and credit slips, for one day of each month. The audits involved reconciling each document's multipart stubs, checking their proper completion and the propriety of signatures, verifying their sequential numbering, and tracing their amounts to the master games worksheet. Any issues, such as unaccounted for slips or variances between the source documents and the master games worksheet, were investigated, documented, and retained. Other audits involved, for example, the recalculation of the win (loss) for one day of each week. Because of the extensive internal auditing procedures, the internal audit organization of MGM MIRAGE,

[9]Normal win percentages in the slot machines area were in the range of 6.5% to 7.5% of slots handle.

headed by Robert Rudloff, vice president of internal audit, employed 63 people.

Bonuses

Results measures were considered in bonuses paid to management personnel. Most executives received annual bonuses averaging about 30% of salary based on both the bottom-line performance of the casino and a set of individual performance objectives. For example, Bill Bingham's annual bonus was based on growth in volume (drop) supplemented with factors that were more difficult to quantify, such as customer relations, employee relations, and/or the successful completion of a casino floor reconfiguration, depending on the focus in any given year. For reasons including lack of control, no bonuses were based on win. Bob Rudloff explained, "We obviously don't want games where the win is *too high*, as that might jeopardize the enjoyment guests derive from gambling and coming into our casino in the first place."

Even though the standard measures of performance were important indicators of success, corporate executives were careful not to place too much emphasis on them because they did not want to encourage casino managers to sacrifice everything for annual bottom-line growth. A good example of a situation where a careful tradeoff was required was customer relations. If a customer had a complaint, casino personnel had to take care to make the customer happy, even at some immediate cost, so that the customer would come back.

There were no bonuses for any other casino personnel, who received only salary and, where applicable, *tokes* (tips). But there were some nonmonetary awards, such as employee of the month and employee of the year. For example, dealers with consistently superior mystery shopper ratings could earn this award. Employees of the year were invited to an annual gala honoring all outstanding employees from across all MGM MIRAGE properties.

Future controls

In response to a request for speculation as to what controls in the casino might look like in the future, casino controller Trent Walker responded:

> In the table games area, we don't have a detailed understanding of what happens at the tables *as it happens* because we can't track the play at the table. We don't really know how much money we have until we count. In other words, we have no way to account for the inventory of cash when it comes to us; we can only do that 24 hours or so later when the cash comes through the count room. The ultimate form of control for us would be to track every play at the tables, as we can with the slot machines because they are *machines*. If a slot machine over- or underperforms, we can shut it down and fix it. Controls in the slot world are virtually real time.
>
> But even slot machines, I must add, are not without their control failures. A couple of years ago, for example, we encountered a slot scam where an individual had figured out a way to put bills in a slot machine, get them validated, thus receiving credit to play, and yet got the machine to spit the bill back. We just have to live with the fact that there are always people out there trying to rip us off. That's just the nature of this business.

Bill Bingham, vice president of table games, added:

> There are new technologies out there that potentially could alter and improve the control environment in the table games area. For example, we could use RFID (radio frequency identification) technology in our chips. If that technology [was] perfected, that could allow us to track every transaction by every customer at the gaming tables. Then we'd be able to capture a lot of information that would be very valuable for decision-making purposes; e.g. average bets, wins and losses, time played. The better we can identify players' betting patterns, the better we can market to our better customers. But RFID is now only about 75% accurate. We'd need it to be close to (if not exactly) 100% accurate to make it worthwhile.

Bob Rudloff, vice president of internal audit, explained:

> We should be able to improve our player ratings. There are essentially four parameters to determine player profiles: the theoretical odds of the game (which we know), the average bet, time played, and the number of decisions (hands) per hour. With this information, we can determine how much a player *should* have won. We currently use this *theoretical* number to comp players. To the extent that we could tie these parameters with precision, however, the better our comp program would perform. A

combination of player cards and RFID technology, for example, would make that possible. We would also be able to easily detect counterfeit chips. These are just some of the potential benefits. With these benefits in mind, some casinos have already begun experimenting with RFID.

But we currently have a wait-and-see attitude, as the costs may outweigh the benefits. One obvious cost is the nontrivial expense of replacing all our chips. But there are probably some more subtle, indirect costs too. For example, what will be the *customer impact* of RFID? Having *too much* information – knowing to the penny who wins or loses how much – isn't always the best for the customer. At some point the customers might lose some entertainment value if we monitor every little thing that happens. And we're not sure that we understand all the privacy implications of this just yet. What if the IRS comes to us and asks for this information? We are in the entertainment business, and so we shouldn't do anything that diminishes customer enjoyment.

Control issues and areas for improvement were always being addressed or contemplated, however. Trent Walker explained:

In the surveillance area, our controls are possibly now about as good as they are going to get. We have cameras trained on every game table, and we cover just about every square inch of the casino floor. This has allowed us to do away with certain old-style controls such as pocketless dealer uniforms and human supervision from overhead catwalks or through one-way mirrors. If we suspect foul play by employees or customers, we can always go back to the tape and verify. We are currently digitizing the surveillance recordings. That will allow us to get rid of the tens of thousands of tapes we currently handle, and it will facilitate the streaming and archiving of the recordings.

In the slot machine area, the *hard count* is about to disappear as everything is almost completely ticket-based now. Eliminating the human element in handling and counting coins is both more efficient from a cost perspective and more effective from a control perspective.

But, there are always the inevitable human errors, such as pit personnel signing a marker for the wrong person. Even though this doesn't happen more than a few times a year, it does happen, and the risk of it happening is higher when volumes are up. We don't fire people for making human errors; instead we work with them to prevent the errors from happening again.

As I said, however, there always are, and will be, people trying to rip us off. There are a lot of hands in the pot – dealers, counters, and money strappers. But we are also getting smarter in catching them. For example, dealers and customers working together have pulled off scams where the dealer *simulates* the shuffle so that the customer can count cards. We've done away with that problem through automatic shufflers and regular updates of the shuffle programs. Customers have tried to scratch key cards with a tiny piece of glass glued to their finger. Improved camera surveillance now can catch that too. All in all, I'd say that our controls are very good. We have gone above and beyond mere compliance with what is required by the GCB. We have learned many valuable lessons where we have been burned over the years.

Bob Rudloff concluded with the following observation:

The industry has changed a lot in the last decade or two. Customers used to be interested in the Las Vegas that offered $2.99 buffets and $49.99 rooms, which were part of a gig to tease people onto the casino floor to gamble. In that era, gaming was where the money was made. Today, most of the MGM MIRAGE properties, and many of the properties of our competitors on the Vegas Strip, don't offer such deals anymore. Now we have the $26.99 buffets and $229.99 rooms, yet occupancy rates have stayed about the same, which is remarkable given that total room numbers have gone up dramatically. This tells me that customer tastes have changed. They don't just come to Vegas anymore to gamble; rather, they are attracted by shopping, dining, spas, shows, and entertainment. They want to have a good time; not just gamble. This has resulted in a shift in revenues from gaming to nongaming. Good controls obviously will always be critical in the gaming side of our business, no matter what the shift in proportion of total revenues; it's just good business sense. Strategically, however, our business is not just about controlling the gaming part of revenues any longer.

Exhibit 1 MGM MIRAGE operating casino resorts

Name and location	Number of guestrooms and suites	Approximate Casino square footage	Slots[1]	Gaming tables[2]
Las Vegas Strip, Nevada[3]				
Bellagio	3,933	155,000	2,409	143
MGM Grand Las Vegas	5,044	156,000	2,593	172
Mandalay Bay[4]	4,756	157,000	1,949	127
The Mirage	3,044	118,000	2,056	109
Luxor	4,403	100,000	1,778	88
Treasure Island ("TI")	2,885	90,000	1,800	64
New York-New York	2,024	84,000	1,867	85
Excalibur	3,990	100,000	1,762	73
Monte Carlo	3,002	102,000	1,726	74
Circus Circus Las Vegas[5]	3,764	133,000	2,364	92
Subtotal	36,845	1,195,000	20,304	1,027
Other Nevada				
Primm Valley Resorts (*Primm*)[6]	2,642	137,000	2,854	94
Circus Circus Reno (*Reno*)	1,572	69,000	1,369	52
Silver Legacy – 50% owned (*Reno*)	1,710	87,000	1,707	68
Gold Strike (*Jean*)	811	37,000	737	15
Nevada Landing (*Jean*)	303	36,000	733	14
Colorado Belle (*Laughlin*)	1,173	50,000	1,167	39
Edgewater (*Laughlin*)	1,356	57,000	1,099	33
Railroad Pass (*Henderson*)	120	13,000	347	6
Other domestic operations				
MGM Grand Detroit (*Detroit, Michigan*)	N/A	75,000	2,841	72
Beau Rivage (Biloxi, Mississippi)[7]	N/A	N/A	N/A	N/A
Gold Strike (Tunica, Mississippi)	1,133	40,000	1,345	48
Borgata – 50% owned (Atlantic City, New Jersey)	2,000	125,000	3,572	133
Grand Victoria – 50% owned (*Elgin, Illinois*)	N/A	34,000	1,100	37
Grand total	49,665	1,955,000	39,175	1,638

This table provides certain information about MGM MIRAGE casino resorts as of December 31, 2005. Except as otherwise indicated, MGM MIRAGE wholly owns and operates the resorts.

[1]Includes slot machines, video poker machines and other electronic gaming devices.
[2]Includes blackjack ("21"), baccarat, craps, roulette and other table games; does not include poker.
[3]Excludes Boardwalk, which closed in January 2006.
[4]Includes the Four Seasons Hotel with 424 guest rooms and THEhotel with 1,117 suites.
[5]Includes Slots-a-Fun.
[6]Includes Primm Valley, Buffalo Bill's and Whiskey Pete's, along with the Primm Center gas station and convenience store.
[7]Beau Rivage sustained significant damage in late August 2005 as a result of Hurricane Katrina and has been closed since. We expect to reopen Beau Rivage in the third quarter of 2006.

Source: MGM MIRAGE 2005 Form 10-K.

Exhibit 2 MGM MIRAGE operating results – detailed revenue information

Year ended December 31	2005 $ (000)	Pct. change	2004 $ (000)	Pct. change	2003 $ (000)
Casino revenue, net:					
Table games	$1,140,053	21%	$943,343	9%	$866,096
Slots	1,741,556	43%	1,218,589	9%	1,115,029
Other	100,042	61%	62,033	10%	56,389
Casino revenue, net	2,981,651	34%	2,223,965	9%	2,037,514
Non-Casino revenue:					
Rooms	1,673,696	84%	911,259	9%	833,272
Food and beverage	1,330,210	58%	841,147	11%	757,278
Entertainment, retail and other	1,098,612	58%	696,117	7%	647,702
Noncasino revenue	4,102,518	68%	2,448,523	9%	2,238,252
Total revenue	7,084,169	52%	4,672,488	9%	4,275,766
Less: Promotional allowances	(602,202)	39%	(434,384)	5%	(413,023)
	6,481,967	53%	4,238,104	10%	3,862,743

Table games revenue, including baccarat, was flat on a same-store basis in 2005. A 4% increase in table games volume was offset by a slightly lower hold percentage, though hold percentages were within the normal range for all three years presented. In 2004, table games volume increased 9%, with particular strength in baccarat volume, up 18%. In both 2005 and 2004, key events such as New Year, Chinese New Year and other marketing events, were well-attended.

Slots revenue increased 8% on a same-store basis, following a 9% increase in 2004. Additional volume in 2005 was generated by the Spa Tower at Bellagio – Bellagio's slots revenue increased over 30% – and the traffic generated by *KÀ* and other amenities at MGM Grand Las Vegas, where slots revenue increased almost 10%. In both periods, MGM MIRAGE benefited from the continued success of our Players Club affinity program and marketing events targeted at repeat customers.

Hotel revenue increased 19% on a same-store basis in 2005. MGM MIRAGE had more rooms available as a result of the Bellagio expansion and 2004 room remodel activity at MGM Grand Las Vegas, and company-wide same-store REVPAR increased 13% to $140 (REVPAR = Revenue per Available Room). This was on top of a 10% increase in 2004 over 2003. The increase in REVPAR in 2005 was entirely rate-driven, as same-store occupancy was consistent at 92%. The 2004 increase was also largely rate-driven.

Source: MGM MIRAGE 2005 Form 10-K.

Exhibit 3 MGM MIRAGE selected financial data

	For the years ended December 31 (in thousands, except per share data)				
	2005	2004	2003	2002	2001
Net revenues	$6,481,967	$4,238,104	$3,862,743	$3,756,928	$3,699,852
Operating income	1,357,208	950,860	699,729	746,538	599,892
Income from continuing operations	443,256	349,856	230,273	289,476	160,440
Net income	443,256	412,332	243,697	292,435	169,815
Basic earnings per share					
Income from continuing operations	1.56	1.25	0.77	0.92	0.51
Net income per share	1.56	1.48	0.82	0.93	0.53
Weighted average number of shares	284,943	279,325	297,861	315,618	317,542
Diluted earnings per share					
Income from continuing operations	1.50	1.21	0.76	0.90	0.50
Net income per share	1.50	1.43	0.80	0.91	0.53
Weighted average number of shares	296,334	289,333	303,184	319,880	321,644
At yearend					
Total assets	20,699,420	11,115,029	10,811,269	10,568,698	10,542,568
Total debt, including capital leases	12,358,829	5,463,619	5,533,462	5,222,195	5,465,608
Stockholders' equity	3,235,072	2,771,704	2,533,788	2,664,144	2,510,700
Stockholders' equity per share	11.35	9.87	8.85	8.62	7.98
Number of shares outstanding	285,070	280,740	286,192	309,148	314,792

In June 2003, MGM MIRAGE ceased operations of PLAYMGMMIRAGE.com, the company's online gaming website ("Online"). In January 2004, MGM MIRAGE sold the Golden Nugget Las Vegas and the Golden Nugget Laughlin including substantially all of the assets and liabilities of those resorts (the "Golden Nugget Subsidiaries"). In July 2004, MGM MIRAGE sold the subsidiaries that owned and operated MGM Grand Australia. The results of Online, the Golden Nugget Subsidiaries and MGM Grand Australia are classified as discontinued operations for all periods presented. The Mandalay acquisition occurred on April 25, 2005.

Source: MGM MIRAGE 2005 Form 10-K.

Exhibit 4 Bellagio Casino Resort: Table games organization chart

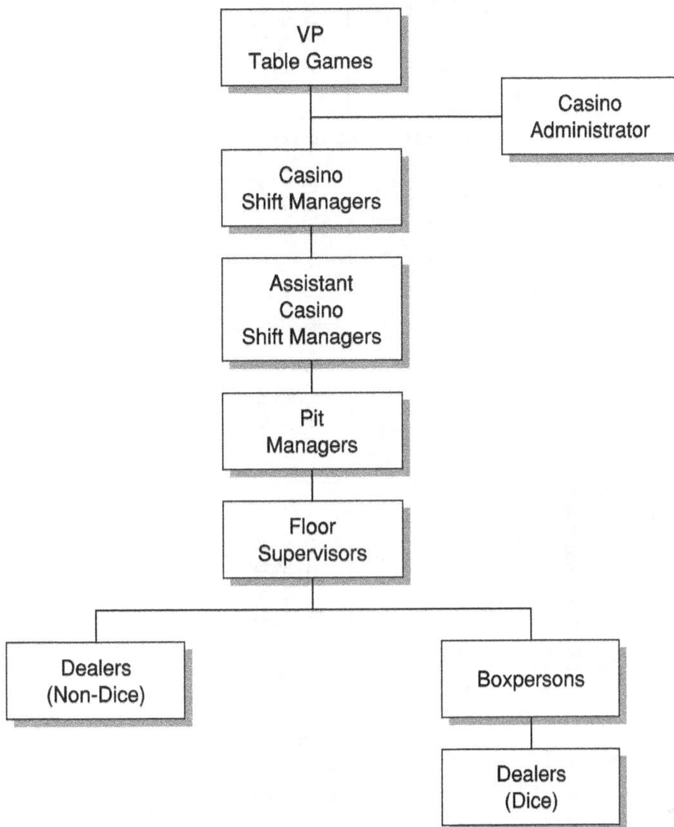

Exhibit 5 Bellagio Casino Resort: Finance organization chart

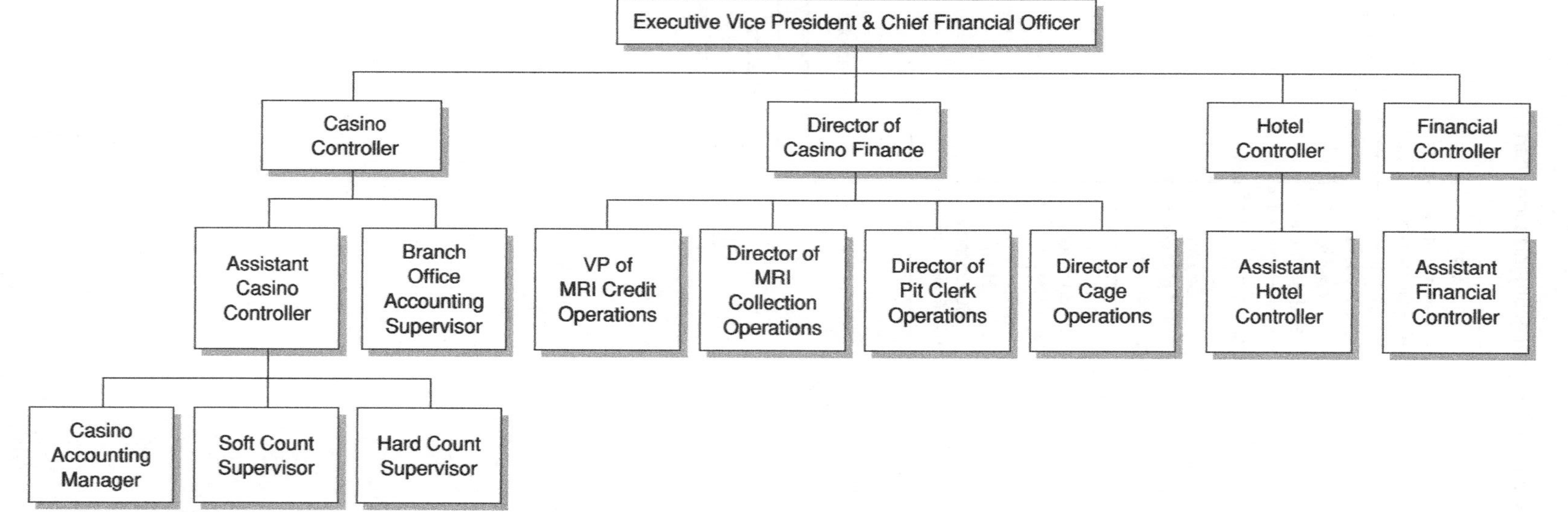

Exhibit 6 Description of Regulations and Licensing by the Nevada Gaming Authorities

The ownership and operation of our casino gaming facilities in Nevada are subject to the Nevada Gaming Control Act and the regulations promulgated thereunder (collectively, the "Nevada Act") and various local regulations. Our gaming operations are subject to the licensing and regulatory control of the Nevada Gaming Commission (the "Nevada Commission"), the Nevada State Gaming Control Board (the "Nevada Board") and various county and city licensing agencies (the "local authorities"). The Nevada Commission, the Nevada Board, and the local authorities are collectively referred to as the "Nevada Gaming Authorities."

The laws, regulations and supervisory procedures of the Nevada Gaming Authorities are based upon declarations of public policy that are concerned with, among other things:

- The prevention of unsavory or unsuitable persons from having a direct or indirect involvement with gaming at any time or in any capacity;
- The establishment and maintenance of responsible accounting practices;
- The maintenance of effective controls over the financial practices of licensees, including the establishment of minimum procedures for internal fiscal affairs and the safeguarding of assets and revenues;
- Providing reliable record keeping and requiring the filing of periodic reports with the Nevada Gaming Authorities;
- The prevention of cheating and fraudulent practices; and
- Providing a source of state and local revenues through taxation and licensing fees.

. . . . .

The Nevada Gaming Authorities may investigate any individual who has a material relationship to, or material involvement with, the registered corporations or any of the licensed subsidiaries to determine whether such individual is suitable or should be licensed as a business associate of a gaming licensee. Officers, directors and certain key employees of the licensed subsidiaries must file applications with the Nevada Gaming Authorities and may be required to be licensed by the Nevada Gaming Authorities. Officers, directors and key employees of the registered corporations who are actively and directly involved in the gaming activities of the licensed subsidiaries may be required to be licensed or found suitable by the Nevada Gaming Authorities. The Nevada Gaming Authorities may deny an application for licensing or a finding of suitability for any cause they deem reasonable. A finding of suitability is comparable to licensing, and both require submission of detailed personal and financial information followed by a thorough investigation. [. . .]

If the Nevada Gaming Authorities were to find an officer, director or key employee unsuitable for licensing or to continue having a relationship with the registered corporations or the licensed subsidiaries, such company or companies would have to sever all relationships with that person. In addition, the Nevada Commission may require the registered corporations or the licensed subsidiaries to terminate the employment of any person who refuses to file appropriate applications. [. . .]

. . . . .

We are required to maintain a current stock ledger in Nevada that may be examined by the Nevada Gaming Authorities at any time. [. . .]

. . . . .

License fees and taxes, computed in various ways depending on the type of gaming or activity involved, are payable to the State of Nevada and to local authorities. Depending upon the particular fee or tax involved, these fees and taxes are [. . .] based upon either:

- A percentage of the gross revenues received;
- The number of gaming devices operated; or
- The number of table games operated.

The tax on gross revenues received is generally 6.75%. A live entertainment tax is also paid on charges for admission to any facility where certain forms of live entertainment are provided.

. . . . .

Because we are involved in gaming ventures outside of Nevada, we are required [. . .] to comply with certain reporting requirements imposed by the Nevada Act. We would be subject to disciplinary action by the Nevada Commission if we:

- Knowingly violate any laws of the foreign jurisdiction pertaining to the foreign gaming operation;
- Fail to conduct the foreign gaming operation in accordance with the standards of honesty and integrity required of Nevada gaming operations;

Exhibit 6 *Continued*

- Engage in any activity or enter into any association that is unsuitable because it poses an unreasonable threat to the control of gaming in Nevada, reflects or tends to reflect discredit or disrepute upon the State of Nevada or gaming in Nevada, or is contrary to the gaming policies of Nevada;
- Engage in any activity or enter into any association that interferes with the ability of the State of Nevada to collect gaming taxes and fees; or
- Employ, contract with or associate with any person in the foreign gaming operation who has been denied a license or a finding of suitability in Nevada on the ground of personal unsuitability, or who has been found guilty of cheating at gambling.

. . . . .

[. . .] Pursuant to a 1985 agreement with the United States Department of the Treasury (the "Treasury") and provisions of the Money Laundering Suppression Act of 1994, the Nevada Commission and the Nevada Board have authority, under Regulation 6A of the Nevada Act, to enforce their own cash transaction reporting laws applicable to casinos which substantially parallel the federal Bank Secrecy Act. Under the Nevada Act, the licensed subsidiaries are required to monitor receipts and disbursements of currency related to cash purchases of chips, cash wagers, cash deposits or cash payment of gaming debts in excess of $10,000 in a 24-hour period, and file reports of such transactions with the United States Internal Revenue Service. The licensed subsidiaries are required to file suspicious activity reports with the Treasury and provide copies thereof to the Nevada Board, and are also required to meet the reporting and record keeping requirements of Treasury regulations amended by the USA PATRIOT Act of 2001.

Source: Excerpts from MGM MIRAGE 2005 Form 10-K.

Exhibit 7 Bellagio Casino Resort: Master games inventory sheet

PIT *4* SHIFT *swing/gyd* DATE *1-17-06*

GAME	IOU	100,000	25,000	5,000	1,000	500	100	25	5	1	TOTAL
RW1					77,000	41,500	17,500	6,100	1,200	100	143,400
RW2					67,000	39,000	16,900	7,925	1,285	90	132,200
BJ1					44,000	25,500	12,900	4,100	600	100	87,200
BJ2						21,000	9,200	2,500	900	100	33,700
BJ3					47,000	22,000	10,000	4,100	1,000	100	84,200
BJ4					39,000	26,500	9,600	2,000	600	100	77,800
BJ5					53,000	33,500	8,500	2,000	700	100	97,800
BJ6					48,000	22,000	11,600	3,175	1,230	95	86,100
BJ7											
BJ8					56,000	27,000	9,100	2,200	1,200	100	95,600
BJ9											
BJ10					42,000	23,500	9,400	2,675	770	55	78,400
BJ11					40,000	31,500	10,100	2,200	700	100	84,600
BJ12					52,000	21,500	11,400	1,300	1,100	100	87,400
BJ13					36,000	30,000	9,500	2,975	1,120	105	79,700
BJ14					33,000	17,000	11,900	2,200	700	100	64,900
BJ15					49,000	21,500	9,200	2,800	860	40	83,400
BJ16					42,000	26,000	8,900	2,325	940	35	80,200
BJ17					40,000	23,500	7,500	2,450	865	85	74,400
BJ18					50,000	20,000	10,300	2,850	740	110	84,000
BJ19					43,000	26,500	9,900	3,525	970	105	84,000
BJ20					57,000	27,500	10,800	3,675	495	130	99,600
BJ21					51,000	18,500	11,200	2,275	1,210	115	84,300
BJ22					50,000	23,000	10,000	4,100	730	70	87,900
BJ23					51,000	25,500	8,300	2,725	755	120	88,400
BJ24					34,000	23,000	9,400	2,125	1,155	120	69,800
BJ25					43,000	24,500	7,400	3,525	785	90	79,300
BJ26					59,000	18,000	7,400	2,425	790	85	87,700
BJ27					33,000	22,500	8,500	3,950	810	140	68,900
BJ28					37,000	27,500	10,200	2,625	470	105	77,900
BJ29					36,000	20,000	9,300	4,500	650	50	70,500
BJ30					50,000	24,500	9,800	4,400	785	115	89,600
WPT1					57,000	26,500	10,600	2,300	955	45	97,400
WPT2					44,000	18,500	10,400	1,900	1,400	100	76,300
WR1					52,000	17,000	8,200	2,200	900	100	80,400
TOTAL											2,797,000

Incoming *John. W. McIntyre 56941*

Outgoing *Beth. C. Chung 23587*

Note: Numbers on this form were disguised to safeguard company restrictions on the release of internal operating data.

Exhibit 8 Bellagio Casino Resort: Fill slip

FILLS BELLAGIO - RESTRICTED COPY 1

DOC. # 7734350

CLERK ID: ROA	PIT 02
DATE: 1/17/06	GAME BJ
TIME: 12:58P	TABLE 05
	CASE SHIFT D
	PIT SHIFT D

	DENOMINATION	AMOUNT
@@@@@@@	100,000.00 ...	.00
@@@@@@@	25,000.00 ...	.00
@@	20,000.00 ...	.00
@@@@@	5,000.00 ...	.00
@@@@@	1,000.00 ...	20,000.00
@@	500.00 ...	10,000.00
@@	100.00 ...	6,000.00
@@	25.00 ...	1,000.00
	5.00 ...	.00
	1.00 ...	40.00
	.50 ...	.00
	.25 ...	.00
		TOTAL 37,040.00

*** NOTIFY SURVEILLANCE ***

Rob Arlington 25891	Gilbert R. Hall 36582
CHIP BANK CASHIER	SECURITY GUARD
Mary L. Comben 68752	Kendall Brooke 65892
DEALER / BOXPERSON	CASINO SUPERVISOR

F 37040

Note: Numbers on this form were disguised to safeguard company restrictions on the release of internal operating data.

Exhibit 9 Bellagio Casino Resort: Soft count room procedures

The soft count supervisor and two count team members had to be present when the soft count room key was obtained from the cage. The soft count supervisor and two count team members had to be present when the keys to remove the full drop boxes from their cart and the keys to remove the drop box contents were obtained from the master vault. The count team then entered the soft count room.

A currency counter was used to count the table game drop proceeds. Immediately prior to beginning the count procedures, a test of the currency counter's accuracy was performed by two count team members using a precounted batch of currency obtained from the master vault consisting of all denominations. The results of the test were recorded on the *grand totals report* produced by the currency counter. The supervisor and one count team member had to sign the report. Quarterly, casino accounting personnel performed unannounced counter tests, the results of which were also documented and maintained.

Each drop box was individually opened and emptied on the count table. The contents of the subsequent drop box to be opened were prohibited from being emptied onto the count table until the previous box's contents had been entirely removed and stored to prevent the commingling of funds between drop boxes. The empty drop box was shown to another count team member and to the surveillance camera to verify that the box was empty. The empty box was then placed in a storage cart. When the storage cart was full of empty drop boxes, it was locked with a padlock. The count team members did not have access to the key for this padlock.

Each drop box's contents were segregated into stacks of currency, chips, and documents. The chips were counted and verified by two count team members, and the chip count was recorded on the back of the so-called *header card*. The header card contained a bar code wherein the table game's pit, game type, and table game number were encoded. The bar code on the header cards were then read by the currency counter's bar code reader and the chip count manually entered into the currency counter.

Currency was prepared for the currency counter and was placed in a rack with the header card. When full, the rack of currency was given to the count team member responsible for operating the currency counter, who placed the currency and header card into the hopper of the currency counter to start the counting. During the operation of the currency counter, count team members other than the count team member operating the currency counter had to witness the loading and unloading of all currency at the currency counter, including rejected currency.[10] The drop box count for each drop box was then individually recorded by denomination and in total in an electronic file generated by the currency counter.

Upon completion of the drop count (currency and chips), the currency counter generated a *master games sheet* that detailed the count by table, denomination, and in total. The master games sheet was then forwarded to a count team member who manually entered the drop count into the computerized *master games worksheet*.

A count team member also individually traced other documents obtained from the drop boxes (fill slips, credit slips, markers) to the master games worksheet. Fill or credit input forms were stapled to their corresponding fill or credit slip. Fill and credit slips also had to be inspected for correctness. Similarly, table inventory sheets reflecting chip inventory counts by table game were examined and traced to the master games worksheet.

Corrections to information, originally input in the computerized master games worksheet, were made by inputting the correct figure. An audit trail of corrections was recorded in the computer. Count team members did not have access to the audit trail file. Correction to information originally recorded by the count team on manual soft count documentation were made by crossing out the error, entering the correct figure, and then obtaining the initials of at least two count team members who verified the change.

Upon conclusion of the table games drop count, the soft count supervisor and one other count team member verified and agreed the currency and chip count to the total count as recorded on the master games sheet and master games worksheet. If the totals did not agree, the error had to be located, corrected, and documented. All count team members then signed the master games worksheet certifying the accuracy of the count.

Currency transfers out of the soft count room during the table games soft count process were strictly prohibited. To prepare a transfer, a three-part *transfer slip* was completed with the amount (by denomination and in total) of funds being transferred, dated, and signed (all copies) by the soft count supervisor and one other count team member. Part 3 of the transfer slip was retained in the soft count room. The cash, chips, and parts 1 and 2 of the transfer slip were transferred to the cage where a cage cashier counted the cash and chips, agreed the total to the amount recorded on the transfer slip, and signed to verify that the amounts agree. The cage cashier retained part 2 of the transfer slip, which was later forwarded to the casino accounting department. Part 1 was returned to the soft count room by a soft count team member, matched and agreed to part 3, and both forwarded to casino accounting.

[10] There were also very stringent procedures to handle rejected currency, which we omit here due to space constraints.

(Continued)

Exhibit 9 (*Continued*)

The cage cashier then agreed the currency and chip transfers as recorded on the transfer slip to the drop recorded on the master games worksheet and signed the master games worksheet verifying that the transfer and drop amounts agree. Any variances had to be reconciled and documented. The master games worksheet then had to be returned to the soft count room by a count team member. The cage cashier then assumed accountability of the drop proceeds.

After the entire count was completed, the soft count supervisor locked the soft count room and returned the drop box keys and drop box cart keys to the master vault, after which the soft count supervisor returned the soft count room keys and the master vault keys to the cage. A count member team then promptly transported the master games worksheet and all supporting documents including the transfer slip directly to casino accounting.

Exhibit 10 Bellagio Casino Resort: Master games worksheet summary report

RUN DATE – 04/28/06	BELLAGIO – RESTRICTED		PAGE – 1
RUN TIME – 10:14:46	MASTER GAMES WORKSHEET SUMMARY FOR 01/17/06		
GAME DESC	*DROP/HANDLE*	*WIN/RESULT*	*%*
CRAPS	168,552	9,452	5.61
BLACKJACK	727,508	–124,752	–17.15
PG POKER	78,278	104,748	133.82
RED DOG	0	0	.00
WHEELS	170,218	48,428	28.45
SINGLE RW	33,710	20,610	61.14
BIG SIX	3,364	1,864	55.41
BACCARAT	461,420	55,425	12.01
PAI GOW	5,800	–120	–2.07
MINI BAC	70,828	6,468	9.13
CARRIB ST	19,581	5,323	27.18
LET RIDE	19,815	4,435	22.38
CASINOWAR	13,632	1,312	9.62
3 CARD PK	56,315	14,155	25.14
SIC BO	0	0	.00
CRZY 4 PK	14,066	106	0.75
PYRMD PKR	0	0	.00
HOLD POKER	6,697	3,517	52.52
	1,849,784	**150,971**	**8.16**

Note: Numbers in this table were disguised to safeguard company restrictions on the release of internal operating data.

Exhibit 11 Bellagio Casino Resort: Table games daily operating report

	BELLAGIO								
	RESTRICTED – DAILY OPERATING REPORT						APRIL 12, 2006 WEDNESDAY		
	2006			2005			BUDGET		
CASINO REVENUE	*Today*	*M.T.D.*		*M.T.D.*	*Variance*	*Var.%*	*M.T.D.*	*Variance*	*Var.%*
PIT	1,336,818	9,424,151		7,017,092	2,407,059	34.3	8,900,800	523,351	5.9
KENO	2,523	22,835		83,937	(61,102)	(72.8)	24,000	(1,165)	(4.9)
CASINO DATA	*TODAY*			*2006 MONTH-TO-DATE*			*2005 MONTH-TO-DATE*		
PIT GAMES:	*DROP*	*WIN*	*WIN%*	*DROP*	*WIN*	*WIN%*	*DROP*	*WIN*	*WIN%*
Baccarat	810,560	511,160	63.1	7,915,818	2,236,938	28.3	7,026,171	2,211,900	31.5
Blackjack	1,240,594	192,664	15.5	23,682,129	2,906,769	12.3	19,770,201	2,268,698	11.5
Craps	762,035	389,435	51.1	8,172,150	2,147,850	26.3	6,825,554	1,376,077	20.2
Mini-baccarat	220,602	8,422	3.8	2,303,889	874,109	37.9	1,648,907	268,340	16.3
Wheels	195,169	39,509	20.2	2,768,677	604,277	21.8	2,070,914	504,128	24.3
Single Wheels	96,865	92,765	95.8	977,110	362,110	37.1	466,963	29,458	6.3
Pai Gow	28,245	(16,305)	(57.7)	439,714	39,814	9.1	423,369	102,565	24.2
Pai Gow Poker	135,457	56,237	41.5	1,078,854	156,774	14.5	865,283	364,233	42.1
Caribbean Stud	20,020	7,465	37.3	321,004	81,570	25.4	384,669	102,279	26.6
Let It Ride	20,140	(1,240)	(6.2)	255,806	58,466	22.9	382,297	100,480	26.3
Casino War	10,760	3,500	32.5	249,191	67,061	26.9	279,498	80,066	28.6
Big Six	4,354	434	10.0	67,070	34,010	50.7	70,411	35,467	50.4
3 Card Poker	61,780	36,460	59.0	974,149	365,069	37.5	930,783	266,134	28.6
Crazy 4 Poker	28,645	7,905	27.6	290,074	72,294	24.9	284,393	74,328	26.1
Pyramid Poker	0	0	0.0	0	0	0.0	17,443	8,436	48.4
Hold 'Em Poker	13,587	8,407	61.9	215,928	61,048	28.3	23,275	0	0.0
Sic Bo	0	0	0.0	0	0	0.0	0	0	0.0
Total Pit Games	3,648,813	1,336,818	36.6	49,711,563	10,068,159	20.3	41,470,131	7,792,589	18.8
LESS:									
Discount Accruals		0			(371,008)			(775,107)	
Promotional Expenses		0			(273,000)			(390)	
Net Pit Games		1,336,818			9,424,151			7,017,092	
KENO	4,630	2,523	54.5	66,892	22,835	34.1	278,971	83,937	30.1
CREDIT DROP%	1,251,500	34.3%		17,935,325	36.1%		14,513,079	35.0%	

Note: Numbers in this table were disguised to safeguard company restrictions on the release of internal operating data.

Exhibit 12 Bellagio Casino Resort: Table games cash drop variance report

Run Date: 04/11/06							PAGE – 2
Run Time: 10:59:15	CASH DROP VARIANCE REPORT FOR 04/10/06 ALL SHIFTS						
PIT/GAME	ESTIMATED DROP						
TABLE	GRAVE	DAY	SWING	TOTAL	ACTUAL DROP	VARIANCE	VARIANCE %
02 BJ 01	0	0	2,500	2,500	1,840	660	35.87
02 BJ 02	0	0	11,000	11,000	11,030	– 30	– 0.27
02 BJ 03	0	0	8,000	8,000	6,630	1,370	20.66
02 BJ 04	0	0	6,500	6,500	4,720	1,780	37.71
02 BJ 05	11,000	13,500	6,500	31,000	32,100	– 1,100	– 3.43
02 BJ 06	7,000	19,000	12,500	38,500	37,480	1,020	2.72
02 BJ 07	6,500	17,000	13,500	37,000	39,220	– 2,220	– 5.66
02 BJ 08	4,000	11,000	22,500	37,500	40,650	– 3,150	– 7.75
02 BJ 09	3,000	9,000	6,500	18,500	21,170	– 2,670	– 12.61
02 BJ 10	6,500	25,000	13,500	45,000	48,680	– 3,680	– 7.56
02 BJ 11	6,000	22,500	13,500	42,000	45,120	– 3,120	– 6.91
02 BJ 12	10,500	4,500	11,000	26,000	30,010	– 4,010	– 13.36
02 BJ 13	0	4,500	4,500	9,000	7,830	1,170	14.94
02 BJ 14	0	12,500	4,500	17,000	14,590	2,410	16.52
02 BJ 15	0	0	0	0	0	0	0.00
02 BJ 16	0	7,000	6,500	13,500	14,430	– 930	– 6.44
02 BJ 17	0	0	0	0	0	0	0.00
02 BJ 18	0	4,500	11,500	16,000	20,720	– 4,720	– 22.78
02 BJ 19	0	2,000	8,000	10,000	13,990	– 3,990	– 28.52
02 BJ 20	14,500	2,500	11,500	28,500	34,970	– 6,470	– 18.50
02 BJ 21	12,500	16,000	9,000	37,500	37,400	100	0.27
02 BJ 22	0	0	4,500	4,500	3,860	640	16.58
02 BJ 23	0	0	0	0	0	0	0.00
02 BJ 24	0	0	0	0	0	0	0.00

Note: Numbers in this table were disguised to safeguard company restrictions on the release of internal operating data.

Exhibit 13 Bellagio Casino Resort: Table games cash drop estimate vs. actual comparison

Gaming Date: 10-Apr-06

			Total
Statistics:	**DROP**	**CASH**	**WIN**
Estimate	3,679,800	1,841,800	607,810
Actual	3,853,027	2,003,027	784,621
Estimate Variance:			
Dollars	(173,227)	(161,227)	(176,811)
Percentage	−4. 5%	−8.0%	−22.5%

Instructions: When the Cash Drop Variance Percentage exceeds 10%, the cause for the variance must be researched and the resulting findings explained in the space provided below. Your response should be received by Casino Accounting within two (2) days of your receipt of this report.

Cash Drop Variance Explanation:

Signature of Responding TG Executive: ______________________

Date: ______________________

Note: Numbers on this form were disguised to safeguard company restrictions on the release of internal operating data.

This case was prepared by Professors Kenneth A. Merchant, Leslie R. Porter, and Wim A. Van der Stede.

CASE STUDY
PCL: A Breakdown in the Enforcement of Management Control

PCL was a leading European consumer electronics, lifestyle, and healthcare company that had entered the Chinese market in 1985. While its consumer electronics business grew steadily in China, the costs of returned sets in its TV division amounted to 5% of the division's total sales in 2008. Even more worrying was that 37% of the returned TVs were of good quality and had been returned without good reason. PCL taskforces set up to study the situation found that control measures designed to handle returns were simply not being carried out by staff and third-party after-sales service centers. What could PCL do to remedy the situation?

The consumer electronics industry in China

With a population of 1.3 billion and rising disposable incomes, China had become the second-largest market for consumer electronics in the world.[1] Analysts forecasted a compounded annual growth rate of 9.8% through to 2014 for consumer electronics, with growing demand for TV sets and computers in smaller cities and rural areas being the main driver.[2] As the market in the big cities had become saturated, market competition had moved increasingly to smaller cities and rural areas. Sales of consumer electronics products in these markets were further enhanced by the government's subsidy program, which offered rebates for purchases of consumer electronic goods in rural areas. Another government program that allowed consumers to trade in old electronic appliances for new ones in nine provincial areas since 2009 had also helped to stimulate demand.

[1] "Consumer Electronics in China," *Euromonitor* (April 2009), online at www.euromonitor.com/Consumer_Electronics_in_China (accessed June 20, 2010).

[2] "China Consumer Electronics Report Q3 2010," *Business Monitor International* (2010), online at www.pr-inside.com/china-consumer-electronics-report-q-r1905491.htm (accessed June 10, 2010).

The television market in China

It was no surprise that China, a country that produced 42% of the world's total shipment of TV sets,[3] had a strong TV market. Domestic manufacturers alone accounted for three-quarters of its liquid-crystal display (LCD) TV market in 2009.[4] Driven by consumers' preference for large-sized TVs and by falling prices, China was forecasted to surpass North America as the largest LCD TV market in the world, with sales reaching 29 million units in 2010, translating to more than 30% in growth year-on-year.[5] The growth would be driven by consumers replacing their cathode ray tube (CRT) sets with LCD sets, especially in third- and fourth-tier cities.[6] International brands faced fierce competition from domestic brands, which enjoyed advantages in both cost control and distribution, and price wars were common as domestic brands lowered their prices to increase their market share. Large retail chains played a critical role in the retail market for consumer electronics in China, and competition for shelf space in such chains was fierce. Manufacturers became involved with the promotions, marketing, and supply chain management of these chain stores in order to build relationships with them.[7] Others opened their own branded stores so they could have a direct hand in shaping consumers' purchase experience.

[3] K. Zhang, "China TV Market to Enjoy Solid Growth in 2014," *iSuppli* (April 26, 2010), online at www.isuppli.com/Display-Materials-and-Systems/MarketWatch/Pages/China-TV-Market-to-Enjoy-Solid-Growth-in-2014.aspx (accessed June 20, 2010).

[4] Ibid.

[5] "Corning: China to Become World's Biggest LCD TV Market," *SinoCast Business Beat* (April 14, 2010), online at www.tradingmarkets.com/news/stock-alert/glw_dtek_corning-china-to-become-worlds-biggest-lcd-tv-market-910387.html (accessed June 20, 2010).

[6] "Overview of China's LCD Market," *GfK Retail and Technology* (March 29, 2010) online at www.gfkrt.com/news_events/market_news/single_sites/005606/index.en.html (accessed June 30, 2010).

[7] I. B. Von Morgenstern and C. Shu, "Winning the Battle for the Chinese Consumer Electronics Market," (September 2006), online at www.mckinseyquarterly.com/High_Tech/Hardware/Winning_the_battle_for_the_Chinese_consumer_electronics_market_1855 (accessed June 20, 2010).

PCL Consumer Electronics – background

PCL was a high-tech multinational company based in Europe. Since its establishment in the late nineteenth century, it had diversified into multiple industry segments. The diversification strained its resources and, consequently, PCL reshaped the organization to focus on the healthcare and electronics sectors. In 2010, it had a sales and service presence and manufacturing sites in more than 100 countries around the world.

PCL's consumer electronics division (PCL Consumer Electronics) was a global player in digital and electronic devices, bringing the latest technology and human-centered designs to the market. Its product portfolio included color TV sets, DVD players, audio products, PC monitors, and PC peripherals. PCL Consumer Electronics had a sales and service presence in more than 50 countries and manufacturing sites in France, Hungary, Belgium, Brazil, Mexico, and Argentina even though it outsourced its production heavily. PCL Consumer Electronics placed a strong emphasis on emerging markets such as China and India. It entered China in 1985, and by 2008, its sales organization on the mainland had grown to 550 people with annual sales of US$752 million (See Exhibit 1).

Repairing the broken system

Returned sets

In 2008, the handling of returned TV sets cost PCL an average of US$6 million, equal to about 5% of its annual TV sales. The costs covered freight from the dealer to PCL's warehouse, repair, and refurbishment at the factory workshop. While PCL spent a hefty sum each year servicing returned goods, about 37% of the returned goods were no-fault-found (NFF) returns, translating to a loss of US$2.2 million for PCL. NFF returns also included demo sets and slow-moving goods that were not supposed to be returned (see Exhibit 2).

The TV return process

After-sales service for PCL's TV division was handled by authorized service centers (ASCs), which were third-party service centers authorized and managed by PCL's after-sales service team. Under China's consumer law, consumers could return a defective TV set to the retailer from whom they made the purchase within five days or exchange it for a new one within 15 days. Retailers sent PCL sets returned by customers to the company's ASCs, which would decide whether to accept the return and repair them. If the defect was serious, the ASC would send the set back to PCL's factory for repair.

Investigation

In response to the high volume of returned sets and high NFF returns, PCL's management appointed the product marketing manager of the TV division, who was also familiar with the return process, to look into the matter so appropriate actions could be taken. He formed a task force that brought together the sales operation manager, the service manager, and the financial controller of the TV business. The team set out to investigate the situation and uncovered a number of causes for the problem.

Neither retailers nor ASCs had been trained in educating customers about product performance or the criteria for accepting returns. Retail stores usually used high-definition signals for product demonstrations, but most consumers used cable TV at home. As a result, consumers often became dissatisfied with the picture quality after they took the TV set home and would try to exchange it for a new set or simply return it. While PCL had established return criteria that were as stringent as those of its competitors, retailers and ASCs often failed to execute them properly, accepting returns without proper screening.

Chain retailers were significant players in China's consumer electronics market, and consumer electronics companies could not maintain their market share without selling through them. Because no international TV brand possessed unique product features or technical advantages that differentiated its products in the market, the manufacturers' best option was to make concessions in their negotiations with chain stores in order to maintain good relationships with them and in turn receive higher visibility at the point of sale. PCL, for instance, cut its profit margins and accepted returns of slow-moving models and demo sets in order to secure prominent display locations in the stores. In addition, PCL salespeople had to meet sales targets and required the support of dealers to achieve these targets. This made it hard for many salespeople to say no to unreasonable returns because doing so might jeopardize their relationship with the dealers.

Moreover, they put little effort into investigating the returns, despite established approval procedures for returned goods.

PCL's after-sales service team, which was responsible for overseeing the ASCs, did not report to the TV division directly, but instead reported to the general manager of the organization, a line of reporting that reduced the incentive for the after-sales team to control TV returns or to monitor the third-party ASCs stringently. Not only did the ASCs fail to inspect the returned sets carefully, but they sometimes faked their inspection records instead of rejecting the return of TV sets. The situation was further aggravated by the fact that PCL had no punishment policy for fraud or incompliance on the part of ASCs.

Action

The team came up with a series of actions based on their initial assessment of the situation. The sales team's annual performance appraisals would be linked with TV returns and the cost of servicing returns, and this new measure was communicated by the TV sales director to all the salespeople. The service manager also communicated to ASCs a new policy whereby they would be fined three times the labor charge for each fake inspection record discovered.

The project team forecasted that their plan would reduce the return rate to 3.5% and the NFF rate to 20% within two months, but their projection did not materialize. In fact, the NFF return rate went up to 40% after two months. Upon further investigation, the general manager and the production manager of the TV division discovered two reasons for the rising rate of NFF returns, despite their efforts. First, the sales team was under enormous pressure to meet their sales targets, which was set at 132% of the sales of the previous year, a rate that exceeded actual market growth. In order to reach their targets, they put pressure on the dealers to increase their purchase volumes, leading to higher inventory levels and tighter cash flow. To counter these problems, dealers negotiated with salespeople to accept returns and to allow exchanges of demo sets and slow-moving goods for new models. The second reason was that the after-sales service team had failed to take punitive action against the ASCs for fake inspection records. There was little incentive for the service team to respond to the ASCs' transgressions, as it did not report to the TV division and its performance indicators were not linked to the amount of goods returned.

Second try

Dissatisfied with the outcome, the general manager of PCL Consumer Electronics appointed the service director, who reported directly to him, to lead the task force. The service director was also given the authority to handle issues that did not usually fall within his scope of responsibilities in order to tackle the problem. Once appointed, the service director put together a new cross-functional team, with each member responsible for a specific area for improving the return rate and NFF return rate, as follows:

- service director – served as team leader;
- service manager – managed the ASC network;
- chief financial officer – responsible for the financial results of the team;
- TV sales operation manager – engaged in dealer management;
- service financial controller – performed service cost computation and analysis;
- TV product manager – concerned with process implementation and improvement.

The team set specific targets:

- TV NFF return rate to be reduced from 40% to 20%;
- TV return and exchange rate to be reduced from 5% to 3.5%;
- total savings of US$1.13 million within six months.

The service director also applied for some US$4,500 as a bonus for the team, to be used for an outing or teambuilding exercise if it could meet its targets. The general manager of the consumer electronics division endorsed the proposal and also incorporated the project targets into the bonus scheme of the team members such that they would lose their annual bonuses if the targets were not met.

The team analyzed the situation and the following actions were drawn up to remedy the situation:

- Given that both the sales team and the ASCs were failing to enforce the established criteria for accepting returned goods, PCL had ended up being more accepting of returned goods than its competitors. To manage the situation, the TV sales operation manager was put in charge of rotating the regional sales managers and salespeople geographically in order to prevent the sales team from becoming too friendly with the dealers.
- The TV sales operation manager and service director were put in charge of ensuring that no models that had been phased out for more than six months would be accepted for return.
- The TV sales operation manager and service director were also put in charge of defining clear and sound criteria for the inspection and acceptance of returned merchandise.
- The TV product marketing manager and service director were put in charge of organizing training on the return process and criteria for all individuals involved in making decisions in the return process.

The team quickly got to work, defining the criteria and monitoring measures to control the return process:

- For goods that were defective upon arrival at the dealers' warehouses, PCL would accept return only if they were functionally defective or there were serious cosmetic failures vis-à-vis PCL's standards for finished goods.
- For defective goods returned within 15 days after purchase by consumers, only functional failures would be accepted as grounds for return.
- Returned goods were to be accepted only after approval by cross-functional personnel.
- Returned goods would be required to come in their original PCL packaging, with all the original accessories.
- Models that had been phased out for more than six months would not be accepted for return or exchange.

PCL's regional service managers and engineers would also visit the top 10 ASCs for returned goods – which together were responsible for 40% of monthly returns – and provide training sessions with detailed working instructions to the ASCs. A new incentive and penalty scheme for ASCs was also drawn up, with the following mandates:

- increased labor charges for inspection of returns;
- penalties for NFF returns;
- quarterly bonuses to those with the highest levels of compliance.

On the sales team side, the TV sales operation manager worked closely with the TV sales directors to draw up a detailed rotation plan. Field salespeople were required to visit top dealers within their respective regions on a weekly basis to solicit feedback and to implement follow-up actions. The plan was fulfilled after seven months and extended to 52% of the salespeople.

The project team met every two weeks for reviews as remedy measures were implemented. Immediate actions were taken to correct any weaknesses that had materialized and warnings were issued to those responsible for them. The team was able to adhere closely to the project schedule.

After six months, the NFF return rate was reduced to 12%, surpassing the team's target of 20%. The return and exchange rates dropped to 3.2%, surpassing the team's 3.5% target. The team did not meet the target of US$1.13 million in savings, though it came quite close at US$1.1 million, and thus the team was awarded its bonus.

Epilogue

After the hard work of PCL's two taskforces, PCL finally managed to bring the issue of the high return rate of its TV sets under control. The work of the two taskforces had revealed a major issue in enforcement within the organization. Even the best strategy or business plan could only be effective if it was properly executed. What could PCL do to ensure that internal control measures would be enforced properly to achieve organizational objectives in the future?

Exhibit 1 PCL Consumer Electronics in China: Organization chart

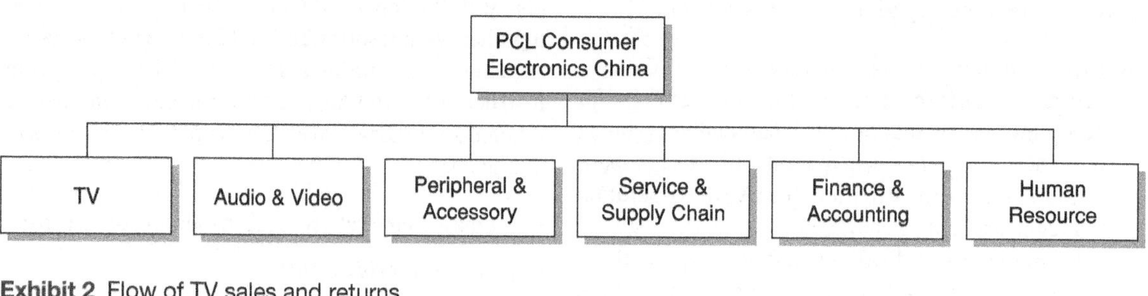

Exhibit 2 Flow of TV sales and returns

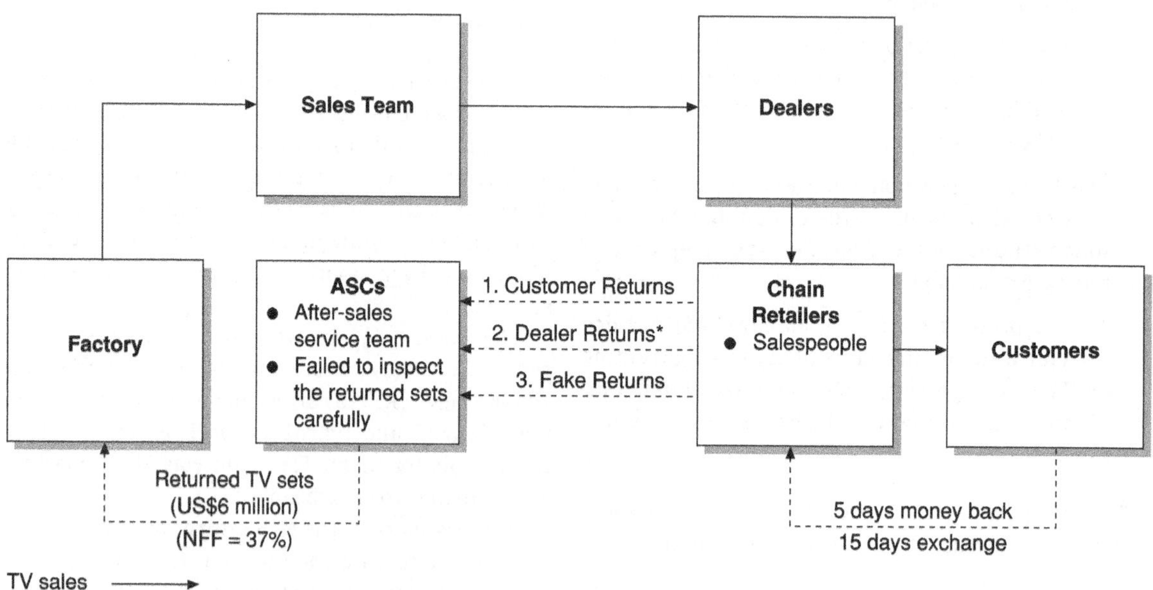

This case was prepared by Grace Loo under the supervision of Professor Neale O'Connor.

CHAPTER 5
Control System Costs

Management control systems (MCSs) provide one primary benefit: a higher probability that employees will pursue organizational objectives. Managers are willing to incur sometimes significant direct, out-of-pocket costs to try to obtain this benefit. But managers must also consider some other, indirect costs that can be many times greater than the direct costs. Some of these indirect costs arise from negative side effects that are inherent in the use of specific types of controls. Others are caused either by a poor MCS design or by implementation of the wrong type of control in a given situation. To make informed cost-benefit judgments, managers must understand these side effects, their causes, and their consequences (costs). Finally, costs may also arise from the need to adapt MCSs to the context in which they operate, which is particularly pertinent in multinational operations. Adaptations to local circumstances can be costly, but not adapting may render the MCSs less effective and give rise to indirect costs.

Direct costs

The direct costs of a MCS include all the out-of-pocket, monetary costs required to design and implement the MCS. Some direct costs, such as the costs of paying cash bonuses (arising from incentive compensation for *results control*) or the costs of maintaining an internal audit staff (needed to ensure compliance with *action-control* prescriptions) are relatively easy to identify. Other costs, however, such as those related to the time employees spend in planning and budgeting activities or preaction reviews, can only be estimated. Even of the time spent, it is hard to estimate how much of it is "value-added." For example, a recent survey of practice suggests that of all the time spent on financial analysis and planning, "only 28% is spent on the analysis that drives insightful business decisions," with the rest being spent on validating data and administering processes.[1]

Many organizations often are unaware of, or do not bother to calculate accurately the size of, all of these direct costs. But all that is required for our purposes is to acknowledge that these costs are not trivial and, thus, should be put against the benefits that MCSs have or are expected to have. This is pertinently illustrated here:

> With the process costs of internal audit [which we discuss in more detail in Chapter 14] for the *Fortune 500* representing between 0.026% and 0.126% of revenue (variable based on company size, industry, and adoption of leading practices), extracting greater value from such an investment is paramount. Moreover, since many Chief Audit Executives (CAEs) still report administratively to the CFO (70% in the *Fortune 500,* according to the 2013 Global

> Audit Information Network Annual Benchmarking Survey), it behooves Finance to equip the function with capabilities to deliver more-informed audit reports. And given the continuing desire of CFOs to play more-strategic roles, having a forward-looking Internal Audit department can be a valuable weapon in their arsenal.[2]

What is more, there is an intricate link between direct costs and indirect costs, as the following quote suggests with regards to the costs for banks to comply with US regulations on financial transactions with countries on the US sanctions list, where:

> "The cost of not being squeaky clean is phenomenal." For example, BNP Paribas's guilty plea to violations of sanctions against Sudan, Iran and Cuba was accompanied by a blockbuster fine of nearly $9bn plus a one-year ban on conducting certain transactions in dollars.[3]

This is a huge indirect cost of the failure of compliance, which has led to more direct costs incurred on internal controls to enhance compliance:

> As a result, costs are rising fast. BNP Paribas, for example, took a £200m charge related to an overhaul of compliance procedures as it responded to its fine by setting up a special unit in New York, aimed at ensuring that it stays on the right side of US rules. Macquarie, the Australian investment bank, announced in May that its direct compliance costs had tripled in three years, to A$320m. HSBC took on 1,500 extra compliance staff in the first half of the year, lifting its compliance spend by about $150m.[4]

Indirect costs

Challenging as estimating the direct costs of control may be, they can be dwarfed by indirect costs of control caused by any of a number of harmful side effects, including behavioral displacement, gamesmanship, operating delays, and negative attitudes, as the example above illustrates and which we discuss further below. Moreover, Chapters 10 and 11 discuss in more detail some of the harmful side effects that commonly arise from the use of financial results controls, especially management short-termism or myopia.

Behavioral displacement

Behavioral displacement is a common MCS-related side effect that can expose organizations to significant indirect costs; it occurs when the MCS produces, and actually encourages, behaviors that are not consistent with the organization's objectives. Behavioral displacement is most common with accountability-type controls (either results or action accountability), where the specification of the results or actions desired is *incongruent*. But some forms of personnel/cultural control can also produce the problem.

Behavioral Displacement and Results Controls

In a results-control system, behavioral displacement occurs when an organization defines sets of results measures that are incongruent with the organization's "true" objectives. For example:

- When companies give their salespeople monthly sales quotas, the salespeople tend to work on the easiest sales, which are not necessarily the most profitable sales or sales with the highest priority.
- When brokerage firms reward their brokers through commissions on client trades, some brokers respond by *churning accounts*, engaging in more transactions than are in the customers' best interests and that run the risk of client dissatisfaction and turnover.

- When companies reward their computer programmers for output measured in lines of code per day, the programmers tend to generate programs with lengthy code even when the company's problems can be better addressed by simpler programs or by off-the-shelf applications.
- When software testers are evaluated in terms of the number of "bugs" they find, the bug count goes up. But more of the bugs found will be minor. Bug counts also create incentives for superficial testing, penalizing testers to take the time either to look for the harder-to-find but more important bugs or to document their findings thoroughly. Bug counts also penalize testers who support other testers through coaching, helping, and auditing.
- When companies reward their research scientists for the number of patents filed, they are likely to see an increase in the number of patents filed. However, this incentive may lead to patent proliferation only and may not enhance, and may even erode, researchers' concerns for the eventual commercial success of their discoveries.

Why do organizations, then, use measures that are not congruent with their true objectives? Most commonly, incongruence arises because organizations focus on easily quantifiable results that lead them to *incompletely* capture all of the desired results. When that is the case, employees are induced to concentrate on the results that are rewarded by the control system and to snub other desired but unmeasured result areas.[5] For example, when a major personal computer (PC) maker started paying its sales reps higher commissions for selling add-on services than for selling PCs, the sales reps became lax about selling no-frills PCs. Sometimes they would even hang up on customers who did not want add-ons. As a result, customer satisfaction went down as did the referral business on which the company had relied for its growth in a highly competitive market.[6]

Similarly, when city officials wanted to tackle overtime in their garbage collection service, they offered the garbage collectors an incentive scheme where they would be paid full time even if they reported back early. It worked. Garbage collectors came back consistently early and received full pay for the shift. Despite this good effect on overtime reduction, however, there was an increase in preventable traffic accidents, missed pickups of garbage, and trucks filled over the legal weight limit. Because the incentive scheme emphasized time, employees nearly exclusively focused on time at the expense of safety, service and obeying work rules.[7]

Garbage collection is not exactly what comes to mind when thinking of *multitasking*, yet even this job is presumably complex enough to be subject to the effects of *distorted incentives* (a form of behavior displacement, as we call it here). Consider, then, the complexity involved in determining appropriate weights on the multiple dimensions of, say, managerial jobs, and one can see how easily incentives can have potentially displacing effects. All told, there are very few jobs, even presumably simple jobs, where what is counted is all that counts – in other words, results controls are almost invariably *incomplete*. If the relative importance of the various aspects of the job is not captured correctly, employees are unlikely to allocate their efforts properly, and outcomes will be distorted. Later chapters offer various possible remedies to this displacement problem, such as by using baskets of measures (Chapter 11) and/or relying on subjective performance evaluations (Chapter 12) to try to cover more completely all the important drivers of performance. The following example nicely summarizes the crux of the issue:

> **"Compensation should reflect the performance of the firm as a whole, *according to the principles*. Assessment areas should include productivity, teamwork, citizenship, communication and compliance." That was true until 2005, when the company determined workers' annual awards "not just on how much business you'd brought in, but also on how good you were for the organization," alleges Greg Smith, a former Vice President, in *Why I Left Goldman Sachs: A Wall Street Story*. "From 2005 until the present day, *the system has become largely mathematical*: you were paid a percentage of the amount of revenue next**

to your name," a figure that could vary from 5 to 7 percent, wrote Smith. "The problem with the new system was that people would now do anything they could – anything – to pump up the number next to their name."[8]

Behavioral Displacement and Action Controls

Behavioral displacement can also occur with action controls. One form of action control-related displacement is often referred to as *means-ends inversion*, meaning that employees pay attention to what they do (the means) while losing sight of what they are to accomplish (the ends). For example, managers who are given an approval limit for capital expenditures have been known to invest in a series of small projects, each of which fall just within their authorization limits. Although the action-accountability controls may not be breached, the resulting pattern of small, incremental investments may be suboptimal.

Sometimes action control-related displacement occurs simply because the defined actions are *incongruent*. As with results controls, this problem arises in an action-accountability context. For example, the PC maker mentioned above also implemented a policy to put a time limit on customer service calls. Specifically, customer service reps who spent more than 13 minutes talking to a customer would not earn their commission. Not surprisingly, service reps began doing just about anything possible to get customers off the phone, such as pretending that the line was not working or just hanging up. As a result, the company's customer satisfaction ratings, once the best in the industry, dropped dramatically and fell below the industry average.[9]

Some action controls cause behavioral displacement because they promote compliant yet *rigid, non-adaptive behaviors*, a pathology commonly associated with *bureaucratic* organizations. For example, US automobile manufacturers focused on elaborate action prescriptions for their assembly workers to try to optimize assembly-line operations. On Japanese assembly lines, in contrast, the control systems in use for assembly workers were much more flexible. Workers were encouraged to experiment with different ways of doing their jobs – for example, by putting the doors on the car before the locks were installed, and then alternating the order to see which was more efficient. By giving their workers more flexibility, the Japanese gained a competitive advantage. Similarly, at Continental Airlines, there used to be a rule for just about everything conceivable in the nine-inch-thick procedures manual known as the "Thou Shalt Not" book. As one company observer noted, "No one could possibly know everything in [the book], so most employees played it safe by doing nothing at all." To overcome the undesired rigidity fostered over time by the rule book, the new management team ceremoniously burned the "Thou Shalt Not" book in the company parking lot to provide a clear signal that, from then onward, employees had "permission to think for themselves."[10] Action controls and bureaucratization can be good in stable environments with considerable centralized knowledge about what actions are desired because they help establish compliant, reliable, and efficient work routines. In changing environments, however, they may hinder the change that is required to stay competitive.

A recent study in Australia suggested that the direct costs of red tape also can be significant:

Global accounting firm Deloitte says internal red tape and self-imposed rules are costing businesses twice as much as government regulations. "Our survey found that the average worker spends essentially a day a week jumping through the hoops of this self-imposed red tape," Chris Richardson from *Deloitte Access Economics* observed. "Much of it is a good thing. To take a simple example, over the past decade, miners and the construction sector have become safer. Industrial accidents have gone down," he said. But not all of it is a good thing. "Partly it's because businesses never look back. You know, they don't do the audit, and they don't ask 'why are we doing this, you know, not just this new rule, but all our rules, do they actually make sense anymore?' What we are saying is that our existing rules

are costing us a fortune; they're not necessarily making us that much better off, or that much less risky."[11]

Behavioral Displacement and Personnel/Cultural Controls

Behavioral displacement can also occur with personnel/cultural controls. It can arise from recruiting the wrong type of employees or providing insufficient training, and when personnel/cultural controls are implemented in the wrong setting, they will be rendered ineffective and encourage unintended behaviors. For example, when Levi Strauss wanted to raise productivity and reduce costs, particularly those incurred by injured workers pushing to make piecework goals, it turned to *teamwork*, which Levi's felt would be more humane, safe, and exemplary of workplace standards in an industry notorious for poor working conditions. The old piecework system – under which a worker repeatedly performs a specialized task (such as attaching pockets or belt loops) and gets paid by the amount of work completed – was abandoned and replaced by teams consisting of 10–35 workers who shared the tasks and were paid according to the total amount of trousers the group completes.

Despite these praiseworthy intentions, however, the nature of the work at Levi's may not be well suited for teamwork. Garment manufacturing consists of a series of specific tasks (pocket setting, belt looping). The speed of these tasks relates directly to a worker's skill for the grueling, repetitive motions involved in stitching fabric. Some workers are much faster than others. Although teamwork was expected to reduce monotony, enable workers to perform different tasks, and reduce repetitive injuries, it failed. When skilled workers were pitted against slower co-workers, the wages of top performers fell while those of lower-skilled workers went up. This not only eliminated savings for Levi's but also caused infighting among co-workers. Longtime friendships were dissolved, and faster workers tried to banish slower ones. Morale was damaged, efficiency dropped, and labor and overhead costs surged. The teamwork concept did not fit the context.[12]

Gamesmanship

We use the term *gamesmanship* to refer generally to the actions that employees take to improve their performance indicators without producing any positive effects for the organization. Gamesmanship is a common harmful side effect faced in situations where accountability forms of control, either results or actions accountability, are used. We discuss two major forms of gamesmanship: slack creation and data manipulation.

Creation of Slack Resources

Slack involves the consumption of organizational resources by employees in excess of what is required to meet organizational objectives. The propensity to create slack often takes place when tight results controls are in use; that is, when employees, mostly at management levels, are evaluated primarily on whether or not they achieve their budget targets (see also Chapter 8). Managers who miss their target face the prospect of interventions in their jobs, the loss of organizational resources, the loss of annual bonuses and pay raises, and sometimes even the loss of their job.

Under these circumstances, managers may look for ways to protect themselves from the downside risk of missing budget targets and the stigma attached to underachievers. One way in which managers keep tight results control from hurting them is by negotiating more easily achievable targets; that is, targets that are deliberately lower than their best-guess forecast of the future. This is called *budget slack*; it protects the managers against unforeseen contingencies and improves the probability that the budget target will be met, thus increasing the likelihood of receiving a favorable evaluation and associated rewards (such as a raise, a bonus, recognition, or a promotion).

On the negative side, the slack obscures true underlying performance and, hence, distorts the decisions based on the obscured information, such as performance evaluations and resource-allocation decisions. That said, slack should not be seen as producing only negative effects. On the positive side, slack can reduce manager tension and stress, increase organizational resilience to change, and make available some resources that can be used for innovation.[13]

In most situations, slack is nearly impossible to prevent. Theoretically, slack is feasible only where there is *information asymmetry*, where superiors have less-than-complete knowledge about what can be accomplished in a given area, and where subordinates are allowed to participate in setting the performance targets for that area. Thus, where performance can be accurately forecast or be set in a top-down manner, it should be possible to prevent, or at least mitigate, slack. But these conditions exist only in rare situations – highly stable environments. If accountability controls are used in other situations, slack must be considered almost inevitable. We discuss various ethical considerations related to slack creation in Chapter 15.

Data Manipulation

Data manipulation involves fudging the control indicators. It comes in two basic forms: falsification and data management. *Falsification* involves reporting erroneous data, meaning that the data are changed. *Data management* involves any action undertaken to change the reported results (such as sales numbers or profits) while providing no real economic advantage to the organization and, sometimes, even causing harm. Data management actions are typically undertaken to make performance look better, such as to achieve a budget target or to increase stock price. However, data management actions can also be undertaken to make performance look worse. Sometimes managers "save sales" for a future period when the current-year bonus has reached its cap. Sometimes they "take a bath" – that is, they make results look worse in bad times (while there are no bonus payouts, anyway) to get a head start on recording an improvement in the subsequent period. Sometimes they report abnormally poor results to try to lower the stock price to coincide with, say, a stock option grant.[14]

Data management can be accomplished through either accounting or operating means. *Accounting methods* of data management involve an intervention in the measurement process. Individuals engaging in accounting methods of data management sometimes violate accounting rules; more frequently, they use the flexibility available in either the selection of accounting methods or the application of those methods, or both, to "manage earnings," as it is often called.[15] To boost earnings, for example, managers might shift from accelerated to straight-line depreciation or change their judgments about accounting estimates (such as about reserves, allowances, and write-offs). IBM corporation used revenues from patent licenses and profits from asset sales to understate the company's reported general and administrative (G&A) expenses, to make the company look "lean" as observers and investors expected it to be.[16] A *Fortune* article called accounting treatments like these, which are consistent with generally accepted accounting principles, "legal, but lousy."[17] Another analyst said: "They've got a lot of ways to beat earnings and they definitely take advantage of it; it's part of how IBM operates."[18]

Operating methods of data management involve the altering of operating decisions. To boost earnings in the current period, managers can, say, try to delay the timing of discretionary expenditures (such as maintenance) and/or try to accelerate sales. These methods affect the size and/or timing of cash flows, as well as reported earnings. Several companies have been charged with booking revenues on sales to distributors (as opposed to waiting until the products have been sold by the distributor), thus taking advantage of the ambiguity in accounting rules on revenue recognition. This rules ambiguity makes "channel stuffing" tempting by persuading distributors to take more product than they really need or want, particularly toward the end of a poor quarter, to help earnings look better than they really are. A recent example occurred at Tesco, a large UK grocer, the analysis of which appears to allow for the possibility of operating as well as manipulating causes of the problems:

> Suppliers make payments to supermarkets that meet certain sales targets for their products, run promotions or place the goods in eye-catching places, such as at the end of aisles. Tesco managers appear to have been too ambitious in forecasting these "rebates." They may also have underreported the costs of stolen and out-of-date produce. *The complexity of Tesco's promotional deals with suppliers may have left too much room for discretion, and honest mistakes, as well as deliberate distortions.* But the risks around accounting for such payments are hardly new. The auditors of several big retailers have amplified their warnings in recent years as rebates have taken up more space on balance-sheets. In its most recent report, in May, Tesco's auditor, PwC, warned of the "risk of manipulation."[19]

Because altering decisions can have adverse effects on real economic value, even when they improve reported accounting income, operating methods of data management can be harmful to the firm in the long term. The actions can harm customer satisfaction (arising from the aggressive sales tactics), employee productivity (arising from the unneeded overtime at quarter's end), and/or quality (arising from postponed maintenance or reduced quality inspections). Manipulation is a serious problem because it can render an entire control system ineffective. If the data are being manipulated, it is no longer possible to determine whether a company, entity, or employee has performed well. The effects of manipulation can also go far beyond the MCS because they affect the accuracy of an organization's information system. If that is the case, management's ability to make good, facts-based decisions will be curtailed. Thus, even though various data manipulation methods are not illegal, they can be costly to the firm in the long term. No wonder, then, that an article in the *Harvard Business Review* called the "earnings game" something that "everyone plays, [but] nobody wins."[20]

Some data manipulation schemes involve outright fraud, however. At Sunrise Medical, four employees at one of the firm's major divisions, including its general manager, engaged in falsifying financial reports. The scheme was intended to disguise a deteriorating financial situation. The company's bonus plan was seen as a major cause of the fraud. The plan paid annual cash bonuses worth up to 50% of salary, but it paid no bonuses in divisions that failed to record a year-on-year earnings increase. It shocked many observers that such a fraud could occur at Sunrise, which "has long presented itself as a values-conscious health-care firm whose employees carry lofty corporate precepts about customers, shareholders and social responsibility on wallet cards."[21] When such frauds come to light, their financial impact can be huge. Reputations are ruined and billions of dollars of shareholder value can be destroyed.

Despite these costs, data manipulation schemes are often fostered by excessive short-term performance pressures and inadequate controls to prevent the dysfunctional side effects, which we discuss further in Chapter 15. In other situations, the blame is laid on the failure of auditors to perform their functions well. Auditors do not always understand the company's business or its accounting methods well enough, or they do not pursue some of the observed improprieties far enough, perhaps in part because of a lack of independence from their clients. The 2008 financial crisis has nudged regulators further toward enacting regulatory and legislative reforms focused on the roles and responsibilities of management and boards of directors in financial reporting as well as the roles and responsibilities of independent auditors in performing their audits of the financial reports. This falls broadly under the realm of corporate governance, which we discuss further in Chapters 13. The role of auditors is discussed further in Chapter 14.

Operating Delays

Operating delays often are an unavoidable consequence of the preaction review types of action controls and some of the forms of behavioral constraints. Delays such as those caused by limiting access to a stockroom or requiring the typing of a password before using a computer system are usually minor and are inevitable (although they can be made more effective and less time-wasting or cumbersome through the use of technology, such as touch IDs or retina-recognition systems). However, other control-caused delays can be major, such as those arising from approvals requiring multiple signatures from managers at various levels in the hierarchy, or from endless memos through layers of higher-ups before anything gets cleared. In these circumstances, required approvals sometimes *straitjacket* operations and, hence, curtail market and customer responsiveness.

To enhance the market responsiveness of its North American operations, Toyota Motor Corporation's president Fujio Cho had the following message for its American division: "It's all yours." In response, Jim Press, executive vice president of Torrance, California-based Toyota Motor Sales USA, noted that, "These days, we don't need so many approvals from Japan; we have more autonomy." The American management used to have to go down to the docks to greet the boats to find out what the new-model-year cars looked like. Now, many Toyota cars and their interiors are designed in the United States. Toyota's president Cho called this a "reinvention" of the carmaker, necessary because the market, especially in the United States, is so competitive. "Any company not willing to take the risk of reinventing itself is doomed," Cho said.[22] This example also dovetails nicely with the next category of MCS costs—*adaptation costs*, and benefits, of tailoring the systems to the local market.

Obviously, where fast action is important, as it is in many competitive markets, decision delays can be quite costly. Delays are a major reason for the negative connotation associated with the word *bureaucracy*. In organizations that tend to place greater emphasis on action controls and suffer these bureaucratic operating delays as a consequence, many MCS changes are motivated by a desire to reduce the burdens caused by these types of controls, which are often seen as *killing entrepreneurship.*

Control-caused operating delays are not an independent problem. They can cause other managerial reactions that are potentially harmful, such as game-playing, or that are undermining the behaviors the controls were designed to keep in check, such as when managers or employees seek the required approvals *after* they spend the money in order to speed up the process; that is, they are said to *act first, apologize later.*

Negative attitudes

Management controls can also cause negative attitudes, including job tension, conflict, frustration and resistance. Such attitudes are important not only because they are indicators of employee welfare, but also because they are often coincident with other behaviors that can be harmful, such as gameplaying, lack of effort, absenteeism and turnover.

The causes of negative attitudes are complex. They may be precipitated by a large number of factors such as economic conditions, personal difficulties, or administrative procedures, which can be cumulative, as suggested by a recent survey of more than 3,000 board members, executives, and managers across 36 countries, indicating that "cumulative pressures" have seen employees engage in accelerating the recording of revenues to meet short-term financial targets; under-reporting costs; and pushing customers to buy unnecessary stock to meet short term sales targets. John Smart, Partner and U.K. head of EY's Fraud Investigation team, said: "The incentives for unethical conduct can be strong given the pressure on pay packets, job security and demand to deliver growth. At the same time, a focus on cutting costs can also weaken the systems and teams in place to prevent and detect these actions."[23]

Negative Attitudes Produced by Results Controls

Results controls can produce negative attitudes. One cause of negative attitudes arises from a lack of employee commitment to the performance targets defined in the results-control system. Most employees are not committed to *targets* they consider too difficult, not meaningful, not controllable, or imprudent (and, of course, illegal or unethical). In the case of a tight results-control system at UPS, for example, commitment sometimes was low because the targets were too difficult, causing employees (e.g. delivery drivers, pilots) to feel too pressured. The company avoided major labor problems apparently because it provided generous salaries. However, a gradual shift by UPS toward more part-time employment and subcontracting over time has triggered strikes protracted in time across different locations amid ongoing negotiations.[24]

Negative attitudes may also stem from problems in the *measurement* system. It is common for managers to complain that their performance evaluations are not fair because they are being held accountable for things over which they have little or no control. (We discuss this issue in more detail in Chapter 12.) Other potential causes of negative attitudes may be associated with the *rewards* (or punishments) associated with the MCS. Rewards that are perceived as inequitable, and perhaps most forms of punishment, tend to produce negative attitudes. Even the target-setting and evaluation processes themselves may produce negative attitudes, particularly when they are implemented with people-insensitive, non-supportive leadership styles. Allowing employees to participate in setting their targets often reduces negative feelings toward results-oriented control systems. (We discuss this further in Chapter 8.)

The collection of factors affecting attitudes is complex. Some evidence suggests that poor performers may react more negatively to better control systems because the limitations in their abilities are easier to discover. More critical, however, are system flaws that could cause negative attitudes in good performers. Attitudes are important MCS outcomes to monitor not only because they have their own value as indicators of employee welfare, but also because the presence of these negative attitudes may indicate the propensity to engage in any of a number of harmful behaviors, such as data manipulation or other forms of gamesmanship, withdrawal, or even sabotage.

Negative Attitudes Produced by Action Controls

Most people, particularly professionals, react negatively to the use of action controls. Preaction reviews can be particularly frustrating if the employees being reviewed do not perceive the reviews as serving a useful purpose. For example, the European investment banking business at Bank of America Merrill Lynch was locked in a clash as former Merrill Lynch managers and Bank of America's top executives argued over how the business should be run. At stake was whether the combined investment business would use the Merrill Lynch-style decentralized model or Bank of America's centralized "command-and-control" model. Specifically, attempts by global banking head Brian Moynihan from Bank of America to remove individual managers' power to rule on matters such as staff compensation and to impose the Bank of America model on Merrill Lynch caused widespread dissent. Prior to the takeover by Bank of America, Merrill Lynch's investment banking business in Europe was largely left to run itself. One London-based former Merrill Lynch manager said: "Moynihan's view is 'we'll do it the Bank of America way and no other,' even though that got them nowhere in European investment banking for the past five years, whereas the Merrill Lynch model, which delegated a lot of authority, has proven very successful over the past 10 years." The spat led to the resignations of more than 40 senior managing directors in London and New York, with more expected.[25]

At 7-Eleven, the global convenience store chain, some managers described the action controls in use in the Japanese locations as "draconian." The company's point-of-sale computer system, which registers every sale at each store location, is used to monitor how much time each manager uses the analytical tools built into the cash register system. Stores are ranked by how often their operators use the system, and if they are not using it "enough," the store managers are told to "shape up." One manager complained: "Sometimes I don't know who's really running the store. It's like being under 24-hour surveillance; it's like being enslaved."[26] Even though 7-Eleven Japan has been called "the world's best-run convenience store chain,"[27] efforts to import the computer-focused action control system to stores in the United States met with stiff resistance because it "goes against American workers' desire for independence."[28] Moreover, although employee-monitoring software (some call it "spyware") may provide what seems useful information, it may undermine employee morale and mutual trust. "If you have to check up on employees all the time, then you probably have bigger issues than just productivity," notes Peter Cheese, managing director of Accenture's talent and organization practice.[29]

Adaptation costs

In addition to direct and indirect costs, further costs related to running effective MCSs may arise from the need to adapt MCSs to the context in which they operate, which is particularly pertinent when operating multinationally, and which we will use as the case in point here. But adaptation costs are also incurred when firms adapt their MCSs across different *strategic business units* (SBUs) or across different business or product/service lines because these have adopted different business unit or competitive strategies. Regardless, adaptations to local circumstances can be costly, and firms may prefer to standardize their systems rather than to adapt them.[30] However, not adapting them may render the MCSs less effective and trigger indirect costs like those we discussed above, for a number of reasons that we discuss in this section.

Adapting MCSs is particularly challenging in multinational environments. Managers of multinational organizations (MNOs) almost invariably face high *information asymmetry* between themselves and personnel in the foreign locations. The foreign personnel have specialized knowledge about their environments (such as about local norms, tastes, regulations, and business risks). The information asymmetry limits the corporate managers' abilities to use action controls, such as preaction reviews, because the corporate managers have limited knowledge to make the needed judgments. MNO managers also face the barriers of distance, time zones, and language, which limit the use of direct monitoring. They cannot easily visit their foreign-based subordinates, although advances in technology have made virtual communications easier. On top of that, they must deal with the significant problem of measuring performance in multiple currencies. All this carries extra costs – costs of operating and adapting the control systems in a multinational environment.

MNOs must understand how they must adapt their management practices, including management control practices, to make them work in each of their international locations. MNOs have similarities with large domestic organizations in that they are usually characterized by a high degree of decentralized decision-making and by management control through financial results controls. That said, controlling MNOs is often more difficult than controlling domestic organizations because MNOs face a multidimensional organizational problem: they are organized not only by function and/or product line, but also by geography. Geographic spread requires managers to be sensitive to each of the national cultures in which they operate and to appreciate different institutional settings and local business environments.

National culture

Some of the effects, benefits, and costs of management controls are universal because, at a certain basic level, people in all countries have similar physiological needs and desires, say, for achievement and financial security. Despite such similarities in people around the world, there are also many differences. One important set of factors with potentially important influences on MCSs can be explained under the rubric of *national culture*.[31] National culture has been defined as "the collective programming of the mind that distinguishes the members of one group or society from another."[32] As such, the national culture concept essentially recognizes that people's tastes, norms, values, social attitudes, personal priorities, and responses to interpersonal stimuli vary across nations. The notion of these differences is quite powerfully expressed in the following quote:

> **"The biggest difference between China and Western countries is that we pursue the goal of getting rich together," Fu Chengyu, head of the country's largest refiner, told reporters. "It doesn't make sense to benchmark Chinese executives against Western – and especially American – executives," said Kjeld Erik Brodsgaard, director of Asia research at the Copenhagen Business School. "They stay in China and move around as civil servants. In a Chinese context they are supermanagers."[33]**

An important factor that contributes to the effectiveness of MCSs is whether the employees perceive them as *culturally appropriate*; that is, whether they suit the shared values maintained by the society in which they operate. When groups of employees perceive things differently, or react to things differently, different control choices may have to be made.

Several taxonomies of national culture have been proposed. The most widely cited taxonomy consists of the four cultural dimensions identified in a study by Geert Hofstede: individualism, power distance, uncertainty avoidance, and masculinity. The *individualism* (vs. collectivism) dimension of national culture relates to individuals' self-concept; that is, whether individuals see themselves primarily as an individual or as part of a group. This affects people's comfort levels with self-interests, their preferences for conflict resolution, and their attitudes toward interpersonal relationships. The *power distance* dimension refers to the extent to which people accept that institutional or organizational power is distributed unequally. Individuals who score high on *uncertainty avoidance* feel uncomfortable when the situation they face is ambiguous. The *masculinity* dimension relates to the preference for achievement, assertiveness, and material success (traits labeled masculine), as opposed to an emphasis on relationships, modesty, and the quality of life (traits labeled feminine).[34]

Hofstede showed that people from different countries vary considerably on these cultural dimensions. For example, the US culture is much more individualistic and more masculine, while the Taiwanese culture is higher in both power distance and uncertainty avoidance.[35] If that is true, then each of the cultural dimensions can be said to have MCS implications. To name just one implication, employees high in individualism are possibly more likely to prefer individual rather than group-oriented work arrangements, performance evaluations, and pay.[36]

But these four dimensions do not explain all aspects of national culture and their differences across countries. For example, one aspect of cross-cultural differences not directly picked up by any of the four Hofstede dimensions relates to corporate goals. Managers in some countries, particularly those in Asia, are often more concerned with the interests of non-owner groups than are US managers.[37] To illustrate, Jack Ma of China's Alibaba emphatically noted that he had said on numerous occasions that he will put "customers first, employees second, and shareholders third" even though he "can see that investors who hear this for the first time may find it a bit hard to understand."[38] Managers running a business for the benefit of many *stakeholders*, and not primarily its *shareholders*, will make different decisions. With regards to MCS design, they are likely to choose, or respond better to, different performance measures (e.g. employee safety) and use different ways of rewarding employees (e.g. job security and employee benefits).

Local institutions

Corporate governance regulations, employment law, and contract law, as well as banking systems and governance interventions, also vary significantly across nations. Just as with national culture, such institutional factors can influence both the design and effects of an organization's MCS. For example, organizations in countries with strong labor unions may find it difficult to provide incentive pay as unions often prefer seniority-based pay systems.

One set of institutional factors with potentially important MCS implications consists of those descriptive of the financial markets in various countries, their importance in raising capital, and the extent of disclosures and types of information they demand.[39] The state of the capital markets in various countries may affect the extent to which firms provide stock-based incentives, such as restricted stock or stock options. Where capital markets are less efficient and/or where trading is thin, stock market valuations are less likely to reflect firm value adequately, rendering stock-based incentives impotent. The quality of the required disclosures of (financial) information by publicly traded firms also varies across countries, in part because of differences in the organization and regulation of their auditing. Just as poor stock valuations may hamper the use of stock-based incentives, so may poor earnings quality affect the use of accounting-based incentives by the parent company for incentive purposes of its managers in some of its foreign entities. The strength of regulation, auditing, and enforcement also may affect managers' abilities and propensities to engage in earnings management. Not all countries require the reporting of quarterly financial performance, which may affect managers' focus on short-term financial performance and, hence, their propensity to engage in myopic decision-making.

Differences in local business environments

Business environments also differ significantly across countries. Elements of these environments can affect environmental uncertainty, inflation, and the availability of qualified personnel. Each of these factors, and many others in this realm, has MCS implications.

Uncertainty

Country-specific environmental uncertainty can be caused by many things. Some countries are inherently riskier places in which to do business. Military conflicts, kidnappings, terrorism, and extortion threats can create major security problems. Some countries are also prone to corporate espionage and theft of corporate secrets by local competitors, perhaps even with the tacit consent of the host government. Risk also differs across countries because of the stage of economic development. As discussed, developing countries tend to have limited access to capital, relatively poor accounting regulation and oversight, weaker legal enforcement of contract violations, and other obstacles to doing business.

Government interventions also affect business risk. Governments have, to a greater or lesser extent, powers that enable them to serve certain objectives. These powers can have major effects on the value of companies' assets and the expected returns on those assets. For example, governments can exercise bureaucratic control in issuing business permits, controlling prices, and restricting currency flows. They can implement laws that restrict foreign firms' activities and/or favor domestic firms. They can design tax laws that redistribute income or affect the value of monetary compensation and other reward arrangements. They can apply constraints through labor policies designed to reduce unemployment such as by rigid labor laws to restrict layoffs.

Inflation

Inflation and fluctuations in inflation, which affect the relative values of currencies, create financial risk. Valued in terms of a fixed currency, high inflation can cause a company's assets or an individual's compensation to deteriorate significantly in value in a short period of time.

Inflation, especially when severe, may require the adoption of some form of inflation accounting, which involves either the expressing of accounts and financial statements in terms of real (rather than nominal) amounts or expressing all assets and liabilities at current (or replacement) values. Or, when less severe, it may require the use of some form of flexible budgeting, to shield managers from uncontrollable inflation risk, or the partial abandonment of accounting measures of performance in favor of some nonfinancial measures.

Talent

Organizations operating in developing countries often face limited availability of skilled and educated personnel. When employees are not highly educated, decision-making structures are usually more centralized, and MCSs tend to be more focused on action controls rather than results controls. Small offices may contain only a few educated people. This makes it difficult to implement one of the basic internal control principles: separation of duties. All told, when talent is in short supply, both the firm's ability to do business and its capacity to affect good control are more likely to be compromised.

Personnel mobility and retention also differ across countries, which the following quote nicely illustrates:

> Japanese workers introduce themselves by their company name first and their own name second, and are far more likely to define themselves by whom they work for than by what they do. This is true even in Japan's most global companies. In the United States you are always 'dating' the company; in Japan, employees 'marry' their company.[40]

When personnel mobility is low, there is less need for implementing long-term incentive plans that motivate managers both to think long term and to stay with the firm to earn their rewards.

Foreign currency translation

MNOs also face currency exchange and translation problems. At first glance, it is not obvious that results controls in MNOs should be complicated by the fact that the firms' profits are earned in multiple currencies. Results controls over foreign entities can be implemented using the same practices employed in most domestic firms, by comparing performance measured in terms of the local currency with a pre-set plan also expressed in the local currency. However, MNOs bear economic risk caused by fluctuating currency values. The values of foreign investments appreciate or depreciate based on the relative values of the home and foreign currencies. Through their performance evaluation practices, MNOs can make their entity managers bear this risk or can shield them from it. The issues involved are discussed further in Chapter 12 regarding uncontrollable factors. The extra measurement noise caused by uncontrollable foreign exchange risk, and various methods of measuring the gains and losses, can affect judgments about the entity managers' performances.

One could argue that entity managers who can influence the amount of the foreign exchange gains or losses should bear the foreign exchange risk. Some entity managers can take actions that have foreign currency implications. Some have the authority to make significant cross-border investments, product sourcing, or marketing decisions. Some have the authority to write purchasing or sales contracts denominated in one currency or another. Some even have the authority to enter into foreign exchange transactions, such as hedging, currency swaps, or arbitrage. But most of these specialized hedging transactions require special skills most operating managers do not have; thus, authority in this area commonly resides with the finance department at corporate.

If corporate managers decide that the managers of their foreign entities should not bear the foreign exchange risk, they can instead use any of four essentially identical methods:

1. Evaluate the manager in terms of local currency profits as compared to a local currency plan or budget.
2. Treat the foreign exchange gain or loss as "below" the income-statement line for which the manager is held accountable.
3. Evaluate the manager in terms of profits measured in home currency, but calculate a "foreign exchange variance" and treat it as uncontrollable.
4. Re-express the home currency budget for the entity in local currency using the end-of-year, not beginning-of-year, exchange rate or some average for the period. This procedure creates a budget that "flexes" with exchange rates.

These are just some examples of the ways in which different situational factors may require adjustments to the MCS, which will trigger adaptation costs and increase complexity. These costs should be outweighed by the benefits of "better" control, however hard such is to estimate because these benefits also include the avoidance or mitigation of some dysfunctional side effects that may occur if the systems are not adapted.

Conclusion

The implementation of virtually all controls, as well as their adaptation to local or situational circumstances, requires companies to incur some direct, out-of-pocket costs. But sometimes those direct costs are dwarfed by the indirect costs caused by any of a number of harmful side effects.

We can make four general observations about the occurrence of these side effects. First, as Table 5.1 summarizes, the harmful side effects are not unique to one form of control. However, the risk of side effects seems to be smaller with personnel controls. Second, some of the control types have negative side effects that are largely unavoidable. It is difficult, or even impossible, for people to enjoy following a strict set of procedures (action accountability) for a long period of time, although the negative attitudes can probably be minimized if the reasons for them are well communicated and if the list is kept to a minimum. Third, the likelihood of severe harmful side effects is greatest when there is either a failure to satisfy one or more of the desirable design criteria or a misfit between the choice of type(s) of control and the situation. Fourth, when controls have design imperfections or when they are inappropriately used, the tighter the controls are applied, the greater are both the likelihood and the severity of harmful side effects.

What makes dealing with these potential side effects difficult is that there is not always a simple one-to-one relationship between the control type and the effect. The need to adapt MCSs to different situations across various business units, with different strategies or operating in

Table 5.1 Control types and possible harmful side effects

Type of control	Behavioral displacement	Gamesmanship	Operating delays	Negative attitudes
Results controls				
Results accountability	x	x		x
Action controls				
Behavioral constraints			x	x
Preaction reviews			x	x
Action accountability	x	x		x
Redundancy				x
Personnel/cultural controls				
Selection and placement	x			
Training	x			
Provision of necessary resources				
Creation of a strong organizational culture	x			
Group-based rewards	x			

Source: K. A. Merchant, *Modern Management Control Systems: Text and Cases* (Upper Saddle River, NJ: Prentice Hall, 1998), p. 224.

different regions of the world, adds to the complexity. Moreover, the existence of the side effects is often difficult to detect. For example, a failure to make the measurement processes more robust in a results- or action-accountability control system only offers the *opportunity* for data manipulation. *Actual* manipulation may not occur until an employee has a personal need for more money; poor performance creates additional pressure to perform; there is a lower chance of being detected or caught; and/or leadership creates a motivation to manipulate.[41] That said, the better organizations can alleviate both the opportunity and motivation for undesired behaviors, the more likely their control systems will have predominantly desired effects and, hence, lower costs.

Even costs can have *hidden* or *indirect benefits*. For example, managers in diversified or multinational corporations are able to learn from potentially desirable practices used in their various businesses or foreign countries. Those practices are known by employees in their entities, and some of those practices can be readily adapted across other entities. Firms that grow by acquisition learn from the management systems, including MCSs, being used in the organizations they acquire. When firms grow by acquisition, they are likely to have to use, at least for a period of time, several variations of MCSs. The MCS variations may persist if they are superior for controlling the acquired businesses, even though it can be costly to maintain multiple sets of MCSs.

Notes

1 *2012 Budgeting, Forecasting, and Planning Survey* (Quantrix, 2012), p. 15.
2 "CFO Insights: Can Internal Audit Be a Command Center for Risk?," *Deloitte* (2014), online at deloi.tt/1OidCMB.
3 "Banks Increase Efforts to Stay on Right Side of Law," *The Financial Times* (September 28, 2014), online at on.ft.com/1hNpwWl.
4 Ibid.
5 This problem is also known as *multitasking* – see J. Roberts, *The Modern Firm* (New York: Oxford University Press, 2004), and other work by John Roberts and colleagues. See also W. A. Van der Stede, "The Pitfalls of Pay-for-Performance," *Finance & Management* (December 2007), pp. 10–13; W. A. Van der Stede, "Designing Effective Reward Systems," *Finance & Management* (October 2009), pp. 6–9.
6 "I Built This Company, I Can Save It," *Fortune* (April 30, 2001).
7 This example is taken from J. Pfeffer and R. Sutton, *Hard Facts, Dangerous Half-Truths and Total Nonsense* (Boston, MA: Harvard Business School Press, 2006), p. 120.

8 G. Smith, *Why I Left Goldman Sachs: A Wall Street Story* (New York: Grand Central Publishing, 2012).
9 "I Built This Company, I Can Save It," op. cit.
10 "Just Think: No Permission Needed," *Fortune* (January 8, 2001), pp. 190–2.
11 "Business Costs Itself Billions in Internal Red Tape," *ABC* (October 28, 2014), online at www.abc.net.au/news/2014-10-29/business-costs-itself-billions-in-internal-red-tape/5849994.
12 "Jeans Therapy: Levi's Factory Workers Are Assigned to Teams, and Morale Takes a Hit," *The Wall Street Journal* (May 20, 1998), p A1.
13 See W. A. Van der Stede, "The Relationship between Two Consequences of Budget Controls: Budgetary Slack Creation and Managerial Short-Term Orientation," *Accounting, Organizations and Society*, 25, no. 6 (August 2000).
14 For various manifestations of such practices, see, for example, M. Jones, *Creative Accounting, Fraud and International Accounting Scandals* (Chichester, UK: Wiley, 2010). See also I. Dichev, J. Graham, C. R. Harvey, and S. Rajgopal, "The Misrepresentation of Earnings," *Financial Analyst Journal*, 72, no. 1 (2016), pp. 22–35, as well as other work by these authors on this issue.
15 See, for example, M. Nelson, J. Elliott, and R. Tarpley, "How Are Earnings Managed? Examples from Auditors," *Accounting Horizons*, 17 (Supplement 2003), pp. 17–35.
16 "Full Disclosure," *Forbes* (April, 2002), pp. 36–8.
17 "Legal, but Lousy," *Fortune* (September 2, 2002), p. 192.
18 "IBM Uses Dutch Tax Haven to Boost Profits as Sales Slide," *Bloomberg* (February 3, 2014), online at bloom.bg/1iVould.
19 "Tesco's Accounting Problems Not So Funny," *The Economist* (September 27, 2014), online at econ.st/1qxwvPw.
20 H. Collingwood, "The Earnings Game: Everyone Plays, Nobody Wins," *Harvard Business Review*, 79, no. 6 (June 2001), pp. 5–13.
21 "Sunrise Scam Throws Light on Incentive Pay Programs," *The Los Angeles Times* (January 15, 1996), p. D1.
22 "In the Driver's Seat at Toyota: U.S. Execs Get more Independence as the Automaker Focuses on Asia and Europe," *The Los Angeles Times* (October 19, 2004), p. C1.
23 "Squeezed U.K. Employees under Increasing Pressure to Commit Fraud," *Ernst & Young* (May 7, 2013), online at www.ey.com/UK/en/Newsroom/News-releases/13-05-07-Squeezed-UK-employees-under-increasing-pressure-to-commit-fraud.
24 See, for example, "UPS Pilots Union Calls for Strike Vote," *The Wall Street Journal* (September 9, 2015), online at on.wsj.com/1hXhn1i.
25 "Power Struggle at BofA Merrill Lynch," *Market Watch* (April 19, 2009), online at www.marketwatch.com.
26 "7-Eleven Operators Resist System to Monitor Managers," *The Wall Street Journal* (June 16, 1997), p. B1.
27 A. Ishikawa and T. Nejo, *The Success of 7-Eleven Japan: Discovering the Secrets of the World's Best-Run Convenience Store Chain* (Singapore: World Scientific, 2002).
28 "Power Struggle at BofA Merrill Lynch," op. cit.
29 "Big Brother Bosses," *The Economist* (September 10, 2009), pp. 71–2. See also "Monitoring the Monitors," *The Wall Street Journal* (August 16, 2010), online at online.wsj.com.
30 See W. Van der Stede, "The Effect of National Culture on Management Control and Incentive System Design in Multi-Business Firms: Evidence of Intra-Corporate Isomorphism," *European Accounting Review*, 12, no. 2 (2003), pp. 263–85.
31 National culture has been deemed an important factor in several literatures, including finance – see, for example, C. S. Eun, L. Wang and S. C. Xiao, "Culture and R2," *Journal of Financial Economics*, 115, no. 2 (February 2015), pp. 283–303.
32 G. Hofstede, *Culture's Consequences: International Differences in Work-Related Values* (Beverly Hills, CA: Sage Publications, 1980), p. 25; G. Hofstede, *Culture's Consequences: Comparing Values, Behaviors, Institutions and Organizations Across Nations* (Thousand Oaks, CA: Sage Publications, 2001). See also www.geerthofstede.nl/dimensions-of-national-cultures (accessed December 2015).
33 "China's State Sector Leaders Embrace Pay Cuts of Up to 60%," *The Financial Times* (October 12, 2014), online at on.ft.com/1fBoBqu.
34 Hofstede, *Culture's Consequences: International Differences*, op. cit.
35 Ibid., Figure 7.1, p. 315.
36 For a sample of several studies in this area, see C. Chow, M. Shields, and A. Wu, "The Importance of National Culture in the Design of and Preference for Management Controls for Multinational Operations," *Accounting, Organizations and Society*, 24, no. 5/6 (July–August 1999), pp. 441–61; and E. P. Jansen, K. Merchant, and W. Van der Stede, "National Differences in Incentive Compensation Practices: The Differing Roles of Financial Performance Measurement in the United States and the Netherlands," *Accounting, Organizations and Society*, 34, no. 1 (January 2009), pp. 58–84.
37 See, for example, "Shareholders vs. Stakeholders: A New Idolatry," *The Economist* (April 24, 2010), pp. 65–6.
38 "Dear Investors: Letter from Jack Ma as Alibaba Prepares Roadshow," *The Financial Times* (September 5, 2014), online at on.ft.com/1JATJ7z.
39 See, for example, C. Leuz, "Different Approaches to Corporate Reporting Regulation: How Jurisdictions Differ and Why," *Accounting and Business Research*, 40, no. 3 (Special Issue, 2010), pp. 229–56.
40 "Insiders and Outsiders," *The Economist* (November 18, 2010), pp. 7–9.
41 B. Litzky, K. Eddleston, and D. Kidder, "The Good, the Bad, and the Misguided: How Managers Inadvertently Encourage Deviant Behaviors," *The Academy of Management Perspectives*, 20, no. 1 (February 2006), pp. 91–103.

CASE STUDY
Philip Anderson

It was three days to month end. Philip Anderson, the Phoenix branch manager of Stuart & Co., the largest brokerage firm in town, was dreading the monthly teleconference meeting with his bosses in New York. Once again his team had failed to deliver on some of the specific product sales targets set for them in the company's sales budget. Specifically, the ratio of in-house to outside product sales of items such as mutual funds and insurance product offerings had not improved from the prior month; his team had not been successful in pushing equity issues syndicated or underwritten by the parent firm to the levels set by his boss a few months earlier; and his team had not increased the overall balance of margin accounts. On the positive side, the number of margin accounts had increased, new clients had been signed up, and overall branch revenues had increased. But Phil questioned how long he would be able to justify not meeting some of the specific targets the firm had given his branch.

Phil began his sales career right after college. His first job was with a cereal producer, as an inside salesman. He switched to the brokerage business after just two years, lured by the potential for higher income and the opportunity to have direct contact with retail clients. Phil was an outgoing individual who had a talent for financial matters, and he looked forward to a job that would allow him to interact with clients directly. Just five months ago, Phil had celebrated his 30th year in the brokerage industry and his 21st year with Stuart & Co. Although he truly enjoyed being a manager and working with his team, some of the other demands of the job were beginning to wear on him. Things had not turned out as he had expected. Phil thought of himself as a hard-working and loyal employee, a good manager, and an ethical businessman. The "compromises" that his career seemed to demand were beginning to trouble him. He did not consider himself a saint, and he knew that his job required balancing conflicting goals, but he wondered how far he could bend without breaking.

Phil started his brokerage career with one of the largest firms in the industry. He moved to Stuart & Co., then a boutique firm, in the hope of breaking free from the high-pressure sales-oriented attitude prevalent in the industry. He thought that the perception that the large firms tried to perpetuate – that their advisors are experts at providing unbiased financial advice – is for the most part wrong. Phil learned firsthand that brokers are paid, first and foremost, to sell products and services. Meeting the financial needs of their clients was not paramount.

Stuart & Co. seemed to be different. It was a firm that emphasized the development of long-term client relationships based upon rendering expert independent financial advice. Its investment advisors were to be trusted counselors to clients on all financial matters. But Phil was also lured by Stuart's compensation package, which included a relatively large fixed salary and a bonus based upon overall branch revenues, growth in the number of ties or relationships (financial, insurance, investment) developed with each customer, and the number of business referrals to other branches.

However, things had changed since he had joined the firm. As the investment and analysis units expanded, the demand on the branch managers to push specific products began to be incorporated into their annual sales budgets. Phil felt that those changes had compromised his ability to deliver investment options suited to his clients' financial situations. They risked the many long-term relationships with clients that he had worked hard to develop and created ethical dilemmas for him and his staff. Phil felt that pursuing some of the new budget goals could result in future financial losses for some of his clients. However, Phil had worked in the brokerage industry and at Stuart & Co. long enough to know that it was dangerous to openly express those concerns to his boss. Additionally, Phil was troubled with the recent scandals in the industry. It was mostly low-level employees like him who were the object of criminal prosecution, not the top executives.

As Phil saw it, his job was to develop and nurture profitable relationships with as many clients as possible, and the specific products and services sold to clients should be dictated by the needs of those clients. Consequently, he could never bring himself to pushing his team to adhere to the firm directives, and this approach had negatively impacted his total compensation in the last few years. Invariably, his annual bonus lagged behind those of other managers at Stuart & Co., even though his branch was one of the largest in the firm in terms of clients, sales volume, and net profits. Phil felt his current situation was unfair. He also was beginning to worry that his failure to meet specific product sales targets was eroding whatever measure of job safety his overall results had given him. To compound the situation, Stuart & Co. had recently been bought by one of the largest brokerage firms in the country, and it seemed that the new hierarchy did not take well to independent-minded managers like Phil who did not aggressively pursue the objectives set out by corporate.

Phil was getting tired of the game but could not see how he could avoid playing it. He was almost 54 years old and was the sole provider for his family. His wife had retired a year before from her teaching job to take care of their three teenage sons. They had just recently bought a 4,000-square-foot home in an exclusive neighborhood of Scottsdale. And last fall, Phil had fulfilled a college dream by buying for himself a brand-new red Corvette. Phil feared that if he allowed his team of advisors to continue focusing on meeting their clients' needs with little regard for corporate targets, more than his discretionary compensation would be at risk.

Phil had many questions and doubts, and few answers. Was he right in allowing his clients' financial goals to take precedence over his own family's financial security? Was he being unreasonable, naive, or impractical? Was there somewhere a proper balance? Was he being too ethical at a time when his family's future should be his primary concern? Or perhaps it was time for him to find another employer that shared Phil's philosophy, if one existed in the brokerage industry? But could he find another good job at his age? Or should he even bother? After all, he had done his part. Maybe it should be the job of some younger managers to champion the cause of service to clients and continue the battle.

This case was prepared by Research Assistant Juan Jimenez and Professors Kenneth A. Merchant and Wim A. Van der Stede.

CASE STUDY
Sunshine Fashion: Fraud, Theft, and Misbehavior among Employees

Shenzhen-based Sunshine Fashion was a Sino-Japanese venture that had grown from merely an OEM export manufacturer of cashmere sweaters to also a retailer with a chain of 220 retail points across China in 2010. In order to manage its retail operation, it had set up regional as well as branch offices to handle stock as well as support and monitor its retail points. Nonetheless, fraudulent behavior among employees had cost the retail chain almost 5% of its domestic sales revenues. The implementation of an ERP system for tracking goods and sales had improved the situation somewhat. What were the challenges that Sunshine faced in trying to control fraudulent behavior among its staff? What additional measures should the management undertake, and how should the remedial measures be implemented to achieve its target?

Company background

Shenzhen-based Sunshine Fashion Co. Ltd. was a Sino-Japanese joint venture founded in 1993. It started out as an OEM[1] export manufacturer of cashmere sweaters and eventually grew to become an integrated manufacturer and retailer with activities that included material sourcing, spinning, dyeing, design, distribution, marketing, and retailing. By 2010, it had three factories, located in

Shenzhen, Shanghai, and Taiyuan of Shanxi province; 220 sales counters in departmental stores across the country; and a workforce of more than 1,000 employees.

Sunshine produced some 300,000 pieces a year for domestic sales, which enjoyed a considerably higher profit margin than its export business. With a turnover of RMB 150 million, domestic sales made up more than two-thirds of Sunshine's business. Sunshine was positioned as a high-end fashion brand in the domestic market with design being the leading factor in determining the sales of its goods. At RMB 3,000 apiece,[2] Sunshine's cashmere sweaters were considered a luxurious item in China.[3]

> We are concerned with the price at which we sell, not how many garments we sell. Volume is nothing for us. If we sell a lot of garments but at a very low price, there is no profit.
>
> *Kitty Li, Sales Manager of Sunshine*

Since the customers of Sunshine were fashion conscious, the value of out-of-season items could fall to as low as one-third of their original price. Sunshine's vertically integrated organization gave it a competitive edge over its competitors. It could complete the product cycle from design to distribution within 20 days, as compared with the three months it took for its major competitor Edor.

The operation

Sunshine's 220 retail counters in departmental stores across the country were managed by 14 branch offices that reported to three regional offices in Beijing, Chongqing, and Nanjing. The three regional offices were all former branch offices promoted to regional offices.

> Before the head office controlled almost everything, the price, the quantity, which branch office was to be allocated how much goods ... These decisions and coordination was concentrated with one person. With three regional companies, [the work] can be separated and it reduces the load on this one person.
>
> *Kitty Li, Sales Manager of Sunshine*

Sunshine had franchised some retail points outside of the major cities but remained cautious about expanding its franchise network out of concern for operational control and brand integrity.

Stock

At the beginning of each season, Sunshine's head office would prepare the stock, tagging each item with barcodes with prices, and send it to the branch offices. The branch offices were responsible for distributing the sweaters to the 220 retail counters and for replenishing the stock at each counter throughout the season. The head office sent the goods to the branch offices by air and sometimes also by courier. Roughly 3% of the goods was lost during transportation. At the end of each season, the branch offices were required to return all leftover stock to the head office and they would be refunded the cost of the returned goods. Over a two month period each year the head office would put ten people to work, counting and inspecting the returned items, repackaging them, and changing the barcodes to a new price if necessary ready for sale in the following season (see Exhibit 1).

Sales

The branch offices and retail points reported information about stock and sales to the head office manually until 1998 when Sunshine implemented an RFID/ERP system. The system networked the branch offices and head office together, and this allowed the head office to receive updates on sales at all the retail points every four hours. Sunshine's RFID/ERP system also stored information about inventory at the branch offices and retail counters, but the information had to be input manually by staff.

Theft and fraud by employees

In 2008, Sunshine faced serious fraud and misbehavior problems by employees with estimated losses of between RMB 9.3 million and RMB 10.5 million, translating to more than 5% of Sunshine's total domestic sales. Although Sunshine's RFID/ERP system provided the head office with an updated point-of-sales situation every four hours, managers who wanted to cheat took advantage of the head office's inability to control discounts and stock at the local level. Sunshine's head office was responsible for setting the price and determining promotional time frames but these time frames were not necessarily followed by all the branch managers. Some branch managers postponed the start date of the promotional period without informing the head office so they could sell sweaters at the original price and pocketed the difference between the sale price and

---

[1] OEM stands for original equipment manufacturer. It refers to manufacturers who produce products for another company that will be retailed under the brand name of that company.

[2] RMB 3,000 = US$451.35 at an exchange rate of $US1 = RMB 6.65.

[3] China's national average GDP per capita of 2007 was RMB 18,665. (*Source*: Statistical Communiqué of the People's Republic, February 28, 2008.)

the discounted price, which was remitted to the head office. Other branch managers reported a higher discount rate to the head office than what was actually the case and pocketed the difference. The situation was further complicated by the fact that the market situation varied widely across China, and each department store had its own policy with regard to the timing of sales promotions.

> It depends on the different department stores. They each have different sales and celebrations and other things. It's hard to control from the head office, they are far away from the office.
>
> *Kitty Li, Sales Manager of Sunshine*

Sunshine had no choice but to allow some autonomy for decisions over promotions and discount rates at the local level, a practice that increased the risk of managers engaging in fraudulent behavior. The branch offices also engaged in a small amount of cash sales and there was no way for the head office to control such sales. The branch managers had total discretion over how much discount they wanted to give in such instances.

Fraudulent behavior was also encouraged by the fact that Sunshine had no mechanism in place to control stock at the local level. While the head office knew how many pieces it sent out to each branch office at the beginning of the season, it had no information on how many of those pieces were at the branch office and how many had been distributed to each retail point at any moment in time. The branch office sent pieces to the retail points almost every day depending on their needs. This made it difficult for the head office to control promotions.

> To check the stock before each promotion is impossible. The promotion each time depends on the different holidays and the policy of each departmental store ... It's hard to take stock before each promotion. We only control the inventory.
>
> *Kitty Li, Sales Manager of Sunshine*

Sunshine's ERP system could not update stock information automatically. It stored stock information, but that information had to be inputted and updated manually. This meant that staff could input the stock information only after a promotion started, giving them an opportunity to sell the sweaters at the original price and pocket the difference. Loss arising from such misbehavior was estimated to cost Sunshine RMB 3 million.

While barcoding the sweaters helped Sunshine to track its products, it had found that the barcodes of some of the sweaters had been changed, which altered the price upward by as much as 50% when the unsold goods were returned to the head office at the end of the season.

> For example, given two garments priced at 1,000 yuan and 500 yuan, respectively, the salesman might sell one piece of 1,000 yuan, and return 500 yuan piece to the head office at the end of the season. The head office knows that the salesman has 1,000 yuan earning. But, if the salesman changes the barcode of the 500 yuan garment to the 1,000 yuan barcode, then on returning the garment and barcode to the head office, the head office thinks that the salesman has only 500 yuan earning (cash). When auditing at the end of the season, the total quantity is not less, but the amount difference who knows?
>
> Every year we have a big quantity and amount of sale, and the price changes all the time (because of festivals, shop anniversary, discount season ...) it's a huge workload to check every barcode, or the boss thinks that is it worth to do so? It's another big cost ...
>
> *Kitty Li, Sales Manager of Sunshine*

Loss due to changed barcodes was estimated at RMB 1.5 million. Sunshine's accounting department visited the branch offices once or twice a year during the sales season to check their stock and their accounts, and the head office also arranged random visits to the retail counters, but to little avail.

Another misbehavior that Sunshine encountered was managers who used the relationship they built up with departmental stores as Sunshine managers to sell their own goods or brands.

> ... these managers, they use their own relationship with the department store manager to begin their own brand and business. Maybe they give money to the manager every year, but this money is from Sunshine, you know, so they use the company's money to set up their own relationship. That's the problem.
>
> *Kitty Li, Sales Manager of Sunshine*

To counter such misbehavior, the president of Sunshine regularly visited department stores with Sunshine retail counters around the country to reinforce the Sunshine brand and to build up a personal relationship with the department stores himself.

> We don't want the branch managers to get too close to one store manager. Once they have good relationship [with the departmental store manager], even better relationship than the general managers from our head office ... they can begin their own brand easily, use this relationship to begin their own business may be at the same time.
>
> *Kitty Li, Sales Manager of Sunshine*

Sunshine rotated the branch managers among the different branches periodically to control their power.

A number of organizational factors also contributed to the rampant fraudulent misbehavior among employees. *Guanxi*, or relationship, with the departmental stores was critical for brands to set up retail points within departmental stores in China, and Sunshine branch managers were often recruited based on the strength of their relationships with the departmental stores rather than their management ability or integrity. With branch managers having an average tenure of two years and a yearly turnover rate of 20%, their weak sense of belonging and loyalty to Sunshine encouraged greed and opportunistic behavior. Branch managers, leveraging the relationships they built with department stores while they worked at Sunshine, often became agents of other brands when they left, turning into competitors of Sunshine.

Branch managers received a fixed monthly salary of between RMB 3,000 and RMB 4,000 and a year-end bonus that was decided solely at the discretion of the general manager. While the standard of living and wage level varied widely across China, the salary of Sunshine's branch managers was generally set on par with Shenzhen, where Sunshine's head office was located and which had one of the highest wage levels in China.[4] Nonetheless, the year-end bonus was decided solely at the discretion of the general manager, and the lack of transparency into how decisions over the bonuses were made gave branch managers little motivation to act in the best interest of the company. To remedy the situation, Sunshine had begun setting sales targets for the branch managers each June based on their location, and the square footage and sales history of the retail points, and awarding year-end commissions to branch managers who could meet their sales target. Under the new system, branch managers could receive commission that was as high as their annual salary if their sales performance was good.

Annual review

Sunshine's management was due to meet soon for its annual review meeting, and employee fraud and misbehavior was on the meeting's agenda. The CEO had decided on a target of reducing the fraudulent behavior to 2% of retail sales. The implementation of the ERP system had given the head office better control over its retail operation, but fraud and misbehavior among employees continued. Li knew that it was impossible to control everything.

> If the manager knows you are to come, he will do something about it. Everything we do is to reduce risk but we cannot control perfectly. If you control them perfectly, they will resign.
>
> *Kitty Li, Sales Manager of Sunshine*

But there must be more that could be done to control such misbehavior. What were the root causes of the staff's misbehavior? What were the strengths and weaknesses of Sunshine's current internal control system? Most of all, what could Li propose to the management to improve the situation? What measures should the management undertake, and how should the remedial measures be implemented? In what order would you implement the recommended actions for Sunshine?

[4] According to the *China Statistical Yearbook 2009*, Shenzhen has the fifth-highest average wage and salary level among the major cities in China after Shanghai, Beijing, Lhasa, and Guanzhou. The average wage and salary of Shenzhen is RMB 43,731, compared to RMB 56,565 in Shanghai. Kunming, which ranks 36th, has an average wage and salary level of RMB 22,432.

Exhibit 1 Sunshine's operational flow for its retail business

	Head office	*Regional offices*	*Branch offices*	*Retail points*
Flow of goods at the beginning of the season	Prepare stock with bar codes and send out at the start of each season. ⇨	⇨	Branch office responsible for replenishing retail points throughout the season. ⇨	
Flow of goods not sold at the end of the season	Head office inspects, counts, and change barcodes if necessary after receiving goods returned. ⇦		Branch offices sent goods not sold back to head office at the end of the season.	
Flow of retail sales information	Receives information via ERP system.	Receives information via ERP system. ⇦	Receives information via ERP system. ⇦	ERP system records sales information. Inventory information has to be input/updated manually.
Discounts/promotions	Determines discounts and promotions.		Branch offices engage in some direct sales and branch managers have discretion in giving discounts in such sales.	Department stores in which retail points are located also make their own discounts/promotion policies.

This case was prepared by Grace Loo under the supervision of Professor Neale O'Connor.

CASE STUDY
Better Beauty, Inc.

In April 2013, Ted Williams, president of Better Beauty, Inc. (BBI), was reviewing the details of his company's performance for the year 2012 and the first quarter of 2013. Overall, performance had not been good. One of the major causes of the poor performance was that the company was missing its cost improvement targets by substantial margins. BBI had put Cost Improvement Programs (CIPs) in place both to help offset some raw material price increases and to offset the effects of price pressures in an increasingly competitive marketplace. Initially, these programs had been quite successful, but in recent years, failure had become the norm.

One major CIP known as the A-53 project, which was the most important CIP for 2013, had not only failed to provide the projected savings, but according to Bryant Richards, the company controller, it might even end up costing the firm money. It was a major cause of BBI's failure to meet its overall CIP goals.

If the A-53 project had been only an isolated incidence, Mr. Williams would not have been quite as worried. In reality, however, it was just one of a long string of CIP project failures. Mr. Williams was convinced that he had to determine the root cause for these major shortfalls. He addressed his staff:

> What is going wrong? We've had problems with a new assembly in toiletries, the start-up of our lean management initiative on the plant floor, and the new formulations for our latest shampoos. These are just this year's problems. Are our problems in the design, testing, and/or implementation of the CIPs? Or perhaps we should reconsider the total cost reduction concept itself. Maybe it has run its course; maybe we've gathered all of the low-hanging fruit. If we cannot do something to reverse this pattern of failure, we will have no chance of achieving our goals!

The company

BBI was a personal care company that sold its products internationally. In the past, the company's primary focus had been on the manufacturing and sales of cosmetics and fragrances. In the last five years, however, in direct response to shifts in the overall market for health and beauty products, more and more of the company's revenue had come from toiletries, hair coloring options, and beauty care tools. In 2012, over half (60%) of BBI's total revenues of just over $1 billion were in the domestic markets (which included Canada and Puerto Rico). The company also distributed products in Europe and Latin America through a direct sales force, and in the Middle East via a broker network.

Up until 2003, BBI, like many cosmetic-focused companies, was managed by its founder, Claudette Beauford. Upon Ms. Beauford's retirement, the management and focus of the company changed substantially. The new president, Ted Williams, had a financial background. He formalized the organizational structure along functional lines, as shown in Exhibit 1. Under its new management team, BBI's strategy broadened to include an expanded product line (toiletries and other health and beauty care products). It also shifted attention away from the company's prior focus on top-of-the-line, or "prestige" products, which earned a premium price in the market, to a more mid-price strategy that emphasized mass market products. The new strategy required an increased focus on the cost efficiencies needed to generate the desired profits.

At first the change in strategy looked promising, but then the company reported operating losses in 2006–2008. In more recent years BBI had been profitable (see Exhibit 2). During this period of strategic change, formal cost reduction and financial targeting procedures were introduced in order to try to keep the BBI's gross margins[1] above 60%, even in a period where some costs were increasing rapidly.

The "easy" cost reductions and improvements caused a significant bump in profits in 2011. But Mr. Williams was concerned that if the company did not find some new cost reductions, profits might turn down again. He was even more convinced that cost improvement projects were the key to maintaining a profitable future for BBI.

Industry trends

In 2013, analysts were estimating that profits in the personal care industry, while sluggish, would improve modestly. Industry volume was expected to rise to $29.2 billion, up about 5% from the $27.8 billion spent at retail in 2012. The 2012 total reflected activity in the major categories of: cosmetics (35%), hair products (24%), shaving products (14%), toilet soaps and deodorants (13%), fragrances (9%), and hand products (5%).

While the 1990s had witnessed robust growth, the recent trends had not been as favorable. Real (inflation-adjusted) shipments had declined, and price competition had increased. Demand for personal care items, considered to be a discretionary purchase, was hurt by the sluggish economic activity in the 2008–2012 period, as well as by the secular changes in the product markets. With less discretionary income available, consumers had cut back on the impulse buying that had been responsible for up to two-thirds of all cosmetics and personal care purchases. The market had improved over the 2010–2012 period, returning BBI to profitability, but margins were still slim.

Relatively flat sales in the 2010–2012 time period had made it possible for BBI and its competitors to

[1] Gross Income ÷ Net Sales.

manage their inventories. That said, there was still intensified competition and price discounting in many lines as competitors sought to gain a higher share of the stagnant personal care market. The discounting at the company level was being augmented by inventory liquidation moves at the retail level, as stores combated overstocking and decreases in overall consumer demand (inflation-adjusted). BBI had sold off one of its operating divisions in 2011 to a competitor, resulting in a one-time improvement in its bottom line. Once the impact of this sale was over, however, BBI's profit trends largely mirrored those of the industry.

The overall softening of consumer demand for cosmetics and fragrances resulted in a slowdown in new product development activity throughout the industry. While established firms were moving to secure their market position, Internet-based sales competitors were springing up with new lines of cosmetics produced in Asia that competed effectively with the traditional personal care companies' integrated production and sales models. In response, many of the traditional companies had implemented lean manufacturing programs in the effort to improve their operating margins. This low-cost, low-waste focus was seen as one way to increase the competitive power of a firm because it provided for greater pricing leverage and the ability to purchase market share through pricing policies. The mature nature of the industry was being reflected in increased competition based on price, the predominant role played by Internet start-ups in setting the trends in new product areas, and an overall profit squeeze. Exhibit 3 shows a retail sales analysis for the personal care industry for the years 2009–2012.

The main trends in the personal care industry, then, reflected the fact that the industry was in the mature phase of the industry life cycle. It also reflected a shift away from fragrances to cosmetics and hair products as the primary areas of competition and growth. While the "prestige" products had held their own during this period, the mid-price product lines were hurt as economy-minded consumers traded down to lower priced or generic products. BBI, having a majority of its products in this mid-price range, was particularly challenged by these trends.

Planning and budgeting

Since he assumed the presidency, Mr. Williams had taken steps to formalize some of BBI's administrative processes and procedures. Long-range planning was still done informally at the top corporate level, and the company's long-range goals and strategies were not communicated in detail to all functional managers.

The annual budgeting process, however, involved several levels of management. Budgeting began in mid-July when top management gave each functional area preliminary targets for its operating and capital budgets. Included in this package was a set of other performance measures specific to the function. For example, marketing managers were given preliminary sales growth targets for each of the various categories of existing products, manufacturing managers were given preliminary cost targets by product category, and R&D managers were given cost improvement targets and timetables for the introduction of new products. The functional managers and their subordinates were expected to coordinate their plans with those of other functional managers and to prepare their plans down to the product level. A series of budget reviews was held in October and early November, and final budgets and performance targets were fixed by mid-November.

During the year, formal performance reviews were conducted on a monthly basis. Managers were expected to be able to explain any major variances in actual versus planned performance to a top executive committee. If significant variances were expected to continue, the budgets were revised, although it was understood by all the managers involved that the original budget would be the standard used to evaluate individual manager's performance at year end.

Capital budgeting

Capital budgeting reviews took place in mid-September. Functional managers presented formal capital appropriation requests to a top management committee. For several years the company had published guidelines suggesting that each project being presented should be justified by showing a two-year payback[2] on invested funds. This short-term focus was emphasized on a continual basis given the increasing price and profit squeeze facing the firm. The guidelines for developing and presenting a capital appropriations request were formalized in the budget manual and included the following instructions for 2013:

1. Budgeted capital spending proposals must be guided by the general trends indicated in the operating

[2] A payback period is the period of time required to recoup the investment.

budget, especially as regards unit (volume) growth and new product introduction.

2. Capacity expansion projects should be restricted to those absolutely necessary to achieve 2013 profit and sales goals and objectives. They must also meet the criterion of providing the appropriate economic returns in a timely fashion.
3. Cost reduction projects should be given a high priority. However, serious consideration will be given by corporate to business constraints at the time approval is requested.
4. Spending of a replacement nature should be deferred unless a serious impediment to operations is threatened.
5. Spending for quality improvement should be considered only if the product's marketability is seriously affected.
6. All non-research expenditures related to marketing of new products are to provide an economic justification and reflect approval by the appropriate senior executive.

Incentive compensation

Incentive compensation was provided annually to managers down to the director level in the firm (one organizational level below vice president). In January, after the audit was finalized, a bonus pool was established as a pre-established percentage of corporate net income. In February, just after the annual performance review meetings, a bonus committee, consisting of the top company officers, allocated this pool to individual managers. The evaluations of performance were done subjectively, but based heavily on objective measures of performance.

In normal years, average bonuses for vice presidents were approximately 50% of base salary. In good years, the bonuses could range up to 100% of salary. The average and maximum bonuses for director-level personnel (one level below vice president) were 60% of those for the vice presidents. Formal performance-dependent bonuses were not paid to personnel below the director level.

Cost reduction program

An important part of Mr. Williams's upgrading of BBI's management systems was the implementation of a formal cost-reduction program supported by a lean management philosophy.[3] Cost reductions were deemed to be of two basic types: cost avoidance projects (CAPs) and cost improvement projects (CIPs).

Any project designed to reduce direct materials costs without a related change in existing products or manufacturing processes was designated as a CAP. The company's CAP goal was an annual 5% reduction in materials costs.

CIPs were projects designed to effect cost reductions through process or product changes, such as reformulation of a product to incorporate less expensive ingredients. The company's budgeting manual explained the CIP goal:

> **Each manufacturing location is to develop and implement Cost Improvement Programs (CIPs) as part of their annual budget package. CIPs are specific action programs directed towards a measurable reduction in existing manufacturing cost levels. The annualized savings from these CIPs should be equal to or greater than 5% of the prior year's total cost of goods manufactured, adjusted for the volume and mix changes. The action programs should encompass all factors of manufacturing, including:**
>
> - **all labor costs associated with manufacturing**
> - **all overhead expenses associated with manufacturing**
> - **only those material costs resulting from:**
>   - **reduced usage and improved yields**
>   - **reduced freight-in costs.**

The Purchasing and Value Analysis departments were most directly responsible for identifying CAP projects. R&D and Engineering were the departments who were directly charged with identifying CIP projects. The CIP ideas, however, had to be implemented by the operating manager most directly affected. In most cases, this manager was in manufacturing.

The CIP/CAP projects were expected to achieve a one-year payback where possible. CIP/CAP projects that did not promise to meet this payback criterion were subjected to close scrutiny by Mr. Williams's staff before approval would be granted.

When the cost reduction program was first introduced, the company realized many important and significant cost savings. In recent years, however, the

[3] Managers following a lean management philosophy consider all expenditures of resources for purposes other than creation of value for end customers to be wasteful and, hence, targets for reduction or elimination.

company had not been achieving its cost improvement targets. The targets and actual results of the cost reductions achieved for each of the years 2009–2013 are shown in Exhibit 4.

An example: The A-53 project

Some of the major problems in the cost reduction program can be illustrated by describing one large CIP project called the A-53 project. The A-53 project involved the substitution of an aqueous aerosol, Dymel-152a/Hydrocarbon, for the existing fluorocarbon mixture.

As a liquefied gas propellant, Dymel-152a had obvious safety and quality benefits over the existing compressed gas fluorocarbon being used. Designed for the low-pressure spray that defined perfume propellants, Dymel-152a had a much lower fill pressure when mixed with fragrance concentrate than the currently used compressed gas alternative. This meant that BBI could eliminate the use of bottles with relatively expensive plastic coatings that had been necessary with compressed gas fluorocarbon currently in use. The plastic coating had been required to ensure the bottles' integrity and to pass industry safety standards, such as stability when placed in a warm water bath. The other advantage was that Dymel-152a was less flammable than the current fluorocarbon blend, providing advantages in both safety and in the production procedures that could be used.

BBI and the other firms in the fragrance industry had used fluorocarbons as propellants almost exclusively up until the mid-1970s, when fluorocarbons were banned by the US government because of concerns about their destroying the ozone layer of the atmosphere. The propellant suppliers who had relied on fluorocarbons as their major sources of revenues were severely affected by the ban. Immediately following the ban, these companies aimed much of their research toward developing a new ozone-safe fluorocarbon propellant. One of these improved gases was currently in use at BBI. That being said, hydrocarbons, especially products like Dymel-152a, were still deemed superior in many ways.

Personnel in BBI's R&D department noted the development of Dymel-152a and immediately saw its potential advantages. They tested the new propellant in simulated production settings and found it superior to the propellants being used. Based on these results, they prepared a Capital Appropriation Request, the summary page of which is shown in Exhibit 5. A summary of their investment analysis is shown in Exhibit 6.

On January 14, 2013, BBI's capital appropriations committee met and approved the money for the A-53 project. Mr. Williams's initial reaction to the project was very enthusiastic, as indicated in the memo shown in Exhibit 7. Shortly thereafter, Don Jacobi (VP-R&D) had people in his department draw up specifications for the use of Dymel-152a on the production line. The propellant switchover was scheduled to take place on March 1, 2013.

Right from the start, the A-53 project ran into several serious problems. One problem was a production delay – the implementation could not be effected until the middle of April. More seriously, though, was when Dymel-152a was put into bottles that were not properly filled with fragrance, it became very unstable. The pressure inside the larger bottles then rose from 40 pounds per square inch (psi) to over 200 psi, a level that the larger-sized bottles (2 oz. and larger) without a plastic coating could not always withstand. As a result, quality control had to reject many bottles because of cracking, and several bottles had even exploded while still in the production area.

Review of the A-53 project

In late April 2013, Mr. Williams called a meeting with his top executives to review the problems with the A-53 project.

Don Kelley (VP-Finance) started the meeting by showing the financial picture. As he handed out the analysis, presented in Exhibit 8, he noted:

> Bryant Richards [BBI Controller] has been following this project very closely. He now estimates that because of the problems we are all aware of – the implementation delay, reduced volumes, higher bottle prices, the problems with the large bottles, and the lost labor efficiency – the 2013 savings will be $319,900, down from the original estimate of $599,600. But if we have to write off our inventory of 3¼ oz. bottles, we will actually lose almost $82,000 on this project this year.

Ted Williams (president):

> This is obviously not good news. Who can explain to me why we've missed the forecast so badly? I would like a few clarifications. First, are these labor charges noted as "additional" going to continue? And, what are we planning to do with the 3¼ oz. bottles?

Frank Martin (VP-Operations):

> This project has been a disaster from the beginning. I was involved in this project at the crucial point – implementation. I heard of the proposed switch from our standard fluorocarbon to Dymel-152a from Don [Jacobi, VP-R&D]. He had pinpointed it as his major cost reduction program for the year. Then when it came time to put the plan in action, research dropped the ball – it became the plant's responsibility to implement the project. Research was claiming the cost reduction but taking no leadership role in putting it in place.
>
> R&D insisted that the glass bottles be handled more carefully to minimize the rubbing of one bottle on another. They said that rubbing is weakening the bottles and making them explode more easily. I think we now know that the rubbing has nothing to do with the problem. Some of the R&D engineers just made that excuse up to cover their failures. They didn't have to bear the incremental costs. We bear the costs of the new procedures they have forced us to follow (see Exhibit 9).
>
> I think we have to continue to incur the additional labor costs until we get a new piece of equipment that will check the fill heights of the bottles before they enter the gas house. We've had some exploding bottles, and I have concluded that the safety factor had to come first, so I've had some people visually checking the fragrance levels before we add the Dymel-152a. We estimate that equipment that would automatically eject low fills would cost approximately $25,000 per line, so for our eight lines that would be an additional capital expenditure of $200,000. If we had this equipment, I think we could save the additional labor costs.
>
> Finally, as to the 3¼ oz. bottles, I'm afraid we're facing a direct write-off here. While we may be able to siphon off some of the product into stronger glass bottles, the rework, scrap, and other problems here will undoubtedly result in significant expense. We're still working on this issue, looking for the best answer.

Don Jacobi:

> Really, all this talk about dropping the ball and glass handling is not addressing what I see as our major concern. If production, namely the machine tenders and line personnel followed our specifications, these issues would not come up. We've known that the glass handling techniques were a long-standing problem, but it wasn't critical before. All the new propellant has done is to decrease our margin of error and it has pinpointed operating deficiencies as a result.

These comments brought the meeting to a boiling point, as Frank Martin exploded:

> Boy! It's easy for R&D to point to us as the reason for the glass problems. I've already altered my whole decorating and glass process. But the real problem here is the gas, not the glass-handling techniques or the way my machine operators do their job! You guys in research still don't know how sensitive this propellant is to variations in the concentrate/propellant ratio, yet you're running around changing procedures in the entire plant without first documenting the characteristics of this gas!

Mr. Williams was disturbed by the conflict between individuals in his top management team, so he thought it was best to adjourn the meeting until the next day to allow tempers to cool. He asked each manager to consider not only the key issues of concern in his own area, but also the future prospects of the company and their role in making this current problem an exception rather than a rule. As they left, Ted sat back and wondered once again where his company was going, and why these CIP projects had begun to go sour:

> We have to stop this pattern of failure, whether it is due to implementation problems, lack of adequate testing, or the CIP/CAP concept itself. Where are we really headed? What has gone wrong with the cost reduction program?

Exhibit 1 Better Beauty, Inc., organization chart

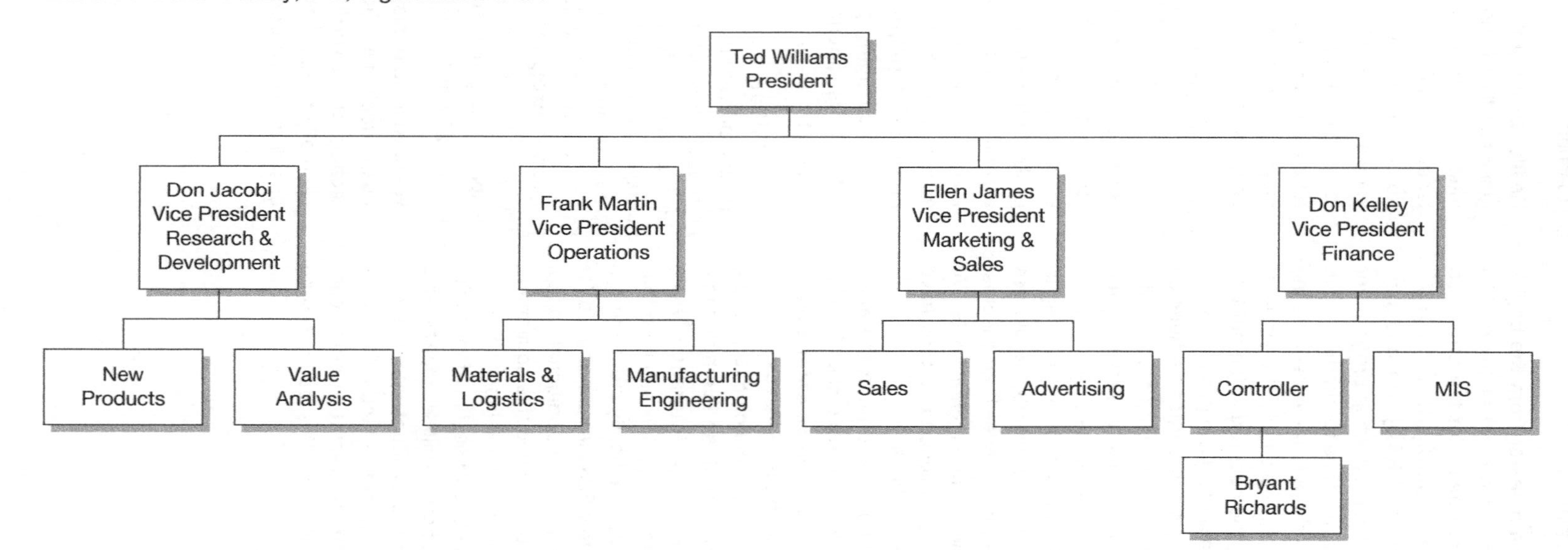

Exhibit 2 Better Beauty, Inc., **Summary Income Statements (in millions)**

	Years Ended December 31						
	2012	2011	2010	2009	2008	2007	2006
Net sales	$1,036.1	$ 991.1	$ 971.9	$1,010.1	$1,025.3	$ 998.6	$ 999.2
Cost of Goods Sold	$ 369.5	$ 341.5	$ 356.0	$ 368.2	$ 379.3	$ 409.1	$ 381.1
Gross Income	$ 666.6	$ 649.6	$ 615.9	$ 641.9	$ 646.1	$ 589.4	$ 618.2
Selling, General & Administrative	$ 292.7	$ 283.1	$ 281.0	$ 318.6	$ 318.2	$ 347.1	$ 618.2
Advertising	$ 203.6	$ 198.9	$ 172.9	$ 195.2	$ 215.3	$ 241.2	$ 217.0
Research & Development	$ 17.9	$ 18.0	$ 17.9	$ 18.2	$ 18.3	$ 18.3	$ 19.6
Profit from Operations	$ 152.5	$ 149.6	$ 144.1	$ 110.0	$ 94.3	$ (17.1)	$ 49.8
Interest expense	$ 0.9	$ 0.5	$ 0.4	$ 1.4	$ 1.5	$ 0.8	$ 4.4
Total Income	$ 153.4	$ 150.1	$ 144.5	$ 111.4	$ 95.8	$ (16.3)	$ 54.2
Interest expense	$ 63.7	$ 67.9	$ 69.8	$ 89.8	$ 102.4	$ 111.6	$ 97.5
Miscellaneous	$ 1.1	$ 0.9	$ 0.4	$ 0.3	$ (0.3)	$ 2.9	$ 6.4
Income taxes	$ 27.6	$ (185.4)	$ 6.2	$ 12.1	$ 5.6	$ 15.1	$ 6.4
Net Income	$ 61.0	$ 266.7	$ 68.1	$ 9.2	$ (11.9)	$ (145.8)	$ (49.4)

Exhibit 3 Better Beauty, Inc., **Retail Sales of Selected Toiletries and Cosmetics (in millions of dollars)**

Products	2009	2010	2011	2012
Hair Products				
Shampoos	$ 2,366.3	$ 2,703.2	$ 2,980.5	$ 3,201.8
Rinses, tints, dyes	$ 904.4	$ 1,014.6	$ 1,454.1	$ 1,697.3
Men's spray & dressings	$ 197.6	$ 189.7	$ 207.8	$ 220.3
Women's hair sprays	$ 872.6	$ 928.3	$ 1,047.1	$ 1,084.6
Home permanent kits	$ 235.5	$ 242.7	$ 266.1	$ 290.9
Hand Products				
Lotions	$ 471.7	$ 518.8	$ 568.2	$ 822.8
Nail polish and enamel	$ 625.4	$ 561.8	$ 601.2	$ 648.5
Cosmetics				
Face creams	$ 1,051.5	$ 1,209.2	$ 1,324.2	$ 1,456.9
Makeup base	$ 1,137.8	$ 1,190.2	$ 1,238.7	$ 1,395.6
Face powder	$ 42.2	$ 260.8	$ 262.0	$ 218.4
Eye makeup	$ 2,823.4	$ 3,490.2	$ 3,411.1	$ 3,701.7
Talc and body powder	$ 138.4	$ 138.4	$ 138.4	$ 145.2
Lipsticks	$ 1,897.8	$ 2,028.4	$ 2,221.5	$ 2,399.2
Liquid facial cleansers	$ 185.5	$ 194.8	$ 408.7	$ 421.0
Fragrance Preparations				
Perfumes	$ 274.8	$ 285.6	$ 300.0	$ 339.4
Toilet water & cologne	$ 1,443.7	$ 1,539.3	$ 1,633.9	$ 2,124.0
Other Toiletries				
Toilet soaps	$ 2,325.2	$ 2,453.9	$ 2,682.9	$ 1,638.8
External personal deodorants	$ 1,463.6	$ 1,710.6	$ 1,844.1	$ 2,034.1
Shaving Products				
Shaving preparations	$ 576.0	$ 615.6	$ 641.1	$ 671.8
After-shave lotions	$ 414.2	$ 455.6	$ 473.8	$ 497.6
Men's cologne	$ 528.1	$ 580.9	$ 633.2	$ 677.6
Shaving accessories	$ 1,749.4	$ 1,909.5	$ 1,942.1	$ 2,112.6

Exhibit 4 Better Beauty, Inc., cost reduction program performance 2009–13

	(in 000s of dollars)				
Cost Reductions	2013	2012	2011	2010	2009
Cost improvement programs:					
Target	$ 4,388	$ 4,452	$ 4,293	$ 4,039	$ 3,752
Actual	$ 2,520*	$ 3,922	$ 4,198	$ 4,049	$ 3,752
Cost avoidance programs:					
Target	$ 3,465	$ 3,528	$ 3,402	$ 3,203	$ 2,982
Actual	$ 3,455*	$ 3,570	$ 3,381	$ 3,203	$ 2,993

* Projected

Exhibit 5

Better Beauty — **CAPITAL APPROPRIATIONS REQUEST**

AR.	M01	956	K
DATE	12/17/12		

1 **CAPITAL CONTROL DATA**

	TOTAL BUDGET	PROJECTS $	CASH (SPENDING)
198—LOCATION BUDGET			
THIS CAR			
CARS TO DATE			

DIVISION ____________

LOCATION ____________

BUDGETED

CAPITAL	Yes	XX	No	XX
P & L IMPACT	Yes	XX	No	XX

VARIANCE

This Project $ ________

Years to Date $ ________

Exchange Rate ________ U.S. $1.00

PROJECT TITLE

2

INVESTMENT IMPACT	**YEARS**	**1**	**2**	**3**	**4**	**5**	**6–10**
With the Project	Sales						
	Net Income A.T.						
Without the Project	Sales						
	Net Income A.T.						
Due to the Project	Sales						
	Net Income A.T.	476.5					
Return on Invest. %		100%					

REASON	C ☒ Cost Reduction (Profit Improvement)	E ☐ Expansion Capacity	Q ☐ Quality Improvement	R ☐ Replacements	S ☐ Safety Security (Regulatory)	O ☐ Other (Specify)______

TYPE	A ☐ Autos	B ☐ Buildings	D ☐ data processing equipment	F ☐ Furniture & Office Equipment	L ☐ Land	M ☐ Machinery And Equipment	O ☐ Other (Specify)______

3 **INVESTMENT SUMMARY**

	AUTHORIZATION	AUDITED ACTUAL
1. FIXED CAPITAL	272,230	
2. WORKING CAPITAL		
3. RELATED EXPENSES (Capitalized)	12,044	
4. TOTAL CAPITAL APPROVAL	284,274	
5. ANNUAL LEASE PAYMENTS NO OF YEARS		
4 **6. TOTAL PROJECT**	392,274	
7. RELATED RETIREMENTS		

8. PAYBACK PERIOD 0.7 YEARS

5 **Description:** Authorization for funds is requested to convert from propane to a **A-53** propellant. With this conversation the first year after tax savings is estimated to be $476,500 due to bulk savings and the elimination of plastic coating on the bottle which was previously required on fills greater than 1 oz. Equipment to handle the new bottles will cost approximately $108,000 and will be purchased through contract with our Tool and Die Supplier. This particular cost is not included in the fixed capital sum of this C.A.R., but it is included in the investment analysis for the return on investment calculations.

6 **APPROVAL**

REGIONS/DIVISIONS/ COUNTRIES	Date			Date	CAPITAL REVIEW BOARD	Date
		Group Contr-oller				
		Group Head				
					Chair-man	

Exhibit 6 Better Beauty, Inc., A-53 project investment analysis

(annualized returns, $000s)	
Material savings	$ 878.8
Additional depreciation	$ (110.3)
Net income before tax	$ 768.6
Tax (38%)	$ 292.0
Net income after tax	$ 476.5
Add: Depreciation	$ 110.3
Net cash generated	$ 586.8
Total Project Expenditures	$ 392.3
Payback period in years	0.7
Return on investment	150%

Exhibit 7 Better Beauty, Inc., president's initial reaction to A-53 project

INTEROFFICE MEMO

DATE: April 14, 2013

TO: Don Kelley [Vice President, Finance]

FROM: Ted Williams [President]

SUBJECT: Cost Reductions

I was delighted to hear from Don that we have certain annual savings of almost $1 million as a result of a new propellant called A-53.

Frank Martin and Don Jacobi are going to make certain this occurs on a timely basis. Please put this down on our list of 2013 savings. Don also believes that we have a prospect to reduce cost on several other products, which on a total savings basis will amount to a lot of money.

Attn: Frank and Don:

Most essential that we find this kind of savings in order to provide the money necessary to build the business in 2013. Please make certain that we take the necessary steps now in order to realize the full effects starting with the end of this year.

Exhibit 8 Better Beauty, Inc., controller's analysis of A-53 project (April 2013)

(000's)	
Original, 2013 lab commitment	$ 586.8
Implementation delayed to April 25th	$ (36.5)
Production volume reduction	$ (54.8)
Material savings below original projection	$ (29.6)
Problems with larger bottles	$ (73.0)
Additional labor costs	$ (73.0)
Net cash flow savings – April revised forecast	$ 319.9
Memo: Inventory exposure (115M pieces of filled 3-1/4 oz. bottles)	$ 401.8

Exhibit 9 Better Beauty, Inc., interoffice memo

Date: April 20, 2013

To: Frank Martin (VP-Operations)

From: Don Jacobi (VP-R&D)

Subject: Revised Glass Handling Techniques

1. Incoming glass shipments from vendor to be pressure-checked by Q.C. as part of incoming inspection procedure.
2. All approved glass receipts released to Container Decorating to be handled in the following manner:
   a. All containers to be removed from corrugated nests, i.e., corrugate nests to be removed from shipping cartons only after all glass has been removed.
   b. Containers to be handled through decorating process avoiding contact with metal edges and minimizing surface contact.
   c. Decorated containers to be placed on lehr belt so as to be able to be packed at discharge end directly off lehr belt avoiding plowing off belt or eliminating need to transfer onto packing belt.
   d. Decorated glass to be spray-coated at discharge end with MYRJ 52S stearate spray being careful to spray only aerosol glass.
   e. All decorated glass to be packed back into corrugate nests, i.e., nests are to be inserted into shipping carton before glass is loaded into carton.
3. In-process pressure checks will be performed by Quality Control after decorating to assure minimum pressure requirements exist in decorated glass. All decorated lots will be released to filling floor based upon those in-process audits.
4. Decorated glass to be handled on filling floor in the following manner:
   a. All containers to be removed from corrugated nests and inserted directly into pucks, i.e., corrugate nests to be removed from shipping cartons only after all glass has been removed.
   b. Containers to be handled through filling process avoiding contact with metal edges and minimizing surface contact prior to cartooning.
   c. Any eight-stage pack must be fully corrugate nested.

This case was prepared by Professors C.J. McNair-Connolly and Kenneth A. Merchant.

CASE STUDY
Fit Food, Inc.

> Our shareholders are demanding better performance from us. Our market valuation has been basically flat for most of the last decade. At the same time, we need to be making larger investments in our future, to develop new products and to augment our sources of organic ingredients. So we need to ratchet up the performance pressure. We need to do better.
>
> *Sean Wright, CEO, Fit Food, Inc.*

Sean made this pronouncement in May 2008 at a management meeting held just after the Fit Food annual shareholders' meeting. The division managers responded to Sean's call to action, but not all of their responses were what Sean had in mind.

The company

Sean Wright founded Fit Food, Inc. (FFI) in 1972. Sean had been working as the VP R&D in a large food company, but he had always wanted to start his own business. In his spare time, he developed a new line of cookies, called "Smart Cookies," that he could advertise as being healthier because they were lower in fat and calories. After many struggles to get Smart Cookies placed in major supermarket chains, by 2000, Sean and his growing team were able to declare proudly that the Smart Cookie brand was being distributed nationally. With more products in development, and taking advantage of the good stock market environment in 2000, Sean launched an FFI IPO. The company's stock was listed on NASDAQ.

By the year 2009, FFI was a medium-sized food company that targeted "tasty-but-healthier" market segments. In 2001, Sean introduced several new snack products and started a Savory Snacks Division. In 2003, he acquired an energy drink company, which became FFI's Sport and Energy Drinks division. By 2009, FFI's annual revenues were approaching $500 million. The company was consistently profitable but heavily leveraged, as Sean had funded the energy-drink acquisition by increasing the company's debt load significantly.

FFI used a divisionalized organizational structure (see Exhibit 1). The general managers of the three relatively autonomous divisions – Cookies & Crackers, Savory Snacks, and Sports & Energy Drinks – reported directly to Sean, the CEO. Each division had its own sales and marketing, production, and R&D departments and a controller. The corporate staff included human resources, MIS, finance, R&D, and legal departments. FFI did not have an internal auditing function. It had outsourced the documentation and testing work needed to comply with the Section 404 requirements of the Sarbanes-Oxley Act. Recently, however, Joe Jellison, FFI's CFO, had suggested that the company was becoming large enough that it should start bringing this work in house.

In 2008, Kristine Trodden was assigned as the external auditing firm partner on the FFI account. Kristine considered FFI not to be a particularly desirable client because of persistent requests to reduce auditing fees amid threats to solicit bids from competing firms.

FFI's board of directors included five members. Sean was the chair. The other outside directors included a small-company CEO, a CFO of a medium-sized public company, a vice president of marketing at a large supermarket chain, and a practitioner in holistic nutrition. All of the outside directors had been suggested by Sean but approved by the board's nominating and governance committee. The board met in person four times a year and also by conference call as needed.

Plans, reviews, and incentives

FFI's planning process began in August when corporate managers sent to each division economic forecasts, other planning assumptions, and preliminary sales targets. The sales targets reflected investor expectations of steady growth. Typically, each division was expected to increase annual revenues and profits by at least 5%.

Over the following two months, division management created formal strategic plans, which included both a strategic narrative and a high-level summary profit and loss statement. The strategic plans were approved by corporate managers in early October. Then division managers developed the elements of their Annual Operating Plans (AOP) for the coming year, which included detailed marketing and new product development plans and pro forma income statements and balance sheets.

Developing the AOPs required many discussions between corporate and division management. The division managers typically argued that they needed to increase their expense budgets to be able to achieve their sales goals, and corporate typically wanted to squeeze expenses to generate increased profits. A fairly standard planning exercise was to ask each division what programs or plans they would cut if their profit budget was cut by 10%. Once these programs were identified, the division managers had to justify adding them back into the budget. Tensions between division and corporate management increased in 2008 because corporate was asking the divisions to increase their growth rates to 7% to allow some new corporate investment initiatives to be funded internally. At the end of the negotiation processes, the AOPs were presented to the board of directors for approval at its meeting held in early December.

During the year, performance review meetings were held quarterly. The focus of the meetings tended to be on explaining variances between revenue and profit performance goals and actual performance. The meetings were quick and painless when performance matched or exceeded expectations, but the tone was dramatically different when the quarterly profit goals were not achieved. Catherine Elliott (marketing manager, Cookies & Crackers Division) explained:

> **Corporate pushes us hard to make our numbers. There is never a good reason for not making our goals. We're paid to be creative and come up with solutions, not excuses. Sean calls it "no excuses management."**

Division presidents and their direct management reports could earn annual bonuses based on achievement of AOP profit targets. The target bonuses ranged from 25% to 100% of the manager's base salary, depending on organization level. No bonuses were paid if division profits fell below 85% of AOP plans. Maximum bonuses of 150% of the target bonus amounts were paid if profits exceeded AOP by 25%. Average bonuses exceeded target bonus levels in seven of the first eight years of FFI's history as a public corporation.

Some corporate managers and division presidents were also included in a stock option plan. FFI stock had performed well in the early 2000s, but virtually all of the gains were lost in the stock market downturn of 2008–2009. Most of the options were underwater.

The recession of 2008–2009 stressed company operations at the same time that Sean was calling for better financial performance. The Savory Snacks Division performed well and achieved the higher growth rates called for in both 2008 and 2009. The other two divisions experienced more challenges, however, as is explained below. (Summary income statements for these divisions are shown in Exhibit 2.)

Sports & Energy Drink Division

The Sports & Energy Drinks Division (Drink Division) was formed in 2003 when FFI acquired a successful, regional energy drink brand. As part of the deal, Jack Masters, the former CEO of the acquired company, became president of the division. Performance in the first few years after the acquisition was good. The targeted drink categories continued to grow; two brand extensions were successfully launched; and Drink Division sales nearly doubled between 2003 and 2006. The division achieved its AOP profit targets easily, and Jack was able to operate without much interference from corporate.

By early 2007, however, Jack saw some clouds on the horizon. The energy drink category was becoming more and more competitive as more players, including some large, well-capitalized corporations, entered the category. At the same time, retailers were consolidating and becoming more powerful, increasing pressure on manufacturers to lower prices. Jack began to worry that he might not be able to deliver the growth that was expected of his division.

2007

Despite Jack's worries, 2007 was another stellar year, with sales growth exceeding even Sean's increased expectations. The category momentum continued, and Jack's brands gained market share, due in part to a successful grassroots advertising campaign.

With performance far exceeding the AOP targets and excellent bonuses assured for the year 2007, Jack thought it would be prudent to try to position the division for success in the future. He met with his management team to discuss his concerns and to come up with ideas to get better control over reported profits. Jack and his team decided on three courses of action. The first was to declare a shipping moratorium at the end of the year, which shifted some sales that would normally have been recorded in 2007 into 2008.

Not all of Jack's managers were happy with the shipping-moratorium plan of action. The production team was unhappy because the moratorium would cause scheduling problems. Some employees would have to be furloughed temporarily at the end of the year to minimize the buildup in inventory. Then, in early 2008, they would have to incur some overtime costs both to accelerate production and to ship the orders that had accumulated. The sales department was concerned that they would have to deal with customer complaints about shipment delays and product outages. Nevertheless, Jack decided to move forward with the shipping moratorium regardless of the costs, which he considered relatively minor.

The second plan was to build up accounting reserves against accounts receivable and inventory balances. In 2007, the Drink Division controller was able to provide a justification for increasing reserves by $1 million over 2006 levels.

The third plan was to prepay some expenses that would have normally been incurred in 2008. Among other things, some facility maintenance programs were accelerated, and supplies inventories were replenished before the end of the year. These items were not material, amounting to expenditures of only about $100,000. But, as Jack noted, "Every little bit helps."

2008

In 2008, some of Jack's fears were realized. As the economy slowed down, consumers became more frugal. The once-exploding energy drink category began to stagnate; competition for market share grew fierce; and margins declined. In addition, there were rumblings of an impending soft drink "obesity" tax that could put even more pressure on profits.

The division was able to make its annual revenue targets in 2008, but the division managers did so by offering an "early order program" developed by the Sales and Marketing Department. Customers were offered discounts and liberal payment terms if they placed orders scheduled to be delivered before the year ended. Discounts ranged from 5% to 20% and customers were given 120 days to pay their invoices without incurring interest, rather than the traditional 30 days. However, Jack learned later that some of the more aggressive salespeople had told customers to accept the shipments now and "just pay us whenever you sell the product."

While sales remained strong, profit margins decreased significantly. In order to make sure the division would hit its AOP profit target, Jack and his controller began to liquidate some of its accounting reserves in the third quarter, and by the end of the year, the reserves were reduced by a total of $1.7 million. The auditors noticed and questioned the change, and brought it to the attention of Joe Jellison, FFI's CFO. Joe looked into the issue and concluded that the new reserve levels seemed justified based on historical performance levels.

2009

Sales started out slowly in 2009, but in the second quarter, the sales team landed a major new national account. Because of the uptake in demand, Jack had now become more concerned about meeting production schedules than he was about achieving sales goals. Thus, the early order program and almost all other promotions and discounts were eliminated.

Jack also told his controller to rebuild reserves, and a total of $2 million in reserves were restored in 2009. Once again the auditors questioned the change, but the controller provided a justification based on uncertainty in the economy and irregularities in some new customers' payment patterns, Jack believed that his division was well positioned for success going into 2010.

Cookies & Crackers Division

The Cookies & Crackers Division (Cookie Division) was built around the "Smart Cookie" product, once FFI's flagship brand. But the Smart Cookie product had been struggling for the last several years. Cookies was a low-growth, low-margin product category with a strong private label presence, though quality health-oriented brands commanded a small price premium. The biggest problem for the Cookie Division, however, was a shift in consumer mindset. In recent years, "healthy" was less likely to be associated with low fat, and more likely to be associated with healthful ingredients such as whole grains, nuts, and natural antioxidants, a trend that the Cookie Division management had largely missed.

Scott Hoyt, the Cookie Division president, had been with FFI since its inception. Scott had a strong background in sales and was credited with selling Smart

Cookie to national accounts, but he was perceived as resistant to change, and his accounting and finance knowledge was relatively weak.

The Cookie Division traditionally relied heavily on a variety of seasonal trade promotions to achieve their volume targets. By 2008, Catherine Elliott, head of the Marketing Department, was concerned that the new required 7% growth rate was probably not attainable without both some aggressive marketing and development of some good new products. During the annual planning process, she made a case for increasing the division's advertising and new product development budgets, but her requests were denied. Sean explained that he did not think the advertising was necessary. He also believed that the projects being funded at the corporate level would yield better returns than the proposed investments in Cookies, and FFI could not afford both investments.

2008

It became obvious early in the first quarter of 2008 that Cookie sales were falling well below the levels forecast in the AOP. The Cookie sales department initiated a promotion to meet the first quarter goals. The specifics of the program were similar to those of the early order program being used in the Drink Division – generous discounts and extended payment terms for early orders. The early order program was implemented aggressively. The sales team was told to contact all of their customers and convince them to take early delivery of product. Many of these contacts were successful. In most cases, the sales staff received written authorization from their customers, but in some cases the authorizations were only verbal.

In the final days of the first quarter, Catherine and Mitch Michaels, head of the Sales Department, asked shipping to work around the clock to ship as much product as possible before the quarter end. In the last hours of the quarter, trucks filled with cookies drove a few blocks away from the loading docks and parked, so that product was technically "shipped" and sales could be booked.

The heavy sales volume at the end of the quarter attracted the auditors' attention. They concluded, however, that the accounting treatment conformed to GAAP (generally accepted accounting principles) since ownership of the product officially changed at the time of shipment.

In the second quarter of 2008, Scott, Catherine, and Mitch knew they had a problem. Second-quarter orders were predictably slow given the amount of extra product that had been shipped in the first quarter. The three managers then decided to ship additional, unordered product to their customers. The additional order volumes were generated either by increasing the quantities of actual orders or by entering orders into the company's billing system twice. When customers complained about the unordered shipments, blame was attributed to human errors, and the sales team was charged with the task of making the unordered shipments "stick." They were offered a number of tools toward that end, such as special pricing and credit terms and product exchanges.

The program worked surprisingly well. Returns increased, but the program still effectively increased revenue by $2.3 million and profit by $460,000. Scott, Catherine, and Mitch were encouraged by the results and praised the sales team for their heroic efforts. They continued the program throughout 2008, being careful to rotate the "mistaken" shipments between customers. At the end of the year, the team managed to deliver 97% of the AOP sales and profits.

2009

During the 2009 AOP process, Scott, along with Catherine and Mitch, made a strong plea to reduce the Cookie Division's revenue goals. They argued that given the weak economy and sluggish category growth, a flat revenue goal, or at most 2% growth, was a more reasonable target. However, Sean was unwilling to lower the goal. He understood the difficulties in the category, but he believed that the setting of aggressive goals and a commitment to achieve them were cornerstones of FFI's success over the years, and he knew that FFI shareholders would be demanding better performance than that.

After the disappointing AOP meeting, Scott called a meeting with his management team to develop new ideas for increasing sales. He thought if the division could make it through 2009 successfully, they would face smoother sailing in 2010 because some new, promising products would be ready for launching. A decision was made to continue the programs used in 2008.

Irene Packard, head of the Production Department, came up with another idea. She thought she could decrease expenses significantly by rewriting contracts with suppliers who supplied both machines and parts. If she could convince suppliers to decrease the costs of parts, and charge the difference to machines, she would be able to capitalize costs that would otherwise have been expensed. Irene estimated that she could reduce expenses by $2.3 million, or $2 million after depreciation. Scott thought this was a good idea. He noted that the cost savings could bring them within striking range of the division's profit goals.

In September, however, one of the junior accountants in the division was feeling unduly pressured to make accounting entries that she felt were not good practice, particularly related to some of the billings that seemed to lack adequate supporting documentation. The managers' justifications for these entries seemed to her to be capricious rather than facts-based. She took it upon herself to discuss the issue with Joe Jellison, FFI's CFO. Joe had one of his assistant controllers examine the accounting practices in the Cookie Division, and he reported finding multiple problems with potentially material financial statement effects. Joe had to decide what to do next. Should he have his people calculate the size of the errors, make the adjusting entries, and fix the processes, or should he, at this point, inform the external auditors and/or the audit committee of the board of directors?

Exhibit 1 Fit Food, Inc.: Organization chart

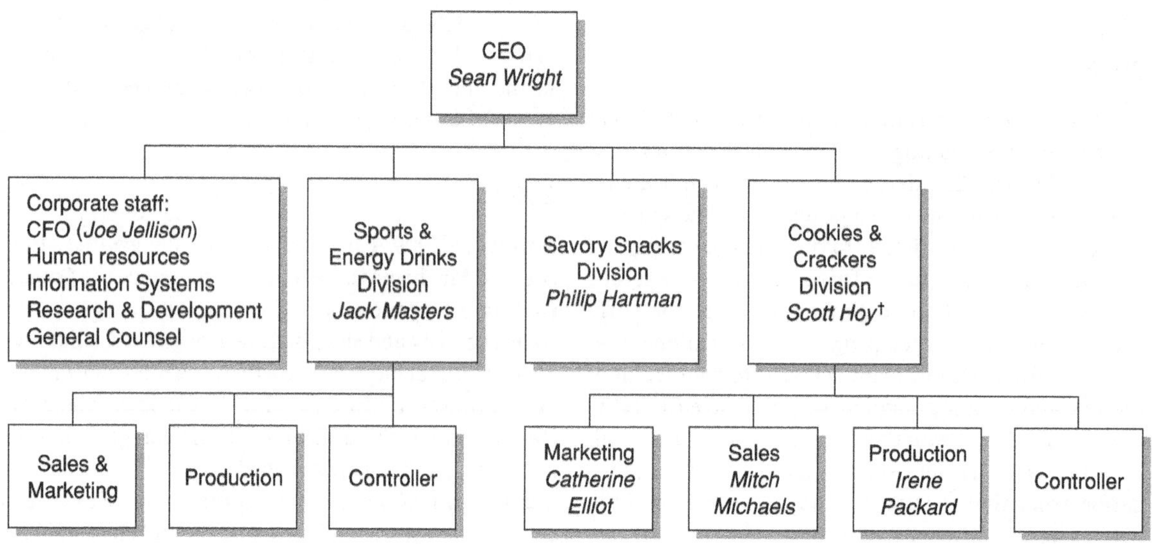

Exhibit 2 Fit Food, Inc.: Income statements for Sports & Energy Drinks and Cookies & Crackers Divisions, FYs ending December 31 ($ millions)

Sports & Energy Drinks Division						
	2007		2008		2009	
	AOP	Actual	AOP	Actual	AOP	Actual
Revenue	$110.0	$125.3	$130.3	$130.5	$137.0	$146.2
Cost of goods	64.0	73.6	75.5	76.6	79.5	87.5
Gross margin	$46.0	51.7	54.8	53.9	57.5	58.7
R&D expense	0.8	1.0	1.0	0.8	1.1	1.0
SG&A expense	18.0	20.0	20.0	19.2	21.0	22.0
Operating Profit	$28.2	30.7	33.8	33.9	35.4	35.7

Cookies & Crackers Division						
	2007		2008		2009	
	AOP	Actual	AOP	Actual	AOP	Actual
Revenue	$130.0	124.5	131.0	127.3	133.0	127.1
Cost of goods	80.6	77.2	81.2	80.2	82.5	76.7
Gross margin	$49.4	47.3	49.8	47.1	50.5	50.4
R&D expense	0.4	0.3	0.4	0.3	0.4	0.3
SG&A expense	20.8	18.8	20.0	18.3	19.0	19.2
Operating profit	$28.2	28.2	29.4	28.5	31.1	30.9

This case was prepared by Professor Kenneth A. Merchant and research assistant Michelle Spaulding.

CASE STUDY
Atlantis Chemical Industries

In late 2011, managers at Atlantis Chemical Industries (Atlantis) were debating whether the company's management systems needed to be changed in response to a major strategic shift that the company was making. The strategic shift involved a significant redeployment of assets away from commodity chemical businesses and toward the discovery of new technologically advanced products that promised higher margins and growth rates.

James Rockman, corporate senior vice president of R&D and chief scientist, was an outspoken critic of the company's current management systems:

> **Our system of evaluating performance based on short-term financial results has trained our operating managers not to take risks. They will not bet on a horse until the race is almost finished and the horse is leading. They tend to think only about the current year's profits, and that is natural because they are rewarded for only incremental improvements. They are penalized for missing budget targets but do not get big rewards for going way over plan.**

Others, however, defended the company's systems, which, they noted, had served the company well over the years. They noted that Atlantis was making large investments in R&D despite the need to maintain a solid earnings record. They were convinced that scientists' natural optimistic biases had to be tempered by a business-oriented focus on the projects' potential for commercial success. These managers suggested that people with market knowledge should be involved intensively and early when new R&D investments were being considered to increase the likelihood that R&D efforts lead to commercial success.

Since the intensity and rancor of the debate had been increasing, it was decided to put this issue on the agenda for discussion at the December 2011 meeting of Atlantis' Executive Committee.

Company background

Atlantis, headquartered in Indianapolis, Indiana, was a large, publicly listed corporation engaged in developing, manufacturing, and marketing a broad range of high-quality chemicals and materials. Its sales reached $6.9 billion in 2010, and it employed 42,000 people in 100 countries.

In 2011, the company had six operating companies (see Exhibit 1 for a partial corporate organization chart). The largest group was Atlantis Chemical Company, the original business, which still accounted for about 50% of total corporate sales.

The Atlantis Agricultural Company, the second-largest group, accounted for 17% of total sales. As shown in Exhibit 1, the Agricultural Company had two operating divisions, Crop Chemicals and Animal Sciences. The Crop Chemicals Division was a leading worldwide producer of herbicides. The Animal Sciences Division focused on animal nutrition and growth products, only a few of which had already been introduced to the market. Exhibit 2 provides summary financial data about these two divisions.

The strategic shift toward faster-growing markets, away from the commodity chemicals that had historically provided most of the company's sales and profits, started in 2005. The 2010 Annual Report stated that:

> **Atlantis is determined to be a leader in its chosen markets, but we must deliver results in the short term as well as generate the resources needed for the coming decades. We will achieve this by aggressively managing good businesses, by inventing and licensing new products that meet customer needs, and by moving out of businesses that prove unable to meet targets.**

One of these targets was explicitly mentioned in both the 2009 and 2010 letters from the CEO to the shareholders: "For the shareholders ... this promise means aiming for a return on equity year after year in the 20% range."

Planning and budgeting

Atlantis used two distinct planning cycles, long-range planning and annual budgeting. The long-range plan, which covered a horizon of 10 years, projected growth rates for operating income, working capital, R&D, and fixed assets for each planning entity.

In June, after senior managers had reviewed and approved the long-range plan, they sent the guidelines contained in the long-range projections to the operating units. The managers of the operating units would then start preparing the following fiscal year's budget (which coincided with the calendar year). The corporate philosophy was that budgets should reflect stretch targets having approximately a 50% chance of being achieved. During October and November, the budgets the operating units submitted were consolidated and presented to, scrutinized by, and negotiated with, senior management. In December, senior management, and then the board of directors, approved the final budget.

Performance measurement

The operating units' primary financial measures of performance were (1) net income, (2) return on capital employed (ROCE), and (3) net cash flow. Net income was defined as operating income less corporate charges, interest, and taxes. ROCE was computed as net income plus after-tax interest expenses divided by average capital employed. Net cash flow was calculated by a formula that adjusted the net income number to reflect actual cash uses and sources (e.g. depreciation, capital expenditures). These measures were intended to reflect the performance of each business unit as if it were a stand-alone company.

The weightings of importance among these measures could vary from year to year, depending on the areas that corporate management identified as critical for each operating unit to focus on. For example, the emphasis on cash flow was higher in the commodity chemical businesses, and that emphasis had been increasing in recent years.

Quarterly performance review meetings focused, in part, on reports comparing actual results to date with budget. Quarterly review meetings were also an opportunity for the managers of the operating units to give an update on any ongoing strategic initiatives, as well as to report any issues affecting the business. The budget served as the basis for incentive compensation and promotions.

Incentive compensation

Atlantis had used a formal annual Performance Incentive Plan (PIP) since 2004. The first step in determining the PIP bonuses was to calculate the size of the bonus pool. This was done by comparing corporate net income with the target set as part of the annual budgeting process. If corporate net income fell below 90% of target, the bonus pool was zero. If performance exceeded the targets by a significant margin, the pool could be as large as 8–10% of corporate net income.

Second, the CEO would provide recommendations regarding allocations of the bonus pool to each profit center to the Compensation Committee of the Board of Directors. These recommendations were based on how well each operating unit in terms of its three financial measures, which were weighted in importance, as compared to its financial targets.

Finally, the bonuses were allocated to individual employees. The employee's job level determined the maximum percentage of salary that could be paid out as bonus, although the CEO could grant exceptions in unusual circumstances. The actual allocation depended on the degree of attainment of annual personal goals. Typically, bonuses for division managers did not exceed 50% of their base salary.

The PIP established that the bonuses would be paid two-thirds in cash and one-third in restricted stock. The restrictions on the company stock continued until Atlantis' total shareholder returns performed at least as well as the average of the Standard & Poor's 500 companies for a subsequent three-year period.

In 2005, the Board approved a new Long-Term Incentive Plan (LTIP). Pursuant to the LTIP, incentive payments depended on the corporation's achieving its goals for earnings per share and ROCE over overlapping three-year performance cycles. The first performance cycle was 2006–2008. However, because of the severe recession that began in 2008, corporate performance had not reached the goals stated in the LTIP, so no payment of long-term awards had been made.

Research and Development Process

As an aid in managing its sizable R&D effort, Atlantis classified R&D activities into three categories. Class I was dedicated to maintaining existing businesses and the supply of technical services. Class II included efforts to expand business assets and markets and to reduce costs of existing processes. Class III activities focused on developing new products. Exhibit 3 illustrates how the company had been increasingly moving its emphasis from Class I to Class III R&D activities, reflecting a growing focus on the introduction of new products.

R&D activities in Class III normally went through three phases of development before commercialization. The first phase began when scientists discovered a new product lead. In biotechnology, a major R&D thrust, this phase involved the major technical efforts to isolate the specific gene responsible for the biological phenomenon under study (e.g. the gene responsible for growth in human cells, for disease resistance in plant cells, or for production of a certain hormone). Once the gene had been isolated, the process of duplicating it in a laboratory setting was greatly facilitated. Laboratory duplication still involved gene splicing techniques, but Atlantis scientists had leading expertise in this area. The first phase of research for new product development could take two or three years to be completed. If successful, it generated a new probe.

The second phase of discovery involved applying the new technical concept or probe to the development of a new product candidate. The discovery phase of R&D was the most technically challenging, and it could take as long as four years. Only if this phase was satisfactorily completed would the R&D activity constitute an ongoing project.

In the third phase, R&D for a new product became a multi-year project focused on commercial and regulatory issues. On the commercial side for biotechnology products, the emphasis was on defining delivery systems (e.g. spray, tablet, or injection), creating marketing programs, and minimizing production costs. On the regulatory side, the tests involved meeting all safety and clinical standards set by regulatory agencies until the product was finally approved for consumer use. Compared with the two other stages, the third stage of development was by far the most expensive and also the longest, often taking five years or more to complete.

R&D costs typically increased sharply as development moved closer to the testing stage for commercial applications. As John Dover, R&D director of the Animal Sciences Division, noted: "It is at least ten times cheaper to discover a new concept than to make it into a product."

Decentralization of R&D activities and assignment of costs

An R&D decentralization study conducted in 2008 concluded that the company should continue to conduct R&D activities in emerging fields, such as biotechnology, at the corporate level, but that the operating units should undertake an increasing role in the effort. As a result, Atlantis management started a major effort to place as much of the R&D activity as possible directly under the control of the operating unit whose business would benefit from the R&D investment. The general managers in charge of the operating units would become responsible for their unit's R&D activities and costs.

The study also developed better bases for further assigning corporate R&D costs to the operating units. Until 2008, for example, most of the R&D costs associated with biotechnology were fully retained at the corporate level; but after the changes, a larger part of these costs were assigned to the operating units.

By 2010, the R&D staffs at the operating unit level were capable of performing most types of R&D activities that were based primarily on existing technologies. When it came to developing new biotech-based technology, however, they were still dependent on corporate R&D. Corporate R&D also provided the operating units some support services, such as bioprocess research and use of analytical laboratories and an information center, on a fee-for-service basis.

Exhibit 4 shows where Atlantis' R&D costs were incurred. The operating units directly controlled about 80% of total R&D costs. Corporate R&D controlled the remaining 20% of total R&D costs, 10% of which was retained at corporate level in 2010 and the other 10% of which was charged back to the operating units, either on a fee-for-service basis (9%) or as an allocation based on net investment (1%). As shown in Exhibit 4, there was a marked increase in the extent of costs charged on a fee basis to the operating units between 2009 and 2010.

The R&D costs retained at corporate related to basic research, which served primarily the chemical and agricultural companies, and within the latter, the Animal Sciences Division. The returns from most corporate R&D investments were quite uncertain. It could be a decade or more between the time of initial investments and the completion of tests required to obtain final regulatory approvals. The regulator demanded extensive, multiyear trials to guarantee that the product would not adversely affect safety when consumed by humans. Most projects also presented significant risks on other dimensions, including technological uncertainties, potential competition from other chemical companies, and the inherent financial hazards associated with substantial investments. As Ron Stovall, controller for the Agricultural Company, explained:

> With many of our projects, we will probably have to invest several hundred million dollars before we have a commercial product. A product has to be a real commercial hit to pay off such major investments. Biotechnology is the highest risk this company has ever taken.

The operating units were not charged for R&D in emerging areas for two main reasons. One was that much of this kind of research was generic. It potentially benefitted several operating units simultaneously. For instance, research on technology for gene splitting could benefit product lines in either agriculture or healthcare and possibly other businesses in ways that were difficult to anticipate.

The other reason for retaining control over biotechnology expenditures at the corporate level was that this investment was crucial for the company's long-term future, and there was a concern that these R&D investments should not be entrusted to the operating units, which operated under short-term pressure. As James Rockman explained:

> Corporate can't afford to fund all the R&D efforts alone. We need to push these costs down to the operating groups that generate enough cash flow to sustain these major investments. The ideal would be for corporate to engage only in the very basic research and to hand a project to the respective operating unit as soon as it reaches a stage when we can start talking about commercialization. The problem is that I have to be sure that there are enough people at the operating level who are really interested in the project. Otherwise, they will cut the R&D funding for the project as soon as they start to feel budget pressure. Operating managers often like to treat R&D expenditures as variable costs.

Effect of profit pressures on R&D

When the consolidated initial budget submissions from the operating units did not reach the corporate profit objectives, as was usual, senior management had to negotiate revisions with the operating unit managers. In December 2009, for example, Greg O'Connor, Atlantis' chairman and CEO, had to raise most operating entities' profit budget targets for 2010 as well as to cut some corporate expense budgets. The operating managers had the discretion to decide how the profit increases would be achieved (e.g. through sales promotions, reductions in the cost of goods sold, or cuts in R&D expenditures).

The corporate R&D group, which was operated as a cost center, was affected. James Rockman had to reduce the 2010 budget for corporate R&D from nearly $93 million to $90.5 million. Exhibit 5 shows the final breakdown of the 2010 R&D budget by cost category.

Most of the operating units also concluded that they had to reduce their R&D budgets to meet the tougher bottom-line targets. For example, John Pastor, president of Atlantis Agricultural Company, reduced his R&D budget by $15 million to a total of $135 million (about 12% of sales). The Agricultural Company divisions—Crop Chemicals and Animal Sciences—in turn revised their R&D budgets to adjust to the new targets. As was his practice, however, Pastor kept a reserve in his budget. This reserve could be used either for important purposes not foreseen at the time the budget was finalized or to cover budget overruns by his operating managers.

When deciding which R&D projects to cut, Pastor, in consultation with his operating managers, considered several aspects of the future potential of the projects in progress. A primary criterion was the level of capital requirements and how they affected the total portfolio of projects. He also assessed qualitative aspects, such as the probability of technological success, the total market potential for the new product, the market share that Atlantis could expect, and the regulatory requirements for final approval. He based his judgments on reports from the operating managers. Current projects, being closer to completion, usually had priority over new ones, which typically represented higher risks to the company.

In his original 2010 budget, Itzhak Rubenstein, general manager of the Animal Sciences Division, submitted a budget proposing additions of 25% in technology expenses. John Pastor vetoed the additions because he felt that, to meet his financial goals, he could not afford any more increases. The Agricultural Company had spent more than 12% of sales on R&D in 2008, and corporate had asked for tighter control over these costs. As a consequence, the Animal Sciences Division was asked to limit its R&D expenditures to a maximum of 50% of its sales. Exhibit 6 shows that even after these budget cuts, the Animal Sciences Division had $35 million in losses in 2009 and a budget of $43 million in losses for 2010.

During the fiscal year, if division managers wanted to spend more on R&D than budgeted, they would first have to consult with their company's president before making any commitments. On the other hand, if the operating managers had unexpected gains during the year, they could negotiate to invest the additional income in projects beyond the original R&D budget, as long as the financial performance targets were met and the actions taken did not result in permanent additions to R&D expense (e.g. people).

Funding new R&D projects

Generally, the closer a project was to the commercialization stage, the more the operating unit bore its costs. However, in the case of pioneering R&D projects, which required developing new technologies, corporate R&D funded the projects directly, with no charges to the operating units. In 2010, for instance, corporate R&D budgeted $42.9 million in R&D costs that it would retain – under the control of James Rockman – to fund new product discovery (Exhibit 6).

There was considerable discussion among the operating units about the use of corporate resources for a centralized R&D effort. The managers in the chemical businesses often felt that corporate management rejected their capital requests and favored the divisions engaged in, particularly, biotechnology research. Some Atlantis Chemical Company managers, who generated substantial cash flow from their mature businesses, had been known to wish secretively that biotechnology efforts would fail so that corporate R&D would release more resources for them to invest in their own businesses.

Some managers of the growing businesses also were critical of the commitment of funds to corporate R&D efforts. They would have preferred to fund and manage R&D, even the technically sophisticated biotechnology discovery efforts, with their own resources. They argued that only with direct responsibility for R&D could they ensure that the projects being worked on were commercially relevant.

James Rockman felt differently, however. He commented on the need for managing emerging technologies such as biotechnology at the corporate level:

> **Operating managers have a strong incentive to think short term, to focus on this year's income, rather than the long-term potential of some R&D investments. If left on their own to fund innovative and risky R&D projects, they would simply choose not to. We could possibly change this short-term focus, or myopia, if we were willing to deemphasize budgets, but we don't seem to want to do that.**

General controversies about R&D funding

Atlantis' chairman/CEO, Greg O'Connor, was personally committed to making the company a leader in biotechnology, but he was also under pressure from the financial community to ensure that Atlantis would report adequate earnings-per-share growth. O'Connor commented on the balance that must be struck between profit goals and R&D requirements:

> **We keep telling scientists that we're in business for the pursuit of products, not knowledge. At the end of the line, everything has to turn into a product. Unless we sell products, nothing happens. But I also know that good research doesn't happen overnight. I tell researchers I pray for patience every night—and I want it right now.**

Greg O'Connor maintained that overfunding is one of the primary mistakes to avoid in industrial R&D:

> **If I look back on the research mistakes we have made, it was usually due to overfunding. If we agree to pay $25 million over three years to see the first tangible accomplishment, and after that time we don't get it, I don't want that project any more. But once the project has surfaced and has gotten up there, it is in the annual report, and it is hard to admit failure.**

Greg and other corporate managers were particularly concerned about the net unallocated R&D cost retained at the corporate level. This was the number that would become part of external reports and that would be closely monitored by the financial analyst community. Atlantis, with a reputation for making sound investments in R&D, wanted to ensure investors would not draw the erroneous impression that R&D expenditures were getting out of control just because more R&D was being funded at the corporate level.

Atlantis had to discontinue a few projects after years of R&D investments because they failed at the commercialization stage. One example occurred in 2008, when a significant project focused on development of a plant growth regulator was terminated. In general, however, the whole area of genetically engineered plants had yielded very impressive scientific progress. The Crop Chemicals Division, for example, had developed some plants that were genetically resistant to common diseases without the need for herbicides.

Itzhak Rubenstein (general manager of the Animal Sciences Division) commented on how the uncertainty associated with R&D exacerbated the conflict among the various objectives he had to face:

> On the one hand, I am supposed to invest in the long run and keep developing new products. I already spend 50% of my total revenues on R&D. But I also have a long-run target to reach a 20% return on equity, and I'm running sizable losses now. So I need to be very careful when allocating current resources. I wish we had a system to evaluate the commercial potential of new R&D investments more thoroughly. Some people believe that if you do good science, the market will follow, but it's not always true.

The corporate R&D group maintained close contact with the operating units to assess the new products' potentials for commercial success. One alternative for increasing discussions of commercial viability earlier in the R&D funding process was to form a commercial development group reporting directly to the CEO (at the same level of authority as Corporate R&D). This commercial group would get involved in all decisions about which research projects to fund. It would raise considerations about market needs, the company's marketing competitive advantages, and assessment of competitive products at the earliest possible stages of the R&D process. Another alternative was to place a commercial staff function at the operating unit level, reporting to the operating general manager. The managers who defended this suggestion asserted that the operating unit was the most knowledgeable about specific customer needs and maintained relationships with possible distribution channels thus being in the best position to assess market potential for new products.

R&D personnel were generally opposed to either of the aforementioned alternatives. They argued that if Atlantis allowed commercial emphasis to interfere with R&D projects at too early a stage, it would thwart most of its opportunities for innovation. As John Dover, director of R&D for Animal Sciences, commented:

> The people responsible for current products are the ones who bring in the cash so that they are also the ones with the most power. The people who do exploratory R&D have very little bargaining power. It is obvious that today's products will always get the division manager's attention. Potential products just don't provide enough motivation.

Other managers defended the current system. Will Carpenter, R&D director in the Crop Chemicals Division, argued that:

> R&D can't be an end in itself. It is a means to get new products so that you can keep growing. But one will always need the financial discipline of controlling costs. And good financial controls are not incompatible with good R&D; they actually force us managers to establish priorities and focus our development efforts in products with the highest potential.

The multiyear nature of R&D projects posed some special financial problems. Some R&D people criticized the current process of annual R&D budgets. John Dover explained:

> All my projects have at least a four-year horizon. Yet, it seems that every year I have to justify myself by asking for funding. What am I supposed to do if I don't get funding for my projects? Why don't they give me funding for four years?

The assignment of corporate R&D costs also was problematic. In 2010, for example, there was considerable debate about how Atlantis would fund the maintenance of the corporate bioprocess development facility, which conducted basic research for several operating units. As stated in the 2010 first quarter report, the Atlantis Life Sciences Research Center, which housed the bioprocess development facility, was "one of the largest and most sophisticated facilities in the world devoted to understanding the chemistry and biology of life." This $150 million facility was dedicated in 2007 and employed approximately 1,200 scientists and support personnel. Until 2010, the bioprocess development facility had been conducting research related to several projects that were later handed over to the operating units. Yet, the problem remained about how corporate R&D would allocate the costs of that facility. The Animal Sciences Division, which typically had used more than half of the bioprocess development facility's capacity, now had fewer projects in progress, and its managers argued that they should pay only for the facility costs directly related to its own projects. From a corporate perspective, however, the facility had to be fully maintained in a state of readiness because Atlantis was deeply committed to biotechnology research and the company had to keep its scientists motivated and fully occupied. The company could not afford to have its scientists sit idle or leave when there was not enough volume to keep the facility fully operative. After several rounds of negotiations, corporate R&D, after curtailing other important research projects, decided to absorb the bioprocess development facility costs that could not be charged to the operating units on a fee-for-service basis.

Don Pattison, the controller for corporate R&D, wondered how the operating unit managers' increasing influence on R&D expenditures would affect the balance between the short-term pressure to meet the annual budget targets and the long-term need to invest in R&D:

> **Does increasing operating unit influence on our key R&D growth programs enhance or mitigate our chances of meeting our goal of becoming an industry leader in innovative, high-quality products? I know there is pressure to level off our R&D spending across the company, including corporate R&D. We have got to make sure we get more bang for our R&D buck in terms of prioritizing those efforts to go after the most promising commercial opportunities if we are going to achieve our new product goals. How can we be sure we have the right incentive system in place so that the operating managers will prioritize these efforts toward increased commercial success?**

These questions reflected senior management's concern about whether Atlantis had a problem in the way it funded R&D. If there was really a problem, what changes should be made to the company's management systems?

Exhibit 1 Partial corporate organization chart

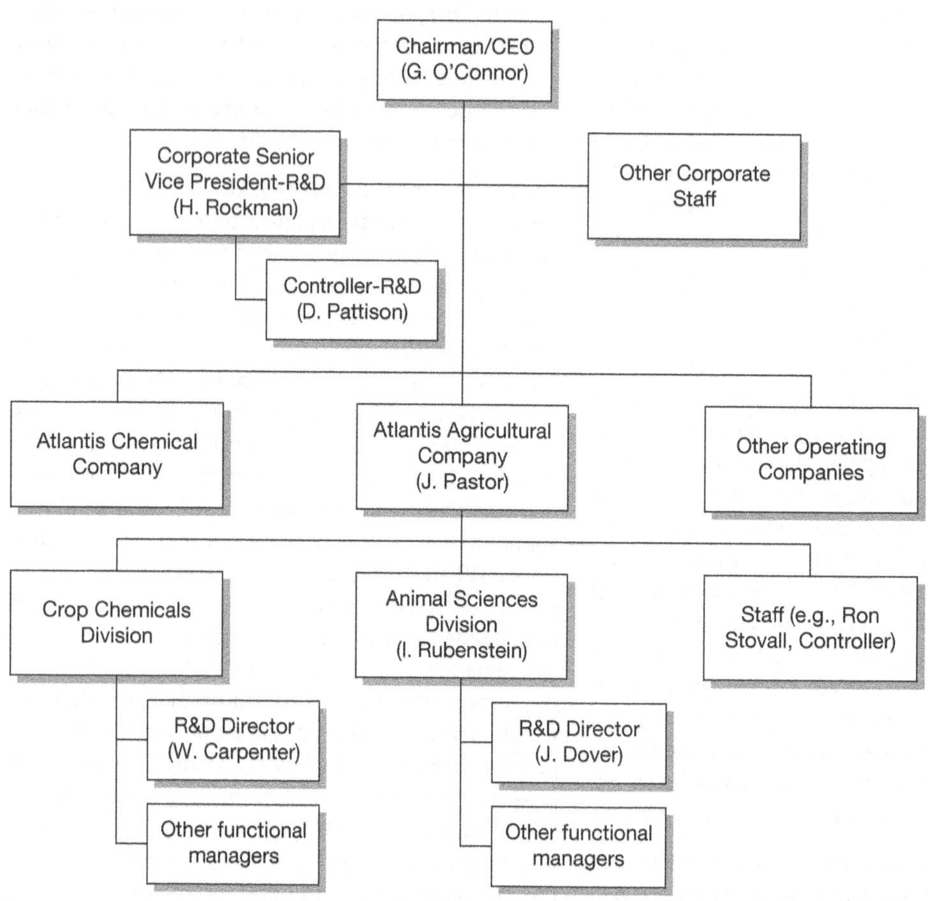

Exhibit 2 Financial highlights of the two divisions of Atlantis Agricultural Company ($ millions)

	Crop Chemicals	Animal Sciences
Sales		
2010	1,067	86
2009	1,073	79
2008	1,256	82
Operating Income (Loss)		
2010	318	(35)
2009	177	(92)
2008	438	(49)
R&D Expenses		
2010	94	41
2009	110	32
2008	107	22

Exhibit 3 Corporate R&D costs by major category (%)

	2010	2009	2009	2007	2006
Class I	26%	27%	29%	32%	32%
Class II	30	23	22	23	24
Class III	40	42	40	35	30
Other*	4	8	9	10	14
Total	100%	100%	100%	100%	100%

*Includes corporate unclassified administrative costs, (e.g., maintenance of the central research laboratory.

Exhibit 4 Distribution of R&D costs between corporate and operating units

	2010 (%)	2009 (%)
Directly controlled and administered by the operating units	80%	80%
Controlled and administered by corporate R&D:		
- Charged to operating units:		
- on a fee-for-service basis	9	4
- allocated as a "corporate charge" based on net investment	1	6
- Reported as part of corporate R&D	10	10
Total R&D Cost	100%	100%

Exhibit 5 Corporate R&D costs, budget vs. actual ($ millions)

	2010 Budget	2009 Actual	2010 Budget minus 2009 Actual Costs
Biotech Product Discovery[1]	$42.9	$40.6	$2.3
Technology Management[2]	2.4	2.4	0
Distributed Research and Development[3]	45.2	49.9	(4.7)
Total corporate R&D	$90.5	$92.9	$(2.4)

[1]Retained by the corporate R&D function and reported as an operating segment.
[2]Allocated to the operating units as an element of corporate overhead.
[3]Charged directly to the operating units based upon measured services rendered and/or negotiated amounts.

Exhibit 6 Animal Sciences Division ($ millions)

	2010 Budget	2009 Budget
Sales	$127	$86
R&D	61	41
Other operating costs	109	80
Operating income (loss)	$(43)	$(35)

This case was prepared by Professor Kenneth A. Merchant.

CHAPTER 6
Designing and Evaluating Management Control Systems

The preceding chapters described the range of management controls that can be used and how they affect behaviors. This chapter discusses a general framework that can be used to design management control systems (MCSs) or to improve those already in use.

The process of designing and improving MCSs requires addressing two basic questions: *What is desired?* and *What is likely to happen?* If what is likely is different from what is desired, then managers must subsequently address the following two MCS-design questions: *What controls should be used?* and *How tightly should each be applied?* The following sections in this chapter describe how to address each of these questions. The chapter concludes with some observations about common management control issues faced when designing or improving MCSs.

What is desired and *what is likely*

MCSs cannot be designed or evaluated without an understanding of what the organization wants the employees to do. *Objectives* and, more importantly, *strategies* that are derived from a good understanding of the organization's objectives often provide important guides to the actions that are expected. A better understanding of objectives and strategies yields a larger set of feasible control alternatives, provides a better chance that each control alternative is appropriately tightly applied, and reduces the chance of producing behavioral displacement problems.

Organizations must determine what is desired, but they also need to try to assess what is likely to happen. This essentially amounts to assessing the likelihood that each of the control problems are present or will occur: lack of direction, motivational problems, or personal limitations. In other words, organizations should ask whether their employees understand what they are expected to do (key actions) or to accomplish (key results), whether they are properly motivated, and whether they are able to fulfill their required roles.

If the likely actions or results differ from the desired actions or results, more or different MCSs might be called for, depending on the severity of the problems and the costs of the MCSs that could be used to solve the problems. In this situation, managers should then address the questions about what MCSs to use and how tightly to apply them.

Choice of controls

The different types of management controls are not equally effective at addressing each of the management control problems. Table 6.1 provides a summary of the control problems each of the types of management controls addresses. It shows, for example, that behavioral constraints do not help solve lack-of-direction problems; hence, if direction is a significant problem in the area of concern, managers will have to consider other forms of control.

The specific set of management controls to be selected from the feasible alternatives should be those that will provide the greatest *net* benefits (i.e. benefits less costs). The benefits of a MCS are derived from the increased probability of success or obtaining the desired outcomes. Since management controls are not costless to implement and operate, these costs must be put against the expected benefits of improved control.

Table 6.1 Control types and control problems

	Control problems		
Control types	Lack of direction	Motivational problems	Personal limitations
Results controls			
Results accountability	x	x	
Action controls			
Behavioral constraints		x	
Preaction reviews	x	x	x
Action accountability	x	x	x
Redundancy			x
Personnel/cultural controls			
Selection and placement	x	x	x
Training	x		x
Provision of necessary resources			x
Creation of a strong organizational culture	x	x	
Group-based rewards	x	x	

Source: K. A. Merchant, *Modern Management Control Systems: Text and Cases* (Upper Saddle River, NJ: Prentice Hall, 1998), p. 253.

Personnel/cultural controls as an initial consideration

In deciding among the many management control alternatives, managers should start by considering how adequate personnel or cultural controls will be, or can be made to be. Personnel/cultural controls are worthy of first consideration because they have relatively few harmful side effects and relatively low out-of-pocket costs. In some cases, such as in small organizations, personnel/cultural controls may provide effective management control by themselves even though they are unlikely to be sufficient.

For example, when Marc Brownstein, president of the Brownstein Group, a small family-run advertising and public relations firm in Philadelphia, decided to take advice from his managers to tackle high turnover (30% per year among a 20-plus-person agency) and low employee morale, he was perplexed when he learned what his employees were asking for. They were not greatly concerned with the levels of salaries or bonuses (although there were some requests for better employee benefits and some "perks" such as office decorations and technology updates). Instead, they wanted to get more involved with the business, such as by having a say about which new accounts the firm should solicit. They also wanted better communication from top management. They felt that Mr. Brownstein did not listen very well and offered little performance feedback. In other words, the important requests were more about communication and decision-making involvement (personnel and cultural controls) than about money (results control). Mr. Brownstein heeded his personnel's advice. Soon after changes were made, the company's billings were at record levels; turnover dropped by half; and, for the first time in its history, the agency won the "Oscar" of the ad world.[1] Many of these changes were not expensive, or cumbersome to implement, yet seemed to produce some good effects.

Even in settings where personnel/cultural controls are not sufficiently reliable by themselves, it is useful to focus on them first because they will have to be relied upon to some extent no matter what other forms of management control are used. Considering personnel/cultural controls first allows organizations to assess how reliable these forms of management control are and, then, determine the extent to which they should consider supplementing them with other forms of control.

Turning to some harder evidence about organizational culture as an important aspect of cultural control, as we discussed in Chapter 3, a recent survey of more than 1,800 CEOs and CFOs around the world provided some striking findings:[2]

> **More than 90 percent of executives said culture is important at their firms, and 78 percent said culture is among the top five things that make their company valuable. But only 15 percent said their own corporate culture is exactly where it needed to be, and 92 percent said they believe improving their firm's corporate culture would improve the value of the company. More than 50 percent of executives said corporate culture influences productivity, creativity, profitability, the value of a firm and growth rates.**

One of the authors of the study, Professor Shiva Rajgopal at Columbia University, added: "Our research provides systematic evidence that effective cultures are less likely to be associated with short-termism, unethical behavior or earnings management to pad quarterly earnings."[3] These are quite significant desirable outcomes for a control system to be able to attain, but equally, let us not ignore that only 15% said that their company culture was where it needed to be, thus underlining both the *potency* as well as the *insufficiency* of culture. Surely, culture is important, but how it can be made more effective to attain good control is poorly understood, where culture is often acclaimed when an organization succeeds, but blamed when it fails.

Because putting one's finger on it is hard, culture is often the "residual" explanation for sustained success or dramatic failure after all the other, more direct reasons or "causes" have been exhausted, such as internal control weaknesses (an action control) or misfiring incentive systems (a results control) in the case of failures. Culture was in that sense an oft-cited reason for the calamity in the financial services sector following the 2009 financial crisis;[4] that said, many organizations have been credited for their strong cultures as well.[5]

Culture was also evoked in the recent Volkswagen "defeat devices" cheating scandal. Interestingly–for reasons related to our inclusive term *personnel/cultural* controls–Andrew Hill, a columnist in The Financial Times, wrote the following in light of the Volkswagen case:[6]

> **The English version of [VW's] statement said it had detected "a mindset in some areas of the company that tolerated breaches of rules." The group was implementing structural reforms, it went on, but it had also initiated a "new mindset."**

"We can have the best people, and a great organization, but we can do nothing without the right attitude and mentality," explained Matthias Müller, the chief executive.

VW's choice of words is instructive. We would have bet that corporate culture–that battered old scapegoat for many scandals–would come in for a further beating.

"Mindset" is in any case a more useful term. It is easy for people to blame bad culture, without themselves feeling any responsibility for the toxic atmosphere. At the same time, each bank, drug company, or defence contractor that promises to clean up its culture, only to mess up again, reinforces the impression that it is hard to change. Mindset is more personal, and plenty of studies show individuals are quite capable of reforming their attitudes and mentality.

All told, then, personnel/cultural controls will be, by themselves, inevitably insufficient. This resonates with the saying that if nobody stole cars, no car would have to be locked. But if no car were locked, somebody would start stealing them. While most employees are probably honest most of the time, there will always be some who are less than totally honest. Organizations therefore cannot fully rely on the absolute righteousness or trustworthiness of their employees. Equally, organizations can hardly count on employees who are so "fascinated by their assignments; jumping out of their skins with excitement about what's next; eagerly pursuing better solutions and new initiatives" that they can rule out using any other types of controls.[7] Therefore, it will be necessary to supplement personnel/cultural controls with controls over actions, results, or both.

Knowing the limitations of personnel/cultural controls, choices among the various forms of action and results controls should depend on the particular advantages and disadvantages each has in the specific setting in question.

Advantages and disadvantages of action controls

Perhaps the most significant advantage of action controls is that they are the most direct form of control. If it is absolutely essential that an action be performed properly the first time (e.g. a significant investment decision), perhaps because the decision is not easily reversible, action controls usually provide the best control because the control-action link is direct. Further, if controls over the actions themselves are judged to be adequate, there is no need to monitor results.

Action controls also provide several other advantages. Action controls tend to lead to documentation of the accumulation of knowledge as to what works best. The documents that are produced (e.g. policies and procedures) are an efficient way to transfer knowledge to the employees who are performing the actions. They also act as a form of organizational memory, so that the knowledge is not lost if, for example, key employees leave the organization.

Action controls, particularly in the form of policies and procedures, also are an efficient way to aid organizational coordination. They increase the predictability of actions and reduce the amount of inter-organizational information flows required to achieve a coordinated effort. As such, they are a key element in bureaucratic forms of organization in a positive sense; that is, in settings where standardization and routinization are desirable organizational attributes.

But action controls have a number of disadvantages. First, there is a severe *feasibility limitation*. As we discussed earlier, excellent knowledge of what actions are desirable exists only for highly routinized jobs. Moreover, there is a tendency, with action-accountability controls in particular, to focus on known or established actions of lesser importance that are easy to monitor, thereby potentially causing *behavioral displacement*, such as the means-ends inversion we discussed in Chapter 5.

A good example is a program that a commercial-industrial laundry company implemented to reduce tardiness and absence, which had hurt its productivity because if one tardy worker falls behind on the job, other workers down the line were left to sit idle. The absence monitoring and reward program did produce one benefit the plant managers were looking for: it reduced the average level of tardiness. But it also quickly emerged that employees ended up "gaming" the program, such as by calling in sick rather than reporting late.[8]

Second, most action controls also often discourage adaptation, innovation, and creativity (of the right kind, unlike the creative "gaming" in the example above). Employees often react to action controls by becoming passive. They develop their work habits based on the work rules they are given. This adaptation may be so complete that they begin to depend on the rules, cease to think about how the processes could be improved, and become resistant to change. In some cases, however, creativity is not required, or indeed not desired. For example, creativity from casino blackjack dealers, airline pilots, or nuclear plant operators is rarely a desired feature. But in other cases, action controls cause significant opportunities for improvement and innovation to be foregone.

Third, action accountability, in particular, can cause sloppiness. Employees who are accustomed to operating with a stable set of work rules are prone to cut corners. For example, in a public embarrassment for the US Air Force's nuclear missile program, two crew members were disciplined for leaving silo blast doors open while they were on duty in an underground facility housing nuclear missiles. Under Air Force regulations, a two-man missile launch crew is required to keep the underground blast door shut when one crew member is asleep during their 24-hour shift. But the crew member was found "derelict in his duties as he left the blast door open in order to receive a food delivery" while the other crew member was on an authorized sleep break.[9] Similarly, airplane accidents have been commonly traced to checklist errors in which the pilots carelessly rushed through their pre-takeoff and pre-landing procedures. These examples illustrate that action controls often cause sloppiness or/or encourage compliance of the "check-the-box" type, rather than the required scrutiny and care to ensure fail-proof operations.

Another situation of sloppiness often arises when various software applications and computer systems require too many different passwords. The users, then, start saving their passwords within spreadsheets or email messages, or change their system preferences to allow them to automatically log into, or stay logged on, the various systems. Circumventing the authentication systems in this way obviously leaves a security gap, the exact opposite result of what was intended. To prevent this from happening, organizations have had to roll out software packages specifically designed so that users can save their passwords securely.[10]

But it is not always the employees who are sloppy, cutting corners, or inattentive. In some cases, organizations have been criticized for not having nearly good enough or tight enough action controls. For example, a recent critique suggested that "nuclear power plants around the world are harboring a 'culture of denial' about the risk of cyber hacking, with many failing to protect themselves against digital attacks," where it was further pointed out that "they are really good at safety; they've got really good physical security, but they have barely grappled with cyber."[11]

Fourth, action controls often cause negative attitudes. Some, perhaps even most, people are not happy operating under them. Some people, especially the more independent, creative types, may leave to find other jobs that allow more opportunity for achievement and self-actualization.

Negative attitudes and frustrations with "bureaucracy" were a common issue with the so-called "ObamaCare" healthcare reforms, or Affordable Care Act–a major reform initiative by President Obama in the United States. Aside from the intentions to increase healthcare coverage and other changes, the new law also:

> **"[...] *turned the heavy flow of government red tape into a gusher.* A 2012 Physicians Foundation survey found that almost four of every five respondents identified too much regulation and paperwork as *a "very important" reason the medical profession is in decline.* With more than 13,000 pages of regulations [...], the Affordable Care Act will make running a**

medical practice *even more stultifying.* In addition to the mountain of paperwork under which they already labor, doctors will be faced with reams of new bureaucratic requirements, such as new Medicare rules governing patient referrals and reporting, new rules governing practice standards, plus tougher civil monetary penalties and criminal sanctions. *None of this will make medicine more attractive or enticing.* The November 9, 2010, edition of Medscape Family Medicine quotes an internist as saying: *"If dealing with Medicare was a headache, dealing with the new bureaucracy will be an intracranial hemorrhage."*[12]

As a further example, perhaps a bit extreme but factual nonetheless, consider how managers at *The South Bend* (Indiana) *Tribune* newspaper ordered the newsroom staff to start writing daily memos detailing their every activity. They did this as the newspaper was scrambling to keep their remaining staffers motivated and productive in the midst of the chaos following a round of layoffs. The purpose of the daily staff memos presumably was to improve communication in order to make the organization as "productive as possible." This was targeted to all reporters, who were instructed to send a daily email to their most immediate editor (and five others) as the last thing to do before they leave for the day. These email "memos" would lay out specifically what the reporters accomplished that day, what they needed to finish or follow up on the next day, and what they planned to do the next day. As such, management believed (or hoped, rather) that the organization would benefit from encouraging communication and sharing information. The editor would be able to tell how busy the reporters had been and, more importantly, what they had accomplished and what they were struggling with. From that, it was expected that "[our] morning planning meetings can be even more efficient." In her guidance as to what the organization was looking for in the memos, Assistant Managing News Editor Virginia Black provided an example of what she wanted by means of a 375-word sample memo that was "mind-numbing in its minute detail." Needless to say, this was received with skepticism among the reporters. As one of them pointed out, "followed to its logical conclusion, this productivity memo thing would produce a never-ending memo loop. Think about it: the last item on your memo must be, 'wrote a memo about how I spent my day,' which, of course, requires you to then write, 'updated my memo to account for memo,' and so on." The reporters could not see how these memos would make the morning planning meetings more efficient. In the meantime, Ms. Black's memo quickly spread through the blogosphere, stirring up plenty of counter-memos (of the sarcastic sort, that is). Someone summarized the ill-fated idea as follows: "Who thought this was a good idea? It would be faster to just tell [us] directly that they believe every single one of [us] is lazy, incompetent and untrustworthy."[13] Clearly, the intended action-accountability measure had created ill will and negative reactions from the independent, creative-minded reporters.

Similarly, in a "battle of humans versus machines," equity traders in one brokerage firm were resisting a push by their firm to impose an ever-increasing amount of computer-based analysis of their trades. Although management may see such "electronic control regimes" as helpful when it comes to monitoring trading desk performance and ensuring regulatory compliance, which has been particularly important following cases of unethical and fraudulent behaviors in banks, others argue that they inevitably will have unintended consequences. One observer noted that traders, who are typically independent-minded, will be tempted to "game the system to produce results that maximize compensation" regardless.[14] Or, as another observer notes: "The traders will be back saying to their compliance officers: There's too much control; let us make money."[15]

But even action control-type electronic or automated systems are not immune to misusage either. One response to the rigging of benchmark rates in banks (such as LIBOR) was to have the indices or benchmarks settled by actual transactions rather than by allegedly "conspiring traders" who sometimes were personally vested in the final outcome, tipping each other off to pending orders, and seeking to get ahead of their clients and profit at their expense. Getting rid of the human factor, where indices would be set on the basis of actual transactions or "real trades" on electronic exchanges, therefore seemed like an obvious solution. But this seemingly comforting solution, however, has been thrown into sharp relief as it appeared that some electronic systems were allegedly also rigged by their capacity to hold trades for hundreds of milliseconds: if the markets moved against the bank in that period, the trades were denied; if they moved in the bank's favor, the trades went through. The article in *The Financial Times* that reported on this issue as paraphrased above was incisively titled: "In modern banking, cheating can be automated."[16]

Finally, some action controls, particularly those that require preaction reviews, are costly. The reviews must usually be performed by individuals who are as well, or more, qualified than those who are taking the actions. Thus, the reviewers must be highly knowledgeable, and their time and services are costly. If they do not take, or have, the time to perform their reviews thoroughly, then the intended control purposes will be rendered moot.

That said, ignorance or lack of time is no defense. As a response to the systemic failures in the financial sector, for example, it has been proposed that executives could be held liable for wrongdoing in activities for which they had responsibility even if they had no specific knowledge of the improper conduct. Professor John Kay put the justification for this as follows:

> **Primary responsibility for rate-fixing scandals lies with those who allowed a culture in which such behavior was seen as normal. This is not to absolve the individuals who actually perpetrated the crimes.**[17]

That said, there is the worry that the requirement that executives have to demonstrate that they had taken all reasonable steps to eliminate wrongdoing might encourage "box ticking" and "paper pushing" rather than substantive action to change organizational culture.[18]

This takes us back to the important point that neither of the various types of control should be seen as individually effective, nor to operate in isolation. It is also pertinent to note how often "culture" was evoked when discussing issues with action controls in the examples from practice above. Action and personnel/cultural controls are intricately related, and so are results controls, to which we now turn.

Advantages and disadvantages of results controls

Results controls also have several advantages and disadvantages. One common advantage is *feasibility*. Results controls can provide effective control even where knowledge as to what actions are desirable is lacking. This situation is typical of many (even most) of the important roles in many organizations. We discuss this more fully in Chapter 2, and return to this also in the context of Chapter 7.

Another advantage of results controls is that employee behaviors can be influenced even while the employees are allowed significant *autonomy*. This is particularly desirable when creativity is required because autonomy allows room for new and innovative ways of thinking. But even where creativity is not important, allowing autonomy has some advantages. It usually yields greater employee commitment and motivation because higher-level personal needs (such as the need for self-accomplishment) are brought into play. Results controls can also provide on-the-job training. Employees learn by doing and by making mistakes. It also allows room for idiosyncratic styles of behavior (such as a unique sales approach, or a personal touch when dealing with employees), which can provide better results than standardization of one approach. Chapter 7 elaborates further on the features of decision autonomy and commensurate results accountability.

A final advantage of results controls is that, as compared to some forms of action control, they are often relatively *inexpensive*. Performance measures are often collected for reasons not directly related to management control, such as for financial reporting, tax reporting, or strategy formulation. If these measures can be used or easily adapted for results controls, the incremental expense of the control can be relatively small.

Results controls, however, have some disadvantages or limitations. First, *congruence* or *alignment* problems may arise due to imperfect knowledge of desirable results. Furthermore, due to *measurement issues*, results measures usually provide less-than-perfect indications of whether good actions had been taken because the measures fail to meet one or more of the qualities of good measures: precision, objectivity, timeliness, and understandability. As discussed in Chapter 2, these congruence and measurement problems are often difficult to fix and, sometimes, even to recognize.

Second, when results are affected by anything other than the employee's own skills and efforts, as they almost always are, results controls impose risk on the employees. This risk is caused by measurement "noise" created by any of a number of likely *uncontrollable factors* (which we discuss further in Chapter 12), including environmental uncertainty, organizational interdependencies, and sometimes just bad luck. Subjecting employees to this risk is often problematic because employees are, to varying degrees, *risk averse*. When organizations make their employees bear risk, they must offer them a higher expected level of compensation (a *risk premium*) compared to when the employees do not bear the risk. Failure to provide the correct premium for the risk borne is likely to lead to employee dissatisfaction, frustration, and perceptions of unfairness, making it difficult for the organization to attract and retain talented employees. Moreover, regardless of whether the correct risk premium is offered, the organization will have to guard against employees' tendencies to take some risk-reducing and/or bonus-maximizing, rather than value-enhancing, actions or decisions.

Third, it is usually impossible to optimize the performance targets set as part of results-control systems (such as budget targets). The targets are often asked to fulfill multiple important, but competing, control functions.[19] One is *motivation-to-achieve*. For this function, it is best for the targets to be *challenging but achievable*. Another is planning. The targets are used to make decisions about levels of cash and inventory to have on hand. For this function, the targets should be *realistic*. A third function is *coordination*. Plans are often treated as commitments and shared among the various entities in an organization so that each entity knows what to expect from the other entities. For this function, the targets should be a *best guess*, or maybe even slightly *conservative*, to make sure they are achieved and no (wasteful) overcommitments of resources take place. Obviously, one set of targets cannot serve all purposes equally well. One or more purposes must be sacrificed if results controls are used. We refer to Chapter 8 for a more detailed treatment of this important target-setting issue and how organizations address it.

Aside from the difficulty involved in setting the right target for the right performance area(s), the measures themselves can be conflicting, and certainly overwhelming, when they are (too) numerous. For example, the Royal College of Nursing (RCN) told an influential group of Members of Parliament in the United Kingdom that "the number of performance targets forced on healthcare professionals must be reduced from 400 to about 15 because staff were being 'bullied' into working harder," and that "the government's demands were 'crazy' and demoralized staff." To remedy the situation, RCN executive director Alison Kitson called on the MPs to scrap many targets and introduce instead focused standards based on skill mix, patient dignity, and clinical outcomes.[20] As we discussed in Chapters 2 and4, a proliferation of measures can lead to confusion and conflicts, making it more likely that the combination of measures will be less congruent with the truly desired results. There clearly is a tradeoff to be made between measurement completeness and congruence.

Similarly, but for an added reason of autonomy, the United Kingdom's home secretary Theresa May told senior police officers that they "had only one target–that is, to reduce crime." She said this in response to criticisms that "micro-management was making a comeback," or, as we said earlier, was risking interference with police officers' autonomy and local knowledge as to how to best provide effective policing and fight crime.[21]

Finally, not all employees like being empowered to produce results as they best see fit. Some employees simply have no desire for autonomy; that is, they enjoy neither the responsibility that these controls impart on them nor the risks to which the controls subject them. However, (self-) selection of employees into jobs that match their skills and ambitions, a form of personnel controls, should mitigate this problem.[22]

Choice of control tightness

The decision as to whether controls should be applied more or less tightly in any particular organization, or in an area within the organization, depends on the answer to three questions: (1) *What are the potential benefits of tight controls?*; (2) *What are the costs?*; and (3) *Are any harmful side-effects likely?*

In any organization, tight control is most beneficial over the areas most critical to the organization's success. The *critical success factors* vary widely across organizations. For example, inventory control is critical in retail superstores because carrying heavy inventories without tight controls amounts to inefficient use of resources without value-added for the customer experience, where the inventory control also must ensure that stockouts do not erode customer experience. Tight inventory control can be implemented by focusing on *key results* if employees can be trusted to determine how to keep inventory near the required service levels, or *key actions* that involve detailed inventory procedures and decision rules. In airlines, seat capacity utilization is one of the critical success factors: Revenue Passenger Kilometers, or RPK, as this *key performance indicator* (KPI) is called (the number of paying passengers multiplied by the number of kilometers flown). Most airlines achieve tight control in this area through extensive preaction reviews over airplane acquisition and replacement decisions.[23]

The potential benefits of tight controls also tend to be higher when performance is poor. For example, in reference to CEO Jack Welch's management style at General Electric, a former manager said, "If you're doing well, you probably have more freedom than most CEOs of publicly-traded companies. But the leash gets pulled very tightly when a unit is underperforming."[24]

What are the costs involved in implementing tight controls? Some forms of control are costly to implement in tight form. As we discussed earlier, tight action controls in the form of preaction reviews, for example, can require considerable top management time to do the reviews. Some other action controls, such as for compliance purposes, can require a lot of information gathering, checking, and reporting time, known colorfully as "paper pushing" for those completing and reviewing the reports. Tight results controls might require extensive studies to gather useful performance standards, or they might require sophisticated information systems to collect and analyze all the required performance data. Chapter 5 deals exclusively with the costs of management control systems, both direct and indirect costs.

Are any harmful side effects likely? All the conditions necessary to make a type of control feasible, such as knowledge about how the control object relates to the desired ends, may not be present. If so, harmful side effects are likely if the control is implemented, *especially* if the control is implemented in tight form. For example, if the environment is unpredictable and the need for creativity is high, such as in hi-tech firms, good knowledge does not exist about either the actions that are needed or the results that should be accomplished. Therefore, neither action nor results control can be said to be clearly effective, and the implementation of either in tight form is likely to cause problems. Tight action controls would likely cause behavioral displacement and stifle creativity. Tight results controls would likely cause problems in selecting the right results measures and setting adequately challenging targets, both of which are difficult in rapidly changing, knowledge-intensive and/or highly innovative settings.[25]

Simultaneous tight-loose controls

In a now-dated but still-seminal management book, *In Search of Excellence*, Peters and Waterman observed that a number of companies they defined as "excellent" employed what they called *simultaneous tight-loose controls*.[26] They observed that the MCSs used in these companies can be considered *loose* in that they allow, and even encourage, autonomy, entrepreneurship, and innovation. But these same control systems can also be called *tight* because the people in the company share a set of rigid values (such as focus on customer needs). Peters and Waterman observed that policies, procedures, and other types of controls are not necessary in these companies because "people way down the line know what they are supposed to do in most situations because the handful of guiding values is crystal clear"[27] and "culture regulates rigorously the few variables that do count."[28] In other words, the MCSs in these organizations are dominated by personnel or cultural control; or they can be said to be tight on objectives and core values, but loose on procedures.

At Southwest Airlines, tight control is presumably achieved by way of a clear *strategic principle*. Herb Kelleher, founder of Southwest, is rumored to have said that "[he] can teach you the secret to running this airline in thirty seconds: We are THE low-fare airline," and that, "Once you understand that, you can make any decision about this company's future as well as I can."[29]

It sounds like nirvana: let culture or a strategic principle provide a high degree of reliance that the employees are acting in the organization's best interest and avoid most of the harmful side effects. But this desirable state is difficult to achieve, as several examples earlier in this chapter have suggested. Many companies are dealing with employees who do not share a single set of values. Then what do managers of organizations without strong cultures do?

It may be possible to approach a similar type of simultaneous tight-loose control even where a strong culture does not exist. This can be accomplished by using tight controls over the few key actions or results that have the greatest potential impact on the success of the organization. More control should be exercised over strategically important areas than over minor areas, regardless of how easy it is to control the latter. None of the controls that might be substituted for culture can be assumed to be free of harmful side effects, but selective use of tight controls may limit these effects. Most individuals can tolerate a few restrictions if they are allowed some autonomy in other areas. In the context of a results-control example mentioned earlier, an organization probably does not need 400 measures if 15 will suffice, and even that may be too many in most situations.

Adapting to change

Most organizations emphasize one form of management control at a given point in time, but they often change their emphasis from one form to another as their needs, capabilities, and environments change. Small companies can often be controlled adequately through the supervisory abilities of founding leaders who develop a staff of loyal employees, centralize most key decisions, and involve themselves personally in detailed reviews of budgets and expenditures. As organizations grow, however, these forms of personnel/cultural and action control may have to be replaced, or supplemented, with other forms of control. As a consequence, organizational growth typically pushes management controls in the direction of increased formalization of procedures for action-accountability purposes and/or development of more elaborate information systems for results-control purposes.[30] In addition to growth, many other situational factors, such as intensifying competition, global expansion, or technological change, inevitably drive organizations to (have to) adapt their management control systems to their changing environments lest they become uncompetitive or even displaced.

Keeping a behavioral focus

What makes the analysis of management controls so difficult is that their benefits and side effects are dependent on how employees will react to the controls that are being considered. Predicting these behaviors is far from an exact science. Significant behavioral differences exist among people in different countries, in different parts of a single country, in different organizations, and in different areas of the same organization. Managers must be aware of such differences because the effectiveness of the management controls used will vary depending on the reactions of the employees involved. As the earlier examples suggest, creative types such as advertising executives or design engineers, and independent-minded or autonomy-seeking types such as managers or traders, tend to react more negatively to action controls than do employees working in production scheduling or accounting. Equally, some employees seem to be relatively highly interested in, and hence motivated by, money as a reward, whereas others are more attracted to stimulating work, autonomy, and challenge.[31]

These differences make the implementation of MCSs particularly challenging, and it is crucial to emphasize that *no one form of control is optimal in all circumstances*. What works best in one organization, or area within an organization, may not work in another. However, it is still important to keep the focus on the people involved, because their responses will determine the success or failure of the MCS. The benefits of management controls are derived only from their impacts on behaviors.

Maintaining good control

What causes control problems so serious that an organization is "out of control"? Although the term seems shattering, this condition is not rare. In addition to the many organizations that no longer exist because their MCSs failed, the list of surviving organizations that have been criticized for poor (or lax) controls is long and often includes even the most "admired" companies by the business press at some point in their history (e.g. "Apple Computer" in the 1990s, which made a remarkably successful and iconic return from the brink in the early 2000s to this day, a transformation marked by a name change to just "Apple Inc.").

The causes of the problems these companies have faced are often diverse. One cause is an imperfect understanding of the setting and/or the effect of the management controls in that setting. An imperfect understanding of the situation is often associated with rapid growth and/or "transformational" or "disruptive" change in their markets.[32] Rapid growth and transformational change often precipitates control problems because it causes the key factors that need to be controlled tightly to change.

Another cause is management's inclination to subjugate the implementation of management controls to other, often more pressing, business demands. This, again, happens often in growth and change situations, which cause managers to delay the development of adequate MCSs, usually while they choose to emphasize marketing or developing the business. The change at venerable Hewlett-Packard from an engineering-led to a marketing-focused company, as well as from a hardware to a services company, is a case in point, and is ongoing with the split into two companies: Hewlett-Packard Enterprise (an IT operations company) and HP Inc. (a maker of PCs and printers).[33] Personal style also makes some managers unwilling to implement proper, or the most suitable, management controls. Entrepreneurs, particularly, often find it difficult to relinquish the centralized control they exerted when their firm was small and wholly owned by them.

Criticisms, however, should be made carefully. While many organizations may have faced MCS weaknesses of various magnitudes, knowing what should be criticized is not unproblematic (including in the examples given in this chapter). It is not easy to keep a finely tuned set of MCSs in place over long periods of time, particularly when the organization is operating in rapidly changing environments. Further, some MCSs that are seemingly inadequate may actually be quite effective because they minimize some harmful side effects. Clearly, there is a tension between trying to fully "regulate" behaviors and allowing some "ambiguity" in the roles of relatively autonomous managers in decentralized entities, where it is difficult for organizations to always make the ostensibly correct tradeoff between *control* and *autonomy*.[34] Organizations often oscillate between one and the other, sometimes overdoing it one way, and then drifting back the other way. In that sense, "optimality" is easy to say, but hard to achieve in constantly changing environments.

Hence, criticisms of MCSs must be made with caution. Controls that seem quite loose may have some unseen benefits, such as in terms of high creativity, a healthy spirit of cooperation, or low cost. Even the suffering of ill effects due to the occurrence of one or more of the control problems does not necessarily imply that a poor MCS was in place. MCSs only reduce the probability of poor performance; they do not eliminate it. Most criticisms should be leveled only after a thorough investigation of the situation. Control is a complex part of the management function. There is no perfect MCS. There is no single best way to accomplish good control. Many control benefits and costs are hard to discern, but for control systems to have desirable effects, organizations must inevitably fine-tune them as the situation calls for, using the best assessments, knowledge, and insights available.

Notes

1 "Self-Evaluation Brings Change to a Family's Ad Agency: Executive Learns to Listen to Employees and Adopt New Work Habits," *The Wall Street Journal* (January 6, 1998).

2 J. R. Graham, C. R. Harvey, J. A. Popadak, and S. Rajgopal, "Corporate Culture: Evidence from the Field" (February 21, 2017), 27th Annual Conference on Financial Economics and Accounting Paper, Duke I&E Research Paper No. 2016-33, Columbia Business School Research Paper No. 16-49, online at https://papers.ssrn.com/sol3/papers.cfm?abstract_id=2805602; "How Corporate Culture Affects the Bottom Line," *Duke's Fuqua School of Business News Release* (November 12, 2015), online at www.fuqua.duke.edu/news_events/news-releases/corporate-culture.

3 Ibid.

4 See, for example, M. Power, S. Ashby, and T. Palermo, "Risk Culture in Financial Organizations," *CARR Research* (Winter 2013), pp. 18–21.

5 Southwest Airlines is the poster child of a firm possessing an acclaimed corporate culture, with many case studies and articles over time devoted to describing and studying it. See, for example, G. Smith, "An Evaluation of the Corporate Culture of Southwest Airlines," *Measuring Business Excellence*, 8, no. 4 (2004), pp. 26–33; M. Thomas, "Strategic Principles at Southwest Airlines," *Strategic Direction*, 31, no. 8 (2015), pp. 10–12.

6 "VW Needs More Therapy to Change Its Flawed Mindset," *The Financial Times* (December 14, 2015), online at on.ft.com/1O4ILtl.

7 "Why I Put My Employees Ahead of My Customers," *Forbes* (June 18, 2010), online at www.forbes.com.

8 "How to Demotivate Your Best Employees," *Forbes* (April 8, 2013), online at onforb.es/10LjBDU.

9 "Missile doors Left Open While Air Force Nuclear Officer Slept," *CNN* (October 24, 2013), online at edition.cnn.com/2013/10/23/us/air-force-nuclear-silo-doors-opened.

10 "Société Générale Bolsters Internal Controls," *Search Security* (May 27, 2008), online at SearchSecurity.com.

11 "Nuclear Power Plants in 'Culture of Denial' over Hacking Risk," *The Financial Times* (October 5, 2015), online at on.ft.com/1iXbLor.

12 "Will the Affordable Care Act Affect Doctors? Yes," *The Heritage Foundation* (June 26, 2013), online at www.heritage.org.

13 "Memo Madness, or, Does Busy Work Increase Productivity?," *Business Week* (February 2, 2009), online at www.businessweek.com.

14 "Traders Sceptical of Electronic Monitoring," *The Globe and Mail* (June 3, 2009), online at www.theglobeandmail.com.

15 "Société Générale Trial Begins This Week," *The New York Times* (June 6, 2010), online at www.nytimes.com.

16 "In Modern Banking, Cheating Can Be Automated," *The Financial Times* (November 20, 2015), online at on.ft.com/1I448Tw.

17 "Ignorance Is No Defence for Misconduct such as PPI and LIBOR," *The Financial Times* (December 8, 2015), online at on.ft.com/1SLUcE4.

18 Ibid.

19 See, for example, S. C. Hansen and W. A. Van der Stede, "Multiple Facets of Budgeting: An Exploratory Analysis," *Management Accounting Research*, 15, no. 4 (December 2004), pp. 415–39.

20 "Too Many NHS Targets Are 'Bullying' Staff, MPs Told," *Nursing Standard* (January 29, 2003).

21 "Police Forces Facing Dozens of New Performance Targets," *BBC News* (September 19, 2013), online at bbc.co.uk/news/uk-24148129.

22 See, for example, D. Campbell, "Employee Selection as a Control System," *Journal of Accounting Research*, 50, no. 4 (September 2012), pp. 931–66.

23 "Dubai Airshow: 'Gulf Three' Deals Will Strike Fear into Rival Airlines," *CNN* (November 19, 2013), online at edition.cnn.com/2013/11/17/business/dubai-airshow-emirates-airbus-quest.

24 "Jack: A Close-up Look at How American's #1 Manager Runs GE," *Business Week* (June 8, 1998), p. 104.

25 See, for example, T. Davila, M. Epstein, and R. Shelton, *The Creative Enterprise* (Westport, CT: Praeger, 2007); T. Davila, M. Epstein, and R. Shelton, *Making Innovation Work: How to Manage It, Measure It, and Profit from It* (Philadelphia, PA: Wharton Business School Publishing, 2006).

26 T. J. Peters and R. H. Waterman, *In Search of Excellence* (New York: Harper & Row, 1982).

27 Ibid., p. 76.

28 Ibid., p. 105.

29 See M. Thomas, "Strategic Principles at Southwest Airlines," *Strategic Direction*, 31, no. 8 (2015), p. 10.

30 See, for example, E. Flamholtz and Y. Randle, *Growing Pains: Transitioning from an Entrepreneurship to a Professionally Managed Firm* (San Francisco, CA: Jossey-Bass, 2000).

31 See, for example, "One-Fifth of American Workers Say Compensation is the Biggest Factor in Work Happiness," *World-At-Work* (September 2, 2014), online at www.worldatwork.org.

32 *Disruptive innovation* is a term coined by Harvard professor Clayton Christensen to describe the relentless competition that established companies can face from new entrants at the bottom of the market; see www.claytonchristensen.com (accessed December 2015).

33 See, for example, "New HP Duo Disappoints on forecast Debut," *The Financial Times* (November 25, 2015), online at on.ft.com/1R5mlaz.

34 See, for example, D. Marginson and S. Ogden, "Coping with Ambiguity through the Budget: The Positive Effects of Budgetary Targets on Managers' Budgeting Behaviors," *Accounting, Organizations and Society*, 30, no. 5 (July 2005), pp. 435–456.

CASE STUDY
Diagnostic Products Corporation

This incentive program is still in its infancy stages, but we believe that we are on the right path. What has amazed us throughout this process is just how difficult it is to achieve a performance bonus program that truly inspires and acknowledges strong performance. I believe that for this reason most enterprises either "settle" for programs that look great on paper but are ineffective in practice, or avoid this type of a program altogether in favor of compensation mechanisms that do not really examine individual performance metrics that are (ironically) most essential to the success of the business plan. Though no plan is perfect, we are determined to develop this program in a way that is first and foremost a benefit to our customers, while addressing our values as a corporation.

James Sorensen, Field Service/Support Manager, Diagnostic Products Corporation

In the second quarter of 2004, Diagnostic Products Corporation implemented a new Performance Bonus Program for its US-based Field Service Engineers (FSEs). The new program provided rewards to FSEs based on their accomplishments, rather than for merely working long hours. The new program was still work in progress, however. Managers were still considering how some of the elements of the program should be structured, and they were not yet able to measure objectively the FSEs' performances in all critical aspects of their jobs.

Diagnostic Products Corporation

Diagnostic Products Corporation (DPC) designed, manufactured, and marketed laboratory instruments and reagents designed for immunodiagnostic testing. The tests were for the diagnosis, monitoring, management, and prevention of various diseases, including thyroid disorders, reproductive disorders, cardiovascular disorders, allergies, infectious diseases, and certain types of cancer. All of DPC's tests were performed in vitro, which is through samples removed from the body, such as blood, urine, tissues, or other bodily fluids.

DPC's products were sold to hospitals, independent clinical laboratories, and physician office laboratories as well as forensic, research, references, and veterinary laboratories. The company sold its products through independent distributors as well as through its own sales force.

Historically, foreign sales accounted for more than 70% of revenues, although in recent years, domestic sales growth had outpaced foreign sales growth. In 2003, the company generated slightly in excess of $60 million in profit after tax on revenues of nearly $400 million (see Exhibit 1). DPC stock was listed on the New York Stock Exchange (symbol: DP).

DPC's primary instrument offering was the IMMULITE series of instruments, which were first introduced in 1993. IMMULITE systems were fully automated, computer-driven modular systems that used specialized proprietary software to provide rapid, accurate test results to reduce the customers' labor and reagent costs. DPC's IMMULITE provided the capacity for walk-away processing of up to 120 samples per hour, on a random access basis, meaning that it could perform any test, or combination of tests, on any patient sample at any time.

DPC had two principal immunoassay platforms (see Exhibit 2). DPC's IMMULITE 2000 addressed the needs of high-volume laboratories, while the IMMULITE served lower volume facilities and niche markets.

The IMMULITE 2000 had an innovative service feature that included a remote diagnostic capability. DPC's service facility could access any IMMULITE 2000 worldwide for the purpose of diagnosing system problems. In 2002, DPC introduced Real Time Service (RTS) on the IMMULITE 2000 system. RTS enabled the IMMULITE 2000 to monitor itself and to proactively contact DPC's service facility if it sensed a potential problem. In this way, DPC was sometimes able to solve a problem before a customer was even aware that it existed.

In early 2004, DPC launched the IMMULITE 2500. This instrument was similar to the IMMULITE 2000 but reduced the time it took to get a result from certain tests, most importantly tests used in emergency rooms to aid in the diagnosis of cardiac conditions. DPC also expected to launch an enhanced version of the Sample Management System (SMS) that would connect to two IMMULITE 2000s or 2500s. The SMS would eventually function as a universal robotic interface that could be linked to almost any of the automated systems available.

The IMMULITE instruments were closed systems, meaning that they would not perform other manufacturers' tests. Accordingly, an important factor in the successful marketing of these systems was the ability to offer a broad menu of individual assays and assay groups; that is, tests that jointly represent decision-making panels for various disease states, such as thyroid disorders or infertility. DPC managers believed that the IMMULITE and IMMULITE 2000 had the most extensive menus of any automated immunoassay systems on the market. In 2004, DPC manufactured over 400 immunodiagnostic test kits (also called reagents or assays). DPC's research and development (R&D) activities continued to focus on expanding the test menus, giving special attention to complete implementations of clinically important assay groups, as well as on developing new generations of instrumentation and software.

In addition to breadth of menu, major competitive factors for the IMMULITE instruments included time-to-results (how quickly the instrument performs the test), ease of use, and overall cost effectiveness. Because of these competitive factors and the rapid technological developments that characterized the industry, DPC devoted approximately 10% of its annual revenues to R&D activities.

DPC was organized functionally (see Exhibit 3). Headquarters were located in Los Angeles, California. Manufacturing facilities were located in New Jersey, California, Wales, and China. DPC also had a distribution network in over 100 countries.

The field service organization

DPC's field service organization was part of its Instrument Systems Division (ISD), based in Flanders, New Jersey. ISD was comprised of DPC's largest manufacturing facility, its instrument R&D function, and its service organizations, which included technical services, service quality management, and US-based field service/support (see Exhibit 4). Technical services personnel provided telephone support to DPC customers and distributors on a 24/7 basis. The service quality management maintained client databases and automated reporting systems, managed regulatory affairs, and administered customer satisfaction surveys.

The field service organization provided on-site support to customers and distributors. The goal of the field service organization was to be on site where needed within 4–6 hours on a 24/7 basis. The visits served multiple purposes, including repairs, installations, preventive maintenance, and instrument removals.

The US field service organization, which included 86 FSEs based in 32 states, was divided into six regions. Most of the FSEs had an associate degree in a technical field, but some had bachelor degrees and/or were trained in the military. Their ages ranged from 25 to 60+. Their average base salary was slightly less than $50,000.[1] The orientation of the DPC field service organization was different from that of some of the company's competitors. DPC operated its field service organization as a cost center, with the emphasis on providing "total customer satisfaction." Some of DPC's competitors ran their field service organizations as profit centers, which sometimes caused them to focus more on cost-cutting rather than customer service.

Field service managers monitored their organization's performance with an extensive array of data that they summarized by product, region, and FSE. These data included repair rates, productivity, call-back rates, incomplete call rates (with reasons), return call rates, MTTR (mean time to repair), MTBF (mean time before failure), travel expense per call, and on-site response time. These data were reported monthly at a Quality Management Meeting.

Preventive maintenance (PM) procedures were an important part of the FSEs' jobs. If a PM was done on time, there was a better chance of the customer having no problems with the instrument. If a PM was not completed to standard, the chance of a "call back" increased significantly, which caused a disgruntled customer and caused DPC to incur more costs. A PM on an IMMULITE instrument took an average of 3.5 hours to complete. On an IMMULITE 2000, a PM took 5.5 hours. Most FSEs completed five to seven PMs per month. The total cost of a service call was significant, as it included direct labor costs, labor-related benefits, travel, and often other field service expenses.

Completing a job on the first visit was another important performance factor. Most customers could not afford to have an instrument down for a few days, or sometimes even for a few hours. If the FSEs did not understand the job they would face in the field, they will not finish it on the first day, and customer satisfaction would be adversely affected. To be prepared, the FSEs should schedule the visit with the customer to reduce the chances that a failure to complete the job was caused by customer time constraints. And they should download the error log and look at the instrument's service history so that they would have the parts they needed with them. As James Sorensen, manager of field service/support, expressed it, "The better the FSEs screen the job, and so the more thorough they are up front, the more likely they are to complete the call on the first visit. Ideally, the FSEs get the 'oh by the ways' on the phone, not at the site."

After each visit FSEs left a short (five-question) satisfaction survey for customers to complete and return. If the customer comments were favorable, they were always shared with the FSE and management. Unfavorable comments were invariably addressed with the customer and the FSE. The vast majority of the field service ratings (over 99%) were in the "very good" and "excellent" categories. But the customer survey return rate was only just above 25%.[2] To get better feedback, DPC hired an outside vendor to conduct phone follow-ups with a random sample of customers starting in January 2005.

Performance-dependent compensation

Because DPC FSEs were exempt employees who were not eligible for overtime, DPC created a Variable Compensation Plan. This plan provided quarterly payments to FSEs for time worked beyond regular working hours. One part of the plan paid the FSEs a monetary "comp unit" for every period of time where a FSE worked for 12 hours or was away from home for 24 straight hours. Long days were common for FSEs as customers' needs were paramount, and some FSEs had to cover customers spread over large regions, so travel time was significant. Extra compensation was also paid for weekend work or for being "on call" during a weekend. In 2003, these extra payments totaled nearly 7% of the FSEs' base pay.

[1] This figure and certain other facts in the case have been disguised.

[2] DPC field service managers believed that the average return rate for similar paper surveys across all industries was less than 10%.

As DPC grew, the field service organization also grew. Approximately 15–20 FSEs were being added each year. The additional staff decreased the need for travel and, consequently, reduced the need to pay comp units.

DPC managers still wanted to provide their FSEs an opportunity to earn extra money, but they thought that the money would be better spent in paying for performance, rather than for hours worked. Managers were particularly concerned that some FSEs who were merely spending too much time on their jobs were earning comp units, while the better FSEs were finishing their jobs early. Sunil Das, manager of regional field service engineering, explained a motivation for change: "We want to acknowledge those who work at a 'superior' level." As a consequence, they designed a new Performance Bonus Program, which was implemented in the second quarter of 2004. The objective of the program was defined as follows:

> **The Bonus Program is designed to measure critical performance metrics of a Field Service Engineer as it pertains to aspects of the job that lead to total customer satisfaction. These metrics target the key facets that increase DPC's value to our customers.**

The new Performance Bonus Program awarded field service engineers both points and money. The money was designed to replace the compensation that was formerly paid in comp units and, hence, to leave the total-compensation packages at competitive levels. But the change was phased in. The comp unit values were reduced by 50% in the third and fourth quarters of 2004 and were eliminated in 2005. The points portion of the program was to be introduced to the field in 2005. Management wanted to take "baby steps" in the implementation of the program and manage each quarter manually until they had a full understanding of the ups and downs of the data.

The awards of points and/or money were based on the FSEs' performance in six areas:

1. **Cross training**. Engineers were awarded 10 "base" points for each instrument that they were qualified to service–IMMULITE, IMMULITE 2000, IMMULITE 2500, SMS–for a maximum of 40 points.
2. **Preventive maintenance (PM) completion**. FSEs earned two points for each PM completed. To earn the points, the PMs had to be both scheduled with the customer and completed on time.

   James Sorenson was confident that the FSEs could not easily manipulate the number of PMs completed, such as by reporting PM completion without actually having done the work. Each PM required a checklist of critical parts that must be changed, and each PM call was automatically tracked in the software. And, Sunil Das added, "When FSEs do a poor job at preventative maintenance, it 'bites them back' in the call back rate" (see below).
3. **Teamwork factor for PMs**. If the region met the specified PM goals for the quarter for instruments covered by warranty and/or service agreement, each FSE in that region would receive the following:

90–96% completed	1% of base quarterly salary, plus 5 points
97–100% completed	2% of base quarterly salary, plus 10 points

4. **Complete first visit**. Complete first visits were defined as service events completed on the first day of the visit. The following proportions of complete first visits were rewarded as follows:

PMs	Repairs
90–99%, 2–11 points 100%, 20 points	85–95%, 1–11 points 96–98%, 18–20 points 99–100%, 24–25 points

   Sunil Das explained that completing service calls on the first day was not always possible, "no matter how hard one tries," due to parts delivery delays and other uncontrollable factors. The DPC national average first-day-completion of PMs was 97%; for repairs it was 93%.
5. **Call back rate**. Call back rates were defined as multiple visits within 30 days of each other where: (1) the same module was worked on; (2) non-PM visits were for the same problem; (3) the subsequent visit was within three days of a PM; and (4) initial and subsequent visits were associated with the same client call. However, subsequent visits in the following categories were not considered call backs: (1) moves; (2) installations; (3) removals; (4) PM; (5) service check list; (6) proactive repair; (7) retrofit; and (8) peripheral.

Some of these exceptions were added after the bonus program was initially implemented. In their early experiences with the program, managers noticed that some of the FSEs that they thought were among their best did not have the lowest call back rates. Sunil Das gave an example:

> One of our sharp engineers noticed during a PM that the hinge on an instrument was a little weak. He went back the next week to fix it, but then we "dinged" him for a call back. So unintentionally we were penalizing an opportunity to "shine" before the customer. Now

we exclude this type of procedure as a proactive repair. It doesn't affect the customer, and the machine is not down. We're trying to get this right. But even the best engineers won't have a 0% call-back rate. We do get some "hard" instrument failures that have nothing to do with the quality of their work.

The rewards for call back rate proportions were set as follows:

IMMULITE			IMMULITE 2000		
Call-back rate	% base		Call-back rate		% base
proportions (%)	Points	quarterly salary	proportions (%)	Points	quarterly salary
10–9	2–3	1.33	20	2–4	1.33
8–7	4–5	1.67	19–17	5–7	1.67
6–5	6–7	2.0	16–14	8–10	2.0
4	10	2.33	13–12	11–12	2.33
3	20	2.67	11–10	13–14	3.33
2	25	3.0	9–7	20–25	4.0
1	40	3.33	6–5	30–35	4.67
0	60	4.0	4–3	40–45	5.33
			2–1	50–55	6.0
			0	60	6.67

A minimum of nine service visits per instrument type had to be attained each given quarter for eligibility. The DPC national average for call backs was approximately 10%, which was less than the industry average of slightly less than 20%.

The new instruments (IMMULITE 2500 and SMS) were not included in this reward schedule. They were too new to have well-established failure rates that distinguished inevitable start-up problems from FSE-related service quality issues. At the end of 2004, only seven FSE specialists were qualified to work on these new products.

6. *Administrative functions.* Managers evaluated each FSE in each of the following performance areas:

1. Customer satisfaction	0–25 points
2. Expense reports	0–25 points
3. Service reports completion	0–25 points
4. Dispatch feedback	0–25 points
5. Synchronization	0–25 points
6. Company car maintenance	0–25 points
7. Conference call roll call	0–25 points
8. Inventory management	0–25 points

The evaluations were based on subjective judgments of data that were monitored centrally. Managers considered several factors deemed important in each area. For example, the *customer satisfaction* ratings were based on both the averages from the customer survey as well as the return rate. The idea was to watch trends in customer survey return rates per FSE (relative to the overall average of about 25%), as some FSEs sometimes neglected to leave a survey for the customer to complete. Past experience had shown, particularly, that some FSEs had tended to "forget" to leave a survey with the customer when they suspected that the customer was dissatisfied about their work. *Dispatch feedback* was based on reports from the service dispatchers. Which FSEs were not accepting calls? Which were "grabbing" them? *Synchronization* ratings reflected the extent to which the FSEs were inputting their service data to the centralized database within 48 hours. FSEs who were never "delinquent" ordinarily received 25 points for synchronization; those who showed a pattern of delinquencies would receive no points and be called in for corrective action.

James Sorensen, manager of field service/support, explained that, "No dollar bonus amounts were attached to performance in the administrative function areas to remove the possibility for perceived favoritism. All we were trying to do when we came up with this was to assess, at the margin, whether someone had put in an honest day's work."

Exhibit 5 shows a quarterly bonus calculation for a hypothetical FSE. This FSE would be paid a bonus of 6.33% of his/her quarterly base salary and would also have earned 261 bonus points.

Field service managers were monitoring the point accumulations as indicators of successes and failures both of their function and those of individual FSEs. They used this feedback to make improvements, such as in the content of training courses and the mentoring of individual FSEs, but they had not yet decided how to attach reward values to the points earned. One possibility that had been mentioned was to invite the top FSE point earner to the annual sales meeting, which was held in the winter in either Hawaii or Arizona. Other possibilities were an awards plaque, a monetary award, and/or a mention in the service newsletter that was distributed company-wide.

Early experiences and plans for the future

At the end of 2004, field service managers were pleased with the initial effects of the new bonus program. From their perspective, the bonus program had introduced a lot more objectivity in the system. Managers had a quarterly, quantitative snapshot of the performance of each FSE. The managers also thought that the bonus program had positive influences on FSEs' behaviors. They saw, for example, decreases in call-back rates, which they attributed to the FSEs paying more care to their jobs and not "trying to rush through the calls."

The field service managers continued to compare the data against the performances of the FSEs whom they thought were the best to make sure the new bonus program was not critically flawed. That's how they discovered, and subsequently added, the new call-back exceptions, as was described above.

At the end of 2004, after much debate, FSE managers decided to make a substantive change. They combined the instrument groups to calculate one overall call back rate per FSE. They concluded that as far as the company was concerned, a call back (regardless of instrument model) is a call back: The expenses incurred are the same, and customers are upset with a call back regardless of the type of instrument they have. The field service managers also decided to have the payout increase based on the number of calls the FSE makes in a given quarter. So FSEs were promised higher payouts for more calls (productivity) and fewer call backs (customer responsiveness), as follows (minimum of 10 calls per quarter):

Calls per quarter	Call-back rate (%)	Payout (% base quarterly salary)	Calls per quarter	Call-back rate (%)	Payout (% base quarterly salary)
10	20	1.0	31–40	20	5.0
	19–15	1.33		19–15	5.67
	14–10	1.67		14–10	6.67
	9–5	2.33		9–5	8.33
	4–0	3.33		4–0	10.0
11–20	20	1.33	41–50	20	6.67
	19–15	2.0		19–15	8.33
	14–10	2.67		14–10	10.0
	9–5	4.0		9–5	11.67
	4–0	5.33		4–0	13.33
21–30	20	3.33	50+	20	8.0
	19–15	4.0		19–15	9.33
	14–10	5.0		14–10	10.67
	9–5	5.67		9–5	12.0
	4–0	6.67		4–0	13.33

While they had proposed the schedule shown above, the field service managers were not yet sure if the payout levels were correct. They were withholding their bonus recommendations to the payroll department while they examined the data further. The fourth-quarter payments were to be made by the end of February 2005.

DPC's field service managers knew that there was "still some wariness" among the FSEs regarding the new program. Many FSEs had expressed concerns. Some FSEs were concerned that the company had "taken something away from them." Others were not sure that they were being held accountable for something "real." And some complained that they were placed at an unfair advantage, as compared to other FSEs, because of their customer mix.

The field service managers knew that they would have to continue to "tweak and massage" the program to get it right, and feedback from the field service force would help the process. They knew that they had to decide how to reward the FSEs' accumulations of "points," something they had promised to do by 2005. And they knew that they had to enhance their performance metrics and, hopefully, move some of the performance areas, such as parts inventory, out of the subjectively assessed "administration" category.

Exhibit 1 Diagnostic Products Corporation: Income statements for years ending December 31 (all data in millions)

	2003	2002	2001	2000
Net sales	381.39	324.09	283.13	247.61
Cost of goods sold	164.36	137.75	120.69	110.52
Gross profit	**217.02**	**186.34**	**162.44**	**137.08**
Research and development expenditures	40.68	36.82	31.45	26.46
Selling general and administrative expenses	99.02	84.15	76.47	70.52
Income before depreciation and amortization	**77.33**	**65.37**	**54.52**	**40.10**
Depreciation and amortization	n/a	n/a	n/a	n/a
Nonoperating income	11.11	3.84	3.30	2.42
Interest expense	n/a	1.22	.01	n/a
Income before tax	**88.44**	**67.99**	**57.82**	**42.52**
Provision for income taxes	26.28	21.08	17.81	12.86
Minority interest	.36	(.40)	.98	1.41
Net income before extra items	**61.80**	**47.31**	**39.03**	**28.25**
Extra items discontinued operations	n/a	n/a	n/a	n/a
Net income	**61.80**	**47.31**	**39.03**	**28.25**

Exhibit 2 Diagnostic Products Corporation: IMMULITE products

IMMULITE 1000

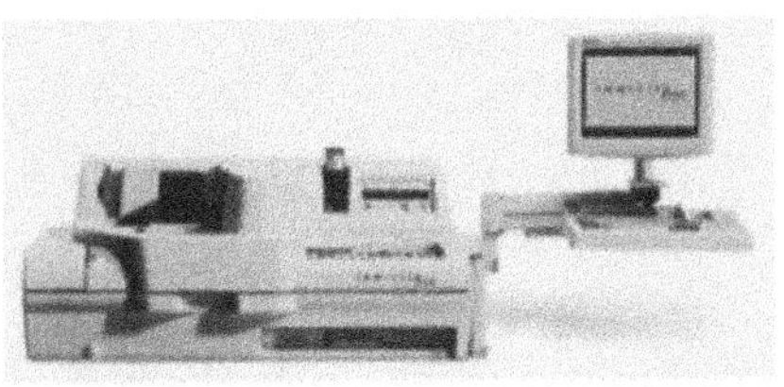

IMMULITE 2000 with Sample Management System (SMS)

Exhibit 3 Diagnostic Products Corporation: Corporate organization chart

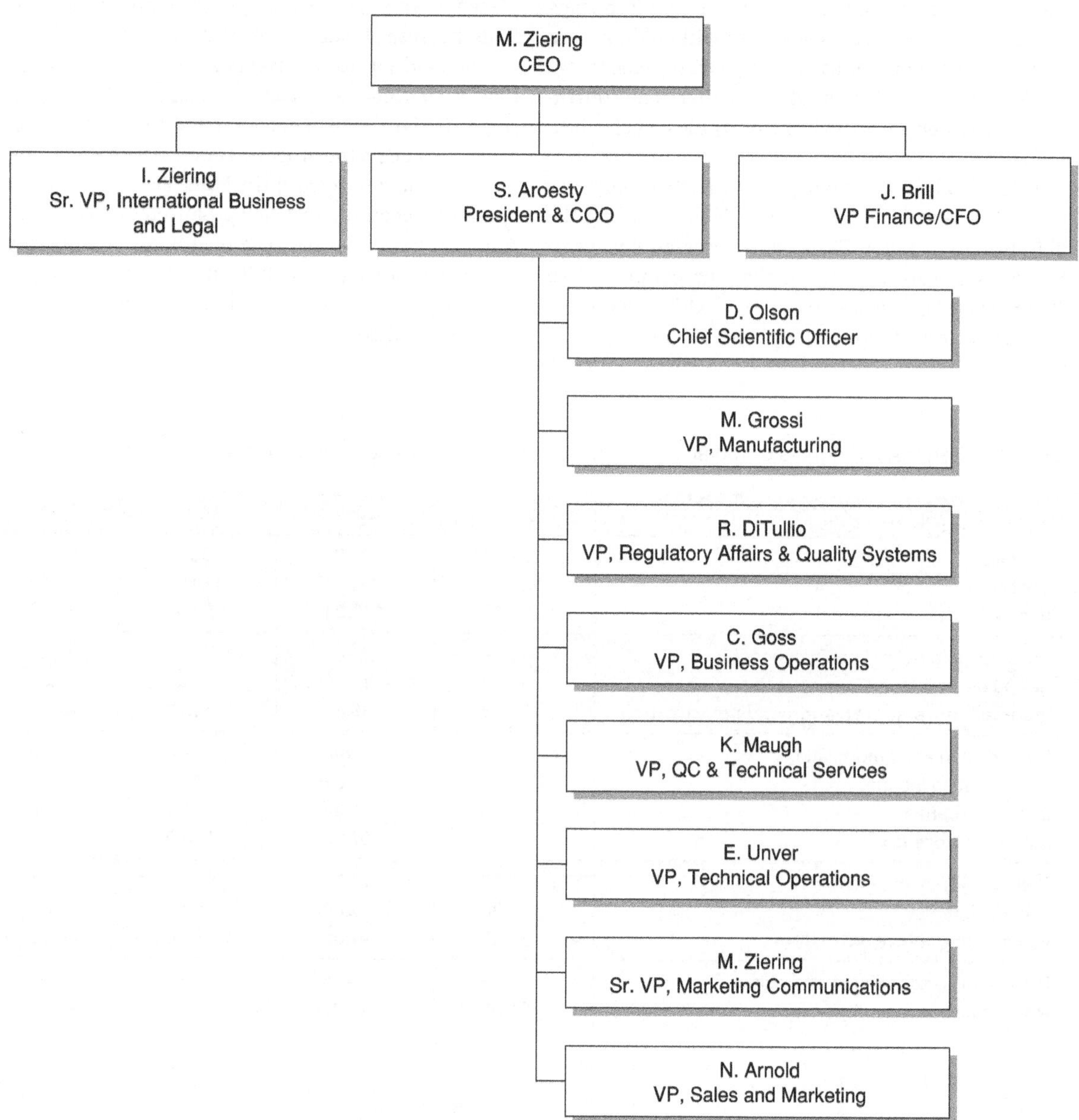

Exhibit 4 Diagnostic Products Corporation: Field service organization

Exhibit 5 Diagnostic Products Corporation: Bonus program reward calculation for a hypothetical FSE

		Points earned	Payout (% base quarterly salary)
Base points	Qualified on IMMULITE and IMMULITE 2000	20	–
PMs completed	10	20	–
Teamwork	97%	10	2
Complete first visit	PMs 95%	7	–
	Repairs 90%	6	–
Call-back rate	IMMULITE 5%	7	2
	IMMULITE 2000 13%	11	2.33
Administration		180	–
Total for quarter		261	6.33%

This case was prepared by Professors Kenneth A. Merchant and Wim A. Van der Stede. Some facts and names have been disguised.

CASE STUDY
Game Shop, Inc.

David McDonald, financial analyst for Game Shop, Inc. (GSI), had just hand-delivered invoices to ExcitoVision, Inc. (EVI), one of GSI's largest customers. He did not have to make such deliveries often, and he hated the task, but he thought this trip was necessary to keep EVI happy. EVI had always been a difficult client to deal with, but the relationship had become much more prickly since GSI had accidentally over-billed EVI for almost $1 million in a recent quarter. The over-billings occurred because of a series of errors, particularly double billings and incorrect calculations of rebates. In fact, GSI almost lost EVI as a customer as a result of this incident. David felt that when he delivered the invoices, he needed to greet the EVI managers "with a bow, and roses and chocolates." In the past few months, David believed that he had made a lot of progress in mending the relationship with EVI and also with some other companies that had suffered because of errors in GSI's billing system.

GSI management knew that the company's billing system needed to be improved significantly. In early 2010, top management had assigned David the task of improving GSI's billing process. He had largely completed the first phase of that task. He had designed new processes, conducted a series of training sessions, and started monitoring billing performance using a new "Billings Scorecard" that contained an extensive array of billing-related performance metrics. David hoped that the new, improved billing system would prove to be effective. The goal was perfection. He noted: "Expectations are high; even one mistake can have huge consequences."

Company background

GSI, founded in 2002, was a leading video game servicing house, providing services to video game publishing companies. GSI converted games from template backgrounds, video, and computer code into finished digital products, mostly DVDs and secure downloadable files. GSI also provided related services such as menu creation, international dubbing, and audio enhancement.

GSI's customers, video game publishing companies, developed or licensed video games, and then financed, distributed, and marketed the games around the world. The video game publishing industry was an oligopoly; it consisted of a handful of very large companies that dominated the market, as well as many much smaller, niche companies. Six game publishing companies accounted for 90% of GSI's revenue.

GSI was divided into 17 profit centers or business units (BUs) (see Exhibit 1). Seven of the BUs were organized around customers, 6 of them focused exclusively on the projects of a single, large customer. The other 10 BUs focused on an area of expertise, such as Creative Content Production and International Dubbing, and worked on projects for numerous customers. The BU managers reported to Kevin Brink, senior vice president of Worldwide Operations and Business Execution, who, in turn, reported to the CEO. Functional departments, such as finance, sales and marketing, legal, and human resources, reported directly to the CEO.

The video game industry was dynamic. GSI employees had to work hard to stay on top of increasingly complex and rapidly changing game features, specifications, and requirements. GSI had a reputation both for production quality and for being able to tackle difficult projects. Kevin Brink explained:

> **Throughout our business we try to create a culture of excellence. One of the signs on my wall says, "Perfect, that is all." Our expectation is perfection, because our reputation can be ruined with just one mistake. Six sigma isn't good enough. We have to operate at 15 sigma, or we go out of business.**

Every month Kevin's office published a 50-page Management Review, which was available to all employees on the company's intranet. The report consisted of dozens of scorecards, focused primarily on product quality. The report created transparency and allowed employees to learn from the reports of failures. Failures were measured and also addressed with a Corrective Action Report (CAR). The CAR outlined the reason for the failure, named the department and/or individual(s) responsible, and prescribed corrective action. CARs linked to an individual employee became part of that employee's permanent record.

Kevin also managed a World Wide Knowledge Base that gave employees around the world access to the most recent work instructions, checklists, forms, and policies. He discouraged employees from sending outdated emails or storing outdated instructions on their PCs. Often when CARs were issued, the failure was at least partially addressed by updating instructions in the Knowledge Base. Kevin believed in knocking out failure modes with smart controls, or, as he explained, "I minimize discretion so that a process cannot continue until the right choices are made. I try to force things to be right."

Billings and revenue recognition

GSI project managers (PMs) were responsible for managing customer projects from start to finish. Their responsibilities included billing. Most PMs had no financial or technical background. All were high school graduates, and some also had a college degree, usually in a liberal arts field. The best of the PMs were smart generalists who were able to juggle multiple priorities.

In addition to the PM, a typical project involved at least eight employees, most of whom had a technical specialty such as video compositing. Projects required quality control personnel as well, usually two focused on the incoming stage of the project and two or three focused on the outgoing stage. Quality control checks were built into the process.

GSI's policy was that no project was to be started without first securing a purchase order (PO) from the customer. The PMs regularly violated that policy, however, with tacit approval from corporate. As one PM explained, "[The big customers] are temperamental. We don't want to upset them." Even starting a project with a PO in hand did not solve all the billing problems. Not all the project contingencies could be foreseen, and overages above the amount specified in the initial purchase order were common in the industry.

Revenue was recognized when it was earned. PMs would estimate the amount they would eventually bill for the work that had been done to date and enter it as accrued revenue. Once the project was billed, the amount changed from accrued revenue to an account receivable. Each PM was responsible for tracking time spent on projects, changes to the projects, and overages. Once the project shipped, the PM was also responsible for compiling a billing packet that the billing department sent to the customer for approval and payment.

Bills, and in some cases even the billing processes, were tailored to each customer. For example, one customer did not allow overages, so they would not sign a PO until the project was completed. The PO, shipping document, and invoice were all sent to this customer at the same time. In a practice somewhat unique to the industry, many customers were not billed when the project shipped, but were given a period of time to review and approve charges after the project was shipped. The period of time allowed varied by customer. Kevin noted, "Sometimes it's as difficult to bill the thing as to build the thing."

Accuracy and timeliness issues

Billing accuracy and timeliness had become increasingly important as the company matured. Kevin was concerned that GSI's reputation for billing was not up to par with its reputation for delivering quality products, and billing problems were causing frictions with important customers. Partly because of the financial reporting and internal control requirements of the Sarbanes-Oxley Act of 2002, most customers were now requesting better invoice accuracy. In addition, as GSI grew, its need for working capital also grew, so it was imperative to get invoices delivered and receivables collected as promptly as possible.

Friction with large customers had revealed some billing issues, and there was additional evidence that problems existed. The PM's accrual estimates could be wildly inaccurate, and there were often several months of accrued revenue sitting on the books. In late 2010, GSI had over $5 million of working capital "trapped in accruals older than 60 days," almost twice GSI's average monthly revenue.

The improvement process

David was assigned the task of improving the billing system. He was given clear project goals: achieve 98% accuracy in accrued revenue calculations and reduce accruals to a maximum of 30 days of sales. If David's project was successful, the accrued revenue amount would decrease from over $5 million to $1.3 million.

In early 2010, GSI management had a brainstorming session to identify the issues. They found that a lot of controls were missing. As a result, some billings were not being turned in. Many that were turned in were inaccurate. Sometimes customers were double billed. PMs were a major cause of the problems. This was understandable, as Kevin noted, "They are busy people. Sometimes they don't get all the details right."

To understand all the root causes of the problem, David built a "fault tree" (see Exhibit 2). The purpose of the fault tree was to diagnose the problem in enough detail so that the solutions would follow from the detailed diagnoses. David's fault tree exercise exposed nearly 100 causes of the inaccuracies and revenue accrual build-ups. These issues could be categorized as system or process issues, customer issues, and management issues.

System/process issues

The billing system had several flaws. Billing paperwork could only be submitted once a week, and reports could take upwards of 10 minutes to download onto a PM's computer. There was also no redundancy in the process. A single employee's vacation could hold up the entire company's billing cycle.

Theoretically, these issues could be addressed with changes to the system, but both the billing and IT departments were resistant to change. David thought that billing department resistance stemmed both from familiarity and comfort with the existing system and, probably, fear of job loss. Billing department personnel had also been burned once by the IT department when it tried to force a new alpha version of a system on them. This system was untested and full of bugs, so hard feelings had been created. The IT department had always given billing projects low priority. Historically, the IT focus had always been on systems designed to improve operations. Financial systems had always been an afterthought.

Customer issues

GSI's policy was that nothing could be shipped without a PO, but some customers refused to issue a PO. They wanted to make changes along the way and have the bill from GSI reflect what was actually shipped. Even where POs were used, they often quickly became obsolete as changes were made to the work orders. Some customers insisted on a lengthy review process before they would approve a bill even though the order had already shipped. Some projects shipped over a long period of time, upwards of one year, but customers would not accept a bill until the final stage of the project was complete.

David accepted that customer behavior could not be controlled completely, but he also believed that PMs and managers could do more to try to influence customer behavior. PMs could try to insist on getting a customer PO. They could also try to get authorization to bill for parts of a job instead of waiting for the entire job to be complete. For example, one BU was able to persuade a customer to pay for international dubbing before the Japanese version, by far the most technical and time-consuming dubbing task, was complete. This shortened the billing cycle on this job from over a year to just four months.

Management issues

Perhaps the biggest issue was that many GSI PMs did not track project changes and simply did not turn in billing paperwork in a timely manner. Some just accrued things randomly. For example, they would declare certain tasks as having been completed, forget what they had done in the prior period, and then bill for them again.

David discovered several causes of this problem. GSI did not have a set of written billing instructions, and many managers did not know how to use the billing tools available to them. In general, PMs did not understand the importance of correct and timely billing, and often were not aware that there was a problem; they assumed several months of accruals were the norm. Managers were also not terribly motivated to spend time on billing. They were much more focused on production. The problem was aggravated during the busy season when some managers complained that they were already in the office until past 11 p.m. every night making sure orders were shipped. Forced to choose between spending time on shipping or billing issues, they chose shipping.

While some of the problems could be seen as failures of specific individuals, David decided to focus on improving the process, rather than focusing on specific individuals' failures. He provided training sessions that included instruction on billing and time management, and he added detailed billing instructions to the World Wide Knowledge Base.

Billings Scorecard

To focus attention on billing performance, David developed a new "Billings Scorecard," a monthly report that tracked each BU's billing performance. David hoped the Billings Scorecard would provide increased visibility about billing performance. Many PMs, and even their bosses, had not cared about billing-related performance in large part because it was not measured or reported. He noted, "We are metrics centric in our culture." David hoped that the scorecard would motivate better billing performance and, in the end, provide the basis for assessing the overall success of his project.

The Billings Scorecard (see Exhibit 3) rated each BU's billing performance in terms of four measures (described below). David converted each of the scores into a 0-to-4-point scale, or "grade."

1. **Percent of sales invoiced = monthly dollars invoiced/monthly dollars sold**

   A perfect score of 1 would mean that every dollar sold was also invoiced. This measure was converted into a grade by multiplying by 4.

2. **Adjusted number of weeks of sales accrued = accruals/(3 months of sales/13) − approval delay**

   A week of sales was approximated using a 13-week average to smooth the value. The measure was adjusted by an approval delay factor that was specific to each customer. Most customers had an approval delay built into their payment systems that allowed them a certain period of time to approve bills before they could be officially billed. The adjusted number of weeks accrued was calculated by subtracting the weeks a customer was allowed for approval from the number of weeks accrued. For example, if a business unit had six weeks of sales accrued, but their customer was allowed three weeks to approve bills, the BU's adjusted weeks of accruals would be three (i.e. 6 − 3). BUs were allowed one week of slack. For each additional week or fraction thereof, one grade point was subtracted from a perfect 4.0 to convert the measure into a grade. So using the example above, a score of 3 would produce a 2.0 or C grade (i.e. 4 − (3 − 1)).

3. **Percent of sales shipped without a PO = sales shipped without PO/sales shipped**

   This measure was only available for the five BUs that used GSI's standard order management system. A perfect score for this measure would be 0; i.e. nothing shipped without a PO. The measure was converted to a grade by subtracting it from 1 and multiplying the result by 4.

4. **Percent of accruals less than 30 days old**

   This measure was a rough estimate of accrual aging. A perfect score of 100% (or 1 in decimal points) would mean that all of the accruals on the books were less than 30 days old. The measure was converted to a grade by multiplying the decimal score by 4 (i.e. 75% or 0.75 would yield a score of 3).

The four grades were weighted equally to produce an overall average. The scores for each BU were published in an email message that was distributed to all BU directors, vice presidents, and senior vice presidents.

Detention

The managers of BUs with a grade of C and below (less than or equal to a 2.0 grade) were called to a "detention" meeting with Tyler Pizer, GSI's vice president of finance. Kevin and David also attended these meetings. During the detention meetings, the participants went through each accrual in detail to determine what was causing a delay. If the delay was caused by client behavior, the problem was noted and communicated to the sales department. If it was caused by managers who were "too busy to bill," David would seek a commitment from the BU director to bill during the current period. Sometimes meeting participants uncovered "phantom" accruals, such as a project that had already been billed or a non-billable project with no accruable value.

Despite the punitive nomenclature, detention meetings were intended to be productive. Sometimes grades were adjusted if it was determined that the poor grades were either caused by incomplete information or were not the fault of the BU employees. David explained,

> The purpose of the detention meetings is to understand and correct the issues in the business unit. The Scorecard is a dialogue opener. In fact, often after discussing a particular BU's performance during detention, we realized that we needed to make a grade change. Sometimes they didn't deserve the D because we were missing the right information. The detention discussions are part of the measurement system analysis.

For example, in June, the BU for Customer 7 received a D grade, mostly because of its very low score on Measure #4 (percent of accruals less than 30 days old). But the BU director, Quinton Ruiz, explained that though there was a low percentage of accruals less than 30 days old, 100% of accruals were less than 60 days old. "We fell a little bit behind because of the busy season, but it hasn't spun too far out of control." The BU's grade was adjusted upward by removing the offending items from the calculation.

Managers of the Creative International Menu BU complained that it was not possible for them to improve their grade on Measure #4. The BU built menus several months in advance of a project completing, but most customers insisted on receiving the bill for menu charges together with the final project. David agreed to factor the menu charges out of Measure #4 in the future.

The Localization BU had similar issues. They could not bill until an entire project with dozens of languages and elements was complete, but they recognized accruals language by language, piece by piece. Tyler and David ultimately decided that due to the nature of their work, the Localization BU could not be expected to earn a grade above 2.0; it was acceptable for them to have significant unbilled accruals.

Sometimes the detention process uncovered simple clerical errors. One business unit called into detention had actually turned in a box of invoices that was misplaced by the billing department, so their grade was also adjusted upward.

P-CARs

David had one other motivational tool at his disposal; he could issue P-CARs (Process Corrective Action Reports) to managers who made billing errors. P-CARs were used to identify software glitches and broken procedures. The P-CARs described where a process went wrong, who the responsible parties were, and what corrective actions should be prescribed. Unlike CARs, which were administered by the human resources department, P-CARs were not noted in an employee's personnel file. The focus of a P-CAR was on the process, rather than the person. Still, no one who was issued a P-CAR was pleased about it.

At the time of the case, David was issuing an average of a few P-CARs per month. He expected that number to decline over time as the broken elements in the processes were repaired. Eventually, he expected most of the errors to come from human mistakes more than from software or process design flaws.

Early results

David was generally pleased with the early results of his billing process improvements and, in particular, the BU managers' responses to the scorecard. He said:

> **Their first reactions might be defensive, but they really do want to understand. They are curious. They want their metrics to go up, and they are intelligent enough to realize that they need to understand the metrics to improve them.**

David expected that the scorecard grades would eventually be used as a "bonus modifier." That is, the grades would be considered by managers in making their judgments about performance. In normal economic conditions, PMs earned an average annual bonus of 20% of salary. However, because the recession of 2008–2009 had adversely affected GSI's performance, nobody within the company had earned any bonuses in the last two years.

In the three months since David had implemented the scorecard and related processes, deferred revenue accruals had dropped by half. Billing error rates had dropped to 0.3%, much lower than the 15% error rates of a year earlier. David expected that billing grades for the following month would be improved, partly because the busy season was over, but mostly because the GSI's CEO had warned BU directors that there would be "dire consequences" if their grades did not increase.

David knew that his mission was far from being complete. The scorecard was still new, and he was open to suggestions for refinements. He still wondered if the scorecard was built on the best measures, and if it made sense to weight them all evenly. He was particularly concerned about Measure #1 because it was distorted by seasonal sales spikes. For example, the BU for Customer #5 had managed to increase its grade to a B− in August, but David knew the improvement was mostly due to declining sales and lagging invoices, not improved billing practices. More generally, David wondered if he would be able to meet his ambitious quantitative project goals without changing customer behaviors. He also wondered if even achievement of those goals would be sufficient in the long run, as the true objective was perfection.

Exhibit 1 Game Shop, Inc.: Organizational chart

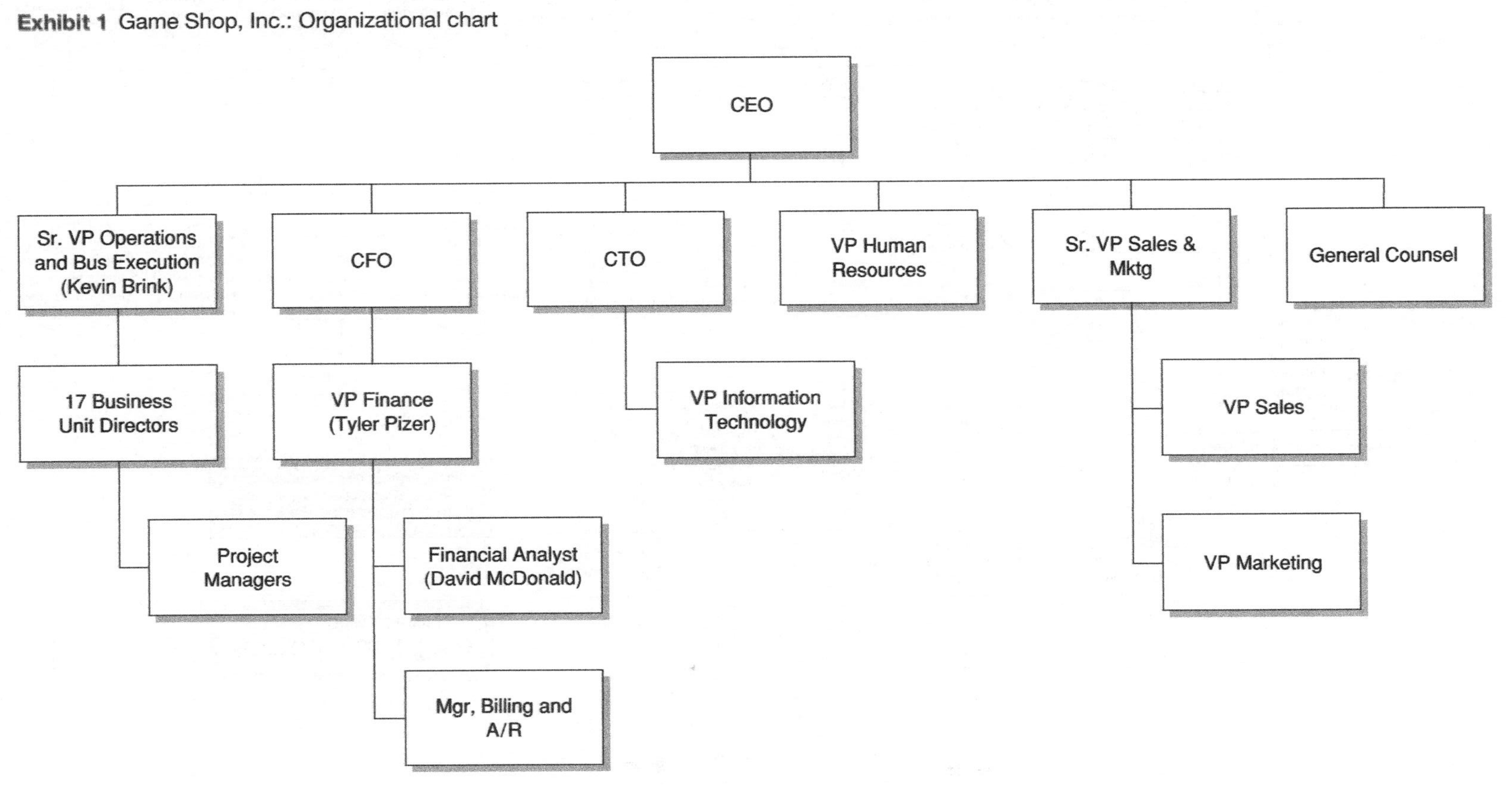

Exhibit 2 Accrual fault tree

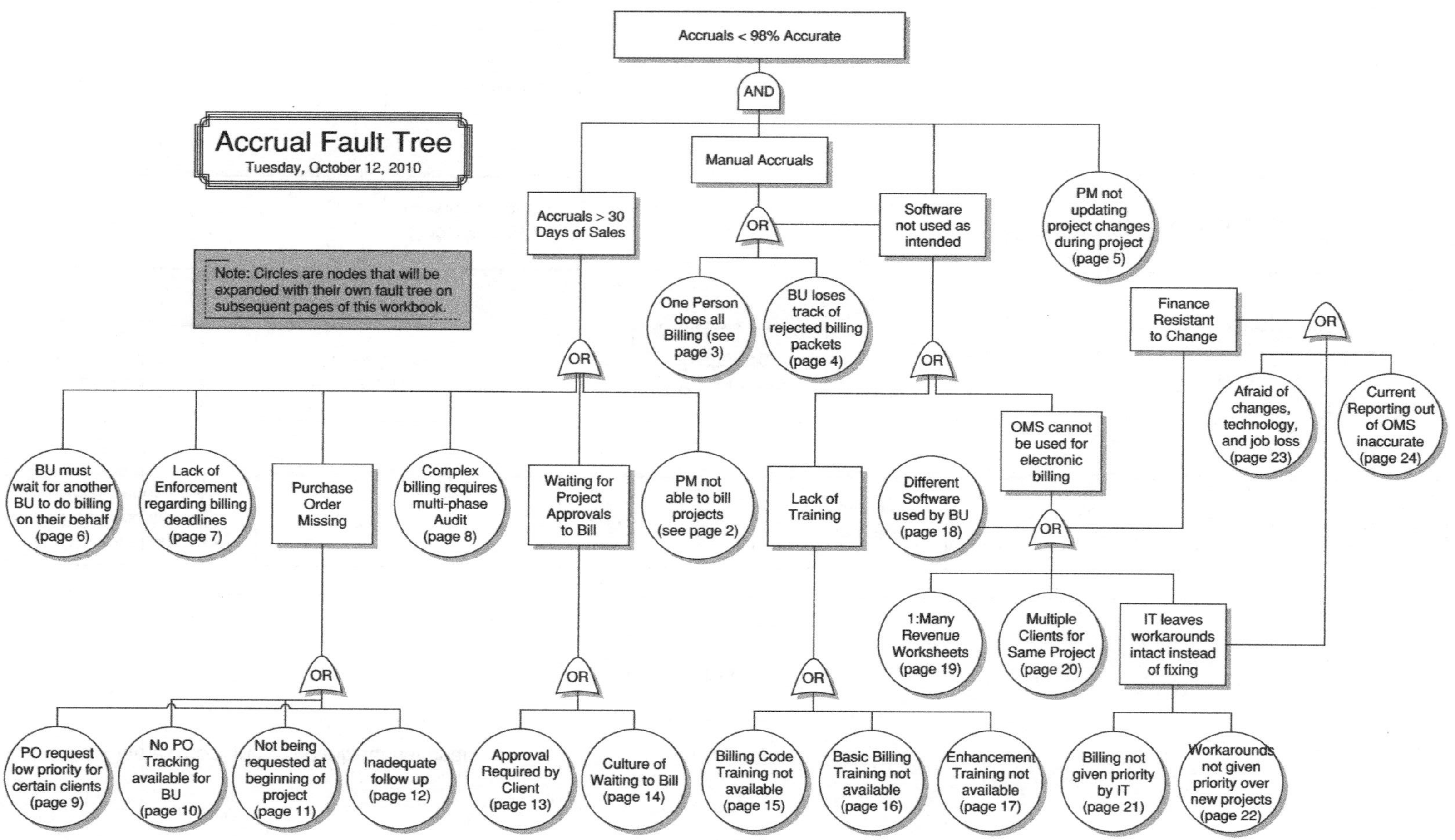

Accrual Fault Tree
Tuesday, October 12, 2010

Note: Circles are nodes that will be expanded with their own fault tree on subsequent pages of this workbook.

Accruals < 98% Accurate
AND
Accruals > 30 Days of Sales
Manual Accruals
Software not used as intended
PM not updating project changes during project (page 5)
OR
One Person does all Billing (see page 3)
BU loses track of rejected billing packets (page 4)
Finance Resistant to Change
OR
Afraid of changes, technology, and job loss (page 23)
Current Reporting out of OMS inaccurate (page 24)
OR
OR
BU must wait for another BU to do billing on their behalf (page 6)
Lack of Enforcement regarding billing deadlines (page 7)
Purchase Order Missing
Complex billing requires multi-phase Audit (page 8)
Waiting for Project Approvals to Bill
PM not able to bill projects (see page 2)
Lack of Training
Different Software used by BU (page 18)
OMS cannot be used for electronic billing
OR
1:Many Revenue Worksheets (page 19)
Multiple Clients for Same Project (page 20)
IT leaves workarounds intact instead of fixing
OR
OR
OR
PO request low priority for certain clients (page 9)
No PO Tracking available for BU (page 10)
Not being requested at beginning of project (page 11)
Inadequate follow up (page 12)
Approval Required by Client (page 13)
Culture of Waiting to Bill (page 14)
Billing Code Training not available (page 15)
Basic Billing Training not available (page 16)
Enhancement Training not available (page 17)
Billing not given priority by IT (page 21)
Workarounds not given priority over new projects (page 22)

Exhibit 2 *(continued)*

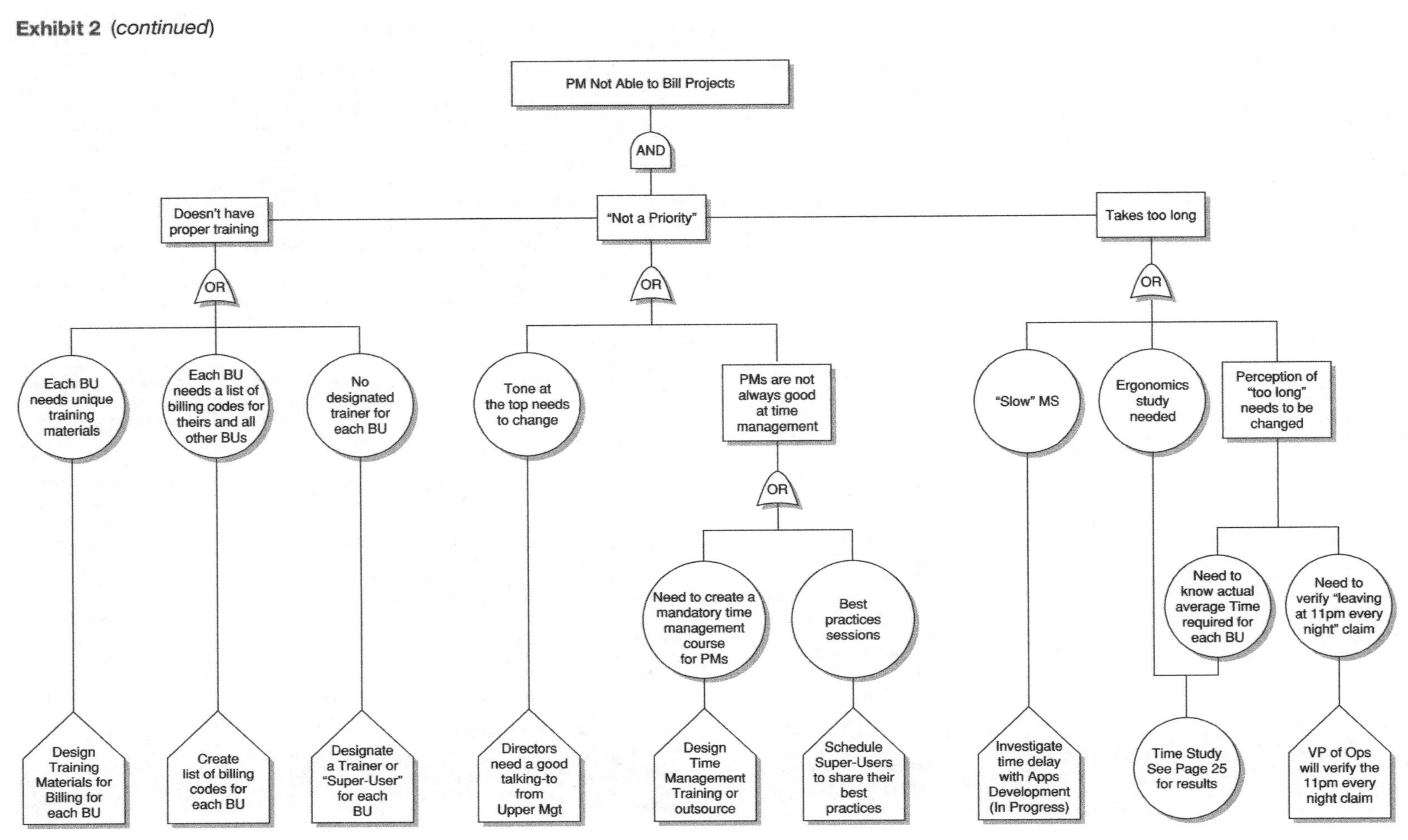

Exhibit 3 The Billings Scorecard (June)

Business unit	June invoiced	June sales	% of sales invoiced	GPA 1	Weeks of sales accrued	Customer approval delay	Adjusted weeks of sales accrued	GPA 2	% shipped w/o PO	GPA 3	% accruals < 30 days Old	GPA 4	Overall GPA	Grade
Customer 1	803.84	2,668.47	0.30	**1.20**	4.5	3.0	1.5	**3.51**	38%	**2.48**	54.7%	2.19	2.34	C+
Customer 2	345.88	762.40	0.45	**1.81**	9.0	3.0	6.0	**0.00**	9%	**3.65**	46.7%	1.87	1.83	C–
Customer 3	1,683.97	1,954.20	0.86	**3.45**	0.6	0.0	0.6	**4.00**	0%	**4.00**	100.0%	4.00	3.86	A
Customer 4	93.28	370.44	0.25	**1.01**	0.0	0.0	0.0	**4.00**	41%	**2.37**	100.0%	4.00	2.84	B–
Creative International Menu	74.82	134.81	0.55	**2.22**	5.1	5.0	0.1	**4.00**		**n/a**	73.8%	2.95	3.06	B
Creative Content Production	295.65	282.19	1.05	**4.00**	2.9	1.0	1.9	**3.11**		**n/a**	61.4%	2.45	3.19	B+
Creative Design	218.48	144.74	1.51	**4.00**	5.0	3.0	2.0	**3.04**		**n/a**	52.9%	2.12	3.05	B
Network Services	197.25	499.41	0.39	**1.58**	6.6	0.3	6.3	**0.00**		**n/a**	59.5%	2.38	1.32	D+
Digital Reference Services	152.13	152.13	1.00	**4.00**	0.0	0.0	0.0	**n/a**		**n/a**	100.0%	n/a	4.00	A+
Audio Services	137.33	137.33	1.00	**4.00**	0.0	0.0	0.0	**n/a**		**n/a**	100.0%	n/a	4.00	A+
International Dubbing	310.46	310.46	1.00	**4.00**	0.0	0.0	0.0	**n/a**		**n/a**	100.0%	n/a	4.00	A+
Customer 5	261.17	275.32	0.95	**3.79**	11.2	0.3	10.9	**0.00**		**n/a**	33.0%	1.32	1.70	C–
Customer 6	94.96	94.96	1.00	**4.00**	0.0	0.3	– 0.3	**4.00**		**n/a**	100.0%	4.00	4.00	A+
Customer 7	504.78	763.12	0.66	**2.65**	17.0	3.0	14.0	**0.00**	39%	**2.42**	13.9%	0.56	1.41	D+
Design, Eng. & Mfg 1	2,098.85	1,515.81	1.38	**4.00**	0.0	2.0	– 2.0	**4.00**		**n/a**	100.0%	4.00	4.00	A+
Design, Eng. & Mfg 2	–	418.93	–	**0.00**	2.7	2.0	0.7	**4.00**		**n/a**	100.0%	4.00	2.67	B–
Localization	918.26	1,827.66	0.50	**2.01**	7.6	4.0	3.6	**1.39**		**n/a**	34.0%	1.36	1.59	C–

Exhibit 4 Scorecard early trends (June–August)

	GPA 1–% of sales invoiced			GPA 2–adjusted weeks of sales accrued			GPA 3–% shipped with PO			GPA 4–% accruals < 30 days old			Overall grade		
Business unit	JUN	JUL	AUG	JUN	JUL	AUG	JUN	JUL	AUG	JUN	JUL	AUG	JUN	JUL	AUG
Customer I	**1.20**	3.19	2.12	**3.51**	4.00	1.60	**2.48**	3.39	3.54	**2.19**	2.72	2.20	**C+**	B+	C+
Customer 2	**1.81**	2.42	3.45	**0.00**	0.00	0.10	**3.65**	3.65	3.70	**1.87**	2.94	2.31	**C–**	C+	C+
Customer 3	**3.45**	4.00	3.99	**4.00**	4.00	4.00	**4.00**	4.00	4.00	**4.00**	4.00	4.00	**A**	A+	A+
Customer 4	**1.01**	2.59	3.94	**4.00**	3.52	3.60	**2.37**	4.00	0.00	**4.00**	4.00	4.00	**B–**	A–	B
Creative International Menu	**2.22**	4.00	3.32	**4.00**	3.97	3.05	**n/a**	n/a	n/a	**2.95**	2.75	3.11	**B**	A–	B+
Creative Content Production	**4.00**	4.00	2.53	**3.11**	4.00	2.92	**n/a**	n/a	n/a	**2.45**	1.34	1.98	**B+**	B+	B–
Creative Design	**4.00**	4.00	4.00	**3.04**	2.82	3.40	**n/a**	n/a	n/a	**2.12**	2.24	1.94	**B**	B	B
Network Services	**1.58**	4.00	3.31	**0.00**	0.76	0.00	**n/a**	n/a	n/a	**2.38**	2.72	0.87	**D+**	B–	D+
Digital Reference Services	**4.00**	4.00	4.00	**n/a**	n/a	n/a	**n/a**	n/a	n/a	**n/a**	n/a	n/a	**A+**	A+	A+
Audio Services	**4.00**	4.00	4.00	**n/a**	n/a	n/a	**n/a**	n/a	n/a	**n/a**	n/a	n/a	**A+**	A+	A+
International Dubbing	**4.00**	3.95	3.47	**n/a**	n/a	4.00	**n/a**	n/a	n/a	**n/a**	n/a	n/a	**A+**	A	A
Customer 5	**3.79**	3.46	4.00	**0.00**	0.00	2.44	**n/a**	n/a	n/a	**1.32**	1.88	1.97	**C–**	C–	B–
Customer 6	**4.00**	4.00	4.00	**4.00**	4.00	4.00	**n/a**	n/a	n/a	**4.00**	4.00	4.00	**A+**	A+	A+
Customer 7	**2.65**	4.00	4.00	**0.00**	0.00	0.00	**2.42**	3.44	3.34	**0.56**	1.47	0.51	**D+**	C+	C
Design, Eng. & Mfg I	**4.00**	4.00	1.48	**4.00**	4.00	2.84	**n/a**	n/a	n/a	**4.00**	3.58	3.91	**A+**	A	B–
Design, Eng. & Mfg 2	**0.00**	4.00	4.00	**4.00**	4.00	4.00	**n/a**	n/a	n/a	**4.00**	4.00	4.00	**B–**	A+	A+
Localization	**2.01**	3.86	2.82	**1.39**	0.18	0.00	**n/a**	n/a	n/a	**1.36**	1.60	1.02	**C–**	C	D+

This case was prepared by Professor Kenneth A. Merchant and research assistant Michelle Spaulding.

CASE STUDY
Family Care Specialists Medical Group, Inc.

On the afternoon of Saturday, January 9, 2010, Dr. Luis Samaniego, president of Family Care Specialists Medical Group, Inc. (FCS), pondered his proposal to revise the FCS physician compensation system. On the following Monday, the six physicians who comprised the Board of FCS would meet to discuss the Group's accomplishments for 2009 and to consider, among other issues, improvements to the compensation system.

The Group's pay scheme had been a continuing topic of discussion for years. FCS had used two very different incentive plans over the past 10 years and management had spent a year discussing possible revisions, but Dr. Samaniego still had concerns. While he recognized that no scheme could be perfect and that whatever choices the Board made would involve tradeoffs, Dr. Samaniego knew that the scheme chosen would have real impacts on the physicians, the Group, and, most importantly, their patients.

Family medicine

Family physicians together with internists comprised the overwhelming majority of primary care physicians in the United States. Primary care physicians normally served as the first point of contact for a patient with an undiagnosed, non-emergent health concern. In addition to acting as the first point of contact, primary care physicians provided ongoing care and facilitated coordination of care for patients who required the services of other medical specialists. In short, they are the people that most of us think of when we think of our trusted family doctor.

Although sometimes referred to as general practice, family medicine is a recognized medical specialty. In the United States, upon receiving medical degrees, newly graduated doctors had to complete a medical residency program before they could be awarded licenses by their state board. Medical schools provided would-be physicians with general medical knowledge and some clinical skills. The residency programs provided more specialized knowledge and clinical skills through years of intensive work treating patients under the close supervision of an attending physician. Across all specialties including family medicine, residency programs were associated with, and primarily conducted in, hospitals.

In March 2009, the Health Resources and Service Administration (HRSA) of the US Department of Health and Human Services designated 6,080 Health Professional Shortage Areas (HPSAs) with an aggregate population of 65 million. The HRSA calculated that an additional 16,585 practitioners would be required to adequately service this underserved population. The American Academy of Family Physicians calculated that to meet the anticipated needs for primary care physicians over the next decade, the United States would need to train 4,449 each year with the goal of increasing the number of family physicians by 39% over the next 10–15 years. However, in 2007, the number of medical students choosing family care residency programs actually declined by 8% from the previous year to just over 1,100.

The consensus explanation for the growing shortage was money. Due to the prevailing system of medical reimbursements in the United States, which primarily paid providers for performance of specific procedures, the average compensation for family physicians was the lowest of any specialty. A study published in the September 9, 2008, issue of the *Journal of the American Medical Association* documented a high correlation between average annual compensation and the number of filled residency positions by specialty. At the low end with average compensation and percentage of filled residency positions was family medicine, with $185,740 and 42%. These compared unfavorably to radiology ($414,875) and orthopedic surgery ($436,481), with the percentage of filled residency positions of 89% and 94%, respectively. These findings were hardly surprising given current studies estimating that the average graduating medical student carried $140,000 in student loan debt.

Wealth and healthcare in Los Angeles

In 2009, Los Angeles County, California claimed nearly 10.4 million residents. In their 2008 annual report on America's millionaires, TNS Financial Services reported that Los Angeles County again topped the list with 261,081 households with net worth exceeding $1 million, excluding the value of their primary residences. The county boasted 108 licensed general acute care hospitals with a total of more than 27,000 beds. Yet, at the same time, the HRSA database listed over 300 of its more than 6,000 Health Professional Shortage Areas within Los Angeles County. For physicians and other healthcare providers, the Los Angeles area offered a wide range of communities and facilities in which to practice. The choice of where to practice and whom to serve significantly affected compensation.

Family care specialists

In 1988, Dr. Samaniego together with six other Latino family physicians formed FCS with the mission of providing high-quality primary care to underserved communities in East Los Angeles (see Exhibit 1). The FCS physicians' strategy for fulfilling their mission developed along two main, complementary lines. First, the Group reached out to the community by growing into four clinical locations: one each in Montebello and Highland Park, as well as two clinics on the grounds of White Memorial Medical Center (WMMC) in the Boyle Heights neighborhood. The larger of the two Boyle Heights clinics provided the physical presence for the other line of the FCS physicians' strategy, which was to provide the faculty for a Family Medicine Residency program.

Indeed, a number of FCS physicians also served as faculty for the Family Medicine Residency program at WMMC. Dr. Samaniego served as the program's director. In 2008, the three-year residency program was ranked first in California by the Office of Statewide Health Planning and Development (OSHPD) for the third straight year. FCS physicians supervised the clinical training of 21 new doctors, graduating seven family medicine specialists each year with the training to meet the needs of underserved communities. Among the two dozen physicians currently in the FCS Group, five were graduates of the WMMC residency program.

The FCS clinicians–24 physicians, five physician assistants, three mental health practitioners, and one family nurse–together with the 21 WMMC residents served roughly 45,000 patients, including 32,000 HMO patients, tallying 80,000 individual patient encounters per year.[1] FCS clinicians at all four locations, together with residents at the WMMC Family Health Clinic, saw patients on a pre-scheduled basis between 8:30 a.m. and 5:00 or 6:00 p.m., Monday through Friday. The Montebello and Highland Park clinics were also open for scheduled appointments each Saturday from 8:30 or 9:00 a.m. until noon. The Family Health Center was open all day, from 8:30 a.m. until 6:00 p.m. on Saturdays (see Exhibit 2).

Across the four clinics there were just over 200 half-day Saturday sessions annually that required coverage, or roughly eight Saturday sessions per physician per year. As a service to the Medical Residency Program, FCS attending physicians provided weekend and off-shift on-call service to the Medical Center. Each on-call shift required the services of two doctors. The role of first on-call attending was more demanding, requiring the attending to field all calls from the residents. The second on-call attending was required only for rounds. Newly hired physicians in their first year with the Group were required to carry a greater number of on-call shifts, as they were deemed necessary for these new physicians to "learn the ropes." Although all FCS physicians carried some on-call shifts, the requirement to do so decreased with seniority.

Even though its clinicians participated in more than 20 private insurance networks, nearly 40% of FCS patients were covered by Medicare and roughly 30% by MediCal, the designation for the State of California Medicaid program (see Exhibit 3). Reimbursement rates from these public programs were generally lower than those from private payers, but these were the constituents that FCS had been formed to serve. For their contribution to the residency program, FCS received a fixed contribution of $1.6 million each year from WMMC. While teaching was a major part of the FCS mission, on an hourly basis it generated less revenue for the Group than clinical care. First-year residents could see on average just four patients per day. Second-year residents could see seven to eight, and third-year residents eight to nine. An FCS attending physician was required to act as a preceptor, supervising the patient care provided by the residents.

[1] Some of the company-specific data presented in this case have been disguised for confidentiality reasons.

In addition to work in FCS clinics and teaching at WMMC, the terms of FCS employment agreements with its physicians required each physician to maintain privileges at a number of other area hospitals. To do so, each physician was required by the hospitals to attend and participate in medical staff meetings and other activities in these facilities, in addition to rendering patient care. Within FCS clinics, the physicians were required to attend medical staff meetings and site quality improvement (QI) program meetings. Beyond the walls of the clinics and hospitals, FCS physicians were expected by the Group to volunteer in the community for about one week each year. All physicians in California were required by the Medical Board of California to complete 50 hours of continuing medical education biannually in order to maintain licensing and certification.

Thus, FCS physicians' time was a precious commodity, and there was a limit to the number of hours each physician could devote to the clinical care that produced revenue for the Group. On average, FCS physicians worked five to six 3.5-hour clinical sessions per week across an average of 46–47 weeks per year per physician. Full-time clinical physicians might see patients as many as seven or eight sessions per week, while physicians with more educational or managerial responsibilities might see patients as few as two or three sessions per week. Other full-time clinicians, such as the Physician Assistants (PAs), saw patients during as many as 10 sessions per week, though PAs saw, on average, 10 or fewer patients per session.

Nonetheless, it was not uncommon for physicians to work part time outside of their main practice. This "moonlighting" was common throughout the industry, not just amongst physicians. Primarily due to concerns about quality and image control, the FCS Group employment contract barred its clinicians from moonlighting except with explicit permission from the practice executive. Dr. Samaniego routinely granted such permission, as the Group's clinicians knew what it took to make requests that would not raise concerns. A moonlighting physician could earn as much as $500 for taking a half-day shift on a holiday, making moonlighting attractive even for very busy physicians.

Not all of the Group's operating margin could be paid out to the physicians and other clinicians. On occasion, unfavorable changes in payers' reimbursement schedules or increases in operating costs forced the Group to operate at a deficit while the Group's management implemented steps to mitigate the problem. During these periods, reserves established during better periods maintained the Group's solvency. Financing constraints dictated that the Group build reserves in order to fund major capital investments in facilities and technology. For example, upgrading its IT infrastructure and purchasing software systems to implement electronic medical record systems could cost a practice the size of FCS's on the order of $1 million. Consequently, the total pool available to fund any clinician compensation program was limited.

The evolution of the FCS physician compensation scheme

In the early days, FCS clinicians were paid fixed salaries. Those more recently hired and less experienced were paid less; the experienced senior clinicians more. However, the salary range had always been relatively narrow. A physician could reach the upper end of the salary scale in five years with the Group. Over time the Group's leadership came to believe that incentives would help drive better achievement of the FCS mission of service and benefit the Group.

Starting in 1994, and for the next six years, FCS operated what they called the Quality Improvement Incentive Program (QIIP). The stated purpose of the QIIP was "to reward behavior that reflects the highest standards in Family Medicine, medical education, and health care service to [FCS] patients and [the] community." The program assigned possible points (weights) to seven categories of quality improvement activities (see Exhibit 4). By design, the total points across the seven categories for each clinician totaled 100. Based on both objective and subjective criteria determined in advance for each category, the clinic medical directors in collaboration with the Residency Program co-directors scored each clinician's degree of achievement in each area.

For example, an individual clinician might have 10 points allocated to the category Provider Meetings. Achievement in this category would be judged by the objective criterion of attendance at both FCS and site provider meetings. Clinicians in attendance were required to sign in at such meetings, and the records were maintained and provided to the practice executives. At the same time, increasingly subjective criteria would also be considered, such as volunteering for special projects, active participation in meetings, and assumption of leadership and responsibility for projects assigned. Hypothetically, the clinician might have been awarded 9 of the 10 possible points for this category. The process would be repeated for each category and the points summed, yielding a score or percentage achievement for that clinician for the period.

Dr. Samaniego and others at FCS believed that small rewards were unlikely to motivate clinicians to modify their behavior. They believed that a figure of one-fifth to one-quarter of compensation was necessary to motivate different behavior. Thus, a fraction of each clinician's potential total compensation equal to between 20% and 25% would be multiplied by the total QIIP score for the period to determine payout of the at-risk portion of that clinician's compensation.

While Dr. Samaniego was satisfied with the motivational dimension of the QIIP, with time it became evident that the program was failing FCS on other dimensions. The WMMC Family Medicine Residency Program was achieving its stated mission, placing nearly half of its graduates into family medical practice in East Los Angeles and most others into underserved communities outside the immediate area. FCS itself was experiencing more difficulty in the competition for its associated program's own graduates. The Group also lost senior clinicians to larger and better-funded competitors in the local market, especially the national leader in managed care, Kaiser Permanente, which employed more than 14,000 physicians and covered more than 3 million patients in Southern California by 2008. Dr. Samaniego was himself a product of Kaiser's residency program.

Under competitive pressure to attract and retain increasingly scarce family medical specialists, FCS scrapped the QIIP in 2001 in favor of a new scheme that rewarded physicians willing to take extra initiative and responsibility in return for higher compensation. Under the new system, FCS would permit its clinicians to work extra hours for FCS, placing the Group on a more even footing with its local competitors for its clinicians' time.

Under the new program, physicians seeking to increase their compensation could indicate their desire for extra sessions prior to the start of each scheduling period. Sessions were scheduled by the practice executive semi-annually, from January through June and from July through December. Schedules were prepared and posted one month prior to the start of each six-month period. Physicians who requested an increased number of weekend sessions at FCS clinics would be paid for these extra sessions at a rate comparable to rates for moonlighting at non-FCS facilities. Further, the "extra" sessions assigned to these physicians would be deducted from the total pool to be shared among all physicians. That is, if five physicians requested an average of four extra weekend sessions for one six-month period, this reduced the pool of sessions to be shared by 20 sessions, bringing the total shared pool to about 80. Consequently, the base number of weekend sessions required of all physicians would be reduced from about four to about three. For their extra effort, the "volunteering" five physicians might increase their compensation by as much as 7–10% for the six-month period. Likewise, on-call shifts would be compensated, though the rate of compensation for on-call shifts ranged from about 85% to less than 50% of that for Saturday clinic sessions, depending on factors such as holidays and first versus second on-call rolls.

To provide a productivity incentive for all of its physicians, with the new program FCS established targets for the number of patients each physician would serve in a typical half-day clinical session. The target number was set at 14 patients per session. On a monthly basis, the Group's information systems began generating a productivity report showing the number of total patient encounters, the number of clinical sessions, and the average number of encounters per session for each physician (see Exhibit 5). Based on the average number of patients per session, a monthly bonus was computed according to the formula $250, $750, or $1,000 when the average was 12, 13, or 14, respectively. The total monthly productivity bonus was prorated by the percentage of time each individual physician dedicated to clinical care each month. So, for example, a physician who consistently achieved a productivity average of 13 encounters/session while devoting half of her time to clinical duties would earn a total productivity bonus of $4,500 over the course of a year.

Under the new plan, it was possible for an ambitious doctor to earn compensation roughly equal to that of physicians employed by larger local competitors. However, base compensation for FCS doctors remained at about the 50th percentile for family physicians in comparable markets based on recent salary surveys, while physicians at the larger local competitors were closer to the 90th percentile. The difference was slightly more than 20% of total compensation. Dr. Samaniego believed that FCS offered other advantages over some larger competitors in the form of greater flexibility and intrinsic rewards, but the Group's continuing challenges with retention left him wondering whether the new compensation system was doing all it could. At the same time, he felt somewhat nostalgic for the QIIP, with its greater emphasis on FCS's mission.

Constraints

The number of patients seen was an imperfect measure of clinical productivity. Some cases were more complex and required more time to deliver high-quality care. Some FCS clinicians specialized in treating certain types of patients who required on average more or less time per patient encounter. OB/GYN cases, for example, took somewhat less time while geriatric cases required more. Also, the financial effect of seeing an additional patient varied widely. Private payers generally compensated FCS at higher rates than Medicare, while MediCal payments were typically only a fraction (e.g. 30%) of private rates. FCS was paid for managed care (HMO) patients primarily on a monthly basis with relatively little or no additional payments for specific patient encounters. Billings were prepared in batches, as many as six weeks apart. When combined with the time payers took to respond to billings, collections lagged treatments by a matter of months. In many cases, collections were received in the name of the patient's primary physician of record, even though the patient may have been seen by another clinician. In any case, FCS would not provide different levels of care to patients with different health plans, making any incentive system based on billings or collections questionable, regardless of the practical problems of implementation.

Moreover, clinicians had more control over the number of patients seen in each session than over the payer mix or average case complexity. Clinicians were given discretion over the maximum number of patients to schedule for a session as well as whether or not to accept patients arriving late for scheduled appointments and those seeking treatment on short notice. Some Saturday clinics were operated on a walk-in basis. However, FCS maintained a policy of not significantly overbooking despite a no-show rate that often averaged as high as 30%.

Direct measurements of the quality of care provided by a given clinician were expensive to collect. As part of each clinic's Quality Improvement program, so-called chart reviews were conducted on a weekly basis. These peer reviews of a very small sample of each clinician's patient encounters were considered to be very powerful motivators, though they were not linked to compensation. In the words of Dr. Samaniego, "It's like a dagger through your heart when one of your peers says 'Hey Louie, you forgot to do X here'."

Various payers measured the quality of care provided based on metrics such as the proportion of diabetic patients covered by the payer's plan that received annual eye exams or of women in targeted groups receiving scheduled mammograms. Bonuses paid to FCS for achieving targeted levels or improvements on such metrics had totaled as much as hundreds of thousands of dollars to as little as a few tens of thousands of dollars in some years. However, achievement of such targets depended heavily on patient compliance as well as on clinical diligence. As with collections, the fact that the same patient might be seen by multiple clinicians made linkage of performance on such metrics to the actions of individual clinicians practically impossible. Likewise, achievement on patient satisfaction surveys were seen as measures of the clinics as a whole more than as measures of individual clinicians.

A better way?

These constraints notwithstanding, Dr. Samaniego believed that the FCS compensation scheme had become overly focused on clinical productivity. Like a number of the other Board members, he felt that the original QIIP had been more balanced and better aligned with the Group's mission. However, patient volume, payer mix, staffing, and productivity drove financial results and, ultimately, what the Group could afford to pay clinicians and staff. Even in the not-for-profit world of hospitals like WMMC, there was a popular aphorism that without margin there is no mission, and despite the importance of their shared mission, FCS had never been a not-for-profit enterprise.

Dr. Samaniego questioned whether the current scheme was effective in achieving even its relatively narrow purpose. While some clinicians now requested additional Saturday sessions and even additional on-call shifts, only a few achieved bonus levels of average patients seen per session on a monthly basis. Further, while the new scheme had helped to narrow the gap between physician compensation at FCS and the local market level, periodic departures of experienced clinicians seeking better pay or hours and the perennial competition to recruit new physicians only highlighted the fact that serving their target communities would never be as lucrative as treating the average patient population in the LA area. Dr. Samaniego felt certain that the FCS compensation scheme could be improved, but he was less certain of how to achieve the right balance.

Exhibit 1 Mission statement

Family Care Specialists (FCS) Medical Corporation

Mission Statement

Family Care Specialists Medical Corporation is dedicated to the maintenance, restoration, and improvement of each family member's health. The medical group provides high quality, compassionate and culturally responsive medical care, and is dedicated to improving community health and the education of family physicians.

Exhibit 2 Locations and hours

Boyle Heights	8:30 a.m.–5:00 p.m. Monday–Friday
Highland Park	8:30 a.m.–5:00 p.m. Monday–Friday 9:00 a.m.–Noon Saturday
Montebello	8:30 a.m.–6:00 p.m. Monday–Friday 8:30 a.m.–Noon Saturday
White Memorial Medical Center Family Health Clinic	8:30 a.m.–6:00 p.m. Monday–Saturday

Exhibit 3 Patient mix

Patient mix by payer and type			
	Percentages		Patients
Managed care			
Medicare HMO	17%		7,650
MediCal HMO	5%		2,250
Private HMO	43%	65%	19,350
Fee-for-service			
Medicare/Medi-Medi *	13%		5,850
PPO	10%		4,500
MediCal	5%		2,250
Other	7%	35%	3,150
		100%	45,000

Exhibit 4 Quality Improvement Incentive Plan (1994–2001)

Quality Improvement Incentive Plan (QIIP)	
"To reward behavior that reflects the highest standards in Family Medicine, medical education and health care service to our patients and community."	
Provider Meetings	10 points
Medical Staff Meetings	10 points
Community Service	10 points
Clinic Site Quality Improvement Program	20 points
Patient Satisfaction Survey	15 points
Site Medical Director	35 points*
Medical Education	
TOTAL	100 points

*Allocated by percentage of physician time spent in clinical vs. education.

Exhibit 5 Sample productivity report

Clinic B: Monthly summary				
	Providers	Total Patients seen	Number of sessions	Patients/session
1.	Clinician One, MD	45	4	11.25
2.	Clinician Two, MD	250	23	10.87
3.	Clinician Three, MD	255	21	12.14
4.	Clinician Four, MD	349	29	12.03
5.	Clinician Five, MD	210	19	11.05
6.	Clinician Six, MD	331	18	18.39
7.	Clinician Seven, PA-C	321	32	10.03
8.	Clinician Eight, PA-C	315	33	9.55
	Totals	**2,076**	**179**	**95.32**

This case was prepared by Professor Kenneth A. Merchant and research assistant David P. Huelsbeck.

SECTION III

Financial Results Control Systems

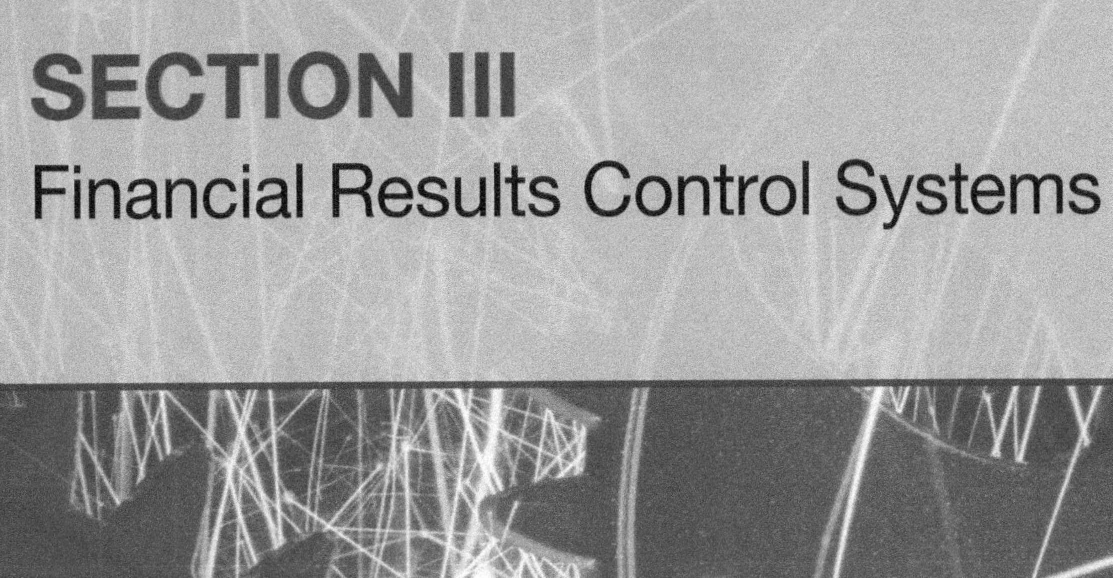

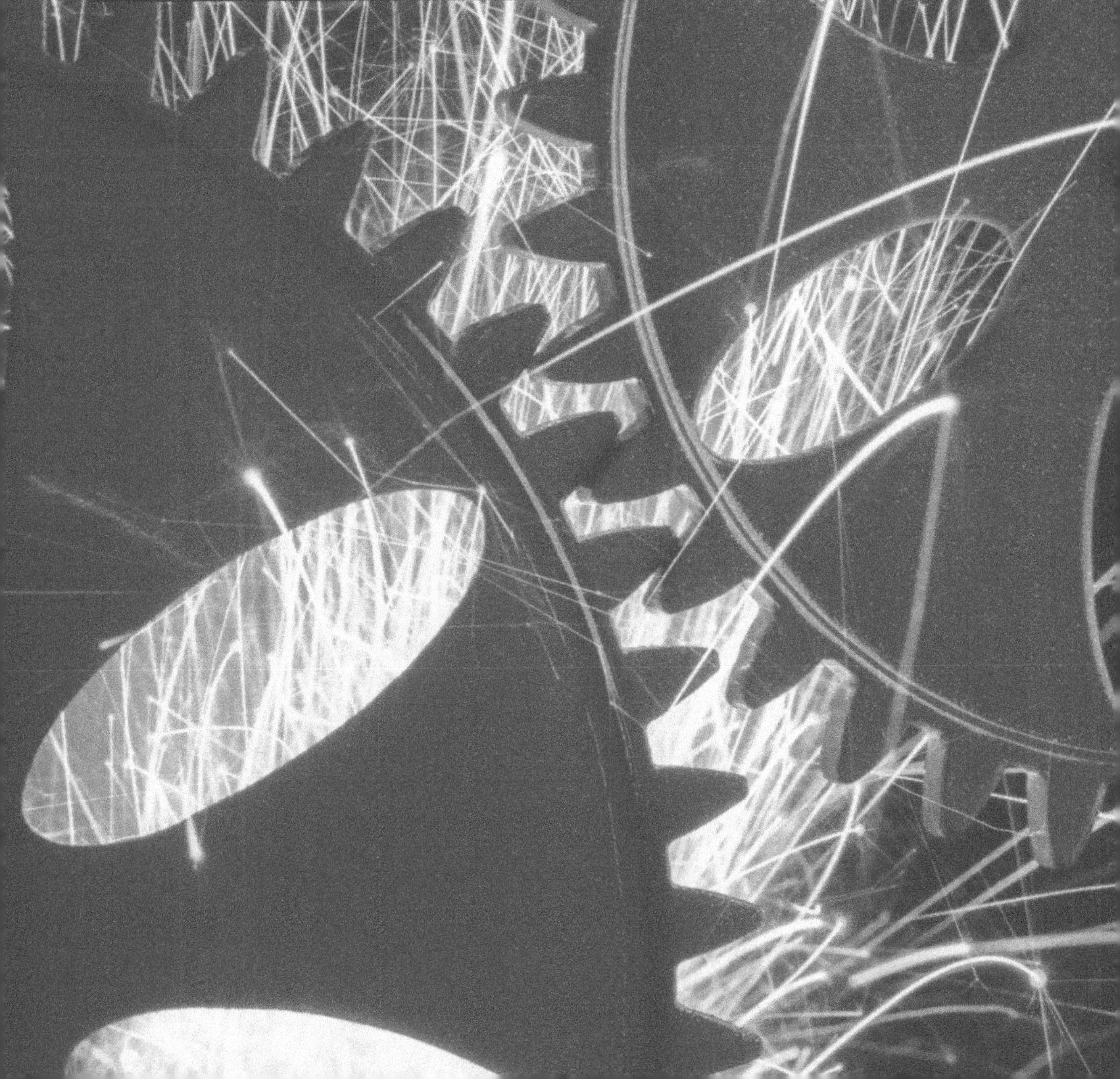

CHAPTER 7
Financial Responsibility Centers

The vast majority of organizations control the behaviors of many of their employees, particularly their managers, through *financial results control systems*. In financial results control systems, results are defined in monetary terms, most commonly in terms of accounting measures such as revenues, costs, profits, or returns (e.g. return on equity). At higher organization levels, financial results control systems often are the most pervasive and dominant form of control.

Financial results control systems have three core elements: (1) *financial responsibility centers*, which define the apportioning of accountability for financial results within the organization; (2) *planning and budgeting systems*, which are used for a number of control-related purposes including the setting of performance targets for evaluating performance; and (3) *incentive plans or contracts*, which define the links between results and various rewards.

This chapter describes the advantages of financial results control systems and then discusses in depth one important element of these systems: financial responsibility centers. It also describes one common problem faced by organizations using multiple financial responsibility centers: the transfer pricing problem. We discuss the other two financial results control system elements (planning and budgeting systems and incentive systems) in Chapters 8 and 9, respectively.

Advantages of financial results control systems

Several good reasons explain the ubiquity of financial results control systems in organizations. First, financial objectives are paramount in for-profit firms. Profits and cash flows provide returns to investors and are among the primary measures outsiders use to evaluate for-profit firm performance. Thus, it is natural that managers of for-profit firms monitor their success in financial terms and use the financial measures to direct their employees' actions toward important organizational ends. Managers of non-profit organizations, too, must monitor finances closely because cash flows usually create significant constraints for their organizations.

Second, financial measures provide a *summary measure* of performance by aggregating the effects of a broad range of operating initiatives across a possibly broad range of markets, products/services, or activities into a single (or a few) measure(s). In so doing, they enhance the comparability of the effects of the initiatives and reduce the possibility of conflicting signals about their importance. The financial measures remind employees that the various operating initiatives they take on, such as initiatives to improve response times, defect rates, delivery reliability, or customer satisfaction ratings, benefit the organization only if they result in improved financial performance. Because financial measures are a comprehensive summary measure of performance, they provide a relatively easy, standardized, and inexpensive way for the organization to evaluate the results of a variety of operational initiatives without necessarily needing to obtain and evaluate the intricate detail of each of the initiatives.

The ubiquity and usability of financial measures is particularly valuable for the management of complex, diversified firms (as we also discussed, and listed several examples, in Chapter 2). Management in these organizations can usually set corporate goals in financial terms, decompose the corporate goals into multiple financial responsibility centers, and then monitor only one (or just a few) results measures – such as, accounting profits or returns and their components (revenues, costs, assets, and liabilities) – which provide a good summary of the effects of most of the actions or decisions needing to be controlled. The managers then do not need to track either the actions that are affecting financial performance (e.g. how time was spent, how specific expenditures were made) or the specific line items that comprise the summary measures of performance (e.g. revenues by product line, cost line items) until problems (such as failures to achieve performance targets) appear in the summary measures. The process of getting involved only when problems appear is also known as *management-by-exception*. In this way, financial results controls reduce the amount of information that top managers need to process and evaluate. At the same time, financial results controls provide a relatively unobtrusive form of management control; that is, they provide control while allowing those being controlled considerable autonomy.

Third, most financial measures are relatively precise and objective. They generally provide significant measurement advantages over *soft* qualitative or subjective information and over many other quantifiable alternatives (e.g. quality or customer satisfaction measures). Cash flow – the primitive financial measure – is relatively easy to observe and measure. Accounting rules, on which most financial measures are built, limit the managers' measurement discretion, improve measurement objectivity, and facilitate the verification of the resulting measures.

Finally, the cost of implementing financial results controls is often small relative to that of other forms of management control. This is because the core financial results control measurement elements are largely in place. Organizations already routinely prepare and transmit elaborate sets of accounting information to government agencies, creditors, shareholders, and other constituencies on either a mandated or voluntary basis. This information can be readily and inexpensively adapted for control uses. In Chapter 10, we provide a further in-depth analysis of the features, as well as the limitations, of financial measures of performance.

Types of financial responsibility centers

Financial responsibility centers are a core element of a financial results control system. The term *responsibility center management* denotes the apportioning of responsibility (or accountability) for a particular set of outputs and/or inputs to an employee (usually a manager) in charge of an organizational entity (the *responsibility center*). Responsibilities can be expressed in terms of quantities of inputs consumed, physical units of output generated, particular characteristics of the production or service process (e.g. defects, schedule attainment, customer satisfaction), or financial indicators of performance in these areas.

Financial responsibility centers are responsibility centers in which the assigned responsibilities are defined at least partially *in financial terms*. There are four basic types of financial responsibility centers: investment centers, profit centers, revenue centers, and cost centers. Table 7.1 shows that these centers are distinguishable by the financial statement line items for which the managers are held accountable in each type of center.

Table 7.1 Typical examples of financial responsibility centers

Selected financial statement line items	Revenue center	Cost center	Profit center	Investment center
Income statement				
Revenue	x		x	x
Cost of goods sold		x	x	x
Gross margin			x	x
Advertising and promotion		x	x	x
Research and development		x	x	x
Profit before tax			x	x
Income tax			x	x
Profit after tax			x	x
Balance sheet				
Accounts receivable				x
Inventory				x
Fixed assets				x
Accounts payable				x
Debt				x

Note: x signifies that the responsibility center manager is (or could be) held accountable for some elements included in that financial statement line item.
Source: K. A. Merchant, *Modern Management Control Systems: Text and Cases* (Upper Saddle River, NJ: Prentice Hall, 1998), p. 303.

Revenue centers

Revenue centers are responsibility centers whose managers are held accountable for generating revenues, which is a financial measure of output. Common examples are sales managers and, in non-profit organizations, fundraising managers.

Revenues, rather than profits, provide a simple and effective way to encourage sales managers to attract and retain customers. However, it will encourage them to make *profitable sales* if, and only if, it can be ascertained that all sales are approximately equally profitable. But if all revenues are not equally "endowed," controlling with a revenue center structure can encourage employees to make "easy" sales rather than those that are most profitable.

Most revenue center managers are also held accountable for some expenses. For example, many sales managers are accountable for their salespeople's salaries and commissions and perhaps some travel, advertising, and promotional expenses. These managers could be said to manage a *net revenue* center. But while these managers are held accountable for both revenues and *some* costs, they should not be considered profit center managers because there is no profit calculation relating outputs to inputs; that is, these revenue centers are not charged for the cost of the goods or services they sell.

Cost centers

Cost (or expense) centers are responsibility centers whose managers are held accountable for some elements of cost. Costs are a financial measure of the inputs to, or resources consumed by, the responsibility center.[1] In *standard cost centers* (sometimes called *engineered cost centers*), such as manufacturing departments, the causal relationship between inputs and outputs is direct, and both inputs and outputs are easy to quantify. Thus, control can be exercised by comparing a standard cost (the cost of the inputs that *should have been consumed* in producing the output) with the costs that were *actually incurred*. Students of cost or management accounting will recall that these comparisons are typically done by way of so-called *variance analysis*.

In *discretionary cost centers* (sometimes called *managed cost centers*), such as research and development departments and administrative departments (e.g. personnel, purchasing, accounting, estates), the outputs produced are difficult to value in monetary terms. In addition, the relationship between inputs and outputs is not well known. Thus, evaluations of discretionary cost center managers' performances often have a large subjective component to them. Control is usually exercised by ensuring that the discretionary cost center adheres to a budgeted level of expenditures while successfully accomplishing the tasks assigned to it.

That said, firms often turn some of their "service departments" such as, say, human resources, into profit centers by allowing them to charge the other divisions for the services they provide (e.g. for hiring employees or running training programs).[2] This works well, however, only when the non-service departments (that is, the *customers* of the service departments) have the freedom to contract these services from external providers; that is, when they are not *captive* to the internal service provider. When this is the case, the service centers have an incentive to provide good service at competitive prices, where this discipline is imputed merely from setting them up as profit centers and thus making them instantly focused on being competitively responsive to the demand for their services (which generates their revenues) in an efficient (cost effective) way. As we will see next, profit responsibility makes managers focused on *both* revenues and costs, and not on each singularly as is the case in revenue and cost centers, respectively.

A good example of this is Cisco, the large technology firm, which in 2014 embarked on the concept of "revenue marketing" aimed at making marketing a revenue center rather than a cost center. Karen Walker, senior vice president of marketing at Cisco, said that "the goal was that making Cisco's marketing division a profit center would drive $10 billion in sales-qualified leads and contribute 10 percent to company's global sales revenues." Simply put, the idea was that marketing would see revenues allocated from generating *new* accounts, but also the cost of generating them, where accounts already mapped to Cisco account managers would not count as net-new business.[3]

Another example can be found in some banks. The Royal Bank of Scotland runs its turnaround division, an entity focused on businesses in default that it has lent to, as an "internal profit center" called the Global Restructuring Group (GRG), with its own profit and loss account based on the incremental income that it generates for the bank less its operating costs. Some have expressed concern about this as "there is clearly a risk that the [profit-driven] interests of the bank will take precedence over those of customers in financial difficulty, particularly in times of limited liquidity and capital constraints," Simon Hart, a banking litigation partner at law firm RPC, said. The assertion is that, "on occasion, although purporting to be acting in the interests of a turnaround, GRG may in fact be acting to retrieve the maximum value for the bank by initiating a recovery or resolution process and thereby actually hastening the failure of businesses."[4]

Profit centers

Profit centers are responsibility centers whose managers are held accountable for some measure of profits, which is the difference between the revenues generated and the costs of generating those revenues. Business terminology often is not precise, and many firms refer to their investment centers as profit centers. But there is a conceptual distinction between profit and investment centers (which we discuss below): profit center managers are held accountable for profits but not for the investments made to generate them.

Profit and investment centers are an important control element of the vast majority of firms above minimal size. Profit centers, however, come in many different forms, some of which are considerably more limited in scope of operations than others. In deciding whether or not a responsibility center manager truly has profit center responsibility, the critical question to ask is whether the manager has significant influence over *both* revenues and costs. Take Bonnaroo, a 100-band jamboree music and arts festival on a farm outside of Nashville, which is run as 16 on-site profit centers, including concessions, merchandise, and even paid showers. The managers of each of the on-site profit centers are responsible not only for gross revenues, but also for the costs they incur to generate the revenues. Maybe due to linking revenues and costs so directly, and assigning responsibility at the profit level, Bonnaroo has been one of the most financially successful music festivals in North America during the last decade.[5]

However, there are variations of full-fledged profit responsibility that organizations can tweak with. One such limited form of profit center is created when *sales-focused* entities are made into profit centers by charging the entity managers the standard cost of the products sold, thus making them accountable for *gross margin*. Even this limited assignment of costs provides the manager with useful information. Decisions, such as about sales and marketing direction and intensity, will be made based on the incremental contribution to the firm (i.e., gross margins) rather than just gross revenues.

Another limited form of profit center is created where *cost-focused* entities are assigned revenues based on a simple function of costs. A typical example exists where manufacturing and administrative departments supply *unique* products or services, for which sometimes external market prices cannot be determined, to internal customers only. Revenues for these entities might be calculated as cost plus a markup. Are these cost-focused entities profit centers? As we have discussed above, it depends on the extent to which the buying entities are *captive*, which they may well be due to the lack of an outside market alternative for these services. But when the assigned prices are reasonably, although imperfectly, set or benchmarked on a value-for-money basis, the service departments will at least be more motivated to produce quality intermediate products, parts, or services; to provide superior delivery schedules; and to provide friendly, hassle-free customer service to generate the *allocated* or *assigned* revenues lest their "internal customers" start complaining about the poor service or make noises to search for alternative suppliers. Thus, even though the revenues are artificially imputed in these cost-focused profit centers, the main idea is to transmit the competitive pressures faced by a firm in the marketplace to its internal service groups. Internal profit centers that do not directly interface with the market and have no control over revenues in a competitive sense are also sometimes called *micro* profit centers.[6] If the entities do not have significant control over the revenues assigned, however, they are merely *pseudo* profit centers. Assigning revenues to these entities to allow a profit figure to be shown is merely a way to charge the buying entities a cost-based approximation of a market price so that their profits are not overstated and can be compared more easily with entities that source externally.

In deciding whether an entity is a profit center, it is not important to consider either whether the entity's goal is to maximize profits or whether any revenues are generated from outside the firm, however. The financial goal of profit centers, such as those in not-for-profit organizations, can be merely to break even. For example, hospitals can adopt a "profit center" structure to relate the costs of patient care in various clinical groups directly to revenues received either from the patient, through insurance payments, from government subsidies, or via other sources (e.g. grants). The primary goal of the "profit centers" in this case is not to maximize profit; instead it is to assess and manage the costs of medical care within the constraints applied by the funds available. Because the managers of these entities allocate resources (costs) in relation to the funds available (revenues), and thus essentially make cost-revenue tradeoffs, they should be considered "profit center" managers, even though that term is rarely used in the not-for-profit sector. Similarly, it is not necessary that a profit center generates revenues from outside the organization. Many profit centers derive most, or even all, of their revenues by selling their products or services to other entities within the same organization. These sales are made at *transfer prices*, which we discuss in detail later in this chapter.

Investment centers

Investment centers are responsibility centers whose managers are held accountable for both some income statement and some balance sheet line items; that is, for both the accounting returns (profits) *and* the investments made to generate those returns. A corporation is an investment center, so top-level corporate managers, such as the chief executive, often are investment center managers. So are the managers of many subsidiaries, operating groups, and divisions in large, decentralized organizations.

Accounting returns can be defined in many ways, but they typically involve a ratio of the profits earned to the investment capital used. The varying definitions cause many different labels to be put on the investment centers' *bottom line*, such as return on investment (ROI), return on equity (ROE), return on capital employed (ROCE), return on net assets (RONA), return on total capital (ROTC), risk adjusted return on capital (RAROC), and many other variations.[7]

Variations

Although the conceptual delineation of the four categories of financial responsibility centers is clear, there can be considerable variation within each financial responsibility type. For example, Table 7.2 shows four quite different responsibility centers, each of which is a profit center even though the breadth of responsibility, as reflected in the number of income statement line items for which the managers are held accountable, varies considerably. *Gross margin center* managers may be salespeople who sell products of varying margins and who are charged with the standard cost of the goods they sell. The "profit" measure gives them an incentive to sell higher-margin products rather than merely generating additional, possibly unprofitable, revenues. The *incomplete profit center* managers may be managers of product divisions but without authority for all of the functions that affect the success of their products or product lines, such as research and development or advertising. *Complete profit center* managers may be business unit managers who are accountable for all aspects of the worldwide performance of their business segment. Similar variations are also common among the other responsibility center types, as the managers are held accountable for more or fewer financial statement line items.

Table 7.2 Four types of "profit" center

Selected financial statement line items	Gross margin center	Incomplete profit center	Before-tax profit center	Complete profit center
Income statement				
Revenue	x	x	x	x
Cost of goods sold	x	x	x	x
Gross margin	x	x	x	x
Advertising and promotion		x	x	x
Research and development			x	x
Profit before tax			x	x
Income tax				x
Profit after tax				x

Note: x signifies that the responsibility center manager is held accountable for that financial statement line item.
Source: K. A. Merchant, *Modern Management Control Systems: Text and Cases* (Upper Saddle River, NJ: Prentice Hall, 1998), p. 306.

Choice of financial responsibility centers

The four financial responsibility center types can thus be contrasted in a hierarchy reflecting the breath of financial responsibility, or the number of financial statement line items for which the manager is held accountable, as shown in Table 7.1. Revenue and cost center managers are held accountable for only one, or sometimes a few, income statement line items. Profit center managers are held accountable for some revenue and some expense line items. Investment center managers are held accountable for a measure of profit that is related directly to the resources consumed by their entity as reflected by line items on the balance sheet.

One important point to keep in mind is that the lines between the financial responsibility center types are not always easy to discern, so responsibility center labels are not always informative. In actual practice, financial responsibility centers can be arrayed on an almost seamless continuum from cost or revenue centers to investment centers. For example, consider the case of manufacturing managers who are held accountable for meeting customer specifications, production quality standards, and customer delivery schedules, in addition to costs. In combination, these non-cost factors may largely determine the company's success in generating revenues, and these managers clearly have to make tradeoffs between costs and factors that affect revenues. But, technically, these managers are cost center managers.

Much more important than the labeling of financial responsibility centers are the decisions that have to be made in designing financial responsibility structures. The important question to answer is: Which managers should be held accountable for which specific financial statement line items? These choices are obviously important because they affect behavior. Managers pay attention to the measures for which they are held accountable.[8] Thus, from a behavioral angle, the answer to the question is relatively straightforward: Hold managers accountable for the line items you want them to pay attention to.

To a large extent, firms' financial responsibility center structures are coincident with the managers' areas of authority. Areas of authority are defined by organization structures and policies that define managers' *decision rights*. In a typical functional organization (Figure 7.1), none of the managers has significant decision-making authority over *both* the generation of revenues and incurrence of costs, so revenues and costs (including the costs of investments) are brought together in a return measure only at the corporate level. The manufacturing, engineering, and administrative functions are typically cost centers, and the sales function is a revenue center. In a typical divisionalized organization (Figure 7.2), division managers are given authorities to make decisions in all, or at least many, of the functions that affect the success of

Figure 7.1 Typical financial responsibility centers in a functional organization

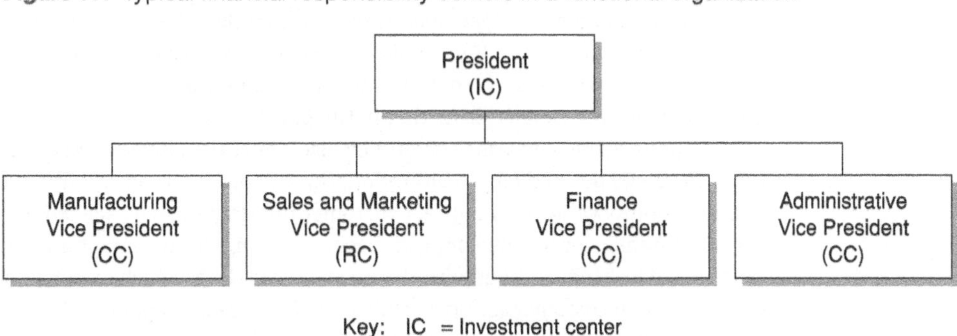

Source: K. A. Merchant, *Modern Management Control Systems: Text and Cases* (Upper Saddle River, NJ: Prentice Hall, 1998), p. 308.

Figure 7.2 Typical financial responsibility centers in a divisionalized organization

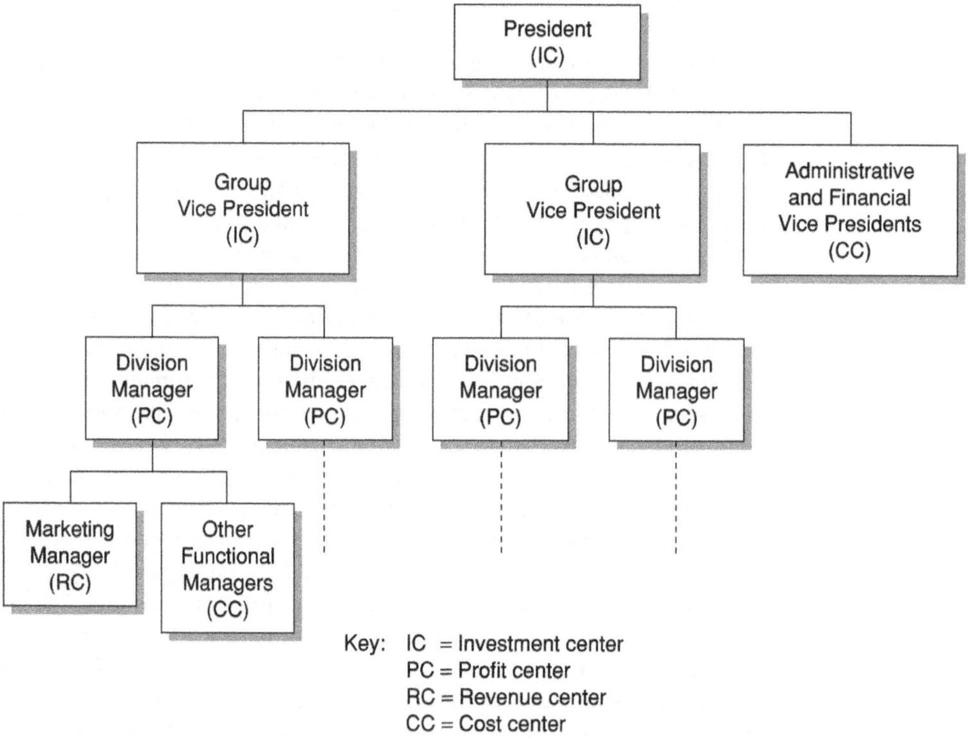

Source: K. A. Merchant, *Modern Management Control Systems: Text and Cases* (Upper Saddle River, NJ: Prentice Hall, 1998), p. 309.

their division. Consistent with this broad authority, each division is a profit center (or investment center) comprised of multiple cost and revenue centers.

Decisions about an organization's structure do not necessarily precede decisions about the type of responsibility centers that should be used; the responsibility structure decision can come first. For example, the desire to have managers make tradeoffs between revenues and costs may lead to the choice of a divisionalized organization structure. As such, there should be a close relationship between decisions about organizational structure and responsibility centers, as that is where *decision authority* and *results accountability* meet.

The desire to have managers pay attention to a particular line item does not necessarily mean that the managers need to have direct and *complete control* over the item, although it should mean that the managers have *some influence* over the line item. Some managers are purposely held accountable for line items over which they have no direct control, such as corporate administrative expenses, to empower them to influence the behaviors of the managers with direct control. We discuss this further in Chapter 12.

Specific strategic concerns sometimes also affect the choice of responsibility center structure. A strategy focused on providing superior customer service may dictate that the managers of responsibility centers with direct customer interfaces (such as customer support) should be held accountable for revenue or profit because having these managers focus just on costs could cause behaviors that conflict with the company's strategy (such as behaviors that reduce costs by skimping on customer service). Alternatively, these managers could be held accountable for costs plus a measure of customer satisfaction.

Some strategies might even suggest that managers not be held accountable for line items over which they clearly have influence. It may be desirable *not* to charge entity managers for the costs of certain activities (such as research and development costs or information technology costs) in order to stimulate greater use, or at least not to discourage use, of these services at the detriment of, say, business development or innovation. If the entity's strategy depends on technological leadership, for example, corporate managers might not want the entity managers to make rigid cost-benefit tradeoffs on every expenditure in this critically important strategic area.

Finally, as business models change, so should responsibility center structures. For example, innovative corporations today are starting to look at energy management in an era of sustainability in a different way, focusing on how energy management can help the business rather than treating it just as a cost. Specifically, companies are finding that they can reduce energy use by investing in projects that can earn tax incentives, create new lines of business, and, in many countries, qualify as a tradable asset in financial markets. A shift in energy management from an "environmental cost" to an "environmental asset" calls for turning a cost into a profit through recycling waste into a source of energy (the excess of which can be sold) as well as through reducing energy usage, which not only saves costs, but also can earn tax incentives and carbon credits worth millions a year. This approach to energy management, in turn, creates the need for a profit center structure where there were previously only costs and risks.[9]

The transfer pricing problem

Profit (or investment) centers often supply products or services to other profit centers within the same firm. When that happens, some mechanism for determining the prices of the transfers must be established.[10] *Transfer prices* directly affect the revenues of the selling (supplying) profit center, the costs of the buying (receiving) profit center and, consequently, the profits of both entities, thus essentially making transfer prices subject to "zero-sum" considerations (that is, more revenue for one is more cost for the other). The impact of these transfer prices depends largely on the number and magnitude of internal transfers relative to the size of each entity. When the amount of transfers is significant, failure to set the right transfer prices can significantly affect a number of important decisions, including those regarding production quantities, sourcing, resource allocations, and evaluations of the managers of both the selling and buying profit centers. Put simply, when this is the case, it ups the stakes in the *zero-sum game* among the transferring entities.

Purposes of transfer pricing

Transfer prices have multiple organizational purposes, and these purposes often conflict. One purpose of transfer prices is to provide the proper economic signals so that the managers affected will make good decisions. In particular, the prices should properly influence both the selling profit center managers' decisions about how much product/service to supply internally and the buying profit center managers' decisions about how much product/service to buy internally. Ideally, then, the decisions that the transferring entities make should be "optimal" not only at their own entity level, but also for the corporation as a whole. Ill-devised transfer prices often do not achieve a global optimum even while being locally optimal – for example, because they cause the buying profit centers to source externally while there is excess capacity for the inputs in the supplying entities elsewhere in the corporation.

Second, the transfer prices and subsequent profit measurements should provide information that is useful for evaluating the performances of both the profit centers and their managers. Transfer prices directly affect the profits of both the selling and buying entities. Ideally, the transfer prices should not cause the performance of either entity to be either over- or understated. Misleading profitability signals can adversely affect allocations of resources within the firm, thus rendering them *suboptimal*. They can also severely undercut profit center managers' motivations because the managers will argue that they are not being treated fairly.

Third, transfer prices can be set to purposely move profits between firm locations. Several factors can motivate managers to use transfer prices in this way. When firms are operating in multiple tax jurisdictions (countries or states), their managers might be motivated to use transfer prices to move profits between jurisdictions to minimize taxes. Corporate income tax rates differ significantly across countries, and managers can set transfer prices to earn profits in relatively low-tax localities to maximize after-tax worldwide profits. Although this particular aspect of the transfer pricing problem is beyond the scope of this chapter, evidence suggests that the maximization of global profits remains a critical consideration of transfer pricing policies in multinational corporations.[11] Clearly, such transfer pricing arrangements that determine how firms' taxable profits are "allocated" between countries is politically controversial. They often make headlines in the press, where Apple, Google, Starbucks, Fiat, and other big-name companies are chastised as tax dodgers, irking their customers and damaging their reputations as socially responsible corporations.[12]

Profit repatriation limitations also may encourage companies to use transfer prices to move profits between entities across country borders. For a number of reasons, including balance of payments problems and a scarcity of foreign currency reserves, some governments prohibit repatriation of profits, either directly or indirectly. Indirect forms of restrictions include distorted exchange rates or high withholding tax rates. When companies are unable to repatriate profits from their entities in foreign countries, they are motivated to set transfer prices to minimize profits in those countries.

Companies also sometimes set transfer prices to shift profits between wholly owned subsidiaries and entities where the profits are shared with, say, joint venture partners. As a matter of fact, transfer prices are for this reason often strictly included and set out in great detail in the joint venture contract to avoid possible expropriation. Sometimes transfer prices are set to move profits to an entity being positioned for divestment in hopes of increasing its valuation and, hence, its selling price.

These multiple transfer pricing purposes often conflict.[13] Except in rare circumstances, tradeoffs are necessary because no single transfer pricing method serves all the purposes well. The usual desire to have transfer pricing mechanisms operate automatically between entities, without frequent interventions from corporate management, provides another transfer pricing complication. Transfer pricing interventions undermine the benefits of decentralization. They reduce profit center (entity) autonomy and cause decision-making complexity and delay. They also increase organizational costs, particularly in terms of the management time needed to review the facts and to reach a transfer pricing "ruling" acceptable to all entities involved. Thus, firms seek to set transfer pricing policies that work without producing major exceptions and disputes.[14]

Transfer pricing alternatives

Most firms use any of five primary types of transfer prices. First, transfer prices can be based on *market prices*. The market price used for internal transfers could be the listed price of an identical (or similar) product or service, the actual price the selling entity charges external customers (perhaps less a discount that reflects lower selling costs for internal customers), or the price a competitor is offering. Second, transfer prices can be based on *marginal costs*, which are approximated as the variable or direct cost of production. Third, transfer prices can be based on the *full costs* of providing the product or service. Both marginal and full cost-based transfer prices can reflect either standard or actual costs. Fourth, transfer prices can be set at *full cost plus a markup*. Finally, transfer prices can be *negotiated* between the managers of the selling and buying profit centers. Information about market prices and either marginal or full production costs often provide input into these negotiations, but there is no requirement that they do so.

On balance, surveys of practice across sources and time seem to suggest that transfers at marginal cost are rarely used and that most companies internally transfer goods or services at either market prices or variations of full costs (e.g. full cost plus markup). In other words, what emerges is that both market price and "cost-plus" methods are the most widely used. Perhaps due to the increased scrutiny and enforcement by the tax authorities of the presumed *arm's-length* principle (see below), most companies use market-based transfer prices for international transfers more often than either cost-based or negotiated transfer prices.[15] We discuss each of the transfer pricing methods next.

Market-based transfer prices

In the relatively rare situation where a perfectly (or at least highly) competitive external market exists for internally traded goods or services, it is optimal for both decision-making and performance evaluation purposes to set transfer prices at competitive market prices. A *perfectly* competitive market exists where the product is homogenous and no individual buyer or seller can unilaterally affect its price.

The case for using market-based transfer prices under competitive conditions is apparent. If the selling profit center cannot earn a profit by selling at the external market price, then the firm is better off shutting that profit center down and buying from an outside supplier, all else equal. Similarly, if the buying profit center cannot earn a profit by buying its inputs at the prevailing market price, then the firm should shut that profit center down and have its selling profit center sell all its outputs to outsiders in the market. Hence, if transfer prices are set at market price, managers of both the selling and buying profit centers are likely to make decisions that are optimal from the firm's perspective, and reports of both of their performances will provide good information for evaluation purposes.

Entities within organizations, however, rarely operate as they would as stand-alone firms in the open market.[16] Therefore, many firms use *quasi* market-based transfer prices by allowing deviations from the observed market prices. The deviations allow for adjustments that reflect differences between internal and external sales. These differences can reflect the savings of marketing, selling and collecting costs, the costs of special terms offered only to external customers (e.g. warranties), or the value of special features, special services provided, or differences in quality standards. Adjustments in market prices also may reflect the belief that the price quoted by the external supplier is not a sustainable competitive price. The price quoted might just be a low-ball bid designed merely to get the first order. The greater the number and size of these adjustments, however, the more the market-based transfer prices are like cost-based prices, and the more difficult the transfer pricing tradeoffs become.

Marginal-cost transfer prices

When intermediate products and services are exchanged internally at marginal cost, it is easy to determine the total contribution generated by the final product or service to the firm as a whole. The total contribution is simply equal to the selling price of the final product or service minus the marginal cost of the last production or service process stage. Although this might be appealing from a cost accounting perspective, and sometimes from a price-setting perspective for short-term pricing decisions, it creates a problem when viewed from a responsibility center perspective. The reason is that the total contribution is not easily traceable to each of the supplying entities, nor do any of the supplying entities even recuperate their full costs, which makes it unfeasible to evaluate them as profit centers. At best, they can be *standard variable cost centers*; that is, their performance evaluation depends on the extent to which their *actual* variable costs for a given output are at or below the standard variable cost. As we have discussed above, this obviously is a very limited form of financial results accountability.

This perhaps explains why the survey sources mentioned earlier indicate that companies rarely use marginal-cost transfers. Indeed, the rarity of use of this method is likely due to the fact that marginal-cost transfers provide poor information for evaluating the economic performance of either the selling or the buying profit center. The selling profit center will typically have to record losses because it bears the full cost of production or provision while receiving in revenue only the marginal costs. Conversely, the profits of the buying profit center will be overstated because it does not have to pay for even the full cost of the transferred goods or services.

Marginal-cost transfer prices also are sometimes difficult to implement. Relatively few companies can measure marginal costs accurately. Direct costs (direct material, direct labor) are not the problem; indirect costs are. Companies that use marginal-cost transfer pricing usually define marginal costs as standard variable costs, but there is no clean break between variable and fixed indirect costs. Indirect cost allocations sometimes are quite arbitrary. Marginal costs also are not always constant over the range of output. Sharp increases in marginal costs may occur if the selling profit center is operating near a capacity constraint.

Full-cost transfer prices

Transfers at *full cost* or *full cost plus a markup* are more widely used. Full-cost transfer prices offer several advantages. First, they provide a measure of long-run viability. For a product or service to be economically sustainable, its full cost – not just its marginal cost – must be recuperated, actually even generating a margin above full cost. Second, full-cost transfers are relatively easy to implement because firms have systems in place to calculate the full costs of production (goods) or provision (services). Finally, full-cost transfers are not as distorting for evaluation purposes since the selling profit center is allowed to recover at least the full cost of production or provision.

Full-cost transfer prices are not a panacea, however. Full cost rarely reflects the actual, current cost of producing the products or the services being transferred. Some of the distortions are caused by poor cost-accounting systems that involve arbitrary overhead cost allocations. In addition, strictly full-cost transfer prices do not provide an incentive for the selling profit center to transfer internally since they include no profit margin. If internal transfers are a significant part of the selling profit center's business, then that entity's profit will be understated. Transfers at *full cost plus a markup*, however, do allow the selling profit centers to earn a profit on internally transferred products or services. They also provide a crude approximation of the market price that can be used in situations where no competitive external market price exists. But because the markup is internally set, such transfer prices are not responsive to changes in market conditions.

Negotiated Transfer Prices

Another transfer pricing alternative is to allow the selling and buying profit center managers to negotiate between themselves. This policy can be effective only if the profit centers are not *captive* to one another; that is, the selling profit center has some possibilities to sell its product outside the company, and the buying profit center has some outside sources of supply. Captivity obviously erodes bargaining power and undermines the negotiations.

Aside from that, negotiated transfer prices often cause several other problems. Negotiating a potentially large number of transactions is costly in terms of management time. Negotiation often accentuates conflicts between profit center managers, and resolution of the conflicts often requires mediation from corporate management. The outcome of the negotiations often depends on the negotiating skills and bargaining power of the managers involved, rather than its likely being economically optimal. If one of the entities has reasonably good outside selling or sourcing possibilities but the other does not, the bargaining power will be unequal. The unequal bargaining power will be magnified if the transaction is a relatively small proportion of the business of one of the entities and a relatively large proportion of the business of the other. The managers of the small-proportion entity will have considerable bargaining power because they can walk away from the transaction without bearing serious consequences. And managers' egos and self-interest can sometimes lead them to try to gain an upper hand in the negotiations over peers with whom they compete for recognition, bonuses, and promotions, even at the expense of the corporation's best interest.

Variations

Researchers have proposed several variations of one or more of the primary transfer pricing methods. All of these variations have some merit and so are worth mentioning, although their actual usage may vary in importance and with circumstances. One possibility is to transfer at *marginal costs plus a fixed lump-sum fee*. The lump-sum fee is designed to compensate the selling profit center for tying up some of its fixed capacity for producing products that are transferred internally. This method has some obvious appeal. It preserves goal congruence because additional unit transfers are made at marginal cost. It preserves information for evaluation purposes because the selling division can recover its fixed costs and a profit margin through the lump-sum fee. It also stimulates intra-firm planning and coordination because the selling and buying entities must discuss the bases for the lump-sum fee.

The major problem with the marginal-cost-plus-lump-sum method is that the managers involved must predetermine the lump-sum fee based on an estimate of the capacity that each internal customer will require in the forthcoming period. If these estimates are incorrect, then the charges will be inaccurate, and the capacity will not be assigned to the most profitable uses. If the selling entity changes all the lump-sum charges after the fact to reflect each customer's actual use of capacity, then the result will be nearly identical to transferring at the full cost of production.

Dual-rate transfer prices are another variation. In this case, the selling profit center is credited with the market price (or an approximation of it), but the buying profit center pays only the marginal (or full) costs of production. This scheme double counts the profits the corporation earns on each transaction. The accounting entries are balanced by putting the difference in a holding account at corporate, which is eliminated at the time of financial statement consolidation.

Dual-rate transfer prices have two basic advantages. First, the managers of both the selling and buying profit centers receive the proper economic signals for their decision-making. The seller receives the market price and is thereby not discouraged to transact internally. The buyer pays only the marginal (or full) cost and, thus, should normally be encouraged to buy internally. As such, the dual-rate transfer pricing method almost ensures that internal transactions will take place, making it possible to maintain a vertically integrated production process.

However, dual-rate transfer prices have disadvantages. Dual-rate transfer pricing can destroy the internal entities' proper economic incentives. Since the buying profit centers pay only marginal (or full) cost, they have little incentive to negotiate with outside suppliers for more favorable prices. Hence, the selling profit centers find it easy to generate internal sales because the transfer pricing policy shields them from competition. Many corporations also dislike to double count profits because it is often difficult to explain to the profit center managers how the double counting has overstated their entity profits. Equally, when the dual rates involve bookings across international borders, the corporation may wish to avoid alarming the tax authorities by the double counting and the retrospective adjustments to the accounts. What may seem merely to be an internal accounting adjustment may not be seen this way by the tax authorities or the regulators and, for this reason, may also not be favored by the firm's external auditors.[17]

Simultaneous use of multiple transfer pricing methods

One potential response to the need to serve multiple transfer pricing purposes is to use multiple transfer pricing methods at the same time. However, it is virtually impossible to use two different transfer pricing methods and simultaneously serve both the decision-making and evaluation purposes because managers make decisions in light of the numbers for which they are being evaluated. Tradeoffs here are usually inevitable.

When firms do use multiple transfer pricing methods, they typically use one method for internal purposes – both decision-making and evaluation – and another method to affect taxable profits across jurisdictions.[18] But the countries in which multinational corporations operate obviously have incentives not to allow these firms to "optimize" reported profits through transfer prices, as they will suffer tax losses if profits are moved out of their jurisdiction. Or they may suffer decreased market competitiveness if the firm manipulates its transfer prices to maintain a monopoly position as a supplier. Therefore, laws often require an *arm's-length* transfer price; that is, a price charged to the associated entity as the one between unrelated parties for the same transactions under the same circumstances. The United States has no restrictions on domestic transfer pricing methods, but the Internal Revenue Service (the US tax authority) disallows the shifting of income with international subsidiaries to avoid US taxes. This is true for many other countries as well. All told, then, it is easier for managers to claim that they are not manipulating reported income to evade taxes if they use the same transfer pricing method for tax purposes as for internal purposes. For this reason, and for reasons of system simplicity, multinational firms sometimes avoid using different transfer pricing methods for domestic and international transfers.

Conclusion

This chapter has provided an introduction to financial responsibility centers and transfer pricing. Financial responsibility centers are one of the core elements of financial results control systems. The definitions of financial responsibility centers are important because they provide managers signals about what financial statement line items they are expected to pay attention to. We discussed how the financial responsibilities usually are congruent with the managers' authorities or decision rights, but there are exceptions. Sometimes managers are held accountable for financial statement line items over which they have no direct authority because the accountability empowers them to influence the actions of those who do have direct authority.

This chapter also discussed how the pricing of goods or services that are transferred from one organizational entity to another often causes problems in the measurement of an entity's financial performance. Except in the rare situation where there is a perfectly competitive external market for the internally traded good or service, no transfer pricing approach can guide profit center managers to make decisions that are optimal from the corporation's perspective and simultaneously provide good information for evaluation. Incentives to move profits between firm locations with different tax jurisdictions cause additional transfer pricing considerations. Transfer pricing methods based on market prices or full costs, and variations thereof, are in common use, but some companies also use negotiated transfer prices. No method is superior in all settings; each has its advantages and disadvantages.

The next chapter discusses planning and budgeting systems, the second core element of financial results control systems. Planning and budgeting systems also have several control purposes, some of which, like transfer pricing purposes, sometimes conflict.

Notes

1 The term *cost center* also has a cost accounting meaning that is different from its meaning here in the context of responsibility center management. Most firms are comprised of many cost centers set up for cost accounting purposes to collect like-type costs and assign them to products and services, but these are not responsibility centers because they focus on cost categorizations rather than lines of authority over expenses by managers in charge of organizational entities with accountability for a cost budget. Firms typically use many more cost centers for cost accounting purposes than for responsibility center control purposes.

2 See, for example, "Study Finds Companies Profit When They Track Product Parts," *Forbes* (December 20, 2013), online at onforb.es/18WTvjT.

3 "Cisco India's New Marketing Initiatives Ramp Up Lead Generation," *CRN* (January 15, 2015), online at www.crn.com.

4 "RBS Finds Itself Back in Hot Water," *The Wall Street Journal* (November 25, 2013), online at on.wsj.com/1ekyZ04.

5 "Who Says the Music Industry Is Kaput," *Business Week* (May 27, 2010), online at www.businessweek.com.

6 R. Cooper and R. Slagmulder, "Micro Profit Centers," *Management Accounting*, 79, no. 12 (1998), pp. 16–18.

7 For a further discussion of return measures and their effects, which we also treat in more detail in Chapter 10, see W. A. Van der Stede, "Discussion of 'The Role of Performance Measures in the Intertemporal Decisions of Business Unit Managers,'" *Contemporary Accounting Research*, 30, no. 3 (2013), pp. 962–9.

8 Ibid.

9 "Why Energy Management Matters to CIOs," *Forbes* (September 15, 2010), online at www.forbes.com.

10 Transfer pricing also applies to transfers involving cost centers. Transfers can be made, for example, at actual or standard cost or at full or variable cost between cost centers. However, since most transfer pricing problems involve profit (or investment) centers, for reasons of simplicity, this chapter refers to both the supplying and buying entities as *profit centers*.

11 See, for example, *Global Transfer Pricing Survey* (Ernst & Young, 2016).

12 Examples are numerous, but for some recent cases, see "Brussels Opens Tax Probe into Apple, Starbucks and Fiat," *The Financial Times* (June 11, 2014), online at on.ft.com/1hJ2Ne7.

13 M. Cools and R. Slagmulder, "Tax-Compliant Transfer Pricing and Responsibility Accounting," *Journal of Management Accounting Research*, 21 (2009), pp. 151–78.

14 See, for example, C. X. Chen, S. Chen, F. Pan, and Y. Wang, "Determinants and Consequences of Transfer Pricing Autonomy: An Empirical Investigation," *Journal of Management Accounting Research*, 27, no. 2 (2015), pp. 225–59.

15 *Global Transfer Pricing Survey*, op. cit.

16 "The Nobel Prize for Economics: The Bigger Picture," *The Economist* (October 12, 2009), online at econ.st/JwM1wM; "The Man Who Showed Why Firms Exist," *The Economist* (September 7, 2013), online at econ.st/161DLgM.

17 For a recent academic treatment of dual transfer prices, see E. Johnson, N. B. Johnson, and T. Pfeiffer, "Dual Transfer Pricing with Internal and External Trade," *Review of Accounting Studies*, 21, no. 1 (March 2016), pp. 140–64.

18 See, for example, S. Anderson, B. Zhou, R. Ghayad, and M. Cragg, "The Interaction of Managerial and Tax Transfer Pricing," *Tax Management Transfer Pricing Report*, 24, no. 17 (January 2016).

CASE STUDY
Kranworth Chair Corporation

In July 2003, Kevin Wentworth, CEO of Kranworth Chair Corporation (KCC), was considering a major reorganization – a divisionalization – of his company's organization structure:

> Like many entrepreneurs, I have always been focused on top-line sales growth, and I have constantly been impressing on my managers to drive sales. My belief was that if you do that, everything else takes care of itself. Up until recently, I think our approach made sense. We had very little competition, and our margins were huge.
>
> Now things are changing. We've got some major competitors who are making headway. I think we needed to take a fresh management approach to

find opportunities to do things better. Our new divisionalized organization structure should help us serve our customers better and maybe force us to eliminate certain markets or products that are not producing results.

But I'm not sure it's working very well. We're seeing some finger pointing between the managers of the newly created divisions and the managers in charge of corporate departments. There is a lot of politics involved in defining the roles, responsibilities, ... and rights, of each of the responsibility centers, and it's not clear to me yet exactly where to draw the lines.

The company

In the early 1980s, Weston Krantz, an avid outdoors person, developed a new design for a lightweight, portable chair that could be stored in a bag and carried anywhere. Convinced that his design had commercial value, in 1987 Weston cofounded Kranworth Chair Corporation (KCC) with his longtime friend, Kevin Wentworth, who had an MBA degree and financial expertise. (The corporation's name was a contraction of the founders' names: Krantz and Wentworth.) KCC was headquartered in Denver, Colorado, in the foothills of the Rocky Mountains. KCC produced a broad line of high-quality and fashionable portable, folding chairs, which were branded as various models of the Fold-it! brand. In its early years, KCC sold its products exclusively to distributors.

Since its inception, KCC had been organized functionally. In 2003, reporting to the cofounders were vice presidents in charge of sales, supply chain, and finance and administration, plus staff managers responsible for advertising and research and development (Exhibit 1).

Over the years, KCC expanded its product offerings. In 2003, it offered an extensive line of folding chairs. The chairs were produced in various sizes and models, including both adult and child chairs, single chairs and loveseats, and full- and beach-height chairs. Some chairs had additional features, such as cup holders, storage pockets, and trays. The chairs were produced at several price points, with varying fabrics, designs (e.g. single vs. double layer), and frame materials. KCC also offered some related products, such as folding tripod stools, ottomans, cots, and stadium seats. KCC also produced custom-designed products. It employed screen-printing artists and seamstresses who applied custom logos, graphics, and lettering to the nylon. KCC products were often seen at corporate trade shows and tailgate parties at sporting events. The company kept track of approximately 1,500 stock keeping units (SKUs) – finished products and various piece parts that the company sold – although about 85–90% of the sales stemmed from only about 40 of the SKUs.

Gradually, KCC built sales by investing in more advertising and by adding other distribution channels. By 2003, it sold some products directly to major retail chains (Wal-Mart, K-Mart, Target), as well as other retailers (e.g. sporting goods stores) of various sizes. It sold to retailers using the KCC sales force, outside reps, and distributors. It also sold custom products directly to corporations and high school or university bookstores and athletic departments. The retail channels provided the highest sales volumes, but those sales were made at lower margins.

In the 1990s, KCC moved its core manufacturing facilities to Mexico and China to take advantage of lower labor rates. Only some assembly ("kitting") and customizing facilities were retained in the Denver location.

In the company's first decade of existence, KCC had little competition. Its chair designs were protected by more than 20 patents. Sales grew rapidly, and average margins were high, in the range of 40–50%, although some margins were sacrificed in later years in order to generate sales from large retail chains.

In 1999, KCC borrowed $30 million because the founders, particularly Kevin, wanted to take a significant amount of cash out of the company. Kevin had become interested in ranching, and he wanted to buy a significantly larger ranch. Ranching had become his passion, and he was spending less and less time at KCC. (For years Weston had spent only a small portion of his time at KCC as he traveled and pursued his various avocations.) The debt service on the loan reduced KCC managers' margin for error. Cash flow was tight, particularly at the slow time of the year – October to January.

Starting in the late 1990s, some significant competitors, mostly from Asian countries, entered the market with comparable chair designs. Despite the fact that most customers perceived KCC as having superior designs and higher quality, and customer satisfaction was high, the higher competition and the worldwide recession of the early 2000s caused sales to flatten and profits to drop. The company's management incentive plan did not pay out in either 2001 or 2002. In 2003, performance was slightly improved. KCC's total revenues were projected to be approximately $70 million, up from $68 million in 2002, and profits were expected to be slightly positive.

Motivation for divisionalization

In 2002, Kevin began to think about changes that might stem from a change in organization structure. He thought that the KCC managers needed to focus more on the quality, and not just the quantity, of sales. To illustrate the point, he described an example in which KCC personnel had aggressively sought business from Target, the large retail chain. In order to develop this retail account, KCC designed a special chair model for Target and offered a special price with a lower gross margin. While Target did sell some Fold-it! chairs, they did not sell many. Part of the reason for the poor sales was that many of Target's outlets did not display the Fold-it! chairs effectively. Instead of displaying them in the sporting goods department, they shelved them wherever they had room. Kevin explained, "I walked into a Target store in a suburb of Denver and found that our products were sitting on the bottom shelf horizontally in the back corner of the Automotive Department, where nobody could ever see them!" Because of the "growth at all costs" philosophy, KCC incurred significant product development and marketing costs and ended up carrying a large amount of inventory; so, overall, the Target account, and some others like it, were very unprofitable. But to develop more focus on the quality of sales, KCC had to develop a stronger customer focus, to understand better customers' needs and wants, and to improve customer service levels.

Kevin also thought that divisionalization, if implemented properly, could help KCC improve its efficiency and asset utilization. He thought that with an improved customer focus, it was almost inevitable that the company could reduce its SKUs, possibly outsource more functions, and generally learn to serve customer needs better while tying up less capital.

Divisionalization alternatives

What kind of divisionalization would be best? Kevin thought first about the relatively conservative approach of merely making the sales function a profit center. This approach would involve charging Sales for the full costs (or, perhaps, full costs plus a markup) of the products they sold. Sales would have to pay for the costs of customizing products and holding inventory. This approach would make Sales more aware of the cost implications of their decisions and, hence, more motivated to generate profitable sales.

But Kevin concluded that KCC should probably go further to create true product divisions. The KCC managers had frequent debates about what products and sales channels were most profitable, but those debates were not informed with hard data. A divisionalization would require some disaggregation of total costs and would facilitate profitability analyses.

If this was done, however, the KCC managers would have to consider how self-contained the new operating entities should be. Kevin wondered, "Should [the product divisions] each have their own supply chain management, sales force, R&D, and human resources functions, or should those resources be shared?"

The obvious product split in KCC was between Retail Products and Custom Products. The Retail Division would focus on the higher volume, standard product sales to retail outlets. The Custom Products Division would focus on the smaller-volume custom sales.

In the approach that Kevin was planning to present to his management team, the two product divisions were to become profit centers. Each entity would be dedicated to its focused core business, but their managers would be free to choose how they did business and what they incorporated into their business model. Reporting to each of the division managers would be managers responsible for sales and marketing, purchasing and inventory control, and finance and accounting. Supply chain, R&D, human resources, and advertising would still be centralized, although these functions would clearly have to work closely with division managers.

Kevin hoped that this new structure would allow the Retail and Custom Products divisions to make some bold, new decisions. The new company focus would also be on creating value, rather than merely growing. For the divisions, creating value could easily mean contracting sales to eliminate unprofitable or marginally profitable products and customers. The best customers, for example, were probably those that bought the most profitable products, placed inventory requirements on KCC that were reasonable and predictable, had a strong credit standing and payment history, and were relatively easy to serve. The divisions might also decide that they should outsource some functions, such as warehousing, which might allow KCC to provide better customer service during the busy seasons and to employ fewer people and assets in the low seasons.

On July 28, 2003, Kevin presented his divisionalization ideas to his management team. Figure 1 shows an excerpt from the presentation he gave.

Figure 1 Excerpt from presentation given by Kevin Wentworth

The new product divisions will be lean, mean fighting machines with a direct purpose and the vision to carry that purpose out. With our [corporate managers'] help, they will look at how they do business now and what they can do better. They will have the opportunity to dream. If we were to start a new product-line business, think of the questions that would have to be answered:

1. How should we staff?
2. How should we source?
3. How should we warehouse?
4. How should we sell?
5. How should we ship?
6. How should we finance?

These are just some of the many questions that a new company has to address.

We have a certain advantage since we already have a baseline. But we also carry along a disadvantage. We have become entrenched in our ways and are the costliest product in the market. If we forced ourselves to completely reevaluate the business, could we significantly reduce costs, provide better customer service, and yield higher operating profits? That answer must be "yes" in order to stay in business in the future. Think of the fabulous business opportunity in front of us!

Some of the KCC managers were enthusiastic about the proposed change. Others thought that the ideas were radical. A few managers were bewildered, as they had never worked in an organization with a divisional structure and had trouble visualizing how it would work. In the ensuing discussion, many questions arose, such as relating to the specifics as to who would be responsible for what and how performance would be measured and rewarded. It was decided that the idea needed more specifics.

A follow-up meeting was held two weeks later. By then most of the managers realized that top management had already made this decision; the company was going to be divisionalized. They then became highly interested in shaping the details of the change. The focus of the second meeting was on defining division management responsibilities.

After considerable discussion, there was general agreement regarding the following general division of responsibilities:

Responsibilities of top management and corporate staff:

1. Overall vision and strategy for the company
2. Financing and other high-level financial matters
3. Engineering, design, and R&D
4. Facilities
5. Legal and intellectual property
6. Supply chain and quality
7. Corporate identity (e.g. public relations, some general advertising)
8. Human resources
9. Information technology
10. Acquisitions and joint ventures

Responsibilities of division management:

1. Overall vision and strategy for their respective markets
2. Development and implementation of divisional annual budgets
3. Staffing
4. Operations, including purchasing of parts and materials specific to respective markets, receiving, warehousing, shipping, and inventory management
5. Controllership and accounting
6. Product-specific advertising and collateral material
7. Information technology support

With this general understanding of the distribution of responsibilities in the company in place, the next task was the development of ideas regarding performance measurement and incentives. This task was assigned to Robert Chang, VP – Finance and Administration.

Performance measurement and incentives

Robert developed a measure that he called *controllable returns*, which was defined as operating income (before tax) divided by controllable assets. To get to operating income, all the division direct expenses were subtracted from division revenues, as were as many of the

[1] If the division (corporate) plan was met, but the corporate (division) plan was not, division management would still receive the divisional (corporate) portion of the bonus.

corporate expenses that could be reasonably allocated to the divisions. The assets deemed controllable by the divisions included their receivables, inventories, and an assigned cost of facilities they used.

Robert proposed an incentive plan that provided 22 managers, down to the director level (one level below division manager), with a cash award based on achievement of annual targets set for controllable return at the divisional and corporate levels. For corporate managers, the bonuses would be based solely on corporate performance. For managers assigned to a division, the bonuses would be based 75% on division performance and 25% on corporate performance.

Robert proposed that the expected payouts be set initially at relatively modest levels. If the annual performance targets were achieved, Kevin and Weston would be paid an award of 40% of salary, division managers would be paid 30%, and managers lower in the hierarchy would be paid 15–20%. No payouts would be made if actual performance was below plan.[1] If actual performance exceeded plan, the payouts could be increased by up to 50%, at the discretion of top management and the company's board of directors.

Robert explained that he proposed the relatively modest awards because the costs of this plan would probably be in excess of $500,000, a significant additional expense for the company. Maintaining competitive total compensation levels was not an issue because KCC managers were currently not accustomed to earning a bonus, since the old sales growth-based incentive plan had not paid out anything in either 2001 or 2002. Plus, Robert thought the company needed to get some experience with setting division-level performance targets and measuring and evaluating performance in a new way before ratcheting the performance-dependent rewards upward while probably reducing the proportion of total compensation paid as fixed base salaries.

These suggestions were discussed in a staff meeting held on October 13, 2003.[2] The major point of dissension was regarding the proposed assignment of some of the corporate expenses to the divisions. Some of the personnel who were slated for assignment to a division complained that they could not control the terms of deals that corporate staff negotiated for them, such as for insurance. Kevin headed off this discussion by explaining that these cost assignments would be built into the performance targets, so they would not affect the actual vs. targeted return comparison. Further, division managers would have near complete freedom of sourcing. If they did not like the services provided to them by corporate staffs, they were free to purchase those services from outside the company.

A follow-up meeting was scheduled for October 27, 2003. That meeting was intended to be used primarily to design the new organization – who would be assigned to what division and in what role (see Exhibit 2). It was hoped that the new divisionalized structure would be completely in place by January 1, 2004, and the first incentives based on controllable return would be paid based on 2004-performance.

Hopes and concerns for the future

Kevin was convinced that the new divisionalized organization structure would give KCC its best chance for future success:

> **Most of us are now convinced that this is a good idea. Although it creates a more complex organization, it will make most of our managers feel more empowered. It will also force us to be more focused on returns, rather than revenues and cost control.**

Privately, however, Kevin expressed concern that this major turning point in the company's history was quite risky.

> **I'm delegating considerable decision-making power to the division managers. If they make mistakes, our business can go down the tubes. The managers will make out all right; they can go find another job. But the fortunes of my family and those of the other major owners would be devastated.**

He had a specific concern about one manager, Joe Yarmouth, the current VP-Sales who would be appointed as general manager of the Retail Division.

> **Joe is in his early 50s, and he has a lot of experience. But most of the experience is in sales, rather than marketing and other functions, and all of his experience before KCC was in big companies – Clorox, Hershey's. Culturally he does not have the small company mindset. He has no experience in**

[2] Sales personnel were still included in a sales-based commission plan. At this meeting the idea came up that the sales commissions should be weighted based on product profitability, but detailed discussion of this idea was deferred.

understanding costs, cash flows, and returns. I think he should have been able to set up more deals that don't require any working capital investment, but he just doesn't think that way.

So Kevin, and indeed most of the KCC managers, looked to the future with both eager anticipation and trepidation.

Early experiences

KCC's early experiences with the divisionalized structure created more concern. The first major initiative of Ed Sanchez, the manager of the new Custom Division, was to propose the procurement of a more sophisticated fabric-cutting machine. This machine would allow the fabric to be cut more efficiently and lower both material and labor costs slightly. A discounted cash flow analysis suggested that this machine was a worthwhile investment. But, Kevin explained:

In my opinion, this investment does not address the real issue in the Custom Division. Our real issue is turnaround time. We have plenty of margin in custom work, but we need to reduce our turnaround time to serve our customers better. I think Ed is turning the wrong dials.

Kevin also knew that in Retail, the newly installed division manager Joe Yarmouth, who had good contacts in the advertising world through his prior jobs, was talking with a new advertising agency about the possibility of a new campaign to advertise retail products more aggressively. Kevin wondered whether this was in the best interest of the company. He commented:

I'm worried about losing economies of scale from dealing with different ad agencies and about what this "go-it-alone" advertising will do to our corporate identity. And in any case, lack of advertising was not the problem we faced at Target; it was product placement!

Joe, in turn, had already been grumbling to Robert about late deliveries and missed sales as well as product returns due to quality problems, which were caused, in his opinion, by vendor problems that were under the purview of Carrie Jennings, the corporate head of Supply Chain and Quality. In the new organization structure, Supply Chain was responsible for obtaining and maintaining an adequate vendor group, primarily in Asia and Mexico, to secure both high-quality subassemblies and on-time delivery, while reducing dependency on any given vendor. The divisions had responsibility only for placing the day-to-day purchasing orders (POs) with these vendors. Joe complained:

If I keep having delivery and quality issues due to problems with our overseas vendors, over which I have no control, I'm sure going to miss my performance target for the year. *I* am the one – not *Carrie* – who feels the pain of lower sales and higher costs due to product returns, because it directly affects the numerator of my controllable returns measure, and thus, *my* bonus that is totally based on it. I have already lobbied corporate to let me have control over vendor negotiations. If they won't do that, they should at least adjust my targets so that my evaluations aren't affected by others' failures. But so far they don't seem to want to listen to me.

Robert estimated that the divisions had about 85% control over their own P&L results. He believed that was significant enough:

Joe's arguments have some merit, but no manager ever controls everything. Our managers need to work with others in the organization within the constraints in which they are placed, to react to a lot of changing conditions, and to deliver the needed results. If Joe can't do this, then we'll find someone else who can.

Robert did not think that corporate managers should make any changes either to the assigned responsibilities or the bonus plan.

Joe had also proposed some other ideas for a leaner Retail business that could potentially affect the design of the Supply Chain function. He wanted to enter into arrangements with large retailers that would provide favorable pricing in return for commitments to take delivery of full containers of finished products right at the port of entry (from either Asia or Mexico). This would eliminate further kitting in the Denver plant and reduce inventory significantly. Kevin thought this could be a good idea, but he was not sure who should take responsibility for working out the details. He was also worried about the politics involved in redrawing the lines of responsibility so early into the new divisionalization.

Another issue that had arisen involved the R&D function. Corporate R&D was responsible for new product designs and refinements. Even though most ideas for new products or product improvements came from the division managers and their sales people in the field, division management did not have much control over which R&D initiatives received priority. Joe Yarmouth commented:

> **There is too much filtering by corporate R&D of the ideas that we feed them. We can't get anything done without Ken Simmons' [R&D manager] blessing, and Ken really takes his orders from Weston [Krantz]. We ought to have more influence. We know our markets better than anyone else in the company, and we are paying for the function. We [the divisions] each fund 50% of the corporate R&D budget. I'm about to take a $150,000 hit for corporate R&D in my 2004 P&L, and what do I get for that? And why do we [the divisions] each have to share the burden equally? I'm also annoyed that Custom is getting a lot more R&D support than I do. Certainly Retail is much larger than Custom, but we're not getting much support from R&D. All they're doing for us are a few tweaks on our standard products.**

Ed Sanchez (Custom), in turn, was complaining that R&D was much too "reactive" to new product features already introduced by competitors, despite the fact that he and his sales people has proposed many ideas for more radical changes.

Under this pressure from the division managers, Kevin was considering whether KCC should allow the divisions to do their own R&D. He knew doing so would solve the problems the divisions managers were complaining about, but he wasn't sure which new problems it might create. Kevin did not like the whining. But he also did not want to undercut the local initiative that the new organization promised to bring to KCC. And in any case, there were pressing issues to attend to on his new ranch.

Exhibit 1 Kranworth Chair Corporation: 2003 organization structure

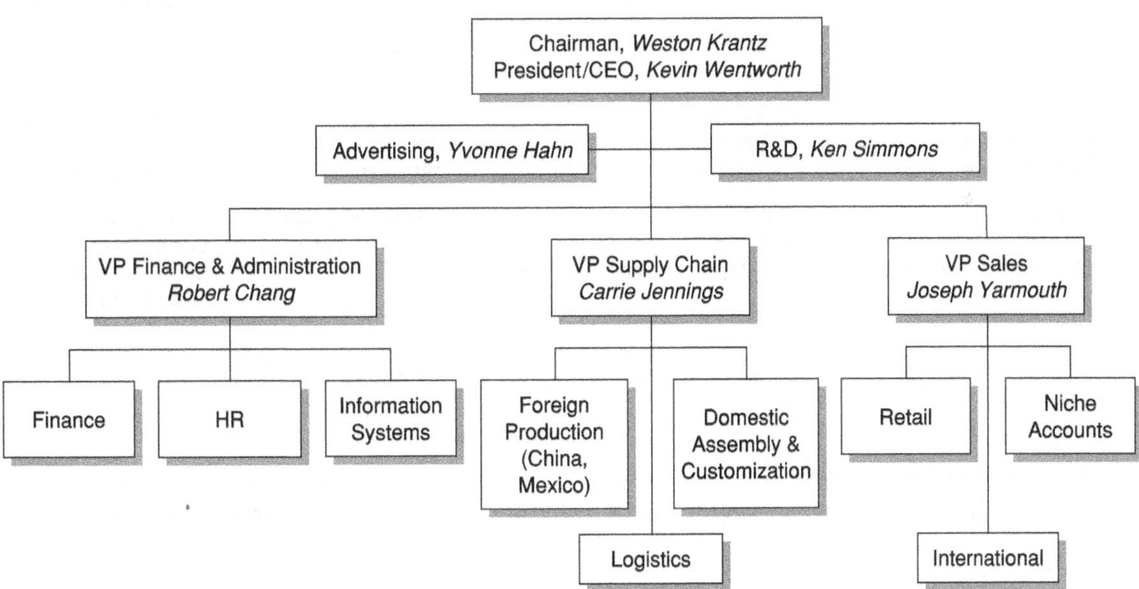

Exhibit 2 Kranworth Chair Corporation: 2004 organization structure

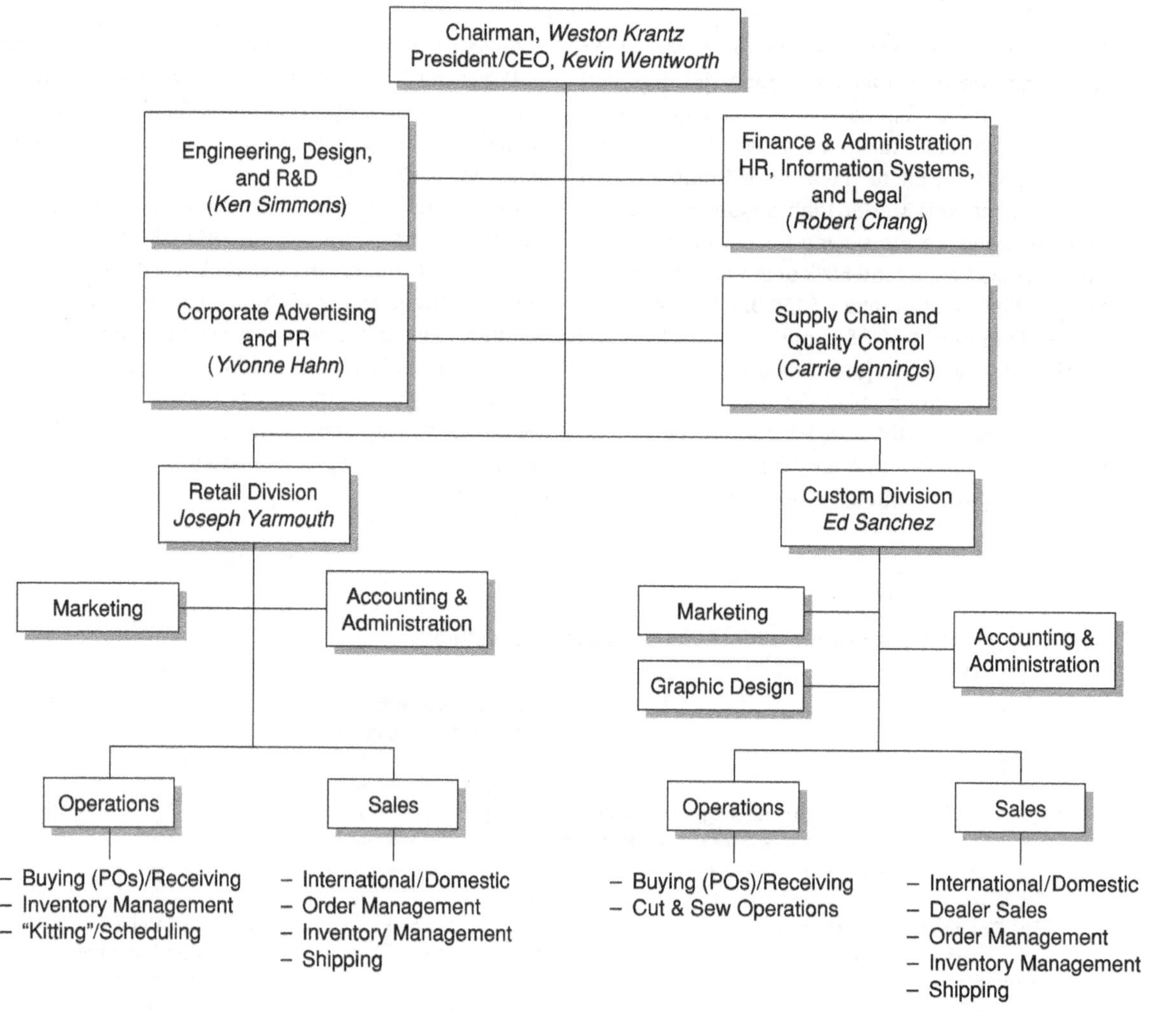

This case was prepared by Professors Kenneth A. Merchant, Wim A. Van der Stede, and research assistant Clara (Xiaoling) Chen.

CASE STUDY
Zumwald AG

University of Southern California
Marshall School of Business
Leventhal School of Accounting
A203-01
Rev. 7-31-15

In August 2015, a pricing dispute arose between the managers of some of the divisions of Zumwald AG. Mr. Rolf Fettinger, the company's managing director, had to decide whether to intervene in the dispute.

The company

Zumwald AG, headquartered in Cologne, Germany, produced and sold a range of medical diagnostic imaging systems and biomedical test equipment and instrumentation. The company was organized into six operating divisions. Total annual revenues were slightly more than £3 billion.

Zumwald managers ran the company on a highly decentralized basis. The managers of each division were allowed considerable autonomy if their performances were at least on plan. Performance was evaluated, and management bonuses were assigned, based on each division's achievement of budgeted targets for return on invested capital (ROIC) and sales growth. Even though the company was partly vertically integrated, division managers were allowed to source their components from external suppliers if they so chose.

Involved in the dispute mentioned above were three of the company's divisions – the Imaging Systems Division (ISD), the Heidelberg Division (Heidelberg), and the Electronic Components Division (ECD).

- ISD sold complex ultrasound and magnetic resonance imaging systems. These systems were expensive, typically selling for £500,000 to £1 million.
- Heidelberg sold high-resolution monitors, graphics controllers and display subsystems. Approximately half of its sales were made to outside customers. ISD was one of Heidelberg's major inside customers.
- ECD sold application-specific integrated circuits and subassemblies. ECD was originally established as a captive supplier to other Zumwald divisions, but in the last decade its managers had found external markets for some of the division's products. Because of this, ECD's managers were given profit center responsibility.

The dispute

ISD had recently designed a new ultrasound imaging system called the X73. Hopes were high for X73. The new system offered users advantages in processing speed and cost, and it took up less space. Heidelberg engineers participated in the design of X73, but Heidelberg was compensated for the full cost of the time its employees spent on this project.

After the specifications were set, ISD managers solicited bids for the materials needed to produce X73 components. Heidelberg was asked to bid to supply the displays needed for production of the X73 system. So were two outside companies. One was Bogardus NV, a Dutch company with a reputation for producing high-quality products. Bogardus had been a longtime supplier to Zumwald, but it had never before supplied display units and systems to any Zumwald division. Display Technologies Plc, was a British company that had recently entered the market and was known to be pricing its products aggressively in order to buy market share. The quotes that ISD received were as follows:

Supplier	Cost per X73 system (£)
Heidelberg Division	140,000
Bogardus NV	120,500
Display Technologies Plc	100,500

After discussing the bids with his management team, Conrad Bauer, ISD's managing director, announced that

ISD would be buying its display systems from Display Technologies Plc. Paul Halperin, Heidelberg's general manager, was livid. He immediately complained to Mr. Bauer, but when he did not get the desired response, he took his complaint to Rolf Fettinger, Zumwald's managing director. Mr. Fettinger agreed to look into the situation.

A meeting was called to try to resolve the dispute. Mr. Halperin asked Christian Schönberg, ECD's GM, to attend this meeting to support his case. If Heidelberg got this order from ISD, it would buy all of its electronic components from ECD.

At this meeting, Mr. Bauer immediately showed his anger:

> **Paul wants to charge his standard markup for these displays. I can't afford to pay it. I'm trying to sell a new product (X73) in a very competitive market. How can I show a decent ROIC if I have to pay a price for a major component that is way above market? I can't pass on those costs to my customers. Paul should really want this business. I know things have been relatively slow for him. But all he does is quote list prices and then complain when I do what is best for my division.**
>
> **We're wasting our time here. Let's stop fighting amongst ourselves and instead spend our time figuring out how to survive in these difficult business conditions.**

Mr. Fettinger asked Mr. Halperin why he couldn't match Display Technologies' price. Paul replied as follows:

> **Conrad is asking me to shave my price down to below cost. If we start pricing our jobs this way, it won't be long before we're out of business. We need to price our products so that we earn a fair return on our investment. You demand that of us; our plan is put together on that basis; and I have been pleading with my sales staff not to offer deals that will kill our margins. Conrad is forgetting that my engineers helped him design X73, and we provided that help with no mark-up over our costs. Further, you can easily see that Zumwald is better off if we supply the display systems for this new product. The situation here is clear. If Conrad doesn't want to be a team player, then you must order him to source internally! That decision is in the best interest of all of us.**

In the ensuing discussion, the following facts came out:

1. ISD's tentative target price for the X73 system was £340,000.[1]
2. Heidelberg's standard manufacturing cost (material, labor, and overhead) for each display system was £105,000. When asked, Mr. Halperin estimated that the variable portion of this total cost was only £50,000. He treated Heidelberg's labor costs as fixed because German laws did not allow him to lay off employees without incurring expenses that were "prohibitively" high.
3. Because of the global business slowdown, the production lines at Heidelberg that would produce the systems in question were operating at approximately 70% of capacity. In the pre ceding year, monthly production had ranged from 60% to 90% of total capacity.
4. Heidelberg's costs included £21,600 in electronic subassemblies to be supplied by ECD. ECD's full manufacturing costs for the components included in each system were approximately £18,000, of which approximately half were out-of-pocket costs. ECD's standard policy was to price its products internally at full manufacturing cost plus 20%. The markup was intended to give ECD an incentive to supply its product internally. ECD was currently operating at 90% capacity.

Near the end of the meeting, Mr. Bauer reminded everybody of the company's policy of freedom of sourcing. He pointed out that this was not such a big deal, as the volume of business to be derived from this new product was only a small fraction (less than 5%) of the revenues for each of the divisions involved, at least for the first few years. And he also did not like the potential precedent of his being forced to source internally because it could adversely affect his ability to get thoughtful quotes from outside suppliers in the future.

The decision

As he adjourned the meeting, Mr. Fettinger promised to consider all the points of view that had been expressed and to provide a speedy judgment. He wondered if there was a viable compromise or if, instead, there were some management principles involved here that should be considered inviolate.

[1] The cost of the other components that go into X73 is £72,000. ISD's conversion cost for the X73 system is £144,000, of which £117,700 is fixed.

This case was prepared by Professors Kenneth A. Merchant and Wim A. Van der Stede.

CASE STUDY
Global Investors, Inc.

> I have a basic "gut" discomfort with the proposition that investment management as a profitmaking function exists only in New York.
>
> *Alistair Hoskins, Chairman/CEO, Global Investors, London*

Bob Mascola, CFO of Global Investors, Inc. (GI), took a last look at his notes as he walked into the conference room where he and the other members of the transfer pricing task force would meet with Gary Spencer, GI's CEO. The transfer pricing task force supervised by Mascola was meeting with Spencer to discuss the latest transfer pricing models that the task force members had identified. Mascola hoped the meeting would result in a final decision about the transfer pricing method that should be used to recognize profits in GI's subsidiaries.

Mascola knew that the meeting would be difficult. On repeated occasions, two of the members of the transfer pricing task force, Alistair Hoskins and Jack Davis, had engaged in heated debates about which transfer pricing model should be selected. Hoskins, the chairman/CEO of GI's London office, believed that regional offices – or at least the regional office he led – should be treated as largely autonomous profit centers so that the value created by these offices would be reflected in their financial statements. However, Davis, GI's corporate vice president of operations, argued that virtually all of the investment strategies used to manage the clients' funds were designed by the research team located in New York. Consequently, Davis believed that the revenues generated by investment activities should be recognized in New York, even if a few investment services were offered by a regional office. The essence of Hoskins's reply to Davis was that expressed in the epigraph.

The company

Global Investors, founded in 1965, was a privately owned investment management company headquartered in New York. A number of directors and executives based in New York, Spencer among them, held majority ownership of GI's outstanding stock. GI, started as a domestic equity investment management firm, had grown to manage US$160 billion for a variety of clients, including corporations, insurance companies, public and private pension funds, endowments, foundations, and high-net-worth individuals.

GI focused on two activities: investment management (which included research, portfolio management, and trading) and client services (which included marketing and investor advisory services provided to institutional investors and independent brokers/dealers). Although the company initially focused on direct sales to institutional investors (such as endowments and pension funds), it was increasingly selling its investment products through independent brokers/dealers who both served wealthy individual investors and invested in GI funds on their behalf (see Exhibit 1). GI generated its investment management revenues by charging a percentage fee for the amount each of its clients invested in GI funds.

GI's investment philosophy differentiated the firm from most of its competitors. Since its inception, GI based all of its investment strategies on financial market theories emerging from academic research. The company developed a prominent New York-based research team composed mostly of PhD-qualified investment experts, who were supported by contracted-for advice from some of the world's most highly regarded academic financial economists.

The company's investment philosophy revolved around the theory that markets are affected by judgmental biases of the market participants. That is, under certain circumstances and for certain time periods, investors, and hence markets, overreact or underreact to information that is publicly available regarding companies' expected risks and returns. Instead of focusing on the valuation of individual securities and actively selecting securities based on their estimated value (as most of its competitors did), GI developed its different funds by focusing more directly on the types of securities that academic research had shown to be undervalued by the market.

As part of its strategy, GI was also committed to lowering its trading costs through economies of scale, technological investments aimed at increasing liquidity, and crossing activities (that is, matching clients' buy and sell requests).

GI focused mostly on equity investments in countries committed to free markets and with reasonably well-functioning capital markets, but it also invested in fixed income and commodity securities. Over the years, GI had expanded its activities throughout Asia, Europe, and the Americas (as shown in Exhibit 2).

GI's subsidiaries

Most of GI's 415 employees were located in New York, but GI also offered its services through four remote subsidiaries (see Exhibit 3). The largest subsidiaries located in Tokyo and London employed 52 and 40 employees, respectively. The other two subsidiaries located in Singapore and San Francisco employed fewer than a dozen individuals each. About 80% of the personnel employed in these offices were dedicated to trading financial assets following guidelines established by headquarters, 15% were dedicated to selling GI's funds, and the rest were involved in operations. Recently, three highly competent senior portfolio managers in Tokyo and four in London had started both to act as subadvisors for the Japanese, Pacific Rim, and European portfolios and to manage a series of trusts for their regional clientele. Many of the sales personnel at those subsidiaries were using these local funds to attract new clients. However, all clients attracted by the subsidiaries, regardless of the location of the subsidiary or the fund they invested in, were assigned a contact person in New York in addition to their local representative. They also received timely information resulting from the internal and sponsored research generated in New York.

GI's subsidiaries were separately incorporated companies. Their ownership composition resembled that of GI's parent company, but additional shares were issued to the subsidiaries' chairmen/CEOs. The chairman/CEO of GI London (Hoskins) owned 23% of the London subsidiary; the chairman/CEO of GI Tokyo (Paul Hashi) owned 5% of the Tokyo subsidiary; and the chairmen/CEOs of GI Singapore and GI San Francisco each owned 3% of their respective subsidiaries.

GI's subsidiaries had historically been treated as cost-focused profit centers, while the administrative departments providing support were treated as cost centers. Expenses and revenues were recorded according to the following accounting model:

1. Expenses (see Exhibit 4, presenting the format of a consolidated statement):
   - Any expenses that could be traced directly to the subsidiaries or the cost centers were recorded in the Direct Controllable Cost category. When expenses could not be directly traced, an allocation method was followed. (The last column of Exhibit 4 describes the allocation bases.)
   - Royalty expenses (paid to academics for developing trading strategies) were charged to the New York office, the center of the firm's investment management activities.
   - Allocations from the cost centers were based on cost center manager estimates of the proportions of the cost centers' services that were consumed by each of the center's internal "clients" (other cost centers or subsidiaries).
   - After the proportions of each cost center's expenses were established, GI utilized a reciprocal cost allocation method, using a system of simultaneous equations, to identify the total costs incurred by each cost center and the dollar amount that should be allocated from each cost center to its "internal clients," both cost centers and subsidiaries.
2. Revenues
   - GI New York retained all of the revenues generated worldwide (from fixed fees charged to the clients based on the amount of money they invested in GI) and assigned GI's subsidiaries a portion of the revenue based on local costs (direct controllable costs and other costs allocated to the subsidiaries) plus a 10% markup over the direct controllable costs.

A report of GI subsidiaries' profits for 2006 is presented in Exhibit 5. The cost-plus revenue-allocation method resulted in a small profit for all subsidiaries. This profit guaranteed that the subsidiaries would comply with capital requirements imposed by local financial authorities. The subsidiaries also used these profit reports both as a benchmark to calculate their taxes and as disclosures to institutional investor clients interested in learning about the financial health of the subsidiary holding their investments. On a few occasions where GI executives discussed the possibility of selling the firm or a subsidiary, the executives also used subsidiary profits to obtain a rough estimate of the worth of each subsidiary (calculated as a multiple of their EBITDA).

Subsidiary profits were not explicitly tied to the managers' compensation. A bonus pool based on GI's total profits was allocated to each executive based on the relative number of bonus points that each had earned. The compensation committee (comprising three members of the board of directors and the vice president of human resources) assigned these bonus points to each executive at the beginning of the year based on its subjective assessments of both the executive's performance in the prior year and his or her contribution to the company.

Alternative transfer pricing models

Some subsidiary CEOs expressed discomfort with the way the firm was calculating their units' profits. During the last quarter of 2006, Hoskins had been particularly vocal in pointing out to Spencer that treating GI's subsidiaries as cost-focused profit centers was wrong. He argued that the resulting profits did not portray a fair picture of the subsidiaries' performance, which could have an adverse effect on the subsidiaries' sales prices, if they were ever spun off. The inaccurate profits also could be viewed negatively by financial and tax regulators in the countries where the subsidiaries were located.[3]

Gary Spencer was not convinced that the current structure created problems that were worth fixing. However, in December 2006, primarily to appease Hoskins, he asked Mascola to create a committee to evaluate the situation, to address both Hoskins' and the tax concerns and, if appropriate, to propose an improved transfer pricing system. Mascola was selected to lead the evaluation process because of his financial expertise, his independence (he did not own any GI stock), and his personality (he was widely regarded as being thoughtful and impartial).

Right after his meeting with Spencer, Mascola began recruiting the people that he believed needed to participate in the process if a new transfer pricing model were to be both well designed and successfully implemented throughout the company. Every person invited accepted the invitation to become part of what became known as the Transfer-Pricing Model Task Force. Mascola chaired the task force, which also included Jack Davis (operations vice president), Michael Freeman (research director), Hashi (GI Tokyo), and Hoskins (GI London).

The task force met periodically over a seven-month period. During that time, they evaluated a number of different transfer pricing alternatives. In an early meeting, Hoskins took the initiative by proposing that GI revenues should be allocated to the subsidiaries using "assets under management" as the allocation base and that the subsidiaries pay a royalty of (around) 50% to New York as compensation for the R&D and trading strategies developed by headquarters. According to his model, the London office would receive 20% of total revenues, since it managed $32 billion of the $160 billion of assets under management at GI (see Exhibit 2). Thus, according to Hoskins, the London office would have been allocated the following revenues in 2006:

	London subsidiary revenues ($000)
Allocated revenues	20% * 619,949.1 = 123,989.8
Minus royalty expense	50% * $123,989.8 = 61,994.9
Net revenues	61,994.9

[3] Many countries' tax authorities were concerned that multinational corporations use transfer prices to shift income out of their country to countries with lower income taxes. Consequently, laws in the United States as well as other countries constrained transfer-pricing policies. For example, Section 482 of the US Internal Revenue Code required that transfer prices between a company and its foreign subsidiaries equal the price (or an estimate of the price) that would be charged by an unrelated third party in a comparable transaction. Regulators recognized that transfer prices can be market-based or cost-plus-based, where the plus should represent margins on comparable transactions.

Tax rates varied significantly across countries: In GI's case, Singapore had the lowest effective tax rate (approximately 20%), followed by the United Kingdom and Japan (25–30%). The United States' subsidiaries paid the highest tax rates (around 40%).

However, Davis and Freeman did not agree that London should record all of those revenues. They argued that the fact that London was managing those funds did not mean they were generating a significant proportion of the value associated with them. Davis argued that, in fact, most of the assets managed by the subsidiaries belonged to New York clients. Further, to manage those assets, the subsidiary employees were just following instructions from headquarters, since the investment management research group in New York was the unit in charge of developing GI's trading strategies. Instead of allocating revenues based on assets under management, Davis believed a more accurate way of allocating revenues would be based on the origin of the clients (the source of the fixed fee revenues generated at each subsidiary), distributed as follows in 2006:

Subsidiary	Asset distribution based on the origin of the clients ($bn)
New York	150.6
London	2.2
Tokyo	4.2
Singapore	1.0
San Francisco	2.0
Total	160.0

Under this proposal, GI London's 2006 revenue would have declined from its actual $26.5 million to a mere $8.5 million and would have resulted in a subsidiary loss of over $16 million.

Totally dissatisfied with Davis's counterproposal, which he considered ridiculous, Hoskins decided to conduct some research to learn whether (and how) GI's competitors were allocating revenues to their subsidiaries. Hoskins learned that the industry standard was to split fee revenues 50–50 between Client Services and Investment Management. Thus, he proposed, GI's business units should be split into these two categories. Half of the revenue would be allocated to Client Services (including two business units: Institutional Investor Sales, and Independent Broker/Dealer Sales), and the other half would be allocated to the Investment Management unit. This would allow GI to treat both activities separately.

Hoskins went on to propose that 50% of the fee revenues be assigned to Client Services based on the revenues generated in each subsidiary (or equivalently, based on the origin of clients, which were directly proportional to the revenues in each subsidiary), while the 50% assigned to Investment Management be allocated based on assets under management. He proposed still to pay a 50% royalty to New York. Under this proposed scheme, Hoskins calculated GI London's 2006 revenues as follows:

	London subsidiary revenues ($000)
Client revenues	1.375% * 50% * 619,949.1 = 4,262.1
Investment management revenues	20% * 50% * 619,949.1 = 61,994.9
Minus royalty expense	50% * $61,994.9 = 30,997.5
Net revenues	35,259.6

Hoskins's new proposal also met with the disapproval of most of the task force members. Although most agreed with the concept of the subsidiaries' recording of revenues from Client Services, Davis reiterated that Investment Management should be considered a New York business unit only, since almost all of the investment strategies were developed at headquarters. Consequently, Davis and Freeman proposed that the fee revenues corresponding to Investment Management (50% of total revenues) be fully recognized by the headquarters office. The subsidiaries, on the other hand, would be reimbursed by headquarters for any expenses related to investment management activities in their units plus a 10% markup if these expenses qualified as direct controllable costs. Using the 2006 financial results, Davis and Freeman estimated that the operating incomes recorded for the different subsidiaries under their proposed model, would be those shown in Exhibit 6.

This model was unacceptable to Hoskins. He argued that the London and Tokyo subsidiaries were actively participating in investment management, and they should be rewarded for the value these activities created. He explained:

> Clearly there is activity under the broad banner of Investment Management in London and Tokyo. The issue is whether our offices add value or not. We are building resources in London on the basis that GI London is at least responsible for the investment management function for locally sourced clients.

We have established an Investment Committee to oversee policies for our fixed income portfolios in the UK and continental Europe as well as for the Irish funds, and we have initiated the development of a local research function. I accept that the local activity is primarily, though not exclusively, one of policy tailoring and implementation rather than original intellectual capital investment, but most companies would regard this as a source of added value.

Hashi supported Hoskins by adding,

Local value-added is not the same for all products or for all clients. It is clear, for example, that GI Tokyo adds little when it simply implements programs of trades suggested by GI New York, but it is also clear that it adds a significant share of value when it is managing money for its own clients in products designed specifically for them using local inputs.

Hoskins also expressed a concern about the effect that not recording the investment management revenues at the subsidiary level would have on external parties. Hoskins believed that local tax authorities might disapprove such treatment, as the profitability from investment management operations would be constrained to 10% or less. He claimed that, in practice, it seemed acceptable that support services (such as those provided by the cost centers) would be transferred at cost (or at a slight markup), but functions that formed part of a group's offering to clients (in this case, client services and investment management) were expected to be transferred in exchange for a proportion of revenues, following an "arm's-length standard."[4] Departures from arm's-length prices could be interpreted by the local authorities as an attempt to shift taxable income out of their countries. Hoskins explained:

Our main competitors in the UK allocate revenues to the location actually carrying out the fund management. The alternative of a cost-plus arrangement, such as we have historically maintained, is probably no longer tenable where we now have local clients from whom we are receiving revenues for local investment activities.

Another external party that Hoskins worried about was his own clients. Hoskins believed that key local clients would be hesitant to appoint GI London to manage their assets if they knew their funds were considered to be managed in New York.

Davis disagreed with Hoskins's and Hashi's contentions. He believed that the contributions made to the local investments managed in London and Tokyo were minimal. Davis argued that the majority of operations at the subsidiaries consisted of selling the investment funds managed in the headquarters or executing a few investment operations, following strategies and guidelines developed by the investment management unit in New York.

Although Freeman agreed that the transfer pricing model should adhere to tax regulations, he believed that the model he and Davis proposed was appropriate. It should not trigger regulators' concerns since it already allowed the subsidiaries to record revenues for the services provided to institutional investor and independent broker/dealer clients (which he considered the main value-added activity performed by the subsidiaries). Additionally, GI's executives believed that the model used to prepare the subsidiaries' financial statements was not all that crucial to other financial regulators since GI was required to report consolidated (rather than subsidiary) financial statements.

The meeting

As Mascola prepared for the meeting with Spencer, he recognized the tensions among the task force members. He had carefully considered the advantages and disadvantages of the models proposed by Hoskins and by Davis and Freeman. He wondered how he could direct the meeting toward a final selection of a transfer pricing model that would both benefit the firm and be accepted by all, or at least most, members of the task force.

[4] "Arm's-length" prices are those charged after bargaining between unrelated persons or those charged between related persons that approximate the result of independent bargaining.

Exhibit 1 Global Investors, Inc.: Total assets under management

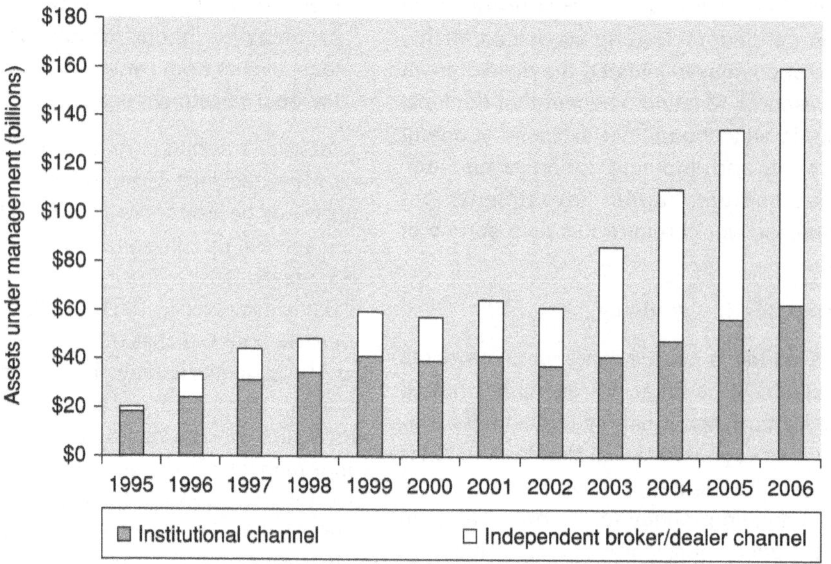

Exhibit 2 Global Investors, Inc.: Types of funds (December 2006)

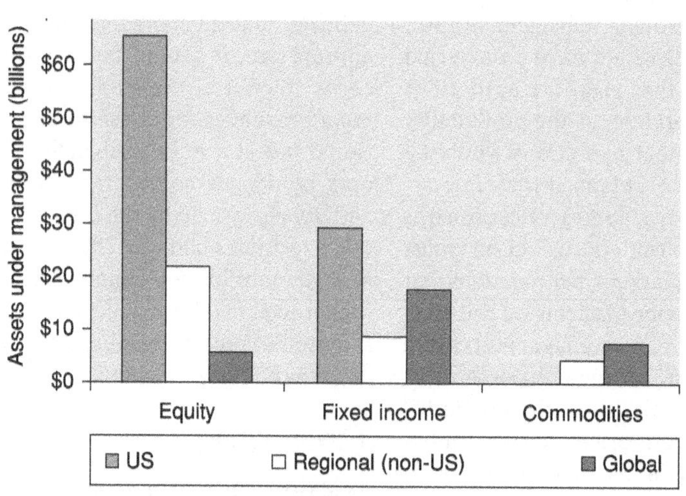

Assets under management by subsidiary (in billions of dollars, as of December 2006)				
Subsidiary managing the assets	**Equity**	**Fixed income**	**Commodities**	**Total**
New York	70.2	36.3	5.9	112.4
London	14.5	14.5	3.0	32.0
Tokyo	6.2	4.0	2.2	12.4
Singapore	2.1	0.3	0.0	2.4
San Francisco	0.0	0.2	0.6	0.8
Total	93.0	55.3	11.7	160.0

Exhibit 3 Global Investors, Inc.: Organizational structure

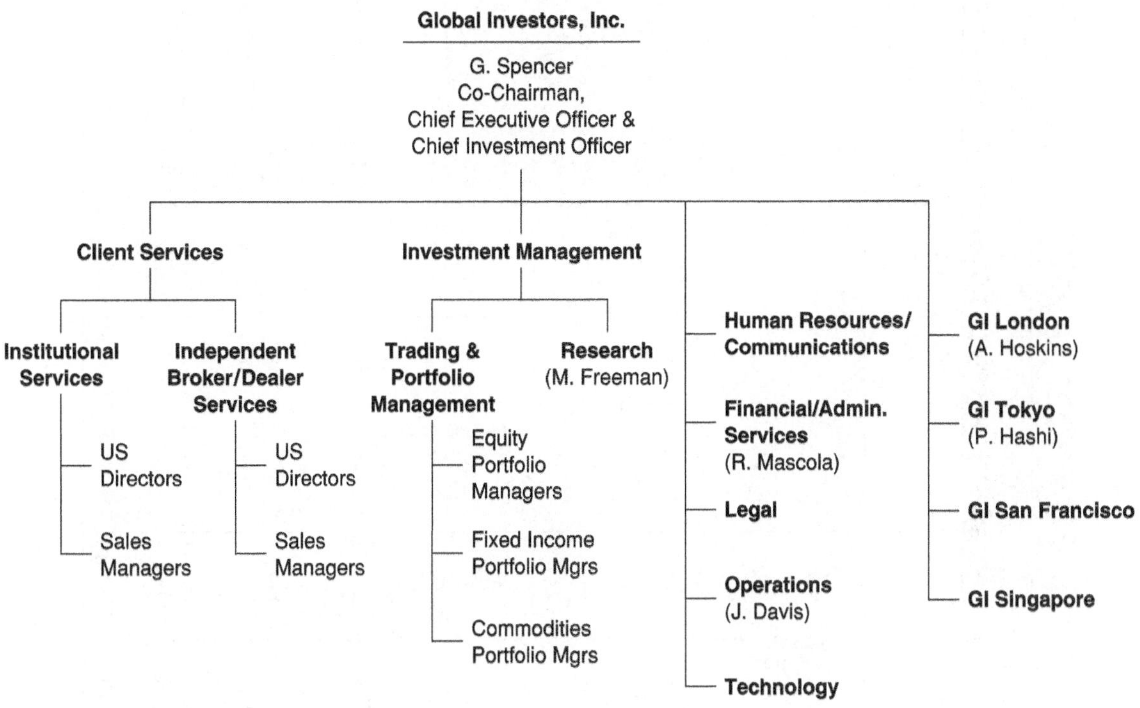

Exhibit 4 Consolidated statement following traditional transfer pricing model

	Business units	Cost centers								
	Headquarters and subsidiaries	**Trading**	**Research**	**Technology**	**Financial services**	**Legal**	**Operations**	**Admin.**	**HR & commun.**	**Allocation if actual is not available**
Fee revenue	yyy	n/a	n/a	n/a	n/a	n/a	n/a	n/a	n/a	
Less: royalties	zzz	n/a	n/a	n/a	n/a	n/a	n/a	n/a	n/a	*Fixed percentage of fee revenues (NY office only)*
Direct controllable costs										
Sales commissions	xxx	xxx	xxx	xxx	xxx	xxx	xxx	xxx	xxx	*50% of the clients' first year fees*
Salaries	xxx	xxx	xxx	xxx	xxx	xxx	xxx	xxx	xxx	*Actual*
Bonuses	xxx	xxx	xxx	xxx	xxx	xxx	xxx	xxx	xxx	*Actual*
Payroll taxes	xxx	xxx	xxx	xxx	xxx	xxx	xxx	xxx	xxx	*Actual*
Employee benefits	xxx	xxx	xxx	xxx	xxx	xxx	xxx	xxx	xxx	*Actual*
Professional fees	xxx	xxx	xxx	xxx	xxx	xxx	xxx	xxx	xxx	*Actual*
Occupancy (rent/utilities)	xxx	xxx	xxx	xxx	xxx	xxx	xxx	xxx	xxx	*Pro rata based on sq. ft.*
Depreciation office equipment	xxx	xxx	xxx	xxx	xxx	xxx	xxx	xxx	xxx	*Actual*
Maintenance	xxx	xxx	xxx	xxx	xxx	xxx	xxx	xxx	xxx	*Actual*
Travel expenses	xxx	xxx	xxx	xxx	xxx	xxx	xxx	xxx	xxx	*Based primarily on reason for trip*
Other administrative:										
Equipment rentals	xxx	xxx	xxx	xxx	xxx	xxx	xxx	xxx	xxx	*Actual*
Advertising	xxx	xxx	xxx	xxx	xxx	xxx	xxx	xxx	xxx	*Actual, or else pro-rata based on revenue*
Bank charges	xxx	xxx	xxx	xxx	xxx	xxx	xxx	xxx	xxx	*Charge to Financial area*
Stationery & supplies	xxx	xxx	xxx	xxx	xxx	xxx	xxx	xxx	xxx	*Pro rata based on sq. ft.*
Meetings	xxx	xxx	xxx	xxx	xxx	xxx	xxx	xxx	xxx	*Pro rata based on sq. ft.*
Gifts	xxx	xxx	xxx	xxx	xxx	xxx	xxx	xxx	xxx	*Pro rata based on sq. ft.*
Postage	xxx	xxx	xxx	xxx	xxx	xxx	xxx	xxx	xxx	*Pro rata based on sq. ft.*
Miscellaneous admin.	xxx	xxx	xxx	xxx	xxx	xxx	xxx	xxx	xxx	*Pro rata based on sq. ft.*
Total direct controllable costs	DCCbu1:DCCbu5	DCCtr	DCCres	DCCtech	DCCfin	DCCleg	DCCop	DCCad	DCChc	

Exhibit 4 *Continued*

	Business units	Cost centers								
	Headquarters and subsidiaries	Trading	Research	Technology	Financial services	Legal	Operations	Admin.	HR & commun.	Allocation if actual is not available
Other allocated costs										
Trading	a1:a5	–	a7	a8	a9	a10	a11	a12	a13	*GI employed a reciprocal allocation method (a system of simultaneous equations) to find the cost allocations (a1,…, h12) and the total costs of the cost centers (A, B, … , H), using for each cost center the following equation: Total Costs = (Direct controllable Costs) + (Other alloc. Costs) e.g. A = DCCtr + b6 + c6 + d6 + e6 + f6 + g6 + h6. In turn, each cost center got reimbursed by allocating its total costs to its "internal" clients (business units or other cost centers) e.g. A = a1 + a2 + a3 + … + a13*
Research	b1:b5	b6	–	b8	b9	b10	b11	b12	b13	
Technology	c1:c5	c6	c7	–	c9	c10	c11	c12	c13	
Financial services	d1:d5	d6	d7	d8	–	d10	d11	d12	d13	
Legal	e1:e5	e6	e7	e8	e9	–	e11	e12	e13	
Operations	f1:f5	f6	f7	f8	f9	f10	–	f12	f13	
Administration	g1:g5	g6	g7	g8	g9	g10	g11	–	g13	
HR & communications	h1:h5	h6	h7	h8	h9	h10	h11	h12	–	
Total direct and allocated costs	TCbu1:TCbu5	A	B	C	D	E	F	G	H	
Reimbursement to cost centers	–	–A	–B	–C	–D	–E	–F	–G	–H	
Profit or loss	Profit or loss	0	0	0	0	0	0	0	0	

Exhibit 5 Operating income using traditional transfer pricing model ($000)

	Business units	Cost centers								
	Headquarters or subsidiaries	Trading	Research	Technology	Financial services	Legal	Operations	Admin.	HR & communic.	Totals
New York										
Global fee revenue	619,949.1									619,949.1
Reimbursement to subsidiaries	(59,529.0)									(59,529.0)
Royalties expense	(41,587.0)									(41,587.0)
Direct controllable costs	(151,411.0)	(27,654.1)	(10,519.1)	(5,966.5)	(6,287.1)	(12,283.7)	(4,620.2)	(2,399.5)	(58,943.0)	(280,084.2)
Other allocated costs to	(111,650.5)	(6,766.5)	(6,315.4)	(2,968.4)	(3,529.5)	(8,866.5)	(2,938.3)	(2,040.5)	(13,071.2)	(158,146.8)
Other allocated costs away	0.0	34,420.6	16,834.5	8,934.9	9,816.6	21,150.2	7,558.5	4,440.0	72,014.3	175,169.5
Operating income	255,771.6	0.0	0.0	0.0	0.0	0.0	0.0	0.0	0.0	255,771.6
London										
Reimbursement from parent[a]	26,507.0									26,507.0
Direct controllable costs	(7,903.7)	(5,231.7)	(163.3)	(23.4)	(1,494.0)	(647.5)	(33.3)	(402.7)	(1,686.4)	(17,586.1)
Other allocated costs to	(16,844.6)	(664.0)	(72.3)	(3.6)	(11.7)	(15.8)	(4.0)	(113.1)	(330.8)	(18,059.9)
Other allocated costs away	0.0	5,895.8	235.6	27.0	1,505.7	663.3	37.3	515.8	2,017.2	10,897.6
Operating income	1,758.6	0.0	0.0	0.0	0.0	0.0	0.0	0.0	0.0	1,758.6
Tokyo										
Reimbursement from parent[a]	20,180.1									20,180.1
Direct controllable costs	(6,452.2)	(6,165.6)	0.0	0.0	(1,028.0)	0.0	(565.3)	(290.6)	(2,707.2)	(17,208.9)
Other allocated costs to	(12,007.0)	(113.9)	(89.3)	(67.6)	(232.8)	(1,080.2)	(417.1)	(96.8)	(1,465.0)	(15,569.7)
Other allocated costs away	0.0	6,279.5	89.3	67.6	1,260.8	1,080.2	982.4	387.4	4,172.2	14,319.4
Operating income	1,720.9	0.0	0.0	0.0	0.0	0.0	0.0	0.0	0.0	1,720.9
Singapore										
Reimbursement from parenta	4,776.1									4,776.1
Direct controllable costs	(1,613.0)	0.0	0.0	0.0	0.0	0.0	0.0	0.0	0.0	(1,613.0)
Other allocated costs to	(3,001.8)	0.0	0.0	(16.9)	(58.2)	(270.1)	(104.3)	(24.2)	(366.3)	(3,841.6)
Other allocated costs away	0.0	0.0	0.0	16.9	58.2	270.1	104.3	24.2	366.3	839.9
Operating income	161.3	0.0	0.0	0.0	0.0	0.0	0.0	0.0	0.0	161.3
San Francisco										
Reimbursement from parenta	8,065.9									8,065.9
Direct controllable costs	(2,233.5)	0.0	0.0	0.0	0.0	0.0	0.0	0.0	0.0	(2,233.5)
Other allocated costs to	(5,609.0)	0.0	0.0	(1.1)	0.0	(289.7)	(3.6)	(56.0)	(178.6)	(6,138.0)
Other allocated costs away	0.0	0.0	0.0	1.1	0.0	289.7	3.6	56.0	178.6	529.0
Operating income	223.3	0.0	0.0	0.0	0.0	0.0	0.0	0.0	0.0	223.3
Consolidated operating income	**259,635.7**	**0.0**	**0.0**	**0.0**	**0.0**	**0.0**	**0.0**	**0.0**	**0.0**	**259,635.7**

[a] The reimbursement from parent is equal to the total costs of the subsidiaries plus 10% of the total direct controllable costs incurred in the subsidiaries.

Exhibit 6 Operating income using Davis and Freeman's proposed transfer pricing model ($000)

Fee revenues by subsidiary		
	Institutional	**Indep. broker/dealer**
New York	227,003.4	356,370.6
London	7,512.0	1,110.5
Tokyo	3,630.4	12,620.6
Singapore	907.6	3,155.2
San Francisco	4,342.3	3,296.5
Total fee revenues	**619,949.1**	

	Business units					Cost centers						
			Investment management									
	Institutional sales	Indep. Broker/ dealer sales	General	Trading	Research	Technology	Financial services	Legal	Operations	Admin.	HR & communic.	Totals
New York												
Fee revenues			619,949.1									619,949.1
Commission revenue/ (expense)[a]	113,501.7	178,185.3	(309,974.5)									(18,287.6)
Investment management reimbursement to subsidiaries			(19,027.7)									(19,027.7)
Royalties expense			(41,587.0)									(41,587.0)
Direct controllable costs	(38,897.6)	(53,415.7)	(59,097.7)	(27,654.1)	(10,519.1)	(5,966.5)	(6,287.1)	(12,283.7)	(4,620.2)	(2,399.5)	(58,943.0)	(280,084.2)
Other allocated costs to	(23,922.9)	(19,229.3)	(68,498.3)	(6,766.5)	(6,315.4)	(2,968.4)	(3,529.5)	(8,866.5)	(2,938.3)	(2,040.5)	(13,071.2)	(158,146.8)
Other allocated costs away	0.0	0.0	0.0	34,420.6	16,834.5	8,934.9	9,816.6	21,150.2	7,558.5	4,440.0	72,014.3	175,169.5
Operating inome	50,681.3	105,540.2	121,763.8	0.0	0.0	0.0	0.0	0.0	0.0	0.0	0.0	277,985.3
London												
Commission revenue/ (expense)[a]	3,756.0	555.3										4,311.3
Investment mgmt reimb from parent[b]			11,068.5									11,068.5
Direct controllable costs	(3,829.5)	(4,074.2)	0.0	(5,231.7)	(163.3)	(23.4)	(1,494.0)	(647.5)	(33.3)	(402.7)	(1,686.4)	(17,586.1)
Other allocated costs to	(2,735.7)	(3,579.9)	(10,529.0)	(664.0)	(72.3)	(3.6)	(11.7)	(15.8)	(4.0)	(113.1)	(330.8)	(18,059.9)
Other allocated costs away	0.0	0.0	0.0	5,895.8	235.6	27.0	1,505.7	663.3	37.3	515.8	2,017.2	10,897.6
Operating inome	(2,809.3)	(7,098.9)	539.5	0.0	0.0	0.0	0.0	0.0	0.0	0.0	0.0	(9,368.6)

(Continued)

Exhibit 6 *Continued*

	Business units					Cost centers						
			Investment management									
	Institutional sales	Indep. Broker/ dealer sales	General	Trading	Research	Technology	Financial services	Legal	Operations	Admin.	HR & communic.	Totals
Tokyo												
Commission revenue/ (expense)[a]	1,815.2	6,310.3										8,125.5
Investment mgmt reimb from parent[b]			4,906.1									4,906.1
Direct controllable costs	(1,862.4)	(4,589.7)	0.0	(6,165.6)	0.0	0.0	(1,028.0)	0.0	(565.3)	(290.6)	(2,707.2)	(17,208.9)
Other allocated costs to	(2,682.6)	(5,034.8)	(4,289.6)	(113.9)	(89.3)	(67.6)	(232.8)	(1,080.2)	(417.1)	(96.8)	(1,465.0)	(15,569.7)
Other allocated costs away	0.0	0.0	0.0	6,279.5	89.3	67.6	1,260.8	1,080.2	982.4	387.4	4,172.2	14,319.4
Operating income	(2,729.8)	(3,314.3)	616.6	0.0	0.0	0.0	0.0	0.0	0.0	0.0	0.0	(5,427.5)
Singapore												
Commission revenue/ (expense)[a]	453.8	1,577.6										2,031.4
Investment mgmt reimb from parent[b]			1,072.4									1,072.4
Direct controllable costs	(465.6)	(1,147.4)	0.0	0.0	0.0	0.0	0.0	0.0	0.0	0.0	0.0	(1,613.0)
Other allocated costs to	(670.6)	(1,258.7)	(1,072.4)	0.0	0.0	(16.9)	(58.2)	(270.1)	(104.3)	(24.2)	(366.3)	(3,841.6)
Other allocated costs away	0.0	0.0	0.0	0.0	0.0	16.9	58.2	270.1	104.3	24.2	366.3	839.9
Operating income	(682.4)	(828.6)	0.0	0.0	0.0	0.0	0.0	0.0	0.0	0.0	0.0	(1,511.0)
San Francisco												
Commission revenue/ (expense)[a]	2,171.1	1,648.3										3,819.4
Investment mgmt reimb from parent[b]			1,980.7									1,980.7
Direct controllable costs	(18.6)	(2,214.9)	0.0	0.0	0.0	0.0	0.0	0.0	0.0	0.0	0.0	(2,233.5)
Other allocated costs to	(192.2)	(3,436.1)	(1,980.7)	0.0	0.0	(1.1)	0.0	(289.7)	(3.6)	(56.0)	(178.6)	(6,138.0)
Other allocated costs away	0.0	0.0	0.0	0.0	0.0	1.1	0.0	289.7	3.6	56.0	178.6	529.0
Operating income	1,960.3	(4,002.7)	0.0	0.0	0.0	0.0	0.0	0.0	0.0	0.0	0.0	(2,042.4)
Consolidated												
Operating income	**46,420.1**	**90,295.8**		**122,919.8**		**0.0**	**0.0**	**0.0**	**0.0**	**0.0**	**0.0**	**259,635.7**

[a]Commission revenue is equal to 50% of the fee revenues generated by the clients of the subsidiary. In New York, the commission expense is equal to 50% of the total fee revenues (allocated to the subsidiaries).

[b]The investment management reimbursement from parent is equal to the total investment management costs of the subsidiaries plus 10% of the investment management direct controllable costs (general/trading).

This case was prepared by Professors Kenneth A. Merchant and Tatiana Sandino.

CHAPTER 8
Planning and Budgeting

Planning, and especially budgeting systems, which are the focus of this chapter, are a pivotal element of financial results control systems. One important output of a planning and budgeting system is a written plan that clarifies where the organization wishes to go (objectives), how it intends to get there (strategies), and what results should be expected (performance targets).

Planning and budgeting systems vary considerably in form and use across organizations,[1] but nearly all commonly involve the setting of financial performance targets used for performance evaluation and incentive purposes, although we will discuss various other purposes of budgeting as well.

According to extensive research by two economists – Nicholas Bloom of Stanford and John Van Reenen of the London School of Economics – setting targets (Chapter 8), rewarding performance (Chapter 9), and measuring results (Chapter 10) are *key to management*. Their study of more than 10,000 organizations in 20 countries suggests that these factors are tightly linked to improved performance measured in terms of productivity, profitability, growth, and survival.[2]

But not every organization does their planning and budgeting well, and not all benefits, and also several issues, arise around the *targets-incentives-measurement* triad, although this triad will be our focus. Some of the organizational benefits of planning and budgeting come from the processes of developing the plans. Planning processes force managers and employees to think about the future, to discuss their ideas with others in the organization, to prepare their projections carefully, and to commit to achieving objectives that will serve the organization's interests. For plans and budgets to serve a useful role, then, the issue is not whether to prepare a plan or budget, but rather *how* to do it.[3]

Purposes of planning and budgeting

Planning and budgeting systems serve four main purposes. Obviously, the first purpose is *planning*; that is, making decisions in advance. Employees tend to become preoccupied quite naturally with their seemingly urgent, day-to-day exigencies. Unless they are encouraged to engage sufficiently in strategic, long-term thinking, they often fail to do so. Planning and budgeting systems provide the needed encouragement. They serve as a potent form of *action control*, forcing managers to propose plans of action when thinking about the future, considering business prospects, resource constraints, and risks. In doing the forward thinking, the managers develop a better understanding of their organization's opportunities and threats, strengths and weaknesses, and the effects of possible strategic and operational decisions. This forward-thinking decision-making process sharpens the organization's responses to its competitive environment.

Decisions regarding strategies, staffing, and operational tactics can be adjusted based on predictions of outcomes before the organization suffers major problems. This is a classic example of what is called *feed-forward control*. Effective planning processes make control systems *proactive*, not just *reactive*. They help managers shape the future, not just respond to the conditions they face and performance they observe.

For example, Berendsen (previously called Davis Service Group), a large public UK-based service contractor that sources, cleans, and maintains industrial textiles, protective clothing, and textiles, considers its good business performance to be, at least in part, "the result of careful budgeting, [which] involves making detailed financial plans for every aspect of the business, identifying risks and ensuring that managers are committed to the outcomes that they have agreed."[4] Similarly, the success of Zara, "the fast expanding, 'fashion-right' company headquartered in the remote northwest corner of Spain in La Coruna," suggests that "if a retailer can forecast demand accurately, far enough in advance, it can enable mass production under push control and lead to well managed inventories, lower markdowns, higher profitability (gross margins), and value creation for shareholders in the short- and long-term."[5] These examples suggest that planning and flexibility or responsiveness do not have to repel, although as we will see, this will depend on the rigidity in the planning and budgeting process; that is, how the plans and budgets are used or how the planning and budgeting is done, rather than the plans and budgets themselves.[6]

A second purpose of planning and budgeting is *coordination*. The planning and budgeting processes force the sharing of information across the organization. The processes involve a top-down communication of organizational objectives and priorities, as well as bottom-up communication of opportunities, resource needs, constraints, and risks. They also involve lateral communication that enhances the abilities of organizational entities (e.g. business units, divisions, functional areas, and administrative units) working together toward common objectives. Everyone involved becomes more informed, so the process is more likely to result in decisions that consider all perspectives. The sales plan is coordinated with the production plan so that shortages or surpluses of inventory and personnel are less likely and resources are synchronized as needed. The production plans are coordinated so that the potentials for bottleneck constraints are minimized. Plans for growth and investments are communicated to the finance function, which takes steps to ensure the needed capital. And so on.

A third purpose of planning and budgeting arises from facilitating *top management oversight*. This oversight occurs in the form of *preaction reviews* (a type of action control discussed in Chapter 3) as plans are examined, discussed, and approved at successively higher levels in the organization before actions are taken. Top management also uses plans as the performance standards used to implement the *management-by-exception* form of control (a type of results control discussed in Chapter 2). The planning and budgeting processes provide a forum that allows the organization to arrive at challenging but realistic performance targets by balancing top managers' wishes for desired performance with lower-level managers' information about possibilities. Negative variances – that is, measured performance below target levels – provide top managers an early warning of potential problems and justification for either reconsidering the organization's strategy or for interfering in the business of subordinate managers.

The final purpose related to planning and budgeting is *motivation*. The plans and budgets become targets that affect manager motivation because the targets are linked to performance evaluations and, in turn, various organizational rewards. As mentioned briefly in Chapter 2, merely telling employees to "do their best" is not nearly as motivating as asking them to attain specific performance targets that are neither too easy nor too difficult to achieve. In an interview with *The Economist*, Gary Latham of Locke and Latham's original *Goal Setting Theory* fame noted that "there is a wealth of evidence that setting well-designed targets does improve employee performance – there have been more than 1,000 academic experiments in goal-setting, of which over 90% have produced positive results." Latham added, "The studies show that an employee with a goal that is clear and simple, and challenging yet attainable, will perform better than one whose only instruction is to do as good a job as possible. Among other things, such a goal helps an individual or team to focus, to evaluate performance, to assess whether to maintain or change course, and to enjoy a sense of achievement when they succeed."[7]

While all performance targets can provide these benefits, this chapter focuses on financial performance targets, which are the most common type of targets derived from firm's annual budgeting processes.

Planning cycles

Organizations often use three hierarchical, sequential planning cycles, which are called *strategic planning, capital budgeting* (or *programming*), and (*operational*) *budgeting.*

Strategic planning

Strategic planning includes the relatively broad processes of thinking about the organization's missions, objectives, and the means by which the missions and objectives can best be achieved, i.e. *strategies*. Strategic planning processes typically involve senior executive corporate and entity managers who are the most broadly informed. They also consider both analyses of the past and forecasts of the future. Although a detailed treatment is outside the scope of this chapter, strategic planning typically involves developing (1) an overarching vision or mission and objectives for the organization as a whole; (2) an understanding of the organization's present position, its strengths and weaknesses, and its opportunities and risks; (3) an agreement about the types of activities or businesses the organization should (and should not) pursue; and (4) a strategy for each of the core activities or businesses the organization has decided to pursue – that is, a plan that sets out the path of action by which each business or entity's objectives will be achieved building on its strengths.[8]

A complete, formal strategic planning process leads to the establishment of the organization-wide strategy as well as, as applicable, strategies for various entities within the organization; identification of resource requirements; and statements of tentative performance goals, usually projected 3–5 or 10 years into the future. Strategic planning provides a framework for the more detailed planning that takes place in the planning cycles that follow, although there is some variation in practice. Recent survey evidence, for example, suggests such variation at least in terms of company size. Not surprisingly, perhaps, the larger the company, the more likely it will engage in both strategic planning and developing or integrating a budget with it each year; whereas 26% of companies with fewer than 50 employees use a budget only, involving (as we will see later) a detailed financial plan with a one-year-only horizon.[9]

Capital budgeting

Capital budgets are situated between long-range, strategic plans and annual budgets. Capital budgeting (also sometimes called *programming*) involves the identification of specific action programs (projects to be implemented or investments to be made) over the next few years (usually 1–3 or 5 years) and specification of the resources each will consume. Programs should translate each entity's strategy, which is generally focused externally, into an internally focused set of activities designed to implement the strategy and, in turn, lead to the achievement of the entity's goals. Programs can be developed at various levels of detail, ranging from that of a complex program covering all the activities necessary for an entity to sell its products in a new geographical territory, down to that of simply purchasing a single new machine for an existing production line. Capital budgeting is constrained in that the program options considered must be consistent with the tentative agreements reached during the strategic planning process. Capital budgeting often involves many people with expert knowledge in areas such as investment analyses, forecasting, and financing. Capital budgeting also typically requires substantially more planning detail than does strategic planning.

The capital budgeting process usually starts with discussions between the entity managers and their subordinates about the programs needed in the near future. As part of this process, managers must inevitably review ongoing programs to judge whether they are fulfilling their intended purposes and whether they should be modified or discontinued. Scarce resources are then allocated to specific programs. Much of the existing theory of resource allocation focuses on allocation of *capital funds*, where the screening and comparisons of potential investments is structured in financial terms using discounted cash flow or similar finance-based analyses, again with some variation in method usage in practice.[10]

However, rarely is resource allocation a mechanical process dependent solely on the financial calculations. Other resources, which may be scarce in the time period being considered and which are more difficult to quantify in financial terms (such as *talent* (human resources), essence of *timing* to reap potential first-mover advantages, and concerns arising from *escalating commitment* due to prior investments), often also influence the final allocation decisions.[11] Moreover, the outcomes of capital budgeting processes are likely also dependent on the track record, preparation, arguing skill, and political power of the managers involved. Managers have to compete for resources. Those making the most persuasive arguments and presentations are generally those whose requests are supported.

A subset of corporate managers is usually involved in reviewing larger program or investment proposals, often as part of a capital or resource allocation committee. These reviews allow the corporate managers another opportunity to communicate corporate priorities to entity managers (helping to alleviate potential *lack-of-direction* problems) and to exercise another preaction review (an action control). They also serve to help lower-level managers, particularly functional managers, understand how their activities fit into the organizational portfolio of activities and how they influence or relate to initiatives in other parts of the organization (again, addressing potential *lack-of-direction* problems). But the reviews also have an important bottom-up communication function: they serve as a forum for lower-level managers to communicate opportunities, threats, and requests for capital funds to the corporate managers. If capital budgeting is done well, the programs receiving resources are individually consistent with corporate objectives and strategies and mutually consistent with other related programs.

(Operational) budgeting

Operational (or annual) budgeting – *budgeting* for short – involves the preparation of a short-term financial plan, a *budget*, usually for the next fiscal year. Budgets match the organization's responsibility structure (see Chapter 7) and provide as much revenue, expense, asset, and liability line-item detail as appropriate. This, unsurprisingly, is how budgeting is defined in a recent survey of practice – as a one-year financial plan of detailed revenues and expenses by organizational entity (responsibility center), where budgeting is shown to be used by 93% of the sampled companies.[12] We suspect that the remaining 7% either comes from survey measurement error or includes responses from companies that have presumably "replaced" budgets or have gone "beyond budgeting," which we discuss later in this chapter.[13] In budgeting, quantitative (particularly financial) data are emphasized.

Every effectively run organization performs the functions of each of the three planning cycles – strategic planning, capital budgeting (programming), and budgeting – although the formality and distinguishability of the cycles vary greatly from one organization to the next. In smaller firms, particularly, one or more of these cycles are usually relatively informal, and many firms combine two, or sometimes all, of these cycles as part of one planning or budgeting process, which they typically do annually. As organizations grow, however, a more elaborate and formal planning process evolves, one closer to a full three-cycle system. In non-profit organizations, the planning processes may be less focused on capital funds, although capital is often a major constraint for them as well, forcing them to consider tradeoffs among various programs and designate available funds annually in their operating budget to well-chosen courses of action that help further their charitable objectives (see Chapter 16).

Target setting

Beyond producing written plans that clarify the organization's goals, strategies, and expected results, plans and budgets become *targets* that affect managers' motivation because the targets are linked to performance evaluations and, often, various incentives (which we discuss in Chapter 9). The use of pre-set performance targets in business organizations is almost universal. We quoted Professor Latham earlier on the robust evidence supporting the positive motivational effects of targets.[14] In addition, budgets are the primary performance target to evaluate performance at managerial levels and to award incentives. Review discussions, which tend to focus on variances between actual performance and targets, can lead to improved understanding of what is, and what is not, working and provide a useful forum for intra-organizational communication. Even in the absence of explicit incentives, managers are motivated to achieve their performance targets if for no other reason than to avoid having to explain to their bosses and colleagues why they missed their targets. For example, China's Haier, the large consumer appliances company, extensively uses a *name-and-shame* approach. Photographs of managers are prominently displayed throughout the company with a red smiley face for good performance and a yellow frowning one for those doing poorly.[15] Moreover, in committing to a target, managers direct attention toward goal-relevant activities. Targets also motivate managers to use the knowledge they have, or discover the needed knowledge, to help them attain the goal.

The most commonly used performance targets at management levels in for-profit organizations arise during the budgeting process, the last stage of the three-cycle planning system. As mentioned earlier, budgeting targets typically are financial in nature, expressed on a fiscal-year or annual basis, match the firm's responsibility center structure, and tie into the annual performance reviews and incentive plans of their managers. For example, the financial targets of profit center managers are defined in terms of profit, or at least in terms of selected line items of controllable revenues and expenses in some combination. For these reasons, our focus in this section is primarily on *financial* performance targets in a *budgeting* context.

Types of financial performance targets

Financial performance targets can be distinguished in a number of ways; that is, whether the targets are (1) model-based, historical, or negotiated; (2) fixed or flexible; and (3) internal or external.

Model-based, historical, and negotiated targets

Performance targets can be (1) derived from a quantitative model of what performance should be, (2) based on historical performance, or (3) derived from a process of negotiation between lower- and higher-level managers.

Model-based targets are derived from predictions of possible performance in subsequent measurement periods. When model-based targets are used in areas where activities are *programmable* (where there is a direct and relatively stable, deterministic causal relationship between inputs and outputs) they are said to be *engineered* targets. For example, in production departments, which are often cost centers, input-output relationships for materials and labor, say, can often be derived directly from the product(ion) specifications. The physical quantities for material and labor requirements can then be turned into financial targets by multiplying the standard quantities by their standard unit costs. But models are also used to try to derive performance targets in contexts other than standard costing applications. For example, firms often develop quantitative models of profit plans at the organization or entity levels, which are built on a financial accounting model and other inputs. Such models inevitably require many forecasts and planning assumptions, such as about the total available market, competitor actions, product mix, prices, and so forth. However, the target that is ultimately adopted arising from such models is often negotiated (which we discuss later in this section) based on the range of outcomes that the model predicts before managers commit to it as the "final" target.

Historical targets are derived directly from performance in prior periods. They sometimes involve what is called *ratcheting*, such as when, for example, a profit center manager is asked to increase profits by 10% over last year's numbers.[16] When budgets are set without taking history as a reference, they are called *zero-based*. Under so-called *zero-based budgeting*, managers must build budgets from scratch rather than base them on the previous year's plan, requiring the justification of every expense. Zero-based budgeting is not commonly used, although it is the preferred budgeting method of private equity companies or activist hedge fund investors after they take control of a company in which they seek major efficiencies through cost cutting – they want every line item and each expense to be justified.[17]

At managerial levels, however, most performance targets are *negotiated* between hierarchical superiors and subordinates, such as when division managers negotiate their profit (or investment) center budgets with corporate. Negotiation is common due to the limitations of model-based approaches and the planning assumptions that they inevitably incorporate (see earlier), as well as due to *information asymmetry* in decentralized organizations. Higher-level managers generally are more knowledgeable about the overall organization's objectives and resource constraints. Lower-level managers generally have superior knowledge about the business prospects and constraints at the operating level. Negotiations about performance targets, therefore, should allow for making use of each level's relative information advantage and induce superiors and subordinates to share at least some of their information.

Tight results control is easiest to implement when targets are engineered because the link between effort and results is direct. Consumption of inputs greater than, or production of outputs lower than, an engineered target indicates a performance problem with little ambiguity. Managers can also use historical targets to affect tight results control if the processes being controlled are stable over time. Tight results control is more difficult when important assumptions about the future are necessary or if negotiation is used, unless the negotiation is tightly constrained by good performance models or good historical performance data. In these latter situations, performance variances from the target might indicate a performance problem, but they also might indicate that the original assumptions were wrong or that the negotiation process was biased.

Fixed versus flexible targets

Another way to distinguish targets is in terms of whether they are fixed or flexible. *Fixed* targets do not vary over a given time period. *Flexible* targets are changed according to the conditions faced during the period. The targets may be set to vary, for example, with changes in the volume of activity, the price of inputs (e.g. oil or rare minerals), interest rates, or currency exchange rates.

Surveys of practice suggest that firms typically use fixed targets (that is, targets that remain *commitments* for the year), but these surveys also suggest that such fixed, annual budget targets can inevitably become obsolete, especially in rapidly changing, competitive environments. In the *Quantrix* survey, three-quarters of the sample companies reckon this to be the case, with more than half the respondents saying they reach that point within the first six months. One-eighth of the respondents even suggest that their budget targets have already become obsolete before the start of the year, whereas one-quarter of the respondents feel that their targets remain useful throughout.[18]

For this reason, many firms "recast" their budget during the year (monthly or quarterly). "Recast" means *reforecast*; not *re-budget* – that is, the original budget targets are not being re-set. Instead, firms reforecast at regular intervals to be able to compare their budgets with the most recent, updated information available, while usually expecting their managers to remain committed to the original budget target. The *Quantrix* survey suggests that, on average, 58% of the sample firms recast their budgets quarterly, with larger firms doing this more frequently, where about one-third of the firms with more than 1,000 employees recast budgets monthly compared to only 19% of companies overall.[19]

Clearly, then, financial targets are fixed in most firms, at least at profit center levels and above. This means that managers are held accountable for achieving their budgets regardless of the business conditions they face, and if they fail to do so, they stand to lose some important forms of rewards, such as their annual bonus.

Where targets are made flexible, this tends to be done at lower organizational levels. Manufacturing (standard cost center) managers, for example, are usually not held accountable for achieving a fixed total cost budget. Instead, their total cost budgets are typically flexible, meaning that their budget varies with the volume of production (e.g. \$350,000 for production of 100,000 units) or involves the use of unit cost standards (e.g. \$3.50 per unit). This is easily demonstrated with an example from the service sector, where the budget (for soap, say) of the manager in charge of the room service unit of a hotel property will be adjusted upward or downward depending on a decline or increase in occupancy relative to the budgeted number of visitors. The hotel manager, however, will not normally have that budget adjusted for variability in occupancy; instead, that person will be expected to manage the property effectively to "hit" the occupancy target and generate the budgeted profit.

Targets can also be made flexible by stating them in terms of *relative performance*; that is, relative to the performance of others facing identical, or at least similar, conditions. Any given manager's performance is evaluated not in terms of the absolute level of his or her own performance, but relative to the performance of others. Most typically, the comparisons are relative to managers in the organization in charge of like entities (e.g. fast food outlets or bank branches of similar size in similar demographic locations). We discuss relative performance evaluations in more detail in Chapter 12.

Internal versus external targets

Almost all planning and budgeting processes involve target-setting approaches that are *internally* focused. Managers consider what is possible within the organization and focus on period-over-period, continuous improvements. But planning and budgeting processes can also involve target-setting approaches that are *externally* focused. This is the case when an organization uses relative performance evaluations and benchmarks its performance and practices with those of other organizations. For example, Volvo, the large truck maker, said that it will set target operating margins for trucks and buses based on the performance of Scania, Daimler, MAN, and Iveco, and its construction equipment and marine engine business operating targets will be benchmarked against those of Caterpillar, Deere, and CNH.[20]

One would expect that firms in competitive environments would engage in at least some form of *benchmarking*. Corus, a large steel maker, used to rely on "tons of steel rolled" as the key measure of performance in its steel plants. This measure, however, did not show whether it met customer needs or whether the steel needed rework because it did not meet quality standards. Therefore, Corus started to monitor and measure how its operations compare with other producers and competitors in the steel industry. This process of benchmarking means that Corus continually reviews its activities to try to become *best-in-industry* instead of just meeting internally generated, often historically determined targets.[21]

Benchmarking can involve comparing the organization's performance against the *best-in-industry* (direct competitors), as in Corus, or *best-in-class* (companies generally recognized for superior performance on the dimension of interest; that is, companies known for their *best practice*). Many aspects of performance can be benchmarked, including specific product or service characteristics (e.g. mean time between failures), specific activities or processes (e.g. customer service), or overall organizational outcomes (e.g. return on assets). When the benchmarking focus is on organizational outcomes (*performance*), rather than on *best practices*, as in the Volvo example, the benchmarks are often used as performance standards for purposes of relative performance evaluations. The idea is that if one aspires to become the best, performance should be compared with the best. (In Chapter 12, we discuss the use of relative performance evaluations for another purpose, that of filtering uncontrollable factors from measured performance.)

Common financial performance target issues

The effects of any results-control system can be undermined if the wrong targets are set or if the targets are not set properly. Two of the most important financial performance target issues are related to (1) the appropriate amount of challenge in a target, and (2) the appropriate amount of influence to allow subordinates in setting targets.

How challenging should financial performance targets be?

The first financial performance target-setting issue is how difficult, or challenging, to make the targets. Should targets be set at *stretch* levels, should they be a *best guess* as to what will happen in the forthcoming periods, or should they be set *conservatively* to help ensure that they will be achieved? The answer to this question depends on the planning process purpose(s) that are emphasized.

For planning purposes, budget targets should be an unbiased *best-guess*. They should equal expected performance; that is, in probabilistic terms, with a 50% chance of achievement – thus, as likely to be missed as to be exceeded. As such, the targets will provide the best decision-making guidance for managers who are planning resource levels without (or less) risk of over- or under-committing resources (such as employee hiring numbers, production levels, and financing) due to either optimistic or conservative performance expectations that may subsequently be either not forthcoming or overshot.

For motivational purposes, however, appropriate target levels should have at least some *stretch* in them. The theory regarding the effects of performance targets on motivation is complex. As management gurus such as Jack Welch and Gary Hamel as well as other pundits have pointed out, if organizations do not set high performance expectations, their employees will not produce superior results.[22] Challenging or *stretch* performance targets push employees to perform at a higher level. They lead to innovation, rather than just incrementalism.[23]

On the other hand, performance targets can be set too high. Research in psychology has shown a fairly consistent, nonlinear relationship between target difficulty and motivation (and, hence, performance), as shown in Figure 8.1.[24] If the targets are perceived as quite easy to achieve, there is virtually no relationship between target difficulty and motivation. People's

Figure 8.1 Relationship between performance target achievability and motivation/performance

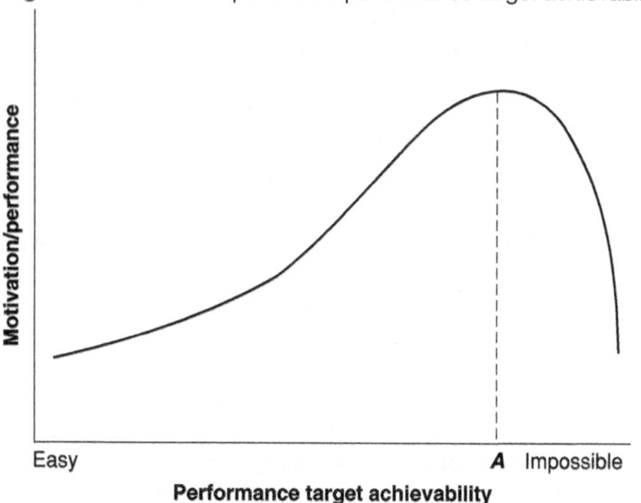

Source: K. A. Merchant, *Modern Management Control Systems: Text and Cases* (Upper Saddle River, NJ: Prentice Hall, 1998), p. 388.

levels of aspiration (and, hence, motivation and performance) are low because they are able to achieve their targets with a minimum of effort, persistence, or creativity. Above a threshold level of difficulty, motivation seems to increase with target difficulty up to the point where people approach the perceived limits of their ability. After that, the relationship levels off and eventually turns down. At high levels of difficulty, most people get discouraged, lose their commitment to achieve the target, and exert less effort – they give up trying. Motivation is highest when performance targets are set at an intermediate level of difficulty, point A in Figure 8.1, which can be called *challenging but achievable.*

Where, specifically, is the point of optimal motivation – the inflection point in the target difficulty-performance relationship? In other words, where do perceptions of excessive difficulty and, hence, lack of commitment to achieve the target set in? The point varies undoubtedly depending on such things as the personalities (such as the degree of confidence and risk tolerance), capabilities, and experiences of the individuals involved. As we will see, it also depends on the setting (such as the degree of uncertainty or the prevalence of uncontrollable factors). This is why some research findings, or sometimes merely anecdotal claims, vary widely in the "recommended" level of challenge that targets should have for "optimal" motivation, ranging from as low as a 25–40% chance of achievement, to as high as an 80–90% chance.

Studies of practice suggest that at corporate and entity (profit center) levels in firms, most annual profit targets are set to be highly achievable. The budget targets are set to be achievable 80% to 90% of the time by an effective management team.[25] These targets should not be described as *easy*, because they require competence and a consistently high level of effort. These highly achievable budget targets have many motivation, planning, and control advantages, as discussed next: increased manager commitment, protection against optimistic projections, higher achievement, reduced cost of interventions, and reduced gameplaying.

Increased manager commitment. Highly achievable budget targets increase managers' commitment to achieve the targets. Most managers operate in conditions of considerable uncertainty; their performance is affected by many unforeseen circumstances. Highly achievable targets protect the managers to a considerable extent from the effects of unfavorable, unforeseen circumstances and allow them few, if any, rationalizations for failing to achieve their targets. They have no choice but to *commit* to achieve their targets regardless of the business conditions faced. This increased commitment causes the managers to prepare their budget plans more carefully and to spend more of their time managing rather than preparing rationalizations to explain away failure to meet them.

Because of the lengthy budget performance period – typically one year in most firms – the costs of a lack of commitment to achieve budget targets are high. If highly difficult targets are set and some negative circumstances arise early in the year, the loss of commitment and decreased motivation may persist for many months. In contrast, if the budget targets are highly achievable, managers can withstand some adverse circumstances, even quite early in the period. They retain the motivation to try to make up for the unforeseen negative effects and are more confident that they will be able to get back on track.

Corporate managers have other possibilities for insuring managers against the effects of unforeseen, negative circumstances. They could shorten the planning horizon and set targets for periods shorter than a year. However, budget target-setting processes are expensive, and profit measures for short-time periods require many inter-period revenue and expense allocations. Another possibility is to *flex* the budget when unforeseen effects arise. However, most profit centers, and sometimes even cost centers, are affected by many unforeseen events, some positive and some negative. It is costly to analyze the effects of each unforeseen effect and make a judgment as to whether and to what extent it should be corrected. For these reasons, highly achievable targets are often seen as the more workable, though imperfect, approach. Here, managers are left to deal both with "the rough" and "the smooth" themselves while maintaining a reasonable expectation, and motivation, that they can meet the target in the end, ups and downs notwithstanding.

Protection against optimistic projections. Highly achievable budget targets protect the organization against the costs of optimistic revenue projections. The first step in budgeting is usually preparation of sales forecasts. Production (or service) levels are then geared to the forecasted level of sales. If the budgets have optimistic revenue projections, managers will be induced to acquire resources in anticipation of revenue (activity) levels that may not be forthcoming. Some of these acquisition decisions are at least partially irreversible. It is often difficult and expensive to shed people and specific assets. It is usually safer to forecast sales and profits relatively conservatively and acquire additional resources only when their need is assured. This conservatism implies that budget targets should be highly, or at least reasonably, achievable.

Higher manager achievement. In the minds of most managers, budget achievement defines the line between success and failure. Highly achievable budget targets are motivating; they make most managers feel like winners. Managers who achieve their budgets are given a package of rewards – bonuses, autonomy, and higher probability of promotion – and their self-esteem is given a boost. Organizations derive advantages when their managers have good self-esteem and feel like winners. Managers who feel good about themselves and their abilities are more likely, among other things, to be eager to work hard, to be entrepreneurial, and to increase their levels of aspiration for the future. In contrast, when managers fail to achieve their budget targets, they live with that failure for an entire year and even beyond, due to the stigma often associated with failure; such frustration is likely to undermine their confidence and commitment, which can be quite costly to the organization. When Tesla, the manufacturer of electronic cars, faced disappointment from analysts about its 2016 forecast for production of 1,600 to 1,800 vehicles per week when the company has said production capacity would be 2,000 per week, Elon Musk, Tesla's founder and chief executive, said: "We don't want to set high expectations – we want winning to feel like winning, if that makes sense."[26]

Reduced costs of interventions. Highly achievable budget targets reduce the costs of needed interventions from higher up in the organizational hierarchy. Most corporations use a *management-by-exception* philosophy. Higher-level managers intervene in the affairs of their subordinate

Figure 8.2 Probability distributions of forthcoming profits for effective and ineffective managers

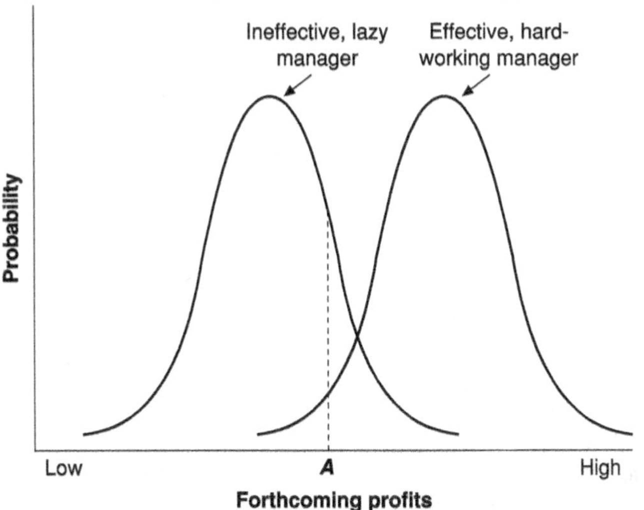

Source: K. A. Merchant, *Modern Management Control Systems: Text and Cases* (Upper Saddle River, NJ: Prentice Hall, 1998), p. 390.

managers only when unfavorable variances from budget signal the need. When 80% to 90% of the managers are achieving their budgets, top management attention is directed to the relatively few situations where the operating problems are most likely and most severe.

Figure 8.2 illustrates this point by showing two probability distributions of forthcoming profits, one for an effective, competent, hard-working manager and one for an ineffective manager. Because the scaling shows better performance to the right, the distribution for the ineffective manager is to the left of that for the effective manager. If the budget target is set at point A, the vast majority, perhaps 90%, of effective hard-working managers will achieve their targets. But a much smaller proportion of ineffective managers, perhaps only 20% given the way this curve is drawn, will likely achieve their targets. Thus, higher-level managers will spend relatively little time intervening in the affairs of effective managers; instead, most of their intervention efforts will be directed at ineffective managers, where it probably should be directed.

Reduced gameplaying. Highly achievable budget targets also reduce the risk of gameplaying. The stakes associated with budget achievement in most firms, which include bonuses, promotions, and job security, are so significant that managers who are in danger of failing to achieve their budget targets have powerful motivations to play games, either with the numbers or through foolhardy decisions (that is, either through accounting or operating methods as discussed in Chapter 5). In other words, and in those circumstances, managers may engage in manipulative actions and decisions to make their performance indicators look more favorable, knowing that their actions or decisions are having no positive effects on real performance and might actually be harming it.[27]

However, the primary risk organizations face by setting highly achievable budget targets is that manager aspirations, and hence motivation and performance, might be lower than they should be, thereby causing the managers to not perform at their best. To mitigate this, organizations can provide incentives to *exceed* budget targets. Figure 8.3 shows a typical results-reward function for entity (profit center) managers. It shows that managers earn all (or sometimes most) of their bonuses by exceeding their budget targets (up to a pre-specified maximum). If the rewards given for exceeding budget targets are sufficiently high relative to those given merely for achieving the budget targets, managers will have incentives not to retreat after the achievement of their budget targets is assured.

Figure 8.3 Typical rewards/results function for a profit center manager

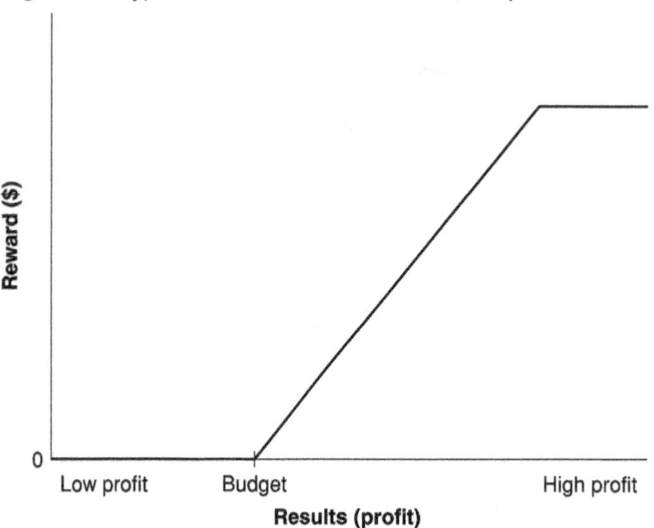

Source: K. A. Merchant, *Modern Management Control Systems: Text and Cases* (Upper Saddle River, NJ: Prentice Hall, 1998), p. 391.

While the use of highly achievable budget targets is the typical observed practice, not all budget targets should be set to be highly achievable. If the firm is in danger of failing or defaulting on a significant loan, corporate managers may set highly challenging profit targets to signal to operating managers the short-term exigency.[28] Top managers sometimes also set high profit targets to limit managers' discretionary investments, both to signal to lower-level managers that the strategy has changed (that is, that short-term profits now have priority over growth) and to enforce that change. They sometimes set high targets because they suspect organizational *fat* or because they want to set up a rationale to replace a manager. They may also set high targets to penalize managers for earning high bonuses or "windfall gains" in prior periods based on good fortune rather than good effort.

Another budget target-setting possibility is to set multiple levels of targets, such as optimistic, realistic, and worst case, each designed to serve a different budget purpose (motivation, planning, or control). This is a budget-focused approach to *contingency, scenario*, or *what-if* planning. The key tension that these approaches try to address is, on the one hand, ensuring that target setting is flexible enough to incorporate uncertainty (to serve the planning purpose) while, on the other hand, preserving the motivational effects of fixed targets (to try to meet the motivational and control purposes).[29]

How much influence should subordinates have in setting their targets?

Another important issue in designing a financial results control system when targets are negotiated is the extent of influence subordinates should be allowed in setting their targets; that is, to what extent should the planning and budgeting process be *top-down* or *bottom-up*? Many organizations lean toward bottom-up target-setting processes at managerial levels. For example, the *Quantrix* survey concludes that "the financial planning and analysis (FP&A) process extends far beyond the FP&A team, as survey respondents report a broad range of managerial input. While it's expected to find heavy involvement from C-level executives and financial executives, companies look for input from departmental, regional, channel, and product managers."[30] Allowing employees to participate in, and to have influence on, the process of setting their performance targets can have several benefits.

Involvement in the setting of targets enhances the focal manager's *commitment to achieve the target*. Those who are actively involved in the process of setting their performance targets are more likely to understand why the targets were set at the levels they were, so they are more likely to accept the targets and be committed to achieving them. A second benefit is *information sharing*. As discussed above, target setting in most firms involves a process of sharing information about local business possibilities and corporate objectives and resources. Managers who are closest to the local business can provide useful information to superiors about both business potentials and risks. Corporate managers can provide information about corporate priorities and constraints. A third benefit is *cognitive*. Allowing participation in target setting has the beneficial effect of clarifying expectations and encouraging managers to think about how best to achieve their targets.[31]

However, all employees, and not even all managers, should always be highly involved in planning and budgeting processes and, in particular, the setting of performance targets. Situations where target-setting processes can be completed effectively in a predominantly top-down manner include the following. First, targets can effectively stem from a top-down process when corporate management has sufficient knowledge of their entity business prospects and issues for setting properly challenging performance targets, or when corporate management has the knowledge that essentially subsumes the knowledge possessed by the entity managers. This occurs most commonly when a given activity or operation is programmable, where targets can be engineered or set with great reliability by projecting historical trends. Related to this, knowledge can also be sufficient for setting performance targets when corporate managers have a good understanding of the local business, perhaps because they formerly ran it and conditions are stable. But even when budgets are prepared in a seemingly bottom-up process, when higher-level managers have this knowledge, they exert greater influence on the final decisions about performance targets, thereby shifting the balance of power in the target negotiation process.

Second, top-down target setting can be effective when higher-level managers have the information available for evaluating performance on a relative basis. For example, they may be managing a large number of relatively homogenous entities operating in a stable environment. These situations exist in some industries, such as where firms manage large numbers of like-concept retailing outlets, including fast food restaurants, car dealerships, or bank branches.

Third, top-down target setting can be effective, and should even be preferred, when lower-level managers are not good at budgeting. Top-down target setting is common in small businesses for just this reason. Small-business operating managers are often technically skilled, but their management and financial education and experience might be limited.

Fourth, top-down target setting should be preferred when lower-level managers' thinking is dysfunctionally bound by historical achievements. Corporate management may know how to set standards according to a learning curve model that has proven accurate in the past; or they may know that a new technology will cause structural changes in the business, thus obsolescing historical performance standards.

Finally, top-down target-setting can be used to try to mitigate biases that lower-level managers are prone to impart to the budgeting process. Biases can lead the organization to set performance targets either higher or lower than is desired. Most operating managers have a conservative bias, and they use the opportunity of involvement in the target-setting processes to set lower targets. Lower targets increase the probability of target achievement, enhance the managers' reward potentials, and make it possible for them to achieve their targets with less effort. But some operating managers, particularly entrepreneurial and sales-oriented managers, may have an optimistic bias. Some managers want a challenge that will give them a feeling of accomplishment. Some want to signal to their bosses that they are aggressive, perhaps to compete for additional resources. Neither such optimism nor pessimism is desirable, and higher-level managers may have the perspective or experiences to mitigate these biases.

While top-down target setting has advantages in some settings, organizations who rely on this type of process must be careful not to forego too many of the benefits of a bottom-up process. Perhaps most importantly, they risk losing their managers' commitment to achieve the targets. Corporate managers may set targets that capable and consistently hard-working managers should be able to achieve with high probability, but if those asked to achieve those targets do not share that perception of achievability, they may be discouraged.[32] The resulting lack of motivation may lead to a low probability of achievement, in which case perception becomes reality.

Planning and budgeting practices, and criticisms

The ways in which planning and budgeting systems are used reflect the outcome of a large number of management design and implementation decisions. Planning and budgeting systems can vary in terms of their planning horizon. Most firms' planning horizons are relatively short: one year or less (22%), two years (10%), three years (29%), four or more years (39%).[33] One key factor affecting firms' planning horizons is the length of the business cycle; that is, the lag between investments and their payoffs. Firms in different industries have very different planning horizons. Those in the power utility industry, say, often plan quite far in the future, 25 years or more. Firms in the retail industry, say, might consider a one- or two-year plan to be adequate. Another key factor in determining the proper planning horizon is uncertainty. Sometimes the future is so uncertain that only short-term plans can be made. For example, a firm in the fashion industry might be able to plan only a season or two ahead, although the example of Zara, the "fast fashion" retailer we mentioned before, is an interesting case in point.

There is also variation across firms in the timing of, and the time devoted to, planning and budgeting. Firms run their long-range planning with greater variation than they run their budgeting, which follows a rather standard, annually recurring pattern familiar to most in large firms. Most firms start their budgeting process four to six months before the end of the fiscal year and complete it during the last two months of the year. The budgeting process takes about four months to complete in most firms. This suggests that budgeting consumes a non-trivial portion of time, over a significant time period each year, of many managers and employees in both line and staff positions. This is confirmed in the *Quantrix* survey. What is more, the larger the company, the more people that are involved. For companies with fewer than 50 employees, 92% report that between 1 and 10 people are involved; for companies with more than 5,000 employees, 31% rely on more than 100 people in the process.[34]

Once the budget is set, firms are unlikely to revise it during the year for evaluation purposes, although they may frequently update it for planning purposes. In the *Quantrix* survey, the majority of respondents reported that they provided "ad-hoc scenarios," a fancy term for revised or additional analyses during the year: 32% reported that they provided between four and six per year, and another 29% reported that they provided one to three per year.[35] But as we discussed earlier, despite these revised, additional, or ad-hoc analyses or scenarios, companies typically require that their managers remain focused on achieving their original budget targets no matter which business conditions they face. This is also the idea behind the use of the term "ad-hoc scenario" by *Quantrix*: an ad-hoc plan to analyze variation to budget or plans and/or to a specific business event or request.[36]

Budgeting is thus costly, particularly in terms of management time. It is not uncommon to hear managers complain that they spend so much time with the budget that they have little time to do any work. They never stop budgeting. That said, it is hard to envision any other way to run large, decentralized organizations with complex reporting structures that inevitably have a high need for coordination and that are managed mainly by the numbers (using results controls) through a management-by-exception approach.

Relatively recently, however, there has been a spate of criticisms of planning and budgeting processes, particularly by the *Beyond Budgeting* movement, asserting, obviously with some justification, that budgets:

- Are rife with politics and gameplaying;
- Produce only incremental thinking and minor modifications to the plans and budgets prepared in the preceding periods;
- Lock the organization into a "fixed plan" and are not responsive to changes in today's fast-moving economy;
- Centralize power in the organization and stifle initiative;
- Separate planning (thinkers) from execution (doers);
- Cause too many costs for too few benefits; and so on.

The more moderate critics make a number of suggestions for improvement involving (relatively minor) modifications to traditional planning and budgeting processes, such as updating plans more frequently (*rolling plan* processes) and using *relative performance standards* and *subjective performance evaluations* rather than relying exclusively on fixed budget targets and pre-agreed incentive formulas. But some of the critics go further, imploring managers to abandon traditional budgeting and to move *beyond budgeting*.[37]

One of the budgeting-abandonment success stories cited by many critics is that of the Swedish-based Svenska Handelsbanken, which eliminated budgets in 1972 and has never looked back to reintroduce them. Svenska Handelsbanken has no annual budgeting process, and it produces no budgets; instead, it evaluates the bank's and its managers' performances by comparing them with measures of competitors' performances on key performance dimensions, such as return-on-capital, cost-to-income ratio, and profit-per-employee. Whereas Svenska Handelsbanken has been successful in managing the firm without budgets, it must be noted that most firms are not in an industry with such homogeneous entities as banking. Therefore, many firms do not have such good relative performance data available to them. Moreover, Svenska Handelsbanken still has to engage in many of the standard planning and budgeting elements described above to fulfill all the other purposes, other than motivation, such as planning, coordination, and facilitation of top management oversight.

The critics are correct, however, that many firms' planning and budgeting processes are ineffective.[38] Designing and implementing planning and budgeting systems is complex and difficult. The purposes for which the systems are needed often conflict, necessitating some difficult tradeoffs.[39] Business conditions are prone to shift, yet it is difficult to adapt plans and budgets quickly. In any case, it is sometimes counterproductive to set performance targets because they can focus employees unnecessarily narrowly, and they can encourage unethical risk taking or earnings management (as will be discussed further in Chapter 15).[40]

The spirit of the *beyond-budgeting* management model can be seen perhaps more as a management philosophy rather than a mere issue of planning and budgeting, or planning and budgeting alone. Its key aim, instead, is to increase the adaptability of organizations. Companies that follow the beyond-budgeting principles tend to have simple organizational structures (or aim to simplify them), flat hierarchies (or aim to make them flatter, less hierarchical), and flexible peer-to-peer networks used to provide and exchange the benchmarking data and share best practices. They operate with an assumption that organizations, like natural systems, are capable of self-organization and self-regulation. Their managers do not require negotiation of fixed performance targets, as is done in a traditional budgeting system. Allocations of resources are event-driven, not calendar-constrained. Allocated resources are not treated as entitlements that must be spent. Unconstrained by a fixed and outdated plan, employees strive to improve their performance relative to their peers or some other benchmark. Creativity and rapid response to customer needs and unpredicted events are encouraged.

However, there are no "quick fixes" when it comes to improving an organization's adaptability and responsiveness in highly competitive, uncertain, and turbulent environments. To improve the design of a planning and budgeting system, or anything that presumably takes its place, managers must be aware of all of the purposes for which the systems can be used and wisely choose the combinations of system elements that best serve these purposes in their settings.

The beyond-budgeting "management model" has been developed and refined as its use has spread to several organizations around the world.[41] That said, many organizations continue to consider budgets as indispensable,[42] although many of them also continually struggle to make them more effective.[43]

The key difficulty is to get the needed flexibility while maintaining the features of plans and planning that stem from drawing managers away from fighting day-to-day fires, encouraging them to think about the future, and helping them shape that future. But as useful as plans and planning can be, when they become *fixated* on a single number or target, they can hinder rather than help and even become detrimental. Even the best laid plans must allow for some, or even any, carefully considered adjustment and flexibility to respond to any of a number of changes in the environment. This can be done, as suggested earlier, and as the setting requires, through updating budgets more frequently, using subjective performance evaluations, rolling forecasts, and possibly other means, some of which we discuss in later chapters, especially Chapter 12. A survey of over 500 senior finance professionals by Deloitte, however, suggests that striking this balance is inevitably difficult, as gleaned, for example, from the following two points:[44]

> *Integrating planning, budgeting and forecasting* – 37% of respondents admitted to a failure to align their planning, budgeting and forecasting effectively. In these circumstances there is a risk that the activities of the organisation will be misdirected, lack focus, alignment and cohesion.
>
> *Using forecasting properly* – 61% of survey respondents recognised the importance of forecasting as a way of compensating for the static nature of budgeting. However, there is a failure to appreciate how forecasting can enhance corporate agility and specifically a lack of understanding of how it fundamentally differs from planning, budgeting and target-setting.

As we said at the start of this chapter, some of the organizational benefits of planning and budgeting come from the processes of developing the plans. For plans and budgets to serve a useful role, then, the issue is not *whether* to prepare a plan or budget, but *how*.[45]

Conclusion

Planning and budgeting systems are potentially powerful management tools that serve multiple purposes. They provide a way of converting managers' visions into an organized set of tactics that are employed throughout their organizations. They provide a standard that can be used to judge organizational success or progress. And they have many behavioral implications, such as regarding the effort invested in thinking about the future and commitment to achieve performance targets.

Many of the criticisms of planning and budgeting systems, such as those made by devotees of the so-called *beyond-budgeting* movement, focus on the flaws of negotiating performance targets. It is true that allowing target negotiations has drawbacks. The negotiating processes are costly, particularly in management time. Hence, firms are willing to engage in the processes relatively infrequently, typically annually. Targets that are fixed that far in advance can easily become obsolete, particularly in fast changing environments. Moreover, allowing negotiation of targets can also enhance gameplaying, such as the reluctance to share private information to be able to create budgetary slack and to maximize incentive payouts associated with achieving the targets. Still, negotiating targets has its advantages, as this chapter has described. Although annual budgets have been criticized for inducing gameplaying behaviors and for being incapable of meeting managers' needs in rapidly changing environments, evidence suggests that they remain in widespread use and continue to play a crucial role in coordinating and motivating employee actions and behaviors.

However, just because an organization prepares a plan does not mean that it is engaging in useful planning. Frequent criticisms voice that strategic planning is overly bureaucratic and absurdly quantitative. Often plans are prepared but not used; they just take up shelf space. For plans to be effective, they must match the business conditions the firm is facing so that they can be used as a near-constant guide for employee actions. The plans should also assign responsibility and accountability for performance. This is an important role for budgets. Budgets turn plans into performance targets that affect employee motivation, particularly because the targets are often linked to performance evaluations and rewards, which we discuss in the next chapter, and which must be implemented judiciously as well to have good effect.

Notes

1 See, for example, *2012 Budgeting, Forecasting, and Planning Survey* (Quantrix, 2012).
2 In addition to the original academic articles and working papers by Bloom, Van Reenen, and colleagues, see "Measuring Management," *The Economist* (January 18, 2014), online at econ.st/1b4aTUl.
3 See, for example, "Companies Get Budgets All Wrong," *The Wall Street Journal* (July 22, 2013), online at on.wsj.com/1OfjJaR.
4 "Planning a Budget (Davis Case Study)," *Times 100* (2010), online at www.thetimes100.co.uk.
5 "Zara's Secret to Success: The New Science of Retailing," *Forbes* (October 14, 2013), online at onforb.es/16ZsH74.
6 See also M. D. Mumford and M. Frese, *The Psychology of Planning in Organizations: Research and Applications* (New York: Routledge, 2015).
7 Quoted from "The Quantified Serf," *The Economist* (March 7, 2015), online at econ.st/1GZAcbw.
8 In large, diversified corporations, the question as to which businesses the corporation should (and should not) be in is often referred to as "(corporate) *diversification strategy*." The individual strategies for each of the businesses that the corporation has decided to pursue are, in turn, referred to as "(strategic business unit) *competitive strategies*."
9 *2012 Budgeting, Forecasting, and Planning Survey*, op. cit., p. 5.
10 See, for example, P. A. Ryan and G. P. Ryan, "Capital Budgeting Practice of the Fortune 100: How Have Things Changed," *Journal of Business and Management*, 8, no. 4 (2002), pp. 355–64. See also U. Götze, D. Northcott and P. Schuster, *Investment Appraisal: Methods and Models* (Heidelberg, Germany: Springer, 2015).
11 See, for example, J. J. Gong, W. A. Van der Stede, and S. M. Young, "Real Options in the Motion Picture Industry: Evidence from Film Marketing and Sequels," *Contemporary Accounting Research*, 28, no. 5 (2011), pp. 1438–66.
12 *2012 Budgeting, Forecasting, and Planning Survey*, op. cit., pp. 3, 5.
13 See also T. Libby and R. M. Lindsay, "Beyond Budgeting or Budgeting Reconsidered? A Survey of North-American Budgeting Practices," *Management Accounting Research*, 21, no. 1 (March 2010), pp. 56–75.
14 "The Quantified Serf," op. cit. See also A. Locke, "Goal-Setting Theory and Its Applications to the World of Business," *Academy of Management Executive*, 18, no. 4 (November 2004), pp. 124–25.
15 "Grow, Grow, Grow," *The Economist* (April 17, 2010), p. 13.
16 For a recent series of papers on the issues of target ratcheting, see J. H. Evans, "A Forum on Ratcheting and Incentives," *The Accounting Review*, 89, no. 4 (July 2014), p. 1195; C. Aranda, J. Arellano, and A. Davilla, "Ratcheting and the Role of Relative Target Setting," *The Accounting Review*, 89, no. 4 (July 2014), pp. 1197–1226; R. J. Indjejikian, M. Matejka, K. A. Merchant, and W. A. Van der Stede, "Earnings Targets and Annual Bonus Incentives," *The Accounting Review*, 89, no. 4 (July 2014), pp. 1227–58; R. J. Indjejikian, M. Matejka, and J. D. Schloetzer, "Target Ratcheting and Incentives: Theory, Evidence, and New Opportunities," *The Accounting Review*, 89, no. 4 (July 2014), pp. 1259–67.
17 See, for example, "Burger King Chief Takes Aim at McDonald's," *The Financial Times* (August 26, 2014), online at on.ft.com/1tHvCIY; "Hedge Fund Manager Bill Ackman Seizes 7.5% Mondelez Stake," *The Financial Times* (August 6, 2015), online at on.ft.com/1DsumCk.
18 *2012 Budgeting, Forecasting, and Planning Survey*, op. cit., p. 8.
19 Ibid., p. 6.
20 "Volvo Aims for Profit Margins at Top of Heavy-Equipment Industry," *Bloomberg* (September 22, 2011), online at www.bloomberg.com.
21 "Continuous Improvement as a Business Strategy: Target Setting (Corus Case Study)," *Times 100* (2010), online at www.thetimes100.co.uk.
22 J. Welch, *Jack: Straight from the Gut* (New York: Warner Business Books, 2001); G. Hamel, *Leading the Revolution*

(Boston, MA: Harvard Business School Press, 2000); S. Kerr and S. Landauer, "Using Stretch Goals to Promote Organizational Effectiveness and Personal Growth: General Electric and Goldman Sachs," *Academy of Management Executive*, 18, no. 4 (November 2004), pp. 134–8.

23 "Grow, Grow, Grow," op. cit., pp. 12–13.

24 As mentioned earlier in this chapter, Edwin Locke and Gary Latham are renowned researchers in the area of goal setting theory. For a recent reflection by them on research in the target-setting area, see E. Locke and G. Latham, "Building a Practically Useful Theory of Goal Setting and Task Motivation: A 35-Year Odyssey," *American Psychologist*, 57 (2002), pp. 705–17.

25 See, for example, K. A. Merchant and J. F. Manzoni, "The Achievability of Budget Targets in Profit Centers: A Field Study," *The Accounting Review*, 64, no. 3 (July 1989), pp. 539–58; and K. A. Merchant, "How Challenging Should Profit Budget Targets Be," *Management Accounting* (November 1990), pp. 46–8.

26 "Tesla Warns Vehicle Sales Target at Risk," *The Financial Times* (August 5, 2015), online at on.ft.com/1W2HaVR.

27 See also M. Jensen, "Corporate Budgeting Is Broken: Let's Fix It," *Harvard Business Review* (November 2001), pp. 94–101; and M. Jensen, "Why Pay People to Lie?," *The Wall Street Journal* (January 8, 2001), p. A32.

28 See, for example, M. Matejka, K. A. Merchant, and W. A. Van der Stede, "Employment Horizon and the Choice of Performance Measures: Empirical Evidence from Annual Bonus Plans of Loss-Making Entities," *Management Science*, 55, no. 6 (June 2009), pp. 890–905.

29 See, for example, W. A. Van der Stede and T. Palermo, "Scenario Budgeting: Integrating Risk and Performance," *Finance & Management*, no. 184 (January 2011), pp. 10–13. See also N. Frow, D. Marginson, and S. Ogden, "Continuous Budgeting: Reconciling Budget Flexibility with Budgetary Control," *Accounting, Organizations and Society*, 35, no. 4 (May 2010), pp. 444–61; "Managing in the Fog," *The Economist* (February 26, 2009), pp. 67–68.

30 *2012 Budgeting, Forecasting, and Planning Survey*, op. cit., p. 12.

31 There is an extensive stream of research in the area of budget participation going back nearly half a century. For a study that speaks to some of the benefits discussed here, among many other studies too numerous to list here, see M. Mahlendorf, U. Schaffer, and O. Skiba, "Antecedents of Participative Budgeting: A Review of Empirical Evidence," in M. J. Epstein and J. Y. Lee (eds.), *Advances in Management Accounting*, 25 (2015), pp. 1–27.

32 T. Libby, "The influence of Voice and Explanation on Performance in a Participative Budgeting Setting," *Accounting, Organizations and Society*, 24, no. 2 (February 1999), pp. 125–37.

33 *2012 Budgeting, Forecasting, and Planning Survey*, op. cit., p. 5.

34 Ibid., p.13.

35 Ibid., p. 7.

36 Ibid., p. 3.

37 See, for example, J. Hope and R. Fraser, *Beyond Budgeting: How Managers Can Break Free from the Annual Performance Trap* (Boston, MA: Harvard Business School Press, 2003); B. Bogsnes, *Implementing Beyond Budgeting: Unlocking the Performance Potential* (London: John Wiley & Sons, 2008). For an academic perspective, see S. C. Hansen, D. T. Otley, and W. A. Van der Stede, "Recent Developments in Budgeting: An Overview and Research Perspective," *Journal of Management Accounting Research*, 15 (2003), pp. 95–116; T. Libby and R. M. Lindsay, "Beyond Budgeting or Budgeting Reconsidered? A Survey of North-American Budgeting Practices," *Management Accounting Research*, 21, no. 1 (March 2010), pp. 56–75.

38 "Companies Get Budgets All Wrong," op. cit.

39 S. C. Hansen and W. A. Van der Stede, "Multiple Facets of Budgeting: An Exploratory Analysis," *Management Accounting Research*, 15, no. 4 (December 2004), pp. 415–39.

40 L. Ordonez, M. Schweitzer, A. Galinsky, and M. Bazerman, "Goals Gone Wild: The Systematic Side Effects of Overprescribing Goal Setting," *Academy of Management Perspectives*, 23, no. 1 (2009), pp. 6–16.

41 For more information, see the *Beyond Budgeting Institute*, online at bbrt.org (accessed December 2015).

42 Libby and Lindsay, "Beyond Budgeting or Budgeting Reconsidered?" Op. cit. See also B. Ekholm and J. Wallin, "Is the Annual Budget Really Dead," *The European Accounting Review*, 9, no. 4 (2000), pp. 519–39; T. Libby and R. Lindsay, "Beyond Budgeting or Better Budgeting?" *Strategic Finance* (August 2007), pp. 47–51.

43 J. Orlando, "Turning Budgeting Pain into Budgeting Gain," *Strategic Finance* (March 2009), pp. 47–51; "How to Better Connect Planning, Forecasting, and Budgeting," *Journal of Accountancy* (February 20, 2014), online at shar.es/1Gxnwf.

44 *Integrated Performance Management* (Deloitte, 2014), online at www.planbudgetforecast.com/report.

45 For an academic study on the use and usefulness of budgeting (in times of economic crisis, for example), see S. D. Becker, M. D. Mahlendorf, U. Schaffer, and M. Thaten, "Budgeting in Times of Economic Crisis," *Contemporary Accounting Research* (2016), in press.

CASE STUDY
Royal Wessanen NV

In early February 2009, Sjoerd Schaafsma, CFO Europe at Royal Wessanen, was pondering on the budget for the remainder of 2009 as well as the strategic outlook for 2010 and beyond. An era with a lot of strategic uncertainty laid ahead. The uncertainty arose not only from the global economic crisis resulting in lower revenue growth, but also from recent corporate decisions to change the company's strategy.

Since the late 1990s, Wessanen's main market of organic food had shown a very satisfying annual growth at well above 10%. Since 2008, however, growth began to slow and had stabilized at less than 5%, thereby no longer meeting corporate expectations. Worse, the economic recession led management to believe that 2009 was likely to show a decline in the market for organic food. Because of the high level of uncertainty, and not ruling out the possibility of negative growth, Mr. Schaafsma considered developing an alternative forecast for 2009 to take into account a "worst-case scenario" of declining revenues. But to effectively pursue this, he knew he needed the support and commitment of the full Executive Board.

Royal Wessanen NV

In the seventeenth and eighteenth centuries, The Netherlands was one of the world's most prominent trading nations, with a huge merchant fleet that carried new and exotic materials between Europe and the far-flung ports of the Far East, the Americas, the Caribbean and Africa. Amsterdam was the hub of this trading activity where many of the ships docked and unloaded their cargoes into the warehouses that lined the River Zaan. One of the owners of those warehouses was Adriaan Wessanen, a renowned trader of that time. In 1765, the 41-year-old Mr. Wessanen teamed up with his 31-year old nephew, Dirk Laan, to trade in "Mustard, Canary and other seeds." The then-new company was called Wessanen & Laan.

By about two-and-a-half centuries later, in 2008, Royal Wessanen NV developed into a group with operations in seven countries in Western Europe and North America. Royal Wessanen NV was listed on the Midcap Euronext stock market in Amsterdam. Revenues were £1.6 billion split 40–60 over Europe and North America, respectively. (See Exhibit 1 for a combined overview of the revenues and EBIT of Wessanen by business and location.)

Wessanen had a two-tier board structure. The Board consisted of the chief executive officer (CEO), chief financial officer (CFO), and president of the North American operations. The CEO also acted as president of the European activities. Under the Executive Board, there were two leadership teams: one for the European and one for the North American markets, respectively (see Exhibit 2).

In the second half of 2008, revenue growth dropped from 10% to below 5%. Key challenges were to keep growing the top line while protecting margins. Stalled, or even declining, growth became a serious business reality. The existing strategy set out to cope with these challenges focused on three differentiating capabilities:

- Strong and focused brands and excellent branding skills;
- Best-in-class distribution services;
- Excellence in category management.

2009 – a year of transformation

In February 2009, the CEO left the company. A member of the Supervisory Board filled the CEO position *ad interim*, while the search for a new CEO was on. At that time, a radical change in the global strategy was announced to increase the company's focus on the European market and concentrate on its leading brands in organic foods. In Europe, Wessanen aimed to become a "one-system" company with considerably more harmonized brands and centralized sourcing. The plan was to eventually divest all US businesses, which consisted of four entities, namely Panos, Liberty Richter, Tree of Life, and American Beverage Company (ABC).

Two business lines – Organic and Frozen – were to constitute the core of the company's operations in Europe. First, Wessanen Europe was a dedicated player in organic food with a strong presence primarily in the Benelux (including, chiefly, Belgium and the Netherlands), the United Kingdom, France, and Germany. The strategy for this business line consisted of a so-called "multichannel approach with channel-specific solutions." Wessanen Europe's two sales channels were grocery stores on the one hand, and Health Food Stores (HFS) on the other hand, with channel-specific solutions ranging from Wessanen-owned brands to private labels. Innovation was key at this time. New brands were launched and existing product ranges were extended or changed with high frequency, with mixed levels of success, however, as is common in fiercely competitive consumer product markets.

Frozen Foods, the second main business line, was involved in the distribution and marketing of snack foods. The Wessanen brand in the Benelux for this was Beckers. Private labels were distributed and sold through the Dutch-based Favory Convenient Food Group, a joint venture with Rabo Private Equity. The activities of the companies in Germany and Italy – Karl Kemper and Righi, respectively – were deemed low on potential synergies with the Benelux frozen food operations. For this reason, they were sold.

In the latter half of the year, the American Panos brands and Liberty Richter were sold, too. The sale of Tree of Life was announced in December 2009, leaving ABC the main operation to divest in the United States. In the summer of 2009, however, irregularities were discovered in ABC's books, resulting in a restatement of its accounts. During that period, the local management team was restructured and a recovery plan to regain profitability was established. The turmoil, however, meant that ABC's divestment plans had to be put on hold.

Evaluating 2009, it seemed that after two difficult years, including poor growth, CEO turnover, and fraud in the American operations, Wessanen had turned a corner and was back on track with a clear strategy going forward. The company had transformed from a widely diversified conglomerate with many house brands, cocktails, snacks, and biological food, to a more focused corporation concentrating chiefly on the European organic and frozen food markets. The reorganization and concentration of activities resulted in an expected drop in revenues from £1.6 billion to approximately £700 million by the completion of the divestment processes (Exhibit 1). That said, it would also result in a strengthened balance sheet due to an improved debt-equity ratio and lower working capital.

The new strategy of less diversification also introduced a stronger dependency on a few core markets, both business- and location-wise. However, stock market analysts pointed to the risks associated with such concentration especially due to the large uncertainty in the development of the organic food market which had not yet taken up much space in a typical consumer's grocery cart.

Planning and control

To enable the Executive Board and the management of the operating companies (OPCOs) to manage and control the organization, Wessanen's internal governance structure was based on a performance framework that consisted of annual budgets and a monthly and quarterly review cycle. All planning and performance reporting was done in Hyperion, an Enterprise Performance Management (EPM) tool from Oracle.

Budgeting was essentially a bottom-up planning process, which was guided by the Executive Board with specific targets on the three KPIs that formed the backbone of the reporting in this company: Net Sales (and by comparison to prior periods, the expected growth in Net Sales), Earnings Before Interest and Taxes (EBIT), and Working Capital.

Net Sales were essentially Gross Sales adjusted for discounts. Net Sales were also sometimes referred to as the "Top Line" or simply "Revenues."

EBIT was calculated from Net Sales by subtracting Cost of Goods Sold (COGS),[1] Marketing, Advertising & Promotion costs, and Sales, General & Administrative costs (SG&A). What is broadly known as SG&A included many detailed line-item accounts, often referred to as "overheads" although not all of these costs were fixed.

Working Capital conformed to its usual accounting definition, including inventory, accounts payable (vendors), and accounts receivable (debtors). Working Capital was turned into a KPI by dividing it by the last three months of Net Sales that was extrapolated for the year by multiplying it times four. This method was chosen

[1] As was customary in accounting terms, revenues minus COGS was also separately reported as Gross Margin.

and introduced in the budgeting process of 2009 to get the best possible match between the working capital closing position of a specific quarter, aligned with the respective Net Sales, and taking into account seasonality effects (see Exhibit 3).

Each September, "Corporate Guidelines for the Preparation of the Royal Wessanen Budget" were issued to the managing directors (MDs), financial directors (FDs), and controllers of the OPCOs by Dick van der Wardt's Corporate Accounting & Control Department. These corporate guidelines communicated the top-level targets (see Exhibit 4). The guidelines also set out the procedures and timetable for the budgeting process as well as the specifications for use of Hyperion. Technical information about interest rates, currency rates, tax rates, and capital expenditures were also provided. The time horizon for the planning process covered the budget year ($t + 1$) as well as the two subsequent years ($t + 2$; $t + 3$). Planning for the second and third years was referred to as the "Strategic Update." The strategic updates were designed to corroborate the espoused strategic plan and to inform corporate management on both the threats and opportunities for the coming years, including their potential effects on P&L and cash flows of the OPCOs in light of their strategic plan. Strategic updates were reported (and entered into Hyperion) with substantially less detail than the detail that was required for budgets.

The budget had to be prepared in a period of approximately six weeks during September–October of each year. As part of this process, Mr. Schaafsma met with the local management teams to discuss the major business challenges on how to establish the required targets. Mr. Schaafsma noted that these meetings usually had "an informal character and were all about important performance drivers, such as the customer portfolio, product portfolio, operational excellence and the quality of the personnel involved in the local business processes."

The budget was reported via two formats. One, based on Hyperion including all the financial data, enabled the Corporate Accounting & Control department to roll up the financials of the different OPCOs to a corporate performance overview. The other was a PowerPoint reporting format which included the main overviews from Hyperion, but also allowed for more commentary. Here the OPCOs had to report their analysis on the changes to prior years and both the presumed risks and upside potentials that were embedded in their forecasts.

In early November of each year, the MD and FD of each OPCO presented their budget to the Executive Board. It was not unusual within Wessanen that corporate "upped" the initially proposed targets by the OPCO managers. In the end, however, the targets were set in agreement with the Executive Board, containing what they believed was the "optimal" amount of stretch. OPCO managers, however, considered their targets "challenging" in most of the years.

The targets for Net Sales, EBIT, and Working Capital were used for the bonus schemes of the MDs of each respective OPCO. Specifically, the annual bonus payments of MDs reflected their OPCO's actual results relative to these targets, including minimum, on-target and stretch target levels. Bonus payouts were calculated as shown in Exhibit 5. The minimum target level was set at 90% of the on-target level, whereas the stretch target level was set at 110% of the on-target level. The three performance targets were weighted 20-40-40 in the bonus scheme; that is, 20% of the bonus potential was based on target achievement of Net Sales, 40% on EBIT, and 40% on Working Capital. Target achievement on each performance measure was independent from target achievement on any of the other two performance measures. In other words, target achievement on each performance measure was strictly cumulative in the determination of the overall bonus payout. Seventy percent of an MD's incentive pay was determined in this way – that is, based on meeting the targets, and hence, determined formulaically. The other 30% was based on an MD's "individual performance," which was assessed subjectively (see Exhibit 6).

The base amount of the incentive pay was 10% of annual salary. The maximum bonus for MDs was set at 25% of salary or 250% of the incentive pay base amount. Thus, for the formulaic part of the incentive, at target performance, an MD earned 70% of 10% of salary. On average, incentive awards at Wessanen amounted to between 5% and 10% of salary. As is customary in most organizations, the remuneration committee (a committee of the Supervisory Board) reserved the right to cap or change incentive payouts on a discretionary basis, but this was done only rarely.

During the budget year, OPCOs had to submit revised forecasts each quarter to provide the Executive Board with a latest estimate of the projected financials for the year. These forecasts were reported next to the budget, which was considered the "fixed plan." This was all done in Hyperion in order to provide the company its "integrated" EPM for which the system was designed. The reforecast for the third and fourth quarter (done at the end of the second quarter, or end of June) also required an update for the subsequent two years on the three KPIs. In September, then, corporate guidance was established for the upcoming year, which was the starting point for the upcoming budget discussions.

Monthly, actual financial performance was reported against the budget-to-date and the latest forecast-to-date. Variances were discussed monthly during half-hour conference calls between the Executive Board, Mr. Schaafsma, and the respective OPCO's MD and FD. Much more extensive face-to-face discussions took place among the same group of people each quarter in order to vet the performance of the previous quarter and the forecast for the remainder of the year. This was called the Quarterly Business Review (QBR). Mr. Schaafsma commented:

> **Our QBRs are not just "talking shops." We require the OPCO managers to make detailed reports in preparation for these meetings. These meetings easily last for two hours, and they are "honest" – sometimes brutally honest. We discuss performance on the financials, based on reporting formats in Hyperion, but we also drill deep into nonfinancial performance indicators to discuss and grasp the current state of the business. These nonfinancials can have to do with credit notes, customer complaints, sick-leave percentages and employee turnover. Any and all exceptions are flagged up and fair game for discussion. Our QBRs are, however, not just about operational performance. We also use them to discuss, and decide as appropriate, the launch of new brands; to evaluate progress on projects; to assess key investments and/or to raise other issues we suspect may be lurking in our OPCOs. All told, the QBRs allow us to spend some "quality time" with our OPCO managers ...**

Finally, two other components of Wessanen's internal control and governance structure were the company-wide Framework of Internal Control (FIC) and the Wessanen Company Code (WCC). The FIC provided a clear overview of the control activities applied to the most important process-level risks of the main business functions. The purpose of these control activities was to ensure effective and efficient operations, reliable financial reporting, and compliance with laws and regulations. In May of each year, the OPCOs were required to perform their annual control self-assessments based on the FIC. The results were communicated to Internal Audit and the Executive Board. A summary was communicated to the Supervisory Board. For any identified control weaknesses, an action plan was put in place by management. Progress on these action plans and follow-ups on any internal audit issues were reported and discussed during the QBRs. A risk and control database was kept to keep track of all the reported risks and improvement or "mitigation" plans.

The WCC provided employees with a set of moral and ethical guidelines for how to do business and how to achieve results in an appropriate manner. It included Wessanen's Mission, Core Values, Business Principles, and Guidelines. The Guidelines dealt with several topics, including information security, insider trading, gifts and favors, bribery and corruption. The WCC also referred to Wessanen's whistle-blowing policy, fraud policy, sustainability policy and applicable authority limits.

Challenging times (early 2009)

To get the management support he knew was required, Mr. Schaafsma urgently requested a meeting with the new interim CEO. The CEO supported the idea to develop a cost-cutting scenario that would "stress test" a possible drop in revenues of 10%. The idea had been floated before in 2008 by the former CEO. At that time, however, the implementation was not pushed through. But by this time around, the economic situation had deteriorated more than it had then, so Mr. Schaafsma felt that it was now-or-never to press on with the idea:

> **Looking back, and happy about having convinced the new CEO, I knew that all eyes were trained on me to take charge of what turned out to be a frenetic process to implement a "hurricane proof" scenario. I was happy to have joined forces with Dick [van der Wardt, VP Corporate Accounting & Control]. The two of us together, with our teams, worked hard to get this done as swiftly as possible.**

Time was running short, though, because revising an annual plan made little sense the further they were down into the year. This was March 2009. The primary objective was to keep EBIT at budget level while anticipating a drop in revenues of approximately 10% relative to the original budget. Given that Net Sales projections were revised down, and given that EBIT targets stayed the same, that implied that budgeted costs had to come down.

Mr. Schaafsma's team developed a model based on what they had determined to be the relevant cost categories. These categories included all expenditures that had a fixed component in them, but at the same time were deemed to have minimal negative impact on potential growth in Net Sales. The marketing, advertising, and promotion budgets were ring-fenced to protect the top line. During this period, management's attention was primarily focused on Net Sales and EBIT. Further reducing Working Capital was, while important, subjugated to the focus on Net Sales and EBIT.

The financial modeling taking into account these parameters was done in close cooperation with Mr. Van der Wardt who facilitated the technical management accounting part of the process by working out the details in Hyperion and Excel. Messrs. Schaafsma and Van der Ward analyzed all cost accounts per country primarily in the SG&A category, and contemplated new targeted cost levels on a line-by-line basis. For example, they scrutinized travel, car fleet, personnel, advisory services, and other expenses related to costs such as warehousing and shipping. As it turned out, on most accounts they simply put down a target to reduce the spending by 10–20%. They also reviewed all Capital Expenditure (CAPEX) projects. For new projects, they kept those that they deemed offered a sufficiently compelling business case to improve EBIT. Most ongoing projects were continued. The last thing they wanted to do was to upset high-impact change programs that focused on improving longer-term profitability. An example of one of the ongoing projects was the European rollout of the ERP system.

Based on the modeling and analysis, guidance was worked out for the local management teams. Mr. Schaafsma explained:

> The influence of our newly installed interim CEO was clear here. He, but also the other board members, understood clearly that action was required. However, they were resolute in their desire to see a scenario that reflected the economic crisis while not jeopardizing potential growth. Their idea was also to safeguard the margins, by reducing SG&A and overheads. The CEO felt strongly that this was the right approach, and somehow reckoned that it would keep the management teams in the OPCOs on board, too.

OPCO MDs and FDs were asked to discuss the guidance with their respective management teams and to come back with plans to meet the targeted lower cost levels. During this process, Mr. Schaafsma had lengthy talks with the local management teams to discuss the impact of the many tough decisions that had to be made. Examples of the actions taken were the renegotiation of vendor contracts, salary freezes, and leaving vacancies open. In some cases, even layoffs were on the table, which made the process in one or two of the OPCOs rather painful for those involved. Mr. Schaafsma observed:

> How the teams handled this challenge varied clearly between those who had dealt with this before and those who had little or no experience with cost cutting. Interestingly, and fortunately to a degree, many of our managers had been groomed in successful companies, and made great careers, during times of mainly growth. They had gotten used to 'the-sky-is-the-limit' sorts of attitudes. They were now facing a new reality. For them, the rather hard-nosed meddling from Corporate came as somewhat of a surprise.

That said, Mr. Schaafsma gathered from the discussions with the vast majority of the management teams that the purpose of the exercise was, all things considered, quite well understood and its necessity not doubted, at least not in conversations with him. "Maybe there is some truth in the proverbial wisdom that 'necessity is the mother of . . .,'" he mused.

The Executive Board was very serious about the process – they considered the space for negotiations as quite limited. For most OPCOs, the "hurricane proof" scenario was completed after only one round of discussions and negotiations. In other cases, the cost saving plans developed by the OPCO's did not meet the Board's expectations. In these cases, Messrs. Schaafsma and Van der Wardt guided the management teams of the respective OPCO to reach the savings in alternative accounts and asked them to stretch further, thus requiring an additional round to converge on an agreed plan.

The numbers were compiled in Excel outside of Hyperion. With the new numbers now available, however, two issues had to be addressed. First, it was not clear how, and as what, to upload the revised numbers into Hyperion. The Hyperion version that the Corporate Accounting & Control department was running could not accommodate two budgets. An upload, therefore, would require an override of the original budget with the newly developed scenario. If the original budget was not replaced, the only way to proceed would be to report the alternative scenario outside of the system by way of an "extra" set of books. But evaluating actual results versus the latest forecast and two budget versions across two systems seemed almost like "too much of a good thing," sighed Mr. Van der Wardt.

The second and possibly more contentious quandary was whether to change the targets in the OPCO managers' bonus schemes. After an already tough reporting for most cost line-items even against the original budget, the Executive Board decided to drop the original budget and to fix the alternative "hurricane proof" scenario into the systems and bonus schemes. "The original budget was history," said Mr. Schaafsma. "It was now hurricane season, and the correspondingly named 'hurricane scenario' became the new plan for 2009."

Fiscal Year 2009 operational results came in close to the hurricane budget. It helped that reorganization costs came in lower than expected. These costs were related to re-organizing the legal entity structure following the split of business lines into Organic and Frozen. Moreover, locations had been rejigged yielding further efficiencies. On the other hand, some layoffs to help reduce overhead had caused one-off staff-related redundancy costs. Advertising and promotion expenditures also were substantially higher than forecast. This was mainly because the interim CEO and Mr. Schaafsma felt the need to boost the retained frozen food brands in the second half of the year to try to grow this business in the face of negative "publicity" from the discontinued brands, which had by themselves, however, helped to streamline costs.

The divestments in North America had been delayed. Tree of Life was eventually sold, but later than planned. The fraud case that had surfaced in ABC in the summer of 2009 required a restructuring, which delayed the timing by which this business could be even put up for sale.

The future

Mr. Schaafsma and Mr. Van der Wardt contemplated on how they could possibly better translate business uncertainty into alternative scenarios of the budget:

> **Should we develop these alternative scenarios beforehand rather than during the year? Would there be enough support in the operating companies to do this even if there was no "hurricane" coming?**

What they obviously could not know is whether the budget would have been met even if it had not been reset ... but would that have been a good thing?

Exhibit 1 Key figures, FY 2008 and FY 2009 (in € million), Royal Wessanen NV

Structure 2008	Structure 2009				
	Revenues			Ebit	
Wessanen Europe (Biological Food)	**Continued**	**2009**	**2008**	**2009**	**2008**
France	Wessanen Europe	€ 493	€ 501	€ 3-	€ 41
Benelux					
United Kingdom	Frozen Foods	€ 120	€ 123	€ 3	€ 2
Germany					
Italy	ABC	€ 90	€ 102	€ 30-	€ 2
Frozen Foods	Non-allocated			€ 14-	€ 8-
Food Group	*Total Continued*	*€ 703*	*€ 725*	*€ 44-*	*€ 37*
Benelux: Backers					
Germany: Karl Kemper → Discontinued					
Italy: Righi → Discontinued	**Discontinued**	**2009**	**2008**	**2009**	**2008**
	Frozen Foods	€ 30	€ 35	€ 2-	€ 1-
North Amerca					
American Beverage Company (ABC)	Panos Brands	€ 36	€ 35	€ 3	€ 3
Panos Brands → Panos Brands					
Liberty Richer → Panos Brands	Tree of Life	€ 817	€ 802	€ 1	€ 11
Tree of Life → Tree of Life	*Total Didcontinued*	*€ 883*	*€ 872*	*€ 3*	*€ 14*

Source: Royal Wessanen NV, *Annual Report 2009*, pp. 12–13.

Exhibit 2 Organization chart, Royal Wessanen NV

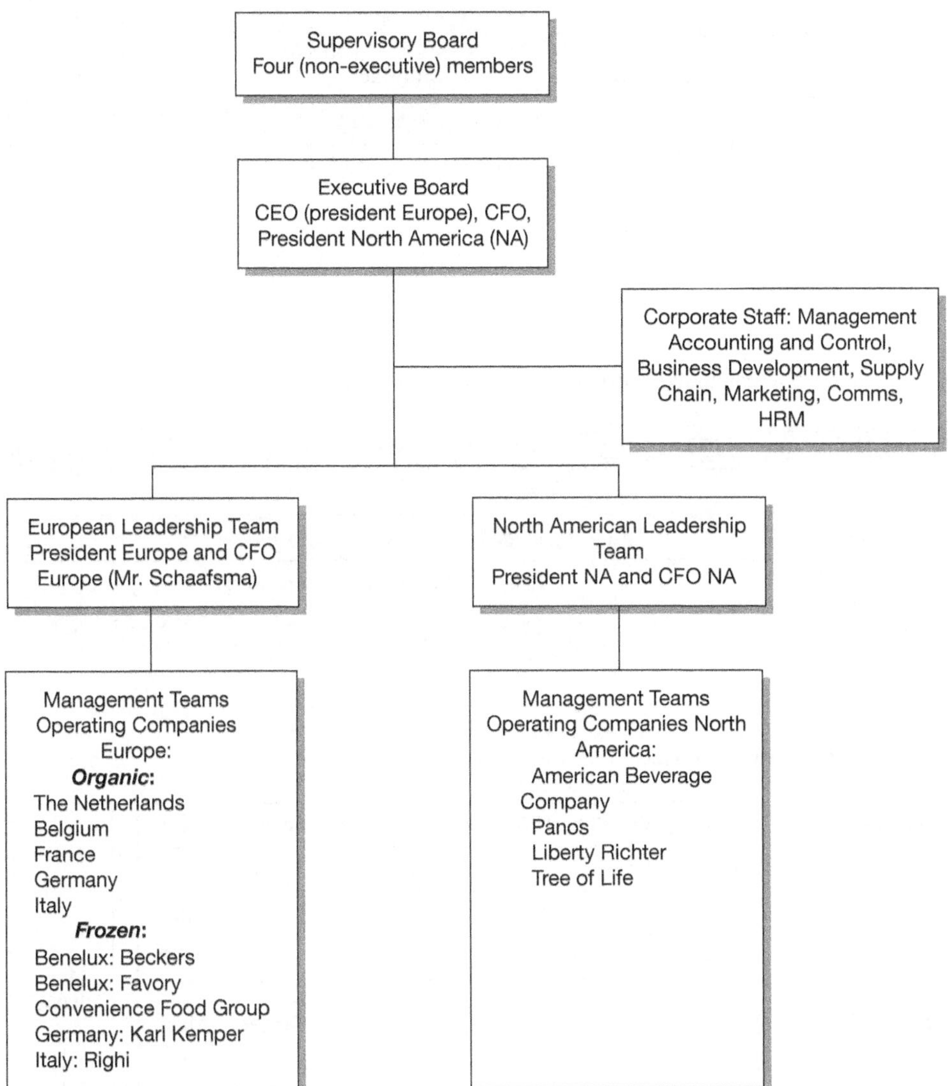

Exhibit 3 Working capital as percentage of sales – new definition for the 2009 budget, Royal Wessanen NV

$$\text{New Working Capital KPI} = \frac{\text{Working Capital at Month End}}{(\text{Actual Month Third Party Net Sales} + \text{Prior 2 Months Third Party Net Sales})*4}$$

Exhibit 4 General budget guidelines for the 2009 budget, Royal Wessanen NV

	Autonomous Sales Growth		EBIT	
In %	Branded	Distribution	Branded	Distribution
Europe	7–8%	5–7%	Based on ROS >10%	Based on ROS >5.5%
North America	7–8%	7–8%	Based on ROS >10.5%	Based on ROS >2.3%

*) ROS = Return on Sales

Exhibit 5 Financial targets incentive calculation scheme Royal Wessanen NV

Resits versus Financial Targets	Financial Targets Incentive Score
Below minimum target	0%
Minimum target to On-Target	Linear increase from 25% to 100%
On-Target to Stretch Target	Linear increase from 100% to 250%
Above Stretch Target	250%

Exhibit 6 Distribution of incentive payment, Royal Wessanen NV

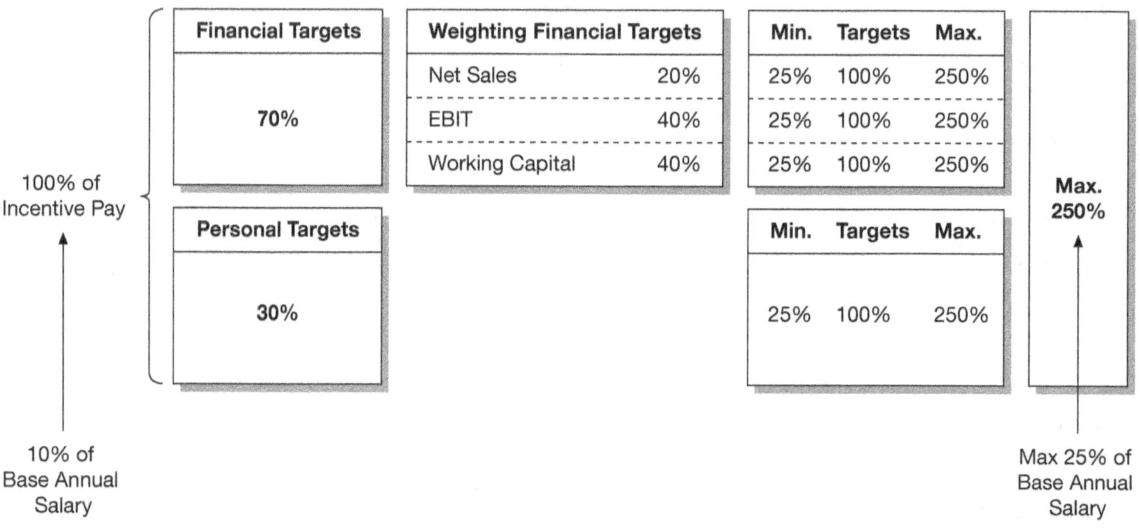

This case was prepared by Professor Wim A. Van der Stede (London School of Economics) and Dimitri Kruik (Erasmus University Rotterdam).

CASE STUDY
The Stimson Company

Henry Stimson, president/CEO of The Stimson Company, a small engineering company and manufacturer of dust control systems and equipment, explained the problem:

> We have a considerable amount of tension present in our professional staff now, with most of the dissatisfaction focused on the project budgeting system. Everybody has strong feelings on the subject. The project leaders and operations people feel that the original estimates made by the sales engineers are not very realistic and, therefore, not very useful for planning workloads and schedules. The sales engineers, on the other hand, feel that a lot of the budget changes are motivated only to produce a zero variance, and that there is not enough thought or effort invested to try to meet the budget.

The company

The Stimson Company (TSC) was founded by Henry Stimson's grandfather. The company was privately held, with the Stimson family still controlling nearly all of the stock. In 2015, annual revenues were approximately $15 million, and the company had just under 130 full-time employees. In the recession of the late 2000s, TSC's financial position was weak, but under Henry Stimson's leadership the finances had strengthened to the point where the company had no long-term debt and was earning modest profits.

TSC's personnel had a particular expertise in providing dust control systems for general industrial applications. The systems filtered the air from machines which generated dust or particulate air pollution and passed the clean air back into the plant. In the past 15 years TSC had generated most of its revenues and profits from clients in the paper industry.

Exhibit 1 shows a picture of a core dust control system component: the separator. Separators and some other system components were more or less standardized products, although they varied somewhat depending on the type of dust generated, the size of the application, and the desired methods of emptying the dust bags. The other components, such as main and branch pipes, hoods and conveyers, had to be custom-designed to fit the customer's equipment and plant layout.

TSC managers preferred to sell complete systems, meaning that company personnel would handle the job all the way from design through installation and test. TSC was the dominant supplier of such systems to the paper industry in the Northwest region of the United States, but company managers were beginning to consider diversifying both into other industries and into other products that would utilize their engineering expertise.

Project management

Because a large proportion of TSC's revenues were derived from a limited number of large-scale projects, project management was very important to the company. Two roles in the organization were specifically project-oriented: sales engineers and project leaders (see organization chart in Exhibit 2). The sales engineers were responsible for the initial customer contact, analysis of the problem, definition of the system concept, selling, original job cost estimating, and pricing. The project leaders were responsible for the detailed technical development (design) of the project and the management of the job from time of order entry to completion. Throughout the remainder of this case, Project 14321 will be used to illustrate the functioning of these roles and the company's management systems.

Project 14321

In 2014, TSC was asked by the Oregon Paper Corporation (OPC) to submit a proposal for a complete dust control system for the converting area of a toilet-paper processing plant. The machines in the converting area took tissue paper from the mill, rolled it into logs 96 inches wide, slit it into widths of 4½ inches, and packaged it for sale. OPC was interested in a dust control system because it would reduce maintenance on the converting machines, make a less dusty product, and keep the plant safely within federal safety standards.

TSC submitted an estimate for the entire job, but for their own internal reasons, OPC asked that the project be broken into two phases. Thus, TSC submitted a phase I proposal for part of the job. This proposal was accepted and TSC began the work. The request for a proposal for phase II, a job which eventually was assigned number 14321, followed as expected.

Proposal

For all potential jobs where the customer was considered serious about adding equipment, the sales engineer prepared formal estimating sheets. These required detailed estimates for each element of direct cost, built up by pounds of material and hours of labor for each system component. These units were converted to dollars by multiplying by standard costs, which the accounting department updated every six months, and by getting quotes for special materials or service.

To get to a *full-cost* estimate, overhead was applied based on pounds of material or hours of labor. Accounting personnel updated annually the 16 overhead rates, eight each for variable and fixed overhead categories.

The price was determined by adding a profit percent onto the full-cost estimate. The company's goal was to maintain a 10–15% net profit margin on sales (before tax). Because time was often limited, Jonathan Hemmer, sales engineer, used a rough rule-of-thumb based on dollars per required volume of air (cubic feet per minute) to estimate the total cost and price for Project 14321. For the breakdown in costs, Jonathan compared this job with a similar, large job completed the year before. Steve Davis, proposals manager, explained:

> **First of all, you have to realize that these estimates involve a lot of guesses. This project is now being installed, but portions of the new OPC building are being remodeled, and the work is not yet finished. Their equipment is not in location. So with this as with many other jobs, we had to estimate it based on their drawings. For more or less standardized components, such as separators, those do not cause a big problem. But for customized components, such as branch lines, the estimates are only guesses.**

To protect the company against these project uncertainties, sales engineers typically added a "contingency" to the estimate. The contingency was done on an entire job and not on an individual component unless the risk was high on a particular section of the job, perhaps because of lack of information about it. The contingency was intended to protect TSC from cost uncertainties. It was not affected by what the market would bear. However, some extra revenue dollars might be added if TSC managers felt the company was in a strong competitive position.

The proposed price of $3,197,640 for the Phase II work was presented to OPC. It was accepted on November 12, 2014, and that is when the project was assigned number 14321.

Project kickoff

On November 13, the project kickoff meeting was held. The primary purpose of this meeting was to transfer the responsibility for the job from the sales engineer, Jonathan Hemmer, to the project leader assigned to the job, Sanjiv Kumar. Also in attendance at the meeting were Steve Davis (proposals manager), Bob Stimson (design manager), Bruce McIntosh (operations manager), Mike Giordano (plant manager), Gary Blasiar (a separator specialist), and Mary Fiore (job cost accountant). Most of the discussion at the two-hour meeting was on technical subjects, such as about what filter media and fan size were required, and the expert team provided their inputs.

After this meeting, Sanjiv, the project leader, planned the project, broke the tasks into work orders starting with the design work, established the schedule, and began the process of coordinating manpower and material needs.

Project control

Control of the project was an ongoing process, with frequent communications required between Sanjiv, the project leader, and personnel in both OPC and the various TSC work areas: design, operations, and installation. Each month, Sanjiv was required to assemble a Job Status Report which showed the percent physical completion at the end of the month and the predicted dollar variance to completion for each element of cost. This report was built up from the work order level and summarized by the project leader to the level of detail provided in the original project budget.

The estimates of percent complete were an important part of the control process because they directly affected the percent of the budget used for comparison with actual expenditures to date and, therefore, the variances. In estimating the percent complete in the design area, Sanjiv used drawings as his gauge. Drawings represented a relatively small element of work, and that work did not normally stretch out over several reporting periods. It was generally not difficult either to estimate how long the work represented by a drawing should take or to judge whether that work was done.

In the fab area, Sanjiv relied on inputs from the fabrication department. Based on their experience and accumulated records, the fabrication department broke down the work orders into individual operations and established standard hours for each operation to come up with a total standard for each work order. Then they looked at how much they had accomplished and calculated the total percent complete on each work order. Sanjiv believed their estimates were generally quite good, better than he could make, but he noted that errors could occur on occasion:

> **For instance, they may say their fabrication is so many percent complete on a given work order, but I know we have already shipped all of it. Or the records may show only 50% of the material on a job has been withdrawn, but they are indicating 100% fabrication.**

Field installation was a bigger problem, since TSC was only beginning the establishment of standards for installation. Sanjiv had to rely on the estimates of installation foremen who were generally optimistic. For example, a foreman might say that he was 99% complete with a work order when the reality was perhaps more like 85%. Since Sanjiv often worked with new foremen, it was impossible for him to judge which were most optimistic and which were relatively pessimistic. But the foremen were able to tell Sanjiv which items on a work order were complete, so Sanjiv had some information on which to apply judgments on the estimates.

The Job Status estimates were input to the computer, and the portion of the budget determined by the percent complete was compared with actual costs to date. Three monthly reports were produced. The Detailed Job Cost Report showed a comparison of actual costs (and labor hours) with fraction of budget (total budget multiplied by percent complete) for variable cost categories only. The Summary Job Cost Report summarized variable costs by component and showed variance-to-date and forecast-to-completion. The Job Cost Fully Accounted Summary summarized variances by component and showed variances to date for variable cost, full cost, and net profit.

The projects were monitored by accounting staff. Shortly after the reports were produced, Mary Fiore, job cost accountant, asked the project leaders for explanations of cost category variances greater than $2,500 appearing during the month and of any obvious errors (e.g. expenses incurred but showing zero percent completion). She was trying to determine whether an actual problem existed or whether, for example, the variance was merely a timing problem or was the result of a recording error. Any large input errors were corrected before the financial statements were produced.

Around the 10th working day of each month, a company-level financial review meeting was held with the key managers in attendance: Henry and Bob Stimson, Charles Cowsill, Bruce McIntosh, Kristina Boyd and Steve Davis. About 30 minutes of this meeting was devoted to a review of the top 6 to 10 projects, which typically covered about 80% of the costs incurred during the month. Mary Fiore would present a summary of the project variances with the explanations provided by the project leaders. The discussion would focus mostly on overall performance, not the specifics of the jobs.

Budget adjustments

A number of budget adjustments were made for Project 14321. **Appendix A** explains the rationale and general procedure for budget adjustments. The following are two illustrative examples of budget adjustments for Project 14321:

A. Blow-back dampers

In December and January, work proceeded on Project 14321, mostly on project design. On January 23, 2015, Sanjiv Kumar submitted a budget adjustment for $7,613 for the inclusion of three blow-back dampers. Normally, the blow-back dampers had to be specifically called out in the budget, since they were unique and required a certain amount of time to be fabricated. However, sales engineering allocated the dollars for the blow-back dampers to M (Main Line), instead of separating them under V (Valves) or some other designation. But because the blow-back dampers were shown in the drawing as part of A (manifold), Sanjiv released them on an A work order. (He later admitted that he should have gone back to sales engineering and requested that the blow-back dampers be shown as part of the manifold.) On the job cost report, these choices made A look bad and M look unnaturally good.

Sanjiv observed, however, that "Even with these dollars allocated to the manifold, the sales engineering estimate was extremely low." It did not include enough pounds for the three blow-back valves. Based on actual drawings, Sanjiv submitted the budget adjustment.

Even after the budget revision, however, when fab actually built the dampers, the actuals were way off budget. Sanjiv guessed that the material requirement calculation done in design from actual drawings failed to include scrap, or it may have been based on metal cuttings of sizes of sheets that did not exist. These differences between estimate, design, and fab showed up as budget variances because a budget adjustment could not be made after work was started. Jonathan Hemmer, the sales engineer, commented:

> I agree that in comparison with what was actually built, the material estimate was low. However, it's my contention that the manifold was over-designed and thus over-built for this application. Before this happened, design should have met with sales engineering to discuss the anticipated variances to attempt to develop corrective action.

B. Platforms

On June 16, a second formal meeting was held. Design had progressed to the point where it was possible to tell operations that they could look for specific work orders on a specific schedule. In attendance at this meeting were Sanjiv Kumar, Bob Stimson, and Bruce McIntosh. The next day, because of what he learned at the meeting, Sanjiv submitted an adjustment which increased the budget by $38,170, the details of which are shown in Exhibit 3. Sanjiv elaborated on the largest item, which individually caused a $39,910 increase:

> In order to estimate accurately, we can't extrapolate directly from past data. We need to look more closely at what's required from the current job. Last year we built a very similar collector and used that as a gauge for estimating. But this collector required a minimum of four platforms that weren't in the estimate ... I think sales engineering basically took their estimate from their old estimate. But not only did they overlook the platforms, we overran their original estimate. They should have looked at the actuals on that job and not reproduced a bad estimate.

Jonathan Hemmer explained from his perspective:

> We have to use last year's job as a guide. Both collectors have 18 hoppers. The configuration is slightly different, and the size of the OPC collector is a little smaller. I checked against the actuals on last year's job when that job was about 98% complete, and the separators were 100% complete at that time Based on that check I estimated we should come in at about 135,000 pounds of material. Allowing for some additional bracing and reinforcing, I forecast the actuals would come in closer to 140,000 pounds. But we are predicting this job will come in at about 165,000 pounds. Not only is the material way off, but installation on last year's job took 2,300 hours, and we're now forecasting 2,800 on this job. The platform will make a difference, but not 500 hours.
>
> We did include some hours for the platforms in the original estimate, although I admit we didn't have anything specific in mind, and that's an obvious shortcoming. We certainly didn't think in the grand scale that was eventually drawn up. I don't know how to explain the extra 25,000 pounds of material. There must be some over-designing. But our original estimate for fab hours was 3,864, and on the latest cost sheets we're running at about 3,000 hours. That's obviously to the good, and it's not consistent with the material overrun.

Scope changes/budget revisions

When a scope change required the customer price to be renegotiated, a budget revision was also required. **Appendix B** describes this price renegotiation and budget revision process in general and the rationale for involving the sales engineer in it. The following are two examples of budget revisions for Project 14321.

A. Move collectors

In February, after the manifold was released for fabrication, Sanjiv, the project leader, provided OPC some additional information about where the collectors would be located on the roof and the static and wind loads that would be imposed on the roof. OPC decided that these loads were unacceptable and asked that the collector be shifted 150 feet north and to the grade level of the building. Even though TSC was well into production at that point, an acceptable alternative for the collectors could not be found. Substantial modifications were required to incorporate the existing manifold with some additional piping that had to be installed. This necessitated a re-estimate of the job, agreement on a new price, and revision of the budget.

Jonathan Hemmer, the sales engineer, was responsible for negotiating the price change. OPC accepted the proposed price increase of $203,500, and Jonathan revised the budget to reflect the needed changes.

A short time later, Sanjiv also submitted two adjustments which increased the budget by just under $47,500 because the final drawings showed the job had expanded beyond where sales engineering had figured.

Since this occurred after TSC had received the additional money from the customer, Sanjiv had to adjust the budget. He explained:

> One of the problems we had with this change, and it happens on occasion, is a definitional problem of where the manifold left off and where the main pipe began. I may report the costs against the manifold, while the sales engineer had figured the budget in the main. The sum total for the manifold and main may be the same, but we would show a variance for each.
>
> We also had a problem with the total dollars budgeted. This is only speculation, but what may have happened here is that sales engineering figured we couldn't ask the customer for all of the dollars for the change and they decided that TSC would absorb part of the cost.

Jonathan Hemmer was not aware of this budget adjustment at the time but he commented on it several months later:

> I wish Sanjiv had let me know what was happening. There is nothing worse than knowing after the fact that, for example, your manifold is 10,000 pounds over budget. It may have ended up that way anyway, but we can't provide suggestions or learn from problems if we don't know about them.

B. Pipework supports

On June 24, another budget revision was necessary. OPC insisted that the pipework did not meet their standard, even though TSC maintained that it met the industry standard. OPC managers felt that the change should be made at no cost to them, since they gave TSC the total job without soliciting competing bids. TSC managers protested. The disagreement was finally settled with a price increase of just $15,000. The total cost estimate, however, which went through as a budget revision, was around $42,500. Sanjiv Kumar commented:

> This revision is a good example of a major problem we have with sales – their budget changes are often painfully slow. In this case, we had known for months that the budget needed revising, and I had to keep prodding them to make the change. These expected changes can often span several reporting periods, and it creates confusion as to whether we should be reporting against the budget or what we expect the budget will be. Sometimes the revision takes so long that the work is done before the revision comes through.

Status at August 2015

From the beginning, Project 14321 had had its share of problems as reflected by the numerous budget adjustments and budget revisions. The Summary Job Cost Report for 14321 at July 31 showed a small unfavorable total variance versus the budget at the estimated 43% complete, caused mainly because of the problems in the collector part of the separator component. Sanjiv Kumar described the current problems and his remaining concerns:

> A gross estimation error has just recently surfaced. The budget for "Material-Sundry" in the S (separator) component is $41,865. We have already spent over $45,000, and our forecast to complete is in excess of $67,500. It could be argued that we should have recognized this problem earlier, but this is also a notable example of poor estimating. I'm going to have to adjust the budget upwards in this area.
>
> We could also have more trouble with the budget for management hours. Each addition to project scope or extension of the project schedule extends the number of reporting periods and increases management time. Since the company has grown, we have progressed from just "doing" a project to "managing" a project, but the budgets haven't reflected this. On a large project, management time can be 20%–22% of the total design budget, but the original budget for 14321 allowed only 4%–5%.
>
> In addition, I'm a little worried about the estimates for getting painting and pneumatic piping done on this particular project. We're not as good as we could or should be at estimating other trades, such as printing, plumbing and electrical, and I'm not sure there are enough dollars in there to get the job done ... And finally, we could always run into some problems in installation.

Since the budget changes had increased the planned costs much faster than the price had been negotiated upward, the project's planned profit margin had slipped from an original 11% to less than 6% (see Exhibit 4), a level considered below the company's desired range of between 10% and 15%. The margin would slip even lower if the budget had to be adjusted upward any further, and Sanjiv seemed to think it would have to be. Steve Davis looked back at the job and summarized his feelings:

> I don't think this was a particularly difficult job. I still feel that in an overall sense our original estimate was accurate, although I will agree that there were numerous discrepancies in the components. At this

point, however, it's even hard to tell that. We may be seeing variances because conservative estimates of percent complete are making the jobs look worse than they really are. Design and fabrication seem to like to hold back a few percent as a hedge against something going wrong or just the unknown.

But more importantly, what seems to be missing is a commitment to bring a job in at the minimum cost possible. If we involved the various groups in setting the budgets, the numbers would be so super-conservative that they would be meaningless. We'd either be planning projects at a loss or we'd be pricing ourselves out of the market. Not all of the budgets set by sales engineering are tight. They should be a target to shoot for; an incentive for superior performance, so we are motivated to search for creative solutions to our problems. We've got to get this commitment internalized because standards of performance aren't available for everything we do. We're not trying to punish anybody, but the company does have to exist, after all.

Appendix A Budget adjustments

Over time, many changes were likely to be made to the system as it was originally planned and estimated. More information would be gathered as to the precise customer requirements, such as for the layout of the exhaust piping, and as company personnel reviewed the technical design, suggestions would be made to improve performance or cut costs.

In addition, while the sales engineers were considered excellent at estimating the total cost of a job, very often their estimates for specific phases of a job (e.g. main, exhausters) were very inaccurate, overestimated for some parts and underestimated for others, and the dollars in the budget would have to be moved between components. The custom elements of the systems, such as branch piping, presented the greatest estimating uncertainty. Some definitional problems also existed, as the boundary between components was not clear. A project leader might build on a branch line work order what a sales engineer estimated as part of the main piping.

The job budgets were intended to reflect the company's best estimate of what it should cost to do the work described. This was because while the projects were in process, the budgets were important tools for planning and control, and after a job was completed, budgets which proved to be accurate were useful as an aid for estimating future similar jobs. As the project unfolded, the detailed breakdown in original budget was likely to become less and less realistic. Thus, the company instituted a budget adjustment procedure to allow the project leader to change the budget to reflect a realistic standard, but with the following constraints:

1. No budget adjustments were allowed once work within a labor category (e.g. design, fabrication, installation) was started within a job section (e.g. separators, main, exhausters), with the exception of general job costs.
2. No budget adjustments were allowed unless the adjustment totaled at least eight hours and 10% of the total hours in the work order.
3. All budget adjustments had to be approved by the operations manager.

Appendix B Budget revisions

If for any reason the customer price had to be renegotiated, such as for a scope change or customer-caused cost overruns (e.g. schedule delay), the sales engineer was notified to prepare a budget revision. This involved a re-estimate of costs, using the same Estimating Sheets used when the project was proposed, and a renegotiation of price. When the price change was agreed upon, the new cost estimate was entered as the revised project budget.

Even though at the time of most of these budget revisions, the project leader's detailed knowledge far exceeded that of the sales engineer on the job, because they had been following progress daily, it was seen as desirable to involve the sales engineer in the budget revision because:

1. More realistic estimates were likely. The sales engineers had been exposed to a broader range of jobs, and they had begun to accumulate a database of standards for recurring operations that could facilitate the estimating process. They were also more skilled at preparing estimates at the concept stage; i.e. before detailed drawings and specification sheets were available.
2. It was a good opportunity to develop the sales engineer/customer relationship because it was a chance to meet without a new sale being the explicit intent. In addition, it would provide a relationship continuity for the customer as the sales engineer may have made agreements regarding the specifications of the system that were not put explicitly in the written agreement.
3. It was a good learning opportunity for the sales engineers. By getting out in the field and seeing how the project was progressing, they could learn, both technically and in their estimating.

Exhibit 1 Anatomy of the Stimson Type C Separator

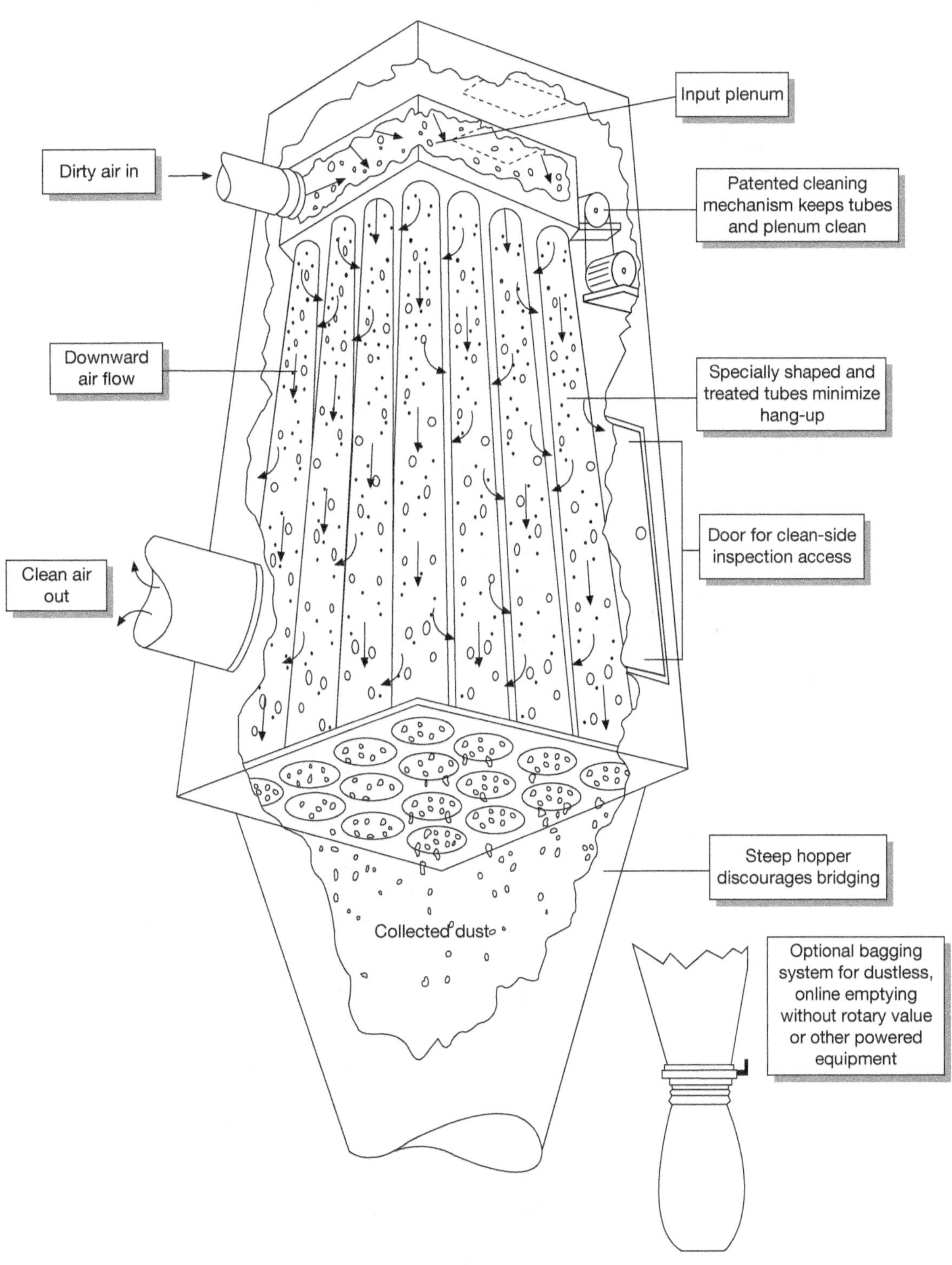

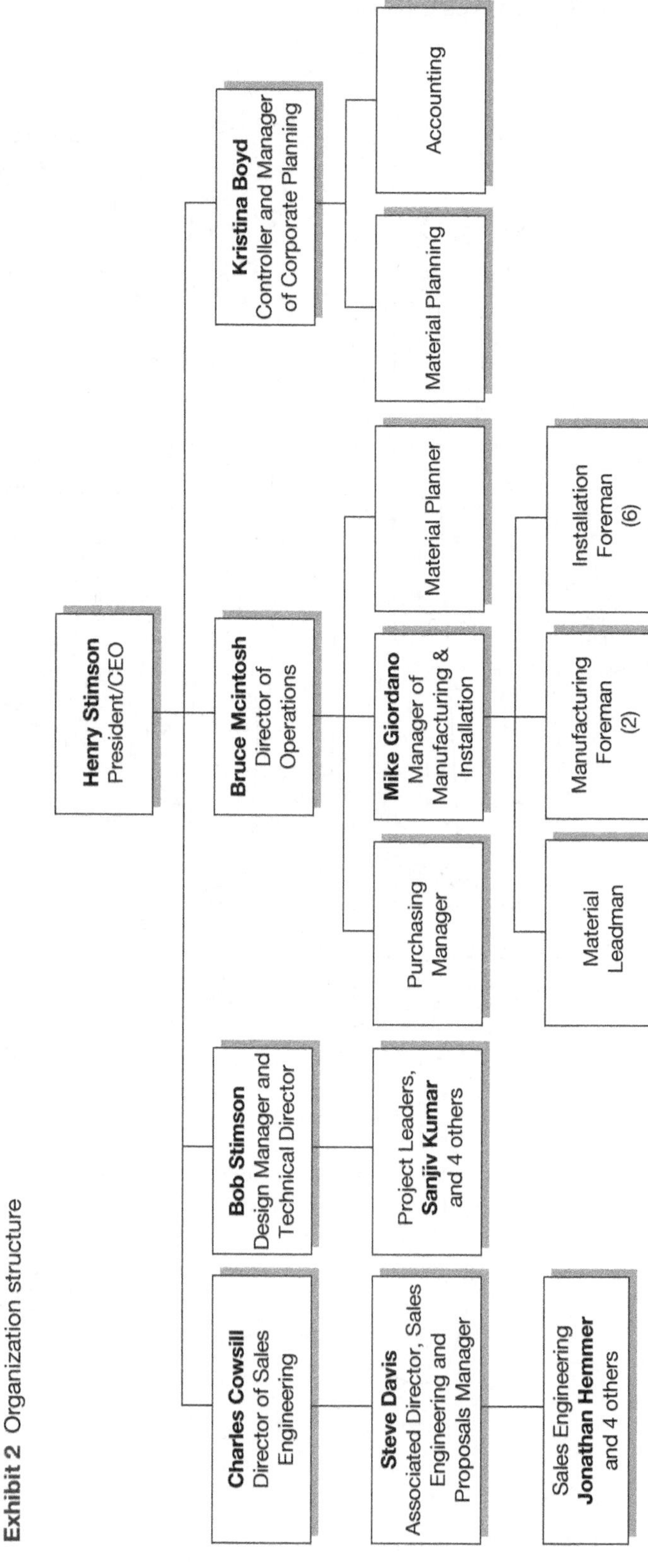

Exhibit 2 Organization structure

Exhibit 3 June 17, 1980 budget adjustment – Project 14321

Component	Increase (Decrease) in Budget	Reason
S	$39,910	Sales had not included enough for access platforms. Fab time estimates were based on performance on 14019 collector which was very similar.
E	(3,543)	Design decided that fan adjustments would be made by fan supplier.
E	(6,340)	Design felt sales had overestimated fabrication time.
B	19,543	Design felt sales had underestimated fabrication time.
A	6,625	Input from the field.
Z	(18,025)	Design reevaluation based on improvement in method of fabricating and installing.
	$38,170	

Exhibit 4 Plan and forecast for Project 14321

	Original Plan	Forecast at 7/31/15
Selling price	$3,197,640	$3,426,248
Variable costs	1,910,288	2,125,680
Contribution margin	$1,287,352	$1,300,568
Allocated fixed overhead	933,603	1,102,898
Net profit	$ 353,750	$ 197,670
Contribution margin %	40.26%	37.96%
Net profit percent	11.06%	5.77%

This case was prepared by Professor Kenneth A. Merchant.

CASE STUDY
Multiple Versions of the Plan

It was a Sunday. The first day of the annual Strategic Planning retreat of the Board of Directors of Anderson Industries, Inc. had finally arrived.

Anthony Rizzo, a young financial analyst, had been working for Thom Thomson, Anderson's recently-appointed chairman/CEO, for the last six months. He had been given the assignment to present the newly developed Corporate Restructuring Program to the Board. Anthony was both excited and nervous.

The Corporate Restructuring Program was one of Mr. Thomson's key management initiatives, largely because Anderson had frequently been criticized for having unusually high expenses. Composed of 83 projects, the program was complex, with many moving parts. However, a key element of the program was to reduce expenses by $100 million while maintaining current revenue levels, thus providing dramatic improvement in a key metric known as the operating expense ratio (operating expenses/revenues). Management viewed this expense reduction goal to be a stretch, but they also considered it necessary, and they wanted to build credibility by demonstrating the company's ability to meet an important goal. The Board of Directors was aware of the program and its objectives, but Anthony's presentation was intended to provide much deeper insight.

The prior week had been unexpectedly easy. Because of Mr. Thomson's desire to avoid any surprises, all of the presentations had been finalized by Wednesday, and the dry run took place on Thursday. On Sunday, Anthony planned to arrive at the hotel early to have a chance to check the meeting room before the presentation. The meeting was to start at 2:00 p.m., and Anthony was one of the first presenters.

Traffic was light, and Anthony was well ahead of schedule. Upon arriving at the hotel, he checked to see if his room was available. He learned that he could not check in for a few hours, but the front desk delivered an urgent message asking him to call Sharon Carpenter, Anderson's head of financial planning, as soon as possible.

On the call, Sharon explained that she had received the newest budget submissions from the business units just before leaving the office on Friday afternoon. Wanting to get a head start on next week's work, she began her review of the company-wide roll-up on Sunday morning. Initially, everything looked fine, but she noticed that a few ratios were a little off. One was the operating expense ratio, so she wanted to inform Anthony before his presentation to the Board. Sharon and Anthony discussed some of the most likely explanations for the exceptions, but lacked the data to reach any conclusions. Sharon commented that the budgeting process tended to be somewhat iterative this early in the cycle, so she almost regretted her decision to take a quick look on Sunday morning. Nevertheless, Sharon and Anthony both knew that some very ambitious goals had been set causing them to be concerned that real slippage had occurred. Focusing on Anthony's presentation, the potential impact was clear. To meet the targeted operating expense ratio, either revenues would have to increase by $25 million, which was unlikely given the current economic conditions, or the expense reductions would have to increase by an additional $15 million, which was slightly less than 2% of total company-wide expenses.

After speaking with Sharon, Anthony asked if the hotel could provide him with space to work. He was led to the hotel engineer's office, a very small office deep in the guts of the hotel. There, he got back on the phone with Sharon, and they considered the alternatives. The focal point of Anthony's presentation could be impacted in a small, but still material, way; they could only speculate about the reasons for the change in projections; and they could not reach Mr. Thomson. Further, time was very short. Should Anthony simply proceed with the presentation as previously approved, should he try to incorporate the new projections into the presentation, should he "hide" the slides showing numbers and try to finesse his way around the issue, or should he be upfront about the uncertainty in the numbers? How would the Board react if uncertainty was demonstrated? How would Mr. Thomson respond if surprised during the Board meeting?

Anthony tried again to speak with Mr. Thomson, who was meeting with the Audit Committee of the Board, but that Committee meeting ran longer than expected. Mr. Thomson rushed to the Board Meeting, flanked by a few of the Audit Committee members, getting there just in time for the scheduled start.

CASE STUDY

Vitesse Semiconductor Corporation

This case was prepared by Fred Magner and Professor Kenneth A. Merchant.

In the semiconductor industry, picking the right R&D investments and then turning those investments into successful products largely determines success. To help with that decision process at Vitesse Semiconductor Corporation, Marty McDermut (CFO) and Patty Heinen (manager of Financial Planning and Analysis) had spent the last several months developing a business model designed to put R&D successes at Vitesse in the proper perspective. The model showed that the company would achieve its long-term goals only if R&D projects generated at least 35% returns. They proposed implementing a minimum IRR hurdle rate of 35% for R&D investments.

In the first resource allocation meeting after they made their proposal, however, Marty and Patty were disappointed that the senior management team had just approved one particular R&D proposal, to build a new Carrier Ethernet product, with a forecast that was much lower than the desired 35% IRR. Marty and Patty tried to make the case against investing in this project, but they lost the argument.

Industry background

Firms in the semiconductor industry face some unique challenges. Significant R&D spending is necessary to drive future revenues and profits. Because new products have limited life cycles, chip manufacturers must continuously develop new products to replace revenues from declining products. In order to grow, they must accelerate new product growth or improve the returns that the new products generate. Most of the spending is focused on applying and extending existing technologies, but occasionally investments are made to try to develop groundbreaking technologies that might open new markets.

Semiconductor chips are components in customers' products, so chip design is guided by the technological advances and changing requirements of those customers. Marketing and sales personnel work closely with existing and potential customers to understand their needs. "Design wins" are often secured before chips are fully developed and available for sale. At the design-win point, customers design the chips into their products, so the chip manufacturers begin to have an idea about how much revenue and profit a specific project will generate. Some risk still exists even after a design win. The customers can drop a product, miss a product cycle, or even introduce new technology too early. Vitesse mitigates its risk by collaborating closely with customers.

Revenues from new products ramp up slowly. Using Vitesse Semiconductors' product lines as examples: Chips sold to phone carriers to include in their routers and switches typically have a 10-year life cycle, with revenues peaking in years 5, 6, and 7. Chips designed for enterprise-level networking devices[1] have shorter, quicker revenue cycles, but revenues typically still do not peak until three years after the product is introduced. (See Exhibit 1 for Vitesse's carrier and enterprise revenue cycles.) Operating margins are lower in the first few years of a product's life cycle because the R&D expenses are recognized immediately, whereas the revenues come later.

Many new products are followed by "derivative" products that build on the earlier technology but are somehow improved in subsequent iterations, for example, with more features, better performance, lower power consumption, and/or lower costs. It is not unusual for a new product platform to generate four to six derivative products. The first product is typically the least profitable because of the high initial development costs, but profit often increases with each derivative. When a new product platform is launched, the rough plan for derivative products is outlined in a "product roadmap."

Chip costs decline over time. The most dramatic cost reductions take place between the first and second year of production. Yields, or the proportion of chips that are found to perform properly, typically improve with volume and experience and can increase by as much as 50% in the second year of production. Costs are often reduced further by lowering material costs and by transferring processing and testing functions overseas.

Vitesse Semiconductor

Vitesse Semiconductor Corporation, headquartered in Camarillo, California, designed and marketed advanced semiconductor chip solutions for the growing network and communication industries. Founded in 1984, Vitesse continued to innovate in response to its customers' demands for more data and more sophisticated devices. The company was known for engineering excellence and developed several industry leading technologies. Vitesse stock was traded on NASDAQ under the symbol VTSS.

[1] Enterprise-level networking devices are used in large companies or enterprises. The word enterprise implies multi-site, multi-server applications. Cisco is an example of an enterprise customer.

In 2006, some former executives at Vitesse were indicted for backdating stock options. The charges were resolved with a $3 million settlement with the SEC. Although there was no guilty verdict or admission of guilt, the scandal was distracting and expensive.

About that same time, the telecom industry began to shift to packet-based Ethernet networking technologies. Vitesse brought in a new management team that included Marty McDermut as its CFO. The new team shut down development of many legacy products and focused its R&D spending on the development of a new line of products based on Ethernet technologies. The move was risky, as Marty explained:

> **There were no new products for three to four years, and Vitesse had to continue servicing its significant debt load at the same time that revenues from its existing legacy product lines were declining. The strategy killed operating margins for a while because all the new products were at the same early stage of the bell-curved revenue cycle.**

The shift to Ethernet turned out to be a good decision, and by 2013, the investment began to pay off. Marty and the rest of the new management team successfully explained the turnaround story to Wall Street analysts by categorizing Vitesse's products as new, mature, or end-of life, and by demonstrating strong revenue growth from new products. Revenues from new products doubled in 2012 and were projected to double again over the next two years, to approach $60 million by 2014.

The communications industry was seeing exponential growth on public and private communications networks. These networks included those used by long-distance, local exchange service providers and wireless service providers ("Carriers"), as well as specialized networks, such as those used by Internet service and over-the-top ("OTT") content providers. Driving the traffic growth was the rapid adoption of data-intensive applications and services such as web access, web-delivered content, Internet Protocol ("IP") video conferencing and telepresence, IP television and, more recently, Cloud storage, Cloud computing, and Software-as-a-Service ("SaaS") by Enterprises. Powerful mobile devices like smartphones and tablets that rivaled and often exceeded the capabilities of desktop machines also consumed these types of services. In the not too distant future, the industry expected that a majority of devices, appliances, sensors, machines, terminals, vehicles, as well as public and private power distribution systems ("Smart-Grid") would all be connected to these ever-expanding worldwide communications networks, leading to what is commonly referred to as the Internet of Things ("IoT"). While all independent, this expanding conglomerate of networks faced common challenges: how to provide service delivery, synchronization and timing, and security.

To address the challenges, packet-based Ethernet networking technologies increasingly formed the basis to deliver these new applications and services. Long present in Enterprise networks, Ethernet was expanding rapidly in both Carrier and Industrial networks, replacing older technologies. In addition, so-called virtualization technologies that started in Ethernet-based Cloud data centers were making inroads into Enterprise and Carrier Ethernet networks, promising even more efficient network resource utilization. Even in Industrial Process Control, Smart-Grid Energy Distribution, Transportation and Automotive networks, the nascent transition from proprietary legacy networks to ubiquitous Ethernet-based networks was taking place. Substantial portions of the Carrier, Enterprise and IoT networks were expected to be rebuilt based on these new technologies over the next 5 to 10 years.

Current Business Plan Review Process

In 2013, Vitesse spent approximately $40 million annually on R&D. Close to 60% of that spending was for salaries, 20% was for other project-specific costs, and 20% was for use of shared resources, such as engineering software. Only the "other project-specific costs" could be reduced without taking drastic measures with long-term consequences, such as layoffs.

R&D assets and spending were allocated to specific projects through the Business Plan Review (BPR) process. Every product derivative was considered a new product and went through the BPR process individually. (See Exhibit 2 for excerpts from the official BPR procedure document.) Marketing initiated the BPR, and the entire executive team was required to approve it before a project could move forward.

Projects were initiated throughout the year, often in response to a customer's need. Some financial discipline was designed into the project selection process; BPRs included detailed revenue and cost projections. Marketing department performance was evaluated, in part, by whether or not new products delivered the revenue and profit projections in the BPRs. But there was no clear financial measure or criteria for selecting projects, or for ensuring that a project's financials were consistent with short- or long-term business plans. Generally, projects were expected to have a 4–5 times ROI[2] or positive NPV at a 20% discount rate, which was thought to be close to the cost of capital for Vitesse. Marty acknowledged, however, that this rate was somewhat arbitrary; 20% was a commonly used hurdle rate, but it was not based on any current analysis specific to Vitesse. The positive NPV guideline was not closely adhered to in the BPR processes, either. Everyone understood that new projects usually returned less than future derivatives, even though that was not explicitly stated or quantified with a lower hurdle rate. Most of the scrutiny during the BPR process was on the marketing and engineering design data, not on the financial data.

The current issue

In 2013, Vitesse was enjoying strong revenue and profit growth driven by R&D investments from prior years. However, the number of new product launches had slowed down significantly in 2012, from an average of 30 new products to less than 10. Management knew that the company had a few "grace" years during which it would continue to realize growth driven by the increasing revenue stream of current products. But a board member asked Marty if the current portfolio of R&D projects could be expected to drive long-term revenue growth at the rates that were forecasted in the long-term business plan. It was a good question. Marty explained,

> **Projects are approved one at a time, but someone needs to be concerned with the bigger picture, the financial implications of the complete product portfolio. In this industry you can make big decisions that dig big holes. You might be OK for a few years, but if you don't have enough new products in the pipeline, you won't be able to sustain growth.**

The difficulty was that the BPR process was somewhat disconnected from the company's business model. Vitesse's business model assumed that new, yet undefined projects would be introduced regularly to replace revenue from obsolete projects. However, the project selection process did not guarantee that revenue from selected projects would be sufficient to meet those long term revenue goals. The 4–5 times ROI and 20% hurdle rate was not informative. Marty and Patty wondered if

[2] ROI was calculated as the 15-year cumulative gross margin divided by R&D investment.

they could develop a more useful benchmark to guide project selection decisions and make sure that investment decisions were consistent with the company's long term business model. Was there a straightforward way to communicate whether or not a project was acceptable?

IRR target development

Marty and Patty's solution was to calculate the IRR on R&D project spending that was assumed in Vitesse's long-term business model. Then they could compare the IRR they calculated from the model to the IRRs that the current portfolio of R&D projects was forecast to generate. If the IRR assumed in the business model was close to the IRR of actual projects, they could infer that they were on track to achieve the model's revenue goals. Perhaps more importantly, the IRR calculated from the model could become a functional hurdle rate for future R&D projects that would link project selection to long-term business goals.

The IRR calculations were based on several assumptions. Patty began with Vitesse's revenue-normalized business model, shown in Table 1.

Patty wanted to calculate the IRR on the model's direct R&D spending, not total R&D spending, since only the direct spending was used in the BPR process. Unfortunately, however, that information was not readily available.

She asked the R&D manager to estimate the percentage of R&D that was direct spending. R&D personnel had been resistant to collecting information for the IRR calculation. They did not want to spend a lot of time gathering data if no one was going to use it. The senior vice president of R&D told Patty, "Unless we use the IRRs to drive behavior, it's just a collection of pretty pictures." Marty and Patty did not disagree; they hoped their analysis would indeed change behavior.

Project Revenue Timing Estimate:

Year:	1	2	3	4	5	6	7	8	9	10
Enterprise	30%	75%	100%	75%	50%	30%				
Carrier	0%	30%	50%	50%	100%	100%	100%	50%	50%	30%
Blended	17%	55%	78%	64%	72%	61%	44%	22%	22%	13%
Normalized to 100%	**4%**	**12%**	**17%**	**14%**	**16%**	**14%**	**10%**	**5%**	**5%**	**3%**

Table 1 Revenue-normalized business model

P&L Model	Model	Minimum	Mid	High
Revenue	100%	100	100	100
Cost of Goods Sold	38–43%	43	41	39
Gross Margin	57–62%	57	59	61
R&D	25–28%	28	27	25
SG&A	15–19%	19	17	16
Operating Income	15–21%	10	15	20

Eventually, the R&D manager provided the needed information. He estimated that 60% of total R&D spending was direct spending on projects. Patty was able to verify that these numbers tied, more or less, to the total R&D spending reported on financial statements.

Patty used two different models for the timing of project investment. In Model 1 the entire investment takes place in Year 0, the year before the investment began generating revenue. In Model 2, the investment is incurred 20% in Year −1, 70% in Year 0, and 10% in Year 1.

Project Investment Timing Estimate:

Year:	−1	0	1
Model 1		100%	
Model 2	20%	70%	10%

To calculate IRR, Patty also had to make some assumptions about how project revenue was distributed over time. Patty followed current projections and assumed that 56% of project revenue followed the quicker enterprise revenue distribution pattern, and 44% of project revenue followed the slower carrier revenue distribution pattern. She weighted revenue patterns accordingly, to develop a blended 10-year revenue distribution.

Patty subtracted the investment from the revenue each year and calculated the IRR on the resulting 10-year income stream. She concluded that R&D project investments should yield IRRs between 35% and 40% to achieve the profit projections in the business model. (See the IRR model in Exhibit 3.) Obviously if the company wanted profit growth rates, the IRRs would have to be even higher. Patty used the same methodology and estimated that target IRRs would have to increase to 43%–47% to achieve 20% profit growth.

Results of the analysis

Patty thought that the results of the analysis were enlightening. The target IRR she calculated was significantly higher than the 20% hurdle rate that was used in the current BPR process, and often higher than the actual IRR new products were generating.

Patty went on to calculate the IRR for all new products and platforms currently on the market. The calculations were based on actual revenue and costs as well as forecasts taken from platform roadmaps. As expected, the IRRs of new platforms were always well below Patty's target, but the IRRs increased with each derivative. (See Exhibit 4 for one example: Ethernet platform IRRs.) Patty also calculated IRRs for entire roadmaps, the weighted IRR for every derivative in a platform, and several fell below the 35% target. (See Exhibit 5 for IRRs of all current platform roadmaps.)

Recommendation

Marty and Patty took their results to the marketing and executive teams and made a strong recommendation to increase minimum project hurdle rates. They argued that a minimum 35% IRR tied to the company's business model was required. This higher IRR rate was necessary to achieve long-term profit plans. They recommended that instead of approving one project derivative at a time, entire platform roadmaps should be approved, but only if the platform met the 35% IRR target. Marty believed that management had to learn to say no to bad investments.

Marty also suspected that marketing low-balled revenue forecasts in the BPR because their performance was evaluated against the BPR revenue targets. Marty hoped the higher hurdle rate would compel everyone involved on a project to commit to higher returns and to figure out how to deliver them, either by reducing costs, expanding markets, or increasing the number of derivatives.

Response

Vitesse's CEO and marketing team were intrigued by the analysis. The actual IRRs of some projects surprised them. Their sense of a project's return had been largely informed only by anecdotal results, so they were interested to learn that, among other things, one large and popular project was not as financially successful as they had previously believed. But even though everyone understood the analysis and its implications, no one seemed in any hurry to formally adopt the 35% IRR target as a new project hurdle rate.

Carrier Ethernet project

The first test came when a BPR for a new Carrier Ethernet product landed on Marty's desk. This was a new product that, if approved, would be Vitesse's first entry into this aspect of the Carrier Ethernet market. Marty and Patty were both in the BPR meeting and argued against its approval because the project did not have a positive NPV even at the 20% hurdle rate, let alone the more meaningful 35% hurdle rate. Even future derivatives were expected to be low margin, falling below the 35% IRR target.

Marketing pushed back, arguing that it was necessary to approve the project for "strategic reasons." If Vitesse did not enter this aspect of the Carrier Ethernet market now, they argued, Vitesse would miss an entire generation of products. It was necessary to take a loss in the short term, so they could build a customer base and keep the door open for more profitable derivatives in the future. Patty understood this argument and did not think it was unreasonable, but she did not want to approve the BPR as it had been presented. She explained:

> **I wasn't completely against moving forward with the new Carrier Ethernet project, but I thought that marketing should take another look at the numbers and commit to higher revenues (and profits). Their forecasts are typically too conservative. And since marketing claimed that earnings from future derivatives would justify the initial loss on the project, I thought they needed to document that. I wanted to see a roadmap.**

As the discussion continued it became evident that no one was willing to kill the project. In addition to the strategic reasons for approving the project, marketing argued that engineering resources were not totally fungible. Different groups had different expertise, and the engineers who would be assigned to this project could not be redeployed immediately to other projects. Marty and Patty eventually conceded, but they insisted that the marketing team at least seriously consider how to increase the project's IRR. Marketing agreed to study the issue, but they made it very clear that they were not committing to a higher revenue forecast in the BPR.

Concerns

Marty and Patty were disappointed that the project was approved even though it did not meet the IRR benchmark that they had worked so hard to develop. It made them evaluate whether or not the IRR benchmark was useful as a tool to assess projects. The IRR calculations relied on forecasts and assumptions, so no one could be sure they were 100% accurate. And even assuming the IRR targets were accurate, Marty and Patty knew that there might be legitimate strategic reasons for pursuing a project. If so, could those be quantified? Certainly a new project could not be expected to meet the same hurdle rate as a later iteration. That was understood by everyone in the organization. Marty and Patty wondered how they could include those considerations into the decision process with an objective measure.

Marty and Patty conceded that IRR target might not be appropriate as a hard cutoff for projects, but they still believed it was a useful tool that could add discipline to the BPR process and could better position Vitesse to meet both its short- and long-term financial goals.

Exhibit 1 Carrier and Enterprise Revenue Cycles

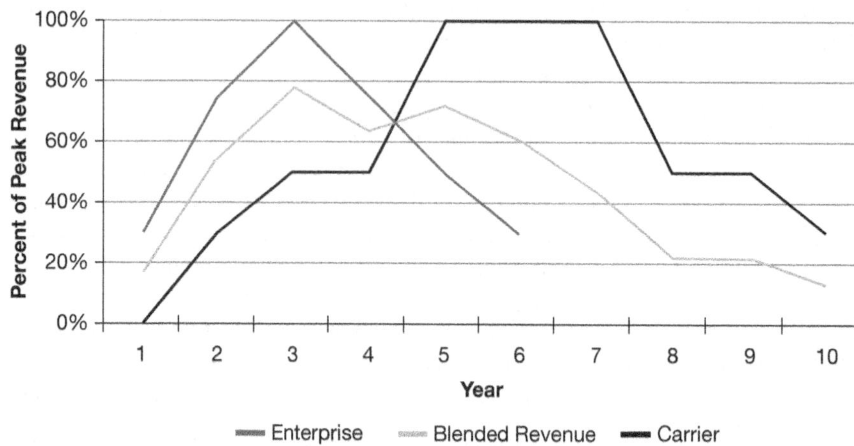

Exhibit 2 Excerpts from the BPR procedure document

VSC Procedure VQPR-1001

Intent

The BPR process is intended to ensure proper product investments, resulting in viable product choices supported with appropriate resources, and to weed out products that are not likely to meet business goals. A BPR meeting is intended to validate the business *for a specific product*, not a market area or broad family of devices.

BPR Presentation Template

The following information provided by the Product Marketing Manager (PMM) shall be presented using the template defined in VQFF-1005:

General market area of the opportunity
Market conditions and target customers
Qualitative description of the product and opportunity
Product Positioning relative to other products, roadmap, division strategy
Competition
Project Priorities List
Risks
SWOT analysis
Sources of data for Workbook numbers
Basis for average sales price numbers

BPR Presenter Workbook

The following information provided by the PMM and the Design Manager shall be presented using the template defined in VQFF-1006:

Top-down analysis of unit forecast with assumptions
Bottom-up analysis of unit forecast with assumptions
Product Cost structure analysis from standard online cost model and/or reviewed by manufacturing
Development Costs & Schedule with assumptions
Units, Revenue, Profit, Time to Money, NPV/ROI calculation

- Typical analysis should assume nominal development schedule, ASP and market share
- Worst case analysis should assume loss of 1 of 3 top customers, plus one additional design spin with associated delay, plus greater ASP erosion and lower unit shipments

Scorecards

Attendees will rate the presented product using the scorecard defined in VQFF-1007. The following 15 factors will be rated on a scale of 1–5:

a. Revenue and Profit
b. Quality of Forecasting Methods (sliding scale with BPR level 0–2)
c. Strategic Alignment
d. Customer Needs
e. Standards or Compliance Issues
f. Competitive Analysis
g. Product Positioning
h. Key Requirements & Priorities
i. Risk Management
j. Market Channels & Key Contacts
k. Management Support
l. Resource Availability
m. Core Competencies
n. Dependency Management
o. SWOT analysis

Forecasting Notes

Accurate forecasting of revenue for a new product is notoriously difficult. Cumulative errors of less than 25% in the four factors of revenue (customers, unit volumes, ASPs and timing of ramps) can lead to results that miss or exceed predictions by a factor of two or more. Optimism in forecasting tends to make most products miss rather than exceed their goals. The presenter of a BPR is responsible for forecasting the target revenue within reasonable limits of accuracy.

Exhibit 3 IRR model

P&L Model	Model	Minimum	Mid	Hgh	Breakeven
Revenue	100%	100.0	100.0	100.0	74.6
COGS		43.0	41.0	39.0	30.6
GM	57–62%	57.0	59.0	61.0	44.0
R&D	25–287%	28.0	27.0	25.0	27.0
SG&A	15–197%	19.0	17.0	16.0	17.0
Opinc	15–21%	10.0	15.0	20.0	0.0

60% R&D is direct project spending

Revenue Multiplier	1.0
Investment Multiplier	1.0
Discount Rate	20%

	Year														
	IRR	ROI	NPV	−1	0	1	2	3	4	5	6	7	8	9	10
Minimum, Model 1	34%	2.04	$7.36		(17)	2.14	7.02	9.92	8.14	9.16	7.74	5.60	2.80	2.80	1.68
Minimum, Model 2	33%	2.04	$5.86	(3.36)	(11.76)	0.46	7.02	9.92	8.14	9.16	7.74	5.60	2.80	2.80	1.68
Mid, Model 1	37%	2.19	$8.61		(16)	2.21	7.27	10.27	8.43	9.48	8.01	5.79	2.90	2.90	1.74
Mid, Model 2	35%	2.19	$6.91	(3.24)	(11.34)	0.59	7.27	10.27	8.43	9.48	8.01	5.79	2.90	2.90	1.74
High, Model 1	41%	2.44	$10.36		(15)	2.29	7.52	10.62	8.71	9.80	8.28	5.99	3.00	3.00	1.80
High, Model 2	39%	2.44	$8.39	(3.00)	(10.50)	0.79	7.52	10.62	8.71	9.80	8.28	5.99	3.00	3.00	1.80
Breakeven	26%	1.63	$2.99		(16)	1.65	5.42	7.66	6.29	7.07	5.97	4.32	2.16	2.16	1.30
Breakeven	25%	1.63	$2.23	(3.24)	(11.34)	0.03	5.42	7.66	6.29	7.07	5.97	4.32	2.16	2.16	1.30

Exhibit 4 Sample platform IRRs

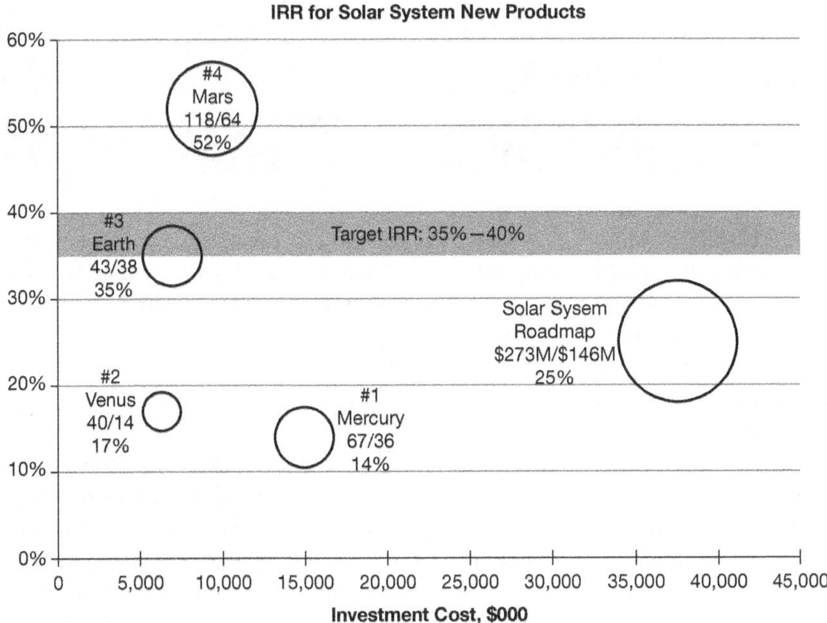

Exhibit 5 IRRs for all current roadmaps

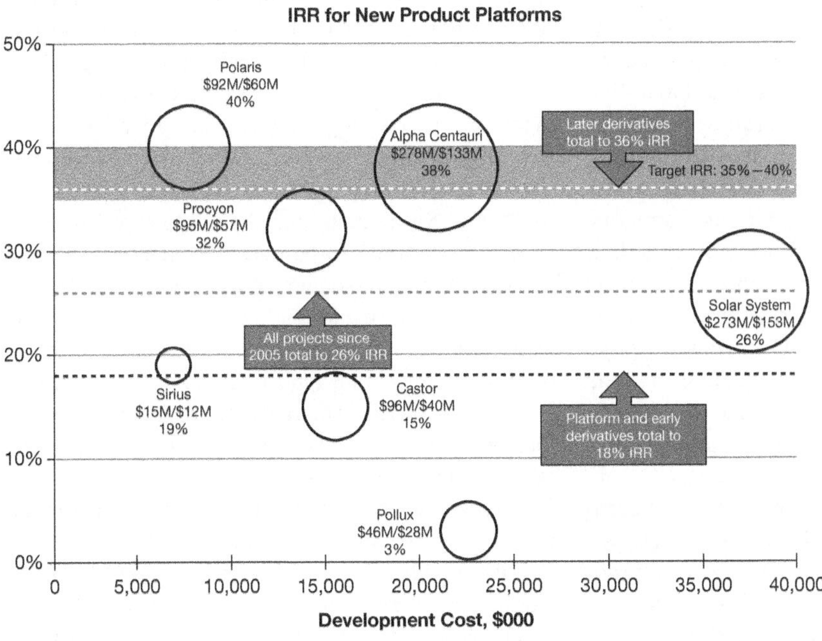

This case was prepared by Professors Kenneth A. Merchant and Marshall Vance and Research Assistant Michelle Spaulding.

CASE STUDY
VisuSon, Inc.: Business Stress Testing

On the evening of Friday, October 10, 2008, Linda Ott sat alone in her office contemplating the year to come. Linda was the founder of VisuSon, Inc. (VSI), a small manufacturer of medical ultrasound equipment, and the only CEO the company had ever had. Linda reflected on the meeting she had had that afternoon with Jonathon Foley, VSI's CFO. At the meeting, they reviewed the company's results for the third quarter just ended and discussed projections for the rest of 2008 and for 2009. The last item on the agenda – the look at 2009 – dominated their discussion and now occupied Linda's thoughts.

Sales were at a record high in the third quarter of 2008. Furthermore, the company's book of confirmed orders provided ample assurance that the fourth quarter, and 2008 as a whole, would continue VSI's established pattern of double-digit growth (see Exhibits 1–3).

But there were dark clouds on the horizon. The Dow Jones Industrial Average had just closed at 8,451, nearly 20% below its level of a week before and down 40% from a year ago. Of more direct importance to VSI, the February collapse of the auction-rate securities market produced some delays in orders and collections, while many US hospitals, VSI's largest group of customers, scrambled to replace their auction-rate debt with alternative sources of capital. Both Linda and Jon believed that this one problem had reduced sales growth for the year by several percentage points from what they had projected at the same meeting a year ago. Both Linda and Jon agreed that a wider credit crisis would negatively impact 2009 sales, but there was no historical precedent on which to base a reliable forecast.

Linda worried about the near-term impact on earnings and the long-term strategic impact of a slowdown while VSI prepared to release its first entirely new product platform in several years. The new platform accounted for nearly 30% of VSI's research and development budget plus more than $10 million in capital expenditures over the last two years. Jon, however, had cautioned against "fixating on sunk costs," as he put it. He believed the company should be focused on cash flow and VSI's own access to financing as much as customer demand. As Linda pored over the numbers and considered various scenarios, she wondered whether Jon might be right.

Ultrasonography

Medical devices for ultrasound imaging (ultrasonography) use high-frequency sound waves to generate graphical representations of soft tissue, organs, and blood flow. This often can be accomplished non-invasively through the application of probes, called transducers, to the surface of the patient's skin. In some important applications, transducers are inserted into body cavities or even into blood vessels to produce better images. Modern ultrasonography equipment is capable of producing moving 3-D images of internal body structures in real time. With the use of so-called Doppler technology and color display, the speed and direction of fluid flow can be accurately measured and displayed. Ultrasonography is generally a less expensive form of radiology than magnetic resonance imaging (MRI) and computed tomography (CT). In contrast to CT and X-Ray imaging, ultrasonography does not expose the patient to potentially harmful radiation. Consequently, ultrasonography has developed into the most common form of radiology for some areas of medicine. Cardiology and obstetrics/gynecology, for example, provide important applications for ultrasonography.

By 2008, the global market for ultrasonography equipment was dominated by four large medical device manufactures that were themselves divisions of global conglomerates. Industry analysts estimated that Philips Healthcare, Siemens Healthcare, GE Healthcare, and Toshiba together controlled approximately 80% of the worldwide market. But the medical ultrasound market remained quite dynamic and innovative with more than a dozen smaller competitors vying for the remaining share. In addition to new and niche competitors from North America and Europe, new entrants into the global market were emerging from other parts of the world, particularly

China. Historically, as smaller competitors established themselves and grew, they were often acquired and absorbed by one of the four dominant players.

Rapidly developing technology and above average growth drove the dynamism of the ultrasonography equipment industry. The US domestic market for medical ultrasound had grown at 4–6% annually for the last decade. Certain segments, especially cardiology and so-called hand-carried ultrasound (HCU), were projected to grow much faster than the overall market. By 2008, industry analysts believed that the US market, which accounted for more than 40% of the global market, had reached saturation. New sales were primarily replacing older technology. In contrast, markets in the developing world were expected to grow at annual rates above 5% for at least the next five to seven years.

Company Background

VSI manufactured its ultrasonography systems at a plant in Apple Valley, California, and sold them worldwide through a network of independent distributors. The firm began as Visutech Partners in 1998, commercializing and licensing novel signal processing and visualization algorithms pioneered by Linda Ott's former academic research laboratory.

After several years of initial development efforts, the fledgling firm signed a licensing agreement with Bainbridge Manufacturing. At the time, Bainbridge was a contract manufacturer of components for the medical ultrasound market. It possessed considerable manufacturing expertise but lacked proprietary technology of its own. Bainbridge hoped to use the licensed technology to move up from lower-margin contract manufacturing into the more profitable market for integrated ultrasonography systems. By the time Bainbridge's new system had won approval from the US Food and Drug Administration, Visutech had merged with a unit of Bainbridge, forming VSI with Linda as the Chief Executive and the former head of the Bainbridge unit as the newly independent firm's Chief Operating Officer. Linda's former principal research collaborator, Dr. Simon Lee, was retained as Director of Engineering (see Exhibit 4).

As a new firm entering a market dominated by much larger firms, VSI chose to target a mid-tier niche. It focused on cardiology applications where it believed its proprietary technology conferred the greatest advantage. VSI targeted its initial offerings well. Within its first six years, its systems were in use in hospitals and medical practices across all 50 states and in most countries in Western Europe. One major competitor responded to VSI's entry into their market by negotiating an agreement under which they resold VSI's top-of-the-line system under their own brand. Though nearly 70% of its revenues still came from the domestic market, with the addition of two global distributors, VSI's expansion into Asia and Latin America had begun.

VisuSon, Inc. in 2008

By the start of 2008, VSI had grown to just over 200 full-time employees. Of this number, roughly half were in manufacturing. The engineering department employed a staff of 25 scientists and engineers supported by a dozen technicians. As most sales were handled through distributors, the sales and marketing staff totaled just 25 employees. The accounting and finance, information technology, human resources and payroll, and legal staffs, all reporting to Jon Foley, made up the remainder.

As medical diagnostic devices, VSI's products were subject to extensive regulations by a number of governmental authorities. Chief among these was the US Food and Drug Administration (FDA). In addition to its role of overseeing and approving pre-clinical testing of VSI's products, the FDA also oversaw registration of VSI's manufacturing facility and compliance with the FDA Quality System Regulation. Consequently, all of VSI's manufacturing employees were required to learn and maintain proficiency with the company's stringent quality control and recording systems. Together with the skills and training required for the manufacturing process, this slowed the process of bringing newly hired manufacturing employees up to full productivity and placed a premium on the retention of skilled employees. VSI's only seasonal or part-time employees were clerical. Accounting and legal temps were used to fill occasional staffing shortages.

Beyond the impact it had on the manufacturing process, regulation drove the new product release process. All of VSI's products were required to obtain pre-market clearance as FDA 510(k) Class II devices before they could be sold in the domestic market. Typically, the process of pre-market notification and clearance for VSI's products required two to three months, but for the most innovative products, it could take substantially longer. For example, the process of earning clearance for VSI's first intravenous transducer catheter required well over a year.

VSI's systems were modular platforms, enabling incremental expansion or enhancement of their functionality. As transducer technology advanced, VSI introduced new and improved probes. These new components could be added to existing platforms. Frequently, this necessitated concurrent upgrades to the processing and control software. Less frequently, VSI upgraded the digital signal processing unit at the core of each system. Since the introduction of VSI's original platform, the Alpha-PD, it had introduced just one new platform, the smaller and less costly Delta-CV. In 2007, both platforms were enhanced and were now marketed as Alpha-PDx and Delta-CVx. Customers with older devices were able to purchase upgrades to bring their existing devices up to the latest standard.

Sales to new customers typically resulted from a lengthy process. In general, the time from initial contact with a VSI distributor to the final delivery and acceptance was between 12 and 18 months. Existing customers periodically purchased new probes or other system upgrades, but even these smaller sales could normally be measured in months from inception to delivery. Platform sales to new customers and often to existing customers were competitive. It was not uncommon for customers to require competing vendors to place equipment at the customer's location for direct comparison and evaluation. For especially promising or demanding accounts, VSI provided not only equipment but staff sonographers to augment the distributor representatives in demonstrating equipment and training customer personnel.

Due to the length of the sales cycle, VSI began each year with a strong indication of the volume of sales to be expected in the coming year. For more than two-thirds of their annual platform sales, the sales cycle was already underway before the beginning of the year. Moreover, VSI kept careful track of its end customers. The company's knowledge of its customers and their applications for its systems were invaluable in forecasting the number who would purchase upgrades. This helped VSI develop quarterly and annual sales targets for its distributors.

The budgeting process

The overall market for medical ultrasound equipment had historically expanded at an annual growth rate of 4–6%, and the market segments on which VSI focused grew at an even faster clip. Thus, from the early years of the firm, VSI's management systems were designed to allow the firm to cope with rapid growth. The budgeting process was a key element of the firm's management system. The budget provided the foundation for VSI's planning, control, and incentive systems.

VSI's planning and budgeting cycle started 13 months prior to the start of the company's fiscal year (see Exhibit 5). It began with the annual meeting of the Radiological Society of North America (RSNA), which was held in late November of each year. This professional conference was well attended by radiologists and other physicians from across North America and beyond. It also featured an exhibit space where virtually all of the radiology equipment vendors came to show their latest offerings. The meeting was an opportunity for VSI to meet with its most important North American distributors, key customers, and prospects. Initial feedback gathered at RSNA allowed VSI sales and marketing to develop business forecasts for the coming year.

Coincident with the RSNA meeting, industry analysts would release their annual updates of market growth, market share, and five-year forecasts. VSI did not rely on these market analyses for forecasting the next year's sales. The state of the sales pipeline and distributor quota commitments were far more useful for near-term sales forecasting. But the market analyses aided VSI's marketing team in planning and positioning the firm and its products for the years beyond.

Engineering managers, together with product managers from the marketing team, would begin finalizing specifics and features for any new products to be introduced at the next year's RSNA meeting shortly after they returned from the current year's meeting. This was necessary as the FDA pre-market certification process required months and needed to be successfully concluded ahead of the next meeting. A detailed understanding of the features of the product line was required in order to anticipate unit costs and relative market competitiveness as well as to develop pricing plans. Engineering personnel, together with specialists in the legal department, were responsible for the FDA 510(k) pre-market notification process. Typically, VSI sought certification from the FDA before pursuing certification from foreign regulators.

By early February, on the basis of the plans provided by the engineering and marketing departments, the manufacturing department would begin to generate bills of materials, labor standards, and cost estimates. Capacity projections and capital equipment requirements were also developed by manufacturing as part of this process. Manufacturing would initiate negotiations with suppliers to meet their anticipated needs for components, subassemblies, and any additional capital equipment required by the manufacturing process. Though underway by midyear, these agreements would not be finalized before December when the budgets were finalized and then approved by VSI's board of directors.

While engineering was navigating the approval process and manufacturing was developing cost estimates, it fell to sales to begin working with the distributors. Although most distributor agreements were renewed each December as part of the quota commitment process, sales worked with the distributors throughout the year. In addition to monitoring current sales activity and achievements toward quota, the sales department worked through a formal review and evaluation process with each distributor of the partnership's performance over the previous year. At the same time, the distributors provided feedback on developing sales leads for the coming year. Together with the distributors, sales would formulate plans to support these sales efforts with VSI demonstration and training staff as well as evaluation equipment. Sales would also begin providing distributors with advanced marketing information concerning forthcoming offerings in order to elicit feedback on anticipated volume and market pricing. Though most distribution and sales agreements included confidentiality clauses, the distribution network was a valuable source of competitive intelligence regarding expected features and pricing by competitors. This information was combined into a preliminary sales forecast provided to the budget committee by mid-August of each year.

On the basis of the preliminary forecast from sales and their own planning effort for any new products, manufacturing developed and submitted a draft labor budget to human resources (HR). The other departments also submitted staffing requests at this time, but the manufacturing labor budget was the most critical. HR was responsible for developing the staffing and training schedule for the coming year. As part of this process, HR reviewed the salary and wage surveys it purchased from consultants to ensure that VSI kept pace with the competitive labor markets. Salaries and wages were a significant cost category for VSI. This information was critical for developing department managers' merit pay budgets for the coming year as well as for refining the direct labor budget. The most intensive phase of the budget process took place each September. By this point in the year, the volume of sales and product mix for the coming year was relatively predictable. Combining the updated sales forecast distributed by the sales department at the beginning of the month with salary, wage, and staffing information provided by HR, department managers developed detailed budgets for their departments using a standardized spreadsheet produced by the Accounting Department. The design of the spreadsheet largely automated the roll-up of department budgets to higher organizational levels. But in the budgeting review processes, changes were inevitably suggested, forcing negotiations and revisions. The budgeting review effort was intensive, but the process was not overly cumbersome because VSI's management consisted of fewer than 20 individuals. Finally, in December, VSI's executive committee, and then the board of directors, approved the consolidated budget.

Management of cash and working capital was a critical issue for this small, rapidly growing company. VSI management and its bankers agreed that the firm should typically hold six weeks of operating expenditures in its cash accounts. In an effort to be responsive to the needs of its distributors and customers, VSI maintained a policy of holding 30–40 days' forward sales in finished goods inventory. Finished goods accounted for just more than 40% of the total value of inventory, with the remainder split about equally between work in process and raw materials. At the other end of its operating cycle, VSI's accounts receivable balance hovered between 60 and 80 days of trailing sales. In an effort to minimize net operating capital, VSI maintained accounts payable and accrued liabilities at the highest levels possible while still taking advantage of all available trade credits for prompt payment. Likewise, expenses were only prepaid when required. Nonetheless, its long operating cycle and high growth rate required VSI to finance this growing investment in working capital through short-term borrowing against the value of its accounts receivable and inventories. Thus, before any budget could be considered viable, it required review and approval by the finance department.

Anywhere from one-third to one-half of the managers' cash compensation was tied to achievement of objectives set by the executive committee and the board at the start of each year. For first-level managers, one-third of cash compensation was considered "at-risk," with the level rising to 50% for Linda. For most managers, achievement of budget objectives was weighted 50% in importance for determining the annual bonus. The remaining 50% was based on achievement of other quantified goals and/or a subjective evaluation of performance.

The new challenge

The budget that Jon Foley delivered to Linda earlier in the day was based on an assumption of 10% revenue growth for 2009 (see Exhibits 6 and 7), a level that had been considered quite conservative just a month earlier. It included plans to bolster Asia/Pacific and Latin American sales support by hiring more account managers and sonographers and by devoting additional demonstration equipment to these markets. While it included no plans for major product releases in 2009, engineering and marketing planned to begin the FDA 510(k) process for approval of the new hand-carried ultrasound (HCU) platform targeted for release in 2010. Recently, the HCU market had grown faster than the cart-based segment where VSI currently competed. Analysts were forecasting an acceleration of the shift toward greater use of HCUs. Linda and the board were eager to enter this new market segment.

With the assumption of 10% growth, most first-level management perceived that they would face tight resource constraints. Manufacturing headcount and manufacturing compensation were budgeted to grow by only 6.4% and 9.0%, respectively. Capital expenditures were actually budgeted to fall significantly as the firm more fully utilized existing capacity. Additional investments were expected to accompany the new HCU platform introduction in 2010. By far the most significant growth in operating expenses would come from expansion of the sales staff, with total compensation expense in sales and marketing budgeted to increase by slightly less than 40%. This was considered an investment required to maximize the potential growth from new product introductions in subsequent years. Growth in engineering head count of 12% and engineering compensation of just over 15% was in equal parts justified by growth in manufacturing capacity and the installed base and by development of the new product line. Finally, the roughly 12% growth in headcount and compensation expense within finance was deemed necessary to support growth in the other three functions.

However, while the strategic importance of growing into new markets and keeping ahead of the technology would not change, continuation of the market's and VSI's high rates of growth could not be assured. The US domestic market was dominated by private not-for-profit hospitals, which rely in part on endowments like those of some private universities. The nearly 40% fall in equity market values was sure to adversely affect such investment portfolios. Government-owned hospitals were already anticipating funding shortages because the slowdown was reducing tax revenues. In addition, the crisis was likely to reduce demand for elective procedures, further reducing all hospitals' revenues and spending. Consequently, analysts were beginning to speculate about a decrease in capital spending by US hospitals of as much as 14% in 2009. Yet, it was unclear how capital spending on radiology generally, and sonography in particular, might be affected. As the bulk of sales in the domestic market were replacements for older technology, many customers could defer purchases.

Customers had already shifted purchases to later in the year during 2008. Linda and others at VSI feared that this pattern could become more pronounced due to the developing recession. With limited workforce flexibility, VSI would be forced to choose between building inventory early in 2009 or risking stocking out later in the year. Fortunately, the sales mix was expected to remain essentially fixed, as it was driven by customers' clinical requirements rather than by financial factors.

As Linda reviewed the spreadsheet Jon Foley had prepared for the 2009 budget, she considered his words of caution. Jon believed that in the short term VSI's fate could be determined by how well they managed cash and by their ability to access bank financing. He felt that all plans should be built upon an assumption of reduced gross debt levels and improved debt ratios. He suggested that they "prepare for the worst and hope for the best," and advocated beginning a policy of "deferring expenditures and wringing cash out of the working capital accounts." Jon argued that committing to plans for growth was risky and that "modest cuts now [could] avert severe cuts later." While Linda had come to rely on Jon's financial expertise, her trusted friend and collaborator, Simon Lee, had privately criticized the CFO as overly cautious and Peter Beeson had on more than one occasion dismissed him as "just a bean counter." In contrast, Tom Nelson, VSI's COO, who had worked with Jon at Bainbridge, never made a significant proposal without having Jon first vet the numbers.

Linda knew that deferring planned investments, let alone cutting back, would limit the company's capacity for growth in 2009 and beyond. Recognizing that any course of action would create some controversy within the management team, she wondered how exposed VSI was to a decrease in sales, which might be imminent. How great a downturn could the company endure without having to make the sort of deep cuts that would choke off future growth? And might VSI's own survival be threatened if market conditions became really unfavorable?

Exhibit 1 Income statements

Income statement	2008 (estimated)	9 months ended 9/30/08	2007	2006
Revenues (net)	$59,766	$44,227	$52,994	$47,443
Cost of goods sold	27,269	20,224	24,806	22,930
Gross margin	32,498	24,003	28,188	24,513
Operating expenses				
Selling	10,663	7,921	9,581	8,705
R&D	7,566	5,744	6,646	5,856
General and administrative	7,458	5,611	7,028	6,673
Operating income	6,811	4,728	4,933	3,279
Interest expense	1,060	773	886	653
Income before tax	5,751	3,955	4,046	2,626
Tax	2,013	1,384	1,416	919
Income before extraordinary items	3,738	2,570	2,630	1,707
Extraordinary items (net of tax)	–	–		
Net income	$3,738	$2,570	$2,630	$1,707

Exhibit 2 Balance sheets

Balance sheet	2008 (estimated)	9 months ended 9/30/08	2007	2006	2005
Current assets					
Cash	$5,930	$5,448	$5,258	$4,701	$4,178
Accounts receivable (net)	12,898	12,153	11,436	10,238	9,093
Inventories	6,767	6,216	6,000	5,371	4,770
Prepaid expenses	2,030	1,835	1,800	1,611	1,431
Total current assets	27,625	25,652	24,494	21,922	19,472
Non-current assets					
Property, plant, and equipment	26,531	26,945	24,108	21,583	19,167
Less accumulated depreciation	6,323	6,353	6,356	6,430	6,483
	20,208	20,592	17,752	15,152	12,685
Other assets	4,282	4,209	3,522	2,988	2,466
	–	–			
Total assets	$52,115	$50,454	$45,767	$40,063	$34,624
Current liabilities					
Accounts payable	4,496	4,348	4,423	3,960	3,516
Notes payable	14,860	14,640	12,040	9,470	6,210
Tax payable	384	253	368	239	111
Accrued liabilities	2,437	2,357	2,397	2,146	1,906
Current portion of long-term debt	339	339	339	339	339
Total current liabilities	22,516	21,938	19,568	16,154	12,083
Non-current liabilities					
Long-term debt	348	433	687	1,027	1,366
Total liabilities	22,865	22,371	20,255	17,180	13,448
Owners' equity					
Common stock	189	189	189	189	189
Additional paid-in-capital	4,546	4,546	4,546	4,546	4,546
Retained earnings	24,516	23,348	20,777	18,147	16,440
Total owners' equity	29,251	28,083	25,512	22,882	21,175
Total liabilities and equity	$52,115	$50,454	$45,767	$40,063	$34,624

Exhibit 3 Statements of cash flows

Statement of cash flows	2008 (estimated)	9 months ended 9/30/08	2007	2006
OPERATIONS:				
Net income	$3,738	$2,570	$2,630	$1,707
Adjustments to reconcile:				
Depreciation and amortization	5,182	3,836	4,275	3,813
Accounts receivable	(1,462)	(717)	(1,198)	(1,146)
Inventories	(767)	(216)	(628)	(601)
Prepaid expenses	(230)	(35)	(189)	(180)
Accounts payable	73	(75)	463	443
Tax payable	15	(115)	129	128
Accrued liabilities	40	(41)	251	240
Cash flow from operating activities	6,590	5,208	5,734	4,405
INVESTING:				
Additions to PP&E	6,509	5,845	5,978	5,482
Acquisitions of technology licenses	1,889	1,519	1,430	1,321
Cash flow used for investing activities	8,398	7,364	7,409	6,803
FINANCING:				
Borrowing of notes payable	14,860	11,510	12,040	9,470
Repayments of notes payable	(12,040)	(8,910)	(9,470)	(6,210)
Long-term borrowing	–	–	–	–
Repayment of long-term debt	(339)	(254)	(339)	(339)
Cash dividends paid	–	–	–	–
Cash flow from (used by) financing	2,481	2,346	2,231	2,921
Net increase (decrease) in cash	$673	$190	$557	$523
	2,481	2,346	2,231	2,921
Cash paid for income taxes	$1,621	$1,122	$1,287	$791
Cash paid for interest	$1,054	$780	$846	$614

Exhibit 4 VisuSon, Inc.: Organization chart

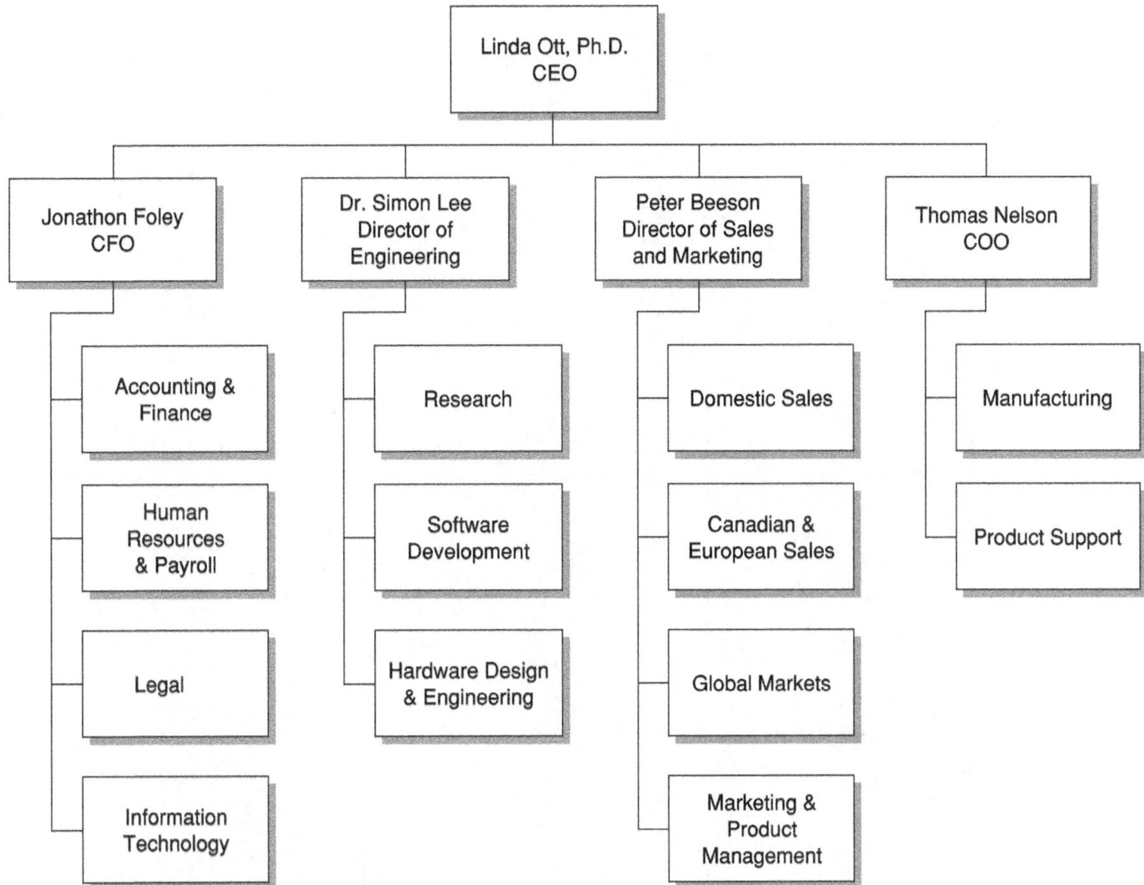

Exhibit 5 Budget timeline

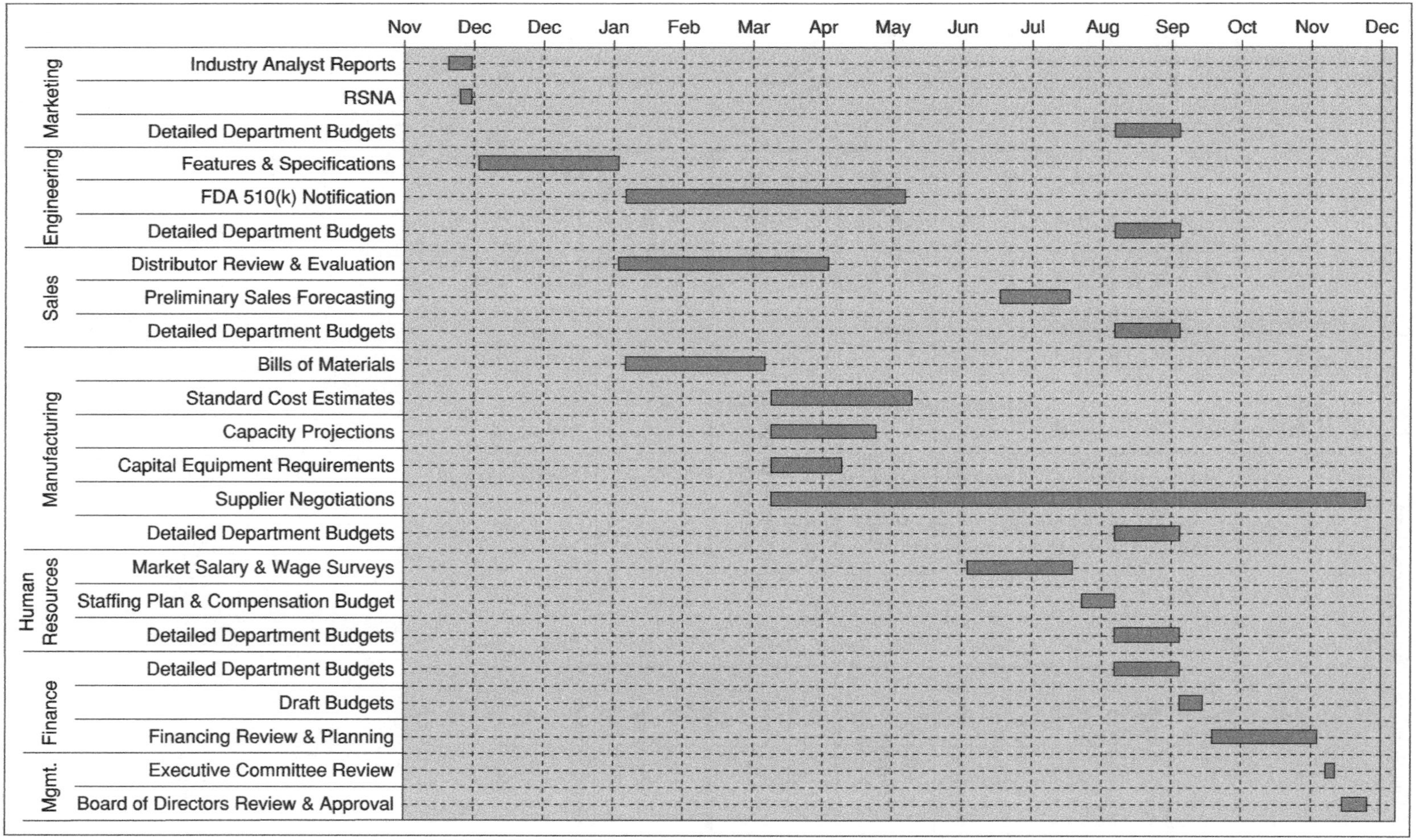

Exhibit 6 Staffing

Staffing Budget	Current FTE	Estimated attrition	Requested FTE	Anticipated need (excess)	Estimated wage increase
Manufacturing:					
Management	4	–	4	–	3.0%
Supervisory	8	1	8	1	2.0%
Labor & Technical	92	4	98	10	2.0%
Clerical	5	1	6	2	0.0%
	109	6	116	13	
Engineering:					
Management	4	–	4	–	3.5%
Science	5	–	5	–	3.0%
Engineering	16	1	16	1	3.6%
Technical	11	1	14	4	2.6%
Clerical	6	1	8	3	0.0%
	42	3	47	8	
Sales & Marketing:					
Management	5	–	5	–	2.0%
Commissioned	4	1	5	2	1.5%
Professional	6	–	9	3	2.7%
Technical	10	2	15	7	3.0%
	25	3	34	12	
Finance Division:					
Management	5	–	5	–	3.0%
Professional	9	1	9	1	3.0%
Technical	6		8	2	1.8%
Clerical	12	2	13	3	0.0%
	32	3	35	6	
	208	15	232	39	

Exhibit 7 Summary budget

2009 Budgeted income summary				Comments and analysis
Revenues (net)			$65,743	10% growth
Cost of goods				
Direct materials		12,742		
Direct labor		6,959		
Manufacturing overhead				
Salary and wages	4,078			Includes $160 for management bonuses
Depreciation and amortization	3,148			Includes $596 on 2009 investments
Miscellaneous	2,919	10,145	29,846	Includes indirect materials, utilities, and maintenance: 74% fixed
Gross margin			35,897	
Operating expense				
Selling				
Salary and wages	2,807			Includes estimated commissions of $965 + $190 management bonus
Marketing and advertising	5,036			85% discretionary / 15% variable
Shipping	1,747			95% variable, based on estimated forward rates
Sales promotion funding	1,972	11,562		Discretionary-variable
Research and development				
Salary and wages	4,934			Includes $210 for management bonuses
Depreciation and amortization	1,712			Includes $430 on 2009 investments
Consulting	1,640			Discretionary
Miscellaneous	39	8,325		Discretionary
General and admin.				
Salary and wages	6,567			Includes $445 for management bonuses
Travel and training	2,060			Discretionary
Depreciation and amortization	791			
Miscellaneous	395	9,813	29,700	Includes $105 of contract labor: 20% variable
Operating income			6,197	
Interest expense			1,250	At assumed rate of working capital growth
Before tax income			$4,947	
Capital expenditure			$5,960	92% for replacements and license renewals

This case was prepared by Research Assistant David P. Huelsbeck and Professor Kenneth A. Merchant.

CHAPTER 9
Incentive Systems

One of the primary principles of effective management is that rewards should be the third thing you work on. Measurements should come second, and both rewards and measurements should be subordinated to performance definition; i.e., clear and unambiguous articulation of what needs to be done.

Steven Kerr, Chief Learning Office, Goldman Sachs[1]

The third major element of financial results control systems deals with the provision of organizational rewards; that is, the design of incentive systems. As per the opening quote above, incentives follow performance definition. Performance definition, described by Kerr as the "clear and unambiguous articulation of what needs to be done," includes both defining desired performance and assigning responsibility for achieving the desired results. Defining desired performance and setting adequately challenging performance targets in the desired performance areas are among the main purposes of planning and budgeting systems, which we discussed in Chapter 8. Designing responsibility centers, which we discussed in Chapter 7, determines the accountability for the desired result areas. Incentive systems, which we discuss in this chapter, tie rewards (and/or punishments) to the performance evaluations. Incentive systems are important because they reinforce the definitions of the desired result areas and motivate employees to achieve and exceed the performance targets. Section IV of this text focuses exclusively on the important topic of performance measurements, which drive the performance evaluations and associated incentives in most organizations.

Hereafter, we use the term *incentives* to refer primarily to things that employees value – (positive) *rewards*. That said, organizations can, and do, also provide some negative rewards, or *punishments* or *penalties*.[2] In an organizational context, however, punishments commonly manifest themselves through an *absence* of positive rewards, such as not being paid a bonus or being passed over for a promotion. Naming and shaming is another type of unpleasant experience (hence, punishment) that employees would rather avoid. For example, at Black & Decker's semiannual meeting of division heads, managers who had met their budget targets sat on the left side of the room, whereas those who had failed to meet their targets were asked to sit on the right in order to explain to the others why they had not met their targets. Mr. Archibald, the executive chairman, explained proudly: "They hate being over on the right. We think this kind of peer competition is motivational." In a similar fashion, China's Haier, the large consumer appliances company, uses naming and shaming by prominently displaying photographs of managers throughout the company with a red smiley face for good performance and a yellow frowning one for those doing poorly.[3]

Table 9.1 lists some of the types of rewards that organizations use. Note that many of these rewards are *non-monetary*. Although it is widely accepted that individuals universally value money, it is equally correct to suggest that monetary rewards are not the only thing that people

Table 9.1 Examples of positive and negative rewards

Positive rewards	Negative rewards (punishments)
Autonomy	Interference in job from superiors
Power	Loss of job
Opportunities to participate in important decision-making processes	Zero salary increase
Salary increases	Assignment to unimportant tasks
Bonuses	Chastisement (public or private)
Stock options	No promotion
Restricted stock	Demotion
Praise	Public humiliation
Recognition	
Promotions	
Titles	
Job assignments	
Office assignments	
Reserved parking places	
Country club memberships	
Job security	
Merchandise prizes	
Vacation trips	
Participation in executive development programs	
Time off	

Source: K. A. Merchant, *Modern Management Control Systems: Text and Cases* (Upper Saddle River, NJ: Prentice Hall, 1998), p. 427

value.[4] When properly chosen, non-monetary rewards will be greatly appreciated by employees, and in many cases, they place a smaller financial burden on the firm. For example,

> **While raises or bonuses are not unimportant, especially in [an] uncertain financial climate, [survey evidence suggests] that workers across a spectrum of ages – from Baby Boomers who have worked hard to reach the peaks of their career, to Generation X'ers struggling to satisfy professional ambitions and personal fulfillment, to Millennials who view work/life balance as their right – are looking for a remix of conventional rewards. Many of these don't cost a dime but pay off in increased engagement, loyalty, and willingness to go the extra mile. For example, when surveyed about the possibility of working remotely, 83% of Millennials and 75% of Boomers say that the freedom to choose when and where they work motivates them to give 110%.[5]**

Therefore, organizations typically do not rely on just a single form of rewards. In many for-profit firms, various monetary incentives in the form of cash or stock usually go up and down with performance. But a manager's autonomy, authority, recognition, and status often do, too. Corporate managers can (threaten to) reduce the decision autonomy of entity managers by refusing to fund investments in entities where performance is poor. In entities where performance is excellent, they can grant managers additional power and increase their recognition within the firm by publicizing the results. Employees who climb the corporate ladder also often are given various *perks* (discretionary rewards), such as the opportunity to travel first class, to pick a larger office, to be given first choice for vacation scheduling, to have a preferred parking spot, and so on.

This chapter first describes the purposes of incentives. It then focuses mainly on monetary incentives to discuss various important incentive system decisions that organizations need to consider, such as about the extent to which the incentives are determined formulaically, the shape of the incentive-performance function, and the form and size of incentive pay. The chapter concludes by providing a set of criteria for evaluating incentive systems.

Purposes of incentives

Performance-dependent rewards, or incentives, provide the impetus for the alignment of employees' natural self-interests with the organization's objectives. They provide three types of management control benefits. The first is *informational*. The rewards attract employees' attention and inform or remind them of the relative importance of often-competing results areas, such as cost, quality, customer service, asset management, and growth. Merely telling employees that customer service, for example, is important might have some effect on their behaviors. But including customer service measures in annual bonus plans is more likely to convince them to emphasize customer service. In other words, the rewards signal which performance areas are important and help employees decide how to *direct* their efforts. For this reason, the informational aspect of incentives is sometimes also referred to as the *effort-directing* purpose.

A pertinent example is the global financial services company, Barclays. Reeling from misselling practices by branch personnel of insurance, loans, and bank accounts, which it believed their commission payments had encouraged, the company decided that "Barclays staff will no longer be paid any commission for selling financial policies," but that "from now on, any bonuses will be dependent entirely on giving customers good quality service" because "the key to Barclays long-term success is the level of service we provide, not how many products we sell."[6] Also in banks, brands have been shown to be shaped less by advertising and marketing than by their customers' experiences. "In such cases, customers get the message only if employees do," which is why some banks, like HSBC, link the pay of some of their employees to indicators of brand health.[7]

The informational purpose of incentives is equally pertinently illustrated by the case when Bob Dudley, the UK oil group's new chief executive at BP, vowed to improve BP's safety culture upon taking the helm following the company's deep-sea oil well disaster in the Gulf of Mexico. To make his point, Mr. Dudley announced that the company had decided that bonuses for the fourth quarter of 2010 would be based *solely* on how employees perform in terms of safety and risk management. BP would honor the existing performance contracts for the first three quarters of the year, but the fourth quarter's performance would be measured "solely according to each business's progress in reducing operational risks and achieving excellent safety and compliance standards," he said. In so doing, Mr. Dudley signaled in no uncertain terms that the company was "absolutely clear that safety, compliance and operational risk management [was to be] BP's number one priority, well ahead of all other priorities."[8]

The second control benefit is *motivational*. Some employees need incentives to exert the extra effort required to perform tasks well; that is, to work hard, do a good job, and succeed.[9] In other words, this purpose of incentives is sometimes also called the *effort-inducing* purpose.

Sometimes even hard-working employees need incentives to overcome their natural aversion to some difficult or tedious actions that are in their organization's best interest, such as working cooperatively with other divisions to resolve customer complaints, making cold sales calls to get more business, preparing paperwork, or training employees. The crucial point here, however, is that the incentive systems are designed to encourage the desired behaviors, and not to crowd them out.[10]

The third control benefit is *attraction and retention* of personnel. Performance-dependent rewards are an important part of many employees' total compensation package. Some rewards are promised because the organization wants to improve employee recruitment (*selection*) and retention, either by offering a package that is comparable or superior to the packages offered by their competitors or in the relevant labor market, or by linking payments to an employee's continued employment. Some firms also overtly offer compensation packages with below-average *base salaries* but with performance-dependent compensation elements (*variable pay*) that provide the opportunity to earn above-average total compensation if excellent performance is forthcoming. These packages tend to appeal to employees who are entrepreneurial, rather than risk averse, and those who are confident about their abilities to achieve. These efforts to use compensation packages to attract and retain the most suitable employees often form a key element of firms' personnel control strategy, as discussed in Chapter 3.

Finally, incentive systems also serve several *non-control purposes*. Incentive systems that are performance-dependent make compensation *more variable with firm performance*. This decreases cash outlays when performance is poor and, thus, smooths earnings, because compensation expense is lower when profits are lower. This purpose is clearly articulated in a recent survey of practice, and inevitably put into the context of the aforementioned attraction and retention purpose:

> "Organizations are under immense pressure to keep costs in line to remain competitive, and as a result, we are seeing more than 90 percent of companies shifting more of their spending to variable pay because this type of strategy enables them to recognize and reward performance without growing their fixed cost," said Ken Abosch [at compensation consultant] Aon Hewitt. "Pay is a top engagement driver for employees, and as the market continues to improve, organizations will need to differentiate through variable pay programs to attract and retain top talent."[11]

Incentive system design choices can also affect a firm's *tax payments*. Some forms of compensation are not deductible for tax purposes, and some deductions are limited. For example, Section 162(m) of the US Internal Revenue Code limits the deductibility of compensation in excess of $1 million paid to an employee unless the compensation qualifies as "performance-based." The intent of this law was to discourage high guaranteed payments to executives in situations where shareholders were not benefiting (presumably because the fixed pay is not performance-based).[12]

Government regulations also affect compensation arrangements in organizations, thus driving another important concern of incentive system design – *compliance*. For example, concerns for compliance were heightened following the financial crisis of 2008, especially in banks, where lawmakers and regulators, although with significant variations across countries, mandated or tinkered with caps on bonuses and deferred bonuses as well as restrictions on how bonuses are paid out (such as, for example, in deferred shares instead of cash).[13] Firms respond to these restrictions by finding ways to maintain competitive compensation packages. The following quote illustrates this: "Banks are now rushing to find ways to maintain overall levels of compensation. With bonuses limited to a small multiple of salaries and banks unwilling to greatly increase their fixed costs, many firms – including Goldman – are hoping to bridge the gap by introducing *role-based allowances*" (italics added).[14] The idea behind these role-based allowances is that they would not qualify as bonuses as defined by the regulator (such as by being based on seniority or "role" instead of on performance) and thus would not count toward the bonus cap, while having some characteristics of bonuses such as being adjustable upward or downward each year. One could therefore maintain that the regulation has led to a new form of compensation – so-called *allowances* – that fall somewhere between fixed pay and bonuses,[15] and which, for this reason, will be closely scrutinized by the regulators.[16]

While this chapter focuses on the management control benefits of incentives, it must be recognized that the control and non-control purposes of incentive systems can, and must, sometimes be traded off against each other. Consequently, observing organizations' incentive practices does not necessarily provide definitive clues as to which incentives they find to be most effective for control purposes.

Monetary incentives

Money is an important form of reward that is often linked to performance, particularly at management levels in organizations. Monetary incentives certainly are not the only form of reward, and they may not even always be the best one, but their use is common. There are three primary ways through which monetary incentives can be provided: performance-based salary increases, short-term incentive plans, and long-term incentive plans. Note that the term "performance-based" is key to distinguishing incentives from entitlements. When we use incentives hereafter, we presume them to be performance- or merit-based, instead of amounts being awarded as cost-of-living adjustments or on the basis of seniority, custom (e.g. a holiday "bonus" depending on salary band rather than performance), or collective bargaining agreements.

That is not to say that there is agreement about the extent to which pay should be performance-based. Indeed, views on this vary widely. For example, a survey in the United Kingdom revealed that, in the private sector, 54% of the responding employees believe that their salary should reflect their own performance, 36% think it should reflect inflation, and 32% feel it should reflect their experience. In the public sector, however, the percentages are 36% performance, 55% inflation, and 33% experience. These variations support the aforementioned *selection* purpose of incentives – that is, different incentive incentives systems will attract, or can be designed to attract, different types of individuals to different types of organizations. Indeed, the survey also suggested that while "public sector workers agreed that private sector workers should be paid based on how well they perform, they are more reluctant to see their own pay linked to individual performance (36%), that of their team (11%) or that of their organization (5%)."[17]

Salary increases

Organizations give, or at least consider, salary increases to their employees typically each year. These salary increases are minimally cost-of-living adjustments. But they can also be seen as an incentive when at least some portion of the raise is merit-based. Salary increases are typically a small proportion of an employee's salary, but they have considerable value because they are not just a one-time or lump-sum payment; instead, they provide a permanent increment because employees' salaries are rarely reduced (although, in years of austerity, further increases may be put on hold).

Salary increases can be seen as an incentive when they are expected to be "earned" through performance or the acquisition of skills that promise improved performance in future periods. Even the Vatican has apparently introduced an "element of incentive" into its salary system, as it takes into account issues such as "dedication, professionalism, productivity and correctitude" when awarding pay raises.[18]

Short-term incentives

Many organizations in the private sector, but also increasingly those in the public sector, in a growing number of countries, use short-term incentives, which include bonuses, commissions, and piece-rate payments. Incentives have become so widespread that some have claimed that they are "overused" and that they "emerge as the first answer to almost every problem" in the sense of:

> **Is the medical system inefficient? Set up a managed care system that provides financial incentives to doctors, insurers, patients, and hospitals. Bad customer service? Provide financial incentives for better customer service. Airplanes not flying on time? Pay employees if the planes fly on time, and so on.[19]**

The primary rationale for variable pay is to differentiate pay; that is, to provide rewards in accordance with an employee's contributions to the organization, hence the notion of *pay-for-performance* or *variable pay*. Such pay is meant to provide the *motivation* for employees to go the "extra" proverbial mile for the "extra" compensation. But such compensation is also *risk-sharing* because the employee (employer) receives (pays) the incentive compensation only when the performance on which it is based has been realized; hence, the notion of *at-risk pay* from the employee's side. For the employer, however, this feature makes compensation expense more variable with performance, where compensation expense is higher (lower) when performance is better (worse), and thus, when the firm can best (least) afford the higher (lower) pay.

Short-term incentives typically provide cash payments (although other forms of payment such as in the form of equity are also possible) based on performance measured over periods of one year or less. The awards are often called *annual incentive pay* or *bonuses*. The awards can be based on the performance of a single individual, or on that of a group of which an individual is a member, such as a work team, a profit center, or even the firm as a whole. Probably the most commonly used performance metrics in annual bonus plans are financial; or to put differently, there are very few bonus plans that would not have at least some financial performance metric included.[20] For example, a division manager's bonus could be calculated as a percentage of the division's profits up to a maximum (e.g. not to exceed, or capped at, half the manager's annual salary). But there are innumerable ways to set *bonus formulas*, the key parameters of which we discuss in more detail in a later section.

In addition to financial measures of performance, the incentive plan can also include bonus payments contingent on achievements in nonfinancial performance areas. For example, 30% of an entity manager's bonus could be based on meeting targets for customer satisfaction and a further 10% based on meeting targets for environmental performance. In some cases, nonfinancial performance is the dominant portion. At Lloyd's and Royal Bank of Scotland, for example, individual sales performance represents only a small fraction (less than 5%) of the bonus of retail banking personnel; the rest is based on customer service and satisfaction levels.[21]

When the bonus formula in annual incentive plans includes multiple performance dimensions, bonuses can be earned, sometimes controversially, due to on-target performance in one or some areas despite poor performance in other areas, and while the firm is making losses or jobs are being cut, say. This happened, to the outrage of shareholders, when the boss of oil firm BP, Bob Dudley, earned a 20% increase in his 2015 compensation while overseeing the firm's biggest-ever operating loss for that year. Ironically, shareholders had, in the prior year, voted in favor of the pay policy that resulted in Mr. Dudley's pay packet for 2015, which was designed to measure his effectiveness in hitting a series of targets such as scaling back capital spending, reducing costs, and maintaining safety.[22] Companies that are concerned about this eventuality can make bonus payments contingent on minimum performance thresholds in all of the bonus formula components and, thus, use one performance measure as condition or a *modifier* for the other. Again, the combinations of possibilities add up to a virtually infinite number of conceivable bonus formulas.

To add further to the variety of bonus plans, some short-term incentive awards are assigned in two steps. First a *bonus pool* is funded, often based on corporate performance and often conditional on meeting minimum corporate performance thresholds. In the second step, the pool is then assigned to individuals, usually through a rating system that provides higher awards to better performers.[23]

All of the major compensation consulting firms provide data on reward practices collected from a large number of firms across industries in a large number of countries around the world. These surveys are not always easy to compare (due to different sample composition in terms of type and size of companies as well as industry and country coverage, plus different survey instruments and incentive system categorizations and valuations taken at different times). Overall, however, these surveys suggest that short-term incentive pay is ubiquitous at management levels with nontrivial payouts relative to base salary for on-target performance, and with a trend of variable pay spreading around the world. However, in addition to a wide variation across countries, industries, and firm sizes and types, the surveys exhibit a wide spread in variable pay across organizational roles and levels. Although it is virtually impossible to draw a line through these findings, perhaps one careful generalization is that both bonus eligibility and magnitude tend to increase with organization level; that is, as employees move up the organizational ladder, they are more likely to be eligible for a bonus and to receive a proportionally bigger bonus, when earned, out of total compensation.

Despite this generalization, variation remains the norm. For example, even though bonuses are typically strongly geared in the financial sector – where, according to data from the European Banking Association, the average bonus for bankers earning more than 1 million can be well over three times fixed pay[24] – some banks, perhaps rare exceptions, do not believe in bonuses. Par Boman, chief executive at Sweden's Handelsbanken, argues that bonuses create a mismatch between short-term incentives and long-term performance:

> **I do not believe you can combine long-term commitment with short-term incentives or you will have a mismatch. That doesn't mean I'm against bonuses in principle, but in our company, we cannot see that they will help us develop the bank in the long-term. It doesn't make sense to pay bonuses in good times and then in bad times tell employees they have to work harder for 30 percent less money.**[25]

Perhaps the key message is that short-term incentive (STI) and long-term incentive (LTI) plans, to which we turn next, should complement each other. In the words of Peter Schloth, Principal with Mercer, a major compensation consulting firm:

> **Properly designed LTI programs should motivate to develop strategies and policies to achieve long-term growth and increase the value of the organization. Effective STI programs should motivate to execute on strategies and policies, and make good operating decisions to maximize performance over the course of a year.**[26]

Long-term incentives

Long-term incentive awards are based on performance measured over periods greater than one year. Their principal objective is to reward employees for their role in creating long-term value. In addition to motivating employees to contribute to the organization's long-term success, long-term incentive awards also aim to attract and retain key talent by making total expected compensation more attractive; by encouraging employee ownership (through equity-based features of the plan);[27] and by tying incentive payouts to service period requirements (to address retention concerns). Long-term incentive awards often are restricted to relatively high levels of management based on the argument that executive decision-making at these levels most directly impacts the long-term success of the organization, although some would object to this argument and call instead for a distributed responsibility for long-term success to everyone in the organization. We will come back to this point when we discuss group rewards.

Long-term incentive plans (LTIPs) come in multiple forms; as with short-term incentive plans, one must be careful to generalize selected features of these plans. There is variation in the period that LTIPs cover (although three to four years is quite common); in the performance metric(s) the plans include; and in the targets that are expected to be achieved over the period. Some LTIPs measure performance in accounting terms, such as earnings per share (EPS), say. The target for these metrics can be *cumulative* over the LTIP period (such as by requiring EPS to be within a given range each year of the performance period in addition to meeting the target at the end of the period), or instead be stipulated as an *end-of-period* target (where the plan requires only that the EPS target is achieved at the conclusion of the performance period regardless of the actual fluctuations in EPS during the period). Some firms implement *consecutive* (end-to-end) LTIPs, meaning that a new cycle begins only at the completion of the previous one. Others opt for *overlapping* performance cycles, where a new plan begins each year; hence, multiple plans are running simultaneously, making it easier to tweak the long-term targets, or even the chosen metrics, each year. Overlapping LTIPs also facilitate enrolling newly eligible employees and new hires each year.[28]

Equity-based plans are another common way to provide long-term incentives. These plans provide rewards based on changes in the value of the firm's stock. Equity-based plans, too, come in many forms, including the following:

Stock option plans

Stock option plans give employees the right to purchase a set number of shares of company stock at a set price (i.e. the exercise or *strike* price) during a specified period of time (i.e. after the options vest but before they expire). Although stock option terms vary across firms, most options are granted *at the money* (i.e. the exercise price is equal to the stock price on the day of grant) with a three- to five-year vesting rate (i.e. one-third, one-fourth, or one-fifth of the options granted, respectively, vest at the end of each of the first three, four, or five years), and a 10-year maturity (i.e. the options expire 10 years after they are granted). When the stock price is above the option exercise price – that is, when the stock options are *in the money* – the employee can exercise the vested options and either hold the shares or sell them with a gain. However, when the strike price of vested options is higher than the stock price, the options are said to be *underwater*. Rather than having motivational effects, underwater options often are a source of morale and retention problems, particularly if the firm's stock price malaise is deemed to persist.

While employees might desire stock options because of the size of the potential gains, stock options also have several attractive features for the granting firms. From an incentive perspective, employees benefit only when the stock price goes up, so stock options motivate employees to work effectively, one would presume, to increase their company's stock price. This improves incentive alignment, as employees benefit only when shareholders benefit; that is, when the stock price goes up and, presumably, value has been created. Moreover, the potential for share ownership associated with stock options also affects alignment by tying some of the employee's wealth to the company's future. Finally, vesting schedules coupled with service-based restrictions that cause employees to forfeit unvested options when they leave the firm are believed to enhance employees' long-term focus on the business as well as retention. Thus, stock options get employees to think more like owners while enhancing retention of talent. Stock options also allow the firm to provide incentive compensation without cash outlay, which makes stock options particularly attractive for cash-constrained firms such as those during start-up but also turnaround, either not yet generating profits or facing losses (and retention concerns).[29] In fact, stock options create a positive cash flow for the firm when employees exercise options (due to the purchase of shares, but also due to a tax-deductible compensation expense in the amount of the difference between the exercise price of the options and the market price of the stock). Moreover, until 2005, most stock option grants did not require the firm to take a charge against earnings. This flaw in the accounting rules provided powerful incentives for firms to grant options rather than to use other forms of compensation that require expensing. As of 2006, however, the most commonly applied accounting rules around the world, including International Financial Reporting Standards (IFRS) and US Generally Accepted Accounting Principles (GAAP), require that the fair value of the stock options at the grant date be estimated using an option pricing model. A detailed discussion of such non-control implications of stock options, however, is outside the scope of this text.

Despite these features, stock options also have several disadvantages. Stock option grants represent a potential future issuance of shares, which creates *dilution* and may put a downward pressure on stock prices (which firms try to counter by committing to share repurchases with the proceeds from the exercise of stock options). Stock options also sometimes motivate managers to undertake riskier business strategies because the managers are rewarded for gains but not penalized for losses. Their risk-taking behavior can increase stock price volatility. Stock options also have been criticized for generating *windfall* compensation due to market-wide stock price improvements rather than strong firm performance. In reverse, however, stock options also can fall *underwater* due to bearish stock market conditions rather than poor firm performance and cause morale and retention problems. Also when the firm is performing poorly and the stock price is subdued, stock options are worth little and, thus, are likely to erode the motivation to perform – ironically, just at a time when it is important for the executives and employees to be motivated the most. Moreover, given the relatively high liquidity of stock options (due to short vesting periods) and, often, the vast amounts of stock options held, executives may be encouraged to take actions that boost stock price in the short term but harm shareholders in the long run after the options have been cashed in. Considering these issues, the premise that stock options contribute to the creation of shareholder value has been actively debated and researched.[30]

Before they became so contested, however, stock options were by far the most prevalent form of stock-based incentives during the 1990s, particularly in the United States and especially in certain industries (e.g. hi-tech). Although stock options remained in play, the years 2003 and 2004 began to show declining grant rates, rising exercise rates, and declining eligibility as firms were increasingly considering alternatives to standard option plans, particularly below the executive/management level.[31] The decline in stock options' popularity around that time, particularly in the United States, coincided with the change in accounting rules that required stock option expensing. But other reasons could help explain stock options' decline, such as the bear stock market in the United States that drove many stock options underwater, as well as investor activism against the ostensibly *excessive pay* that stock options helped provide during the boom. Investors also scorned the dilution effects of the large amounts of stock options that were being granted.

Differences in stock option use have existed, and continue to persist, across countries, however. Firms in Britain and France, for example, make use of stock options, whereas firms elsewhere in Europe have a preference for full-value share awards (see below). That said, use of stock options, never so widespread in Europe as in America, appears to be declining in most countries.[32] With the decline in stock option usage, however, other forms of equity-based compensation have become more prominent, including *restricted shares* and, especially, *performance awards*.[33]

Restricted stock plans

Employees eligible for restricted stock do not have to spend cash to acquire the stock, as the shares of stock are given to them; but selling those shares is restricted for a specified period of time (five years, say) and contingent upon employment at that time. In other words, the employee has full ownership rights over the shares, including voting and dividend rights; but the shares are subject to sale restrictions and/or risk of forfeiture until the vesting event occurs, that is, until completion of the service period.

Restricted stock obviously provides a reward for increases in stock price, although the stock itself also has value when the stock price is flat or even declines (unlike stock options that only provide a reward when the stock price exceeds the exercise price). Because *full-value stock awards* like restricted stock have less risk than stock options, the firm can issue fewer shares as it would when using stock options instead, thus causing less dilution. On the other hand, restricted stock has been derided as a *giveaway* or pay-for-*pulse* (rather than pay-for-*performance*). This is because the stock has some value (even if the stock price declines), and the restrictions on selling the stock disappear merely with the passage of time and continued employment during that time; that is, with the completion of the service period. For this reason, restricted stock is said to better serve *retention* purposes and benefits stemming from *ownership*, rather than *motivation* per se.

Performance stock or option plans

To mitigate the "giveaway" feature of restricted stock and bolster the pay-for-*performance* rationale, some firms have resorted to *performance awards* by making their stock grants contingent on the achievement of stock or non-stock goals over a specified period. In this way, *performance stock* shares are restricted stock shares that vest upon the achievement of specific performance targets and not merely the completion of a service period. Until the specific performance target has been achieved, the shares are subject to sale restrictions and/or forfeiture contingent on continued employment. Once vested, the performance shares usually are no longer subject to restriction.

Similarly, *performance options* are alternative stock option plans that make vesting or exercise of the options contingent on improvements in stock performance or the achievement of certain stock or non-stock targets. Performance options can come in different forms. *Premium options* have exercise prices greater than the stock price on the grant date. *Indexed options* have exercise prices contingent on performance relative to a peer group of firms. *Performance-vested options* link the vesting of the options to the achievement of performance targets, such as return on equity, earnings per share, or other financial or operating measures (e.g. sales growth).

Examples can be varied, such as for performance stock option plans that contain both premium pricing and performance vesting. Regardless of the variations, the key idea behind these alternative stock option plans is to provide stronger incentives to maximize shareholder value by raising the bar for stock price improvements before the options become exercisable (as is the case with premium and indexed options) or by raising the bar on the conditions to vest and, thus, earn the stock (as is the case with performance-vested options). However, as is true for all incentive plans that require the setting of performance targets, triggers, or thresholds, doing so effectively is a key challenge. When the performance conditions are set too leniently, the performance stock or option plans will be seen as merely providing giveaways. But when they are set too tough, they can have other undesired consequences, such as excessive risk taking, discouragement, and/or turnover.

There are many other possible long-term incentive instruments, but most are variants of stock option, restricted stock, or performance stock/option plans. For example, both restricted stock and performance stock plans involve granting stock. But sometimes firms provide awards in *units* instead of actual shares. For example, at the Coca-Cola Company:

> Performance Share Units (PSUs) provide an opportunity for employees to receive common stock if the specified performance measure [i.e. compound annual growth in economic profit] is met for a predefined performance period [i.e. over three-year periods – 2012–14, 2013–15, 2014–16, 2015–17, etc.]. PSUs generally are subject to an additional holding period. PSUs generally vest 100% after four years (three-year performance period followed by a one-year holding period).

However,

> The PSUs for the 2013–2015 performance period will have zero payout because the pre-established economic profit growth target was not met. As with the two prior PSU programs, no compensation will be realized for this portion of long-term incentive compensation.
>
> [For the 2014–16 period, the Company's 2016 proxy statement states that] Through December 31, 2015, payout is projected above the target level. Company performance over the remaining year of the performance period [2016] will determine the number of shares earned, if any. Results will be certified in February 2017.
>
> [And, for the 2015–17 period, the Company's 2016 proxy statement states that] Through December 31, 2015, payout is projected near the target level. Company performance over the remaining two years of the performance period [2016 and 2017] will determine the number of shares earned, if any. Results will be certified in February 2018.[34]

Performance share units are thus granted in units instead of actual shares, where each unit awarded usually represents the value of one share of stock. But PSUs only entitle the employee to stock upon vesting, and as the example illustrates, when the vesting is performance-based – and thus when these are so-called *performance shares* – they may not always result in an award. (Moreover, as recipients of PSUs, employees usually have no ownership rights until vesting, since no shares are actually issued until that point.)

Another variation of equity-based long-term incentives are *Stock Appreciation Rights* (SARs). SARs are similar to options in that the eligible employees benefit from appreciation in the company's stock price. They are different in that the employees do not have to spend cash to acquire the stock. Instead, without acquiring the stock, employees just receive the amount of any increase in stock price over the specified period. But like stock options, the employee typically can exercise the SAR at any point after vesting but before expiry. When the SAR is exercised, the firm pays the employee cash (cash SARs), stock (stock SARs), or a combination of both, in an amount equal to the stock's appreciation since the date of grant.

As with short-term incentive plans, the variety of long-term incentive plans is infinite, which should caution against making any seemingly simple generalizations or patently effective prescriptions. That said, evidence suggests that equity-based incentives have grown historically to a recent plateau, as follows:

> The percentage of pay tied to the stock market for CEOs of US companies was negligible in the early 1980s, rose to about one-quarter in the early 1990s, peaked at roughly one-half in the early 2000s, and remains near 40% today.[35]

Another discernable trend perhaps is the decrease in the use of stock options and the increase in performance-based plans. Consistent with this, the aforementioned 2016 proxy statement of Coca-Cola explicitly states that they "adjusted the mix if equity compensation to use fewer stock options and more performance share units" in line with their compensation practice or principle where "the vast majority of pay is to be performance-based and not guaranteed." David Hofrichter, principal and business development leader of Hewitt's Executive Compensation

Consulting practice, echoes this by opining that, indeed, "Compensation Committees now want something for [their LTIP grants]; [which] they are expressing [...] through performance plans that target key metrics and support the strategy of the organization."[36]

Incentive system design

In the following sections, we discuss three related incentive system design choices: the extent to which the rewards are determined formulaically, the shape of the incentive-performance function, and the size of incentive pay.

Incentive formula

The types of rewards provided and the bases on which they are awarded are commonly communicated to the incentive plan participant by means of an *incentive formula* and described in an incentive contract that might be written in great detail. However, the rewards sometimes can also be assigned *subjectively* instead of completely formulaically. Subjectivity almost inevitably plays some role for decisions about promotions and job assignments. But subjectivity can also be part of annual bonus assignments in the following ways: (1) all or part of the bonus is based on subjective judgments about performance; (2) the weights on some or all quantitative measures are determined subjectively; or (3) a subjective performance threshold or *override* is used, in which case a subjective determination as to whether or not to pay a bonus is made.

Subjectivity can be used for a number of reasons. It may be difficult to describe the bases for the rewards and/or their weightings from a large set of evaluation criteria prior to the performance period. Keeping the contract flexible can mitigate motivating employees in directions that turn out to be no longer appropriate as conditions change. When the contract is left flexible, employees are encouraged to keep doing their best and not give up in the face of an impossible performance target or, in reverse, coast once the target is achieved. And, keeping the bases for rewards vague can reduce employees' propensities to manipulate the performance measures.[37]

The use of subjectivity in contracting, however, can affect employee risk. It can *decrease* risk if it allows adjustments for the effects of factors that are outside the employee's control (which we discuss in greater detail in Chapter 12). But the use of subjectivity can also *increase* employee risk. First, with implicit contracts, employees bear the risk that their evaluators might evaluate them on different bases from what they were assuming when they made their decisions; that is, subjective evaluations are prone to *hindsight bias*. Second, if employees do not *trust* their evaluators to make informed and unbiased performance assessments, subjectivity can result in employee frustration, demotivation, and friction. Finally, when evaluations are subjective, employees may attempt to inappropriately influence their evaluators for better evaluations. These problems, however, are reduced if the employee and the evaluator develop a working relationship with greater mutual trust, which has been shown to be critical for the effective implementation of completely or partially subjective performance evaluations.[38]

Shape of the incentive function

When the reward promises are *formulaic*, the link between rewards and the bases on which they are awarded is often determined by a rewards-results or *pay-performance function*. This was illustrated in a budget setting in Chapter 8 (Figure 8.3), showing that bonuses are typically promised only over a restricted performance range; that is, the function has lower and upper reward cutoffs, and it is linear in shape (although sometimes with kinks) between the cutoffs.[39]

At profit center levels, most firms set a *lower cutoff* or *threshold* in their short-term incentive contracts. Below some significant fraction (e.g. 80%) of targeted annual performance (which is typically the budget), managers do not earn incentive pay for performance. Organizations set a lower cutoff because they do not want to pay any bonuses for performance they consider mediocre or worse. The fraction of the target set as the lower limit varies, among other things, with the predictability of the target; that is, it tends to be a lower fraction when predictability is lower. An *upper cutoff* or *cap* on incentive payments also is commonly used; it means that no extra incentive pay is provided for any additional performance above the cutoff. The caps are typically set at a percentage of the annual performance target, such as 150% of budget. Upper cutoffs can be considered for a number of reasons, including the following:

1. A concern that the high incentive payments might not be deserved because of *windfall gains* (unforeseen good luck);
2. A concern that employees will be unduly motivated to take actions to increase current period performance at the expense of the long term; in other words, produce results that are unsustainable (which was the stated reason for the cap on bonuses for banks in the European Union, a rule that limits bonuses of high-earning bankers to the same level as their salaries or twice the amount with shareholder approval, to "curb the high bonus multiples that European lawmakers say contributed to excessive risk taking in the run-up to the financial crisis");[40]
3. A desire not to pay hierarchically subordinate employees more than hierarchically higher employees or managers, thus maintaining *vertical compensation equity*;
4. A desire to keep total compensation somewhat consistent over time so that employees are able to sustain their lifestyle and, thus, to mitigate "feast-or-famine" volatility in pay year over year; and,
5. A concern about a possibly faulty plan design, the risk of which is greatest when the plan is new.

Size of incentive pay

Because employees almost invariably value money, a significant proportion of variable pay should motivate them to achieve the performance goals. Further, compensation packages that offer significant performance-contingent pay (*at-risk pay* or *pay-for-performance*) are likely to attract employees who are confident about their abilities to produce superior results and/or are more willing to accept risk. In that sense, the type of compensation package offered serves an *employee selection* role.

However, the most important consideration regarding the high use of variable pay is that if performance is not totally controllable by the employees, then the incentive system inevitably imposes risk on them (hence the term *at-risk pay*). Employees, therefore, will want to be compensated for bearing that risk; that is, their compensation *in expectation* must be higher than what it would be when offered a fixed salary. If the organization fails to provide the *risk premium*, which is an additional compensation expense, it will find itself unable to compete for talent in the labor markets.

Criteria for evaluating incentive systems

Each incentive plan – being one of many possible variations, as we have seen – should be carefully evaluated on all of its features individually and collectively; that is, as a package. This should be done regularly as circumstances change, as seems to be "best practice" in many firms, as suggested by Andrew MacLeod, head of pay research at Aon Hewitt:

> Rather than debating the philosophical point of whether or not bonus plans work, companies seem to be more focused on assessing whether they are working in reality and

improving their design to make them more likely to succeed. Ninety-four percent of our study's respondents now have a review process in place, with a big increase in the use of cost/benefit analysis.[41]

Setting aside infinite variations in specific incentive plan designs, the following criteria can be used as overall principles when evaluating an incentive system.

First, the rewards should be *valued*. Rewards that have no value will not provide motivation. However, reward tastes probably vary across individuals. As compared with top executives, lower-level managers are likely more interested in protecting their autonomy and in improving their prospects for promotion in addition to the size of their short-term income (after their base salaries are assured). Employees later in their careers are probably more concerned about job security. And so on. Overall, studies suggest that the reasons people join and stay with an organization are broader than compensation alone, including the satisfaction that comes from the work they do and the role they have, the long-term opportunities for development and advancement, and the feelings of belonging to an admirable organization that shares their values.[42] Reward tastes also vary across countries due to many factors, including culture, stage of economic development, and differences in tax and regulation, although evidence suggests that these differences are diminishing and that the world is getting flatter when it comes to incentive pay.[43] Nonetheless, some differences at various levels will remain, and if organizations can tailor their reward packages to their employees' preferences, then they could possibly provide the control benefits of incentives more effectively. Such tailoring is costly, however, and firms often opt to administer a single organization-wide incentive system (or, at most, just a few systems).

Second, the rewards should be large enough to have *impact*. If rewards that are valued are provided in trivial amounts, the effect can be counterproductive. Employees can be insulted and react with such emotions as contempt and anger.[44] Reward visibility may affect impact. If rewards are visible to others, the motivational effect is enhanced by a sense of pride and recognition.

Third, rewards should be *understandable*. Employees should understand both the reasons for and the value of the rewards. Organizations can incur considerable expense in providing potentially valuable rewards, but if employees do not understand them well, the expense will not generate the desired motivational effects.

Fourth, rewards should be *timely*. Delay in providing the rewards after the performance is said to dilute their motivational effects. Prompt rewards also increase the extent of any learning that takes place from receiving the reward and connecting it to the performance for which it was given.

Fifth, the effects of the rewards should be *durable*. Rewards have greater value if the good feelings generated by the granting of a reward are long lasting; that is, if employees remember them.

Sixth, rewards should be *reversible*. Performance evaluators often make mistakes, and some reward decisions are more difficult to correct than others. Promotions, for example, are difficult to reverse.

Finally, rewards should be *cost efficient*; that is, all else equal, incentives should achieve the desired motivation at minimal cost. As the quote earlier in this section suggests, however, many organizations now seem to have a review process in place, with a big increase in the use of cost-benefit analysis.

Monetary incentives and the evaluation criteria

How well do the monetary rewards that many organizations provide satisfy the reward evaluation criteria? Monetary rewards can have potent impacts on employees' behaviors because virtually everyone values money. Money can be used to purchase goods and services that can satisfy each employee's most pressing desires. A vice president in a human resources consulting firm expressed this advantage in colorful terms, "You can't pay orthodonture bills with crystal from Waterford."[45] Put differently, "working for cookies is not an option."[46] Money also has important symbolic values. It reflects achievement and success, it accords people prestige, and it sometimes even serves as a proxy for some people's estimation of their self-worth.

However, the observation that employees almost without exception value money does not necessarily imply that higher incentives will lead to higher performance. Indeed, studies suggest that there may be an inverse U-shaped relationship between effort levels and incentive intensity, indicating that ever higher incentives may actually result in a decline in performance or produce unintended consequences. Those consequences stem from dysfunctional behaviors and "gaming" of the performance metrics to increase "measured" performance and personal wealth at the expense of long-term value creation or "real" performance improvements[47] (various examples of which we discussed in the earlier chapters). This is anecdotally expressed in the following quote from John Cryan, chief executive at UBS, a global bank:

> Mr Cryan not only noted that overall levels of compensation in his industry remain too high. He also pondered whether bonuses really spur his banking colleagues to the elevated levels of productive effort such inducements are supposed to extract. In his own case, Mr Cryan said the answer was no. "I will not work any harder or any less hard in any year, in any day because someone is going to pay me any more or less," he observed.[48]

This echoes the view of Jeroen van der Veer, the former boss at Shell, an oil major:

> If I had been paid 50 per cent more, I would not have done [my job] better. If I had been paid 50 per cent less, then I would not have done it worse.[49]

Of course, these gentlemen were very well paid, which may affect their marginal utility for money and thus how "much" they value it. That said, various monetary rewards sometimes also fail the impact criterion. Merit raises, for example, are typically quite small for most employees, so total raises look small in times of low inflation. But even bonuses may suffer from impact or, worse, lead to demotivation when expected but not earned:

> The impact of a cash bonus is often short-lived. Staff quickly start to think of it as a permanent part of their compensation. The following year they quite naturally become upset if their bonus turns out to be lower.[50]

Moreover, the performance evaluations on which the merit raises are based typically are infrequent, kept confidential, or communicated to employees in quite vague terms, thus leaving them ambiguous (thereby affecting understandability) and possibly failing to provide a sense of recognition. Indeed, the annual performance reviews on the basis of which merit raises are typically determined have recently been increasingly debated in terms of their effectiveness to properly motivate employees.[51] To quote from a *Harvard Business Review* article:

> In a survey Deloitte conducted recently, more than half the executives questioned (58%) believe that their current performance management approach drives neither employee engagement nor high performance. [What is more, tallying] the number of hours the organizations were spending on performance management – they found that completing the forms, holding the meetings, and creating the ratings consumed close to *2 million hours a year.*[52]

Another common issue arises when firms that fall on hard times "flatten" pay, inadvertently or not. Because it is difficult to cut an employee's pay, poor performers are merely given no raises or bonuses, and the penalty to these employees is low. But lowering the payments to the top performers is where it hurts, often leading to perceptions of inequity, demotivation, and increased turnover, unhelpfully, among the most valuable employees.

On the other hand, some forms of monetary incentives, such as stock options, have been said to have "too much" impact. Stock options have often been granted in large numbers to, particularly, higher-level employees or executives. Due to the large number of stock options typically granted and held by top executives, and exacerbated by relatively short vesting periods, the executives may be encouraged to take actions that affect stock price in the short term but harm shareholders in the long run. For example, an action that can slightly affect stock price downward at the time of a stock option grant, or boost stock price at the time of a stock option exercise, can make a huge difference for the stock options to be subsequently "in the money" or yield a greater payout at exercising, respectively, when applied to a very large number of stock options. In other words, pay can be significantly impacted by short-term movements in stock prices, thus encouraging executives to take measures to affect stock price rather than to maximize shareholder value in the long term (by which time they may have left the firm). In that sense, and due to the potential short-term impact that stock price may have on the potential value and payout from stock options, these instruments are, in fact, working against their intended purpose – that is, to have the executives focused on the long term rather than to take actions that affect short term. This illustrates that, indeed, impact is a powerful criterion for incentives to have; but equally, when impact directs behaviors in ill-aligned ways, it can be detrimental.[53]

Because incentive contracts sometimes are quite complex (as are many long-term incentive plans, such as performance stock plans) or even ambiguous (when they include the use of subjectivity), and because performance-related feedback is infrequent, incomplete, and/or biased, employees often fail to understand the reasons why they are given the rewards (or the size of their rewards). When the rewards fail the understandability criterion, they are less likely to produce the desired effects. Stock options are often said to be ill-understood by employees, especially at lower organizational levels. Regarding performance rating issues, such as completeness and/or biases, particularly in annual performance reviews, a Deloitte report cites work in psychology that found that only one-fifth of the variance in employee performance ratings reflects the employee's actual performance; the larger part reflects other factors, particularly *rater* perceptions (three-fifths of the variance) and other *noise*:

> **Assessing someone's *skills* produces inconsistent data. Objective as *I* may try to be in evaluating you on, say, strategic thinking, it turns out that how much strategic thinking *I* do, or how valuable *I* think strategic thinking is, or how tough a rater *I* am significantly affects my assessment of your strategic thinking.**[54]

Monetary rewards vary in their timeliness. Piece-rates used in some production settings are possibly the timeliest. Sales commissions are perhaps a close second. The most common period for performance reviews, however, such as for salary increases and bonuses, is annual. Long-term incentive awards – those based on multiyear performance – are less timely. It has been suggested that the mental discount rate employees apply to delayed rewards is greater than the time value of money. Or, as Peter Boreham, a director at Hay Group, put it: "Once you go beyond three years [as is commonly the case with long-term incentive plans], the mental discount that executives put on rewards gets very large; any longer and it becomes a lottery ticket."[55] One survey study estimates that incentive pay is discounted compared to fixed pay by about 10% for cash bonuses and 50% or more for deferred bonuses and long-term incentives.[56] Hence, extending the time horizon of incentives, which has been increasingly called for to enhance a focus on the long term, is not costless given the rather large mental discount that people attach to delayed payouts.

Following the 2008 financial crisis, a common trend in the calls for change was to defer bonus payments because "deferring bonus payments helps companies to control short-termism," said Vicki Elliot, a worldwide partner at Mercer. "It means that a portion of the bonus is payable to employees in installments based on subsequent company and/or business unit performance. This *claw-back approach* sends the message that the bonus isn't finally determined until company or business unit performance is sustained."[57] In other words, deferring some of the bonus payments should prevent employees from pocketing bonuses when they misleadingly appear to be doing well and keeping the money when their firm subsequently suffers or even collapses. "There has been too much focus on payments that are very short-term focused, people who pick up the tab for short-term profits, without having to bear the costs of long-term impairments," said Stephen Green, chairman of HSBC, a global bank.[58]

Another way to possibly mitigate the short-term focus of some incentive systems while circumventing the cost of the "mental discount" that comes with deferred payments is to consider *risk-adjusted measures* as the basis for bonus determination. However, the vast majority of banks (and likely nonfinancial firms as well) admitted that they lack "reliable methods to measure the risks they are running" and had to "work out how to phase compensation to make sure it reflects the risks being taken over a long period."[59] Some banks have considered paying bonuses in contingent bonds (rather than cash), which are "wiped out" if the bank's capital ratio [a key indicator for a bank's survival] falls below a predefined threshold, which should curb incentives to take excessive risk.[60] But even though the employees own the bonds, they may value them less than cash. As we will see in the next chapter, there are indeed no easy solutions to overcome the ubiquitous myopia problem.[61] And, this is not only a problem in banks, although the crisis clearly has put a spotlight on their incentive systems. For example, several Chinese cities and counties dropped gross domestic product (GDP) as a performance metric for government officials in an effort to shift the focus to protecting the environment and reducing poverty:

> The move, which follows a directive issued by top leaders, is among the first concrete signs of China switching its blind pursuit of economic growth at all costs towards measures that encourage better quality of life. Analysts say that adherence to GDP as a performance metric – thus linking it to local officials' promotion – has contributed to environmental degradation and urban sprawl as officials encouraged heavy industry and bulldozed agricultural land to build housing developments.[62]

This latter example is one of promotion-based incentives, which are durable. Most monetary rewards, in contrast, particularly small ones, are not. In many cases, salary increases are "lost in the paycheck" – they are quickly spent and forgotten (see also earlier quotes above). One survey found that 29% of employees who earned bonuses used them to pay bills; 18% "admitted they couldn't remember where the money went." The report concluded that, for most employees, "[cash] bonuses have no lasting value."[63] Durability can perhaps be improved if the award is given but restricted for a period of time, such as with an award of restricted stock (or contingent bonds, as in another example above), because the employee can see the reward, and can value it, but cannot spend it. This benefit of durability would also apply to the deferred bonus schemes that firms ponder, thus involving a tradeoff against the possible cost due to mental discounting. In contrast, some non-monetary rewards, such as a promotion or a recognition that goes on one's CV, are quite durable (although they tend to be less or not reversible).

Indeed, monetary rewards also vary in their reversibility. Bonus awards are reversible because they are typically contingent on performance in a single period. Salary increases, on the other hand, provide an almost guaranteed increment because pay cuts are rare. But some question whether even bonuses are truly reversible. Employees come to expect them, and if there is no payout, they will be frustrated, especially if it happens because the company is not doing well. Recall the quote here from Handelsbanken, arguing that "it doesn't make sense to pay bonuses in good times and then in bad times tell [employees] they have to work harder for 30 percent less money."[64] Or, as Tidjane Thiam, chief executive of Credit Suisse, a global bank, muses:

> Remuneration is a "battle ground." [And although he] is not against bonuses for his investment bankers, if pay goes up and down with performance, but, "it's the 'and down' that they don't accept."[65]

Finally, monetary rewards tend to be expensive. The value provided to the employees is a direct cost to the firm. Some other forms of rewards, such as titles, recognition, interesting job assignments, or prized parking spots are much less expensive, yet they can have value to employees.

Although monetary rewards do not satisfy all the evaluation criteria equally well, the criteria are not all equally important, either. As such, monetary rewards possibly are quite effective in satisfying the most important criteria. In particular, money is highly valued, so monetary awards attract most employees' attention. That is not to say that monetary rewards are not sometimes overused or that they could not be better designed.[66] As we have shown, such design considerations inevitably will involve tradeoffs among the various criteria.

Group rewards

Team or group rewards certainly have advantages; they were discussed in Chapter 3 as one the methods by which personnel/cultural controls can be implemented. But they also have some significant disadvantages. Group rewards often do not provide *direct* and strong incentive effects. They provide a direct incentive only if the individuals to whom the rewards are promised perceive that they can influence the performance on which the rewards are based to a considerable extent. Group rewards also create the potential for *free riding*. In larger teams, particularly, some team members can slack off and suffer little adverse effects on the rewards earned.

As such, stock-based plans, one prominent form of group rewards, provide direct incentives only for the small number of managers at the very top of publicly held firms who presumably can influence their firm's stock price in a meaningful way. When lower-level employees are included in stock-based plans, their compensation is made more volatile and uncertain, but their motivation is not proportionally affected.

Group rewards can produce a beneficial form of cultural control, however. Team members may monitor and sanction each other's behaviors and produce improved results. Comments like, "Get to work; you're hurting my profit sharing!" are evidence that cultural control – mutual monitoring – is working. It is this benefit and the avoidance of some dysfunctional effects of individual rewards that group rewards can provide.

Some firms have used group rewards very effectively over long periods of time. For example, all employees (or "partners," as the company calls them) at John Lewis, a large UK retailer, share in the company's profit, which in some years amounts to several weeks up to two months' worth of salary for each employee, depending on company performance. "Today's results reflect the collective hard work of our partners," said Charlie Mayfield, John Lewis chairman. "While not a universal panacea, [our collective performance-based bonus plan] clearly underpins the partnership's performance," he added.[67] Other firms have variations of group rewards through share ownership. For example, Slater & Gordon, a stock-exchange-listed Australian law firm, commented on its employee stock ownership plan as being designed to "encourage staff retention, improve performance, and align employee and shareholder incentives."[68]

Conclusion

Incentives are an important part of the results-control arrangements used to direct employees' behaviors. Rewards that can be linked to measures of performance or subjective performance evaluations come in many forms. It is widely, but not universally, believed that monetary rewards are important for motivation. However, a wide range of other forms of rewards, such as praise, titles, recognition, promotions, and so on, also can be potent motivators while being cost efficient and having advantages in terms of satisfying the various other evaluation criteria that we discussed.

Incentive contract design presents problems that are far larger than just the choice of rewards, however. For example, tailoring rewards to employees' individual preferences would seem to be effective, but that benefit has to be weighed against the potential for employees' perceptions of inequities and the cost of contract administration. Similarly, it is well recognized that organizations' total compensation package must be competitive to attract and retain talented employees. If a portion of the compensation package, such as base salary, is not competitive, perhaps because cash is in short supply during the start-up phase of a new venture, then the incentives-performance function for the variable portion of pay may have to be adapted to compensate, or alternative forms of compensation such as stock options may have to be provided.

Perhaps the safest advice that can be proffered is that incentives should be sufficiently meaningful to offset other motives employees have to act in ways that are contrary to the organization's best interests, but the rewards should not be greater than those necessary to provide the needed motivation. An incentive system will not create value for the organization unless the incremental value of the increased performance generated by the incentives exceeds the associated compensation and administration expense. Organizations also have to worry about implementing an incentive system that encourages behaviors that do not lead to the desired outcomes. Many incentive systems have *unintended consequences* that can actually destroy value, such as by encouraging results that maximize incentive pay in the short term while jeopardizing the long-run viability of the organization. If that is the case, it may be better to have no incentive system than to have a bad one. The literature is littered with examples of incentives having unintended consequences. This is, in a perverse sense, testimony that incentives work – that is, they encourage employees to produce results. But if poorly designed incentive systems encourage employees to produce the wrong results or do the wrong things in the wrong way, then strong incentives will only get the organization off track, and sometimes even ruin the firm, more quickly.

Notes

1 S. Kerr, "Executives Ask: How and Why Should Firms and Their Employees Set Goals," *Academy of Management Executive*, 18, no. 4 (November 2004), pp. 122–3.

2 For recent research on incentive schemes including penalties, see for example W. A. Van der Stede, A. Wu, and S. Y. Wu, "The Reinforcement Effect of Bonuses and Penalties," *Working Paper* (2016); M. H. Christ, K. L. Sedatole, and K. L. Towry, "Sticks and Carrots: The Effect of Contract Frame on Effort in Incomplete Contracts," *The Accounting* Review, 87, no. 6 (November 2012), pp. 1913–38; T. Hossain and J. A. List, "The Behavioralist Visits the Factory: Increasing Productivity Using Simple Framing Manipulations," *Management Science*, 58, no. 12 (2012), pp. 2151–67.

3 "Cut-and-Build Archibald," *Forbes* (September 23, 1996), p. 46; "Grow, Grow, Grow," *The Economist* (April 17, 2010), Special Report, p. 13.

4 For examples of recent research on non-monetary incentives, see S. M. Lourenço, "Monetary Incentives, Feedback, and Recognition – Complements or Substitutes? Evidence from a Field Experiment in a Retail Services Company," *The Accounting Review*, 91, no. 1 (January 2016), pp. 279–97.

5 S. A. Hewlett, "Attract and Keep A-Players with Nonfinancial Rewards," *Harvard Business Review* (May 24, 2012), online at hbr.org/2012/05/attract-and-keep-a-players-wit.

6 "Barclays Abolishes Commission Bonuses for Branch Staff," *BBC* (October 10, 2012), online at www.bbc.co.uk/news/business-19902562.

7 "What Are Brands For?," *The Economist* (August 30, 2014), online at econ.st/VPofD5.

8 "BP Links Bonuses to Safety Performance," *The Financial Times* (October 18, 2010), online at on.ft.com/1QueezM.

9 There is a large literature on this, but for a review of research examining the effects of monetary incentives on effort and performance, see S. E. Bonner and G. B. Sprinkle, "The Effects of Monetary Incentives on Effort and Task Performance: Theories, Evidence, and a Framework for Research," *Accounting, Organizations and Society*, 27, no. 4/5 (May–July 2002), pp. 303–45. Another good review or overview article with further references is T. Chamorro-Premuzic, "Does Money Really Affect Motivation? A Review of the Research," *Harvard Business Review* (April 10, 2013), online at hbr.org/2013/04/does-money-really-affect-motiv.

10 An interesting article in this regard, as its title aptly suggests, is U. Gneezy, S. Meier, and P. Rey-Biel, "When and Why Incentive (Don't) Work to Modify Behavior," *Journal of Economic Perspectives*, 25, no. 4 (Fall 2011), pp. 191–210.

11 "U.S. Organizations Report Highest Compensation Spend in 39 Years," *Aon Media Center* (August 26, 2015), online at aon.mediaroom.com/news-releases?item=137290.

12 See, for example, "IRS Releases Final Regulations Under Section 162(m)," *Harvard Law School Forum on Corporate Governance and Financial Regulation* (April 9, 2015), online at corpgov.law.harvard.edu/2015/04/09/irs-releases-final-regulations-under-section-162m.

13 See, for example, "Regulations and Lower Returns Put Pressure on Pay and Bonuses," *The Financial Times* (April 24, 2014), online at on.ft.com/QGRu8v; "SEC Proposes Rules on Executive Pay and Performance," *The New York Times* (April 29, 2015), online at nyti.ms/1OEoKcQ; "Bonus Reforms to Come under Glare of Financial Stability Board," *The Financial Times* (November 8, 2015), online at on.ft.com/1WK47e6.

14 "Goldman Sachs Pioneers Plan to Deal with Bonus Cap," *The Wall Street Journal* (January 30, 2014), online at on.wsj.com/1czchTr.

15 "City Bankers to Evade EU Bonus Cap with 'Role-Based' Allowances," *The Financial Times* (April 13, 2014), online at on.ft.com/Q4eMoO.

16 "EU Bank Watchdog Signals Crackdown on Allowances," *The Financial Times* (June 13, 2014), online at on.ft.com/1on9CDS.

17 "Majority of Public Sector Employees Have Reservations about Performance-Related Pay, Reveals CIPD," *HR Magazine* (January 16, 2013), online at www.hrmagazine.co.uk.

18 "Vatican Unveils Merit-Based Pay," *BBC* (November 22, 2007), online at www.bbc.co.uk.

19 J. Pfeffer and R. Sutton, *Hard Facts* (Boston, MA: Harvard Business School Press, 2006), p. 129.

20 See, for example, "Aon Hewitt: Bonus Schemes in Europe Back on Track" (September 23, 2014), online at www.consultancy.uk.

21 "Lloyds Says Customer Service Key to Future," *The Financial Times* (December 12, 2013), online at http://on.ft.com/1kDQavb.

22 "Pay Dirt," *The Economist* (April 23, 2016), online at econ.st/26gMsSS.

23 For an academic treatment of "bonus pools," see M. Ederhof, M. V. Rajan, and S. Reichelstein, "Discretion in Managerial Bonus Pools," *Foundations and Trends in Accounting*, 5, no. 4 (2011), pp. 243–316; and W. A. Van der Stede, "Review of 'Discretion in Managerial Bonus Pools,'" *The Accounting Review*, 88, no. 1 (January 2013), pp. 351–4.

24 "Goldman Sachs Pioneers Plan to Deal with Bonus Cap," *The Wall Street Journal* (January 30, 2014), online at on.wsj.com/1czchTr.

25 "Bank Chief Champions Case for Fixed Pay," *The Financial Times* (February 18, 2010), online at on.ft.com/1rseOF3.

26 "Key Differences Exist between Long- and Short-term Executive Incentive Awards," *Mercer* (March 10, 2015), online at www.mercer.com.

27 For an academic article on this topic, see U. Von Lilienfeld-Toal and S. Ruenzi, "CEO Ownership, Stock Market Performance, and Managerial Discretion," *The Journal of Finance*, 69, no. 3 (June 2014), pp. 1013–50.

28 See, for example, "Key Differences Exist between Long- and Short-Term Executive Incentive Awards," *Mercer* (March 10, 2015), online at www.mercer.com.

29 See, for example, M. Matejka, K. A. Merchant, and W. A. Van der Stede, "Employment Horizon and the Choice of Performance Measures: Empirical Evidence from Annual Bonus Plans of Loss-Making Entities," *Management Science*, 55, no. 6 (June 2009), pp. 890–905.

30 See, for example, B. Hall and K. Murphy, "The Trouble with Stock Options," *Journal of Economic Perspectives*, 17, no. 3 (Summer 2003), pp. 49–71; "Do Stock Options Improve Performance?," *CalBusiness* (Spring–Summer 2010), pp. 8–9. See also D. Aboody, N. Johnson, and R. Kasznik, "Employee Stock Options and Future Firm Performance: Evidence from Option Repricings," *Journal of Accounting and Economics*, 50, no. 1 (May 2010), pp. 74–92; "US Chief Executives Hoard Good News for Stock Sales," *The Financial Times* (September 7, 2014), online at on.ft.com/1oUm9Jb; A. Edmans, L. Goncalves-Pinto, Y. Wang. and M. Groen-Xu, "Strategic News Releases in Equity Vesting Months," *Working Paper* (2016), online at papers.ssrn.com/sol3/papers.cfm?abstract_id=2489152.

31 See, for example, Watson Wyatt Worldwide, *Stock Incentives: Moving toward a Portfolio Approach* (2005) and Deloitte & Touche USA LLP, *2005 Stock Compensation Survey* (2005).

32 "Pay Attention," *The Economist* (June 12, 2008), pp. 77–8.

33 "Last Gasp for Stock Options?," *The Wall Street Journal* – CFO Journal (August 26, 2013), online at http://blogs.wsj.com/cfo/2013/08/26/last-gasp-for-stock-options. See also "Five Trends in Stock Compensation," *HR Times* (March 20, 2014), online at hrtimesblog,com.

34 The Coca-Cola Company, online at www.coca-colacompany.com/content/dam/journey/us/en/private/fileassets/pdf/investors/annual-meeting/TCCC-2016-Proxy-Statement.pdf.

35 M. J. Mauboussin and D. Callahan, "A Long Look at Short-Termism: Questioning the Premise," *Journal of Applied Corporate Finance*, 27, no. 3 (Summer 2015), pp. 70–82.

36 "Hewitt Study Shows Long-Term Incentives in Executive Compensation Packages Are Back – but with a Catch," *Aon Hewitt* (August 5, 2010), online at www.hewittassociates.com.

37 For an overview, see J. Bol, "Subjectivity in Compensation Contracting," *Journal of Accounting Literature*, 28 (2009), pp. 1–24.

38 For a detailed discussion and further references to this literature, see M. Gibbs, K. A. Merchant, W. A. Van der Stede, and M. E. Vargus, "Determinants and Effects of Subjectivity in Incentives," *The Accounting Review*, 79, no. 2 (April 2004), pp. 409–36.

39 See also K. J. Murphy, "Performance Standards in Incentive Contracts," *Journal of Accounting and Economics*, 30, no. 3 (December 2000), pp. 245–78; X. Zhou and P. Swan, "Performance Thresholds in Managerial Incentive Contracts," *Journal of Business*, 76, no. 4 (October 2003), pp. 665–96.

40 "Regulations and Lower Returns Put Pressure on Pay and Bonuses," *The Financial Times* (April 24, 2014), online at on.ft.com/1JFJxum.

41 "Bonuses Are Back, but with Tighter Rules and Better Targets," *Aon Media Center* (September 17, 2014), online at aon.mediaroom.com/news-releases?item=137052.

42 "Companies Using Employee Engagement to Attract, Retain Top Talent," *Industry Week* (July 2, 2010), online at www.industryweek.com; D. Scott and T. McMullen, *The Impact of Rewards Programs on Employee Engagement*, Hay Group & World-at-Work (June 2010).

43 K. Abosch, J. Schermerhorn, and L. Wisper, "Broad-Based Variable Pay Goes Global," *Workspan* (May 2008), pp. 56–62.

44 "Forty-One Percent of Employees Say They Would Be Insulted by a Low Bonus," *World-at-Work* (November 3, 2010), online at www.worldatwork.org.

45 "Bonus Question: Cash Rewards or Gifts? Experts Are Divided," *The Los Angeles Times* (May 30, 1999), p. C5.

46 "Bonuses Are Bad for Bankers and Even Worse for Banks," *The Financial Times* (January 25, 2016), online at on.ft.com/1WJF8Ju.

47 See, for example, K. Pokorny, "Pay – But Do Not Pay Too Much: An Experimental Study on the Impact of Incentives," *Journal of Economic Behavior and Organizations*, 66, no. 2 (May 2008), pp. 251–64; D. Ariely, U. Gneezy, G. Loewenstein, and N. Mazar, "Large Stakes and Big Mistakes," *Review of Economic Studies*, 76, no. 2 (April 2009), pp. 451–69; see also W. A. Van der Stede, "The Pitfalls of Pay-for-Performance," *Finance & Management* (December 2007), pp. 10–13.

48 "Bonuses and the Illusion of Banking Performance," *The Financial Times* (November 25, 2015), online at on.ft.com/1LAeYRs.

49 "Bonuses Are Bad for Bankers and Even Worse for Banks," op. cit.

50 Ibid.

51 See, for example, "Meritocracy without the Numbers," *Strategy + Business* (September 22, 2015), online at strat.bz/SbPkwJU; "Why GE Had to Kill Its Annual Performance Reviews after More than Three Decades," *Quartz*, online at qz.com/428813; "The Measure of a Man: Reports of the Death of Performance Reviews Are Exaggerated," *The Economist* (February 20, 2016), online at econ.st/1U9VifD.

52 M. Buckingham and A. Goodall, "Reinventing Performance Management," *Harvard Business Review* (April 2015), online at hbr.org/2015/04/reinventing-performance-management.

53 See, for example, J. Efendi, A. Srivastava, and E. Swanson, "Why Do Corporate Managers Misstate Financial Statements? The Role of Option Compensation and Other Factors," *Journal of Financial Economics*, 85, no. 3 (September 2007), pp. 667–708; "CEOs Strategically Time News Releases for Their Own Benefit," *LSE Business Review* (March 22, 2016), online at blogs.lse.ac.uk/businessreview/2016/03/22/ceos-strategically-time-news-releases-for-their-own-benefit.

54 M. Buckingham and A. Goodall, "Reinventing Performance Management," *Harvard Business Review* (April 2015), online at hbr.org/2015/04/reinventing-performance-management.

55 "Hard to Get," *CFO Europe* (April 2009), pp. 38–41.

56 "Making Executive Pay Work: The Psychology of Incentives," *PwC Report* (2012), online at www.pwc.co.uk.

57 "Financial Organizations Shuffling Compensation Programs," *World-at-Work* (January 14, 2010), online at www.worldatwork.org. See also "UBS Extends Deferred Bonus Plan," *Bloomberg* (January 23, 2015), online at bloom.bg/1Bjucbk; "Moody's Urges Slower Bank Bonus Payouts," *The Financial Times* (December 9, 2014), online at on.ft.com/131jzOy.

58 "HSBC Chief Backs Bank Pay Reform," *BBC* (September 13, 2008), online at www.bbc.co.uk.

59 "Banks, Aware of Discord on Pay, Work to Adjust, a Survey Finds," *The Wall Street Journal Europe* (March 30, 2009), p. 3.

60 "UBS Extends Deferred Bonus Plan," op. cit.

61 R. Gopalan, T. Milbourn, F. Song, and A. V. Thakor, "Duration of Executive Compensation," *The Journal of Finance*, 69, no. 6 (December 2014), pp. 2777–2817.

62 "Small Chinese Cities Steer Away from GDP as Measure of Success," *The Financial Times* (August 13, 2014), online at on.ft.com/1rpzRqj.

63 "Bonus Question: Cash Rewards or Gifts? Experts Are Divided," op. cit.

64 "Bank Chief Champions Case for Fixed Pay," *Financial Times* (February 18, 2010), online at on.ft.com/1rse0F3.

65 "Bonuses Are Bad for Bankers and Even Worse for Banks," op. cit.

66 See also W. A. Van der Stede, "Designing Effective Reward Systems," *Finance & Management* (October 2009), pp. 6–9.

67 "John Lewis Staff Get £151m Bonus," *BBC* (March 11, 2010), online (www.bbc.co.uk); see also "TSB Freezes CEO Pay, Pledges Free Employee Shares in IPO," *Bloomberg* (June 5, 2014), online at bloom.bg/1GCxXK0.

68 "Slater & Gordon Offers One Million Shares to Employees," *The Law Society Gazette* (July 11, 2014), online (www.lawgazette.co.uk).

CASE STUDY
Harwood Medical Instruments PLC

Harwood Medical Instruments PLC (HMI), based just outside of Birmingham, England, manufactured specialty medical instruments and sold them in market niches that were becoming increasingly competitive and price sensitive because of pressures to reduce healthcare costs. HMI was organized into nine divisions each run by a general manager. Over the years, HMI had grown both organically and by acquisition. Six of the divisions had been acquired by HMI within the past decade.

All of HMI's divisions sold medical products to hospitals, laboratories, and/or doctors, so the need for product quality and reliability was high. The divisions varied significantly, however, in terms of the degree to which their success depended on, for example, development of new products, efficiency of production, and/or customer service.

Bonuses for division general managers were paid semi-annually. Up to the year 2009, these bonuses were calculated as 1% of division operating profits.

HMI's managing director, Andy Guthrie, had concerns, though, that the operating profit measure was too narrowly focused. He had been reading articles about performance measurement and decided to implement a "more balanced" scorecard. In November 2009, just before introducing a new bonus plan, Mr. Guthrie explained to his chief financial officer that he was willing to pay out higher bonuses than had been paid historically if improved performance warranted doing so.

The new plan provided a base bonus for division general managers of 1% of division operating profits for the half-year period. This base bonus was adjusted as follows:

- Increased by £5,000 if over 99% of deliveries were on time; by £2,000 if 95–99% of deliveries were on time; or by zero if less than 95% of deliveries were on time.
- Increased by £5,000 if sales returns were less than or equal to 1% of sales, or decreased by 50% of the excess of sales returns over 1% of sales.
- Increased by £1,000 for every patent application filed with the UK Intellectual Property Office.
- Reduced by the excess of scrap and rework costs over 1% of operating profit.
- Reduced by £5,000 if average customer satisfaction ratings were below 90%.

Exhibit 1 Harwood Medical Instruments PLC

Operating results for the Surgical Instruments and Ultrasound Diagnostic Equipment Divisions, 2010 (£ in 000s)

	Surgical Instruments Division		Ultrasound Diagnostic Equipment Division	
	1st half of 2010	2nd half of 2010	1st half of 2010	2nd half of 2010
Sales	£42,000	£44,000	£28,600	£29,000
Operating profit	£4,620	£4,400	£3,420	£4,060
On-time deliveries	95.4%	97.3%	98.2%	94.6%
Sales returns	£450	£420	£291	£289
Patent applications filed	0	1	4	8
Scrap and rework costs	£51.1	£45.0	£39.7	£28.2
Customer satisfaction (average)	78%	89%	81%	91%

If the bonus calculation resulted in a negative amount for a particular period, the manager received no bonus. Negative amounts were not carried forward to the next period.

Exhibit 1 shows results for two representative HMI divisions for the year 2010, the first year under the new bonus plan. The Surgical Instruments Division (SID), one of HMI's original businesses, sold a variety of surgical instruments, including scissors, scalpels, retractors, and clamps. The markets for these products were mature, so growth was relatively slow. Not much innovation was needed, but controlling costs was critical. The Ultrasound Diagnostic Equipment Division (Ultrasound), which was acquired in 2007, sold and serviced ultrasound probes, transducers, and diagnostic imaging systems. The ultrasound market promised excellent growth and profits if the division could keep its sophisticated products on the cutting edge technologically and control both product development and production costs effectively.

In 2009, the total annual bonuses for the year earned by the managers of SID and Ultrasound were approximately £85,000 and £74,000, respectively.

This case was prepared by Professor Kenneth A. Merchant.

CASE STUDY
Superconductor Technologies, Inc.

In October 2003, Martin (Marty) McDermut, Senior VP, CFO, and Secretary of Superconductor Technologies, Inc. (STI), was reflecting on some issues related to his company's compensation and incentive systems. He had multiple concerns. Marty knew that STI's most important asset was its people, and he was worried about employee retention. STI's stock price was stuck far below its historical highs, so most of the options that had been granted to employees were "underwater." Without the prospects of significant rewards, some of the company's key people might be "ready to bolt." He wondered, "What can we do so that these things that we have put in place don't vanish?"

Marty also worried that some of the incentive system elements might motivate some behaviors that were not in the shareholders' best interest. One specific concern of this type was that top management would be too motivated to try to sell the company to cash in the large numbers of options that they had been granted. He sighed:

> **These things have tremendous motivational effects, but they can really get you in trouble if you don't think the issues all the way through.**

Company history and strategy

Superconductor Technologies, Inc. was founded in Santa Barbara, California, in 1987 by Nobel Prize winner Dr. J. Robert Schrieffer, who teamed up with three venture capitalists to form a company to capitalize on a scientific breakthrough known as high-temperature superconductivity (HTS) technology. In the mid-1990s, STI managers decided to focus their application of HTS technology on the wireless communications industry. In 1997, STI began the transformation to an operating company with the launch of its first commercial product, the SuperFilter®. M. Peter Thomas, a wireless-industry veteran, was hired as CEO.

By 2003, STI was the global leader in developing, manufacturing, and marketing HTS products for wireless communication networks. STI's products incorporated patented technologies that extended network coverage, increased capacity utilization, and improved both the uplink and downlink radio frequency signals, thus lowering the incidence of dropped and blocked calls. They also enabled higher wireless transmission data rates while reducing operators' capital and operating costs. Over 3,000 STI systems had been installed worldwide, making STI the clear leader in the HTS wireless network optimization technology marketplace. STI's successes stemmed largely from its technological developments, including patented thin-film technologies and unique software design and simulation tools. It planned to exploit its management, engineering, and manufacturing expertise to maintain and expand its market leadership in radio frequency enhancement solutions.

In 2003, STI, which had nearly 300 employees, was organized into two main operating entities. One was located in Sunnyvale, California, at the former site of Conductus, a company acquired in December 2002. People at the Sunnyvale location were primarily involved in research, some of which was funded by the federal government on a cost-plus basis. The other operating entity was located in Santa Barbara, California. Personnel at the Santa Barbara location were responsible for the company's commercial applications.

STI management looked at the year 2002 as a "watershed year," even though STI reported a net loss of $19.5 million that year (see financial statements in Exhibits 1 and2). The reason was the increased market acceptance of STI's products, which was expected to fuel further revenue growth and bring the company closer to profitability. In its entire 17-year history, STI had never made a profit. In 2002, STI also completed a multimillion-dollar expansion of its production facilities in Santa Barbara to ramp up production and further improve product quality.

Since 2001, STI revenues had grown quite rapidly. In 2003, revenues were expected to be nearly $50 million, up from $22 million in 2002. In both 2002 and 2003, STI was named one of the "Technology Fast 50" companies in the Los Angeles area.

STI was considered to be a consensus-driven company. As Marty McDermut phrased it, "People buy into our major decisions before we go ahead." Plans were developed on a bottom-up basis. Performance was reviewed monthly, and the forecasts for the remainder of the year were updated quarterly.

STI went public in March 1993 (NASDAQ: SCON), with 1.5 million shares offered at $10 per share. In an eight-week period in early 2000, STI's stock price shot up above $100, but it came down as quickly as it had risen. Most of the time since then, the stock had been trading below $5 per share (see Exhibit 3).

Still, STI's future looked bright. In 2003, approximately 150,000 wireless communications base stations were deployed in the United States alone, providing service to nearly 140 million people.[1] The number of US subscribers to mobile services had been growing at 14% per year, and the average monthly minutes of use per person was growing at an annual rate of 26%. The combined effect of more subscribers and more minutes of use resulted in an exponential increase in total wireless communications traffic. That growth was expected to continue, and the greater wireless traffic had also led to a rise in radio frequency interference, resulting in more dropped and blocked calls and origination failures, outcomes that negatively affect customer satisfaction. Consequently, the wireless operators had continuing needs to find new, cost-effective ways to increase network traffic while improving network performance. STI's products, which could be employed at a fraction of the cost of building more base stations, were designed to be part of the solution to the industry's delivery problems.

Elements of management compensation

The compensation package for STI's top 30 people, those down to the director level (one level below vice president), was comprised of three elements:

1. **Base salary.** STI set its salaries at competitive levels. For most employees, including top executives, annual salary increases were in the range of 0–5%.
2. **Cash bonuses.** All top STI executives were included in a bonus plan that provided cash awards based on

[1] The global numbers were nearly one million base stations serving more than one billion customers.

Table 1 Key elements of corporate "Performance Scorecard"

Cash	Number of employees
Sales	Warranty expenses
Profits	Inventory
Timing of sales	Yield
Receivables (days outstanding)	Gross margins
On-time delivery performance	Product reliability

the achievement of a weighted combination of corporate and individual objectives. The targeted bonus awards varied by organization level, from 25% to 40% of base salary.

Up through 2002, all bonuses were based exclusively on corporate performance. The compensation committee of the board of directors reached a judgment about corporate performance by comparing results measured in terms of the elements of a "performance scorecard" (see Table 1) with expectations.

The performance evaluation judgments did not automatically weight all the measurement elements equally in importance. Ken Barry, VP-Human Resources and Environmental Health & Safety, suspected that sales (revenue growth) was by far the most important criterion considered by the compensation committee. He postulated that the judgments about bonuses might come about as follows:

Let's see ... they met the revenue target; ... they didn't earn as much profit as we'd expected; ... but, they didn't have any major operational problems internally or externally, ... and they signed a big deal ... so, taken together, that probably warrants a bonus equal to potential for the year ...

Ken concluded that what it really came down to in normal years was for the compensation committee to decide whether to award a bonus at 80%, 100%, or 120% of the target bonus. Because the Board met with the key executives about four times a year, Ken believed that they had sufficient knowledge to make these bonus decisions, although the evaluations were undeniably subjective.

Before 2002, everyone received the same, undifferentiated bonus potential percentage. In 2002, however, the compensation committee concluded that some executives had performed better than others. They decided that these differences should be recognized by basing some of the bonus awards on individual performance. They decided to base the bonuses 75% on corporate performance and 25% on individual performance.

Each executive's individual performance was evaluated in terms of achievements in 4–9 performance areas tailored to the individual's areas of responsibility. Examples of achievements that were considered in the evaluations of specific individuals included:

- Successfully accomplish a project milestone;
- Reduce costs of products manufactured;
- Establish a needed line of credit;
- Maintain receivables at a level equal to or less than 28 days outstanding;
- Make significant new hires/retain valued employees;
- Maintain safe workplace (no lost-time accidents).

The evaluations of individual performance were linked to bonus awards as follows:

Evaluation	% of target bonus earned
Exceeded objectives	37.5
Met objectives	25
Partially missed objectives	12.5
Substantively missed objectives	0

When the compensation committee was not sure of its evaluations, they generally asked for more information or for an explanation from the "team leader," CEO Peter Thomas, before making the final call.

3. **Stock options.** Annually, almost all STI employees were given stock options. The purpose of the options was to promote the success, and enhance the value, of the company by linking the personal interests of participating employees to those of the company's stockholders and by providing such employees with an incentive for outstanding performance. The details of the stock option plan had been modified somewhat over the years, but all the options granted were 10-year options, and they vested over either four or five years.

The number of options granted varied depending on organization level, tenure, and individual performance. Lower-level employees were given only a few, perhaps only 200, options per year. Top management received thousands of options annually. Exhibits 3 and 4 provide detail on the option grants given to STI's top five executives.

Ken Barry estimated that in a normal year, about 10% of the workforce (30 employees, say) did not receive stock options, for one of three reasons, each of which explained the treatment of about 10 of the excluded employees. The first reason was because some employees did not meet performance expectations. Ken added, "By not meeting performance expectations I mean that we usually let these employees go within the next year." Second, some employees were not given the annual allotment of options for equity reasons. Some of them, for example, had recently received extra options because they had been promoted. And third, extra options were not provided to employees hired during the last quarter of the year.[2]

Implementation of the compensation plans

In 2001, STI failed to achieve its revenue plan by a narrow margin. All STI executives were given 80% of their target bonus.

The year 2002 was not a good one. STI did not come close to achieving its aggressive revenue plan. The STI plan was set at $32 million, and the actual revenues for 2002 were $22 million. In July 2002, management implemented a salary cut of 10% for the top 10 executives. At the end of the year, no bonuses were paid, and virtually all the options that had been granted previously were underwater.

In March 2003, STI's board approved a 2003 Equity Incentive Plan that reserved six million shares for issuance to key employees, directors, and consultants of the company. Two million of these shares were reserved for the top 20 executives. This plan replaced other stock option plans created in 1992, 1998, and 1999. It was designed both to help ensure that STI did not lose its key employees and to drive employees to focus on having the company become profitable. Becoming profitable was important because management wanted to raise more money, but they were told that would be difficult until and if the company started earning profits.

The 2003 Equity Incentive Plan provided 10-year options to be awarded on January 1, 2004, with "cliff vesting" after five years.[3] However, this plan also included a unique feature, a promise of accelerated vesting – 50% on January 1, 2004, and 50% on January 1, 2005 – if the company was profitable in the fourth quarter of 2003 and if the profits were judged to be sustainable.[4]

In January 2003, the executives whose salaries had been cut had their salaries reinstated to prior levels. They were not given back pay, however.

Issues for the future

Both Marty McDermut and Ken Barry raised issues about the incentive packages that STI should use in the future. If accounting rules regarding stock options were changed to require the immediate recording of the value of the options as an expense, as seemed likely to happen, should that cause the company either to discontinue the granting of options or to restrict their use, perhaps only for top executives? Should the company instead substitute restricted stock, or some combination of restricted stock and options? Marty did not think that the solution would be just to provide higher bonus payments because those payments would cause "a big hit to the P&L."

Particularly if the use of options was to be restricted, Ken Barry thought that the company would need more deferred compensation options, mechanisms that

[2] All employees were given stock options when they were first hired.

[3] That is, all the options would vest on January 1, 2009.

[4] Without the cliff vesting feature, the accelerated vesting in this plan would have had a significant accounting implication. The original fixed price options did not require the recording of any compensation expense because the options were granted at the market price at the time of grant (*Accounting Principles Board Statement 25, Accounting for Stock Issued to Employees*, October 1972). However, without the cliff vesting provision, a change in terms, in this case the acceleration of vesting, if it happened, would require STI to record compensation expense in accordance with the "variable method" (*FASB Interpretation 44, Accounting for Certain Transactions Involving Stock Compensation: An Interpretation of APB Opinion No. 25*, March 31, 2000). Under variable accounting, compensation expense is recognized based on the excess of the underlying stock's market price over the exercise price on the exercise date. Then, prior to the exercise date, compensation expense is estimated each period. It varies with the movement in the price of the company's stock in comparison to the exercise price. Therefore, if a company changes the terms of its stock option grants, it is subject to the uncertainty of how much compensation expense it will have to record, not only during the vesting period of the option, but until the option is actually exercised by the employee. If the company's stock performs well, the company will probably have to take a hit to earnings.

would allow the company to spread the employees' compensation over 5, 10, or even 15 years. Deferred compensation approaches had tax benefits for the employees, and they allowed the company to save cash during its most rapid growth period.

Related was a concern about the appropriate short-term/long-term balance of the incentive package. Should STI link the much desired annual profit objective more strongly with incentives, or should the company continue to be patient in its positioning of the firm for long-term success? Ken also was not sure whether the assignments of the rewards should be less subjective after the firm became profitable.

Ken had also started thinking about issues that the company would face when it expanded internationally. STI had no foreign employees as yet, but Ken knew that incentive approaches varied markedly around the world. He wanted to be prepared to give recommendations to management when and if the international expansion took place.

Exhibit 1 Superconductor Technologies, Inc.: Income statement data for years ending December 31 ($ millions)

	2002	2001	2000	1999	1998
Net sales or revenues	22.40	12.39	9.96	7.12	7.98
Cost of goods sold	17.36	8.49	13.92	5.54	10.79
Depreciation, depletion, and amortization	1.93	2.14	1.79	1.31	0.94
Gross income	**3.11**	**1.77**	**-5.75**	**0.27**	**-3.74**
Selling, general, & admin expenses	18.90	18.90	15.09	10.88	5.44
Other operating expenses	0.00	0.00	0.00	0.00	0.00
Other expenses – total	38.18	29.52	30.80	17.72	17.16
Operating income	-15.79	-17.13	-20.85	-10.60	-9.18
Extraordinary charge – pretax	3.80	0.98	0.13	0.00	0.00
Nonoperating interest income	0.22	1.05	0.81	0.02	0.08
Earnings before interest and taxes (EBIT)	**-19.37**	**-17.06**	**-20.17**	**-10.58**	**-9.10**
Interest expense on debt	0.15	0.15	0.48	0.30	0.06
Pretax income	-19.51	-17.20	-20.66	-10.88	-9.16
Income taxes	0.00	0.00	0.00	0.00	0.00
Net income before extra items/preferred div	**-19.51**	**-17.20**	**-20.66**	**-10.88**	**-9.16**
Extra items & gain(loss) sale of assets	0.00	0.00	-10.61	0.00	0.00
Net income before preferred dividends	-19.51	-17.20	-31.27	-10.88	-9.16
Preferred dividend requirements	1.76	2.60	2.20	1.36	0.27
Net income available to common	**-21.27**	**-19.80**	**-22.86**	**-12.24**	**-9.43**

Exhibit 2 Superconductor Technologies, Inc.: Balance sheet data for years ending December 31 ($ millions)

Assets	2002	2001	2000	1999	1998
Cash and ST investments	18.19	15.21	31.82	0.07	0.31
Receivables (net)	3.41	1.45	3.69	1.59	1.94
Total inventories	6.35	5.73	3.78	2.75	2.72
Raw materials	1.84	1.39	1.09	0.43	0.82
Work in progress	3.14	2.95	1.96	1.69	1.67
Finished goods	2.01	1.40	0.72	0.63	0.24
Progress payments & other	–0.65	0.00	0.00	0.00	0.00
Prepaid expenses	0.00	0.00	0.00	0.00	0.00
Other current assets	0.56	0.60	0.50	0.45	0.17
Current assets – total	28.50	22.98	39.79	4.85	5.14
Long-term receivables	0.82	0.00	0.00	0.00	0.00
Property, plant & equipment – net	11.09	5.22	4.99	4.10	5.11
Property, plant & equipment – gross	23.74	16.24	14.34	12.15	12.10
Accumulated depreciation	12.65	11.03	9.35	8.05	6.99
Other assets	25.74	1.96	1.98	2.14	2.25
Deferred charges	0.00	0.00	0.00	0.00	0.00
Tangible other assets	0.49	0.28	0.11	0.21	0.18
Intangible other assets	25.25	1.68	1.88	1.93	2.07
Total assets	**66.15**	**30.16**	**46.76**	**11.09**	**12.51**
Liabilities & shareholders equity					
Accounts payable	5.89	2.70	2.00	1.80	2.40
ST debt & current portion of LT debt	1.55	0.28	0.24	2.16	0.81
Accrued payroll	1.05	0.84	0.90	0.67	0.58
Income taxes payable	0.00	0.00	0.00	0.00	0.00
Dividends payable	0.00	0.00	0.00	0.00	0.00
Other current liabilities	3.50	0.41	0.46	0.24	0.00
Current liabilities – total	12.00	4.23	3.60	4.87	3.79
Long-term debt	0.57	0.27	0.51	0.75	0.93
Other liabilities	3.23	2.00	4.24	0.00	0.00
Total liabilities	**15.80**	**6.50**	**8.35**	**5.62**	**4.72**
Preferred stock	0.00	37.53	0.00	20.34	8.98
Common equity	50.34	–13.87	38.41	–14.87	–1.20
Common stock	0.06	0.02	0.02	0.01	0.01
Capital surplus	154.74	73.34	110.65	32.21	35.01
Other appropriated reserves	0.00	–2.28	–4.52	0.00	0.00
Retained earnings	–104.46	–84.95	–67.75	–47.09	–36.22
Total liabilities & shareholders equity	**66.15**	**30.16**	**46.76**	**11.09**	**12.51**
Common shares outstanding (thousands)	59,823.55	18,579.16	17,823.16	7,739.22	7,722.59

Exhibit 3 Superconductor Technologies, Inc.: Stock performance Copyright 2003 Yahoo! Inc. http://finance.yahoo.com/

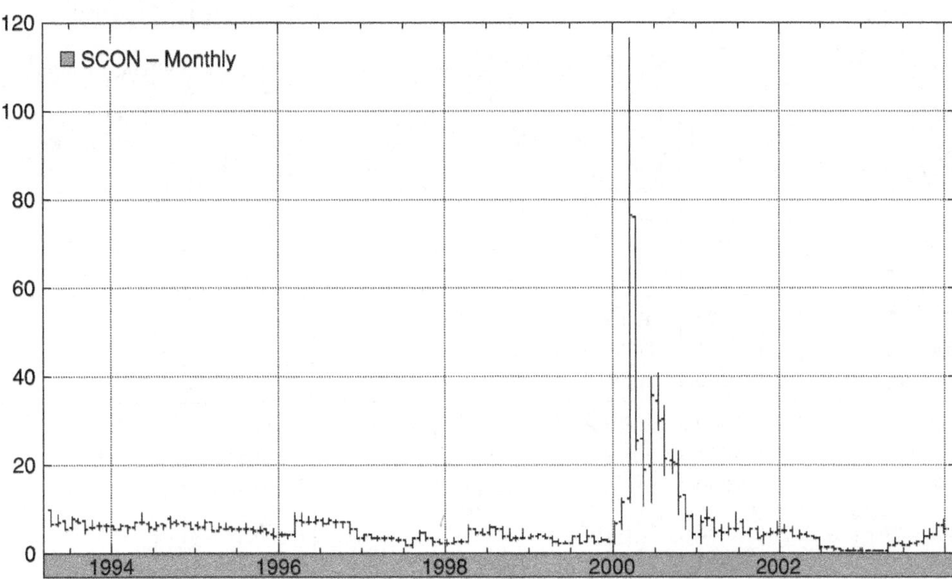

Exhibit 4 Superconductor Technologies, Inc.: Executive officer compensation

The following table sets forth all compensation received for services rendered to the Company in all capacities during the fiscal years ended December 31, 2002, 2001, and 2000 by the Company's Chief Executive Officer and the four executive officers other than the Chief Executive Officer whose total salary and bonus for fiscal year 2002 exceeded $100,000.

		Annual compensation			Long-term compensation	
Name and principal position	Year	Salary ($)	Bonus ($)	Other ($)[1]	Securities underlying options (#)	All other compensation ($)[2]
M. Peter Thomas	2002	303,854	–	–	125,000	1,980
President and Chief	2001	300,014	72,000	–	75,000	2,323
Executive Officer	2000	285,394	70,000	–	250,000	1,290
E. Ray Cotten	2002	194,997	–	–	57,750	6,180
Senior Vice President,	2001	209,467	30,172	–	7,300	7,250
Business Development	2000	195,582	28,080	–	20,000	3,810
Robert B. Hammond	2002	208,394	–	–	57,750	690
Senior Vice President and	2001	205,945	29,628	–	3,650	809
Chief Technical Officer	2000	194,613	27,675	–	40,000	690
Robert L. Johnson[4]	2002	186,267	–	–	66,000	690
President, STI Wireless	2001	182,163	26,244	–	38,350	809
Systems, North America	2000	116,462[4]	20,048	–	100,000	504
Martin S. McDermut[5]	2002	194,961	–	–	43,750	690
Senior Vice President,	2001	193,895	23,310	–	43,750	809
Chief Financial Officer and Secretary	2000	167,212[5]	24,975	43,374[3]	100,000	398
Charles E. Shalvoy[6]	2002	277,052	–	–	–	–
President and CEO	2001	264,992	56,644	–	153,000	–[7]
of Conductus	2000	250,185	66,250	–	200,000	–

[1]Excludes certain perquisites and other amounts that, for any executive officer, in the aggregate did not exceed the lesser of $50,000 or 10% of the total annual salary and bonus for such executive officer.
[2]Term life insurance premiums.
[3]One-time relocation expenses.
[4]Mr. Johnson joined the Company in April 2000.
[5]Mr. McDermut joined the Company in February 2000.
[6]Mr. Shalvoy joined the Company in December 2002. All compensation paid by Conductus prior to acquisition of Conductus by the Company. Mr. Shalvoy is the President of the Conductus subsidiary and an Executive Vice President of Superconductor Technologies, Inc.
[7]Because Conductus provided group term life insurance for its employees and named executive officers on an aggregate basis, Conductus is unable to determine the amount of term life insurance premiums paid by Conductus for Mr. Shalvoy during the 2002, 2001, and 2000 fiscal years.

Source: *STI Proxy Statement*, May 23, 2003

Exhibit 5 Superconductor Technologies, Inc.: Option grants to executives in 2002

The following table sets forth certain information regarding stock options granted during the fiscal year ended December 31, 2002, to each of the executive officers named in the table under "Executive Officer Compensation – Summary Compensation Table."

	Individual grants				Potential realizable value at assumed annual rates of stock price appreciation for option term[3]	
Name	Number of securities underlying options granted[1]	% of Total Options granted to employees in fiscal year[2]	Exercise price ($/share)	Expiration date	5% ($)	10% ($)
M. Peter Thomas	125,000	15%	5.60	2/4/2012	385,930	950,563
E. Ray Cotten	57,750	7%	5.60	2/4/2012	178,300	439,160
Robert B. Hammond	57,750	7%	5.23	1/23/2012	178,300	439,160
Robert L. Johnson	66,000	8%	5.23	1/23/2012	190,307	468,736
Martin S. McDermut	43,750	5%	5.23	1/23/2012	126,151	310,715
Charles E. Shalvoy[4]	–	–	–	–	–	–

[1]Except as set forth herein, each option vests over a four-year period at the rate of ¼th of the shares subject to the option at the end of the first 12 months and 1/36 the of the remaining shares subject to the option at the end of each monthly period thereafter so long as such optionee's employment with the Company has not terminated.

[2]Total number of shares subject to options granted to employees in fiscal 2002 was 851,975, which number includes options granted to employee directors, but excludes options granted to nonemployee directors and consultants.

[3]The Potential Realizable Value is calculated based on the fair market value on the date of grant, which is equal to the exercise price of options granted in fiscal 2002, assuming that the stock appreciates in value from the date of grant until the end of the option term at the compounded annual rate specified (5% and 10%). Potential Realizable Value is net of the option exercise price. The assumed rates of appreciation are specified in rules of the SEC and do not represent the Company's estimate or projection of future stock price. Actual gains, if any, resulting from stock option exercises and common stock holdings are dependent on the future performance of the common stock and overall stock market conditions, as well as the option holders' continued employment through the exercise/vesting period. There can be no assurance that the amounts reflected in this table will be achieved.

[4]Mr. Shalvoy joined the Company in December 2002 and did not receive any options from the Company in 2002, although he did receive options from Conductus in 2002 prior to the acquisition.

Source: STI Proxy Statement, May 23, 2003.

This case was prepared by Professors Kenneth A. Merchant and Wim A. Van der Stede.

CASE STUDY
Raven Capital, LLC

In late December 2009, portfolio managers at hedge fund Raven Capital, LLC had just finished delivering annual performance reviews and year-end bonuses to their staffs. They spent considerable time and effort trying both to allocate bonuses fairly and to keep employees happy. But those two goals were sometimes in conflict. Every year some employees were surprised by the amount of their bonuses. Some of the surprises were positive, but inevitably some were negative.

CFO Julie Behrens reflected on Raven's performance evaluation and incentive compensation plan:

> **Hedge funds like ours have access to lots of data. We have many performance measures and indices that we can use for benchmarking purposes. But interestingly, our incentive plan is not purely quantitative. We consider the performance metrics, but none of them gives us a complete picture of an employee's contribution to the company. The management team makes our evaluation system work with painstaking qualitative adjustments. Still, I wonder if we should make at least a portion of our incentive plan more formulaic.**

Industry background

Hedge fund managers pursue absolute returns on their underlying investments. The investments can be any combination of financial vehicles, including stocks, bonds, commodities, currencies, and derivatives. Sometimes hedge fund managers hold cash, sell short, and/or buy or sell options or futures.

The word "hedge" means to manage risk. Risks come in many forms, such as inflation risk, market risk, interest rate risk, currency risk, sector risk, and regional risk. Hedge fund managers are experts in designing hedging positions for most perceivable risks, making a true hedge fund less risky than a traditional long-only investment fund, at least in theory. But each hedge fund is unique. Different hedge funds use different mixes of investment vehicles, and their strategies vary significantly from conservative to highly speculative.

Hedge funds differ from other managed funds in a few key areas. Hedge fund investors are typically required to have high income, high net worth, and demonstrated investment knowledge. Because hedge funds manage money for a limited range of sophisticated, accredited investors, they operate with fewer regulations than other funds. They are less restricted in their use of leverage and are distinguished from mutual funds by a greater flexibility in investment strategies. Hedge fund management companies are typically organized as limited partnerships. The manager acts as the general partner, and the investors act as the limited partners.

Most hedge fund companies use the same business model. They derive revenue from two sources: management fees and incentive fees. Management fees, typically 1–2% of assets under management (AUM), are earned regardless of performance. Incentive fees, collected annually, are performance-based, typically totaling 20% of a fund's return above a "high water mark," the highest level of value the fund ever had for each investor. If a fund loses money, its managers are not penalized, but they cannot collect further incentive fees until the fund surpasses its high water mark; i.e. until the losses are recovered. The high water marks are different for each investor, depending on the point at which they invested their monies. (See Exhibit 1 for a simple high water mark example.) Hedge funds typically use the management fees to cover their operating expenses. Incentive fees are normally distributed to staff as bonuses.

The year 2008 was an extremely challenging year for the hedge fund industry. The S&P 500 index dropped 37%, the credit markets tightened, and investors around the world fled to safe investments. AUM at hedge funds fell sharply due to trading losses and redemptions, as investors rushed to liquidate their assets. A record number of hedge funds closed in 2008. By 2009, the S&P 500 rose 24%, regaining some of the prior year's losses. According to several indexes that track hedge fund performance, hedge funds that survived 2008 were up 18%

or more in 2009, making it the best year for hedge fund performance since 2003. However, almost half of all hedge funds were still below their high water marks at the end of 2009.

Raven Capital, LLC

Investment strategy

Raven Capital, LLC was founded in 1999 by Maxwell (Max) Stoneman. Total AUM in 2009 were slightly less than $1 billion. Raven's funds bought and sold long and short positions in domestic equities. Raven managers focused their investments in industries – financial, energy, technology, consumer products, and healthcare – in which they had years of expertise and many management contacts. Their heaviest investment weights were in the financial and energy industries.

Almost half of Raven's AUM came from "funds of funds" – funds that invested in portfolios of different hedge funds. Another 33% came from pension and retirement funds, and 18% came from high net worth individuals. Only 1.5% came from foundations and endowments. (See Exhibit 2 for a chart of capital sources by investor type.)

As a traditional hedge fund, Raven made investment decisions based on fundamentals, not short-term momentum, arbitrage opportunities, or expectations of superior predictions of macroeconomic trends. Analytical horse power was considered key to Raven's success. Raven managers sought superior returns based on a thorough understanding of strategic, financial, and competitive dynamics of companies and industries, as well as selective entry and exit points. Specifically for long positions, Raven targeted both growth companies and solid companies that were currently out of favor. Raven also took short positions in companies that they perceived had fundamental problems, aggressive accounting and overstated earnings, and/or stock prices that reflected unrealistic earnings expectations.

Raven's approach was disciplined. Managers were cognizant of macroeconomic trends, but macro trends did not materially alter the overall strategies, long/short exposures, or industry focus. As portfolio manager Jeffrey Lomintz put it, "We do what we say we're going to do within the bands that are prescribed because we want to have product integrity." Raven funds had tight net exposure targets (long exposure plus the absolute value of short exposure). Net exposure for their long/short funds was typically 40%–55%.

Organization

Raven's 17 employees were organized into two groups, Investment Management and Business Operations. Max Stoneman was the general manager and CIO of Raven. Together with Jeffrey Lomnitz, Max also managed the Investment Management Group. Max and Jeffrey acted as Raven's portfolio managers (PMs), managing 100% of the firm's assets. They supervised the analysts and traders who comprised the balance of Investment Management. Julie Behrens managed Business Operations. (See Exhibit 3 for an organization chart.)

The analysts were industry specialists who closely studied and monitored the publicly traded companies in their industry. They studied financial statements, interviewed management, and ran models, working to identify inflection points in companies' business models. Analysts frequently championed stocks for inclusion in Raven funds, and made entry and exit price recommendations. They were also responsible for monitoring stocks once investments had been made in them.

As PMs, Jeffrey and Max were responsible for "pulling the trigger" on stock picks. They considered analysts' inputs, and decided which stocks to buy at what price, and how to size the positions. The analysts perceived the PM's investment styles as being somewhat different. One was described as wanting to be a "home run hitter." The other was said to take "smaller cuts at the ball because he did not like volatility."

The traders were responsible for executing buy and sell orders at the portfolio managers' target prices. Hitting target prices could be difficult, especially for illiquid stocks or to buy and sell orders large enough to move the stock price. Traders made use of relationships and negotiations with executing brokers to obtain favorable pricing.

Raven was a relatively small firm. Most of its employees lived in the same neighborhood, and knew each other socially as well as professionally. Employee tenure at Raven was higher than the hedge fund industry average.

Performance

For over a decade, the Raven Capital team had delivered superior risk adjusted returns for the investors who entrusted their monies to the company. For example, Raven's Flagship Fund (the Fund), the firm's oldest, had an annualized return since inception of 14.8%, as compared to a 7.3% annualized return for the S&P 500 firms in that period. In approximately 70% of the months when the market was down, the Fund's values either increased or were down less than the market declined. (See Exhibit 4 for the Fund's monthly fund risk report.)

But 2008 was a year for the record books on the downside. Though Raven funds beat the overall market, they lost significant absolute value. The Fund dropped 27% (the S&P dropped 37%). While technically the job of a hedge fund was to participate when the market went up, and lose less when the market went down, many clients had an expectation that the fund would never lose money, let alone a significant amount of money.

Raven's liquidity terms were much more liberal than those of many hedge funds. Raven funds did not have lock-ups or gates.[1] For example, if a fund had a gate of 15%, and investors requested withdrawals totaling 25% of the fund's assets, fund managers could legally refuse all withdrawals exceeding 15%. Investors desperate for cash sold their assets that were liquid regardless of performance, and the funds entrusted with Raven were liquid. That liquidity policy contributed significantly to the decline of Raven's AUM in 2008 as investors needed to get cash fast.

By the end of 2009, both the markets and Raven funds turned a corner. The Fund was up 36% and had exceeded its high water mark. But despite the investment gains, the firm's AUM had not returned to anything near their historical levels. By the end of 2009, Raven's AUM were only 41% of what they had been at the beginning of 2008.

Analyst compensation

Raven analysts earned a minimum base salary of $180,000 plus an annual bonus granted at the discretion of management. Bonuses fluctuated significantly but generally ranged from approximately $150,000 upward to several million dollars.

Raven's incentive fees earned became the annual bonus pool. The bonus pool was split two-thirds to Investment Management and one-third to Business Operations, as was traditional in the industry. Within Investment Management, the PMs typically took a standard percentage of the pool, and the balance was allocated to the other employees.

[1] *Lock-ups* restricted withdrawals of the original investment in a hedge fund for a period of time. *Gates* limited the percentage of a fund's assets that could be withdrawn during any redemption period.

The bonus allocation decisions were made subjectively by the management team, Max and Jeffrey (the two PMs) and Julie (CFO). They considered many quantitative measures but applied considerable judgment in deciding what quantitative factors to consider and how to weight the multiple indicators in importance. Jeffrey explained, "Most importantly we need a process that is fair and repeatable."

The bonuses were awarded based on a combination of company, team, and individual performance. For evaluating analysts, the primary quantitative evaluation measure was an analyst performance report (see Exhibit 5) that was updated monthly and closely tracked by all members of the Raven team. The performance of every stock that an analyst "touched" was coded, and the monthly profits or losses from those stocks were tracked in the report.

Though the management team knew that at least some analysts would prefer to be awarded bonuses based entirely on quantitative measures, they recognized several difficulties with a strictly formulaic approach. First, analysts could only choose stocks within their industry of expertise, so their performance could be helped or hindered by industry performance. Though theoretically their performance could be measured against an industry benchmark, managers believed that in practice it was very difficult to find a robust index.

Second, exposure to short or long positions could have a significant effect on performance as well. It may well have been in an analyst's best interest to take only long positions in a rising market, but Raven strategy often required somebody to "take shorts for the team."

Finally, analysts could "touch" stocks in several ways that were not reflected in the stock performance report. For example, if an analyst made a stock recommendation, but the PM chose not to buy a position, the stock was not tracked on the report. Several analysts kept track of those stocks on their own, to receive credit for good picks even if they did not become part of a fund. Equally, if an analyst made a "save" by recommending getting out of a position, it was not directly reflected in the report, either. Analysts could clearly also make bad calls that the PM chose not to implement. Jeffrey explained, "I could follow an analyst's recommendation to buy a stock at $10 and ignore his recommendation to sell at $15. If I ultimately sell at $18, who gets the credit? The analyst had a good idea but he told me to sell the stock earlier, and I didn't, so we made even more money. That's one area where the performance evaluations get murky."

Ultimately, company performance drove bonuses, since the company couldn't pay out more than it earned in incentive fees. Max explained,

> There are years where everyone is overpaid. If the firm has a great year and you have horrible performance, you'll be overpaid. But in years like this year, everyone is underpaid. You may have done well, but fees were lower because we had to get up to our high water marks again. There were not as many dollars to go around. But my memory is not that short.

Management used a "mental carry forward" to compensate people they felt had been overpaid or underpaid in prior years. Managers also adjusted bonuses based on qualitative factors. For example, they considered whether analysts wasted time with poor recommendations. Jeffrey explained, "Some analysts use a dart board approach. If you throw enough darts, you'll eventually hit the board, but it puts the burden on the PMs to sort through all those ideas."

From the analysts' perspective, Raven's evaluation method, while not perfectly visible, was generally seen as fair. The analysts were not oblivious to the economics of the business. They were aware of how much the company earned each year, and had a general idea of what they deserved as a bonus. While they sometimes believed their bonus award was not completely fair compared with other analysts, the differences were generally not huge. As analyst Winston Hill put it, "we're not underpaid by 50%." Winston explained further:

> I don't know the mad science behind how Max comes up with some of his performance metrics. I'm sure he runs the numbers a number of different ways. There is an art to this as well as a science ... Everyone thinks that Max and Jeffrey are fair people. This model would not work if there wasn't a trust factor.

Having such a subjective process was not the industry norm. Many other hedge funds did use a formulaic approach, most typically awarding a pre-negotiated percentage of fund returns as an annual bonus. Winston reflected, "The great thing about that is you know exactly what you make."

Concerns

Each year seemed to present unique evaluation challenges. Julie listed some of the questions that had to be addressed:

> What is the firm making? How are the funds doing? How should we evaluate employee contribution? Should we pay for tenure? How much of the bonus pool should go to those working in administration?

Reflecting on the 2009 year-end performance reviews, the Raven management team had some concerns. They feared that bonus expectations had become unmanageable. They valued their analysts and wanted to keep them happy. High water marks had made this year unusually difficult for Raven and for hedge funds in general. But because fund returns were high, some analysts felt entitled to bonuses similar to the record amounts earned in 2007. And, as Max and Jeffrey both noted, "Most employees overrate their performances and overvalue their worth." In the past, it was not uncommon for analysts who were unhappy with their compensation to jump to companies with more assets or to start hedge funds of their own, but that possibility had become far less likely given the state of the industry.

Max and Jeffrey were also concerned that they were not accomplishing much in the way of evaluating and improving performance through the review process. During their reviews, analysts paid careful attention to the bonus award, but were unable to focus on anything else. One possibility that Julie had suggested was to move performance reviews to September, to separate performance discussions from the awarding of bonuses, which would still be done in December.

Exhibit 1 Hypothetical high water mark example

	Pool at beginning of period	% return	$ return	Pool at end of period	Incentive fee earned at rate of 20% of fund returns
Year 1	$800,000	+25%	+$200,000	$1,000,000	$40,000*
Year 2	$1,000,000	−20%	−$200,000	$800,000	$0
Year 3	$800,000	+10%	−$80,000	$880,000	$0
Year 4	$880,000	+25%	+$220,000	$1,100,000	$20,000**

*($1,000,000 – $800,000) × 0.2 = $40,000
**($1,100,000 – $1,000,000) × 0.2 = $20,000

Exhibit 2 Raven assets under management by investor type (as of 7/1/2009)

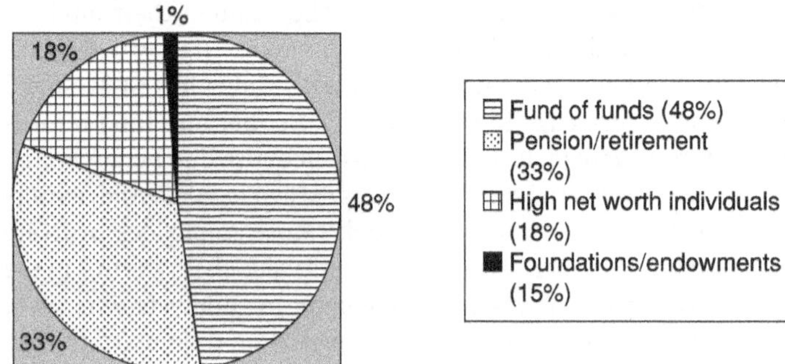

Exhibit 3 Organizational chart

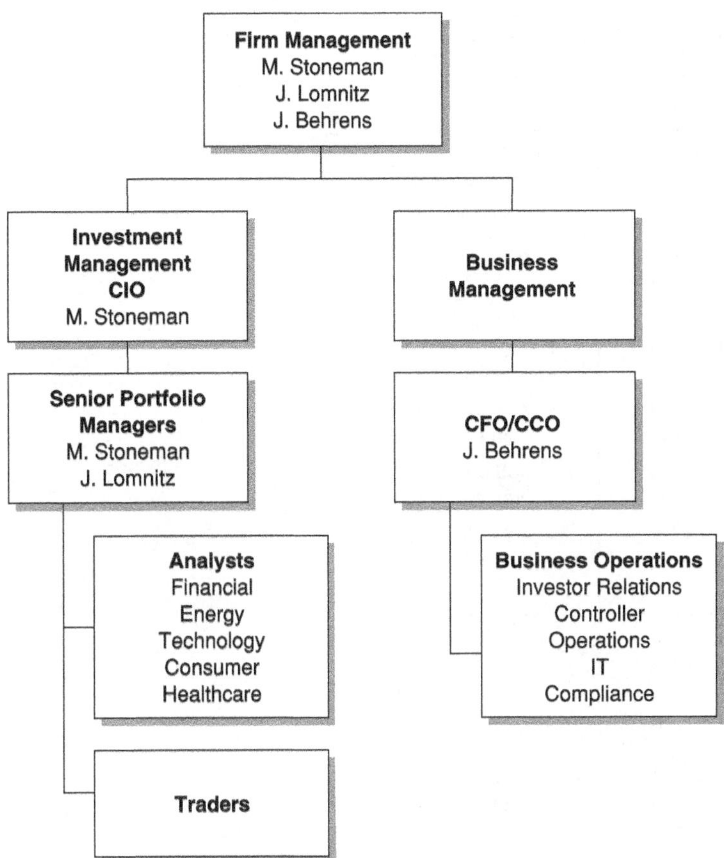

Exhibit 4 The fund risk report

Statistical Highlights		
Firm AUM	$732M	
Fund AUM	$128M	
Returns Since Inception	**Fund**	**S&P 500**
Cumulative	687.50%	182.70%
Annualized	15.11%	7.34%
General Summary	**MV**	**Delta Adj.**
Equity ($)	$131,557,936	–
LMV ($)	$119,262,214	$131,035,077
SMV ($)	($61,414,565)	($73,739,807)
Gross Exposure	$180,676,779	$204,774,884
Net Exposure	$57,847,649	$57,295,270
LMV (% Equity)	90.65%	99.60%
SMV (% Equity)	(46.68%)	(56.05%)
Gross Exposure (% Equity)	137.34%	155.65%
Net Exposure (% Equity)	43.97%	43.55%
1 day VaR 95%	$1,392,438	–
1 day VaR 99%	$2,111,171	–
Position Info.	**Long**	**Short**
Top 25 positions	74.88%	(30.21%)
# of Positions	53	63
Days Liquidity (Fund)	0.70	0.12
Turnover	15.58%	35.68%
Risk Metrics	**Fund**	**S&P 500**
Standard Dev.	3.87%	4.60%
Standard Dev. Ann.	13.42%	15.94%
Sharpe Ratio	0.85	0.55
Downside Dev.	2.53%	3.49%
Sortino Ratio	1.30	0.30
Benchmark Comps	**Fund**	**S&P 500**
R^2	54.44	1.00
Beta	0.62	1.00
Alpha (Since Inception)	574.63%	–
Correlation	0.74	1.00

(Continued)

Exhibit 4 *Continued*

Definition of risk metrics	
Alpha	The Y-intercept of the security characteristics line. The specific benchmark used in the Monthly Fund Risk Reports is the S&P 500 with dividends reinvested.
Annualized standard deviation	(Monthly standard deviation) × (square root of 12).
Beta	With ra denoting the rate of return of asset A and rp denoting the rate of return of referencing benchmark, beta can be expressed as beta(a) = covariance (ra,rp)/ variance (rp).
Correlation coefficient	Correlation coefficient pX,Y between two random variables X and Y, with standard deviations sigma (X) and sigma (Y) is defined as pX,Y = covariance (X,Y)/(sigmaX sigmaY).
Downside deviation	The standard deviation of the returns that are less than the minimum acceptable return (MAR).
Hard to borrow	This is defined by our broker as MV of short equities for which we receive less than our cold rate.
Liquidity	The day's liquidity for each position is calculated by dividing the shares held by 30% of the average 20-day trading volume. The day's liquidity for the firm or fund is based on the weighted average of firm or fund holdings.
R^2	R-squared, coefficient of determination, in linear regression, which is employed here, R-squared is simply the square of the correlation coefficient.
Sortino Ratio	Investment return-risk free (ROR)/downside deviation. The downside deviation is relative to a user-specified minimum acceptable return (MAR), which in the case of the fund risk report is 0.
Standard deviation	The square root of variance.

Exhibit 5 Analyst performance report

Long portfolio

Month to month profit/loss in $ millions (profit and loss defined as realized plus changes in unrealized)

Analyst	Jan	Feb	Mar	Apr	May	Jun	Jul	Aug	Sep	Oct	Nov	Dec	2009
MS	22.6	−1.3	29.3	21.7	8.1	−13.4	−11	7.7	32.6	30.5	−31.4	−8	87.4
BS	5.4	0.5	7.1	1.8	13.3	−5.6	−6.2	7.3	5.3	10.7	2.5	−1.2	40.8
JL	9.8	−1.5	13.8	11.7	16.1	7.8	−17	24	22.1	16.6	−30.4	1.6	74.6
NK	3.7	−0.5	−4.3	2.8	0.7	4.2	−9.8	3.1	4.6	9.7	−0.2	−3.0	11.07
WH	8	2.1	−1	8.3	12.1	−10.7	−2	−1.2	−1.1	−0.6	−1.6	−1.4	11.02
CF	0.2	−0.1	−0.1	0.1	−0.01	−0.2	−0.1		−0.1	0.1	−0.03	0.1	−0.31
CIM	−1.4	−0.4	2.3	2.5	3.4	0.5	0.7	−0.8	0.02	1.2	−0.6	−0.01	7.4
IPOS		0.27			0.2	0.4	0.5	0.3	−0.01	0.05	0.09		1.73
GOLD	−1.2		−0.8	−0.1	−0.4	−0.3	0.5	−0.5					−2.8
TOTAL	46.8	−0.7	46.4	49.1	53.2	−17.3	−44.7	40.7	64.1	71.4	−61.2	−12.3	235.4

Short portfolio

Month to month profit/loss in $ millions (profit and loss defined as realized plus changes in unrealized)

Analyst	Jan	Feb	Mar	Apr	May	Jun	Jul	Aug	Sep	Oct	Nov	Dec	2009
MS	13.8	6.9	29.9	4.5	5.8	−9.7	19.8	13.8	36.2	50.2	4.8	9.8	185.8
BS	0.9	−0.8	−0.3	−5.9	4.9	−0.9	7.8	9.6	6.9	15.3	11.1	0.1	48.8
JL	2.6	9.6	16.9	4	11.4	14.5	−15.2	27.4	13.9	4.7	−14	12.8	88.7
NS	3.3	1.5	−2.4	−0.4	−1.7	3.1	−8.6	0.7	3.2	6.4	8.8	−5.6	8.3
WH	3.8	5	−2	−2.4	2.1	−11.9	1.7	−0.3	−1.1	−0.6	−1.6	−1.4	−8.7
CF	0.2	−0.1	−0.1	0.1	−0.01	−0.2	−0.1		−0.1	0.1	−0.03	0.1	−0.3
CIM	−1.3	−0.3	2	2.1	2.9	0.9	0.8	−0.8	−0.2	1.2	−0.1	−0.2	7.1
IPOS		0.3			0.2	0.4	0.5	0.3	−0.01	0.1	0.1		1.7
GOLD/SPYS	−4.7	4.4	−4.5	−7.5	−7	1.6	7.7	−3.7	−3.6	−0.01	5.6	0.7	−11.3
TOTAL	18.3	26.6	39.5	−5.2	18.5	−1.6	14.2	47.4	56.8	80	17.8	16.9	329

(Continued)

Exhibit 5 *Continued*

Total portfolio

Month to month profit/loss in $ millions (profit and loss defined as realized plus changes in unrealized)

Analyst	Jan	Feb	Mar	Apr	May	Jun	Jul	Aug	Sep	Oct	Nov	Dec	2009
MS	−8.8	8.3	0.6	−17.2	−2.3	3.8	30.8	6.1	3.5	19.7	36.2	17.8	98.5
BS	−4.4	−1.3	−7.3	−7.7	−8.4	4.7	14	2.3	1.5	4.7	8.6	1.3	8.0
JL	−7.2	11.1	3	−7.7	−4.7	6.8	1.8	3.4	−8.2	−11.9	16.5	11.2	14.1
NK	−0.3	2	1.9	−3.2	−2.4	−1.1	1.2	−2.5	−1.4	−3.4	9	−2.6	−2.8
WH	−4.2	2.9	−1	−10.6	−10	−1.3	3.6	0.8					−19.7
CF													
CIM	0.03	0.1	−0.3	−0.4	−0.5	0.4	0.2	0.03	−0.2	0	0.5	−0.2	−0.3
NC													
SPYS	−3.5	4.4	−3.8	−7.5	−6.6	1.9	7.2	−3.2	−3.6	−0.01	5.6	0.7	−8.5
TOTAL	−28.4	27.3	−6.9	−54.3	−34.7	15.6	58.9	6.7	−7.3	8.6	79	29	93.6

Analyst	2009 profit	% of 2009 profit	Allocated capital ($ millions)	% of allocated capital	% return on allocated capital
MS	234.59	71.3%	800	33%	29.3%
JL	88.71	27.0%	800	33%	11.1%
NS	8.31	2.5%	300	12%	2.8%
WH	−8.66	−2.6%	300	12%	−2.9%
CF	−0.31	−0.1%	2	0%	−15.3%
CIM	7.09	2.2%	30	1%	23.6%
IPOS	1.73	0.5%		0%	
GOLD/SPYS	−11.26	−3.4%	190	8%	−5.9%
TOTAL	329.03	100%	2422	100%	13.6%

This case was Prepared by Professor Kenneth A. Merchant and research assistant Michelle Spaulding.

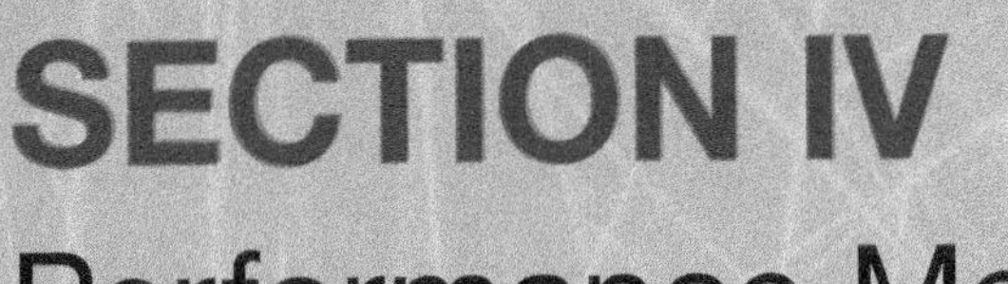

SECTION IV

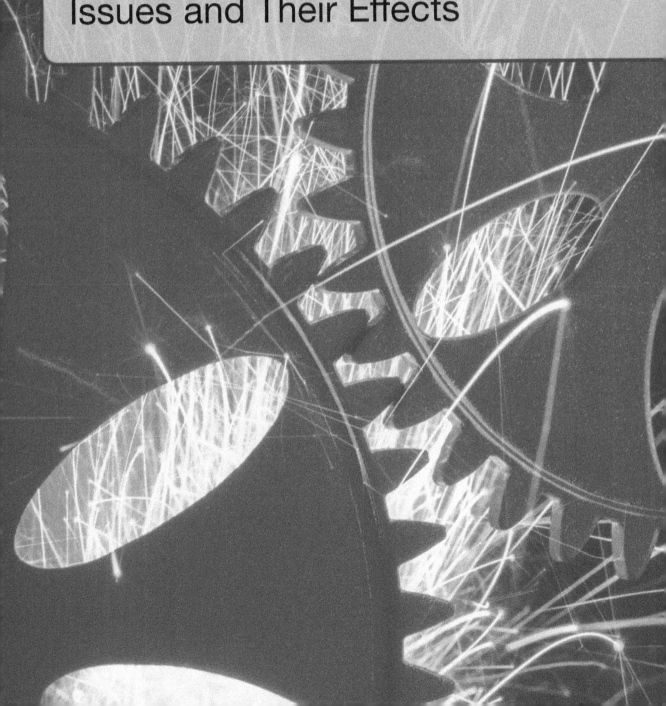

Performance Measurement Issues and Their Effects

CHAPTER 10
Financial Performance Measures and Their Effects

The primary objective of for-profit organizations is to maximize shareholder (or owner) value, or *firm value* for short. Thus, the results-control ideal would be to reward employees for their contributions to firm value. However, because direct measurements of the contributions by employees to value creation are rarely possible, firms have to look for measures that proxy for this ultimate objective and resort to results-control alternatives to either reinforce desired behaviors where the proxies leave gaps or mitigate undesired consequences that may arise from relying on the proxies.

A commonly cited management "truism" is that *what you measure is what you get*. As discussed in Chapter 9, this truism is particularly pertinent when the performance measures are linked to incentives that reinforce the attainment of the measured performance. But which performance measure(s) should be used? At managerial levels in organizations, job responsibilities are both broad and varied. In common jargon, managerial jobs are said to be *multitasking* in nature. Reflecting this task variety, the list of measures used in practice to motivate and evaluate managerial performance is long. That said, the list of measures can be classified into three broad categories. Two of these categories include summary financial measures of performance, expressed either in market (stock price) or accounting terms, and the third category includes combinations of measures.

The *summary measures* reflect the aggregate or *bottom-line* impacts of multiple performance areas (e.g. accounting profits reflect the aggregate effects of both revenue- and cost-related decisions). The first category of summary measures contains *market measures*; that is, those that reflect changes in stock prices or shareholder returns. The second category contains *accounting measures*, which can be defined in either residual terms (such as net income after taxes, operating profit, residual income, or economic value added) or ratio terms (such as return on investment, return on equity, or return on net assets). These two categories of summary financial (market-based or accounting-based) measures of performance are the focus of this chapter. These measurement categories represent *financial* measures of performance because they are either denominated in currency (e.g. quarterly profits of $19.2 million); as a ratio of financial numbers, such as $0.12 earnings per share (EPS) or 12% return on equity (ROE); or as a change in financial numbers, such as 11% earnings growth.

The third measurement category consists of *combinations of measures*. These combinations can involve the use of either type of summary measures, or both, plus some *dis*aggregated financial measures (e.g. revenues, expenses) and/or *nonfinancial* measures (e.g. market share, customer satisfaction, employee turnover). We discuss the use of combinations of measures in Chapter 11. In both chapters, we use the evaluation criteria introduced in Chapter 2, notably *congruence, controllability, precision, objectivity, timeliness, understandability*, and *cost efficiency* to evaluate and to compare and contrast each measurement category.

Most organizations base their higher managerial-level results controls to a great extent on summary accounting measures of performance. Earlier chapters (particularly Chapters 2 and 7) elaborated the reasons why accounting measures of performance are in such common use. They have some significant advantages over other measurement alternatives. In particular, at minimal incremental cost, they provide a useful summary of the results of the many actions and decisions that managers take. It must be recognized, however, that even the best accounting measures are not perfect; they are only surrogate or proxy indicators of changes in firm value.

The use of accounting performance measures as a proxy for changes in firm value creates various control problems. This chapter describes one of the most significant problems accounting measures cause: a tendency to make managers excessively short-term-oriented, or *myopic*. This chapter also discusses the issue of *suboptimization*, a form of behavioral displacement caused particularly by the use of accounting-based ROI-type (ratio or return) measures. Chapter 11 focuses on how the myopia problem can be alleviated, at least to some extent. A whole chapter is devoted to this subject because of its importance and complexity. The final chapter in this section, Chapter 12, discusses how to handle problems caused when employees are held accountable for results they cannot completely control.

Value creation

It is generally understood that the primary objective of for-profit organizations is to *maximize the value of the firm*, subject to some constraints, such as compliance with laws and adequate concern for employees, customers, and other stakeholders.[1] As Michael Jensen, a financial economist, phrases it, "200 years' worth of work in economics and finance indicate that social welfare is maximized when all firms in an economy attempt to maximize their own total firm value."[2] Ideally, then, to reflect success properly, performance measures should *go up when value is created and go down when it is destroyed.*

We hasten to add, however, that while the arguments presented in this chapter are based on the assumption of value maximization as the ultimate organizational objective in the context of for-profit corporations, we realize that corporations have responsibilities to a broader set of stakeholders, including employees, customers, suppliers, and society, and that fulfilling these stakeholder responsibilities is both important and requires tradeoffs. Although it is beyond the scope of this chapter to debate the question about the ultimate (balance of) objective(s) of corporations, the evaluation framework presented in this and earlier chapters, and the *congruence* criterion in particular, can be used to evaluate performance measures no matter which objective(s) an organization pursues. The framework can be conceptually applied even to non-profit settings (as we discuss in Chapter 16), where the organizational purposes (e.g. to provide healthcare, education, or affordable housing) are not directed toward maximizing shareholder value. But even where value maximization is the key objective, concerns related to sustainability and corporate social responsibility, for example, also need to be addressed; we also discuss this in Chapter 16.[3]

Returning to the strict context of "firm value" as alluded to by Jensen, the value of any economic asset can be calculated at any specific time by discounting the future cash flows that the firm is expected to generate, where the discount rate reflects the time value of money and risk. Thus, employees can, all else equal, increase value by increasing the size of future cash flows, by accelerating the timing of those cash flows (due to the time value of money), or by making them more certain or less risky (thus allowing a lower discount rate). The change in firm value over any given period is called *economic income*. Therefore, *maximization of economic income* is an alternative way of phrasing the basic corporate financial objective of value maximization. As we will see, *economic income* is different from *accounting income*, and the difference has important management control implications.[4]

Market measures of performance

One way of assessing value changes is by using market measures of performance, which are based on changes in the market value of the firm or, if dividends are also considered, return to shareholders. The value created (return to shareholders) can be measured directly for any period (yearly, quarterly, monthly) as the sum of the dividends paid to shareholders in the measurement period plus (or minus) the change in the market value of the stock. For publicly traded, exchange-listed firms whose stock is traded in actively traded and properly regulated capital markets, the *market value* of the firm is generally viewed as the closest, although imperfect, measure of (hence, proxy for) the firm's *true intrinsic value*. As we have seen in Chapter 9, firms often employ a variety of stock-based compensation plans, such as stock option and restricted stock plans, which link incentive payments to stock price. In this way, employees who are eligible for equity-based compensation plans are rewarded for generating shareholder returns as defined above, or at least its most significant component – changes in the value of common stock.

In that sense, market measures have broad appeal in part because they provide relatively direct indications of changes in firm value. Such measurement *congruence* allays political pressure that outsiders otherwise might bring on the company. Who is to complain if managers share rewards in synch with those enjoyed by the firm's owners? If the market value changes are measured in terms of recent transaction prices in an actively traded, efficient market, the market measures also have other advantages. For publicly traded, exchange-listed firms, market values are available on a *timely* (daily) basis. They are *precise* (no or little random error) and relatively *accurate* (no or little systematic biases, assuming an efficient information environment), and the values are usually *objective* (not manipulable by the managers whose performances are being evaluated; or, at least, not nearly as manipulable as some other measures).[5] They are *understandable*, at least in terms of what the measures represent. And, they are *cost effective* because they do not require any company measurement expense.

Market measures do have limitations, however. First, market measures suffer from *controllability* problems. They can generally be affected to a significant extent only by the top few managers in the organization, who have the power to make decisions of major importance. They say little about the performances of individuals lower in the organization, even those with significant management responsibilities, except in a collective sense. Individually, the efforts of virtually all employees below the very top level of management usually have an infinitesimally small impact on stock prices, which is captured pertinently by the following quote: "So many things can affect stock-price performance that have nothing to do with the individual employee – employees may actually be demotivated upon realizing that it can be like a lottery; we should only ask employees to control things they can influence, like earnings."[6] Or in the view of Warren Buffett, the legendary investor:

> **Buffett doesn't like what he calls *lottery ticket* arrangements, such as stock options, in which the ultimate value could range from zero to huge and is *totally out of the control of the person whose behavior we would like to affect*. Instead, goals should be *tailored to the economics* of the business, simple and measurable, and *directly related to the daily activities of plan participants*.[7]**

But even for the top management team, market measures may be far from being totally controllable. Stock market valuations are affected by many factors that the managers cannot control, such as changes in macroeconomic activity (economic growth), political climate (e.g. election results), monetary policy (e.g. interest rate policy), industry events, and actions of competitors (e.g. a major oil spill), as well as the general stock market mood (bearish or bullish). When this is the case, stock prices are less informative about even top-level managers' performances. Therefore, one reason why accounting information is important in incentive contracting is that earnings can shield executives against the *noise* inherent in firms' stock prices.[8]

It is possible, however, to "improve" the market measures to make them more informative of the controllable elements of performance, such as by using *relative performance evaluations* (RPE). For example, managers can be held accountable for generating market returns greater than those of the overall market or greater than those of a chosen peer group of companies. When done well, and consistent with efficient contracting, RPE firms select peers that allow effective removal of common risk and improve fairness in compensation.[9] (We discuss methods of making adjustments for the effects of uncontrollable factors in more depth in Chapter 12.)

Second, market values do also not always reflect *realized* performance; instead, the values merely represent *expectations*, and it can be risky to base incentives on expectations because those expectations might not be realized. Indeed, markets can overreact to news (in either direction, positive or negative), such as to the appointment of a new chief executive or to news about a merger or a major project, or even to regular earnings announcements.

For example, Microsoft chief executive Steve Ballmer said that he was "surprised" by the market reaction to the software giant's web search deal with Yahoo. Microsoft's share price was hammered on Wall Street. "Watching the market reaction, nobody gets it," Mr. Ballmer said, even though he argued that the deal was a win-win strategic partnership that would create economic value for the shareholders of Yahoo and Microsoft.[10] Similarly, when Molycorp, owner of the largest rare-earths deposit outside China, said it needed more time to file its annual report so the company would be able to determine the size of a "substantial" goodwill write-down, Jonathan Hykawy, an analyst for Byron Capital Markets Ltd., said that he was "surprised by the ferocity of the market reaction to the news – this charge is non-cash, so would not of itself impact the company's production ramp or prospects in any way."[11]

Who is right – Mr. Ballmer and Mr. Hykawy, or the markets – is hard to tell in advance, but it shows that managers' and market expectations are not always aligned, and that expectations are not to be equated with realizations. Market valuations do not always fully reflect the underlying value of the firm; hence, decisions or transactions on any given day, such as stock option grants or exercises, can be affected by the difference. Worse, as we have discussed in Chapter 9, the possibility for such differences may even trigger *opportunistic* motivations by the executives to try to affect stock prices coincident with certain decisions or transactions, such as by selectively disclosing information to which the markets are expected to (over)react either with a downward or upward effect on stock prices, to bring about more favorable conditions for the granting or exercising of stock options, respectively.[12]

A third and related problem with market measures of performance is actually a potential *congruence* failure. Markets are not always well informed about a company's plans and prospects and, hence, its future cash flows and risks. This hampers the use of market valuations as a proxy for firm value. For competitive reasons, companies may treat information about R&D productivity, pricing and sourcing strategies, product and process quality, and layoff intentions, say, as confidential. Market valuations cannot reflect information that is not available to the market. If sizable rewards are linked to market valuations, managers might be tempted to disclose this information to affect valuations, even if such disclosures could harm their company.

But even market valuations with well-informed participants might not always be correct. Over the years, a number of valuation *anomalies* – such as the "Monday effect" and the "January effect," just to name two – have been documented, although these tend to be relatively small and temporary in duration. More significant for incentive purposes are some other, larger market imperfections and lags; these are particularly likely, and more likely to be significant, in markets where stocks are not as actively traded. For example, in developing countries, suggestions to reward managers based on stock market valuation changes are met with skepticism. Because regulations in certain countries are not as well established and not as well enforced as those in developed countries, managers can time or slant their disclosures to affect market valuations, and large investors can manipulate the markets.

This, therefore, raises a fourth problem with market measures – that is, their *feasibility* in certain circumstances. Market measures are also only readily available for publicly traded firms; they are not available for either privately held firms or wholly owned subsidiaries or divisions,[13] and they do not apply to non-profit organizations.

To summarize the limitations, market measures are only *available*, and hence reasonably feasible, for publicly traded firms. They are largely *uncontrollable* by any employees except the top few individuals in the management hierarchy. Even for those few individuals, the measures are buffeted by many uncontrollable influences, making the market measures *noisy* indicators of performance. And, changes in stock price on any given day can be misleading for several of the reasons discussed above. All told, then, a company's stock price at any point in time can be a poor guide to long-term value, and thus, although an emphasis on shareholder value seems highly congruent conceptually, the use of short-term changes in stock price as a proxy for it can cause problems. One of these problems is that, even though relying on market measures should align managers' incentives with the long-term value of the firm, they not always will. Worse, they can even create adverse incentives.

But several studies have documented positive effects of market-based measures and associated incentives, such as of stock options (also discussed in Chapter 9) on, say, innovation which is an inherently long-term endeavor requiring appropriate risk taking, even when used at lower, non-executive levels in the organization.[14] Thus, there is no one-size-fits-all approach, and there are tradeoffs. But an exclusive reliance on market measures is likely ineffective, even where the benefits are believed to exceed the drawbacks because, inevitably, market measures do have limitations.

These limitations of market measures cause organizations to look for surrogate measures of performance. Accounting measures, specifically accounting profits and returns, are the most important surrogates used, particularly at management levels below the very top management team.

Accounting measures of performance

Traditionally, most organizations have based their managers' evaluations and rewards heavily on standard accounting-based, summary financial measures. Accounting-based, summary or *bottom-line* performance measures come in two basic forms: (1) *residual* measures (or *accounting profit* measures), such as net income, operating profit, earnings before interest, tax, depreciation and amortization (EBITDA), or residual income; and (2) *ratio* measures (or *accounting return* measures), such as return on investment (ROI), return on equity (ROE), return on net assets (RONA), or risk-adjusted return on capital (RAROC). These measures are typically derived from the rules defined by standard setters for financial reporting purposes.

Summary accounting-based measures have some appealing advantages. They satisfy many of the measurement criteria. First, accounting profits and returns can be measured on a *timely* basis (in short time periods) relatively *precisely* and *objectively*. Accounting rules for assigning cash inflows and outflows even to very short measurement periods have been set and described in great detail by accounting rule makers, such as the International Accounting Standards Board (IASB) or the US Financial Accounting Standards Board (FASB). It is possible to measure accounting profits in short time periods, such as a month, with considerable precision. Precision stems from the existence of accounting rules, and hence, different people assigned to measure the profit of an entity for any given period will arrive at approximately the same number. We say *approximately* because the accounting rules require some judgment, such as about certain liabilities or the depreciable lives of certain types of assets, just to name two. Further, for large firms or publicly traded firms, but also for privately held firms that require bond or equity capital, independent auditors provide, mandatorily or voluntary, an objectivity check of the accounting calculations. Objectivity is important when incentives are linked to measures because it eliminates, or at least sharply reduces, the potential for arguments about measurement methods where judgments need to be made about the accounting treatment.

Second, as compared with other quantities that can be measured precisely and objectively on a timely basis, such as cash flows, shipments, or sales, accounting measures are at least conceptually *congruent* with the organizational goal of profit maximization, where *profit* is an archetypal accounting construct. In this respect, accounting profits provide an advantage over cash flows because accounting accruals are designed to provide a better matching of cash inflows and outflows over time.

Third, accounting measures usually can be largely *controlled* by the managers whose performances are being evaluated. The measures can be tailored to match the authority limits of any level of manager, from the CEO down to lower management levels. As such, entity managers are typically held accountable for fewer of the income statement and balance sheet line items that they can control, compared to managers with more authority higher in the organizational hierarchy (as we discussed in the context of responsibility centers in Chapter 7). Because of this, the profit performance of an entity within the organization is almost certainly more controllable by the entity manager than the change in the company's overall stock price. Accounting profits also are not, or not as severely, affected by some of the uncontrollable factors discussed above that affect stock prices.

Fourth, accounting measures are *understandable*. Accounting is a standard course in every business school, and managers have used the measures for so long that they are well familiar with what the measures represent and how they can be influenced, at least at a conceptual if not fully accounting-technical level.

Finally, accounting measures of performance are *inexpensive* because most firms have to measure and report financial results to outside users already, certainly when they are publicly traded, but also in many countries when they exceed a certain size and require auditing (see above). Even when these conditions do not apply, to obtain funding of any kind (debt or equity) requires the reporting of at least some financial information to the fund providers, who will do a due diligence or an audit of the numbers and the overall viability of the organization.

For all these reasons, pioneer business baron Alfred P. Sloan may have had a point when he proclaimed that "no other financial principle with which I am acquainted serves better than [accounting] rate of return as an objective aid to business management."[15] Nonetheless, accounting measures of performance are far from perfect indicators of firm value and value changes. While research has shown that the correlations between annual accounting profits and stock price changes are positive,[16] they are not a perfect surrogate and, thus, only imperfect proxies for economic income.[17]

In some types of firms, accounting profit measures are essentially meaningless. A good example is start-up firms. These firms almost inevitably report significant accounting losses early in their life cycle. The losses are just an artifact of conservative accounting rules that require the immediate or rapid expensing of long-term-focused business-building investments (such as investments in R&D and product and market development). In these cases, which include virtually all start-up firms, managers are not, or should not be, greatly concerned with short-term accounting profits (or rather losses) because the need for a long-term focus reduces the degree of *congruence* between earnings and firm value.

More generally, *measurement congruence*, or the correlation between accounting profits and firm value, increases with the length of the measurement period, which suggests a tradeoff between the congruence and timeliness measurement evaluation criteria. The increasingly higher correlations with increasingly longer measurement windows occur primarily because accounting profits provide a lagged indicator of economic income. Changes in economic income are often reflected only some time later in the profit measures. How much later depends on what caused the economic income change and what type of accounting measurement rules is being used.

There are thus various reasons why accounting profit measures fail to reflect economic income perfectly. Many things affect accounting profits but not economic income, and vice versa. First, accounting systems are *transactions-oriented*. Accounting profit is primarily a summation of the effects of the transactions that took place during a given period. Most changes in value that do not result in a transaction are not recognized in accounting profit. When a firm receives a patent or regulatory approval for a new drug, the expectation of economic income is affected; but there is no transaction, no accounting entry, and, thus, no effect on accounting income.

Second, accounting profit is highly dependent on the *choice of measurement methods*. Multiple measurement methods are often available to account for identical economic events. Depreciation accounting choices (straight-line vs. accelerated methods) are but one example. These methods also often require making judgments, such as in this example, about the depreciable lives of the assets. Longer lives spread the costs over more years and thus affect the accounting profits recorded over those years.

Third, accounting profit is derived from measurement rules that are often *conservatively biased*.[18] Accounting rules require slow recognition of gains and revenues but quick recognition of expenses and losses. For example, accounting rules define strict criteria that must be satisfied before revenue (and the associated profit) can be recognized, and expenditures on intangible assets are generally expensed immediately. Thus, accounting measures do not always match revenues and expenses well, and this problem is particularly acute where measurement periods are shorter than the firms' investment payoff horizons.

Fourth, profit calculations *ignore some economic values* and *value changes* that accountants feel cannot be measured accurately and objectively. Investments in major categories of companies' intangible assets, such as research in progress, human resources, information systems, and customer goodwill, are expensed immediately. Consequently, these types of assets do not appear on the balance sheet. The omission of intangible assets occurs even though, for many companies, these types of assets are much more important than the old industrial-era-type assets of property, plant, and equipment.[19] The physical assets of companies like Apple, Google, and Facebook, for example, are only a relatively small portion of each company's total market value. Profit also *ignores the costs of investments in working capital*. Managers sometimes increase their sales and profits by making poor investments in extra inventory, the costs of which do not appear on the income statement.

Fifth, profit reflects the cost of borrowed capital (through interest deductibility) but *ignores the cost of equity capital*. Firms earn real income only when the returns on capital are greater than the cost of that capital, and ignoring the cost of equity capital overstates the difference between returns and costs (that is, profit). This omission is serious because equity capital is typically more expensive than borrowed capital, and the cost of equity capital is even higher for companies with risky (volatile) stocks. Failure to reflect the cost of equity capital also hinders comparisons of the results of companies with different proportions of debt and equity in their capital structures.

Sixth, accounting profit *ignores risk and changes in risk*. Firms, or entities within firms, that have not changed the pattern or timing of their expected future cash flows but have made the cash flows more certain (less risky) have increased their economic value, and vice versa. This value change is not reflected in accounting profits.

Finally, profit figures also *focus on the past*. Economic value is derived from future cash flows, and there is no guarantee that past performance is a reliable indicator of future performance.

The multiple reasons why accounting income and economic income diverge have caused some critics to make strong statements against the use of accounting performance measures. Most managers, however, have found that the advantages of accounting measures outweigh their limitations, and they continue to use them. But they must be aware that motivating managers to maximize, or at least produce, accounting profits or returns, rather than economic income, can create a number of behavioral displacement problems. *Myopia* is probably the most potentially damaging. Managers who focus on accounting profits or returns measured in short periods tend to be highly concerned with increasing (or maintaining) monthly, quarterly, or annual profits. When managers' orientations to the short term become excessive – that is, when they are more concerned with short-term profits or returns rather than with long-term value creation – the managers are said to be myopic, which we discuss in the next section.

In summary, then, the major failure of accounting measures of performance is in terms of the congruence criterion for evaluation. Accounting measures do not reflect changes in economic values well, particularly in shorter measurement windows. They also suffer some controllability problems, although less than market measures; but these problems can be addressed using the same methods that can be used to adjust the market measures, which we discuss in more detail in Chapter 12. Accounting measures, however, rate highly in terms of the other evaluation criteria – timeliness, accuracy, understandability, cost effectiveness, and feasibility.

Investment and operating myopia

Accounting performance measures can cause managers to act myopically in making either investing or operating decisions. Holding managers accountable for short-term profits or returns may induce managers to reduce or postpone investments that promise payoffs in future measurement periods, even when those investments have a positive net present value and meet other criteria to make them worthwhile. This is *investment myopia*.

Investment myopia stems directly from two of the problems with accounting measures described above: their conservative bias and their ignoring of intangible assets with predominantly future payoffs. Accounting rules do not allow firms to recognize gains until they are realized; that is, until the critical income-producing activities (such as a sale) have taken place and the earnings can be measured in an objective, verifiable way. On the other hand, the rules require firms to begin recognizing costs when the investments are made. The understatement of profits in early measurement periods is magnified because accounting rules are purposely conservative. Projects with uncertain returns and little liquidation value, such as R&D projects and employee development and customer acquisition initiatives, must be expensed as the costs are incurred, and capital investments must be expensed over periods that are typically shorter than those in which returns will be realized.

The motivational effect of these measurement rules is perverse because managers who are motivated to produce accounting profits or returns can (in the short term) do so by *not* making worthwhile investments. By not making the investments, the managers reduce expenses in the current period and do not suffer the lost revenue until future periods. Even worse, the quest for short-term profits and returns sometimes induces managers to engage in manipulative *earnings management* practices, such as not booking *operating* expenses immediately, but instead pushing them into the future as *capital* investments. We discuss such manipulative behaviors in more detail in Chapter 15, but the following indicative excerpt highlights this:

> "A large fraction of CEO pay appears unrelated to periodic value creation," said Lars Helge Hass, Jiancheng Liu, Steven Young and Zhifang Zhang, the authors of a report on pay at FTSE 100 companies by CFA UK, a society of investment professionals, and Lancaster Business School. *Relatively simplistic performance measures such as Earnings per Share (EPS) and Total Shareholder Return (TSR) continued to dominate the measures against which executives' performance was benchmarked* over the period [10 years from 2003 to 2013]. Value-based metrics that related performance to the cost of capital were rarely used. [...] *The report said the dangers of over-reliance on such measures of executives' performance were well documented and included: investment myopia, earnings manipulation*, excessive risk-taking, and threats to organizational culture.[20]

Managers can also boost current period profits and returns by destroying goodwill that has been built up with customers, suppliers, employees, and so on. They can force employees to work overtime at the end of a measurement period to finish production so that the product can be shipped and the revenues and profits booked. But if the product is of lower quality, customer satisfaction (and future sales) may diminish; the costs of service repairs or customer returns may increase; and some employees may be demotivated and tempted to leave. As the excerpt above suggests, such actions and decisions may ruin the organizational culture.

Another common "trick" is known as *channel stuffing*, which involves boosting near-term sales by extending lower prices to distributors, encouraging them to load up while potentially hurting later sales. These are examples of *operating myopia*, sometimes also colloquially referred to as "shipping bricks and other tricks." These are examples of employees and organizations (through their culture) becoming "too aggressive, too focused on the short term, and too disconnected from the needs of customers."[21]

In many cases, determining whether managers are acting myopically is difficult. For example, in 2014 when IBM, the information technology giant, announced a $1 billion global restructuring with major job cuts in its US home market to maintain the company's earnings growth in the face of flagging revenues, some analysts started to question whether IBM's pursuit of five-year earnings targets, which were long seen as a mark of financial discipline, may have led to an excessively short-term focus on profits. To quote one analyst, "many investors expect IBM to hit its $20 EPS target [for 2015], but remain concerned about the long-term health of the business." This was in part because the cuts followed disappointing sales, which added to concerns on Wall Street that IBM was missing out on some of the fastest-growing markets in cloud computing. The firm's view – unsurprisingly, perhaps – was that this was not the case, stating that "IBM continues to rebalance its workforce to meet the changing requirements of its clients, and to pioneer new, high-value segments of the IT industry." Was the company acting myopically for the sake of hitting its earnings targets, by slashing costs but eroding its capacity to move effectively into new high-growth markets? Or, was it instead competitively positioning itself to achieve exactly that? It is hard to tell, and judgments as to whether the cuts were myopic clearly varied.[22]

The IBM example illustrates the difficulty of making judgments that involve short-term versus long-term tradeoffs. We discuss several ways to address the myopia problem in Chapter 11. But first we turn to another set of problems created by relying on return-on-investment (ROI) measures of performance, a specific form of accounting performance measure that is commonly used in large, divisionalized firms.

Return-on-investment measures of performance

Divisionalized organizations are comprised of multiple responsibility centers, the managers of which are held primarily accountable for profit or some form of accounting ROI, as discussed in Chapter 7. The divisionalized form of organization dates back to the 1920s, when it was introduced in the DuPont Company, but its use spread particularly quickly after World War II as one response to increased organizational size and complexity. To this day, the divisionalized form of organization is used by many firms above minimal size requiring delegation of decision authority.

Referring to Chapter 7, divisionalization and decentralization are related concepts, but the two words are not synonymous. An organization is said to be *decentralized* when authority for making decisions is pushed down to lower levels in the organization. All divisionalized organizations decentralize authority, at least to some extent, in specified areas of operations, notably a line of business or a geographical area. But the converse is not true – not all decentralized organizations are divisionalized. When decentralization is effected along functional lines of authority (such as production and marketing), the responsibility centers are usually cost and revenue centers, not profit or investment centers (divisions).

Divisionalization provides several advantages. Large, complex organizations are not able to control behaviors effectively with action-dominated control systems involving, for example, the direct guidance of a central manager or the enforcement of standard operating procedures by a central administration. No central management can know everything about a complex organization's many product-market combinations and operational capabilities and constraints. Even if it could, it would take time for central management to direct its attention to each issue that arises, become informed about the details, and reach a decision. Decision-making would be unnecessarily delayed, even if it were informed.

When an organization is divisionalized, local managers become experts in their products and markets, and they are able to make informed decisions more quickly. Because they control their own success to a significant extent, the local managers are likely to be more motivated and entrepreneurial. Their involvement in decision-making helps them acquire experience that will benefit them as they move to higher organization levels through promotion. Top management's time becomes available to focus on strategic decisions.

Divisionalization is not without its problems and challenges, however. Many of the issues, particularly, relate to the problems created by the measurement of performance in terms of ROI.

Return-on-what?

ROI is a ratio of the accounting profits earned by the division divided by the investment tied up in the division. Divisionalized corporations typically use some form of various types of ROI measures to evaluate division performance.

Variances from plans can be analyzed using formula charts (*ROI trees*) such as the one shown in Figure 10.1. Such analyses might show that a division's actual ROI of 15% was below the planned level of 20%, even though sales profitability (profit as a percent of sales) was on plan but asset turnover (sales divided by total investment) was below target:

Planned ROI (20%) = profit as percent of sales (20%) x asset turnover (1.0)

Actual ROI (15%) = profit as percent of sales (20%) x asset turnover (0.75)

Figure 10.1 Formula chart showing relationship of factors affecting ROI

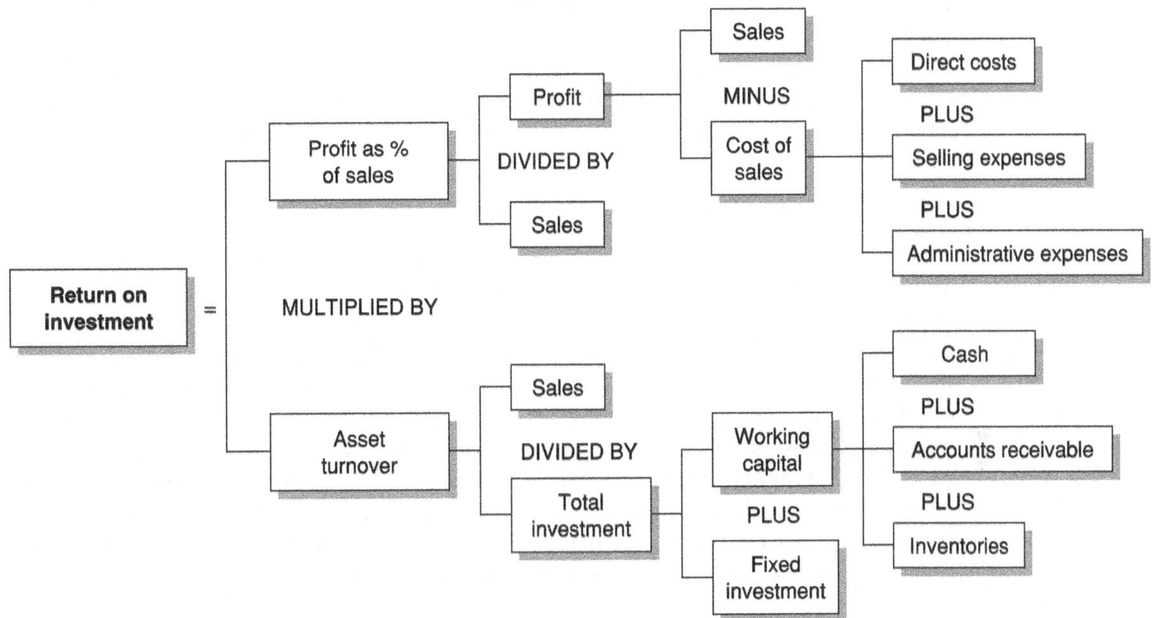

Source: K. A. Merchant, *Modern Management Control Systems: Text and Cases* (Upper Saddle River, NJ: Prentice Hall, 1998), p. 543.

The measures can then be further decomposed to understand whether, in this example, the variance was due primarily to a decline in sales or more capital tied up in a specific kind of assets.

ROI formula charts are also useful for linking performance at various organizational levels. The chart can be expanded out to the right to show specific measures that can be used for control purposes down to the lowest levels in the organization. Sales performance can be disaggregated into sales volume and price factors. These factors can be further disaggregated by product, geographical region, customer segment, or sales team.

The actual forms of ROI-type ratios that companies employ vary widely, as do the labels companies put on their bottom-line investment center measures. Among the most common are *return on investment* (ROI), *return on equity* (ROE), *return on capital employed* (ROCE), and *return on net assets* (RONA). For a specific entity or division, firms might use *return on controllable assets* (ROCA) to take account of the assets or capital that the entity or division managers can control commensurate with the investments that they are authorized to make. In these ratios, both the numerator and denominator can include all or just a subset of the line items reflected on the corporate financial statements. The profit measure in the numerator of the ROI calculation can be a fully allocated, after-tax profit measure, or it can be a before-tax operating income measure. Similarly, the denominator can include all the line items of assets and liabilities, including allocations of assets and liabilities not directly controlled by the division managers; or it can include only controllable assets, which generally include, at a minimum, receivables and inventories. The variations are innumerable.

ROI-type measures are in widespread use because they provide several advantages. First, they provide a single, comprehensive measure that reflects the tradeoffs managers must make between revenues, costs (the balance of which translates into profit), and investments. Second, they provide a common denominator that can be used for comparing returns on dissimilar businesses, such as divisions and outside competitors, or types of investments. Third, because they are expressed in percentage terms, they suggest that ROI figures are comparable to other financial returns, such as those calculated for stocks and bonds, although such a direct comparison should be qualified (as we explain later). Finally, because ROI measures have been in use for so long in so many places, virtually all managers understand both what the measures reflect and how they can be influenced, by changes in both the numerator and denominator.

Problems caused by ROI-type of measures

Relying heavily on ROI measures in a results-control system can cause some problems, however. One problem is that the numerator in the ROI measure is accounting profit. Thus, ROI has all the limitations of profit measures, such as the tendency to produce management myopia, the common form of behavioral displacement, which we address further in Chapter 11. A second limitation is a tendency for the measures to induce *suboptimization*. A narrow focus on ROI can lead division managers to make decisions that improve division ROI even though the decisions are not in the corporation's global best interest; that is, decisions that appear locally optimal (in the division) may not be globally optimal (for the firm). Finally, ROI measures sometimes provide *misleading signals* about the performance of the investment centers (divisions) because of difficulties in measuring the fixed asset portion of the denominator. These misleading signals can cause poor investment and performance evaluation decisions, as we explain below.

Suboptimization

ROI measures can create a suboptimization problem by encouraging managers to make investments that make their divisions look good even though those investments are not in the best interest of the corporation. Put simply, this problem arises because division managers are unlikely to propose capital investments that are expected to yield returns below their divisional return targets, even if those investments are good from the company's perspective. Table 10.1 shows a simplified suboptimization example of this type. Assume the corporate cost of capital is 15%. If an investment opportunity arises promising a 20% return, the investment should be made (assuming the opportunity is consistent with the firm's strategy and other considerations). The manager of Division A, whose performance targets reflect historical performance of 10%, would be willing to make this investment, but the manager of Division B, operating at 40%, would not.

Conversely, ROI measures can cause managers of unsuccessful divisions to invest in capital investment projects that promise returns below the corporate cost of capital. This problem is illustrated in Table 10.2, which changes the Table 10.1 example only slightly by assuming the corporate cost of capital is 25%. In this situation, Division A would be willing to make this investment promising a 20% return, even though this investment does not cover the corporation's cost of capital.

Unless managers guard against these problems, the effect of situations like the examples shown in Tables 10.1 and 10.2 is that the firm's capital will gradually be allocated away from its most successful or, at least, highest-earning divisions and toward its least successful divisions, which is incongruent with the objective to maximize firm value, all else equal.

Where division managers have the authority to make financing decisions (to finance their investment decisions), ROI-type measures can also lead to suboptimization at that level. For example, return-on-equity (ROE) measures may induce managers to use debt financing (i.e. to reduce the equity put into the denominator of the ratio). This may push their entity's leverage to levels in excess of the desired corporate leverage.[23]

Misleading performance signals

Difficulties in measuring the denominator of the ROI measure, particularly pertaining to fixed assets, can provide misleading signals about the performance of an investment center (division).

Table 10.1 Example of suboptimization: failure to invest in a worthwhile project

Assume: corporate cost of capital = 15%		
Base situation	**Division A**	**Division B**
Profit before tax	$100,000	$400,000
Investment	$1,000,000	$1,000,000
Return on investment	10%	40%
Assume an investment opportunity that is good for the company: invest $100,000 to earn $20,000/year.		
New situation		
Profit before tax	$120,000	$420,000
Investment	$1,100,000	$1,100,000
Return on investment	10.9%	38.2%

Source: K. A. Merchant, *Modern Management Control Systems: Text and Cases* (Upper Saddle River, NJ: Prentice Hall, 1998), p. 545.

Table 10.2 Example of suboptimization: investment in a project that is *not* worthwhile

Assume: corporate cost of capital = 25%		
Base situation	**Division A**	**Division B**
Profit before tax	$100,000	$400,000
Investment	$1,000,000	$1,000,000
Return on investment	10%	40%
Assume an investment opportunity that is *not* good for the company: invest $100,000 to earn $20,000/year.		
New situation		
Profit before tax	$120,000	$420,000
Investment	$1,100,000	$1,100,000
Return on investment	10.9%	38.2%

Source: K. A. Merchant, *Modern Management Control Systems: Text and Cases* (Upper Saddle River, NJ: Prentice Hall, 1998), p. 546.

The asset values reflected on the balance sheet do not always represent the economic value of the assets available to managers for earning current returns. The assets were added to the business at various times in the past, under varying market conditions and varying purchasing power of the monetary unit. As such, the book values of the various assets accumulated over time on the balance sheet may say little about the economic value of the assets; that is, their ability to generate future cash flows. Nonetheless, many firms use net book values (NBV) to compute divisional ROI. When NBV is used, ROI is usually overstated. The overstatement is larger if the entity includes a relatively large number of older assets. Assuming inflation, the NBV of older assets are below their replacement values because they were bought in a period of lower prices, but even without taking inflation into account, also because they have been depreciated longer.

This ROI-overstatement problem is illustrated in Table 10.3. Assume that Divisions C and D are identical operating units except that Division C purchased most of its fixed assets many years ago and Division D has mostly new assets. For the sake of simplicity, assume there have been no technological advancements; that is, the old assets perform the same tasks as efficiently as the new assets (because if not, there could be productivity gains that need taking into account). Profit before depreciation is identical, but Division D's depreciation is twice that of

Table 10.3 Example showing ROI overstatement when denominator is measured in terms of net book value

	Division C	Division D
Profit before depreciation	$110,000	$110,000
Depreciation	$10,000	$20,000
Profit after depreciation	$100,000	$90,000
Assets (net book value)	$500,000	$3,000,000
ROI	20%	3%

Source: K. A. Merchant, *Modern Management Control Systems: Text and Cases* (Upper Saddle River, NJ: Prentice Hall, 1998), p. 547.

Division C, so C's profit after depreciation is slightly higher. But C's ROI is dramatically higher than D's, mostly because its assets have a lower NBV. The difference between 20% and 3% ROI is not real; it is an artifact of the measurement system.

Another quirk of ROI measures is that ROI calculated using NBV automatically increases over time if no further investments are made. This is illustrated in Table 10.4. Assume that Division E is operating in a steady state, earning an ROI of 12% in year 1. Because the assets are being depreciated, the ROI increases to 13.3% in year 2, and 15% in year 3. This ROI increase is not real, either.

These measurement quirks can cause managers who are using ROI-type measures to make poor decisions:

- They encourage division managers to retain assets beyond their optimal life and not to invest in new assets that would increase the denominator of the ROI calculation. (This dysfunctional motivational effect is exacerbated when the managers expect their job tenures to be short, illustrating another channel through which the myopia problem operates.)
- They can contribute to the problem illustrated in Tables 10.1 and 10.2; that is, the tendency for capital allocations to be distorted.
- If corporate managers are unaware of these measurement effects or do not adjust for them, they can cause distortions in evaluating division managers' performances.

Measuring fixed assets at gross book value (GBV) – that is, gross of depreciation conventions that are used for financial reporting purposes – minimizes some of these problems because GBV

Table 10.4 Example showing increase in ROI due merely to passage of time

	Division E		
	Year 1	Year 2	Year 3
Profit before depreciation	$110,000	$110,000	$110,000
Depreciation	$50,000	$50,000	$50,000
Profit after depreciation	$60,000	$60,000	$60,000
Assets (net book value)	$500,000	$450,000	$400,000
ROI	12%	13.3%	15%

Source: K. A. Merchant, *Modern Management Control Systems: Text and Cases* (Upper Saddle River, NJ: Prentice Hall, 1998), p. 547.

is closer to replacement value than is NBV. In periods of inflation, as is almost always the case (although, in recent years, only moderately so in most advanced economies), old assets valued at gross book value are still expressed at lower values than new assets, so ROI will still be overstated. Another possibility is to use "adjusted NBVs" by depreciating the assets commensurate with their economic lives, where the rate of depreciation can be different (slower or faster and/or nonlinear) from the depreciation rates used or allowed for financial accounting or taxation purposes. This takes the productivity of the assets into account, which may be more crucial in times of rapid technological change but low inflation.

A final potential problem is that ROI measures create incentives for managers to lease assets rather than buy them. Under some accounting rules,[24] leased assets accounted for on an operating-lease basis are not recognized on the balance sheet, so they are not included in the ROI denominator. Managers can increase their divisional ROI by gaming the system in this way. Of course, corporations can easily include the capitalized value of assets employed in division ROI calculations even when those leases are not required to be capitalized for financial reporting purposes. This adjustment avoids this potential problem, but adjustments are costly and may complicate the administration of different books for different purposes. The idea of "adjusting" accounting measures of performance, however, leads us to the next section.

Residual income measures as a possible solution to the ROI measurement problems

A number of researchers and consultants have argued that the use of a residual income measure can help overcome the suboptimization limitation of ROI. *Residual income* is calculated by subtracting from profit a capital charge for the net assets tied up in the entity or division (investment center). The capital is charged at a rate equal to the weighted average corporate cost of capital. Conceptually, one could adjust the capital charge rate for each investment center's risk, thus making the performance measurement system consistent with the capital budgeting system. (In the interest of focus, we do not carry this suggestion through in our discussion below because it does not change the basic residual income calculations; it just causes them to be matched to the risk profile of each of the divisions.)

If the residual income charge is made equal to the required corporate investment rate of return, then the residual income measures give all division managers an equal incentive to invest, thereby addressing the suboptimization problem inherent in ROI measures. Regardless of the prevailing levels of return in each of the divisions, the division managers are motivated to invest in all projects that promise internal rates of return higher than, or at least equal to, the corporate cost of capital (again, *all else equal*, thus ignoring any strategic or other considerations and options).[25] This is illustrated in Table 10.5, showing a modified version of Table 10.1 with a row added for residual income. In both divisions, residual income is increased if the worthwhile investment is made.

Residual income also addresses the financing-type suboptimization problem. By considering the cost of both debt and equity financing (by using a weighted average corporate cost of capital), residual income removes the managers' temptations to increase their entity's leverage through debt financing.

Residual income does not address the distortions often caused when managers make new investments in fixed assets, however. Many desirable investments initially reduce residual income, but then the residual income increases over time as the fixed assets get older and are depreciated.

Table 10.5 Example of suboptimization with residual income: failure to invest in a worthwhile project

Assume: corporate cost of capital = 15%		
Base situation	**Division A**	**Division B**
Profit before tax	$100,000	$400,000
Investment	$1,000,000	$1,000,000
Return on investment	10%	40%
Residual income	$(50,000)	$250,000
Assume an investment opportunity that is good for the company: invest $100,000 to earn $20,000/year.		
New situation		
Profit before tax	$120,000	$420,000
Investment	$1,100,000	$1,100,000
Return on investment	10.9%	38.2%
Residual income	$(45,000)	$255,000

Source: K. A. Merchant, *Modern Management Control Systems: Text and Cases* (Upper Saddle River, NJ: Prentice Hall, 1998), p. 548.

One consulting firm, Stern Stewart & Company, recommends a measure called *Economic Value Added* (EVA™) that combines several of the modifications to the standard accounting model in a residual income-type measure.[26] The generic EVA formula is:

EVA = Modified Net Operating Profit After Tax − (Modified Total Capital × Weighted Average Cost of Capital)

The word "modified" refers to many adjustments to standard accounting treatments, such as the capitalization and subsequent amortization of intangible investments such as for R&D, employee training and advertising and the expensing of goodwill. Just which modifications should be implemented in any given situation is subject to judgment. The *weighted average cost of capital* reflects the weighted average cost of debt and equity financing.

Because it addresses some of the known weaknesses of accounting profit or return measures, EVA should better reflect economic income than accounting profit does in many settings. It should mitigate the investment myopia problem discussed above because it involves capitalization of the most important types of discretionary expenditures managers might try to cut if they were pressured for profits (such as on R&D, employee training and customer acquisition). EVA also has all the advantages of a residual income-type measure.

It must be recognized, however, that despite its name, EVA is still only is a proxy at best for economic income. It does not address all of the problems that differentiate accounting income from economic income, although the proposed adjustments to the accounting numbers should attenuate the gap. In particular, EVA still reflects primarily the results of a summation of transactions completed during the period, and thus, the past, while economic income reflects changes in *future* cash flow potentials. This is an especially pertinent issue for firms that derive a significant proportion of their value from future growth. Joel Stern, now chairman of Stern Value Management in New York, would argue though that this is a matter of using an appropriate rate of return for risk, suggesting that value management essentially "involves both selecting an appropriate measure of corporate performance and also a required rate of return for risk in achieving that corporate performance, [thereby] providing a way of measuring performance year-by-year contemporaneously."[27]

EVA also has some other measurement limitations. It suffers from *objectivity* problems as the EVA adjustments require considerable judgment. Managers therefore can bias EVA just as they can accounting numbers. EVA also is probably not differentially affected by any of the usual *controllability* problems. EVA, however, is more likely to create some additional *understandability* problems, as the measures can be complex and are not as widely familiar. Many of the firms that have decided not to use EVA or similar types of measures developed mainly by consulting firms, such as *Cash Flow Return on Investment* (Holt Value Associates), *Total Business Return* (Boston Consulting Group), *Economic Profit* (McKinsey & Co.) or *Shareholder Value Added* (LEK/Alcar), or which have tried such a measure and then abandoned it, seem to have done so mainly because of understandability failures.[28] The survey of FTSE 100 companies by CFA UK and Lancaster Business School that we quoted from above also states that "value-based metrics that relate performance to the cost of capital are rarely used."[29] Maybe this is because, despite some key features, implementing these measurement systems can be quite *expensive*, requiring considerable assistance from consultants and systems and management development and training time.

In summary, EVA may have better congruence characteristics in some industry settings when a carefully chosen (and not too complex) set of adjustments are made to the traditional accounting profit measures. EVA also exhibits the features of any generic residual income measure. That said, and perhaps not surprisingly, EVA is hardly a measurement panacea, an ideal that, as we discussed, is hard for any measure to meet.

Conclusion

The primary goal of managers of for-profit firms should be to maximize shareholder or firm value, which is a long-term, future-oriented concept. Short-term accounting profit and return measures provide imperfect, surrogate indicators of changes in firm value. *Management myopia*, an excessive focus on short-term performance, is an almost inevitable side-effect of the use of financial results control systems built on accounting measures of performance. In the next chapter, we discuss six alternatives that can be used individually or in combination to eliminate or reduce myopia.

In this chapter, we also discussed the issue of *suboptimization*, another form of behavioral displacement caused particularly by the use of accounting-based ROI-type measures. Managers who still rely on ROI-type measures do so probably because the conceptual weaknesses of ROI are well understood and the potential suboptimization problems can be monitored through the company's capital budgeting and strategic planning processes. Managers of highly profitable divisions can be encouraged to make more investments, and proposed investments from less profitable divisions can be scrutinized carefully. And even the managers evaluated by these measures should understand that when they "run down" their business by not investing in it or by not replacing their old assets will eventually hamper their ability to generate revenues from these assets, thereby hurting the numerator of their ROI measure, assuming of course that they plan to be around long enough in the company for that to be a worry of them. In that sense, ROI measures have, only over time though, a self-disciplining mechanism built into them.

It is true that the suboptimization problems can be avoided or mitigated to some extent through the investment review processes, as well as through their inherent self-disciplining mechanism. By using these processes, companies can use ROI-focused results control systems with some degree of effectiveness. One might ask: Why use a measurement system that works effectively only in conjunction with bureaucratic oversight and processes (or other balancing control mechanisms) that are needed to prevent managers from taking undesirable actions? The answer to that question in many settings is that the net benefits of such a system are greater than those of several other feasible alternatives. There is no panacea, and better control is likely to arise from a set of mutually reinforcing and balancing mechanisms. An all-purpose performance measure (or performance measurement system) that meets all control objectives effectively without triggering any potentially harmful side effects simply does not exist.

Notes

1 See, for example, "Shareholders vs. Stakeholders: A New Idolatry," *The Economist* (April 26, 2010), online at econ.st/KA1p7h.
2 M. Jensen, "Value Maximization, Stakeholder Theory, and the Corporate Objective Function," *Journal of Applied Corporate Finance*, 14, no. 3 (Fall 2001), p. 11.
3 For an interesting example and perspective on the "corporate social responsibility" of firms in light of "shareholder value maximization," see "Maximizing Shareholder Value: The Goal That Changed Corporate America," *The Washington Post* (August 26, 2013), online at wpo.st/8EXX1.
4 See, for example, "Analyse This," *The Economist* (April 2, 2016), online at econ.st/1V9hSFB.
5 See, for example, "CEOs Strategically Time News Releases for Their Own Benefit," *LSE Business Review* (March 22, 2016), online at blogs.lse.ac.uk/businessreview/2016/03/22/ceos-strategically-time-news-releases-for-their-own-benefit; see also G. Gong, L. Y. Li and J. Y. Shin, "Relative Performance Evaluation and Related Peer Groups in Executive Compensation Contracts," *The Accounting Review*, 86, no. 3 (May 2011), pp. 1007-1043.
6 "Options for Everyone," *Business Week* (July 22, 1996), p. 84.
7 "Warren Buffett's 9 Rules for Running a Business," *CNBC* (November 11, 2014), online at cnb.cx/1Hk7L9q.
8 For a seminal article on this issue of the choice of performance measures in incentive contracts, see R. A. Lambert and D. F. Larcker, "An Analysis of the Use of Accounting and Market Measures of Performance in Executive Compensation Contracts," *Journal of Accounting Research*, 25 (Supplement, 1987), pp. 85–125.
9 See, for example, "Peer Benchmarking and Trends in Executive Compensation," *Audit Analytics* (November 19, 2015), online at www.auditanalytics.com/blog/peer-benchmarking-and-trends-in-executive-compensation.
10 "Microsoft CEO Surprised at Yahoo Deal Reception," *Reuters* (July 31, 2009), online at www.reuters.com.
11 "Molycorp Delays Report to Determine 'Substantial' Writedown," *Bloomberg* (February 28, 2013), online at www.bloomberg.com.
12 See, for example, D. Aboody and R. Kasznik, "CEO Stock Option Awards and the Timing of Corporate Voluntary Disclosures," *Journal of Accounting and Economics*, 29, no. 1 (February 2000), pp. 73–100; A. Edmans, L. Goncalves-Pinto, Y. Wang, and M Groen-Xu, "Strategic News Releases in Equity Vesting Months," *Working Paper* (2016), available at papers.ssrn.com/sol3/papers.cfm?abstract_id=2489152.
13 See, for example, B. Schindler, "Understanding Private Company Incentive Pay Practices," *Workspan* (March 2008), pp. 44–8; The Rise and Fall of the Unicorns: Some Private Technology Firms Are Having Trouble Justifying Their Lofty Valuations," *The Economist* (November 28, 2015), online at econ.st/1Ne7TLM.
14 See, for example, X. Chang, K. Fu, A. Low, and W. Zhang, "Non-executive Employee Stock Options and Corporate Innovation," *Journal of Financial Economics*, 115, no. 1 (January 2015), pp. 168–88.
15 A. P. Sloan Jr., *My Years with General Motors* (Garden City, NY: Doubleday, 1964), p. 140.
16 See, for example, B. Lev, "On the Usefulness of Earnings: Lessons and Directions from Two Decades of Empirical Research," *Journal of Accounting Research*, 27 (Supplement 1989), pp. 153–92; and "Are Earnings Reports Obsolete?" *Stanford Business* (October 6, 2015), online at stanford.io/1LhJ6kv.
17 See, for example, R. M. Bushman, A. Lerman, and X. F. Zhang, "The Changing Landscape of Accrual Accounting," *Journal of Accounting Research*, 54, no. 1 (March 2016), pp. 41–78.
18 For an academic review paper on the issue of accounting conservatism, see A. Mora and M. Walker, "The Implications of Research on Accounting Conservatism for Accounting Standard Setting," *Accounting and Business Research*, 45, no. 5 (Special Issue, 2015), pp. 620–50.
19 B. Lev, *Intangibles: Management, Measurement, and Reporting* (Washington, DC: Brookings Institution Press, 2001); C. D. Ittner, "Does Measuring Intangibles for Management Purposes Improve Performance? A Review of the Evidence," *Accounting and Business Research*, 38, no. 3 (May 2008), pp. 261–72. See also R. M. Bushman, A. Lerman, and X. F. Zhang, "The Changing Landscape of Accrual Accounting," *Journal of Accounting Research*, 54, no. 1 (March 2016), pp. 41–78.
20 "Top Managers' Pay Reveals Weak Link to Value," *Financial Times* (December 28, 2014), online at on.ft.com/1CODoYe.
21 "Barclays Cuts 3,700 Jobs in Restructuring," *Financial Times* (February 12, 2013), online at on.ft.com/12I9AKS.
22 "IBM Braced for Fresh Job Cuts," *The Financial Times* (February 28, 2014), online at on.ft.com/1kyGFyN.
23 See, for example, "The Best Way to Measure Company Performance," *Business Week* (March 5, 2010), online at www.businessweek.com. See also W. A. Van der Stede, "Discussion of 'The Role of Performance Measures in the Intertemporal Decisions of Business Unit Managers,'" *Contemporary Accounting Research*, 30, no. 3 (Fall 2013), pp. 962–9.
24 Accounting rules for leases can vary by jurisdiction and change over time. For a recent change in the accounting rules for leases under IFRS, see "IFRS 16 Leases: Project Summary and Feedback Statement," *IFRS* (January 2016), online at ifrs.org.
25 See, for example, J. J. Gong, W. A. Van der Stede, and S. M. Young, "Real Options in the Motion Picture Industry: Evidence from Film Marketing and Sequels," *Contemporary Accounting Research*, 28, no. 5 (Winter 2011), pp. 1438–66.
26 G. B. Stewart, III, *The Quest for Value* (New York: HarperCollins, 1999); J. M. Stern, J. S. Shiely, and I. Ross, *The EVA Challenge: Implementing Value-Added Change in an Organization* (New York: Wiley, 2003).

27 "Joel Stern on SVM," *The Economist* (April 30, 2016), online at econ.st/1NAKhTR.

28 See, for example, B. Birchard and A. Nyberg, "On Further Reflection," *CFO Magazine* (March 1, 2001).

29 "Top Managers' Pay Reveals Weak Link to Value," *Financial Times* (December 28, 2014), online at on.ft.com/1CODoYe.

CASE STUDY
Behavioral Implications of Airline Depreciation Accounting Policy Choices

Most managers have significant discretion in choosing their accounting policies. The managers of some companies choose sets of policies that are relatively "conservative"; others choose sets that are relatively "liberal." Conservatism results in delay of the recognition of some revenues or gains and/or acceleration of the recognition of some expenses or losses. Liberal accounting policies do the opposite. The effect of conservatism is that profits are reported later than they would have been had more liberal accounting policies been adopted.

If one wants to determine whether an airline company is being conservative or liberal in its choice of accounting policies, one obvious place to look is in the area of accounting for property, plant, and equipment (PP&E). PP&E usually constitutes more than 50% of the total assets of an airline. Interestingly, airlines' accounting policies for PP&E vary significantly.

Consider, for example, the aircraft depreciation practices used at four major airlines:

Delta Air Lines:[1]

- Straight-line over estimated useful lives
- 20- to 32-year life (from the date the equipment was placed in service)
- Residual value = 5% to 10% of cost

American Airlines:[2]

- Straight-line
- 16- to 30-year life
- Residual value = 5% to 10% of cost

Singapore Airlines:[3]

- Straight-line
- 15- to 20-year life
- Residual value = 5% to 10% of cost

Lufthansa:[4]

- Straight-line
- 20-year life
- Residual value = 5% of cost

Other facts:

1. An aircraft can fly indefinitely, assuming the aircraft is maintained properly.
2. The cost of maintaining an aircraft tends to increase over time. Exhibit 1 shows a typical function relating

[1] Source: Delta Air Lines, Inc. Form 10-K for the year ended December 31, 2015. From July 1, 1986, to April 1, 1993, Delta's policy had been to depreciate equipment to residual values (10% of cost) over a 15-year period. Prior to July 1, 1986, the company's policy was to depreciate equipment to a 10% residual value over a 10-year period.

[2] *Source*: American Airlines Group, Inc. Form 10-K for the year ended December 31, 2015. Prior to January 1, 1999, AMR used an estimated useful life of 20 years and a residual value of 5%. For the year ended December 31, 1999, the effect of this change was to reduce depreciation expense by approximately $158 million.

[3] *Source*: Singapore Airlines Annual Report for the year ended December 31, 2015. From April 1, 1989 to April 1, 2001, Singapore's policy had been to depreciate over a 10-year period to a residual value of 20% of original cost. Prior to April 1, 1989 at Singapore Airlines, the operational lives of the aircraft were estimated to be 8 years with 10% residual values.

[4] *Source*: Lufthansa Group Annual Report for the year ended December 31, 2015. Prior to March 2014, Lufthansa depreciated its aircraft over 12 years to a residual value of 15% of cost. See R. Weiss, "Lufthansa Changes Dividend Formula on Plane-Depreciation Switch," *Bloomberg* (December 10, 2014).

the cost required to maintain the airframes of commercial jetliners, commonly referred to as the "maturity factor," as the jetliners' cumulative flight hours increase.

3. The useful economic life of an aircraft is finite, but it is often difficult to estimate. Some DC-3 aircraft are still flying cargo routes commercially, even though this aircraft made its debut in 1935. But these aircraft, and some that followed them, such as the Boeing 707, which had its maiden flight in 1957, are no longer competitive for use in passenger markets.
4. New aircraft prices tend to rise over time. Fair market values for *used* aircraft decrease over time, but unless the aircraft are made obsolete by a technological breakthrough in new aircraft, which is rare, the values tend to decrease slowly. Some aircraft maintain 90% or more of their original value even after decades of use. Used aircraft values do fluctuate sometimes significantly depending on, for example, market demand and supply conditions in the air travel and aircraft production industries, technological innovations, and changes in laws (e.g. governing noise pollution or allowable tax deductions). However, rarely do used aircraft market values drop below 50% of their original purchase price.
5. In many countries, including the United States, the rules governing the depreciation allowable for tax purposes are quite different from those that determine the depreciation that can be taken for financial reporting purposes. The tax rules allow ultra-conservative accounting to ensure that companies do not have to pay the tax before they have collected cash from their customers. Corporations should and do take advantage of these rules and depreciate the aircraft as quickly as possible to defer the taxes that need to be paid (assuming positive income).

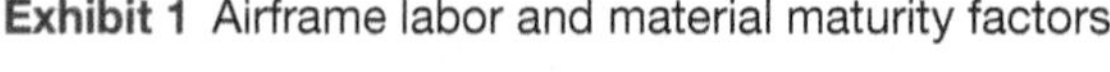

Exhibit 1 Airframe labor and material maturity factors

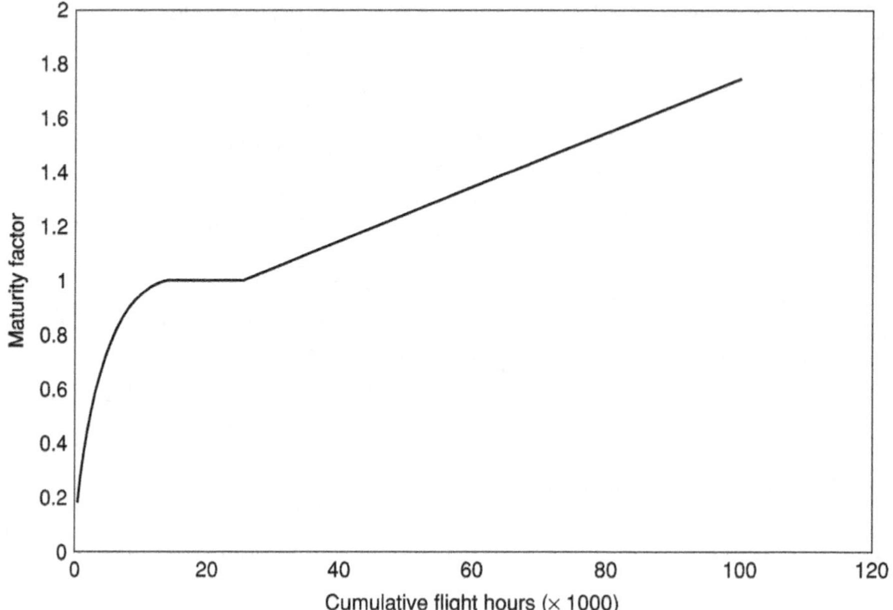

This case was prepared by Professor Kenneth A. Merchant.

CASE STUDY
Las Ferreterías de México, S.A. de C.V.

> We had been operating our company like a family, but maybe we're too big to operate that way. I think some of our people have gotten lazy, and our performance has suffered. That is why I asked for the design of a new incentive compensation plan. We need to be more competitive to survive. I want our people to focus on what they can do to improve company performance, and if we're successful, I am quite willing to share a good proportion of the proceeds of our success.
>
> —*Fernando Gonzalez Chairman and CEO, Las Ferreterías de México, S.A. de C.V.*

The company

Las Ferreterías de México, S.A. de C.V. (Ferreterías) was the second-largest retailer of lumber, building materials, and home improvement products and equipment in Mexico. Ferreterías operated 82 stores in Mexico City and throughout most of the northern regions of Mexico. Each of Ferreterías' stores offered between 10,000 and 20,000 stock keeping units (SKUs) in a retail sales area, an outside lumberyard area, and a garden center. The total store areas ranged from 10,000 to 35,000 square feet.

Ferreterías was founded in 1902 in a suburb of Mexico City by Fernando Gonzalez' grandfather. Over the years, the company added more locations. It was listed on the Mexican Stock Exchange in 1983. In 2012, Ferreterías had sales of 2,210 million pesos and profits of almost 120 million pesos (see summary financial statements in Exhibits 1 and 2).[1]

Starting in the late 1980s, Fernando Gonzales launched a major company expansion to take advantage of the growth in the Mexican economy. He thought that his company needed to emulate the methods of the large American homebuilding retailers, such as Home Depot and Lowe's, in order to survive. Thus, improving market share and improving operating efficiencies became Ferreterías' strategic priorities.

The store managers enjoyed considerable autonomy. They were responsible for hiring, firing, and supervising their store's personnel. While the stores had the same architectural designs and some basic stock keeping requirements, the individual store managers were allowed to adapt their merchandise offerings, their inventory levels, and their advertising and promotional activities to their local markets, which were quite diverse. The store managers were given considerable latitude to reduce prices to move excess inventory or to meet competition. They were responsible for making credit-granting decisions, although for large accounts they were expected to ask finance personnel at headquarters to perform a credit check. And some aggressive store managers tried to generate new business by calling on prospective customers themselves.

The 82 stores were organized into nine geographical regions. The regional managers, each of whom was a former store manager, provided oversight and advice. Their role was seen as an important part of the management structure because most of the store managers had little formal education. Only a few were college educated, and few of those had formal business education. Each region also contained a regional sales office with specialists who worked with larger customers, primarily larger contractors, in selecting materials and estimating costs. Sales to these customers, however, were made through the store nearest to the job.

The corporate staff of Ferreterías provided a range of centralized functions, including purchasing, human resources, marketing, real estate, and investor relations. Inventory was shipped to the stores from one of three regional warehouses.

[1] At the time of the case, one Mexican peso was worth approximately US$0.08.

All Ferreterías' employees were paid a base salary or hourly wage plus a bonus based on a share of the company's overall profits. These bonuses were small, usually in the range of 2% to 5% of base salary, depending on organization level. In addition, Fernando Gonzalez typically provided some discretionary bonus awards to employees whose performance in a given year was exemplary. Generally, however, these types of bonuses were not considered to be effective at motivating behavior, as was indicated in the comment by Mr. Gonzalez presented at the beginning of the case.

A new incentive plan

In July 2012, Mr. Gonzalez hired a consulting firm to design a new performance-based compensation plan. He asked his chief financial officer and head of human resources to assist the firm with its work.

Mr. Gonzalez's original intent was to include all company salesmen, buyers, and managers in the new incentive plan. After a series of interviews, however, the consulting firm reported that it would not be easy to measure the performances of either salesmen or buyers. While most customers were assigned to one particular salesperson, it was difficult to assess whether a sale came from the assigned salesperson's efforts. Many customers had dealt with Ferreterías for years, and they placed their orders regardless of whether or not they received a call from a Ferreterías salesperson. Some of the large contractors had also established personal relationships with one or more corporate or regional staff, and oftentimes they called their friends for advice, rather than relying on the salesperson formally assigned to them. Measuring the performances of the buyers was similarly problematic. The primary aspect of buyer performance that could be measured – the prices paid for items purchased – was affected by many factors over which the buyer had little control. These included the order size and market conditions. Because of these measurement problems, the consultants concluded that the measures that could be tracked would not provide meaningful bases on which to assign bonus awards. They recommended that they work first on designing an incentive plan for managers, which included the individual store managers (82), regional managers (9), and corporate staff managers (5). (Neither Fernando Gonzalez nor his chief operating officer was to be included in this plan; the compensation committee of the company's board of directors determined their bonuses.)

All other employees would continue to earn the same profit sharing awards that they had been earning. Those included in the new management incentive plan would no longer earn the profit sharing awards.

The consultants' suggestion for the management incentive plan included the following features:

1. **Bonus pool.** A total bonus pool would be created according to the following formula: 4 million pesos plus 8% of the corporate income before bonuses and taxes in excess of 120 million pesos. The total bonus pool would be divided into three classes as follows:

Store managers	70%
Regional managers	15%
Corporate staff managers	15%

2. **ROI measure of performance.** The bonus pools would be assigned to managers based on their entity's return on investment (ROI), defined as bonus-eligible revenues minus expenses divided by total store investments. The following guidelines were provided to facilitate the calculation of the ROI for bonus purposes:
   - The **revenues** eligible for bonuses included all shipments from the store except those stemming from sales orders written by regional or headquarters personnel.
   - The **expenses** include all direct store costs and all regional and headquarters costs. The costs of significant regional and headquarters activities traceable directly to a given store (e.g. cost of preparing a customer credit report, cost of a building upgrade) would be charged directly to that store. All other costs would be allocated to the stores. Activity-based allocations would be used where possible, such as in using the stores' relative proportions of receipts into inventory to allocate purchasing expenses. All other expenses would be allocated based on a proportion of bonus-eligible store revenues.
   - The **investment** at each store would include the annual average of the month-end balances of cash, inventory in stock, accounts receivable associated with the bonus-eligible revenues, equipment, furniture, fixtures, buildings, and land. (If the property is rented, the rent would be recognized as an expense.)
3. **Allocation of the bonus pool.** The store managers' bonus pool would be divided among the store managers based on their relative proportion of

bonus units earned. All managers whose stores earned at least 5% ROI would earn one bonus unit. For each full percentage point above five, the managers would earn an additional bonus unit, up to a maximum of six bonus units.

In 2012, the distribution of the stores' ROI was as follows:

ROI	N
< 5%	6
5–6%	6
6–7%	9
7–8%	11
8–9%	20
9–10%	15
10–11%	8
11–12%	4
> 12%	3
	82

For store managers who had been in that position for less than the full year and managers who transferred between stores during a year, bonus units would be assigned by the relevant regional manager(s) by applying the basic bonus unit award philosophy as closely as possible.

The regional managers' bonus pool would be divided among the regional managers based on a proportion of the bonus units earned by the stores in their region divided by the total bonus units earned by all stores.

The allocation of the corporate staff bonus pool would be decided by Fernando Gonzales based on the corporation's annual ROI performance.

4. **Form of the awards.** Bonuses were to be paid in cash as soon as the financial statements were prepared and audited and the amounts could be calculated.

Concerns before implementation

As Mr. Gonzalez looked over the consulting firm's design, he had some concerns. First, it was obvious to him that the new plan would increase the company's compensation expense. How much would that expense increase, and would the benefits of the plan be worth that expenditure? Second, he knew that he would have to be the one to announce the implementation of the plan. He had to anticipate what his managers' reactions would be. What were they mostly likely to complain about? Is this plan fair to all of the managers? And, finally, he still lamented the fact that personnel in the regional sales and corporate purchasing organizations were not included in this plan. If their individual performances could not be measured objectively, was there some other way he could motivate them and reward them for performing their roles, which were critical to the company's success?

Exhibit 1 Las Ferreterías de México, S.A. de C.V. income statement as of 12/31/2012 (Ps 000)

Net Sales	2,216,540
Costs of Sales	1,582,670
Gross Margin	633,870
Selling, General and Administrative Expenses	377,580
Depreciation Expense	65,740
Interest Expense	14,320
Total Expenses	457,640
Earnings before Taxes	176,230
Income Tax Provision	58,240
Net Earnings after Taxes	*117,990*

Exhibit 2 Las Ferreterías de México, S.A. de C.V. balance sheet as of 12/31/2012 (Ps 000)

Assets	
Current Assets	
Cash and Cash Equivalents	79,880
Short-Term Investments	5,430
Accounts Receivable	16,550
Merchandise Inventory	387,550
	489,410
Property, Less Accumulated Depreciation	857,650
Long-Term Investments	8,720
Other Assets	14,060
Total Assets	*1,369,840*
Liabilities	
Accounts Payable	211,260
Other Current Liabilities	57,860
Long-term Debt	384,350
Other long-term liabilities	67,140
	720,610
Shareholder' Equity	
Preferred Stock ($10 par; 300,000 shares issued)	30,000
Common Stock ($20 par; 1,000,000 share issued)	200,000
Retained Earnings	419,230
	649,230
Total Liabilities and Shareholder Equity	*1,369,840*

This case was prepared by Professors Kenneth A. Merchant and Wim A. Van der Stede, with the research assistance of Sung-Han (Sam) Lee.

CASE STUDY
Industrial Electronics, Inc.

> My division had another great year last year. We all worked hard, and the results were there. But again we got no reward for our hard work. It's very frustrating
>
> *– Division manager, General Products Division, Industrial Electronics, Inc.*

Industrial Electronics, Inc. (IE) produced a wide range of electronic equipment, including signal sources, test equipment, communications systems, and various piece parts and subassemblies such as motors, generators, and probes. Total annual sales were in excess of $8 billion. IE's stock was listed on the New York Stock Exchange.

The company's objective was to maximize shareholder value. In most of its business areas, IE had to be innovative to stay ahead of the competition. However, price competition was also significant, so the company also had to maintain tight control over costs.

The company was organized by product line. Its 16 relatively autonomous divisions were managed as profit centers. The division managers reported to one of four Business Group managers who, in turn, reported to the company's CEO.

Thirty managers, including all line managers at the level of division manager and above plus key corporate staff managers, were eligible for an annual management bonus award. (Many lower-level employees were included in a separate "management-by-objectives" incentive plan.) The management bonuses were based on company-wide performance. Each year, a bonus pool equal to 10% of the corporation's profit after taxes in excess of 12% of the company's book net worth was set aside for assignment as bonuses to managers. This amount was divided by the total salary of all the executives eligible for a bonus. This yielded an "award per dollar of salary." The maximum bonus paid was 150% of salary.

Historically IE's managers had been earning bonuses that ranged from of 30% to 120% of salary, with the average approximately 50%. But because of the recession in the prior two years, the bonus pool was zero.

Complaints about the management bonus system had been growing. Most of them stemmed largely from division managers whose divisions were performing well, even while the corporation as a whole was not performing well. These managers believed that the current bonus system was unfair because it failed to properly recognize their contributions. The quote cited at the beginning of the case was representative of these complaints.

In response, top management, with the assistance of personnel in the corporate Human Resources and Finance departments, proposed a new management bonus plan with the following features:

1. Bonuses would be determined by the performance of the entity for which each manager was responsible. That is, division manager bonuses would be based 100% on division performance; group manager bonuses would be based 100% on group performance; and corporate manager bonuses would be based 100% on corporate performance.
2. For bonus award purposes, actual performance would be compared with targets negotiated during IE's annual budgeting process. IE's philosophy was to try to set budget targets at "threshold" levels that were likely to be achieved if the management teams performed effectively. Corporate managers knew that IE was a "high tech" company that operated in many business areas in which there was significant operating uncertainty. It was often difficult to forecast the future accurately. They thought that the relatively highly achievable budget targets provided the operating managers with some insurance against an operating environment that might turn out to be more harsh than that seen at the time of budget preparation.
3. Each division would be given an "economic profit" objective equal to budgeted operating profit minus budgeted operating assets multiplied by 12%, which

was assumed to be approximately IE's weighted average cost of capital. For example, a division with an operating profit budget of $100,000 and budgeted operating assets of $500,000 would be given an economic profit objective of $100,000 – 60,000 = $40,000.

4. The actual investment base was calculated as follows:

Cash	Assumed to be 10% of cost of sales
Receivables and inventories	Average actual month-end balances
Fixed assets	Average actual end-of-month net book values

5. If an entity's actual economic profits were exactly equal to its objective, the manager would earn a bonus equal to 50% of salary. The bonus would increase linearly at a rate of five percentage points for each $100,000 above the objective and be reduced linearly at a rate of five percentage points for each $100,000 below the objective. The maximum bonus would be 150% of salary. The minimum bonus would be zero.

Tis case was prepared by Professor Kenneth A. Merchant.

CASE STUDY
Haengbok Bancorp

In 2009, Haengbok Bancorp, one of Korea's smaller nationwide banks, opened its first foreign branch in New York. It opened the branch for multiple reasons. This would be an important step in fulfilling Haengbok's objective of being an international bank. Having a US presence would allow the bank both to provide better support to its Korean partners and to generate additional business from primarily US-based Korean-owned, but also related, businesses. Most of Haengbok's customers were small and medium-sized businesses, but many of those businesses had some international operations. In addition, having some employees based overseas would allow the bank to be better informed about worldwide banking trends.

Haengbok managers knew that the competition for US-based Korean customers was fierce. Many Korean banks, some of them much larger than Haengbok, had well-established operations in the United States. Nevertheless, they thought the time was right to open the US branch because many smaller businesses were having difficulty raising capital as a result of the financial crisis. The branch was located in New York both because it was the largest US money center and because the New York–New Jersey metropolitan area contained a relatively high concentration of Korean-owned and oriented businesses.

Haengbok's New York branch was a wholesale operation. The primary goal was to make US dollar loans to Korean or US companies. To limit foreign exchange risk, the branch had to raise all of its money, except for a small capital contribution from Haengbok Bancorp, in the US money markets. Only a few retail accounts were maintained for the convenience of Haengbok's multinational clients. No special services were offered to build the retail side of the business. Check-clearing services were outsourced to a major US, New York-based bank.

Management of the branch

Hyun Ki Kim, an experienced Haengbok account manager previously based in Seoul, was appointed as senior manager of the New York branch. Mr. Kim quickly hired five experienced account managers with track records of success at other banks in the United States. The account managers began identifying clients in need of loans. For the most part, the account managers were assigned defined geographical territories to develop. Two were based on the East Coast, two on the West Coast, and one in the Midwest. However, two of the account managers had had significant, specific prior industry experiences, and they were given responsibility for developing opportunities with a few specifically identified prospective clients in those industries that were located outside their assigned territory.

Mr. Kim knew that the account managers he hired had varied corporate experiences and operating styles, but that did not concern him at all. He put few constraints on their activities. He told the account managers that he did not care how they identified and cultivated their clients as long as they eventually "booked good deals."

For monitoring and incentive purposes, Mr. Kim set each account manager up as a "mini profit center." Their profit centers were credited with the interest earned on the loans initiated, and they were charged for the expenses incurred, including the cost of funding the loans. This was not the system used by Haengbok Bancorp in Korea, but Mr. Kim thought that such a system was needed to encourage the account managers' entrepreneurialism, which would be needed to be able to grow the branch rapidly.

In addition to their base salaries, which branch studies showed to be slightly below comparable bank averages, the account managers were paid a bonus of 10% of the aggregate profits generated in their mini profit centers each year. They were not penalized for aggregate losses that might be incurred in any given year, but it was understood that losses would not be tolerated for extended periods of time. The bonuses were paid out in full in cash shortly after the fiscal year end. Mr. Kim thought that after the account managers had built their loan portfolios to their envisioned levels, their total compensation would be more than competitive with those of the established banks.

Mr. Kim thought that as the branch matured, he might begin to set goals for each account manager and to provide bonuses based on achievement of those goals, but in the start-up phase, he did not have enough knowledge of either the market potentials or the account manager capabilities to set meaningful goals. He worried that short-term profits provided only an imperfect measure of success in the wholesale banking industry. For one thing, the loans were typically granted for terms of 5 to 10 years, and no loan ever granted had a zero chance of default. But he thought that the rather rudimentary system put in place would suffice during the branch's start-up period. A more sophisticated reward system would probably emerge over time.

Managing time productively was a critical skill for the account managers. In all the geographical territories, the number of potential clients was huge. But competition was also stiff. Many Korean banks, including Hanmi, Nara, Wilshire, Center, Saehan, Pacific City, Shinhan, Woori, and Mirae, were already well established in the United States, and some Korean-oriented businesses also raised money from non-Korean banks. The Haengbok account managers had to identify and solicit business from their best prospects. The best clients were businesses who wanted larger loans with higher spreads and, importantly, also had the ability to pay the loans back. The account managers also had to consider both the costs of finding the prospects, analyzing their situations, and preparing the loan applications and the probabilities of getting the loans approved.

After the account managers identified loan prospects, they prepared a credit application. The loan application package needed to include a description of the client and its business, the proposed use of the loan funds, the proposed loan terms (e.g., size, payments, fees, security, covenants), and an analysis of the loan's risk. Risk was addressed in many ways, but market prospects and the client's financial statements were always considered.

Applications for loans less than $1 million could be approved by Mr. Kim. If the proposed loan exceeded $1 million, the application had to be approved by the branch's Credit Committee, which was comprised of Mr. Kim, the branch CFO/treasurer, and two of the most experienced account managers. If the proposed loan exceeded $5 million, then the Haengbok Bancorp Corporate Credit Committee, based in Seoul, would also have to give approval before the loan could be made.

After loans were made, they were reviewed on a regular basis by management, national bank examiners, and external auditors. Management also regularly monitored clients for signs of possible problems, which might be indicated by declining business conditions, violations of covenants, and missed payments.

A rejected loan application

In early 2010, Jae Lee, an account manager assigned to the southwestern US territory, submitted a credit application for an $11 million, seven-year term loan for Far East Trading Corporation (FETC), a company that had significant business activities in Korea. The pricing included a 1% fee at closing and a variable rate of 5% above the prime lending rate. The loan was fully collateralized with inventory. Because of the size of the loan, Jae spent considerable care in preparing the application. He was pleased with it:

> **I thought this was a good deal for Haengbok. I priced it with a relatively large spread, so we were going to make good money over the life of the loan. FETC is a good company that has been in business for many years, and it has an experienced management team. They have found good business opportunities even in the current recessionary period. So I concluded that the loan was relatively low risk.**

The branch's Credit Committee, of which Jae was not a part, quickly approved the loan. At the time, committee members noted that Jae's application was well prepared and that they trusted Jae's judgments about the merits of the deal. Jae happened to be one of the more experienced account managers. He had worked for several years for two major US banks before joining Haengbok's New York branch.

Since the proposed size of the loan exceeded $5 million, the application also had to be approved by the corporate Credit Committee in Seoul. When the corporate committee met, Jae joined part of the meeting by telephone. The committee members asked Jae a number of questions asking for both clarifications and more detail. Jae thought that he was able to answer all the questions satisfactorily.

A couple of days later, however, Jae and Mr. Kim were informed that corporate had decided that the loan should not be made. The committee spokesman explained that the problem was not with either Jae's analysis or the loan terms. A concern arose because some members of the Credit Committee had heard allegations that FETC was involved in some transfer pricing disputes with the tax authorities. These disputes could lead to protracted legal costs, possibly hefty fines, or an expensive settlement. While they could not confirm the allegations and did not know if the legal settlements, if any, might hinder FETC's ability to meet its cash flow obligations, when it came time to vote on this application, a majority of the committee members decided to err on the side of caution.

This case was prepared by Professor Kenneth A. Merchant.

CASE STUDY
Corbridge Industries, Inc.

In 2016, Corbridge Industries, Inc. (Corbridge) was starting a process that could lead to major changes in its planning and measurement systems. Chantal Coombs, vice president of planning, explained:

> **The basic thrust of what we are starting to do is very simple, although it has potentially major ramifications. We are changing the basic decision rules by which we evaluate our plans and our accomplishments. We have become convinced that for Corbridge, at least, the traditional accounting measures such as net earnings or return on net assets, are neither good criteria on**

which to base decisions, nor reliable indicators of performance.

The primary objective of our company is to create value for our shareholders. We believe that stock values, like the values of all economic resources, depend on investors' expectations of future cash flows, discounted for time and risk. Consequently, we think that in evaluating possible actions, it is more important to focus on the possible impacts of our decisions on future cash flows and risk, rather than estimating the impact on the accounting indicators. In addition, we think that it makes sense to judge our performance based on what we accomplish for our shareholders—meaning the amount of value we generate for them.

The company

Corbridge was a midsize but diversified company with $2.2 billion in annual sales of specialized, business-to-business supplies to some large manufacturers mainly in the midwestern United States. The company had experienced robust growth in both revenues and earnings over the years (see Exhibit 1).

Corbridge was organized into four business groups: Semiconductor, Electrical Products, Industrial Products, and Custom Products. The Semiconductor Group (SG) (2015 sales of $561 million, four divisions) designed, manufactured, and marketed a broad line of semiconductor components, including electronic sensors (e.g. photodiodes), memory devices, microprocessors, and transmission devices (e.g. fiber optics, speech synthesis chips). The Electrical Products Group (EPG) ($507 million, five divisions) produced assorted components or various subcomponents for generators and motors, circuit breakers and electrical connectors. The Industrial Products Group (IPG) ($774 million, six divisions) sold a wide range of components including custom engineered ball, roller, and slider bearings, precision engine parts, mechanical seals, industrial laminates, and some other nonwoven materials. The Custom Products Group (CPG) ($310 million, four divisions) designed, manufactured, and distributed products that used in-house technologies for small-order, sometimes one-off specialized components for the military and space technology sectors among others. A financial comparison of these groups is presented in Exhibit 2. The groups' 19 divisions were, in turn, divided into 70 product departments, each with profit-center responsibility.

In 2016, the compensation of a typical manager was expected to be approximately 60% salary and 40% performance incentives. The performance incentives were based 75% on operating income less a capital change (i.e. residual income), and 25% on the accomplishment of specific KPI (key performance indicator) targets.

Corbridge was a growth-oriented company with relatively young management. Most general managers had an engineering education and either technical or marketing experience, or both. The average age of the division managers was approximately 41. Tom McDowell, the chair of the board, was only 51. Top management was interested in maintaining at least moderate levels of overall internal growth and in acquiring companies with operations that complemented Corbridge's portfolio.

Planning processes

Planning at Corbridge was intended to be a bottom-up process. The strategic planning process started in March with headquarters sending general planning guidelines to the business units. These guidelines included an economic forecast and some preliminary estimates of the resources the company would make available to each business unit. The department managers (and lower-level managers where appropriate) were expected to propose their own goals and strategies. They were asked to prepare three-year plans with the emphasis on market analysis and identification of strategic alternatives. Quantitative data (including financial) were required in only summary form.

These plans were then reviewed at successively higher organizational levels. The Corporate Management Committee (CMC) reviewed the plans and evaluated the total portfolio of businesses early in September. The CMC rarely made material changes to the strategic plans at this time: changes were usually made only if the resource position changed or if an acquisition or divestment was imminent.

After CMC approval of the strategic plan, the department managers prepared detailed operating plans (budgets) for the next year. The operating plans included targets for sales growth, profit margins, and operating earnings and were intended to be consistent with the strategic plans. The operating plans were also reviewed at successively increasing organizational levels, usually with only minor modifications being made.

The shareholder value model

In the early 2010s, corporate staff began experimenting with a model called V-Plan as an aid in evaluating strategic plans. V-Plan was developed by a management consulting firm, with the help of some leading academics in the fields of finance, accounting, and business planning.

At the heart of V-Plan was a discounted cash flow (DCF) model, which, with the input of estimates of future cash flows and factors for discounting time and risk, could be used to place a value on any business entity at any point in time. For strategic planning purposes, V-Plan could be used to value an entity given the assumptions behind any of a number of different strategic alternatives. A particular strategy was considered to generate a positive value for shareholders only if it increased the business entity's cash flows in a manner sufficient to more than offset new investments that might be required. Cash flows (and value) might be generated by, for example, increasing the volume of sales, increasing the contribution generated by each incremental sale, or reducing the amount of investment tied up in working capital as compared to the levels in the base period. In concept, V-Plan was identical to capital-investment-analysis models based on the net present value (NPV) method. But with V-Plan, all cash outlays that were required to implement a strategy were considered, not just capital investments, which typically composed only a small fraction of the total.

History of use of the shareholder value model

Prasad Vepa, director of corporate planning, described how Corbridge came to incorporate V-Plan in its planning processes:

> **By all the traditional accounting measures, our performance over the last two decades was excellent. Take any measure you want – sales growth, earnings growth, return on equity, return on assets, and earnings per employee – they all indicate we had done very well. Our shareholders, however, hadn't really derived any benefit from this *success*. In 2013, our market value was essentially where it was in 2004, even though stocks in the S&P 500 had averaged about 8% returns in this time period. And although we increased our dividends as earnings increased, this never provided shareholders with a return greater than 4%.**
>
> **In 2013, the merger and acquisition people in our corporate planning department were involved in a lot of value analyses. We were using pretty sophisticated models which helped us analyze the determinants of value – cash flow potentials and risk – under various business and economic assumptions, so that we could put a value on business segments we were considering buying or selling. In our planning meetings, my group saw the need for the same types of analyses. One choice our management was often faced with was whether to acquire an existing business or to build one by allocating resources to one of our existing business units. Thus, it was natural that we began to use cash flow-based value models in our planning analyses.**

Corbridge first applied the shareholder value models to the plans submitted during the 2014 planning process. The operating managers were not involved in the actual use of the models; corporate staff just took the numbers in the plans and plugged them into the models. The purpose of this exercise was not to use the output in decision-making, but just to get some familiarity with the problems that might arise when the models were used to compare internal business units.

In the first year, the corporate planning staff used the model's cash flow-based estimates of changes in *intrinsic shareholder value* at the corporate level and compared them with Corbridge's actual changes in market value over the period 2009–13 and the year 2014. The model's estimates were quite accurate. They showed that the corporation's net cash returns during the 2009–13 period were actually not sufficient to increase shareholder value, but that the plans for 2014, if they were achieved, would do so. And, indeed, at the end of 2014, when the plans had been achieved, the total Corbridge market value had risen to over $750 million, up from the $550 million level where it had been for virtually the entire prior decade.

At this time, top-level Corbridge managers indicated that they were very comfortable with these findings. Tom McDowell (chairman) stated that the value concept supported intuitive feelings he had had.

Later in the year, V-Plan was given a real credibility boost. At year-end 2014, Corbridge stock was selling at about $32 per share, and at midyear 2015 it was around

$40. In June 2015, Rick Aubrey, an analyst in the Corporate Planning Department, used V-Plan to analyze Corbridge's financial performance and concluded that despite continuing improvement in the accounting numbers, company performance did not justify the higher stock price. Rick estimated that by year-end the stock price would be around $31 per share if the company maintained its current strategy and performance came in as projected. This estimate was shown to the high-level corporate managers, but they did not choose to alter company strategies at that time.

At year-end, with everything going according to plan, Corbridge stock was selling at $30. Rick observed:

> You can't depend on the model showing that kind of accuracy consistently. We have to make a number of assumptions and approximations; nobody really knows how the stock market will respond at any given time; and the market does not have access to the confidential information I used in my analysis. But the theory behind the model is correct; the intrinsic value of our company should depend on the size, pattern, and uncertainty surrounding the cash flows we expect to be able to generate in the future.
>
> The success of this forecast was very important. It gave the model credibility. Everybody is used to thinking in terms of sales and earnings growth, and we have always used those numbers to plan with, even though they are not very good numbers on which to base our decisions or to judge our success.

V-Plan and strategic planning

Rick went on to describe how the model could be used to support Corbridge's planning efforts:

> Let me show you some examples of why I think we should use V-Plan in our planning processes. Here is a situation where operating managers might be discouraged from investing in, or even proposing, good strategies because of their adverse impact on accounting earnings [Exhibit 3]. Schedule 1 shows pro-forma income statements for a three-year period in which I've assumed no real growth but 10 percent inflation, which I know is unrealistic in the current day and age, but bear with me—this is just to make my point and for ease of computation and dramatic effect. I've called this Strategy 1; it can be considered a base case or a maintenance strategy.
>
> Now, suppose a manager identifies a strategy which requires an investment of $5 million in marketing expenses in each of the next three years (2016–18) but which promises five percent real growth in 2017 and 2018. The projected income statements for this alternative (Strategy 2) are shown in Schedule 2.
>
> The implication should be clear. With a projected decline in earnings in 2016, this strategy will probably suffer an early death. The division manager will be reluctant to propose it because top management is not likely to look at it enthusiastically and, furthermore, if the strategy were implemented it would adversely affect his bonus.
>
> From the shareholder's standpoint, however, this is a good plan. The cash flow and shareholder value numbers are shown in Schedule 3. As per our standard conservative procedure, I've assumed the operating cash flows will remain constant at the 2018 level in perpetuity. But even so, the value numbers make it obvious that our shareholders would want us to invest in this plan. An analysis would show that the internal rate of return is over 30 percent.
>
> The accounting biases can also operate in the opposite direction—that is, a decision that promises excellent profits can be bad for the shareholders. Here is such an example [shown as Strategy 3 in Exhibit 4].
>
> I've taken the same base case (Schedule 1) and this time assumed that a manager has identified an investment of $25 million in capital equipment and working capital that would increase the operating margin from 20 to 22 percent. This provides an improved profit picture (Schedule 2), but this is actually a bad investment that yields less than the 18 percent cost of capital that I've assumed. The net effect is to reduce the value of the earning assets in this business unit by almost $5 million (Schedule 3).
>
> These are very simple examples, of course, but I can assure you that these patterns occur in some of the plans submitted by our operating units. Let me show you one example. During the 2015 planning process, one of our divisions proposed a strategy which showed sharp increases in both sales and earnings [Exhibit 5]. From these numbers, it is easy to conclude that this is a pretty decent plan. In truth, however, it is not.
>
> Using V-Plan, I calculated that the pre-strategy value of this division (net of liabilities) is approximately $500,000. But if this strategy is implemented,

I figure that the value of this division would actually be a negative $1.2 million [Exhibit 6]. This is true because the strategy requires a considerable up-front investment for items which do not show up in the income statement for some time. I conclude that implementing this strategy would cause a decrease of $1.7 million in the intrinsic value of this division and the value of Corbridge stock. And if anything, my calculation may be optimistic because for this business segment it would be easy to justify using a risk-adjusted discount rate greater than the 18 percent that I used in making these calculations. The 18 percent is the overall corporate weighted-average cost of capital, and this particular business unit is probably one of the riskiest businesses in our portfolio.

I think we should seriously consider selling this business, assuming someone would be willing to pay something close to the $500,000 that it is worth right now. We certainly should not be investing the money proposed in this plan. The increased sales and earnings picture is misleading; this plan will actually be very costly to our shareholders.

Let me make one qualification, however. I am not suggesting that impact on shareholder value should be the only criterion we should look at when we make our strategic resource allocation decision. What I am suggesting is that impact on shareholder value should be an important financially-oriented criterion and that it is far superior to looking at projections expressed in traditional accounting terms.

Change in statement of objectives

At the end of 2015, the wording of Corbridge's primary statement of objectives was changed to read as follows:

The primary objective of Corbridge Industries is to increase shareholder value. This will be accomplished by focusing on markets where the Company has or can capture a major share, by developing a higher-than-average flow of successful new products, and by continuing to emphasize productivity of Company personnel and assets.

Formerly, the primary objective had been "to grow and to improve profitability." This change in the wording of the statement of company objectives was not brought about by the V-Plan directly, but it was motivated by the same logic that the model used.

The future of the shareholder value model

Corbridge planned to work with and to refine the shareholder value model and eventually to spread its use throughout the organization. Tom McDowell (chairman) promised to use V-Plan and related models "more intensively and extensively."

A number of important issues remained to be solved, however. One issue was the planning horizon. In making the value calculations, all cash flows, no matter how far into the future, had to be considered, but the Corbridge operating plans only included three years of data. To work around this limitation, the planning staff had been making the assumption that the operating cash flows in the last year of the plan would remain constant in perpetuity, in the absence of information to the contrary. While the most immediate cash flows had the largest value impact because of discounting, this assumption was subject to obvious criticisms, particularly for those divisions with products with relatively short product life cycles. Thus, to improve the accuracy of V-Plan's calculations, one possibility that had to be considered was an extension of the planning horizon, from three years to five, or perhaps even longer.

A second issue was whether the plans should reflect a single point estimate of future results or whether they should reflect a range of possible outcomes and an assessment of the likelihood of each. V-Plan's value calculations were intended to reflect the *expected value* of the future cash flows, and the model could easily accommodate probabilistic cash flow estimates. However, several senior managers thought that single-point estimates were necessary for control purposes, so that managers could be held responsible for achieving a specific plan.

Risk presented another problem. Corbridge's early uses of the model used the same discount factor – the corporate average cost of capital – in all analyses. If Corbridge had been highly vertically integrated and in a single market, this might have been acceptable, but the corporate planning staff felt that the various business units faced quite different levels of risk. Quantifying the amounts of risk faced in order to reflect them in the discount rates used in the value calculations was not straightforward, however, and more thought would have to be given to this issue before use of the model was made more widespread.

A fourth issue was the speed of implementation, meaning how fast to involve managers at each organization level in the use of the model. Because they were convinced of its worth, top management was inclined to use the impact-on-shareholder-value criterion for evaluating plans immediately. This might, however, cause frustration and conflict if the lower-level managers did not understand the bases on which the decisions were being made. All managers were familiar with the NPV concept because they were required to use it in preparing their capital investment proposals, but it was not clear whether they could easily transfer their knowledge of this basic concept to the preparation of entire operating plans.

Finally, if impact on shareholder value became an important criterion in strategic decision-making, another issue would arise; that is, whether or not to link a value-related performance criterion – impact on shareholder value – to the management reward system. To reinforce the shareholder value concept, some portion of management compensation could be made contingent on value increases – either of the corporation as a whole or of specific business units. The question was: should this be done, and if so, how soon?

Exhibit 1 Corbridge financial results 2004–2015 ($ million)

	2015	2014	2013	2012	2011	2010	2009	2008	2007	2006
Net sales	2,152	1,841	1,577	1,334	1,139	1,025	883	762	647	533
Net earnings	110	96	84	71	61	50	44	38	33	28
Capital expenditures	98	86	57	59	59	35	40	45	36	19
Market value (ave.)	755	769	544	526	551	619	581	563	625	662
Ratios (%)										
Increase in sales	16.9	16.7	18.2	17.1	11.1	16.1	15.8	17.8	213	16.5
Increase in net earn.	14.6	14.2	18.3	16.4	21.9	13.6	15.8	15.2	17.8	21.7
Net earn. as % of sales	5.1	5.2	5.3	5.3	5.3	4.9	5.0	4.9	5.1	5.3
Dividends as % of net earn.	29.7	27.4	25.7	26.2	24.1	20.7	19.2	21.8	22.5	24.9
Ret. on ave. shareholder equity	15%	14.6%	14.6%	13.5%	12.9%	12.0%	12.2%	11.9%	11.6%	11.1%

Exhibit 2 Financial comparison of major business groups

	2015	2014	% Change
Semiconductor			
Net sales	$561	$428	31.1
Net earnings	6	5	20.0
Electrical Products			
Net sales	$507	$469	8.1
Net earnings	28	27	3.7
Industrial Products			
Net sales	$774	$701	10.4
Net earnings	63	56	12.5
Custom Products			
Net sales	$310	$243	27.6
Net earnings	13	8	62.5
Corbridge Total			
Net sales	$2,152	$1,841	16.9
Net earnings	110	96	14.6

Exhibit 3 Example showing discouragement of a good investment ($ million)

Schedule 1: Projected Income Statements, Division A, Strategy 1 (Base Case)				
		Forecast		
	Actual 2015	2016	2017	2018
Sales	$200	$220	$242	$266
Variable operating expenses	160	176	194	213
Depreciation	10	11	11	12
Discretionary expenses	20	22	24	27
Total expenses	190	209	229	252
Profit before tax	10	11	13	15
Income tax (40%)	4	4	5	6
Profit after tax	$6	$7	$8	$9

Schedule 2: Projected Income Statements, Division A, Strategy 2 (Real Growth)				
		Forecast		
	Actual 2015	2016	2017	2018
Sales	$200	$220	$253	$291
Variable operating expenses	160	176	202	233
Depreciation	10	11	11	12
Discretionary expenses	20	27	29	32
Total expenses	190	214	243	276
Profit before tax	10	6	10	15
Income tax (40%)	4	2	4	6
Profit after tax	$6	$4	$6	$9

Schedule 3: Value Calculations				
Annual Cash Flows	2016	2017	2018	2019 and beyond
Strategy 1	$18	$19	$21	$21
Strategy 2	15	17	21	24

Value of Division A on December 31, 2015 at 18% (ignoring liabilities)
Strategy 1 $102.3 million
Strategy 2 $108.1 million

Exhibit 4 Example showing encouragement of a bad investment ($ million)

Schedule 1: Projected Income Statements, Division A, Strategy 1 (Base Case)				
		Forecast		
	Actual 2015	2016	2017	2018
Sales	$200	$220	$242	$266
Variable operating expenses	160	176	194	213
Depreciation	10	11	11	12
Discretionary expenses	20	22	24	27
Total expenses	190	209	229	252
Profit before tax	10	11	13	15
Income tax (40%)	4	4	5	6
Profit after tax	$6	$7	$8	$9

Schedule 2: Projected Income Statements, Division A, Strategy 3 (Improve Operating Margins)				
		Forecast		
	Actual 2015	2016	2017	2018
Sales	$200	$220	$242	$266
Variable operating expenses	160	172	189	208
Depreciation	10	12	13	14
Discretionary expenses	20	22	24	27
Total expenses	190	206	226	248
Profit before tax	10	14	16	18
Income tax (40%)	4	6	6	7
Profit after tax	$6	$9	$10	$11

Schedule 3: Value Calculations				
Annual Cash Flows Investment	2016	2017	2018	2019 and beyond
Strategy 1	$18	$19	$21	$21
Strategy 3 $(25)	21	23	25	25

Value of Division A on December 31, 2015 at 18% (ignoring liabilities)

Strategy 1 $102.3 million

Strategy 3 $ 97.4 million

Exhibit 5 Division A, Strategy X: Projected income statements ($ million)

	2016	2017	2018
Sales	$74	$89	$106
Expenses	70	84	99
Profit before taxes	4	5	7
Income taxes	2	2	3
Profit after taxes	$2	$3	$4

Exhibit 6 Division A, Strategy X: Shareholder value calculations ($ million)

Present value of earning assets at end of implementation of strategy	$16.8
Less: Present value of investment required	(7.9)
Less: Market value of debt (net of monetary assets)	(10.1)
Present value of division if strategy is implemented	(1.2)
Less: Pre-strategy value of division	.5
Shareholder value contribution of strategy	$(1.7)

This case was prepared by Professor Kenneth A. Merchant.

CASE STUDY
King Engineering Group, Inc.

In early 2016, managers at King Engineering Group, Inc. (King), a large engineering and construction company, were striving to strengthen the links between corporate and business unit goal setting. Their task was somewhat unique because King was privately owned by an employee stock ownership plan (ESOP). In May 2016, Jim Anderson, King's chief financial officer (CFO), described the challenge:

> **Our goal, like that of all corporations, is to maximize value for our investors. But King is essentially an investment maintained by a pension plan; the funds just happen to be invested in engineering and construction assets. What performance should our owners reasonably expect? Should we compare our performance against that of our publicly traded competitors or other pension plans? And how can we best get all of our business units working toward the achievement of our corporate goals?**

The company

George E. King founded King Engineering in 1946. By the year 2016, King was a large full-service engineering and construction firm, with over 11,000 employees and nearly $1.5 billion in annual sales.

King was headquartered in Oklahoma City, Oklahoma, but its operations were global. King had three main business units (see organization chart in Exhibit 1). The Transportation Group (approximately 20% of total company sales) built highways, bridges, and rail and transit systems. The Energy & Chemicals (E&C) Group (40%) offered design and construction services for oil and gas field refineries, power generation facilities, and chemical plants. The Infrastructure & Technology (I&T) Group (40%) built projects in 16 different market sectors, including shopping centers, dams, resorts, airports, and telecommunication infrastructures. The I&T Group also provided environmental services, such as the monitoring of air and water quality and construction of municipal waste treatment plants. In a typical year, King's operations encompassed approximately 3,000 projects, the budget for some of which exceeded $1 billion. The significant projects totaled about 200 in the Transportation Group, 60–70 in E&C, and 200 in I&T.

King's organization structure also included three regional organizations beyond its North American market (Europe, Middle East, Africa & South Asia (EMEASA); Latin America; and Asia Pacific). King's regional management worked closely with the global business units to support international customers, to coordinate King's in-country resources with local partners, and to mobilize King's global workforce to provide the technical capabilities required on the projects.

In the late 2000s as a result of the great recession, the engineering and construction industry underwent some significant changes. These included firm consolidations (mainly because many firms were performing poorly) and an acceleration of the shift (particularly in energy and chemicals markets) from cost-plus contracts toward fixed-price business. King, which traditionally had been among the more conservative players in the industry, responded successfully by cutting costs, outsourcing non-critical engineering skills, and developing greater marketing efforts. Over time, King had also restructured its corporate business portfolio through both internal development and acquisitions. In October 2015, the company announced an intention to sell the E&C Group, which generated about 25% of total company sales, but a buyer had not yet been identified.

In light of these changes, King developed a strategy of delivering more than traditional ("blue-collar") engineering, construction, and program management. The company instead moved to try to deliver more "turnkey solutions," which involved financing, engineering, procurement, construction, operation, and maintenance capabilities on a global scale. These changes required King to bear more risk. Since more of these projects were based on fixed-price rather than cost-plus contracts,

King bore the cost-control and schedule risks. In some projects, King was even providing customers with "back-end guarantees." For example, the customers would buy kilowatts from King at a fixed price, rather than just paying for construction of a power plant, so King was bearing the performance risks. In some of the projects, the risks were shared with a joint-venture partner.

Ownership by an Employee Stock Ownership Plan (ESOP)

King had always been privately owned. But in 1984, to create liquidity for the original owners and to take advantage of some newly created tax changes, King's managers created an Employee Stock Ownership Plan (ESOP) and had the ESOP buy all of the company stock. After 1984, King Engineering had only one shareholder: the ESOP trust.

ESOPs are employee benefit plans that make employees of a company the owners of the stock in that company.[1] ESOPs are required by law to invest primarily in the securities of the sponsoring employer. All employees are automatically members of the ESOP, and they build up a "beneficial interest" over time. King employees' ESOP interests are fully vested after seven years, and they receive a lump sum payout at retirement.

ESOPs provided two tax-related advantages. First, since ESOP contributions are tax deductible, a corporation that repays an ESOP loan in effect gets to deduct principal as well as interest from taxes. Second, dividends on ESOP stock that are paid to employees are also tax deductible. Moreover, when King's ESOP was formed, US federal tax law allowed lenders to exclude 50% of the interest earned on loans to ESOPs from its taxable income. This gave rise to so-called "leveraged ESOPs," such as that in place at King, and used as an important element of corporate finance. In a leveraged ESOP, the company borrows money from a bank or other qualified lender and then, in turn, lends it to the ESOP. The ESOP can use the funds to buy either existing stock or new stock from the company. Competitive markets forced the lenders to pass some of these savings on, so ESOPs were able to borrow money at favorable rates.[2]

ESOPs also provide advantages in that they give employees a significant ownership stake in their company. This ownership stake can improve the company's culture and lead to performance gains.

Despite the advantages of the ESOP, not all of the employees were happy with the change in ownership. When the King ESOP was formed, several employee groups filed a class action lawsuit against King and its officers and directors. They maintained that they had little say in the decision, that the plan disproportionately benefited higher-level executives, and that the buyout left the ESOP with all of the debt but none of the decision-making power. The final appeal was heard in 1991, and the settlement favored King's position.

Accounting performance measures

The generic income statement used in the construction industry is in the following format:

	Revenues
minus:	Direct contract costs (materials, labor, and overhead)
=	Gross profit
minus:	General and administrative expenses (G&A)
=	Net operating income

In its early years, King's managers' main focus was on the revenue line. The problem with this approach was that the varying mix of the contracts in which King was involved often produced misleading revenue trends and revenue-based ratios. Some of King's contracts, such as some oil exploration projects, were set up to run all the revenues generated by the project through King's accounting records, but King's profit as a percentage of those revenues was very small. In others, all project revenues flowed to the client's records, and King's records reflected only the smaller amount of revenues earned directly from King's efforts, which yielded proportionally good margins. For yet others, King earned significant royalty payments but had no costs associated with them.

In the early 2000s, when a new management team assumed control, King's managers changed their focus. They made greater use of the following four measures:

Gross Profit Sold (GPS): the excess of anticipated revenue from contracts booked during a period over anticipated direct contract costs.

[1] ESOPs are quite common. In 2015, the National Center for Employee Ownership estimated that there were approximately 7,000 ESOPs in existence in the United States covering about 13.5 million employee owners (or about 8.5% of the US workforce). For more information on ESOPs, see www.esop.org.

[2] This provision in the tax law no longer exists.

Gross Profit Produced (GPP): the excess of revenue over direct contract costs for a given accounting period.[3]

Overhead (OH): included the indirect non-contract expenses incurred in the various administrative units (e.g. corporate, division).

Net Operating Income (NOI): gross profit minus overhead.

King's managers started closely monitoring two key performance ratios: the GPP/GPS conversion ratio and the GPP/OH divergence ratio. The *GPP/GPS conversion ratio* emphasized the fact that sales (GPS) do not mean much unless they actually get consummated (GPP). The *GPP/OH divergence ratio* was meant to keep overhead spending in check. In combination, the two performance ratios were in place to encourage managers to get "productive" sales (GPP) that generate bottom-line profitability (NOI) with an efficient use of resources (OH). The mechanics underlying the use of these ratios are discussed further below.

Planning and budgeting processes

King's planning and budgeting processes focused on the development of an annual plan. King did little long-term operational planning because of the difficulty of accurately seeing very far into the future. Jim Anderson (CFO) said, "Twelve to eighteen months' visibility is the most you really get." One major planning limitation was that the economy-wide changes (such as growth in GDP or changes in population demographics and consumer demand) that could be forecast reasonably accurately, and that were useful for planning purposes in many firms, were not the drivers of King's business opportunities. Those were largely driven by discrete political, legislative, and economic events that were difficult to predict, and they were affected by changes in commodity prices (particularly oil). As Jim Anderson explained, "Could anybody predict the fall of the Iron Curtain? Could anyone foresee the Iraq War and its aftermath? Did anybody know in 2000 where the 2016 Olympics would be held?" While King's managers made some longer-term projections, Jim Anderson described only the company's targets for the next year as "good." He called targets for the second year out "guesswork," and targets for the third year out as outright "fiction."

Up until 2014, King's financial planning process was like that used in many corporations. Corporate executives did not communicate any overall corporate performance benchmarks to the business units. They provided only a few planning parameters (e.g. expected average salary increases). The business units then developed largely bottom-up financial plans. Corporate management reviewed the bottom-up plans and typically "squeezed some more profit out." Bill Houchin, president of the I&T Group, reflected on the old planning process:

> **The outcomes were really corporate-imposed business unit targets. Where did these numbers come from? I really don't know. My best guess is that they were trend-based. Corporate managers would ask line managers to do better than they had done the prior year. But not all of these plans were realistic. Some business units really had to stretch to make their numbers, and sometimes they compromised their future in doing so.**

In 2014, the new management team made significant changes to the planning and budgeting process. The major changes were:

- A more scientific corporate goal-setting process backed by a "sales-to-share price model" that translated share price growth goals into corporate financial targets.
- An interactive process designed to produce greater convergence between the corporate and business-unit targets.
- A focus on allocation of discretionary investment monies, which were called "free money" because the business units did not bear the cost of the investment.

Each of these elements is described in the following explanations of the corporate and business unit planning processes.

The corporate goal-setting process

King's goal was to "maximize share price" for its ESOP trust. Since no market-determined share price existed, King had a stock valuation done annually by an outside consulting firm, which compared King's financial performance with that of the company's major publicly held competitors: Fluor, Amec Foster Wheeler, Parsons, ICF International, Jacobs, Morrison Knudsen, Stone & Webster, Stantec, and URS Corp. This analysis yielded

[3] King's managers also monitored a measure of **Gross Profit Backlog** (GPB), which was cumulative Gross Profit Sold less the Gross Profit Produced in the current period plus/minus backlog adjustments (e.g. stemming from projects falling out of backlog or contract term renegotiations). As such, GPB was a measure of the profit potential of the projects in backlog.

revenue, EBIT, and EBITDA multiples that were used, along with judgment, to compute an "equivalent share price" for King stock.

As part of the annual planning process, King's corporate managers set an annual share price growth goal that, in recent years, had been 15%. Jim Anderson (CFO) explained:

> **Like all corporations, we want to grow. But we have trouble funding and staffing growth. Our expenses tend to be front-loaded, but our revenue is slow to be collected, and the pool of qualified professionals is limited. We think that 25% growth is probably too much. That would also reveal a number of organizational constraints involving people, particularly managers and professionals. So we have been happy with 10–15%.**

The share-price-growth goal was translated into financial performance targets that could be used to guide corporate and operating managers in their decision making and performance monitoring activities. Jim Anderson was in the process of developing a sales-to-share price model that would serve this purpose. The model, which is illustrated in Exhibit 2, assumes a desired 15% increase in share price end-of-year 2015 to end-of-year 2016 (from \$19.46 to \$22.38). The model then calculates the NOI needed to produce that target share price.

The calculations shown in Exhibit 2 needed to be extended to create OH and GPS targets for the year 2016. NOI is GPP minus OH. Jim Anderson believed that GPP and OH had to diverge by 20%, that is, *the GPP/OH divergence ratio* must be about 1.20. Then GPP is the sum of NOI and OH. To calculate GPS, another calculation was necessary to account for the fact that not all anticipated contracts would actually be fulfilled: *the GPP/GPS conversion ratio*. For 2016, Jim Anderson set the GPP conversion target at 97%, roughly the historical average. Thus, the GPS target was the GPP target divided by .97. Here is a numerical example that illustrates the logic linking OH, GPP, and GPS targets with the targeted share price:

Target Share Price for 2016 (assuming 15% growth)	\$22.38	(from Exhibit 2)
Corresponding Target NOI	[1] \$21,980	(from Exhibit 2)
OH-target for 2016	109,900	(=[1]÷ .20)
GPP-target for 2016	[2] 131,880	
GPS-target for 2016	\$135,959	(=[2]÷ .97)

While Jim Anderson was convinced that he was on the right track in developing this model, he also acknowledged the current model parameters were not reliable. King's business had changed so dramatically in recent years, for example, by the shift toward more fixed-price rather than cost-plus contracts. Jim concluded that he really had only two good data points – the annual results since 2014 – that he could use for model estimation purposes.

The business unit planning process

At the same time the corporate target-setting process was taking place, the business unit managers prepared their bottom-up plans. In June, the Group managers asked their subordinates (profit and cost center managers) to put together "baseline" projections for the next year. The baseline projections assumed a continuation of current operations and some inflation, but no new investments.

The base-line projections contained "factored" estimates of forthcoming GPP. Projects that were currently "in hand" or in the process of being consummated were included in the plan at a 100% certainty level. Expected additional tasks stemming from existing contracts were included at a 90% certainty level. All other "prospective contracts on the sales horizon" were weighted by a specific "probability of capture," which might be as low as 5%. Then, based mostly on historical trends, a layer of unidentified work – project development opportunities that arise on a day-to-day basis and could not yet be foreseen – was added.

Profit center managers were also asked to propose up to two levels of incremental investment, generally 2% and 5% higher than current levels. These incremental investments had to either contribute to King's existing strategy or lead the business units to move in new and useful directions. For example, one incremental investment that was funded led to King's recent move into running the vehicle emissions inspection program for the state of Oklahoma. This program was an offshoot of King's air quality business in its environmental profit center. The investment proposals had to include a solid investment analysis, including estimates of future cash inflows and an estimated return.

Some managers took this opportunity to propose new investments. Others decided they had no prospects that would pass corporate scrutiny, so they did not propose anything.

Corporate review processes

In early September, after internal group reviews, the budget and investment proposals were submitted to corporate. Corporate managers first reviewed them for "reasonableness." Then the plans were discussed in a weeklong meeting held toward the end of September. One focus of this planning meeting was on the forecasts and probability estimates of newly identified projects.

If the consolidation of the business unit plans fell short of achieving the corporate targets, the management team would collectively have to figure out who would have to "step up" to, possibly, reduce overhead. If the consolidation showed a surplus, the managers would have to decide whether to accept the surplus. About this process, Jim Anderson said, "setting business targets here is no different from what happens elsewhere. There is a lot of sandbagging and horse-trading."

At the end of this process, corporate managers created planning reserves to protect against the chance of business units not achieving their targets. The sum of the business unit plans was designed to exceed the corporate target.

Another focus of the planning review meeting was the investment proposals. To support the investment initiatives that they considered worthy, corporate managers gave out what they called "free money." The money was considered "free" because the investment was not charged to the business units. However, after investments were approved, the returns forecast in the investment proposals were added to business units' plans for the subsequent years.

Some operating managers thought the forecast augmentation catch to the "free money" was a high cost. Bill Houchin (president of the I&T Group) explained:

> **Although the money is "free" for one year, it is allocated with the clear understanding that we turn it into GPP in the following years. We are held fully accountable for the cash flows and returns in our investment proposals, which means that what we said we "could achieve" suddenly becomes what we "must achieve." The challenge is even greater because there is a vote on the investments to approve. The investments that are at the top of the list seem to be those that return the money fast, so that forces you to accelerate your forecasts of the returns. And then these returns don't count toward your GPP growth goals; they're incremental to that. I understand that there must be accountability, but you can't get someone to the edge of the envelope if there is a significant downside to taking risk.**

The final business unit plans were due in November. Corporate managers typically made a few final adjustments before seeking board approval. The business plans became final by mid-December.

Management incentives

In addition to the typical subjective performance reviews that were used for salary adjustment purposes, King used two formal performance-dependent incentive plans – a Management Incentive Plan and a Long Term Incentive Plan.

Management Incentive Plan (MIP)

Several hundred employees were included in the MIP, from corporate officers down to project managers, functional managers, and key employees in overhead departments. Employees' MIP target bonuses ranged from 75% of base salary at the executive level (corporate officers) to 10% of salary at lower organizational levels (e.g. functional managers).

The criteria for which bonuses were given had changed significantly over the years. Prior to 2013, the MIP placed a high weighting of importance on control of overhead. In 2013, the new CEO responded to divisions' requests to "let us manage our costs." He placed more weighting on GPS and deemphasized the rewards that could be earned directly by controlling overhead expenses. However, the divisions "went crazy on spending" without generating sufficient additional NOI.

In 2014, the MIP was changed to include two performance factors – GPS and NOI. But corporate managers learned quickly that some operating managers were not good at managing NOI. Since then corporate managers sought to improve operating managers' financial management skills. Jim Anderson explained that, "the sales-to-share-price models on which I have been working, as well as the use of the GPP/GPS and GPP/OH ratios, have actually been quite helpful in explaining to our managers the relationship between GPS, GPP, NOI and, ultimately, share price."

In 2016, the MIP rewards for the highest level managers (down to group presidents) were based on achievement of corporate (or group) GPS and NOI targets. Lower-level general managers (regional presidents and lower-level profit center managers) were given GPS and OH targets.

The 2016 MIP plan also allowed more subjectivity in performance evaluations, up to 30% in some situations, rather than less than 10% in the older plans. The importance weighting of the subjective element of the performance evaluation was increased to encourage greater cross-organizational synergy and cooperation. Corporate managers believed that some managers had not aggressively sought business opportunities that required cross-organizational cooperation. They also knew that the heavy bonus emphasis on measured division performance had led to some "non-value-added" activities, such as the charging of unfair transfer prices on borrowed or shared resources.

Bill Houchin (president of I&T) explained that the overall corporate targets provided limited guidance to him in setting targets for his eight profit centers:

> Goals given to you at an aggregate level don't necessarily make much sense lower in the organization. Our standards have to be much more pragmatic. They have to be based on controllability and achievability.
>
> Take the 15% growth goal. That's the CEO's vision for the company. But Transportation is and should be growing at a 25% rate. Similarly, if you look at our businesses you will see great variation in GPP/OH ratios. In aviation we get a ratio of about five – and infrastructure is even higher than that – whereas it is only about one, or less, in most of the environmental business. These are all successful operations; it's just the nature of their businesses. For example, we don't have a lot of overhead in aviation because we don't have to invest in local sales and support offices to get jobs: its clients contract with us from anywhere in the world.

Bill went on to explain that in the subjective evaluation of his people he considers a variety of "soft" objectives. These included the extent to which managers worry about management development (succession planning) and training; the extent to which they "lead" (as opposed to merely "manage") their unit; and the extent to which they cooperate with other units within I&T as well as King in total.

While the subjective component of the performance evaluations could be weighted up to 30%, Jim Anderson wondered if this feature of the plan was having the desired effect. He thought that the subjective evaluations tended to be significantly influenced by objective measures:

> Are you likely to get a good discretionary bonus if you seriously missed your financial targets? I don't think so. People are people, and evaluators may not always be able to make this disconnect. In my view, the subjective component should be used to evaluate orientation to corporate-wide goals. Our company has grown largely through acquisition. We have generally kept the businesses separate, and they have not worked well together.

Although the aforementioned MIP criteria were to be used as general guidelines for the provision of annual incentive payments, corporate allowed the business units to design their own MIP-programs, subject to a sanity check at corporate. For example, the MIP reward function within the I&T Group looked approximately as shown in Exhibit 3. In I&T, MIP participants would earn some bonus money if the performance for which they were being held responsible exceeded a threshold, defined as 90% of the target.

The bonuses earned for exceeding targets were not great. About this aspect of the plan, Jim Anderson said, "We are pretty conservative. We are willing to pay for good performance, but today's GPS may not be profitable for years down the road, and in some cases it might not be profitable at all. We can't just open-end the bonus payments."

There was one catch. If the corporation did not achieve 100% of its NOI target, then the use of all formulas was suspended. Any bonuses given in such circumstances were discretionary.

The performance targets were set to be achievable with good performance. Jim Anderson noted that "A few people meet all of their targets; most meet most of their targets." Bill Houchin concurred with this judgment. He explained:

> I don't mind a stretch, but I don't want it to be too severe. If we plan for 2–4% growth, I can roll with some fluctuations in the business and still make it. If my goals ask for 12–15%, we'll have to crank down on investment. You end up just hurting yourself.
>
> I think that my people are about 90% confident that they can meet the 90% threshold. In my view, achieving the threshold should be "certain with effort." That is, if you work hard and make good decisions, you will make it. Hunting dogs make their targets; lap dogs don't.
>
> The probability of achieving full target, on the other hand, should be perceived as "slight." If my

people get to 120% or more of their target, then there is clearly something wrong with my target setting. Although rewards are capped, exceptional performance can always be taken care of through discretionary bonuses.

Long Term Incentive Plan (LTIP)

The LTIP was designed to encourage key employees of the corporation to remain in King's employ and to motivate them to exert maximum effort to achieve the corporation's long-term goals. LTIP awards, which were paid in cash, were based on three-year performance. In 2014, when the LTIP was first adopted, about 70–80 people were included, roughly down to one level below the managers of the major profit-and-loss units.

The primary performance criterion in the LTIP was King's share price growth. In each new performance cycle, each individual included in the plan was awarded a substantial number of performance units (depending on organizational level). A performance unit was a contingent right to receive a cash amount in the event certain performance criteria were achieved. For each cycle, the board of directors decided the list of employees who would participate in the plan, the value of a performance unit, the number of units to be granted to each participant, and the performance criteria/targets.

The payments vested over the three years following the completion of a performance cycle at the rate of one-third per year. Payments were made in January after they vested. A new performance cycle started each year, so three cycles were in progress simultaneously. A participant in any cycle, however, might or might not be granted performance units for a different cycle or cycles. No LTIP payments had yet been made because the first performance cycle, which started in 2014, was not yet complete.

Bill Houchin believed that the LTIP was less of an incentive plan and more of an attempt to replicate the stock option plans used in publicly traded companies:

This is truly "blue smoke and mirrors." We don't think about it as much as we do about the MIP. I understand the payouts from the LTIP can be very significant, and people who are in the plan are grateful. But I look at the potential awards as a windfall. After all, our individual impacts on King's share price are relatively small. If the market is up and we happen to be in a window that allows us to take advantage of it, then that's great.

If we shed our E&C business, we will have more control over the LTIP rewards because what will be left in the corporation will be more predictable. It won't be as affected by the swings in oil prices. So there will be a lot more accountability on our part. I would also say that the LTIP is a powerful tool to change attitudes towards more of a King mentality, so it's good from that standpoint.

Concerns for the future

Jim Anderson thought that King had made progress in its attempts to translate the share price concerns of its retirees or near-retirees into measures that would drive the business unit managers to find ways to drive share price. But he knew more work had to be done, and he had some significant questions and concerns:

First, is there some way to take the subjectivity out of our share price targets? We have tended to compare our performance with those of our closest industry competitors, but 50% of the firms in this industry, particularly those whose business is somehow connected to oil production, are doing relatively poorly at the current time. Should we be thinking instead about what return our investors need? Or should we consider what other pension plans or investment funds are providing?

Second, to what extent should we consider our shareholder groups' retirement needs or concerns? We are a relatively old company; the average age of our employees is 47. But we're really comprised of two significant age groups. We didn't hire much in the early 2000s when our business was not doing well, so the 36–45 age group is largely missing. Age makes a big difference in thinking about pension plans. A 59-year-old engineer wants low risk. A 25-year-old, on the other hand, if he or she thinks about the pension plan at all, is willing to tolerate high risk in exchange for a high expected long-term return. How should we blend these concerns? Should these concerns affect where we invest our money? We also have 6,000 ESOP participants who are no longer employed at King. How highly should we weight their concerns?

Third, is there a flaw in this whole system? The parameters in the sales-to-share price model are based on very few data points. If we could retrofit the sales-to-share-price model using real, historical data, but taking out the effects of the structural

> changes in our business over the years, would we generate meaningful results? Would this model work in another industry? I want to be able to go to the board and explain that we have not just dreamed this up.

Some other King employees, particularly those with some financial sophistication, were also concerned about the exclusive reliance on financial volume measures like GPS, GPP and OH, instead of return measures like Return on Assets (ROA), or even a broader set of financial and non-financial measures. The manager of E&C's Global Business Development area elaborated:

> I think our biggest problem is that we don't have a good return measure for our profit centers. We need to work on an ROA measure. Right now there is no way to assess an investment or exit strategy. For example, I used to think we were investing too much in Chemicals which, I thought, had changed to a commodity business. Now I am happy that it is seen as a commodity business. But financial assets are not the key. Intellectual assets – people – are more important. So I don't know if it's a financial calculation we need.

Jim Anderson agreed:

> Some critics have pointed out that the current "size" measures, for example, do not reflect the use of assets and their ability to generate cash flows and that GPS lags sales effort (although it is a good leading indicator of future GPP and NOI). Okay, but if we use return-type measures, what should be in the denominator? We need to look broader than financial assets. Our value is in people and intellectual capital, not just receivables. Some others have pointed out that our overhead numbers are not fully activity-based, and at times in the past they believe this has caused some of our cost-based prices to be non-competitive. And some have argued that we should be looking at some non-financial performance measures, such as measures of political involvement, public relations exposure, joint efforts, and win rates. There are lots of things we might be working on.

Exhibit 1 King Engineering organization chart

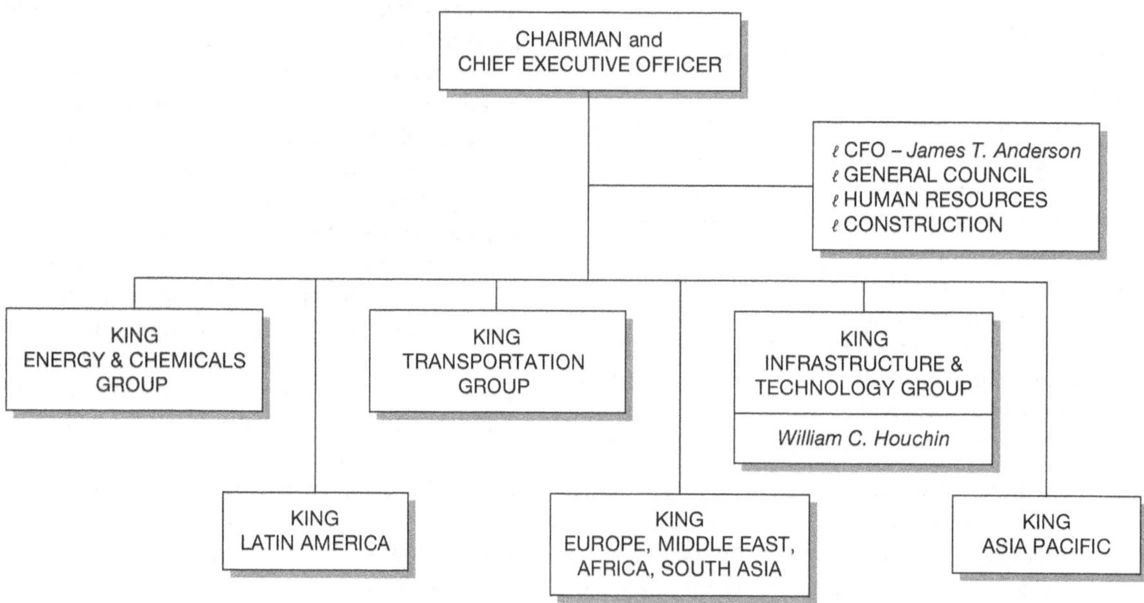

Exhibit 2 King Engineering illustration of sales-to-share price model calculation assuming a desired 15% growth in share price

	2015 (actual)	2016 (plan)
Price/share	$19.46	$22.38
x #shares outstanding	41,699	41,699
= capitalization value	$811,523	$933,224
÷ P/E multiple	17.6	17.6
= earnings	46,109	53,024
+ tax	10,849	12,476
+ interest expense	15,000	13,000
= EBIT	71,959	78,500
– other income	5,000	5,000
– excess ESOP contribution[4]	49,066	51,520
= NOI	17,893	21,980

[4]King's contribution rate to the ESOP was approximately 15–20% of eligible compensation, which was significantly higher than the typical 6–8% range in other ESOP companies. Excess ESOP was an adjustment made by the valuation consultancy to compare King with its major competitors that, regardless of whether they are ESOPs or not, typically returned a lower proportion of earnings to shareholders.

Exhibit 3 King Engineering illustration of the MIP reward function used in the I&T Group

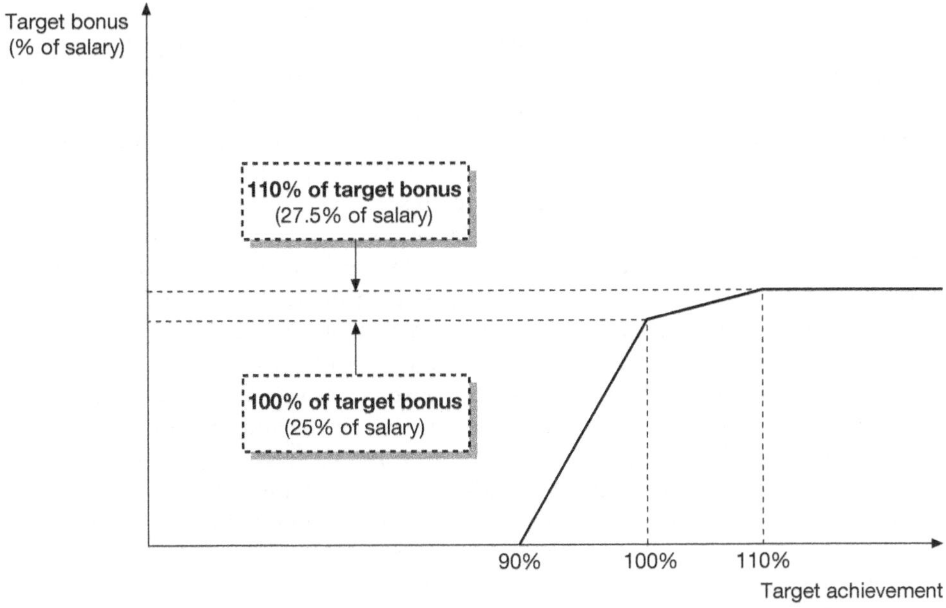

CASE STUDY
Berkshire Industries PLC

> We had to do something different. The company was doing great according to all the performance indicators we monitored, and our managers were earning nice bonuses, but the shareowners weren't benefiting.
>
> *William Embleton*

William Embleton, managing director of Berkshire Industries PLC, explained why his company had implemented a new incentive system based on an "economic profit" measure of performance starting in the year 2000. In 2002, however, Berkshire managers were questioning whether their new system had had its desired effects. The new economic profit measure did not seem to be any better in reflecting shareowner returns than did the old measure – accounting earnings – on which Berkshire managers had previously focused. And the new system was causing some management confusion and a perceived unfairness issue. Mr. Embleton had to decide whether to modify the new system, and if so how, or to replace it with something else.

The company

Berkshire Industries PLC (Berkshire) was founded in 1852 as a brewery serving local pubs. Over the years it had grown, both internally and by acquisition. In 2002, Berkshire was a medium-sized, publicly held corporation focused on the beverages and snack foods industry. It had annual turnover of about £500 million and it employed nearly 3,500 people in six countries. Berkshire was listed on the London Stock Exchange. The company headquarters was still located in Manchester, England, where the company was founded.

Berkshire had four operating divisions: beer, spirits, soft drinks, and snack foods. The managing directors of each of these divisions had considerable autonomy because Berkshire operated in a decentralized fashion. The small headquarters staff was primarily responsible for coordinating the finance, human resources, and various administrative functions (e.g. legal, information systems).

Measurement and incentive systems

Since the company had gone public, the primary performance emphasis at Berkshire had been on corporate earnings per share (EPS). The company's long-term EPS growth target was 8%, but the target was modified each year based on anticipated market conditions and pending acquisitions, if any.

The company's annual planning process was a bottom-up process, which first involved the operating divisions proposing their earnings targets for the year and their means of achieving them. The division's draft plans were consolidated and compared with Berkshire's corporate EPS growth target. Typically, the difference between the divisions' plans and the corporate target was material. This "planning gap" was eliminated in a series of discussions among corporate and division managers, typically by increases in some or all divisions' targets.

Because top management considered it so important to meet analysts' EPS expectations, they also established a corporate "profit reserve" of approximately 10% of planned earnings. This reserve was established to ensure that the corporation would achieve its targets even if one, or perhaps even two, of its divisions failed to achieve their targets. If, later in the year, management determined that the company would achieve its targets, they would release this reserve to the Investments Committee for spending on discretionary projects, most of which had relatively long-term payoffs. But in 2000 and 2001, none of this reserve was released to the Investments Committee. All of it was turned in to meet the corporate EPS targets.

Senior managers at Berkshire, a group of about 40 people, participated in an annual incentive compensation plan. Performance was evaluated based on achievement of earnings targets in the entity to which the manager was assigned: a division in the case of division-level personnel or the entire corporation in the case of corporate-level personnel. The target bonuses ranged from 20% to 90% of base salary, depending on the manager's level of seniority. The plan allowed for subjective overrides of bonus awards if superiors, or the compensation committee of the board of directors in the case of top management, felt that performance shortfalls were caused by factors beyond the manager's control.

The motivation for a new incentive plan

In 1999, Berkshire's board of directors asked William Embleton to explore the desirability of a new performance measurement and incentive system based on an "economic profit" measure of performance, a concept that had received many popular reviews in the management press.

The board's motivation for a new plan stemmed from two concerns. First, they were concerned that managers' interests were not aligned with those of shareowners. They were particularly concerned that EPS was not a good measure of performance in the new era where the management mantra had become "maximization of shareowner value." They noted that while Berkshire's EPS had been improving steadily, at an average annual growth rate of 9% in the last decade, the company's shareowners had not benefited. The company's share price had increased only slightly over that period of time.

Second, the board wanted to force more objectivity into the performance evaluation and reward system. Some board members believed that too many subjective bonus awards were being made, giving managers bonuses even in years where their entity did not perform well. One effect of allowing subjective judgments was that bonus awards were only loosely correlated with the realized operating performances. Another effect was a lot of misspent time, as managers engaged in "politicking." They tried to convince their evaluators that they had performed well, even though the results were disappointing. The board members in favor of change thought that a new incentive system should place sharp limits on the use of subjectivity in granting bonus awards, if not eliminate it entirely.

The new system

In response to the board's request, William Embleton asked three consulting firms to submit proposals for an engagement to design a new measurement and incentive system. After a series of meetings, the Berkshire management team and board selected the large New York-headquartered firm of Corey, Langfeldt and Associates (CLA). The consulting engagement was staffed by CLA associates based in London.

The CLA approach was based on the firm's proprietary "economic profit" measure of performance. The CLA formula for economic profit was:

$$\text{Economic profit} = \text{Adjusted Net Operating Profit after Taxes} - \text{Capital} \times \text{Cost of Capital]}$$

Net operating profit after taxes (NOPAT) excluded all nonoperating noncash charges, such as depreciation, amortization, asset write-offs and write-downs, and reserves. Cost of capital was determined annually for each business unit based on the yield on long-term government obligations plus a risk premium calculated based on an assumed capital structure and risk factor (β value) for comparable peer firms. Since Berkshire's business units were all seen as being in relatively stable industries, all were given the same cost-of-capital rate of 10%.

In each of their engagements, CLA would propose a specific combination of adjustments to NOPAT to make the economic profit measure "better," to better match costs and benefits and, hence, to improve the relationship between economic profits and share prices. The CLA system designers had identified well over 100 adjustments that might be used in certain situations. But in Berkshire's case, the consultants proposed only two adjustments because they wanted "to keep the model simple." First, they suggested that the company's consumer advertising expenses should be capitalized and amortized on a straight-line basis over three years. The current year's expense was added back to operating profits, and the capitalized amount was added to net operating assets. Exhibit 1 shows an example.

Second, the CLA consultants suggested that the goodwill that had arisen from the company's acquisitions should not be amortized.[1] Hence, they suggested that cumulative goodwill which had been amortized to date should be added back to net operating assets, and all goodwill amortization expense should be added back to operating earnings.

In their presentations, the CLA consultants explained that their economic profit measure was superior to all other measures, particularly accounting earnings, that Berkshire could use. The consultants presented charts showing that their measure of economic profits was highly

[1] In the United Kingdom, companies can disclose goodwill amortization charges on the income statement, and they can also present goodwill-adjusted earnings per share figures.

correlated with returns to shareowners in a broad range of corporations. Thus, they claimed, it is the one measure that provides "the right signals to management all the time." Motivating managers to maximize their entity's economic profit would induce them to invest in their entities' futures. They would make all investments promising returns greater than the corporation's cost of capital. It would also motivate them to recognize the full cost of tying up the company's capital and, hence, to reduce their employed assets where the returns are inadequate.

Knowing their competition, the CLA consultants also directed some of their critique at systems that tried to link management incentives to elaborate combinations of measures. The multiple-measurement systems, they explained, were usually hopelessly complex. The systems typically incorporated measures that were not directly linked with shareowner value. They included performance concepts that were vague (for example, personnel development) and supported by weak measures. And they rarely made the trade-offs among the multiple measures clear. The overall effects were diffusion of management attention and loss of understandability and accountability.

The CLA consultants also recommended against the implementation of a stock-based incentive program. They pointed out that stock prices are affected by many external factors and are highly volatile in the short term. They further explained that stock-based incentives are not an effective tool for motivating division- and lower-level managers who can have, at best, a modest impact on share prices.

The measurement focus of the CLA presentation was highly convincing to some of the board members. One remarked:

> **This is what we need, one simple measure that goes up when shareowner value is created and that goes down when value is destroyed. If we get our managers focused on this measure, they will be working in the best interest of our shareowners. With earnings, we just don't know what we're getting.**

A second element of the CLA system involved the automatic ratcheting of performance targets. In the CLA system managers were compensated directly for improving their entity's economic profits. In the first year, the performance targets were set based on a projection of the unit's historical economic profit growth rate, if that growth rate was deemed to be good performance, multiplied by 75%. Thereafter performance targets were set automatically based on improvements from the actual performance of the prior year. Each business unit's performance target was ratcheted up (down) by 75% of the amount by which actual performance exceeded (fell short of) the unit's prior year's performance. The CLA consultants explained that this method of setting targets avoided the need to renegotiate performance targets each year and, hence, the politics and gameplaying that was almost inevitably associated with these negotiations. It also incorporated the desired management philosophy of continuous improvement.

A third element of the system was the explicit elimination of payout thresholds and caps. Managers were assigned a target bonus, a fixed percentage of base pay, that would be earned if their units just achieved their performance targets. These targets were increased slightly from the bonus levels that were earned under Berkshire's old system to encourage managers' acceptance of change. The target bonuses ranged from 20% of base salary for functional managers within a division to 100% for Berkshire's managing director. If the units exceeded their performance targets, managers would earn larger bonuses. The slope of the line determining the payoffs for each level of economic profit was based on each unit's historical growth rate. This slope was intended to remain the same from year to year, although it was subject to board review. The maximum bonus that could be earned was unlimited (see Exhibit 2).

The fourth element of the system was a "bonus bank" that was intended to reduce manager risk by smoothing out the bonus awards, to reduce managers' short-term gaming behaviors, and to improve manager retention. If a unit's economic profit performance exceeded the performance target, the "excess" bonus earned (calculated as the slope of the payoff function times the amount by which the actual economic profit exceeds the target) was credited to the bonus bank. Managers were then paid their target bonus plus one-fourth of the amount in the bonus bank. If economic profit fell below the target amount, a negative entry (obtained as the slope of the payoff function times the amount by which the actual economic profit fell short of the target) was made to the bonus bank. If managers changed divisions, their bonus bank amounts would follow them. Managers who left Berkshire voluntarily forfeited the amounts in their bonus bank accounts.

Problems and concerns

While Berkshire's board members' and managers' hopes were high after the company's introduction of the new economic profit system in 2000, early experiences with the system were disappointing. The new system had caused several problems and concerns. The board and the top management team were considering whether the system needed fixing. Some even questioned whether the new system should be continued.

One problem was that the new system had created considerable management confusion, which persisted even after all the operating managers had attended a series of training sessions. Corporate managers thought that the operating managers would quickly learn how the economic profit measure worked, since their bonuses now depended on it. But a number of the managers seemed not to understand how the economic profit measure was computed, and some of them continued to manage their entities based on their old earnings-based management reports.

A second problem was discouragement and demotivation in the Spirits Division (Spirits). In both 2000 and 2001, economic profits in Spirits were poor. In the recessionary times, consumers were drinking less spirits. With consumer demand down, some of the Spirits Division's competitors cut prices significantly and Spirits had to match their reductions. This had a disastrous effect on margins. Spirits failed to achieve both its 2000 performance target and its ratcheted-down 2001 target, by wide margins. As a consequence, bonus awards for Spirits managers were significantly below target levels, and all Spirits managers had sizable negative balances in their bonus bank accounts.

Ian Dent, Spirits' managing director, asked William Embleton for some special adjustments. He requested that the Spirits Division performance targets be adjusted retroactively to reflect the economic conditions that were actually faced. He did not think it was fair for his managers to suffer the negative effects of factors over which they had no control. He explained that his team had worked very hard in the trying conditions they had faced, and they had made the hard decisions that were called for, including cutbacks in discretionary expenses and layoffs. He also requested that the economic profit system not be applied to his division because it was not responsive to changing market conditions. Ian was worried that his division would suffer some significant management losses because of his managers' negative bonus bank balances.

A third problem was a widely shared perception of a basic failure of the economic profit measure itself. Overall, Berkshire's performance, as measured in terms of economic profit, seemed excellent. Economic profit had improved since 2000, but the company's stock price had actually declined over this period (see Exhibit 3). The CLA consultants had sold the new system based on a promise of a high correlation between the company's economic profit numbers and returns to shareowners, but to date, at least, the economic profits did not seem to be moving in parallel with the stock price. The shareowners had not benefited.

Exhibit 1 Example showing effect of capitalization and amortization of consumer advertising expenditure (£000s)

		First year of use of new system			
		1998	1999	2000	2001
Advertising expense as reported on income statement		900	1,200	1,800	2,400
Amortization for economic profit report	1998	300	300	300	
	1999		400	400	400
	2000			600	600
	2001				800
Advertising expense on economic profit report				1,300	1,800
Cumulative advertising expense (on income statement)		900	2,100	3,900	6,300
Less: cumulative amortization (economic profit report)		300	1,000	2,300	4,100
Capitalized advertising for economic profit calculation of capital for economic profit report				1,600	2,200

Exhibit 2 Link between economic profit performance and bonus awards

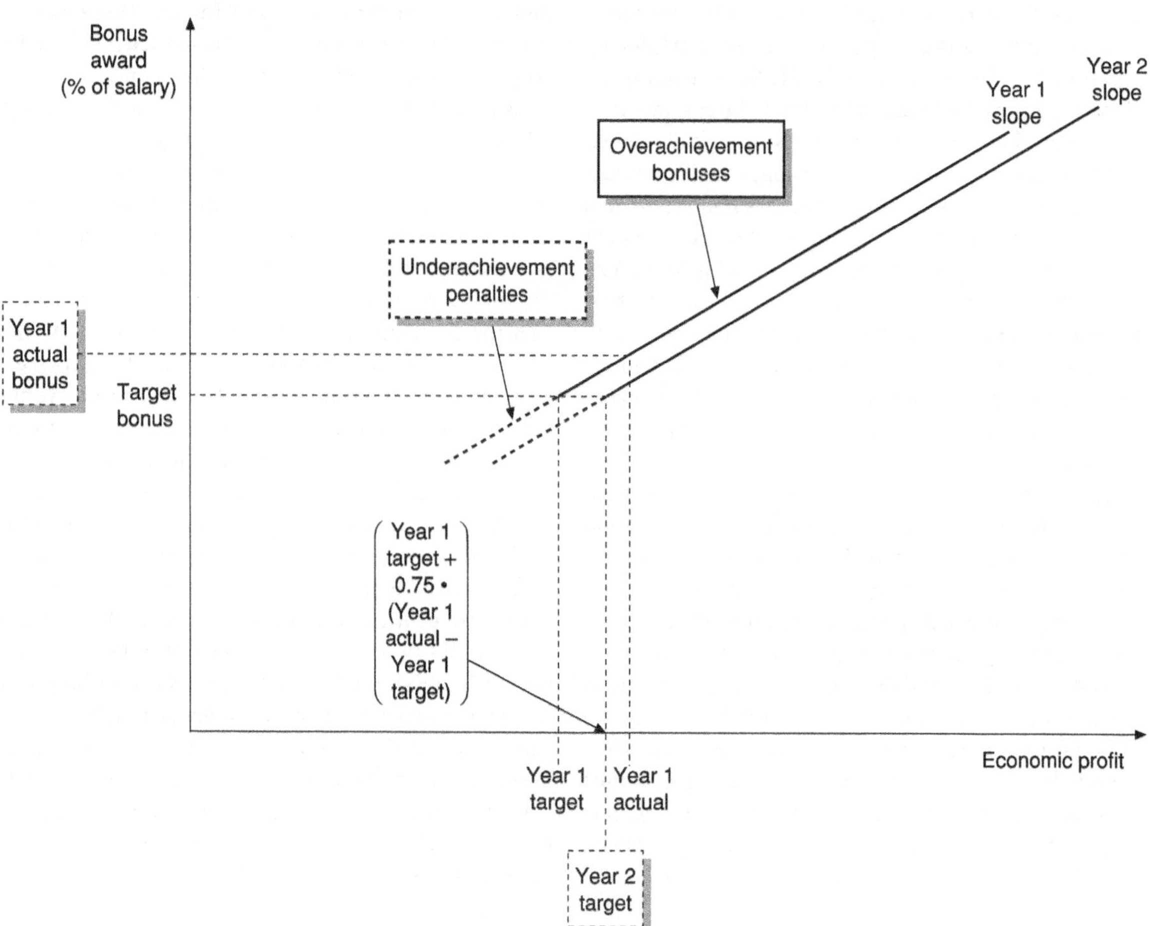

Exhibit 3 Berkshire Industries' earnings, economic profit, and stock price, 1997–2002

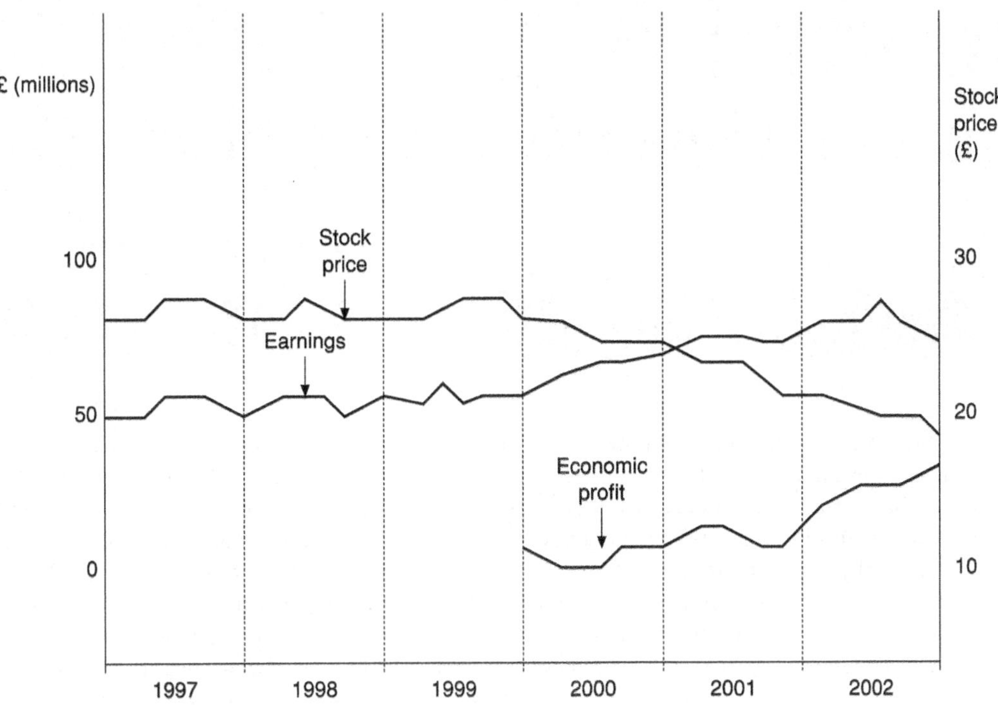

This case was prepared by Professors Kenneth A. Merchant and Wim A. Van der Stede, with the research assistance of Xiaoling (Clara) Chen.

CHAPTER 11
Remedies to the Myopia Problem

In Chapter 10, we explained how the use of financial results controls that emphasize current-period accounting profits can cause managers to become excessively short-term-oriented, or *myopic*, in their decision-making. Myopia is a well-known dysfunctional side effect of financial results control systems. In this chapter, we first discuss the pressures that cause managers to act myopically. We then discuss six financial results control remedies that can be used to alleviate the myopia problem. These remedies include: (1) reducing the pressure for short-term profits; (2) using preaction reviews (action controls) to control developmental, long-term investments; (3) lengthening the horizon over which performance is measured and rewarded (using long-term incentives); (4) changing what is measured (other proxies for shareholder value creation instead of accounting income); (5) adjusting or improving accounting measures to better reflect economic income; and (6) replacing (or complementing) accounting measures with (nonfinancial) value drivers of performance (that is, using *combination-of-measures systems*).

Pressures to act myopically

Managers, particularly top-level managers, must understand the ever-present tension between short-term and long-term results and continually guard against unwise tradeoffs between them. What promotes one often hinders the other, or so it may seem. Every manager must continually strive for both, performing well today while, at the same time, developing the business for a sustainable future. As Peter Drucker is credited to have said, a manager "must keep his nose to the grindstone while lifting his eyes to the hills, which is quite an acrobatic feat."[1] "Lifting the eyes to the hills" is particularly hard when managers believe that the stock market will react vigorously to short-term earnings reports. Managers, then, may be inclined to take steps to maintain a smooth, steady earnings growth pattern and to meet or beat market earnings expectations at almost any cost.[2]

To suggest that stock markets react only to earnings, however, is an overstatement at best and misguided at worst. Research indicates that stock markets also react to announcements of strategic significance, such as investments in capital or research and development (R&D) projects, new management hires, and mergers and divestments. In other words, if management is deemed to be taking sound long-term decisions, the market seems to be able to compound into its valuations what the long-term impacts on earnings will be, even though the results may not be reflected fully – or even adequately – in short-run profits with immediate effect. Indeed, as we discussed in Chapter 10, stock valuations should reflect estimates of businesses' long-term cash generation potentials even though they are imperfect estimates, as we also discussed.[3]

Nonetheless, pressures for short-term results remain present. Acting myopically is one common response to the pressures arising from the belief in the need to prop up short-term profits. Another common response is to engage in *gamesmanship*, such as by altering judgments about reserves, which we discuss in more detail in Chapter 15. But here is an example to illustrate this point, as well as whether or not the market properly responds to the reported accounting profits:

> Many banks have been "releasing" reserves against bad loans since the worst of the crisis passed and the economy began recovering. That money flows to the bottom line, helping some banks boost earnings at a time when lending and trading profits have been soggy. [...] The releases are "masking some horrible operating performance," said Mike Mayo, a banking analyst at Crédit Agricole. "The bottom line is your earnings power is decreasing." As banks write off bad loans as uncollectable, they are releasing reserves they no longer need to cover those loans. When those charge-offs exceed new funds being added to reserves, there is a net release of reserves. That money is booked as income. [...] Banks say the reserve releases are justified by declines in bad loans and the economy's improvement. The releases are permissible under accounting rules. [...] But analysts note the releases aren't high-quality contributors to earnings, because they aren't generated by the banks' core businesses and can't be repeated indefinitely. "It's cotton candy," said Matt McCormick, a portfolio manager and banking analyst with Bahl & Gaynor Investment Counsel in Cincinnati. "It looks good, but it's not going to be substantial for you." [...] Reserve releases don't drop directly to the bottom line, because they become income that must be taxed. But the earnings contribution at some banks is substantial.[4]
>
> "At some point you run out of reserves to release, and you can't cut more costs without cutting loans," says Josh Rosner, an industry analyst with Graham Fisher in New York. Among the four largest U.S. banks, Bank of America has received the biggest boost from releasing reserves: the move helped it turn $11.8 billion in losses since 2010 into $11.4 billion in profit. Citigroup, which reported $40.4 billion in net income over that time, would have booked about half that amount without the accounting benefit. [...] Analysts say rampant use of the reserves has made profit reports virtually meaningless. [But] not all investors may feel the same way. JPMorgan rose 25 percent in the last 12 months. Citigroup is up 27.5 percent over that time, while Wells Fargo gained 31.3 percent and Bank of America surged 44.6 percent. "Bank earnings are a joke," says Paul Miller, a bank analyst at FBR Capital Markets in Arlington, Virginia. "They are very poor quality, but investors are just embracing them."[5]

Myopia and gamesmanship are the two most common forms of what is generally referred to as *earnings management*. Some companies are known for earnings management. For example, an article in *Fortune* explained that,

> [...] though earnings management is a no-no among good-governance types, [General Electric] has never denied doing it, and GE Capital [GE's large capital division that has helped finance GE's vast array of businesses] is the perfect mechanism. Since financial assets are, under normal conditions, far more liquid than tangible assets, the company can buy or sell them in the final days of a quarter so that reported earnings rise with comforting smoothness, right in line with Wall Street expectations." As such, GE Capital "has become such a necessary part of GE's legendary earnings results that General Electric could not perform as well or consistently if anything happened to it," according to Michael Lewitt, President of Harch Capital Management, a hedge fund.[6,7]

Some chief executives, however, appear to steadfastly object to such pressures and simply refuse to smooth or manage earnings, and over the long term, their companies' stock performance does not seem to have been hurt by it. For example, Progressive, an Ohio-based insurance company, seems to have maintained strong stock performance even though its chairman, Peter Lewis, refused to try to smooth earnings zigzags: "It is not honest," he said. "Besides, when companies manage their earnings they mar their own business intelligence: the accounting stuff that is required to smooth things out causes management to mislead itself."[8] Another example is Amazon, the giant electronic commerce company, whose boss Jeff Bezos has defied the critics of short-termism by resolutely taking a long-term view and proclaiming the following:

> "Amazon will continue to make investment decisions in light of long-term market leadership considerations rather than short-term profitability considerations or short-term Wall Street reactions." The company continues to invest heavily today, consistent with this principle, and investors have accorded the business an astonishingly high market capitalization while reporting remarkably little current profits.[9]

Another excerpt presumably gives the lie to critics of short-termism:

> Amazon went public in 1997, then worth $438m. It now has a market cap of $315bn. A brutally short-termist market would require that such exponential growth be underpinned by a steady stream of cash return. Amazon has [...] never paid a cent in dividends. But surely it has a history of strong profits, at least? General Electric, whose market cap Amazon recently overtook for the first time, earned $15bn last year. Amazon has earned a cumulative $2bn in the last 20 years. [...]. Then it must have consistently met analysts' expectations? It has fallen short in 13 of the last 20 quarters, and yet over that period the stock has risen 300 per cent. [...] Twenty years later, it is still that promise of future cash flows that keeps investors bidding up the stock. [Contrast this with] IBM that has adhered to the supposed Wall Street orthodoxy of cutting costs, leveraging up and paying big buybacks and for a while the stock outperformed. But recently the outperformance ended. The complaint of Stanley Druckenmiller, a hedge fund investor, *was not that there was insufficient financial engineering but that the company had not invested for growth.*[10]

Nonetheless, it seems to take resolve, and even perhaps some stubbornness, to resist pressures to act myopically. Therefore, it is important to have an effective management control system (MCS) in place to help mitigate myopia whether it stems from real or presumed capital market pressures. In addition to the approaches discussed in Chapter 10 to try to offset the tendencies of accounting measures of performance that may inflict myopia, we discuss a further six lines of defense here.

Reduce pressures for short-term profit

Sometimes the best myopia-avoidance solution might be merely to relax the pressure for generating short-term profits. The reductions in pressure can be affected in either of two basic ways. The weighting placed on the annual (or quarterly) profit targets can be reduced, perhaps even to zero; while other, longer-term performance indicators, such as market share or technical breakthroughs, are emphasized. At Johnson & Johnson, for example, the large and successful healthcare and pharmaceuticals company, profits are not directly linked with rewards:

> Our company philosophy is to manage for the long term. We do not use short-term bonus plans. Salary and bonus reviews are entirely subjective and qualitative and are intended to reward effort and give special recognition to those who have performed uniquely.[11]

Alternatively, the short-term profit targets can be made easier to achieve. Profit targets that are more highly achievable create some room for managers to be preoccupied by longer-term initiatives. The risk of doing so, however, is that relaxing short-term profit pressure may trigger slackness – a loss of concentration on short-term results – without necessarily a sharper long-term focus. Therefore, when relaxing the pressures for the short term, the managers whose pressures are being relaxed must be trusted; otherwise (or in addition), the needed pressure must be imparted in other ways, such as through timely nonfinancial performance evaluations (which we discuss further in this chapter).

A curious example of this, and the importance of an appropriately balanced focus on targets and other criteria, can also be found in sports. For example, in China,

> [...] an investigation into the country's sports administrator condemned the "blind pursuit" of athletic success. [Specifically,] China's State General Administration of Sports will abolish the practice of rewarding provincial teams and coaches for their medal hauls. Instead, it will put more weight on "multiple criteria including public participation in sports and cost efficiency of public sports investments" [after] the country's sports administrator concluded that "the unscrupulous, illegal and fraudulent pursuit of gold medals not only distorts the spirit of sport but hurts career development and national interests." [However,] athletics experts said gold medals were not the problem so much as the lengths coaches and athletes were willing to go for them. "It is not wrong to focus on gold medals in competitive sports, the essence of which is to jump higher, run faster and be stronger," said Tan Jianxiang, a sports professor at South China Normal University. "But they shouldn't be connected to sports officials' promotions or make them richer. The value of gold medals has been twisted."[12]

A more conventional example is found in banking. Stuart Gulliver, chief executive of HSBC, a global bank, said that:

> [...] the bank had changed the incentive schemes for staff in its retail and wealth management business to switch them from earning a commission on each product sold to a "balanced scorecard" of performance targets, adding that [among other factors] this had reduced revenue but "the quality of revenue that remains is significantly higher as the risk of customer redress is greatly reduced [presumably as a result of less aggressive sales tactics]."[13]

Control investments with preaction reviews

To control *investment myopia*, some companies find it useful to use financial results controls to reward improvements in short-term *operating performance* only. The costs of longer-term investments are "taken out of the equation" and considered *below* the income statement line for which the managers are held accountable. Therefore, managers feel no pressure, or less temptation, to cut these investments to boost short-term profits. The key to implementing this approach is to distinguish between *operating expenses*, which are necessary to produce current-period revenues, and *developmental expenses*, which are incurred in order to generate revenues in future periods. If this distinction can be made, the profit center managers are asked to maximize *operating income* – that is, they are asked to focus on current period sales and costs – which are good indicators of short-term performance. The managers are asked to propose ideas for developmental investments that will produce revenues and profits in future operating periods. The quality of those investment ideas and the payoffs from the expenditures is then monitored with other forms of control, such as preaction reviews of expenditure or investment proposals through so-called *capital budgeting* rounds, and by monitoring of progress and accomplishments against predefined milestones (as discussed in Chapter 3).

Some companies use variations of this approach, such as by not charging operating units for some developmental expenses that benefit them. Instead, they fund certain types of business development at higher organization levels (such as corporate or business group levels) until the investments begin to generate revenues in order to cushion lower-level entities' earnings from the impact of these expenses.

Other firms have split themselves into what could be called *today* businesses and *tomorrow* businesses. In the today businesses, managers are charged with making their businesses lean, efficient, and profitable in their competitive environment. Managers of tomorrow businesses are charged with developing new business opportunities (such as products and markets) that might someday augment or replace the existing today businesses. Today businesses are controlled through tight financial results controls. Tomorrow businesses are controlled with a combination of nonfinancial performance indicators and action controls. A good example is Google. In late 2015, Google was restructured into a company called Alphabet, where the "old" Google is Alphabet's *today business* that generates dollops of cash, and where the "other companies that are pretty far afield" are its *tomorrow business*, requiring huge cash injections. In the words of Larry Page and Sergey Brin, co-founders of Google, the rationale for setting up Alphabet was explained as follows:

> Google is not a conventional company. We do not intend to become one. As part of that, *[we make] bets in areas that might seem very speculative or even strange when compared to our current businesses.* [...] We did a lot of things that seemed crazy at the time. Many of those crazy things now have over a billion users, like Google Maps, YouTube, Chrome, and Android. [...] We are creating a new company, called Alphabet. [...] Alphabet is mostly a collection of companies. *The largest of which, of course, is Google. This newer Google is a bit slimmed down, with the companies that are pretty far afield of our main internet products contained in Alphabet instead.* What do we mean by far afield? Good examples are our health efforts: Life Sciences (that works on the glucose-sensing contact lens), and Calico (focused on longevity). Fundamentally, we believe this allows us more management scale, as we can run things independently that aren't very related. [...] *We will rigorously handle capital allocation and work to make sure each business is executing well.* [...] Sergey and I are seriously *in the business of starting new things.* Alphabet will also include our X lab, which incubates new efforts like Wing, our drone delivery effort. We are also stoked about growing our investment arms, Ventures and Capital, as part of this new structure. [...] *We are excited about getting more ambitious things done, taking the long-term view,* empowering great entrepreneurs and companies to flourish, [and] investing at the scale of the opportunities and resources we see.[14]

In less invasive variations than the complete restructuring of Google, however, the approach of separating and protecting developmental expenditures has two major limitations. One is that a clear distinction between operating expenditures and developmental expenditures may not exist, or that the distinction can be blurred. For example, manufacturing process improvements and market development programs will probably provide benefits (cost reductions or additional revenues) in current *and* future periods. Consequently, managers have some latitude to incur expenses either above or below the operating margin line, and they can use this latitude to game the system. In particular, when their entity is performing well in comparison with budget targets, they can choose to fund development expenditures within their current operating budget.

Another limitation of this approach is that it passes final decisions about which developmental expenditures to fund to corporate management. Relative to entity managers, corporate managers in large, diversified corporations, particularly, are almost inevitably less well informed about the prospects of each specific business and the desired type and level of funding. This may harm the quality of resource allocation decisions to key investments in the future. On the other hand, corporate managers may squander, or be seen to squander, resources on "pet peeve" or "moonshot" projects that never materialize and are relegated as mere distractions.[15]

Extend the measurement horizon (use long-term incentives)

Lengthening the period of measurement is a third alternative for improving the congruence of the accounting measures of performance. As discussed in Chapter 10, the longer the period of measurement, the more congruent the accounting measures of performance are likely to be with economic income (changes in shareholder returns). One way to enhance congruence is by providing incentives tied to performance measured over longer periods; that is, by providing long-term incentives.

Even Christine Lagarde, managing director at the International Monetary Fund (IMF), weighed in on this issue, as *The Financial Times* outlined:

> [...] banks need to *shake up bonus-heavy pay structures* and attack corporate cultures that encourage excessive short-term risk-taking, opining that *pay practices needed to encourage the long-term performance of banks and other companies rather than short-term gains*, and that shareholders needed to be given a bigger say on pay while banks should have the power to claw back pay and bonuses in the event of misconduct or changes in performance. "Regulation alone cannot solve the problem," Ms. Lagarde said, adding that "whether something is right or wrong cannot simply be reduced to whether or not it is permissible under the law; what is needed is a culture that induces bankers to do the right thing, even if nobody is watching."[16]

On the point of shareholder "say" on the issue, one of the world's biggest fund managers, Fidelity, a top 10 shareholder in a third of the FTSE 100 groups as well as several European companies, added its voice and took aim at the long-term incentives of chief executives in an effort to tie executive pay more closely to the performance of the company. In particular,

> [...] *Fidelity wants companies to increase the time executives must hold shares from three years to five before they are allowed to sell. That is intended to encourage long-term planning rather than "quick fix" policies with only short-term benefits.* Dominic Rossi, investment chief for equities at Fidelity, said: "Extending holding periods for a minimum of five years is easy to operate. It will result in a far better alignment between executive compensation and the longer-term performance of the company."[17]

As discussed in Chapter 9, long-term incentive plans come in a variety of forms, but they usually provide rewards either for stock appreciation or for the attainment of performance targets, such as earnings per share (EPS) or accounting returns such as return on investment (ROI) or return on equity (ROE) measured over a three- to five-year period. One study suggests that long-term incentive (LTI) plans are in common use and exhibit the following features:

- Not only are LTI plans in common use, companies also have been re-examining the mix of components and appear to have increased performance-based awards while de-emphasizing stock options and time-based restricted stock (see Chapter 9 for a discussion of the difference between the two).
- Moreover, the survey suggests that the most prevalent metrics used in performance-based LTI plans are return measures, such as ROI, TSR (Total Shareholder Return) and EPS.

- Most companies use at least two metrics, where TSR is used most frequently.
- Companies also use LTI metrics that reflect key measures of success in their industry. For example, the automotive industry frequently uses cash flow as a metric, focusing executives on liquidity to manage the significant cash requirements associated with the industry. In the pharmaceutical and technology industries, where the success of a company's pipeline and current product offerings is reflected in their stock price, TSR is more frequently used.
- Furthermore, many companies use a two-pronged approach of measuring performance against both internal goals and relative to an external benchmark such as by using a peer group (see also Chapter 9).
- The study concludes that "this continued shift towards performance-based LTI compensation reflects an effort by companies to respond to shareholder feedback and align executives' pay with performance."[18]

Long-term incentive plans are adopted to lengthen managerial horizons and, thus, to attenuate management myopia. To have these effects, however, the expected payoffs from long-term incentives must reflect the additional discounting that employees apply to deferred compensation. As discussed in Chapter 9, one survey study estimated that incentive pay is discounted compared to fixed pay by about 10 percent for cash bonuses and 50 percent or more for deferred bonuses and long-term incentives.[19] Hence, extending the time horizon of incentives has a cost in terms of providing higher payoffs in expectation. If the firm fails to compensate for this, it will provide motivational effects that are still skewed toward the short term. But giving the long-term incentives too much weight, or making them potentially too lucrative, also causes problems, as examples in Chapter 9 suggested and as the following quote reinforces:

> Linking compensation to share price has been viewed as a way to make sure the interests of the CEO and other top managers are aligned with those of shareholders. In recent years, however, the system has encouraged executives to take actions that boost share price in the short term but hurt shareholders and other stakeholders later, after the executive has cashed out.[20]

This is why other features of long-term incentive plans have been increasingly adopted (or been mandated as is the case, among others, for bankers in Europe). One such feature comes in the form of so-called *claw backs*, which allow bonuses or other incentive payouts to be rescinded if long-term performance is poor (or when it turns out that pay stemmed from *managed*, manipulated performance, misconduct or material errors, or if performance suffers from a severe downturn from a risk management failure). Even short-term incentives, like bonuses, can be given a long-term feature by paying them not in cash but in some greater or lesser fraction in deferred shares to allow for these to be recouped or clawed back in future years if performance suffers.[21] Or some incentives could be paid out in so-called *performance bonds*, where when future performance tanks, the bonds would be forfeited; in the case of banks, the debt could be used to help recapitalize a bank that fell into difficulties (where the bonds would then automatically convert into equity).[22] These are all relatively new features of incentive plans or incentive instruments whose principal purpose is to ensure that employees and managers act in the longer-term interest of the company.

Another issue to be addressed in designing accounting-based long-term incentive plans is the performance standard. Firms commonly use the numbers included in the long-term strategic plan as the standard. But this practice can cause problems. It can drive much of the creative thinking out of strategic planning, and it may make managers conservative in their aspirations (out of fear to be held against meeting those aspirations), exactly what most firms would not wish their strategic planning processes to suffer from.

Measure changes in value directly

A fourth possible remedy to the myopia problem is to try to measure *economic income* or shareholder value creation directly by estimating future cash flows and discounting them to the present value. This direct measurement of the value of an entity can be made both at the beginning and the end of a measurement period. The difference between the beginning and ending values is a direct estimate of the value created during the period, and thus of economic income.

The idea of measuring economic income directly and then using it in a financial results control system to motivate managers' behaviors is fraught with difficulties, however. Hence, this remedy to myopia suffers from feasibility. Will the cash flow forecasts prove to be accurate? Who should prepare the forecasts? Certainly some measurement difficulties need to be faced, but some believe that measuring changes in economic income directly might be workable within usable levels of accuracy in some situations (although likely rather infrequently).

Estimating future cash flows is not a new management concept. Most companies have considerable experience in preparing estimates of future cash flows and in reviewing the estimates for reasonableness. Analyses of future cash flows are a standard part of investment and acquisition proposals, and some companies are also accustomed to using discounted cash flow methods for strategic planning purposes. Discounting cash flow estimates is also an important part of several accounting rules (such as those related to long-term receivables, leases, asset impairments, and pension liabilities), despite the importance accountants place on measurement precision. One of the significant trends in accounting actually seems to be a greater tolerance for this so-called softer, forward-looking, but potentially more relevant, data.

That said, measurement precision and objectivity are significant stumbling blocks to the use of direct measures of economic income. If rewards are linked to the cash flow estimates, managers may be tempted to bias their estimates. These biases could perhaps be controlled by having the estimates prepared, or at least reviewed, by an independent third party, such as a consulting firm or auditor. To do their work, however, these outsiders would have to be given access to considerable amounts of information, and the process would undoubtedly be expensive. Nonetheless, if these problems can be overcome, direct estimates of economic income (changes in cash flow potentials) could be given some practical use in results-control systems, at least on a less frequent basis (e.g. every three years rather than annually).

Improve the accounting measures

A fifth approach to mitigate investment myopia involves changing the measurement rules to make the accounting income measures *better*; that is, more congruent with economic income. These improvements address one or more of the deviations between accounting income and economic income.

Some measurement improvements provide a better matching of revenues and expenses. Companies can choose depreciable lives for fixed assets that are close to the useful economic lives of the assets, not conservatively short, as is typical. Similarly, companies can capitalize all, or at least more, categories of expenditures made for the express purpose of generating cash flows (revenues or cost savings) in future periods (developmental expenditures). Capitalization of investments, such as for R&D, customer acquisition, and employee development, will provide a better matching of revenues and expenses if the future cash flows (revenues) are forthcoming from these investments, as they should if the investments are good ones.

Some measurement improvements recognize profits (and losses) more quickly, which makes the performance indicators timelier. The value changes are recognized as soon as they can be measured or estimated, rather than waiting for the completion of a transaction. Variations of this concept already exist, such as in *mark-to-market* accounting in certain industries (e.g. banks), where certain assets on the balance sheet are held at their market value rather than their historical cost. This causes profits and losses to be recorded when the changes in value are observed and not just when the assets are sold.[23] Oil companies are another example, where the timing of the value changes could anchor on when oil or gas is discovered, which is commonly several years in advance of the production of the reserves and, hence, the cash flows to the firm and the accounting recognition of the gains.

Another possible adjustment involves charging depreciation for older assets that for financial reporting purposes are considered fully depreciated, suggesting they no longer have a cost. Charging depreciation recognizes the economic value of these assets that are still in use and provides proper signals, and incentives, that managers should replace the assets when the decline in the assets' service potentials warrants the replacement.

Some accounting measure improvements are designed to reflect the company's entire cost of capital, not just the cost of debt through its interest deductibility. Companies concerned about this problem include an imputed cost of equity capital on their income statements. Other accounting measure improvements are designed primarily to improve the denominator of return-on-investment measures (as discussed in Chapter 10). For example, some companies put all of their entities' leases on the balance sheet regardless of whether they qualify under the prevailing accounting rules as capital leases.[24] Note that such adjustments to accounting measures of performance, and many more, are akin to those originally proposed by Stern Stewart & Company (now Stern Value Management), the consulting firm that recommends the Economic Value Added (EVA) measure (also discussed in Chapter 10).

However, most of these measurement improvements deviate from the applicable accounting rules and, hence, their implementation will cause the performance reports used for management control purposes to differ from those prepared for financial reporting purposes. The accounting measure improvements, then, necessitate the use of a third set of financial records, a management set, to supplement the books designed for financial reporting and tax purposes. Managers must be aware that these improvements, then, are not without costs. There are added processing, reporting, and reconciliation costs, and possibly costs of confusion that might not be inconsequential.

Measure a set of value drivers

The short-term, backward-looking, transactions-based orientation of accounting measures (discussed in Chapter 10) can be balanced by focusing also on other performance measures that are more future-oriented. For example, well-chosen nonfinancial measures can provide signals about what is likely in the future. Accomplishments in areas such as R&D, new product development, product quality, and customer satisfaction are often *value drivers* and hence, *leading indicators* of future financial performance. Thus, *supplementing* the accounting measures with some combination of these value drivers can be used to mitigate managers' tendencies to prop up short-term financial measures at the expense of future performance. Indeed, many firms have found it useful to focus on a set of value drivers in their measurement systems. Because carefully selected value drivers are leading indicators of forthcoming cash flows and profits, value drivers focus managers' attention on actions and decisions they should worry about today in order to create (or not destroy) value in the reasonably distant future.

One commonly used measurement combination is of market and accounting measures, each of which we discussed separately in Chapter 10. This particular combination of measures is often a key element of *performance stock* or *performance options* that we discussed in Chapter 9, and which also create long-term incentives, a myopia-problem remedy that we discussed above.

A second commonly used measurement combination involves the use of either summary accounting measures or specific, disaggregated financial elements (e.g. revenues, expenses, margins, assets, and liabilities), or both, with any of a number of *nonfinancial* measures (e.g. product quality, yields, customer satisfaction, and days since last lost-time accident). These combinations can be as simple as including a second parameter in an incentive contract. A division manager's bonus, for example, might be based 50% on return on assets and 50% on sales growth in units. But measurement combinations can also be quite complex.

Numerous stylized combination systems with a variety of trade names have been developed and publicized in recent years, such as *Performance Prisms*[25] and *Balanced Scorecards*,[26] just to name two. Kaplan and Norton's Balanced Scorecard is undeniably the most widely adopted of these. Specifically, it proposes a combination of short-term measures and leading indicators framed into the following four perspectives:[27]

- Financial perspective: *How do we look to shareholders?* Examples of measures in this category include operating income and ROE.
- Customer perspective: *How do our customers see us?* Examples of measures in this category include on-time delivery and percent of sales from new products.
- Internal perspective: *What must we excel at?* Examples of measures in this category include cycle time, yield, and efficiency.
- Innovation and learning perspective: *Can we continue to improve and create value?* Examples of measures in this category include time to develop next generation, new product introductions versus competition.

The first perspective is primarily short-term-oriented and financial in nature, whereas the other three entail prominent categories of nonfinancial, leading indicators of future financial performance.

The generic concept of combination-of-measures systems is not new, however. Many companies have used a variety of measures of value drivers. In the 1950s, when General Electric was decentralizing its organization into over a hundred profit centers, its managers developed a measurement system comprised of eight key measures: short-term profitability, market share, productivity, product leadership, employee attitudes, personnel development, public responsibility, and balance between short-range and long-range objectives. The eighth item was not a measure, but a reminder that the short/long-term balance was indispensable. GE's managers ran their complex organization using this set of key performance indicators for much of the 1950s and 1960s.[28]

Similarly, given the importance of new product development at 3M Corporation (now 3M Company or just 3M), all 3M divisions were required to have new products account for at least 30% of their sales. At Emerson Electric (now Emerson), 10% of division (profit center) managers' bonuses was tied to keeping their plants union-free, which they believed was critical to maintain the needed flexibility to implement product and process innovations.[29] In the airline industry, important value drivers have traditionally included measures of on-time performance, mishandled baggage, ticket over-sales, and in-flight service, all of which are believed to affect customer satisfaction.[30] Empirical evidence, much focused on customer satisfaction, appears to support the premise that some nonfinancial measures are significantly associated with future financial performance and contain additional information not reflected in past financial measures.[31]

The core idea behind combination-of-measures systems is that if the organization tracks the right set of leading indicators and gives them proper importance weightings, then profits will inevitably follow. Some studies document that both nonfinancial and financial performance improve following the implementation of performance measurement and incentive systems that include nonfinancial performance measures.[32] But to make the value-driver sets effective, managers must carefully consider which leading indicators to use and how the chosen indicators should be weighted, individually and in total.

In essence, then, a measurement combination approach including leading indicators of future performance, or value drivers, should reflect the economic effects on shareholder value of specific management accomplishments and failures more quickly than do accounting measures. Hence, holding managers accountable for some combination of leading indicators shifts the balance of incentives toward longer-term concerns because it forces the managers today to make tradeoffs between short-term profits and the drivers of future profits. As such, this balancing of short-term and long-term concerns can be seen as an attempt to make the performance indicators more *timely*. This is desirable because financial performance measures are generally thought to be lagging indicators of performance. The goal is to provide the information needed in a *feed-forward* control system, which strives to alert managers of potential problems before they unravel in poor financial performance.

Besides the forward-looking feature, another key argument supporting the use of measurement combination approaches is that no single measure, no matter how good it is, can reflect organizational performance sufficiently well to motivate proper management decision-making. As such, the multiple measures might provide a more *complete*, and hence more *congruent*, reflection of performance by capturing aspects of performance that are not reflected, or are not weighted highly enough in importance, in a summary performance measure. Measurement combinations are also more *flexible*. With summary financial measures, every dollar of inflows (revenues) and outflows (expenses) is weighted the same in importance. As a consequence, valuable information can be lost in the aggregation. If, however, the summary measures are decomposed, different financial elements can be given different weightings of importance. For example, revenues from new products can be weighted more highly than those from mature products, and, if it is appropriate, controlling general and administrative expenses (overheads) can be given greater importance than controlling raw material costs.

Another version of the completeness argument reflects a *stakeholder* view of the firm. That is, market and accounting measures reflect mainly the interests of the organization's financial claimants; the shareholders or owners. Hence, other measures can help reflect the interests of other stakeholders, which might include employees, customers, suppliers, conservationists, governments, and society at large (which we discuss further in Chapter 16).

Finally, combination-of-measures systems can address an *understandability* problem that exists in some settings. Some managers do not understand fully or near-completely what they should do to increase their entity's value. Combination-of-measures systems give managers greater direction than do the systems based on summary performance measures, either market or accounting in nature. If the combination systems are well designed, they impart a better understanding as to what should be done to create value. The (presumed or tested) causal linkages in a balanced scorecard,[33] for example, provide managers with some guidance as to what they must do to influence the financial performance measures, which are at the end of the *causal chain*. In the words of Kaplan and Norton:

> [A] properly constructed balanced scorecard should make explicit the sequence of hypotheses about the cause-and-effect relationships between outcome measures and performance drivers of those outcomes. Every measure selected for a balanced scorecard should be an element in a chain of cause-and-effect relationships that communicates the meaning of the business unit's strategy to the organization.[34]

But while balanced scorecard systems provide guidance to managers as to how to produce the desired ends, they can also erode their sense of decision authority.

Do these combination-of-measures systems work? Conceptually, it is difficult to argue against the combination-of-measures idea. They are flexible. If a summary performance measure has a weakness (e.g. too short-term oriented), managers can add another measure that minimizes that weakness (e.g. one that emphasizes returns in the future, such as new product development successes or building market share).[35] If the combination of those two measures leaves out a concern for the environment, a measure can be added that induces managers to have that concern. And so on. Combination-of-measures systems are in widespread use, which suggests strongly that many companies have found them useful. However, because combination-of-measures systems exist in so much variety, with a large number of possible measures that can be included, they may be difficult to validate in terms of their effectiveness. That said, the following quote indicates their prevalence across sectors, including financial services:

> Vishal Khosla, executive director at EY, said some companies were developing more sophisticated ways to measure executive performance. "We are increasingly seeing financial services firms, particularly those within the banking industry using approaches like the balanced scorecard to measure performance," he said. "This approach uses a mix of both financial and non-financial metrics that are linked to the strategic goals of the firm, and also take account of a range of risk measures."[36]

Inevitably, some companies' combinations-of-measures systems are not effective. Some companies uncritically implement boilerplate frameworks of measures without much consideration as to whether those frameworks fit the specific situation in which they are used. Other companies focus on the wrong measures. For example, managers of a fast food company thought that employee turnover was a key performance indicator, but subsequent analyses revealed that what explained the differing profitability of restaurants was, specifically, the turnover of supervisors, not that of front-line employees.[37] Even when the correct measurement concept is identified, decisions must still be made as to how to measure that concept. For example, in a retail environment, should customer satisfaction be measured by a survey of customers, by ratings from mystery shoppers, or in terms of a measure of customer retention?

Another difficult question to address is how many measures are needed to define performance completely, or at least completely enough. For example, balanced scorecard systems are said ideally to contain 23 to 25 measures.[38] For motivational purposes, however, 20 or more measures are probably too many. When so many measures are used, each of the individual measure's importance is likely to become diluted, thereby causing employees to not pay sufficient attention to the measures with low(er) weights as a consequence.

Perhaps not surprisingly because of the ease of working with summary financial performance measures, one study by a compensation consulting firm found that where companies use a balanced scorecard, the financial dimension of performance – one of the four performance dimensions – is weighted heavily, 55% of the total in their sample of balanced scorecard firms.[39] Should this seemingly heavy weighting of financial measures be considered *balanced*? Will the lesser emphasis on the nonfinancial measures be sufficient to mitigate myopic behaviors induced by the financial measures?

There is also some evidence that managers may apply their own implicit weights to the various measures. For example, one study documented that even after a large financial services firm implemented a balanced scorecard system, most of the company's managers continued to base performance evaluations on factors other than those included in the balanced scorecard.[40] Other studies found that cognitive biases or information overload may cause evaluators to overemphasize the common measures, those used throughout an organization or based on a common methodology, as compared to the unique measures included in a balanced scorecard.[41]

The importance weightings would be difficult to set even if the performance factors were independent, but they are not. Many, if not most, of the performance factors *interact*. For example, consider just two factors – labor productivity and production throughput. Throughput can be increased by working employees harder, but at some point fatigue sets in, causing productivity to decrease. Similar tradeoffs occur with many of the combinations of measures that might be considered.

Many of the payoff relationships are also *nonlinear*. For example, customer satisfaction may be particularly important if a company has not been paying attention to it. At some point, however, after the firm has spent enough on customer satisfaction, or maybe even overspent, further improvements in customer satisfaction are not good investments. Greater satisfaction beyond that point might not generate any additional sales. The inflection point is hard to determine.

Generally, the weights placed on the various performance indicators must vary across organizational settings and must be aligned with the strategy. The weights also must be adjusted over time as conditions change, and they must vary depending on the quality of the measures and the cost of measuring. If the weights are ill-calibrated, the combination-of-measures system will have the same effect as if the wrong measures were chosen, meaning that the weighted combination of measures does not reflect, or is *incongruent* with, the organization's objectives.

Finally, *costs* should be considered. The cost of designing and implementing a simple combination-of-measures system involving the use of just a few measures that are already in existence might be minimal. In many organizations, however, the development of a balanced scorecard often involves consultants to help with both the development and implementation processes and possibly the development of new measures. Some individual measures can also be quite expensive to use. It is expensive to administer customer satisfaction surveys, to employ mystery shoppers to evaluate operations from a customer perspective, or to conduct safety audits. But some of these costs are already incurred (e.g. safety audits) for other purposes (e.g. health and safety compliance), and increasingly more structured and unstructured data are available – for example, about customers – harvested from social media and other "big data" channels.

Conclusion

As discussed in Chapter 10, the primary goal of managers of for-profit organizations should be to maximize shareholder value. Value is a long-term concept. Short-term accounting profits and returns provide imperfect, surrogate indicators of shareholder value changes (economic income). Management myopia, an excessive focus on short-term performance, is an almost inevitable side effect of the use of financial results control systems built on accounting measures of performance.

Myopia can be mitigated at top management levels by holding these managers accountable for increasing market valuations. Shares of stock are priced, although surely also imperfectly, based on a corporation's expected future cash flows, not just on current-period results. But the task of reducing myopia is more difficult at middle and lower management levels. This chapter described six alternatives that can be considered to mitigate myopia. None of the alternatives is a panacea. Still, it is important to understand where each of the alternatives falls short of perfection and how those shortfalls can be addressed. Choosing the "right" amount of pressure for short-term results to apply, the "right" control mix to use, and/or the "right" measurement alternative to adopt requires detailed analyses and complex judgments. Each approach has advantages and disadvantages, but when applied effectively, it will enhance the understanding of the role everyone plays in creating value, motivate and reward accordingly to create it, and mitigate behavioral displacements.

Notes

1 P. F. Drucker, *The Practice of Management* (New York: Routledge, 2011), revised Classic Drucker Collection edition, p. 296.

2 "Corner Office Thinks Short Term: Managers' Focus Is to Hit Targets, Smooth Earnings, Sacrificing Future Growth," *The Wall Street Journal* (April 14, 2004), p. C3. See also J. Graham, C. Harvey, and S. Rajgopal, "The Economic Implications of Corporate Financial Reporting," *Journal of Accounting and Economics*, 40, no. 1–3 (December 2005), pp. 3–73; I. D. Dichev, J. R. Graham, C. R. Harvey, and S. Rajgopal, "Earnings Quality: Evidence from the Field," *Journal of Accounting and Economics*, 56, Nos. 2–3 (Supplement, December 2013), pp. 1–33.

3 For a more extensive treatment of the question of whether capital markets inculcate short-termism, see M. J. Mauboussin and D. Callahan, "A Long Look at Short-Termism: Questioning the Premise," *Journal of Applied Corporate Finance*, 27, no. 3 (Summer 2015), pp. 70–82.

4 "Banks Depleting Earnings Backstop," *The Wall Street Journal* (February 3, 2012), online at on.wsj.com/ypN061.

5 "The Accounting Wizardry behind Banks' Strong Earnings," *Bloomberg* (January 14, 2014), online at bloom.bg/1mc0IcA.

6 "GE under Siege," *Fortune* (October 15, 2008), online at money.cnn.com/magazines/fortune.

7 Under the leadership of Jeff Immelt, GE's chief executive, the company has in recent years been divesting most its non-industrial portfolio, including its media and finance entities, to re-focus on its core industrial roots, where most of its GE Capital divestiture had been completed by late 2015 when it sold its commercial lending and leasing businesses with roughly $32 billion in assets to Wells Fargo, a large bank. See "Last Big Chunk of GE Capital Sold to Wells Fargo," *Fortune* (October 13, 2015), online at for.tn/1VPTIlQ.

8 "Executive Critical of 'Managed' Earnings Doesn't Mind if the Street Criticizes Him," *The Wall Street Journal* (April 16, 1999).

9 Quoted from Mauboussin and Callahan, "A Long Look at Short-Termism," op. cit., p. 77.

10 "Unicorns Beware: Markets Get It Wrong on Tech Valuations," *The Financial Times* (November 13, 2015), online at on.ft.com/1iYJIoa.

11 R. Simons, "Codman & Shurtleff, Inc.: Planning and Control System," Harvard Business School Case No. 9-187-081, p. 8.

12 "China Seeks End to Gold Medal Fixation," *The Financial Times* (January 27, 2015), online at on.ft.com/1CuiPiv.

13 "HSBC Suffers 20% Fall in Profits," *The Financial Times* (May 7, 2014), online at on.ft.com/1s29h5M.

14 "G is for Google," *Larry's Alphabet Letter* (August 10, 2015), online at abc.xyz/investor/founders-letters/2015 or at abc.xyz.

15 See, for example, "Crazy Diamonds: Billionaires Are Funding Lots of Grandiose Plans," *The Economist* (April 30, 2016), online at econ.st/1NWiDf0.

16 "Christine Lagarde Calls for Shake-up of Bankers' Pay," *The Financial Times* (May 6, 2015), online at on.ft.com/1hgJZCY.

17 "Fidelity Challenges Companies on Long-Term Incentives," *The Financial Times* (September 22, 2013), online at on.ft.com/1J3jvM7.

18 *Changing Practices in Executive Compensation: Long-Term Incentive Plan Design* (Compensation Advisory Partners, 2015), online at www.capartners.com/uploads/news/id209/capartners.com-capflash-issue66.pdf.

19 *Making Executive Pay Work: The Psychology of Incentives* (PwC, 2012), online at www.pwc.co.uk.

20 "Incentives for the Long Run: An Executive Compensation Plan That Looks Beyond the Next Quarter," *Knowledge@Wharton* (May 27, 2009), online at knowledge.wharton.upenn.edu. See also A. Edmans, L. Goncalves-Pinto, Y. Wang, and M Groen-Xu, "Strategic News Releases in Equity Vesting Months," *Working Paper* (2016), online at papers.ssrn.com/sol3/papers.cfm?abstract_id=2489152.

21 See, for example, "Five Trends in Stock Compensation," *HR Times* (March 20, 2014), online at hrtimesblog.com; "UK Bankers Face Tough Bonus Clawbacks," *The Financial Times* (July 29, 2014), online at on.ft.com/1k5Te8U; "SEC Proposes Rules on Executive Pay and Performance," *The New York Times* (April 29, 2015), online at nyti.ms/1OeoKcQ.

22 "BoE's Mark Carney Urges Banker Bonus Overhaul," *The Financial Times* (November 17, 2014), online at on.ft.com/1oXyG5d.

23 For a broader and recent discussion, see C. Laux and C. Leuz, "The Crisis of Fair-Value Accounting: Making Sense of the Recent Debate," *Accounting, Organizations and Society*, 34, Nos. 6–7 (August–October 2009), pp. 826–34.

24 As mentioned in Chapter 10, accounting rules for leases can vary by jurisdiction and change over time. For a recent change in the accounting rules for leases under IFRS, see "IFRS 16 Leases: Project Summary and Feedback Statement," *IFRS* (January 2016), online at ifrs.org.

25 A. Neely, C. Adams, and M. Kennerley, *The Performance Prism* (London: Financial Times/Prentice Hall, 2003).

26 See, for example, the core text R. S. Kaplan and D. P. Norton, *The Balanced Scorecard* (Boston, MA: Harvard Business School Press, 1996). But also see R. S. Kaplan and D. P. Norton, "The Balanced Scorecard: Measures that Drive Performance," *Harvard Business Review* (July–August 2005), pp. 172–80; and several other articles by these authors on the balanced scorecard during the last two decades, such as R. S. Kaplan and D. P. Norton, "Having Trouble with Your Strategy? Then Map It," *Harvard Business Review* (September–October 2000), pp. 3–11. For a historical account by one of the co-developers of the balanced scorecard, see R. S. Kaplan, "Conceptual Foundations of the Balanced Scorecard," *Harvard Business School* (Working Paper 10-074, 2010).

27 Kaplan and Norton, *The Balanced Scorecard*, op. cit.

28 See, for example, R. Greenwood, *Managerial Decentralization: A Study of the General Electric Philosophy* (Lexington, MA: D.C. Heath, 1974).

29 "A Knight with Thick Armor for IBM," *Business Week* (August 23, 1993).

30 B. Behn and R. Riley, "Using Nonfinancial Information to Predict Financial Performance: The Case of the U.S. Airline Industry," *Journal of Accounting, Auditing & Finance*, 14, no. 1 (Winter 1999), pp. 29–56; A. Davila and M. Venkatachalam, "The Relevance of Nonfinancial Performance Measures for CEO Compensation: Evidence from the Airline Industry," *Review of Accounting Studies*, 9, no. 4 (December 2004), pp. 443–64.

31 For a classic academic article on this topic, as the title suggests, see C. D. Ittner and D. F. Larcker, "Are Nonfinancial Measures Leading Indicators of Financial Performance? An Analysis of Customer Satisfaction," *Journal of Accounting Research*, 36 (Supplement, 1998), pp. 1–35. For a recent, related article, see C. X. Chen, E. M. Matsumura, J. Y. Shin, and S. Y. Wu, "The Effect of Competition Intensity and Competition Type on the Use of Customer Satisfaction Measures in Executive Annual Bonus Contracts," *The Accounting Review*, 90, no. 1 (January 2015), pp. 229–63.

32 See, for example, R. Banker, G. Potter, and D. Srinivasan, "An Empirical Investigation of an Incentive Plan that Includes Non-Financial Performance Measures," *The Accounting Review*, 75, no. 1 (January 2000), pp. 65–92.

33 See, for example, D. P. Huelsbeck, K. A. Merchant, and T. Sandino, "On Testing Business Models," *The Accounting Review*, 86, no. 5 (September 2011), pp. 1631–54.

34 Kaplan and Norton, *The Balanced Scorecard*, p. 31. For Kaplan and Norton's point in this quote on "communicating the meaning of the strategy to the organization," see, for example, D. Campbell, S. M. Datar, S. L. Kulp, and V. G. Narayanan, "Testing Strategy with Multiple Performance Measures: Evidence from a Balanced Scorecard at Store 24," *Journal of Management Accounting Research*, 27, no. 2 (Fall 2015), pp. 39–65.

35 See, for example, M. J. Gibbs, K. A. Merchant, W. A. Van der Stede, and M. E. Vargus, "Performance Measure Properties and Incentive System Design," *Industrial Relations: A Journal of Economy and Society*, 48, no. 2 (2009), pp. 237–64.

36 "Top Managers' Pay Reveals Weak Link to Value," *The Financial Times* (December 28, 2014), online at on.ft.com/1CODoYe.

37 C. D. Ittner and D. F. Larcker, "Coming Up Short on Nonfinancial Performance Measurement," *Harvard Business Review*, 81, no. 11 (November 2003), pp. 88–95; See also G. Cokins, "The Promise and Peril of the Balanced Scorecard," *Journal of Corporate Accounting and Finance*, 21, no. 3 (March–April 2010), pp. 19–28.

38 D. P. Norton, "BEWARE: The Unbalanced Scorecard," *Balanced Scorecard Report* (March 15, 2000).

39 Towers Perrin, "Inside the 'Balanced' Scorecard," *Compuscan Report* (January 1996), pp. 1–5.

40 C. D. Ittner, D. F. Larcker, and M. W. Meyer, "Subjectivity and the Weighting of Performance Measures: Evidence from a Balanced Scorecard," *The Accounting Review*, 78, no. 3 (July 2003), pp. 725–58.

41 M. Lipe and S. Salterio, "The Balanced Scorecard: Judgmental Effects of Common and Unique Performance Measures," *The Accounting Review*, 75, no. 3 (July 2000), pp. 283–98; R. D. Banker, H. Chang, and M. Pizzini, "The Judgmental Effects of Strategy Maps in Balanced Scorecard Performance Evaluation," *International Journal of Accounting Information Systems*, 12 (2011), pp. 259–79; Y. Chen, J. Jeremias, and T Panggabean, "The Role of Visual Attention in the Managerial Judgment of Balanced-Scorecard Performance Evaluation: Insights from Using an Eye-Tracking Device," *Journal of Accounting Research*, 54, no. 1 (March 2016), pp. 113–46.

CASE STUDY
Catalytic Solutions, Inc.

We're a young company, and this is an exciting place to work. But the work is intense. People are here at work 24 hours a day, seven days a week. Our employees would probably be motivated even without our bonus plan. But the plan is still important. It is a tool to focus people's attention on the right things ... Being a young company, we're still in a "preprofit" stage of operation. Thus our performance measures are primarily nonfinancial. The nonfinancials are what we need to pay attention to.

Michael Redard, Vice President of Finance and Administration for Catalytic Solutions, Inc., was commenting on his company's performance measurement and incentive systems. Mike was confident that his company's systems were working effectively, but he also knew that the systems would have to evolve significantly over time as the company grew and matured.

Company history and strategy

Catalytic Solutions, Inc. (CSI) was founded in Santa Barbara, California, in 1996 by Steve Golden and Bill Anderson. Steve, who had a PhD in material sciences, developed a new coating formulation and proprietary manufacturing processes that produced catalytic converters with better performance and substantially lower prices than competing products. Catalytic converters are used to reduce the pollution caused by combustion engines. Bill, formerly the CEO of a publicly held company, had over 30 years of experience as a senior executive. He became the CEO of CSI shortly after raising seed money to finance the first few years of operation.

Exhibit 1 presents a timeline of the company's early history. CSI's first patents were issued in 1999 and its first sales were recorded as CSI started producing converters for stationary engines. These early sales proved that the technology was viable. But CSI's managers' immediate goal was to supply converters to the huge automotive sector that spent over $7 billion (estimate for 2001) on catalytic converters, primarily because of tightening worldwide emissions regulations.

CSI's technological advantage was mainly due to the fact that its converters used 50–80% less Platinum Group Metals (PGMs) than did competitors' converters. Standard converters typically contained large amounts of PGMs platinum, palladium, and rhodium. As pollution standards became increasingly stringent (Exhibit 2), the demand for, and the price of, PGMs had risen dramatically (Exhibit 3). In 2001, about 60% of the world supply of PGMs was used to produce converters. Further, there was uncertainty about the supply of palladium, most of which came from Russia. The average converter cost per vehicle tripled between 1990 and 2001, becoming the third-largest automobile component cost after the engine and transmission. The savings resulting from CSI's lower usage of PGMs could range from $40 for a small-vehicle converter to as much as $200 for those used in large sports utility vehicles (SUVs). In an industry where manufacturers "kill for pennies," this presented an enormous cost saving potential. At the same time, CSI's proprietary technology was shown to have superior performance characteristics. CSI converters were able to withstand extremely high temperatures in exhaust systems and meet increasingly stringent emissions standards worldwide.

For years, three companies had dominated the supply of catalytic converters to the automobile market. However, CSI managers thought that the risk of one of these companies being able to appropriate CSI's technology was relatively low, for several reasons. First, CSI had patent protection. CSI had been issued two patents, and three others were pending. (Each patent establishes a protection period of 17 years.) Second, CSI had developed some innovations, such as the coating composition and a proprietary manufacturing process, that CSI managers thought would be hard to imitate, even based on a finished product analysis (reverse engineering). Third, CSI continued to expend significant resources to improve its technology and to maintain its lead. And finally, suppliers to the automobile industry faced substantial barriers to entry. It had taken CSI several years to get established in the auto industry. New entrants copying CSI's technology would face similar challenges and would not be able to demonstrate a substantial cost advantage over CSI.

Suppliers for new platforms had to cooperate with car manufacturers several years before new models were launched. Winning a new original equipment (OE) commitment translated into sales, but with a one- to five-year lag, depending on the customer and the platform. In the meantime, CSI had to work closely with the engine development teams of major car companies. Strict schedules had to be met during several rounds of preparing, testing, and shipping samples. Consistency and perfect quality were crucial. Further, it was a prerequisite for auto industry suppliers to obtain the QS-9000 quality certificate, which was a more demanding equivalent of the ISO-9000 certification. It was hard to obtain business without demonstrating technical skills, a commitment to flawless production, and reliable on-time deliveries.

CSI managers were also in the process of developing applications for other markets. One was the growing light duty diesel market, which, management estimated, would total $2.2 billion by 2008. Outside the transportation industry, the power-generating sector was likely to become the next major opportunity. More stringent emission regulations required pollution reductions of more than 50% of the existing standards by as early as 2003. The market for natural gas turbine converters was estimated to grow to nearly $1.3 billion by 2008. Other markets could include alternative fuel vehicles and fuel cells that may someday revolutionize the transportation industry.

Early successes

CSI's early revenue stemmed largely from sales in the auto industry after-market, a $50 million market for converter replacements. OE commitments were to follow.

Honda Motor Company became the early OE adopter. It started evaluating CSI's technology in 1999, and in October 2000 it took an initial 10% stake in CSI. Production for the Honda Stepwagon model began in December 2000. Two additional vehicle programs were added in 2001. In late 2001, CSI was assigned to a high-volume platform for General Motors scheduled to begin in 2004. In early 2002, the company signed a strategic agreement with Ford to evaluate several high-volume platforms. By this time, CSI was cooperating at some level with most of the major automakers of the world.

In June 2002, CSI received the *Gratitude Award for Excellency in Research and Development* by Honda Motor Company. During a special award ceremony at CSI, Mr. Tsuneo Tanai, senior vice president/general manager of Honda R&D Americas, Inc., stated:[1]

> **In early testing, everyone at Honda was very impressed by the great performance of the CSI product. Honda realized the huge potential that this technology promised. On behalf of Honda, I would like to express my deepest gratitude to everyone at CSI.**

This award attested to CSI's success in the early years of the company's existence. CSI's converter product had won acceptance in one of the toughest markets in the world. Mike Redard explained: "It is extremely hard to penetrate the automotive market, change is slow in this industry."

CSI's product design had clearly won acceptance from the industry. The next step was to get ready to produce several million perfect quality converters each year. Production quality was important because the auto market was unforgiving.

The company in 2002

Most of CSI's senior management team had been with the company for several years (see Exhibit 4). The newest member was CFO Kevin McDonnell, who joined in 2002. CSI's board consisted of three of the executive officers and four outside directors.

In 2000, CSI employed 38 people. That number grew quickly to 110 in 2001, and 125 in 2002. In 2002, about half of the employees worked in manufacturing and quality control; one-third were engineers assigned to R&D, and the rest were in sales and administration. Given that the main part of the research had been carried out earlier, recent efforts concentrated largely on the development of applications in close cooperation with the customers. Many of the engineers were new, young PhDs with little industry experience. The company policy was to attract open-minded people who were not burdened with taken-for-granted approaches established in the converter industry. Mike Redard explained: "This is an exciting place to work with lots of opportunity, but there is also an element of risk due to the early stage of the company. We tend to attract ambitious people who are comfortable taking some risks."

People came to CSI because they believed in its future success. They were highly committed and hard working. Further, there was a strong spirit of team membership and cooperation, and personnel turnover was relatively low. CSI's human resource practices were designed to encourage this cooperation and to attract long-term employees. Managers were closely involved with operations and knew their employees well, which contributed to the collective spirit and informal culture.

As CSI was preparing for mass production, however, it became clear that some more formal managerial structures and policies were necessary. The company needed measurement devices to keep track of progress on a number of dimensions. The emphasis was mainly on nonfinancial performance indicators. Critical drivers of long-term success were quality, on-time delivery, and production efficiency. It was also crucial to win new sales commitments from OE car manufacturers. CSI managers believed that the initial focus on nonfinancial targets would later translate into financial success.

Getting new OE commitments was the responsibility of top executives. Suppliers' reputations and prices were the key determinants of success in the bidding process. Reputation was important because each OE commitment required several years of development work that had to meet the high standards of the auto industry. CSI also had to demonstrate significant cost savings over its more established competitors in order to have a good chance of winning new contracts. CSI's bids were based on estimates of unit costs derived from product specifications provided by the customer.

CSI's sales had climbed steadily through 2001, but the company was still perhaps a year or two from becoming profitable. The managers hoped to issue a public stock offering within a few years, but there was no

[1] *Source:* http://www.pressreleasenetwork.com/pr-2002/june/mainpr1280.htm.

pressure to rush the IPO. The company had adequate capital to fund its immediate product and process development and operating needs. In January 2002, it raised $29.6 million from private sources.[2] And with the public stock market valuations quite low in 2002, the cost of raising capital from private sources was not significantly higher than could be expected in a public stock offering.

Compensation systems

Every employee's compensation package consisted of three components: base salary, stock options, and a bonus (since 2001). **Base salaries** were set to be at or slightly below the industry median. Mike Redard noted that "In many instances people who joined CSI from larger, established companies took a pay cut to do so." The spread between the top and bottom salaries in the company was not large, and salary raises were modest, typically in the 4 –5% range.

The first year they joined CSI, each employee was given **stock options**. These options vested over the first four years at 25% per year and expired 10 years after granting (or within 30 days of leaving the company). While a formal plan for annual stock option grants had not yet been implemented, follow-on grants were awarded on an ad hoc basis to ensure that employees' stock holdings were in line with their current position and contribution to the company. The value of the stock option component varied substantially depending on tenure, position in the company and value to the organization.[3] By 2002, employees (most of them were hired during the 2000 –2002 period) had on average accumulated value in stock options worth 50% of their annual salary. The employees, in total, owned on a fully diluted basis about 24% of CSI shares.

One problem that Mike Redard had observed regarding the options was that "many people don't understand them and don't know how to value them." The options were, indeed, difficult to value. They could become quite valuable if the company went public and was successful. But they could also become near worthless if the company did not go public or if its performance languished.

The **annual bonus** plan was put in place in 2001 to communicate the importance of some short-term goals to employees and to align their interests with firms' objectives. Some employees also appreciated the cash bonuses, which were more immediate and "tangible" than the stock options. The target bonus could be from 5% to 15% of an employee's base salary depending on level within the company. All bonuses were awarded based on corporate, not individual, performance because, as Mike explained, "We want a team effort. We all win or all lose together."

Each year the senior managers discussed what elements they should be focusing on, why focus on those elements was important, and what weight each element should carry. These discussions established the list of performance areas on which the bonus assignments would be based. Because reliable, objective measures were important, managers recognized that the company needed to make rapid progress in improving some of its systems of measurement.

Exhibit 5 shows the performance areas linked to bonuses in 2001. The measures reflected company-wide achievements in three areas: receipt of new OE commitments, execution of existing business, and building of infrastructure.

1. In the area of **OE commitments**, managers identified a number of specific programs that CSI felt they had the opportunity to bid for in 2001. If the manufacturer made the order commitment to CSI, CSI employees would earn a designated portion of their target bonus. The two largest of these programs were given an importance weight of 20% each. This meant that if customers committed to both of these programs, employees would earn 40% of their target bonus amount just from this result. Also identified were three other large programs, each of which would add 10% of the target bonus and two smaller programs each with a weight of 5%. Each additional, significant, unidentified OE commitment would add 5%, up to a maximum of 15%, of the target bonus. If all of these OE commitments were made in 2001, CSI employees would earn 95% of their target bonuses. These programs were given a high weighting of importance because, as Mike Redard explained, "absent some problem, an assignment means you are designed into the vehicle platform, thus providing a high degree of visibility to future revenue."
2. **Execution of existing business** was assessed in terms of two elements: shipment volumes to two major customers and shipment quality. Maximum shipments to each major customer could produce 40% of the target bonus. The measures of quality were scrap, shipment errors, and on-time delivery. For each of these measures, performance ranges were set to result in bonuses of minus 5% to plus 5%

[2] This and other financial and operational figures in the case are disguised.

[3] The exercise price of stock options was based on independent valuations obtained during recent financing rounds.

for scrap, minus 10% to plus 5% for shipment errors, and zero to 10% for on-time delivery performance.

3. Finally, in 2001, the **building of infrastructure** referred to the attainment of QS-9000 certification. If this certification was attained, employees would earn 20% of their target bonuses.

Overall, the performance targets were set so that employees would have "a decent shot" at earning 100% of the target bonus. Performance ranges were set to allow bonus assignments to range from 0 % to 215% of the target amounts, but Mike Redard explained that if the actual bonus earned was extreme, say either 20% or 200% of the target bonus, then "you'd have to question whether the performance targets were set correctly."

In 2001, after what Mike Redard described as "a lot of hard work," actual performance resulted in employees earning 117.9% of their target bonus. New OE commitments accounted for 50% of the total, execution for 32.9%, quality for 15%, and QS-9000 certification for 20% (see Exhibit 5). The QS-9000 quality certificate was actually awarded to CSI in January 2002, but since the timing was so close to the end of the year, management counted it as a successful accomplishment of the goal for 2001.

Mike Redard explained that management reserved the right to make subjective adjustments to the bonus plan, and this QS-9000 timing issue was one example where they exercised that right. But he quickly explained that: "We don't want to make subjective changes to provide rewards when the company has clearly not achieved its targets. Our employees understand that there can be some variance in the bonus awards. There will be good years and bad years."

In 2002, the performance areas linked to bonus awards were changed, as is shown in Exhibit 6. **Financial targets**, with a weight of 0 – 60% of the target bonus, were added. The focus was on increasing revenues and reducing operating losses. As in 2001, CSI continued emphasizing new **OE commitments** (0 –105% of the target bonus) and **quality** as reflected in scrap, shipment errors, and on-time delivery (total weight of minus 15% to plus 20% of the target bonus). **Building infrastructure** was defined in 2002 as the upgrading of production to full automation, increasing safety standards, and obtaining QS-14001 certification (total weight 0 –20%). Having the automated production line operational by the end of 2002 was a major challenge. Nevertheless, management had little doubts that the target would be met because it had to be – mass production was crucial for future growth.

CSI executives knew even this new list of measures omitted some important performance indicators. For example, it did not include a measure of new patents. While patents were unquestionably important, this particular measure was not included in the bonus plan because patents occurred infrequently and were the focus of only a few people in the company. But more importantly, CSI managers believed strongly that too many indicators would leave employees uncertain as to where the priorities should be. Mike Redard thought that the optimum number of measures was 4–6.

The performance targets for 2002 were again set so that 100% of the target bonus was realistically achievable. Entering the last quarter of 2002, the projected outcome for the year was for payments of 75–100% of the target bonus.

In addition to these three compensation elements, Mike Redard explained that management had additional ways of rewarding top performers, including special raises and promotions.

The future

Overall, Mike Redard and the rest of the CSI management team was confident that the company's compensation system, and in particular its bonus plan, was fulfilling its objectives:

> We have benefited from the variety of backgrounds of our management team. We all worked for different companies with different compensation policies, and we all have experience with both good and bad bonus systems. The nice thing about working for CSI is that here we have the chance to do it right from the start. Sure, we are still wrestling with how many performance measures to include and which ones are most relevant, but I think the overall structure is working. The bonus plan communicates in simple terms to our employees what is important ...
>
> We met most of our targets last year and I think in general people are quite happy with the bonus they received.

Mike expected that the financial measures would probably account for about 30% of the target bonus in 2002. He thought that the importance of financial measures would probably increase in the future as CSI became closer to becoming a public company. However, he also said he "would be shocked if their importance ever exceeded 50%."

Exhibit 1 Company history

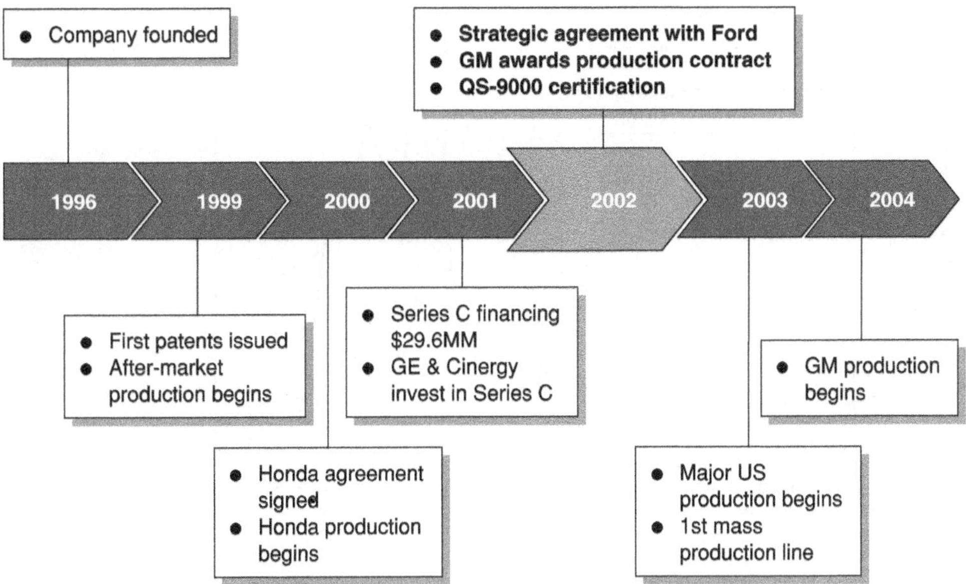

Exhibit 2 Tightening NO_x emissions* standards in the United States

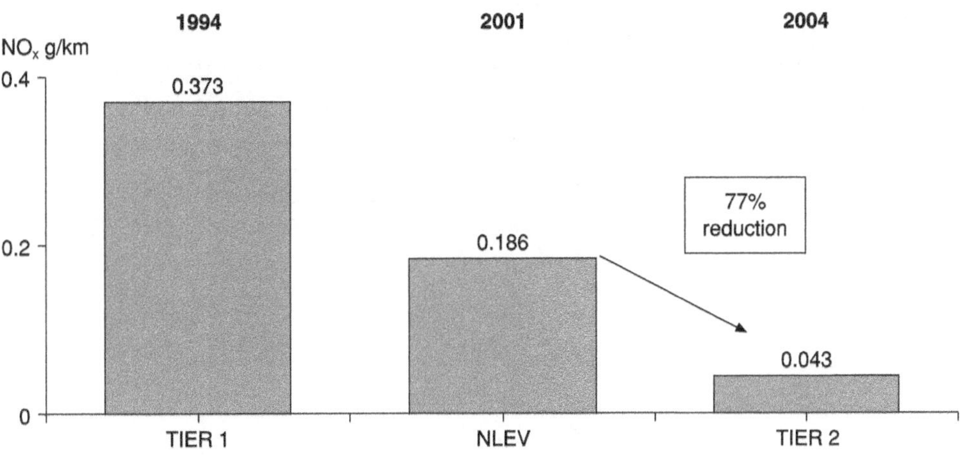

*NO_x (nitrogen oxide5) emissions are a major cause of smog problems in large cities.

Exhibit 3 Volatile cost of metals

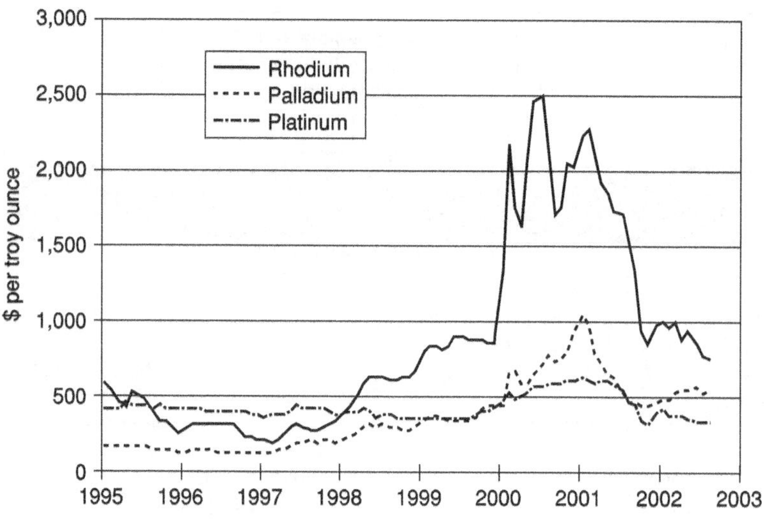

Exhibit 4 Management team

Stephen Golden, PhD	CTO, Chairman, Cofounder
William Anderson	CEO, Cofounder
Daniel McGuire	President, COO
Kevin McDonnell	CFO
Michael Redard	VP, Finance and Administration
Timothy Truex, PhD	VP, Technical Marketing
Steven Shotwell	VP, Operations and Manufacturing

Exhibit 5 2001 bonus objectives and actual results

	Target bonus %	Actual result %
OE program commitments[1]	0–95	50
Execute existing business		
Unit shipments[2]	0–80	32.9
Quality[3]	(15)–20	15
Build infrastructure	0–20	20
Total	215%	117.9%

Objective	Target bonus %
[1]**OE program commitments**	
New program A	5
New program B	5
New program C	10
New program D	10
New program E	10
New program F	20
New program G	20
Other OE commitments	each 5% (max. 15%)
[2]**Shipments**	
Customer A	0–40
Customer B	0–40
[3]**Quality**	
Scrap	(5)–5
Shipment errors	(10)– 5
On-time delivery	0–10

Exhibit 6 2002 bonus objectives

	Target bonus %
Financial	0–60
Revenue	
Operating income	
OE program commitments	0–105
Quality	(15)–20
Scrap	
Shipment errors	
On-time delivery	
Build/improve infrastructure	0–20
Mass production	
QS-14001 certification	
Safety	
Total possible	205%

This case was prepared by Professors Michal Matějka, Kenneth A. Merchant, and Wim A. Van der Stede.

CASE STUDY
Dortmunder-Koppel GmbH

In February 2014, Dortmunder-Koppel GmbH (DKG), a large privately held German conglomerate, instituted a new long-term incentive plan in its US subsidiary. This incentive plan provided cash awards for key managers whose business units were able to meet the targets set in their long-term strategic plans, Alfred (Al) Harris (Senior VP-US Finance & Administration) explained why the plan was established and what he saw as the major risk:

> The new long-term incentive plan is designed as an integral part of our compensation package, and we also expect it to have some positive motivational effects. In particular, we are hoping that it will reinforce the message that we are interested in managerial thinking that extends beyond just concerns for quarterly or annual earnings.
>
> I have some worries, though, that the new plan might not accomplish what we want, and might even be counter-productive. We are a highly decentralized firm, and the instructions we send to our division presidents about how they are to do strategic planning emphasize that we want it to be a creative process. We say: "We want you to do some 'blue-sky' thinking. You tell us, as an entrepreneur, where you want to take the business. Be creative. Be ambitious. Assume the money is there." But we haven't always been consistent. When the divisions come in with their plans, we are prone to say: "This is ridiculous. There's no way your business will quadruple in four years. Go back and be more realistic." And now we are saying that the managers' long-term compensation is based on the strategic planning numbers. We may be eliminating any chance of getting the blue-sky thinking the company wants and really does need.

The company

DKG, headquartered in Dortmund, Germany, consisted of a portfolio of manufacturing and service businesses in eight industry groups. The groups were quite varied, including, for example, packaging products (e.g. glass containers), pumps, farm machinery, metal products, shipping, and information services. (Summary financial figures are shown in Figure 1.)

DKG was managed by a three-member Executive Committee, consisting of the controlling stockholder and his representatives, and a five-member Board of Management (Exhibit 1). Each Board of Management member had both line and staff responsibility, with responsibility for one or more of the eight industry groups and one or more staff functions (see Exhibit 2). The industry groups were each run by a group president who was responsible for from five to seven product divisions. DKG's 44 divisions were largely self-contained businesses that were organized on a functional basis, with manufacturing, marketing, R&D, and finance managers reporting to the division president.

Although DKG had operating facilities in 14 countries, a significant proportion of the company's business was in the United States. In 2014, five of the eight industry groups and 19 of the 44 divisions were headquartered in the United States. The US legal entity accounted for approximately 50% of DKG's sales and 70% of net income. Most of the US operations had been part of a publicly held company that was acquired in 2003.

DKG's divisions were quite diverse. Some of their markets were rapidly growing. Others operated in

Figure 1 Summary financial information (US$ millions)

	2013	2012
Consolidated Sales	4,701	4,791
Net Income	165	321
Cash Flow	285	435

more mature markets. Most of the divisions were pursuing "build" strategies, seeking growth while trading off short-run profitability and long-run competitiveness. Two divisions were having to slash prices to maintain market share in competitive markets. A few other divisions were pursuing "harvest" strategies, maintaining margins but losing market share. However, if they were generating satisfactory financial returns, they were not currently being considered for divestment.

Planning processes

The company's annually recurring planning processes were divided into two distinct cycles: strategic planning and operating planning.

Most of the strategic planning was done at the division level, with very few guidelines provided to the divisions by corporate. The division presidents were expected to analyze their strengths, weaknesses, opportunities, and threats and to present proposals to top management as to what they wanted to do over the next five-year period. The plans might involve investments, acquisitions, and/or divestments.

The strategic plan was not required to be submitted in any particular format, but it was expected that it would be in narrative form, backed up by a small set of supporting numerical schedules. (Exhibit 3 provides an outline summary of the planning package submitted by one of the Metals divisions as part of the most recent 2014–2018 planning process that took place in 2013; the 2014 strategy planning exercise for the 2015–2019 planning horizon was still ongoing.) Presentations of the strategic plans were made to the group presidents and the Board of Management in the spring and early summer.

After the strategic plans had been approved, the divisions began working on their operating plans. The operating plans were expressed in terms of income statements and balance sheets for the coming year by month. The operating plans were reviewed by the group president, the Board of Management, and headquarters staff in late September or early October.

The operating plans were intended to be detailed expressions of the first year of the strategic plans, but that mapping was not always exact. Al Harris explained:

> **A casual observer might conclude that the operating plans bear no relation to the first year of the strategic plans. But anywhere from 3–6 months have passed between the time the strategic plan is put together and the time when the operating plan is prepared, and a lot can change over that period. The operating plans reflect the new information. I would also say that it is generally true that the operating plans are more conservative – or "realistic" if you prefer – than the strategic plans, sometimes significantly so.**

The compensation package

The compensation package that DKG offered its management personnel varied significantly by location. For personnel in the industry groups based in Europe, compensation consisted almost entirely of salary. In its US-based groups, however, DKG offered its management personnel base salaries that were competitive, but not on the high side. It relied on incentive pay to make its total compensation packages competitive. The company offered two incentive plans – a short-term plan and a long-term plan – that paid cash awards based on "business unit" (a term with a specific meaning, explained further below) performances as compared to plans.

Short-term incentive plan

The short-term incentive plan (STIP) provided annual cash awards based on the level of return on investment (ROI) achieved by the business unit to which the individual was assigned (again, explained further below). ROI was defined as pretax, pre-interest operating income divided by the net book values of assets less current liabilities. About 150 managers were included in the STIP, including most managers down to one or two levels below division presidents.

As part of the operating planning process, the Board of Management member responsible for each division or group established a range of ROI performance that would qualify for the short-term incentive awards. Performance below the lower (threshold) level would qualify for no awards; in company terminology, the payout factor would be 0.0. Performance at the upper (maximum) level, would qualify for twice the normal award (payout factor of 2.0). No extra awards would be paid for ROI above this level. The payout factor increased linearly with ROI between the threshold and maximum levels. The ROI target in the operating plan was generally near the middle of the threshold-maximum range.

At normal performance levels (payout factor of 1.0), the STIP was designed to pay the following percentages of salary:

Expected Payout	
Organizational Level	(% of salary)
Group President	65%
Division President	50
Functional Manager	35

Long-term incentive plan

The long-term incentive plan (LTIP) provided cash awards to approximately 60 high-level general and staff managers. Payouts were based on sales growth and ROI performance over a longer period, generally four years, again as compared to the targets established during the planning processes. Further details on the LTIP are provided later in the case.

The weighting of the elements of compensation

The payouts were set to provide compensation in approximately the following proportions for a division president:

Salary	50%
STIP	25%
LTIP	25%

For higher management (e.g. group presidents), salary was a lower proportion of total compensation; for lower management, it was a higher proportion.

History of long-term incentives

DKG's US businesses had had an LTIP since the 1980s (before being acquired by DKG). Up until 2009, the LTIP was a performance share plan. Under this plan, participants, who included personnel down to division presidents and key staff personnel, were assigned a number of hypothetical shares of phantom stock and were paid biannually (i.e. every two years) for growth in the value of the stock over the prior four-year period. Typical two-year awards were 100–150% of annual salary.

After DKG acquired the US-based public company, the performance share plan was continued, except that the payoffs were based on total corporate earnings instead of stock price because the shares were no longer publicly traded. The payouts were calculated with the assumption that the DKG price-earnings ratio would be equal to, and remain equal to, that of the public company at the point in time when the shares ceased to be traded.

In the Great Recession of 2008–2009 and beyond, however, the performance share plan fell on hard times. Business was so bad that the entire share issues were wiped out for long periods of time. This led DKG management eventually to replace the performance share plan with another type of LTIP plan.

The new LTIP

The new long-term incentive plan, announced in 2014, was designed (1) to link motivation and rewards to the achievement of long-term strategic goals at the group and division levels, and (2) to provide payouts that, when combined with base salary, annual incentives, benefits, and perquisites, would provide the competitive total compensation opportunities required to attract and retain talented executives.

A. Participants and payout levels

Participants included the group and division presidents and key headquarters staff personnel. In addition, group presidents could nominate other individuals for inclusion in the plan. These would be people who had made important contributions, who had significant responsibilities, and/or who had high potential. These nominations were subject to the approval of the Compensation Committee of the Board of Directors. In 2014, the total number of participants in the plan was 60 (2% of the exempt workforce in the United States.).

The payouts varied by level in the organization. The expected payouts were as follows:

Organizational Level of Participant	Expected Payout (% of salary)
Group president	65%
Division president/senior headquarters staff	50%
Functional manager	35% or 25% (depending on role)

B. Performance measures

Payouts were based on: (1) growth in sales, and (2) return on investment (ROI) in the business unit to which the individual was assigned over the performance cycle (normally four years). *Sales growth* was measured on a cumulative, compound basis over the length of the performance cycle. *ROI* was averaged over the years in the performance cycle.

C. Definitions of business units

Each division was not defined as a unique business unit for purposes of assigning LTIP awards. Some divisions were grouped together into what were called "natural complementary work units." For example, one work unit called "Glass Containers" included four glass container-related divisions. Jerry Chapin (President – Packaging Products Group) explained why this was done:

> Our glass container divisions are essentially in the same business; they just operate in different regions of the country. One of our objectives in combining them in the long-term incentive plan was to get the managers to think in terms of a national glass business, rather than as a regional business. More of that kind of thinking would help us improve our facility and equipment utilization and our service to national accounts.

At the time the plan was started (February 2014), 13 business units were identified. These included 12 operating units plus New York staff, as follows:

1. Packaging Products Group
    2. Glass Containers (4 Divisions)
    3. Corrugated Containers (1 Division)
4. Electrical and Construction Products Group
    5. Plastic and Foam Products (2 Divisions)
    6. Electrical Products (2 Divisions)
7. Fluids Systems Group
8. Metal and Automotive Products Group
    9. Automotive Products (2 Divisions)
    10. Metal Products (2 Divisions)
    11. Commercial Vehicles (1 Division)
12. Information Technology Group
13. New York Staff

D. Performance cycle

Despite the fact that the strategic plans were prepared with a five-year horizon, the long-term incentives were generally based on a four-year performance cycle. Lisa Kozlowski (Director – US Personnel) explained the rationale for this choice:

> There are two reasons for the four-year performance cycle. First, a four-year performance cycle keeps us in line with industry practice. The surveys we have gathered show that most companies with long-term incentive plans have used either a three- or four-year cycle. Second, the performance share plan we were replacing had a four-year performance cycle, and we didn't see any need to change.

In addition to the first normal four-year performance cycle (2014–2017), there were two shorter, "special" cycles, one covering 2014–2015 and the other 2014–2016. This was done to help retain key personnel who had not received payments from the discontinued performance plan. Al Harris noted:

> We were really able to add the special cycles to replace the awards we had lost only because we're privately held. If we were a public company, we'd have had to issue a proxy statement, and it would have been a difficult thing to explain.

E. Payout factors

The method of determining the long-term incentive payout factors was similar to that used for determining the factor for the short-term awards. During the planning process, a payout range was established for each performance measure, and the extreme points on this range determined the line from which the payout factors would be calculated.

Payout factors were set at 1.0 if the sales growth and ROI targets in the strategic plan were achieved. Generally the targets were set in the middle of the range from minimum to maximum. However, the responsible Board of Management member could decide that the plan's target was either tough or easy and recommend to the corporate Compensation Committee that the performance range be skewed in one direction or another. Lisa Kozlowski explained:

> Assume a business unit planned an ROI of 20%. A normal payout range might be 14–26% because the threshold is generally set about 30% below plan

and the maximum is set about 30% above. But it is rare that ROI targets are set below 15%, which is what we assume as our cost of capital,[1] so the range would probably be set at 15–26%.[2]

Further assume, however, that the responsible Board-of-Management member judged this plan to be optimistic or particularly challenging. He might then choose to skew the payout range downward, perhaps to 15–22%. He would be saying: "This is really a tough plan. If they make 20% ROI, I would be very pleased." Then if this unit actually achieved the 20% ROI, the payout factor would be approximately 1.4, or 70% of maximum. [This example is shown in graphical form in Exhibit 4.] The opposite would also be true, as if the plan was conservative, the range might be set from 17–29%.

There are different ways to skin a cat. We could keep rejecting a plan because it's too loose or too tough, or we can make this type of adjustment to the incentive plan to take care of the problem. We have been making the same kind of adjustments to the targets for the STIP for years.

F. The Award Calculation

The actual cash award was determined by multiplying the individual's award potential (i.e. assigned percentage of salary) by a weighted average of the payout factors achieved in sales growth and ROI. Exhibit 5 shows a sample calculation.

The weighting between sales growth and ROI was set differently in different business units to reflect the relative importance of each, given the unit's strategy. Growth-oriented units had a higher weighting on sales growth, while mature units had a higher weighting on ROI. For example, the following chart shows how the weightings were set for the rapidly growing Information Technology Group and the more stable Fluids Systems Group:

Group	Sales Weighting	ROI Weighting
Information Technology	60%	40%
Fluids Systems	30%	70%

One final feature was included in the award calculation. In the event that a unit's actual ROI was below the cost of capital, penalties were assessed according to the following schedule:

Amount ROI Below Cost of Capital	Reduction in Award
1 percentage point	25%
2 percentage points	50
3 percentage points	75
4 percentage points	100

It was expected that the assessment of penalties would be a rare occurrence.

As an incentive to encourage a manager to transfer from a healthy business unit to one in a turnaround situation, DKG provided a guarantee that for the first two years the payouts from the LTIP would be no less than what they would have been in the business unit they left.

Long-term incentives for US headquarters personnel

For headquarters personnel (e.g. staff), the LTIP awards were based on a payout factor calculated as follows:

- Ninety percent was based on a simple average of the payout factors of the five US-based groups, with no upper limit to the performance range considered.
- Ten percent was based on control of headquarters expense. Performance was rated at 1.0 at the budgeted level, 0.0 at 110% of budget, and 2.0 at 90% of budget.

Managerial judgment allowed

Provision was made for applying managerial judgment if it was felt that the actual performance as indicated by either measure was distorted by extraordinary circumstances. Recommendations for judgments were to be made by the group president of the affected business unit to the Board of Management and the Compensation Committee of the Board of Directors.

Al Harris explained why these after-the-fact judgments were allowed:

We always have to keep in mind what we are trying to do: We are trying to motivate operating managers to make good business decisions. Uncontrollable

[1] The cost of capital assumed for purposes of calibrating the expected returns in the long-term incentive plan could be changed annually. In 2014, it was set conservatively high. Indeed, Al Harris estimated that in the most recent period, 2013, the company's marginal cost of capital was approximately 9.5%.

[2] For the sales growth measure, it was rare that the threshold was set below zero.

factors can distort the measures so much that they become motivationally useless.

For example, one of our groups does a significant amount of business in China. We are forecasting continuing weakness in the Chinese yuan, and if that happens, it will have a tremendous negative effect on that business. If we didn't adjust the numbers, personnel in that group could lose the awards of several of four-year cycles in addition to their annual incentive. We're trying to be fair. There are always going to be judgments that will have to be made.

Concerns

DKG management felt obligated to make changes to their old compensation package because, as Al Harris explained, "A high proportion of our compensation is based on incentives, and our package was not really competitive when the old performance share plan zeroed out."

But Al went on to describe two of his major concerns:

As I mentioned before, are we going to cause managers to become more conservative? Are we going to discourage really creative long-range thinking?

As a senior financial executive, I also worry about whether we have good control over our performance measures. We don't have an internal audit function, and the compensation of the most senior people who should be performing this control function is based on the same measures used to reward the managers. Is this a case of putting the "fox in the chicken house?" Do we have a significant risk of bias without the necessary controls?

However, Al concluded, "This plan has only just been put in place. It would be unreasonable to think we could get everything perfectly right from the start. I expect that we will be in the process of evaluating what we're doing for many years to come."

Exhibit 1 Organization structure

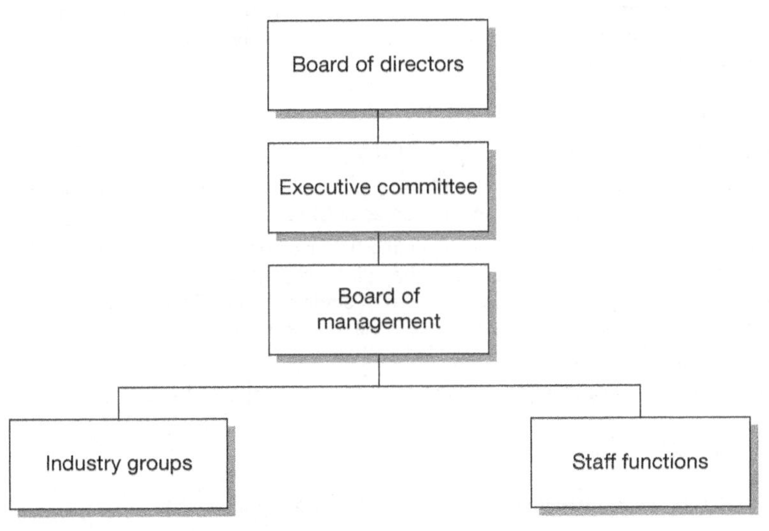

- Agricultural and Farm Machinery (6, $636)
- Shipping and Transport Services (5, $726)
- Equipment Leasing and Services (5, $291)
- Metal and Automotive Products* (5, $543)
- Packaging Products* (5, $345)
- Electrical and Construction Products* (6, $573)
- Fluids Systems* (5, $690)
- Information Technology* (7, $204)

- Finance
- Control and Administration
- Legal
- Tax
- Planning and Corporate Development
- Personnel and Labor Relations

* Headquartered in New York

Note: Numbers in parentheses show the number of division in each operating group, and 2013 sales in US$ millions.

Exhibit 2 Responsibilities of Board of Management members

	Responsible for:	
Board of Management Member	**Industry Groups**	**Staff Functions**
Eckhard Klein	Agricultural and Farm Machinery	Finance Control
Karl Schusster	Shipping and Transport Services	Legal Tax
Gerhard Haussmann	Equipment Leasing and Services	Planning and Corporate Development
Harold (Hal) Johnson*	Metal and Automotive Products Packaging Products Electrical and Construction Products	US Personnel and Labor Relations
James Pernecky*	Fluids Systems Information Technology	US Headquarters Staff

*Based in New York

Exhibit 3 Outline of strategic plan submitted by a metals division in 2013

1. Mission and Strategic Thrust for the 2014–2018 planning horizon (3 pages).
2. Market and Competitive Analysis (9 pages of narrative, 3 tables of figures). This section discussed market sizes and trends for each of the two major product lines, key customers, industry capacity and a competitor analysis, including strengths weaknesses and plans. The charts showed:
   1. DKG market share (1990–2018).
   2. Industry capacity by manufacturer (2009, 2012, 2015, 2018).
   3. Key customer analysis--volume and DKG market share (2011, 2012, 2018).
3. Internal Analysis (4 pages). Discussion of capabilities in areas of marketing, product development, production, and human resources. Also one section on degrees of integration with other areas of DKG.
4. Strategy (5 pages). Started with discussion of specific objectives, including 8% average growth rate, 15% market share, 8% return on sales, and 50% return on investment before tax. Then discussion of strategic alternatives (e.g. maintain, broaden product offerings, forward integration) and the selection of strategy made. Concluded with list of specific actions that would have to be accomplished in order to implement the chosen strategy.
5. Financial Summary (5 schedules with 3 page-up pages).
   1. Sales, Profit, Return on Investment, Cash Sources and Uses, and Employee Count (2008–2018)
   2. Summary Balance Sheet (2012–2018)
   3. Sales and Profit Comparison (2011 vs. 2012)
   4. Capital Expenditure Summary (2012–2018)
   5. Market and Sales Forecast (2012–2018) – market size, market share, competitor assumptions.
6. Organization (1 page organization chart)

Exhibit 4 Determining long-term payout factors – example

Assume: A performance range of 15–22%
Actual performance = 20%

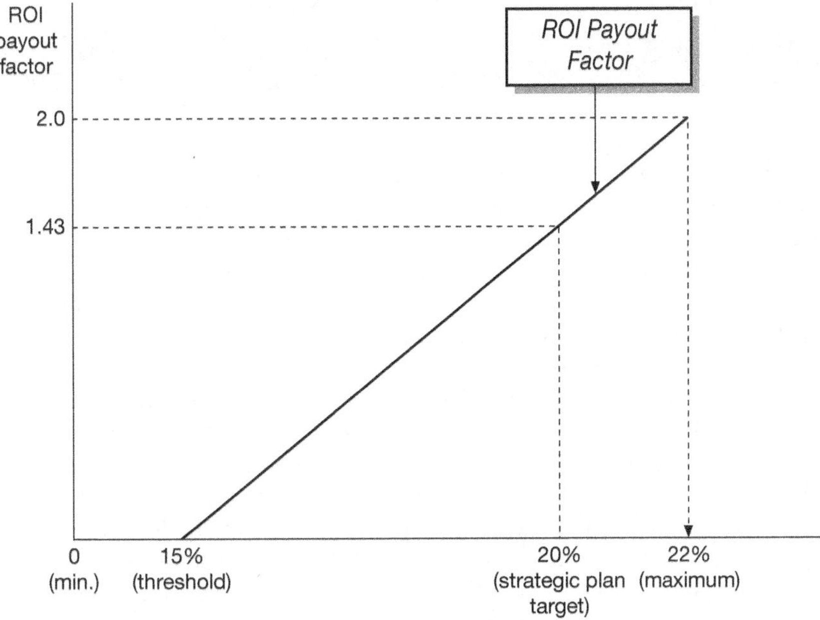

At 20% ROI, the Performance Factor = 1.43 (interpolated)

Exhibit 5 Long-term incentive award – calculation example

Assume: (1) Individual assigned 100% to a business unit with performance weighted 30% sales growth and 70% ROI (2) Expected payout for this individual: 50% of salary = $120,000

Performance factor	Target award	Target	Maximum	Actual achieved (over 4 years)	Rating achieved	LTIP amount payable
Sales growth	$36,000	2%	6%	4%	1.5	$54,000
ROI	$84,000	18%	23%	18%	1.0	$84,000
						$138,000

This case was prepared by Professor Kenneth A. Merchant.

CASE STUDY
Johansen's: The New Scorecard System

Jill Landon's palms were starting to sweat. It was the morning of Johansen's annual performance summit, and she was still unsure about what overall performance rating to give Jared Clark. It was clear from the data that he deserved the highest rating on the financial, strategy, and leadership initiatives on the new scorecard. But his performance this year in customer service fell far short of the level required by the guidelines in the new scorecard system. Based on the data, she did not think she could justify more than a "meets expectations" rating of 3 for Clark's customer service rating. As a result, she knew that Clark would be ineligible for the best overall performance rating of 5 and, subsequently, would not receive the maximum bonus possible. In fact, based on the new system, he would receive a lower bonus than he did last year if given a 4 overall this year (Exhibit 1).

Landon knew the importance of the company's new scorecard system. Although Clark's scorecard suggested that he should receive an overall rating of 4, the thought of giving Clark anything less than a 5 overall was difficult to stomach. Landon was Johansen's Southwest regional manager; and Clark had been her best store manager for a number of years. She had never seen another store manager who could deliver the financial performance that he could year after year. Landon's own annual performance evaluation was based primarily on the sales and financial performance of the Southwest region, performance that was affected greatly by what happened in Store 51; she was grateful for a manager like Clark, since her own future promotion and compensation prospects depended on continuing to turn in top results.

Landon recalled a conversation she had with Clark the previous November. When Clark informed her that one of Johansen's largest national competitors was planning on opening a store in the same mall as Store 51, her immediate thought was, "This is our highest-performing store in the region. How will this affect sales?" Clark then proceeded to tell her that he had been approached by the competitor to be the store manager for this new store. Clark also detailed the generous increase in salary he had been offered, as well as the opportunity for larger annual bonuses. Despite the appealing offer, he shared that he loved Store 51 and Johansen's because of the corporate culture and the positive encouragement and interest in his success as a store manager that he had received over the years. The potential for higher pay was understandably attractive, however. He also remarked that he hoped Landon would bear this in mind when evaluating his performance and when the company considered which store managers to promote within the company. Landon was concerned about the competitive threat, but relieved that Clark was forthcoming about it and seemed open to working things out so that he could remain at Johansen's.

Background

Johansen's, a large high-end department store, first opened its doors in New York City in 1950. Founded on the principle of superior customer service, Johansen's quickly found success and expanded its stores across the country. Johansen's built its reputation and brand on putting the customer first and offering an unparalleled level of customer service. This core value was integral to maintaining its position as the premier high-end retailer for decades.

As of 2014, Johansen's had 121 stores across 32 states. Due to its growth over the years, Johansen's was divided into five regions: Northeast, Southeast, Midwest, Southwest, and Northwest (Exhibit 2). Each region had a regional manager who oversaw all the store managers in that region. Generally, Johansen's promoted from within, and it was not uncommon for an associate at one store to be promoted to manager of another. At the store manager level, it was more typical for a promotion to regional manager to occur within the same region, but there were instances in which a store manager from one region was promoted to regional manager of another region.

In 2006, Johansen's was facing financial difficulties. As a result, most of the senior executives were replaced. The new leadership team was eager to drive across-the-board improvements in financial performance. To this end, a financially based incentive system was implemented. Johansen's store managers were the "boots-on-the-ground" employees, and were critical to driving sales; Johansen's believed in empowering its employees, and store managers had a great deal of autonomy and control over their stores. They had little to no influence over store location – and consequently customer demographics – and other major store investments. But they had the ability to influence sales levels, and they affected the in-store customer experience, determined individual store marketing and sales promotions, handled individual store merchandising, and were responsible for training and developing employees. As a result, the leadership team considered the stores to be profit centers and decided that store managers would be rated and compensated based on three key financial metrics for their stores: same-store sales growth, gross margin, and net income.

Although Johansen's saw a modest improvement in its financial performance early on, by 2012, the company's financial performance had stagnated again (Exhibit 3). Management commissioned a study to figure out why Johansen's was facing financial difficulties once more. The study provided three key insights. First, it became clear that Johansen's industry-leading position was far from assured. It used to be that Johansen's main competition was from other retail stores. Now, however, Johansen's faced additional competition as more and more Internet retailers emerged. E-commerce had been growing faster than any other retail sector since 2008 and, as a result, was consuming an ever-greater share of retail spending. Exhibit 4 shows the growth trends for e-commerce and total retail sales, as well as for department stores and apparel. Like most retailers, Johansen's did have an online presence, but only a marginal percentage of its revenue came from online sales. Nearly all Johansen's sales came from in-store purchases due to the robust customer experience that appealed to shoppers. Moreover, given the e-commerce retailers' cost structures, Johansen's knew it was unlikely to be able to successfully engage in a price war, placing an even greater emphasis on its in-store experience going forward. Second – and to make matters worse – recently published market research that was reviewed as part of the study indicated that a rival company's customer service was superior to that of Johansen's. This news seriously jolted upper management. Certainly, improving financial performance had been essential to this new leadership team, and to varying degrees the team had succeeded in this regard. Delighting customers had always been Johansen's key value proposition, however, and the prospect of losing this important differentiator caused great angst among senior managers. Finally, an analysis of detailed financial and employee data suggested that cost-cutting efforts that led to greater profitability may also have fueled customer service–related compromises. When the leadership team implemented the incentive program focused on financial metrics in 2006, it had assumed managers knew that customer service was at the heart of the company's identity. Now, the leadership team was convinced that an overemphasis and focus on financial performance had eroded performance around its key success factor, customer service.

The leadership team was determined to make any necessary changes to restore Johansen's position as the premier customer service provider in the industry, while also continuing its trend of improved financial performance. Superior customer service had always been associated with the company's name, and it was an even more important success factor considering the growth in e-commerce. To ensure a customer experience that pulled patrons away from the Internet and into Johansen's retail locations, it was imperative that the company refocus its efforts along this dimension. The leadership team agreed that incentives drive behavior, and it became clear that the financially driven incentive system needed to be overhauled.

The new performance measurement and incentive compensation system

After much discussion and analysis, the leadership team agreed that a new performance measurement and incentive system was needed. The leadership team reflected on the role of the company's store managers and decided to implement a new assessment tool that it called the "scorecard system." Under the new system, store managers would be assessed across four categories: financial, customer service, leadership, and strategy. The store managers would receive a rating for each of these individual categories on a 1-to-5 numerical scale: 1 conferred a "below expectations" rating, 3 a "meets expectations" rating, and 5 an "exceeds expectations" rating.

1. *Financial:* The regional manager worked with the corporate finance department to establish year-over-year (YoY) sales-growth and profitability targets for the individual stores.[1] These targets included a baseline target that stores had to hit in order to achieve the "meets expectations" rating. These baseline targets appropriately accounted for each store's unique demographics; as such, stores that had more favorable demographics could be expected to have more aggressive baseline goals. In addition, a stretch target was issued by the corporate finance department that, although achievable, would require an impressive performance to meet. If met, however, it would qualify stores and managers for the maximum rating of "exceeds expectations" in this category.

2. *Customer Service:* The company had always measured customer service through customer surveys. The surveys were developed, administered, and analyzed by a third party to preserve the integrity of the questions and the results. Every customer had the opportunity to take the survey – instructions were featured on the bottom of the receipts printed at checkout. Sales associates often circled the instructions with a highlighter to draw the customer's attention to them. Customers who took the survey would be eligible for a monthly drawing to win a $500 gift card redeemable at any Johansen's store. Until 2005, customers who wished to take the survey called a toll-free number and provided numerical answers to a sequence of questions using the telephone keypad. In 2005, this changed, and the receipts instead directed customers to a website so that they could take the survey online. The survey had 10 questions about the customer's in-store experience. Each of the questions allowed the customer to answer on a scale from 1 to 5, with 5 being the best score. The scores for the 10 questions were averaged to get an overall survey score. All the overall survey scores for an individual store were then averaged to get a customer satisfaction score at the store level. In addition, customers had an opportunity to provide qualitative feedback at the end of each survey. Company-wide, the response rate of the survey in 2012 was 18.5%, and the average customer satisfaction score was 3.6.

   In this category of the scorecard, store managers were evaluated quantitatively and qualitatively. First, the regional manager considered the store's survey response rate. Managers whose stores achieved less than a 12% response rate could earn a maximum of a "meets expectations" rating in the customer service category, even if the feedback was positive. This constraint was part of the system because in cases of particularly low response rates, the sample size was considered too small for the data to be meaningful. Second, the regional manager considered the average customer satisfaction score for the store. To get a 5 rating in customer service, store managers needed to get an average customer satisfaction score of 4.4 or higher. Third, the regional manager made a subjective assessment of the qualitative customer feedback that the store received.

3. *Leadership:* Johansen's believed in 360-degree feedback, which the human resources (HR) department administered annually. HR forwarded the results of the exercise to regional managers so they could factor those results into a store manager's leadership rating. HR also communicated turnover and employee complaint information to the regional managers so that this too could be factored into the leadership rating. The regional manager weighed all the information received from HR to determine what rating to give the store manager in this category.

4. *Strategy:* The purpose of this element of the scorecard was to achieve cohesiveness and alignment throughout the company. Store managers were subjectively evaluated by the regional manager on promotion of the Johansen's brand and branded merchandise, and also the implementation of corporate initiatives such as inventory management, training, merchandising mix, and initiatives from corporate (e.g. inventory management and employee training).

After assigning a rating for each of the four dimensions, the regional manager gave the store manager an overall rating, also on a 1-to-5 scale. Ultimately, the

[1] Johansen's had company-wide sales, profitability, and same-store sales-growth targets. Company sales goals could be met in one of two ways: same-store sales growth or adding new stores. At the individual store level, however, sales growth and same-store sales growth would be redundant metrics.

overall rating determined a store manager's bonus (Exhibit 5). Additionally, when regional manager positions became available, store managers who had the highest performance ratings were the first ones considered for promotion.

But the overall rating was not a simple average of the ratings in the four categories of the scorecard. Rather, it was a subjective rating by the regional manager that was supported by the underlying individual ratings in each category and the following corporate guidelines. In order for a store manager to receive an overall rating of a 5, he or she needed to be rated at least a 3 in all four categories, achieve a 5 in three of the four categories, and achieve a 4 or higher in the customer service category. Requiring a store manager to get at least a 4 in the area of customer service emphasized Johansen's renewed focus on this key success factor.

The new system was rolled out company-wide and implemented beginning January 1, 2013. It initially received mixed responses from the regional managers. Those who had been with the company for several years were relieved to see that corporate management was working to restore Johansen's original culture and character. But some regional managers resisted the new system and were quite reluctant to buy in. The skeptics, having always exceeded their financial goals, were concerned that their performance evaluation under this new system would be adversely affected by nonfinancial, "soft" metrics. Moreover, many of these managers had been promoted or hired during the period when improving financial performance was the company's number-one goal, and they now felt vulnerable to a system that didn't fully appreciate their unique skill sets, which were more geared toward running highly efficient, financially savvy stores.

The new scorecard system: Early success

The time had come for Johansen's first annual performance review under the new scorecard system. Despite the lack of buy-in from some of the regional managers, the leadership team believed that the new system had proved successful so far. During the first three quarters, most regions showed both increased profitability – as a result of growth in revenue – and increased customer satisfaction scores. It appeared that Johansen's was on its way back to the top!

The Store 51 dilemma

Store 51, located in the Southwest region, generated annual revenue of $150 million in 2013, the highest in the region and the sixth highest in the United States (see Exhibit 6 for a financial summary of Store 51 compared with the average Johansen's store). Store 51 typically led the region in sales due to its advantageous location in Orange County, California. The store was located in a shopping center that had numerous upscale shops and restaurants but no direct competitors to Johansen's. Store 51 was also a flagship store, resulting in a number of advantages for it. First, given its status and history in the area, it had a very loyal customer base. This helped drive the second advantage: extensive, detailed historical customer data. This data provided Store 51 with a heightened understanding of and insight into its customers and, consequently, provided great merchandising advantages. Additionally, the surrounding neighborhoods were very affluent; this resulted in people who entered Store 51 generating higher-than-average revenue per transaction than those in most other Johansen's stores.

Despite its continued success, Store 51 was in an interesting predicament. The store manager, Jared Clark, was known as one of the best store managers in the country. Under the old performance system, he exceeded every financial metric and received the highest store manager bonus possible every year; his record was pristine. Under the new scorecard system, Clark still exceeded the financial targets. The new system, however, revealed several issues regarding Clark's performance as a manager that had previously gone undetected by Landon as the Southwest regional manager. In the first and second quarters under the scorecard system, Landon noted particularly high employee turnover (45%) and relatively low customer satisfaction scores of 3.2 and 3.4, respectively, at Store 51. She approached Clark to discuss these shortcomings, and was relieved to find that he was receptive to the feedback.

Clark was able to modestly improve his customer satisfaction score in the third quarter, and the latest results for the fourth quarter indicated further improvement. Per usual, Store 51's financial performance was well above that of the other stores in the region. But Clark's performance in customer service remained below the company average, even with his improvement throughout the year. Another complicating element that needed to be considered was the relatively low customer survey response rate (the highest it had been in 2013 for Store 51 was 7% in the fourth quarter). It was not particularly surprising that Store 51's response rate was less than the average, since the older, wealthier demographic of Orange County was less likely to go online and fill out a survey (Exhibit 7). Landon could not help but wonder, however, whether the low survey participation rate for Store 51 was the root of Clark's low customer service scores. Perhaps if the sample size was larger, Clark would be able to achieve a higher rating in the customer service category, making him eligible for the overall rating of 5. Or was the fundamental customer base inherently disadvantageous to Store 51's customer service score? Based on the feedback through the survey, the majority of survey participants only took the survey when upset.

Landon was faced with a dilemma: How should Clark be rated this year? (See Exhibit 8 for Clark's scorecard.) At Johansen's annual performance summit, regional managers and the managers of several corporate functions (finance, customer service, and HR) discussed overall regional performance and store manager ratings (see Exhibit 9 for information about these managers). Landon knew that regardless of the rating she gave Clark, she would have to justify it to all these managers at the performance summit, as well as to Clark afterward.

Exhibit 1 Johansen's: The new scoreboard system, Southwest regional manager

Jared Clark's historical and projected annual compensation

	2012		2013	
Jared Clark's salary:	$85,000		$91,000	
+bonus				
Overall rating = 3	10%	$8,500	10%	$9,180
Overall rating = 4	25%	$21,250	25%	$22,950
Overall rating = 5	40%	$34,000	40%	$36,720

Exhibit 2 Johansen's: The new scoreboard system, Johansen's regional breakdown

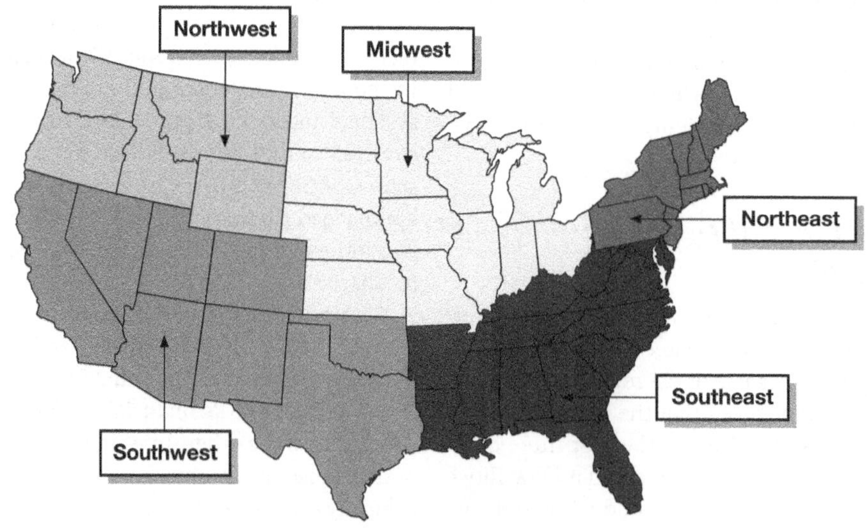

Source: Author adaptation of "Blank USA, w territories," posted to public domain under Creative Commons (CC BY-SA 3.0) by "Lokal_Profil," February 12, 2007, https://commons.wikimedia.org/wiki/File:Blank_USA,_w_territories.svg (accessed May 13, 2014).

Exhibit 3 Johansen's: The new scoreboard system, Johansen's financial overview

	2013	2012	2011	2010	2009	2008	2007	2006	2005
Net sales	$8,300	$7,790	$7,800	$7,600	$6,610	$6,600	$7,000	$6,725	$6,612
Cost of goods sold(COGS)	$5,400	$5,140	$5,130	$4,950	$4,350	$4,390	$4,500	$4,350	$4,166
COGSas % of net sales	65.1%	66.0%	65.8%	65.1%	65.8%	66.5%	64.3%	64.7%	63.0%
Gross profit	$2,900	$2,650	$2,670	$2,650	$2,260	$2,210	$2,500	$2,375	$2,446
Gross profit as % of net sales	34.9%	34.0%	34.2%	34.9%	34.2%	33.5%	35.7%	35.3%	37.0%
SG&A expenses	$1,950	$1,830	$1,830	$1,750	$1,650	$1,650	$1,675	$1,650	$1,621
SG&A expenses as % of net sales	23.5%	23.5%	23.5%	23.0%	25.0%	25.0%	23.9%	24.5%	24.5%
EBT	$950	$820	$840	$900	$610	$560	$825	$725	$825
Taxes (40%)	$380	$328	$336	$360	$244	$224	$330	$290	$330
Net income	$570	$492	$504	$540	$366	$336	$495	$435	$495
Net income as % of net sales	6.9%	6.3%	6.5%	7.1%	5.5%	5.1%	7.1%	6.5%	7.5%

Source: Created by author.

Exhibit 4 Johansen's: The new scoreboard system, historical retail industry trends

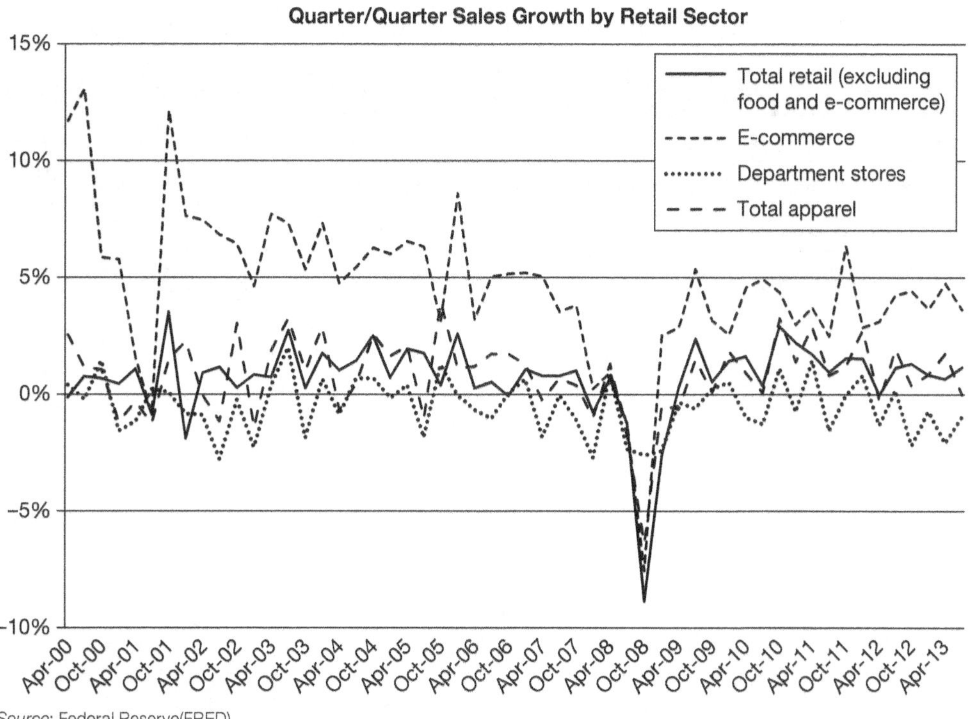

Source: Federal Reserve(FRED)

Exhibit 5 Johansen's: The new scoreboard system, store manager compensation and bonus structure

	2012	2013
Average store manager salary:	$73,000	$76,650
Bonus as a % of salary		
Overall rating = 3	10%	10%
Overall rating = 4	25%	25%
Overall rating = 5	40%	40%

Source: Created by author.

Exhibit 6 Johansen's: The new scoreboard system, Johansen's store financials ($ in millions)

2013	Johansen's	Average Store	Store 51
Sales	$8,300	$68.60	$150.00
Gross profit	$2,900	$23.97	$60.00
Gross profit %	34.94%	34.94%	40.00%
YoY sales growth (a)	6.41%	4.49%	5.50%

(a) YoY Sales Growth for the company as a whole came from two sources: same-store growth and new stores.
Source: Created by author.

Exhibit 7 Johansen's: The new scoreboard system, Johansen's customer demographic

	Johansen's	Store 51
Average customer age range	24–55	32–64
Average customer annual household income	$100,000	$135,000
Average sales/square foot	$408	$772
Average store size	160,000 sq. ft.	195,000 sq. ft.

Source: Created by author.

Exhibit 8 Johansen's: The new scoreboard system, Johansen's scorecard for Store 51's manager

Store Manager: Jared Clark **Evaluation Period:** January 1–December 31, 2013
Store Number: 51
Region: Southwest
Regional Manager: Southwest regional manager

Rating Summary

	Financial	Customer Service	Leadership	Strategy	**Overall**
Rating	5	3	5	5	**5**

Rating Explanation and Justification:

Category 1: Financial (quantitative)

Store managers must meet the "baseline target" to achieve a rating of 3.
Store managers must exceed "stretch target" to achieve a rating of 5.

	Q1'13	Q2'13	Q3'13	Q4'13
Profit: -Baseline target met? -Stretch target exceeded?	 Y Y	 Y Y	 Y Y	 Y Y
YoY sales growth: -Baseline target met? -Stretch target exceeded?	 Y Y	 Y Y	 Y Y	 Y Y

Additional note: *This year, aggressive financial stretch targets were set for Clark'sstore. Clark exceeded the stretch targets and achieved figures well beyond expectations.*

Financial Rating: 5

Category 2: Customer Service (quantitative and qualitative)

Store manager must achieve a survey response rate of 12% to receive a rating of 4 or 5.

	Q1'13	Q2'13	Q3'13	Q4'13
Response rate	3.5%	3.7%	5.5%	7.0%

Store manager must achieve a store customer satisfaction score of 4.4 to receive a rating of 5.

	Q1'13	Q2'13	Q3'13	Q4'13
Customer satisfaction score	3.2	3.4	3.7	4.1

Qualitative assessment: *Although Clark did not achieve the 12% minimum customer service survey response rate, his customer service performance improved throughout the year. In the first quarter, the feedback was generally negative; customers were able to find the merchandise they demanded, but were very unsatisfied with the customer service. In Q2, I spoke to Clark about the importance of customer service. He was receptive to the feedback, and saw an increase in survey response rate (from 3.7% in Q2 to 5.5% in Q3). Additionally, the feedback from customers was not overwhelmingly positive, but certainly was not as negative as it had been in the first half of the year. In Q4, Clark's performance increased again. The survey response increased to 7%, and customers had positive things to say about Store 51.*

Customer Service Rating: 3

(continued)

Exhibit 8 *(continued)*

Category 3: Leadership (qualitative)

Questions to consider when rating store manager: Were there many employee complaints? What was the nature of the complaints? Isolated incidents or ongoing issues? Was there an increase in turnover throughout the time period being assessed? What was the nature of the 360-degree feedback? Was store manager interested in developing leadership skills?

Qualitative assessment: *Clark's turnover was notably high at 45% during the first half of the year. In Q3 and Q4, however, turnover was reduced to 33%, a turnover figure better than the corporate average of 35%. There were 23 employee complaints throughout the year. 17 of them were from the same two employees, however. This does not necessarily imply that Clark's leadership was poor; the high volume of complaints from two individuals could simply indicate a mismatch in personalities. Those two employees voluntarily left Johansen's in November. Clark's 360-degree review was highly positive for the most part.*

Leadership Rating: 5

Category 4: Strategy (qualitative)

Questions to consider when rating store manager: Did store manager actively promote the Johansen's brand? Was branded merchandise in high-visibility areas throughout the store? Were corporate initiatives implemented? Was store manager proactive in seeking corporate guidance and initiatives?

Qualitative assessment: *Clark exceeded my expectations in this area. He regularly asked me about new corporate initiatives and how he could best implement them in Store 51. Clark also worked hard to enhance the Johansen's brand. He engaged members of his team and store managers across the Southwest region to brainstorm ways to promote Johansen's as a whole and also Johansen's branded merchandise. Clark is the strongest Johansen's corporate ambassador in the Southwest region.*

Strategy Rating: 5

OVERALL RATING: __________

Exhibit 9 Johansen's: The new scoreboard system, managers attending the performance summit

Corporate Human Resources Manager Don Harold

Last year, Harold was ready to leave Johansen's. After six years, his job had become monotonous, the company was struggling, and morale was low. He was just starting to look at opportunities elsewhere when senior management announced an overhaul of the existing performance measurement system. The company had been too focused on financial performance, and had lost sight of its strong customer service value proposition. The new scorecard system was an effort to bring the company back to its core values. Harold was offered a promotion within human resources to develop and implement the scorecard system. This was exactly the type of opportunity that he was looking for, so he eagerly accepted the promotion and stopped looking for other positions.

As much as the change in responsibilities was refreshing, it was challenging to develop the new system. While crafting it, Harold had his own performance assessment in mind. He would be evaluated and compensated based on the successful implementation of the new system, buy-in from employees, and changes made after system implementation. He wasn't sure exactly how those factors would be measured, but he did know that his boss would do the evaluation after seeking input from other constituents to get their assessment about the implementation process and general support of the system design, as well as reflecting on the extent of changes needed after the first year under the system. Harold was eligible for a one-time bonus of up to 30% of his salary based on the outcome of that review. He worked hard to come up with the best system possible, and he thought it was truly a stellar system.

Corporate Customer Experience Manager Mitch Dougan

After several years at Johansen's, Dougan was given the opportunity to become the company's first customer experience manager. This position was created alongside the development of the new scorecard system, and was considered instrumental to Johansen's return to its core value of premier customer service.

In this role, Dougan's main objective was to improve customer service across the company. He would be evaluated and would be eligible for a bonus based on the increase in customer service survey response rates, and also the customer satisfaction scores and qualitative feedback received through the surveys. He hoped that the new scorecard system would help boost the scores. He was very enthusiastic about the company's renewed focus on customer service, as well as his new opportunity to shine in this role.

Corporate Finance Manager Marjorie Thompson

This year, Thompson was celebrating her 15th anniversary with Johansen's. She started as a finance intern when she was in college and had moved up the finance ranks over the years. During her tenure with the company, she saw several years of stellar financial performance. In 2005, however, she watched the company's financials, as well as her bonus, start to stagnate. Johansen's began to recover after implementing a financially based incentive system, but that recovery was short-lived. Then the company implemented the new scorecard system, and Thompson was worried about what would happen as a result. She just wanted to see the company return to an exceptional financial standing.

Although Thompson was in finance, she was quite in tune with the stores in the different regions, and she had strong relationships with the regional and store managers. She recently caught wind of a rumor that a Johansen's competitor tried to recruit Store 51's manager, Jared Clark. Given that Clark's financial performance exceeded that of any other store manager's performance in the region, she was deeply concerned about the possibility that Johansen's could lose Clark to a competitor. Thompson saw Clark as a real star, and few store managers had been able to turn in the stellar financial performance that he had over time. Thompson believed that the company needed managers like him, particularly since her performance evaluation depended on the company's financial performance.

Other regional managers (Northeast, Midwest, Southeast, Northwest)

The annual performance evaluation of the regional managers was based in large part on the sales and financial performance of each region, and these regional managers considered themselves fortunate to have these top performers managing stores in their regions. They knew that these star performers were counting on the new scorecard system to rate them fairly.

The top-performing store manager in each of these regions excelled in all areas of the scorecard, including customer service. Depending on the region, the top store manager achieved a customer service survey response rate from 18% to 19%, had an average customer satisfaction score from 4.4 to 4.6, and received positive qualitative feedback from those responses. Each of them truly deserved an overall rating of 5.

This fictional case was prepared by Professor Luann Lynch, Jennifer Forman (MBA '14); and Graham Gillam (MBA '14).

CASE STUDY
Mainfreight

Mainfreight, a large international logistics company with headquarters in Auckland, New Zealand, managed its performance without preparing annual budgets as most other companies did. At Mainfreight, budgets were believed to distract managers' attention away from their day-to-day business.

Company background and organization structure

Mainfreight was founded in 1978. Its stock was listed on the New Zealand stock exchange in 1996. In 2012, the company had 214 autonomous branches operating in 14 countries, including New Zealand, Australia, the United States, Asia, Europe, and Mexico. The company had been profitable since its founding. In 2012 it generated NZ$1.8 billion in revenues; it employed over 5,000 team members[1] (see Exhibit 1 for key performance data); and it was named New Zealand Company of the Year.

Mainfreight offered a full supply chain solution, from managed warehousing to international and domestic freight forwarding. The company was organized into three main divisions: Domestic Freight, Air and Ocean (international freight) and Logistics. It did not own any trucks, ships, or airplanes. Instead it relied on a network of owner-drivers and air, rail, and shipping freight handlers to deliver its consignments.

The company's organization structure was flat, with just four hierarchical levels between front line team members and the Group Managing Director (GMD). Team members reported to branch managers; branch managers to general managers;[2] and general managers to the GMD, who reported to the Board.

The organization was highly decentralized, but all organization units had clearly defined responsibilities and reporting lines. Managers' decision-making authority was also constrained by certain policies, such as limits on the levels of expenditures that could be authorized at each management level. As one manager explained – "there is a rule that no one commits themselves to a lease over a $100,000 per annum without Director approval" – which is no small threshold by most companies' standards.

The small central support team included the Human Resources (HR), Information Technology (IT), and Finance functions. No centralized marketing function existed because the executive team believed that delivering freight on time provided sufficient marketing for the company. All support service costs were fully allocated to branches.

At Mainfreight the "branches are king." Branch teams were accountable for providing quality service to customers. The branches had relatively stable fixed costs and focused on managing the direct or variable costs of shipments.

The branch managers treated their branches as their own businesses. The branch managers were acknowledged to be the most knowledgeable about local markets and conditions and were authorized to make decisions about issues such as pricing, service offerings, delivery modes, and hiring. Overall, the branch managers were expected to have their "fingers on the pulse" and to make decisions that would have a positive impact on margins and profitability.

Decisions to open and close branches were made by the general managers. They decided, for example, when and where to open and close branches based on the prevailing conditions and knowledge of their markets.

Company culture

Mainfreight described itself as "a special company with special people." It viewed its philosophy of business, stated in its Three Pillars (see Exhibit 2), as a key contributor to its success. Selected principles derived from

[1] The company use the term team member instead of employee.

[2] Country managers had been introduced in some parts of the world, but not yet in New Zealand. General managers of each division reported to their respective country managers who reported to the Group Managing Director.

this philosophy that underpinned Mainfreight's approach to business include:

- Capitalism creates the profits needed to improve living standards for owners, employees, and communities. To generate profits, keep managers' attention focused on the drivers of performance.
- Every branch of the business needs to generate profits. Provide managers with autonomy and trust them to make decisions that are in the best interest of the company.
- Centralized control processes, budgets, and bureaucracy are ineffective and time consuming, and divert management's attention away from the business. Avoid hierarchy and bureaucracy at all costs.
- Team members have valuable contributions to make and may be the future managers and directors of the company. Provide opportunities for team members to grow and promote from within.
- Success is the result of teamwork. Share the rewards of success with the whole team.

The Mainfreight culture was intendedly egalitarian and supportive. The company provided a familial, nurturing environment in which everyone won or lost together. Few distinctions were made between managers and team members, and everyone shared open plan offices, parking spaces, lunch facilities, and the annual bonus. This culture established the foundation for the company's performance management system. The company tolerated honest mistakes but expected team members to learn from their mistakes and to avoid repeating them.

The executive team recognized that they were charged with maintaining the organizational culture through coaching, mentoring and encouragement. Here is a representative quote from an executive:

> **When you have got that devolution going on, it is not about a head office control environment. It is about a cultural environment. The one job I think I have got to do is to maintain that culture, to maintain that enthusiasm and that passion that the people have to grow this business into something more than what it is now.**

Mainfreight's top executives saw themselves as providing team members with an opportunity to help build a 100-year-old company and to share in the excitement of creating an organization that was trying to make a difference, to its customers, employees, and communities. As one executive described it:

> **We want these young people to understand the Mainfreight culture which is so exciting. It's exciting to be in a business that is going for the moon all the time.**

All the executive managers had worked their way up through the business and were very knowledgeable about operations. They regularly visited branch offices and "walked the talk."

The performance management system

Budgets were not part of Mainfreight's performance management system (PMS) because they were believed to distract managers' attention away from day-to-day business, as was mentioned in the introduction to this case. One manager explained:

> **Business moves quickly today, things change on a weekly basis. To distract a branch manager, to ask him to pore over a set of [budget] numbers, while real business is happening on his doorstep, means the manager is ignoring or cannot get to real business.**

The company believed that by providing quality service to customers and maintaining team morale, profits would look after themselves. Mainfreight's PMS focused on enabling managers to perform their roles, as one manager surmised:

> **Basically, you are left to it. They are monitoring how you are performing based on your financials. It is like any business right? But there is also ... the culture of the business, the audit score, the morale, all those things that impact intangibly on the bottom line profit. We talk about quality, culture, and profit in that order.**

Goals and strategies

Mainfreight's aspirational, medium-term goal was to become New Zealand's largest company by size and market capitalization by the year 2028. The specific milestones and targets to be achieved along the way were specified in its 2012 Annual Report (see Exhibit 3).

Mainfreight did not have formal strategic plans but it was clear about its strategic direction. Managers did not create detailed strategic plans because they believed sufficient guidance was provided by the company's overall objective – to grow by continually increasing profits. The GMD described the company's views on strategy in this way:

> [Why have] a strategic plan that was written in March and not applicable in October? ... Does Mainfreight have a strategic plan? No it does not. Does Mainfreight understand its strategic direction? Definitely it does.

Strategic directions evolved through regular discussions between executive managers, which were informed by their discussions with branch managers. Strategic considerations were integrated into wider discussions, as explained in the following quote:

> We have two Country Manager meetings a year. These are normally in March and October, and these just precede a Board meeting. So we have one or two days of Exec or Country Manager meetings, and then that's followed by a two-day Board meeting ... that's when the strategy for the year, or the next six months is promulgated ... then the Board would spend time in general business discussing what we believe to be right or wrong in a particular business direction.

The outcome of these discussions was shared understandings of the company's strategic intentions, rather than formal plans. According to one member of the executive team:

> The overall strategy is to continue to grow, to be in many of the right places, to determine what those right places are in the world, and generally to open international Air and Ocean-type operations.

The strategic intent that emerged from these regular conversations was not fixed. It remained fluid and could be adjusted quickly if required. For example, Mainfreight's intended strategy for entering the European market was via Air and Ocean services. What actually happened was that the executives learned that a European freight operation was for sale, albeit one with minimal Air and Ocean business, and they decided to acquire it.

Mainfreight's "emergent" approach to strategy meant that there was little separation between planning and action. Both activities occurred in rapid succession. Planning was simply a continuous consideration and response to current opportunities. Hope et al. (2011, p. 211) described this approach to planning as typical of the processes found in what they called "Beyond Budgeting organizations," in this way:

> Strategy making via this process is less reliant on sophisticated tools than on fast, relevant (actionable) information and responsible people who know what is expected of them and what to do in any given situation.

Performance standards

Mainfreight's executive team used heuristics to set performance expectations. The overall company goal was to grow profit by 15% per year, and branches are expected to set targets in line with this standard. This influence of profit expectations on branch target setting was explained by one executive in this way:

> We do not do budgets but the branch managers create targets ... they know we think anything less than 15 percent is failure. They do not set targets in sales or gross profit or expenses, they do it in pretax profit. They just produce one number.

The executive team also established standards for key performance indicators (KPIs), such as profit growth, percent of accounts receivable to sales, percent of aged debtors, number of claims for damage, number of consignment notes raised, percentage of on-time deliveries and number of credits raised. For example, the following quote identifies the targets set for the number of claims expected for a given consignment volume:

> We measure the number of consignments before you have one claim. On an outwards [consignment] if you get greater than fifteen hundred consignments ... before there is a claim then you are considered to have met the target. And it is about three thousand on an inward [consignment].

The branches set annual profit targets within the overall guidelines provided by the executive team. The target-setting process was relatively brief, generally completed within one day. Branch managers, in consultation with their teams, identified a realistic net profit target for the upcoming year. Last year's performance and current business conditions were considered when setting the target. Branch managers informed their respective general managers of the proposed target, and those that were reasonably challenging and achievable are approved. Once approved, the targets become notional contracts. They were signed by every team member in the branch – from the kitchen lady to the branch manager – and then framed and hung on the office wall. The company performance target was simply the aggregation of the branch targets.

Reporting

Mainfreight's PMS was supported by information systems that provided consistent and transparent information. All levels of the company reported the same information, in the same format, using the same classifications for revenues and costs.

Weeklies were the key mechanism for keeping performance on track. They resembled abbreviated profit-and-loss statements (see Exhibit 4), showing actual performance for the previous week, including revenues, direct costs, gross margin, an aggregated figure for routine overheads, and non-standard overheads. Preparation of the weeklies took no more than two hours.

Every Monday, branch managers phoned their weekly results through to their respective general managers[3] and posted the results on the Quality Board in the shared lunch facilities for the entire team to see. The weekly conversation took place directly between managers; it did not involve the accountants or any other intermediaries. General managers consolidated the branch information and in turn phoned the divisional results through to the Group managing director (GMD). The format was the same as that used at the branch level (see Exhibit 4). The results reported at this level reflected the overall performance by division and country. The GMD made the overall results available to members of the executive team and the Board by Tuesday afternoon.[4] At the start of each week, every person in the company was aware of corporate performance for the preceding week.

Everyone, from the front line to the Board level, scrutinized the weekly information to identify emerging trends and to develop appropriate responses. The company defined a trend as any change in margin that persisted for three consecutive weeks. The aim was to resolve margin issues within four weeks. This process was explained in the following quote:

> We are concerned if we start to see a trend. For us, three weeks is a trend. So the first week might indicate that there's a hiccup. Managers start asking some questions during the second week to identify why this is happening. If it continues the third week we know there's a trend here, and we've got to act on that.

Branch managers gauged their current performance (weekly, monthly, or quarterly) in comparison to the results achieved in the corresponding period of the previous year. The aim was to always improve on prior periods' performance. This approach eliminated the need for rolling forecasts or periodic budgets; the prior period figures provided a natural baseline from which to improve performance. In the words of team members:

> People say we have got to measure to make changes. And we do measure. Instead of comparing against the budget, we compare against last year.
>
> • • •
>
> The weekly forecast just becomes your budget – it is just that it is dynamic, it is live and in real time. You are comparing to real time things.

The importance of the weeklies for managing the business was described by one executive as follows:

> We do not do quarterly forecasts; the weeklies suffice. We are more focused on the day-to-day business and the annual profit looks after itself. We do not need to know what the next quarter will look like because we have last year's. So the branch managers know when they have big weeks coming up and that they have to meet them.

Mainfreight managed its operations with its weeklies, so it was critical that those figures were accurate. As one team member explained:

> We monitor those tolerances and see how good they are. We treat additional profit from weeklies with the same disrespect as we do under profit when compared to it ... the accuracy of the weeklies is paramount. It is our barometer of our business and unless you get it right, you can't act on it to make the changes.

Monthlies

Monthly accounts were produced by the accountants towards the latter half of the month following the one

[3] As the company expanded, the process for weeklies was slightly modified. Country managers were introduced, and general managers reported to country managers. They, in turn, accumulated the branch results and reported them to the group managing director.

[4] Traditionally, results were known by Monday evening but with operations now spread throughout the world results are not available until early Tuesday afternoon.

being reported. A separate profit-and-loss report was produced for every branch. Accountants used the monthlies to verify the accuracy of the branch weeklies. The weekly figures provided by branch managers were expected to be accurate to within plus or minus 1% of the monthly results. All discrepancies, either favorable or unfavorable, were queried.

Branch managers reviewed the monthlies and verified whether transactions coded to their branch's general ledger belonged there. Through this process they maintain detailed control over all their costs. One branch manager explained the process in this way:

> As a manager you get to know your business, down to [the] financials. You can say to me, "Hey, why is this [account] up? ... Why has that [account] come down?" I can tell you. I go through those numbers. We live these numbers; we own these numbers.

Apportionment of shared revenues

The nature of the company's operations meant that interactions between branches, both within and between countries, was required in order to deliver customer consignments. Given that branch performance was assessed on its margins, it was imperative to have a "fair" apportionment of revenues earned on each consignment between branches. For Domestic operations, a centrally-determined allocation schedule was used to determine inter-branch allocations. Sending branches were required to allocate prescribed amounts to receiving branches for the services they provided, such as handling and delivery, to complete the delivery. This procedure ensured that receiving branches were able to cover their actual costs and generate a profit. This approach avoided cross-subsidization and ensured that at all times branch managers sold at the real cost to make margins.

Resource allocation

Mainfreight allocated resources dynamically, meaning that it committed resources as, and when, required. Managers at different levels could commit to varying levels of expenditure up to the limit authorized by the executive team. Before committing additional resources, branch managers spoke to their general manager. During these typically brief conversations, branch managers justified how additional funds would be used. General managers considered the broader implications of the resourcing requests and gave immediate approval to any that seemed justified. There were no formal approval processes to follow or paperwork to complete. The contrast between this approach and traditional budgeting is highlighted in the following quote:

> With budgets, people get so focused on saying we cannot do this because there is nothing left in the budget. We just do not have that. We just get on and do it. It works.

Performance evaluation

Mainfreight used performance comparisons of financial and nonfinancial KPIs to assess how well branches, divisions and countries were performing. Inter-branch comparisons matched branches on type of operations, revenue and size before assessing profit performances. This meant that branch performance was compared to the performance of its peers. It was called a "buddy branch comparison."

League tables (branch rankings) were used to compare the relative performance of branches with respect to KPIs. For example, a league table on claims performance is shown in Exhibit 5. These results were circulated to all branches. These tables showed a company-average figure, and branches knew that if their performance fell below the average their bonus would be negatively affected. The use of ranges was explained as follows:

> We use ranges to assess performance with respect to key indicators. This is what you said you were going to achieve, and this is what the norm is. Then there's a spread below and above. ... It is not that you have to achieve a specific target ... you can actually achieve more.

Inter-country comparisons were also made. A member of the executive team explained how country comparisons are handled:

> We can look at the margins in each business, in each country and know who is performing and who is not. In fact in some categories we will compare country by country, compare them side by side on the P&L sheet. We can do a comparison of costs, margins and revenues, and categories of revenue.

The comparative measures of performance enabled Mainfreight to benchmark its branches and divisions. It did not, however, benchmark itself against competitors.

The preference for internal benchmarking was explained in the following quote:

> **At the end of the day, we do not do too much comparison with competitors. We are thinking about our business, not what theirs might be. The important thing is the expectation of our own performance.**

The key measure used to assess how well the company was doing overall was return on revenue (ROR). The GMD explained the importance of this measure to the company:

> **I see ... things like return on investment, return on equity, debt-to-equity ratios ... What is [our] return on equity? ... it is not a measure that I refer to ... we measure this business in return on revenue, and we have some guidelines on what we want for return on revenue, and our return on revenue measure is ... at the profit before tax line. We have a set of guidelines that we apply, the 5 to 7 percent return for Air and Ocean, 10 to 12 percent for Domestic, and 15 to 20 percent for Logistics. Those are the key financial measures, which we manage this business on, on both a weekly and monthly basis.**

Financial rewards

Mainfreight's bonus system applied to all team members. The two separate-but-interrelated components of the bonus scheme were the base bonus and the discretionary bonus. Profitable branches earned a base bonus equal to 10% of branch net profit. This bonus was shared evenly among all team members who were employed for at least twelve months, regardless of their role in the branch.

The base bonus was adjusted by the discretionary bonus calculation. The discretionary bonus considered a range of performance indicators, including profit growth, debtors, claims and damages. Profit growth was assessed in relation to what the branch could reasonably have been expected to earn given the prevailing conditions. Branch performance on the remaining indicators was assessed in relation to peers and average levels of performance. A branch could increase (or decrease) the discretionary bonus by one or two percent of branch net profit depending on its relative performance on the selected indicator. Branches' performances on claims per consignment (see Exhibit 5) were also considered.[5] Branches whose performance was above the average increased the discretionary bonus amount; those below the average had their discretionary bonus reduced.

Nonfinancial rewards

The company acknowledged the efforts of the team in a variety of ways. Plaques were given to branches that achieved their profit pledges or that won the branch-of-the-year award. Similar awards were given to individuals who were long serving members of the team and those who were acknowledged as top achievers. The plaques are publicly displayed on the walls of branch offices. Team members also received tokens of appreciation such as hams at Christmas or a bucket of apples during the year.[6]

The company continually acknowledged the contribution of the team members to its success. The names of all team members were listed every year in the company's Annual Reports. In 2009, they were even printed on the cover. Similarly, the names of all team members, with their length of service, were listed in the published corporate histories.

Cash management

Cash management was a key focus for the performance management system. A key reason for running weekly profit reports was to make sure that the billing was done each week. Billings had a direct and positive impact on cash flow. The history behind sending billing statements each week is explained as follows:

> **We had all the invoices on the statement every Friday night . . . Every cent that we could possibly charge out was charged out then. The freight industry has a history, may it never change, of charging weekly and trying to get paid weekly. We do [still] get paid on some weekly cycles . . . the railways always charged weekly, the ships always charged weekly. It was just one of those global traditions, and there was absolutely no point in trying to break it.**

The KPI for accounts receivable ensured that once customers were billed, managers made sure that the

[5] Number of consignments completed before a claim is made, for both inward and outward consignments.

[6] The company has had to adapt these New Zealand-grown practices to other locales. The company had to find ways of giving appropriate to specific countries.

accounts were paid on time. The pressure to collect accounts on time was tied to Mainfreight's policy of paying owner-drivers and creditors on time. The impact of on-time payments was explained as follows:

> **At Mainfreight we have a philosophy of paying our creditors on the 20th of the month, every month. We pay our drivers on the 15th of the month, every month. That forces us to collect our money . . . If you pay on time, you have to collect your money on time, and you cannot allow your credit terms to be extended.**

Mainfreight managers also believed that strong companies earn profits based on good customers. They wanted customers who valued quality service and were willing to pay for it, on time (Davies, 2003, pp. 60, 102). The company was not interested in, and actively avoided acquiring customers who wanted only the cheapest service. In their words, "Silly rates lead to silly margins and should be avoided." One executive explained this philosophy as follows:

> **Some customers like [one large retailer] live in the swamp . . . so we will not quote for them. We tend not to quote for the breweries unless it is strategic . . . Until recent times we have not shown any interest in supermarkets . . . They want cheap and ever cheaper service.**

These disciplines – bill weekly, pay on time, and manage the margins earned from individual customers – contributed to the company's cash management discipline.

Issues

Mainfreight had not prepared a traditional annual budget since its founding. The founder, a qualified accountant, set out to create a non-bureaucratic, non-hierarchical, decentralized organization. He had always viewed budgets as a waste of time, and he wanted to avoid them at all costs.

The Mainfreight performance management system was not perfect. Company managers were facing a few issues. There was some tension in the organization because the divisions' bonus potentials were not equal. In particular, team members in the Domestic Freight division could earn bonuses in the thousands, if not tens of thousands. The potentials in the Logistics division were much lower because of the high capital investments costs charged to the profit-and-loss statements. And there was a perception on the part of some managers that some branches found it easier to achieve their performance targets than others.

However, no team member had ever suggested that Mainfreight should introduce a traditional annual budgeting system.

Further Readings

Davies, K. 2003. *With Passion Anything is Possible. Mainfreight – An Insight* (Auckland: David Ling Publishing Limited).

Davies, K. 2013. *Ready Fire Aim: The Mainfreight Story: How a Kiwi Freight Company Went Global* (Auckland, New Zealand: Random House New Zealand).

Hope, J., Bunce, P., & Roosli, F. 2011. *The Leader's Dilemma: How to Build an Empowered and Adaptive Organization without Losing Control* (San Francisco, CA: John Wiley & Sons Ltd.)

O'Grady, W., & Akroyd C. 2016. The MCS Package in a Non-budgeting Organisation: A Case Study of Mainfreight. *Qualitative Research in Accounting & Management*, 13, no. 1, pp. 2–30.

Exhibit 1 Mainfreight performance

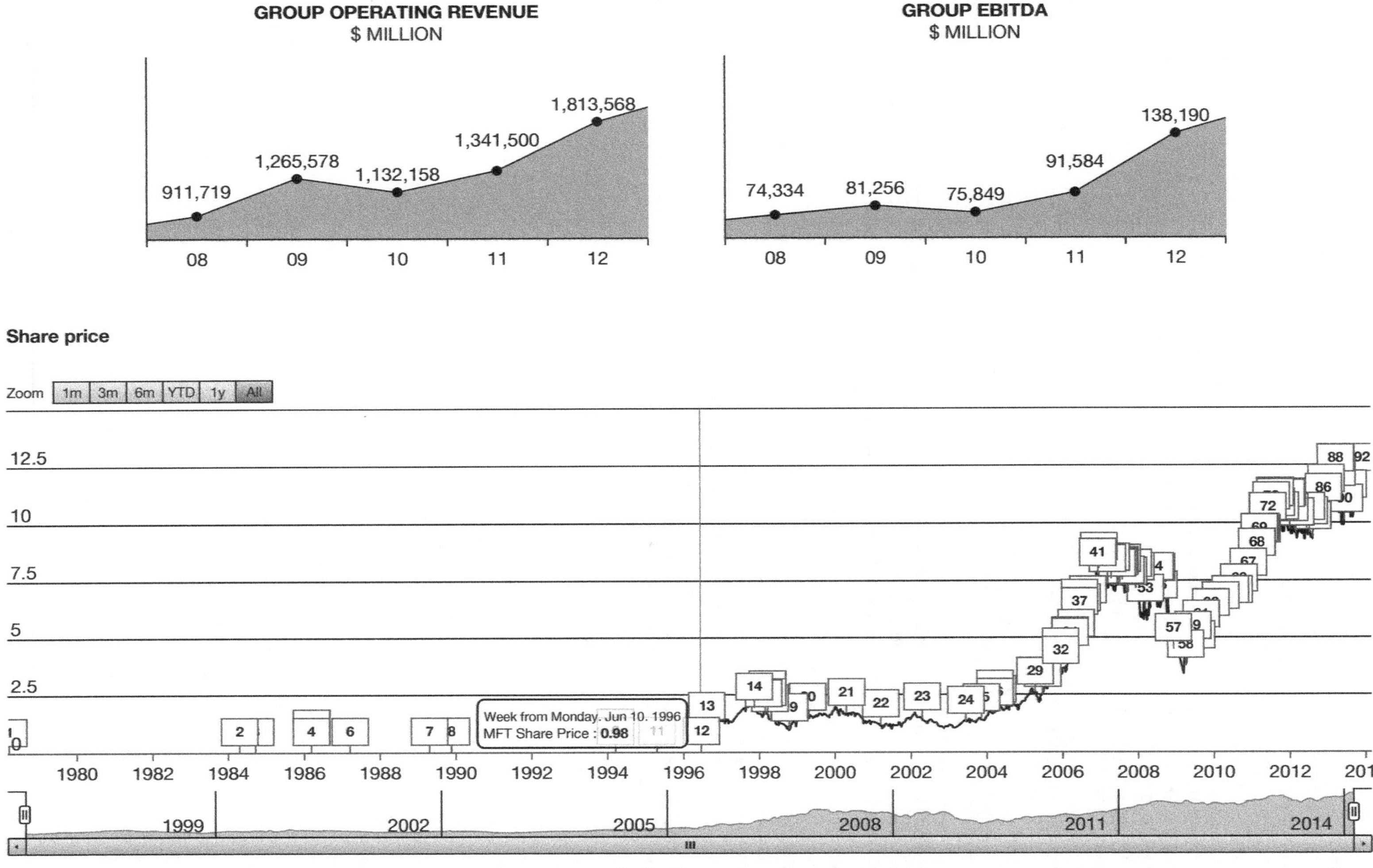

An interactive chart showing key milestones and share price for Mainfreight can be found at http://www.mainfreight.com/global/en/global-home/investor-centre.aspx

Exhibit 2 Mainfreight culture and values

Culture
Under-promise, over-deliver
Keep reinventing with time and growth
Education is optional, learning is compulsory
Let the individuals decide
Keep it simple
Tear down the walls of bureaucracy, hierarchy and superiority
Avoid mediocrity – maintain standards and beat them
Look after our assets
Immaculate image and presentation
Promote from within
No job descriptions
Integrity – how it affects other people

Family
Eat together – use mealtimes as a discussion time
Listen to each other
Share the profits and the successes
Openly discuss problems and openly solve them
Don't beat up your brothers and sisters
Have respect – seek it from others and show it by actions

Philosophy
One-hundred-year company
Profit comes from hard work, not talk
We are driven by margin, not revenue
Train successors, so that you may advance
An enduring company is built by many good people, not a few
We are here to make a positive difference, as well as a dollar
We "care" for our customers, environment and community base
Total quality management
Ready, fire, aim

Exhibit 3 Mainfreight targets and target status

TARGET	STATUS
2013	
• Revenue of US$400 million in Mainfreight USA and number of owned branches doubled from 12 to 24	• Revenue in the 2012 financial year US$208 million. Owned branches now number 33
• CaroTrans located on five continents	• On target, currently Asia, North America, South America, and Australia. European branch to open mid-2012
• Mainfreights is KiwiRail's largest customer in New Zealand	• Developing; currently 4th on their customer list
• Mainfreight Austraia operations have doubled revenue to AU$600 million	• On target, currently Australian revenue is AU$391 million
• 12 branches in our Asian network	• Currently 10
• Asian interests produce profit before tax of $l0 million	• Likely by 2018
• Another five branches opened in our Australian Domestic business	• Two new branches opened in past year: Albury and Sunshine Coast
• European Air and sea operations profitable	• On target
• Mexican and Canadian branches profitable	• On target - both to open in 2012
• Further European network expansion	• Finland and Moscow branches opened 2012; additional Eastern Europe branches expected
2014	
• Mainfreight USA has revenue of US$500 million earning a rate of return of 7%	• Likely by 2018
• We have a branch network established throughout Southeast Asia	• Likely to located in three Southeast Asia countries in 2012
• Asian interests produce sales revenues in excess of $100 million earning a return on revenue of 7%	• Likely by 2015; Current revenue including related party sales NZ$56 milion (or US$45 million)
• European Air & Sea operations developed in Eastern Europe	• On target
2015	
• Sales revenue exceeds $2 billion	• Likely to be achieved in 2013.
• Our American and European interests earn more profit than our Austral and New Zealand operations	• Expect this to be achieved in 2018 to allow our American interests the opportunity to develop further
• Over 300 branch localions around the world	• On target
• Located six European countries	• Completed through the acquisition of the Wim Bosman Group in April 2011
• Located in three South American countries	• Established in Chile through CaroTrans; ongoing focus to extend development
• Branch network extends throughout Asia including a presence in India	• Asian development continues including a Southeast Asian presence; India opportunities continue to be explored
2016	
• sales revenues exceed $3.0 billion	
• European revenues exceed £500 million	• Likely by 2018
• More branches opened in Eastern Europe	• Allready in Polland, Romania, Russia - new branches opened in Finland
• Asia/Europe and USA/Europe trade lanes are our largest by volume and revenue	
• Located in all European countries	• A little ambitious, howenver we will try hard!

(continued)

Exhibit 3 Mainfreight targets and target status (*Continued*)

TARGET	STATUS
2017	
• Mainfreght has a will-established Intrenational network trading between Europe, USA, South America, and Asia/Pacific • 85% of revenue is earned outside of New Zealand	
2028	
OUR 50TH YEAR OF BUSINESS MAINFREIGHT BECOMES NEW ZEALAND'S LARGEST COMPANY BY SIZE AND MARKET CAPITALISATION. JUST IMAGINE!	

Source: Mainfreight's 2012 Annual Report. See http://www.mainfreight.com/global/en/global-home/investor-centre/report-library.aspx.

Exhibit 4 Format of weekly performance reports

	Branch A Weekly results	%	$	$	
			This year	Last year	
1	Sales				
	Allowances from Sending branches				
2	Less: Direct Costs				
	Allowances to Receiving branches	%			%
	Pick Up & delivery	%			%
	Linehaul Total	%			%
3	Gross Margin	%			%
4	Standard Overheads				
	Extra overheads				
	Salaries				
5	Weekly Profit	%			%
6	No. of consignments				
	Total cubic metres				
	Total tonnage				
7	Branch Manager's comments				
	Insights on mix, events, weather, etc				
	Notes on Sales & Margin performance				

Division Weekly Results				
	This year	Last year	Gross Margin	L/Haul Margin
Week Ending				
Branch A				
Branch B				
Branch C				
...				
...				
...				
...				
...				
...				
...				
...				
...				
...				
Branch XYZ				

Exhibit 5 Branch league table on claims performance

Claims Performance							
Outward Consignments Per Claim				Inwards Consignments Per Claim			
Branch	To March 2012	To Sept 2011	To March 2011	Branch	To March 2012	To Sept 2011	To March 2011
Chem Auckland	1756	1892	1667	Chem Auckland	5680	6755	4670
Rotorua	1158	1068	1166	Chem Christchurch	3470	2255	1746
Whangarei	1081	1318	571	Blenheim	2264	3147	1800
Chem Christchurch	1032	930	584	Palmerston North	1589	1832	1267
New Plymouth	936	799	759	Owens Auckland	1502	1810	1401
Napier	750	799	697	DF Auckland	1399	1529	1337
Mt Maunganui	744	892	551	Mt Maunganui	1345	1385	964
Dunedin	695	855	1009	MF Auckland	1266	1196	1060
Palmerston North	676	704	897	Taupo	1179	1178	1362
MF Hamilton	655	753	655	Napier	1168	914	1327
Blenheim	649	617	505	New Plymouth	1160	1170	1083
MF Auckland	627	662	639	*Total Company*	*1084*	*1155*	*1106*
Owens Auckland	617	676	607	MF Hamilton	1063	1568	1110
Total Company	*582*	*612*	*576*	Owens Christchurch	1022	1339	877
MF Wellington	581	592	515	DF Christchurch	969	1098	1320
MF Christchurch	532	574	444	Whangarei	969	1164	598
DF Auckland	473	486	652	MF Wellington	898	826	1026
Invercargill	396	409	366	MF Christchurch	887	844	1102
Owens Christchurch	379	431	348	Nelson	814	802	713
DF Christchurch	349	348	445	Rotorua	762	1136	1183
Nelson	319	384	343	Invercargill	635	677	1108
Taupo	221	386	244	Dunedin	616	668	846

This case was prepared by Professor Winnie O'Grady.

CASE STUDY
Statoil

We have a management model that is very well-suited to dealing with turbulence and rapid change. It enables us to act and reprioritize quickly so that we can fend off threats or seize opportunities. This is much more difficult in a "traditional budget" world.

Helge Lund, CEO, Statoil

Statoil, the large Norwegian energy company, used an innovative performance management process called "Ambition-to-Action" to translate the company's overall strategies into strategic objectives, key performance indicators, needed actions, and individual goals. It combined two management concepts – the "balanced scorecard" and "beyond budgeting" – in a unique way.

The implementation of the Ambition-to-Action process had taken a long time, but by 2010 it had been fully implemented across Statoil. In August 2010, Bjarte Bogsnes (Vice President, Performance Management Development), reported that:

One of our core values is to challenge accepted truths. We threw out our annual budgeting process back in 2005. In 2010, we decided to throw out the calendar. We are for instance implementing event-driven dynamic forecasting. No longer do we require any forecasts to be prepared at any fixed time, and the planning horizons vary depending on the business or operation. We are striving to make our entire process – strategic planning, target setting, action planning, forecasting – totally dynamic, done as needed. We want our management process to be business-driven, not calendar-driven. This is not accounting. Our aim is to create the conditions required for teams in Statoil to perform to their full potential.

The new Ambition-to-Action process had already provided many benefits. But Bjarte acknowledged that some Statoil managers were still uncomfortable with the Ambition-to-Action process. "It's a long journey, and it should be. Changing mind-sets is not a quick fix," he said.

Company background

Statoil, headquartered in Stavanger, Norway, was a large, multinational energy company.[1] The company was formed in 1972 by the Norwegian government and was wholly state owned until 2001 when its shares were listed on both the Oslo and New York stock exchanges. After the 2007 merger with the oil and gas division of Hydro, a Norwegian competitor, Statoil became the world's largest offshore energy producer, the world's third-largest seller of crude oil, and Europe's second-largest gas supplier. Statoil was also the largest company based in Scandinavia measured by market capitalization (nearly US$70 billion) and annual sales (US$70 billion). The company employed 20,000 people in 34 countries.

Statoil's original focus was on the exploration, production, and development of oil and gas on the Norwegian continental shelf. The company's distinctive competency was deep water offshore drilling in harsh environments. Over the years, it diversified into refining and retailing of petroleum products and production of alternative forms of energy, such as wind power. In October 2010, Statoil spun off its retail business to create a separate public corporation, Statoil Fuel & Retail.

Statoil's strategy was to grow its long-term oil and gas production profitably while gradually building a position in renewable energy production. The oil reserves on the Norwegian continental shelf, on which the company had relied for many years, were being depleted. International growth was a key strategy. Statoil managers knew that the company was entering a new, more competitive, and more unpredictable era, so faster responsiveness to change was deemed critical.

The Statoil organization structure was relatively flat. It consisted of six main business units: (1) Exploration & Production – Norway; (2) Exploration & Production – International; (3) Natural Gas; (4) Manufacturing &

[1] More information on the company can be found at www.statoil.com.

Marketing; (5) Projects & Procurement; and (6) Technology & New Energy (see Exhibit 1).[2]

Ambition-to-Action

Statoil's Ambition-to-Action was a process that was designed to provide integration from organizational strategy to employees' actions, while providing sufficient freedom and flexibility. It was designed around five basic principles:

1. Performance is ultimately about *outperforming peers.*
2. *Do the right thing* in the actual situation, guided by the *Statoil Book*,[3] the Ambition-to-Action, decision criteria and authorities, and sound business judgment.
3. Within this framework, *resources* are made available or allocated case-by-case.
4. Business follow up is *forward looking* and *action* oriented.
5. Performance evaluation is a *holistic* assessment of delivery *and* behavior.

Strategic objectives, performance indicators, and actions

The Ambition-to-Action process was built around a key performance indicator (KPI) scorecard system that was originally introduced at the company in 1997. In 2002, additional information was added to the KPI-dominated scorecard – a mission, strategic objectives, and needed actions – to provide a broader and richer language for describing and evaluating performance than could be provided by focusing just on KPI measures. Bjarte Bogsnes explained:

> Ambition-to-Action is the cornerstone of how we manage our business. It is how we exercise leadership, and it is the core of our business review meetings. It is a much better tool than a budget for integrating the strategic processes with financial and operational measurement activities and people processes. A budget cannot provide a holistic approach to management as it has a narrow financial focus, and accounting numbers are getting more distant from our business. Because oil prices are so volatile, accounting reports tell us very little about performance unless we benchmark. You can't read strategy out of a budget, but you can read strategy out of a good scorecard.

All the Ambition-to-Action information was displayed together on a single page. Exhibit 2 shows an Ambition-to-Action example, that for the entire corporation. The overall mission is shown at the top: "Globally competitive – an exceptional place to perform and develop." The left column shows the *strategic objectives*, which answered the question: "Where are we going?" The center column showed the *performance indicators*, which answered the question: "How do we measure progress?" The right column described the *key actions* to be taken, which answered the question: "How do we get there?"

The corporation's two key financial performance indicators were relative total shareholder return and relative return on average capital employed (RoACE). Exhibit 3 shows backup detail for these two KPIs, which compare Statoil performance with that of the other major energy companies.

Exhibits 4, 5, and 6 show other examples of Ambition-to-Action documents. These examples are for organizations at Levels 2 and 4 in the Projects & Procurement organization and at Level 3 in the Exploration & Production – Norway organization. The examples show the wide variety in the chosen strategic objectives and KPIs.

In 2010, over 1,100 Ambition-to-Action documents were in use within Statoil. Managers were encouraged to try the Ambition-to-Action process, but there was no corporate mandate imposing its use. Most, but not all, organizational entities above a certain size used it. The number of Ambition-to-Action documents had grown significantly over the years, more than doubling in just the last two years, simply because most Statoil managers wanted to use the process.

The *strategic objectives* were designed to describe "what success looks like on a medium term time horizon." To test the objectives they had developed, managers were asked to consider the following questions:

- Do they provide clear guidance and direction?
- Are they written in a language that makes you tick, without too many buzzwords?
- Do they support each other (cause and effect, from people and organization to finance)?

[2] Statoil announced a new organization effective January 1, 2011, that carved out North America as a seventh major business unit.

[3] The *Statoil Book* explained the company's most important operating principles, policies, and requirements. It set standards for "our behavior, our delivery and our leadership."

- Is the time horizon right, within an appropriate delivery period?

The lists of *performance indicators* (KPIs) were organized using five perspectives, the four traditional balanced scorecard perspectives – finance, market, operations, and people and organization – plus a fifth perspective of particular importance to Statoil: health, safety and environment (HSE). Statoil's conventional order for display of the perspectives was different from that of the standard balanced scorecard. Instead of starting with the financial perspective at the top, Statoil placed the people and organization perspective on top, followed by HSE, operations, and market, ending with finance. This was done to secure sufficient focus on the performance drivers found in the first four perspectives, as Finance was seen as the ultimate consequence of performing well in the other perspectives.

The managers of each entity selected the set of KPIs that they believed would work best for their organization. There were relatively few attempts to use the same KPIs at multiple levels of the organization if it did not make sense to do so, although some corporate entities from time to time tried to "push" their own favorites. Managers were aware of the strategic objectives, performance indicators, and actions of the entities above them in the corporate hierarchy, as all of this information was made available on the common management information system (MIS) that maintains all Ambition-to-Actions. But Statoil did not want a mechanical "cascading" of the objectives, performance indicators, and actions throughout the organization. What they wanted was for each entity to run its own strategy process and to "translate" higher-level strategies into strategy themes that were actionable at each organization level. The goal was to secure ownership and have local teams manage themselves effectively in their local environment while moving in the right direction as defined by the strategies of entities higher in the organizational hierarchy. The measures were changed to fit the circumstances being faced, as Baard Venge (Controller, Drilling & Well) explained: "We change measures when strategy changes or when we find better ones. If a measure is easy to manipulate, it is useless. We take it out."

Statoil wanted managers to define KPIs that were *relative*, rather than absolute. Relative KPIs linked inputs with outputs (e.g. cost per barrel) and, where possible, they compared the organization's performance with some benchmarks – performance relative to other entities. Statoil managers thought that relative KPI targets were more robust and "evergreen," meaning that they did not need to be updated as often. They also drove performance by stimulating a competitive mindset and peer pressure to perform and encourage learning from the best performers and the sharing of best practices. Regarding the question as to how challenging to set to targets, Geir Slora (senior vice president, Drilling & Well) clarified, "We want achievement of the targets to be possible. In most cases we are not aiming at world records. We are aiming at being in the top 25%."

Bjarte Bogsnes noted:

> Absolute KPIs, such as a cost figure, is just measuring one side of the equation and is not in relation to what you want to get out of those costs. Is meeting an absolute cost target good or bad? Well, it depends on what you get back from those costs. Perhaps you should have spent more, as you lost value by missing business opportunities by not doing so. Or maybe you should have spent less because some expected opportunities did not come true. In any case, you will only know afterwards and not beforehand what the "right" cost level is. It is however not possible to find good relative KPIs in all areas, so we also use absolute cost targets. These should however be set at an overall level, not a detailed level, to secure flexibility for teams to take the right decisions.

Finally, the *actions* listed on the Ambition-to-Action documents were those considered to be the most important for achievement in the areas of performance reflected by the KPIs.

Regarding the advice he tended to give managers who were working on their Ambition-to-Action documents, Bjarte Bogsnes proffered:

> Teams must spend quality time defining strategic objectives before moving on to the KPIs. The strategic objectives translate strategy into success using language that people understand. When scorecards only show KPIs, what strategies do they communicate? Making strategy more concrete through strategic objectives can also reveal lack of clarity in the strategy ...
>
> Don't search for the perfect KPI; it doesn't exist. I've spent 10 years looking for it. There are good KPIs and good combinations of KPIs, but there's no perfect KPI. The problem is that we often forget what the "I" in KPI stands for – *indicator*. It's only an

indication of whether we are moving towards our strategic objectives. It's not a goal by itself. Therefore, de-emphasize KPI targets and heighten objectives and actions.

The Ambition-to-Action documents were intended to be updated only as required, not on a periodic (e.g. annual) basis.

Performance targets, forecasts, and capital allocations

Statoil previously used a traditional annual budgeting process but, inspired by the beyond budgeting principles,[4] the company's Executive Committee approved its discontinuance on May 9, 2005.[5] Statoil managers had many reasons for believing that budgeting was harmful to the corporation; for example:

- The budget forced three different purposes into one set of numbers – target setting, forecasting, and resource allocation – hurting the quality of each purpose as these are different things. The budget as a forecast became biased because the same number also served as a target, or as an application for resources. An ambitious sales target cannot be the same number as a 50/50 sales forecast.
- The budget became obsolete shortly after it was prepared because the assumptions on which it was prepared were no longer accurate. Nonetheless, some operating managers tended to view the budgeted costs as entitlements that should be spent anyway: "Nobody ever gives anything back." Other operating managers were limited by the cost budget ceiling that prevented them from doing additional things that would be value-creating.
- Detailed budgets became centralized micro-management of highly competent and educated knowledge workers, which the company claimed were its most important asset.
- Managers spent a lot of budget review time looking backwards, explaining variance, rather than focusing on the future. Even though the budget reference points became more irrelevant as the months in the year went by, they were still compared with actual costs monthly with "accounting accuracy."
- Budgeting was done on an annual cycle, but an annual cycle is not optimal for all parts of Statoil's business. For some that is too often, but others should be evaluating performance and reforecasting more frequently.
- The budget preparations were predicated on the assumption that financial capital is the main constraint. In many areas of Statoil, other constraints, particularly expertise (human resources), were more salient.

Bjarte Bogsnes explained that all these problems with budgeting undermined the power of their scorecards:

A key reason why many scorecard implementations fail is because they compete with the budget as a management tool, which confuse the organization over what's the most important. As long as we had both, the budget normally won because it had the longest tradition, and managers were most familiar with it. When we removed the budget, no one was in doubt about the role of the scorecard. We got an amazing turbo-charging of the process.

The Ambition-to-Action process is shown in diagram form in Exhibit 8. The process started with strategic planning. Strategic themes and issues out to a 10-year horizon were discussed when needed as well as at the

[4] Beyond budgeting is a management model aimed at overcoming the problems caused by traditional budgeting. The model, first developed at the Swedish bank Handelsbanken, has been developed and refined as its use has spread to several other organizations around the world, including Toyota, Southwest Airlines, Whole Foods Markets, and Nokia.
The aim of the beyond-budgeting management model is to increase the adaptability of enterprises. Exhibit 7 shows the 12 core beyond-budgeting principles. The first six principles are focused on taking the right leadership actions to address the drivers of change. The second six principles align management processes with leadership actions. Companies that follow the beyond-budgeting principles have simple organizational structures, flat hierarchies, and flexible peer-to-peer networks. They operate with an assumption that organizations, like natural systems, are capable of self-organization and self-regulation. Their managers do not require negotiation of fixed performance targets, as is done in a traditional budgeting system. Allocations of resources are event-driven, not calendar-driven. Allocated resources are not treated as entitlements that must be spent. Unconstrained by a fixed and outdated plan, employees strive to improve their performance relative to their peers or some other benchmark. Creativity and rapid response to customer needs and unpredicted events are encouraged. The 12 principles are closely inter-related. Beyond-budgeting proponents caution that adopting a few principles while ignoring the others could lead to unsatisfactory outcomes.

[5] Bjarte Bogsnes noted that "When you work with external partners [companies on large projects, say], you are often required to provide traditional budgets. When you aren't preparing budgets to operate internally, this can be confusing for those managers who have this external interface. So, we haven't completely eradicated budgets for those purposes." Baard Venge agreed: "It is hard to be dynamic if our partners are not also dynamic. Most of them want to see an annual budget."

two Executive Committee meetings held each year. The ambition statements and strategic objectives developed out of the strategy discussions. They remained relatively stable over time.

Statoil managers separated the functions typically served by traditional budgeting processes – target setting, forecasting, and resource allocation – from each other in order to help improve the quality of each of these activities. Statoil used three distinct processes separated in time, or by KPIs used, to accomplish these very different purposes.

Performance *target setting* was done first. Performance targets were set to be both ambitious and, if possible, relative. Ideally, relative targets both connected inputs with outputs (e.g. cost per unit of production) and allowed performance comparisons with that of other like organizations (e.g. "above average in the industry"). For example, targets for the health, safety and environment measure of "serious incidence frequency" (SIF) commonly used in the exploration areas of the company were set relative to other like-entities within Statoil. Relative performance targets provided several advantages: there was no need to negotiate targets each year; managers set more ambitious targets for themselves because no one likes to be a laggard; and they motivated managers to be interested in learning from those who performed better on a relative basis.

Forecasts were designed to reflect expected outcomes, to provide early warnings of problems that might be occurring so that corrective actions could be taken if necessary. Statoil managers knew that there would always be noise in the forecasts, but they wanted the forecasts to be honest and unbiased. The forecasts were intended to reflect expected outcomes realistically, whether favorable or unfavorable. When visibility into the future was poor, the forecasts could include scenarios and ranges of outcomes.

The frequency, lead time, and time horizon of the forecasts were intended to be driven by the business – not the calendar. In the first years of use of Ambition-to-Action, however, the process was more calendar-driven. Entities did strategic planning, KPI selection and target setting in the spring; action planning and forecasting in the fall, and performance evaluations at the end of the year.

Thus, starting in 2010 and 2011 respectively, Statoil changed the process to require use of *dynamic* (or *event-based*) *forecasting and target setting.* Bjarte Bogsnes explained that, "An event is either something that happens around us or an action we take ourselves that has an effect that should be reflected in our targets and forecasts." Deciding when to update was a local manager decision. Forecasts were updated when an "event" happened or when important new information became available, but the time horizon was whatever local managers believed was relevant for their entity. Forecast updates were noted in a *forecast log* that was available for everyone to see in the MIS system. Strategic objectives, KPI selection, and target setting could be changed when necessary. However, major changes required approval one level up; minor changes were only reported as information. If changes affected other entities, the entity initiating the change was responsible for informing those entities. Changing targets did not happen frequently, but they were intended to happen at natural points in time instead of directed by the calendar. Performance evaluation still took place once a year as before, but against Ambition-to-Actions that varied from very stable to very dynamic.

As a result, Statoil's forecasts were approximately correct at all times, rather than being correct only at one fleeting point in time as is true in companies with a traditional annual planning and budgeting process. But since the targets were set to be ambitious and the forecasts were made to be realistic, it was common to have a gap between the two sets of numbers. This was seen as natural, as managers aimed high but had a realistic view of where they were.

Forecasts were not intended to be performance commitments, because targets had been set earlier. Cost forecasts were also not applications for resources for funds, as discussed next.

Allocations of resources at Statoil were not a mechanical function of either targets or forecasts. Managers had the freedom to commit resources up to limits defined by their scope of responsibility. The definition of a limit was however significantly redefined.

The problem with the conventional annual budget process was that it forced entities to decide on funding once a year, not only the total level but also the funding composition, which was not always the right time. Statoil did still allocate funds to projects or major decisions involving costs, but only when the project was ready for a decision. Additional allocations were made dynamically, when the resources were needed, rather than far in advance as was typically done in a periodic budgeting process. Resources were "in principle" available whenever they were needed, if the project was good enough and if fresh forecasting information indicated sufficient capacity. "The bank is open year round," Bjarte Bogsnes exclaimed, "but you can still get a no on your request for money."

The intention with dynamic resource allocation was to cause a different managerial mind-set. Instead of asking "Do I have the budget for this?" managers should ask whether spending the money was the right thing to do. Was it within their decision authority, could they justify the expenditure, was the spending necessary, and, last but not least, was the spending within the framework defined by Ambition-to-Action? This framework might include KPI targets like profit targets, unit cost targets or an overall absolute cost target. Some entities had no cost KPIs at all, instead addressing cost through strategic objectives or actions, combined with a continuous monitoring of their own actual spending development.

Business reviews

Performance reviews provided a structured assessment of actual performance. The reviews focused on the Ambition-to-Action documents, which were produced monthly. Each document (examples are shown in Exhibits 2, 4, 5, and 6) provided a quick summary of recent performance. The circles to the right of each performance indicator and each action showed whether forecasted (not actual) performance was meeting targets or schedules. A circle with a plus sign (coded green) indicated yes; one with an exclamation point (colored yellow) was questionable; one with a minus sign (coded red) indicated no. The arrows to the right of the circles indicated if the last forecast update reflected a positive or negative trend since the last reporting period. This format created much more forward-looking business reviews.

The reviews typically started with an evaluation of KPIs and necessary action performance vs. targets. This was not as straightforward as it might first appear, as Geir Slora (senior vice president, Drilling & Well) explained:

> We can live with some red circles, as we look at the reasons for misses. Were there unforeseen problems? If the KPIs are all green, we get suspicious that the manager was too conservative in target setting. For example, one manager in the drilling business was able to show "all green" on his Ambition-to-Action because his cost targets were set in absolute terms. His entity was able to come in below the cost targets because they failed to do all the drilling that was expected for the period which, of course, was not good. At the end of the day, all we really want to see is whether the organization is headed in the right direction.

As a matter of fact, comparing the performances vs. targets was only a starting point. More important were the answers to the following five questions to "pressure test" the KPI results:

- *Did the KPI results contribute to the strategic objectives?* What were they unable to pick up? If we look beyond the KPI results, how would we evaluate performance?
- *How ambitious were the targets?* With hindsight, would we say that they were stretched?
- *Were there changes in assumptions that should be taken into account?* Were the results affected by a tail-wind or head-wind that had nothing to do with performance?
- *Were agreed-upon or necessary actions taken?*
- *Were the results sustainable?* Or had the managers made themselves look better in the short run at the expense of the long run?

Eldar Saetre, the CFO, said:

> Some uninformed observers might fear the prospect of cost anarchy. I disagree. Many businesses within Statoil have KPI targets on profitability and/or unit costs, benchmarked against peers where possible. Here, costs are managed by setting unit (rather than absolute) cost targets. Entity managers cannot spend wildly without a return or a good business case. In other areas we give overall guiding on acceptable cost levels. Across all businesses, we monitor cost trends carefully, at least monthly, and intervene at any time if a negative trend has no good explanation.

Individual performance evaluations

Individual performances evaluations were done holistically and with the advantage of hindsight. All Statoil employees had individual goals for both delivery (*what*) and behavior (*how*). Performance was judged 50% on delivery, as defined by Ambition-to-Action, and 50% on behavior and living up to Statoil values. Delivery performance was evaluated subjectively, taking into consideration relevant hindsight information. Statoil used 360-, 180-, and 90-degree behavior evaluations plus a people survey and day-to-day observations to learn how managers and employees were living up to the company's values. Delivery and behavior evaluations were each scored on a 1–5 scale and weighted equally in determining salary increases and bonuses on top of the common bonus for everybody, which was linked to Statoil's financial performance vs. competitors.

Elder Saetre explained:

> We have broken the automatic link between fixed KPI targets, performance evaluation and bonuses, not just by introducing behavior as a key element, but also by broadening our definition of delivery. Delivery used to be solely defined by KPIs, but they seldom provide the whole picture. That is why you need a more holistic assessment. We now look at Ambition-to-Action as a whole and make qualified judgments with hindsight. It takes a few years for employees to understand how it works, but then it can be very credible.

Implementation

KPI-dominated scorecards were first introduced as a local initiative on one of the offshore platforms in the late nineties. Their popularity grew rapidly, both sideways and upwards in the organization, and by 2003 all of Statoil used them. Then the broader Ambition-to-Action process was introduced, emphasizing also strategic objectives and actions. In 2005, the company abolished traditional budgets, starting out with some pilots. The 2007 merger with Hydro, which added 10,000 people in new roles in a new organization, meant starting all over again in many entities. In 2010 the decision was taken to kick out the calendar.

Statoil managers did not wait until they had nailed down every detail. They designed the major features of the system and implemented it. They knew they were entering unfamiliar territory and did not believe that everything could be designed up front.

Some Statoil employees were worried about the change, as Bjarte Bogsnes recalled:

> The skeptical ones fall in two categories. Some are skeptical because they are confused. These just need time to learn and understand. But there will always be a group of hard-core skeptics that you cannot convince up front. Instead of arguing against them, tell them you accept that there is a risk that it will not work. But what is actually the risk if throwing out budgets fails? Most companies can go back to budgeting overnight. Nobody will have forgotten how to do it. So ask them to compare that minimal downside risk with the upside if it works as intended. That tends to calm people down.

By 2010, the Ambition-to-Action process was fully operational throughout Statoil. All of the major business units had implemented the process, and virtually all senior managers thought that it was a success. Exhibit 9 summarizes the major changes from the old command-and-control management style to the new more dynamic and flexible style.

Corporate managers did not impose the Ambition-to-Action process on any entity. They concluded that local managers needed to have the freedom to adapt the principles and practices of the process to fit their entity's needs, and they needed to find it useful themselves. If they did not, they would not use it anyway. Corporate managers needed to impose only enough structure to maintain a coherent vision and direction from the top to the bottom of the organization. They asked only that if the process was being used, all the documents be kept fully up-to-date at all times. They did try to communicate the purposes of the process and stood ready to train the managers to use it more effectively. They expected that as the managers became more comfortable with the system, its use was likely to increase and improve.

Even though all the major entities had chosen to implement Ambition-to-Action, not all implementations were equally effective. The quality of implementation at lower organization levels, particularly, was uneven because the levels of understanding, quality, and commitment varied considerably. Some managers used the process as it was designed, as a "leadership tool." But others used it merely as a "reporting tool," as a budget in disguise. Numerous problems were apparent. For example, some of the strategic objectives and KPIs were poorly chosen or defined or not changed often enough. Some performance standards were absolute when they could have been relative. Some KPIs and performance targets were dictated to subordinates by higher-level managers through cascading processes. Some important performance qualities, such as "capabilities and competencies" in an internal consulting entity, could not be measured effectively.

Too many forecasts were only updated with a year-end horizon. Too many targets had end-of-December delivery dates.

The future

It was inevitable that refinements to the process would be made over the years. The company was just beginning to incorporate risk heat maps into Ambition-to-Action. Bjarte Bogsnes thought that the system could become even more dynamic. In 2010, action planning, resource allocations, and forecasting were all done dynamically, and from 2011 setting the strategic objectives, determining the KPIs and KPI targets would also be event- and business-driven. Looking forward Bjarte thought that, for example, performance evaluations might also be more closely linked to the completion of projects or activities.

He added:

> I still have my dark days when I observe practices or behaviors reflecting what we wanted to leave behind. My medicine is, however, both simple and effective. I think back to how things were when we started out some years ago. If we can make similar progress in the coming years, we will have moved mountains.

Exhibit 1 Statoil: Organization chart

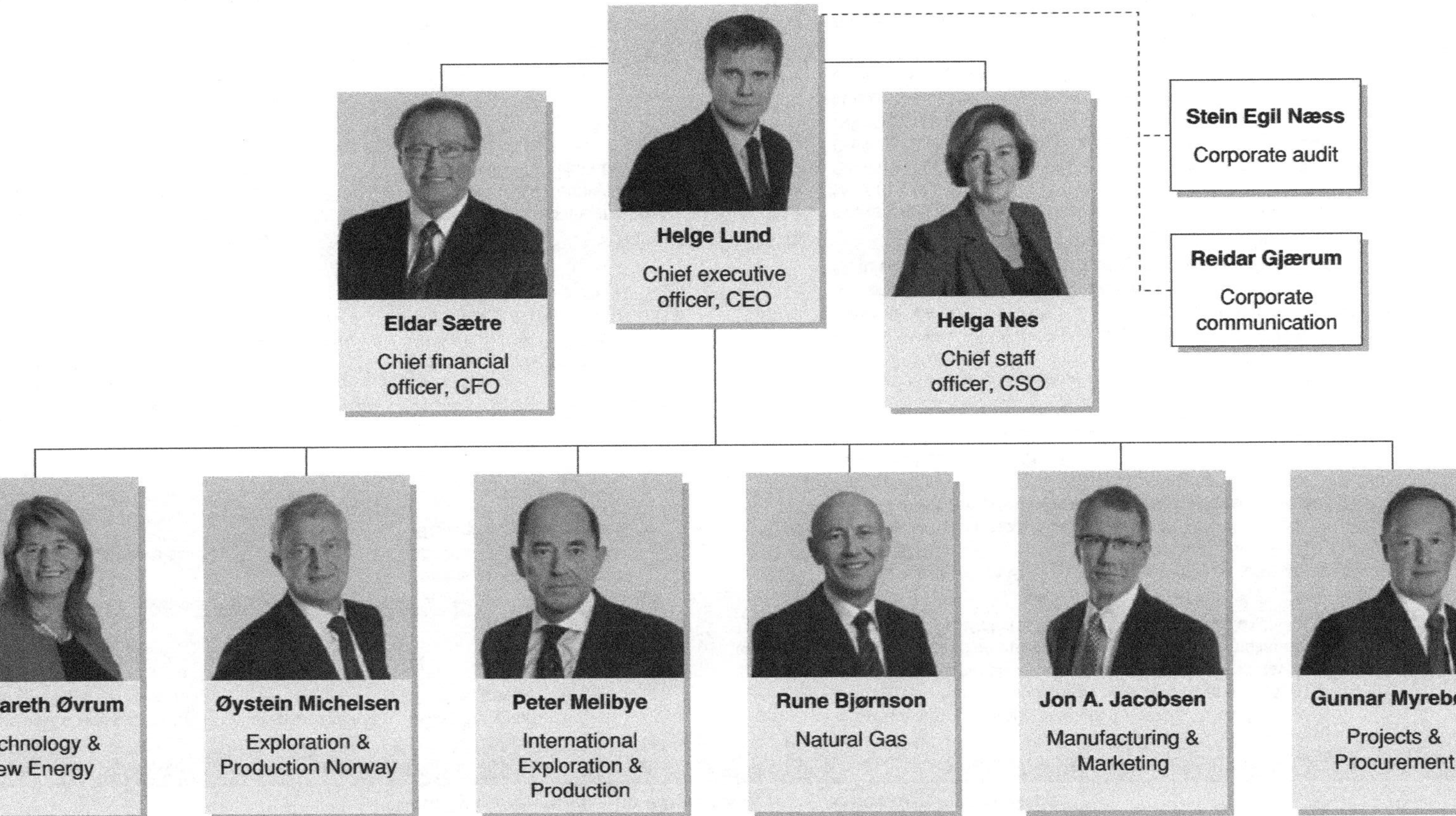

Exhibit 2 Ambition-to-Action example – Statoil Corporation

Globally competitive – an exceptional place to perform and develop

Strategic objectives	Performance indicators	Actions (top 5)
People and organisation		
A values-based and performance driven organisation	Living the values	Ensure a strong position in talent markets (31.12.2010)
Secure compliance and learning	P@S process	Build a global organisation and common processes (31.12.2010)
		Accelerate people and leadership performance and development (31.12.2010)
		Continued focus on ethics and anti-corruption compliance (31.12.2010)
		Prepare for the Statoil 2011 organisation (20.12.2010)
Health, safety and environment		
Industry leader in HSE	Serious incident frequency	Ensure active use of HSE risk management in all activities at all levels (01.10.2010)
Industry leader in carbon efficiency	Climate	Improve technical integrity at our plants (11.01.2011)
	TTS Observations and actions	Secure a working environment promoting health and well-being (31.12.2010)
		Make climate ambition and strategy operational in the short, medium and long time frame (31.12.2010)
		Analyse and learn from GOM accident and recommend actions (01.03.2011)
Operation		
Operational and functional excellence	PE EPN	Deliver Peregrino and Leismer Demo as well as a road-map for oilsands (31.12.2010)
Apply technology to create value	Production oe Statoil Share	Ensure successful NCS integration process and value capture (31.12.2010)
High quality and cost efficient project development	Production cost (NOK/boe)	Implement actions to reach NCS Production / PE target (31.12.2010)
	Finding cost exploration (USD/boe)	Implement fast-track approach to develop NCS resources (31.12.2010)
		Mature and add value to GoM paleogene resource base (31.12.2010)
Market		
Exploration success among the best in the industry	New resources (equity, mmboe)	Actively secure petroleum business activities in Northern areas of the NCS (31.12.2010)
Maximise value creation through our value chains	Reserves to DG3 (equity, mmboe)	Create opportunities from exploration strategy (31.12.2010)
Secure competitive long term value creation	Downstream NOI (NOK bn)	Drive communication and stakeholder dialogue to strengthen reputation (31.12.2010)
		Mature Shah Deniz value chain (31.12.2010)
		Optimise value from gas flexibility and contract modernisation (31.12.2010)
Finance		
Competitive shareholder return and profitability	Relative RoACE	Actively manage cash position and balance sheet (15.12.2010)
Realise the full potential from the merger	Relative Shareholder Return	Drive overall cost performance according to targets (31.12.2010)
Retain financial robustness		Mature relevant inorganic and restructuring opportunities such as Peregrino, Marcellus and Shakespeare (31.12.2010)

Exhibit 3 Relative Statoil performance

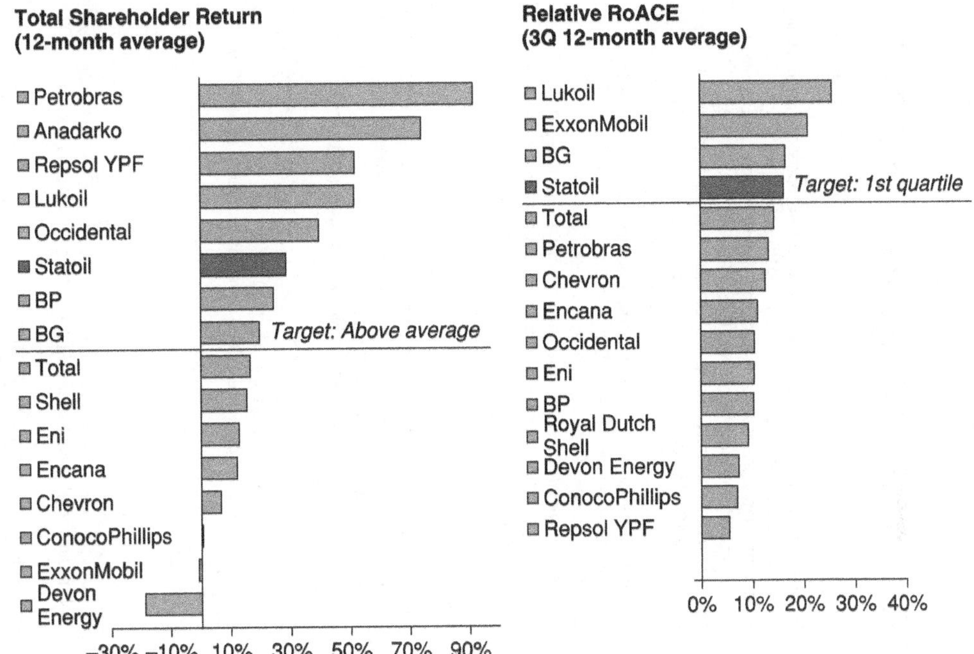

Exhibit 4 Ambition-to-Action example – Exploration & Production-Norway, Drilling & Well Organization (Level 3)

Professional delivery and innovation

Strategic objectives	Performance indicators		Actions (top 5)	
People and organisation				
Competitive edge through a value based and performance driven culture An efficient organisation with clear roles, responsibilities and best practice work processes	Indicator for safe and efficient operations Manning on/offshore People@Statoil process	(+) ⇨ (+) ⇨ (+) ⇨	Actively use the P@S-process for development, deployment and reward (30.11.2010) Ensure alignment with the standardized operational model and secure safe, compliant and efficient operations (30.11.2010) Further develop a professional relationship with the unions and together ensure a good working environment (30.11.2010) Optimize organisational competence, capacity and flexibility (30.11.2010) Prioritize leadership- and leadership team development in EPN (10.12.2010)	(+) (+) (+) (!) (+)
Health, safety and environment				
Prevent unintentional discharges to sea and reduce the environmental impact of any environmental incidents Secure a working environment that promotes well-being and good health Strengthen risk management in order to achieve an high HSE level	TRIF Accidental oil spills Accidental spills other Well control incidents SIF Falling objects	(−) ⬊ (−) ⇨ (−) ⬈ (−) ⇨ (−) ⬊ (!) ⬈	Strengthen HSE culture, risk management and compliance (31.12.2010) Total risk assessment in D&W (30.09.2010) Verification of well control equipment (15.11.2010) Ensure satisfying technical integrity of our facilities (31.12.2010) Risk management of safety issues focusing on prevention of incidents related to crane and lifting operations and Falling Objects (31.12.2010)	(+) (!) (+) (+) (+)
Operation				
Develop D&W to a competent supplier of drilling and well solutions by utilising our values and talents to the full potential	Production EPN – SØA Rig availability Ops(f) Total Drilling Performance m/day Intervention success Completion success	(−) ⬊ (+) ⬈ (−) ⬈ (−) ⬈ (+) ⬈ (+) ⬈	Assessment of 2011 – wells (15.10.2010) Business units to analyze the high level of downtime (30.09.2010) Risk- and contingency planning with management involvement (30.05.2010) ✓ Performance management through measurement, daily/weekly target setting and accountability (A-standard) (30.09.2010) Defined customer–supplier relationships with mutual clarification of expectations (31.12.2010)	(!) (!) (+) (!) (+)
Market				
Environmental relations: D&W will be presented as an efficient vendor of wells. Reputation – develop a good reputation.	Number of new wells	(−) ⇨	Customer and supplier meetings (30.06.2010) IOR potential – D&W proactive in idea development phase of AMAP (VC) (30.11.2010)	(+) (+)
Finance				
More for less	Total cost ex rig rate per meter Variance cost and time new wells	(−) ⬊ (−) ⬊	D&W reduce total spending by 3 BNOK – BU's to propose concept (01.12.2010) Initiate inventory project (01.10.2010) ✓	(!) (!)

Exhibit 5 Ambition-to-Action example – Projects & Procurement (Level 2)

Building for Tomorrow. Together.

Strategic objectives	Performance indicators	Actions (top 5)
People and organisation		
PRO Leadership implemented and demonstrated through a commercial mindset and culture A value-based and performance-driven organisation	Deployment GPS Living our values P@S process	Strategic workforce planning – operational people and competence strategy (30.06.2010) Increase quality in project deployment (30.06.2010) Evaluation of future manning needs and priorities (30.04.2010) Improve quality of P@S process, clarify and implement roles and responsibilities (30.12.2010) Increase quality of project teams (30.09.2010)
Health, safety and environment		
Industry Leader in HSE PRO Leadership implemented and demonstrated through HSE top performance in operational line	Serious Incident Frequency SIF benchmark – projects TRIF benchmark – projects	Improve work processes and establish standard A for HSE management in projects (01.12.2010) Secure a working environment promoting health and well-being (30.10.2010) Ensure active use of HSE risk management in all activities at all levels (01.12.2010) Implementation of revised HSE requirements in procurement (01.10.2010) Stimulate energy optimization prior to DG2/3 (01.10.2010)
Operation		
Implemented platform for compliance, standardisation and industrialisation Successful completion of projects	Estimate development Estimate Development Benchmark Main milestones Mitigating red risks Progress benchmark	PEOPS (01.12.2010) Sheringham Shoal contingency plan (30.09.2010) Sheringham Shoal Schedule Risk Analysis (31.08.2010) ✓ Frame agreements (01.06.2010) Top 10 risk register 2010 (15.12.2010)
Market		
Best value for Statoil in a global supplier market A professional and commercially oriented project provider	Customer Satisfaction	Define expectations and content of PEOPS discussions in PRO MC (30.04.2010) ✓ Establish a structured interaction between PRO and the customers (12/31/2010) Execute PEOPS improvement program (12/31/2010)
Finance		
Top 30% performer among peers within projects and procurement	Estimate development – early phase. DG2 → DG3 Procurement synergy impact PSR Strategic rig capacity vs license committed capacity Value Capture	Enforce commercial mindset in PRO (01.03.2010)

Exhibit 6 Ambition-to-Action example – Projects & Procurement, Sheringham Shoal (Level 4) (Offshore Wind)

Sheringham Shoal: Creating sustainable energy and shaping the future

Strategic objectives	Performance indicators	Actions (top 5)
People and organisation		
A project organisation known for open, friendly and truthful communication	Work environment survey	Execute self assessment of working environment within project team (31.12.2010)
Develop wind farm competence through project execution		Two teambuildings yearly (31.12.2011)
Health, safety and environment		
Zero harm to people and environment	SIF	HSE Program and HSE Activity list (31.12.2011)
	Harmful discharge to sea	Establish and follow up Authority plan (31.12.2011)
	TRIF	HSE reviews and monitoring plan (31.12.2011)
		Dropped objects campaign (31.12.2011)
		HSE training (VC) (01.03.2011)
Operation		
Pursuing opportunities, ensuring predictable results	Estimate Development	Top 10 risk register (31.03.2012)
Combine Statoil's offshore experience with best practise from the wind industry	Main milestones	Target cost actions (31.03.2012)
	Progress	
Market		
Develop stakeholder relations	Claims from contractors	Monitor interface register and avoid delay to agreed dates (31.12.2011)
Pursue cost reduction and optimisation opportunities	Timely consent approval	Timely closing of Variation orders (31.12.2011)
Finance		
Build cost awareness throughout the entire value chain	SOX Compliance	Execute SOX self assessment yearly (31.03.2012)

Exhibit 7 The 12 principles of beyond budgeting

Change in leadership	Change in processes
1. **Values** – Govern through a few clear values, goals, and boundaries, **not** *detailed rules and budgets.*	7. **Goals** – Set relative goals for continuous improvement, **don't** *negotiate fixed performance contracts.*
2. **Performance** – Create a high performance climate based on relative success, **not** *on meeting fixed targets.*	8. **Rewards** – Reward shared success based on relative performance, **not** *on meeting fixed targets.*
3. **Transparency** – Promote open information for self-management, **don't** *restrict it hierarchically.*	9. **Planning** – Make planning a continuous and inclusive process, **not** *a top-down annual event.*
4. **Organization** – Organize as a network of lean, accountable teams, **not** *around centralized functions.*	10. **Coordination** – Coordinate interactions dynamically, **not** *through annual planning cycles.*
5. **Autonomy** – Give teams the freedom and capability to act; **don't** *micro-manage them.*	11. **Resources** – Make resources available as needed, **not** *through annual budget allocations.*
6. **Customers** – Focus everyone on improving customer outcomes, **not** *on hierarchical relationships.*	12. **Controls** – Base controls on relative indicators and trends, **not** *on variances against plan.*

Exhibit 8 A pictorial representation of the Ambition-to-Action process

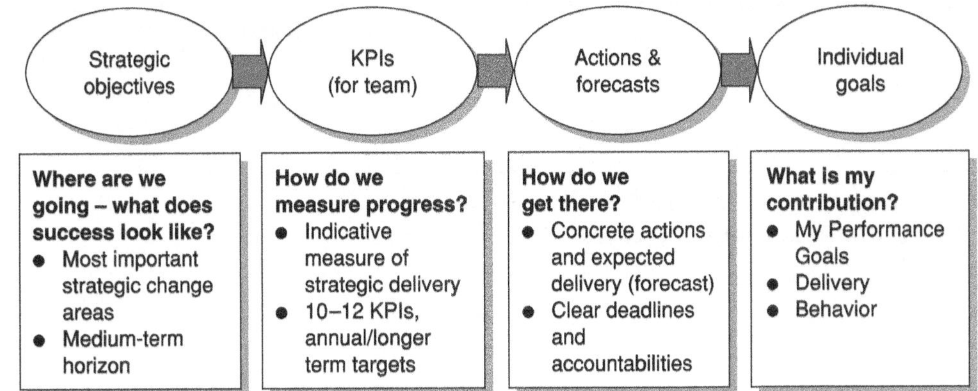

Strategic objectives
KPIs (for team)
Actions & forecasts
Individual goals
Where are we going – what does success look like?
• Most important strategic change areas
• Medium-term horizon
How do we measure progress?
• Indicative measure of strategic delivery
• 10–12 KPIs, annual/longer term targets
How do we get there?
• Concrete actions and expected delivery (forecast)
• Clear deadlines and accountabilities
What is my contribution?
• My Performance Goals
• Delivery
• Behavior

Exhibit 9 Summary – "a *systematic* change of the *whole* process"

	"Annual command and control"		*More dynamic & flexible* *A new performance language*
Target setting	• Equal to plan – "what we can deliver" • KPI targets • Absolute targets	⇨	• Aspiration driven – "what we must deliver". Targets before plan • "Ambition-to-Action" • Relative targets
Planning	• Plan = target, forecast and resource allocation • Gaps vs. targets hidden • One outcome only • Very detailed	⇨	• Plan = forecast only (actions and *expected* performance) • Gaps vs. targets visible • Main uncertainty spans • Less detailed
Resource allocation	• Annual pre-allocation through budgets • Budgets "an entitlement – my money"	⇨	• Resources available when needed, but within KPI targets + mandates + decision criteria. Monitoring of development
Business reporting	• Backward looking • Variance vs. YTD budget	⇨	• Forward looking • Forecast vs. targets, and actions to close gaps
Evaluation/rewards	• Only based on budgets and KPIs	⇨	• A broader evaluation: "Ambition to action" + Behavior

---

This case was prepared by Professor Kenneth A. Merchant and Wim A. Van der Stede.

CHAPTER 12
Using Financial Results Controls in the Presence of Uncontrollable Factors

The effects of unpredictable, uncontrollable events have been ubiquitous following the 2008–2009 financial crisis that caused widespread volatility and wreaked havoc on strategies, decisions, and business plans far beyond the bankers' wood-paneled offices on Wall Street or London's City. But there are many other examples, just to mention some:

- The closure of most of the airspace over Europe for several days in mid-April 2010 on concerns that ash from the Eyjafjallajokull volcano in Iceland could damage aircraft engines also spread far and wide, like the ash, to affect a variety of economies, sectors, and businesses. Airplanes were grounded, which severely disrupted businesses not just in the airline industry, but also in tourism, deliveries, supplies, and so forth.
- Then, a few days later, came the Macondo oil well blowout in the Gulf of Mexico, also known as the BP or Deepwater Horizon oil spill, and the temporary offshore drilling moratorium that was imposed because of it. This severely impacted not only BP, but also the entire oil industry and related sectors as knock-on effects became apparent.
- In March 2011, the Fukushima nuclear disaster in Japan caused Germany to shutter its nuclear reactors, casting a dark cloud over the future of Japan's nuclear fuel industry and, indeed, many other countries' nuclear fuel ambitions and plans.[1]
- In October 2012, Hurricane Sandy, the deadliest and most destructive hurricane of the then Atlantic hurricane season, and the second-costliest hurricane in US history, significantly disrupted business, leaving insurers and re-insurers with a bill of over $25 billion.[2]
- In July 2014, still reeling from the disappearance of flight MH370 in March, Malaysia Airlines received news of another flight, MH17, crashing in Ukraine. An unprecedented two crashes of the same airline in the span of four months – a tragedy without comparison. Malaysia Airlines is still flying but struggling to survive because, regardless of fault, customers deserted the airline.[3]
- The Ebola outbreak in West Africa in the summer of 2014, which was not contained until late 2015, hit many African economies where they were most vulnerable – the tourism industry – as travelers reconsidered trips to popular destinations as far away from the Ebola-struck countries as Kenya and South Africa.[4]
- And then there was the tumbling of the oil price by more than a third in 2015 extending a drop by half in 2014, which changed just about any plan of any economy and business that depended on oil in some nontrivial way.

And the list goes on. Business is rife with uncontrollables; events that could not have been predicted with reasonable confidence or accuracy in terms of either their likelihood, timing, impact, or magnitude.

Against this backdrop, consider the following, rather less significant, situation. The manager of a hi-tech subsidiary of a medium-sized, publicly traded firm was asked to grow annual sales and profit by 20% during the upcoming fiscal year. After the budget was prepared, however, a large client-company that was projected to buy more than 15% of total output from the subsidiary faced financial difficulty and, later in the year, went out of business. As a consequence, the subsidiary's actual performance was flat, and the subsidiary missed its budget target by a substantial margin. Almost everyone familiar with the situation agreed that, although bankruptcy is a common occurrence in fast-growing, hi-tech industries, it was virtually impossible to forecast at budget time that this customer would have gone out of business as quickly as it did. (Actually, several of the events mentioned above cause firms, and not just those in the industries directly affected, to go out of business in a short period of time, which are the ripple effects through which the turmoil spreads. For example, "one Thai insurance company that had booked a trip to Cape Town to reward its biggest earners canceled the trip for 1,500 people," said Barry Hurter, the chief executive of South Africa's ERM Tours, which runs excursions that include safaris and corporate retreats.)[5] Should you expect the subsidiary manager to have had a contingency plan for such occurrences? Should the subsidiary manager be held accountable for not meeting the budget target? Would you forgive this subsidiary manager for the poor performance? Would that forgiveness include allowing the subsidiary manager to keep this job? Earn a salary increase? Collect a bonus?

If one adheres to the *controllability principle* in a strict sense, one would give the subsidiary manager in this situation all, or most, of the eligible rewards. The results shortfall was not the subsidiary manager's fault. The controllability principle, which was introduced in Chapter 2, states that employees should be held accountable only for what they control. A measure is totally controllable by an employee if it is affected only by the employee's actions or decisions. The logic behind the controllability principle is obvious: Employees should not be penalized for bad luck. Nor should they be given rewards for mere good luck.

To implement the controllability principle, performance evaluators can reduce, and sometimes even eliminate, some of the distorting effects of uncontrollable factors on measured performance. This chapter discusses several ways in which this can be done. Use of such distortion-reducing procedures is rarely unproblematic, however. Many important results measures, particularly at managerial levels in an organization, are only *partially* uncontrollable. Even though the measures are affected by occurrences outside the managers' control, such as supply shortages, changing cost factors, competitors' actions, or even business calamities, managers can take actions to *react* to these factors to try to mitigate their impact on the results measures. If managers are protected against the uncontrollables, they might not be motivated to wield the influence they have or could have. Moreover, even when it is clear that a given factor is largely uncontrollable, the extent of the distortion in the results measures because of it is often difficult to estimate. Combined, then, organizations must determine both whether and to which extent they should adjust the results measures for the influence of uncontrollable factors.

Dealing with the effects of uncontrollable factors is also prone to misjudgments. Organizations sometimes fail to protect managers from the effects of uncontrollable factors when they should be protected; and sometimes they do protect them when they should not. Sometimes the protections that are provided are ill-conceived. If judgments about how to deal with uncontrollables are not made correctly, the advantages of results controls will be diminished, and potentially serious morale problems can arise from poor results-based performance evaluations.

In the following sections, we discuss the problem of evaluating performance when measures are affected by uncontrollable factors. It presents the basic rationale for the controllability principle and describes the types of uncontrollable factors that can be faced. It then discusses the various methods organizations can use to implement the controllability principle and the applicability, advantages, and disadvantages of each of the methods.

The controllability principle

Several related arguments explain why employees should not be asked to bear uncontrollable business risks. Organizations that hold employees accountable for uncontrollable factors bear the costs of doing so because the vast majority of employees are *risk averse*; that is, employees prefer that their performance-contingent rewards stem directly from their efforts and not be affected by the vagaries of uncontrollables.

To illustrate risk aversion, assume the following two compensation contracts. The first provides a fixed salary of €100,000 per year. The second provides an opportunity to earn €200,000 if a performance target is met, and all involved agree that the likelihood of meeting the target is 50%. If the target is not achieved, however, there will be no compensation. The expected value of both contracts is €100,000, but most people will choose the fixed salary, the guarantee of €100,000 because they do not want to bear the risk of earning nothing.

People's degrees of risk aversion vary with personal and various other characteristics such as career type and stage. Although it is hard to generalize, sales and marketing personnel perhaps are, or are said to be, relatively more risk tolerant than are accounting and finance personnel, who are said or believed to be more prudent and who may have self-selected into accounting, auditing, and control-related jobs because of that trait. For salespeople, on the other hand, accepting to work on commission rather than salary may be some indicator of their relative risk tolerance. Compared to mid-career colleagues, say, employees at the start of their career – who still can recover from a job mishap if it were to happen, and who may have no dependents to provide for, no mortgage payments, or other major financial commitments yet – are more likely to tolerate more risk or even seek risk, depending on their personality and ambitions. So, too, are people at the other end of their career, who may have become independently wealthy through years of hard work and strong earnings power, although for them reputation concerns are still likely to affect their attitudes toward risk.

The extent of a person's risk aversion can be assessed by varying the parameters in the earlier example. For example, if the amount of the salary guarantee was lowered to €90,000, some relatively risk-tolerant (less risk-averse) people would be tempted enough by the higher expected value of compensation of the performance-contingent alternative (€100,000) that they would be willing to take the 50% risk of earning nothing. If the salary guarantee was lowered to €80,000, another group of people would be willing to take the risk. But the key point is that employees, on average, cannot be taken to be risk neutral.

Risk aversion is the basis for the primary argument supporting the controllability principle. Firms that hold risk-averse employees accountable for the effects of factors they cannot completely control will bear some costs of doing so. First, to compensate for the risk, firms will have to provide risk-bearing employees with a higher expected value of compensation. If they fail to do so, the firms will bear some costs in alternate forms, such as an inability to hire talented employees, a loss of motivation from their employees, and, probably eventually, turnover.

Second, firms holding employees accountable for uncontrollables will bear the costs of some employee behaviors that seek to lower their exposure to uncontrollable factors, possibly at the expense of firm value. Employees may fail to develop or implement ideas for investments that are in the firm's best interest but that involve some risk. They may also engage in gameplaying behaviors, such as managing earnings or creating budgetary slack, to protect themselves against the effects of the uncontrollable factors.

Third, firms may bear the cost of lost time, as employees whose performances are evaluated in terms of measures that are distorted by uncontrollable influences are prone to develop excuses. They will spend time arguing about the extent of the distortions, at the expense of doing their jobs. The scheming, discussions, and "politicking" are not only unwelcome, but they may trigger needless job-related stress and tension.

To a feasible extent, then, business risks should essentially be left with the business owners. Owners are better able to bear the risk as investors or because they have chosen to do so by virtue of being entrepreneurs. Unlike employees, owner-investors can diversify risk in their investment portfolios. Owner-entrepreneurs' rewards stem directly from the risk-bearing function they perform, and choose to perform, as their fortunes go up and down with the success or failure of the business.

Types of uncontrollable factors

Before describing the methods managers can use to control for the distorting effects of uncontrollable factors, it is useful to categorize the types of factors that can be, to a greater or lesser extent, uncontrollable by management. They include (1) economic and competitive factors, (2) *force majeure*, and (3) interdependencies.

The first uncontrollable factor includes a broad range of *economic and competitive factors* that affect one or more results measures. One important results measure – profit – is affected by many factors that change: consumer demand, product/service prices, and/or the costs of doing business (factor costs). Among the factors that affect consumer demand and prices are business cycles, competitor actions, changing customer tastes, customer boycotts, changing laws and regulations, and foreign exchange rates. Among the factors that affect costs are the supply and demand of raw materials, labor and capital, foreign exchange rates, regulations, and taxes. Virtually every other results measure also can be affected by multiple, uncontrollable economic and competitive factors. For example, company stock prices are affected by market cycles, rumors and investor tastes, or even moods. On-time delivery measures can be adversely affected by supply shortages and changing customer demands. Customer satisfaction measures can be affected by, among other things, the quality of the products and services provided by competitors or the arrival of an online competitor with quite a different business model to essentially meet the same customer need.[6]

Changes in economic and competitive factors are difficult for performance evaluators to deal with because, although most of these factors appear to be uncontrollable, managers can and should usually make responses to these changes to positively influence the results measures. When raw material prices increase, managers can consider substituting alternate materials. When the cost of capital increases, they can consider delaying capital investments and reducing inventories. When exchange rates change, they can consider sourcing or selling in different countries. When customer tastes change, they can alter their product design or change their marketing strategy. Indeed, responses such as these are a key part of being a *manager*. As a consequence, most evaluators do not buffer managers from changes in economic and competitive factors, although they might take steps to have the organization share some of the risk with the managers, such as by corporate hedging to try to mitigate fluctuations in raw material prices.

A second type of uncontrollable factors includes unpredictable and abnormally severe events caused by natural or other forces, commonly referred to as *force majeure* (or *act of nature* and *act of God*, although with varying meanings and interpretations under different systems of law). Such "major forces" are large, unexpected, one-off uncontrollable events such as hurricanes, earthquakes, floods, riots, terrorist attacks, key executive deaths, and, if they are not caused by negligence, fires, accidents, major installation breakdowns, thefts, and so on. Most acts of nature involve negative surprises, but positive surprises sometimes also occur. For example, while hurricanes and other natural calamities can destroy many businesses (and business plans) in their path, they create opportunities for others, such as construction firms, manufacturers of power generators and drywall, and self-storage companies[7] as well as insurance companies.[8] And while severe weather can keep airplanes grounded at a huge cost in lost business and subsequent damages, they boost hotel bookings in the airport's vicinity. Similarly, while the above-mentioned volcanic ash cloud grounded airlines, P&O cross-Channel ferries and Eurostar trains were fully booked, and a group of businesspeople paid a taxi driver £700 to take them from Belfast to London after they became stranded.[9]

Many organizations are inclined to protect employees from the downside risks caused by *force majeure*, but only if the events are deemed to be clearly uncontrollable and if steps are taken by the managers to recover from the adversity as expeditiously as possible. Moreover, in some cases, controllability itself is at question, as controversy can develop over the cause of, say, fires, accidents, breakdowns, or thefts. Also potentially contentious is the extent to which a manager could have reduced exposure to these effects by purchasing insurance protection or other risk-transfer solutions.

Even some of the most unprecedented, uncontrollable events, such as the 9/11 terrorist attacks on the United States, needed an immediate response from management. Within days of the attacks, Boeing Company, the aerospace giant, scaled back production in its commercial airplanes unit while planning for faster growth in defense-related units. Similarly, Bill Marriott, chairman and chief executive of Marriott International, a global hotel group, made his first cost-cutting decision on the afternoon of September 11 by canceling the firm's advertising based on the expectation that panicked customers were going to have fear of flying and would stay away from hotels in droves for at least several weeks.[10] Similarly, many companies are investing heavily to protect themselves from the effects of weather. Better forecasts and better scenario planning helped insurer Swiss Re to spread its risk better and FedEx to route its planes more robustly to deliver packages with minimal delays.[11] These examples illustrate clearly that managers must *respond* even when mostly uncontrollable events happen. While the events themselves are uncontrollable, managers have *influence* over the effects that will be felt, and good managers should be expected to respond to the best of their abilities.

A third and quite different type of uncontrollable factor is caused by *interdependence*. Interdependence signifies that an entity is not completely self-contained, causing the measured results of the entity to be affected by other entities within the organization. Interdependencies can be pooled, sequential, or reciprocal.

Pooled interdependencies exist where an organization's entities use common resources or resource pools, such as shared staff or facilities (e.g. shared human resources support, shared research, and development). Pooled interdependencies raise the question whether managers should be put at risk for the poor performance of shared resource pools, such as corporate staff activities on which they must rely. In many large firms, managers in the resource-dependent entities are protected from cost increases by the terms of an annual contract, negotiated during the annual planning process, which stipulates the services to be provided and their costs. The expected costs are impounded in a fixed allocation rate, and unexpected rate increases cannot be passed on to internal customers until the next contract negotiation. But they are not necessarily protected from the poor performance of the shared activity.

Sequential interdependencies exist when the outputs of one entity are the inputs of another entity. Organizations that are high in sequential interdependence are vertically integrated firms, such as paper and steel companies. *Reciprocal interdependencies* are bidirectional sequential interdependencies. That is, organizational entities both produce outputs used by other entities and use inputs from them. Reciprocal interdependencies are high in some related-diversified firms. Most corporations deal with both sequential and reciprocal interdependencies by setting up internal *transfer pricing* systems that try to approximate the conditions found in external markets. These systems, which we discussed in Chapter 7, make these interdependencies act much like the economic and competitive uncontrollables described above, and evaluators then can deal with them in much the same way.

Another type of interdependency stems from *interventions from higher-level management*. Higher-level managers can force a decision on an entity manager and, in so doing, significantly affect a results measure linked to one or more forms of rewards. For example, corporate managers might order a division to sell to a particular customer at a money-losing price in return for other benefits that will accrue to other entities in the firm. Corporate managers can also affect results measures simply by not approving decisions initiated by an entity manager. They might not approve a proposed expenditure or a production schedule change. If these decisions are imposed on the entity managers, some organizations will make an adjustment for such arguably uncontrollable interventions. Others, however, argue that these interventions are not always totally uncontrollable. The entity managers might be involved in the discussions leading up to the decision and should, therefore, be held responsible for the effects of the negotiations and deliberations with their corporate superiors over which they could be expected to have had some influence.

Controlling for the distorting effects of uncontrollables

Managers can reduce (and sometimes even eliminate) some of the distorting effects of some of these uncontrollable factors by using either or both of two complementary approaches. *Before* the measurement period begins, they can define the results measures to include only those items that employees can control or at least only those items over which they have significant influence. *After* the measurement period has ended, they can calculate (or estimate) and adjust for the effects of any remaining uncontrollable factors using techniques such as variance analysis, flexible budgeting, relative performance evaluations, or subjective performance assessments. Both of these methods of controlling for the effects of uncontrollable factors have costs. These costs must be balanced against the benefits of reducing the risks employees must bear.

Controlling for uncontrollables *before* the measurement period

Two primary methods can be employed to control for uncontrollables before the measurement period: purchasing insurance and design of responsibility structures.

Insurance

Many uncontrollable events, such as physical damage to company assets, employee-caused damage, product liability suits, employee errors and misappropriations, riots, and vandalism, are insurable. A detailed discussion of insurance generally, and insurable events and insurance policies specifically, is outside the scope of this text. However, the key concept underlying insurance is that the company (the insured party) accepts a known relatively small "loss" (cost) in the form of a regular payment in exchange for being covered by the insurer for possibly large (although relatively unlikely) losses. Insurance might, therefore, be especially pertinent for what are sometimes called "low frequency – high impact" events. As such, the key benefit from purchasing insurance derives from a transfer of risk from the insured to the insurer.

Responsibility structures

The controllability principle underlies most of the logic guiding the design of responsibility structures. In Chapter 7 on financial responsibility structures, we presented a key concept in the design of responsibility centers, which is but a slight modification of the controllability principle: *Hold employees accountable for the performance areas that management wants them to pay attention to.*

Table 12.1 Entity income statement broken down by controllable and non-controllable items

	$
Sales	xxx
Less: variable costs	(xxx)
Sales margin	xxx
Less: controllable division expenses	(xxx)
Controllable profit	xxx
Less: non-controllable division expenses	(xxx)
Less: allocations of central expenses	(xxx)
NET PROFIT	xxx

This general concept is widely applied. Organizations do not hold salespeople or production managers accountable for the results of corporate financing or major asset acquisition decisions. There is no need for these managers to pay attention to these decisions that clearly fall outside of their purview, and thus outside of their control.

Performance reports often separate controllable from uncontrollable items. As an illustration, Table 12.1 shows such an itemized performance report with four profit measures. A control system built on this report would hold the profit center manager responsible for *controllable profit*. Everything below the controllable profit line is deemed to be uncontrollable by that manager. In other words, companies thus aim to "match" an entity manager's *scope of decision authority* with the line item for which they hold the entity manager accountable.

But are the items below the controllable profit line really uncontrollable? Maybe not entirely, thus raising the issue: When should managers be expected to pay attention to things over which they have less than complete control? In other words, can there be grounds for charging entity managers with the effects of corporate financing decisions or corporate research and development (R&D)? Assigning them the costs as a line item on their entity's budget or profit-and-loss statement would, in effect, hold them accountable for that line item. If these managers are not involved in the corporate decisions regarding financing and R&D, say, and if there is no need for them to be aware of how much the corporation is spending on interest expense or R&D, then there is no need to assign them a share of those costs.

As an alternative example, should entity managers be assigned a share of corporate administrative (overhead) costs, such as those incurred in the corporate personnel and information systems departments? Here, the answer may be yes. Charging these costs is likely to empower the entity managers to challenge the size of the costs and the quantity or quality of the services rendered in exchange for the costs. In other words, allocating these overhead costs to the entities will stimulate the entity managers to put pressure on the corporate overhead departments to control service costs and to provide "competitive" services. These charges, however, violate the strict controllability principle, but they are consistent with the rule presented above; that is, to hold managers accountable for the performance areas you want them to pay attention to. You want them to exercise some *influence* even though they have less than direct control over these areas.

When employees are held accountable for many performance areas over which they have little influence, the organization will bear the increased costs of making employees bear the risk. At some point, these costs outweigh the benefits. As such, this approach is bounded by the limits of holding employees accountable for *too many* things over which they have *too little* influence.

Controlling for uncontrollables *after* the measurement period

Removing the distorting effects of uncontrollable factors from the results measures can also be attempted *after* the measurement period (but before the assignment of rewards). This can sometimes be done *objectively* (through numerical calculation) using variance analysis, flexible performance standards, or relative performance evaluations. Alternatively, it can be done *subjectively* through exercising evaluator judgment. There are benefits and costs to each approach.

Variance analysis

In MCS applications, variance analysis is a systematic approach or method designed to explain why actual results differ from predetermined standards, budgets, or expectations. They can help segregate controllable from uncontrollable variances and help explain who should be held accountable for the controllable variances, which are either positive (favorable) or negative (unfavorable) variances.

Variance analysis techniques as applied to manufacturing operations are described in great detail in every cost accounting textbook. To explain why actual manufacturing costs are different from standards, variance analysis distinguishes material, labor, and overhead cost variances and then breaks each down into price, mix, yield, volume, and potentially other variance components. (Most cost accounting textbooks explain these variances, and the formulas for calculating them, in great detail.)[12] The variance analysis technique can be usefully applied to many settings other than production, however, as it essentially involves varying one performance factor at a time from expected to actual levels within a computational model to see what caused overall actual performance to differ from expected performance.

As an illustration, Table 12.2 shows how variance analysis can be applied to a sales territory in a foreign country. Assume that managers have determined that sales are largely dependent on four factors (industry volume, market share, price in local currency, and the currency exchange rate), and so they prepare a sales plan (a model) based on estimates of each of these factors. At the end of the measurement period, almost inevitably, actual sales will be different from the plan. An analysis such as that shown in Table 12.2 can then be developed to understand the bases of the sales variances.

The original sales plan is reflected in the left-hand column of Figure 12.2, which shows the planned or budgeted value for each of the key factors. The first analysis involves changing one of

Table 12.2 Application of variance analysis to a sales entity

Sales plan	Actual Ind. Vol.	Actual MS	Actual Price	Actual Ex. Rate
Expected industry volume (IV_B)	**IV_A**	IV_A	IV_A	IV_A
Planned market share (MS_B)	MS_B	**MS_A**	MS_A	MS_A
Planned price (local currency) (PLC_B)	PLC_B	PLC_B	**PLC_A**	PLC_A
Planned foreign exchange rate (FX_B)	FX_B	FX_B	FX_B	**FX_A**
	Ind. Vol. Variance	Market Share Variance	Sales Price Variance	Exchange Rate Variance

A = actual
B = expected, planned, or budgeted

the factors from the planned to the actual value. Figure 12.2 separates the effect of industry volume first.[13] The difference between the sales plan and the amount shown using actual industry volume is the *industry volume variance*. The second analysis changes a second factor, here market share, from the planned to the actual value, while holding the previously changed value (industry volume) at actual. This identifies a *market share variance*. This process continues for each of the remaining two factors, identifying a *sales price variance* and an *exchange rate variance*, respectively. The sum of the four variances will equal the total *sales variance* (the amount by which actual sales are different from the sales plan). This is illustrated with numbers in Table 12.3.

Variance analyses such as these separate uncontrollable from controllable factors in explaining the difference between actual and planned results. In this example, the industry volume and currency exchange variances would probably be considered uncontrollable, whereas the market share and price variances should be controllable by a sales entity manager. If that is the case, specific individuals (or groups of individuals) can be held accountable for the controllable variances; that is, in the above example, it is likely that the market share and price variances are deemed to fall within the responsibility of the sales entity. However, further analyses might show that the accountability for these variances should be shared with other departments or entities, such as engineering (product design) or production (production quality, schedule attainment) because there may have been scheduling or customization issues, say, which caused sales volumes to be lower than expected. The exchange rate variance might be the responsibility of the corporate finance function if this department is in charge of currency hedging. If not, this variance might be considered uncontrollable on the whole.

Table 12.3 Illustrating the Table 12.2 example with a set of numbers

Assume:
IV_b = 2 million
IV_a = 2.4 million
MS_b = 10%
MS_a = 8%
PLC_b = 0.90
PLC_a = 1.10
FX_b = 1 home currency: 1 foreign currency
FX_a = 1.2 home currency: 1 foreign currency

Sales (in home currency)
Planned = 180,000 (2m × 10% × 0.9 × 1)
Actual = 253,440 (2.4m × 8% × 1.1 × 1.2)
Total Sales Variance = 73,440 favorable

Variances (in home currency)

Industry volume variance = **36,000 favorable** (the plan called for 10% of 2m industry volume which turned out to be bigger at 2.4m, hence 200,000 vs. 240,000, or 40,000 units higher at the expected price of 0.9 = 36,000)

Market share variance = **43,200 unfavorable** (the budget assumed a 10% share of 2.4m, but the entity only achieved to obtain 8%, hence 240,000 vs. 192,000, or 48,000 units less at the expected price of 0.9 = 43,200)

Price variance = **38,400 favorable** (the budget expected to sell 192,000 units at a price of 0.9, but the entity managed to sell at a price of 1.1, hence the difference between 172,800 and 211,200, or 38,400)

Foreign exchange variance = **42,240 favorable** (the budget expected a 1:1 currency exchange of the entity's sales of 211,200 in foreign currency, but the home currency weakened to 1.2:1, hence a favorable currency translation of 42,240)

Flexible performance standards

Flexible performance standards, which we introduced in Chapter 8, can also be used to protect managers from the effects of uncontrollable factors. Flexible standards define the performance that employees are expected to achieve *given the actual conditions faced during the measurement period*. To refer to the example above, flexible performance standards might be made to vary with some of the pertinent uncontrollable factors – for example, the sales entity's budget would be "re-calculated" at the prevailing exchange rates rather than the initially expected exchange rates.

In this way, *flexible* (or "*re-calculated*") *budgets* can be particularly useful when there is a dominant input factor whose cost has changed beyond normal variations, such as due to, say, oil price fluctuations that materially affect factor costs. This situation is not descriptive of many industries, however. That is, even though production costs in many firms vary with, say, direct material cost, few production processes are dominantly dependent on any given material or input. Therefore, firms conventionally expect that managers will be able to manage or compensate unfavorable price movements for some materials against favorable price movements for some other materials. Or, if that is not the case, they expect that managers will be able to somehow mitigate the adverse effects of unfavorable price movements. That said, in periods where oil prices unexpectedly drop by more than half in a year, such as in 2014–2015, flexible budgets that re-calculate the plan at prices that better reflect the new reality can be useful and avoid frustration of managers held accountable against targets materially impacted by these factors, assuming that indeed they are largely uncontrollable and have fluctuated beyond normal ranges.

When environments are less predictable and managers wish to embed various assumptions about the future into their planning, they sometimes engage in what is called *contingency, scenario*, or *what-if* planning exercises. For example, some banks have set up contingency plans to account for the possibility of any nation exiting the European Union's common currency, the euro:

> **"We've been doing some contingency work to ensure that we have a robust system and ability to absorb shocks if on a Sunday night a sovereign decides to leave the euro," Carl Norrey from JPMorgan in London said – "the probability of a country exiting the euro is no longer zero."[14]**

General Electric also does extensive contingency planning around scenarios including the spread of the financial woes to more markets and the possibility of a breakup of the euro:

> **"We're putting in contingencies for everything we can think of," GE Capital Chief Executive Mike Neal said. "You'd be nutty today to have a large European business and not be gaming for something like that."[15]**

Similarly, Coca-Cola had contingency plans ready to adapt its World Cup sponsorship in Brazil if unrest and protests about the high level of spending on the World Cup compared with public services were to return to the streets:

> **"We hope there [will be] no unrest," Coke's Executive Vice President Joe Tripodi said from Atlanta. "But we recognize these things happen. You always have to be smart to have all kind of Plan Bs, Plan Cs and Ds to prepare for any contingency. And if certain things happen you might have to change [...] your marketing. [...] The world we live in now is full of disruption, frequent chaos and change all the time," he added. "So, as a company and as a brand if you are not prepared to respond, then you aren't going to survive."[16]**

Proponents of contingency planning maintain that it improves a company's ability to cope with (possibly radical) variations in key aspects that impact on the business, allows dealing with complex risk and control issues, and prepares to take pre-emptive action. In other words, it prepares organizations to respond to "known unknowns"—possible events that they are aware can happen or have a non-zero chance of occurring but whose impacts are hard to estimate with precision. As such, scenario planning provides another way to apply flexible performance standards. At the beginning of the measurement period, managers prepare plans for several reasonable scenarios. At the end of the period, managers are then held accountable for achieving the plan associated with the scenario that actually unfolds.[17]

However, drawing up plans for a range of scenarios is not costless, particularly when done frequently, such as for annual budgeting purposes. That said, and perhaps due to recent events that had become nearly unthinkable in living memory, such as the bankruptcy of major banks, "people are trying to move beyond historic notions that tail risk events are so infrequent on the one hand, and so extreme on the other hand, that there is nothing you can do about them," said Eugene Ludwig, founder of the Washington-based risk management firm Promontory Financial Group.[18]

Another way to make performance standards more flexible is simply to update them more frequently. Any time a performance standard is set, there is a chance that the assumptions underlying the preparation will prove to be inaccurate, rendering the standard obsolete. Obsolete standards subject managers to uncontrollable risks. Potential obsolescence is easy to see in a budgeting context. Budgets are prepared under the assumption of a given set of planning parameters, such as economic forecasts. The budget targets then remain fixed for the duration of the planning horizon (typically one year). The managers are at risk for all the *forecasting errors*; that is, they are asked to achieve their budget targets regardless of the conditions actually faced.[19] To mitigate this, firms might evaluate managers' performances monthly or quarterly (rather than annually) and then prepare an updated, hopefully more realistic, budget for the next month or quarter. *Rolling budgets* are an application of this approach, where there is a "constant" 12-month budget window even though it is updated each month or quarter by adding a month or quarter as each month or quarter passes. As such, the 12-month budget is "rolling forward" on a monthly or quarterly basis.

But updating standards more frequently is not a panacea, either. One problem is cost. Updating standards can be time-consuming depending on how elaborate the budget preparation process is. Measuring results in short time periods also creates some other potential problems. It is not always possible to determine in a short time period whether the results generated by some individuals, such as managers or research scientists, are good or bad. As such, the short time horizon may exacerbate the myopia problem by introducing even shorter "windows" or time horizons, as we discussed in Chapter 11.

Relative performance evaluations

Another method of protecting employees from the distorting effects of uncontrollable factors is by way of *relative performance evaluations* (RPE). RPE means that employees' performances are evaluated not in terms of the absolute levels of the results they generate, but in terms of their results relative to each other or relative to those of their closest outside competitors. For RPE to be effective, all parties in the comparison or *peer group* must be performing roughly the same tasks and/or face roughly the same sets of opportunities and constraints. These conditions are sometimes met in companies with numerous comparable entities, such as in banks with many like-branches and fast food chains with many like-restaurants.

Consider a pizza parlor example. When at one time the price of mozzarella cheese rose sharply, the increase caused a profit squeeze at virtually all pizza parlors because cheese accounts for nearly half of a pizza's cost, and pizza prices are roughly fixed. As a spokesman for Domino's Pizza put it, "customers are accustomed to 'three-digit pricing' – people buy lots more pizza at $9.99 than at $10.99."[20] Consequently, profits at virtually all pizza parlors fell sharply over this period. If the evaluations of the managers of pizza outlets were based on their achievements vis-à-vis pre-established targets, such as budget targets not flexed with the change in cheese prices (as discussed above), then all the managers would be evaluated as poor performers. If those evaluations were linked to rewards, then presumably, these managers' bonuses would be quite low, if not zero. But in this case, since all pizza outlets suffered the same uncontrollable shock, their performances can be compared relative to each other. As such, RPE would be an easy way for large pizza chains to adjust for the effects of this uncontrollable economic factor.

In most settings, however, good comparison groups do not exist, which may explain why RPE is not in widespread use, at least in a formal, objective sense. That said, the RPE *concept* often does influence subjective performance evaluations or justifications for target adjustments after the fact. Changes in targets with hindsight are often made with reference to *industry effects*. In a loose sense, this is RPE where the comparison group is the company's relevant industry. It is not *formal* RPE, however, in the sense that targets were not RPE-based in the original plan but rather adjusted *after the fact* in an arguably *discretionary* way to reflect unforeseen industry changes, which takes us to the next section.[21]

Subjective performance evaluations

Many *subjective performance evaluations* take into consideration all the logic embodied in the objective methods of adjusting for uncontrollables. However, instead of making a formal, numerical calculation, the evaluator makes a judgment as to whether the results generated reflect strong or poor performance. Proper subjective performance evaluations have undeniable advantages.[22] Most importantly, they can correct for flaws in the results measures. As we have seen in earlier chapters, particularly Chapters 2 and 7, results measures rarely reflect controllable performance completely and accurately. Therefore, a rigid linking of evaluations to results measures inevitably implies penalizing employees for bad luck and rewarding them for good luck. When adding judgment, evaluators can use both the results measures and their knowledge of the situations faced by the employees to evaluate whether they performed well in any given period.

Subjectivity in evaluations creates its own problems, however. First, in applying judgment, subjective evaluations vest a source of power in superiors over their subordinates, which may create tension and resentment.

Second, subjective evaluations are prone to biases.[23] One such bias is known as the *outcome effect*, where the evaluator's knowledge of other results influences the performance evaluations even though the results may *not* be informative of the evaluatee's performance.[24] Another possible bias is known as the *hindsight effect*, where evaluators with knowledge of results tend to assume information about the pre-result circumstances that was not available to those being evaluated when they faced the circumstances. In other words, hindsight effects arise when an evaluator sees events that have occurred as being more controllable then they were when they took place; that is, the bias arises from inaccurate assessments of reality *ex post facto*.[25] Thus, while subjectivity is intended to lower employees' reward-related risks, it can sometimes raise the risk of performance evaluations that are unfair, inconsistent, or biased.

Third, subjectivity often leads to inadequate, or perhaps even no, feedback about how performance was evaluated. This lack of feedback inhibits learning and mitigates the motivation of the evaluatee to improve performance in subsequent periods.

Fourth, even when the evaluations are fair, employees often do not understand or trust them. A mere perception of bias, whether accurate or not, can create morale and motivational problems. This is particularly salient when the evaluators *renege* on reward promises that were (presumably) made but not documented in writing.

Fifth, subjectivity often leads to creation of an *excuse culture*. Humans seem to have an inherent trait that causes them to make excuses for poor performance. This trait has been studied in psychology under the rubric of *attribution theory*, which maintains that individuals tend to attribute their success to their own efforts, abilities, skills, knowledge, or competence, while they attribute their failures to bad luck, task difficulty, or a variety of other external or situational factors at least partially out of their control. In other words, they tend to make excuses when things are not going well. In an excuse culture, instead of focusing on generating good results and being committed to achieving targets, employees spend considerable amounts of time making excuses and lobbying their evaluators for forgiveness of poor or mediocre results. They aim to beat the evaluation system rather than to work within it. These negotiation processes, as well as the appeal processes through which the employees often contest their performance evaluations, distract employees from the real tasks at hand.[26]

Finally, and as a consequence of many of the issues raised above, if they are done well, subjective performance evaluations can be expensive, especially in terms of the time committed by both the evaluators and evaluatees. Evaluators must often spend considerable time informing themselves about the circumstances their subordinates faced during the performance period. If performance targets were not reached, the evaluators must sift through considerable information that will enable them to separate legitimate reasons from excuses. If performance exceeds targets, they must assess whether good luck rather than effort explains the high performance, an exercise for which they are unlikely to receive much sympathy from the employees being evaluated. And, if the performance evaluations are rather negative, evaluators must be prepared for dealing with a fair dose of disgruntlement.

Other uncontrollable factor issues

Organizations face other issues when considering adjustments for uncontrollables. One is the *purpose* for which the adjustments are made. Uncontrollables should not be treated identically for all reward purposes. Evaluators are likely to be more forgiving or willing to give the benefit of the doubt for longer when considering job retention decisions. However, evaluators are likely much less forgiving and more resolute when considering annual incentive pay, such as when determining bonus amounts. If performance is down, organizations are less likely to have the financial resources to pay the bonus, so employees are asked to share the pain.

A second issue regards the *direction* of the adjustments. Most evaluators seem to adjust for uncontrollables after the measurement period *asymmetrically*; that is, they make their adjustments in one direction only: to protect the employees from suffering from bad luck, but not to protect the owners (shareholders) from paying out undeserved rewards for good luck. The evaluators find it difficult to deny rewards, particularly bonuses, to employees when the organization has done well. Moreover, the managers face no pressure to make downward adjustments in rewards for good luck because the employees do not raise the issue, while the owners (shareholders) probably are not aware of the issue. Even if they are aware, they are already benefiting from the good performance. So who is to complain?

Conclusion

The controllability principle, holding employees accountable only for what they can control, seems so simple, yet implementing it is far from unproblematic. There are many complications. Most results measures are only partially uncontrollable, and estimating the extent of uncontrollability is often less than an exact science. Moreover, organizations want employees to respond properly to many factors that influence the measures even if these factors are partially uncontrollable. As such, the controllability principle or, perhaps more accurately, the *influenceability principle* – hold employees accountable for what they can sufficiently influence – provides good general guidance.

When decisions are made to protect employees from the effects of uncontrollables, each of the methods for doing so involves tradeoffs. If the adjustments are made after the performance period has ended, some of the advantages of having fixed, preset performance standards will be lost. Adjustments that involve subjective judgments can create bias, inconsistency, and challenge. If complex procedures are implemented to deal with the many types of possible uncontrollable factors, simplicity is lost, raising the possibility that some employees will fail to understand what they are being asked to achieve. Regardless of the complexity, the stakes are high, as significant problems can arise if uncontrollables are not dealt with properly.

Notes

1 See, for example, "Fukushima Accident Has Ripple Effect in Worldwide Nuclear Industry," *The Asahi Shimbun* (November 26, 2013), online at fukushimaontheglobe.com/the_earthquake_and_the_nuclear_accident/3146.html.

2 See, for example, "Sandy's Insurance Bill Estimated at $25 Billion for Industry," *The Wall Street Journal* (January 3, 2013), online at on.wsj.com/ZYm7tq.

3 See, for example, "Can Malaysia Airlines Survive MH17 Disaster?" *The Guardian* (July 18, 2014), online at gu.com/p/4v3n2/stw; "Recovery Phase: Two Years after Flight MH370 Vanished Malaysia's Flag Carrier Is Still in Trouble," *The Economist* (April 2, 2016), online at econ.st/1ZNtdvB.

4 See, for example, "Ebola Virus Outbreak Threatens Africa's Tourist Industry," *The Wall Street Journal* (August 19, 2014), online at on.wsj.com/XxTp3e.

5 Ibid.

6 Depending on the nature of the new competition, this is sometimes called "disruptive innovation," a term coined by Harvard professor Clayton Christensen – see www.claytonchristensen.com/key-concepts (accessed January 2016).

7 "Sandy to Boost Construction Jobs as Rebuilding Spurred," *Bloomberg* (October 31, 2012), online at www.bloomberg.com/news/articles/2012-10-31/sandy-to-boost-construction-jobs-as-rebuilding-spurred.

8 "Natural Disasters Help Insurance Industry Grow in Asia," *South China Morning Post* (November 6, 2014), online at www.scmp.com/business/banking-finance/article/1349000/natural-disasters-help-insurance-industry-grow-asia.

9 "Volcanic Ash Keeps Flights across Europe Grounded," *The Guardian* (April 17, 2010), online at www.guardian.co.uk.

10 "Uncertainty, Inc.: CEOs Find There Is No Playbook for War and Ailing Economy," *The Wall Street Journal* (October 16, 2001), p. A1.

11 "Getting Ahead of the Weather," *Fortune* (February 7, 2005), pp. 87–94.

12 Variance analysis is covered in great detail in C. T. Horngren, S. M. Datar, and M. V. Rajan, *Cost Accounting: A Managerial Emphasis*, 15th ed. (Upper Saddle River, NJ: Prentice Hall, 2014).

13 The order in which the factors are analyzed is not important. The actual variance amounts may be slightly different because of the placement of what is referred to in some textbooks as the "joint variance." Regardless of the ordering, the total variance will be explained, and the magnitude of each of the variances will be indicative of the effect of that factor on the total.

14 "Euro Exit Risk Prompts JPMorgan to Set Up Contingency Plans," *Bloomberg* (July 25, 2012), online at www.bloomberg.com/news/articles/2012-07-25/euro-exit-risk-prompts-jpmorgan-to-set-up-contingency-plans-1-.

15 "GE: Best Approach for Continent Is to Pull Back," *The Wall Street Journal* (May 31, 2012), online at on.wsj.com/1AreQjz.

16 "Coca-Cola to Soften Marketing if Unrest Hits World Cup," *USA Today* (April 2, 2014), online at usat.ly/1igfOGf.

17 W. Van der Stede and T. Palermo, "Scenario Budgeting: Integrating Risk and Performance," *Finance & Management*, no. 184 (January 2011), pp. 10–13.

18 "Pimco Sells Black Swan Protection as Wall Street Markets Fear," *Bloomberg* (July 20, 2010), online at www.bloomberg.com/news/articles/2010-07-20/pimco-sells-black-swan-protection-as-wall-street-profits-from-selling-fear.

19 See, for example, "Companies Get Budgets All Wrong," *The Wall Street Journal* (July 22, 2013), online at on.wsj.com/1OfjJaR.

20 "Pizza Chains in Cheese Squeeze," *The Los Angeles Times* (September 3, 2001), p. C4.

21 See, for example, "Long-Term Incentive Plans with Relative Performance Measurements," *Compensation Advisory Partners* (January 9, 2012), online at www.capartners.

com/news/78/61/Long-term-Incentive-Plans-with-Relative-Performance-Measurements.

22 For an overview, see J. Bol, "Subjectivity in Compensation Contracting," *Journal of Accounting Literature*, 28 (2009), pp. 1–24. See also M. Gibbs, K. Merchant, W. Van der Stede, and M. Vargus, "Determinants and Effects of Subjectivity in Incentives," *The Accounting Review*, 79, no. 2 (April 2004), pp. 409–36.

23 See, for example, F. Moers, "Discretion and Bias in Performance Evaluation: The Impact of Diversity and Subjectivity," *Accounting, Organizations and Society*, 30, no. 1 (January 2005), pp. 67–80.

24 See, for example, D. Ghosh, "Alternative Measures of Managers' Performance, Controllability, and the Outcome Effect," *Behavioral Research in Accounting*, 17 (2005), pp. 55–70.

25 See, for example, S. A. Butler and D. Ghosh, "Individual Differences in Managerial Accounting Judgments and Decision Making," *British Accounting Review*, 47, no. 1 (March 2015), pp. 33–45.

26 This statement was the subject of a research article focused on examining *excuse cultures*: F. Larmande and J. P. Ponssard, "Fishing for Excuses and Performance Evaluation," *Review of Accounting Studies*, 19, no. 2 (June 2014), pp. 988–1008.

CASE STUDY
Olympic Car Wash

The Olympic Car Wash Company owned and operated 30 car washes in Belgium. The general managers of each of the 30 locations reported to Jacques Van Raemdonck, Olympic's chief operating officer.

At the end of each quarter, Jacques had to evaluate the performances of each of the car wash locations. His evaluations determined the size of a bonus pool that was allocated to personnel at the location. If the location achieved its budgeted profit target, €3,000 was put into the bonus pool. The pool was also augmented by €1 for every €10 the location exceeded its profit target.

However, the bonus contract gave Jacques the right to make subjective adjustments for the effects of factors he deemed outside the control of personnel at the location. In the past few years, Jacques had made such adjustments for the adverse effects on revenue of construction taking place on the street just in front of one car wash location and to cover the costs of vandalism at another location.

By far the largest uncontrollable factor that Jacques had to consider was, however, the weather. In particular, sales volume dropped sharply when it rained, and it rained frequently in Belgium. The budget, which was updated quarterly, was prepared based on an assumption of hours of good weather. Inevitably, though, those assumptions were not accurate.

During the recent spring quarter, it rained many more hours than were assumed in the company's budget, and actual profits for all of the locations were far below the budgeted profit level. The results for the Aalst location are shown in Figure 1. Figure 2 shows

Figure 1 Profit vs. budget for Aalst location for spring quarter

	Budget	Actual	Variance
Revenue	€184,000	€124,080	€(59,920)
Variable expenses (50% of revenue)	92,000	62,040	29,960
Fixed expenses	53,820	55,000	(1,180)
Total expenses	145,820	117,040	28,780
Profit	38,180	7,040	(31,140)

Figure 2 Operating statistics for Aalst location for spring quarter

	Budget Assumption	Actual
Average number of vehicles washed in a good weather hour	23	24
Average revenue per vehicle	€10.00	€11.00
Total hours in quarter	920	920
Hours of bad weather	120	450
Hours of good weather	800	470

some operating assumptions and statistics for the quarter. The Aalst location is open every day, 10 hours per day, when it is not raining. The car wash employees are paid the legally required minimum wage plus a fixed amount for each car wash completed, so labor costs are largely variable with revenues.

How large should the bonus pool be for the Aalst location?

This case was prepared by Professors Kenneth A. Merchant and Wim A. Van der Stede.

CASE STUDY
Beifang Chuang Ye Vehicle Group

On January 1, 1999, the municipal government of Beijing (People's Republic of China) mandated a new vehicle emission control standard. The new law, in essence, required all passenger vehicles sold within the Beijing city limits to be equipped with a fuel injection system, rather than an older carburetor system.[1]

This new law did not come as a surprise to the managers of Beifang Chuang Ye Vehicle Group, a large group of companies that included four automobile dealership locations in Beijing. They had become aware of the impending new law about a year earlier. However, like most other Beijing dealers and the manufacturers who supplied the vehicles, they did not believe that the Beijing government would actually enforce the new law. But it did! The government would not register any vehicles that did not meet the new, tighter emission standards. As a consequence, in early 1999 the Beifang dealers had no cars meeting the legal requirements to sell. In January 1999, their new car sales fell to zero.

Now, in early February 1999, Ming Zhou (vice director and general manager) had to decide, among other things, whether he should compensate his dealership managers and sales personnel as if this unfortunate external circumstance had not happened or whether they should be made to share the company's losses, and if so, to what extent.

The company

Beifang Chuang Ye Vehicle Group (Beifang) was a holding company comprised of 14 companies, most of which operated in segments of the transportation market in northern China. Among the Beifang companies were three taxi companies (operating 3,600 vehicles), a car rental company, an automobile association (with 160,000 members in northern China), an advertising company, a

[1] A similar law was made effective across the entire People's Republic of China on September 1, 2001.

vehicle importer, three automobile dealerships, and an automobile repair company.

Beifang was formerly 100% owned by the Chinese central government, but the company was privatized. By the year 2000, the government owned only 10%. The other 90% was owned by private investors, the most prominent of which were members of Ming Zhou's family.

The three automobile dealerships were all 100% privately owned. The largest dealership company, Beijing Munitions Vehicle Trade Head Company (Beijing Munitions), sold and serviced four brands of vehicles, all of which were manufactured in China: Volkswagen, Citroën, Jeep, and Jin Bei. It maintained four locations in the greater Beijing area. Beijing Munitions had 90 employees. It also had indirect responsibility for the personnel servicing its customers' Citroën vehicles. However, the Citroën service personnel were formally considered employees of one of the car rental companies, which maintained a fleet of 2,000 Citroën vehicles.

The other two automobile dealership companies sold new cars only.[2] North Zhi Xing Car Trade Head Company, with 20 employees, sold imported cars (particularly Volkswagens and Audis) at one Beijing location. Qun Xing Car Lian Suo Dian, with 70 employees, sold domestic vehicle brands from locations in the Changan area in the northeast of China.

All of the dealership companies were organized by function. Beijing Munitions had a general manager and managers of sales, accessories, service, parts, marketing, and administration. The other two companies had fewer departments because they were just sales companies.

Net profit was the primary performance measure tracked within Beifang. Until 1999 all of the dealership companies were profitable. The dealerships were also all growing at healthy rates, 20% or more annually. Beifang managers predicted that the growth rate would increase significantly, particularly for imported brands of vehicles, if and when China was granted admission to the World Trade Organization.

Employee compensation

In each of the car dealership companies, an incentive compensation pool was created based on the company's net profit performance, as shown in Table 1.

Taking money from this pool, the general manager of each company was expected to earn about 2% of the company's total net profit (8% of the total bonus pool) if the company just achieved its net profit target. He[3] would earn 1.5% of the profit if profit was positive but below target. And he would earn 4% of the profit if profits exceeded the target. The general managers decided how to allocate the remainder of the bonus pool to their subordinates.

The bonus potentials were a significant proportion of total compensation. The general managers' monthly base salaries ranged from 7,000 to 10,000 yuan.[4] In typical years their total monetary compensation ranged from 160,000 to 200,000 yuan. In the best year the highest-paid general manager earned 360,000 yuan. The managers were also given some fringe benefits, including an apartment and a car.

The sales manager in Beijing Munitions earned a monthly base salary of 8,000 yuan, plus a car, which is all he earned if net profit targets were not met. If the targets were met, he would earn approximately 10,000 yuan per month.

The entire bonus pool would not necessarily be paid out immediately each month, however. Beifang and dealership company managers could, and typically did, reserve up to 3% of the pool both to provide lunar new year "bonuses," which were typically one month's base salary, and to smooth out the month-to-month and year-to-year fluctuations in incentive payments.

The net profit targets were set based on history and expected market changes. The target-setting processes started in early November with the submission of bottom-up budgets. The negotiation process culminated in an annual planning meeting held near the end of December. The targets could be, and typically were,

Table 1 Calculation of bonus pool

Monthly net profit	Bonus pool share of total net profit
< 0	0
> 0 but < target	25%
> target	27%

[2] Separation of the functions of new car sales, used car sales, and car servicing was still the norm in China, although some large dealerships, such as Beijing Munitions, were beginning to combine the activities. Still, even Beijing Munitions was not involved in used car sales or financing and insurance.

[3] In all cases, the general managers were male.

[4] One yuan equals approximately US$0.12.

revised each half-year. The monthly bonuses in the second half of the year were based on the revised targets.

Decisions to be made

In February 1999, Ming Zhou had to make a number of immediate decisions. He did not expect any cars to be available for sale until March at the earliest. The dealership companies were all losing money, and it was already obvious that they would not achieve their annual net profit plans. These losses were coming right out of Mr. Zhou's personal wealth, and that of his partners. Because Beifang was somewhat diversified, the company could stand to bear the losses in the dealerships for a short period of time. But should it?

Mr. Zhou had empathy for his employees. This problem was not their fault. They did not have great personal wealth, and most of them had families to support. Should he keep his employees on the payroll, prepare a revised plan, and then reward them if the revised plan was achieved? Should he keep them on the payroll but at a lower salary rate, perhaps even down to the government-mandated salary of approximately 500 yuan per month? Or should he lay off all or some off the employees until cars were available to be sold? If he did the latter he would still have to pay them the government-mandated unemployment rate of approximately 300 yuan per month, and he would risk the possibility that many of them would find alternative employment, as the Beijing economy was quite healthy.

This case was prepared by Professors Thomas W. Lin, Kenneth A. Merchant, and Wim A. Van der Stede.

CASE STUDY
Hoffman Discount Drugs, Inc.

In January 2016, a small fire broke out in the backroom of a pharmacy in Downey, California, owned and operated by Hoffman Discount Drugs, Inc. The fire department concluded that the fire was started by a fault in the store's electrical system. Luckily, the sprinkler system worked and fire damage was held to a minimum. However, the water from the sprinklers damaged some of the inventory. Jane Firstenberg, the store's general manager, completed a Damage Report, which described the situation and calculated the resulting losses. The losses were calculated as follows:

Total losses incurred
= value of inventory lost + cleaning expenses
+ payroll used in clean-up process

The losses incurred were not charged to their ordinary line item (for example, payroll). Instead, they were charged to an account called "Non-insured Losses." In this case, the loss totaled $17,440.

Jane was discouraged when she saw the amount of the loss. If the loss had been greater than $20,000, a corporate adjustment would have been made to offset the effects of this "uncontrollable event" for net income bonus purposes. But since the loss was less than $20,000, no adjustment would be made. Jane commented:

> This really hurts. My store is having a great year in sales, but our margins have been down. Now this. This loss might cause us not to achieve our net

income objective for the year. We were right on the edge as it was. It takes a lot of sales to make up for a nearly $20,000 loss. I was looking forward to a nice bonus check. Even worse, if our bonuses are cut, I'm worried I may lose part of my management team. A couple of them have already been considering offers from competitors.

The company

Hoffman Discount Drugs, Inc. (HDDI) was a large retail drug store chain, which operated over 400 stores located throughout the Western United States. It operated over 200 stores in the Southwest region, which included Southern California, Arizona, and Nevada. HDDI stores were typically located in large shopping centers that also included a large supermarket chain store.

HDDI's recent performance had been mixed. For the last few years, sales levels had been increasing and were currently the highest in the company's history. However, because of intense competition in the company's major markets, operating earnings were barely above break-even. In late 2015, HDDI's president was fired, after only two years on the job, and Matt LeGeyt was appointed president.

Matt immediately started negotiating with several major insurance carriers to have HDDI be the sole distributor of prescriptions to individuals who hold policies with those carriers. By obtaining those prescription distribution rights, Matt believed HDDI stores would benefit from increased customer traffic. But Matt believed HDDI's real key to success was to improve operations at the store level. He thought the company needed more effective local marketing, better customer service, and more efficient operations. He did not want to change the company's decentralized mode of operation, however. He believed it was potentially one of HDDI's advantages over its more centralized competitors.

Store operations

A typical large HDDI store carried $2 million of inventory, served nearly 900,000 customers per year, and generated annual sales of approximately $20 million and net income of $1 million. In computing net income, all corporate expenses except interest and income taxes were traced or allocated to the stores. In addition, the stores were charged a carrying cost on their inventory based on an annual approximation of the corporation's marginal cost of capital.

HDDI stores offered a wide range of products. The average percentage of total store sales was as follows:

Category	% of Sales
General merchandise	64%
Pharmacy	29
Liquor	7
Total	100%

General merchandise items included health and beauty aids, detergent and soap products, baby supplies, greeting cards, toys, and seasonal items.

Many functions, such as purchasing, human resources, investor relations, and real estate, were centralized within HDDI, and inventory was shipped to the stores from one of three regional warehouses. Each store had the same basic look, and each store was required to carry a basic set of pharmacy-related inventory.

Other than these constraints, however, the stores were relatively autonomous. Store managers were allowed to adapt their merchandise offerings to their local market. Therefore, stores located near the beach stocked many sun- and water-related items, such as sunscreen, beach towels, and boogie boards. Those located near retirement communities carried large stocks of age-related items, such as pain killers, laxatives, and blood pressure monitors. And those in neighborhoods dominated by upper-income professionals with young families carried large stocks of baby- and child-related products, as well as videocassette recorders, stereos, and cameras.

The store managers were also allowed to make decisions about local advertising. That is, they selected the amount and type of local advertising (newspaper, radio, and television), although newer managers typically asked for and received considerable guidance in this area from corporate specialists and their district managers. A typical large store spent nearly $800,000 per year on local advertising.

Store management bonus plan

HDDI's policy was to pay store-level managers salaries that were slightly below market levels but to provide bonus opportunities that made the total compensation package competitive. The bonuses were intended to motivate the managers to work hard and to act in the company's best interest.

The HDDI Store Management Bonus Plan was based on achievement of pre-determined objectives for sales and net income for each store.[1] These objectives were set in a "top-down" fashion. In a series of discussions which considered historical performance, demographic and competitive trends, and corporate initiatives, corporate and regional managers established sales and profit objectives for the corporation. They then broke these objectives down into objectives for the three regions. The regional managers, in consultation with the district managers, disaggregated the objectives into districts. And the district managers then had the responsibility to set objectives for the individual stores in their districts.

Because the company was constantly adding some new stores and improving some store locations, the corporate, regional, and district objectives were usually increased, typically by an average of 4% to 7% annually. But the growth objectives for individual stores were generally more modest. Sometimes store objectives would even be lowered as would be the case, for example, if the major supermarket store in the HDDI store's shopping center was closed.

The objectives for each store were disaggregated into monthly periods using historical seasonality patterns and, if necessary, some management judgment. Each month during the year, store managers received reports comparing their store's sales, net income, and inventory performance with their objectives for the month and the year-to-date. Line-item detail was also provided for analysis purposes.

HDDI's fiscal year ended March 31. In early March, at the end of the company's annual planning process, each member of each store management team was presented with a Store Management Compensation Letter (see example in Exhibit 1). Managers had to signify receipt and understanding of this letter by signing a copy of the letter and returning it to the corporate Human Resources Department.

The Management Compensation Letters listed the individual's base salary, bonus objective, and total compensation objective. The bonus objectives were set as follows:

Role	Bonus objective (% base salary)
General manager	15–20%
Assistant general manager	7–10%
Assistant manager	3–5%

The managers would earn their bonus objective if they exactly achieved their predetermined sales and net income objectives.

The bonus objective was broken down into a net income (before bonus) objective and a sales objective. Reflecting HDDI's belief in the importance of high profits, the net income objective was given three times the weight of the sales objective. That is, 75 percent of the bonus was based on achievement of net income objectives. The other 25 percent was based on achievement of sales objectives.

Exhibit 2 shows the description of the bonus plan as provided annually to participants. The bonus earned based on net income performance was calculated by adding/subtracting a percentage of the variance to/from the net income bonus objective according to the following formula:

$$B_N = O_N + A = O_N + (V \times S)$$

where:

B_N = bonus earned based on net income performance

O_N = net income bonus objective

A = adjustment to net income bonus objective

V = net income variance = actual net income minus net income objective

S = sharing percentage (see below)

The sharing percentage depended on the manager's level in the store, as follows: general manager (10%), assistant general manager (3%), assistant manager (1.5%). These percentages were set to reflect the different levels of responsibility associated with each job.

The effect of this net income bonus formula was that for every dollar of income the store earned above its predetermined objective, the general manager earned in bonus 10 cents more than his/her bonus objective.

[1] The only other compensation plan offered to store- and lower-level employees was a stock purchase plan. Employees could have a portion of their check withheld for the purpose of purchasing stock. The stock was sold to the employees at the current market price, but the employees would not have to pay any commission fees on their purchases.

Conversely, for every dollar actual income fell below the objective, the general manager earned 10 cents less than his/her bonus objective.

The sales portion of the bonus was based on the percent of annual sales objective achieved. The effect on the bonus objective was determined by using one of the charts shown at the bottom of Exhibit 2. The chart on the left was used if net income before bonus was above budget; the chart on the right was used if net income before bonus was below budget. These two charts differ only when sales exceed budget. If sales exceeded the objective but net income was below budget, then the managers' sales bonuses were set at lower limits.

Exhibit 3 shows a bonus calculation example.

Shortly after the midpoint of the appraisal period (that is, at the end of the 26th week of the year), HDDI gave each manager a bonus check equal to one-half of the expected year-end bonus. This was done to provide the managers more timely reinforcement in hopes that they would stay focused throughout the entire year. This aspect of the plan seemed to work. Managers who received a large interim check were excited and were motivated to earn another large check at year end. Those who received a small check were motivated to make up the difference in the second half of the year.

Adjustments for uncontrollable events

HDDI corporate managers reserved the right to make subjective adjustments to bonuses earned in case actual performance was distorted by uncontrollable events. They considered only three types of uncontrollable events: natural disasters (for example, fires, floods, earthquakes), robberies, and rioting and looting. In larger (AAA classification) stores, adjustments were considered only if the damage resulting from the uncontrollable event exceeded $20,000. Events causing less than $20,000 damage were considered to be *immaterial*. Losses were considered only individually, not cumulatively, but in any case it was quite rare that an individual store would experience more than one or two uncontrollable events in a single year.

One example of an uncontrollable event was described in the introduction to this case. Here are three others:

1. In November 2015, heavy rains and a stopped-up sewer drain caused flooding around the HDDI store in Van Nuys, California. The store suffered approximately $16,000 in inventory damage as water came into the stockroom, and cleanup expenses totaled $4,000 more. A more serious problem, however, was that a sinkhole developed in the major street artery in front of the store, and the street was closed for three days for repairs. The store manager argued that customers' difficulties in getting to the store caused sales for the month to be down more than $200,000, costing the store approximately $12,000 in net income. Corporate managers readily agreed to an adjustment for the inventory damage, but their opinions were mixed as to whether to make the adjustment for the "lost profits" because they thought the estimates were *soft*. However, they eventually did agree to an income adjustment totaling $6,000.
2. In December 2015, an armed robbery occurred in an HDDI store in Glendale, Arizona. Since only $380 was stolen, no adjustment was made for bonus purposes.[2]
3. In April 2013, a neighborhood Cinco de Mayo party got out of hand. Looters stole nearly $400,000 worth of merchandise from a store in East Los Angeles and caused another $100,000 in structural damage to the building. Corporate managers awarded the managers of this store their full bonus objectives as was their policy when stores suffered "heavy" damage.

Management concerns

Matt LeGeyt, the new president, who believed the company's key to success was in improving store operations, had already expressed interest in conducting a thorough evaluation of the Store Management Compensation Plan. When Jane Firstenberg complained to her superiors about unfairness of the situation described in the introduction to this case, HDDI managers agreed to move this task up on the agenda. The corporate Human Resources Department was asked to conduct a thorough analysis of the plan and to present their recommendations at the July management meeting.

[2] The losses associated with robberies averaged less than $500. Store managers were generally able to limit the amount of robbery losses by following the company policy of collecting money from the cash registers at regular intervals.

Exhibit 1 Store management compensation letter

Ralph Williams
General Manager
Store #142
Store Classification: AAA

PERSONAL AND CONFIDENTIAL

The following pertains to your assignment for fiscal year 2016 as of 03/31/16

BASE PAY:	$88,800
BONUS OBJECTIVE:	$15,800
TOTAL COMPENSATION OBJECTIVE:	$104,600
THE PERFORMANCE RATING USED FOR PAY REVIEW PURPOSES WAS:	08

25% OF YOUR BONUS OBJECTIVE IS BASED ON STORE SALES AND 75% IS BASED ON BUDGETED NET INCOME BEFORE BONUS.

YOUR STORE IS CURRENTLY ON THE REGULAR PLAN (Refer to your 2016 Store Management Compensation Booklet for Plan details)

MINIMUM % OF BONUS OBJECTIVE PAYABLE:	0%
MAXIMUM % OF BONUS OBJECTIVE PAYABLE:	500%

The following information pertains to your Store Management assignments for fiscal 2016 to date and your most recent salary history:

EFFECTIVE				ANNUAL COMPENSATION OBJECTIVE					
					BONUS		STORE	NIBB[3] BUDGET	
DATE	STORE	DIST	POSI.	BASE	OBJECTIVE	TOTAL	CLASSIFICATION	SALES BUDGET	PLAN
03/31/16	142	LO2	GM	88,800	15,800	104,600	AAA	1,745,554 21,400,286	REG.
02/03/15	142	LO2	GM	85,200	15,800	101,000	AAA	1,745,554 21,400,286	REG.

PRIOR COMPENSATION HISTORY:

02/04/15	142	GM	85,200	13,600	98,800
04/23/14	89	AGM	62,200	4,800	67,000
03/26/14	111	AGM	62,200	4,800	67,000
01/29/14	111	AGM	56,400	4,800	61,200
03/27/14	111	AGM	56,400	4,000	60,800
01/31/14	111	AGM	54,800	4,000	58,800
12/06/13	111	AGM	54,800	3,000	57,700
03/29/13	89	AM	52,000	2,000	54,000

These are the facts according to our records as of this date. Changes after this date will be sent to you in a separate carrier. No other considerations or adjustments will be made at any time unless stated and authorized in writing by the Regional Vice President of Operations.

If any of this information varies from what you understand your compensation plan to be, please contact your District Manager immediately for an explanation. Otherwise, please confirm your understanding of this information (including Appendix A, which is attached to your Store Management compensation letter, and the bonus payment table) by promptly signing one page of this letter and returning it to the Corporate Human Resources Department within two weeks.

I understand the compensation program explained above and have received a copy of Appendix A and understand the contents.

Signed:____________________ Date:________________

[3]NIBB = net income before bonus

Exhibit 2 Net income/bonus function for regular plan

This plan is broken down into two pieces - NET INCOME BEFORE BONUS and SALES. The minimum payout is 0 and the maximum is 500% of your bonus objective for the combined pieces.

NET INCOME BEFORE BONUS (NIBB) PORTION OF BONUS OBJECTIVE:

Bonus calculations are based on variance from budget. Your NIBB bonus objective will be adjusted by the amount of the variance multiplied by the sharing rates as follows:

GENERAL MANAGERS	+or– 10.0% OF VARIANCE
ASSISTANT GENERAL MANAGERS & SENIOR MERCHANDISE ASSISTANTS	+or– 3.0% OF VARIANCE
ASSISTANT MANAGERS, MERCHANDISE ASSISTANTS & SERVICE MANAGERS	+or– 1.5% OF VARIANCE

SALES PORTION OF BONUS OBJECTIVE

Bonus calculations are based on the percent of Sales budget achieved using the following charts:

If Net Income before Bonus is Above Budget:		If Net Income before Bonus is Below Budget:	
% of Sales Budget Achieved	% of Sales Objective Earned	% of Sales Budget Achieved	% of Sales Objective Earned
90.0%	0.0%	90.0%	0.0%
91.0	10.0	91.0	10.0
92.0	20.0	92.0	20.0
93.0	30.0	93.0	30.0
94.0	40.0	94.0	40.0
95.0	50.0	95.0	50.0
96.0	60.0	96.0	60.0
97.0	70.0	97.0	70.0
98.0	80.0	98.0	80.0
99.0	90.0	99.0	90.0
100.0	100.0	100.0	100.0
101.0	120.0	101.0	110.0
102.0	140.0	102.0	120.0
103.0	160.0	103.0	130.0
104.0	180.0	104.0	140.0
105.0	200.0	105.0	150.0
106.0	220.0	106.0	160.0
107.0	240.0	107.0	170.0
108.0	260.0	108.0	180.0
109.0	280.0	109.0	190.0
Max. 110.0	300.0	Max. 110.0	200.0

In the event a person transfers into a store, earnings are referred as the higher of the person's adjusted earnings after a transfer of the store's adjusted earnings.

DEDUCT 5% FROM THE PAYOUT ON SALES FOR EACH 1% STORE EARNINGS ARE BELOW 97%; DEDUCT 5% FROM THE PAYOUT ON STORE EARNINGS FOR EACH 1% ACTUAL SALES ARE BELOW 100%.

Exhibit 3 Bonus calculation example

Assume:

General manager			
Base salary	$90,000	Bonus objective break-down:	
Bonus objective	16,400	Net income	$12,300
Total compensation objective	$106,400	Sales	4,100

Net Income portion of bonus:

actual 2015 net income	$1,990,082
minus 2015 net income objective	1,517,872
variance	472,210
sharing percentage	10%
adjustment to NI bonus objective	$ 47,221

net income bonus objective + adjustment = net income bonus earned
$12,300 + 47,221 = $59,521

Sales portion of bonus:

actual 2015 sales	$19,285,820
2015 sales objective	18,608,946
actual % objective	103.6%

Since the store achieved its net income objective, use the left-side chart in Exhibit 2. Interpolating on the chart, the percent objective earned is 172%.

sales bonus objective × percent objective earned = sales bonus earned
$4,100 × 172% = $7,052

Total compensation earned:

Base salary	$ 90,000.00
Net income bonus earned	59,521.00
Sales bonus earned	7,052.00
Total compensation	$156,573.00

This case was prepared by Professor Kenneth A. Merchant.

CASE STUDY
Howard Building Corporation, Inc.

Paul McGunnigle, CEO of Howard Building Corporation, a large general contracting company, described the difficult balance his company faced between generating profits on its projects and maintaining good relationships with its customers and subcontractors:

> **We have to make profits on our projects. Profits are the lifeblood of every company. If costs on a project increase, the money can only come from three sources: the client, the subcontractors, or us.**
>
> **But I don't want our project managers to be solely focused on profits at the expense of relationships. We have always prided ourselves on the idea that we make key decisions based upon success and not profit, with the belief that success ultimately leads to profit in the long run. Decisions based primarily on profit quite often diminish success, which in turn diminishes opportunity. Ours is a long-term strategy. If at the end of a project, clients, architects, and subcontractors won't give us a positive recommendation, then the project was not a success, even if it was profitable.**
>
> **If we make mistakes, such as underbidding, we live with those mistakes and learn from them. On the other hand, I also don't want to make it too easy for the project managers to let Howard Building Corp. absorb every cost increase. Sometimes they need to push back.**

The Company

Howard Building Corporation (HBC) was a privately-owned, commercial general contracting company, founded in 1983 by Gary Conrad, Paul McGunnigle and Michael Howard, with offices in Los Angeles and Costa Mesa. In the 30+ years since HBC opened its doors, the company grew from a small business with 15 employees and annual revenue of $3 million, into an industry leader with 160 employees and annual revenue of approximately $300 million. Employee turnover at HBC was extremely low.

HBC specialized in tenant improvement (TI) projects. TI projects altered the interior of an existing structure to meet the needs of a tenant. TI projects could be more complicated than building from the ground up because the existing structure imposed constraints. On the other hand, TI projects did not require lengthy entitlement procedures and were therefore much quicker and usually more profitable than ground-up projects. HBC was a TI industry leader, particularly in the entertainment and technology industries, and had a recent emphasis in the growing healthcare industry. HBC was the winner of multiple IIDA (International Interior Design Association) Awards including, most recently, Best Leisure and Entertainment Project (2014) and Best Large Project (2015).

HBC employees' actions were guided by five core values:

1. Every transaction must be fair for all.
2. We look forward to every challenge with confidence.
3. We build what no one has built before.
4. We embrace our role as leaders in the industry.
5. We are good citizens in our community.

The core values permeated the attitudes and decisions of HBC's loyal, long-term employees. HBC was particularly known for treating sub-contractors well and paying them quickly, as Mike Howard explained:

> **We have a very good rapport with subcontractors. They know they will be paid and even forwarded money if needed. Our relationship with subcontractors allows us to request and receive their very best foreman.**

Project Management Teams

HBC derived revenue from a relatively small number of large projects, about 100 projects per year. Managing each project well, from the initial bid to completion, was critical to success. The construction industry was highly competitive. Typical gross profit margins were 8-10%. Anything beyond that was available only on very small projects. The low margins left little room for error without significant financial impact.

Each project was managed by a team composed of a Project Executive, a Project Manager (PM), an Assistant Project Manager or Project Engineer, and a Superintendent (SI). The **Project Executive** was a high ranking executive, the President, CEO, or one of three SVPs, who was assigned to the project. The Project Executive attended monthly project meetings and was kept informed throughout the building process. A Project Executive was typically assigned to 10 to 20 projects per year.

The **Project Manager** (PM) was ultimately accountable for the success and profitability of an assigned project, and was responsible for the project from design to completion. Specific responsibilities included maintaining positive relationships with all parties, developing the project budget and preparing bids, preparing and maintaining project schedules, executing contracts with subcontractors, managing inspections by government agencies, managing change orders, and monitoring the superintendent on the project. A PM typically managed three projects per year.

PMs at HBC earned a generous base salary. They were also eligible for an annual bonus of 10% of any profit earned above a base profit requirement. So, for example, if a PM's base profit expectation was $500,000 per year, and s/he had an exceptionally good year, bringing in $800,000 in profit, then he/she would earn 10% of $300,000, or a $30,000 bonus. Bonuses were almost always awarded strictly according to the formula. If they were adjusted due to unique circumstances, the adjustment was always in the PM's favor.

The bonus was usually a relatively small part of the total compensation by design, according to PM Craig Roalf:

> **The owners don't want us to be mercenaries. They want us to do the right thing for our customers. I've been with this company for 30 years. It's not something that's a question in my mind or anyone else's mind what you want to do. You want to do a good job, you want a successful project, and you want to show profitability at the end of it.**

The **Assistant Project Managers** or **Project Engineers** assisted the PMs with their duties, primarily the dissemination of information. They also provided technical support to the superintendents.

The **Superintendent** (SI) reported both to the PM and his/her functional manager, the General Superintendent. The SI worked onsite, overseeing work, and making sure everything was done correctly, according to scope documents and codes. The SI was responsible for maintaining schedules and communicating with all parties if the schedule changed. The SI was not responsible for the project budget and was not compensated based on project profitability. The SI's primary responsibility was ensuring that work was done correctly.

LA Prep Project

To illustrate the functioning of HBC's project management systems, the history of one project will be described. The customer for this project was LA Prep, which was to be a new food-business incubator in Los Angeles. The project would convert an existing building located in the Lincoln Heights area of Los Angeles into 50,000 square feet of commercial kitchen spaces for lease to wholesale food producers. Lincoln Heights was a low income, mostly Hispanic, geographical area located just east of downtown Los Angeles. The new facility would be equipped with everything a new food producer might need: areas for food storage, a demonstration kitchen, and a staffed warehouse for receiving and logistics. L.A. Prep would also provide its tenants group buying opportunities, health department approvals, and expedited wholesale licenses.

By the time LA Prep contacted HBC, it had already signed its anchor tenant—LA Kitchen, a philanthropic organization that had signed a contract to lease 20,000 of the 50,000 square foot facility. LA Kitchen had an innovative business model of its own: It reclaimed food that would otherwise be wasted, and trained youths just exiting foster care and older adults just released from prison in culinary trades. The reclaimed, prepared food was distributed to local social service organizations.

In early 2014, on the recommendation of their architect, managers of LA Prep asked HBC to bid on a TI project. HBC managers viewed the LA Prep project as an exciting, high profile opportunity. LA Prep's groundbreaking business model had been featured in local news stories as well as in a story in *The Wall Street Journal*[1] as a catalyst for job growth in Los Angeles. Los Angeles city officials were similarly enthusiastic about LA Prep, both for its prospects for stimulating job growth in the Lincoln Heights area of the city and for the positive publicity the LA Prep venture was creating. They happily cooperated with LA Prep, partnering with the company to create new health and building codes for the project.

But HBC managers also viewed the LA Prep project as very complex. Paul McGunnigle (CEO) described it as "a logistical nightmare." There were unique electrical requirements, health requirements, and many unknowns. An unusually high number of subcontractors, over 25, would be required to complete the project.

The project was further complicated by financial constraints. LA Prep had a fixed budget that was not large enough to do everything they needed to do, and they had loan covenants that prevented them from securing additional financing.

Craig Roalf, one of HBC's most experienced and strongest technical PMs, was assigned to the L.A. Prep project. Also appointed were Deanna Rott as Project Engineer, and Gary Scharrer as Superintendent. Both Deanna and Gary were also highly experienced in their respective roles. Mike Howard was assigned as the Project Executive.

Bid/Contract

HBC responded to LA Prep's request on March 7, 2014. The bid, called a Letter of Intent, was given to LA Prep in the form of a "Guaranteed Maximum Price (GMax)," subject to additions and deductions that might be enacted by Change Orders. If the costs exceeded the GMax for reasons not due to an agreed upon change order, then HBC would be contractually obligated to absorb the costs without reimbursement by LA Prep. The GMax was, as the name stated, the guaranteed maximum price HBC would charge LA Prep for the completion of the project.

HBC was proud of its pricing process, as was explained on the HBC website:

> **We deliver preliminary pricing that is the most thorough in the industry. Every component needed to build a project is priced through our extensive network of pre-qualified subcontractors, offering clients a construction budget that reflects current market costs, not just estimates. This avoids surprises later and ultimately results in project savings.**

HBC personnel built the GMax starting with an estimate of the Cost of Work. The goal was to make this estimate as accurate as possible. The estimate was based on an extremely detailed bottom-up budget that included material costs and proposals from subcontractors for every component of the project. However, as was typical in the industry, the project drawings were only about 70% complete when the bid and GMax were developed. Where the details were missing, costs were estimated using square foot-based rules-of-thumb. (See Exhibit 1 **Budget Cost Summary** for the summarized Cost of Work estimate.)

Added to the Cost of Work to arrive at the GMax were General Condition Costs, a Profit/Fee, Insurance Costs, and a Contingency. Here are explanations of the terms whose meanings are not self-evident:

- **General condition costs** were recurring costs necessary to operate a construction site that were billed to the customer at an agreed upon rate per week for the agreed upon duration of the project. General condition costs typically included on-site project supervision, equipment rentals, safety programs, and other general recurring costs. (See Exhibit 2 **General Conditions Breakdown.**) The General Condition Cost Breakdown also identified general costs that were not included in the General Condition Cost rate, but instead would be directly reimbursed by the customer. Typical "reimbursables," as these costs were called, were utilities, permits, and printing costs.

  Project duration was an important variable in estimating the GMax. If the project duration expectation was exceeded, general condition costs would go over budget. If a project delay was caused by the client, HBC had a contractual right to place a "delay claim" on the project, thus increasing the General Condition costs of the project. The duration of the LA Prep project was contracted at 20 weeks.

- A **Contingency** was added as a protection against uncertainties, to shield the company in case costs came in higher than originally budgeted. Typically 5-25% of the value of the project was set aside as a contingency. If more information was available at the time of setting budgets, the contingency was set at the low end of the range. Contingencies were necessary

[1] http://www.wsj.com/articles/food-accelerators-and-the-10-bag-of-pasta-1420590268

Figure 1 Calculation of GMax

Cost of Work (Exhibit 1)	$6,393,178
General Condition Costs (Exhibit 2)	119,537
Fee/profit (2.5% of costs incl. General Conditions)	162,818
Insurance	66,755
Subtotal	$6,742,288
Contingency (approx. 5% of Subtotal)	347,475
Total Budget (GMax)	$7,089,763

for every project, but they were especially important for the LA Prep project because costs on this project were more uncertain than they would be for a more standard building concept. If the contingency budget was not used, per the contract, 75% would be returned to LA Prep and 25% to HBC.

For the LA Prep project, the GMax was calculated as shown in Figure 1. Historically, HBC achieved its project budget targets about 90% of the time.

HBC managers knew that customers also typically budgeted their own construction contingencies for scope changes that might arise as the project progressed.

Change Orders and Budget Adjustments

Inevitably, projects did not go exactly as planned. Customers often changed their specifications as the project unfolded, necessitating **Change Orders.** And, of course, unforeseen problems were discovered. These uncertainties did not phase Paul McGunnigle, as he explained:

> **There are always issues and problems on large building projects. This business is all about managing problems. If the projects ran themselves no one would need us. A good PM will communicate change orders early, and give reasons ahead of time, not excuses afterwards.**

For the LA Prep project, over 100 change orders were documented on a change order log. This was a not an atypical number of change orders for a project of this size. HBC and LA Prep were able reach payment agreements for about 70 to 80 of the change orders. However, as the project neared completion and L.A. Prep funds and HBC contingencies were depleted, the negotiations became more difficult. Relationships became more strained.

The five change orders detailed below represent typical situations that required change orders. These examples are illustrative of the dynamics of the project, constraints provided by the contractual agreements, and relationships between HBC and LA Prep personnel.

1. Change Order (CO)#2

CO#2 was a customer-directed scope change. Since the drawings were only 70% complete when the project was bid, it was not a surprise that a CO was required once the final drawings were issued for construction. Once the drawings were finalized, the city issued plan check and corrections, and the changes were priced.

Pricing COs could be a time-consuming exercise, as project Superintendent, Gary Scharrer explained:

> **We study the final drawings for any changes in scope. Once we identify changes, we could apply square-foot-based unit cost rules-of-thumb and price the changes very quickly. However, since the mid-1980s we have involved outside construction management companies in the process to minimize project costs. But sometimes they are inexperienced, and this pricing exercise takes much longer. Schedules have also been significantly condensed in the 30 years I've worked in the industry. Projects that used to take six months, are now expected to be completed in four months. So it is easy to get behind schedule.**

The changes on CO#2 touched 15 trades. They resulted in significant increases in the cost of MEP (mechanical, electrical, and plumbing), particularly, but also some other project elements. The architect, engineers, and HBC project manager worked together to design the changes as cost effectively as possible, but the final result was a cost increase of $224,572. LA Prep agreed to pay a majority of the cost: $217,593. HBC volunteered $6,979 from its contingency budget to subsidize the cost of this CO. This change process delayed the entire project by two weeks.

Craig Roalf chose not to make a "delay claim." While it would have been within HBC's contractual rights to place the claim, it would not have been the cultural norm to enforce rights so rigidly, especially at the beginning of a project, with a large contingency budget still available.

2. CO#4

CO#4 began with an RFI (request for information) from a subcontractor. The subcontractor had received drawings that showed an 8" high platform for an exhaust fan on a flat roof, but the actual roof of the building was sloped, not flat. Structural upgrades were deemed necessary, resulting in a redesign and scope change. The engineers, architect, and PM worked together to value-engineer the redesign down from an initial cost of $63,000 to only $12,000. LA Prep approved and paid for this change. But this change also caused more delays, as Gary explained,

> **RFIs often slow projects down. The outside engineering company is contractually obligated to respond to RFIs in a timely manner, but it doesn't always happen. Some engineering companies are better than others.**

3. CO#10

CO#10 was necessary because the cost of building an elevator came in much higher than HBC had originally estimated. HBC received only one proposal from a subcontractor in time to be included in the Cost of Work calculations and GMax bid. Unfortunately the subcontractor's proposal was for a 3,000 pound freight elevator. They were unable to deliver the 5,000 pound freight elevator that was necessary for the LA Prep project. HBC was forced to use a much more expensive vendor, resulting in a $39,164 increase. HBC paid for this increase from its contingency budget.

4. CO#78

CO#78 was caused by vandalism. HBC had just installed the service entrance for water, and the copper piping was exposed in preparation for the final plumbing inspections. This was in a period when copper prices were at an all-time high. Two days before the scheduled inspection, vandals cut the copper pipes that had just been installed. HBC immediately replaced the pipes and built a security cage to protect the copper from vandalism, at a cost of $3,655. HBC issued CO #78 after the work had been completed, but LA Prep "declined" the work, and refused to pay for it.

At this point in the project, HBC had already contributed the entire contingency to prior COs, as Mike Howard explained:

> **We knew that LA Prep's budget was tight from the beginning and they did not have a large contingency of their own for scope changes. So at some point in the project, we offered the contingency fund to them to use as they saw fit. In retrospect that was a mistake. They took advantage of our generosity.**

The $3,655 for CO #78 came out of HBC's profit.

5. CO#94

CO#94 was caused by a timing issue. The LA Prep project required temporary power from July 2014 to March 2015, until permanent power became available. Power was clearly stipulated in the contract as LA Prep's financial responsibility. Craig Roalf explained: "We assume that the power, parking, and water necessary for construction are to be provided by the owner at no cost to the General Contractor." Power was not included in the general condition rate. It was to be billed to and reimbursed by LA Prep on a monthly basis as the actual expense was realized. A CO was necessary because HBC did not receive the bill from the power company until April 2015. Temporary power had not been included in the monthly billings to LA Prep. The total cost of the temporary power for the nine-month period was $11,099.

LA Prep refused to approve this CO, arguing that because they had not been informed of the expense in a timely manner, they had made other decisions with the money that had been available. Craig acknowledged that although ethically LA Prep should have paid for the utility charges, they were within their legal rights to refuse payment, because they were not informed of the costs as stipulated in the contract. And LA Prep insisted that they were out of money. The $11,099 came out of HBC's profits.

About this CO and others like it, Mike Howard commented:

> **[L.A. Prep] starting taking our contract literally. For example, if the CO was not in in 10 days, they would automatically reject it. They were desperate for every piece of change they could get. When these kinds of things happen, the relationship suffers.**

Billing

HBC billed LA Prep every month by applying a percentage of work complete to each line item in the contract, as revised by agreed upon change orders. The percentage of work complete was determined by the Project Manager for each line item of the budget, and certified by the project architect. The total amount due was calculated for each line item by multiplying the revised contract amount for the line item by the percentage of work complete. Previous payments and retainers were subtracted from the total amount due to determine the amount due for the current month. (See Exhibit 3 **Application and Certificate for Payment for an example of a monthly billing.**)

LA Prep was not informed about, nor was it concerned with, subcontractor costs and the actual cost of work. They were billed strictly according to the cost of work contracted, revised only by change orders. HBC bore the risk and reward of the actual cost of work coming in higher or lower than contracted. For example, if the revised contracted amount for asphalt paving was $26,000 and the actual subcontractor's costs for asphalt came in at $28,000, HBC could only charge LA Prep $26,000. HBC would lose money on that particular line-item. On the flip side, if for example the cost of insulation was contracted at $75,000 and the actual subcontractor costs came in at $71,000, HBC could still charge LA Prep the full contracted amount of $75,000 for completed insulation work.

Project Control

Perhaps the most important control tool was the Variance Report, used internally by HBC to track project profit (see Exhibit 4). The Variance Report was updated every month. It summarized the financial impact of the COs for the period. The COs were reflected in the report as changes to the contract price for a line item, depletion of the contingency fund, or depletion of the contracted profit, depending on the agreement made in the COs. Column (A) in Exhibit 4 shows the original contract amount for each line item. Column (B) shows the contract price revised by change orders, i.e. the revised amount LA Prep agreed to pay HBC by line item. This report also tracked changes to the subcontractor costs (commitments) for each line item during the same period. Column (C) shows the subcontractor cost originally budgeted by HBC for each line item. Column (D) shows the revised subcontractor cost after all subcontractor change orders, i.e. the revised amount Howard agreed to pay its subcontractors by line item.

HBC's profit was the difference between the revised contracted price and the revised subcontractor commitment for each line item (B-D), plus 25% of whatever remained of the contingency fund and 100% of whatever remained of the contracted profit. In the case of this project, the difference between the agreed upon price to LA Prep and cost of subcontractor work was $(217,060). The remaining contingency fund was $0, and the remaining contracted profit was $176,294, resulting in a net profit (loss) of $(40,766).

Changes that reduced the projected profit required approval and signature of the Project Executive. These changes were referred to as a "X" costs. The most common "X" costs were subcontractor changes that increased the cost of work above what was contracted. For example, Exhibit 4 shows an "X" cost for steel. The contract with LA Prep was revised up by $41,416, but the subcontractor cost increased by $45,359, $4,421 more than what was charged to the client, requiring executive approval. Executive approval was also required before any unused line items could be returned to the customer, if overall project profitability was already in jeopardy. For example, per Exhibit 4, landscaping was removed from the contract and the entire line-item was returned to the customer. This reimbursement required executive approval. Paul explained,

> Once a contract is signed, any change that diminishes profit must be signed by the Project Executive. PMs cannot just move money from another line item that came in under budget. This provides some incentive to charge clients appropriately if they have made a scope change.

Meetings were held weekly to discuss project issues. In attendance were the PM, Project Engineer, and SI, as well as the outside architect and engineer hired by LA Prep and LA Prep management. Mike Howard, the HBC Project Executive, also attended meetings occasionally, about once a month. RFIs and the response (or lack thereof) were documented in meeting minutes. Exhibit 5 shows excerpts from the minutes of a weekly meeting.

Craig Roalf explained the benefit of involving the Project Executive for the duration of the project:

> The Project Executive knows what is going on. They understand the tenor of meetings and the impetus and rationale for decisions that are made. There are no big surprises at the end of the project.

Mike Howard explained one of his roles in the project meetings:

> Sometimes managers do not push hard enough or clearly state the drop dead date for decisions by clients that are necessary to keep the project on track. In that case, I pull the PM aside outside of the meeting to discuss my concern.

HBC posted several other key project management documents on the Project Exchange, a web page created for each project and accessible to the customer as well as to HBC employees. The Project Exchange was updated weekly with images of the construction-in-progress, an updated project schedule, the RFI and Change Order logs, as well as monthly meeting minutes.

Final Accounting

In the end, the duration of the project was 45 weeks, as compared to an initial estimate of 20 weeks. And, as is shown in Exhibit 4, HBC lost $40,766 on the project.

Exhibit 1 Budget Cost Summary

LA Prep
210 and 230 W. Ave. 26
Los Angeles, CA 90031

Budget #: 14-020
Date: 3/7/2014
RSF: 55,846

WEEKS PROJECTED ON SITE: 20

BUDGET COST SUMMARY			
Trade #	**Description**	**Trade Cost**	**Per SF**
01400	Surveying	$ 12,500	$ 0.27
01800	Finish Clean up	$ 21,932	$ 0.63
02001	General Sitework	$ 32,850	$ 0.70
02500	Site Demolition	$ 120,390	$ 2.15
02510	Grading & Earthwork	$ 10,000	$ 0.27
02201	Asphalt Paving	$ 20,210	$ 0.42
02410	Underground Utilities	$ 80,379	$ 3.76
02480	Landscaping	$ 20,000	$ 0.45
02300	On-Site Concrete	$ 180,060	$ 3.49
03200	Reinforcing Steel & Rebar	$ 13,560	$ 0.24
04100	Masonry	$ 61,700	$ 1.18
04400	Stone	$ 10,500	$ 0.27
05100	Steel	$ 258,700	$ 6.14
05580	Sheet Metal	$ 26,114	$ 0.14
05700	Ornamental Metal	$ 68,450	$ 1.32
06132	Rough Carpentry	$ 101,800	$ 1.37
06400	Arch. Woodworking	$ 20,800	$ 0.07
07200	Insulation	$ 54,420	$ 1.21
07500	Roofing	$ 28,250	$ 1.24
08200	Doors/Frames/Hardware	$ 152,080	$ 2.87
08800	Glazing	$ 55,700	$ 1.13
09250	Drywall	$ 470,713	$ 9.15
09300	Ceramic Tile	$ 68,580	$ 1.49
09500	Acoustical Ceiling	$ 111,832	$ 3.92
09680	Flooring	$ 230,568	$ 5.46
09900	Painting	$ 196,776	$ 5.45
10426	Signage	$ 4,574	$ 0.12

(*Continued*)

BUDGET COST SUMMARY			
Trade #	Description	Trade Cost	Per SF
10800	Toilet Partitions	$ 32,683	$ 0.57
11131	Projection Screens	$ 630	$ 0.01
11160	Dock Equipment	$ 2,100	$ 0.04
11450	Kitchen Equipment	$ 378,519	$ 16.46
14200	Elevators	$ 100,102	$ 1.79
15300	Fire Sprinklers	$ 63,461	$ 1.81
15350	Fire Extinguishers	$ 4,060	$ 0.05
15400	Plumbing	$ 1,099,983	$ 25.81
15500	HVAC	$ 1,246,810	$ 25.05
16001	Electrical	$ 1,002,213	$ 22.40
16600	Fire/Life Safety	$ 29,179	$ 0.81
	Total	**$ 6,393,178**	

Exhibit 2 General Conditions

PRECONSTRUCTION PERIOD (12) WEEKS			
Cost Category	**Weekly Rate**	**# Of Weeks**	**Totals**
Project Executive	No Charge	12	No Charge
Project Manager	No Charge	12	No Charge
Project Engineer	No Charge	12	No Charge
Project Administrator	No Charge	12	No Charge
Subtotal	No Charge	12	No Charge

CONSTRUCTION PERIOD (20) WEEKS			
Cost Category	**Weekly Rate**	**# Of Weeks**	**Totals**
Project Executive	Inc. in Fee	20	Inc. in Fee
Project Manager	Inc. in Fee	20	Inc. in Fee
Assistant Project Manager	Inc. in Fee	20	Inc. in Fee
Project Engineer	$420	20	$8,400
Superintendent (Exterior)	$2,200	20	$44,000
Superintendent (Interior)	$1,800	20	$36,000
Laborers	$500	20	$10,000
Project Administration	Inc. in Fee	20	Inc. in Fee
Direct Expenses			
• Field Office & Supplies	Included	20	Included
• Communication & Electronic Equipment	$65	20	$1,300
• Temporary Protections/Barricades	$80	20	$1,600
• Rubbish Removal	$320	20	$6,400
• Safety Program/Equipment	$120	20	$2,400
• Small Tools/ Misc. Equipment	$192	20	$3,837
• Fencing	$280	20	$5,600
• Field Inspections	Included	20	Included
Reimbursables			
• Reprographics for Bid Set and Construction Set • Permits, Plan Check, Agency, Impact and/or Utility Fees • Distribution, Postage & Mailing			
Subtotal	$5,977	20	$119,537
Should the schedule be extended during the construction period for reasons beyond the responsibility of HBC, the weekly General Conditions cost shall be **$5,977.00**			
TOTAL GENERAL CONDITIONS			**$119,537**

Exhibit 3 Application and Certificate for Payment

APPLICATION AND CERTIFICATE FOR PAYMENT | **AIA Document** G702

TO:	LA PREP PROPERTIES, LLC 400 MT. WASHINGTON DRIVE LOS ANGELES, CA 90065	APPLICATION NO: 8 PERIOD TO:	 1/31/15
FROM:	HOWARD BUILDING CORPORATION 707 WILSHIRE BLVD., STE 3750 LOS ANGELES, CA 90017-3506	INVOICE NO: CONTRACT DATE:	8307 3/10/14

Application is made for Payment, as shown below, in connection with the Contract. Continuation sheet, AIA Document G703, is attached.

ORIGINAL CONTRACT SUM	$	7,089,763.00
Net Change by Change Orders	$	48,012.00
CONTRACT SUM TO DATE	$	7,137,775.00
TOTAL COMPLETED & STORED TO DATE	$	5,856,648.74
RETAINAGE	$	551,171.94
TOTAL EARNED LESS RETAINAGE (Line 4 Less Line 5 Total)	$	5,305,476.80
LESS PREVIOUS CERTIFICATE FOR PAYMENT (Line 6 From Prior Certificate)	$	4,356,137.75
CURRENT PAYMENT DUE	$	949,339.05
BALANCE TO FINISH, PLUS RETAINAGE (Line 3 less line 6)	$	1,832,298.20

CONTRACTOR: HOWARD BUILDING CORPORATION	
BY:	
CRAIG ROALF PROJECT MANAGER	DATE 1/30/15
ARCHITECT'S CERTIFICATE FOR PAYMENT In accordance with the Contract Documents, Based on on-site observations and the data comprising the above application, the Architect certifies to the Owner that to the best of the Architect's knowledge, information and belief the Work has progressed as indicated, the quality of the work is in accordance with the Contract Documents, and the Contractor is entitled to payment of the AMOUNT CERTIFIED.	**AMOUNT CERTIFIED** .... **ARCHITECT:** By:______________________Date__________ This certificate is not negotiable. The AMOUNT CERTIFIED is payable only to the Contractor named herein. Issuance, payment and acceptance of payment are without prejudice to any rights of the Owner or Contractor under this contract.

Exhibit 3 Application and Certificate for Payment *(Continued)*

LA PREP

APPLICATION NO.	8
INVOICE DATE	1/30/2015
PERIOD TO	1/31/2015

DESCRIPTION OF WORK	REVISED CONTRACT AMOUNT	WORK COMPLETED		TOTAL COMPLETED TO DATE	% COMPLETE	BALANCE TO FINISH	RETAINAGE
		PREVIOUS APPLICATION	THIS PERIOD				
Contingency	61,282.00					61,282.00	
Insurance	70,003.00	46,887.36	10,550.10	57,437.46	82.05	12,565.54	
Bond	1,253.00	419.00	834.00	1,253.00	100.00		
Surveying	12,500.00					12,500.00	
Finish Clean-Up	21,932.00					21,932.00	
General Sitework	32,850.00		16,788.00	16,788.00	51.11	16,062.00	1,678.80
Site Demolition	144,441.00	132,025.00	2,850.00	134,875.00	93.38	9,566.00	13,487.50
Grading & Earthwork	10,000.00		9,414.00	9,414.00	94.14	586.00	941.40
Asphalt Paving	25,865.00	1,100.00	13,270.00	14,370.00	55.56	11,495.00	1,437.00
Underground Utilities	153,519.00	5,900.00		5,900.00	3.84	147,619.00	590.00
Landscaping	20,000.00					20,000.00	
On-Site Concrete	226,033.00	225,458.00		225,458.00	99.75	575.00	22,545.80
Reinforcing Steel & Rebar	13,560.00		13,560.00	13,560.00	100.00		1,356.00
...	...	...	...	...		...	...
HVAC	1,281,835.00	989,173.45	236,833.71	1,226,007.16	95.64	55,827.84	12,600.72
Electrical	1,070,416.00	860,422.10	160,769.80	1,021,191.90	95.40	49,224.10	102,119.19
Fire/Life Safety	29,179.00	14,589.50	8,753.70	23,343.20	80.00	5,835.80	2,334.32
General Conditions	119,537.00	81,666.65	16,416.46	98,080.11	82.05	21,456.89	
Fee	170,809.00	114,407.65	25,741.13	140,148.78	82.05	30,660.22	
Totals	7,137,775.00	4,807,776.32	1,048,872.42	5,856,648.74	82.05	1,281,126.26	551,171.94

Exhibit 4 Final Variance Report

	OWNER CONTRACT			SUBCONTRACTOR COMMITMENT			
	Owner Contract (A)	Total Changes	Revised Owner Contract (B)	Original Subcontractor Cost (C)	Subcontractor Change Order	Revised Subcontractor Cost (D)	Variance/ Profit (B-D)
General Conditions	$ 119,537	$2,662	$122,199	$315,439	$15,742	$331,181	**$ (208,982)**
Insurance	$ 66,755	$5,496	$ 72,251	$ 53,421		$53,421	**$ 18,830**
Surveying	$ 12,500	$ (8,086)	$4,432	$2,200	$2,,233	$4,433	**$ (1)**
Finish Clean Up	$ 21,932	-	$ 21,932	$ 21,932	-	$ 21,932	**-**
General Sitework	$ 32,850	$ (85)	$ 32,765	$32,365	$3,143	$ 35,508	**$ (2,743)**
Site Demolition	$ 120,390	$25,551	$145,941	$123,713	$23,101	$146,814	**$ (873)**
Asphalt Paving	$ 20,210	$5,655	$25,865	$20,210	$7,805	$28,015	**$ (2,150)**
Underground Utilities	$ 80,379	$ 90,656	$ 171,035	$ 143,929	$27,106	$171,035	**-**
On-Site Concrete	$ 180,060	$ 57,186	$ 237,246	$ 180,060	$ 58359	$ 238,419	**$ (1,173)**
Landscaping	$ 20,000	$ (20,000)	–				**-**
Steel	$ 258,700	$41,416	$ 300,116	$259,178	$45,359	$304,537	**$ (4,421)**
Rough Carpentry	$ 101,800	$ 20,458	$122,258	$100,869	$ (1,919)	$98,950	**$23,308**
Insulation	$ 54,420	$ 21,034$	$75,454	$50,197	$21,118	$71,315	**$4,139**
Doors/Frames/Hardware	$ 152,080	$85,902	$ 237,982	$152,080	$85,326	$237,406	**$ 576**
Drywall	$ 470,713	$ 124,420	$ 595,133	$ 470,713	$127,331	$598,044	**$ (2,911)**
Acoustical Ceiling	$ 111,832	$ (6,681)	$ 104,971	$ 111,832	$ (6,571)	$ 105,261	**$ (290)**
Flooring	$ 230,568	$ (4,070)	$ 226,498	$229,686	$ (1,612)	$ 228,074	**$ (1,576)**
Painting	$ 196,776	$ (13,601)	$183,175	$196,776	$ (10,141)	$ 186,635	**$ (3,460)**
...	...	...	...	...	...	...	...
Elevators	$ 100,102	$46,948	$147,050	$137,932	$11,051	$148,983	**$ (1,933)**
Fire Sprinklers/Extinguishers	$ 63,461	$13,442	$76,903	$63,461	$13,442	$76,903	**-**
Plumbing	$ 1,099,983	$186,212	$1,286,195	$1,099,983	$197,877	$1,297,860	**$ (11,665)**
HVAC	$ 1,246,810	$93,747	$1,340,557	$1,246,810	$93,827	$1,340,637	**$ (80)**
Electrical	$ 1,002,213	$137,733	$1,139,946	$ 1,002,213	$154,761	$1,156,974	**$ (17,028)**
Fire/Life Safety	$ 29,179	–	$ 29,179	$ 29,179	–	$ 29,179	**–**
Subtotal	$ 6,579,470	$ 549,191	$7,128,661	$6,438,068	$907,653	$7,345,721	**$ (217,060)**
Contingency	$ 347,475	$ (347,475)	–				**–**
Contracted Profit/OH	$ 162, 818	$13,476	$176,294				**$176,294**
Total Original Contract	$ 7,089,763	$215,192	$7,304,955				**$ (40,766)**

Exhibit 5 Excerpt from Weekly Meeting Minutes

LA PREP	Meeting Date:	2/17/15
Project Meeting Minutes #38	Next Meeting	Tuesday, Feb 24, 2015 @1PM

ITEM	RESP	DISCUSSION
1.4	INFO	**Drawings Status & Plan Check Changes** 2-3-15 – There may need to be a revision to civil drawings due to changes in the basement 2-10-15 Delta #10 was received last week from Civil Engineer. Delta #11 expected shortly **2-17-15 Delta 11 has not been issued**
1.6	HBC	**Submittal Process** 2-10-15 HBC to submit quarry tile along with floor sealant **2-17-15 HBC submitted Via by hand and is waiting SAA's approval. HBC has already received owner approvals on tile and sealant submittals.**
1.7	SAA	**RFI Process** 2-3-15 RFI's 152 and 153 are still pending 2-10-15 RFI's 152 and 153 have been answered. RFI's 154, 155, and 159 are outstanding. **2-17-15 RFI 154 has been answered. RFI's 155 and 159 are still outstanding.**
1.9	HBC	**Schedule/Long Lead Items/3 Weeks Look Ahead** 2-3-15 March 6th is current move in date. However there are electrical requirements that are holding up projects from receiving electrical. 2-10-15 All corrections have been made with Electrical with the exception of the newer rated 3R battery closet that is still being reviewed. DWP pushed on schedule to Friday **2-17-15 Waiting on doors to be keyed. Keying is scheduled on Thursday by LAP. Schedule is being delayed daily by not having electrical.**
1.12	LAP	**Pay Application** 2-3-15 Pay Application was sent back to HBC with comments. HBC is waiting on December payment. LAP said it was approved today and will be sent out. 2-10-15 Dec payment received. Jan pay application has been revised and approved. **2-17-15 LSP is looking for Pay App # 6 releases.**
27.0	HBC	**Veggie Washer** 1-27-15 LA Prep has stated that a 2 ½" is good enough and this is what should be used 2-3-15 LAK has asked for stub outs only as an option 2-10-15 All items were carried in alternatives. HBC has suggested running waste and underground at a minimum. **2-17-15 LAK does not want to proceed with Veggie washer. Item Closed.**
33.0	HBC	**Color Choice for the Building** 2-3-15 A color has been selected as CL 1466 Flat. LAP still waiting on changes. 2-10-15 HBC to submit. **2-17-15 LAP had not received a price change per its request.**

The above constitutes our understanding of the content and conclusions of the meeting. All attendees are requested to review this report and direct any errors or omissions in writing with 7 calendar days or these minutes will be presumed correct as written. Items deleted from the minutes are those determined by attendees as to be that they are resolved or required no additional action.

Prepared by: ______________________ Date 2/11/15

Deanna Rott, Project Engineer

Research Assistant Michelle Spaulding and Professor Kenneth A. Merchant prepared this case.

CASE STUDY
Bank of the Desert (A)

In late 2001, Annette Lo, president of Branch Network of the retail banking division of Bank of the Desert (BoD), a large regional bank, was pondering the adequacy of the bank's branch performance measurement and evaluation system. Having the right performance indicators was important because BoD had an aggressive sales culture. Annette and her management team focused much of their attention on improving the performances of branches that were not achieving their growth targets. The performance evaluations were also important because they affected the assignments of annual bonuses for branch personnel.

Annette's discomfort with the bank's current system stemmed from several sources. She had heard grumbling from some of the branch managers, particularly about their performance targets. At least some of the branch managers did not understand how their targets were set, and those who thought that their targets were unfair were prone to complain about them. Annette had also heard claims that the bank's performance measures and evaluations, which were more sensitive to customer acquisition than to customer retention, had led to relatively high "customer churn" rates.

Annette discussed her concerns informally with Dave Phillips, a consultant friend. Dave said that it sounded to him like the system did have some significant weaknesses. BoD's performance measures both seemed to be incomplete and not to direct management attention to the areas with the greatest payoff potential. Annette decided that she should conduct a thorough review of the system.

The company

Bank of the Desert, headquartered in Phoenix, Arizona, was a diversified financial services company that provided banking, insurance, investments, mortgage, and consumer finance services to customers located throughout the southwestern region of the United States. BoD competed in virtually every segment of the financial services industry and, in its regional market, it was among the market leaders in many. In 2001, BoD's size ranked it among the largest US banks. It had assets of approximately $30 billion and more than 10,000 employees.

BoD managers had observed the wave of consolidations in the banking industry, which were motivated to increase profits through greater economies of scale, but they were highly motivated to keep BoD independent. They believed that BoD could serve its customers best by remaining a smaller bank focused on the needs of the fast-growing Southwest region. To discourage potential acquirers so that they could remain independent, BoD's managers knew that they needed to keep the company's stock price high. Thus, they set an aggressive 10% annual earnings-per-share growth rate target. BoD had not managed to meet this target each and every year, but it had reached the target over the long term: the bank's annualized growth rate since 1990 was 11.1%.

BoD's Retail Banking Division offered a full range of deposit, investment, loan and insurance products to consumers and small businesses in metropolitan and community markets. It served nearly 2 million households through the third-largest retail banking network in the region, with approximately 250 branches and 2,700 automated teller machines (ATMs). Net income from retail banking exceeded $800 million in the year 2001. The division's mission was to satisfy all of its customers' financial needs and to help the customers succeed financially. The major components necessary to turn this vision into reality were all in place.

While some important decisions, such as regarding branch locations, product offerings, pricing, and promotions, were made at division headquarters, the day-to-day operations of the division were highly decentralized (see organization chart in Exhibit 1). Each of the regional presidents was responsible for approximately 50 branches, so the time they had available to help any one branch was limited. Thus, personnel in the branches were responsible for identifying their own customers and satisfying those customers' needs for financial services. Division-level staff provided some product training, marketing, and financial analysis support.

Performance measures and incentives

For managers at the top of the retail division's management hierarchy, from the division president down to the regional presidents, the performance measurement and incentive system focused on financial performance, in particular *growth in profits*. As mentioned above, BoD's profit growth target was 10% per year. During BoD's annual planning and budgeting process this overall target was disaggregated into targets for the branch network and each region. Given the importance of the branch network to BoD's total profits, the division and branch network annual profit goals were typically very close to 10%. In recent years the profit growth goals for the *regions* had varied, however, from 7% to 13% depending, particularly, on each region's economic prospects and the number of new branches that would be opened in that region.

Although BoD produced an extensive set of profit reports down to the level of individual branches, product types (e.g. demand deposits), and customers, profits were seen to be largely uncontrollable at the branch and lower organization levels. Branch profits were highly affected by interest rates. The branch managers also had little or no control over many of the revenue and expense items on the branch income statements. For example, the branch managers had no control over decisions regarding product offerings, prices, or facility leasing costs. Division-level managers even set branch staffing levels, which they did based on volumes of transaction activity.

What the branch managers could control, however, was the management of their employees for the purpose of generating bank revenues. Thus BoD's branch incentive compensation system focused on what were perceived to be the two most important, controllable profit drivers at the branch level. Both were revenue-focused. The first measure included in the incentive system was the *number of product sales*, scaled by the number of full-time-equivalent employees (FTE) in the branch to make the measure comparable across branches of different size. Product sales included both sales to new customers and new accounts opened by current customers. The measure was *number* of sales, rather than the profitability of the sale, because the profits of any given sale to the bank could vary significantly, for example depending on how much customers eventually deposited in an account or how long they kept the account open. But new sales were very important to the branch because they could provide a stream of profits to the bank that could last many years.

The second measure included in the incentive plan was the *cross sell/total retail accounts ratio*. "Cross sell" was defined as the proportion of customers who purchased products in more than one product category (e.g. loans, deposit accounts, mortgages, credit cards) per customer. The cross sell ratio was seen as a useful indicator of the effectiveness of the branches' marketing and sales efforts.

All performances within the division were evaluated by comparing actual results relative to targets set during the annual planning process. The goal-setting process was primarily top-down. In September of each year, BoD's corporate-level managers sent preliminary global profit targets to division managers. These preliminary targets were designed to ensure that the bank achieved its minimum 10% annual profit growth rate. Division-level staff then set preliminary goals for each region and branch, primarily by extrapolating trends in the branches' past performances. These preliminary goals were consolidated, reconciled with the bank's target for the division, and presented to the top management team. Top management made adjustments based on their knowledge of market trends and promotion and investment plans for the year. Then the goals were presented to the branch managers, whose inputs led to a final round of negotiations.

At the end of the year, bonuses were paid to branch personnel based on their percent achievement of targets for the number of product sales per FTE (weighted 75%) and cross sell/total retail accounts ratio (weighted 25%). The number of product sales measure was given a higher weight because it was seen to be a more important driver of total profits. No bonuses were paid on performance dimensions where performance was below target. Personnel whose branches exactly achieved their targets would earn bonuses ranging from 10% to 50% of base salary. If performances exceeded targets by 50% or more, personnel could be paid bonuses of up to twice the target bonus levels.

Exhibit 1 Bank of the Desert organization chart – Retail Banking Division

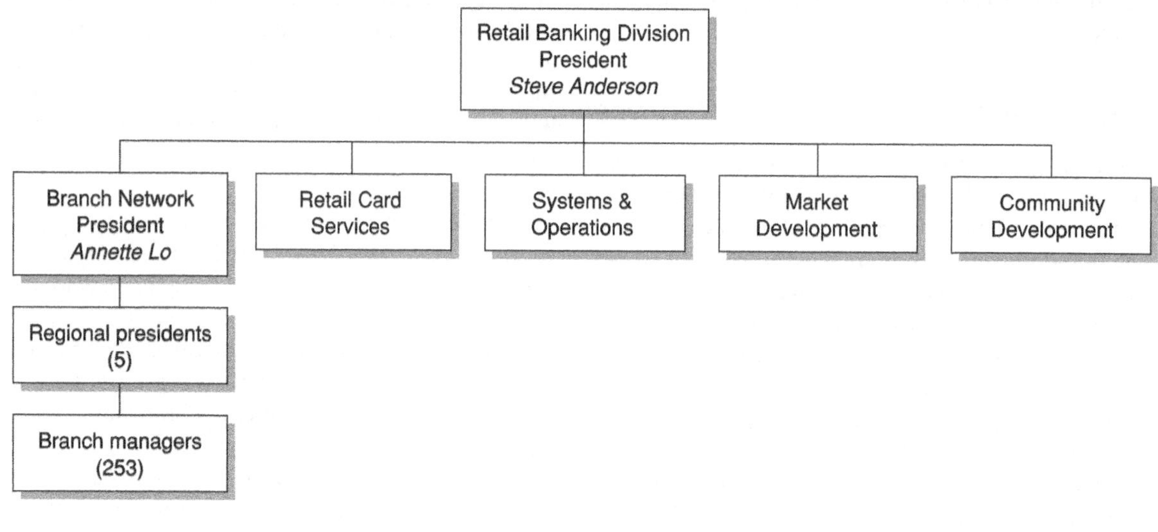

This case was prepared by Professors Kenneth A. Merchant, Wim A. Van der Stede, and research assistant Xiaoling (Clara) Chen.

CASE STUDY
Bank of the Desert (B)

In October 2001, Annette decided to hire a management consulting firm to evaluate BoD's system of branch performance measures and evaluations. Dave Phillips, an experienced partner, was the lead consultant on the job. At the end of a four-month examination period Dave's consulting team presented its preliminary findings.

The consultants' findings startled Annette and her management team. Among other things, the consultants presented a list of the "10 branches with the largest improvement opportunities." Surprisingly, that list included several branches that the BoD management team thought were among its best performers. The manager of one of these branches had even been recently singled out for promotion.

Annette knew that the consultants' findings would have to be studied very carefully. If they were correct, major changes would probably have to be made to the bank's performance measurement and evaluation system.

Performance standards

One of the consulting team's recommendations was that each branch's performance should be compared with what they called its *market opportunity potentials*, rather than with budget targets that were primarily extrapolations from the past. The consultants argued that large performance increases relative to past performance might only indicate low starting points. Market opportunity potentials, instead, would reflect the level of performance that each branch should reasonably be able to reach given its size, location, and operating conditions.

But how should those potentials be measured? BoD's branches were quite diverse. They operated in many different locales, some urban, some suburban, and some in small towns. Some of the branches were located in affluent communities, and some were located in poor communities. Some were old, established branches, and some were newly opened. And some had served customers for many years, while others served more transient communities. After considerable discussion the consulting team concluded that the branch performance potentials varied most significantly with the number and mix of customers in the regions they served and that market potentials could be measured reasonably accurately on that basis.

BoD staff had previously analyzed a broad range of customer demographics and behavior patterns and classified the bank's retail customers into 30 customer types, which they summarized into 10 broad segments, which included categories such as "Well Off," "Newly Secure," and "Future Potential." The customers in these categories varied in terms of their mix of purchases of various products and services and in current and future profit potentials.

The consulting team took these data on the mixes of customer types served by each of the 253 branches and, using a sophisticated statistical clustering program, grouped the branches into 10 clusters. The clusters were labeled:

1. Young Professionals	6. Old Wealth
2. Experienced Investors	7. New Investors
3. Middle-Class Workers	8. Small Branches
4. Transaction Customers	9. Small Business Banking
5. New Wealth	10. Priority Banking

Branch clusters 1 through 7 were based solely on the mix of consumer segments. For example, the average branch in the "Old Wealth" cluster (6) was comprised of 17.4% of "Well Off " customers, 11.5% of "Newly Secure" customers, 42.5% of "Future Potential" customers, 1.8% of "Core Bankers," 0.7% of "Traditional Bankers," 8.1% of "New Investors," 7.3% of "Getting There" customers, 6.7% of "Checks and Mortgages" customers, 0.7% of "Middle Stable" customers, and 3.3% of "Anomalies and Unclassified" customers.

Information on consumer characteristics was unavailable for some specialized branches. These branches were clustered based on balance sheet and transaction characteristics. Clusters 8 through 10 fell into this category. Among them, cluster 8 included branches with less than 3,500 customers, and clusters 9 and 10 were highly focused branches.

The branch clustering was important because it could be used to set more reasonable performance standards. Branch performances could be compared only with the performances of other BoD branches in the same cluster, i.e. those facing roughly the same business environment.

The consultants decided to set the branch performance standards based on the current performance of the *average* branch in each cluster. Dave Phillips explained:

> We did not want to pick some theoretical performance standard. It's too easy to argue with those. We chose to set standards based simply on how the average branch in each cluster was currently performing. The opportunity for improvement, then, was simply calculated based on bringing the poor-performing branches up to average. Everybody can understand that. Once they pick that "low hanging fruit," then maybe the bank managers can get more sophisticated and figure out how to move the higher-performing branches up.

Performance opportunity metrics

Another key element of the consultants' engagement involved the development of a metric that could be used to distinguish the high and low performing branches in each cluster. They decided to take a customer focus. They based their performance model on the simple logic that the bank, and indeed any business, can improve its profits by: (1) acquiring new customers; (2) improving the profit potential of each of its customers (e.g. by selling them multiple products and, particularly, the most profitable products); and (3) retaining each customer as long as possible. They called the combination of the first two factors the *market opportunity.* They called the third factor the *customer retention opportunity.*

The team also sought to develop metrics that would quantify both opportunities on a common measurement dimension – profits. They thought that the common metric would help division managers bridge the gap between the financial performance focus at upper management levels and the operational focus at the branch level.

A. Market opportunity metric

Each branch's market opportunity was the product of two factors: a customer value mix opportunity and a market penetration opportunity. Underlying the calculation of the *customer value mix opportunity* were some cost accounting analyses that had recently been conducted by BoD staff. These analyses estimated profitability by product and by customer. The *product profitability* analyses estimated the average profits the bank earned from the sale of each of a broad range of products. These included, for example, loans of various types, current accounts, savings accounts, credit cards, and certificates of deposit with various maturity lengths. Only averages could be estimated because the profitability of bank products can be dramatically different depending on how the customers use the products. For example, some current account customers maintain large balances; others do not. Some make considerable use of tellers for their transactions, while others use only the relatively inexpensive automated teller machines (ATMs). And some manage their accounts carelessly (e.g. bouncing checks), making it possible for the bank to charge them fees, while others do not.

Customer profitability was based on the profitability of the mix of products purchased by customers of different types. The customer profitability analysis first involved ranking the 10 customer types described above in terms of desirability (i.e. both current profitability and growth potential). These categories were then reclassified into one of four more aggregate categories. Category 4 included all unprofitable customers. This category included, surprisingly, 18% of all the bank's customers. Category 3 included customers who generated some profits but who, because they offered limited growth potential, were not the type that bank managers wanted their line officers searching for. Categories 1 and 2 included the "outstanding" and "excellent" customer types. BoD managers only sought customers in Categories 1 and 2. The consultants calculated that the Category 1 and 2 customers, which comprised only 25% of the BoD's customers, provided 84% of the Retail Banking Division's total profits.

Based on these analyses and data on the mix of products purchased by customers in Categories 1 and 2, the consultants calculated a "standard profit per household," that is, what a branch could be expected to earn by attracting one more customer in either Category 1 or 2.

For example, Branch 188 served a total of 6,075 households, but only 19% were in the top two tiers (outstanding or excellent) in terms of profitability, as compared to the average percentage of top-tier customers in its cluster of 21%. Thus, Branch 188 can be said to have a customer value mix opportunity of 2%. The difference in profitability between the top two tier customers (outstanding and excellent profitability) and bottom two tier customers (moderate and potential profitability) is \$543 for Branch 188. Therefore, the customer value mix opportunity of 2% translates into a profit potential of about \$66,000 (i.e. 0.02 × 6,075 × \$543, rounded).

The other element of the market opportunity metric, the *market penetration opportunity*, was more difficult to calculate. BoD had never measured market penetration or share at the branch level. The branch and ATM network was designed so that the individual service locations would work in a complementary manner to serve customers and to capture market share. Thus bank managers did not believe that the market share of any particular individual location was particularly meaningful. However, BoD staff had previously defined 48 distinguishable "market areas" served by the bank's branches. The consulting team used these data and calculated BoD's penetration rate in each market area by dividing the BoD retail households in the market area by the total potential households in that particular market. They then assumed that the penetration rate was the same for all BoD branches located in this market area.

For example, there were 135,176 households in the South Tucson area of Arizona (market area 1), in which Branch 188 was located. Within this market area BoD served a total of 32,442 households, so BoD's penetration rate was 24%. This figure was compared to BoD's overall average penetration rate of 29%. This led to the conclusion that the BoD branches in the South Tucson market area had a penetration opportunity rate of 5%.

Branch 188 currently served 6,075 households. Assuming that the branch's customer mix stayed the same at an average profit per household of \$132, if the branch could increase its market penetration by 5%, thus bringing in an additional 304 households as customers, it could expect to earn an additional profit of about \$40,000 (i.e. 0.05 × 6,075 × \$132, rounded).

The total market opportunity was the sum of the customer value mix opportunity and the market penetration opportunity. For Branch 188, this was approximately \$106,000.

B. Customer Retention Opportunity Metric

The consultants knew that good customer service was one of the primary profit drivers in a bank branch and, indeed, most types of businesses. But BoD did not have good measures of customer satisfaction or customer feedback. It did, however, track a primary outcome of good customer service – customer retention. From the bank's customer retention statistics, the consulting team calculated the profit opportunity that would be derived from improving each branch's customer retention rate to the average of its cluster. The formula was:

Customer retention profit opportunity = number of households currently served × retention improvement opportunity (%) × number of years of improved retention[1] × cluster average customer profit opportunity

For example, Branch 188 has a customer retention rate of 81.2%, as compared to the average retention rate in its cluster of 82.8%. Branch 188's customer retention opportunity, then, is 1.6%. Branch 188 serves 6,075 households in total and the profit per household is $132. Therefore, in dollar terms Branch 188's customer retention opportunity is $38,000 (i.e. 0.016 × 6,075 × $132 × 3, rounded).

The case of Branch 992

To illustrate how the new proposed evaluation systems yielded results that contrasted with those of the evaluation system BoD was currently using, consider the consultants' conclusions regarding the performance of Branch 992. Branch 992 had been in operation for 36 years, and it served a total of 9,128 households.

Based on the operational metrics used for incentive purposes, Branch 992 had a cross sell/total retail accounts ratio of 95.3% and 5.6 sales per FTE per day, as compared to a target cross sell ratio of 93% and 5.4 sales per FTE per day. Since it exceeded both of its targets, Branch 992 was considered a superior performer under BoD's current evaluation system; it was ranked 44th best of the 253 branches.

Under the consultants' proposed evaluation system, however, Branch 992 was not ranked nearly as highly. In fact, in terms of the opportunity metrics, it was ranked 218th out of the 253 branches.

[1] Assumed to be 3. This is to recognize that retention improvements generate streams of profits over more than a single year.

Table 1 Branch 992 performance vs. cluster 5 averages

	Cluster 5 average	Branch 992
Customers in top 2 tiers (%)	31.5%	24.1%
Customer retention (%)	88.2%	87.6%

Under the proposed segmentation Branch 992 belonged to cluster 5 ("New Wealth"). As shown in Table 1, Branch 992's performance was below the cluster average for both the customer mix and customer retention metrics. The penetration rate in Branch 992's market area was 28%, as compared to the overall bank average of 29%, so Branch 992 also failed to achieve that performance standard.

The consultants translated these performance opportunities into dollars and concluded that if Branch 992 could be brought up to average performance its profits would increase by $411,068 (27.5%) from a stronger customer value mix; $14,932 (1%) from better market penetration; and $26,317 (1.8%) from increased customer retention. With a total profit opportunity of $452,318, Branch 992 had the largest opportunity for improvement in the "New Wealth" branch cluster. It was far from being a top performer!

The consultants' presentation

Dave Phillips presented his report to BoD's retail division management on February 4, 2002. He described his team's approach and the rationale behind it. He showed that the new approach would lead to some significant differences in branch evaluations. Branch 992 was one of the examples that he presented. And he concluded his presentation with some overall statistics about how much money BoD had been "leaving on the table." Dave claimed that bringing the weaker performing branches in each cluster up to average would yield an additional bank profit of about $8.8 million from the customer value mix opportunity, $5.9 million from the market penetration opportunity, and $4.2 million from the customer retention profit opportunity. Taken as a whole, the division's profit would increase by approximately $18.9 million (7%), just from bringing all the poor-performing branches up to the current average within each cluster.

The division managers were stunned by the consultants' overall conclusions and, especially, by some of the specific branch examples. They wondered why the consultants' findings suggested that maybe they should be thinking about firing a branch manager, the one of Branch

992, whom they were preparing to promote because his branch had consistently met its performance targets.

In the days following the meeting Dave noted that the bank managers quickly started asking useful questions that they had not been asking, such as: Why do some branches do so well on the metrics we have been using but so poorly on the opportunity metrics? How should we be setting goals? If we implement this system, will the improvement automatically happen, or would we have to do something else to bring the poor performing branches up to at least average performance levels?

Dave knew that his team's analysis was not the final answer. They had completed only the first phase in what would have to be a lengthy analysis and change process. Nonetheless, Dave thought that they had achieved their primary purpose, which was to stimulate the BoD managers to ask some of the right questions. He considered the opportunity metrics primarily as a diagnostic tool that was particularly valuable for internal learning and improvement. However, he also thought that the opportunity metrics would encourage the branch managers to take a broader view of the business and focus their attention on the dimensions of performance that were critical to the long-term success of the company. In Dave's words:

> **They are in the earliest stages of figuring out the implications of seeing their business from this new perspective. Over time they will refine the perspective, and will begin to relate my findings to their day-to-day behavior. But the most important thing to note is that they were stunned. That was the primary value. I showed them that their perceptions of performance and their decision-making processes were less effective than they had thought because they didn't have a complete context for either.**

However, Dave pointed out to the bank managers that while his system was relatively simple it might not be the ultimate answer to all their evaluation problems. The analyses were based on a number of marketing and cost accounting analyses. Even if these analyses were correct today – which Dave's team assumed they were at face value – the studies would have to be updated on a regular basis. He also pointed out that the three suggested metrics (customer mix, market penetration, customer retention) did not define branch performance completely. For example, those metrics did not reflect how well branch managers controlled the expenses that they could control or how well they developed their employees' skill sets. Bank managers would have to decide whether focusing only on the three suggested metrics would cause branch managers to ignore other important but unmeasured aspects of their jobs.

Decisions to be made

Annette and BoD's other retail bank managers knew they had to make some important decisions. Was the consultants' approach superior to the system they had been using? If it was superior, how fast should they try to implement it? They had already communicated the terms of the 2002 bonus plan, using the old evaluation criteria, to branch personnel. Could they change now? If so, how would they explain the new system to the branch personnel? What should they do next?

This case was prepared by Professors Kenneth A. Merchant, Wim A. Van der Stede, and research assistant Xiaoling (Clara) Chen.

CASE STUDY
Fine Harvest Restaurant Group (A)

In March 2013, Ralph Martin called Karen Williams for an appointment. Ralph was the manager of Restaurant #036, a Fine Harvest restaurant located in Grandview, Missouri. Karen was the president and CEO of the Fine Harvest Restaurant Group (hereafter "Fine Harvest"), a chain of 246 companyowned restaurants. Ralph was livid. He had just received his performance evaluation from Joe Simmons, his immediate superior, the Kansas City area manager. The evaluation was not good, and Ralph learned that he would not be earning a bonus for the year 2012. Ralph had already expressed his anger to Joe, but on further reflection, Ralph decided that he would not just passively accept the evaluation. He felt able to express his anger and frustration directly to Karen because he had known her for a long time. He was one of the first employees Karen and her husband, Robert, hired when they founded the Fine Harvest Restaurant Group in 1994. Despite the gap in the management hierarchy, Karen agreed to meet with Ralph. The meeting was scheduled for April 2, 2013.

At the April meeting, Ralph bluntly laid out his complaint. He explained that performance evaluation was not fair.

> My employees and I worked our butts off all year. We did the best we could. In fact, I think we did the best that could be done. You know I'm a good manager. I've proven it over many years. And now for me to get this slap in the face ... well, it's just not fair. And this is a particularly bad year to not get a bonus. My wife's been out of work because she has been ill, and I've got two kids in college.

Ralph also explained that he had been talking with some other restaurant managers, and they too did not trust the company's performance evaluation system. Many of them did not want to complain, because they perceived they had earned part of their bonuses out of luck.

The company

Fine Harvest Restaurant Group, headquartered in St. Louis, was one of the largest family-owned businesses in the United States. Over the last 18 years, Fine Harvest had grown from a single location to a national company with 246 outlets in 27 states, predominantly in the Midwestern and Western regions of the United States. It had about 4,250 employees and approximately $289 million in annual sales.

Since its founding, the privately held Fine Harvest dramatically outperformed its competitors. Same-store sales, a common industry measure of growth, had increased almost every year since 2001, with a 7.3% jump in 2007. The only year in the last decade when same-store sales did not increase was during the recession of 2008, when same-store sales remained steady. Fine Harvest also continued to add to its growth by opening new restaurants. In 2012, Fine Harvest recorded annual revenues approaching $290 million, capping five consecutive years of growth at a compound annual rate of 14.2%.

Fine Harvest's core menu offerings focused on sandwiches and salads. At Fine Harvest, the customer could choose from a wide selection of attractively displayed sandwich and salad choices a-lacarte or order one of four meal types (chef salad, soup and sandwich, salad unlimited, and vegetable burger), also known as "combination platters." For larger parties, customers could order party platters that served 10–12 people.

The founders also believed that Fine Harvest's success was due in part to the flexibility the restaurants provided by adapting to a variety of operating environments. Since its founding in 1994, Fine Harvest had broadened its operations from the St. Louis area to 27 states, and management had aggressive plans for continued expansion.

Fine Harvest was one of the first quick-service chains to open restaurant locations inside of a supermarket and was also testing drive-through locations in several markets. Fine Harvest strategically positioned its restaurants in four sites:

1. Shopping center cafeterias;
2. Key intersections and downtown areas;
3. University campuses, airports, casinos, resorts, and stadiums;
4. Major supermarkets and retailers.

Fine Harvest made a significant investment in each location. Its in-house architectural and construction team oversaw each step of development to ensure a high quality of design and construction. In addition, it made sure that its restaurants accommodated the specific criteria of each location while still maintaining the operational and visual elements characteristic of Fine Harvest.

Both owners, Robert and Karen Williams, remained actively involved with their company on a daily basis as chairman and president/CEO, respectively. They believed that much of their success was due to their active involvement in the daily operations of each restaurant. There were no plans to offer franchises in the near future.

Organization structure

As shown in Exhibit 1, the executive committee of the Fine Harvest organization consisted of seven people: founder and chairman of the board (Robert Williams); president and CEO (Karen Williams); chief financial officer; vice president of human resources, vice president of marketing, senior vice president of operations; and senior vice president of restaurant development. Three vice presidents reported directly to the chief financial officer in the functional areas of business planning, accounting and finance, and information systems. The senior vice president of operations supervised the work of the vice president of purchasing, the executive chef, and the director of food and beverages.

Thirty four geographical area managers, each supervising between 4 and 11 restaurants, also reported on a regular basis to the vice president of operations, and reported summary results to the members of the executive committee on a quarterly basis. The area managers were responsible for administering the management and staff training programs, setting performance targets for the restaurants, and overseeing the performance of the restaurants. The area managers were primarily held accountable for the achievement of the financial goals.

The staff of a typical Fine Harvest restaurant consisted of a general manager, one or two assistant managers, and approximately 12 to 15 hourly employees. The general manager of each restaurant was responsible for the day-to-day operations of that restaurant, including sales, costs, hiring, training, ordering, inventory, and marketing. The general manager ensured that the restaurant provided excellent customer service, maintained high-quality food, and met financial and operational goals. The assistant managers were responsible for purchasing, maintaining product quality, and controlling food and kitchen labor costs.

Budgeting and performance measurement systems

Fine Harvest's goal-setting process was primarily top-down. In October of each year, Fine Harvest's top executive committee set preliminary profit margin targets for each of the area managers. These targets were based on historical projections, plans for new restaurants in each area and the committee members' knowledge of market trends and the competitive environment. They were also designed to ensure that the company achieved its desired minimum of 12% annual growth in profits.

The area managers then set tentative financial targets for each restaurant. At the restaurant level, restaurant margin was the fundamental indicator of performance. Restaurant margin was calculated as the difference between a given restaurant's revenues and its expenses. Interest expense, taxes, and rent or leasing expense were excluded from the margin calculation. This was done because the restaurant managers had little or no input into decisions about financings and restaurant locations.

In setting restaurant margin targets, the area managers generally extrapolated from the restaurants' historical performances. However, they also took into consideration new information that they were aware of, such as local population growth rates, highway construction plans, and competition. These preliminary restaurant targets were consolidated, reconciled with the executive committee's target for the area, and presented to the executive committee.

At the end of the year, bonuses were paid to area managers and restaurant managers based on their percent achievement of targets for the restaurant margins. No bonuses were paid where performances were below targets. If performances exceeded targets by 50% or more, the managers could be paid bonuses of up to twice the target bonus levels. Salary increases and promotions also depended primarily on the achievement of the financial targets.

Fine Harvest managers believed that the most important factor affecting growth prospects for a restaurant was the population growth rate in the surrounding area. Restaurants located in communities that were growing rapidly grew faster than those in declining communities. For analysis purposes, Fine Harvest grouped their restaurants by area in which they operated and estimated the growth rate for each area. They then compared each restaurant to its peers as well as the performance of the entire system.

The performance evaluation of Restaurant 036

Ralph had worked on the Grandview downtown restaurant for five years. Before he took over, the profit margins of this restaurant had never exceeded 3.5% since its opening in October of 2000 and were often in the red. During his tenure, Ralph brought the profit margins up from 3.4% in 2007 to 8.8% in 2012. He had achieved most of this improvement in the first two years, during which profit margins increased at an average 30.5% annual growth rate. But according to Ralph, the restaurant could not sustain this rate indefinitely, since all the main improvements had been already implemented. The profit margins had increased only 8.4% in the last year (from 8.12% in 2011 to 8.8% in 2012).

Ralph complained to Karen that the targets set by Joe Simmons assumed that the restaurant could increase its profit margins indefinitely and at an unrealistic rate. "Instead of rewarding us for turning around this restaurant, Joe has frustrated our efforts by imposing ever increasing targets. I feel like a donkey following a carrot on a stick." Ralph also complained that Simmons did not understand how downtown restaurants operated. "Downtown restaurants are less profitable than restaurants operating in malls or supermarkets."

Karen's indecision

Karen was not sure what to make of Ralph's complaint. On one hand she worried that Ralph would lose motivation or would even leave the company if she did not revise his performance evaluation. Ralph was one of the most loyal, capable, and hard-working employees that Karen had encountered, and she could not afford to lose a manager like him. On the other hand, Fine Harvest had a no-exceptions policy when it came to performance evaluations. Karen understood well that bending the rules for one employee would threaten the credibility of the company's performance evaluation system, which had produced exceptional results since it was implemented in 2005.

Karen also worried that the frustration expressed by Ralph was a symptom of a wider-spread problem. She had already heard that some managers were unhappy with their bonuses because they asserted their targets were too challenging and she was concerned that some of the managers who were not complaining might have too easy targets. As the restaurant group grew larger and operated in increasingly diversified markets, Karen was suspicious that she was losing touch. She wondered whether the performance evaluation system, which had served the company well for almost two decades, needed to be modified. How could she know when the targets set were too easy or too challenging? What changes, if any, could she implement to improve the current system?

Exhibit 1 Fine Harvest Restaurant Group organization chart

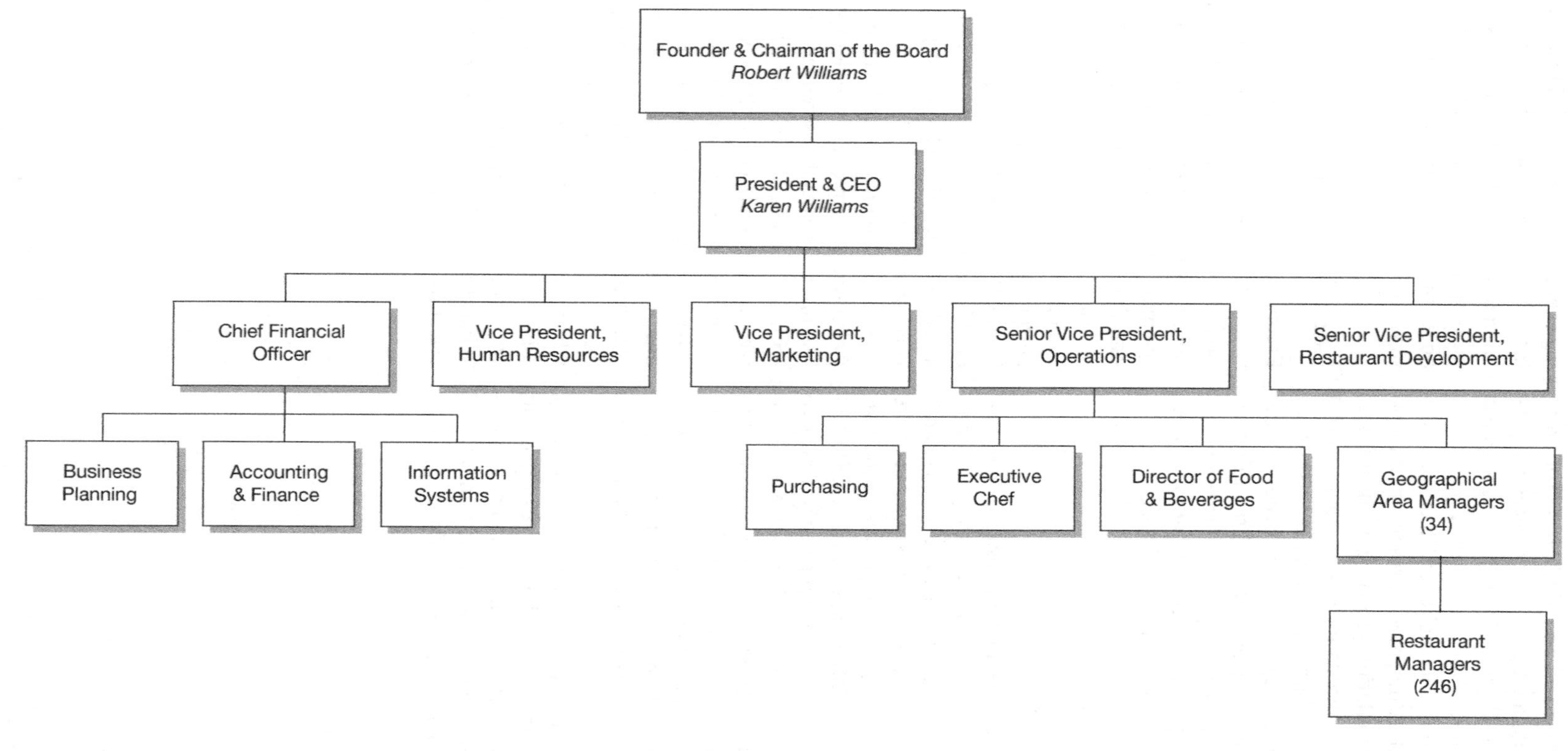

This case was prepared by Professors Xiaoling (Clara) Chen, Kenneth A. Merchant, Tatiana Sandino and Wim A. Van der Stede.

CASE STUDY
Fine Harvest Restaurant Group (B)

In May 2013, Karen Williams, president and CEO of the Fine Harvest Restaurant Group, (hereafter "Fine Harvest"), had a discussion with Mike Henderson, a consultant friend, about her concern that her company's performance measurement and evaluation system may have become obsolete. Karen recounted to Mike her interaction with a trusted restaurant manager (Ralph Martin) who had recently claimed that the performance evaluation system was unfair. The restaurant manager complained that all of the restaurants were expected to be similarly profitable, despite significant differences in their operating environments, and that the system penalized profit margin growth, since performance improvements were followed by increases in future profit margin targets (a problem commonly known as ratcheting). Karen recognized that it was difficult to set accurate profit margin targets for the increasing number of restaurants operated by Fine Harvest (246 outlets as of 2013).

Mike agreed with Karen's view that the target setting processes were not keeping up with the evolution of the company. Mike suggested that Karen adopt a "relative performance evaluation" (RPE) procedure to set the right targets. Karen vaguely remembered from her executive MBA classes at the Olin Business School in Washington University that in an RPE system, managers' performances were evaluated not in terms of the absolute levels of their organizations' results, but rather in terms of their results relative to the results of peer organizations facing the same sets of opportunities and constraints. Karen thought this might be a good idea and decided to use Mike's help in performing a thorough analysis of the system before she took any actions.

Consulting engagement

Cluster analysis and performance standards

Mike and his consulting team claimed that by comparing each restaurant's performance with its peers' performances, rather than with budget targets that were primarily extrapolations from the past (with limited adjustments for expected population growth and market trends), Fine Harvest would be able to set performance goals that reflected the level of performance that each restaurant should reasonably be able to reach given its location and operating conditions. The consultants argued that the company's tradition of setting similar profit and profit growth targets across the board was deeply flawed because the restaurants operated in areas with different profit potential and performance increases relative to past performance might only indicate low starting points.

The consultants found that the Fine Harvest restaurants were actually quite diverse, despite the fact that they operated in areas where the average demographics of the population were similar to each other. Some operated in mature markets while others operated in developing markets. They also operated in different venues. Some of the restaurants were located in shopping malls, some on university campuses, and some were drive-through restaurants. Some were old, established restaurants, and some were newly opened.

The consulting team set out to identify clusters of restaurants operating in approximately the same business environment. They proposed that restaurant performances be compared only with the performances of other Fine Harvest restaurants operating in the same cluster. Karen already told Mike that area growth rate was just one of a few factors shaping the operating environments of the restaurants. To gain more insight into the best segmenting scheme for the 246 Fine Harvest restaurants, Mike asked Karen her intuition about the dimensions on which restaurant performance potentials varied most significantly.

Drawing on her own extensive experience with the restaurants and some inputs from other members of the top executive committee, Karen came up with three criteria: the type of venue, the stage of development of the market, and the dining style mix. The type of venue refers to the operating environment of the restaurant. For example, a restaurant could be operating in a shopping mall, a strip mall, or in a downtown area. It could also be a drive-through operation. The stage of development of the market captures the degree to which the market is mature. A restaurant could be located in a new, developing, or mature market. The dining style mix refers to the relative proportion of eat-in vs. take-out orders among all meal orders.

Venue type was chosen as a criterion because it was one of the primary drivers of customer behavior. For example, people ordered different things, and often had a different propensity to buy drinks in mall locations vs. at stand-alone street locations. The stage of development of the market was selected as an additional criterion since it had an impact on volume and growth. Karen also chose eat-in vs. take-out mix as a criterion, since this had an impact on labor productivity and drink sales.

Karen had thought of other criteria such as infrastructure investment and square footage of restaurants, but these two criteria were largely subsumed by the "venue type" criterion. She also considered the average daily traffic generated by the mall/supermarket as a potential clustering criterion, but she decided to take account of traffic directly, due to the existence of fairly accurate "hard" data.

Karen was not very confident that her intuitive criteria could best characterize the market potentials for the different restaurants. The consulting team offered to conduct a cluster analysis based on the criteria suggested by Karen and her management team. If their data analysis showed that the resulting clusters differed significantly on key performance dimensions, then the criteria would receive some empirical support.

The consulting team identified five different types of venues: shopping mall, strip malldowntown, drive-through, and nontraditional. The data revealed that the market took a relatively short period of time to develop for all restaurants except for drive-through restaurants. For this reason, the consultants decided to segment only drive-through restaurants based on their stage of market development. Dining style mix could be either primarily eat-in dining or a mix of eat-in and take-out dining. The combinations of restaurant characteristics along these dimensions yielded 10 clusters:

1. Drive-through, new
2. Drive-through, developing
3. Drive-through, mature
4. Shopping mall, eat-in dining
5. Shopping mall, mixed dining
6. Strip mall, eat-in dining
7. Strip mall, mixed dining
8. Downtown, eat-in dining
9. Downtown, mixed dining
10. Nontraditional (e.g. campuses, airports, casinos, stadiums)

The consultants decided to calculate the average performance outcomes of the restaurants in each cluster and then compare the averages across the 10 clusters. If the average performance on different metrics proved to be significantly different across clusters, Karen's intuition would prove to be sound.

Performance metrics

The consultants' next task was to develop metrics that could be used to measure the performance outcomes of Fine Harvest restaurants. After interviewing the top executives at Fine Harvest, the consultants identified "sales composition" and "labor productivity" as the main controllable components that could affect each restaurant's profit margin according to the following formula:

$$\text{Profit Margin} = \text{Revenue} - \text{Labor Cost} - \text{COGS (Cost of Goods Sold)}$$

Most of the executives agreed that the employees had little control over the volume of meals they sold, given that customer demand was largely determined by the restaurant's location. A lengthy analysis led the consultants to propose three metrics that they thought reasonably captured the key performance dimensions over which the restaurant managers and employees had control.

The first two metrics captured the sales composition component. These metrics were related to cross-selling and super-sizing, which represented two of the limited means available to the restaurants for increasing revenue profitability, given that they could not control the menu items or pricing. The first metric, product

Table 1 Cluster averages on key performance dimensions

Cluster name	Product Profitability Metric (profit/meal)	Drink Incidence Metric (#drinks/meal)	Labor Productivity Metric (labor-hrs/meal)
Drive-through, new	4.193	0.5124	0.1758
Drive-through, developing	4.182	0.4823	0.1334
Drive-through, mature	4.194	0.4891	0.1252
Shopping mall, eat-in dining	4.267	0.7052	0.1121
Shopping mall, mixed dining	4.248	0.6414	0.1081
Strip mall, eat-in dining	4.269	0.6573	0.1181
Strip mall, mixed dining	4.223	0.6575	0.1027
Downtown, eat-in dining	4.229	0.6610	0.1267
Downtown, mixed dining	4.278	0.5554	0.1266
Nontraditional	4.108	0.6131	0.1299

profitability, estimated the average profits the restaurant earned from the sale of each meal (that is the price per meal minus the cost of goods sold per meal).[1] The second metric, drink incidence, tracked the amount of cross-selling by calculating the average number of drinks sold with each meal. Because drinks generally brought in higher profits than the food items, the consultants believed that all else equal, restaurants selling more drinks would have a higher profit margin.

The third metric, labor productivity, was an expense measure that Fine Harvest was currently using in accounting calculations. It was measured as the number of labor hours per meal. Having examined a large variety of costs Fine Harvest was tracking, the consultants believed that labor costs represented the primary cost pool for the restaurants. As a result, restaurants that were better able to manage labor costs would bring in more profits. Indeed, the consultants' analysis showed that labor costs accounted for about 50% of the variability in the profitability of each restaurant.

[1] The costs of goods sold per meal were calculated as the total costs of the prepared foods divided by the total number of meals. The total costs of the prepared foods were equal to:

- Beginning inventory, plus purchases, minus ending inventory (where inventory included food ingredients, utensils, and other kitchen supplies used to prepare and serve the food)
- Plus depreciation of kitchen equipment,
- Plus a charge for utilities and kitchen space.

Labor costs and drink costs (which included the costs of drinks and cups) were NOT included in this calculation. Likewise, drink prices were not included in the price per meal.

Initial results from the consultants' analysis were summarized in Table 1. Using a statistical package, the consultants showed that the 10 clusters differed significantly on at least one of the key performance dimensions, which led them to conclude that Karen's intuitions were valid. These results had important implications. As restaurants operating in different environments had substantially different performance potentials, restaurant managers should get differential performance targets.

Performance opportunities

Since the initial analysis confirmed Karen's intuitions, the consultants suggested that the next step would be to set the current performance of the *average* restaurant in each cluster as the performance standard for all the restaurants in that cluster. Mike's experience had taught him that average benchmarks were straightforward. In his words, "Employees find it difficult to argue with their superiors, when their superiors request that they do not perform 'below the average.'"

The consulting team also sought to develop metrics that would quantify the opportunities on a common measurement dimension – profits. They thought that the common metric would help restaurant managers bridge the gap between the financial performance focus at upper management levels and the operational focus at the restaurant level.

A. Product profitability opportunity

The product profitability analyses estimated the average profits the restaurant earned from the sale of each meal. The consultants used the average meal profit for each cluster as the benchmark for that cluster. The difference between the actual average meal profit and the benchmark represented the product profitability opportunity. This opportunity was then multiplied by the number of meals sold for each restaurant to obtain the dollar amount of profit opportunities.

For example, Restaurant 001, opened in December 2009, sold an average of 32,129 meals per quarter. Restaurant 001 belonged to the Drive-through/Developing cluster and had an average meal profit of $4.264 as compared to the average meal profit of $4.182 in that cluster. Thus, according to the consultants' analysis, Restaurant 001 outperformed the other restaurants in the same cluster and therefore did not face a meal profitability opportunity.

Restaurant 011, opened in April 2012, also belonged to the Drive-through/Developing cluster. In contrast with Restaurant 001, Restaurant 011 faced a product profitability opportunity since it had an average meal profit of $4.121, which was lower than the average meal profit of $4.182 in that cluster. Thus, Restaurant 011 could be said to have a meal profit opportunity of $0.061. The number of meals per quarter for Restaurant 011 was 44,457. Therefore, meal profitability opportunity of $0.061 translated into a profit potential of about $2,700 (i.e. 44,457 × $0.061, rounded to the nearest hundredth). In other words, assuming that the number of meals sold per quarter by Restaurant 011 stayed the same, if the restaurant could increase its average meal profit by $0.061, it could expect to earn an additional profit of about $2,700.

B. Drink incidence opportunity

As with the product profitability opportunity metric, the consultants set the average number of drinks per meal for each cluster as the benchmark for all the restaurants in the cluster. The difference between the actual average number of drinks per meal and the benchmark was the drink incidence opportunity. This opportunity was then multiplied by the profit per drink and the number of meals sold for each restaurant to obtain the dollar amount of drink-related profit opportunities.

Take Restaurant 001 as an example again. Restaurant 001 sold an average of 0.5211 drinks per meal as compared to the average 0.4823 drinks per meal for the Drivethrough/Developing cluster. Restaurant 001 again outperformed the other restaurants in the same cluster, and thus, did not face a drink incidence opportunity.

Restaurant 011, however, faced a big drink incidence opportunity. This restaurant sold an average of 0.3341 drinks per meal, falling below the Drive-through/Developing cluster average of was 0.4823 drinks per meal. Thus, Restaurant 011 had a drink incidence opportunity of 0.1482. Considering that the number of meals per quarter for Restaurant 011 was 44,457 and that the profit per drink was $1.10, the drink incidence opportunity of 0.1482 translates into a profit potential of about $7,200 (i.e. 0.1482 × 44,457 × $1.10, rounded to the nearest hundredth). In other words, assuming that the number of meals sold per quarter and the profit per drink for Restaurant 011 stayed the same, selling an additional 0.1482 drinks per meal, would bring in an additional profit of about $7,200.

C. Labor productivity opportunity

Labor productivity was measured as the number of labor hours per meal. The difference between the actual average number of labor hours per meal and the benchmark was the labor productivity opportunity. This opportunity was then multiplied by the cost per labor hour and the number of meals sold for each restaurant to obtain the dollar amount of labor-related profit opportunities.

For example, Restaurant 001 used an average of 0.1320 labor hours for each meal sold, as compared to the benchmark of 0.1334 labor hours for the Drive-through/Developing cluster. Thus, Restaurant 001 did not face a labor productivity opportunity. Instead, Restaurant 011 used 0.1349 labor hours for each meal sold, which exceeded the benchmark of 0.1334 for the cluster, resulting in a labor productivity opportunity of 0.0015 per meal. The labor cost per hour was $7.765. Therefore, the labor productivity opportunity of 0.0015 translated into a profit potential of about $500 (i.e. 0.0015 × 44,457 × $7.765, rounded to the nearest hundredth). In other words, assuming that the number of meals sold per quarter and labor cost per hour stayed the same, if Restaurant 011 could decrease its labor hours per meal by 0.0015 hours (or about 5.4 seconds), it could expect to make an additional profit of about $500.

The total profit opportunity was the sum of the product profitability opportunity, the drink incidence opportunity, and the labor productivity opportunity. For Restaurant 001, this was $0, but for Restaurant

011, this was approximately $10,400 (i.e. $2,700 + $7,200 + $500). The dollar amount of profit opportunity was divided by the total number of meals per quarter to obtain the profit opportunity per meal. Thus, Restaurant 001 had a profit opportunity per meal of $0, while Restaurant 011 had a profit opportunity per meal of 23.4 cents (that is, $10,400/44,457 = $0.234/meal).

The cases of Restaurants 011 and 036

To illustrate how the proposed target-setting and performance evaluation systems yielded results that contrasted with those of the current system, the consultants presented the cases of Restaurant 011 and Ralph Martin's Restaurant 036 to the executive committee.

Based on the current budgeting and performance evaluation system, Restaurant 011 achieved a profit margin of 26.7%, exceeding the 23.5% target for the current year. Thus, restaurant 011 had a 114% achievement of the store margin target. Compared with the other restaurants, Restaurant 011 was considered a good performer under Fine Harvest's current evaluation system; it was ranked 77th best of the 246 restaurants.

Ralph's Restaurant (#036) was opened in October of 2000 and served 33,932 meals per quarter. Its quarterly revenue was about $229,034. The restaurant reported a profit margin of 8.8% which was way below its 18.5% target, resulting in a 48% achievement of the store margin target. Under the current system, Ralph's Restaurant performance was ranked on the lowest quartile; falling in the 189th position relative to the other 246 restaurants.

Under the consultants' proposed budgeting and performance evaluation system, however, the performances of Restaurants 011 and 036 were ranked significantly differently. In fact, in terms of the dollar amount of profit opportunities, Restaurant 011 was ranked 229th, while Restaurant 036 was ranked 59th out of the 246 restaurants. In terms of the profit opportunities per meal, Restaurant 011 was ranked 184th, while Restaurant 036 was ranked 60th.

Under the proposed segmentation, Restaurant 011 belonged to the Drivethrough/Developing cluster and Restaurant 036 belonged to the Downtown Mixed Dining cluster. As shown in Table 2, Restaurant 011's performance fell below the Drive-through/Developing cluster averages in every dimension, while Restaurant 036 reported a number of drinks and labor hours per meal that were better than the "Downtown Mixed Dining" cluster averages.

With a total profit opportunity of $10,400, Restaurant 011 had the second-largest opportunity for improvement among the 33 restaurants in the Drive-through/Developing cluster. In contrast, Restaurant 036 was the best performer among the 6 restaurants in its cluster, and had limited opportunities for improvement. Increasing the restaurant's profit per meal up to the cluster's value would allow the restaurant to increase its profits by $879. Once the targets were set right, Restaurant 011 turned from a good performer to a poor performer, while Restaurant 036 turned from a poor performer to a good performer dramatically.

Decision time

The consultants' analysis suggested that Fine Harvest had not been setting the right targets. The existing system did not seem to set targets according to the performance potential of restaurants operating in vastly different environments. At the scale in which Fine Harvest was operating, Karen could no longer rely on her intuitions and personal observations to adjust the historically based targets to the realities of each of the restaurants.

As for the new performance measurement system, Mike argued that the valuable outcomes from this new system were twofold: first, it forced the area managers to consider how to use the measures. It offered an organizing principle about what to show to the restaurant

Table 2 Performance of Restaurants 011 and 036 and corresponding cluster averages

	Profit per meal	Number of drinks per meal	Number of labor hours per meal
Restaurant 011 (Drive Thru, Developing)	$4.121	0.3341	0.1349
Drive Thru, Developing Cluster Averages	$4.182	0.4823	0.1334
Restaurant 036 (Downtown Mixed Dining)	$4.252	0.6200	0.1175
Downtown Mixed Dining Cluster Averages	$4.278	0.5554	0.1266

managers and how to focus the restaurant managers' attention on the key aspects that needed improvement. Second, the relative performance measures highlighted the opportunities for improvement, whereas the traditional performance measurement system did not focus managers' attention on opportunities.

Mike and his consulting team claimed that bringing the weaker-performing restaurants in each cluster up to average would yield an additional quarterly profit of about $286,600 from the product profitability opportunity, $415,000 from the drink incidence opportunity, and $387,100 from the labor productivity opportunity. Taken as a whole, Fine Harvest's profit would increase by approximately $1,088,700 (roughly 8% of the company's profit), just from bringing all the poor-performing restaurants up to the current average within each cluster.

It was time for Karen and her management team to make some important decisions. They had three options. First, they could change the history-based target-setting process to one based on RPE. Second, they could keep the current budgeting and performance evaluation system and merely employ the data analysis as an attention-directing tool to help restaurant managers focus on the right aspects of the business. Third, they could keep the current budgeting and performance evaluation system but find ways to improve the accuracy of the target setting. Which alternative would be the best for Karen and her management team? If they decided to adopt the system proposed by the consultants, how fast should they try to implement it and what problems would arise in the implementation process?

This case was prepared by Professors Xiaoling (Clara) Chen, Kenneth A. Merchant, Tatiana Sandino and Wim A. Van der Stede.

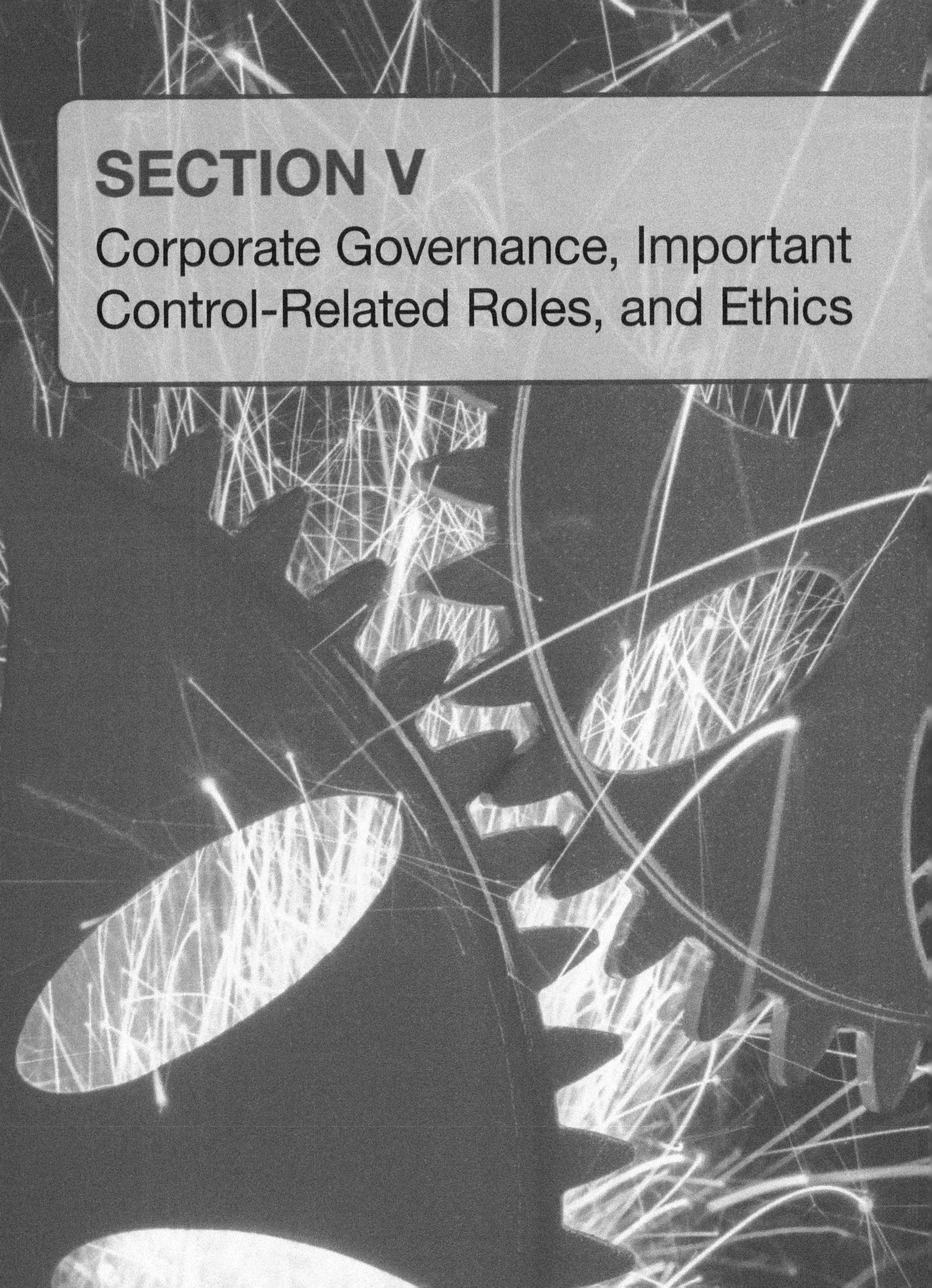

SECTION V

Corporate Governance, Important Control-Related Roles, and Ethics

CHAPTER 13
Corporate Governance and Boards of Directors

The term *corporate governance* refers to the sets of mechanisms and processes that help ensure that companies are directed and managed to create value for their owners while concurrently fulfilling responsibilities to other stakeholders (e.g. employees, suppliers, and society at large). Many institutional and organizational arrangements (including regulations, laws, and norms) and processes have corporate governance effects, and their effects vary considerably across countries. In Anglo-American economies, the primary governance mechanisms are provided by equity markets and the structures that support them or result from them. These include laws and regulations, boards of directors, external auditors, governance ratings, and takeover threats. In some Western European and Asian economies, relatively more governance influence is provided by concentrated ownership patterns, such as the *Keiretsu* in Japan, the *Chaebols* in Korea, institutional investors in India, and state ownership in China. Governance in German companies is heavily influenced by national banks, insurance companies, and labor unions. Scandinavian countries rely more on social norms and expectations. Islamic countries rely on *Sharia* law.[1]

Beyond the institutional setting, including legal and social influences, corporate governance practices in all countries are influenced by what is thought to be "best practice." Some of the broad pronouncements about best practice are based on the recommendations of expert panels, such as the Cadbury Committee in the United Kingdom and the Treadway Commission in the United States.[2] Lists of best practices are published by the many corporate governance ratings organizations, such as ISS, the Corporate Library, and Governance Metrics International; by professional organizations such as the National Association of Corporate Directors in the United States; and in publications by many recognized or self-appointed experts.

The knowledge about best practices comes almost exclusively from developed economies in the West. Corporate governance in emerging markets is generally seen to be less well developed, and accompanying legal enforcement tends to be weak.[3] However, even in developed economies, knowledge of what constitutes best practice, either in general or in any specific setting, is incomplete. In the meantime, regulations are frequently changing. Corporations and boards of directors must do the best they can in environments that are often dynamic.

Corporate governance systems and management control systems (MCSs) are inextricably linked. A corporate governance focus is slightly broader than a MCSs focus. A MCSs focus takes the perspective of top management and asks what can be done to ensure the proper behaviors of employees in the organization. The corporate governance focus is on controlling the behaviors of top management (the so-called C-suite executives) and also, although less directly, those of all the firm's other employees. The links between corporate governance and MCSs are obvious. Changes in corporate governance mechanisms and practices will usually have direct and immediate effects on MCS practices and their effectiveness.

Primarily because of the major business scandals that were uncovered in the early 2000s – including Enron, WorldCom, Tyco, Parmalat, and Royal Ahold, just to name a few; the mismanagement, misreporting, and fraud that contributed significantly to the 2008 financial crisis; and other more recent abuses, such as late trading, market timing, manipulations in trading of financial instruments and commodities, and option backdating – interest in corporate governance has skyrocketed.[4] This chapter provides a brief introduction to this complex and broad subject.

The chapter begins by providing an overview of the legal and regulatory environment within which corporate governance practices must operate. The regulations are difficult to summarize because they vary considerably across legal jurisdictions; and even within a single jurisdiction, they are fragmented. For example, many of the regulations are specific to an industry (such as banks) or to a goal (such as accurate financial reporting). The US Sarbanes-Oxley Act of 2002 is described in some detail in this chapter because it is the most significant piece of legislation affecting corporate governance practices to be passed in the United States since the Securities Act of 1934. Its importance also extends beyond US borders because it has inspired, and is similar to, other corporate governance reforms that have taken place around the world in recent years. The chapter then discusses the roles of boards of directors and, particularly, boards' audit and compensation committees. Chapter 14 discusses two other important organizational roles with both corporate governance and MCS significance, those of controllers and auditors.

Laws and regulations

Corporations are legal entities. As such, they are subject to the laws and regulations of the government jurisdictions in which they operate and those of the stock markets on which their shares are traded. Corporate governance approaches and mechanisms vary widely across countries. Generally, however, the world is said to be divided into two corporate governance orientations: the Anglo-American system that focuses on the primacy of shareholders as the beneficiaries of fiduciary duties, and the Continental European/Japanese system that has a broader concern also for the rights of other stakeholders. But even within these two broad types of systems, considerable variation exists in the governance mechanisms used (e.g. board composition and structure) and the contexts in which the mechanisms must work (e.g. laws, extent of merger-and-acquisition activity).[5]

The legal system in the United States creates a *fiduciary obligation* for managers and directors to act in the best interest of shareholders. The directors, the elected representatives of the shareholders, are charged with overseeing the actions of management. Since the shareholders are viewed as the residual claimants of the cash flows generated, the primary goal is to maximize the value of the corporation. As we discussed in Chapter 10, value creation is a long-run, future-oriented concept, so it can easily be seen that treating all stakeholders well is also in the long-term interest of the shareholders. In the United States, corporations are incorporated in a given state and are bound by the laws and court decisions of that state. The Chancery Court in Delaware is particularly influential because many large corporations are incorporated in that state.

The US federal government began regulating financial markets and their participants (e.g. corporations, securities exchanges, brokers, dealers, and advisors) after the stock market crash of 1929. The US Congress passed the Securities Acts of 1933 and 1934 that, among other things, created the Securities and Exchange Commission (SEC), the agency primarily responsible for enforcement of US federal securities laws. These acts require that publicly traded corporations disclose certain types of information on a regular basis to the SEC, to the company's shareholders, and to prospective investors. The disclosures are intended to promote efficiency and transparency in the financial markets and to provide the additional benefit of discouraging bad behavior.

The Continental European/Japanese system of governance is aimed at ensuring that the corporation is managed for the good of the enterprise, its multiple stakeholders, and society at large. The shareholders are only one of many affected stakeholder groups. One important effect of this legal difference is in the composition of the boards of directors. Large German corporations, for example, are required to have a two-tier board structure, one that provides strategic oversight and another that provides operational management oversight. In German corporations with more than 2,000 employees, the strategic oversight board must be comprised of equal numbers of employees and shareholders' representatives.[6] In Japan, banks are often represented on the boards of directors of companies with which they do business.

Regardless of their home country, all corporations are bound also by the rules and regulations of the stock exchange on which their shares are traded. Large exchanges, such as the New Stock Exchange (NYSE) and NASDAQ in the United States, the London Stock Exchange (LSE) in the United Kingdom, or Deutsche Börse in Germany, maintain extensive sets of rules to regulate their listed companies, to prevent manipulative practices, and to promote fair principles of trade.

Overall, then, corporations are subject to a complex array of laws and regulations designed to direct and constrain their activities. Many parties independent of management and the board of directors monitor corporate governance practices. These include auditors, regulators, analysts, credit-rating agencies, self-appointed watchdogs, and whistle-blowers, among others.

An important example of legislation specifically aimed at strengthening corporate governance generally, as practiced in the United States, is the Sarbanes-Oxley Act of 2002, to which we now turn.

The Sarbanes-Oxley Act

In July 2002, in response to some major corporate failures, most notably Enron and WorldCom, the US Congress passed the Sarbanes-Oxley Act (SOX). SOX imposed new requirements on corporations listed in the United States and their auditors. The explicit goal of SOX was to improve the transparency, timeliness, and quality of *financial reporting*. But since improved controls over financial reporting also have management control implications, understanding the elements of SOX, and also those of other financial reporting regulations, is crucial for those interested in MCSs.

SOX has had effects beyond US borders. All companies registered with the SEC must comply with SOX whether their headquarters are based in the United States or abroad. In addition, some countries, such as Canada and Japan, have adopted regulations similar to SOX.[7]

Figure 13.1 provides a summary of some of the key provisions of SOX. Among other things:

- The *external auditing* industry, which was formerly self-regulated, became highly regulated by the federal government. SOX created the Public Company Accounting Oversight Board (PCAOB) and gave it the authority, with oversight from the SEC, to set auditing standards and to monitor auditors' actions. (We discuss the role of auditors in more detail in Chapter 14.)
- The members of audit committees of companies' boards of directors are required to be independent and financially literate.

Figure 13.1 Key provisions of the Sarbanes-Oxley Act of 2002

Section(s) of the Act	Key Provision(s)
101 102 104	Creates the Public Company Accounting Oversight Board (PCAOB) to oversee the audit of public companies. • The PCAOB will register accounting firms that audit public companies. • It has the authority to establish standards for auditing, quality control, ethics, and independence relating to the preparation of audit reports. • It will conduct a continuing program of inspections to assess the degree of compliance of each registered public accounting firm with professional standards. • It will hold disciplinary proceedings and impose sanctions against firms whose acts, practices, or omissions violate the Act, the Board's rules, professional accounting standards, or the federal securities laws.
105	Increases penalties for accountants who fail to testify, produce documents, or cooperate with an investigation.
201	Prohibits auditors from providing certain non-audit services (including bookkeeping, financial information systems design and implementation, appraisal or valuation services, actuarial services, internal audit, management, human resources, investment advice, legal services) to the companies they audit.
202	Requires audit committee pre-approval of all services provided by audit firm.
203	Requires lead and second (review) audit partner rotation every five years.
204	Increases required communications between auditors and audit committee on critical accounting policies and practices, alternative accounting treatments, and other material written communications with management.
206	Requires a one year "cooling-off" period if audit firm employees who worked on the account are hired by the client into certain key financial oversight positions. Their former firm is prohibited from performing any audit services for the new employer for one year.
301	• Gives audit committee sole authority for the appointment, compensation, and oversight of auditors and approval of any significant non-audit work. • Limits audit committee membership to independent directors. • Requires development of channels of communication for complaints from whistleblowers and others to the audit committee.
302	Requires management (CEO and CFO) certifications that: • They reviewed financial reports (quarterly and annual). • Financial statements do not contain any untrue statements or omission of material facts and that they fairly present the financial condition and results of the operations of the company as of, and for, the periods presented in the report. • They are responsible for the company's internal controls, have designed the controls to that material information is made known to them, have evaluated the effectiveness of the internal controls, and have presented their conclusions about the effectiveness of the internal controls in the report. They evaluated the disclosure controls and procedures as of period end and disclosed any material changes in internal control during the period. • They disclosed to auditors/audit committee if control deficiencies and/or fraud exist.
304	Includes a "claw-back" provision requiring CEOs and CFOs to forfeit certain bonuses received and profits realized on the sale of securities following a financial report that is later restated due to material non-compliance with securities laws as a result of misconduct.
402	New company loans to directors or executive officers are prohibited.
404	• Requires that annual report include management's assessment of the effectiveness of the company's internal control over financial reporting. • Auditors must attest to and report on management's internal control assessment.

Figure 13.1 *(Continued)*

Section(s) of the Act	Key Provision(s)
406	Requires annual disclosure as to whether the company has adopted a code of ethics for its CEO and senior financial officers (e.g., CFO, controller). If it has a code, it must make it publicly available. If it does not have a code, it must explain why it does not.
407	Requires company to disclose whether it has a financial expert on the audit committee and if not, to explain the reasons why it does not.
409	Requires "rapid and current" disclosure of material changes in financial condition or operations.
802 806 807 902 906 1102 1007	Increases penalties. Imposes fines of up to $5 million and/or up to 25 years imprisonment for such actions as: • The knowing alteration, destruction, or concealment of documents with the intent to impeding an official investigation; • For retaliation against whistleblowers; • For knowingly or willfully filing a false certification; • For willful violations of various white collar criminal laws.

Source: The full text of the act can be accessed on the Public Company Accounting Oversight Board website: pcaobus.org/About/History/Documents/PDFs/Sarbanes_Oxley_Act_of_2002.pdf.

- Senior company managers, usually the CEO and CFO, are required to certify that they had reviewed their company's quarterly and annual financial statements; that the financial statements are fairly presented, with no untrue statements or omissions of material facts; that they acknowledge responsibility for disclosure controls and procedures and internal controls over financial reporting; and that they have evaluated those controls and procedures and disclosed any material changes or deficiencies to the auditors and audit committee. Penalties for fraud and for obstructing an investigation were broadened and made more severe.

One of the most significant provisions, and clearly the most expensive one, was contained in the internal control-related section of the act, Section 404. Even prior to SOX, good internal controls were said to be good business practice. Not only did good controls help ensure fair and accurate financial reporting, but they helped ensure that managers would have good information with which to make their business decisions, and they helped reduce the incidence of fraud and loss of assets. Sarbanes-Oxley made good internal controls a legal requirement, at least for companies publicly traded in the United States.

Section 404 mandated a formal evaluation of the effectiveness of a company's internal controls by both management and the company's external auditor and formal written opinions about the effectiveness of those controls. In doing this evaluation, managers and auditors are required to examine a broad range of internal controls over financial reporting, including policies and procedures, audit committee effectiveness, integrity and ethical behavior programs (which we discuss in Chapter 15), whistle-blower programs, and tone at the top (see also Chapter 3).

The existence of a single *material weakness* – a deficiency in internal control so major that it could result in a material misstatement of a company's actual financial situation (see definitions in Figure 13.2) – requires managers and auditors to conclude that the company's internal controls are not effective. Companies have no obligation to disclose the existence of any deficiency less severe than a material weakness, although they and their auditors are required to evaluate them to determine whether they could result in a material weakness.

Figure 13.3 shows the 2015 conclusion by Microsoft Corporation's CEO and CFO about the effectiveness of their company's internal control system.

Figure 13.2 Definitions of control deficiencies

A *control deficiency* exists when the design or operation of a control does not allow management or employees, in the normal course of performing their assigned functions, to prevent or detect misstatements on a timely basis. A deficiency in *design* exists when (a) a control necessary to meet the control objective is missing or (b) an existing control is not properly designed so that, even if the control operates as designed, the control objective is not always met. A deficiency in *operation* exists when a properly designed control does not operate as designed, or when the person performing the control does not possess the necessary authority or qualifications to perform the control effectively.

A *significant deficiency* is a control deficiency, or combination of control deficiencies, that adversely affects the company's ability to initiate, authorize, record, process, or report external financial data reliably in accordance with generally accepted accounting principles such that there is more than a remote likelihood that a misstatement of the company's annual or interim financial statements that is more than inconsequential will not be prevented or detected.

A *material weakness* is a significant deficiency, or combination of significant deficiencies, that results in more than a remote likelihood that a material misstatement of the annual or interim financial statements will not be prevented or detected.

Source: PCAOB Auditing Standard No. 2, *An Audit of Internal Control over Financial Reporting Performed in Conjunction with an Audit of Financial Statements*, online at pcaobus.org/Standards/Auditing/Pages/Auditing_Standard_2.aspx.

Figure 13.3 CEO and CFO certification of effectiveness of the internal control system of Microsoft Corporation

Under the supervision and with the participation of our management, including the Chief Executive Officer and Chief Financial Officer, we have evaluated the effectiveness of our disclosure controls and procedures as required by Exchange Act Rule 13a-15(b) as of the end of the period covered by this report. Based on that evaluation, the Chief Executive Officer and Chief Financial Officer have concluded that these disclosure controls and procedures are effective.

REPORT OF MANAGEMENT ON INTERNAL CONTROL OVER FINANCIAL REPORTING

Our management is responsible for establishing and maintaining adequate internal control over financial reporting for the company. Internal control over financial reporting is a process to provide reasonable assurance regarding the reliability of our financial reporting for external purposes in accordance with accounting principles generally accepted in the United States of America. Internal control over financial reporting includes maintaining records that in reasonable detail accurately and fairly reflect our transactions; providing reasonable assurance that transactions are recorded as necessary for preparation of our financial statements; providing reasonable assurance that receipts and expenditures of company assets are made in accordance with management authorization; and providing reasonable assurance that unauthorized acquisition, use or disposition of company assets that could have a material effect on our financial statements would be prevented or detected on a timely basis. Because of its inherent limitations, internal control over financial reporting is not intended to provide absolute assurance that a misstatement of our financial statements would be prevented or detected.

Management conducted an evaluation of the effectiveness of our internal control over financial reporting based on the framework in *Internal Control – Integrated Framework (2013)* issued by the Committee of Sponsoring Organizations of the Treadway Commission. Based on this evaluation, management concluded that the company's internal control over financial reporting was effective as of June 30, 2015. There were no changes in our internal control over financial reporting during the quarter ended June 30, 2015 that have materially affected, or are reasonably likely to materially affect, our internal control over financial reporting. Deloitte & Touche LLP has audited our internal control over financial reporting as of June 30, 2015; their report is included in [Figure 13.4].

Source: 10-K Report, Microsoft Corporation, 2015, Item 9A: Controls and Procedures.

Figure 13.4 shows the 2015 opinion of Deloitte regarding Microsoft's financial statements and internal control over financial reporting. The two internal control opinions are consistent: both express the opinion that Microsoft's internal controls were effective, meaning that no material weaknesses were found and no combination of the significant weaknesses that might have been found could have caused a material misstatement of the company's financial statements.

Figure 13.4 External auditor's opinion on Microsoft Corporation's financial statements and internal control over financial reporting, for fiscal year 2015 (ended June 30, 2015)

To the Board of Directors and Stockholders of Microsoft Corporation

Redmond, Washington

We have audited the internal control over financial reporting of Microsoft Corporation and subsidiaries (the "Company") as of June 30, 2015, based on criteria established in *Internal Control – Integrated Framework (2013)* issued by the Committee of Sponsoring Organizations of the Treadway Commission. The Company's management is responsible for maintaining effective internal control over financial reporting and for its assessment of the effectiveness of internal control over financial reporting, included in the accompanying Report of Management on Internal Control over Financial Reporting. Our responsibility is to express an opinion on the Company's internal control over financial reporting based on our audit.

We conducted our audit in accordance with the standards of the Public Company Accounting Oversight Board (United States). Those standards require that we plan and perform the audit to obtain reasonable assurance about whether effective internal control over financial reporting was maintained in all material respects. Our audit included obtaining an understanding of internal control over financial reporting, assessing the risk that a material weakness exists, testing and evaluating the design and operating effectiveness of internal control based on the assessed risk, and performing such other procedures as we considered necessary in the circumstances. We believe that our audit provides a reasonable basis for our opinion.

A company's internal control over financial reporting is a process designed by, or under the supervision of, the company's principal executive and principal financial officers, or persons performing similar functions, and effected by the company's board of directors, management, and other personnel to provide reasonable assurance regarding the reliability of financial reporting and the preparation of financial statements for external purposes in accordance with generally accepted accounting principles. A company's internal control over financial reporting includes those policies and procedures that (1) pertain to the maintenance of records that, in reasonable detail, accurately and fairly reflect the transactions and dispositions of the assets of the company; (2) provide reasonable assurance that transactions are recorded as necessary to permit preparation of financial statements in accordance with generally accepted accounting principles, and that receipts and expenditures of the company are being made only in accordance with authorizations of management and directors of the company; and (3) provide reasonable assurance regarding prevention or timely detection of unauthorized acquisition, use, or disposition of the company's assets that could have a material effect on the financial statements.

Because of the inherent limitations of internal control over financial reporting, including the possibility of collusion or improper management override of controls, material misstatements due to error or fraud may not be prevented or detected on a timely basis. Also, projections of any evaluation of the effectiveness of the internal control over financial reporting to future periods are subject to the risk that the controls may become inadequate because of changes in conditions, or that the degree of compliance with the policies or procedures may deteriorate.

In our opinion, the Company maintained, in all material respects, effective internal control over financial reporting as of June 30, 2015, based on the criteria established in *Internal Control – Integrated Framework (2013)* issued by the Committee of Sponsoring Organizations of the Treadway Commission.

We have also audited, in accordance with the standards of the Public Company Accounting Oversight Board (United States), the consolidated financial statements as of and for the year ended June 30, 2015, of the Company and our report dated July 31, 2015, expressed an unqualified opinion on those financial statements.

/s/ DELOITTE & TOUCHE LLP

Seattle, Washington

July 31, 2015

Source: 10-K Report, Microsoft Corporation, 2015.

The documentation and testing of internal controls as required by Section 404 is expensive. Estimates of the total cost of compliance in the first year were as high as $35 billion.[8] General Electric alone spent $30 million in the first year of 404 compliance.[9] But the costs of compliance declined significantly in year two – an average reduction of 44% for larger companies (those with a market capitalization over $700 million).[10] Those declines resulted because most of the documentation of existing controls was completed in year one, and all involved parties became more familiar with the new requirements. In addition, the PCAOB and SEC provided additional guidance both to auditors and companies regarding best ways to comply with Section 404.

While the costs of compliance are significant, SOX affected companies' MCSs in positive ways. It improved companies' internal control structures, audit committees' confidence in the company's internal controls, and companies' ability to prevent and detect fraud. However, even following all the tenets of SOX will not guarantee an infallible control system. In fact, most experts have concluded that the extreme examples of fraud and corporate failure that motivated legislators to pass SOX would have occurred even if SOX had existed at the time. For example:

> **The existence of SOX would not have, and does not now, prevent fraudulent acts from being perpetrated, does not prevent pervasive internal and external collusion to cover up the fraud, and does not prevent decisions being made at the highest levels inside a company in contravention of stated corporate practices and policies.[11]**

But while it is not perfect, SOX has had significant effects on the activities and responsibilities of all those in financial reporting- and control-related roles. In the remainder of this chapter, we discuss one of the most important roles, that of members of boards of directors and, in particular, the boards' audit and compensation committees.

Boards of directors

In publicly traded companies, shareholders typically diversify their risks and own a portfolio of shares in numerous firms. Individually, they rarely have an incentive large enough to devote the time and resources necessary to ensure that management is acting in the best interest of the shareholders. The solution is for shareholders collectively to delegate their authority to monitor management's actions to a *board of directors*.

Boards of directors (and also corporate officers) have a fiduciary duty to foster the long-term success of the corporation for the benefit of shareholders and also, particularly when insolvency is threatened, debt holders. In the United States, this basic fiduciary duty is deemed to have multiple elements:

1. *Duty of care* – duty to make/delegate decisions in an informed way;
2. *Duty of loyalty* – duty to advance corporate over personal interests;
3. *Duty of good faith* – duty to be faithful and devoted to the interests of the corporation and its shareholders;
4. *Duty not to "waste"* – duty to avoid deliberate destruction of shareholder value.

All of these duties are defined by, and enforced through, the US legal system. In court cases involving all but the duty of loyalty, directors are somewhat protected by the *business judgment rule*. This rule is a legal presumption that a corporate fiduciary has endeavored in good faith to exercise care in the corporation's interest. It places the burden on the party complaining of breached duty to prove gross negligence.

To carry out their responsibilities, boards must ensure that they are independent and accountable to shareholders, and they must exert their authority for the continuity of executive leadership with proper vision and values. Boards are given ultimate control over management. They are singularly responsible for the selection and evaluation of the corporation's chief executive officer (CEO), and they also must ensure the quality of senior management (the corporate executives). Boards also should review and approve the corporation's long-term strategy and important management decisions, such as the design of compensation plans that motivate management to achieve and sustain superior long-term performance.

Boards of directors have two main control responsibilities. First, they safeguard the equity investors' interests, particularly by ensuring that management seeks to maximize the value of the shareholders' stakes in the corporation. Second, they protect the interests of other stakeholders (such as employees, suppliers, customers, competitors, and society at large) by ensuring that the employees in the corporation act in a legally and socially responsible manner. Among other things, they help ensure fair financial reporting, fair compensation, fair competition, protection of the environment, and proper conduct of business by the corporation overall.

Many characteristics of boards and their members can affect their effectiveness. It is widely believed, and hence legally required, that a majority of board members should be *independent* of management. Interlocking directorates, situations where board members serve on each other's boards, is one particular problem many have lamented. Charles Elson, director of the Center for Corporate Governance at the University of Delaware, commented as follows on the "clubby nature" of boards, where companies' boards are populated with business partners and individuals with direct financial ties:

> Directors shouldn't be consultants. Their only financial ties to the companies they oversee should be through stock ownership, and they should own enough company stock that if they lost it, it would really hurt.[12]

Lack of independence from management is one red flag for the lucrative CEO pay packages that many have criticized.[13] However, there is likely an inflection point because "full" independence also may not be desired for "optimal" board functioning, for two reasons among others:

> First, full independence deprives the board of spontaneous and regular access to the firm-specific information of other senior executives. Second, full independence eliminates the first-hand exposure of future CEOs to board-level discussions of strategy, which steepens the learning curve for eventually promoted candidates.[14]

Board members should also be competent and must be able to devote the needed time to the role. One consultant described an extreme situation:

> [The] worst board [I've ever seen] was five people strong, and two of them had to be brought in on stretchers. One was 87 [years old] and one was 83. They just laid them on a table in the back of the room, and that's how they got their quorum.[15]

In another example, the alleged state of the board was described as follows:

> [This] entrenched, *incompetent* Board has become a refuge for failed CEOs and we believe these Directors will say and do anything as they attempt to cling to their thrones. The Directors are focused on their own interests at the expense of shareholders, cannot be entrusted to lead [the company] and do not deserve a single vote after having destroyed $9 billion of value.[16]

But some board members are ineffective because they are serving on too many boards for the time they have available. Sometimes, boards also suffer from significant rotation of board members, leaving a board with a relative lack of experience and/or tacit knowledge. This was alleged to be the case at Tesco, the giant UK supermarket group:

> According to two people familiar with the company's leadership, part of Tesco's current problem is the structure of the board and executive committee. Many top executives and board members have left in the past three years and have been replaced by people lacking the experience to stand up to [the CEO], they said.[17]

That said, length of service inevitably has an inflection point somewhere between serving "too long" and "not long enough." As an example of where that inflection point may lie, the UK regulator has put it at nine years, "since at that point the U.K. code says non-executive board members can no longer be assumed to be independent of the company."[18]

The many examples of board failures illustrate that firms should be concerned about the functioning of their boards.[19] There is a burgeoning literature on the functioning of corporate governance systems and boards of directors. However, corporate governance systems are complex, and how the various governance mechanisms interact with one another and with characteristics of the situations in which they operate to produce good (or bad) outcomes is not well understood. Many research findings conflict. These conflicts reflect the incomplete state of knowledge in this complex area.[20]

In the meantime, board members have to do the best job they can.[21] But in deciding how to structure their activities and how to act, boards of directors should follow some basic principles. First, they must comply with the relevant laws and regulations. To ensure this compliance, they often have to rely heavily on their company's lawyers both to inform them of the relevant laws and to educate them about the implications of those laws. If they are accused of wrongdoing, they will be judged in light of the extent they upheld their duties of care, loyalty, and so on.

Second, board members should try to follow what they believe to be best practice. Consultants often play an important role in spreading and advocating such (various) practices. That said, board members should keep in mind that so-called experts often provide conflicting advice. Equally, evidence in many basic board-related areas, including the desirability of splitting the chairman and CEO roles,[22] the optimum amount of equity involvement by board members, the right set and mix of board member skills, and the right board size, is still equivocal.

For possible guidance, board members could also examine the criteria used in any of the many corporate governance ratings. Among the most commonly cited ratings are those published by Institutional Shareholder Services (ISS), Standard & Poor's (S&P), and GMI (formerly Governance Metrics International). A company's ISS Corporate Governance QuickScore is based on an analysis of nearly 200 factors in four key governance "pillar" areas: board structure, compensation/remuneration, shareholder rights, and audit. The S&P Corporate Governance Score is based on scoring committee consideration of over 100 indicators of corporate governance arrangements. GMI's ESG (environmental, social, governance) score is based on an analysis of 150 key metrics. The relative weights of these key metrics vary depending on market, regional, ownership and sector differences. The details of all of the rating methods are proprietary, but it is possible to discern or infer what these organizations consider important for good corporate governance.

However, there is surprisingly little correlation among the indexes the rating firms compile, and their validity has been called into question.[23] Some prominent examples suggest that the relationship between the ratings and performance is tenuous at best. For example, just before major governance failures were uncovered at Fannie Mae, S&P gave Fannie Mae a 9 out of 10 rating and a "gold star" for its corporate governance practices, and just before major fraud problems surfaced at HealthSouth, S&P indicated that the company outperformed 92.3% of its industry peers. These ratings, and the guidelines on which they are based, are not totally reliable, although that does not imply that good corporate governance is not important.[24]

The final guide to director behavior must involve judgment. Oftentimes, there is no specific law that must be followed, and the best-practice advice is conflicting, vague, or unreliable. Still, directors must endeavor to make the right choices. Many of these examples involve situations where directors are not quite comfortable with something in the company, but they also do not want to overstep their bounds to interfere in the day-to-day management of the company. Where should the line be drawn between the management and oversight roles in the organization? For example, if the board asks the CEO for a management succession plan, but some board members are not comfortable with some of the choices of successors, how forcefully should they voice their objections?

Boards put in place a number of structures and processes that enable them to carry out their responsibilities effectively. Some issues are delegated to board committees both because many issues are too complex and too time-consuming for the entire board to address, and because delegation allows directors to make maximum use of their expertise. The board can delegate certain decisions to the relevant committee, or it can ask the committee to study the issue and develop recommendations to bring to the full board.

Most corporations have at least the following standing committees: audit committee, compensation committee, and nominating and governance committee. Some also have other committees that fit the needs of the company's industry or operating situation. These might include some combination of finance, investment, technology, public policy, environment, innovation, corporate social responsibility, digital/social media, and/or risk management committees.

The following sections discuss two virtually universal board committees with significant management control-related responsibilities: audit committees and compensation committees.

Audit committees

Audit committees provide independent oversight over companies' financial reporting processes, internal controls, and independent auditors. They enhance a board's ability to focus intensively and relatively inexpensively (without involving the full board) on the corporation's financial reporting-related functions, and also sometimes risk management activities. Although detailed regulations vary across countries, in most developed capital markets, audit committees are required to be comprised of outside (non-executive) or *independent* directors with a further requirement that they be *financially literate.*[25]

An audit committee's charter typically specifies the scope of the committee's responsibilities and how it carries out those responsibilities, including structure, processes, and membership requirements. Audit committees establish procedures for handling complaints regarding accounting, auditing, and internal control matters, including procedures for the confidential, anonymous submission by employees of concerns regarding questionable accounting practices. Audit committees also are typically responsible for the appointment, compensation, retention, and oversight of the work of the external auditors. SOX mandates these responsibilities in publicly traded corporations. The external auditors, in turn, discuss and address the quality, not just the acceptability, of the company's accounting principles with the audit committee.

Audit committees are intended to be informed, vigilant, and effective overseers of their companies' financial reporting processes and internal control systems. As such, audit committees generally assume the board's responsibilities relating to the organization's financial reporting, corporate governance, and control practices. In the financial reporting area, audit committees provide assurance that the company's financial disclosures are reasonable and accurate. In the corporate governance area, audit committees provide assurance that the corporation is in compliance with pertinent laws and regulations, is conducting its affairs ethically, and is maintaining effective controls against fraud and employee conflicts of interest. In the corporate control area, audit committees monitor the company's management and internal control systems that are designed both to safeguard assets and to employ them to achieve established goals and objectives. In fulfilling these responsibilities, audit committees hire the company's external auditors and monitor their performance. They maintain lines of communication between the board and the company's external auditors, internal auditors, financial management, and inside and outside counsel. Since they have limited resources directly available to them, audit committees must rely on the resources and support of other groups within the organization, particularly the internal auditing function.[26]

Independence from management, in both fact and appearance, is one essential – and, in many countries, legally required – characteristic of an audit committee. Before SOX was passed in the United States, company CEOs were known to select the audit committee members, determine their rotation policies, define their duties, routinely attend their meetings, and review and approve reports given to the audit committee. Such direct influence by the CEO or other key executives, such as the CFO, poses an obvious threat to the independence of the audit committee in their oversight role. Indeed, many corporate fraud cases involve the CEO or CFO, or both. When independence is lacking, employees and auditors will be reluctant to bring serious problems to the committee's attention, and the committee's effectiveness will be severely undermined. But other factors, such as directors' financial expertise and tenure, also affect the strength of the safeguards that audit committees provide.

The foci of audit committee oversight have changed significantly over the years. SOX placed a premium on documentation and testing of internal controls. The 2008 financial crisis caused many audit committees to broaden their charters to include a focus on oversight of management's risk management practices, broadly defined. The focus is often no longer just on financial statement risk. Many audit committees now also provide oversight of their companies' scenario planning, enterprise risk management, and investment risk decisions. Cybersecurity, in particular, is a growing concern for audit committees, risk committees, and entire boards.[27]

While more research on audit committee effectiveness is needed, it is clear that audit committees and their processes must be adapted to the requirements and resources of their company and board. That said, some common practices suggest that audit committees ascertain to do the following:

- Gain support and direction from the entire board of directors.
- Use agendas and follow formal work programs; keep minutes of meetings and distribute them to the full board of directors; schedule meetings in advance so participants have time to prepare.
- Have at least three members, but not too many more so that all members can be active participants.
- Ensure that the committee is comprised of the "right" individuals. Define the members' responsibilities and expect members who no longer contribute appropriately to step down. Ensure that all members are independent of management, financially literate, and engaged.
- Meet at least four times per year, including a pre-audit meeting and a post-audit meeting. (Some experts consider the frequency and duration of meetings to be highly reliable indicators of audit committee effectiveness.)
- Send a clear instruction to the independent auditor that the board of directors, as the shareholder's representative, is the auditor's client and that management is not. (This is a legal requirement of Sarbanes-Oxley.)
- Review all financial information; review interim, as well as annual, financial reports.

- Discuss with the independent auditor their qualitative judgments about the appropriateness, not just the acceptability, of the organization's accounting principles and financial disclosure practices.
- Go beyond a "check-the-box" orientation to compliance with legal requirements. Deal with the real issues of developing effective oversight and risk management practices.
- Be proactive. Participate in setting policies. Monitor the corporate code of conduct and compliance with it. Ensure that the internal auditing involvement in the entire financial reporting process is appropriate and properly coordinated with the independent auditor.
- Secure access to resources as needed, such as for responding to crises or conducting special investigations.

Compensation committees

Most publicly traded companies delegate the important issues related to compensation to a board *compensation committee* (sometimes called a remuneration committee) comprised solely of independent directors. New York Stock Exchange rules, for example, require the formation of such a compensation committee.

Compensation committees deal with issues related to the compensation and benefits provided to employees, particularly top executives. In some companies, the compensation committee also provides oversight regarding the design and operation of retirement plans, although in other companies this function is delegated to an investment committee of the board.

Compensation committees have fiduciary responsibilities for ensuring that the company's executive compensation programs are fair and appropriate to attract, retain, and motivate managers and reasonable in view of company economics and the relevant practices of comparable companies.

Compensation committees typically rely on the company's human resource function for staff support. In addition, because the design of compensation plans can raise many complex issues, many of which we discussed in Chapter 9 – such as relating to performance measures, types of compensation (e.g. cash and stock options) and compensation structures (e.g. performance thresholds and vesting provisions), external and internal compensation equity, and legal and tax considerations – compensation committees often employ outside consultants to provide data or expertise that the company does not have internally. Consultants often conduct industry compensation benchmarking studies and provide advice regarding the design of compensation plans. Compensation committees should retain full responsibility for overseeing the work of any compensation consultants they hire.[28]

Much criticism is currently being directed at compensation committees.[29] Some of this criticism stems from the large compensation, severance, and/or retirement packages that have been offered to top executives. Examples of companies that have been scorned for "excessive pay" have been in the business press almost daily, especially since the financial crisis of 2008, when public outcry turned to the pay packages of "greedy bankers." Further criticism is leveled at boards who seem either unwilling or powerless to rein in the pay of their executives. A 2015 survey of directors by the accounting firm BDO suggested that US company boards still had trouble controlling the size of CEO compensation.[30] Other critics are more concerned with the weak links in many companies between rewards and performance. Criticism is likely when the executives are well compensated not only when their performance is seen as poor in an absolute sense, but also when economic conditions are good even though their companies' performance lagged behind those of their closest competitors.[31] Beginning in 2018, public companies are required to report the ratio of CEO companies to median employee pay, although the BDO survey showed that 74% of the directors responding thought that this ratio is neither meaningful nor helpful. Senior management compensation and the functioning of compensation committees will undoubtedly continue to be a focus for additional regulation in the corporate governance arena.

Conclusion

This chapter has provided a brief introduction to the complex topic of corporate governance. It discussed the laws and regulations that govern its practice and the important control-related roles played by members of boards of directors and, particularly, its audit and compensation committees. Boards of directors are important parts of companies' corporate governance systems and, hence, MCSs. Laws and regulations require some practices deemed desirable, such as the independence of board members who serve on audit and compensation committees. But laws and regulations cannot define everything. In the best-run corporations, what is not defined by laws and regulations is shaped by a desire to emulate what is commonly called "best practice." The problem is that there is far from universal agreement as to what constitutes best practice. Multiple governance rating agencies define sets of practices that they deem to be best practice, but their suggested best practices do not always agree. Many books and articles provide advice about aspects of corporate governance, but those ideas, too, do not always converge.

Although boards are important, there are limits to what they can do. It is common to blame boards of directors when companies suffer improprieties and ethical lapses. But independent directors serve their organizations only part time. They provide only oversight, although they should do so effectively. Good corporate governance must depend on managers' building a culture of integrity that involves an open and candid relationship with their engaged and supportive-but-challenging boards.

Also, one must remember that boards of directors and their committees consist of groups of individuals. Each individual has unique perceptions and understandings of roles and responsibilities. Thus, the functioning of these bodies depends heavily on group dynamics, which includes concerns such as how the agendas are set, how issues are presented, how people get along, and whether members tolerate confrontation and/or compromise.[32] These are complex issues, and much is yet to be learned about what makes boards and board committees effective.

Notes

1 See, for example, R. I. Tricker, *Corporate Governance: Principles, Policies and Practices* (Oxford: Oxford University Press, 2015); *Global Trends in Corporate Governance* (New Delhi: Deloitte, 2015), online at bit.ly/1X3ddWH; C. de Kluyver, *A Primer on Corporate Governance* (New York: Business Expert Press, 2013); W. Judge, "Corporate Governance Mechanisms Throughout the World," *Corporate Governance: An International Review*, 18, no. 3 (2010), pp. 159–60; K. Balachandran, A. Dossi, and W. Van der Stede, "Corporate Governance Research in 'The Rest of the World,'" *Journal of Accounting Auditing & Finance*, 25, no. 3 (Fall 2010), pp. 523–9.

2 See, for example, *The U.K. Corporate Governance Code* (Financial Reporting Council, September 2014), online at frc.org.uk/Our-Work/Publications/Corporate-Governance/UK-Corporate-Governance-Code-2014.pdf; *Committee of Sponsoring Organizations of the Treadway Commission* (COSO), online at www.coso.org, and, specifically, *The COSO Financial Controls Framework* (2004 version) and the original 1992 COSO Report: *Internal Control – An Integrated Framework*.

3 J. J. Chen. *A Primer on Corporate Governance: China* (New York: Business Expert Press, 2015).

4 See, for example, N. Rajagoplan and Y. Zhang. "Recurring Failures in Corporate Governance: A Global Disease?," *Business Horizons*, 52 (2009), pp. 545–52; R. B. Lamm, "The Shape of Things to Come in Corporate Governance," *The Securities Edge* (August 27, 2014), online at goo.gl/v98BFG; "String of Scandals Puts Japanese Investors on Edge," *The Financial Times* (May 29, 2016), online at on.ft.com/1U4zG0t.

5 See, for example, J. Coffee, *Gatekeepers: The Professions and Corporate Governance* (New York: Oxford University Press, 2006), particularly Chapter 4.

6 De Kluyver, *Primer on Corporate Governance*, op. cit.

7 See, for example, P. Ali and G. Gregoriou, *International Corporate Governance after Sarbanes-Oxley* (New York: Wiley Finance, 2006).

8 "How Much Is It Really Costing to Comply with Sarbanes-Oxley?" *The Wall Street Journal* (June 16, 2005), online at on.wsj.com/1sjGwrq.

9 L. Rittenberg and P. Miller, *Sarbanes-Oxley 404 Work: Looking at the Benefits* (Altamonte Springs, FL: The Institute of Internal Auditors Research Foundation, January 2005).

10 CRA International, *Sarbanes-Oxley Section 404 Costs and Implementation Issues: Spring 2006 Survey Update* (Washington, DC: CRA International, April 17, 2006).

11 S. Ernst, "CPA Corner: Sarbanes-Oxley and Corporation Fraud – Does One Size Fit All?" *AICPA CPA Insider* (May 8, 2006).

12 "Safeguards Failed to Detect Warnings in Enron Debacle," *The Los Angeles Times* (December 14, 2001), online at articles.latimes.com/2001/dec/14/news/mn-14906.

13 For this alleged problem with corporate governance and boards as well as many other issues, see, for example, L. Bebchuk and J. Fried, "Pay without Performance: Overview of the Issues," *Journal of Corporation Law*, 30 (2005), pp. 647–73; L. Bebchuk and J. Fried, *Pay without Performance: The Unfulfilled Promise of Executive Compensation* (Cambridge, MA: Harvard University Press, 2004).

14 O. Faleye, "The Cost of a (Nearly) Fully Independent Board," *Journal of Empirical Finance*, 31 (June 2015), pp. 49–62.

15 "Now Hear This," *Fortune* (May 2, 1994), p. 16.

16 "Casablanca Capital Blasts Cliffs Board for Fabrications, Material Omissions and Mischaracterization of Facts," *Business Wire* (June 23, 2014), online at goo.gl/doIHtG.

17 "Slow to Respond, Tesco Now Pays the Price," *The Wall Street Journal* (June 22, 2014), online at on.wsj.com/1srX142.

18 "Long-Serving Non-Executives Are on the Wane in the UK," *The Financial Times* (December 28, 2014), online at on.ft.com/1AXzPwO.

19 See, for example, D. Barton and M. Wiseman, "Where Boards Fall Short," *Harvard Business Review* (January–February 2015).

20 See, for example, D. Larcker, S. Richardson, and I. Tuna, "Corporate Governance, Accounting Outcomes, and Organizational Performance," *The Accounting Review*, 82, no. 4 (July 2007), pp. 963–1008. See also "Corporate Constitutions," *The Economist* (October 28, 2010), p. 74.

21 See, for example, "From Cuckolds to Captains: Corporate Boards Are Playing a More Prominent Role in Steering Companies," *The Economist* (December 7, 2013), online at goo.gl/UehfY3.

22 See, for example, "Schroders Criticized for Elevating Michael Dobson to Chairman," *The Financial Times* (March 3, 2016), online at on.ft.com/1UAKKGT.

23 See, for example, R. M. Daines, I. D Gow, and D. F. Larcker. "Ratings the Ratings: How Good Are Commercial Governance Ratings?," *Journal of Financial Economics*, 98, no. 3 (2010), pp. 439–61; and M. Ertugul and S. Hegde, "Corporate Governance Ratings and Firm Performance," *Financial Management* (2009), pp. 139–60.

24 "How Good Are Commercial Corporate Governance Ratings," *Stanford Business* (September 1, 2009), online at stanford.io/1pjDBXJ.

25 See, for example, US Securities and Exchange Commission, *Final Rule: Standards Relating to Listed Company Audit Committees: Rel. No. 33-8220* (December 18, 2007), online at www.sec.gov.

26 For a more detailed discussion of the audit committee charter, see publications by the major accounting firms, such as Deloitte & Touche, *Audit Committee Resource Guide* (Deloitte, 2010), online at www.deloitte.com.

27 *Corporate Board Survey Results: 2015 Trends and Insights* (Chicago: JWC Partners, January 2015); and *Governing for the Long-Term: Looking Down the Road with an Eye on the Rear-View Mirror* (New York, PwC, 2015).

28 See, for example, C. S. Armstrong, C. D. Ittner, and D. F. Larcker, "Corporate Governance, Compensation Consultants, and CEO Pay Levels," *Review of Accounting Studies*, 17, no. 2 (June 2012), pp. 322–51.

29 "Executive Pay Committee Chair in the Hot Seat," *The Financial Times* (May 2, 2016), online at on.ft.com/1TGhrRq.

30 *The BDO Board Survey* (BDO USA, September 2015).

31 "What Directors Think," *Corporate Board Member* (Special Supplement, 2009), p. 16. See also "Is a Pay Revolution Nigh? And If Not, Should It Be?," *The Financial Times* (May 8, 2016), online at on.ft.com/1TxUI7l.

32 See, for example, K. Merchant and K. Pick. *Blind Spots, Biases and Other Pathologies in the Boardroom* (New York: Business Expert Press, 2010).

CASE STUDY
Arrow Motorcar Corporation

Harry Standell, a member of the board of directors of Arrow Motorcar Corporation (Arrow), had a lot on his mind as he drove to the office. It was March 22, 2016, the day Arrow's board had agreed to ask formally for the resignation of the company's president/CEO and founder, Billy Ray Repko. Billy Ray had already been informed that if he did not resign, he would be fired. Harry hoped that Billy Ray would step down gracefully and not provoke a confrontation. Billy Ray had been the mastermind of the company for many years. But now Harry believed the board had little choice but to remove him because Arrow was in a crisis. Arrow was not able to pay either its employees or its payroll taxes; checks were bouncing; and outstanding accounts payable were being ignored. Harry and the other board members were convinced that the crisis was the result of Billy Ray's management style and excessive spending and that it was the board's moral and legal obligation to the company's shareholders to remove him as president and CEO.

When Harry arrived at the Arrow offices, however, he was greeted by security staff barring entry to the building. His efforts to enter the building through a rear entrance were futile because the locks had been changed. Billy Ray had barricaded himself inside the building. Clearly this was not going to be an amicable management succession process. Billy Ray had declared war.

Arrow and the exotic sports car industry

Arrow Motorcar Corporation designed, manufactured, and sold exotic sports cars. Cars are defined as exotic by their price range (in the $200,000–$400,000 range and over); their speed (in excess of 160 mph); their driving performance; their technologically superior, high-performance components; their extensive use of hand manufacturing; and their appearance. Exotic sports cars are offered to a select, wealthy clientele. Arrow management estimated that the total worldwide market for exotic sports cars was approximately 6,000 vehicles per year. The company's major competitors were Ferrari and Lamborghini, who together dominated the market. Arrow, located in Montgomery, Alabama, was the only US-based manufacturer of exotic sports cars.

Formerly a stock car racer, Billy Ray Repko subsequently earned a college degree in aeronautical engineering. Billy Ray's vision was to marry his two interests by designing an automobile using the finest aerospace technology. For Billy Ray, performance was paramount; cost was no object. He believed that he could find buyers who appreciated, and could pay for, automobiles constructed with his avant-garde, uncompromising approach to automobile design.

Arrow's standard model, powered by a 6.0 liter, all-aluminum engine with twin turbochargers that generated over 600 horsepower at 5,700 rpm, was priced at $448,000. It could accelerate from 0 to 60 mph in 3.9 seconds and reach speeds of 260 mph. The car made considerable use of aerospace technology, including advanced composite materials for body panels, military specification electrical systems, and advanced tactical fighter instrumentation and head-up displays. It also contained numerous safety and luxury features, such as an integrated roll cage, energy-absorbing crush zones, a spacious, hi-tech, jet-aircraft-like leather cockpit, and a state-of-the-art sound system.

From 2000 to 2010, the company operated as Arrow Car, a privately funded limited partnership founded by Billy Ray Repko. Arrow Motorcar Corporation was formed in September 2010. Billy Ray sold approximately 35% of the company's stock for $12 million to a collection of his family members and friends.

Arrow delivered its first car to a paying customer in September 2013, and as of March 2016 it had sold a total of 13 cars, to an international clientele. In its peak month, the company employed 45 people. Because of its low sales volumes, however, Arrow had reported substantial financial losses since its inception (see statements of operations in Exhibit 1). In an attempt to build volume, Arrow was developing two other models, a roadster and coupe. Billy Ray Repko wanted to price these models in the $700,000–$800,000 range, but some of the members of the board of directors thought the new models should be more modestly priced, at perhaps around $200,000.

The board of directors

At its incorporation in 2010, Arrow had three members on its board of directors. Billy Ray was the chairman. Harry Standell was a financial consultant who had been a consultant to Arrow Car at the time of its formation. Barry Rosenfeld worked for the bank from which Arrow had obtained some loans.

The Board's primary role was to act as a fiduciary body, to oversee management decisions and protect shareholders' interests. The board helped Billy Ray develop the company's strategy, and it ratified major financial and policy decisions, such as advertising and promotion budgets. When actual expenses were greater than budgeted expenses (as they often were), Billy Ray Repko, in his role as president, had to explain the variances to the other board members. Although the outside board members recognized that Billy Ray's effectiveness as president would probably decline as the company grew in size, they had not concerned themselves with a succession plan, partly because the company was so small and partly because Billy Ray would be strongly opposed to such an action.

The board of directors met quarterly on a regular basis. Additional special meetings were called occasionally to deal with specific issues, such as the signing of corporate documents. Arrow management rarely provided information to board members prior to the meetings, but they shared considerable data and progress reports during the meetings. The atmosphere of the board meetings was generally congenial.

In 2014, Phil Jacobs was added to the board of directors. Phil was an attorney and a longtime associate of Billy Ray. According to Harry:

> **Billy Ray wanted to shift the balance of power on the board. By 2014 Barry and I were not agreeing with him on some of the things that he wanted to do. He was getting voted down in some situations, and he wasn't particularly happy about that. I think he felt bringing Phil in would help shift the balance in his favor a little bit.**

Early signs of trouble

In June 2013, Robert Smith was hired as vice-president, finance. Robert quickly began to feel uncomfortable with Billy Ray's management style. Robert said:

> **Billy Ray hires good people who think they will be able to make a difference. But it didn't take me long to realize that he doesn't give anyone the freedom to be effective.**

Robert thought Billy Ray was excessively focused on raising money and promoting the company while neglecting attention to engineering and production. He also believed that Billy Ray's management style, which was shaped by "a compulsive, obsessive personality and a foul mouth," imposed undue stress on employees. Robert confronted Billy Ray about his concerns, but was not able to change either Billy Ray's priorities or his management style. Robert informed the board members of his concerns, but he received no support. For many months, Robert felt he was the sole voice of dissent, noting that "obviously Billy Ray hand-picked most of the board."

Until 2015, the outside board members were not seriously concerned about Billy Ray's management style, although they considered him eccentric. Harry explained that:

> **At some point in his schooling, Billy Ray must have stayed up all night preparing for an exam or a presentation and received an "A" for his effort. Since then he has decided that's the way life works, that if you let everything wait until the last minute and cram all your preparation into two days, you get better performance than if you spread it out over the month beforehand. That's how he functioned.**

In retrospect, Harry attributed much of the outside board members' support of Billy Ray to the fact that most of the information they received was designed to elicit agreement. He said:

> **Billy Ray was literally a master of giving everybody, including the board, just enough information to support the conclusion he wanted them to reach. The boardroom presenters were well coached, and we never received all of the relevant information.**

The board finally took serious issue with some of Billy Ray's management actions early in 2015. Within three months of joining the board, Phil Jacobs became a strong adversary of Billy Ray because of some issues brought to his attention by Arrow employees. In an executive session of a board meeting, he charged that Billy Ray was misusing expense reports, using company funds for personal home improvements, and participating in other forms of self-dealing at the company's expense. The board asked Robert Smith to look into these issues. Three weeks later, a board meeting was called to formally discuss the charges and to decide on a course of action. Phil Jacobs called for Billy Ray's immediate removal.

But Phil did not get the board's support. The outside board members did not think the charges of illegal activity could be substantiated. Robert Smith did a study but found no evidence that Billy Ray had diverted any company assets to personal use. He did question approximately $15,000 of items charged on Billy Ray's American Express card because he had provided inadequate documentation. But Billy Ray explained that all the expenses were legitimate because, as the president of an exotic car company, he "had an image to maintain."

The board did conclude that Billy Ray had participated in some questionable business deals. For example, Billy Ray lent an associate $25,000 of company money, which was secured by a personal note made payable to himself. He also negotiated a lease at a below-market price and attempted to re-lease the property to Arrow at the market price. The board insisted that Billy Ray charge Arrow the lower price for the lease, arguing that he should not realize personal gain at the expense of the company. Billy Ray reluctantly succumbed to the board's wishes on the lease issue. And since the loan was repaid and neither of these deals ended up hurting Arrow, the directors felt these items did not warrant Billy Ray's termination. Harry said:

> **By this time I think the Board was actually concerned about Billy Ray's management style, how he ran things, and about his excessive spending, but he hadn't done anything illegal. He also had an employment contract (see excerpts in Exhibit 2) which says he's allowed to be a bad manager. He just isn't allowed to do anything illegal.**

The outside directors also believed it was not in the company's best interest for them to agree with Phil Jacobs's call for firing Billy Ray because there was no obvious successor. In Harry's words:

> **One of the concerns at that time was that Phil had no Act II. Act I was "get rid of Billy Ray!" Act II was, "What do we do now?" There had to be something in place as far as I was concerned. You don't just throw the guy out. You have to have a plan to move forward.**

One outcome of this board meeting, however, was an agreement to change the process for reimbursing Billy Ray for personal expenses. Previously, Arrow had paid Billy Ray's entire credit card bill. After the meeting, Billy Ray was required to submit formal expense reports to the accounting department.

Later that year, Phil Jacobs resigned from the board and later died. He was replaced on the board by Aiden West, a self-employed consultant and businessman, and another long-time associate of Billy Ray Repko.

A Malaysian investor

In June 2015, Arrow obtained $2.1 million in financing from Zafran Megat, a Malaysian investor. Mr. Megat bought 4 million shares at $.40 and also paid $118,000 for an option to buy an additional 6 million shares at $.50. Mr. Megat advanced the money to Arrow before completing a due diligence review. The board members perceived this quick advance quite unusual and not business-like, but they later discovered that Mr. Megat customarily did business on the basis of trust.

Included in Mr. Megat's purchase agreement was the right to appoint a director to the board. Thus a fifth director, Dan Zuraidi, was added to protect Mr. Megat's interests in the company. Billy Ray had said that Mr. Megat insisted that the board not be increased in size, thus leaving him only a 20% vote, so Barry Rosenfeld resigned to make room for Mr. Megat's director, leaving the board still comprised of four members. But the remaining board members later found out that Billy Ray had lied to them. Billy Ray and Mr. Megat had never discussed the board-size issue.

In the summer of 2015, Billy Ray negotiated a new employment contract. It included an option to buy 1 million shares of stock at $.265, which was the value an outside appraisal firm put on the company's stock on the date the option was issued.

By December 2015, Arrow was out of money again, and some employees had to be laid off. Mr. Megat was unwilling to exercise his stock purchase option, but he agreed to exercise Billy Ray's stock option if Billy Ray would transfer that option to him. Mr. Megat sent $265,000 to Arrow in accordance with this agreement. But then, despite an agreement signed to the contrary, Billy Ray tried to renege on this deal, claiming that he had not intended that his option be transferred but just used as collateral for a loan. This disagreement breached the Malaysians' trust in Billy Ray. After this point, they had no interest in making additional investments in Arrow, but they did keep Mr. Zuraidi on as a director to protect the money they had already invested.

Events leading to Billy Ray Repko's termination

As Arrow's financial position worsened, tension between Billy Ray and the board of directors increased. The company's payroll taxes for the period September through December 2015 were not paid on time. This caused a discussion over disclosures in the company's financial reports for the fiscal year ended September 30, 2015. According to Harry:

> Although the financial reports were required by the bank to be filed within 90 days of the fiscal year-end, Billy Ray would not allow it to be filed with the required disclosure that we hadn't paid our payroll taxes. But I would not allow it to be filed without that disclosure. So Billy Ray and I compromised. We had a sales prospect who was expected any day to give us a $100,000 check as a deposit on a car. That money could be used to pay the payroll taxes. We decided to let the financial reports be late.

In February 2016, Harry was invited to Billy Ray's house for a baby shower for the accounting manager who was preparing to go on maternity leave. This was his first visit to the house, and when he arrived, he was shocked to find the house was decorated in "modern Arrow." Cabinets, floor tiles, and wall tiles were all identical to those used in Arrow headquarters. Harry recalled:

> When I went into the house, I couldn't quite believe it. I looked around and saw what looked like a mirror image of our office. On Monday morning, I said to Robert Smith, I know you've examined all of the company invoices, but I have now been in Billy Ray's house and you're never going to convince me that company money wasn't used in that house. I don't know how we're going to prove it, but I will guarantee you that he has diverted company assets.

That same month, Robert Smith informed the board that in the opinion of the heads of the marketing, finance, and production departments, the business plan Billy Ray was showing potential investors was "wildly optimistic." He believed that Billy Ray's continued use of the business plan to solicit funds could be construed as being fraudulent.

By March, Arrow's financial position was critical. Employees weren't being paid; the financial reports still had not been issued because the payroll taxes had not been paid; $14,000 in checks had bounced; and remaining accounts payable were being ignored. But Billy Ray was focused on other things: he and some of his managers were out of the country, at the Geneva car show.

Harry was ready to take action. He was convinced that with Billy Ray as CEO, Arrow was headed for disaster. But before Harry could take any action against Billy Ray, he needed Aiden West's support. Aiden had also become increasingly disenchanted with Billy Ray. Aiden had been trying to assist Arrow in obtaining financing, but he was finding it difficult to do so because the potential investors he had contacted did not trust Billy Ray. Harry brought up the issue over lunch. He explained:

> Aiden talked about his inability to raise any money because of Billy Ray's management style. I told him about my concerns regarding the probable diversion of funds. I also explained that I had pulled out a couple of Billy Ray's American Express bills and found out that the procedure we thought had been put into place had not been implemented. Billy Ray instead told the accounting department that they were now to pay off from only the face page of the bill. They were no longer going to get all account detail.

Harry and Aiden agreed to call the company's outside counsel for advice. The lawyers acknowledged that the board did have authority to terminate Billy Ray for cause, and they further acknowledged that there appeared to be sufficient cause, most particularly the fraudulent business plan and diversion of company assets. Harry called Mr. Megat, and he agreed to support the other outside board members in their decision to terminate Billy Ray.

Harry hand-delivered to Billy Ray a notice for a special board meeting to be held on Friday, March 18, 2016. This notice, which contained no explanation of the purpose of the meeting, was given 24 hours in advance of the meeting, as was required by company by-laws. After receiving this notice, Billy Ray called Mr. Megat, who told him that the purpose of the meeting was to terminate Billy Ray as president. Billy Ray immediately called Aiden West and demanded an explanation.

Aiden and Billy Ray met for nearly the entire day on Wednesday, March 16. Harry was there for part of the day. At this meeting, Aiden confirmed what Mr. Megat had said and added that the board planned to give him the opportunity to resign in the best interest of the shareholders. If Billy Ray chose to resign, the board would send out a press release explaining that Billy Ray had wanted to devote himself to creative aspects of the business. If Billy Ray chose not to resign, the board would terminate him and sue him for conversion of funds.

Billy Ray questioned both why this was happening and why now. He said he needed to go to New Jersey for discussions with a dealership, and he had a financing meeting set up in New York. But Aiden and Harry did not want him to make the trip. They did not think he should act as president and CEO when he was soon to be fired, and they did not want him to raise money by using the fraudulent business plan.

Finally, Billy Ray asked that the special board meeting be postponed for 30 days. The board members refused this request, but they did agree to postpone until Monday to give Billy Ray the weekend to decide if he would resign or be terminated. The meeting was scheduled for Monday, March 21, at 5:00 p.m. On Monday morning, Billy Ray responded by moving into the headquarters' building and barring all outsiders, including the board members, from the building.

Exhibit 1 Statements of operations

	Years ended September 30			September 12, 2010 (Inception) to September 30, 2015 (Cumulative)
	2015	2014	2013	
Sales, net	$ 1,287,866	$ 754,800	$ 20,000	$ 2,062,666
Cost of sales	974,966	579,800	20,000	1,574,766
Gross profit	312,900	175,000	–	487,900
Costs and expenses				
Salaries and wages	917,350	1,533,199	1,253,554	4,251,037
Rental expense	96,358	112,972	128,558	529,088
Utilities expense	91,793	116,578	64,264	316,575
Research and development	1,275,841	718,346	2,340,818	4,878,034
Depreciation and amortization	429,394	466,316	241,437	1,266,813
Advertising and promotion	566,121	535,023	655,194	1,890,137
Professional fees	613,015	324,411	580,852	1,833,288
General and administrative	528,275	917,726	427,820	2,153,405
Warranty expense	27,564	31,157		58,721
Provision for loss contingency	–	33,167	–	633,167
Abandonment of property and equipment		234,911		234,911
Total costs and expenses	4,545,711	5,623,806	5,692,497	18,045,176
Other income (expense)				
Other income	231,299	88,489	214,179	836,211
Other expense	(35,400)	(15,862)	(26,373)	(119,523)
	195,899	72,627	187,806	716,688
Net loss	$ (4,036,912)	$ (5,376,179)	$(5,504,691)	$(16,840,588)
Net loss per share	(0.39)	$ (1.11)	$ (1.90)	
Weighted average common shares outstanding	10,245,056	4,832,556	2,890,329	

Exhibit 2 Excerpts from Billy Ray Repko's employee contract

EMPLOYMENT AGREEMENT

EMPLOYMENT AGREEMENT, effective July 1, 2015, by and between ARROW MOTORCAR CORPORATION, a Delaware corporation (the "Company") and BILLY RAY A. REPKO (the "Employee").

WHEREAS, the Company has, prior to the date of this Agreement, employed the Employee as the Company's President, and

WHEREAS, the Company desires to continue to employ the Employee on a full-time basis, and the Employee desires to be so employed by the Company, from and after the date of this agreement.

NOW THEREFORE, in consideration of the mutual covenants contained herein, the parties agree as follows:

Article I
EMPLOYMENT DUTIES AND BENEFITS

Section 1.5 Expenses. The Employee is authorized to incur reasonable expenses for promoting the domestic and international business of the Company in all respects, including expenses for entertainment, travel and similar items. The Company will reimburse the Employee for all such expenses upon the presentation by the Employee, from time-to-time, of an itemized account of such expenditures.

Section 1.6 Employee's Other Business. Employee shall be allowed to participate in outside business activities provided (i) such activities do not interfere with Employee's performance of his duties as a full-time employee of the Company; and (ii) the outside business is not a Business Opportunity of the Company, as defined herein. A Business Opportunity of the Company shall be a product, service, investment, venture or other opportunity which is either:

(a) directly related to or within the scope of the existing business of the Company; or
(b) within the logical scope of the business of the Company, as such scope may be expanded or altered from time-to-time by the Board of Directors.

Article II
COMPENSATION

Section 2.1 Base Salary. The Company shall pay to the Employee a base salary of not less than the amount specified on Schedule 1. This amount may be adjusted for raises in salary by action of the Board of Directors.

Section 2.2 Bonus. The Employee shall be entitled to receive a bonus at such time or times as may be determined by the Board of Directors of the Company.

Article III
TERM OF EMPLOYMENT AND TERMINATION

Section 3.1 Term. This Agreement shall be for a term which is specified on Schedule 1, commencing on its effective date, subject, however, to termination during such period as provided in this Article. This Agreement shall be renewed automatically for succeeding periods of one year on the same terms and conditions as contained in this Agreement unless either the Company or the Employee shall, at least 30 days prior to the expiration of the initial term or of any renewal term, give written notice of the intention not to renew this Agreement. Such renewals shall be effective in subsequent years on the same day of the same month as the original effective date of this Agreement.

Section 3.2 Termination by the Employee Without Cause. The Employee, without cause, may terminate this Agreement upon 90 days' written notice to the Company. In such event, the Employee shall not be required to render the services required under this Agreement. Compensation for vacation time not taken by Employee shall be paid to the Employee at the date of termination.

Section 3.3 Termination by the Company With Cause. The Company may terminate the Employee, at any time, upon 90 days' written notice and opportunity for Employee to remedy any non-compliance with the terms of this Agreement, by reason of the willful misconduct of the Employee which is contrary to the best interests of the Company. Upon the date of such termination, the Company's obligation to pay compensation shall terminate. No compensation for vacation time not taken by Employee shall be paid to the Employee.

(continued)

Exhibit 2 *Continued*

Schedule 1
Duties and Compensation

Employee: Billy Ray A. Repko

Position: President and CEO

Base Salary: $275,000 per year, payable bi-weekly and quarterly performance payment equal to 10% of improvements over annual budget as approved by Board from time to time

Bonus: As determined by the Board of Directors

Term: December 31, 2020

Duties and Responsibilities: Supervision and coordination of all operations of the Company; supervision of all other operating officers of the Company.

This case was prepared by Professor Kenneth A. Merchant.

CASE STUDY
Golden Parachutes?

A special conference-call meeting of the compensation committee of the board of directors of Database Technologies, Inc. (DTI) was scheduled for the morning of February 23, 2007. DTI, headquartered in Sunnyvale, California, was a leader in database-related software. The company's main products helped customers monitor, forecast, and manage data growth in enterprise resource planning (ERP) system environments.

The main agenda item for the special compensation committee meeting was discussion and possible approval of a proposed Change in Control Severance Agreement. In November 2006, a large, European-based technology company had expressed interest in acquiring DTI. Because of this inquiry, John Hoffman, DTI's chairman/CEO, had asked Alan Adamson, chair of DTI's compensation committee, to have his committee consider the implementation of a severance agreement. Mr. Adamson agreed. There was some urgency to the request because DTI management expected to receive the formal acquisition offer sometime in the first half of 2007.

After a series of discussions with Mr. Hoffman and Mr. Adamson, DTI's outside counsel drew up a proposed severance agreement. The agreement, if enacted, would provide payments under certain conditions (explained below) to a "select group of management or highly compensated employees" of DTI. Included in this select group were five executives: DTI's CEO, COO, CFO, chief technology officer (CTO), and general counsel/secretary.

The materials sent to the committee members in advance of the meeting explained that the severance agreement was –

> intended for the benefit of both the key DTI executives and the company. It would protect the executives against significant negative personal as well as financial consequences that could result from a change in control. Further, having this severance agreement in place would help to keep the executives employed and focused on shareholders' interests, rather than on their own interests. That is, it would help to ensure that the company would be

able to rely upon the executives to continue in their positions without concern that they might be distracted by the personal uncertainties and risks created by the possibility that they might lose their jobs.

Under the terms of the severance agreement, the named executives would be entitled to receive benefits if the executive received a Qualifying Termination following a Change in Control of the company. *Change in Control* was deemed to have occurred as of the first day that 40% or more of the then-outstanding voting securities changed hands. A *Qualifying Termination* was deemed to have occurred if any one or more of the following events occurred within a 24-calendar-month period following the date of a Change in Control:

1. An involuntary termination of the executive's employment for reasons other than Cause. *Cause* was defined as the occurrence of either or both of the following: (a) the executive's conviction for committing a felony or (b) the executive's willful engagement in misconduct that is significantly injurious to the company.
2. A voluntary termination of the employment by the executive for Good Reason. *Good Reason* was defined as the occurrence, without the executive's express written consent, of any one or more of the following:
   a. A material reduction in the nature of status of the executive's authorities, duties, and/or responsibilities or a diminution of the executive's reporting relationship.
   b. A reduction in the executive's base salary.
   c. A reduction in the executive's relative level of participation in and relative level of coverage in the company's employee benefit plans. (The company can eliminate and/or modify existing programs, but the executive's level and amounts of coverage under all such programs must be at least as great as is provided to executives who have the same or lesser levels of reporting responsibilities within the company's organization.)
   d. The executive is informed by the company with less than 180 days' notice that his/her principal place of employment for the company will be relocated to a location that is greater than 35 miles away from the executive's principal place of employment for the company immediately prior to the Change in Control.
3. The company or any successor company repudiates or breaches any of the provisions of the Severance Agreement.

The executive's right to terminate employment for good reason was not affected by the executive's incapacity due to physical or mental illness.

Each Qualifying Termination would entitle the affected executive to receive:

1. A lump-sum payment equal to twice (2×) the executive's highest annualized base salary in effect at any time on or before the effective date of termination.
2. A lump-sum payment equal to twice (2×) the highest aggregate bonus(es) paid by the company to the executive for any one of the three full fiscal years of the company immediately preceding the executive's effective date of termination.
3. A lump-sum payment equal to the portion of the executive's account under the company's qualified retirement plan, nonqualified deferred compensation plan, or any other supplemental retirement plan that has not become vested as of the effective date of termination. Included in this provision was an immediate vesting of all of the executives' stock options.
4. A continuation of the executive's car allowance or other company perquisites for 24 months following the effective date of termination.
5. A continuation of the executive's and his/her family's medical coverage, dental coverage, and group term life insurance for 24 months following the executive's effective date of termination.
6. A reimbursement of up to $18,000 for outplacement services obtained during the 24-month period following the effective date of termination.
7. If the payments exceeded the safe harbor amount set by the US Congress, the payments would be "grossed up" so that the executives would not have to pay an excise tax sometimes referred to as a "golden parachute" tax.[1]

[1] If the present value of the severance payments ("parachute payments") exceeded three times the individual's average annual compensation in the most recent five taxable years, a federal "golden parachute tax" would have to be paid. This tax legislation was passed to try to discourage what the US Congress considered to be "excessive" severance payments. The amount of the golden parachute tax was calculated as 20% of the excess of the parachute payments over the executive's average base salary over the prior five-year period.

If the company grossed up the payment, the paid tax amount would also have to be treated as part of the parachute payment, and a golden parachute tax would have to be paid on this amount also. As a consequence, grossing up the payments could be quite costly. The need to pay taxes on the excess and the need to pay additional taxes on the gross-up amounts was sometimes likened to a dog "chasing its tail."

The executive would not be entitled to receive severance benefits if employment terminated, regardless of the reason, more than 24 months after the date of a Change in Control.

An estimate of the amounts that would be paid to the five key executives if the payments were triggered in 2007 is shown in Exhibit 1. CEO John Hoffman was the only executive who would be subject to the so-called golden parachute tax. John's proposed severance payments exceeded the allowed base amount because when John was recruited to DTI, he had been given a large number of options with a 10-year vesting period. If a Change in Control occurred, all of these options would immediately vest. The value of these options would comprise approximately half of the Change in Control Payments that John would be paid.

The materials sent in advance of the meeting presented a statement that most companies of DTI's size or larger had such an agreement in place, with the range of severance payments typically set between one and a half to three times the executives' base salary plus bonuses. However, the committee members were not provided with any formal benchmarking data.

A committee member's reactions

As Dennis Feingold, one of DTI's three compensation committee members, read the proposed severance agreement, he had mixed feelings about it. Dennis believed that the purposes of such plans were valid. DTI's interests could be badly hurt if key executives, fearing for their jobs, left the company before the acquisition was consummated. Most, if not all, of these executives would probably not be retained by the management of the acquiring company. A severance agreement would probably keep them on the job until the end, and the payments would probably enable them to sustain their lifestyles until they could obtain another comparable job.

Dennis had particular empathy for DTI's CTO, who was recruited to DTI just a few months earlier from a firm located in New York. Losing his job not long after a disruptive personal relocation would be difficult for the CTO and his family.

Dennis was not particularly concerned about the total cost of the severance payments. While the severance payments would reduce the acquisition price, they probably were not large enough to have a negative effect on the consummation of the transaction itself. Even if all of the severance payments were paid, the total cost would probably only be about $12 million, not a large amount of money in comparison with the company's acquisition price, which probably would be close to $2 billion.

But Dennis did have some concerns about the payments. Some of the individual payments would be quite large. Some of these executives were already quite wealthy, and they would be given millions of dollars more in severance payments. Dennis knew that shareholders did not have to approve such payments and probably would not even become aware of them, but he was concerned that if they, or rank-and-file employees, became aware of them, there would be some resentment.

Dennis also asked himself whether the company's performance warranted these payments. While the company's stock price had risen over the years, by most objective metrics DTI's performance in recent years could be rated only mediocre, perhaps slightly below the median as compared to similar technology-intensive companies. A part of him thought that, with the exception of the newly hired CTO, the executives had been amply rewarded for their efforts over the years. In return, perhaps they should owe loyalty to the company.

Dennis wondered why these five employees, as key as they were, should have severance arrangements different from those of any other employee in the company. Other corporate officers (e.g. VP-operations, VP-sales and marketing, VP-human resources, controller) were not included in the severance agreement. In fact, Dennis noted that since no DTI employees were represented by a union, all DTI employees had always been considered to be employed "at will," meaning they could be fired at any time without cause.

Dennis knew that severance payments were a political hot button. Many management critics had focused much attention on what they perceived as "outrageous" management compensation packages, with large severance payments and potential payments seen as part of the problem.[2] Dennis knew that some corporate governance rating agencies and other "watchdogs" would be observing. He did not want to see DTI listed as being

[2] In 2005 the average parachute payment for CEOs of the top 100 US corporations was $28 million. Some payments were much larger, such as the $188 million that Gillette's CEO James Kilts received when his company was sold to Procter & Gamble, and the $162 million that William McGuire, CEO of United Health, would receive if his company were sold. See, for example, "Examining the Largest Golden Parachutes," *Harvard Law School Forum on Corporate Governance and Financial Regulation*, online at corpgov.law.harvard.edu/2012/02/26/examining-the-largest-golden-parachutes/; and M. Brush, "You're Fired. Here's Your $16 Million," *MSN Money* (April 9, 2003), moneycentral.msn.com/content/p44954.asp.

among a "rogue's gallery" of firms whose boards did not exercise their fiduciary responsibilities in the compensation area. Dennis was also concerned about his personal reputation. He enjoyed his board service and wanted to serve on other boards.

On the other hand, Dennis knew that if he raised objections, the other committee members would undoubtedly point to the fact that most companies have a severance agreement, and the terms of this agreement probably should be judged as reasonable by current corporate standards. Dennis himself, the CEO of a large company in the food processing industry, was covered by a severance agreement. His was not quite as lucrative as the one being proposed at DTI, but Dennis certainly did not want to go on record as being against severance agreements.

So, as Dennis prepared to go to the meeting, he was mulling over all of these issues, which accumulated into one big question. Should he just "go along" with the other two compensation committee members and vote to approve the severance agreement as proposed, or should he voice his concerns? If the latter, how forcefully should he press his concerns if the other committee members did not immediately agree with him?

Exhibit 1 Estimate of DTI parachute payments if paid in 2007 ($000)

Executive	Change in control payment	Excess parachute payment	Total payment
CEO	$4,474	$1,670[3]	$6,144
COO	2,110	–	2,110
CFO	1,685	–	1,685
CTO	1,400	–	1,400
General counsel	623	–	623
Total	$10,292	$1,670	$11,962

[3] **Test for the need for a golden parachute tax payment:**

Total change in control payments	$4,474
Safe harbor amount (3x limit)	3,402
Difference	$1,072 (Since the difference is positive, a golden parachute tax must be paid.)

Calculation of the amount of the golden parachute tax:

Total change in control payments	$4,474
Base amount (ave. salary over last 5 years)	1,134
Excess parachute	3,340
Golden parachute tax (20%)	668
Grossed up golden parachute tax	$1,670

This case was prepared by Professors Kenneth A. Merchant and Wim A. Van der Stede.

CASE STUDY
Pacific Sunwear of California, Inc.

As a publicly owned company in the United States, Pacific Sunwear of California, Inc. (PacSun) was required to comply with the provisions of the Sarbanes-Oxley Act of 2002 (SOX). Among other things, SOX required top management to test their company's system of internal controls and to certify that it is effective. It also required the company's external auditors to conduct independent tests of those controls and to express their independent opinion about the effectiveness of the company's system.

In 2006, after their second year of complying with SOX, PacSun management looked back and concluded that the process had provided a few benefits, but they thought that the compliance costs far exceeded the benefits, at least to the company. With the compliance processes now well controlled and the costs of compliance having been sharply reduced, they were turning their attention back to issues of more business relevance, such as business continuity planning and, more generally, controlling business risks.

The company

PacSun's mission is to be "the leading lifestyle retailer of casual fashion apparel, footwear and accessories for teens and young adults." The company's origins were as a small surf shop that started in 1980 in Newport Beach, California. The company was incorporated in August 1982, and it went public in 1993. Its stock is traded on NASDAQ using the symbol PSUN. By 2006, PacSun was a large company, with annual sales of almost $1.4 billion (see Exhibit 1). Over the years, the company's stock was split 3-for-2 six times, and was one of the fastest-growing stocks on the NASDAQ stock exchange.

PacSun operated chains of mostly mall-based stores with three distinct retail concepts. As of July 29, 2006, it ran 826 PacSun stores, 102 PacSun Outlet stores, 201 d.e.m.o. stores and six One Thousand Steps stores, for a total of 1,112 stores located in all 50 states of the United States and Puerto Rico. PacSun and PacSun Outlet stores specialized in board sport-inspired casual apparel, footwear, and related accessories. d.e.m.o. specialized in fashion-focused streetwear. One Thousand Steps, a new concept started in 2006, targeted 18- to 24-year-old customers and featured an assortment of casual, fashion-forward, branded footwear and related accessories.

In its stores, PacSun offered a wide selection of well-known board-sport-inspired name brands, including Quiksilver, Roxy, DC Shoes, Billabong, Hurley, and Volcom. The company supplemented the name brand offerings with its own proprietary brands. The company had its own product design group that, in collaboration with the buying staff, designed the proprietary brand merchandise. The company also had a sourcing group that oversaw the manufacture and delivery of its proprietary brand merchandise with manufacturing contracted out both domestically and internationally.

PacSun's merchandising department oversaw the purchasing and allocation of its merchandise. Its buyers were responsible for reviewing branded merchandise lines from new and existing vendors, identifying emerging fashion trends, and selecting branded and proprietary brand merchandise styles in quantities, colors, and sizes to meet inventory levels established by company management. The planning and allocation department was responsible for management of inventory levels by store and by class, allocation of merchandise to stores, and inventory replenishment based upon information generated by its merchandise management information systems. These systems provided the planning department with current inventory levels at each store and for the company as a whole, as well as current selling history within each store by merchandise classification and by style.

All merchandise was delivered to the centralized distribution facility in Anaheim, California, where it was inspected, received into its computer system, allocated to stores, ticketed when necessary, and boxed for distribution to its stores or packaged for delivery to its Internet customers. Each store was typically shipped merchandise three to five times a week, providing it with a steady flow of new merchandise. The company used a national and a regional small package carrier to ship merchandise to its stores and Internet customers. The company occasionally used airfreight to ship merchandise to stores during peak selling periods.

PacSun's expansion pace was steady and fast. In 2005, the company opened 115 net new stores, which included 67 PacSun stores, 12 PacSun Outlet stores, and 36 d.e.m.o. stores, and also expanded or relocated an additional 34 existing stores.

The store operating structure was relatively flat. Each store had a manager, one or more co-managers or assistant managers, and approximately 6–12 part-time sales associates. District managers supervised approximately 7–12 stores. Regional directors supervised approximately 6–10 district managers.

District and store managers and co-managers participated in a bonus program based on achieving predetermined metrics, including sales and inventory shrinkage targets. The company had well-established store operating policies and procedures and an extensive in-store training program for new store managers and co-managers. It placed great emphasis on loss prevention programs in order to control inventory shrinkage. These programs included the installation of electronic article surveillance systems in all stores, education of store personnel on loss prevention, and monitoring of returns, voids, and employee sales. As a result of these programs, PacSun's historical inventory shrinkage rates were below 1.5% of net sales at retail (0.6% at cost).

PacSun's merchandise, financial, and store computer systems were fully integrated. Its software was regularly upgraded or modified as needs arose or changed. Its information systems provided company management, buyers, and planners with comprehensive data that helped them identify emerging trends and manage inventories. The systems included purchase order management, electronic data interchange, open order reporting, open-to-buy, receiving, distribution, merchandise allocation, basic stock replenishment, interstore transfers, inventory, and price management. Company management used weekly best/worst item sales reports to enhance the timeliness and effectiveness of purchasing and markdown decisions. Merchandise purchases were based on planned sales and inventory levels and were frequently revised to reflect changes in demand for a particular item or classification.

All of the PacSun stores had a point-of-sale system operating on in-store computer hardware. The system featured bar-coded ticket scanning, automatic price look-up, electronic check and credit/debit authorization, and automatic nightly transmittal of data between the store and corporate offices. Each of the regional directors and district managers could instantly access appropriate or relevant company-wide information, including actual and budgeted sales by store, district and region, transaction information, and payroll data.

The company's culture was lean and frugal. To illustrate, PacSun's CFO explained, "We never succumbed to management entitlements. Very few employees have company paid-for Blackberries, cell phones, and credit cards. No one travels by first class airfare."

Complying with Section 404 of the Sarbanes-Oxley Act of 2002

As a company whose securities were sold publicly in the United States, PacSun was bound by the provisions of the Sarbanes-Oxley Act of 2002. PacSun was first obligated to comply with the full provisions of SOX in its 2004 fiscal year (ended January 29, 2005).

The most difficult and expensive provisions in the act to comply with were those contained in Section 404. Section 404 dealt with internal controls over financial reporting (ICOFR) – the processes that are designed to ensure the reliability of the financial reporting process and, ultimately, the preparation of financial statements. Section 404, with later clarifications by the SEC and the PCAOB, required management to (1) accept responsibility for the effectiveness of the company's ICOFR; (2) evaluate the effectiveness of the company's ICOFR using suitable control criteria;[1] (3) support the evaluation with sufficient evidence, including documentation of the design of controls related to all relevant assertions for its significant financial statement accounts and disclosures; and (4) present a written assessment of the effectiveness of the company's ICOFR as of the end of the company's most recent fiscal year. The company's CEO and CFO personally had to certify the results of the evaluation.

[1] Most companies and auditors, including PacSun and PacSun's auditor (Deloitte & Touche LLP), relied on the language, concepts, and evaluation criteria described in the integrated internal control framework developed by the COSO (Committee of Sponsoring Organizations).

As part of its assessment, management had to determine if identified internal control deficiencies – individually or in combination – constituted significant deficiencies or material weaknesses. An internal control *deficiency* exists when the design or operation of a control does not allow management or employees, in the normal course of performing their assigned functions, to prevent or detect misstatements on a timely basis. An internal control deficiency may be either a design or operating deficiency. A *significant deficiency* is a control deficiency, or combination of control deficiencies, that adversely affects the company's ability to initiate, authorize, record, process, or report external financial data reliably in accordance with generally accepted accounting principles such that there is more than a remote likelihood that a misstatement of the company's annual or interim financial statements that is more than inconsequential will not be prevented or detected. A *material weakness* is a significant deficiency, or combination of significant deficiencies, that results in more than a remote likelihood that a material misstatement of the annual or interim financial statements will not be prevented or detected. The existence of even a single material weakness is grounds for an *adverse* 404 opinion.

Management then communicated the findings of their tests to the external auditor. The company's auditors then had to attest to management's assertion on the effectiveness of internal controls – whether they had done enough work to have the basis to express their opinion – and to express their own opinion. If management had not fulfilled its responsibilities, the auditor was required to issue a disclaimer opinion.

The first year – FY 2004

The PacSun SOX compliance process for FY 2004 began in mid-2003. At that time, the company had a lean accounting staff and had not previously had an internal audit function. The company created its internal audit function in mid-2003 (one manager) and outsourced the initial direction of the 404 compliance work to a Big-4 auditing firm as an "audit consultant."[2] By late 2004, the internal audit function had been expanded to include a director, a manager, and two staff auditors. The audit consultant designed a five-step process:

1. *Scope and plan the evaluation.* This required scoping the entire internal control evaluation process. What controls and locations/units would be included in the study? What would be the approach, milestones, timeline? What resources would be needed?
2. *Document the controls.* All of the controls over relevant financial statement assertions related to all significant accounts and disclosures had to be documented. Documentation of controls could take many forms and could include a variety of information, including policy manuals, process models, flowcharts, job descriptions, documents, and forms.
3. *Evaluate the design and operating effectiveness of the controls.* Tests of the key controls had to be designed and carried out, and the results of the tests had to be documented.
4. *Identify, assess, and correct deficiencies.* Findings should be communicated and deficiencies corrected, if possible.
5. *Report on internal control.* Management had to prepare a written assertion about the effectiveness of internal control over financial reporting.

The audit consultant and PacSun personnel identified 21 major business processes that the company used, such as involving property, plant and equipment, payroll, and taxes (see Exhibit 2). Each of the processes was assigned an "owner," and deadlines were set for the development of detailed process narratives.

The documentation included detailed descriptions of the process objectives, the risks that threatened achievement of the objectives, the controls used to minimize the risks, and the process owners who were responsible for maintaining and documenting the process. The process narratives varied significantly in length depending on the complexity of the process. For example, some supply-chain narratives were 20–25 pages in length, while the equity narrative was only five pages in length.

Each of the 21 major business processes was disaggregated into subprocesses. Exhibit 3 shows the business objectives, and risks for the Merchandise Accounting process, a part of major process number 9 (Supply Chain Processes/Merchandise Accounting) (see Exhibit 2). The narrative of the process is shown in Exhibit 4. The two controls associated with this subprocess that were designated as *key* are shown in bold type in this narrative.

[2] The company could not have outsourced the work to its primary auditor. Doing so would have compromised the primary auditor's audit independence.

In FY 2004, a total of 238 key controls were identified across the 21 major business processes (as is shown in Exhibit 2). PacSun's CFO explained:

> We did a good job in year one paring down the number of key controls. (Some big companies have identified 10,000 or more key controls.)[3] But our task was also easier than that of some other companies. We have a simple business model; a simple organization; and all of our major operations are located in Anaheim.

PacSun and the audit consultant's personnel jointly performed the tests of the controls.

In FY 2004, one significant deficiency was identified by company management. This deficiency was caused by a variance between PacSun's accounting and that suggested in a February 2005 interpretation letter from the SEC's chief accountant. This new interpretation affected virtually all firms in the retail industry. The CFO explained:

> There were several parts to the problem. First, when most retailers buy a store in a mall, they sign a 120-month lease. They start construction three months before opening but do not have to pay rent expense until the store opens. The SEC, though, decided that the lease should be expensed over 123 months. Second, if we received a landlord incentive allowance, which is designed to help us fund improvements, we treated that allowance as a reduction in capital expeditures, rather than a deferred lease incentive liability. The SEC ruled that it should be treated as a deferred lease incentive liability and amortized as a reduction in rent expense rather than as a reduction in depreciation expense, as we had been doing.
>
> The adoption of the new accounting policy resulted in an immaterial reduction in net income of less than $25,000 for each period presented. However, these corrections did result in multi-million dollar reclassifications between rent expense (within cost of goods sold) and depreciation expense (within selling, general and administrative expenses), cumulative adjustments to the property, plant and equipment and deferred rent amounts on the balance sheet, and reclassifications between cash flows from investing activities and cash flows from operating activities on the company's statements of cash flow.

The CFO explained what these changes meant from his perspective:

> In 2005, we had to restate our prior two years' financial statements, which resulted in no material change to net income. What purpose did that restatement serve? I think the fact that we caught and fixed the problem is indicative of good internal control. But auditors judge restatements as deficiencies. But what type of deficiency? Here there is no consistency in the auditing industry. Two of the Big-4 firms, judged this particular type of restatement as only a significant deficiency. The other two judged it to be a material weakness.

Certifications

Section 302 of SOX required both the company's CEO and CFO to personally certify the "appropriateness of the financial statements and disclosures contained in the periodic report" and to guarantee that "financial statements and disclosures fairly present, in all material respects, the operations and financial condition of the issuer." Exhibit 5 shows the CFO's certification that appeared in the company's 10-K for FY 2004. About the certification requirement, the CFO said, "I feel confident about my certifications here."

PacSun top management required their subordinates to share the certification responsibility. All PacSun officers (vice president level or higher) were required to certify that the controls in their area were effective (see Exhibit 6). Process owners also had to sign a similar certification (see Exhibit 7). The CFO noted that there was no resistance to the sharing of the certification requirements. He said, "This should not just be an accounting exercise; you've got to get the whole organization engaged."

In FY 2004, PacSun received "clean" opinions from its external auditors, Deloitte & Touche, LLP, both for the fair presentation of its financial statements and for the effectiveness of the company's internal control system (see Exhibit 8).

[3] A survey commissioned by the Big-4 accounting firms found that the average number of key controls identified in year one of Section 404 compliance by larger firms, those with over $700 million in capitalization, was 669. For smaller firms, those with a market capitalization between $75 million and $700 million, the average was 262 key controls (CRA International, *Sarbanes-Oxley Section 404 Costs and Implementation Issues: Spring 2006 Survey Update*, Washington, DC, April 17, 2006, pp. 4–5). PacSun's market capitalization was greater than $1 billion.

The year 2 process – FY 2005

In the second year of complying with SOX Section 404, the process was much easier. Everybody involved – audit consultant, PacSun, and primary auditor personnel – had already been through the process once. Most of the needed documentation had already been created. Rather than involving the audit consultant's personnel, the testing of controls was done by the PacSun internal audit staff, which had now grown to four persons. The testing was spread more evenly throughout the year, as the company was able to anticipate better what needed to be done. And the primary auditor was able to combine its financial statement opinion work with the 404 audit.

In SOX year two, most companies were able to make significant reductions in the number of key controls they tested,[4] but PacSun's reductions were relatively small. The number of key controls tested was reduced from 238 to 222 in FY 2005, only a 7% reduction. The CFO explained that this was not surprising to him. He argued that PacSun had a tight, effective control system even before SOX was implemented; the control environment at PacSun was not particularly complicated because the company operated primarily from a single business location and, from a control perspective, had a simple business model; and PacSun and the audit consultant personnel did a good job in identifying the key control points in the first year.

But in FY 2005, the company discovered a new significant internal control deficiency. The issue related to the accounting for the liabilities created by the company's loyalty program called "Pac Bucks." In the Pac Bucks program, shoppers earn $25 in Pac Bucks for each $50 they spend. To use their Pac Bucks, the shoppers must spend at least another $50 in the stores within a set period of time. In FY 2005, the external auditors concluded that PacSun's accounting was not recognizing the liabilities and expenses in the proper accounting quarter (the full fiscal year was unaffected). This accounting problem was deemed to be a significant deficiency, but not a material weakness. In FY 2005, PacSun received clean financial statement and 404 opinions.

The costs of complying

The cost to PacSun of SOX compliance was significant. Exhibit 9 shows an estimate of the costs of 404 compliance and, for comparison purposes, the costs of the annual financial statements audit for fiscal years 2004 and 2005. These figures show that in FY 2004 the total cost of compliance – financial statement audit and 404 compliance – was an estimated $2 million, of which only a small portion of the cost was attributed to the standard financial statement audit. In year two, the costs declined by almost 40%. This reduction is comparable to that reported by other companies.[5]

But there were also some other, implicit costs. For example, the CFO noted that SOX had made it more burdensome to serve on the Audit Committee of the Board of Directors. At PacSun, the Audit Committee played an active role in the SOX 404 compliance process. While PacSun's director of internal audit, reported administratively to the CFO, he reported functionally directly to the Audit Committee. The director of internal audit met with the Committee five times a year and had conference calls with the committee members at least once a quarter. The CFO noted, however, that the relationship with the Audit Committee had become much more formalized, and time-consuming in a sense, due to SOX. "What took 30 minutes a couple of years ago takes 2–3 hours now. Everyone now asks checklists of questions. If you don't ask the questions, there is no record; and you need to create the record."

There also were costs associated with training. Although PacSun did not have a formal, dedicated SOX training program for rank-and-file personnel, several SOX orientation sessions were offered in combination with other training programs, such as for store personnel.

Management reflections and plans for the future

Overall, PacSun management thought that the costs of the SOX compliance process far exceeded the benefits. The CFO explained:

> **There were some benefits. When you go through an elaborate documentation process, it is inevitable that you will see some gaps and some redundancies. We did plug some gaps in our payroll and**

[4] A survey found that larger companies (those with greater than $700 million in market capitalization) reduced their numbers of key controls tested by more than 19%, from 669 in year one to 540 in year two (CRA International, 2006, p. 4).

[5] Large companies (those with greater than $700 million in market capitalization) reported that their total costs of complying with SOX Section 404 declined from $8.5 million in year one to $4.8 million in year two, a reduction of almost 44% (CRA International, 2006, p. 3).

information systems areas. Most of the changes we made involved better segregation of duties. For example, we had some payroll clerks who had access to too many systems. But the process was very expensive and, for the most part, not very useful for us. This company has always been tightly controlled, so we did not uncover any major issues, and the process forced us to create a lot of documentation that was not needed.

I also wonder about the effectiveness of this legislation for its intended purposes. This process will not stop crooks from being crooks. For example, it won't stop people from doing off-balance sheet transactions ...

When asked if the public disclosure of the significant internal control deficiencies had an effect on the company's stock price, the CFO responded that he could not detect any.

Going into year three of the SOX process, the role of the PacSun internal audit function was evolving. The focus of the first two years of its existence was on financial reporting and ensuring compliance with SOX. In FY 2006, the focus was shifting to a broader focus on controlling business risks. The department was spending a lot less time on SOX compliance and a lot more time worrying about business continuity planning. It was also preparing to conduct some operational audits.

Exhibit 1 Pacific Sunwear of California, Inc.: Consolidated statements of income and comprehensive income

	(in thousands, except share and per share amounts)		
FISCAL YEAR ENDED	January 28, 2006	January 29, 2005	January 31, 2004
Net sales	**$1,391,473**	**$1,229,762**	**$1,041,456**
Cost of goods sold, including buying, distribution and occupancy costs	884,982	781,828	668,807
Gross margin	**506,491**	**447,934**	**372,649**
Selling, general and administrative expenses	309,218	277,921	244,422
Operating income	**197,273**	**170,013**	**128,227**
Interest income, net	5,673	1,889	732
Income before income tax expense	202,946	171,902	128,959
Income tax expense	76,734	64,998	48,759
Net income	**$126,212**	**$106,904**	**$80,200**
Comprehensive income	$126,212	$106,904	$80,200
Net income per share, basic	$1.69	$1.41	$1.05
Net income per share, diluted	**$1.67**	**$1.38**	**$1.02**
Weighted average shares outstanding, basic	74,758,874	75,825,897	76,595,758
Weighted average shares outstanding, diluted (See notes to consolidated financial statements.)	75,713,793	77,464,115	78,849,651

Source: Pacific Sunwear of California, Inc. Annual Report 2005.

Exhibit 2 SOX 404 compliance project process index as of 2/10/2005

Reference		*Business process*	*Narrative*	*Owner*	*Key controls*
1	A	Control environment	–		11
2	B	IT general controls	1/16/2004		25
3	C	Budgeting process/financial planning	11/9/2004		2
4	D	General ledger maintenance	11/9/2004		13
5	E	Retail store operations and retail accounting	7/26/2004		8
6	F	Retail IT	11/9/2004		7
7	G	Retail store leasing acitvities	11/9/2004		5
8	H	General accounting	11/9/2004		8
9	I	Supply chain processes/merchandise accounting	11/30/2004		32
10	J	PP&E	11/9/2004		9
11	K	Accounts payable – merchandise	12/3/2004		21
12	L	Accounts payable – non-merchandise	1/19/2004		2
13	M	Payroll	11/22/2004		31
14	N	Treasury	1/19/2004		11
15	O	Debt	1/19/2004		4
16	P	Goodwill	7/19/2004		2
17	Q	Consolidation process	11/9/2004		2
18	R	Taxes	11/9/2004		22
19	S	Legal matters	7/9/2004		2
20	T	Equity	1/19/2004		17
21	U	Financial reporting process	10/25/2004		4
					238

Exhibit 3 Objectives and risks of the merchandise accounting process

PROCESS DOCUMENTATION: MERCHANDISE ACCOUNTING
PROCESS OWNER:
EFFECTIVE DATE: MAY 25, 2005

CONTENTS:

A. Control Objectives
B. Risks Which Threaten Objectives
C. Computer Information Systems

A. CONTROL OBJECTIVES:

1. To initiate, process and accurately record appropriate purchases reserves for sales returns, markdowns, chargebacks, vendor allowances, transfers, adjustments (to units and prices) and related liabilities.
2. Develop and maintain relationships with suppliers that meet company requirements.
3. Obtain quality merchandise on a timely basis.
4. Ensure inventory is properly safeguarded from damage or theft.
5. Inventory settings within system are complete.
6. Only valid inventory master file information has been captured in the system.
7. Accurately record physical and cycle count adjustments.
8. Approve and accurately record price changes and unit adjustments.
9. All inventory movement between the distribution center and stores (and from store to store) are recorded completely and accurately.
10. Proper presentation of inventory related line items are reflected on the financial statements.

B. RISKS WHICH THREATEN OBJECTIVES:

A. Poor quality merchandise is not identified timely.
B. Reserves for sales returns, markdowns and vendor chargebacks are not adequately reflected in the financial statements (e.g. the reserve for sales returns does not reflect actual return rates).
C. The Company obtains poor quality merchandise and/or obtains it at a different time than needed.
D. The Company selects suppliers that fail to meet standards.
E. Configured tolerances for physical inventory re-counts are inadequate. Adjustments may be inaccurate and/or posted by inappropriate users. Physical and cycle counts, significant adjustments are not investigated for root-cause.
F. Changes in prices are not authorized and/or are not automatically activated, resulting in inaccurate prices assigned to products.
G. Improper cutoff procedures result in inaccurate inventory and liability balances at period-end.
H. Inadequate receiving procedures and system content allow for the receipt of unauthorized purchases.
I. Inadequate monitoring of imports in transit result in inaccurate inventory and liability balances.
J. DC outbound shipments are not reconciled to receipts at stores resulting in missing/damaged goods not properly reflected on the financial statements.
K. Inventory accounts (including RTV's) are not reconciled timely resulting in inaccurate inventory's AP balances.
L. Inventory is not properly safeguarded from damage or theft.
M. Shortages/discrepancies identified are not monitored or reflected in inventory balances and/or root-cause are not identified and addressed in a timely manner (e.g. supplier failing to meet standards, employee picking inaccuracies, etc.).
N. Financial statement presentation and disclosures is inaccurate and/or misleading.
O. Inventory movements between distribution center and the stores or between stores monitored, reconciled, or are not properly recorded.
P. Inappropriate inventory system settings may impact financial statements.
Q. Incomplete or duplicated master data could prevent the initiation or completion of transactions.
R. Slow moving inventories are not identified in a timely manner.
S. Vendor allowances are being allocated to the wrong class of inventory or to the wrong vendor, and/or allowance amount is improperly calculated.

C. COMPUTER INFORMATION SYSTEMS:

Island Pacific, PKMS, Travado POS System

Exhibit 4 Narrative describing the process and controls surrounding distribution center receiving, a merchandise accounting subprocess

SUBPROCESS: DISTRIBUTION CENTER RECEIVING

Once the PO is EDIed to the vendor, the vendor then fills the PO and requests an Advance Shipping Notice (ASN) from Pac Sun. The ASN details out what Pac Sun expects to receive at the case level detail (it is similar to the vendor's shipping document or packing slip). Currently, Pac Sun has vendors on two different types of EDI: (1) SPS Commerce EDI and (2) Traditional EDI. SPS Commerce is a web based EDI tool that allows the vendor to look at the PO online, input their shipping information online, and if the shipping parameters are within predefined tolerance levels, Pac Sun will automatically generate an ASN for the vendor.

The system will not accept any ASNs outside of the predefined tolerance levels without a manual override of the system (SCP6). Only Store Planning and Allocation Managers (SPAMs), the Sr. Programmer Analyst, and the Import Assurance Coordinator, at the direction of the buyer, have the ability (and the system access within the EDI user maintenance IP profile control) to perform these types of override (CP7).

With Traditional EDI, the vendor is subject to the same business rules regarding quantity and price that determine if the shipment is within tolerance, and if it is, an ASN is generated. The Senior Programmer Analyst monitors all transactions to ensure that none are hung up in the system. (SCP8) If an ASN is hung up, the Senior Programmer Analyst will contact the buyer so that the vendor can be contacted and any issues resolved. Once both Pac Sun and the vendor have accepted the ASN, all of the PO history can be seen in IP and the vendor can print labels for the cartons that will be delivered to Pac Sun.

The PKMS system is based on only allowing one SKU per case. PKMS can also handle prepacks (merchandise prepackaged in a set size run – for example, 5 small, 10 medium, 20 large, 12 x-large in a single prepack). The system has a subfile that identifies prepacks. Prepacks are still only allowed one SKU per box and they will show up in the system as size 1111 (instead of a valid size code). In the IP system, the prepacks are exploded into the individual sizes and everything is seen by individual SKU. PKMS takes care of all of the warehouse instructions regarding packing and picking of the merchandise. The PKMS software generates transactions called PIX's to bridge PKMS and IP. Based on instructions generated from PKMS, the PIX will update IP. A Never Ending Program (NEPS) is constantly running that scoops all of the instructions out of PKMS to IP using PIX's so that IP is continuously being refreshed and updated with the most recent movement activity in the warehouse.

When a valid ASN is accepted, it allows the vendor to call the distribution center (DC) and schedule a delivery appointment (CP9). When the goods arrive, the trucking company buzzes in at the security gate. In PKMS, the first PIX is the receipt of the merchandise.

Merchandise is only received and accepted if there is a valid PO, ASN and delivery appointment (CP10). In order to be able to enter the docking facility and be assigned a door number, the truck driver must provide a valid ASN/PO and have a delivery appointment. Once the security guard and the receiving office validate everything, the truck is instructed to go to a particular door. The truck is parked, the documents are presented to the receiving personnel and the truck is unloaded and the cartons scanned by RF gun. The RF scan creates a PIX in PKMS and a receipt in IP. PKMS records the number of cartons received and the units in each carton, which is then bridged (via a PIX) into the IP system. The IP system then automatically closes the PO if the PO has been filled (SCP11). **A receipt number is generated in IP (next available number in the sequence) and a purchase is generated in the stock ledger (SCP12).** The stock ledger represents the perpetual inventory record for the chain. This process helps to ensure that merchandise received is recorded accurately and all merchandise received is recorded.

A predetermined level of test cartons is set (currently set at every 10th carton) whereby the carton is opened on the dock to verify that the ASN agrees to the carton contents (SCP13). PKMS will instruct the receivers to conduct random audits of cartons by prompting them after a carton has been scanned. The receiving of the goods cannot continue until this audit has been completed and the information regarding the quantities in the carton have been input into the RF gun. This predetermined level can be adjusted at the vendor level if it has been determined that a vendor has a high incidence of discrepancies. If certain checks fail, then the carton will be segregated to the rework area to be resolved with the vendors. At this point, there is a 100% review of the shipment prior to it being received in the system (i.e. the entire contents of the trailer are sent to the rework area for review prior to receipt). Any unusual items are forwarded to one of the DC Supervisors who investigates the differences and ensures correct treatment.

Rejected merchandise is adequately segregated from good merchandise and regularly monitored to ensure timely return to vendors (CP14). If merchandise is known to have problems from the outset (i.e. no ASN) they are sent to the "hospital." Items in the hospital have been physically received, but they are not recorded in IP. (See discussion regarding proper cutoff below.) The hospital is the troubled goods area where the inventory is reviewed to determine whether it can be reworked or if it should be returned to the vendor. The buyer is contacted if the goods are damaged and the buyer obtains a return authorization (RA) number from the vendor. DC personnel (the RTV Supervisor) contact the buyer for RA information for merchandise in RT (RTV) status. Once an RA# has been received, the goods are shipped and PKMS and IP inventory are relieved.

Exhibit 4 *(Continued)*

Although the goods have been physically received, items in the hospital have *not* been received in the IP system due to the fact that there is something wrong with them. In order to ensure that all items are properly recorded in inventory at any quarter- or year-end cutoff warehouse management and either the Merchandise Accounting Manager or the Assistant Controller – Merchandise Accounting physically inspect the hospital area at these cutoff dates noting the PO information for merchandise in the hospital area so that the goods can be accrued for. (CP15). A reversing journal entry is posted to accrue the PO quantity and cost for the goods in the hospital area that have not been systemically received in IP.

Exhibit 5 CFO financial statement and internal control certification

I, _________, certify that:

1. I have reviewed this annual report on Form 10-K of Pacific Sunwear of California, Inc.;
2. Based on my knowledge, this report does not contain any untrue statement of a material fact or omit to state a material fact necessary in order to make the statements made, in light of the circumstances under which such statements were made, not misleading with respect to the period covered by this report;
3. Based on my knowledge, the financial statements, and other financial information included in this report, fairly present in all material respects the financial condition, results of operations and cash flows of the registrant as of, and for, the periods presented in this report;
4. The registrant's other certifying officer and I are responsible for establishing and maintaining disclosure controls and procedures (as defined in Exchange Act Rules 13a–15(e) and 15d–15(e)) and internal control over financial reporting (as defined in Exchange Act Rules 13a–15(f) and 15d–15(f)) for the registrant and have:
   a) Designed such disclosure controls and procedures, or caused such disclosure controls and procedures to be designed under our supervision, to ensure that material information relating to the registrant, including its consolidated subsidiaries, is made known to us by others within those entities, particularly during the period in which this report is being prepared;
   b) Designed such internal control over financial reporting, or caused such internal control over financial reporting to be designed under our supervision, to provide reasonable assurance regarding the reliability of financial reporting and the preparation of financial statements for external purposes in accordance with generally accepted accounting principles;
   c) Evaluated the effectiveness of the registrant's disclosure controls and procedures and presented in this report our conclusions about the effectiveness of the disclosure controls and procedures as of the end of the period covered by this report based on such evaluation; and
   d) Disclosed in this report any change in the registrant's internal control over financial reporting that occurred during the registrant's most recent fiscal quarter (the registrant's fourth fiscal quarter in the case of an annual report) that has materially affected, or is reasonably likely to materially affect, the registrant's internal control over financial reporting; and
5. The registrant's other certifying officer and I have disclosed, based on our most recent evaluation of internal control over financial reporting, to the registrant's auditors and the audit committee of the registrant's board of directors (or persons performing the equivalent functions):
   a) All significant deficiencies and material weaknesses in the design or operation of internal control over financial reporting which are reasonably likely to adversely affect the registrant's ability to record, process, summarize and report financial information; and
   b) Any fraud, whether or not material, that involves management or other employees who have a significant role in the registrant's internal control over financial reporting.

Date: April 7, 2005

____

Senior Vice President and Chief Financial Officer

Exhibit 6 Officer quarterly disclosure certification

I, ______________________, certify that:

1. I have brought to the CFO's attention everything that I believe might be important for purposes of disclosure in the Company's financial statements, including those filed with the Securities and Exchange Commission;
2. I am not aware of any material transactions (over $5,000) or agreements that I have not already reported to Finance via the monthly accrual sheet or other mode of communication;
3. I have not entered into any transactions or agreements on behalf of the Company that are in violation of the Company's policies, including the Company's Code of Ethics;
4. I have not made any false statements of material fact or intentionally omitted facts that would make the information underlying the Company's financial statements misleading as to any material fact;
5. I am not aware of (a) any fraud involving management or employees who have significant roles in the system of internal control or any fraud involving others which could have a material effect on the financial statements, (b) any violations of laws or regulations whose effects have not been considered for disclosure in the financial statements or as a basis of recording a loss contingency, (c) any communications from regulatory agencies concerning noncompliance with or deficiencies in financial statements, or (d) any failure to comply with contractual agreements where such failure would have a material effect on the financial statements that has not been discussed or for which a provision has not been recorded; and
6. I know of no plans or intentions that may materially alter the valuation of any Company assets or liabilities.

____

Signature

____

Date

Exhibit 7 Process owner certification

I, ______________________, certify that:

1. I am the designated Process Owner for the processes listed below and, as such, I am responsible for maintaining the adequacy and accuracy of the Process Narrative which serves as the documentation of disclosure controls and procedures and internal control over financial reporting for those processes. I am responsible for the following processes:

   ________________ ________________

   ________________ ________________

   ________________ ________________

2. The process narratives on file with the Internal Audit department for my designated processes accurately document the internal control over financial reporting in existence at the end of the quarter covered by this certification.
3. I have disclosed to the Director of Internal Audit any change in internal control over financial reporting that occurred during the most recent fiscal quarter that has materially, or is reasonably likely to materially affect internal control over financial reporting.
4. I have evaluated the effectiveness of the internal control over financial reporting for my designated processes and have concluded that such controls and procedures were effective as of the end of the quarter covered by this report.
5. Based on my evaluation, I have disclosed to the Director of Internal Audit any control deficiencies in the design or operation of internal control over financial reporting which are likely to adversely affect the company's ability to record, process, summarize, and report financial information.
6. I have disclosed to the Ethics Review Team or the Audit Committee any fraud, whether or not material, that involves management or other employees who have a significant role in the company's internal control over financial reporting.

____

Signature

____

Date

Exhibit 8 Report of independent registered public accounting firm, FY 2004

To the Board of Directors and Stockholders of
Pacific Sunwear of California, Inc.
Anaheim, California

We have audited the accompanying consolidated balance sheets of Pacific Sunwear of California, Inc. and subsidiaries (the "Company") as of January 29, 2005 and January 31, 2004, and the related consolidated statements of income and comprehensive income, shareholders' equity, and cash flows for each of the three years in the period ended January 29, 2005. These financial statements are the responsibility of the Company's management. Our responsibility is to express an opinion on these financial statements based on our audits.

We conducted our audits in accordance with the standards of the Public Company Accounting Oversight Board (United States). Those standards require that we plan and perform the audit to obtain reasonable assurance about whether the financial statements are free of material misstatement. An audit includes examining, on a test basis, evidence supporting the amounts and disclosures in the financial statements. An audit also includes assessing the accounting principles used and significant estimates made by management, as well as evaluating the overall financial statement presentation. We believe that our audits provide a reasonable basis for our opinion.

In our opinion, such consolidated financial statements present fairly, in all material respects, the financial position of Pacific Sunwear of California, Inc. and subsidiaries as of January 29, 2005 and January 31, 2004, and the results of their operations and their cash flows for each of the three years in the period ended January 29, 2005, in conformity with accounting principles generally accepted in the United States of America.

We have also audited, in accordance with the standards of the Public Company Accounting Oversight Board (United States), the effectiveness of the Company's internal control over financial reporting as of January 29, 2005, based on the criteria established in *Internal Control – Integrated Framework* issued by the Committee of Sponsoring Organizations of the Treadway Commission and our report, dated April 4, 2005, expressed an unqualified opinion on management's assessment of the effectiveness of the Company's internal control over financial reporting and an unqualified opinion on the effectiveness of the Company's internal control over financial reporting.

As discussed in Note 2, the accompanying consolidated financial statements as of January 31, 2004 and for the years ended January 31, 2004 and February 1, 2003 have been restated.

Deloitte & Touche LLP

Costa Mesa, California
April 4, 2005

Exhibit 9 PacSun estimated audit and SOX compliance costs, FY 2004 and FY 2005 ($000)

	FY 2004	FY 2005
Primary auditor		
Standard financial statement audit	240	225
SOX 404 audit	470	345
Audit consultant		
Documentation and testing – non-IT	100	
Documentation and testing – IT	600	70
PacSun		
Setting up the Internal Audit dept.; started with SOX implementation	200	315
Other costs (rough guess by CFO)	500	300
Total financial statement audit and SOX 404 compliance costs	$2,110	$1,255

This case was prepared by Professors Kenneth A. Merchant, Wim A. Van der Stede and research assistant Fei Du.

CASE STUDY
Entropic Communications, Inc.

In 2009, Entropic Communications, a small but growing semiconductor company headquartered in San Diego, California, was implementing a new Enterprise Risk Management (ERM) process. Lance Bridges, Entropic's VP/general counsel, had taken the lead in developing the process and was coordinating its implementation. The first full process cycle was completed at the end of 2009. Lance was contemplating how effective it had been.

Lance was sure that the process had raised issues, stimulated discussion, and resulted in some tangible measures to mitigate risk. But he had a few areas of concern. He thought the risks that were identified might have been better aligned with company objectives. He knew that some department heads had not taken the process seriously. He was not sure either if there had been enough communication between departments or if the departments had applied risk scores consistently. Lance also wondered if a process like ERM might be most helpful in dealing with already known risks, and less useful for identifying and analyzing new risks that could arise in the dynamic industry in which Entropic operated. And he was unsure of the value of the final output of the ERM process – a risk management matrix. Some managers in the company had shown little or no interest in it. As Entropic headed into 2010, Lance was considering how the company might improve the process going forward.

Company background

Entropic Communications, Inc. was a fabless semiconductor company (meaning that it specialized in the design and sale of hardware devices while outsourcing the fabrication or "fab" of the devices to a specialized manufacturer) focused on ground-breaking system solutions for connected home entertainment. Entropic was incorporated in Delaware in 2001 and went public in 2007. The company's stock traded on NASDAQ under the symbol ENTR. In 2009, revenues totaled $116 million (see Exhibit 1). At the end of 2009, Entropic employed approximately 300 people. The organization was structured by functional department (e.g. sales, marketing, engineering, human resources).

Entropic sold products in four product lines: home networking, DBS outdoor unit solutions, broadband access, and TV tuners. Entropic's home networking solutions enabled service providers to deliver multiple streams of high definition (HD) video throughout the home using the existing coaxial cable infrastructure. Applications of this technology allowed end users to download and share or "place-shift" video and personal content (e.g. photos, games) throughout the home. A demonstration of Entropic's home networking solutions can be seen at www.entropic.com/products/mocaanimation.htm. Entropic's DBS outdoor unit solutions supported multiple tuners and simultaneous reception of multiple channels, from multiple satellites, over a single cable. Formerly each tuner required a unique cable, but with Entropic technology, a single cable could support 12 tuners. The simplified cabling structure allowed satellite broadcasters to roll out new services without expensive installation and retrofitting, while improving aesthetics for the homeowner.

Entropic's broadband access solution was a cost-effective delivery system for broadband data, video networking, and voice services, designed to deliver "last kilometer" connectivity to customers in areas with fiber optic networks that terminated up to 600 meters from their home.

Entropic also sold silicon tuners with support for multiple analog and digital standards for terrestrial and cable applications.

Most of Entropic's customers were original equipment manufacturers (OEMs) that sold equipment incorporating Entropic technologies to service providers, such as telecommunications companies (e.g. Verizon), cable companies (e.g. Comcast), and direct broadcast satellite (DBS) companies (e.g. DISH Network, DirecTV). Entropic worked closely with OEMs and service providers to develop customized solutions, and to increase the adoption of solutions that included Entropic technology. In 2009, four OEM customers accounted for 58% of Entropic's net revenues.

Entropic's products all provided technological advantages, but they competed in extremely dynamic markets characterized by rapid technological advancements, evolving industry standards and new demands for features and performance of multimedia content delivery solutions. Many of Entropic's competitors had longer operating histories and significantly more resources.

Enterprise Risk Management

In 2010, risk was a hot topic in business management. Throughout the preceding decade, stricter regulatory compliance requirements, rating agency attention, and risk reporting requirements all promoted interest in the subject. Enterprise Risk Management (ERM) emerged as one of the leading management tools used to address risk.

A string of accounting scandals, most notably Enron and WorldCom, led to the passage of the Sarbanes-Oxley Act in 2002. Sarbanes-Oxley focused on internal controls related to fraud, compliance, and financial reporting risks. Under Section 404 of the act, management was required to produce an annual "internal control report" verifying the effectiveness of internal controls over financial reporting. To meet the compliance requirements, many managers organized their documentation and tests of internal controls using the Internal Control Framework developed by the Committee of Sponsoring Organizations of the Treadway Commission (COSO).

In 2004, COSO developed a framework for Enterprise Risk Management that incorporated the widely used Internal Control Framework, but addressed a much broader range of risks. ERM encompassed operational and strategic risks, as well as the more easily defined financial, reporting, and compliance risks. COSO defined ERM as "a process, effected by an entity's board of directors, management and other personnel, applied in strategy setting and across the enterprise, designed to identify potential events that may affect the entity, and manage risk to be within its risk appetite, to provide reasonable assurance regarding the achievement of entity objectives." The COSO framework categorized objectives as strategic, operational, reporting, and compliance. The framework outlined eight "components" or process steps to analyze, manage, and monitor risks (see Exhibit 2). The ERM framework was designed to align a corporation's actual risk exposure with its risk appetite. The goal of ERM was to reduce negative surprises and improve risk response decisions, ultimately improving an enterprise's financial performance.

In 2008, the global financial crisis led many to question whether risk was being adequately addressed in financial institutions specifically, but also in publically traded companies more generally. Standard and Poor's Rating Services (S&P) had incorporated risk management into their ratings for financial and insurance companies since 2005. In the latter part of 2008, they began to incorporate ERM discussions into regular meetings with nonfinancial companies as well. After interviewing more than 300 nonfinancial companies, they released preliminary findings regarding ERM in July 2009 (see Exhibit 3).

In early 2010, the Securities Exchange Commission (SEC) amended its proxy statement requirements to require a discussion of the board's role in risk oversight. (See Exhibit 4 for SEC's final rule.) The stated purpose was to "improve corporate disclosure regarding risk, compensation and corporate governance matters when voting decisions are made." While a formal ERM process was not specifically required, the new SEC rule put pressure on boards and management to create a structured risk management process of some kind and in some form.

It was in this environment that Entropic's management decided to implement ERM, in part to help the board of directors discharge its fiduciary duties. Entropic's finance department already reported financial risks to the board's audit committee quarterly; the board reviewed operational risks in connection with the SEC filings quarterly; and the board regularly discussed strategic risks at quarterly Board meetings, but Lance believed a more comprehensive summary of the company's risk assessment and management practices would be helpful. Lance had completed a risk management process for the legal department because he wanted an organized, systemic approach to identify and address risks in his area of responsibility. Lance presented his method and findings to the audit committee of the board in the fall of 2008, and recommended rolling out the process to the entire company the following year. Patrick Henry, Entropic's president and CEO, agreed with Lance's recommendation, so Lance embarked on the creation of a comprehensive ERM process at Entropic.

The ERM process at Entropic

Implementing an ERM process generally involved five steps: event identification, risk assessment, risk response, communication, and monitoring.

Event identification

Lance began the event-identification process with the risks discussed in the SEC 10-K filings (see summary in Exhibit 5). Like all publicly traded corporations, Entropic was required to disclose its risk factors, including business, financial, and liquidity risks, in its annual report on Form 10-K. Lance sorted those risks by department and then charged each department head to develop a more comprehensive list of risk events for their respective department, using his list as a starting point.

Each department approached the event identification task slightly differently. Some used frameworks to make the process more systematic and comprehensive. Human Resources developed a matrix of functional department (benefits, payroll, recruitment) and the life cycle of an employee (recruit, hire, separation) as a framework for identifying risks. Marketing chose to identify risks by functional department, by product line, and by risk type (competitive, company, and customer risks). Legal used a risk template from an outside source to make certain its list was comprehensive. The departments that were not as engaged in the process relied heavily, and in some cases exclusively, on Lance's initial list of risks. The final output was a catalog of almost 150 potential risk events, sorted by department. (See Exhibit 6 for an excerpt from the Risk Management Matrix.)

The department heads who invested time in the process believed that it was helpful to go through the event identification exercise, although most agreed that the process itself was more useful than the output. Many found it beneficial to spend time analyzing the business in terms of risk. They believed that the process provided assurance that known risks were clarified and were being addressed. For example, Lance was able to pinpoint and clarify legal obligations in areas that he did not deal with every day (e.g. facilities and certain labor laws) and to make sure that those risks were being monitored by an appropriate department manager.

Most of the risks identified were well known. The lack of new findings was not usually considered a failure of the process, but was more often attributed to management already actively addressing risks. As Patrick Henry stated, "If there had been big surprises, it would have meant we were asleep at the wheel." However there was some acknowledgement that there could be flaws inherent in the process itself. Suzanne Zoumaras, VP Human Resources, explained, "The list is only as good as the people who create it. The same people who create a list of risks, aren't going to be surprised by it."

Risk assessment

Risk assessment or quantification involved prioritizing and rating the potential severity of the risks. To that end, Lance developed a simple two-dimensional scoring method that was used by all of the departments. To locate each item on a "risk heat map," a severity score and a likelihood score were assigned to each risk event. The product of the scores became the overall score. Severity and likelihood were quantitatively defined, as explained in Figure 1 below. Severity was defined in terms of cash impact. Likelihood was defined in terms of a probability of occurrence in a given timeframe.

Figure 1 Risk heat map

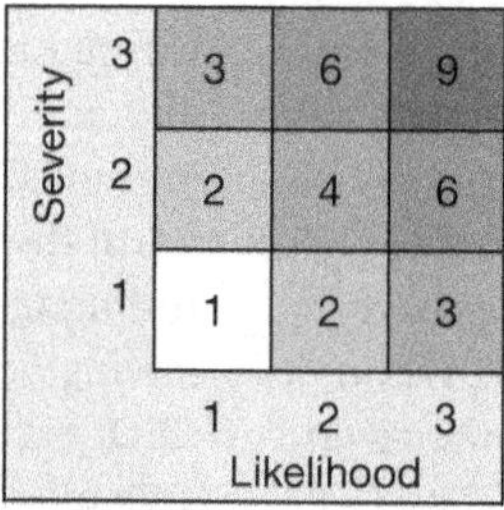

Severity scale

1 = Not significant (likely annual cash impact from risk occurring < $1 million)
2 = Significant but not material (likely annual cash impact from risk occurring is $1–$3 million)
3 = Material (likely annual cash impact > $3 million OR likely to affect stock price)

Likelihood scale

1 = Unlikely to occur in the next 12 months
2 = Potential for minor occurrences in the next 12 months
3 = Minor occurrences happening now OR potential for significant occurrences in next 12 months

Entropic considered the risk events independently; there was no attempt to identify or quantify correlations between them. Every department used the same scoring system, but the scoring was done solely within each department. Individual risk scores were not aggregated into an overall company risk score that could be tracked over time. Top management had no enthusiasm to introduce an aggregate score into the process.

Most managers were happy with the scoring system. They found it easy to implement and useful. In some cases, quantifying risks helped department managers realize that they didn't have high-level risks. In other cases, quantifying risks enabled managers to prioritize and focus. As Vinay Gokhale, Senior VP – Marketing and Business Development, explained, "Having metrics really helped. Otherwise it would have just been a big worry session." Nevertheless, Lance wondered if everyone applied the scoring method consistently and rigorously. He suspected that some participants might have just backed into the numbers they wanted.

Mitigation measures were summarized in a Risk Management Matrix for risks with a score of 4 or less. The 16 risks with scores of 6 or 9 received more attention, and in some cases risk-mitigation programs were initiated or improved.

Risk response/control activities

In most cases, mitigation plans were designed to reduce risk. For example, the legal department identified the lack of a formal document-retention policy and related procedures for preserving or destroying documents as a risk. As part of the risk response effort, IT and Legal collaborated, ultimately developing a Document Retention Policy that was subsequently implemented at Entropic. As a direct result, emails were moved to a new server and were only retained for one year rather than indefinitely, resulting in potentially significant savings and enhancing the company's ability to comply with electronic discovery orders in litigation. In Human Resources, ERM stimulated a higher level of compliance to existing standards. For instance, Human Resources developed measures to ensure that job descriptions were updated when people changed positions internally.

In other cases, a choice was made merely to accept certain risks. One of the few risks assessed as 9 was competitive risk, specifically relating to inadequate information on competitor's plans and products. Although managers at Entropic aggressively sought public information on competitors, they recognized that often reliable competitive information was just not available or hard to come by in the emerging industries in which they operated. This risk was accepted as inherent to the business. As Patrick explained, "Any company with a viable business model has competitive risk. You can't mitigate it completely, unless you have a tiny uninteresting market."

A third option, avoiding a risk by eliminating the risky event altogether, was not employed by any of the departments.

Communication

The majority of communication throughout the process took place between Lance and the department heads. No company-wide meeting dedicated to discussion of either the ERM process or the output was scheduled. Informally, however, some of the issues identified in the ERM process made their way into discussions at other formal company-wide meetings, such as the Annual Operating Plan (AOP) meetings. In December 2009, Lance presented the final output – the Risk Management Matrix with a summary of mitigation measures – to Patrick Henry and Entropic's Board of Directors.

Monitoring

The last step in the process was to decide how risks would be monitored on an ongoing basis. Lance and Patrick agreed that it would probably make sense to monitor existing risks on a semi-annual basis and to update the Risk Management Matrix on an annual basis.

Departmental participation

Department heads were given flexibility to tailor their department's level of participation in the ERM process to fit their departmental needs. As a result, the amount of commitment to the process varied greatly from department to department.

The Engineering department was at one end of the spectrum. Engineering already had a robust quality control process in place that governed not only manufacturing but also new product development and testing processes. Consequently, engineering managers saw the ERM initiative as largely "make-work." The department's culture, which stressed innovation and creativity, tended to resist formal process and bureaucracy.

Management in the Finance department didn't see a great need for ERM, either. In 2008, the Finance department had updated its internal controls to comply with requirements imposed by Sarbanes-Oxley and the SEC for public companies. As a result, the department had recently been through a detailed review of its risk management practices. With regard to this new ERM process, CFO David Lyle explained,

> It's not something that we put a lot of time into. When you're a smaller company and you have a smaller department, you tend to have fewer resources than are needed to do everything you need to do. A separate ERM program is lower on the priority for this department because we don't have a lot of time to spend on it. But I'm a huge fan of process. I don't want to discount its value, just because I didn't participate so much in it. We already manage risk well. We talk about risk every day. I just don't think Lance's forms helped us.

On the other end of the spectrum were Human Resources and Marketing, two departments that participated actively in ERM and that found it useful. Suzy Zoumaris explained, "I'm a process person; having the right processes and controls in place frees me up to do more strategic things."

Patrick Henry was not troubled by the varying levels of commitment to the ERM process. Participation in the ERM process had no bearing on performance reviews or capital allocations. Patrick had a pragmatic perspective. He was not interested in championing processes for process sake. He recognized the need for good systems, but was also cognizant of the downside of adding too much process too quickly. He explained,

> It's important to layer on process at the right thickness and to scale it appropriately to the size of the company. One of the key benefits of being a small company is speed of decision making. We don't want to become too bureaucratic and become a slave to process, as opposed to designing processes that serve us.

Final thoughts

Lance and Patrick were largely satisfied with the ERM process. They thought that the time spent going through the process was valuable and reasonable. But they didn't see a pressing need to further expand or elevate ERM in the near future.

Lance considered improving the process by changing to the COSO organizing framework – strategic, operational, reporting, and compliance risks – to identify and describe types of risk in future iterations. He thought that categorizing risks by objective could help particularly in identifying risks that intersected multiple departments. He also considered improving the process through further work on the back end of the process, particularly analyzing how risks were interrelated and the extent to which mitigating or addressing one risk might increase other risks or lead to new risks not previously identified.

Despite Lance's and Patrick's overall satisfaction with ERM, they recognized some of its limitations. The process was redundant for some departments. Not all risks could be mitigated. In fact, the most severe risk was inherent to the business. Not all risks could be anticipated; in the same year that ERM was implemented, Entropic mitigated a serious business risk that was not on the ERM matrix. A service provider insisted on using technology that Entropic engineers were sure would not meet quality standards. Entropic management could refuse the service provider's request, or move forward with a sub-optimal solution, but either way they ran the risk of losing an important customer. Entropic management was ultimately able to work out a solution, but the risk of losing the service provider's business dwarfed any of the risks in the ERM matrix. Patrick felt strongly that responding well to surprises was as, or more, important than trying to identify and mitigate everything upfront. Nevertheless, Entropic planned to continue to refine and use the ERM process in the future.

Exhibit 1 Entropic Communications, Inc., income statements (2005–2009)

	Years Ended December 31				
	2009	2008	2007	2006	2005
	(in $ thousands, except per share data)				
Consolidated Statement of Operations Data:					
Net revenues	$116,305	$146,033	$122,545	$41,471	$3,719
Cost of net revenues	57,399	79,411	76,196	31,099	1,979
Gross profit	58,906	66,622	46,349	10,372	1,740
Operating expense:					
Research and development	45,161	55,769	35,235	11,601	9,574
Sales and marketing	13,955	16,262	10,348	4,112	2,247
General and administrative	10,868	12,752	8,685	2,192	1,846
Write off of in-process research and development	–	1,300	21,400	–	–
Amortization of intangible assets	16	2,735	2,634	–	–
Restructuring charges	2,173	1,259	–	–	–
Impairment of goodwill and intangible assets	208	113,193	–	–	–
Total operating expenses	72,381	203,270	78,302	17,905	13,667
Loss from operations	(13,475)	(136,648)	(31,953)	(7,533)	(11,927)
Other income (expense), net	142	229	31	482	(269)
Income tax (benefit) provision	(93)	(49)	44	–	–
Net loss	(13,240)	(136,370)	(31,966)	(7,051)	(12,196)
Accretion of redeemable convertible preferred stock	–	–	(118)	(126)	(89)
Net loss attributable to common stockholders	$(13,240)	$(136,370)	$(32,084)	$(7,177)	$(12,285)
Net loss per share attributable to common stockholders – basic and diluted	$(0.19)	$(2.01)	$(2.47)	$(1.66)	$(3.70)
Weighted average number of shares used to compute net loss per share attributable to common stockholders	69,834	67,733	13,011	4,325	3,317

Source: 2009 Form 10-K.

Exhibit 2 COSO Enterprise Risk Management integrated framework – objectives and components

This enterprise risk management framework is geared to achieving an entity's objectives, set forth in four categories:

- *Strategic* – high-level goals, aligned with and supporting its mission
- *Operations* – effective and efficient use of its resources
- *Reporting* – reliability of reporting
- *Compliance* – compliance with applicable laws and regulations

Components of enterprise risk management

Enterprise Risk Management consists of eight interrelated components. These are derived from the way management runs an enterprise and are integrated with the management process. These components are:

- *Internal environment* – The internal environment encompasses the tone of an organization, and sets the basis for how risk is viewed and addressed by an entity's people, including risk management philosophy and risk appetite, integrity and ethical values, and the environment in which they operate.
- *Objective setting* – Objectives must exist before management can identify potential events affecting their achievement. Enterprise Risk Management ensures that management has in place a process to set objectives and that the chosen objectives support and align with the entity's mission and are consistent with its risk appetite.
- *Event identification* – Internal and external events affecting achievement of an entity's objectives must be identified, distinguishing between risks and opportunities. Opportunities are channeled back to management's strategy or objective-setting processes.
- *Risk assessment* – Risks are analyzed, considering likelihood and impact, as a basis for determining how they should be managed. Risks are assessed on an inherent and a residual basis.
- *Risk response* – Management selects risk responses – avoiding, accepting, reducing, or sharing risk – developing a set of actions to align risks with the entity's risk tolerances and risk appetite.
- *Control activities* – Policies and procedures are established and implemented to help ensure the risk responses are effectively carried out.
- *Information and communication* – Relevant information is identified, captured, and communicated in a form and timeframe that enable people to carry out their responsibilities. Effective communication also occurs in a broader sense, flowing down, across, and up the entity.
- *Monitoring* – The entirety of enterprise risk management is monitored and modifications made as necessary. Monitoring is accomplished through ongoing management activities, separate evaluations, or both.

Source: ERM – Integrated Framework, Executive Summary, September 2004.

Exhibit 3 S&P Progress Report: Integrating Enterprise Risk Management analysis into corporate credit ratings, July 22, 2009, preliminary findings

Based on our discussions, we note that:

- The level of adoption, formality, maturity, and engagement of ERM varies widely within and across sectors and regions. We haven't seen many companies provide clear examples of definitions for risk tolerance or risk appetite. While that's not surprising (since ERM is still relatively new), a preliminary conclusion could be that many companies find it difficult to ensure uniform behavior across the enterprise.
- Many companies exhibit an active management of risks with ongoing risk reviews and the assessment of high-impact/high-probability risks.
- The way the risk management function fits in the organizational structure indicates how integrated a company's approach is to risk management. We observe that "silo-based" risk management, focused only at the operational managers' level, continues to be prevalent.
- There appears to be a link between transparency and disclosure and companies' confidence about ERM; many companies have been willing and able to provide considerable detail about risk management practices.
- Companies with a true enterprise-wide approach to ERM appreciate the importance of going beyond only quantifiable risks or even top 10 risks. They increasingly understand the importance of emerging risks.
- Companies often facilitate their ERM execution via separate structures, with associated roles and responsibilities clearly defined. The ERM function's reporting line is typically to the CFO or the CEO, often with a direct line of communication to the board of directors, commonly to the audit committee. However, we have also seen numerous examples of risk-management structures that lack stature and influence in their organizations.
- Companies in industries with more quantifiable and hedgeable risks are generally more comfortable discussing ERM, but they tend to focus on controls of those specific risks. Examples include: energy, pharmaceuticals, agribusiness, and some manufacturers.

Just as a company's introduction of ERM is unlikely to radically change its current decision-making processes, we don't see ERM analysis radically altering our existing credit rating opinions. We expect its value to be incremental in many cases, negligible in a few, and eye opening in some.

Exhibit 4 SEC rule amendments, summary and excerpt

PROXY DISCLOSURE ENHANCEMENTS AGENCY: Securities and Exchange Commission.

ACTION: Final rule.

SUMMARY: We are adopting amendments to our rules that will enhance information provided in connection with proxy solicitations and in other reports filed with the Commission. The amendments will require registrants to make new or revised disclosures about: compensation policies and practices that present material risks to the company; stock and option awards of executives and directors; director and nominee qualifications and legal proceedings; board leadership structure; the board's role in risk oversight; and potential conflicts of interest of compensation consultants that advise companies and their boards of directors. The amendments to our disclosure rules will be applicable to proxy and information statements, annual reports and registration statements under the Securities Exchange Act of 1934, and registration statements under the Securities Act of 1933 as well as the Investment Company Act of 1940. We are also transferring from Forms 10-Q and 10-K to Form 8-K the requirement to disclose shareholder voting results.

EFFECTIVE DATE: February 28, 2010

C. New Disclosure about Board Leadership Structure and the Board's Role in Risk Oversight

3. Final Rule

The final rules also require companies to describe the board's role in the oversight of risk. We were persuaded by commenters who noted that risk oversight is a key competence of the board, and that additional disclosures would improve investor and shareholder understanding of the role of the board in the organization's risk management practices. Companies face a variety of risks, including credit risk, liquidity risk, and operational risk. As we noted in the Proposing Release, similar to disclosure about the leadership structure of a board, disclosure about the board's involvement in the oversight of the risk management process should provide important information to investors about how a company perceives the role of its board and the relationship between the board and senior management in managing the material risks facing the company. This disclosure requirement gives companies the flexibility to describe how the board administers its risk oversight function, such as through the whole board, or through a separate risk committee or the audit committee, for example. Where relevant, companies may want to address whether the individuals who supervise the day-to-day risk management responsibilities report directly to the board as a whole or to a board committee or how the board or committee otherwise receives information from such individuals.

Exhibit 5 Risk factors identified and described in Entropic's 10-K report

Investing in our common stock involves a high degree of risk. Before deciding to purchase, hold or sell our common stock, you should carefully consider the risks described below in addition to the other cautionary statements and risks described, and the other information contained, elsewhere in this Annual Report and in our other filings with the SEC. The risks and uncertainties described below are not the only ones we face. Additional risks and uncertainties not presently known to us or that we currently deem immaterial may also affect our business. If any of these known or unknown risks or uncertainties actually occurs, our business, financial condition, results of operations and/or liquidity could be seriously harmed. In that event, the trading price of our common stock could decline and you could lose some or all of your investment.

Risks related to our business

We have had net operating losses for several years, had an accumulated deficit of $242.0 million as of December 31, 2009 and only recently became profitable, and we are unable to predict whether we will remain profitable.

We face intense competition and expect competition to increase in the future, with many of our competitors being larger, more established and better capitalized than we are.

We depend on a limited number of customers, and ultimately service providers, for a substantial portion of our revenues, and the loss of, or a significant shortfall in, orders from any of these parties could significantly impair our financial condition and results of operations.

If we fail to develop and introduce new or enhanced products on a timely basis, our ability to attract and retain customers could be impaired, and our competitive position may be harmed.

Our results could be adversely affected if our customers or the service providers who purchase their products are unable to successfully compete in their respective markets.

If the market for HD video and other multimedia content delivery solutions based on the MoCA standard does not develop as we anticipate, our revenues may decline or fail to grow, which would adversely affect our operating results.

Even if service providers, ODMs and OEMs adopt multimedia content delivery solutions based on the MoCA standard, we may not compete successfully in the market for MoCA-compliant chipsets.

The semiconductor and communications industries have historically experienced cyclical behavior and prolonged downturns, which could impact our operating results, financial condition and cash flows.

Our operating results have fluctuated significantly in the past and we expect them to continue to fluctuate in the future, which could lead to volatility in the price of our common stock.

Our operating results may be harmed if our 2009 restructuring plan does not achieve the anticipated results or causes undesirable consequences

Adverse U.S. and international economic conditions have affected and may continue to adversely affect our revenues, margins and profitability.

The success of our digital broadcast satellite outdoor unit products depends on the demand for our products within the satellite digital television market and the growth of this overall market.

Market-specific risks affecting the digital television, digital television set-top boxes and digital television peripheral markets could impair our ability to successfully sell our silicon tuners.

The success of our silicon tuners is highly dependent on our relationships with demodulator manufacturers.

The market for our broadband access products is limited and these products may not be widely adopted.

We intend to expand our operations and increase our expenditures in an effort to grow our business. If we are not able to manage this expansion and growth, or if our business does not grow as we expect, we may not be able to realize a return on the resources we devote to expansion.

Any acquisition, strategic relationship, joint venture or investment could disrupt our business and harm our financial condition.

We may not realize the anticipated financial and strategic benefits from the businesses we have acquired or be able to successfully integrate such businesses with ours.

The average selling prices of our products have historically decreased over time and will likely do so in the future, which may reduce our revenues and gross margin.

Our product development efforts are time-consuming, require substantial research and development expenditures and may not generate an acceptable return.

Our products typically have lengthy sales cycles, which may cause our operating results to fluctuate, and a service provider, ODM or OEM customer may decide to cancel or change its service or product plans, which could cause us to lose anticipated sales.

Fluctuations in the mix of products we sell may adversely affect our financial results.

If we do not complete our design-in activities before a customer's design window closes, we will lose the design opportunity, which could adversely affect our future sales and revenues and harm our customer relationships.

(continued)

Exhibit 5 (*Continued*)

Our products must interoperate with many software applications and hardware found in service providers' networks and other devices in the home, and if they do not interoperate properly, our business would be harmed.

Our customers may cancel their orders, change production quantities or delay production, and if we fail to forecast demand for our products accurately, we may incur product shortages, delays in product shipments or excess or insufficient product inventory.

Our ability to accurately predict revenues and inventory needs, and to effectively manage inventory levels, may be adversely impacted due to our use of inventory "hubbing" arrangements.

We extend credit to our customers, sometimes in large amounts, but there is no guarantee every customer will be able to pay our invoices when they become due.

We depend on a limited number of third parties to manufacture, assemble and test our products, which reduces our control over key aspects of our products and their availability.

When demand for manufacturing capacity is high, we may take various actions to try to secure sufficient capacity, which may be costly and negatively impact our operating results.

We believe that transitioning certain of our silicon products to newer or better manufacturing process technologies will be important to our future competitive position. If we fail to make this transition efficiently, our competitive position could be seriously harmed.

We rely on sales representatives to assist in selling our products, and the failure of these representatives to perform as expected could reduce our future sales.

Our products may contain defects or errors which may adversely affect their market acceptance and our reputation and expose us to product liability claims.

We depend on key personnel to operate our business, and if we are unable to retain our current personnel and hire additional qualified personnel, our ability to develop and successfully market our products could be harmed.

If we fail to comply with environmental regulatory requirements, our operating results could be adversely affected.

Certain of our customers' products and service providers' services are subject to governmental regulation.

Our failure to raise additional capital or generate the significant capital necessary to expand our operations and invest in new products could reduce our ability to compete and could harm our business.

Our costs have increased significantly as a result of operating as a public company, and our management is required to devote substantial time to comply with public company regulations.

Our effective tax rate may increase or fluctuate, and we may not derive the anticipated tax benefits from any expansion of our international operations.

Our ability to utilize our net operating loss and tax credit carryforwards may be limited, which could result in our payment of income taxes earlier than if we were able to fully utilize our net operating loss and tax credit carryforwards.

If we fail to manage our exposure to global financial and securities market risk successfully, our operating results could be adversely impacted.

Risks related to our intellectual property

Our ability to compete and our business could be jeopardized if we are unable to secure or protect our intellectual property.

Our participation in "patent pools" and standards setting organizations, or other business arrangements, may require us to license our patents to competitors and other third parties and limit our ability to enforce or collect royalties for our patents.

Any dispute with a MoCA member regarding what patent claims are necessary to implement MoCA specifications could result in litigation which could have an adverse effect on our business.

Possible third-party claims of infringement of proprietary rights against us, our customers or the service providers that purchase products from our customers, or other intellectual property claims or disputes, could have a material adverse effect on our business, results of operation or financial condition.

Our use of open source and third-party software could impose limitations on our ability to commercialize our products.

Because we license some of our software source code directly to customers, we face increased risks that our trade secrets will be exposed through inadvertent or intentional disclosure, which could harm our competitive position or increase our costs.

Risks related to international operations

We expect a significant portion of our future revenues to come from our international customers, and, as a result, our business may be harmed by political and economic conditions in foreign markets and the challenges associated with operating internationally.

Our products are subject to export and import controls that could subject us to liability or impair our ability to compete in international markets.

Exhibit 5 *(Continued)*

Our third-party contractors are concentrated primarily in areas subject to earthquakes and other natural disasters. Any disruption to the operations of these contractors could cause significant delays in the production or shipment of our products.

Risks related to ownership of our common stock

Our stock price is volatile and may decline regardless of our operating performance, and you may not be able to resell your shares at or above the price at which you purchased such shares.

Future sales of our common stock or the issuance of securities convertible into or exercisable for shares of our common stock may depress our stock price.

Anti-takeover provisions in our charter documents and Delaware law might deter acquisition bids for us that you might consider favorable.

Our principal stockholders, executive officers and directors have substantial control over the company, which may prevent you and other stockholders from influencing significant corporate decisions and may harm the market price of our common stock.

If securities or industry analysts publish inaccurate or unfavorable research about our business, our stock price and trading volume could decline.

We do not expect to pay any cash dividends for the foreseeable future.

Our stock may be delisted from The NASDAQ Global Market if the closing bid price for our common stock is not maintained at $1.00 per share or higher.

Source: Entropic, Inc. 10-K for fiscal year ending Dec 2009.

Exhibit 6 Risk management matrix

Note: The following matrix is an excerpt from the matrix created by Entropic. Actual likelihood and severity scores assigned by the company have been disguised.

	Risk Description	Likelihood	Severity	Risk Score
Engineering	Failing to follow industry "best practices" in product development & designs	2	2	4
	Risk of missing a design window due to product development delays	2	3	6
	Being unaware of requirements for or failing to obtain government certifications related to our products (e.g., compliance with FCC standards, safety regulations for consumer products)	1	1	1
	Risks re: our products failing to achieve timely certification by a standards body or an operator	2	2	4
	Risk that our products will not interoperate fully with software or hardware in a customer's product or a service provider network	2	2	4
	Risks re: failing to acquire the most appropriate chip design software tools	1	3	3
	Infringing patents held by third parties	1	3	3
	Infringing third party copyrights	1	2	2
	Risk of currency fluctuations increasing our cost of labor in overseas development sites	1	1	1
Operations	Product quality – unanticipated warranty returns	2	3	6
	Export control (proper permits and licenses, export of encrypted product, US Gov't boycotts)	1	3	3
	Product quality – low manufacturing yields	2	2	4
	Risk of cost increases from our suppliers that cannot be passed on to customers	2	2	4
	Risks of supply constraints	2	2	4
	Inadequate inventory controls or inability to sell products in inventory due to how they are marked or manufactured	2	2	4
	Product quality – latent defects	1	3	3
	Risk that our MRP systems will prove inadequate for our needs or fail to provide necessary functionality	1	3	3
	Failing to comply with environmental regulations (worldwide)	1	2	2
	General product safety	1	1	1
	Risks of supply interruption (e.g., act of god or war)	1	1	1
	Risk of currency fluctuations affecting our cost to build product	1	1	1
	Failing to maintain ISO certification or pass customer quality audits	1	1	1
Marketing & Business Development	Assuring that product features, costs and availability date meet customer requirements	2	3	6
	Assuring that length of product life cycle and sales volume will be sufficient for required ROI	1	2	2
	Pricing products to achieve target gross margins	3	2	6
	Accurately assessing market size and forecasting market share for the company's products	2	2	4
	Risks re: customer acceptance of products (performance, bugs, integration, documentation, etc.)	1	3	3
	Risks associated with penetrating new markets or new applications	2	2	4
	Inadequate G2 on competitor's products, plans	3	3	9
	Infringement of trademarks held by third parties	1	1	1
	Loss of key customer or operator relationships due to personnel changes	2	3	6
	Building excessive inventory	1	2	2

Exhibit 6 *(Continued)*

	Risk Description	Likelihood	Severity	Risk Score
Sales	Failing to accurately forecast product demand, future orders, deployment rates and inventories of customers/operators	2	2	4
	Not being able to accurately track existing orders or price commitments	1	2	2
	Risks associated with use and management of sales reps and distributors	1	2	2
	Risks associated with long sales cycles	1	2	2
	Sales seasonality	1	1	1
	Loss of relevant personnel	3	1	3
	Conflicting Sales/Marketing service models	2	3	6
	Shipment Terms & Conditions disputes	1	2	2
	Risks associated with customer collections & disputes	2	2	4
	Risks associated with contract violations & disputes	1	2	2
	Failure to meet customer audit requirements	1	1	1
	Failure to hire qualified regional Sales/TAM personnel	1	2	2
	Product quality/customer returns	1	2	2
CTO	Risks associated with participation in standards bodies (MoCA, ITU, etc.) – Notice of IP, RAND license obligations	2	2	4
	Risks associated with identifying and addressing competing technologies and evolving industry standards	2	3	6
	Failure to timely identify new and emerging markets and complementary technologies	2	3	6
	Failure to develop core technology competencies over the long term	1	3	3
Human Resources	Negligent hiring/background checks	1	1	1
	Risks related to "on-boarding" new employees and consultants	1	1	1
	Compliance with immigration laws at hire and ongoing	1	1	1
	Workplace safety and health	1	1.5	1.5
	Health and benefit plans	1	1	1
	Privacy protection for employees	1	2	2
	COBRA Administration	1	1	1
	Discrimination and Sexual Harrassment in the workplace	1	1	1
	Risks related to "exiting" employees and consultants	1	1	1
	Retaliation/wrongful discharge	1	2	2
	Recruiting risk	1	2	2
	Risks associated with identifying resource needs early enough to timely fill them and ensuring all required competencies are identified	1	2	2
	Retention risk	2	2	4
	Employee compliance with laws	1	1	1
	Ethical business conduct	1	1	1
	Compliance with labor laws	1	1.5	1
Facilities	Facilities planning risk	1	2	2
	Design & maintenance risks	1	1	1
	Special needs risks (e.g., cooling for computer servers, rooftop use, network infrastructure, etc.)	1	2	2
	Compliance with (i) building codes, (ii) local regulations & (iii) lease obligations	1	1	1
	Workplace safety and health	2	2	4
	Physical security & monitoring of premises	1	2	2
	Use & disposal of hazardous materials	1	1	1

(continued)

Exhibit 5 *(Continued)*

	Risk Description	Likelihood	Severity	Risk Score
IT	Risk that company proprietary information will be compromised due to hacking or industrial espionage	2	2	4
	Theft/misuse of proprietary information by current or former employees and consultants	2	2	4
	Service gaps, unscheduled computer downtime or slow network impacting productivity	1	1	1
	Disaster recovery (e.g., earthquake/fire)	1	3	3
Finance and Accounting	Financial statements/earnings management and manipulation	1	3	3
	Risk that all transactions are not accurately recorded or accounted for	1	3	3
	Adequate accounting controls (Sarbane-Oxley internal controls of financial reporting)	1	3	3
	Adequate disclosure controls	1	2	2
	Awareness of new accounting rules or pronouncements	1	1	1
	Changes in accounting policies required by auditors	1	1	1
	Revenue recognition issues	1	3	3
	Collection of revenues from customers who take goods on credit	3	2	6
	Theft risk for cash accounts	1	1	1
	Cash management – loss of principal/illiquidity	1	2	2
	Taxes – awareness of tax obligations	1	1	1
	Taxes – timely and accurate domestic & int'l filings	1	1	1
Legal	Antitrust & Trade Reg. Compliance; FCPA Compliance	1	3	3
	Litigation – patent infringement (including customer indemnification claims)	2	3	6
	Litigation – wrongful termination; discrimination; whistleblower claims	1	2	2
	Litigation – warranty or product defect claim	2	1	2
	Contracts – creating binding obligations without proper review or authorization	2	2	4
	Contracts – onerous contract obligations, breach of contract	2	2	4
	Awareness of new laws or regulations affecting the company	1	3	3
	Retention of Documents During Litigation	1	3	3
	Management/destruction/return of third party confidential information	1	2	2
	Obtaining, maintaining and enforcing intellectual property rights (includes patents, trademarks, trade secrets) in the US and in foreign countries	2	3	6

This case was prepared by Professor Kenneth A. Merchant and research assistant Michelle Spaulding.

CASE STUDY
Bio/Precise Medical Devices, Inc.

In early February 2012, Herb Marshall, CFO at Bio/Precise Medical Devices (BPMD), was reviewing the February operating report submitted from the manager of BPMD's Chinese subsidiary. On page 3 of a six-page report he saw a vague reference to consulting payments that had been made. Since he did not remember any consulting engagements having been authorized for China, he asked Steve Jefferson, BPMD's chairman/CEO, about the payments. Steve did not know anything about such payments, either, so they started asking questions. They discovered that salespeople in BPMD's Chinese subsidiary had been providing kickbacks to buyers for many years. The Chinese country manager said that everyone provided such kickbacks, and there was no problem with the practice. But Herb and Steve immediately ordered that no more kickbacks be paid.

The kickback amounts were relatively small, and they were not material to BPMD's consolidated financial statements in any accounting period. All the payments had been accounted for as expenses. However, the kickbacks presented a serious problem because they probably constituted a violation of the bribery provisions of the US Foreign Corrupt Practices Act (FCPA). If these illegal acts were detected by US government regulators, BPMD could be subject to severe financial and business penalties, and some of its employees could also face significant fines and even imprisonment.

A major portion of the agenda for the meeting of the board of directors held in late February 2012 was devoted to a discussion of what to do. At this meeting, lawyers from BPMD's outside law firm, who specialized in FCPA-related issues, laid out the options regarding disclosure. They explained that since BPMD had discovered the problem itself and since the amounts were immaterial, the company had no obligation to disclose the violations to the regulators. It was possible, and maybe even probable, that regulators would never become aware that any violations ever existed. But, they advised, if BPMD did not self-report the violations and the regulators found out about them through another source, the penalties would probably be much more severe than if the company self-reported. In any case, steps needed to be taken to ensure that no BPMD employees ever made such "facilitating payments" again.

The company

BPMD developed, manufactured, and sold a range of medical devices and technologies used to treat an array of heart and artery diseases and disorders. The products included coronary and peripheral stents and other angioplasty products and related delivery systems, heart valve replacement technologies, cardiac ablation devices, implantable cardiac resynchronization devices, and various other diagnostic and monitoring tools for heart-related problems. BPMD sold its products in nearly 50 countries around the world. Sales had been growing at an annual rate of about 20%, and 2010 revenues totaled just over $500 million. BPMD launched its IPO in 2000, and its stock was listed on NASDAQ. The company's worldwide headquarters was located in Seattle, Washington.

BPMD's Chinese subsidiary, located in a suburb of Shanghai, employed about 90 full-time personnel, about 30 of whom were in the sales department. The sales department had one national sales manager for China and four regional sales managers. About 80% of the company's sales in China were made by BPMD employees. The other 20% of sales were generated by third-party sales agents or distributors representing BPMD in, particularly, some of the smaller cities in China. Most of BPMD's revenue in China was derived from sales of products to existing customers.

The US Foreign Corrupt Practices Act

The FCPA prohibits individuals and entities from offering to pay, paying, or authorizing the payment of "money or anything of value" directly or indirectly (i.e.

through an agent) to foreign officials for the purpose of "obtaining or retaining business." It is one of the most significant and feared pieces of legislation for companies operating abroad.

The term foreign official included all employees of governments (whether they were elected, appointed, or hired, and paid or unpaid), political parties, party officials and candidates, and officers of state-owned companies. The act made it unlawful to make a payment to a third party while knowing that all or a portion of the payment will go directly or indirectly to a foreign official. The term "knowing" included both conscious disregard and deliberate ignorance that a corrupt payment or offer will be made. Intermediaries could include joint venture partners or agents. There was no *de minimus* exception to the FCPA's prohibition on corrupt payments to foreign officials. The FCPA also required companies covered by the provisions to make and keep books and records that accurately and fairly reflect the transactions of the corporation and to devise and maintain an adequate system of internal accounting controls.

The FCPA was passed in 1977 in response to widespread perceptions that corruption, and in particular bribes to foreign government officials for the purpose of securing business or otherwise gaining an improper business advantage, was a serious and possibly growing problem. An influential investigation by the US Securities and Exchange Commission (SEC) conducted in the mid-1970s found that over 400 US companies had made over $300 million in questionable or illegal payments.

Subsequently, Congress became concerned that the FCPA was putting US companies at a competitive disadvantage. In 1988, the act was amended to make the provisions applicable to foreign firms and persons who cause, directly or through agents, an act in furtherance of such a corrupt payment to take place within the territory of the United States. Congress also directed the Executive Branch to commence negotiations with the Organization of Economic Cooperation and Development (OECD) to try to convince the country's major trading partners to enact legislation similar to the FCPA. In 1997, almost 10 years later, the United States and 33 other countries signed the OECD Convention on Combating Bribery of Foreign Officials in International Business Transactions.

The U.S. Department of Justice (DOJ) "is responsible for all criminal and civil enforcement of the anti-bribery provisions with respect to domestic concerns and foreign companies and nationals," while the US Securities and Exchange Commission (SEC) "is responsible for civil enforcement of the anti-bribery provisions with respect to issuers." If the FCPA's "anti-bribery provisions" were violated, the following penalties could be imposed:

- The corporations were subject to a fine of up to $2,000,000 for each violation or twice the benefit sought from making the corrupt payment.
- Individuals (e.g. officers, directors, agents) could be fined up to $100,000 and imprisoned for up to five years for each violation.

For violations of the "accounting and recordkeeping provisions" of the FCPA:

- Cases involving negligent record keeping and nothing more can subject the individuals involved to fines of up to $5,000 per violation and companies up to $50,000 per violation.
- Intentional violations prosecuted criminally by the Department of Justice (DOJ) can result in fines of up to $5 million and 20 years in jail per violation for individuals, and up to $25 million in fine per violation for companies.

Other considerations:

- Companies are prohibited from indemnifying their officers and employees against liability under the act.
- Firms or individuals found in violation of the FCPA could be barred from doing business with the federal government.
- FCPA enforcement authorities often couple FCPA charges with allegations of violations of other federal statues, including those regarding money laundering, tax fraud, or racketeering.
- The FCPA investigations often take years. All relevant documents are thoroughly reviewed. All employees involved in the transactions are subjected to detailed interviews by outside counsel. Every inconsistency is probed, often involving multiple rounds of interviews. To the managers involved, the process can feel "interminable and invasive."[1]

The FCPA was intended to have, and indeed had, an enormous impact on the way American firms conducted

[1] A. G. Murphy, *Foreign Corrupt Practices Act* (Hoboken, NJ: Wiley, 2011), 27.

their business. Several firms whose employees or agents paid bribes to foreign officials were the subject of criminal and civil enforcement actions, resulting in large fines and suspension and debarment from federal procurement contracting, and some of their employees and officers were sentenced to jail. To avoid such consequences, many firms implemented detailed compliance programs intended to prevent and to detect any improper payments by employees and agents. However, a 2011 Deloitte study found that only 29% of executives surveyed were "very confident" that their company's anti-corruption program would prevent or detect corrupt activities.[2]

FCPA enforcement efforts were increasing sharply. In 2011, a total of 48 enforcement actions enforcement actions were initiated by the DOJ or the SEC,[3] as compared to 74 in 2011, but only 40 in 2009 and 33 in 2008.[4] Many US corporations, including such icons as Avery Dennison, McDonald's, IBM, Whirlpool, Avon, and Rockwell Automation, found themselves connected to bribery cases in just China alone.

FCPA-related fines – paid either to the DOJ or the SEC, depending on the type of case – were larger and were increasing. The largest FCPA case involved Siemens, which paid the US regulators $800 million in fines and disgorgement of profits to settle alleged violations of the FCPA. The statutory calculus in this case permitted a fine of up to $2.7 billion, but the government agreed to the lesser amount because of Siemens' substantial cooperation in the case.[5] Siemens also paid the German authorities more than $1 billion for the same conduct, and it paid its lawyers and forensic accountants hundreds of millions of dollars to conduct the investigations and to negotiate the settlements. Eight of the top 10 monetary settlements in FCPA history were reached in 2010. Just a more recent examples: in 2011, Alcatel-Lucent settled a FCPA case involving bribes in nine countries in Africa, Asia, and South America for $137 million, and Johnson & Johnson agreed to pay $77 million to settle a bribery case in Iraq.

[2] Deloitte, "Anti-Corruption Practices Survey 2011: Cloudy with a Chance of Prosecution?," available at http://www.deloitte.com/assets/Dcom-UnitedStates/Local Assets/Documents/FAS_ForensicCenter_us_fas-us_dfc/us_dfc_fcpa compliance survey report_090711.pdf.

[3] P. Ploeger, M. Somsen, and R. Lamp, "2011 FCPA Enforcement Actions Reach Second-Highest Level," De Brauw Blackstone Westbroek N.V. (February 1, 2012)."

[4] T. C. Cimino, J. A. Zubaira, R. C. Jennings, R. T. Copenhaver, W. Hayman, and M. A. Nelson, "Foreign Corrupt Practices Act Trends," *The National Law Review* (September 8, 2011).

[5] Murphy, *Foreign Corrupt Practices Act*.

Some individuals found in violation of the act were also being sentenced to jail; the longest sentence to date was 87 months.[6] Both the DOJ and the SEC were devoting increasing resources to FCPA enforcement, so the increased pace of FCPA prosecutions was seen as likely to continue.

The violation at BPMD

The investigation of the "consulting payments" launched in February 2012 revealed that the kickbacks were being paid to doctors and personnel who controlled the medical device purchasing decisions of certain hospitals. Most of these hospitals were owned by the government of the People's Republic of China, which meant that the hospital employees were "Chinese government officials."

Further investigations revealed that the improper commissions made were typically 3–5% of the gross sales generated by the contracts, but sometimes they were as high as 20%. The commissions had been made since at least late 1999 and over the years totaled over $1.6 million (see Table 11). Most of the payments were paid in cash and hand-delivered by BPMD salespersons to the person who controlled the purchasing decisions for the particular hospital department. A few payments were delivered by mail or wire transfer. All of the payments were authorized by the subsidiary general manager. These payments were recorded in the accounting records as either (translated from Chinese): (1) sales commissions for customers, or (2) sales consulting fees.

It was also determined that some other expenses, such as for client meals and entertainment, might also have been in violation of the FCPA. But because of poor documentation, it was difficult to determine the size of this additional potential problem.

Legal explanations

At the October board meeting, lawyers from BPMD's law firm explained that violations of the FCPA were serious. Management certainly needed to ensure that these practices never occurred again. These steps would inevitably involve a combination of new management in China, new procedural controls, and employee training sessions.

[6] J. Legum, "Trouble for Murdoch: Feds Collecting Billions in Fines, Sending Executives to Jail for Corruption Abroad," *Think Progress* (July 11, 2011).

Table 1 BPMD "sales commission" or "sales consulting" payments made to Chinese government employees

Year	Amount of commission payments
1999	$7,242
2000	$31,997
2001	$43,851
2002	$36,265
2003	$86,582
2004	$99,203
2005	$120,045
2006	$138,999
2007	$179,360
2008	$275,286
2009	$300,305
2010	$319,681
Total	$1,638,816

The lawyers explained that BPMD had no obligation to disclose the violations to the regulators. But they also noted that penalties were typically much lighter for companies that did self-report their violations.

If BPMD did self-report the violation, then the company would be subject to significant penalties plus sizable legal defense costs. Almost certainly, the company:

- Would have to pay a significant fine, up to twice the gross gain resulting from the offense. Almost all sales in BPMD's Chinese operation were to government-owned hospitals. (BPMD's net profits earned in China over the 12-year period of the violations totaled approximately $3.5 million.)
- Would have to bring in a new management team in the Chinese subsidiary and charge them with responsibility for oversight of compliance with the FCPA.
- Would have to hire an independent compliance expert, likely an external forensic accounting firm, to investigate the problems, to recommend a system, including policies and procedures, codes of conduct, employee training, and disciplinary mechanisms relating to FCPA compliance, and to monitor BPMD's ongoing activities in China to ensure FCPA compliance. The focus of the firm's attention could be limited to China, or it could be extended to BPMD's operations particularly in other regions or countries that pose high risks of corruption, or perhaps even worldwide. The firm would probably be required to continue its extra compliance activities for a period of years. The total cost would be in the millions of dollars.
- Would be placed on probation for a multiyear period. Additional FCPA violations during the period of probation would be dealt with harshly.

Less certain were:

- The consequences to individuals involved in the violations. The general and sales managers in China, and possibly the US-based manager to whom the Chinese subsidiary reported could be subject to fines and imprisonment.
- The effect on BPMD's US business. The company could be barred from selling products to federal government-owned hospitals. Such sales constituted about 15% of the company's sales in the United States.

Board decisions to be made

After the lawyers had finished their presentation and left the boardroom, the BPMD board began to engage in a vigorous discussion of the issues. Perhaps the most important, and most immediate, issue that had to be decided was whether to self-report the violation. Potentially BPMD could clean up the control and record-keeping problems internally before the government regulators found out about them. But what would that require? If the company did self-report the violations, the regulators would tell company management what needed to be done, but those steps might not be the same ones that management would chose voluntarily.

This case was prepared by Professor Kenneth A. Merchant.

CHAPTER 14
Controllers and Auditors

This chapter discusses the roles and challenges of personnel in two important corporate governance- and management control system (MCS)-related roles that both require financial measurement expertise: controllers and auditors. Personnel in these roles *within the firm*, such as corporate and division controllers and internal auditors, must serve two important roles. One role is *management service*, which involves helping line managers with their decision-making and control functions to help create firm value. The other role is *oversight*, which involves ensuring that the actions of everyone in the organization, especially the managers, are legal, ethical, and in the best interest of the organization and its owners. Fulfilling both roles often creates *tension*, as these two roles can, and often do, conflict. This chapter discusses this conflict and some other issues faced in making individuals in these roles effective.

The chapter also discusses the control roles of *external* auditors, who provide an important independent check on managers' financial reporting, disclosure, and internal control practices. They face a different set of role conflicts, those between the need to serve their clients, the need to serve the public interest, and the need to earn profits for their own employer, the audit firm.

Controllers

The finance and accounting functions in a corporation are typically managed by a person with the title of *chief financial officer* (CFO) or *vice president finance* (VP Finance). (Terms vary across countries. In the United Kingdom, the term *finance director* is typically used for this role.) In recent times, particularly since the early 2000s, this role has gained in status.[1] For example, Fazal Chaudhri, group financial director at Exelco, a Belgian diamond concern, said the crisis has done his job profile "a favor" – where once local managers would wait for him to approach them about performance, Mr. Chaudhri now fields calls from throughout the organization seeking strategic advice, he said.[2] "In an economy in which access to credit and the financial health of the business is a major area of focus, it does make sense for the CFO to be involved in important decisions the company is making," another executive said.[3] In other words, the crisis may have strengthened the importance of the financial executive's *management service* role. It, and the corporate scandals of the early 2000s, have also strengthened the importance of the financial executive's *oversight* role. For example, the passing of the Sarbanes-Oxley Act in the United States added status, but also risk, to the senior financial officer role in publicly held firms because CFOs must co-sign both the financial statement certifications and the opinions as to the effectiveness of their firm's internal control systems.

Figure 14.1 Corporate financial management roles

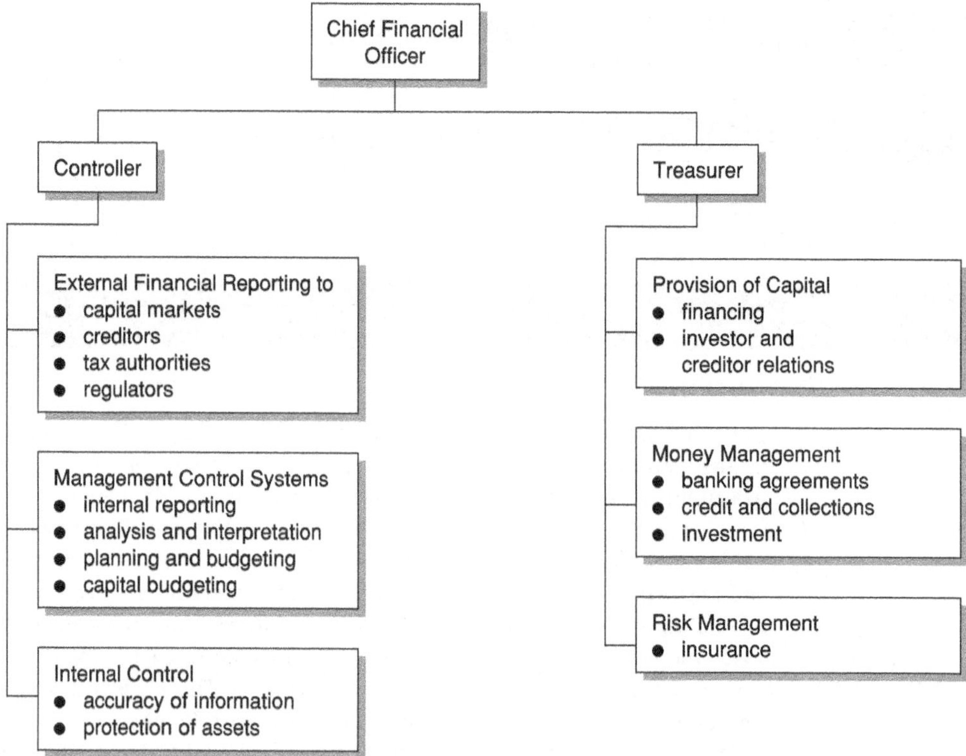

Source: K. A. Merchant, *Modern Management Control Systems: Text and Cases* (Upper Saddle River, NJ: Prentice Hall, 1998), p. 640.

As Figure 14.1 shows, the senior financial executive role commonly encompasses two domains, which typically exist in larger firms as specific roles with dedicated personnel for each: controller and treasurer. (In smaller firms, these roles may be combined.) The *controller* function deals primarily with financial record-keeping, reporting, and control. The *treasury* function deals primarily with raising and managing capital. The treasury function is generally highly centralized. The controllership function is often decentralized in large divisionalized corporations, with controllers in most or all of the profit centers (business units, divisions) and some of the larger cost centers (e.g. manufacturing plants).

Controllers play key roles in line management and in the design and operation of a management control system (MCS). They are the financial measurement experts within their firm (or their entity), and most of them are key members of the management team. As such, they are involved in preparing plans and budgets, challenging operating managers' plans and actions, and participating in a broad range of management decisions, including allocating resources, pricing, setting policies regarding receivables and payables, making acquisitions and divestments, and raising money.[4]

Evidence suggests that controllers have become more and more highly involved in helping managers make good business decisions:

> The CFO is increasingly being called upon to weigh in on much more strategic decisions involving the company, including everything from transactions to providing assessments

of emerging markets and analyses that go far beyond looking at the books and determining whether there will be enough cash to support investment.[5]

"It began with the trend of increased regulation and the introduction of Sarbanes Oxley. A lot of CEOs realized they didn't have the expertise to deal with that and turned to their CFOs," says Tracy Riley, national managing partner for PwC Canada's assurance practice. "At the same time, they were also dealing with a proliferation of data and the need to gain insights about that data. The CFO has been in the middle of all that, and increasingly CEOs expect their finance group to take ownership of it. As we get more into business expansion on a global basis and managing the risk that comes with it, the opportunity for the CFO to play an increased role grows."[6]

Or, as another article suggested, "Coming into the 21st century, financial professionals saw the emphasis of their responsibilities shift from recording various aspects of a corporation's financial health to joining top executives in a broad-based partnership."[7] But being highly involved in management decision making or becoming a "business partner" is not a substitute for the other important role controllers must play as their entity's "chief accountant" – that is, their "oversight" and "scorekeeping" role. They, and their subordinates, record transactions, prepare performance reports, and fulfill financial, tax, and government reporting obligations. They establish and maintain internal control systems that help ensure both the reliability of information and the protection of the company's assets. Depending on the organization, the controller also might supervise the internal audit and management information system functions. The same article, then, not surprisingly, also cautions that "as [the financial professionals] become ever closely connected with the business, they must also ensure to not become subservient to it."[8]

Indeed, as chief accountants for their entities, controllers must stay appropriately *independent* of their entity managers. They have a *fiduciary responsibility* to ensure that the information reported from their entity, particularly that of a financial nature, is accurate and that the entity's internal control systems are adequate. They have a management *oversight responsibility* to inform others inside and outside the organization, such as the relevant regulator or industry watchdog, if individuals in their entity are violating laws or ethical norms.

Can controllers who are highly involved as part of the management team maintain the requisite degree of independence to fulfill their fiduciary and management oversight responsibilities effectively? In other words, can controllers *wear two hats*, one of a *team member* and *confidant* and the other of a *watchdog* or *police cop*? In one sense, controllers' fiduciary responsibilities are quite consistent with their management oversight responsibilities – both sets of responsibilities require a constructively critical mind-set and a sense of independence from management:

"If you think about what CFOs are good at – what's in their DNA – they are disciplined, detailed, they have integrity – these are the traits needed to implement any large-scale program that involves change," says Don Rupprecht, finance effectiveness leader, PwC Canada. "The financial crisis showed that those traits could be used outside of finance."[9]

That said, the fiduciary and management oversight responsibilities can conflict with the controllers' management service responsibilities, and if not that, they certainly can create tension. Indeed, survey evidence of over 5,000 financial professionals from countries across the globe suggests that the respondents recognized "concerns" from their expanding roles, ranging from increased pressure from management to fears about their own objectivity.[10]

It is often claimed that *corporate controllers* put the interests of their corporate management, with whom they are closely connected as a management team, before the interests of the shareowners and other stakeholders. Similarly, *business-unit* or *division controllers* (*entity controllers*, for short), those located in a decentralized entity such as a business unit, division, or operating unit, can easily become personally or emotionally attached to their local, decentralized entity and the people they work with in the entity. They want to be part of the team; or, as they sometimes say, they may *go native*. Indeed, entity controllers who are included in an incentive compensation plan based on entity performance can have motivations to "go along" with their entity management and, worse, condone gamesmanship that affect the results measures they are assumed to oversee and report to corporate. To maintain the integrity of the controller's role, firms can, and probably should, implement several additional safeguards to ensure that controllers fulfill their management oversight and fiduciary duties effectively.

First, audit committees of boards of directors and internal auditors can be used to oversee the controller function. Audit committees were discussed in Chapter 13, and the roles and activities of internal auditors are discussed below. Second, controller behaviors can be shaped through personnel or cultural controls, such as selection and training. Some controllers have better judgment, have a better sense of ethical integrity, and are better able to function effectively in situations with strong role conflict than others. Individuals who are subject to professional standards may be good choices for controller positions. For example, the American Institute of Certified Public Accountants (AICPA) bolstered its professional code of ethics by requiring CPAs who work in corporations (rather than in public accounting) to report material misstatements of their company's financial statements to their superiors. If the superiors fail to respond, the CPA should report the misstatements to the company's outside auditors or to regulators such as the Securities and Exchange Commission (SEC). Professional codes such as this one add weight to the fiduciary responsibility of controllers, who are also CPAs. Finally, training programs can remind controllers of their multiple responsibilities and give them the interpersonal skills useful in maintaining the proper balance between their management service and their management oversight and fiduciary roles.

Designing incentive systems that do not create temptation is a third way to ensure that controllers fulfill their management oversight and fiduciary duties effectively. In particular, controllers probably should not be rewarded for performance defined by measures they can manipulate.

Finally, some firms have found that *solid-line* reporting in the controller's organization is effective for controlling entity controllers' activities. As shown in Figure 14.2, solid-line

Figure 14.2 Possible reporting relationships in the controller's organization

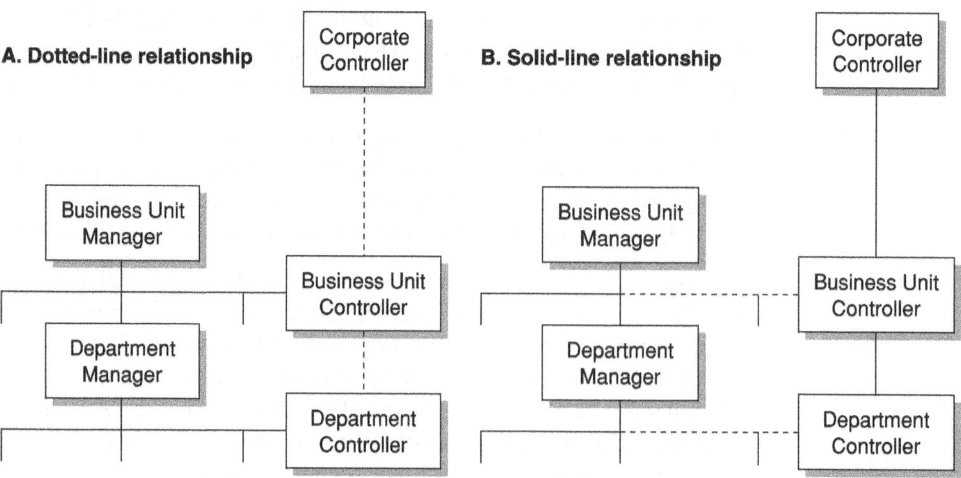

Source: K. A. Merchant, *Modern Management Control Systems: Text and Cases* (Upper Saddle River, NJ: Prentice Hall, 1998), p. 642.

reporting means that the entity controller's primary reporting relationship is to the corporate controller (or, in the case of a lower-level operating unit, a higher-level entity controller). In this controllership structure, the corporate controller – not the local entity managers – determine the entity controller's tasks, priorities, and performance evaluations.

Solid-line reporting is designed to reduce the personal attachment between entity controllers and the local entity management to which they are assigned. It signals to the entity controllers that their most important roles are to protect the corporation's assets and to ensure that financial reports are accurate. This reminder is perhaps more important if the entity is located at great distance from headquarters. But for all entity controllers, it provides a heightened emphasis on their management oversight and fiduciary responsibilities. The downside of solid-line reporting, however, is a potential reduction in the quality of the entity controller's management service function. Entity controllers reporting on a solid-line to corporate can come to be viewed in the local entity as *corporate spies* rather than as members of the entity management team, which can cause role confusion and stress.[11]

All told, then, designing an effective controllership function is both difficult and important, where the role itself is inevitably challenging:

> **Increasingly, CFOs are stepping up and volunteering to drive change, asserts Don Rupprecht of PwC. "They aren't waiting to be tapped. They are calling for better metrics, better decision making in the field based on data. They are calling for more insight and analytics and they are volunteering to lead the effort. This is becoming the norm and will only continue."[12]**

Auditors

When the word *audit* is mentioned, most people think first of either a *financial audit*, in which a public accounting firm expresses an opinion about the fairness of presentation of a company's financial statements, or a *tax audit*, in which government auditors test to see if taxpayers have followed the laws and reported taxable income truthfully. Historically, these common audit forms have played only limited roles in management control systems, whereas other types of audits, such as *internal audits*, *operational audits*, and *performance audits*, have been seen as much more critical to the effective operation of internal control systems. Nonetheless, since the passing of the Sarbanes-Oxley Act in the United States, for example, the external financial audit, in particular the portion of it that is designed to express an opinion on the effectiveness of a company' system of *internal controls*, has become more relevant for MCSs.

Audits

An audit can be defined as a *systematic process* of (1) *objectively obtaining and evaluating evidence* regarding *objects of importance*, (2) *judging* the degree of correspondence between those objects and certain *criteria*, and (3) *communicating* the results to relevant users. This definition is broad so as to cover all types of audits. It is useful to elaborate on the meaning of the key (italicized) terms.

The phrase *systematic process* is used to connote the fact that audits are not done randomly. They involve an orderly sequence of interrelated steps, all designed with one or more audit objectives in mind. Every audit starts with what is commonly called a planning phase, which involves developing an understanding of the established criteria of the groups who will use the audit report and the required scope of the audit. The planning phase is used to design an audit program that identifies the specific tasks to be performed and, if appropriate, the schedule for starting and completing each task and the persons assigned to each task.

The second phase of the audit process, which is typically the most time-consuming, involves *obtaining and evaluating evidence*. This process is *objective* because auditors are, by definition, independent of those being audited. Non-independent reviews, such as superiors inspecting the work of their subordinates for which they are also held responsible, are not audits, despite the obvious similarities. Depending on the focus and scope of the audit, the evidence gathering may involve some or all of the following: observation, interviews, reviews of reports, re-computations, confirmations, and analyses. As evidence is gathered, alterations to the original audit program may be necessary.

Differences in the *objects of importance* provide the major reason for the varied labels put on different types of audits. Compliance audits are designed to test for compliance with rules about behavior or results, such as specific company policies, laws, or loan covenants. Marketing audits focus on the effectiveness and efficiency of the marketing function. Financial statement audits provide a basis for the external auditors to express an opinion as to whether the financial statements fairly present the financial status and performance of the entity involved.

The third phase of an audit requires a *judgment*, based on the evidence, as to whether (or to what extent) the criteria have been met. While these judgments are professional and evidence-based, they are inevitably fallible because, in all but the simplest situations, some probability exists that the judgments will subsequently be proven incorrect. For example, all of the evidence necessary to make an infallible judgment may or will not be available, or the judgment may involve an assessment about an uncertain future.

The *criteria* for comparison can vary widely across audit types. They may be very narrow and specific, such as those used in procedure-related compliance audits (e.g. requirement of two signatures on checks). Or they may be no more specific than a vague definition of a desired characteristic, such as related to the "efficiency" of a given process or function or the extent to which the process or function meets some "value for money" criterion.

Communicating the results to relevant users concludes the audit process. The audit report is the primary tangible product of the audit. At a minimum, the audit report describes the evidence examined and presents an opinion as to whether the established criteria were met. In issuing the report with the stated opinion, the auditor, in essence, assumes responsibility for the opinion, with the risk of economic or reputation loss if the opinion is subsequently determined to be incorrect. Sometimes the report highlights areas where improvements can be made, and it may go as far as to make specific recommendations.

External and internal auditors

Auditors can be classified as either external or internal. *External auditors* are primarily prized for their independence, meaning that that they have no financial or other interests in the auditee (the firm being audited by the auditor or audit firm) except, strictly, performance of the audit itself.[13] Those performing financial audits (described below) are generally accountants employed by a public accounting firm or so-called *audit firms*. They have professional training and experience and are licensed by a professional association. Those executing performance audits (described later in this chapter) are employed by a public accounting or consulting firm. These auditors can have any of a variety of backgrounds, including in general management, risk management, finance, information systems, engineering, or computer science.

Internal auditors are employees of the company they are auditing. They are often referred to as "the eyes and ears of management." Internal audit staffs can operate with either narrow or broad charters, and the breadth of charter is one of the major determinants of the size of the staff. A narrow charter, which would necessitate a relatively small internal audit staff only, leads to mostly compliance audits and performance of some functions for the external auditors (such as preparation of audit schedules and documentation of internal controls) to reduce external audit fees. At the other extreme, some staffs operate with a broad charter that can include many forms of performance auditing, involvement in the design and improvement of business processes and internal control systems, and other forms of what would usually be classified as management consulting.

The size of internal audit staffs varies widely across firms. Small firms typically have no internal auditors. Large firms may have a small or a large staff. Internal audit, however, is often prone to "cuts" in difficult economic times, ironically when firms might benefit most from the audits. For example, the following two reports lament the cuts to public sector internal audit budgets:

> The [internal audit] budget decreases in local government mean that there is a significant risk that some internal audit functions will get to a point where they no longer have the resources to do the work necessary to give a robust annual opinion. This in turn puts the objectives of the organization at risk.[14]
>
> Cuts to some public sector internal audit budgets are an issue. [...] The Chartered Institute of Internal Auditors (IIA) warns that, at a time of major restructuring, a large proportion of the public sector may be unnecessarily vulnerable to serious financial or operational failures, without adequate arrangements in place to spot potential dangers and put plans in place to minimize their impact.[15]

These quotes suggest that internal audits, especially when broader in scope, which they increasingly are, can play important roles in organizations, be they public or corporate:

> Internal auditors help organizations to manage the wide range of risks facing them, including for example: financial and fraud risks; data security risks; and health and safety risks. They help the board and management identify and address risk management, internal control and corporate governance issues before they become a problem.[16]
>
> Internal auditors of financial companies are to get a new U.K. code of conduct, aimed at securing them increased resources and respect, while getting them to focus more sharply on risk management. [...] Internal auditors have traditionally focused primarily on fraud prevention. But there is a growing view that the department should also monitor the way banks measure and manage a variety of risks, including credit risk, market risk and even environmental issues. [...] "Analysis of the financial crisis and more recent problems in the banks emphasizes the need for internal audit to be at the heart of corporate governance. To enable this, all parties with an interest in the governance of financial institutions need more specific guidance on the role of internal audit," said Roger Marshall, director of the Financial Reporting Council and chair of the audit committee of Old Mutual, an insurer.[17]

Internal auditor backgrounds vary with their staff's charter. Many internal auditors have an accounting background, but as internal audit charters have broadened, many firms' audit staffs have become more diverse and include, among others, information system specialists, computer experts, and consultants. Moreover, and mainly because the charter of internal audit can be so varied, internal audit functions frequently turn to subject matter experts to assist in audit coverage requiring deeper knowledge of the specific business, process, or function. What most internal audit staffs have in common, however, is that they are typically headed by experienced professionals having titles such as chief audit executive, head of internal audit, or variations thereof.

Most internal auditors have ties to a professional association that sets professional standards, adopts a code of ethics, develops a common body of knowledge for internal auditors, and runs certification programs leading to the qualification of "Certified Internal Auditor" (or a variation thereof). In the United States, there is the Institute of Internal Auditors, and its UK equivalent is the Chartered Institute of Internal Auditors, mentioned earlier in this chapter. Many other countries have similar professional bodies.

Organizationally, the internal audit function operates in a staff capacity and almost always reports high in the organization, at least to the corporate controller or CFO/VP Finance. However, experts recommend that the internal audit staff should report directly to the audit committee of the board of directors to enhance their independence, credibility, and visibility:

> **For example, the new standards [in the United Kingdom] advise that the appropriate reporting line for Heads of Internal Audit in public sector organisations is to the audit committee, with administrative reporting to the chief executive. But 28% of Heads of Internal audit in local government said their teams report to the Chief Financial Officer (CFO). The IIA says that this could create a conflict of interest, potentially limiting internal audit's ability to be completely objective in fulfilling its scrutiny of financial controls, which also fall into the remit of the CFO.[18]**

Finally, many internal audit functions are said to be still heavily stuck in the past, focusing on financial and compliance audits (see below), presumably still the hallmarks of the heightened regulatory and compliance era (such as triggered by Sarbanes-Oxley in the United States). One US survey suggests that only 13% of respondents indicated that their departments allocated at least 25% of resources to strategic and business audits (which we categorize as *performance audits* below), while a majority (57%) assigned this degree of resources to traditional financial audits. The survey also suggests, however, that strategic, business, and operational audits are among the fastest-growing areas of internal audit focus.[19] This perhaps echoes the sentiments in a survey in the Asia Pacific region about the role of the finance function more generally:

> **According to nearly two-thirds of the CEOs surveyed, technology was the largest factor determining the future role of the CFO. Cloud computing and social media are offering CFOs a chance to "leverage technology in new ways," said Geoff Wilson, chief operating officer for the Asia Pacific region at KPMG. Nevertheless, roughly 40% said strict regulation impedes the CFO's focus, although about the same percentage saw it is an opportunity to pull ahead of competitors.[20]**

Once again, this illustrates the tussle and tension between the compliance and business roles that staff in these roles must effectively and reliably navigate.

Common audit types

While the mechanics and techniques are basically the same among all types of audits, the motivations and end results are different. This section briefly describes some of the most common types of audits that serve various control purposes.

Financial audits

In a financial audit, independent, external auditors are asked to express an opinion as to whether the financial statements prepared by management are fairly presented in accordance with applicable accounting standards, such as International Financial Reporting Standards (IFRS) in many countries or Generally Accepted Accounting Principles (GAAP) in the United States. The guidelines that external auditors must follow in performing an audit in the United States are known as Generally Accepted Auditing Standards (GAAS). These guidelines are established by the Public Company Accounting Oversight Board (PCAOB), which was born out of the Sarbanes-Oxley Act. Similarly, International Standards on Auditing (ISAs) are developed by the International Auditing and Assurance Standards Board (IAASB) of the International Federation of Accountants (IFAC). These acronyms aside, financial audits essentially provide a tool by which outside regulators (such as stock exchanges and government bodies) can enforce standards for the preparation and presentation of accounting information to interested parties outside the organization, which is critically important for the efficient functioning of capital markets as well as the public sector, among other purposes. A detailed discussion of financial audits, however, is outside the scope of this text.

Compliance audits

Organizations are responsible for complying with many laws, rules, procedures, and administrative policies set down by various authorities. In a compliance audit, the auditors are asked to express an opinion as to whether actual activities or results are in compliance with the established standards, rules, and regulations. As such, compliance audits generally involve a narrower scope of investigation than do other types of audits. Despite the narrower scope, compliance audits nonetheless often unearth fraud and irregularities, even though that is not their primary purpose. Both external and internal auditors perform compliance audits. Compliance audits vary widely in the amount of evidence to be gathered and the auditor expertise needed. Audits for compliance with more complex rules, such as some tax laws, may require considerable specialized knowledge and substantive professional judgment.

Performance audits

Performance audits go by various names such as *operational audits*, *management audits*, or *strategic audits*. They provide an overall evaluation of the general performance, or some specific aspect of the performance of an activity, function, entity, or company and its management. Performance audits can be performed by broad-scope internal auditors or external auditors in a consulting role. The criteria for comparison are vague in many performance audits, often only loosely referring to assessing an activity, function, or entity's effectiveness. Accordingly, an important part of performance audits often involves defining the criteria in more specific terms. In many cases, the scope is usefully limited by virtue of focusing on a specific activity, function, or entity, or a specific performance dimension thereof (e.g. quality, delivery, information systems). In addition to making a judgment as to whether performance meets the set criteria, performance auditors usually also produce an important by-product through identifying areas for improvement. Although performance auditors generally have broader training and experience than other types of auditors, they typically also turn to internal or external subject matter experts, depending on the needed coverage on any given assignment. The audit reports may be directed to management, government regulatory agencies (such as environmental protection agencies), or related parties in the context of certain contractual or business partner arrangements.

The value of audits

Audits create value in two primary ways. First, the audit report adds credibility to the information provided to user groups. The auditors provide an independent check against criteria reflecting user needs for whom presumably the knowledge as to whether or to what extent the criteria have been met is valuable. As a by-product of this evaluation process, auditors often provide what can be an equally valuable benefit through identifying areas for improvement and making specific recommendations where practices need to be redressed or issues addressed. These recommendations can deal with minor procedural changes or major management policy changes. Some argue, however, that recommendations should not be part of the audit function. They reckon that giving advice compromises audit independence, if not in the first audit, certainly in all audits performed by the same auditors after the recommendations are (or are not) implemented. The independence particularly of external auditors, who often also provide performance audits, tax services, or various types of consulting to their clients as an extension of their financial statement audits, has been a thorny issue and the subject of increased regulatory attention.[21]

The second benefit of audits comes not from the audit itself, but from the *anticipation* of an audit. Knowing that an audit will or might take place can strongly motivate the individuals involved to conform to the standards they reckon the auditors will use in their evaluation. "Everyone performs better if they know someone is looking over their shoulder. When you put out the word that no one is looking, it's an invitation to disaster."[22] But this may also explain the general "negativity" about audits, as exemplified by the following survey evidence:

> While many organizations say they have improved their internal audit capabilities, a survey from PwC finds the progress hasn't been enough to keep pace with the increasingly risky and complex business landscape. The survey of more than 1,900 chief audit executives, internal audit managers, members of senior management and board members found that 55% of senior management reported that they do not believe internal audit adds significant value to their organization, and nearly 30% of board members believe it adds less than significant value.[23]

Regardless of these views, audits are clearly not equally valuable in all situations. One factor that affects the potential value of an audit is the importance of the area audited. The greater the potential consequences (the higher the stakes), the greater the audit's potential value. Audits are also potentially more valuable if the probability is high that the established criteria either are not being met or would not be met in the absence of the audit. Finally, audits are potentially more valuable when other control mechanisms are not feasible. For example, reviews by independent auditors are necessary when the user group is not able to satisfy itself directly as to whether the established criteria have been or are being met. This inability may be caused by the complexity of the subject matter, physical remoteness, institutional barriers preventing access to some of the evidence needed (such as in a joint venture), or just reasonable suspicion that self-interest (of those being audited) will prevail over the interests of the relevant user group(s) in the absence of an independent, objective audit.

Audits can be valuable tools in many management control situations. Auditors can serve as the "eyes and ears" of management in assessing what is happening within the organization, and they can also share their expertise by providing recommendations for improvement. For management purposes, the potential value of an audit is greatest if the criteria used for comparison are those set by management. Audits commissioned by outsiders, such as financial or environmental audits, are designed to serve the interests of those outsiders, although the auditors may provide some observations of use to management. But even for those audits, the benefits can come in seemingly unexpected ways. For example, a report commissioned by the UK government (to decide if emissions reporting will be mandatory) found that companies that measure their carbon emissions do not find the exercise arduous or expensive – some even said it brings benefits. Just over half the firms surveyed said reporting emissions carried a net benefit for their business. Indeed, although there may be no obvious direct benefits from the act of reporting emissions, reporting emissions forces a company to measure them first; that does bring benefits, as measuring emissions produces an incentive to reduce them, which might be done by spending less on energy.[24]

Another benefit is the avoidance or mitigation of costly, harmful, sometimes even calamitous outcomes. If internal audits (and controls) are effective at avoiding or minimizing harm, then this benefit is inevitably hard to measure. But it can be significant, considering that "internal auditors advise on the management of risks including fraud, data security, and health and safety; [...] they aim to help the board and management identify issues *before they become a problem*; [...] and they help reduce the risks of serious problems causing financial loss or exposing the organization to regulatory or legal action."[25]

Where audits are feasible, they can be an important alternative or supplement to other management control mechanisms, such as direct supervision or incentives, and they can help assess the effectiveness of the controls (including whether they produce any harmful side effects) and/or the degree of compliance (especially with action controls). Audits can test whether the desired behaviors were in fact taken and document any unintended consequences. Auditors can usually reach an informed judgment by examining just a small proportion of the relevant evidence. And, in some situations just the threat of an audit can be a powerful deterrent against undesirable behavior.

But audits have limitations. One is that they are done only on a periodic basis and thus offer little protection against problems occurring in the interim except to the extent that they provide a deterrent effect. This limitation of audits is pertinent in situations where something must be done properly the first, or every, time. Audits also can create negative reactions, such as defensiveness, especially when individuals feel their integrity is questioned or their autonomy is jeopardized. Audits can be costly. They consume considerable time from expert auditors, as well as from company employees who have to prepare information for the auditors to review. Moreover, audits can assess only the past. Thus, audits of one-time occurrences have value only if they provide some useful insights about situations that might occur in the future.

All told, audits are invaluable in many situations and have likely increased in importance to the point where, just as with CFOs and controllers, chief audit executives (CAEs) are being called to become "strategic business partners" alongside the senior executive team given their expertise in risk and given how risk has become a core focus of boards and senior executives.[26] Or, as one commentator idealizes this, "for companies to maximize the strategic contributions of the CAE, however, they must have both a *business-aware* auditor and an *audit-aware* board and leadership group."[27] But the elevation of the role of auditors, as the quote suggests, implies that *business-aware auditors* will face similar role duality, and possibly role conflicts, as controllers do in the execution of their management *service* versus *oversight* roles.

Conclusion

This chapter focused on the important control-related roles of controllers and auditors, both internal and external. These are challenging roles. Auditors, for example, must examine business processes and employees' work (such as the work of accountants, managers, and so forth) in a limited amount of time and make judgments as to whether the work meets the set standards. Some standards, such as those defining significant and material internal control weaknesses (as described in Chapter 13) or fairness of presentation, are sometimes ill-defined and inevitably require judgment. The controller and internal auditor roles are particularly challenging because they involve an inherent conflict of interest. Individuals in these roles are asked to serve their organization and its management while at the same time fulfilling a management oversight role on behalf of the organization's owners and other stakeholders. Their role may require them to take actions that are quite costly to their organization in the short run, such as exposing a fraudulent financial reporting scheme. It takes strong, courageous individuals with excellent interpersonal skills to perform such roles effectively. But building and maintaining a strong finance function is an important foundation of a management control system, and where firms manage to effectively navigate the various role conflicts, they stand to benefit from significant positive spillover effects.[28]

Notes

1 See, for example, "McKinsey Global Survey Results: How Finance Departments Are Changing," *The McKinsey Quarterly* (April 2009), online at www.mckinseyquarterly.com.

2 J. Karaian, "Business Outlook Survey," *CFO Europe* (April 2, 2009), pp. 13–14.

3 "CFOs Have Bigger Roles Than Ever Before – and They Like It That Way," *Forbes* (August 2, 2013), online at onforb.es/17iola9. See also "Asia Pacific CEOs Say Role of CFO Increasingly Important," *The Wall Street Journal* (December 9, 2014), online at blogs.wsj.com/cfo/2014/12/09/asia-pacific-ceos-say-role-of-cfo-increasingly-important.

4 See, for example, *The New Value Integrator: Insights from the IBM Chief Financial Officer Study*, IBM Global Business Services (March 2010).

5 "CFOs Have Bigger Roles Than Ever Before," op. cit.

6 "How the Financial Crisis Transformed the CFO from Bean Counter to Change Agent," *Financial Post* (October 16, 2014), online at natpo.st/1P9mgPX.

7 See, for example, W. Van der Stede and R. Malone, "Accounting Trends in a Borderless World," Chartered Institute of Management Accountants (November 2010), online at www.cimaglobal.com. See also J. Banks, "Value Creation – Support Network," *Excellence in Leadership* (November 2010), pp. 12–15; Institute of Chartered Accountants in England and Wales, *The Finance Function: A Framework for Analysis* (2011); H. Chang, C. D. Ittner, and M. T. Paz, "The Multiple Roles of the Finance Organization: Determinants, Effectiveness, and the Moderating Influence of Information System Integration," *Journal of Management Accounting Research*, 26, no. 2 (2014), pp. 1–32.

8 Van der Stede and Malone, "Accounting Trends in a Borderless World," op. cit.

9 "How the Financial Crisis Transformed the CFO from Bean Counter to Change Agent," op. cit.

10 Van der Stede and Malone, "Accounting Trends in a Borderless World," op. cit.

11 V. Maas and M. Matejka, "Balancing the Dual Responsibilities of Business Unit Controllers: Field and Survey Evidence," *The Accounting Review*, 84, no. 4 (July 2009), pp. 1233–53.

12 "How the Financial Crisis Transformed the CFO from Bean Counter to Change Agent," op. cit.

13 There is an ongoing debate as to whether, or the extent to which, the provision of non-audit services by audit firms impairs auditor independence. See, for example, M. Causholli, D. J. Chambers, and J. L. Payne, "Does Selling Non-Audit Services Impair Auditor Independence? New Research Says, Yes," *Current Issues in Auditing*, 9, no. 2 (December 2015), pp. 1–6.

14 *Governance and Risk Report 2014* (Chartered Institute of Internal Auditors, 2014), online at www.iia.org.uk/media/1042498/0819-gov-risk-report-25-11-14.pdf.

15 "More than a Third of Public Sector Organizations Do Not Have Fully Effective Risk Management Mechanisms," *Chartered Institute of Internal Auditors* (December 18, 2013), online at iia.org.uk.

16 Ibid.

17 "New Code of Conduct for Internal Auditors," *The Financial Times* (September 9, 2012), online at on.ft.com/1ITZHuu.

18 "More than a Third of Public Sector Organizations Do Not Have Fully Effective Risk Management Mechanisms," op. cit.

19 See, for example, *Business Upheaval: Internal Audit Weighs Its Role amid the Recession and Evolving Enterprise Risks*, PricewaterhouseCoopers (2009), online at www.pwc.com.

20 "CFOs Have Bigger Roles Than Ever Before," op. cit.

21 See, for example, Causholli, Chambers, and Payne, "Does Selling Non-Audit Services Impair Auditor Independence?," op. cit.

22 "UC Sues Official over Alleged Embezzlement," *The Los Angeles Times* (August 25, 1995), p. A3.

23 Survey Roundup: Executives on Analytics, Internal Audit," *The Wall Street Journal* (April 4, 2014), online at blogs.wsj.com/riskandcompliance/2014/04/04/survey-roundup-executives-on-analytics-internal-audit-value.

24 "Carbon Counting Is 'Good for Business,'" *BBC* (November 30, 2010), online at www.bbc.co.uk.

25 "Auditors Blow Whistle on Inadequate Procedures for Reporting Crises," *The Financial Times* (February 23, 2014), online at on.ft.com/1fBCgxC.

26 "Social Media Risks Create an Expanded Role for Internal Audit," *The Wall Street Journal* (August 6, 2013), online at deloitte.wsj.com/riskandcompliance/2013/08/06/social-media-risks-create-an-expanded-role-for-internal-audit.

27 "Leadership in the Risk-Intelligent Organization," *Business Week* (September 30, 2010), online at www.businessweek.com.

28 Chang, Ittner, and Paz, "The Multiple Roles of the Finance Organization," op. cit.

CASE STUDY
Don Russell: Experiences of a Controller/CFO

In February 1991, Don Russell, chief financial officer (CFO) at Eastern Technologies, Inc. (ETI) was mulling over a critical decision. Don had joined ETI only 14 months earlier and had gradually become convinced that the company's financial accounting was excessively aggressive. He thought a sizable correcting entry should be made immediately. But if the correction was made, ETI would report a large loss that would trigger violations of debt financing covenants and place the company's survival in jeopardy.

ETI's chairman and president were strongly against making the correcting entry. They reminded Don that the company had a plan to shore up its operations and to get cheaper financing in place and that the plan needed time to work. But Don was not convinced that top management's plan was viable.

Don felt that ETI's accounting reports were misleading to decision-makers both outside and inside the company. This caused him particular concern because he had seen the dangers of manipulating earnings reports at his previous employer. But he knew that if he forced the change now, he would lose his job. Even if ETI survived, he was sure he would be fired for "not being a team player." As he noted to an observer:

> It is frightening to know that you're going to be out the door almost immediately after you make the decision. It's even more frightening to me right now because I've just gone through a divorce and remarriage, and now I've got six kids and annual alimony payments of $60,000.

He also thought about the effect the decision would have on the value of the tens of thousands of ETI stock options he had been given. The options would be worth several hundred thousand dollars when exercised, and half of them could be exercised in two months.

Early career

Don Russell joined the audit staff of the Chicago office of Touche & Young (T&Y) in July 1973 immediately upon graduation from the University of Illinois. His advancement was rapid. In 1983, he was promoted to senior manager and was given indications that he was on track toward partnership. Over the 1975 – 80 period, Don attended DePaul University's evening MBA program and earned his degree in management information systems. T&Y gradually shifted his work responsibilities to take advantage of his systems expertise. By 1984 Don's time was split almost equally between auditing and systems consulting.

In 1985 Don left T&Y to become corporate controller for Cook & Spector, Inc. (C&S), a large ($4 billion sales) consumer products division of Queen's Industries, a major British corporation. C&S had been acquired by Queen's in 1984. Don was familiar with C&S because it was one of his major audit clients. He explained why he decided to take the job:

> When the headhunter first approached me about the job I wasn't interested. C&S had an antiquated accounting system. It was a huge company, but they still had a manual accounts receivable system. They did no planning; no budgeting. It was ridiculous. But C&S's top managers told me, "You have carte blanche to make whatever changes you think are necessary. You have complete control." So I was intrigued by the challenge.
>
> It was also a great career opportunity. C&S was a large, reasonably profitable corporation with some outstanding brand names. And my job was significant. I had 250 people working for me. I reported to the CFO, and the only other person reporting to him was the Treasurer who had eight people working for him. So I thought I would probably be next in line for the CFO job.

Controllership experiences at Cook & Spector

Systems development activities

Don started at C&S in August 1985. He spent his first six months planning the changes he wanted to make to the firm's accounting information systems. Then over the next three years he implemented major changes. He changed the chart of accounts so that the firm could produce profit and loss statements down to the product level; the new system had 500,000 account/cost center combinations. He installed new general ledger, accounts receivable, and accounts payable systems that would operate in a modern database environment. And he implemented a standard cost system in the firm's 42 factories. About the cost system change, he observed, "C&S had had only an actual cost system. The monthly costs fluctuated wildly and weren't useful. They didn't provide a reflection of what was going on."

After the accounting systems were computerized, Don found it easy to reduce costs in the controller's department. He reduced his accounting staff from 250 to 110 and saved the company over $4 million per year.

Earnings management activities

In 1985, for a variety of reasons, C&S's profit performance was running $45 million ahead of the $200 million plan. To *save* the profit for periods when it might be needed, Don established several types of large reserves. For example, C&S had been aggressive in expensing the acquisition costs incurred as part of the Queen's acquisition process, so Don set up a large reserve ($53 million) for taxes, in case the IRS disallowed the expense deductions. He also set up reserves for unknown liabilities because, "Everybody realized that the company had a poor accounting system." Don believed at the time that the reserves were justified and that, "It's better to be safe than sorry. If it turns out that we were overly conservative, it's no big deal."

These reserves had to be spread across the 34 line items in the income statements of each of the over 600 product lines in 60 divisions in a way that would not attract the attention of the analysts on Queen's corporate staff or the auditors. Don accomplished this task without significant questions being raised.

In 1986, company sales and profits were below forecast and top management told Don they wanted to use some of the reserves. They said they wanted to report an 8% increase in earnings and to increase significantly the amount of expenditures on new product development to help the company grow in the future. Don was able to free up the reserves to satisfy these requests.

Corporate recognition

Don's superiors were ecstatic about his efforts. He had modernized the company's accounting systems; had saved the company $4 million in overhead annually; and had demonstrated great skill in managing the accounting profit numbers. After a year with the company, he was promoted to vice president/controller.

Don was flushed with success:

> Every management meeting I was held up as the ideal. I remember one top-level meeting when they flashed my picture on the screen and said, "Follow this guy's lead. This is the way you should manage your department." One time the president called me *the Monet of the accounting profession.*
>
> My head was exploding. At T&Y they keep telling you you are worthless to keep you there and to keep your salary down. All of a sudden I'm important, and I'm making a lot of money. After I had been at C&S six months I gave them my six-month plan, and I got a $30,000 bonus right there on the spot. I was in shock. I had never had that much free money in my life. Plus I was involved. I attended all the key management meetings.

Concerns about earnings management

During his third year at C&S, Don began to have concerns about his manipulations of reserves. He said:

> I hadn't really thought much about my manipulations of reserves. I thought I was being a team player. This is how the company had been run for years. It had a record of 33 consecutive years of increasing quarterly earnings. But real results, with recessions and everything else that happens, don't happen that way. So I hadn't invented earnings management at C&S, although we were probably now doing it on a grander scale than had been done before.
>
> But it suddenly dawned on me that something was horribly wrong. We were pristine in reporting for taxes because I sent my tax manager to the operating units to make sure real data were going to the IRS. But we didn't care if real data were going to Queen's. All of a sudden we had two years that weren't comparable and we really didn't know where we were. When people looked back at trends they were looking at distorted numbers. And because we spread the reserves around we had distorted all the product P&Ls.

Don attempted to drain the reserves out of the product-level profit and loss statements, but the complexity was overwhelming because each of the 60 divisions and over 600 product lines would now have two P&Ls each. Plus the draining provoked a number of arguments with the operating managers because the divisions had been manipulating the numbers on their own. They had not really spent the promotion expense by product as was reported, and they had their own buried reserves. In fact, the division reserves probably totaled more than those created at corporate. So even if Don could eliminate the distortions he had caused, the product statements that would result still would not yield accurate information.

Don's concern about the earnings management activities rose in 1988:

> The year 1988 looked like another down year and everybody was saying, "We need more product development because last year's development didn't work." And the president, of course, was saying we need another 8% increase in income.
>
> I told the president that we can't allow the reserves within the division. Every year we'd have something like a $200 million target, but we'd have $40 million in reserves ready to help us. So everybody would get their bonuses; the executive parking lot was filled with BMW 750s and Mercedes. I was doing well also. My regular salary was around $130,000, but my total compensation was nearly $230,000.
>
> While the company was reporting profits, I thought we were headed in a downward spiral. The old products were still extremely profitable, but we were spending a huge amount of money on new products and were disguising the fact that the new products were a lot less profitable. There was no linkage between bonuses and a strategic plan, just a link to an accounting number that was not tied to a plan. It was just an accounting game. We were getting our bonuses for nothing – actually worse than nothing because we were making bad decisions.

Attempts to change the company's financial goals and measurement system

To improve company decision-making and reduce the temptations to manage earnings, Don decided to try to change C&S's financial goals and measurements system. He was particularly concerned that the potentially lucrative bonuses, ranging up to 70–100% of base salary, were based on operating profit numbers that were too easy to manipulate.

He began a fact-finding study. He began interviewing all the C&S division heads on his own and soon realized that the company was not doing any real strategic planning. He found that company planning involved just settling on a set of revenue and profit numbers that looked reasonable. C&S operating managers were unwilling to tell Queen's about their real plans, such as for new products, because they were worried that they would *have egg on their face* if they weren't able to accomplish their plans.

Among the questions Don asked in the interviews was, "What are the most important decisions you make on a monthly and annual basis, and what information do you use in making those decisions?" The manager of the largest operating unit said, "On a monthly basis, one of the most important decisions I make is how much profit to recognize."

Don's reaction:

> I was floored. This is one of the most senior managers in a huge company, and he was telling me that one of his most important decisions is how to manipulate the numbers. His operating decisions are secondary. His first role, he viewed, was to give the president the profit number he wanted that month.
>
> And this guy wasn't unique. Everyone else I talked with reinforced this message. Managers who missed their monthly budget targets would take a lot of flak. The president would quickly call them and ask, "What are you doing? How are you correcting the problem? Cut your advertising! Fire some people!..." This drilled into me what happens when you allow manipulations. People don't focus on real problems.

Don planned to take his interview observations to the president and tell him:

> We've got a big problem here because we're not managing the company the way we should be. We're spending four times the amount of product development and capital expenditures we need because it's easy to get Queen's to approve them. But Queen's assumes we are making good decisions, and we're not.

But Don wanted to be able to propose an alternative, and he set out looking for "the Holy Grail of more reasonable financial reporting."

Don learned that some companies were experimenting with an approach to planning that focused on changes in shareholder value. This focused measurement attention on hard numbers – cash flows – rather than the easily manipulatable operating profit. He studied these approaches and proposed their use to top management, but they were completely opposed to any changes. They did not understand why they would want to make such a drastic change when the company and its management team were doing so well.

The decision to leave

As the pace of accounting systems change slowed, Don's job became more routine, and he became bored. He began listening for other career opportunities. He thought he wanted to become a chief financial officer so that he could work more in finance areas where he had had no experience. And he thought he would like eventually to move into a line management position.

In early 1989, a headhunter approached Don with an opportunity to interview for the position of CFO of Eastern Technologies, Inc. (ETI), a public communications services company. ETI was growing rapidly and was raising large amounts of money both from banks and direct placements. He was interviewed for the job and accepted it when it was offered. He joined ETI on December 1, 1989.

CFO experiences at Eastern Technologies

The company

ETI, headquartered in Stamford, Connecticut, was founded in 1978 as a cable television firm. It had several cable franchises in New England and the New York metropolitan area. The company had been profitable since the early 1980s. It went public in 1984 with an initial offering price of $11.00 per share. For the 1988 fiscal year (ended June 30), revenues were $30 million and profits were just above $1 million. The 1988 year-end stock price was $8.75.

In 1987, ETI's founder, a skilled electronics engineer, decided to diversify the company's operations into the fast-growing area of satellite broadcasting. This business involves sending broadcast signals, such as from a concert or a sporting event, to a broadcast satellite that relays the signal to a network of large dish antennas on the ground. These antennas then distribute the signals to users, such as local television stations.

To finance the construction of antennas and distribution networks throughout the Northeast, ETI raised considerable bank financing. By the end of 1987, ETI's debt–equity ratio was 4 to 1, but management figured the company still needed $10 million of additional capital. They approached a prominent investment banking firm to make a bond offering. The investment bankers showed ETI management how easy it was to raise money with high-yield bonds, and the company eventually made a much larger offering – of $25 million. When the bonds sold, the company had considerable cash but a debt–equity ratio of 6 to 1.

ETI management used the extra cash to accelerate the expansion of facilities and to acquire a Baltimore-based broadcasting firm of similar size to ETI. Growth exploded as the company signed more and more long-term contracts with customers. Revenues totalled $81 million in 1989, almost three times the 1988 level. But after-tax profits were just under $1 million, as the company had to book a large loss in the fourth quarter of the year to cover *one-time start-up problems* with the new technology.

ETI made another acquisition in February 1990. This was of a Southern California-based consulting firm that provided specialized communications services primarily to firms in the defense industry. The two acquired companies were run as largely autonomous divisions within the ETI corporate structure.

Transition of power

When Don joined ETI his major concern was whether ETI's president, Joe Blevins, would allow him autonomy in his CFO role. Joe was a former T&Y audit partner who had joined ETI in 1987. But Don found Joe's approach to the transition of power to be quite reasonable. Joe asked Don to focus his initial attention on improving the company's operating systems: ETI had no computerized systems, no planning, and no budgeting, and the controller was weak. But Joe let Don sit in on the discussions with bankers and investment bankers to help him learn the treasury functions that he would eventually assume.

Don quickly found that ETI's financial focus was on earnings per share, and he vowed to change the focus to cash flow. Joe said, however, "You don't really understand the market. I'll listen to your thoughts, but EPS is what the analysts care about. Cash flow may be the latest *voodoo* thought, but it's not very realistic." Still, Don thought Joe would be open-minded, and he believed he could convince Joe to change.

Don, however, had a lot of work to do before he could focus on changes in the company's planning and measurement processes. He focused his attention first on ETI's chart of accounts. Billing was done manually, and expenses were assigned only to highly aggregated accounts. For example, the company paid huge bills for satellite rental and telephone services with no attempt to trace the expenses to contracts or even product lines. Another complicating factor: many of the charges were not billed regularly, so expenses had to be accrued. But the bases on which the accruals were done were not well thought out, and the company's monthly profit figures fluctuated wildly. Don knew he could not prepare a credible budget without a better understanding of where the expenses were coming from and what lines of business were more profitable than others. That understanding required a better accounting system. He wanted eventually to be able to produce reliable budgets and operating reports at department, and even project, levels of the organization.

Changing the chart of accounts proved to be a difficult process because few people in the company understood what Don was trying to do. The controller was not supportive. He was comfortable with the current chart of accounts and liked the fact that it was easy to work with. Don observed that, "It didn't matter to him that it did not provide meaningful information. He thought of accounts just as pots that you throw expenses into. If you make the system more complex the assignment of expenses takes more thought."

Don also had to spend time integrating the systems of the newly acquired subsidiaries. He found ETI to be much more dynamic than C&S. At C&S he had time to plan what he wanted to do. At ETI he had to implement changes quickly and hope to fine-tune the systems later.

ETI's first budgeting process

Don led ETI through its first formal budgeting process in June–July 1990. Most of the numbers work was done by accounting personnel after they had consulted with the operating managers. Budgets were prepared for each division using the categories in Don's new chart of accounts.

When the budget for fiscal year 1991 was consolidated, it showed a $2 million loss. But nobody was sure if the budget was realistic. This was the first budget that had been prepared at the division level, and no division-level historical reports were available for comparison purposes. It also quickly became apparent that budgeting mistakes had been made. For example, management soon discovered that a major contract had been left out of the budget. Operating managers had failed to pass the information to accounting personnel, and two months into the year, some significant unbudgeted expenses had to be paid.

ETI's financial reporting strategy

After the budget was prepared, Don began an analysis of why the budget showed a loss for FY 1991 even though ETI had been reporting profits for years. It became obvious to him that the satellite communications business was in reality very unprofitable. ETI had been reporting profits because the company had implemented an extremely aggressive financial reporting strategy. Joe Blevins had a theory that all start-ups are unprofitable in the beginning and that aggressive accounting policies are necessary to make the company look profitable so that money can be raised. The profits catch up later.

Joe used a number of methods of boosting earnings, including the following:

1. Virtually all repairs and maintenance were capitalized. Because there was so much development going on, Joe's position was that all the engineers' and technicians' time was spent working on construction or making modifications that add capability to the equipment. Therefore, all the costs were capitalizable.
2. Most interest was capitalized because it was deemed to be the cost of financing the construction in progress. For example, Don found that "We had deferred $3.5 million in interest for construction of a new video control center. We claimed it hadn't been put into service until May 1990 because we were still getting the bugs out of it, but it had actually been up and running since mid-1988 and certainly met the GAAP criterion of substantially complete." Don also found that "Nothing ever came out of construction in progress. They just kept capitalizing more and more interest."
3. Most equipment was being depreciated on a 12-year life. But electronic equipment, which comprised the bulk of the equipment, probably has a maximum five-year life, and some of the expensive tubes have a maximum 24-month life.
4. As many expenditures as possible (for example, travel) were classified as being related to one of the acquisitions so that they would add to goodwill and be amortized over 40 years instead of being expensed immediately. Also, if any parts of the acquired businesses were suffering operating losses, those losses were capitalized. On the other hand, a gain of over a half million dollars on the sale of a portion of a communications relay station acquired

in an acquisition was recorded directly as profit instead of as an adjustment to the price of the acquisition. Don noted, "We told the auditors we were just selling the rights to that asset since the buyers obviously couldn't take the asset with them. The auditors swallowed hard but accepted it."

The auditors had not objected strenuously to ETI's financial reports because they did not understand the technology. Satellite communications was a relatively new business that was just starting to grow. Few equipment retirements had taken place as yet, so it was difficult to tell what the true equipment lives were. Don found out that, "When the auditors asked questions about the 12-year depreciation lives Joe would always point to the large antennas and say, 'They will be there for 100 years.' That's true, but not much of the company's equipment cost is in the antennas."

Don also noted:

> The auditors had a feeling that there were some repairs and maintenance being capitalized, but they never really found it. When they did their investigations the engineers would tell them, "We're just fine-tuning the equipment, getting it ready to use." The auditors weren't thorough enough. If they had studied it carefully they would have found, for example, that it takes $400,000 per year to maintain each of the fancy video tape decks. If the company doesn't do the maintenance Sony won't guarantee the machines.

By the end of FY 1990, Don judged that of the $10 million in capital additions for the year, $3.5 million was in interest and another $2 million was for items that should have been classified as repairs and maintenance expense and engineering salaries. If those expenses were moved to the income statement, ETI would show a huge loss. But as long as ETI management could get funds for more capital additions, they would keep deferring those expenses.

Year end 1990

Don went to Joe and proposed a large accounting adjustment, of nearly $2 million, approximately twice the amount ETI would otherwise report as 1990 profit. But Joe was in the middle of an important series of negotiations that had begun in 1989 with National Telephone Corporation (NTC), a large telecommunications company. NTC had offered to buy a new offering of ETI stock at a substantial premium over market prices and to allow ETI to participate as a partner in the start of a whole new type of business – satellite telephone communications. This business, which was in an early development stage, involved having special telephones manufactured by NTC send a signal to a satellite positioned to handle such transmissions. The satellite would relay the call to a ground station that fed it into the regular phone network. This business was seen to have a large potential market in providing easy telephone communications to remote areas and to passengers in airplanes throughout the world. NTC was attempting to set up a worldwide satellite communications network and was promising to give ETI the East Coast franchise. ETI managers knew that the NTC deal was important both for the opportunity to enter a new business and for the infusion of cash that would allow the retirement of some expensive bonds.

So when Don proposed the accounting adjustment, Joe said,

> No! No! No! You don't understand. We've got NTC going to hand us an enormous amount of money, and that will solve the problem. We must report the profits they're expecting or they'll back away from us. Let's get through this year and digest these acquisitions. Our interest costs will be lower next year because we will be able to renegotiate our loans. Let's focus on the future. I'll talk to the auditors.

Don attended the meeting with the auditors, but said, "I had to leave the room because it was so outrageous."

The auditors gave the ETI 1990 financial statements an unqualified opinion, although they told the board of directors that the statements were *pushing the edge on aggressive reporting*. In response to a question about how the auditors approved the statements, Don replied:

> When I was at T&Y I felt relatively certain that nobody could get anything by me. By the time I'd left C&S I realized that auditors provide *no* safety net. There is no way you can have relatively untrained people (even those with up to five years' experience), no matter how many you have, come up against financial people in a company with similar backgrounds but with a lot more experience and a full year to decide how they want to shape the financial picture they want to present to the world.
>
> I think Joe also had an effect on the auditors. He has an explosive personality. I have watched him call the auditors, even the partner, into his office and literally shriek at them. He grossly overreacts

to things; he's not emotionally mature. I think they're afraid of him. Even when they realize their mistakes they feel a natural pressure to go along to keep their client afloat. They hope it works out.

Even though Don felt ETI should not be reporting as it did, he knew he did not know what the proper accounting should be because he had spent his time focusing on improving the company's systems. Furthermore, he felt that the problem would be fixed in 1991 as a lot of goodwill amortization and depreciation of equipment put in service would have to be recognized as expense. Don was also appeased because management had agreed to limit expenditures, and Joe had finally agreed to let him change the company's measurement focus from EPS to cash flows.

Don wrote the management discussion and analysis section of ETI's 1990 annual report. In it he indicated that fiscal year 1991 would be a year of restructuring, that the company would be amortizing its expenses over a much shorter period and, consequently, that profits would be much lower. His feeling at the time:

I felt that I had done a reasonable job of telling people what was going on. I was signalling that the trend should not be plotted from these results. I thought if people looked at cash flows they would understand what was going on. We had disclosed how much interest we had capitalized. I thought that someone who was smart and took the time would be able to draw the right conclusions from our disclosures.

Fiscal year 1991

The budget proved to be reasonably accurate in the first quarter of fiscal year 1991, and Don was convinced that the company would actually report something close to the $2 million loss that had been forecast unless changes were made. He showed his analysis to top management and made them promise to make significant cuts in expenditures. They committed to cut people and travel, to delay the capital additions, and even to sell some assets.

But at the end of the second quarter (January 1991) the manager of the satellite video division dropped his $3.5 million operating profit projection for the year to $1.5 million, so company profits were now forecast at a $4 million loss for the year. Don visited the presidents of all the divisions and asked them to raise their profit forecasts for the year, but they said that was impossible. For example, the president of the most profitable division said he had made a bad error and fired a couple of salespeople and his sales were below plan. Plus he said he had budgeted an aggressive level of sales that he had known from the beginning he could not deliver.

Don was now quite concerned. The rest of ETI's top management team still did not put great faith in the budget numbers, and they had not cut costs as sharply as Don would have liked. And they still believed that the negotiation with NTC pointed the way to the company's future. Don knew their stance perpetuated the pressures for aggressive financial reporting.

Don wondered what he should do. Should he continue to work on improving the company's accounting and budgeting systems and keep trying to convince top management that ETI had a serious financial problem on its hands? Or should he force the issue by making the accounting adjustment and hope that the company (and his job) survived the loss?

This case was prepared by Professor Kenneth A. Merchant. The case describes a real situation, but the facts have been disguised, and any resemblance to actual people or events is unintentional.

CASE STUDY
Desktop Solutions, Inc. (A): Audit of the St. Louis Branch

In 2015, a team of auditors from the Internal Audit staff of Desktop Solutions, Inc., an electronic distributor, audited the St. Louis branch of the Operations Group. Their audit report included the following overall judgment:

> **In our opinion, the St. Louis branch's administrative process was *unsatisfactory* to support the attainment of branch business objectives.**

The auditors noted that many of the branch procedures were working effectively, but they found that major deficiencies existed in the branch's equipment control and order entry processes.

This case focuses on the areas of the audit that led to the unsatisfactory audit judgment. It describes what the auditors did, what they found, and how management responded.

Desktop Solutions, Inc.

Desktop Solutions produced a broad line of printing and scanning systems for desktop printing/publishing applications. In 2015, the company's revenues were well over $800 million (see Exhibit 1). The company's printers and scanners were available for rental or purchase. All rental plans in the United States included maintenance, service, and parts. For equipment purchase, Desktop Solutions offered financing plans over two- to five-year periods with competitive interest rates. Some equipment was sold with trade-in privileges. The company also sold supplies, such as toner, developer, and paper.

Desktop Solutions' worldwide marketing and sales organization marketed directly to end-user customers. The company also used some alternate channels, including retail stores, direct mail, and sales agents. And it maintained worldwide networks of regional service centers (for servicing products) and distribution centers (for sales of parts and consumable supplies).

Operations Group

The Operations Group (OG) was the North American sales, marketing, and service operation within Desktop Solutions' Operations Division. Within the OG, the most important line organizations were the branches. They represented Desktop Solutions' direct interface with customers and were responsible for fulfilling all their equipment and servicing needs.

Until the late 2000s, the management of the branches in OG had been highly decentralized. The decentralized organization was abandoned in the late 2000s and early 2010s in favor of a functional type of organization, which allowed for more direct control over branch functions by regional headquarters. Under the functional organization, each branch was run by three parallel functional managers – a branch sales manager, a branch control manager (or branch controller), and a branch technical service manager – each of whom reported directly to the respective functional manager at the regional level (see Exhibit 2). The sales manager was responsible for all sales and leasing of Desktop Solutions products in the branch territory. The control manager was in charge of all the internal operating, administrative, and financial reporting systems, such as order entry, accounts receivable, equipment control, and personnel. The technical service manager was responsible for the installation, servicing, and removal of sold and leased equipment.

The most difficult challenge with the new functional organization was maintaining good communication between personnel in the different functions of the branch. Frequent and effective communications were also important for achieving customer satisfaction, which was the most important branch success factor. Good communications were required to ensure that equipment would be installed promptly, that billings would be accurate, and that problems would be resolved with a minimum of hassle.

Internal audit

Internal audit had been a centralized function at Desktop Solutions since 2000. The function was centralized in order to increase auditor independence and to improve the professionalism of the staff. In 2015, the internal audit organization consisted of 15 people, headed by Steve Kruse, who reported to the chief financial officer, Scott Pepper.

Two features of the Desktop Solutions Internal Audit (IA) organization were unique as compared with the internal audit groups in most corporations. First, the IA personnel had diverse backgrounds, and internal audit was not considered a career objective for most of them. The accounting/auditing personnel, who predominated on many corporate internal audit staffs, were in the minority; only three of the IA personnel were CPAs. The others were trained in a variety of disciplines, including engineering, marketing, computer science, and liberal arts. Nine of the staff came into IA from outside Desktop Solutions. An initial assignment in IA was perceived as a good introduction to the company and a good training ground for moving into line operations. Most staff auditors did, in fact, move into the operations side of the company after gaining a few years' IA experience.

Second, the IA charter was very broad. The listing of IA functions (see Exhibit 3) showed that IA was expected to be involved in the development, not just the testing, of operational and internal controls. Exhibit 4 describes the different types of audits the IA staff performed and the allocation of audit resources among them in 2015.

Most of the audits were planned at headquarters, as part of the review of the company's controls. However, IA also received requests for services from line managers. In recent years, the number of such requests had exceeded IA's capacity. Balancing the needs for regular audit cycles with the needs for special services requested was the difficult part in preparing the IA plan. Audit plans were approved by the audit committee of the board of directors, which was given regular progress reports throughout the year on each audit.

After executing an audit, IA staff gave formal presentations to senior line management detailing their results and recommendations. They also followed up at a later date to see if the deficiencies had been corrected and the recommendations had been implemented.

Audit of the St. Louis branch

The St. Louis branch was selected for audit in 2015 for three reasons. First, the 2015 Master Audit Plan called for a number of large branch audits. The St. Louis branch, which served customers in Missouri, Illinois, and Kansas, was one of the largest of OG's 52 branches. In 2015, it earned revenue of $15.2 million and had a sale/lease equipment inventory of 7,710 machines. Second, a 2013 audit of the St. Louis branch had uncovered deficiencies in branch equipment control, and IA management thought this would be a good time to verify if improvements had been implemented. And third, a new branch control manager (branch controller) was recently hired, and the audit would give the new control manager a chance to work with the auditors and learn about the branch's systems and problems. The IA audit team and the new controller arrived at the St. Louis branch on the same day.

The objective of the audit was to determine whether the branch administrative/control processes were well defined, executed, and managed to ensure: (1) controlled and documented equipment movement and tracking; (2) timely and accurate order entry; (3) proper customer billing and adjustment; and (4) effective collections activity.

On the St. Louis audit, like most branch audits, the auditors focused most of their attention on equipment inventory and accounts receivable. These were the two largest branch balance sheet items, and both were under the direct control of the branch managers.

Equipment control/billing

Equipment control (EC) involved the tracking of equipment movements in and out of the branch's physical inventory and the simultaneous triggering of changes in customer billings. EC was critical to the branch's ability to schedule, deliver, and install machines for Desktop Solutions customers, and to be paid for the equipment the customers used.

The key control personnel in EC were the order administrators (OAs), the equipment administrator (EA), and the schedulers. The OAs were responsible for editing incoming orders, entering the orders into the computer system, keeping track of the orders after they were sent to scheduling, and processing the install transactions (install date, serial number, meter reads).

The EA was responsible for the accuracy of inventory records, and the timely resolution of equipment discrepancies that delayed orders (thus billing) from being completed. The EA maintained the Non-Revenue Report (NRR), a computer-generated inventory listing (by equipment serial number) of all branch equipment not installed at a customer location. The NRR was updated daily with information about new installations and cancellations. At the beginning of each month, the EA took a physical inventory of all equipment at the warehouse, matched it with the NRR, and reconciled the differences. Equipment on the NRR not found at the warehouse was reclassified as uninventoriable (lost). If it was not found within 90 days, the branch was charged for the net book value of the lost equipment. The process for cancellation and deinstallation of equipment was very similar.

The schedulers matched the orders with the equipment shown as available on the NRR. A target delivery date (ideally two days) was transmitted to the rigger who delivered the equipment (by serial number indicated).

Exhibit 5 shows a simplified flow chart of the process used in the St. Louis branch for order-entry and installation of the high-end printing and scanning systems. Personnel in the control function of the branch played a central communication role, transmitting the order information from the sales representatives to the rigger (warehouse) personnel and branch technical service personnel. They also processed the information about installations so as to trigger the customer billing.

Some low-end systems were delivered and installed by the sales representatives (reps). When this was done, the equipment control process was simplified because the rep was responsible for delivering the order paperwork and the printer serial number to the OA for entry into the computer system.

While their operations were quite similar, the branches used slightly different administrative processes and personnel roles. OG management elected not to use a detailed, centralized set of administrative processes for all branches. They preferred allowing the branch managers to tailor their branch's processes to the local conditions.

Audit procedures

The audit fieldwork at the St. Louis branch took a team of four auditors approximately two months to complete. Exhibit 6 describes the tests performed on the equipment control process. About 40% of the audit time was devoted to equipment control procedures. Initially the IA personnel conducted background interviews with key branch personnel. They also reviewed organization charts and prepared detailed flow charts of the order entry, scheduling, and equipment control processes. This was done to understand how the branch operated, to determine the degree of compliance with company procedures, and to determine the efficiency of branch personnel. Potential problem areas were noted for special attention during the audit fieldwork.

In addition to equipment control, the auditors also tested several other areas, including customer billings for equipment, supplies, and servicing (for accuracy and timeliness), price plan conversion (for compliance with company procedures), order entry and cancellation processes (for accuracy and efficiency), credit and collections, and order-to-installation time lag. Each of these areas represented a cycle or process activity which was important to the operation of a branch.

Findings – equipment control

The auditors found that management failed to define responsibilities clearly or hold the EA accountable for his performance. Branch management was not involved in the monitoring and maintenance of the equipment control process. And control management did not maintain effective contact with marketing and service management to ensure that the equipment control process was operating properly. Exhibit 7 describes some of the deficiencies found.

However, the branch was rated "very good" in other areas. The auditors noted that the negative impacts from the deficiencies in the equipment control area seemed to be effectively minimized:

> **Although the delayed equipment transaction processing contributed to incorrect billings and an increased rate of costly billing adjustments, overall the billing function was sufficiently well organized and controlled to be able to absorb the pressures generated. The billing adjustments reviewed were highly accurate, and resolution of customer inquiries was satisfactory. The credit and collection program was well administered; performance budgets were consistently met; and adjustment and write-off activity was well controlled.**

Recommendations and follow-up

On July 14, 2015, the audit team presented a final listing of the recommendations to the branch managers. Shortly thereafter, they prepared a formal audit report to all OG management responsible for the St. Louis branch operations.

In the audit report, the auditors presented a list of 46 recommendations. Most of the recommendations were directed to the new branch control manager, and generally related to one or more of the following:

1. The reconciliation between the physical inventory and the inventory records (NRR) should be completed;
2. The deficient equipment processes should be studied, refined, and documented; and
3. The individuals involved in equipment control should be given clearly defined responsibilities and be held accountable for the accuracy of the equipment reports and billings.

Ultimate responsibility for correcting deficiencies rested with line management (branch managers), not with IA. Company policy required the branch managers to prepare an action plan to address each of the deficiencies and recommendations made in the audit report. The last written response to the auditors' recommendations came from the St. Louis branch control manager on December 15, 2016. He addressed each of the auditors' recommendations and noted that most of them had already been implemented.

Company policy also required that someone independent of both IA and branch management be assigned to monitor progress in implementing the audit recommendations. In OG, this was usually someone from the headquarters finance staff.

Reactions

Martha Sorensen (IA manager) reflected on the audit:

> The St. Louis branch had been recognized for some time as a problem branch. In most of the branches, many of the systems and administrative procedures go back to the days when the branches were run by a single branch manager, and the branches that were not well run in those days tended not to get going well when we switched to the functional organization. So going into this audit, we had a good idea we would find some problems, and the results of the audit confirmed this judgment. I hope we're now well on the way to getting the problems ironed out.

Phil Phillips, Region 3 manager, responded to the disclosure of the St. Louis branch's ongoing equipment control problem:

> We can't blame these problems on the system because it works well in other branches. The problems occur for a combination of reasons including people, management, the sheer volume of work that was handled, and the fact that St. Louis is larger and has a more diverse organization structure than most of the other branches. These all create problems. We believe the problems are manageable but it will take time to whittle away at them. We're making progress, but at this point we have not given the St. Louis branch a specific time deadline to clear up all their problems.

Exhibit 1 Summary income statements, Desktop Solutions, Inc. (in $ millions)

	Year Ended December 31	
	2014	2015
Operating Revenues		
Rentals and services	$456.2	$524.4
Sales	313.2	352.6
Total operating revenues	769.4	877.0
Cost and Expenses		
Cost of rentals and services	203.2	232.4
Cost of sales	155.8	161.2
Research and development expenses	51.8	60.2
Selling, administrative and general expenses	289.2	319.6
Total cost and expenses	700.0	773.4
Operating Income	69.4	103.6
Other Income (Deductions), Net	(18.8)	(4.8)
Income before Income Taxes	50.6	98.8
Income Taxes	13.6	27.2
Income before Outside Shareholder's Interests	37.0	71.6
Outside Shareholder's Interests	7.1	11.8
Income from Continuing Operations	29.9	59.8
Discontinued Operations	5.2	2.4
Net Income	$35.1	$62.2

Exhibit 2 Operations Group organization chart

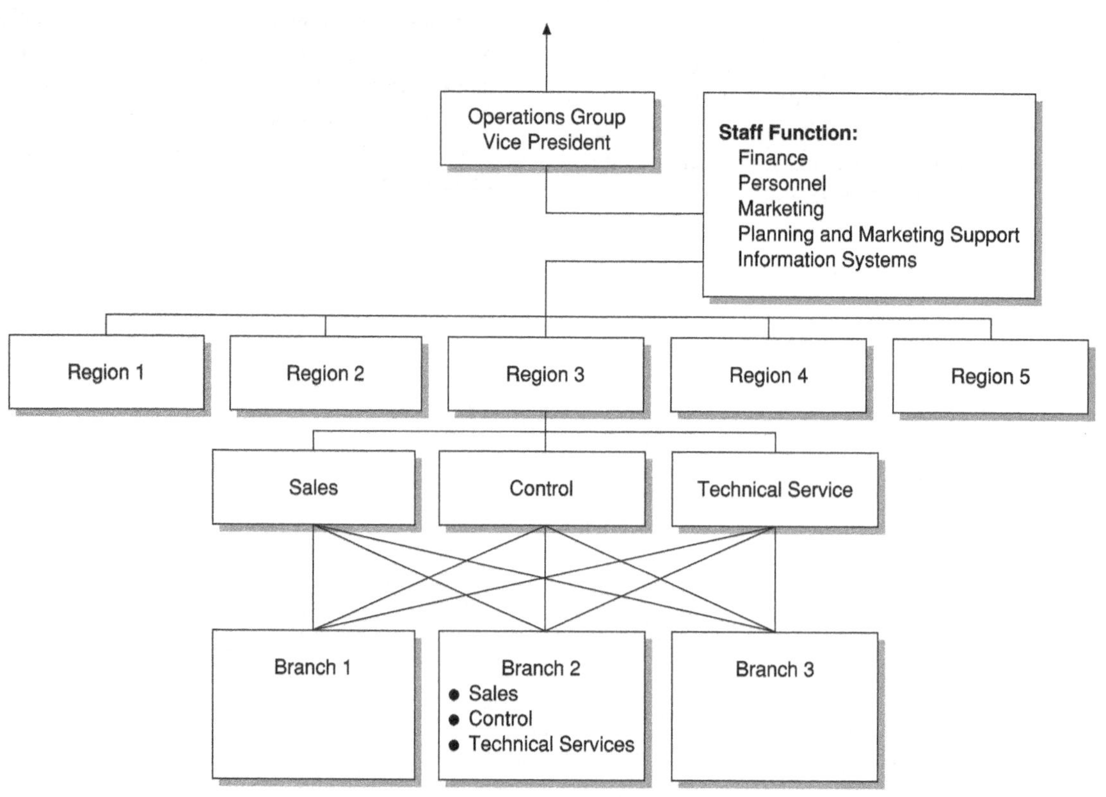

Exhibit 3 Internal audit functions

1. Develop and implement a program of operational, financial, and information systems audits that best meet the requirements of the corporation; assure the integrity of operational and internal controls in protecting the assets of the company and improve operational effectiveness.
2. Assist corporate and operating unit management in identifying and developing operational, financial, and systems policies and procedures necessary to accomplish the goals and objectives of the corporation; evaluate activities through audit report findings and recommend actions to eliminate problems uncovered during audits.
3. Perform special audits in any functional area and for all levels of management as required.
4. Present the audit plan and related audit findings to the Audit Committee of the Board of Directors and corporate management.
5. Coordinate external audit activities and control-related audit fees. Ensure an optimum balance between internal and external audit work in fulfilling the basic audit objectives and obtaining annual certification of Desktop Solutions' consolidated financial statements.
6. Develop new concepts of auditing responsive to the changing business and technological environment within Desktop Solutions and maintain a professional staff skilled in the required disciplines.

Exhibit 4 Audit types and 2015 plan for allocation of resources

Control Environment Audits (24% of resources in 2015)
Control Environment audits evaluate the organizational arrangements; financial planning and analysis; personnel policies and practices; and policy definition and communication within operating organizations. The objective is to assess the basis on which responsibility is assigned, accountability is determined, performance is measured, and overall specific controls are established.

Business Entity Audits (39%)
These are reviews of specific business cycle controls in a business entity such as a branch or small to medium subsidiary.

Business Cycle Audits (17%)
These are reviews of the seven business cycle as set forth in the Desktop Solutions Compendium of Internal Controls to determine if the overall and individual cycle control objectives stated there are being met. The overall objectives tested are: authorization; accounting transaction processing; and safeguarding of corporate assets. The cycle reviews will also include reviews of applicable control environment functions and tests of supporting computer controls.

Financial Audits (11%)
Financial audits, unless otherwise indicated, are in direct support of the annual audit by our external auditors and represent independent evaluation for the purpose of attesting to the fairness, and reliability of the financial data.

Systems Audit (8%)
System audits are pre-implementation and post-implementation reviews and data center audits. Pre-implementation audits consider the integrity, control, performance, security and conformance with policies and standards of each system reviewed during the design and development process. Post-implementation audits determine whether cost and performance objectives are met and test the system's integrity, including controls, in its live environment. Audits of data centers assess overall performance and the data control function and address security, scheduling and utilization, control, documentation, organization, training and cost effectiveness.

Exhibit 5 Simplified flow chart of order entry and installation for high-end systems

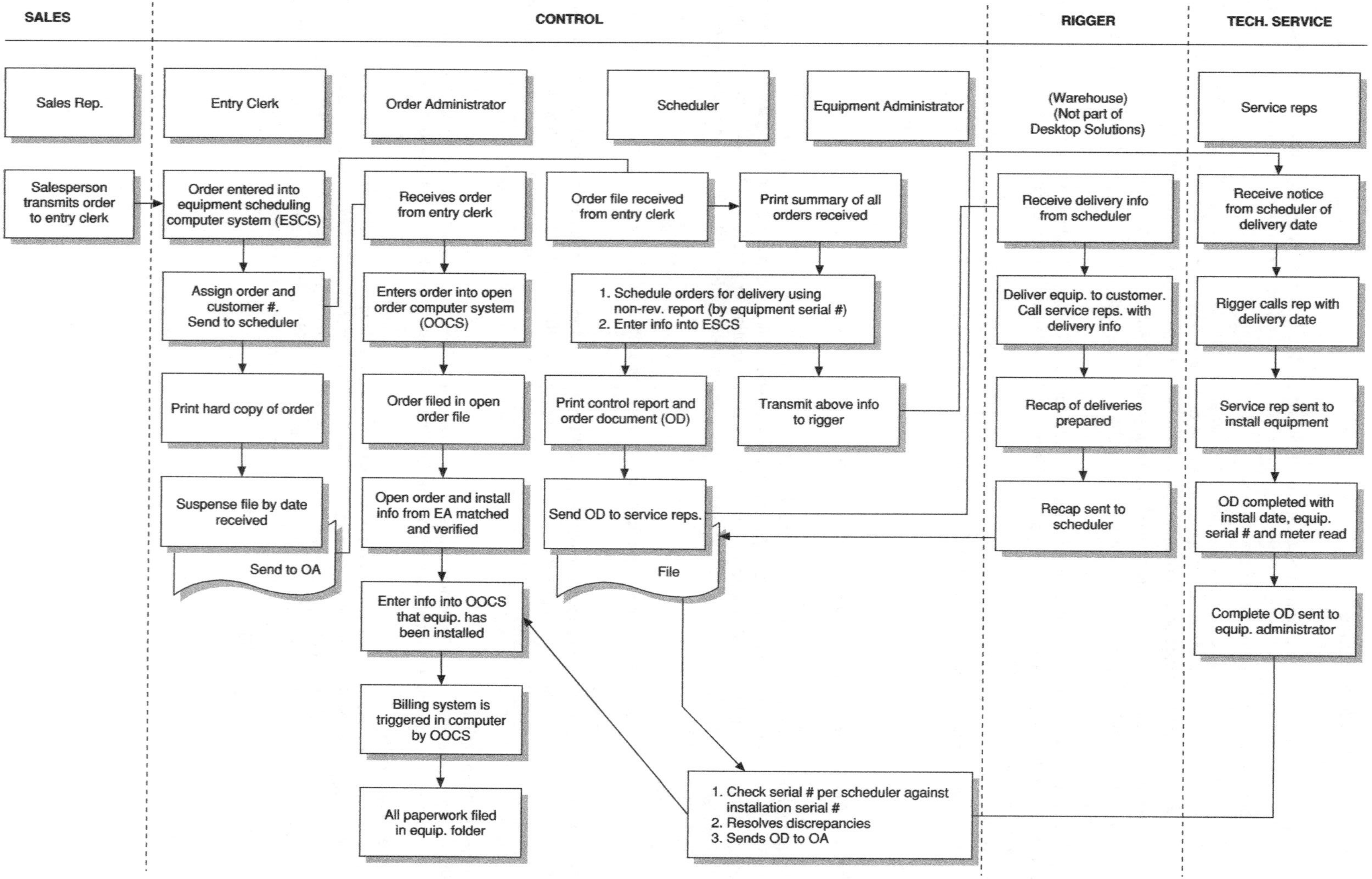

Exhibit 6 Audit tests performed on equipment control at the St. Louis branch

1. ***Physical inventory***. A total sample of 1,387 equipment units was examined, including a complete (100%) examination of the units of one single product. The audit team recorded all the serial numbers of the sample units found at the rigger (warehouse) and matched the numbers with those shown on the NRR. Serial numbers not matching up were given to the equipment administrator for reconciliation.
2. ***Scheduling process***. The auditors examined the paperwork for a sample of 243 installations to see how the schedulers notified the riggers about what equipment to install.
3. ***Install lag test***. A sample of 46 machines was examined for the timeliness of the steps in the order-to-install process, including how long the sales reps held on to orders before submitting them, how long the OAs took to enter the order correctly, how long it took the schedulers to get the machine out to the customer site and then the delay before the technical service reps installed the machine; and how long the OAs take to enter the final install information correctly into the system to trigger the billing process.
4. ***Cancel lag test***. A sample of 33 cancellations was examined for proper adherence to contract terms and cancellation policies. The auditors were looking to see if the customer cancellation notification policy was followed, if the stop billing date was appropriate, if the removal charges were correctly billed, and if the processing was done on a timely basis.
5. ***Low-volume copier installations***. A sample of 23 low-volume copier installations was examined to see if transmission of information from the sales reps to the OAs was adequate.
6. ***Trials***. A sample of 22 machines out for customer trial was tested for adherence to company duration guidelines and approval procedures.

Exhibit 7 Partial list of internal audit findings at the St. Louis branch

1. The responsibilities of branch personnel were found to be slightly unusual in order entry and scheduling/equipment control. Some special order transactions (e.g., maintenance agreements, price plan conversions) were processed by customer service assistants, not OAs. The OAs did not track orders through the order-to-install process. And the information about installations and status changes went to the EA, instead of the scheduler, as at most other branches.
2. The physical inventory of 1,387 mainframe and sorter units showed over 633 discrepancies when compared to the NRR. Seven weeks after the audit results were turned over to the branch, the EA had only reconciled 382 of these items, leaving 251 items unreconciled: 76 units potentially lost, 15 units potentially found, and 160 location and/or status discrepancies. At other branches, 95–100% of the inventory discrepancies were typically reconciled within the first two weeks.
3. The schedulers had learned they could not rely on the NRR, so they kept their own equipment inventory records. They manually assigned serial numbers to incoming orders. To move equipment quickly, they sometimes directed the rigger to deliver products directly from the receiving dock before the serial numbers had been recorded in the branch's inventory by the EA. They kept track of movements in or out of the inventory based on information received from service personnel, but the auditors found that this listing was also inaccurate.
4. It took seven days on average from the date a machine was installed to the time the system recognized it as a valid install so that billing could begin. In addition, some documentation was missing: three of the 46 sampled had no credit approval; two had no service agreement; four had no valid installation date stamp.
5. The cancellation procedure was not working effectively. One hundred machines that had been returned by the customer and sent to the refurbishing center had not been noted as canceled by the OAs, and this number had increased sharply in the prior three months.
6. The low-end printing equipment was not well controlled. Units to be delivered by the sales reps were taken from regular inventory, rather than from a special pool of machines in "consignment to sales" status. In nine cases (39%), the sales reps did not send the serial numbers of the equipment to the OAs. In one case, the rigger tried to deliver a machine to a customer who had received his a week before from the sales rep.
7. Of the machines out for customer trial, only three of the 22 tested complied with company policy, and five had no approval signature. For four successful trials (i.e., the customer wanted to keep the machine), the ending date was recorded improperly, resulting in 29 days of unbilled rental revenue. For eight unsuccessful trials, the removal was scheduled two days past the trial expiration. Four trials were extended without approval. The average length past the normal trial duration was 17 days, while the average length past the extension deadline was 9.5 days.
8. Management failed to define responsibilities clearly or hold the EA accountable for his performance. Management did not get involved in the monitoring and maintenance of the equipment control process. Finally, control management did not maintain effective contact with marketing and service management to ensure that the equipment control process was operating properly as it affected those areas.

This case was prepared by Professor Kenneth A. Merchant with the assistance of Howard Koo.

CASE STUDY
Desktop Solutions, Inc. (B): Audit of Operations Group Systems

In September 2015, Don Lindsay, the newly appointed manager of the Systems department of the Operations Group (OG) of Desktop Solutions, Inc., believed that some deep-rooted problems were hindering his unit's operational effectiveness. Systems had a long-standing reputation as being expensive and resistant to change, and systems planning in OG was generally recognized as deficient. As one manager put it:

> **Don's predecessor tended to allow the user organizations to tell him what to do. The Systems personnel work closely with the various users, so closely, in fact, that it really became a direct-line relationship to the user managers and a dotted-line relationship to the Systems managers. That does not allow for a very effective operation because you really don't have control of the organization. All the users had their own parochial demands. They built their own databases, and there was very little sharing of files even between individuals in the same branch. The result was that the number of Systems personnel needed to meet the increasing number of user needs ballooned. People became resistant to change, and they were protective of what they had created. Virtually no planning or coordination was occurring.**

Don thought that personnel from Desktop Solutions' corporate Internal Audit (IA) staff could help him by providing an independent opinion as to how well Systems was performing, identifying problems that might have gone unnoticed, and making suggestions for improvement. He also thought that an audit with recommendations for change would increase the support he would get from upper-level OG management and user organizations for implementing changes. He therefore requested a special audit from the IA organization. The purpose was to assess OG-Systems' ability in performing its centralized system support functions.

OG-Systems

Systems was a centralized systems support organization charged with two primary tasks: (1) maintaining and enhancing existing OG information systems; and (2) planning and implementing replacement systems. Because of OG's diversity, these tasks were formidable. OG had 10 regional offices responsible for a total of 52 branch offices. Each region and branch operated their own unique information systems with different procedures and databases. Requests for system maintenance and development could come from any of several management levels in the user organizations (i.e. branch or regional offices), and they were allowed to go directly to the first-line (lowest-level) Systems managers responsible for their particular systems.

In 2015, Systems' budget was $31.6 million, of which about 60% was to be spent on systems maintenance, planning, and development, and the rest was to be spent on data processing operations. All work was fully charged back to the user organizations. Systems employed 155 people, 93 of whom were directly involved in code-creation activity (i.e. programmers, analysts).

The Systems organization, which reported directly to the OG vice president, was divided into three parts: Operations, Planning and Systems Architecture, and Control and Administration. The Operations organization was responsible for creating new software and running three regional data processing centers. The Planning and Systems Architecture organization was responsible for long-range planning of both software and hardware. It also provided technical expertise to user organizations and reviewed all new system designs for hardware compatibility. The Control and Administration organization was responsible for financial planning, analysis and reporting.

Audit procedures and findings

The OG-Systems audit was planned and executed by two auditors who spent approximately 1,600 hours each on the entire project. One of the auditors had an extensive systems background, and was familiar with the operation and history of the Systems organization. Exhibit 1 describes the audit steps performed and the percent of time spent on each.

The auditors confirmed that systems planning and coordination in the OG organization were inadequate. They observed that many systems implementation decisions were being made at lower levels of management of the user organizations without reference to related decisions in other areas. They found that Systems did not guide and coordinate the systems and programming personnel in the user organizations in the development of long-range or annual work plans, but they concluded that this problem was partly beyond the control of the Systems organization. One of the comments in their report was, "Generally, the current OG group-level business planning process does not result in formal management-approved output that is sufficiently integrated and detailed to direct a long-range systems development process."

To improve systems planning, the auditors suggested that OG senior management should:

1. Designate an information controller in each functional area to be responsible for providing an interface between strategic business planning and strategic systems planning. This person would also be responsible for integrating information needs within the function and between functions and for ensuring that all systems development activities flowed through OG-Systems. Once senior OG management had decided on a strategic business direction and the information needs, Systems personnel could develop compatible systems within each user organization to satisfy those needs.
2. Establish a process of recording and reporting of systems benefits to improve systems investment appraisal decisions and performance evaluations.

They suggested that the vice president of OG-Systems (Don Lindsay) should:

1. Establish and document responsibilities and procedures to ensure that the systems/user interface took place as needed and at the appropriate managerial levels within each organization.
2. Prepare detailed descriptions of the automated portions of the existing OG information processing cycles to support OG function and group-level business process planning. These documents should also be analyzed in order to identify opportunities to integrate existing processes and resources and to reduce costs.
3. Develop and maintain a description of the OG Systems Architecture, including hardware, software, databases, and networks, which is sufficiently detailed to guide Systems planners in the development of the Long Range Systems Plan, as well as to direct operations managers in the development of application systems.
4. Establish and document responsibilities and procedures to ensure that Systems planners develop a Long Range Systems Plan based on an understanding of the OG Long Range Business Process Plan, the OG Systems Architecture, current OG information cycles, and future business requirements.
5. To ensure the promotion of the Long Range Systems Plan, ensure that the first year of the Long Range Systems Plan be sufficiently detailed to serve as the next year's Annual Work Plan; assign accountability for the execution of the Annual Work Plan to management in the user organizations; establish and document procedures to ensure the review and approval by the Systems planning staff of adjustments to the Annual Work Plan; and assign specific responsibility within the planning function for review of all new applications systems for adherence to the Long Range Systems Plan.

In the area of line operations, the auditors concluded that a diversity of operational practices existed within Systems, due to "a general lack of discipline and definition in operational practices within user first line operations, as well as the absence of common operational procedures, measures and tools at the group level." This diversity restricted management's ability to monitor and assess the quality and efficiency of software production activities, hindered the realization of economies of scale.

The auditors also concluded that key elements of the software creation process were not sufficiently controlled to ensure the efficient production of high-quality software products. To remedy these deficiencies, they presented a long list of specific recommendations. These included suggestions for developing and implementing procedures for job requests and authorizations, scheduling jobs, ensuring better software security, and evaluating and documenting changes.

Management reactions

The reactions to the audit were generally favorable. Larry Parton, manager of OG Planning and Systems Architecture, expressed his feelings:

> You can treat auditors either as outsiders or as a resource for management. Desktop Solutions has a very strong audit staff, and we like to take advantage of their expertise. We have some problems, and we have an awful lot to gain by asking them to come in and do an audit. That is the way we treated it and that is the way it turned out. We needed an independent look at what we were doing, and the audit group gave us that.

Don Lindsay was also satisfied:

> The reason I invited corporate audit to come in and do this audit was relatively straightforward. I had my own diagnosis of the problems in the Systems Department and an action plan for solving then. I just needed to get someone else's perception of the problems and their recommendations. IA is really the only group we have to do this kind of work. They are not a Gestapo organization; they are a support group that has the ability to get into this kind of work.
>
> I feel very good about the audit report. I agree with their base identification of the issues. They confirmed my analysis. I don't feel they came up with a lot of strong recommendations, however. I think the solution to many of our problems is a better focus on systems planning within the entire OG, and that is something that I, by myself, cannot solve. That is probably the single most important issue in OG, and the audit report dealt with it only superficially. It discussed planning but seemed to place more emphasis on day-to-day operating issues.
>
> It was not my original intention to use the audit report as additional leverage to plead my case, but that has certainly turned out to be an important benefit. After we realized how deeply ingrained our problems were, we realized that we had to use every means available to get the message across. The audit report was one such forum.

Exhibit 1 Audit steps performed and the percent of time spent on each on the OG-Systems audit

1. *Scoping* (30%). Conducted preliminary independent interviews with users and Systems managers about their systems procedures and working relationships.
2. *Planning* (15%). Reviewed the results of the scoping phase and discussed them with Don Lindsay. Formulated a model of how the operations work and developed a set of problem hypotheses. Developed fieldwork questionnaires.
3. *Fieldwork* (25%). Sent questionnaires to a sample of involved or affected personnel, including 11 first-line managers and 10 analysts and programmers, all in the Systems organization, and 12 first-line user managers. Followed up the questionnaires with personal interviews and prepared a summary of responses. Interviewed five second-line and three third-line Systems managers and prepared a summary of these responses.
4. *Clearing and Summarizing* (15%). Verified interview responses where necessary. Developed conclusions drawn from fieldwork summaries and proposed recommendations. Presented conclusions and recommendations to OG-Systems management.
5. *Formal Report to Systems Management* (15%). Prepared formal written audit report with conclusions and recommendations for Systems management (Don Lindsay).

This case was prepared by Professor Kenneth A. Merchant with the assistance of Howard Koo.

CASE STUDY
Andrew G. Scavell, Chief Risk Officer

In November 2013, Andrew G. Scavell, chief risk officer at maritime operator LP&F Cargo Ltd., was pondering:

> **What is the risk manager's role? Should it be just about preventing bad things from happening—*dangers*? Or should the scope of risk management include wider commercial challenges—*opportunities*, which may have bigger impacts—positive impacts, that is—than the dangers?**

"I think both," he sighed, "as long as the CRO stays well clear of 'acculturating' – of going native to put it bluntly – with the executives running the business."

In his 19 years at the company, Andy had not always been in charge of risk. Risk and risk management became Andy's purview when he was promoted to become the company's CRO, LP&F's first, in 2009. Since then, Andy had kept busy establishing risk management as a full-fledged C-suite function. This, however, had not just been about setting up risk management systems. Andy's key challenge had been to try to have everyone embrace risk management rather than it being seen as merely a bureaucratic nuisance, a rationalizing afterthought, or something for which the company could take out insurance.

The company

LP&F Cargo Ltd. (LP&F) was a maritime operator formed over the years through several mergers of smaller operators as the industry grew and sea lanes expanded, yet competition intensified, capital requirements deepened, margins narrowed, and risks soared. Only two of the original operators' names were still captured in the company's acronym (La Porta & Finch), but many others had been swallowed up, integrated with the then-existing fleet and operations, and their former company names (gradually) discarded.

LP&F wasn't one of a handful of "super" maritime (container ship and tanker) operators like Maersk or Evergreen, although it was considered a strong second-tier contender for a broad range of services, some of which rather specialized and tailored to specific customer needs. For example, LP&F's fleet contained several purpose-built vessels to carry products to exacting care requirements with respect to handling, stowing, ventilation, and in-transit inspections. In both the dry and liquid shipping business, LP&F had established a reputation for control of conditions in the hold. At the same time, and to strengthen its position in this unforgiving business, LP&F also had to retain scheduling flexibility, necessitating capital investments in interchangeable vessels.

LP&F publicized itself as a provider of integrated transportation solutions for dry and liquid goods, offering services that included mainly transportation by vessel, terminal handling, and storage. The company's customers, which included mostly manufacturers (but also some traders) using or processing these materials (including lumber, plywood, wood pulp, paper, ferrous and non-ferrous metals, chemicals, petroleum products, oils, and a variety of other break-bulk cargoes), relied on LP&F's speciality infrastructure to move and store these products around the globe. LP&F's 10 largest customers accounted for approximately 65 percent of its revenues in 2013.

Slightly over half of the cargo transported by LP&F was carried under long-term contracts, which, despite the term, typically covered periods of one year, though there was increasing pressure to negotiate longer-term contracts. The remaining half was priced on the spot market, where the effects of market conditions on shipping rates were felt instantaneously. For 2012, total revenues were just shy of £1.3 billion, up nearly one quarter from 2010, continuing a slow but steady recovery from the deepest of the recession felt in 2009 following the onset of the global financial and economic crisis in 2008 (see Exhibit 1). Tonnage carried was up from 2011, too, for the first time since 2008. Due to a decline in freight rates since 2009, margins and profits were down, although these had begun to recover from 2012 mainly due to cost efficiencies and a readjustment of the fleet through both vessel disposals and new orders as appropriate. But because of this recovery, shipping companies had again begun to hurry to place orders for vessels while they were cheaper to build (due to overcapacity in shipbuilding yards around the world), more environmentally friendly, and more fuel efficient, and thus, cleaner and cheaper to operate. Supply of shipping capacity, however, had again begun to outpace demand, which showed in the results for 2013. Andy expected that in 2014 the company would barely break even, if not show a loss, the first in his entire career with LP&F.

Economically, the fortunes of the industry, and thus those of the company, were directly affected by trends in world trade. With the downturn since 2008 came excess capacity, rising costs, and falling freight rates. Too many ships were competing for too little cargo, causing freight rates to plunge to levels that scarcely covered operating costs. Specialization softened the blow for LP&F somewhat, yet cost efficiency (pertaining to the running costs of a vessel) and asset utilization (pertaining to the life over which a vessel was able to earn revenue) were pressing as ever, the latter especially due to limited financing for new vessels. Ironically, overcapacity gave operators more leeway to dock vessels for maintenance with good effect on asset preservation. It also allowed operators to "slow steam" vessels, thereby improving fuel efficiency, although for a specialized, customized cargo-handler like LP&F, this often was not an option. But to LP&F's advantage, customers often had less choice of operators to handle their cargo due to specialization. Indeed, in LP&F's segment, its customers normally did not have shipping needs that could be easily handled on the spot market or that were easily switchable from one long-term contract with a given operator to another.

That said, managing costs remained difficult due to erratic fuel prices as one of the main operating costs, while fixed costs remained high. Indeed, unfilled capacity was "sunk" in the sense that once a vessel left port, any excess space was wasted and irredeemable for the entire voyage, which sometimes took weeks to complete. Global trade imbalances triggered by the economic downturn also plagued the industry, where vessel operators faced increasing difficulties to fill capacity on both the outbound and return legs of the voyage. Due to the asymmetrical demand for capacity, operators vied aggressively for business.

The industry, and thus the company in response, also had changed in perhaps more intangible ways. Since about the 1990s, possibly traceable to the Exxon *Valdez* oil tanker environmental disaster in 1989, there seemed to have been an avalanche of complex and evolving systems of regulation and a jumble of rules and security measures imposed by national, regional, and international maritime administrations and trade bodies. These regulations of course had to be complied with, although a culture of voluntary alertness to risk issues probably was more effective than merely reluctantly responding to regulation.

The chief risk officer

Andrew (Andy) G. Scavell had a BA with honors in politics and history. After qualifying as a Chartered Accountant, he worked in an old-style merchant bank in the City of London for two years; after which he moved to one of the bank's shipping subsidiaries where he stayed for two years. He then went to work for another international shipping company (now LP&F) in their UK office, first in the treasury/corporate finance department (six years), followed by eight years as the Group Financial Controller (during which he obtained his corporate treasury's qualification). In 2009, Andy became the head of Enterprise Risk Management, at which time he had just obtained his executive MBA from Aston Business School. Everyone referred to Andy as the CRO, however, which became his official title from 2010.

Thus, in 2009, LP&F began to focus on implementing Enterprise Risk Management (ERM). Introducing ERM into LP&F was something that the shareholders and the board wanted but, at the same time, did not know what form it should take. This was part of the journey to be charted by Andy; a journey along a road with some junctures that needed careful thought.

CRO role?

First, there was the role of the CRO itself, the job description for which eventually emerged as shown in Exhibit 2. Specifically, there was some discussion about what exactly the CRO's role was to include, and who the CRO should report to. Should the CRO be "independently" responsible for identifying all the key risks and their applicable mitigations? If so, would that detract from management's role and responsibilities to the shareholders? Or should the CRO rather be seen as "non-executive management" whose role it was to oversee that management had appropriate processes and procedures in place so that the company could manage its risks (such as by way of scenario planning, risk mapping, and other standard risk tools)? In principle, however, Andy felt very strongly that "risk processes have to work with the business, and not the other way around." Put differently, he reckoned that, at least in LP&F's business, strategy drives risk.

Thus, Andy felt that strategic issues had to be par for the course for the CRO:

> Strategic issues are one of the key uncertainties that matter in any organization. Companies regularly fail because of a failure to manage them. My description of the CRO role is that of "non-executive management" – a bridge between the non-executive directors and management [which he sketched to look like the diagram shown in Exhibit 3].

Andy rambled on:

> A *spy*? I can understand why one might suggest that, but no! A difficult role that requires the trust of both the board and management, without being a patsy to either. A NED [non-executive director] will meet three or four times a year and interact with management, but even if they met eight times a year it wouldn't be enough. You need a *guardian* who sits with management all the time. Like a shadow CEO? No, non-executive. The CEO has a completely different role; managing the business day to day, trying to grow the business, and manage risk. The role of the CRO is to challenge management about the assumptions that they make; the biases that they have. I may have a different opinion about what management intends to do, but I am no *fortune teller*. What is important is that the senior managers have challenged themselves and that a robust process has been undertaken, and that the assumptions that they have made are known and reasonable. So I explain and give assurance to the board. That is what NEDs require from me, their non-executive counterpart in management.

Risk appetite?

Second, although the board had no strong sense about how to put risk management in place, they seemed initially absorbed by the notion of "risk appetite," as so many boards were when risk management began to gain prominence, and especially following the 2008 global financial and economic crisis. But, as Andy remarked, the process they had in mind for setting the risk appetite appeared to be back-to-front; that is, risk appetite was seen as the first thing they felt they now needed to think about; the thing that drove everything else; the line in the sand that could not be crossed. Andy suspected that this back-to-front approach was due to misreading the wording of umpteen governance codes, maintaining something along the lines that "*the board and management are responsible for determining the nature and extent of the significant risks it is willing to take in achieving its strategic objectives.*"

If "achieving" was to be taken as read, and not to be misread as "setting," then Andy was of the opinion that "*the board and the management of a company are responsible for setting the strategic objectives of the organization and ensuring that it has the relevant core competencies, capabilities, policies and procedures to effectively implement the strategic goals and manage the risks that arise from the strategic choices made,*" or something rather along those lines. In other words, Andy was of the view that the board and senior management should develop the strategy of the organization first, and then assess the related risks. This was not to suggest that he thought this was strictly one-directional, however. But although he acknowledged inevitable feedback loops, again, he put strategy first, musing that:

> I don't believe that a company consciously seeks risk as a goal – namely, "We want to take more risk." Boards and management seek *profit* – now and in the future, and as part of this pursuit comes risk, which has to be managed. The approach of setting a risk appetite is the inverse; namely asking companies what risk they would be prepared to take – i.e., they are seen as *risk seekers*. Instead, as part of the business strategy discussion/review, the company has to understand/assess the risks that could arise in trying to execute that strategy. As a result, the risk appetite becomes fluid, more dynamic, and perhaps confusing – a far cry from the "immutability" and predetermined nature that risk appetites are usually billed as.

Risk measurement?

Third, although the board was keen on risk measurement, Andy was no big fan of an obsessive focus on quantification *per se*, or quantification in isolation, for several reasons. First, Andy argued that risks can and will change frequently, which can easily result in the company spending too much time trying to put "numbers" on a risk rather than effectively managing the risk. Second, Andy was of the view that it was simply and practically very difficult to calculate accurate numbers for most risks. Many risks were "intelligent guesses of what the future could bring" at best. Shipping also did not give rise to "big data" especially around the likelihood of an event arising. How risks in the future impact cash flows constituted an assessment that was highly subjective. Andy added:

> Of course, one can perform Monte Carlo simulations over the DCF [discounted cash flow] figures and derive a range of numbers and probabilities. In the end, though, I am not sure that the resulting numbers will mean much. To give an example, in 2012, we had a buyer for a vessel for US$70m. We withdrew. In 2013, when we really wanted to sell that vessel, all we could fetch for it was US$15m. We sold. And that is only one small piece — the salvage value—that goes into a standard DCF model.

Andy's related concern was that seemingly accurate risk numbers might create an "illusion of control" that the risk was being managed. Instead, he argued that it was a company's failure to understand the nature of the risks that they were taking, and not their ability to set the correct numerical level of the risk, that was the more fundamental problem. That said, Andy quipped that:

> I absolutely understand the desire, and need, to create risk measures, but sometimes no number is better than *any number too soon* in the process of describing and understanding the risks. When the initial likelihood estimates and/or dollar impacts are seen as low, the risk can become quickly dismissed. I guess the opposite holds, too, where risks become seen as ominous even though they may not be. To avoid that risk measures become risks themselves, one has to be inevitably cynical about their accuracy, at least in our business, although I respectfully submit that the banks in 2008 probably learned that lesson the hard way, too.

Risk management practice

So where did all this take the company, then? If they could not fully conceptualize how risk management should work in theory, would they be able to make it work in practice?

In simplified form, and consistent with Andy's general views on risk management, the objective of performing ERM was "to allow management to make better decisions to have better outcomes." Risk management was therefore to be strategy-driven and include both opportunities as well as dangers. Risk management was also to be "effectively embedded" in the organization, for which Andy had to design a process. Andy believed that the process established both horizontal and vertical embeddedness.

To enable horizontal embeddedness, Andy devised a group risk register that was aligned with the group's strategy. LP&F had a rolling three-year strategic planning horizon, meaning that they planned three years out each year in their executive strategy round. Whereas this seemed a relatively short horizon, Andy explained that, "this is because we don't really much change what we do; only how we do it." Indeed, LP&F was not a diversified group. They did not change the type of service they provided. The main focus was on the type, mix, and duration of the shipping contracts (on the revenue side) and operating efficiencies (on the cost side). Capital expenditure decisions inevitably were an important part of the strategy discussions; "99.9 percent of LP&F's CapEx is at the group level – buying, selling and upgrading vessels. There is no CapEx at the trade [local office] level, and the 0.1 percent that is there is rolled up in their budgets," Andy added.

The group risk register, an excerpt of which is shown in Exhibit 4, contained a dozen key risks categorized into financial, strategic, organizational, and operational risks. For each risk, the table showed the likely cause of the risk; its anticipated effect; an assessment of its likelihood and impact;[1] the presence of proactive

[1] "Impact" was rated using 1 (very low) for a gain/loss up to $25k [250k] at business unit [group] level; 2 (low) for a gain/loss between $25-100k [250k–1m] at business unit [group] level; 3 (medium) for a gain/loss between $100-400k [1–4m] or a significant injury to a person at business unit [group] level; 4 (high) for a gain/loss between $400k and $1m [4–10m] or a single fatality or permanent disability, or significant impact on the operations, environment or reputation at business unit [group] level; and 5 (very high) for a gain/loss greater than $1m [$10m] or a potentially disastrous effect or accident (multiple fatalities) or an operational, environmental or reputational catastrophe at business unit [group] level. "Likelihood" was rated using 1 (very low) if the gain/loss was very unlikely to occur before 18 months' time; 2 (low) if the gain/loss was likely to occur in the long term (between 12 and 18 months); 3 (medium) if the gain/loss was likely to occur in the medium term (between 6 and 12 months); 4 (high) if the gain/loss was likely to occur in the short term (within the next 6 months); and 5 (very high) if the gain/loss was virtually certain to occur and could happen now. Using these scores for gains and losses separately allowed constructing a heat map for opportunities and dangers, respectively.

controls; any residual risk after such proactive controls were considered; and any further reactive mitigations that were deemed necessary. The register also listed and tracked any issues that needed attention and/or actions that were required.

Under financial, the risk register listed the risk shown in Exhibit 4, but also "earnings and cash flow volatility resulting from IR, FX, and Freight rate exposures," which was rated as a gross risk of 5 × 5 = 25 and as a residual risk of 2 × 5 = 10. Proactive controls for this risk consisted of hedging policies, use of a wide range of derivatives, formal counter-party limits and monthly treasury reviews. Reactive mitigations encompassed reconciliations of treasury systems with accounts, monitoring of contract closings, and formal audits and board reviews.

Just as one other example of another type, the register listed the operational risk of "not operating safely – LP&F vessels," rated as a gross risk of 3 × 5 = 15; a residual risk of 2 × 3 = 6; and covering proactive controls such as monitoring of vessel performance, stevedores and crew training, port vessel inspections, preventative maintenance, and vessel whistle-blowing hotlines. The effects of risk in this area included disrupted cargo operations, loss of customers, reputational damage, injury and death of crew, damage to cargo and increased insurance costs. One of the reactive mitigations was root cause analysis.

Overall, the gross risks on the register as at the end of 2013 were rated ranging from 12 to 25, with the residual risks ranging from 3 to 15, indicating that they believed that proactive controls were effective in alleviating the listed risks but not in eradicating them. However, a risk that demonstrated a sustained low residual risk through robust controls would eventually be moved off of the risk register. All the risks on the register were also visually presented on a standard risk heat map, with the "red hot" risks being those that were deemed highly likely with possibly severe impacts.

Updates and revisions to the risk register followed along in pace with the strategic planning cycle. However, Andy admitted that the risk register was actually quite stable as, indeed, if the selected risks were reliably "key" risks, and if the firm's business model did not change drastically, as it didn't, then one should not expect the group's risk register to change drastically in any given year. That said, Andy evinced that the risk register was up to date and closely scrutinized by the board and management alike. The risk register was part of the papers of every board meeting, in addition to it being discussed at least five times during the year with senior management in Risk Review meetings which Andy conducted.

Vertical embeddedness of risk was achieved bottom-up. The main planning tool at the local office level – that is, in the trade offices, as they called them at LP&F – was the budgeting process, which was accompanied with Quarterly Business Reviews (QBRs) and, importantly, "Must Achieve Plans" (MAPs), of which risk considerations were an integral part. Budgets for each trade office were drawn up each year in consultation with the Head Office to ensure synchronicity with the firm's overall strategic plan. Budget targets were fixed for the year, but progress against plan was scrutinized in great detail, again between the local trade office managers and corporate, on a quarterly basis in the QBRs.

Importantly, each trade office also had to draw up a set of key "Must Achieve Programs" (MAPs) at budget time. Each trade office (e.g. in Rio, Shanghai, Tampa, Vancouver) had between 3 and 6 MAPs. An example is shown in Exhibit 5. From gleaning the 12-point MAP template guidance in Exhibit 5, it is clear that MAPs were in a way surrogates for strategic planning at the local level (e.g. see guidance #1 and #2), and that, crucially, MAPs covered both opportunities and risks or "dangers" (#3 and #4). Further, risk identification (#6), risk mitigation (#7), and risk assessment featured prominently in estimates of the likelihood that a given MAP would be achieved (#8). Each MAP had an owner (#5), needed to detail procedures and processes to achieve it (#7), and required an estimate of its US$ impact (#9). Plans of action and their timing (#10) were regularly reviewed (as part of the QBRs) and updated (#11 and #12).

Reviews of budgets and MAPs, and the insights and action plans that arose from them during extensive discussions during QBRs, in turn, were fed back into the strategic planning exercise each year at corporate. Andy participated in some, but not all, QBRs and consolidated all local MAPs into a pivot table which provided him insights useful for monitoring and/or starting discussions at corporate to update and revise the group risk register. Andy updated his pivot table on the same quarterly cycle as the MAPs were reviewed in QBRs. In Andy's pivot table, each MAP was one record that contained a MAP's reference number, location, owner, description, opportunity, danger, estimate of achievement, US$ impact, risks, actions and status. Andy's pivot table listed 29 current MAP records in Q4 of 2013 worth US$488.55 in estimated impact, a non-trivial proportion of LP&F's gross revenues.

A sample bonus plan for a trade office general manager is shown in Exhibit 6. Thirty-five percent of this manager's annual bonus, which can be up to 58.5% or seven months' worth of salary, was based on individual performance (the other 65% of the bonus was based on company performance). Andy reckoned that the individual performance component of the bonus was nearly exclusively based on an evaluation of a manager's performance and initiative in light of his or her MAPs, as indeed the rating criteria shown in Exhibit 6 suggested.

At his level, as CRO, Andy analyzed risks as follows. If a new risk was identified, the first step was to determine whether it was ongoing. The purpose of this was to decide whether a process or procedure needed to be put in place to manage the risk. Piracy risk was an example of this. This was a danger for which LP&F previously had no procedure to properly manage it. Therefore, for a period of time, until they had an operational and robust procedure in place, piracy risk was included on the company's risk register. After an anti-piracy procedure had been put in place and was deemed effective (consisting of crew training; fitting vessels with fences; extra watchmen and armed guards on board; higher sailing speed; vessel convoy formations; coordinated communication with onshore security forces; insurance, and so on), this danger was taken off the company risk register as the risk was being managed by the business as part of their daily operations. However, if any level of residual risk was deemed to increase, it could be moved back onto the company's risk register.

Andy did the same whenever LP&F did "something new." For example, in one Southeast Asia location, LP&F converted a vessel into a floating warehouse which was used as a platform to load cargo from land and from there onto ocean-going vessels. For any such new activity, Andy would carry out a full risk assessment and issue procedures and action plans to be monitored until the activity became stable and part of routine operations. This often involved taking outside advice given the complexity and risks of many of these activities, including, but not only, health and safety issues. New customers, new routes, new cargos, and so on, also always underwent detailed risk assessments.

LP&F did not have separate Key Risk Indicators (KRIs); instead, they had several Key Performance Indicators (KPIs) which they used as "inverted" KRIs. The key measures for a shipping company included, essentially, gross profit per day per vessel (the so-called "voyage result") and various operational cost and productivity measures per vessel and/or by cargo type (e.g. metric tons per day). At firm level, the weighted average shipping contract coverage (in years) also was considered a key measure. Meeting delivery dates for customers and accidents, near-misses and safety were considered key nonfinancial information. Key accounting controls comprised debtor days, creditor days, number of credit notes issued, and, inevitably, any changes in voyage results. It was decided that given that these were the key day-to-day performances that had to be managed, then these same numbers could be used as KRIs. Andy opined that "management was averse to risk management being seen in the business as merely another 'IT project' or just another 'reporting requirement.'"

Encounters with risk

From Andy's experience, the biggest causes of bad outcomes were the following (whether related to dangers or failure to manage opportunities):

a. Assumptions made were invalid;
b. Risks were too readily discounted;
c. Outcomes were not seen as symptomatic of underlying risks; and/or,
d. Execution risk.

Incorrect assumptions

Andy recalled several instances where they got the assumptions wrong, such as when they were falsely thinking that the markets they competed in wouldn't change, which he also dubbed the *risk of complacency*. An instance of this occurred when LP&F tendered for a major contract with an existing customer. The customer nudged LP&F to try and come up with another way to provide the service they were offering. However, when they tendered, they offered the same type of service, because:

> We did not want to change, making the incorrect assumption that no existing player had the size to take this contract from us despite being aware that we were one of three companies tendering, and that we did not know who the third company was. We were wrong. Another company snatched the contract from us, and worse, entered our market as a viable competitor on other contracts as well.

Andy also recalled the following example:

> At the top of the shipping boom we considered hedging a significant proportion of our income

stream for the next 1 to 2 years. Despite distressing signs (e.g. new vessels being built and problems in the financial markets), we decided, however, that it was too risky, or rather "too prudent" I reckon, to lock in lower, but still excellent, returns. We were wrong. The shipping markets collapsed.

That said, Andy felt that LP&F had significantly different challenges regarding risk assessment than, say, the banking and actuarial world had, where there were a lot of data to use. In shipping, in contrast, the problem was that the data populations were relatively small. As a result, determining the probability of an event was very subjective. The impact, if an event occurred, was much easier to determine. This made objective risk assessment a challenge. Andy lamented that,

Risk discussions often are a contest of the strongest personalities, although perhaps one factor that often has a big sway is when a risk has already inflicted a competitor. Then the risk becomes real – we exhale a sigh of relief and quickly consider our own mitigations.

Risks being discounted

An example of this was a discussion about an environmental issue with eucalyptus trees in South America. These types of trees were used to make pulp, which LP&F transported. As a matter of fact, LP&F was one of the largest transporters of pulp from South America (which was the lowest cost producer in the world because the trees grew quicker there than anywhere else in the world due to climatic factors). This type of cargo used about 30–50% of LP&F's vessel fleet capacity. The risk raised was about what would happen if eucalyptus trees suffered from disease and died. If that were to occur, all of LP&F's pulp shipping contracts would be null and void (due to the *force majeure* clause in the contract). Andy recounted:

At first, this risk was dismissed as fanciful, but it was pointed out that a similar risk had happened in the Northern hemisphere with pine trees. Then it was challenged as being the customers' problem until the issue of the *force majeure* clause came up. Again the business executives tried to dismiss it, stating that the customers must have plans to deal with this, and that we could rely on these plans (even though we didn't know anything about these plans). Eventually the business accepted that it was a risk and that it could bankrupt the company, and so this risk needed mitigation. In the end, we took out additional insurance to cover this type of eventuality, which would reduce the financial impact.

At LP&F, they had similar risk discussions about political risks in the Middle East, as the company had a number of shipping contracts where specialized vessels that cannot be used for another purpose had to sail through the Strait of Hormuz. If the strait were closed, then the shipping contracts would be null and void due to *force majeure*, and vessels could not be used in other activities to generate income. As above, the main mitigation was insurance, although in this case LP&F was able to introduce other mitigations as well, such as emergency stocks (of the cargo) and use of other discharge ports.

Incidents (and accidents) not seen as symptomatic of underlying risks

Andy recalled that senior management often tended to see risks as arising from employees lower down in the organization who were not doing what they should be doing; not following the procedures. Andy made two observations. First, while in the shipping business human errors and accidents on a vessel or in ports occurred with nontrivial frequency, they *did not usually* tend to create significant strategic risks. That said, such events *could* have a major impact. Second, and most importantly, the root cause of such events had to be identified, rather than just putting out fires when such events occurred. Someone needed to try and "see a trend" if there was one across a series of seemingly isolated incidents or accidents.

Sure, someone *made an error*, but such errors are more likely to occur when a captain is promoted "over his head" or, as may be the case in some locations more than in others, when equipment and contract labor conditions are poor and threaten safety cargo work.

Execution risk

This risk is related to the inability to implement effective mitigations to risks that had been identified. This problem arose, particularly, due to a major reorganization of the group which resulted in limited management time being available to focus on events that had not yet happened, but if they would, whose impact could be significant. Andy proffered that for an organization to effectively manage risk (uncertainties that are important), the present must be "stable" enough otherwise the company will just be focusing on fire fighting and not plan enough for the future. Andy called this the *risk of inattention*. But, of course, he added that "when the present is too stable, you run into the *risk of complacency*."

The future

To date, all the risk reporting and business risk discussions at LP&F took place through the business planning and quarterly business review processes. This was intentional to reinforce the point that managing risk was part of every manager's "day job" and not a separate activity done as and when time was available or when specifically requested by corporate. Andy also thought that it was important to embed risk management into the day-to-day business by not using KRIs, but instead using KPIs as their equivalent. However, this raised the issue regarding what the role of the CRO/Risk Manager should be. Andy's view was that,

> CROs/risk managers must develop into non-executive management whose role is to challenge the executive team about the bases on which they are making decisions, and to support a robust strategic risk identification process. I am not an expert in many, if even any, of the decision areas that our business managers face, but I can offer an independent risk perspective. I don't know anything about eucalyptus trees, but I had a sense that the source of risk was the same as one that had actually occurred in another hemisphere with another kind of tree. And when we spot important risks, I can source in external advice if we don't have any internal reference point or experience, and above all, I can try to make sure that we have quality discussions about the risks instead of, or at least in addition to, just putting numbers on risks and then carry on as usual. And having been a finance person for most of my early career has given me a broad overview of the business.

Asked if indeed finance is the best training ground for a CRO, Andy paused:

> Interesting question! The two key things for a CRO are to be involved early enough, yet not getting sucked into the executive. An operations person could make for a good CRO ... certainly to have a handle on the business, but maybe at the risk of lack of independence. But not a commercial person, I don't think ... typically not familiar enough with the guts and whole of the business. A CRO must be able to engage with everyone in all key areas.

Andy had also recently started to submit certain MAPs "Existing Controls in Place" (#7 in Exhibit 5) to internal audit. If an internal audit finds that the procedures, processes, contracts, and/or measures that are currently in place are, say, only effective 50% of the time, then that is a more objective assessment than some of the estimates that may have been initially made in earlier drafts of the MAP. But not only that, Andy hoped that such audits would help him identify robust and transferable practice, in addition to it becoming merely just another "traffic light" and/or "blame shifting" system, although it did give a good sense of how well controls were being implemented.

Andy also was adamant that risk processes have to work with the business, and opined that presumably "integrated" ERM systems that can be sourced off the shelf were just too generic – "they put risk before business," he lamented.

Andy felt, however, that he was behind the curve on "big data" and, although he was wary of uncritical quantification, he imagined that big data could be brought to bear to unearth patterns of risk, or indeed, opportunities for that matter, too. One problem that came to mind was port congestion, where valuable vessel capacity is wasted just waiting, especially when LP&F is not paid to wait. "But if we know the location of every vessel headed for a given port, and we have data on wind speeds, navigation routes, weather patterns, stevedore schedules, and what not, couldn't we predict and accordingly adjust better," he wondered? "Maybe we'd learn something about 'black swan' risks, too, such as impacts of global warming on our business and port operations."

Finally, as was fashionable since the crisis, Andy commented that LP&F was looking into being more specific about their risk appetite. But then he quickly added that he rated behavioral biases related to both assumptions and symptoms, if not about the actual recognition of some risks, as the greatest challenge to overcome. "A lot of it is very subjective," he exclaimed.

Exhibit 1 LP&F Cargo Ltd., selected financials (in GBP 000s)

	Years ended December 31,				
	2009	2010	2011	2012	2013
INCOME STATEMENT DATA (selected):					
Total revenues	£ 1,455,859	£ 1,071,456	£ 1,200,211	£ 1,299,524	£ 1,255,275
Voyage related expenses	(725,225)	(509,393)	(581,172)	(613,006)	(717,963)
Vessel operating expenses	(229,983)	(204,648)	(201,205)	(201,317)	(198,518)
Time charter rental expenses	(187,390)	(131,790)	(157,692)	(121,962)	(137,032)
Depreciation and amortization	(84,530)	(79,501)	(75,603)	(86,401)	(65,280)
Gain on disposal of assets	39,590	3,180	4,320	12,970	12,840
Selling, general and administrative expenses	(100,580)	(73,150)	(75,600)	(86,401)	(80,250)
Income from operations	167,740	76,154	113,259	203,407	69,072
Income from affiliates	37,451	10,602	25,920	5,400	7,383
Interest expense, net	(26,751)	(16,961)	(27,253)	(29,160)	(37,450)
Other income (expense)	(20,331)	49,822	(8,104)	(4,321)	(3,794)
Provision for income taxes	15,178	(7,355)	3,218	(6,670)	(3,000)
Net income	173,287	112,262	107,041	168,656	32,211
BALANCE SHEET DATA (at period end, selected):					
Cash and cash equivalents	£ 269,264	£ 367,903	£ 168,118	£ 161,586	£ 148,497
Property, plant and equipment, net	792,443	884,071	972,258	899,426	965,959
Total assets	1,365,942	1,519,032	1,470,355	1,383,937	1,472,014
Total debt	287,831	683,948	631,804	477,361	642,011
Shareholders' equity	764,421	610,713	695,680	622,498	614,536
CASH FLOW DATA (selected):					
Capital expenditures	£ 117,700	£ 10,165	£ 30,240	£ 88,457	£ 46,440
EBITDA	255,788	152,475	184,543	276,839	121,512
EBITDA margin	17.6%	14.2%	15.4%	21.3%	9.7%

Exhibit 2 LP&F Cargo Ltd., chief risk officer job description

Reporting to:	Holding Company Board (with an administrative dotted line to the CEO)
Key Working Relationships:	Executive Management Operational Management Finance Director
Main Purpose of Job:	To develop and lead the Risk Management and Assurance function of LP&F with the aim of: • Enabling the efficient and effective governance and management of significant risks – Enterprise Risk Management (ERM); • Providing assurance that the key risks of the group are being appropriately identified, assessed, managed and monitored – that Management have appropriate plans in place to reduce the level of residual risks to an agreed level within an acceptable timescale; • Providing assurance that the key 'building blocks' of ERM and internal controls are in place and operating effectively in all key business processes; • Consolidating/coordinating the efforts of all providers of assurance on the adequacy of the controls framework in LP&F so that an overall picture can be provided to Management and the Audit Committee; and, • Supporting Management in discharging its Corporate Governance responsibilities with regards to the identification and management of risk.

Key Tasks:	• To develop and maintain a risk management and assurance plan which effectively discharges the scope of risk management and assurance activities as set out in the Audit Committee remit. The plan should be submitted annually to the Audit Committee for approval.
	• To maintain effective liaison with Management to ensure that:
	  • Effective processes are in place to identify and manage all key risks of the business;
	  • Any necessary amendments to risk management and assurance plans are made resulting from changes in the risk profile of the business;
	  • The results of review work are understood and appropriately actioned by Management; and,
	  • Best risk management and internal control practices are shared within the group.
	• To have oversight responsibility for risk governance and assurance.
	• To identify staff with appropriate skills to effectively complete the risk management and audit plan. (NB: this may also involve coaching non-audit staff to allow them to effectively participate in delivering the overall audit plan.)
	• To provide Executive Management and the Audit Committee with regular reporting summarizing risk management and assurance reviews and findings; including progress in implementing agreed recommendations as well as an overall assessment of the control environment and how this is changing within the group.
	• To liaise closely with the group's external Auditors and other providers of assurance and to coordinate effort and ensure that all key risks are appropriately assessed.

Accountability:	The performance of the CRO will be formally assessed on an annual basis by the Board based on feedback gathered from Management and the interaction with board members.

Exhibit 2 (*Continued*)

The Person:	• Graduate Qualified Accountant. • MBA from a respected business school. • Age 40+. • Minimum 10 years post qualification experience gained in a management position in either: • LP&F; • a major international company; • a major audit firm; with: • Proven communication skills both orally and in writing; • Initiative and a proactive approach to problem solving; • Ability to exercise commercial judgment when assessing risks against the need for control; • Credibility at Management and Board level; and, • Experience of the Shipping Industry would be useful although this is not considered essential.

Exhibit 3 LP&F Cargo Ltd., "back-of-an-envelope" organization chart

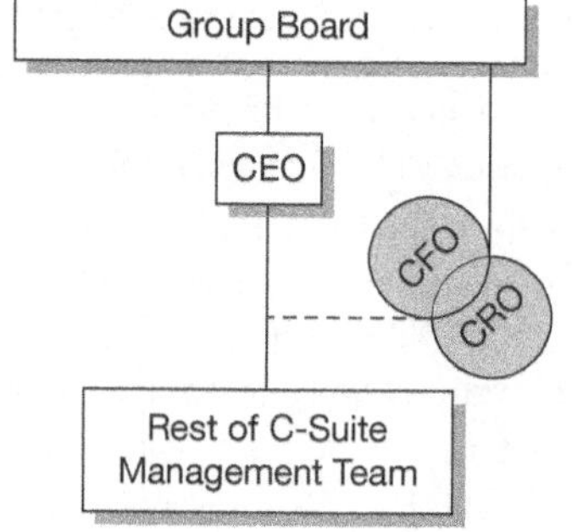

Exhibit 4 LP&F Cargo Ltd., excerpt from LP&F's group risk register

Risk	Non-compliance with Antitrust Competition (ATC), Antibribery & Corruption (ABC), Sanctions, Tax and Legal (Permits and Licences) Legislation											
Risk Area	Finance											
Causes	Lack of procedures	Lack of training	Complex business	Non-experts making decisions	Inexpe-rienced personnel	High personnel turnover	Lack of clear communica-tion on 100% compliance					
Resulting in	Prosecution, fines, imprisonment	Reputational damage	Loss of customers	Unable to access/ operate in certain markets	Unable to execute business strategy	Harder to access finance	Ejected from MACN	Ejected from SSI	High legal fees			
Gross Risk	Likelihood = 3		Impact = 5		Total = 15							
Proactive Controls	Annual ABC training	ABC policy	Tone from the top	Board reporting papers/ discussions	Personnel training	Tax officer	External audits	ABC audits	Formal personnel reference checks	Formal personnel appraisals	Professional qualified teams	Pay good salaries
Residual Risk	Likelihood = 1		Impact = 5		Total = 5							
Reactive Mitigations	ABC audits	Replace personnel	Disciplinary action	External audits	Updated message	Updated policy	Updated training	Insurance				
Issues/ Actions Required	ATC policy requires update	ATC training update and module in voyager	Take out insurance to cover costs of ABC/ATC investigation?	Tax officer to support MPK?								

Exhibit 5 LP&F Cargo Ltd., "Must Achieve Program" template

1. **Must Achieve Program.** This is the goal that is imperative for LP&F to achieve in the next twelve months. The MAP can be realizing an opportunity or preventing a danger from arising; however, it is likely to be something that contributes to the achievement of LP&F's strategy.
2. **Why is the MAP Critical?** This describes why the objective is a MAP, as opposed to a day-to-day action; eg, how the MAP contributes to the attainment of LP&F's strategy. However, not all MAPs will necessarily be of strategic significance. For example, the MAP could be to comply with safety/regulatory requirements.
3. **Opportunity.** This is where the MAP arises from pursuing and realizing an opportunity.
4. **Danger.** This is the type of MAP where LP&F has benefited from preventing (a) bad event(s) from arising.
5. **Owner.** This is the LP&F person who is directly responsible for achieving the MAP.
6. **Risks and Type.** The risks are events that could prevent the MAP from being achieved or assist in its achievement. Trying to articulate the type of risk will help us in ensuring that they are actively managed. The management of these risks will primarily be achieved by determining what actions must be completed (see #10 below).
7. **Existing Controls in Place.** These are the procedures, processes, contracts and/or measures that are currently in place, or will be used as a matter of course, to ensure that the MAP is achieved.
8. **Current Assessment of the MAP.** This is an evaluation of how confident we are of achieving the MAP given the risks identified and the existing controls in place (see #6 and #7 above). The level of confidence is expressed is percentage terms – eg, a confidence level of 90% means that we are extremely confident that the MAP will be achieved, whilst a confidence level of 10% indicates that we had little or no confidence. A confidence level of 50% means that we are highly uncertain that the MAP will be achieved.
9. **Impact of Achieving the MAP.** This is an estimate the US$ impact of achieving the MAP. The main reason of estimating the US$ impact is to ensure that we are correctly utilizing our finite resources. However, it should be noted that not all MAPs will necessarily have a US$ impact. For example, a MAP that required us to widen our customer base may not increase our net income, but instead change our risk profile. Likewise, a MAP relating to regulatory compliance may not have a US$ impact.
10. **Action Plan/Dates.** These are the additional actions that have been identified as being necessary to be completed for us to achieve the MAP.
11. **Status of Actions.** This is the status of the actions (see #10 above) at the time of the quarterly update assessment of the MAP.
12. **Quarterly Update of MAP status.** This is a subsequent quarterly assessment of the likelihood of achieving the MAP and the current estimate of the US$ impact of doing so, after taking into account the actions that have been achieved to date.

Exhibit 5 *(Continued)*

1. Must Achieve Program (MAP): 2014	**Improve ELA** [Europe–Latin America] **trade by finding ways to expedite voyages and increase carrying capacity**	
2. Why is MAP Critical?	**With outbound trade results under increasing pressure, results need to improve to support ELA round-voyage result**	
3. Opportunity: Yes	4. Danger: Yes	5. Owner: PBK

6. **Risk(s) and Type:**
   - Expected increasing competition on spot cargoes (oversupply of tonnage)
   - Port congestion (especially for pulp, which forms the majority of available cargoes)
   - Brazilian economy (in case growth drops)
   - Shifting trade patterns, eg, Europe losing out to Asia & US as cargo supplier
   - Scheduling limitations/tightness of program preventing time for inbound cargo
   - Accommodating larger vessel types, eg, Flex IIs need cargo on board to fit under existing loading spouts in Spain

7. **Existing controls/measures in place to help achieve the MAP**
   - Relationship with existing COA [Contract of Affreightment] partners and extension of COAs achieved during 2012 (two core customers extended through April 2015)
   - Identified areas of possible improvement:
     a) round voyage coordination with LP&F Rio + Program
     b) cargo clearance issues in Brazil (causing delays for malt cargoes)
     c) increased storage capacity in Santander (investigating Rubb Shed cost)
     d) potential port switch from Recife to Portocel (increasing draft/intake)
   - A healthy level of spot market activity will bring us closer to market opportunities (3rd ship a month critical for this)

8. **Current Assessment of MAP**: Likelihood of achieving the MAP = 100%
   Improvements will certainly be made, but likelihood of achieving some goals are very strong (eg, RV coordination) whilst others less so (eg, switch to Portocel)

9. **Impact of Achieving MAP**: Up to about US$2m
   Breakdown as follows:
   a) One third of 32 voy saving 1 day ballast, 11 voy × 1 day × ($15,000 + FO) = $350,000
   b) 10 days saved × $15,000/day = $150,000
   c) 6 calls × 12,000 mt / 5,000 vs 7,500 mt/d = 5 days × ($15,000 + wharfage) = $125,000
   d) 6 calls × 10,000 mt additional cargo × $25/mt = $1,500,000

10. Action Plan/Dates required to achieve MAP		11. Status of Actions
Q1 Make detailed plan Q2-4 Implement plan		
12. Quarterly update of MAP	**Likelihood of achieving MAP**	**Impact of achieving MAP**
Q1 2014	%	US$
Q2 2014	%	US$
Q3 2014	%	US$
Q4 2014	%	US$

Exhibit 6 LP&F Cargo Ltd., template senior business management bonus plan

MEMO

To: Andres Almodovar
From: Benjamin Stevensen
Chairman, LP&F Cargo Ltd

Date: 28 November 2013

LP&F BONUS PLAN 2014

This memo is to introduce and confirm your participation in the LP&F 2014 bonus plan.

The purpose of the LP&F bonus plan is to recognize **above-target** performance.

The plan has two components:

i. **Company Performance**
ii. **Individual Performance**

The relative weight of these components for you is as follows:

Award criterion	Category III
Company Performance	65%
Individual Performance	35%

The Plan

The plan structure, eligibility and award criteria will be subject to annual review and revision.

The plan may be subject to revision in the event of changes in tax jurisdiction, dividend policy, capital structure, accounting principles, mergers/major acquisitions, major changes in the ownership and/or financing of the fleet.

Whilst LP&F has established a bonus plan for 2014, it is subject to annual review and the opportunity to participate in this type of plan should not be considered as guaranteed in future years.

Eligibility

Participating employees will qualify to receive a variable bonus payment based on their 2014 total gross salary under the following criteria:

- Provided they have completed their probationary period
- Provided they are in active employment during the bonus year
- Provided they have not resigned as of December 31, 2014
- Provided they are employed by LP&F or a Company in the LP&F Group as of December 31, 2014 (Note that in redundancy cases eligibility criteria will be separately confirmed)
- Provided their performance review has been completed and submitted for review

Bonus Calculations

The value of the award will be calculated on a pro-rata basis in the following circumstances:

- When an employee is not in active employment (ie, due to long-term sickness absence or maternity leave)
- When an employee has less than 12 months employment with the Company during the bonus year
- When the employee moves into a different Category during the bonus year
- When an employee receives a salary adjustment during the bonus year
- When an employee is made redundant with an effective termination date prior to December 31, 2014

Exhibit 6 *(Continued)*

Company Performance Component

There are five objectives with targets which form the Company performance component:

Objective	Weighting
1. To achieve a net income target	30%
2. To reduce SG&A levels vs 2013 budget	25%
3. Generate new business revenue	20%
4. To develop business niches to deliver a minimum Return on Investment (ROE) of 12%	15%
5. To achieve a reduction in the costs of OpEx	10%

Payout levels for the Company performance component will be determined after Company performance for the fiscal year is known and following approval of FY2014 audited accounts.

Further information about these objectives is contained in Appendix I.

Hurdle

The Company component of the plan is designed to trigger 2014 payments only when a net result of £37.5 million is achieved.

Individual Performance Component

The assessment of individual performance will be based on the fulfillment of pre-agreed individual objectives that form part of your documented annual performance plan. These objectives must be stretch objectives which go beyond the day-to-day requirements of your role, and they must have defined targets and measures that can be used to evaluate performance. An approved copy of your performance plan should be held on MyLP&F (the HR Information System) for you to qualify for this part of the bonus program.

Your performance will be reviewed and evaluated with your immediate manager as part of the annual performance appraisal process and signed off by the next level manager. The table below shows the award level for the individual performance element of the bonus plan based on the achievement of objectives that exceed day-to-day requirements of your role.

Overall Evaluation	Definition/Explanation	Pct. of Bonus Paid
Exceptional Performance	Has exceeded all expectations, has made a significant noteworthy contribution to the Department/Company. Usually this contribution was not planned and goes beyond the normal scope of the individual's role.	96–100%
Exceeded all Objectives	All objectives have been exceeded. The employee has contributed significantly over and above the requirements of the role; results exceed the measures/targets that were agreed.	90–95%
Priority Objectives Exceeded	All the important heavily weighted objectives have been exceeded and other objectives have been met. Performance is above the requirements of the role, shows initiative, taken on additional responsibility and little or no supervision is required.	80–89%
Some priority objectives exceeded	Some, but not all, of the highly weighted objectives have been exceeded, requires very little supervision, has taken on increased responsibility.	70–79%
All objectives achieved, takes initiative	All objectives and targets have been achieved with minimum supervision; results are of a high standard, takes responsibility, uses initiative, acts responsibly.	60–69%
Objectives achieved, meets requirements	Objectives have been achieved; performance is good and meets expectations and requirements of the role.	50–59%
Less than 50% of objectives achieved	Some, but not all, requirements for the role have been met; requires guidance/assistance on an ongoing basis. New hire/newly appointed to the role.	zero
No objectives achieved	Performance below requirements, employee requires constant guidance/assistance and work may need to be checked on a regular basis to ensure accuracy or compliance. Not showing initiative.	zero

(continued)

Exhibit 6 *(Continued)*

Targeted Size and Limitations of Total Bonus Payments

The total combined bonus award (the sum of the two components) will be limited as a maximum percentage of salary, as below.

Award Maximum	Category III
Maximum percent of salary	58.50%
Equivalent months' salary	7
Company component – maximum award as percent of salary	37.50%
Individual component – maximum award as percent of salary	21.00%

This case was prepared by Professor Wim A Van der Stede.

CHAPTER 15
Management Control-Related Ethical Issues

Managers involved in designing and using management control systems (MCSs) should have a basic understanding of ethics. Ethics is the field of study that is used to prescribe morally acceptable behavior. It provides methods to distinguish between "right" and "wrong" and to systematically determine the rules that provide guidance as to how individuals and groups of individuals should behave. Its systematic nature goes beyond what even thoughtful people do in making sense of their own and others' moral experiences.

Ethics is important to understand for managers involved with MCSs. Ethical principles can provide a useful guide for defining how employees should behave. Further, employees' ethics are an important component of personnel and cultural controls (which we discussed in Chapter 3). If good ethics can be encouraged in an organization, they can substitute for, or augment, actions controls (Chapter 3) or results controls (Chapter 2). In the aggregate, the ethical principles that employees follow help define the organization's core values and, hence, its corporate culture and work climate.

Ethics is a difficult subject for many managers to understand. Many managers' basic discipline training is in economics or business.[1] Two common assumptions in economics are that rational people should act to maximize their own self-interest and that the primary purpose of employees in for-profit organizations is to maximize shareholder value.[2] Ethics, however, provides alternative assumptions about how people should, and do, behave. It assumes that ethical individuals must consider the impact of their actions on other *stakeholders* – those affected by their actions – including employees, customers, suppliers, local communities, and other users of shared resources, such as people and animals, that might be affected by corporate use of land, water, and air.

Ethical behavior and value-maximizing behavior are not equivalent. While the commonly cited aphorism "good ethics is good business" is usually true, it is not always true. Good ethics do not always "pay off" for the individuals or organizations involved, and definitely not always in the short term. Ethical individuals sometimes must take actions that are not in their own self-interest, and/or not in their organization's owners' best interest, due to some legitimate interests of other stakeholders. Employees must be accountable to these non-ownership stakeholders as well, and no group, not even owners, automatically has priority over the other stakeholders. Indeed, it is the struggles between being selfish and doing "what is right" that provides the most interesting and important ethical issues that must be considered.

It would be comforting to think that people will be rewarded, at least in the long term, for doing the right things. But that does not always happen. Many employees who do what is right sometimes earn lower bonuses, are passed over for promotions, or are even fired. Miscarriages of justice like these have led to the passing of laws (such as the whistle-blower protection provisions in the Sarbanes-Oxley Act) to protect the rights of employees who were doing the right things. Conversely, employees who act unethically often benefit from their unethical actions. Sometimes they are not caught, and sometimes their bosses are complicit in the unethical practices, look the other way, pressure them, or even reward them for doing the wrong things.[3] The following quote illustrates some form of this:

> **Whenever you see a company where the CEO takes an active, ongoing interest in how transactions are accounted for, that's a huge red flag [for aggressive accounting]. Chief executives need to run the business, they don't need to run the accounting.[4]**

The potential for personal sacrifice while acting ethically is reflected in many codes of professional conduct. The preamble of the Code of Professional Conduct of the American Institute of Certified Public Accountants (AICPA) states, "The Principles call for an unswerving commitment to honorable behavior, even at the sacrifice of personal advantage."[5] But when are the ethical principles so important that they dominate natural self-interest concerns? This is a core ethical question.

This chapter provides an introduction to the complex subject of ethics. It discusses how to conduct good ethical analyses and why they are important, the reasons why people behave unethically, and where MCS-related ethical issues are commonly found. The chapter concludes with some suggestions for encouraging ethical behavior in organizations.

Good ethical analyses and their importance

Unethical behaviors are costly to individuals, organizations, markets, and societies. They create needs for extra laws and standards from governments and regulatory agencies, and extra rules, reviews, or supervision within organizations. These extra enforcement mechanisms are incomplete, imperfect, and expensive, and have the typical drawbacks of rigid action controls. Good ethics is the glue that holds organizations and societies together. In the words of Christine Lagarde, managing director at the International Monetary Fund (IMF):

> **Regulation alone cannot solve the problem. Whether something is right or wrong cannot be simply reduced to whether or not it is permissible under the law. What is needed is a culture that induces bankers to do the right thing, even if nobody is watching.[6]**

Lapses in ethics are often precursors of more serious problems, such as fraud. Mark Carney, governor of the Bank of England, refers to this more generally as "ethical drift":

> **The traders who rigged LIBOR worked in a clubby, laddish atmosphere, a world removed from the woolly commitments to good behavior set out in banks' mission statements.[7]**

An example of ethical drift is "aggressive" financial reporting, which many interpret as less than ethical but maybe not quite illegal, and which often appears to be one step on a "slippery slope" that eventually culminates into costly, fraudulent activities. As Warren Buffett, chairman of Berkshire Hathaway, put it:

> **Once a company moves earnings from one period to another, operating shortfalls that occur thereafter require it to engage in further accounting maneuvers that must be even more "heroic." These can turn fudging into fraud.[8]**

Indeed, many of the worst corporate failures had aggressive accounting practices in common in the years leading up to their eventual ruin.[9] And, even if aggressive accounting practices do not lead to ruin, they can be costly.[10] We have given numerous examples throughout this text, such as the opening examples in Chapter 1, which prove this point.[11] To add another example, Tesco, the United Kingdom's biggest supermarket chain, was said to be "consistently aggressive – Tesco had a more aggressive policy than its peers with regard to revenue recognition, depreciation and property-profit allocation."[12] In late 2014, Tesco faced the worst crisis in its 95-year history when it announced it had overstated its expected profits by £250 million, "prompting the suspension of four senior executives and wiping more than £2 billion off the value of the supermarket behemoth, bringing its share price to an 11-year low as regulators with the power to impose unlimited fines hovered."[13]

Just as they need good skills in their technical disciplines in order to make good business judgments, managers need good ethical reasoning skills to make good ethical judgments. Senior managers themselves should know how to behave so that they can serve as *moral exemplars*, or role models, within their organizations. This is the foundation of what is commonly referred to as *tone at the top*, which we discussed in Chapter 3.

Top management should also design their MCSs to promote moral points of view and ethical behaviors. A number of highly specific controls, including some policies and procedures and elements of measurement and reward systems, stem from ethical analyses. But these controls need to be supplemented with some other controls that help ensure ethical behaviors in areas where totally precise organizational prescriptions are impossible, including training sessions, sets of values, codes of conduct, and credos that help employees identify, appreciate, and assess ethical issues.[14]

Second, ethical issues often are addressed with simplistic rules, such as "always tell the truth," "do no harm," or "do unto others as you would have them do unto you." Such simple, conscience-based rules work only when the values of the person invoking the rule are shared by the others who are or might be affected. As a consequence, they rarely provide guidance for ethical behaviors in specific (management control) situations because people's values often vary widely.

Ethical models

The first challenge in adapting ethical thinking to managerial settings is in recognizing the existence of the ethical issues that do or might exist. The ethics literature includes numerous normative models of behavior. Almost all of these models recognize that, in a social context, ethics is about how actions affect the interests of other people. Every ethical issue involves multiple parties, some of whom benefit while others are harmed, slighted, or put at risk by a particular action. The characterizations of harm, slight, or risk are made in terms of one or more ethical principles, rules, or values that are embedded in the various normative models of behavior. The following sections describe briefly four commonly cited ethical models – utilitarianism, rights and duties, justice/fairness, and virtues.[15] Each model has merits, but none is perfect; each has its own limitations.

Utilitarianism

Using the *utilitarianism* (or *consequentialism*) model, the rightness of actions is judged on the basis of their consequences.[16] Adopted by many businesses because of its tradition in economics, utilitarian-type thinking has been embedded in many public policy decision procedures, such as welfare economics and cost-benefit analyses. In this model, an action is morally right if it maximizes the total of good in the world; that is, if it produces at least as much *net good* (benefits less costs and harms) as any other action that could have been considered. Sometimes this objective is phrased as *the greatest good for the greatest number of people*. Utilitarianism does not mean that the right action is the one that produces the most good for the person performing the act, but rather the one that produces the most good for all parties affected by the action.

Utilitarian models have some obvious limitations, however. Quantifying *net good* is difficult because the benefits of some actions or decisions, such as job satisfaction, freedom from stress, or a risky possibility of additional profits at some time in the future, are difficult to measure, aggregate, and compare across individuals. Further, using utilitarian-type reasoning makes it easy to sacrifice the welfare of a few individuals for the benefit of others. For example, in a famous case from the 1970s, Ford Motor Company's management decided not to do a safety retrofit of the company's Pinto subcompact car to prevent the gas tank from rupturing in rear-end collisions. They used the logic that the expensive retrofit of 11 million Pintos would save only a maximum of 180 deaths, so it would not be cost effective from a societal point of view. Nonetheless, some people did die in horrible, fiery accidents.[17]

Rights and duties

The rights and duties model maintains that every individual has certain moral entitlements by virtue of their being human. Commonly cited basic rights in most modern societies include the rights to dignity, respect, and freedom. Some societies also accept that people should have welfare rights, such as the right to be educated and to have access to healthcare and good housing. Regardless of what is on the list, every right that an individual has creates a duty for someone else to provide, or at least not to interfere. So if an individual is said to have a right to privacy, then others have a duty not to interfere with that person's privacy. If top management has a right to be given informative performance reports, then the managers or employees reporting to them have the duty to provide those reports. In other words, rights and duties need to be *mutually* observed by those participating in the group to which those rights and duties apply.

The rights and duties model has some significant limitations. It is sometimes difficult to get agreement as to what rights different individuals or groups of individuals should have. Rights can proliferate. They can also conflict. Do smokers have the right to smoke, or do others have the right to be free of second-hand smoke? Does management have a right to receive totally informative performance reports, or should those reporting to them have the right to retain some of their private information to themselves in order to, for example, protect themselves from some risk, such as a potential risk of dismissal?

Justice/fairness

The justice or fairness model maintains that people should be treated the same except when they are different in relevant ways. Most societies conclude that *processes*, not necessarily outcomes, should be fair. Most people are not concerned when an already wealthy person wins a lottery if the process was fair. Having a fair process, such as in evaluating employee performance, depends on such things as impartiality and consistency. This may explain why alleged pay inequality inside organizations is, unlike the lottery example, not always accepted as fair. This view is illustrated by opinions such as "trust in business will be damaged by the perception that an executive 'elite' is reaping all the rewards from economic growth," and "all employees should share in a company's success and gaps between those at the top and low and middle earners cannot just get wider and wider," suggesting that the pay-setting and/or performance evaluation and incentive systems and processes are improper.[18]

Treating people the same except when they are different in relevant ways needs proper calibration. People differ in many ways. Thus, determining which of these differences should be considered relevant is a core issue that must be addressed in applying the justice/fairness model. Employees may not be concerned when their compensation packages differ when it arises from differences in the nature of the job. It is seen as fair for people with jobs that are more difficult, more stressful, or riskier to be paid commensurately. But some may not deem it fair for people who have greater needs, such as a single parent, to be paid more than others performing like jobs by virtue of being a single parent. They feel such hardship needs should be taken care of elsewhere, such as through government support programs.

Another limitation of the justice/fairness model is that it is easy to ignore effects on both aggregate social welfare and specific individuals. Perceived justice for one group may harm another group. For example, when pharmaceutical companies are ordered to pay large damages to plaintiffs who allegedly suffered ills even in cases where there is little direct evidence of the drugs causing those ills, could one submit that justice has been done for the plaintiffs but not for the companies?

Virtues

A final commonly used model of moral behavior is rooted in *virtues*. Prominent examples of virtues are integrity, loyalty, and courage. Individuals with *integrity* have the intent to do what is ethically right without regard to self-interest. Integrity has many components, including honesty, fairness, and conscientiousness. *Loyalty* is faithfulness to one's allegiances. People have many loyalties, including to other persons, organizations, religions, professions, and even causes. When loyalties conflict, their relative strength dictates how the conflict is resolved. *Courage* is the strength to stand firm in the face of difficulty or pressure.[19]

Virtues are often reflected in both professional and corporate lists of values, credos, and codes of conduct. For example, the Statement of Ethical Professional Practice from the Institute of Management Accountants (IMA) is organized into four areas of virtue: competence, confidentiality, integrity and credibility.[20] The Financial Executives International's Code of Ethics also uses virtue concepts as it requires members to conduct their business and personal affairs with honesty and integrity.[21] Similarly, the document describing the Code of Conduct for Google (now Alphabet) starts by describing the company's informal corporate motto – "don't be evil" (which was changed to "do the right thing" for Alphabet).[22] It then goes on to describe a number of corporate principles or values. In the area relating to "Serving Our Users," Google employees are asked to have their actions guided by the following principles: *usefulness* (of products, features, and services), *integrity*, *responsiveness* (to users), and *taking action*.[23] Parts of many corporate codes of conduct define how individuals ought to behave; in other words, in terms of duties. Virtue theory does not deal directly with duties, although often duties can be derived quite logically from virtues.

Virtues provide their own *intrinsic rewards*. Virtuous individuals appreciate, and hence pursue, these rewards. But not all employees in organizations should be taken as virtuous *prima facie*, which is why other forms of controls are necessary. As such, publicized sets of virtues can be a valuable part of an organizational control system. However, action controls, such as policies and procedures, cannot always be made both specific and complete. This limitation is reflected in Google's Code of Conduct:

> **It's impossible to spell out every possible ethical scenario we might face. Instead, we rely on one another's good judgment to uphold a high standard of integrity for ourselves and our company. We expect all Googlers to be guided by both the letter and the spirit of this Code. Sometimes, identifying the right thing to do isn't an easy call. If you aren't sure, don't be afraid to ask questions of your manager, Legal or Ethics & Compliance.**[24]

Virtues fill in the gaps and provide guidance as to what is the right thing to do. They are an element of personnel or cultural control.

Virtue-based approaches, however, also have limitations. One problem is that the list of potential virtues is long. For example, in addition to those mentioned in the codes mentioned above, one might consider character, generosity, grace, decency, commitment, frugality, independence, professionalism, idealism, compassion, responsibility, kindness, respectfulness, and moderation. Critics of the virtue model argue that it is not obvious which set of virtues should be applied in any given setting. In addition, some characteristics considered virtues can actually impede ethical behavior. Courage, for example, is sometimes essential to commit fraud, and respect for elders (superiors) might actually stop someone from exposing a fraud. It is also difficult to know whether particular virtues exist in any individuals, how to develop virtues in individuals and groups of individuals, and how to recognize when day-to-day pressures are eroding the virtues.

Analyzing ethical issues

Good ethical behavior needs to be guided by more than opinions, intuitions, or gut feeling. Where the ethics of an action is in question, individuals should structure their situational analysis by using a proper reasoning or decision model. Various models exist, but most involve the following steps:

1. **Clarify the facts.** What is known, or what needs to be known, to help define the problem? The facts should identify what, who, where, when, and how.
2. **Define the ethical issue.** What about the situation causes an ethical issue to be raised? This logic should be phrased using the terms of one or more of the ethical models. Which *stakeholders* are harmed or put at risk? Are there conflicts over *rights*? Is someone being treated *unfairly*? Is someone acting dishonestly (lacking *integrity*)?
3. **Specify the alternatives.** List the alternative courses of action, including those that represent some form of compromise.
4. **Compare values and alternatives.** See if there is a clear decision. If one course of action is so compelling, then the analysis can be concluded.
5. **Assess the consequences.** Identify short- and long-term, positive and negative consequences for the major alternatives. This step will often reveal unanticipated results as, for example, short-term benefits will be shown to be dwarfed by long-term costs.
6. **Make a decision.** Balance the consequences against the primary ethical principles or values and select the alternative that best fits.

It is important to recognize that different people can consider identical situations and reach different conclusions even after structuring their decision processes equally carefully and thoroughly. This can occur because they prioritize the various ethical principles differently. None of the ethical models is perfect and complete, and the models sometimes lead to different conclusions. That insight is important by itself. Managers need to be open to different approaches because different people will be viewing and judging their actions through different lenses.

Why do people behave unethically?

People behave unethically for several reasons. One reason is *ignorance*. Managers who do not understand ethics, or who do not analyze the issues carefully, can make any of a number of mistakes that can lead to high probabilities of unethical behaviors within their organizations. They sometimes fail to recognize some ethical issues when they arise. One common problem is that managers sometimes equate ethical and legal issues; they conclude that if an action is not illegal, it must be ethical. This is clearly not true. For example, it is possible to conclude that many forms of earnings management are unethical, even though they might not be illegal. While many laws do indeed prohibit immoral practices, it is impossible to write laws to prohibit all unethical behaviors. Lying is usually considered immoral; however, laws prohibiting lying would be hard and inefficient to enforce. As a consequence, lying is against the law only in the most important circumstances, such as perjury.

But many people behave unethically at times even when they fully understand that what they are doing is wrong. There are some people who unscrupulously act as *bad apples*. They are essentially dishonest. For them, the burden of good ethics is greater than what they are willing to bear. Those who work in the field of fraud often refer to the so-called "10-80-10 rule," which maintains that approximately 10% of the population will be dishonest. These bad apples are contrasted with the two other categories. The bulk of the population (80%) is honest most of the time but can be tempted to be dishonest if opportunity and need arise simultaneously. The other 10% are honest under all circumstances, even in situations where they are sure they will not get caught.

Why someone – those in the 80% category – might act unethically can be understood in reference to the well-established *fraud triangle* model (Figure 15.1). Fraud is just an extreme form of unethical behavior. The three legs of the triangle are opportunity, motivation, and rationalization. Generally, all three of these factors have to be present at the same time in order for someone to commit fraud. *Opportunity* is created, most commonly, in situations with poor internal controls, little supervision, and not much checking, such as by auditors. The *motives* for committing fraud can be greed or the need for money. But the motives can also be non-monetary, such as caused by pressures to perform, which can be internally or externally generated. And fraud is encouraged by rationalizations. People committing fraud generally know that what they are doing is wrong, but they often find *rationalizations* to justify their behaviors. These rationalizations include such justifications as "if we don't manage earnings this quarter, we'll have to lay off some valued employees"; "aggressive financial reporting may not be totally honest, but everyone does it – we're only shooting ourselves in the foot if we don't"; "I shouldn't be taking office supplies home for the kids, but some of my colleagues are doing much worse things than I do, and it isn't really hurting anybody"; "we're uncomfortable about the aggressive

Figure 15.1 The fraud triangle

The Fraud Triangle
➢ Internal Controls
• None in place
• Not enforced
• Not monitored
• Ineffective
➢ Too much trust
➢ No "tone at the top"
➢ No segregation of duties (do more with less)
➢ Increased span of control = less review
➢ No management oversight/ knowledge
Opportunity
Rationalization
Motivation
➢ "The company owes me, I am underpaid."
➢ "Everyone else is doing it."
➢ "If they don't know i'm doing it, they deserve to lose the money."
➢ "I did it for a noble purpose."
➢ "Nobody will miss the money."
➢ "I've made this company a lot of money"
➢ "I didn't get the bonus I deserved"
➢ "I lost income due to stupid management policies."
➢ "I'm just borrowing the money. I'll pay it back."
➢ "I didn't personally benefit."
- Debt
- Greed
- Vices: gambling, drugs
- Pressure to perform
- Too much work

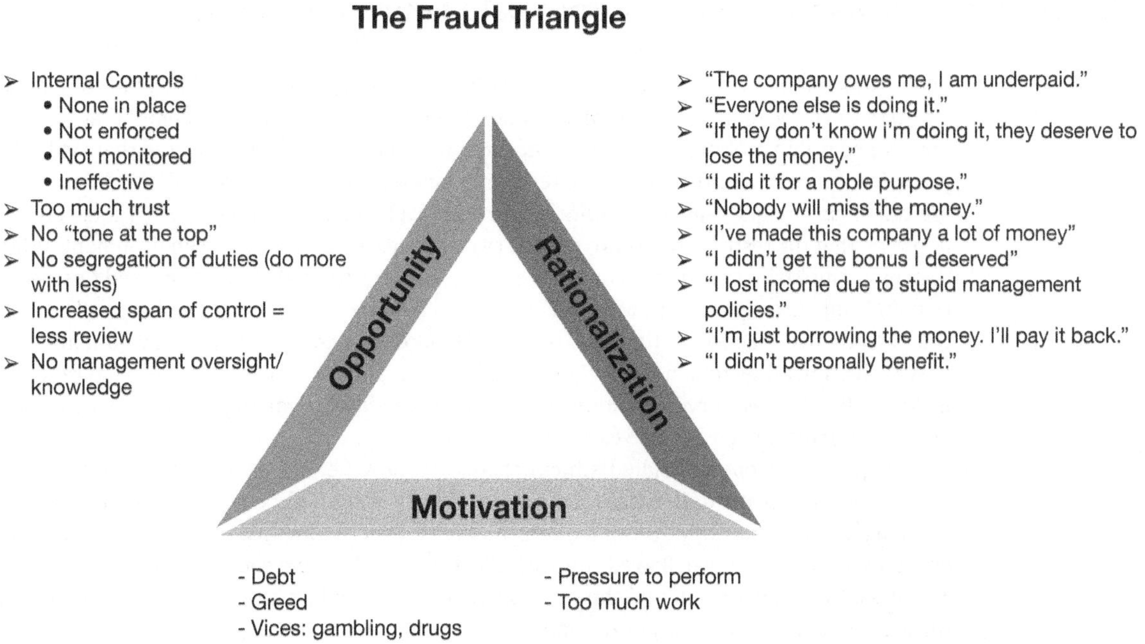

estimates of our tax liabilities, but we decided as a team that this was all right"; and "my boss knows about it – she said we'll be ok." Some of these rationalizations stem from a poor corporate culture. Fraudulent and unethical behaviors are contagious.

The rationalizations, and the subsequent unethical behaviors, are more common in people who lack *moral courage*. These people know they are doing something wrong, but they do not have the strength to do the right thing despite fear of the consequences. It is well known that those who insist on acting ethically can suffer any of many negative consequences, including shame, ostracism, and even dismissal. People with poorly formed ethical beliefs and/or little moral courage may easily "capitulate." Those who wish to build up their moral courage should clarify their core values – those values they are willing to uphold regardless of the consequences.

Those who recognize that they do not have the needed moral courage should choose their work environments carefully. They should choose environments in which it is unlikely they will be pressured into decisions that require good ethical judgment. They may not be suitable for the financial controller-type jobs we discussed in Chapter 14, as indeed one commentator noted that for these jobs around the globe:

> [I don't] know of a senior financial professional who is not under pressure from others around their organization. The difference may be that in the West they face pressure from the executives to show bigger returns for stock markets, whereas in the East they may be under pressure from a powerful majority shareholder to pinch profits from minority shareholders. But they are always between a rock and a hard place. The rock and the hard place are just different parties.[25]

Unethical actions that are not fraudulent differ slightly from fraudulent actions because those acting unethically might not be aware that they are doing something wrong. They might be ignorant or *morally disengaged*. They might not recognize an ethical issue when they face one, such as when they have an *unconscious bias* (which causes them to discriminate, say), so their conscience does not stop them from behaving unethically. They do not even need a rationalization.

Some common management control-related ethical issues

Many ethical issues arise in the context of MCSs. Some people even use ethical arguments to question the basic foundations of management "control" and "capitalist systems" that "coerce" management into making decisions on "economic" grounds (only). They argue that "value" is put before "values" and that corporate restructurings and downsizings aimed at reducing costs are unethical because they put profits before employee and societal welfare. Others counter, however, that the restructurings are necessary responses to changes in the environment. While they may cause pain to displaced employees, they help ensure that the restructured businesses remain competitive and, thus, able to gainfully employ their remaining employees. They call this "creative destruction" – that is, a painful yet necessary condition for innovation and progress, affecting all sectors, not just the for-profit sector, and for which the underlying rationale is that welfare is best served by not propping up old models but making the new ones work.[26] (We discuss this further to some extent in Chapter 16.)

Such political economy-related ethics debates are, however, not within the scope of the following sections. Instead, in what follows, we identify and briefly discuss four narrower, but common and important, MCS-related ethical issues: (1) creating budget slack; (2) managing earnings; (3) responding to flawed control indicators; and (4) using controls that are "too good." These issues are important, and the analyses required to deal with them are representative of those that could be used to analyze similar issues that might arise.

The ethics of creating budget slack

As discussed in Chapter 8, many performance targets, particularly those used at managerial organization levels, are negotiated as part of annual budgeting processes between those who are ultimately held accountable for meeting the budget and their managers, those one step up in the organization chain or hierarchy. Negotiation processes provide opportunities for those proposing their budget to "game" the process; that is, to distort their positions in order to be given more easily achievable targets against which they subsequently will be evaluated and on the basis of which they typically stand to earn performance-contingent rewards.[27] This distortion is often colloquially referred to as *sandbagging* or *creating slack*. As we discussed in Chapter 5, building slack into budgets is quite common. But is it ethical?

When employees create slack, they are exploiting their position of superior knowledge about their entity's prospects. They are failing to disclose to their superiors all of their available information and informed insights and, as such, are presenting a distorted picture of their entity's business. Therefore, creating budget slack can be deemed in violation of several of the obligations listed in the Statement of Ethical Professional Practice of the Institute of Management Accountants.[28] For example, the credibility standard requires management accountants to "communicate information fairly and objectively."

Analysis from the tenets of utilitarianism also suggests that slack creation constitutes an ethical issue. Typically, those creating budget slack will benefit personally from it. Slack protects them against unfavorable occurrences such as an increase in costs, thus mitigating the probability that performance targets would be missed and performance-based rewards left unearned. If the reward-performance function is continuous (i.e. not capped), slack will also increase the size of the rewards that will be earned. Whereas these benefits accrue to those creating the slack, the slack creation can be costly to other stakeholders, especially the firm and its owners. Budgets containing slack are often less than optimally motivating. When achievement of the target is assured, employee effort may be waning. Moreover, exceeding the target may be deemed unwise because it may trigger a higher, more difficult target for the following period. This is called target ratcheting.[29] Employees and managers may not work as hard, they may make unnecessary expenditures to consume the excess, or they may be motivated to play games to "save" the profit not needed in the current year. Slack creation also can be deemed less than correct from the standpoint of the users of the budget submissions – higher-level management – as they will rely on the information in the budget to make investment, resource allocation, and performance evaluation decisions that will become distorted.

On the other hand, some arguments can be raised to support the position that slack creation is ethical, or at least can be seen as justifiable. Many managers argue that creating slack is a rational response within a *results-control* system. They do not view slack as a distortion but as a means of protecting themselves from the downside risks of an uncertain future. Viewed this way, slack serves a function identical to that of the accepted management accounting practices of variance analysis and flexible budgeting, both of which are used to eliminate the effects on the performance measures of some uncontrollable factors (see Chapter 12), and in so doing shield managers from the risk these factors create. This protection from risk is particularly valuable in firms that treat the budget targets as "hard promises" or "performance commitments" with little or no tolerance for missed targets, or "underperformance" with possible dismissal as a consequence when it occurs. In the same way, some managers argue that budget slack is sometimes necessary to address the imbalance of power that is inherent in hierarchical organizations. It offers protection or "insurance" against evaluation unfairness that may arise from imperfect performance measures or evaluation errors or biases by superiors.

Finally, managers who defend slack creation also often point out that it is an accepted practice in their organization's budget negotiating process. Managers at all levels of the organization negotiate for slack in their budgets, and everyone is aware of the behavioral norm. Indeed, they point out, many senior managers were promoted into their positions precisely because they were good at negotiating for slack and, hence, for achieving their budget targets consistently over time. In many organizations, superiors may actually (implicitly) encourage their subordinates to create slack because they also benefit from it. The superiors' targets are usually consolidations of the targets of their subordinates, so they enjoy the same reduction in risk and increase in the expected values of their rewards as the slack creators. When creation of slack is widespread and the practice is encouraged, can we say that the organizational culture is encouraging unethical behavior? Or, does it indicate that in this community, at least, slack creation is rationalized as an acceptable behavioral norm?

Combined, then, in making judgments as to whether slack creation is ethical in any specific setting, many factors must be considered, including the following:

- How good the performance measures are (the extent to which they reflect underlying performance and are unaffected by factors the managers cannot control).
- Whether budget targets are treated as a rigid promise from managers to the corporation.
- Whether the manager's intent in creating the slack primarily reflects self-interest.
- Whether (or how much) superiors are aware of the slack.
- Whether the superiors encourage the creation of slack.
- Whether the amount of slack is "material."
- Whether the individual(s) involved are bound by one or more of the sets of standards of professional conduct. (Most accountants are, whereas most managers are not.)

The ethics of "managing earnings"

A second ethical issue involves the data manipulation problem discussed in Chapter 5. A common form of manipulation is *earnings management*, which includes any action that changes reported earnings (or any other income statement or balance sheet item) while providing no real economic advantage to the organization and, sometimes, actually causing harm. Generally, earnings management actions are designed either to *boost* earnings, such as to achieve a budget target or increase stock price, or to *smooth* earnings patterns to give the impression of higher earnings predictability and, hence, lower risk. Some actions might also be designed to *reduce* earnings, such as to "save" profits for a future period when they might be needed, or to lower stock price to facilitate a management buyout, or to lower the strike price just before a stock option grant.[30]

Earnings management can be deemed unethical for several reasons. First, when the actions are not apparent to either external or internal users of financial statements or the reported information more generically, those engaging in earnings management are deriving personal advantage through deception. This is pertinently expressed in the following excerpt:

> **It would be very helpful to know where people push the boundaries. If all companies could be ranked in terms of aggressiveness or conservative accounting policies, as judged by their auditors, then that would be helpful information. [...] If they're pushing the envelope, you want to know about it. If they're pushing the envelope and technically you can't qualify, we don't find out.[31]**

Second, professional managers and accountants can be said to have a duty to disclose fairly presented information. Indeed, most professional associations state so in their codes of ethics. Specifically, the IMA code referenced above requires to "disclose all relevant information that could reasonably be expected to influence an intended user's understanding of the reports, analyses or recommendations."[32] Hence, the distortions can be interpreted as not being consistent with a professional's obligation to report and disclose information credibly.

Third, the rewards earned from managing earnings are not fair when the reported performance is only cosmetic, not real. This is the reason for recent changes in compensation practices that have so-called *claw backs*, which allow bonuses or other incentive payouts to be rescinded if in retrospect these appeared to have been based on *managed* or manipulated performance.[33]

Managers may have several justifications for managing earnings, however. They might be using their private information about company prospects to smooth out some meaningless, short-term perturbations in the earnings measures to provide more, rather than less, informative performance signals to financial statement users. As with slack creation, they might argue that they take these actions merely to protect themselves from rigid, unfair performance evaluations. They might also take actions that make it unnecessary for them to take other, possibly more damaging actions, such as suspending research and development expenditures.[34] Some earnings management actions are easy to rationalize in this way.

Curiously, most people judge *accounting methods* of managing earnings more harshly than *operating methods* even though the purposes of the two earnings management methods are identical, and the economic effects of the operating methods are typically far more costly to the firm.[35] As discussed in Chapter 5, *accounting methods* of managing earnings involve the selection of accounting methods and the flexibility in applying those methods to affect reported earnings. *Operating methods* involve the altering of actual operating decisions, such as the timing of sales or discretionary expenditures. Clearer standards for judging accounting performance (i.e. accounting standards) could explain this finding. As such, employees may be less likely to engage in earnings management (or other questionable behaviors) when they believe it violates *established rules*, which accounting standards are, suggesting that people use clarity of laws, rules, standards, or procedures as a basis for reaching an ethical conclusion.

Several situational factors are likely to influence judgments as to whether earnings management actions are deemed (un)ethical, including (1) the direction of the manipulation (boost, shrink, or merely smooth earnings); (2) the size of the effect (materiality); (3) the timing (quarter- vs. year-end, random timing vs. immediately preceding a bond offering or stock option grant); (4) the method used (adjusting reserves, deferring discretionary expenditures, or changing accounting policies); (5) the managers' intent regarding the informativeness of the numbers (and disclosures); (6) the clarity of the rules prohibiting the action; and (7) the degree of repetition (one-time use vs. ongoing use even after a warning).

Making judgments about earnings management is complex, although in so doing, it is probably judicious to err on the side of caution rather than rationalization. Speaking out against what he deemed unrelenting earnings management practices, Arthur Levitt, former chairman of the Securities and Exchange Commission (SEC), called these practices so serious that "we need to embrace nothing less than a cultural change."[36] The incidence and size of various corporate scandals and failures, including in major financial institutions such as Bear Stearns and Lehman Brothers in only the first decade of the twenty-first century, seem to have proven him right.[37]

The ethics of responding to flawed control indicators

Results targets and action prescriptions provide signals to employees as to what the organization considers important, be it profits, growth, quality, or any other desired performances. When the targets and prescriptions are not defined properly, they can actually motivate behaviors that employees know are not in the organization's best interest. The employees earn rewards for doing what they are *asked to do*, not what they know they *should do*, and the organization suffers. Indeed, many fraud cases involve employees taking unethical and illegal actions that they perceive to be "necessary" for their company to thrive or survive, sometimes under pressure from higher-ups,[38] but about which they are too ashamed or embarrassed to tell their relatives. This is pertinently expressed in the following quote from a letter by Matthew Lee, a Lehman Brothers senior vice president who believed "senior management" may have violated their own internal code of ethics by misleading investors and regulators about the true value of the then-firm's assets:

> **"I believe the manner in which the firm is reporting [certain] assets is potentially misleading to the public and various governmental agencies," Mr. Lee wrote.[39]**

Mr. Lee addressed his letter to the then-CFO, among others, only days before he was ousted from the firm.

We discussed one common flawed-response example in detail in Chapter 11 – that of *myopia*. It occurs when companies place a high emphasis on the achievement of short-term profit targets, even though some profit-increasing activities (such as reducing investments in employee development, customer acquisition and loyalty, or R&D) may diminish shareholder value in the long run. Relevant to the discussion here, managers who engage in myopic behaviors often know that they are curtailing long-term value or even causing long-term harm to their entity and their company; yet, perhaps under pressure, they decide to do it anyway.

What should employees do if they know the results measures or action prescriptions are flawed? Should they act to generate the results for which they will be rewarded, or should they sacrifice their own self-interest in favor of what they believe to be "truly" best for the organization? When they face this conflict of interest, most employees will choose to follow the rules of the reward system, perhaps while lobbying to get the measures changed. This behavioral norm might not be ethical. Financial professionals have standards of ethical conduct (duties) that require them to further their organization's "legitimate interests." For example, Financial Executives International's Code of Ethics requires its members to "Act in good faith, responsibly, with due care, competence and diligence, without misrepresenting material facts or allowing one's independent judgment to be subordinated."[40]

Managers and employees not bound by those professional standards perhaps should be bound by a sense of loyalty (a virtue) to their organization. But not everyone is. This is the reason why, applied to the banking sector, some financial markets have taken drastic steps to try to boost ethics in their country's financial services. In the Netherlands, for example, top bankers must already swear an oath to behave with integrity, and the industry body will extend the oath to cover bankers at lower levels.[41]

The ethics of using control indicators that are "too good"

Another ethical issue relates to the use of control indicators that are *too good*. Highly, perhaps excessively, tight control indicators have been made possible by advances in technology. For example, computer surveillance programs that allow companies to monitor their employees' personal computer screens, data use, and Internet traffic are widespread today. Supervisors can listen in on employees' sales calls; cameras can record all the actions some employees take; computers can count the number of keystrokes by data entry clerks and telephone operators to gauge productivity; and location devices can track an employee's whereabouts throughout the workday.[42] A recent example from Credit Suisse, the Swiss-based global bank, illustrates this trend very well:

> **In truth, errors and misbehavior happen everywhere. In a well-run institution, though, managers spot problems early. Then measures are taken to limit the damage and make amends. Culture is key, but so are resources. [...] In that context, Credit Suisse's announcement makes perfect sense. It has joined forces with Palantir, a CIA-backed artificial intelligence firm, to use data-driven behavioral analysis to root out rogue traders and insider dealing. Mr. Thiam [the bank's chief executive] says he wants to change Credit Suisse's culture. *But if his employees don't feel comfortable admitting to problems, at least his bank will soon be a lot better at catching them.*[43]**

What is the ethical issue? The number of correct keystrokes and reports of employees' locations-by-time may be good results measures in certain situations. They may describe what the organizations want from their employees, and they can be measured accurately and on a timely basis. That said, there is a fine line between the employer's right to monitor and the employees' rights to autonomy, privacy, or freedom from oppressive controls that suggest they are working in *electronic sweatshops*. Thus, questions relevant to determinations of whether use of such measures is ethical probably include:

- Is the use of the measures disclosed to employees?
- Are safeguards in place to protect the collected data?
- Are safeguards in place to ensure that the data are used for their intended purposes only (e.g. for quality monitoring of customer calls, or for monitoring employees in training, not experienced employees)?
- When supervisors use these tight controls, do they emphasize quality rather than just quantity ("grab everything")?

But some companies also make the news with allegations of subjecting their employees to conditions that presumably resemble an era of *physical sweatshops*. For example, when 11 employees committed suicide in a short period, the Taipei-based company Foxconn "was introduced to much of the world in the worst terms imaginable – as an *industrial monster* that treats workers like machines [...] to make products like the iPhone at seemingly impossible prices." For the image-conscious businesses that Foxconn supplies, including IBM, Cisco, Microsoft, Nokia, Sony, HP, and Apple, the suicides were a public-relations nightmare and a challenge to the "off-shoring strategies" that were essential to their bottom lines.[44] But whether Foxconn's controls were "too tight" is actually difficult to judge. "[Foxconn] pays workers on time and for overtime according to the regulations, and that's why workers always queue to work there," said Geoffrey Crothall, spokesman for Hong Kong-based China Labor Bulletin, a worker-rights organization, adding that "despite [...] the intense nature of the work, it's still better than a small workshop with no guarantee you'll get paid."[45] An anonymous former employee said: "The factories themselves are top notch although they are fairly intense working environments. Westerners would find it very difficult to work there."[46]

Clearly what is acceptable to some is not acceptable to others, and, as the last quote suggests, views may differ across (national) cultures. What is clear, however, is that when controls are "too good" or "too tight" – or "oppressive," as some would argue – they are likely to induce unintended and/or undesirable consequences, such as by triggering job-related tension and even stress-related health complaints. This may be especially true for action controls; indeed, at Foxconn, it was said that "obviously work is tiring and there's pressure; there are lots of rules here."[47] But results controls can also be "too tight" in that they induce myopia and pressures for earnings management, as we discussed earlier in this chapter and elsewhere in this text.

Spreading good ethics within an organization

Ethical progress within an organization typically proceeds in stages. In an early stage, when the organization is small, the organization becomes an extension of the founder or the top management group. The founder acts as a role model, setting the ethical tone, and is usually able to monitor employees' compliance with that tone.

In later stages of development, organizations implement more formal *corporate ethics programs*. These programs include three main elements. First is a set of policies, codes, and values that define how the organization wants its employees to act. These policies might originate first in a set of memoranda from top management, but in larger organizations, they evolve into formal policy manuals and codes of ethics or codes of conduct. Some of the behavioral prescriptions might be quite specific, such as "accept no gifts greater than $50 in value." But necessarily, because not every possibility can be foreseen, some guidance is quite general. It is common to list a set of organizational values that employees are expected to live up to, such as the virtues mentioned earlier in this chapter.

Second is a set of programs designed to ensure that employees understand the specific policies and to help them think through ethical issues that are not specifically spelled out in the written prescriptions. Oftentimes, companies ask their employees to sign a statement certifying that they understand and will abide by the rules. At Boeing, the large aircraft manufacturer, employees are asked to certify annually that they will adhere to the company's Code of Conduct, which outlines the ethical business conduct required of employees in the performance of their company responsibilities. The company website explains that "Individuals certify that they will not engage in conduct or activity that may raise questions as to the company's honesty, impartiality or reputation or otherwise cause embarrassment to the company."[48]

Reinvigorating a code of conduct is also sometimes an effective way to reinforce change, to send a clear signal. This happened when Antony Jenkins, boss of Barclays, the UK-based global bank, told the bank's 140,000 employees to sign up to a new code of conduct, or leave.

Following from this, good ethics programs must involve some enforcement mechanisms, which include monitoring and application of sanctions where called for. The monitoring might be informal, such as is done by direct supervisors, or it might involve formal investigations by internal or external auditors, or even law enforcement agencies.

The codes also might need updating from time to time, even though the underlying principles of good ethical conduct may remain largely the same. For example, at Google, the document that lays out the company's "Ten Things" of their corporate philosophy states right at the top: "We first wrote these '10 things' several years ago. From time to time we revisit this list to see if it still holds true. We hope it does – and you can hold us to that."[49]

Even the best laid-out codes of ethics and signed employee certification statements may not be sufficient. Consider the following excerpt from the Statement of Vision and Values Principles of a large publicly traded corporation:

> Because we take our responsibilities to our fellow citizens seriously, we act decisively to ensure that all those with whom we do business understand our policies and standards. Providing clearly written guidelines reinforces our principles and business ethics. [Our] employees at all levels are expected to be active proponents of our principles and are trained to report without retribution anything they observe or discover that indicates our standards are not being met.
>
> Compliance with the law and ethical standards are conditions of employment, and violations will result in disciplinary action, which may include termination. New employees are asked to sign a statement indicating that they have read, understand and will comply with this statement, and employees are periodically asked to reaffirm their commitment to these principles.

Which company, do you reckon, espoused these principles and required signed statements certifying understanding and compliance with the principles? It was Enron, a corporation now held up as the epitome of corporate evil![50]

This Enron example shows that merely having a set of ethical standards and rules and taking steps to ensure that employees have read them is not sufficient. The standards must be made operational. Top management must set a credible tone at the top, and they must endeavor to maintain a good internal MCS so that potential violators know that there is a good chance that they will be caught. Monitoring should be done by both employees' superiors, colleagues (mutual control), and internal auditors. Violators of the rules should be sanctioned. These sanctions help give employees the courage to resist counter pressures. Companies also often appoint a designated ombudsperson to help employees facing ethical issues.

Tone at the top can be an effective form of cultural control when it is consistent, and supervision and mutual monitoring can be effective when given teeth in an otherwise trusting organizational climate. Under effective corporate cultures, ethical behaviors are "shaped" rather than merely "enforced" from time to time, often after a major violation has occurred and damage has been done.

Conclusion

This chapter has provided a brief introduction to the topic of ethics as it relates to the design and use of MCSs. To create the right ethical environment, management must have moral expertise and know where and how to provide it.

The sampling of issues discussed in this chapter should have made it obvious that many ethical issues are MCS-related, and many important ethical issues do not have black or white answers. One cannot conclude unequivocally that, for example, creating budget slack is always unethical or that controls are too tight to be ethical. The "greyness" of the judgments makes it all the more important for managers to subject the various ethical issues to a formal analysis. That said, many situational factors must be considered in making ethical judgments. For example, judgments of what is ethically acceptable vary across national cultures, suggesting that multinational companies wishing to achieve similar levels of ethicalness across entities located in different countries will have to rely on different sets of controls.

Employees face many pressures and temptations that can cause them to act unethically. They can easily bow to performance deadlines and crises, reward temptations, pressures for conformity, and even counterproductive orders from their bosses. Unless managers act to deflect these pressures and temptations on a fairly consistent basis, their company's ethical climate will be weakened. Managers must help guide the behaviors of their employees who are incapable of thinking through ethical issues (distinguishing right from wrong) themselves. They must understand how and why individuals will reach different ethical conclusions, and, importantly, they must take a stance as to how they want employees in their organization to behave.

Every organization has an ethical culture or climate of some sort; either good, bad, or mixed. It is important for managers to build a good ethical climate, one that respects the rights, duties, and interests of stakeholders inside and outside the firm. An organization that fosters unethical behaviors from its employees, even those that benefit the company in the short run, will probably eventually find itself the victim of its own policies. Such organizations are more likely to attract people who feel comfortable bending the rules; they may even entice sincere people to bend the rules. Bad cultures are contagious. Yet, weakened or poor ethical climates can lead to unethical behaviors that can damage or destroy individual and organizational reputations. Once ethical climates are weakened and reputations are damaged, they can be quite difficult to rebuild.

Notes

1 See, for example, H. Mintzberg, *Developing Managers, Not MBAs* (Harlow, UK: Financial Times/Prentice Hall, 2005).

2 See, for example, "Shareholders vs. Stakeholders: A New Idolatry," *The Economist* (April 24, 2010), online at econ.st/KA1p7h; "Maximizing Shareholder Value: The Goal That Changed Corporate America," *The Washington Post* (August 26, 2013), online at wpo.st/8EXX1.

3 See, for example, "Scathing Report Says Toshiba CEOs Had Role in Accounting Scandal," *The Financial Times* (July 20, 2015), online at on.ft.com/1KgFnZB.

4 "Ebix's Raina Loses Magic Touch as U.S. Probes Accounting," *Bloomberg* (June 20, 2013), online at www.bloomberg.com.

5 American Institute of Certified Public Accountants, *AICPA Code of Professional Conduct* (see, for example, on page 5 of the version most recently available as of this text edition on October 26, 2015), online at www.aicpa.org/Research/Standards/CodeofConduct.

6 "Christine Lagarde Calls for Shake-Up of Bankers' Pay," *The Financial Times* (May 6, 2015), online at on.ft.com/1hgJZCY.

7 "A Bigger Stick," *The Economist* (June 13, 2015), online at econ.st/1MsDNRB.

8 See "Why Honesty Is the Best Policy," *The Economist* (March 9, 2002), online at econ.st/JxdsXd.

9 See, for example, "Findings on Lehman Take Even Experts by Surprise," *The New York Times* (March 12, 2010), online at nyti.ms/1UFar9L.

10 See, for example, "Accounting Scandal Set to Shake Up Toshiba," *The Financial Times* (July 16, 2015), online at on.ft.com/1fMNz7h.

11 See also "Bankers Not Only Ones Pushing Ethical Boundaries," *The Financial Times* (September 25, 2015), online at on.ft.com/1FmAXiS.

12 "Tesco Was Warned in 2010 about 'Aggressive Accounting,'" *BBC* (September 25, 2014), online at www.bbc.co.uk/news/business-29364273.

13 "Tesco in Crisis: UK Managing Director among Four Executives Suspended after Exposure of Accounting Scandal," *The Independent* (September 22, 2014), online at www.independent.co.uk. See also "Not So Funny: Booking Revenues, Like Comedy, Is All about Timing," *The Economist* (September 27, 2014), online at econ.st/1qxwvPw.

14 See, for example, "A Bigger Stick," op. cit.

15 For an overview and more detailed treatment of some of these ethical models, see J. Gaa and R. Ruland (eds.), *Ethical Issues in Accounting* (Sarasota, FL: American Accounting Association, 1997). See also J. Driver, *Ethics: The Fundamentals* (Oxford: Wiley-Blackwell, 2006).

16 See also, J. Driver, *Consequentialism* (New York: Routledge, 2011).

17 See, for example, D. Birch and J. Fielder, *The Ford Pinto Case: A Study in Applied Ethics, Business, and Society* (Albany, NY: State University of New York Press, 1994).

18 See, for example, "Executive Pay '180 Times Average,' Report Finds," *BBC* (July 14, 2014), online at www.bbc.co.uk/news/28286264; "City Leaders Urge Radical Reforms of 'Unfair' Executive Pay," *The Financial Times* (May 8, 2016), online at on.ft.com/1T5Qnel.

19 See also J. Gaa and R. Ruland, "Ethics in Accounting: An Overview of Issues, Concepts and Principles," in Gaa and Ruland, *Ethical Issues in Accounting*, op. cit.

20 The Statement of Ethical Professional Practice from the IMA is available at www.imanet.org/tools-and-resources/ethics-center (accessed May 6, 2015).

21 The Financial Executives International (FEI) Code of Ethics can be found at www.financialexecutives.org/about/FEICodeofEthics.pdf (accessed May 6, 2015).

22 "Alphabet Drops Google's Famous 'Don't Be Evil' Motto," *Fortune* (October 25, 2015), online at for.tn/1j93MVV.

23 See Google Code of Conduct at abc.xyz/investor/other/google-code-of-conduct.html. The Alphabet version can be found at abc.xyz/investor/other/code-of-conduct.html (as accessed on May 6, 2015).

24 See Google Code of Conduct, op. cit.

25 Chartered Institute of Management Accountants, *Global Perspectives on Governance: Lessons from East and West* (2010), p. 8, online at www.cimaglobal.com.

26 See, for example, "Creative Destruction," *The Economist* (June 28, 2014), online at econ.st/1v8uCMm.

27 See also M. Jensen, "Corporate Budgeting Is Broken: Let's Fix it," *Harvard Business Review* (November 2001), pp. 94–101; M. Jensen, "Why Pay People to Lie?" *The Wall Street Journal* (January 8, 2001), p. A32; and "Companies Get Budgets All Wrong," *The Wall Street Journal* (July 22, 2013), online at on.wsj.com/1OfjJaR.

28 Statement of Ethical Professional Practice, *IMA*, op. cit.

29 For an academic treatment of budget ratcheting, see R. J. Indjejikian, M. Mat jka, K. A. Merchant, and Wim A. Van der Stede, "Earnings Targets and Annual Bonus Incentives," *The Accounting Review*, 89, no. 4 (July 2014), pp. 1227–58, as well as the other papers in this issue of *The Accounting Review* titled "A Forum on Ratcheting and Incentives."

30 For a more extensive discussion of earnings management practices, see C. Mulford and E. Comiskey, *The Financial Numbers Game: Detecting Creative Accounting Practices* (Chichester, UK: John Wiley & Sons, 2002). See also J. Graham, C. Harvey, and S. Rajgopal, "The Economic Implications of Corporate Financial Reporting," *Journal of Accounting and Economics*, 40, no. 1–3 (December 2005), pp. 3–73; I. D. Dichev, J. R. Graham, C. R. Harvey, and S. Rajgopal, "Earnings Quality: Evidence from the Field," *Journal of Accounting and Economics*, 56, nos. 2–3 (Supplement, December 2013), pp. 1–33; and A. Edmans, L. Goncalves-Pinto, Y. Wang and M Groen-Xu, "Strategic News Releases in Equity Vesting Months," *Working Paper* (2016), online at papers.ssrn.com/sol3/papers.cfm?abstract_id=2489152.

31 "Assurance Today and Tomorrow," *PwC* (2012), online at www.pwc.com/gx/en/audit-services/publications/assets/pwc-global-investor-survey.pdf.
32 Statement of Ethical Professional Practice, *IMA*, op. cit.
33 See, for example, "Five Trends in Stock Compensation," *HR Times* (March 20, 2014), online at hrtimesblog.com; "UK Bankers Face Tough Bonus Clawbacks," *The Financial Times* (July 29, 2014), online at on.ft.com/1k5Te8U; "SEC Proposes Rules on Executive Pay and Performance," *The New York Times* (April 29, 2015), online at nyti.ms/1OeoKcQ.
34 See, for example, J. Graham, C. Harvey, and S. Rajgopal, "Value Destruction and Financial Reporting Decisions," *Financial Analysts Journal*, 62, no. 6 (November 2006), pp. 27–39.
35 K. Merchant and J. Rockness, "The Ethics of Managing Earnings: An Empirical Investigation," *Journal of Accounting and Public Policy*, 13, no. 1 (Spring 1994), pp. 79–94. For another study of how ethical judgments of earnings management vary across different user groups (shareholders vs. non-shareholders), see S. Kaplan, "Further Evidence on the Ethics of Managing Earnings: An Examination of the Ethically Related Judgments of Shareholders and Non-Shareholders," *Journal of Accounting and Public Policy*, 20, no. 1 (Spring 2001), pp. 27–44.
36 A. Levitt, *The Numbers Game*, Speech at New York University Center for Law and Business (September 28, 1998).
37 See, for example, "Findings on Lehman Take Even Experts by Surprise," *The New York Times* (March 12, 2010), online at nyti.ms/1UFar9L. See also "Bankers Not Only Ones Pushing Ethical Boundaries," *The Financial Times* (September 25, 2015), online at on.ft.com/1FmAXiS.
38 See, for example, "WorldCom Official Tried to Quash Employee's Accounting Concerns," *The Wall Street Journal* (August 27, 2002), p. B6.
39 "Lehman Insider's Letter Warned about Violating Code of Ethics," *The Wall Street Journal* (March 20, 2010), online at on.wsj.com/1zkM59z.
40 Financial Executives International Code of Ethics, *FEI*, op. cit.
41 "Banking Conduct Body Faces Rocky Road to Reform," *The Financial Times* (May 19, 2014), online at on.ft.com/1jOhPbk.
42 See, for example, H. J. Wilson, "Wearables in the Workplace," *Harvard Business Review* (September 2013), online at hbr.org/2013/09/wearables-in-the-workplace; "Tracking Workers' Every Move Can Boost Productivity – and Stress," *The Los Angeles Times* (April 8, 2013), online at www.latimes.com/la-fi-harsh-work-tech-20130408,0,6413037.story; "A High-Tech New Way for Your Boss to Follow You Everywhere," *Bloomberg* (August 1, 2014), online at bloom.bg/1TTKSOI; "Wearables at Work: The New Frontier of Employee Surveillance," *The Financial Times* (June 8, 2015), online at on.ft.com/1IB7dz1; "Banks Listen in to Traders' Banter for Evidence of Market Abuse," *The Financial Times* (February 14, 2016), online at on.ft.com/1odkTb1.
43 "Credit Suisse Spooked by What Lurks Within," *The Financial Times* (March 25, 2016), online at on.ft.com/1RAT5Vt.
44 "Everything Is Made by Foxconn in Future Evoked by Gou's Empire," *Business Week* (September 9, 2010), online at www.bloomberg.com.
45 Ibid.
46 "Foxconn Suicides: 'Workers Feel Quite Lonely,'" *BBC* (May 28, 2010), online at www.bbc.co.uk.
47 Ibid.
48 See Boeing's website at www.boeing.com/principles/ethics-and-compliance.page, and specifically www.boeing.com/resources/boeingdotcom/principles/ethics_and_compliance/pdf/english.pdf for the document that employees sign.
49 See www.google.com/intl/en/about/company/philosophy (accessed May 6, 2015).
50 Enron's Code of Ethics (July 2000), online (no longer available).

CASE STUDY
Two Budget Targets

In the three years since he had been appointed manager of the Mobile Communications Division (MCD) of Advanced Technologies Corporation (ATC), Joe supervised the preparation of two sets of annual budget numbers. When ATC's bottom-up budgeting process began, Joe instructed his subordinates to set aggressive performance targets because he believed such targets would push everyone to perform at their best.

Then, before Joe presented his budget to his superiors, he added some *management judgment*. He made the forecasts of the future more pessimistic, and he added some allowances for *performance contingencies* to create what he called the *easy plan*. Sometimes the corporate managers questioned some of Joe's forecasts and asked him to raise his sales and profit targets somewhat. However, MCD operated in a rapidly growing, uncertain market that Joe understood better than his superiors, and Joe was a skillful and forceful negotiator. In each of the past three years, the end result was that the targets in the official budget for MCD were highly achievable. MCD's performance had exceeded the targets in the easy plan by an average of 40%, and Joe earned large bonuses. Joe did not show his superiors the targets his subordinates were working toward, but some of Joe's direct reports were aware of the existence of the easy plan.

In his subjective evaluations of his subordinates' performances for the purposes of assigning bonuses and merit raises, Joe compared actual performance with the aggressive targets. In the last three years, only approximately 25% of the aggressive targets had been achieved. Joe did not fire any of his managers for failing to achieve their targets, but he reserved the vast majority of the discretionary rewards for the managers who had achieved their targets.

This case was prepared by Professor Kenneth A. Merchant.

CASE STUDY
Conservative Accounting in the General Products Division

The year 2015 was a good one for the General Products Division (GPD) of Altman Industries, Inc., a large industrial products manufacturer. Sales and profits in the division were significantly above plan due largely to unexpectedly brisk sales of a new product introduced at the end of 2014. The good fortune induced Robert Standish, the GPD general manager, to think about how he could save some of the profits for periods in which he might need them more. He believed that GPD's plan for 2017 would be tough to achieve because the corporation as a whole was not doing well, and corporate managers would expect GPD to show growth even above this year's abnormally high sales and profit levels. In addition, already in September 2016, Robert was sure that his division's 2016 profit would exceed the level above which no additional bonuses were awarded for higher performance – 120% of plan. Robert wanted to save some of the 2016 profits so that he could report them in a year in which they would augment his bonus and those of his direct reports.

Robert asked his staff to do what they could before the end of the year to "stash some acorns" that he could use in future years. He suggested to Joanne, his controller, that she start preparing the pessimistic scenarios that could be used to justify the creation of additional reserves and start thinking about how expenses could be accelerated and revenues could be deferred at year-end.

Joanne was uncomfortable. She reminded Robert that because of continuing order declines, Altman executives were looking for ways to report higher, not lower, profits in the current year and that if that situation did not turn around quickly, layoffs were threatened.

But Robert explained that GPD would still be reporting very high profits; he just wanted to save a portion of the excess above plan. And in any case, GPD could not help the corporation much because it was such a small part of the entire corporation.

This case was prepared by Professor Kenneth A. Merchant.

CASE STUDY
Education Food Services at Central Maine State University

Pam Worth, Manager of Education Food Services at Central Maine State University (CMSU), is meeting with a researcher to explain some apparent discrepancies in last year's budgeted figures and the actuals. The researcher, a faculty member at another university, is doing field studies in the food service business. Pam is explaining why she always tries to hide some slack in her numbers when she prepares her budget. She says that it is her understanding that she is just doing what others in her company and in her industry do. She agreed to speak to the researcher only with guarantees of strict confidentiality.

> I like to have a moderate cushion in my budget. The stakes are high. If I make my budget my performance review will be good, almost regardless of whatever else I do during the period, and I will earn my 20% bonus. If I miss my budget without valid reasons I may not be allowed to keep my job.
>
> More than that, however, the cushion in the budget allows me to do a better job. I don't have to worry that my staff is working at peak efficiency all the time, so I don't have to supervise every action. That is better for the staff, also; they hate it when I'm looking over their shoulders. The cushion also allows me to buy things that I can use to provide the university with better service. For example, this year I was able to buy several portable bars that we have used already for some parties.

Pam, an accounting graduate of Northern University, is an employee of Contract Food Services Corporation (CFSC), a large corporation that provides food on a contract basis to universities, hospitals, and businesses. Pam runs a profit center that provides services only to one university – CMSU. Her operation provides food at two major, on-campus cafeterias serving 12,000 students and nearly 2,000 faculty and staff. Pam also has responsibility for the vending machine business on campus, and her employees sometimes provide catering services for on-campus business meetings. Pam's operation employs 59 regular employees and between 150 and 180 students on a part-time basis. Annual revenues are slightly in excess of $3 million.

Relations between CFSC and CMSU are governed by a contract that is renegotiated each January for the following academic year. The contract defines the responsibilities of each party. For example, CMSU administrators are given the power to review and approve CFSC's service plans and prices. The university provides all equipment costing over $100. CFSC sets the menus and hires the employees.

The contract also defines limits on the profits CFSC can earn from the CMSU operation. CFSC earns 100% of the profits from the food operation up to a limit of 10% profit on sales. Beyond that limit, profits are split equally with CMSU. The contract is set this way as an incentive to CFSC managers to provide extra quality and services after they have ensured themselves a reasonable profit.

Budgets are prepared on a bottom-up basis. In July, corporate headquarters personnel send planning guidelines and assumptions (e.g. employee benefits, inflation) to all operating units. The operating managers forecast their customer counts, which determines their food requirements, and then estimate their operating costs for the 18-month period starting in January. Since the university owns the buildings and equipment, the bulk of CFSC's costs are for food and labor.

After the units' budgets are prepared, a series of budget *challenge* rounds are held to review the numbers at successively higher CFSC consolidation levels – district, region, division, group, and corporate. If the numbers meet the managers' profit expectations, the budgets are accepted. Typically, however, each of the managers in the hierarchy is asked to raise his or her profit targets. These requests lead to a series of meetings designed to explore whether revenue projections should be raised or cost projections cut. The size of these profit increase requests are not predictable, but in recent years they have ranged from zero to 15%.

Pam explains that she routinely hides some cushion in both labor and food costs:

I can build the budget cushion in a lot of places. This year for example:

- I kept the proportion of meals served on board contracts (which are more lucrative for us) equivalent to last year's level even though I know that proportion will be growing because the trend is to have more students living on campus.
- I planned for a number of labor hours at $7.15 when I knew that I would hire students for those hours, and students don't earn that much.
- I planned no efficiency improvements when I know we almost always improve our efficiency. There is a learning curve in this business. My superiors know about this learning curve too – they ran operations just like this – but they don't object to my having a cushion. It is to their advantage to have me meet my budget too.

These types of things add up. I put just enough in so that I am sure I will be able to meet my budget targets even after corporate management squeezes some of my cushion out in their reviews.

I know more about what is happening at CMSU than anyone else. My bosses can't come here and check every assumption that I have in the plan. They don't have the time. My immediate boss, for example, is responsible for nine units spread over a fairly large geographic area.

You can easily identify new managers – they submit budgets that are realistic. Experienced managers build in pads for themselves. It's a bit devious, sure, but it's not theft. It's just playing with projections. The money's there. Besides, if you don't build a cushion for yourself you're not going to survive for long in this business.

This case was prepared by Professor Kenneth A. Merchant.

CASE STUDY
The "Sales Acceleration Program"

In early October, Priscilla Musso, general manager of the Specialty Products Division (SPD) of Consolidated Furniture Corporation (CFC), was studying the division's third quarter financial reports. Sales were running significantly below plan, and it became quite clear to Priscilla that SPD would need strong performance in the last quarter of the year in order to reach its annual profit target. Meeting budget was very important to Priscilla and her management team because they were included in CFC's lucrative executive bonus program, and they would lose all of their bonus opportunities if SPD did not achieve the profit targets.

To brainstorm for ideas, Priscilla called her management team together. At first the managers on the team expressed only discouragement. Everybody had been working hard, but the market was softening, and competitors were being very aggressive.

Then, after some delay with nobody else suggesting any options, Jonathan Robbins, SPD's manager of sales and marketing, suggested that the division could implement a new sales program to pull some sales that might ordinarily be made next year into the current year. Any customers who accepted delivery in the fourth quarter would not have to pay their invoice for six months. (Normally payments in the industry were to be made within 30 days.)

Priscilla's first reaction was favorable; this program might, indeed, achieve the desired result. But she asked the members of her team for their reactions.

Shirley Covey, manager of human resources noted that if this program was successful, it would probably cause SPD's employees to have to work overtime at the end of the year, and that was something they traditionally did not want during the holiday season. But Priscilla reminded Shirley that the employees would be paid time-and-a-half for all the overtime hours that they worked.

Priscilla asked Bill Bennett, SPD's controller, if this program would violate any accounting rules. Bill said there would be no problem recording the sales as long as the items were shipped and billed before December 31. The accounting would be consistent with GAAP. But Bill cautioned that this program was probably only providing a short-term, cosmetic profit improvement. While it might well make the current year look better, it would probably cause significantly lower sales to be recorded in the first quarter of next year. So next year the division would start in a deep hole. They would be scrambling all year to trying to dig themselves out of that hole, with no guarantees that they could pull it off. It was just postponing the problem. In addition, Bill reminded the team that this program would be very expensive. On top of the overtime expense that would have to be incurred in the production areas, the program would greatly increase SPD's accounts receivable. CFC was currently paying about 12% on its lines of credit, so this increase in working capital would be quite expensive for the corporation.

But Priscilla cut Bill short. She reminded him that CFC did not allocate interest expenses to SPD, so she was not particularly concerned about the corporation's increased borrowing costs. She was more worried with her superiors' negative reactions if she did not make this year's profit plan than she was about their reactions to her allowing the receivables' balance to increase in the early part of the year. And while she acknowledged that they might be creating a problem for next year, she suggested it would be best to worry about that problem when, and if, it became real.

With no other options on the table to solve the current year's budget problem, the SPD managers decided, unanimously, to implement what they called the "Sales Acceleration Program."

This case was prepared by Professor Kenneth A. Merchant.

CASE STUDY
The Expiring Software License

On September 30, Jianxin (Jimmy) Wu, manager of the Information Systems Department for Southwest Industries (SWI), was in panic mode. SWI was a medium-size manufacturer of portable shelters, tents, and awnings. Jimmy was panicking because the company's Citrix software had just died. Because of his oversight, an invoice had not been paid, and the SWI's license to use the software had expired.

Jimmy knew that something had to be done very quickly. Many of the company's information systems users, who were situated at three different locations, relied heavily on the Citrix software. All of SWI's applications ran under Citrix. The Citrix software gave all employees access to the SWI applications they needed no matter where they were, as long as they had access to the Internet. The Citrix license renewal would cost $3,600, but going through the purchasing department to get a requisition issued would take several days. The users could not be without the Citrix capability for that long.

Then Jimmy thought about using his purchasing card. The card, which worked like a credit card, was intended for small purchases, not including travel, hotels, or food. SWI issued the card to some of its key personnel to avoid the costs of processing the paperwork required for many small, incidental purchases. The company only had to make one single payment to the credit card company, and the credit card company did all the processing.

The maximums placed on Jimmy's card were $2,000 for any single purchase, and $5,000 per month. Jimmy knew that these limits were strictly enforced. Personnel in the accounting department scanned the bills monthly looking for violations. But Jimmy thought that he could get Citrix to split the bill in two, and then the accounting department personnel would not raise any objections.

With no other apparent options at hand, Jimmy decided to try to use his card to renew the license. The Citrix salesman agreed to charge the card in two transactions of $1,800 each. The license was renewed quickly, and few of SWI's Citrix users were ever aware that there had been a problem.

This case was prepared by Professors Kenneth A. Merchant and Leslie R. Porter.

CASE STUDY
Wired, PLC

Don Sperber was the CFO of Wired, PLC, the Thailand subsidiary of Wunderphone, a large telecommunications company based in Germany. Wunderphone owned 70% of Wired. The other 30% was listed on the Bangkok stock exchange and publicly traded. Wunderphone was also a public company and was listed on the NYSE as well as the Frankfurt stock exchange. Wired was a relatively small subsidiary of Wunderphone in terms of revenue. With US$2 billion in annual revenue, it represented less than 4% of Wunderphone's total revenue, which exceeded US$50 billion annually. However, Wired was important to Wunderphone because it operated in an emerging market and had better earnings growth potential than many of Wunderphone's larger subsidiaries, which operated in more mature and more saturated markets.

Don, a US native, enjoyed living in Thailand and working at Wired:

> **My job was exciting. Here I was, early in my career, the CFO of a public company. I loved the people I worked with. And the telephone industry was dynamic. I had the opportunity to head up major initiatives, such as debt refinancings and mergers and acquisitions. It was fun.**

Don was also involved in investor relations and spoke to equity analysts from investment firms regularly about Wired's financial position and earnings trends.

Early in 2012, Don was working on the acquisition of a wholesaler that bought cell phone minutes from Wired and resold them to the public for a profit. Wired management planned to integrate vertically so that the company could bring the retail margins from cell phone minute sales onto its income statement. This acquisition would increase Wired's revenues by approximately 6%.

Steven Sarit, Wired's CEO, asked Don to have Wunderphone's capital expenditure committee review the acquisition proposal. This committee met often, and it typically approved expenditures with minimal administrative effort. If approved, then this transaction could be accounted for as an ordinary capital expenditure.

Don argued, however, that the proposed transaction was a business acquisition. The proposal should be submitted to the mergers and acquisitions committee and, if approved, it should be accounted for as a business combination. He explained that the accounting rule governing the transaction was IFRS Statement #3. If Wired had planned to buy an asset that did not constitute a business, such as a customer list, the asset purchase could be treated as a capital expenditure. But Wired planned to purchase assets constituting an entire operating business. Further, the acquisition contract specified that the transaction was to be a "business" (rather than an asset) acquisition. If the transaction were to be treated as an asset purchase, under Thai law Wired would not assume the acquired company's customer contracts. Continuing the target's customer relationships after the acquisition was critical to the success of the transaction.

But Steven was not ready to give up. He escalated the issue to Philip Behrens, Wunderphone's CFO. Philip explained to Don that it was better for the company to record the purchase as an ordinary capital expenditure. The cell phone market had matured, and the industry's growth rate had stalled. Industry analysts were scrutinizing earnings growth and trends closely. Earnings derived from a business combination would not be valued as favorably as "organic" growth. Philip naturally wanted earnings to be valued as favorably as possible. He told Don and Steven to find a way to "get this done as an asset purchase."

Steven was agreeable, but Don pushed back, arguing that the transaction involved an earn-out, which he maintained was almost impossible to reconcile with an asset purchase. Still, Philip was sure that with a little creativity, Don could work out a way to account for the transaction as a capital expenditure. The conversation became quite heated, and both parties finally agreed to get an opinion from the accounting firm hired to assist in the due diligence on the transaction. This firm agreed with Don, that they could not credibly classify the transaction as an ordinary capital expenditure.

While he was relaying this news to Philip, Don thought that he would add a practical constraint to the argument. He told Philip that the finite amount of money in the capital expenditure budget had either already been spent or earmarked for real and necessary projects.

Philip thought that the budget issue was a minor hurdle that could be overcome and, unconvinced about Don's conclusion about the accounting treatment, Philip took the accounting issue to the independent accounting firm hired to audit Wired's financial statements. The partner at the auditing firm consulted his firm's technical experts, and they concluded that the issue was "gray." Since the acquisition target was reselling minutes they had bought directly from Wired, they thought that perhaps a theoretical argument could be made to support an asset purchase.

That was all Philip needed to hear. Philip told Don that the debate was over. Philip was Don's superior, and he wanted the transaction treated as a capital expenditure. He expected Don to figure out how to make it happen.

Don was at a crossroads. He believed the accounting treatment was just plain wrong, and he did not want any part of it, but his signature was required on the financial statements. He wondered if he could get in trouble if the accounting was done as Philip wanted. He was also worried that Philip would fire him if he continued to challenge him or if he refused to comply.

This case was prepared by Research Assistant Michelle Spaulding and Professor Kenneth A. Merchant.

CASE STUDY
Mean Screens USA, Inc.

Donna Stoneman was the CFO of Mean Screens USA, Inc. Headquartered in Seattle, Mean Screens USA was the sales and distribution division of Mean Screens, Ltd., a privately owned Chinese company founded in 2007 that produced inexpensive LCD screens manufactured in China for sale in the US market. By 2009, rapid growth necessitated a significant infusion of capital. A decision was made to spin off a portion of Mean Screens USA in an IPO.

Since the beginning of the company, Donna had worked together closely with Thomas Yee, Mean Screens USA's division president, to build the division. She continued to play an instrumental role in the company's subsidiary initial public offering (IPO) process, travelling around the world to describe the investment opportunity to potential investors.

However, Donna was troubled by the earnings projections that Thomas had instructed her to present. She felt the forecast was extremely aggressive. She was uncomfortable presenting numbers that she did not think were realistic, and she was concerned that there would be a backlash from investors if Mean Screens USA failed to meet the projections. She expressed her concerns to Thomas who agreed to lower the projections slightly, but he still kept them well above what Donna believed was realistic.

Donna decided to accept Thomas's revised numbers. She felt she had done all she could, as she explained:

> **The earnings projections were not officially under my jurisdiction. I really had no authority to change them. And by definition forecasts are not black and white. It was possible that Thomas's numbers were on target.**

A successful IPO was launched in May 2009, and Mean Screens USA, Inc. was listed on NASDAQ. Mean Screens, Ltd. retained 51% of the public shares of the subsidiary. In the first fiscal year, however, as Donna had feared, Mean Screens USA missed its profit projections by more than 30%.

Thomas was alarmed by the shortfall. He asked Donna what they could do to increase earnings so that the company's financial statements would mirror the forecasts, and in this way pacify the new investors. His first idea was to deem some receivables as obviously collectable to avoid setting up reserves. Donna thought that the idea was ridiculous. She told Thomas that she could not falsify financial statements for any reason. Thomas insisted that there was no falsification. The setting up of reserves was a gray area of accounting that depended on judgment. Donna explained that the company was now public, and the audits would be more thorough. The auditors would surely insist on the establishment of reserves for uncollectible receivables.

Thomas was persuaded that perhaps this plan was impractical, so he suggested another possibility. He suggested that they postpone the writing off of inventory that had likely become obsolete. Again, Donna rebuffed his request.

Thomas was becoming increasingly angry at Donna's refusal to work with him. He threatened her bonus and even told her that the long-term viability of the company was at stake. Donna was sickened. She began to wonder if Thomas was naïve or just unethical. She was unwilling to sacrifice her own principles and integrity, not to mention her CPA license, but she began to fear that her job was on the line.

The reserves issues had still not been resolved when Thomas came to Donna with a third request that he hoped would appease his most important investors. He wanted to ask the parent company for favorable transfer prices for a year or so in order to shift some earnings from the parent company to the subsidiary. He would agree to reverse the favorability of the transfer prices when Mean Screens USA could afford higher prices.

Donna did not even know how to respond. Was Thomas this ignorant about financial reporting requirements, or was he just basically dishonest? If the latter, she had to consider whether or not she wanted to work for someone who was capable of such dishonesty. But she was also worried about her bonus and, ultimately, her job. She had a family to support, and with the country in a severe recession, it would probably not be easy to find another job.

Tis case was prepared by Research Assistant Michelle Spaulding and Professor Kenneth A. Merchant.

CASE STUDY
Lernout & Hauspie Speech Products

> This case is a tragic blow not just for Belgium but also for all of Europe. It shows how badly we need much greater transparency and a sense of corporate governance. For too long, banks and businesses did not feel they should be held accountable to shareholders. That has to change.[1]
>
> *Philippe De Buck, Executive Director, Belgium Federation of Industries*

Mr. De Buck was referring to the demise of Lernout & Hauspie Speech Products (L&H), which had been considered a world leader in speech-recognition technology and one of Belgium's most promising hi-tech companies. The company declared bankruptcy in October 2001 after the discovery of a massive accounting fraud that implicated many L&H managers, including the top management team. Like many others, Mr. De Buck wondered how this could have happened and what might be done to avoid other scandals like this in the future.

[1] William Drozdiak, "Lost in the Translation; Voice-Recognition Firm's Failure Holds Painful Lesson for Europeans," *The Washington Post* (December 17, 2000).

The company

The entrepreneurs

L&H was founded in 1987 when Jo Lernout, then a sales executive with the Belgian arm of Wang Laboratories, Inc., grew intrigued by an early Wang voice-mail system. The system was not selling well because many Europeans still had rotary phones and could not use them to select amongst the voice-mail choices. Mr. Lernout's idea was to create software that allowed users to make voice-mail selections by speaking into the phone. He set up a company to commercialize speech technology. Pol Hauspie, who owned a small firm that made accounting software, joined him. Belgium seemed a good location from which to operate the company because the country was home to many software engineers fluent in multiple languages. The two partners based their company in Ieper, Belgium.

To finance the business, Mr. Hauspie sold his software firm and Mr. Lernout sold his house. Mr. Lernout, an ebullient chain-smoker with ruddy cheeks and a mop of sandy-blond hair, recalled in an interview that convincing his wife "was the hardest road show I've had."[2] The company barely survived several early financial crises. At one point, it couldn't make the payroll and bailiffs came to seize property, Mr. Lernout recalled. But he seemed to thrive on crisis. One of his favorite sayings is, "The grass is always greener on the other edge of the precipice."[3]

Starting any new company is difficult, but two factors helped L&H survive in its early years. The first was Belgium's national pride. Like much of Europe, Belgium envied America's great hi-tech engine of wealth. And now here were two guys with ambitions to turn a rural corner of Flanders into a Silicon Valley of language technology. In L&H's early years, Flanders, Belgium's Dutch-speaking region, formed a tax-exempt zone in Ieper – which gradually became known as the "Flanders Language Valley" – and showered L&H with research grants. The Flanders regional government became a major L&H investor through a venture capital arm. During one of L&H's cash crunches, it guaranteed 75% of a bank loan to the company. "Without that," Mr. Lernout says, "we would have gone broke."[4] Stefaan Top, a Belgian venture capitalist, says the combination of ambitious entrepreneurs and a government that sorely wanted "a local tech champion was a combustible mix – it was dangerous."[5]

The second was a series of complex financing plans dreamed up by Mr. Hauspie. The taciturn former tax accountant set up an intricate holding-company structure that let the founders retain control while selling various minority interests. Devising such structures is "Pol's forte," Mr. Lernout says. "He's very creative. Legally it's all right, and it helps you survive."[6]

In late 1995, the company went public with a listing on the NASDAQ Stock Exchange, even though it had never been profitable and had just a few million dollars in annual revenue. As with many hi-tech firms, the hope lay in a glittering future. "Natural speech interface is the next technology wave," one securities analyst wrote, "a potential multimillion dollar market."[7] L&H's managers dreamed of creating software that would let computers effortlessly understand human speech, speak back, and translate among the world's tongues.

The company seemed to face many challenges. Technical development was painstakingly slow, as the systems had to cope with many different accents and speech patterns, not to mention the need to sort out homonyms such as "wait" and "weight." And industry demand was sluggish. Many rivals struggled. One, Kurzweil Applied Intelligence, Inc., in Massachusetts, imploded after auditors found that its managers had faked a large proportion of the company's sales. Another Massachusetts rival, Dragon Systems, Inc., eked out only slow growth in the mid-1990s. At L&H, however, sales quadrupled in 1996 to $31 million. Though some small acquisitions produced part of the growth, L&H seemed to be relying on sales to customers with which it had financial ties.

Over the years, many of L&H's customers received investments from Flanders Language Valley Fund (FLV Fund), a venture-capital pool that Mr. Lernout and Mr. Hauspie helped create the year L&H went public. Mr. Lernout and Mr. Hauspie were directors of the fund's management arm until 1997, and even afterward they maintained considerable sway over its affairs. Michael Faherty, a former L&H salesman in the United States, says he and others were encouraged to

[2] Mark Maremont, Jesse Eisinger, and John Carreyrou, "Muffled Voice: How High-Tech Dream at Lernout & Hauspie Crumbled in Scandal," *The Wall Street Journal* (December 7, 2000), p. A1.

[3] Ibid.

[4] Ibid.

[5] Ibid.

[6] Ibid.

[7] Ibid.

refer potential customers who were cash-poor to the FLV Fund. "If FLV invests $1 million in the customer," he says, "it was understood that we'd get about $300,000" [in the form of license fees paid by that customer to L&H].[8] Though the FLV Fund denied financial links between L&H and FLV, the close dealings between the two were evident to some informed parties from the start. In 1995, for example, FLV took a 49% stake in the Belgian unit of Quarterdeck Corp., a high-flying California software company. This Belgian unit became L&H's largest customer, accounting for 30% of revenue that year, and Quarterdeck in California accounted for another 6.5% of L&H's sales.[9]

The CEO

In late 1996, Gaston Bastiaens was hired as L&H's president and CEO. Mr. Bastiaens was an engineer who led the failed Newton project at Apple Computer, Inc. But he flourished at L&H. Around the time Mr. Bastiaens joined L&H, the company discovered a new and unusual source of revenue: its own research-and-development needs. This required an intricate accounting maneuver, one that L&H had continued to lean on throughout its tenure as a public company. L&H knew it was trailing competitors in developing software to recognize words spoken at an ordinary clip. "If we didn't catch up, we were cooked," Mr. Lernout recalled in an interview. "But we couldn't catch up, because we didn't have enough R&D dollars."[10]

The solution was to start a company and have it contract with L&H to develop the software. L&H said it gathered outside investors to fund the start-up, called Dictation Consortium, NV. But L&H employees wrote its business plan and did the software work under contract. When the software was finished, L&H had an option to buy the Dictation Consortium at a profit to the investors. The arrangement ensured that L&H could claim to be growing at a rapid pace. Dictation Consortium provided L&H with $26.6 million in revenue in 1996 and 1997, about one-quarter of its 1996 sales and 19% of its 1997 sales. Since Dictation Consortium bore the R&D costs, they didn't burden L&H's bottom line. In 1998, L&H bought Dictation Consortium for $40 million, gaining control of the software it so badly wanted. Since Dictation Consortium had few assets and almost the entire price represented goodwill, it could be amortized over seven years, further shielding L&H's bottom line.

Buoyed by such deals and a spate of fresh acquisitions, L&H's revenue mushroomed to $211.16 million in 1998, more than double 1997's. The stock soared. Mr. Lernout and Mr. Hauspie became entrepreneurial celebrities, Belgium's answer to Microsoft's Bill Gates and Paul Allen.

With the stock price up, Mr. Bastiaens bought technology leaders such as Kurzweil Technologies, Inc., a speech-recognition company in Wellesley Hills, Massachusetts, and Mendez Translation Group of Brussels, Belgium. In 1997, a year after he came on board, Mr. Bastiaens landed an important investor: Bill Gates. Microsoft invested $45 million in L&H, ending up with an 8% stake. The early Microsoft investment gave L&H much needed credibility and revenues. In 1999, Intel invested $30 million in L&H and formed a venture with it to develop e-commerce and telecommunications products.

Though all seemed well from the outside, internally there were continuing glitches with L&H's technology. A 1998 presentation Mr. Lernout gave to French executives in Paris turned into a debacle when the software failed to recognize many words, an L&H insider recalled. "The bottom line was that the technology wasn't ready and the market wasn't ready," this person says, "but management had to deliver every quarter."[11] Under Mr. Bastiaens, it did. L&H kept reporting growth. Its sales rose 63% in 1999 to $344 million. Its Asian sales exploded to more than $150 million from less than $10 million in 1998. In March 1998, its stock hit $72.50, up 2,500% from its initial offering price four and a half years earlier.[12]

However, financial analysts had been suspicious of L&H's financial results as far back as 1997. In February 1997, Lehman Brothers' Brian Skiba issued a report, claiming that L&H's growth in the United States and Europe was much lower than investors had assumed, and that the company was not coming clean. Mr. Bastiaens denied it, but in a conference call, he refused to give a geographic breakdown of sales.[13] Still, investors ignored financial analysts' warnings and applauded the year-2000 acquisitions of Dictaphone, based in Stratford, Connecticut, and Dragon Systems, of Newton, Massachusetts. The future did, indeed, look bright. L&H seemed to have

[8] Ibid.

[9] Ibid.

[10] Ibid.

[11] Ibid.

[12] Ibid.

[13] Ibid.

a lock on some of the best speech-recognition software, and the company was powerfully positioned as the Web migrated into phones and cars, where people would talk to machines and machines would talk back. At the time, Mr. Bastiaens assured anybody who would listen, "This market is going to explode."[14] With the purchase of the company's two main US rivals, L&H was suddenly a software company with $1 billion in annual sales, and it was poised to follow SAP and Nokia Corp. into Europe's technology elite.

The Dictaphone purchase, however, meant more than half of L&H's business was in the United States. This obliged the company to file detailed accounts with the SEC. Analysts learned that sales in Korea had soared from a mere $97,000 in 1998 to $58.9 million in the first quarter of 2000, some 52% of the total sales of the company. Suspecting an attempt to pump up results, investors began to dump the stock in 2000.[15]

The Wall Street Journal report

In August 2000, *The Wall Street Journal* reported that some Korean companies L&H described as customers denied doing business with it, while some others said they had bought less than L&H said they had:

> In all, the *Journal* contacted 18 of about 30 companies claimed by L&H as customers. Three of the companies said they weren't, in fact, L&H customers ... Three more companies said their purchases from L&H over the past three quarters were smaller than figures provided by Mr. Bastiaens or Sam Cho, vice president of L&H Korea. One additional company said it is in a joint business with L&H that produces considerably less revenue than L&H claims. Officials from an eighth company initially said it had formed a joint venture with L&H and that the joint venture, not the company itself, had purchased products from L&H...
>
> Of the other 10 companies, three confirmed they were customers but wouldn't give the size or timing of their purchases. Officials at another six confirmed total purchases totaling $450,000 to $5.5 million in the period since [September 1999]. One company says it signed a $10 million contract with L&H and paid in May 2000.
>
> All told, of the 12 companies that responded to inquiries about their purchases from L&H in the period since [September 1999], the revenue tallied roughly $32 million. From all of its customers in Korea, in 1999 and the first quarter of 2000, L&H posted $121.8 million of Korea sales, and it had said that it expected second-quarter revenue from that country to exceed the first quarter's $58.9 million.[16]

L&H responded with a statement saying that comments attributed to L&H customers were "misquoted or factually incorrect" and that other information in the article was "distorted."[17] To buttress its case, L&H commissioned a mid-year audit by KPMG.

After the Korea scandal broke, Mr. Bastiaens rushed to restore confidence. He contacted several of the Korean customers interviewed for the *Journal* story, and they publicly said they were misquoted. A trip to Korea was arranged for two financial analysts, both of whom were impressed with the company's business there. "I met customers and saw L&H products really being used," says Kurt Janssens of KBC Securities in Brussels.[18] Most important, Mr. Bastiaens asked for the KPMG special audit. "He wouldn't be so stupid as to ask for an audit if he had something to hide," says Pierre-Paul Verelst, an analyst at Brussels brokers Vermeulen Raemdonck.[19]

By this time, founders Lernout and Hauspie thought Mr. Bastiaens had become a liability. On August 25, 2000, he was replaced with John Duerden, a British-born US citizen who had worked at Xerox Corp. and Reebok International, Ltd., before running Dictaphone.[20] In November 2000, L&H admitted for the first time that "mistakes and irregularities" had slipped into the annual accounts. Mr. Hauspie resigned as an officer, and in March 2001, Mr. Lernout was dismissed. In November 2000, L&H filed for bankruptcy protection.[21]

Discovery of a massive fraud

In January 2001, Philippe Bodson replaced Mr. Duerden as L&H's chief executive, and PricewaterhouseCoopers

[14] William Echikson and Ihlwan Moon, "How to Spook Investors," *Business Week* (September 18, 2000), pp. 69–72.

[15] Ibid.

[16] Mark Maremont, Jesse Eisinger, and Meeyoung Song, "Tech Firm's Korean Growth Raises Eyebrows," *The Wall Street Journal* (August 8, 2000), p. C1.

[17] Mark Maremont, "Lernout & Hauspie Shares Fall 19% as It Attacks Article," *The Wall Street Journal* (August 9, 2000), p. A16.

[18] Echikson and Moon, "How to Spook Investors."

[19] Ibid.

[20] Ibid.

[21] "Dossier Lernout en Hauspie," *De Standaard* (January 2011), online at www.standaard.be.

(PwC) was brought in for an investigation. The PwC report was released on April 6, 2001. It revealed that 70% of the nearly $160 million in sales booked by L&H's Korean unit between September 1999 and June 2000 were fictitious. In an effort to earn rich bonuses tied to sales targets, the Korean unit's managers developed highly sophisticated schemes to fool L&H's regular auditor, KPMG International. One especially egregious method involved funneling bank loans through third parties to make it look as though customers had paid when in fact they had not.

L&H's new chief executive, Philippe Bodson, said that upon learning of PwC's findings he "was very impressed by the level of sophistication" of the fraud and "the amount of imagination that went into it."[22]

To fool auditors, L&H Korea used two types of schemes. The first involved factoring unpaid receivables to banks to obtain cash up front. Side letters that were concealed from KPMG gave the banks the right to take the money back if they couldn't collect from L&H Korea's customers. Hence, the factoring agreements amounted to little more than loans.

The second, more creative scheme was set in motion after auditors questioned why L&H Korea wasn't collecting more of its overdue bills from customers. L&H Korea told many customers to transfer their contracts to third parties. The third parties then took out bank loans, for which L&H Korea provided collateral, and then "paid" the overdue bills to L&H Korea using the borrowed money. The upshot is that L&H Korea was paying itself. When the contracts were later cancelled, L&H Korea paid "penalties" to the customers and the third parties to compensate them "for the inconvenience of dealing with the auditors."[23]

The probe also found that the bulk of L&H Korea's sales came from contracts signed at the end of quarters, so managers could meet ambitious quarterly sales targets and receive large bonuses. For instance, 90% of the revenue recorded by L&H Korea in the second quarter of 2000 was booked in 30 deals signed in the final nine days of the quarter. But L&H Korea was forced to subsequently cancel 21 of those contracts because the customers – most of them tiny start-ups – didn't have the means to pay.

The fraud appears to have begun in earnest when L&H bought a small Korean firm called Bumil Information & Communication Co. in September 1999 and put Bumil's management, headed by Joo Chul Seo, in charge of L&H Korea. L&H Korea, which had been reporting negligible sales until then, recorded nearly $160 million in license revenue between the time Bumil was acquired and June 30, 2000. Mr. Seo made $25 million from the sale of Bumil to L&H and earned another $25 million in bonuses for meeting sales targets while at the head of L&H Korea.[24]

Where were the auditors?

In the aftermath of the accounting scandal at L&H, angry investors turned their gaze on KPMG International, the giant accounting firm that audited L&H's books and gave the company clean opinions in 1998 and 1999. KPMG also gave a clean 1999 opinion regarding the accounting for L&H's South Korean operations, where sales had grown improbably to $62.8 million from just $245,000 in the previous year. Michael G. Lange, a partner at a Boston law firm that was leading one of the shareholder lawsuits seeking class-action status against L&H, said that the accounting irregularities at L&H "were so pervasive and included so many aspects of the business" that "there had to be red flags" that KPMG auditors missed.[25]

KPMG, in its defense, accused the former top management of L&H of signing off on revenue over-inflation tactics, of lying about key business structures within the company, of influencing others to give false information to KPMG auditors, and of orchestrating a campaign to minimize their involvement in the events that had led to the calamitous downfall of the company. In April 2001, a few hours before the release of an abridged version of PwC's report, KPMG filed a lawsuit against L&H's former management in a Belgian court. The complaint alleged that former senior L&H executives "deliberately" provided "false or incomplete information" to KPMG and conspired to obstruct the firm's audits.[26]

In its complaint, KPMG said that L&H's former top management "was fully aware and actively involved in the irregularities and that these people have wittingly given false information to KPMG."[27] KPMG alleged that

[22] John Carreyrou, "Lernout Unit Book Fictitious Sales, Says Probe," *The Wall Street Journal* (April 9, 2001), p. B2.

[23] Ibid.

[24] Ibid. According to the PwC report, investigators have been unable to track down Mr. Seo since L&H fired him in November 2000. Mr. Bodson said Mr. Seo was last spotted in China.

[25] Mark Maremont, "KPMG, Former Auditor of L&H, May Draw Investor Ire," *The Wall Street Journal* (January 18, 2001).

[26] Robert Conlin, "KPMG: Lernout & Hauspie Top Management Lied," www.CRMDaily.com (May 11, 2001).

[27] Ibid.

Mr. Hauspie was implicated in a scheme to illegally raise money for a fund he participated in. The scheme involved a complex web of Korean banks, L&H subsidiaries, and Joo Chul Seo, the company's former head of Korean operations. KPMG also alleged that the company co-founder Jo Lernout, at the very least, participated in the campaign to conceal information from its auditors.

In addition, KPMG commented that the practice of inflating revenues was a common one at L&H. "Afterwards [referring to a period in 1999] it appeared that the antedating of contracts to increase the turnover of the relevant quarter was common practice," said the KPMG report.[28] "The company, on a regular basis, increased its turnover of a particular year or quarter by means of various kinds of irregularities."[29]

The aftermath

In April 2001, Mr. Lernout and Mr. Hauspie were arrested in Belgium and placed under custody for nine weeks on charges of forgery and market manipulation. The arrests came after a new round of audits uncovered an additional $96 million in fictitious sales, which brought the tally of fake sales from early 1998 to mid-2000 to $373 million, or 45% of reported revenue.[30]

L&H was declared bankrupt in October 2001 after the commercial court in Belgium rejected the company's request for bankruptcy protection. US-based Scansoft purchased the speech technology and kept some L&H personnel in employ, but the name L&H was axed.

KPMG and its Belgian affiliate settled a lawsuit for $115 million brought against it by shareholders. KPMG stated that they settled to avoid a protracted legal trial, and maintained that they had acted appropriately in their audit of L&H at all times.[31] The court hearings started in May 2007 against Mr. Lernout, Mr. Hauspie, and 19 others, including former senior corporate and subsidiary managers. In September 2010, a Belgian court found the company's co-founders, Mr. Hauspie and Mr. Lernout, as well as former CEO Bastiaens and another senior manager, guilty on various charges relating to financial fraud, including falsification of annual accounts, forgery, and market manipulation. Mr. Hauspie, Mr. Lernout, and the senior manager were all sentenced to five years in prison, of which three years effective and two years probationary. Mr. Bastiaens was sentenced to two years effective imprisonment. Under Belgian prison terms, however, they were unlikely to have to clock any jail time.[32]

While KPMG was cleared, its partner responsible for the accounting supervision at L&H was fined €2,478.93. The court declared that the professional fault held against him was not intentional, but he was found guilty of negligence.[33]

These charges, however, covered the criminal liability of those involved in the company's fraud only. The question of compensation was to be tackled in pending civil proceedings, which were slated to start by the end of 2011.[34]

[28] Ibid.

[29] Ibid.

[30] John Carreyrou, "Lernout & Hauspie Figures Are Arrested," *The Wall Street Journal* (April 30, 2001).

[31] Mark Maremont, "KPMG to Settle Suit over Audit of Lernout," *The Wall Street Journal* (October 8, 2004).

[32] Charles Forelle, "Lernout Founders Guilty of Fraud," *The Wall Street Journal* (September 2, 2010), p. B1; Mark Eeckhaut, "L&H-Toplui Wellicht Nooit Naar de Cel," *De Standaard* (September 22, 2010); www.deminor.com (September 23, 2010).

[33] www.deminor.com (September 23, 2010).

[34] Ibid.

Appendix 1 Appendix to the August 8, 2000 *The Wall Street Journal* report

A Kick from Korea		
Lernout & Hauspie's sales by region or country for the three months ended March 31, 2000 ($000). The company's South Korean business soared after an acquisition in September 1999.		
	1999	2000
Europe (excluding Belgium)	22,435	19,748
United States	20,154	19,939
Belgium	14,739	9,178
Singapore	10,430	501
Other Far East	2,853	2,396
South Korea	97	58,932

Source: *The Wall Street Journal* (August 8, 2000), p. C1.

Appendix 2 10 steps to Chapter 11

A Lernout & Hauspie chronology	
June 30, 2000	L&H reveals that nearly all of its overall growth in recent quarters came from South Korea and Singaporean business.
Aug. 8, 2000	*The Wall Street Journal* reports that some Korean customers claimed by Lernout & Hauspie do no business with the company. Others said their purchases were smaller than L&H reported.
Aug. 25, 2000	CEO Gaston Bastiaens steps down; former Dictaphone CEO John Duerden steps in. The company's stock falls 9% to $31.
Sept. 20, 2000	The SEC launches a formal investigation of L&H's accounting practices.
Sept. 22, 2000	*The Wall Street Journal* reveals that 25% of L&H's 1999 revenue came from start-up companies that it helped create.
Sept. 25, 2000	Europe's Easdaq launches a formal investigation into L&H.
Sept. 27, 2000	L&H issues a profit warning for the third quarter.
Nov. 9, 2000	L&H says it will revise financial statements for 1998, 1999, and the first half of 2000 to make up for past accounting "errors and irregularities"; co-chairmen Jo Lernout and Pol Hauspie resign their executive posts; trading of L&H stock is suspended.
Nov. 16, 2000	The company's accounting firm KPMG International withdraws its audits of 1998 and 1999 results.
Nov. 29, 2000	L&H files for Chapter 11 bankruptcy protection along with its Dictaphone unit, after $100 million is discovered missing in the firm's South Korean unit.

Source: *The Wall Street Journal* (November 30, 2000), p. A3.

Appendix 3 Accounting for auditing problems – recent large settlements paid by auditors

Auditor	Company audited	Year	Allegations	Settlement amount ($ millions)
Ernst & Young	Cendant	1999	Inflated revenue, understated expenses	$335
Ernst & Young	Informix	1999	Inflated revenue	$34
Arthur Anderson	Waste Management	1998	Overstated assets and other accounting problems	$75
Coopers & Lybrand*	Centennial Technologies	1998	Bogus sales	$20

*Now part of PwC.
Source: *The Wall Street Journal* (January 18, 2001), p. C1.

This case was prepared by Professors Kenneth A. Merchant, Wim A. Van der Stede, and research assistant Xiaoling (Clara) Chen. The case was revised with the help of Professor Martine Cools.

CASE STUDY
Ethics@Cisco

> A strong commitment to ethics is critical to our long-term success as a company. The message for each employee is clear: any success that is not achieved ethically is no success at all. At Cisco, we hold ourselves to the highest ethical standards, and we will not tolerate anything less.
>
> —*John Chambers, CEO, Cisco Systems, Inc.*[1]

Cisco Systems, Inc. (Cisco), a large, multinational networking technology company headquartered in San Jose, California, won multiple awards for its ethics program, known internally as Ethics@Cisco. For example, as it had each year since 2008, Cisco was honored in 2012 as one of the World's Most Ethical (WME) companies by the Ethisphere Institute, an international think-tank dedicated to the creation, advancement and sharing of best practices in business ethics and corporate social responsibility. The Ethisphere website explained that the WME designation "recognizes companies that truly go beyond making statements about doing business "ethically" and translate those words into action." Similarly, Cisco's program was named in both 2009 and 2010 by *Corporate Secretary* magazine as the "The Best Overall Governance, Compliance and Ethics Program" in the large-capitalizationcompany category.

Phil Roush (Vice President – Governance, Risk and Controls) explained that Cisco's ethics program

> **... not only demonstrates the Company's effort to be a good corporate citizen, it also provides a competitive advantage. It signals to potential customers how seriously we take ethical conduct, and it translates into how Cisco approaches all of our internal and external interactions.**

[1] http://www.cisco.com/web/about/citizenship/ethics/index.html

Company background

Cisco was the world leader in networking technology for the Internet. The company designed, manufactured, and marketed a broad range of Internet Protocol (IP)-based networking and other related products and services primarily to customers in the communications and information technology industries located around the world. The company's diverse product portfolio included storage, web conferencing, routing, digital video, wireless, switching, and voice technology. Cisco had a significant market share in each of its product categories. The company distributed and sold its products through a large network of channel partners and resellers.

Cisco was founded in 1984 by a married couple, two scientists from Stanford who invented the multi-protocol router so they could send messages to each other from separate office buildings. Ever since then, the company's focus had been "connecting lives." The company's stock became publicly traded on February 16, 1990.

Cisco's growth was rapid. In fiscal year 2011 (ended July 31, 2011), the Company had annual revenues exceeding $43 billion (see Exhibit 1), and it employed approximately 65,000 people in almost 500 different offices in over 165 countries. Cisco spent over $5 billion – roughly 13% of its revenue – on R&D. Its workforce was highly educated: one-third of the employees were engineers, and another onethird were in sales.

The Cisco culture emphasized open communication, innovation, and trust. Phil Roush explained,

> **When I joined Cisco, many executives indicated that this is a company that is built for speed and that we have a high-trust environment. John Chambers [CEO] often refers to the employees as being part of the Cisco family. But in a family of 65,000 co-workers you're going to have some issues arise. You better have some rules, and some accountability, that help facilitate the speed and high-trust environment. Proper governance processes can actually assist a company in moving more rapidly.**

Ethics@Cisco

The Ethics@Cisco program was designed to ensure that all Cisco employees adhere to a very high standard of business and professional conduct. Cisco had only one ethics policy that was applied globally.

The company, however, faced some quite unique and difficult challenges in attaining its compliance and ethics goals. Cisco was a large company with a relatively young workforce with many different cultural norms and languages. Cisco continued to grow rapidly, and much of the company's growth came from acquisitions. Since 2000, Cisco had acquired 105 companies, all of which had to be assimilated into Cisco's culture and processes. As a hi-tech firm operating in a dynamic environment, the company had a "freewheeling spirit" that sometimes needs to be reined in. Perhaps not surprising for a networking company, 85% of Cisco's workforce worked "virtually," regularly working from home or on the road. And much of the Cisco business was sold through channel partners in over 180 countries who were regularly presented with a wide variety of gift giving and receiving conundrums on a regular basis. The partners also presented a challenge in that their actions were more difficult to monitor than were those of employees.

The three core elements of the Ethics@Cisco program were (1) a Code of Business Conduct (COBC); (2) an extensive employee awareness, training and certification program; and (3) internal investigations. These are described below.

Cisco's ethics program was over 15 years old. Previously the program was administered by the Human Resources (HR) department. In 2005, a dedicated, three-person Ethics Office assumed responsibility for this function. In 2012, this office was composed of senior manager Jeremy Wilson, program manager Joel Mark, and marketing communications manager Ruth Savolaine. The Ethics Office's mandate was to drive awareness of Cisco's ethics policies.

In its early years, the Ethics Office reported to Human Resources. In 2008, it became part of Governance, Risk and Controls, which reported to the Finance department. In August 2012, the Ethics Office was moved to become part of a new centralized Compliance department reporting to Cisco's General Counsel. According to Cisco's benchmarking studies, this latest reporting structure was consistent with best practices across publicly held companies. The General Counsel had the oversight on driving the ethics programs and policies.

The Code of Business Conduct

The cornerstone of the Ethics@Cisco program was a Code of Business Conduct (COBC).[2] The COBC was designed to help every Cisco employee understand how to make ethical decisions that were consistent with the company's values as well as with applicable laws and regulations. The core company values underlying the COBC were integrity, respect, open communication, social responsibility, diversity, and empowerment.

Among the specific topics covered in the COBC were sharing concerns, respecting others, using resources responsibly, avoiding conflicts of interest, understanding gift and entertainment policies, protecting Cisco assets, following the law, and adhering to internal financial and accounting policies. The COBC included some specific policies, such as the requirement of pre-approvals for the giving and receiving of gifts valued at US$100 or more, but it also included many more general decision-making principles. The wording in the COBC was mostly general, but it was supported by detailed policies in some areas of activity. The COBC was published in English and 12 other languages.

To make the COBC easily understandable, with low use of jargon, the key principles necessary to demonstrate the company's commitment to integrity were summarized in the COBC in ten "I statements" (see Exhibit 2).

The COBC also included an ethics decision tree that was designed to help employees think through difficult ethical issues (see Exhibit 3). The decision tree helped employees find laws and policies that might apply in the situation they are facing and to ask important questions and/or seek guidance from managers, the Ethics Office, or the legal department before they take action.

Financial employees had an additional Code of Conduct that included more specific financial reporting guidelines and a requirement to be a role model of ethical behavior (see Exhibit 4).

Prior to 2007, the COBC was a static document written in legal terms that could be challenging for a non-lawyer to understand and apply to real life situations. Between 2009 and 2011, the ethics team completely overhauled the document with the goal of bringing the COBC "to life." They shortened it, made it more readable, and added more color and graphics. They replaced legal jargon with text written at a more elementary reading level. They also included practical "what if" examples to make the COBC more relevant to the issues employees faced every day (see Exhibit 5).

In 2012, the Ethics Office team brought the COBC onto an online portal and made it into an interactive eBook, with pages that appeared to turn, intuitive pop-ups, embedded videos, and purposeful animation. Employees were able to ask questions and engage in a two-way dialogue with experts on the ethics team. They could also disclose gifts and potential conflicts of interest using an online reporting tool. The team hoped that with these changes employees would view the COBC as a practical reference tool that could be used whenever they faced an ethical issue.

Ethics awareness, training, and certifications

Cisco used many methods to help ensure that all employees (and partners and agents) were aware of, and understood, the COBC. These included electronic display boards, websites, a management portal, a discussion forum, and various forms of training.

Most companies' ethics training is live, but most all of Cisco's training was done online, due to the company's highly virtual workforce. Annually, employees were required to go through interactive training that took about 20 minutes. They answered ethics questions using the COBC as a reference and received instant feedback if they answered assessment questions incorrectly. The training also included two brief videos that used humor to communicate two key messages: (1) the COBC is robust and easy to use, and (2) there are several ways to get ethics assistance at Cisco. These videos were shown with subtitles for employees whose native language was not English.

In 2012, the videos received positive employee feedback, with 87% of employees reporting that the videos enhanced or somewhat enhanced their understanding of the COBC and the resources available to them. One of the training videos, an ethical-mindset video aimed at new managers, won a Gold Medal in 2011 from the New York Festivals International TV & Film Awards® in the category Internal Use Training Videos.

On request, the Ethics Office developed targeted, job-specific training for individual business units. For example, a five-minute anti-bribery video was produced specifically for employees who interacted with government officials. Other targeted training videos focused on conflicts of interest, ethics for sales associates, new hires, new managers, antitrust, and anticorruption. These topic- and role-specific videos were very targeted and short, because it was known that most

[2] The complete document is shown at http://files.shareholder.com/downloads/CSCO/2047645290x0x563236/f8c558b8-11dd-4f32-89cd-7b9da77895d1/Cisco_Code_of_Business_Conduct_FY12.pdf

people's attention spans are short, and resistance to training increases sharply after about 10 minutes. The videos explained where additional information could be found. The Ethics Office also ran special awareness campaigns, such as an end-of year campaign reiterating the company's gift policies.

Annually, all Cisco employees were required to certify that they had reviewed, understood, and agreed to abide by the COBC. Certification was a condition of employment, and failure to sign the certification document provided grounds for corrective action, up to and including termination of employment where permissible by law.

Before 2009, the COBC certification was not mandatory. In 2009, however, the ethics team obtained a mandate from the Audit Committee to have all employees sign the certification annually going forward. Personnel in the Ethics Office and department managers used Ethics Connect, a proprietary tool that provided instruction, created records of employees who had signed the COBC and agreed to abide by it, and sent targeted email messages to those who had not yet fulfilled their certification obligation. After a five-week campaign ending in early June, COBC certifications were received from 100% of Cisco employees.

Initially there was some resistance to the certification requirement, not because the content of the COBC was objectionable, but because the idea of something being mandatory was a cultural shift. This was one of Cisco's first global mandates. Jeremy Wilson (Ethics Office manager) explained that, "The last one percent (600–700 people) created a bit of a challenge as they were not familiar with the process."

Tone from the top also played a large part in driving ethical behavior. Prat Bhatt (Corporate Controller) reflected,

> Training has a positive impact, but the effects are short-lived. Some people think that training is a check-the-box exercise that everyone has to do. Controls and processes can be circumvented. If you don't have the tone and culture to support ethics, with public hangings for wrong-doing and recognition for doing the right things, the rest is superficial. What I've found unique about Cisco is the culture and the tone, which is set from all the way at the top with the CEO.

Internal investigations

A 24-person Internal Investigation group also reported to the Compliance department. Sixteen members of the group were investigators responsible for investigating employee fraud. These investigators had backgrounds in accounting, auditing, and law enforcement. The cases they investigated ranged from expense fraud to deal manipulation, diversion, and corruption.

Approximately 100 investigation cases were open in a typical quarter, but on average only about 10% of those cases were actionable. Many cases were initiated in the employee online incident reporting tool. Some reports were malicious, such as occurred when vendors "threw mud at each other." Sometimes reports were valid, but they were not supported with strong enough evidence to warrant disciplinary action. In those instances, the internal investigations personnel attempted to get more details from the whistle-blower. Even if they were not able to prove wrongdoing, they could use the incident to evaluate and perhaps improve internal controls. Many cases were identified as a result of Sarbanes-Oxley (SOX) control testing. For example, one expense audit uncovered a $200,000 expense fraud scheme that was successfully investigated. An employee had found a way to log in as her boss to approve her own expense reimbursements.

When Internal Investigations were able to substantiate that there had been an infraction of the COBC or local laws, employees were disciplined. If theft was involved, Internal Investigations made an attempt to obtain voluntary restitution from the employee rather than involving outside law enforcement. Depending on the infraction, employees could be terminated or receive verbal and written warnings. In order to avoid unfair termination lawsuits in the United States, Cisco employees were only terminated if they violated a specific, published policy. Written warnings provided useful documentation should a second infraction be committed. In other countries it could be even more difficult to legally terminate employees because of strong labor protection laws. Typically, very few employees were terminated for policy violations or other improper actions. All incidences of fraud were reported to the Audit Committee, even if the infraction was committed by someone below the Vice President level.

Sarbanes-Oxley compliance

Cisco relied on strong SOX compliance teams to ensure ethical behavior in some important areas of activity, including financial reporting, antitrust, bribery, and insider trading. Kristin White headed a team of 18 professionals responsible for financial and business process controls, reporting to Prat Bhatt (Corporate

Controller). The Information Technology (IT) organization owned its own SOX controls and had its own 18-member team, reporting to the Chief Information Officer (CIO) of IT/Risk Management. These teams were responsible for understanding the US SOX requirements and SOX-like requirements in other countries, and they strove to maintain consistent controls internationally. These teams partnered heavily, and monitored the effectiveness of almost 1,000 key controls. In addition to performing standard SOX duties, the SOX compliance teams made sure that controls were in place in companies that Cisco acquired, in new project venture areas, and in international expansion initiatives.

According to Kristin, working on SOX was rewarding at Cisco because of the company's strong ethics. "Cisco has embraced SOX compliance," she explained. "It's part of the DNA of the company, and it is highly visible." According to Kristin, John Chambers, the CEO of Cisco, took controls very seriously. He was committed to spending quality time reviewing the information and processes to ensure accuracy and adequacy of their public reporting, and he expected his senior managers to highlight issues and let him know if they had any concerns.

Operation of the System

The Ethics@Cisco system encouraged employees who were unsure as to how to act in any circumstance to escalate questions to higher levels of management without fear of repercussion. Difficult ethical questions were often escalated all the way to the General Counsel. Van Dang (Senior Vice President, Regulatory and Compliance), explained:

> **There is an escalation process. People opinion shop. If they don't get the answer they like and they don't agree, they go up the chain and appeal to higher levels of management because lower level managers are less likely to take risks. In some companies if you escalate you lose your job, but not at Cisco. It's a very open company. Employees can go directly to a higher-level manager.**

If employees did not want to get talk with someone in the management hierarchy to get advice on an ethical issue and/or to report a potential problem, they had several other options. They could correspond with personnel in the Ethics Office or use an email alias that sent a message directly to the Audit Committee of the Board of Directors, an anonymous online incident reporting tool, or a multilingual telephone hotline. More than 84% of reports and questions came through email or online sources, with more than 60% being handled by the Ethics Office directly.

The number of ethics calls made at Cisco had been fairly stable at approximately 100–150 calls per quarter. The total number of calls was aligned with those at other hi-tech companies, at less than 1% of the workforce size. Of the calls made, more raised questions (60%) than allegations (40%). The top five call categories were:

1. Policy Issues (policy interpretation/application)
2. Employee Relations (harassment, intimidation, discrimination)
3. Conflicts of Interest – general
4. Conflicts of Interest – gifts
5. Conflicts of Interest – personal relationships

Financial reporting breaches were alleged less than once per year.

The ethical issues raised tended to spike around times of training, annual certification, and special events. For example, Cisco was the technology sponsor of the 2012 London Olympics, so Cisco employees fielded many requests for tickets or special event access, and questions arose. After the ethics team introduced a video showing an employee reporting a second job, there was a 700% increase in disclosures of outside jobs. Cisco had also developed an online disclosure tool to automate the exception-approval process.

The COBC made it very clear that retaliation against whistle-blowers would not be tolerated. The culture at Cisco also supported open discussion, as evidenced by the fact that 82% of people who reported ethics violations or asked ethics questions chose to identify themselves.

Cisco was trying to automate some portions of the control processes. For example, they were considering flagging some forms of reimbursements for an automatic review.

An example: gift acceptances

Most of the guidelines in the COBC were derived from Cisco's values. It was not possible to provide specific rules for every type of situation that might be encountered. The guidelines needed to be interpreted and applied to the specific situations faced. Acceptable behaviors in areas presenting frequent or serious risks were spelled out in more detail.

For example, employees' accepting gifts from suppliers was a common risk area. It was known that in the past some employees had not reported gifts they had received, and some had even sold them on eBay.

The gift-acceptance guidelines explained in the COBC were:

- Have no obligation or expectations (stated or implied)
- Be made openly
- Have reasonable value, defined as less than US$100 per source per year
- Conform to the giver/reviewer's rules
- Be appropriate, legal and accurately documented.

Any exception had to be approved in writing by the Ethics Office. Some gifts could require approvals from a Vice President in the relevant organization or a Human Resources (HR) manager.

With inquiries about gift acceptances, there were three plausible answers: (1) acceptable, (2) unacceptable (the gift must be returned), or (3) the gift may be accepted, but the employee must turn it over to Cisco for public display or donation. Those approving the requests tried to adhere to the COBC guidelines while also trying to allow for reasonable special circumstances.

The multiple channels for grants of exceptions made ethics feedback easily accessible, but could occasionally cause confusion. In one instance, a supplier gave a watch to 200 people in the same department. Only six of those 200 employees asked permission to accept the gift, but because some asked the Ethics Office, some asked HR, and some asked the Vice President in their own organization, they received three different answers. When these discrepancies were discovered, follow-up meetings were held to provide a better understanding of the process and to implement a uniform approach.

Evidence of effectiveness

Annually, Cisco conducted an internal survey of all 65,000+ employees to get feedback on key aspects of the Company's culture. Results from the 2012 survey reflected well on the ethics program (see Exhibit 6). Among other things, on this survey 91% of the employees reported that they were confident that Cisco took ethical business concerns seriously.

Overall, there was a strong sense of pride in Cisco's ethics program. Phil Roush observed:

> It starts with the well-defined "tone at the top" on the expectations of ethical conduct of Cisco's employee base. From those expectations, it cascades out to all of the Company on our approach to business and how we deal with the inevitable questions and unique situations that arise when you do business in over 100 countries.
>
> We still have opportunities to raise awareness across a very diverse and geographically dispersed population. Plus, there are always new questions and concerns that do come up, for example how to consistently address the various forms of social media that are prevalent today. We want our employees to embrace the new technology that is available, but do it in a way that does not expose the Company to negative consequences.
>
> If we do meet with the SEC [U.S. Securities and Exchange Commission] or the DOJ [U.S. Department of Justice], and they inquire about Cisco's Ethics program – we feel that there are many proof points of how seriously we take the expectations on ethical behavior. No company will likely be perfect, but I am confident Cisco has a strong process.

Exhibit 1 Cisco Systems, Inc., income statements (2010–2012)

(In millions, except per-share amounts)	FY 2012 Year Ended July 28, 2012	FY2011 Year Ended July 30, 2011	FY2010 Year Ended July 31, 2010
NET SALES:			
Product	$ 36,326	$ 34,526	$ 32,420
Service	9,735	8,692	7,620
Total net sales	46,061	43,218	40,040
COST OF SALES:			
Product (a), (b) & (d)	14,505	13,647	11,620
Service (a)	3,347	3,035	2,777
Total cost of sales (a), (b) & (d)	17,852	16,682	14,397
GROSS MARGIN (a), (b) & (d)	28,209	26,536	25,643
OPERATING EXPENSES:			
Research and development (a) & (c)	5,488	5,823	5,273
Sales and marketing (a) & (c)	9,647	9,812	8,782
General and administrative (a) & (c)	2,322	1,908	1,933
Amortization of purchased intagible assets (b)	383	520	491
Restructuring and other charges (d)	304	799	
Total operating expenses (a)-(d)	18,144	18,862	16,479
OPERATING INCOME (a) - (d)	10,065	7,674	9,164
Interest income	650	641	635
Interest expense	(596)	(628)	(623)
Other income (loss), net	40	138	239
Interest and other income, net	94	151	251
INCOME BEFORE PROVISION FOR INCOME TAXES (a) - (d)	10,159	7,825	9,415
Provision for income taxes (e)	2,118	1,335	1,648
NET INCOME (a) - (e)	$ 8,041	$ 6,490	$ 7,767
Net income per share:			
Basic (a) - (e)	$ 1.50	$ 1.17	$ 1.36
Diluted (a) - (e)	$ 1.49	$ 1.17	$ 1.33
Shares used in pre-share calculation:			
Basic	5,370	5,529	5,732
Diluted	5,404	5,563	5,848
Cash dividends declared per common share	$ 0.28	$ 0.12	

Exhibit 2 Ten "I" statements in the Code of Business Conduct

Cisco "DNA"	• I am ethical • I know the Code
Values/Integrity	• I share my concerns • I respect others
Four Core Ethics Areas	• I use resources responsibly • I avoid conflicts of interest • I understand policies related to gifts and entertainment • I protect what is ours
Foundational	• I follow the law • I am accurate and ethical with our finances

Exhibit 3 Ethics decision tree

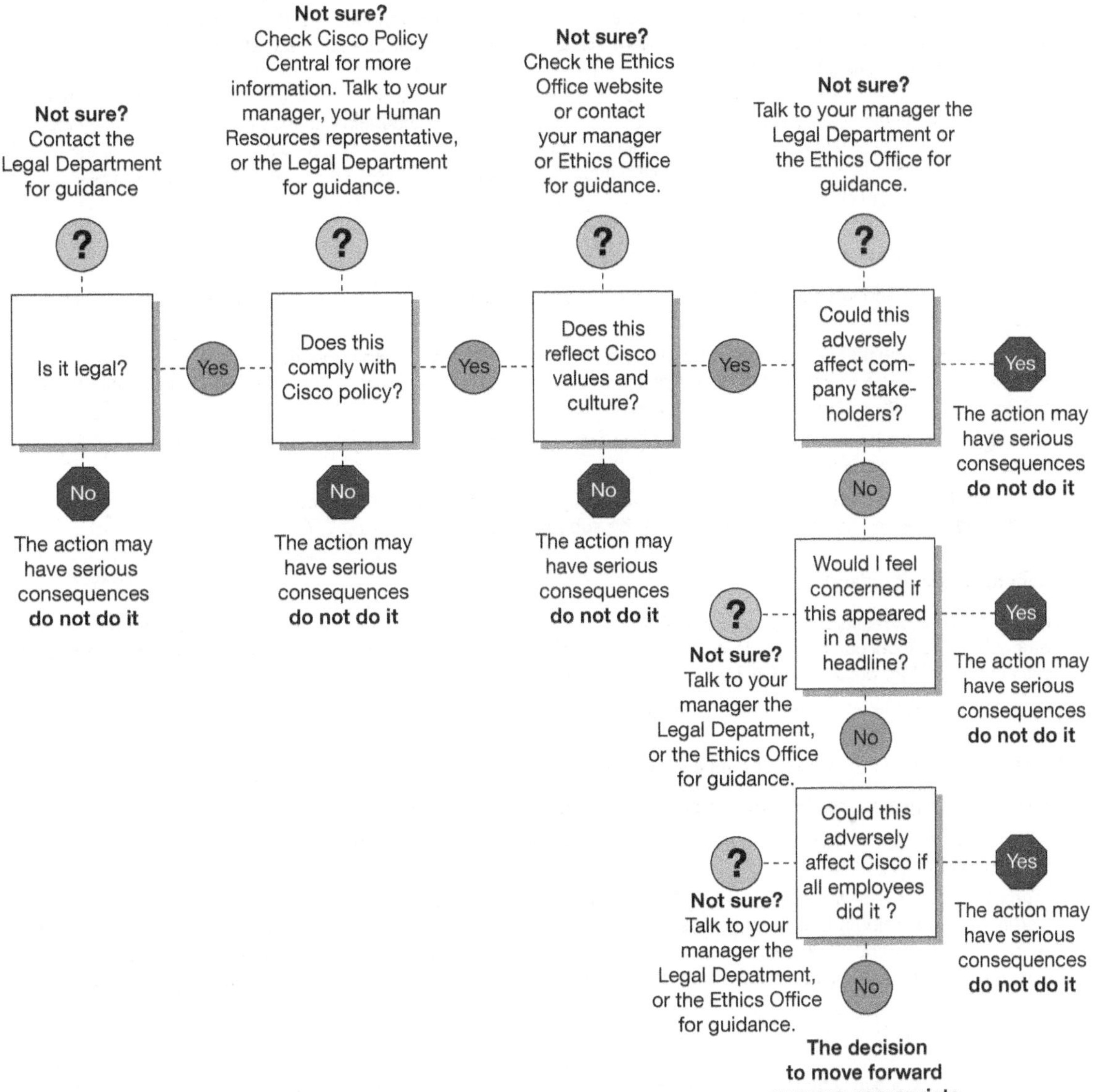

Source: Cisco Code of Business Conduct

Exhibit 4 Special ethical obligations for employees with financial reporting responsibilities (revised Feb 2012)

All employees have an obligation to abide by the Cisco Code of Business Conduct (COBC), which includes adhering to all internal financial and accounting policies. There are also special ethical obligations that apply to employees with financial reporting responsibilities.

Our Chief Executive Officer (CEO), Chief Financial Officer (CFO) and Finance Department employees must adhere to the following principles and also foster a culture throughout the company that helps to ensure the fair and timely reporting of Cisco's financial results and condition. Because of their special role, the CEO, CFO and all members of the Cisco Finance Department are bound by the following Financial Officer Code of Ethics, and each agrees that he or she will, in his or her capacity as an employee of Cisco:

Integrity and Compliance

1. Act with honesty and integrity, avoiding actual or apparent conflicts of interest in personal and professional relationships
2. Provide information that is accurate, complete, objective, relevant, timely, and understandable to help ensure full, fair, accurate, timely, and understandable disclosure in reports and documents that Cisco files with, or submits to, governmental agencies and in other public communications
3. Comply with the rules and regulations of federal, state, provincial, and local governments, and of other appropriate private and public regulatory agencies
4. Act in good faith, responsibly, and with due care, competence, and diligence, without misrepresenting material facts or allowing his or her independent judgment to be subordinated

Protecting Information and Assets

5. Respect the confidentiality of information acquired in the course of doing his or her work, except when authorized or otherwise legally obligated to disclose information; confidential information acquired in the course of his or her work will not be used for personal advantage
6. Achieve responsible use of and control over all assets and resources employed by or entrusted to Cisco

Personal Accountability and Serving as a Role Model

7. Share knowledge and maintain skills important and relevant to stakeholders' needs
8. Proactively promote and be an example of ethical behavior as a responsible partner among peers, in the work environment and the community
9. Promptly report to the Vice President of Governance, Risk, and Controls (GRC) and/or the Chairman of the Audit Committee any conduct that he or she believes to be a violation of law or business ethics or of any provision of the COBC, including transactions or relationships that reasonably could be expected to give rise to such a conflict. (Note: It is against Cisco policy to retaliate against an employee for good-faith reporting of any potential or actual Code violations.)

Violations

Violations of the Financial Officer Code of Ethics are serious. A violation, including a failure to report potential violations by others, will be viewed as a severe disciplinary matter and may result in personnel action, including termination of employment.

Stakeholder and Public Reporting

If anyone believes that a violation of the Financial Officer Code of Ethics has occurred, please contact Cisco Legal, the Ethics Office, or the Audit Committee of the Board of Directors.

The Financial Officer Code of Ethics is complementary to the Cisco Code of Business Conduct and does not replace responsibilities all employees have under the Cisco Code of Business Conduct and Cisco policies.

Exhibit 5 Examples provided in the COBC

What If...

What if my manager is exerting pressure to "make the numbers work?"

Your responsibility is to be honest and accurate. If you feel pressured to do otherwise, contact the Ethics Office, Legal or Human Resources. You may also contact the Audit Committee of our Board of Directors. If you feel uncomfortable going through internal channels, you can call the multilingual Cisco Ethics Line anytime, night or day, worldwide.

What if I am asked to book a deal without a purchase order?

All deals must be accompanied by a purchase order from a customer. These sales records ensure that our finances are accurate and protect the company from fraud. Refer to the Global Bookings Policy for the required elements of a purchase order.

What if I am asked to create a deal to sell a product or service to a reseller who I know is not authorized to receive it, or for purposes other than for which a specific discount was given for competitive reasons?

This could result in product diversion to the "grey market" causing damage to Cisco's legitimate resellers and possible service abuse. If you believe that product/service is being sold outside the approved deal, contact Brand Protection and the Ethics Office.

What if I am asked to structure a deal where the customer can choose only high discounted products?

Such a situation is called "cherry picking" and is not allowed. This can also result in discount leakage and potential product diversion. Refer to your Finance controller or the Ethics Office if you believe you are being asked to structure a deal in this way.

Source: Cisco Code of Business Conduct

Exhibit 6 Results of pulse survey

Year	# of Employee Respondents	Q: I can voice my opinion without fear of retaliation	Q: I know where to go to report ethics concern or question	Q: I have confidence Cisco takes ethical business concerns seriously	Q: My mgt team sets a good example of values, culture and COBC
2012	53,306	78%	87%	91%	84%
2011	55,158	75%	83%	90%	81%
2010	50,490	72%	83%	91%	81%
2009	47,245	65%	79%	92%	84%

This case was prepared by Research Assistant Michelle Spaulding and Professors Kenneth A. Merchant, Leslie Porter, and Lori Smith.

SECTION VI

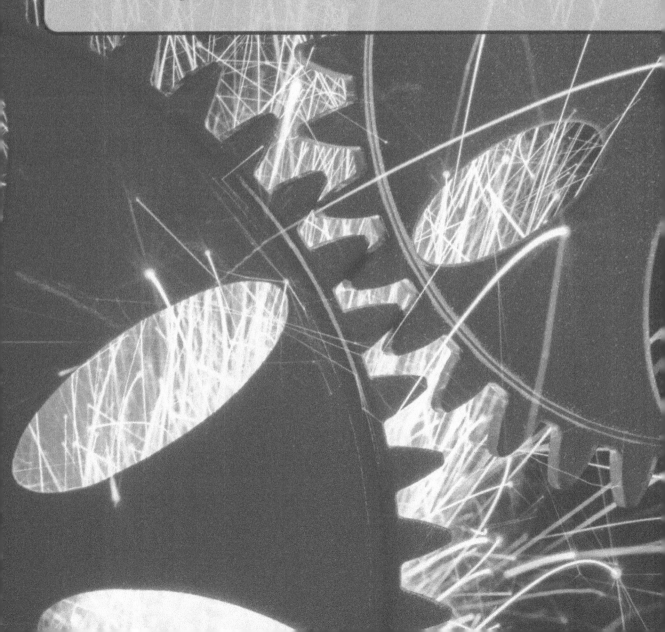

Management Control when Financial Results Are Not the Primary Consideration

CHAPTER 16
Management Control in Not-for-profit Organizations

In this final section and chapter, we turn our attention to management control systems (MCSs) in *organizations where financial results are not the primary consideration or objective*. As we discussed earlier, particularly in Chapter 10, the primary objective of *for-profit* organizations is to maximize shareholder (or owner) value – *firm value*, for short – subject to some constraints, such as compliance with laws and adequate concern for employees, customers, and other stakeholders. In such *for-profit* organizations – which are typically referred to as *firms*, *companies*, or *businesses* in a conversational sense, or *corporations* in a legal sense – profit is rarely the only, but it is still the dominant or primary, objective.

Many corporations actively engage with a broad range of stakeholders; set targets related to environmental and social goals such as carbon reduction or investments in education or community development;[1] and report on these activities under the rubric of *sustainability* or *corporate social responsibility* (CSR),[2] or in the form of *triple bottom lines* (related to their economic, natural, and social capitals),[3] either as stand-alone reports or as part of their annual reports. An often-cited corporation in this regard is Unilever.[4] Several studies have examined whether CSR or similarly termed *non-profit* initiatives by corporations are substantive or symbolic,[5] lead to real beneficial environmental or social impacts,[6] and/or add value for the firm.[7] Studies to date have provided early and mixed evidence. But regardless of the strength or balance of evidence, corporations have responsibilities to a broader set of stakeholders, including employees, customers, suppliers, and society, and fulfilling these stakeholder responsibilities is both important and requires tradeoffs. It also requires effective MCSs that properly *align* every employee's actions and behaviors with the intended balance of the firm's objectives with proper accountability, as we have discussed throughout this text. The following quote pertinently summarizes the changed focus in recent years in this regard:

> While in the past it was common for CSR to reside in the purviews of marketing or communications, this is beginning to shift amid criticism that companies might be using their initiatives as a form of 'greenwashing', i.e., to build reputations not backed by substance. Instead companies are moving toward business units having ownership [over sustainability] at the highest levels, with sustainability teams providing guidance and support. [. . .] Companies at the forefront in this area integrate ESG [environmental, social, governance] considerations into overall strategic planning and identify a few areas that are the most relevant to the long-term health of the business. [. . .] They voluntarily issue sustainability reports using the Global Reporting initiative framework.[8]

However, not every corporation is willing or intends to subjugate every social or environmental objective to the primacy of economic value maximization. That is, some organizations "do good" for reasons stronger than what is justified by "doing well" or for reasons other than that "it pays" or "is profitable" to do good. Here are two examples:

> Messrs. Gilbert and Houlahan, friends as undergraduates at Stanford University, helped start the basketball shoe and apparel company AND1. As the company grew, co-founder Gilbert and president Houlahan emphasized financial success along with corporate social responsibility: the firm paid employees respectable wages, donated 5% of profits to charity, and made sure factories in China met their standards. The company was generating close to $250 million in annual revenue when it was sold to American Sporting Goods in 2005. *Gilbert and Houlahan were personally enriched – but disempowered: they watched their effort to create an innovative business model vanish under the new owners.* [. . .] Gilbert and Houlahan were not alone. Ben & Jerry's, known for its ice cream and its social responsibility, was sold to Unilever in 2000. Although some board members had misgivings, *they voted for the sale because Vermont, like most states, required the board to act in the interest of the shareholders, which meant accepting Unilever's exceptionally lucrative offer.*[9]

To protect their "triple bottom line" of combined financial, social, and environmental performance even as companies switch owners and/or struggle with shareholder pressure for returns or dividends, some firms have changed their standard incorporation as a *C corporation* to a "benefit" incorporation or *B corporation*. As opposed to standard corporations, the crucial feature of B corporations is that they allow their boards and managers to sacrifice shareholder value for the greater good. However, this requires that they specify their social and environmental goals in their corporation's bylaws; that they have their sustainability and corporate social responsibility strategies certified as credible and transparent by a third party (such as B Lab);[10] and that they publish an annual report that measures how well these goals are being met. When they meet these criteria, B corporations are allowed to shift their firm's emphasis from shareholder value to stakeholder value.[11] When this is the case, and for such an alternative pursuit of objectives to be effective, these firms' MCSs will have to be aligned accordingly to create the desired goal congruence.

But B corporations, while still *corporations*, may exhibit certain characteristics that place different demands on the standard MCSs as discussed throughout this text. For example, they may attract, or wish to attract, employees that are motivated to work for organizations that especially care about social and environmental causes and impacts. They are also likely to have unique and strong organizational cultures (see Chapter 3). These and other characteristics are likely to have implications for the types of incentives, say, that these firms put in place (as discussed in Chapter 9).

Corporations, B corporations, and not-for-profits

In *C corporations*, *investor-owned corporations*, or *corporations* for short, the owners (shareholders) of the firm exercise control by voting for its directors who provide control over management (as discussed in Chapter 13). The residual earnings of the firm belong to the owners and management is responsible primarily to the shareholders for the profitability of the firm. In other words, the primary goal of investor-owned corporations is shareholder value maximization. In contrast, and as explained in the last section, *benefit (B) corporations* allow boards and managers to sacrifice shareholder value for the greater good under specified conditions (as listed earlier, but which vary by jurisdiction of incorporation). A third broad type of corporation is often referred to as *not-for-profits* (sometimes also called *tax-exempt corporations*). *Not-for-profits* differ principally from investor-owned corporations because they have no shareholders, and no single individual or body of individuals has ownership rights to the firm's residual earnings or exercises control of the firm. Instead, control is exercised by what is typically called a *board of trustees*. The primary goal of most not-for-profit organizations generally takes the form of a mission, such as to offer education, pursue cancer research, or provide healthcare.

In prior chapters, we focused on MCSs in for-profit organizations (*corporations* of the first type, but also by reasonable extension to *benefit corporations* of the second type, which adopt a more explicit focus or priority on supplemental social and environmental objectives). Not-for-profit organizations, however, deserve some specific focus because they are in some ways quite different from the other types of corporations. They are also important. Not-for-profit organizations fill a number of important societal roles. All (or virtually all) government organizations, museums, labor unions, and political and fraternal organizations are not-for-profit organizations. Many, if not most, schools and hospitals are, too. Collectively, not-for-profit organizations comprise a considerable portion of the economy the world over.

That said, even not-for-profit organizations have many things in common with their for-profit brethren. Most of them provide services (or, less commonly, products) and have to compete with other organizations to be the chosen provider. They have professional managers who develop objectives, strategies, and budgets. Many not-for-profit organizations are large, and so their managers delegate authority and hold their employees accountable in specific performance areas. But not-for-profit organizations' MCS alternatives and challenges are often quite different from those faced by "pure-play" or "benefit-type" for-profit organizations. This chapter focuses on these differences. Despite the finer-grained distinctions among corporations that we have elaborated above, we do this under the broad rubric of differences between "for profit" and "not-for-profit" organizations in the next section. But the lines can be blurry, as the following quote suggests:

> **Companies recognize that aligning with non-profit organizations makes good business sense, particularly those non-profits with goals of economic prosperity, social well-being and environmental protection.[12]**

Key differences between for-profit and not-for-profit organizations

Ironically perhaps, but strictly speaking, the defining difference between for-profit and not-for-profit organizations does not lie in how much profit they can generate, but instead in how it is distributed. A not-for-profit organization's profit cannot be paid out to the owners or anyone else associated with the organization; instead, it must be dedicated to the purpose or mission of the organization. Hence, the major defining characteristic of a not-for-profit organization is the *organization's purpose*; its mission or goal. As such, a not-for-profit organization typically has as its primary purpose to provide some kind of public service. The not-for-profit category, however, includes a large and diverse set of organizations, so the types of services provided vary widely. They can be charitable, religious, scientific, educational, or even political. Included in the not-for-profit category are *governmental organizations* and their various institutions, authorities, agencies, and programs. Also included are a large number of private organizations operated for *public benefit*, such as museums, hospitals, universities, and schools. Some not-for-profit organizations, such as religious organizations and charitable foundations, serve various *private benefit* purposes. And some, such as cooperatives, and labor, fraternal, trade, and homeowners' associations, are operated for the *mutual benefit* of their members.

Unlike for-profit organizations, not-for-profit organizations do not have any outside equity interest. However, like all corporations, they do have to generate revenues to fund their operations. Many not-for-profit organizations earn revenues by selling services or products, such as by charging admissions to see a museum exhibit or a theatrical presentation. Others are given money by a third party in exchange for providing their service. For example, a government entity might provide a school a fee or subsidy for every child enrolled in the school. However, money (that is, cash flows and surpluses of revenues over expenses) is only a constraint; it is not normally the overriding goal of a not-for-profit organization. That said, some entities within not-for-profit organizations do have goals to earn profits. For example, governments run lotteries, hospitals run gift shops, and universities sell books, meals, and athletic tickets. In earning their profits, they compete with for-profit organizations. But whatever profits they earn are meant to be used to further the organizations' overriding purpose and not to be paid out to the owners or anyone else associated with the organization. Not-for-profit organizations do not pay dividends. All the resources they acquire must be used to further the organizations' primary purpose.

In sum, all not-for-profit organizations have in common the above *purpose* and *profit distribution* (ownership) characteristics. However, although not-for-profit organizations are sometimes perceived as relatively small organizations working for altruistic purposes, such as food banks and community charities staffed by a small number of dedicated managers and unpaid volunteers, being not-for-profit does not necessarily mean being small or being charitable. Many not-for-profit organizations are major employers, and a large part of the revenues they generate is needed to cover their expenses or overheads. In other words, besides the not-for-profit purpose and the lack of shareholders, it is often difficult to tell some of these not-for-profit organizations from their for-profit counterparts. Nevertheless, not-for-profit organizations tend to have some characteristics with MCS implications that apply to them far more than they apply to for-profit organizations. The following sections describe these characteristics and their MCS implications.

Goal ambiguity and conflict

As discussed at the outset in Chapter 1, MCSs should be designed to enhance the probability that the organization's goals will be achieved, and assessments about MCS effectiveness should be predicated upon judgments of the likelihood (or degree of) goal achievement, regardless of whether these goals are primarily financial or a balance of financial, social, and environmental goals. Although put somewhat simplistically, goal clarity exists, or is more likely to be commonly shared or understood, in for-profit organizations by virtue of their value-maximizing mantra.[13] Furthermore, although again somewhat simplified, managers of publicly traded firms particularly can obtain timely feedback on their goal achievement by monitoring their firm's stock performance and comparing it to that of their competitors and the overall market.

This level of goal clarity, however, does usually not exist in not-for-profit organizations. Many *constituents* typically have an interest in the organization, its goals, and its performance. But these constituents often do not agree; their values and interests conflict. The board of trustees of a museum may perceive their primary goal as to inspire a diverse public through the collection and exhibition of works of art of the highest quality. Other stakeholders, such as the local community and government officials, might be more interested in having the museum present exhibitions aimed at children. Still others, such as religious leaders, might be most concerned about whether or not the art is, in their view, socially and morally acceptable. Resolving these conflicts and differences in perceptions requires unique decision-making mechanisms.

Conflict is also inevitable in government organizations. These organizations are often directed from a number of sources, including the executive, legislative, and judicial branches of government and, possibly, from various levels of government, some national and some local. Law enforcement agencies, for example, have to respond to laws passed and rulings made by all levels of legislatures. Their funding, and their consequent accountability, may also be to multiple authorities. Managers of these organizations face external pressure because the press and public in democratic societies have access to considerable information. Some key officials may face reelection pressures and, thus, feel a need to please campaign donors and the public at large. This diffusion of direction and potential conflict greatly complicates management generally, and goal congruence in management control specifically. At best, it causes goal complexity; at worst, it triggers conflict and confusion.

As an example, consider the Los Angeles Department of Water and Power (DWP), which had long regarded itself more as a private company than as the city's public utility, causing a chronic source of tension with city officials. The city controller had repeatedly accused DWP officials of wasting hundreds of thousands of dollars on community events, staff perks, and parties. DWP officials, however, rebutted that the city bureaucrats just misapprehend the organization, which at the time raised more than $3 billion in revenues for the city annually. "The parties may seem like unnecessary expenses, but they are essential for supporting the community and boosting the morale of DWP employees," said the utility's general manager. Separately, the state attorney general filed a claim against the DWP, alleging that the utility gouged customers during the energy crisis by overcharging ratepayers, to which DWP management retorted that "[we] sold power for less than the maximum but more than the cost." Although the DWP received high marks for power quality and reliability, customer service, price, value, and company image in an independent survey by J.D. Power and Associates, city officials and DWP management seemed to disagree about the organization's goals. "They are neither behaving like a Fortune 500 company that is accountable to shareholders, nor like a public utility that is accountable to ratepayers," said the city controller. But even city officials disagree, as one councilman said: "[The DWP] takes in $3 billion worth of people's money; who wouldn't expect them to give some back to the community."[14]

Without clarity as to what goals should be achieved and how tradeoffs among them should be made, it is difficult, if not impossible, to judge how well the organization's control system or, indeed, how well the management team, is performing. Some not-for-profit organizations struggle with these fundamental problems of goal ambiguity and conflict. That said, goal ambiguity must be addressed to establish an effective control system while reflecting the legal, regulatory, policy, and resource environment within which the particular not-for-profit organization operates.

Difficulty in measuring and rewarding performance

Even if not-for-profit organizations' goals are quite clear, managers of these organizations typically do not have at their disposal any single, quantitative bottom-line performance indicator, like the profit and return measures available to corporations. The degree of achievement of the organization's overall goals – the provision of quality service to its constituents – usually cannot be measured accurately in financial terms. If a hospital's goal is to save lives or to cure the ill, for example, how is success to be judged? By time to attend to patients brought to the emergency ward? By survival rates among emergency patients experiencing heart attacks? By cancer cure rates? Or should there be measures of prevention rather than merely curing? And how about costs? And because one focus can be compromised in favor of another (e.g. cost vs. care; prevention vs. cure), what importance is to be placed on each? The following excerpt illustrates the multitude of problems faced when trying to adequately measure performance in a healthcare setting:

> The Obama administration's goal of tying more Medicare payments to the quality – not the quantity – of health care by 2018 has intensified the debate over how "quality" is defined and measured. Many doctors, hospitals, insurers and cost experts want to move away from the myriad quality metrics that largely measure process – from tracking the percentage of patients with chest pain who get an aspirin in the ER, to how hair is removed from ambulatory surgery patients – toward broader measures that assess patient outcomes. [. . .] The National Quality Forum, a non-profit advisory group, submitted recommendations on 199 performance measures for Health and Human Services to consider in 20 federal programs. [. . .] Many of the proposals seek to better align measures among various programs and replace narrow process-oriented metrics with "measures that matter." For example, one recommendation would replace individual metrics on the percentage of diabetes patients who get foot exams, eye exams and blood-glucose checks with a composite measure of diabetes control. [. . .] But some doctors question whether the measures that exist can adequately measure quality. [. . .] And there is little agreement on what measures matter most or are more likely to produce good value. "In many areas of patient care, we do not yet have high-quality outcome measures with enough specificity to drive improvement" [and] "measurement fatigue is a real problem in hospitals" [where] "to me, the only metric that matters is, did you get better?" [. . .] Some have complained that safety-net hospitals are being unfairly penalized because low-income patients may be sicker and have less support at home, which would require adjusting some measures for socioeconomic status. And, [. . .] there are problems capturing data across multiple hospitals: "When people have surgical complications, they are unlikely to go back to the same hospital where they had the surgery done."[15]

Without a small set of quantifiable performance indicators, the tasks of management and management control become more complicated. It becomes difficult to:

- Measure organizational performance in light of the overall goals and, thus, to use results controls (including performance-based incentives) even at a broader organizational level;
- Analyze the benefits of alternative investments or courses of action;
- Decentralize the organization and hold entity managers accountable for specific areas of performance that relate exactly or precisely enough to the organization's overriding goal; and,
- Compare the performances of entities performing dissimilar activities.

Boards of trustees or overseers and regulators of not-for-profit organizations have been especially criticized for their lack of focus or inability to measure performance. They have been censured for failing to determine "what matters most" or, as in the example above, to effectively measure "what got the patient better."

Interest in increasing the use of performance measurements by public-service organizations and in disseminating more such data to the general public has been growing, however. The goal of these initiatives is to supplement the traditional input-focused measures (such as expenditures and staffing levels) with results-oriented measures (such as output, quality, and timeliness), and in so doing, to improve governmental efficiency and effectiveness by increasing public managers' accountability.[16] Such "government accountability" and public management "reforms" have been introduced in almost all sectors of government in many countries around the world.

One must caution, however, that an increased focus on measurement may produce some of the same dysfunctional side effects that are also common in for-profit organizations, such as behavioral displacement (concentration on the areas measured to the exclusion of other important but unmeasured areas) and gaming (misrepresentation of data). For example, "some quality metrics [have been] removed from consideration when a high percentage of physicians score well or 'topped out' on them," thus curtailing their potency to demonstrate improvements.[17]

However, some studies have provided evidence of beneficial effects or other positive externalities of performance measurement in some not-for-profit settings. For example, one study of managers in not-for-profit hospitals found that performance measurement and associated incentives attracts managers who are more talented at balancing the books (financial performance) while achieving not-for-profit objectives.[18] A number of not-for-profit organizations also have reported success with combination-of-measures approaches (e.g. balanced scorecards) to manage their operations effectively.[19]

Survey evidence suggests that not-for-profit and government organizations are keenly interested in incentive-compensation practices. For example, according to the 2016 Vivient Consulting and World-At-Work survey, over three-quarters of the sampled US not-for-profit and government organizations make significant use of short-term cash incentives (STIs) to motivate and reward employees, although long-term incentive (LTI) usage is rare, with only about one-sixth of these organizations using them (compared to over half of the privately held organizations in their sample). More than four-fifths of the non-profit and government organizations said their annual incentive plans were effective and that they will continue using them. The survey concluded that "STI budgets at non-profit/government organizations are starting to approach the levels reported by the private, for-profit organizations."[20]

All told, then, when carefully designed, and when adequate performance measures can be found, performance measurement and incentive systems might have many similarities between for-profit and not-for-profit organizations, both in their purported functional, but possibly also dysfunctional, effects.

Accounting differences

The financial statements prepared by not-for-profit organizations vary widely from those used in for-profit organizations in both form and content. A comprehensive standard for general-purpose external financial statements provided by not-for-profit organizations did not exist in the United States until the Financial Accounting Standards Board (FASB) issued Financial Accounting Statement No. 117 in 1993 (FAS 117). Up until that time, some not-for-profit organizations provided consolidated financial statements whereas others did not. Some not-for-profit organizations provided cash flow information, but most did not. FAS 117 was intended to improve the relevance, understandability, and comparability of not-for-profit organizations' financial statements. Since then, financial statement standards for not-for-profits have been issued and updated globally, such as under the auspices of International Financial Reporting Standards (IFRS) and other standard setters.[21]

The individual accounting standards used by not-for-profit organizations for operating transactions also have historically been different from those used in for-profit corporations, such as for depreciation, for example. Most experts, however, now conclude that the accounting principles used in not-for-profit organizations should be similar if not identical to those used in for-profit organizations, with one exception: not-for-profit organizations need separate accounts, called funds, to segregate operating transactions from contributed capital transactions.

For-profit organizations acquire their resources by selling stock, borrowing money, and earning profits through the selling of the goods and services they provide. Their managers can use those resources in any legal way they wish. Most of the resources obtained by not-for-profit organizations, on the other hand, are donated or granted to the organization. The terms of the donation or grant can *restrict* the purposes for which those resources can be used. The restriction may involve use of the resources for a specific purpose (such as to conduct cancer research), a particular type of expenditure (such as for a new building), or a particular time period (such as only until or not before a given date).

Ensuring that each of these donations or grants is used only for its intended purpose places extra demands on the managers of not-for-profit organizations. Some of these restrictions are legal obligations; others are moral obligations from the organization to the donor. To satisfy the extra dimension of accountability that these restrictions involve, most not-for-profit organizations use *fund accounting*. Fund accounting separates resources restricted for different purposes from each other. Each fund has its own set of financial statements: balance sheet and statement of changes in fund balances. Each not-for-profit organization also has a *general fund* that is used to account for all operating transactions and resources not included in any of the restricted funds.

Most not-for-profit organizations prepare consolidated financial reports. The fund accounting counterpart of the for-profit organizations' income statement (which can be called a *statement of activities, operating statement*, or *statement of income and expenses*) provides important information about the financial performance of the not-for-profit organization. Figure 16.1 shows a representative example of a consolidated statement of activities, in this case for the University of Southern California (USC).[22] The statement shows that USC, a private university, raised over $4.24 billion in revenues in its 2015 fiscal year, but nearly $200 million of those revenues were restricted, either temporarily or permanently (the two middle columns). Expenses totaled nearly $4 billion. Thus, USC was able to invest the surplus of about $262 million in its assets, most particularly buildings and various other kinds of restricted and unrestricted investments.

The statement of activities is quite informative because if resource inflows are persistently less than resource outflows, the not-for-profit organization will not survive. On the other hand, inflows that exceed outflows consistently by too great a margin is not by itself desirable, either. It may indicate that the organization is not fulfilling its primary mission as well as it could with the resources it has available to it.

External scrutiny

Most not-for-profit organizations do not directly serve, and do not have to answer to, a group with ultimate authority, like a shareholder group. They do, however, have to answer to a number of external constituencies, often including donors, government entities, alumni, and even society at large to some extent. These external constituencies often are demanding. This is natural because most not-for-profit organizations were established precisely to provide valuable social services, and as a consequence, they are often held to a higher standard.[23] In that context, performance reports can provide valuable information that helps the constituents make informed choices, such as regarding which school to send their children to, which hospital to entrust their health with, or which charity to donate their money to. To help inform the public, websites have been developed, such as Charity Navigator (www.charitynavigator.org), which claims to be "America's premier independent charity evaluator, [which] works to advance a more efficient and responsive philanthropic marketplace by evaluating the financial health of America's largest charities."

Figure 16.1 Consolidated statement of activities, University of Southern California, for the year ended June 30, 2015

		Year Ended June 30, 2015			
		Unrestricted Net Assets	Temporarily Restricted Net Assets	Permanently Restricted Net Assets	Total Net Assets
	Revenues				
1	Student tuition and fees	$1,710,225			$1,710,225
2	Less financial aid	(460,276)			(460,276)
3	Net student tuition and fees	1,249,949			1,249,949
4	Endowment income	45,527		$432	45,959
5	Investment and other income	14,360		205	14,565
6	Net appreciation (depreciation) in fair value of investments	33,565	$73,090	(2,214)	104,441
7	Contracts and grants	455,177			455,177
8	Contributions	248,837	124,011	164,917	537,765
9	Sales, services and other	217,457			217,457
10	Auxiliary enterprises	308,515			308,515
11	Health care services	1,310,882			1,310,882
12	Present value adjustment to annuities payable		37	(2,033)	(1,996)
13	Net assets released from restrictions/ redesignations	161,063	(164,473)	3,410	
14	Total Revenues	4,045,332	32,665	164,717	4,242,714
	Expenses				
15	Educational and general activities	2,415,602			2,415,602
16	Health care services	1,300,218			1,300,218
17	Depreciation and amortization	198,357			198,357
18	Interest on indebtedness	66,178			66,178
19	Total Expenses	3,980,355			3,980,355
20	Increase in Net Assets	64,977	32,665	164,717	262,359
21	Beginning Net Assets	3,417,909	1,966,794	2,077,885	7,462,588
22	Ending Net Assets	$3,482,886	$1,999,459	$2,242,602	$7,724,947
	Nature of specific net assets				
23	Designated	$808,017			$808,017
24	Externally restricted		$53,802	$25,422	79,224
25	Pledges		327,070	321,549	648,619
26	Unexpended endowment income	214,053			214,053
27	Annuity and living trusts		54,168	88,222	142,390
28	True endowment and net appreciation		1,564,419	1,807,409	3,371,828
29	Funds functioning as endowment	1,337,683			1,337,683
30	Debt service funds	86,322			86,322
31	Invested in plant	1,036,811			1,036,811
32		$3,482,886	$1,999,459	$2,242,602	$7,724,947

The accompanying notes are an integral part of this statement.

High societal expectations lead to high demands for accountability, as we have seen earlier. Sometimes benefactors, or the general public, bring direct political pressure on the organization. If an organization is perceived not to be performing effectively or appropriately, donations can be withheld, and managers and boards of trustees can be forced out of office. Government regulators can shut the organizations down or place additional restrictions on them.

For example, when the Los Angeles convention center's occupancy rate dropped by over 10 percentage points in a given year, city officials, hotel owners, and regional business advocates rapidly pressed for changes and reforms at the Visitor Bureau, the not-for-profit group responsible for renting the city-owned convention center and promoting regional tourism. The various constituents threatened to monitor the bureau's activities more closely, set performance benchmarks, or else cut ties with the Visitors Bureau.[24] They pressured the non-profit organization to act fiscally responsibly.

And when the American Red Cross – an affiliate of the International Red Cross network, which had rolled out a global disease prevention program with a strong anti-smoking component – refused to stop accepting donations from tobacco companies, officials at the parent company said that the US group risked damaging not only its own reputation, but that of the entire global humanitarian network. "We have been very clear about the potential reputational damage not just for them but for all of us," and although "we have not taken the route of public condemnation, [. . .] we continue 'to put pressure' on the American Red Cross to change its policy." Pressure on the American Red Cross was coming from other fronts as well. Some of the largest US public health advocacy organizations, including the Public Health Law Center and Action on Smoking & Health, wrote to the American Red Cross president urging the organization to stop taking tobacco donations.[25] Clearly, the extra scrutiny from parties often external to the organization places extra control system-related demands on not-for-profit organizations and on their managers and boards of trustees.

Members of not-for-profit organizations' boards are sometimes selected, however, for reasons that do not always pertinently qualify them to exercise organizational oversight optimally. For example, they may have been selected because they are potentially large donors to the organization or because they have held high-ranking government or other positions but in unrelated areas. In addition, most not-for-profit trustees are paid little or nothing (or are barred to be paid) for their services, so they may be less committed to, or more easily distracted from, their tasks. Although not-for-profit governance has been tightened generally, the consequence is that, as one set of authors concluded, "Effective governance by the board of a not-for-profit organization is a rare and unnatural act."[26] When the organization's internal oversight comes up short, direct pressure is more likely to be brought from external constituencies.

The sometimes-intense external scrutiny can also shape some decision-making processes, including some MCS-related processes. Planning and budgeting processes are likely to be more important and more time-consuming because the external parties must be heard and their concerns must be accommodated. Management and employee compensation in not-for-profit organizations is also often subject to considerable political pressure. In the words of a Los Angeles city official who commented on the city's review of employee bonuses: "A big piece of the process is not just money; it's inspiring confidence. People don't have confidence [city officials] are spending tax dollars wisely. You've got to be hyper-focused in the attention to detail."[27]

A related concern, and one which naturally transitions into our next section, is that "in the charitable sector, there tends to be more trust and less scrutiny [. . .] the Achilles heel in the charitable sector is that people appear to be more trusting and have less internal controls and oversight; that is a weakness."[28]

Employee characteristics

Employees of not-for-profit organizations often have some characteristics that distinguish them from those in for-profit organizations, and those characteristics can have both positive and negative control implications. The sizes of the compensation packages of employees in many not-for-profit organizations are not competitive with those offered at for-profit organizations. This can cause control problems if employee quality is diminished, as one of the main control problems – personal limitations – may be more salient. For example, when an audit revealed that the Los Angeles County Department of Mental Health had sloppy bookkeeping, weak controls over its expenditures, and spotty compliance with county contract regulations, the department's chief deputy director replied that "it was essentially a lack of training and [. . .] we need to make sure that our staff understands what the requirements are and follow them."[29]

To address some of the personnel-related control problems, the mayor of Los Angeles and other city leaders have defended large salaries to lure top managers away from private companies, while government critics have called these high salaries "an outrageous waste of taxpayer money". The mayor, however, stood by his policy of hiring good people and holding them accountable, even "if that means paying top dollar – if you think it's expensive to hire talented people, try hiring untalented people; it's penny wise and pound foolish," the deputy mayor said.[30] Many not-for-profits also face retention issues and lack formal employee retention strategies to address them. For example, one survey suggests that,

> The vast majority of nonprofits surveyed (90%) do not have a formal strategy for retaining staff despite many indicating that staff retention is an organizational challenge. Interestingly, according to survey respondents, the top three functional areas experiencing the most growth are also the top three functional areas experiencing the greatest challenges with retention (direct services, program management/support, and fundraising/development, respectively).[31]

On the other hand, not-for-profit organizations often attract employees who can be highly committed to their organization's goals. Such employees may find it more intrinsically rewarding to pursue their organization's goal, whether that is providing shelter for the homeless, food for the hungry, or a cure for AIDS, compared to creating value for shareholders in an abstract, dispassionate sense. Some not-for-profit employees even work with an idealistic fervor. When such employees are attracted and can be retained, their high commitment minimizes the other control problems: lack of direction and lack of motivation. Control, then, can be more easily achieved through personnel/cultural means.

Conclusion

Control in not-for-profit organizations exhibits both similarities with, and differences from, control in for-profit organizations. The basic needs for good control are the same. Managers of not-for-profit organizations have to address the same set of control problems – lack of direction, lack of motivation, and lack of ability (personal limitations) – as do their for-profit counterparts. They also have basically the same set of control tools – action, results, and personnel/cultural controls – at their disposal. They also face many of the same problems, including the need to implement goal-congruent performance measurement and incentive systems, and the need to avoid many of the same dysfunctional side effects that we discussed elsewhere in this text. And as an earlier quote suggested, the reverse is also true, where for-profit corporations recognize that espousing some non-profit principles and practices can make good business sense, particularly related to goals of social well-being and environmental protection in addition to economic prosperity.[32]

However, MCSs in not-for-profit organizations are sometimes not as well developed as those in for-profit organizations for a number of reasons, such as relating to the types of personnel that they attract and manage to retain, as well as resource constraints and public or even political pressure, to name a few. On the other hand, many larger and perhaps more professional not-for-profit organizations implement many of the control features used in for-profit organizations.

That said, MCSs often must differ appreciably in not-for-profit organizations. Managers of these organizations often find that a command-and-control style of management is not effective. They must spend considerable time managing elaborate, open decision processes designed to build consensus. Even then, the decisions often get tied up in lengthy approval processes involving multiple regulators, overseers, and interest groups. Managers cannot easily define results measures and motivate behavior through financial incentives. The goals are not always clear; the important results are often difficult to measure; internal auditors cannot just be ordered into a department to do a performance audit; and the provision of incentives may be unfeasible or unaffordable. There are no stock options to offer as long-term incentives. Bonuses are often specifically prohibited by law or labor contracts, and if not that, subject to public scrutiny and scorn.

There are, however, several success stories that suggest lessons not-for-profit managers can learn from for-profit managers. Richard Riordan, a successful businessman who went on to serve two terms as the mayor of Los Angeles, implemented mission statements for various departments and formal results-oriented performance evaluations backed up by, in some cases, merit pay. A study revealed that his city officials – "executives," as he called them – ranked among the most richly compensated public officials in the country. Mr. Riordan's organizational changes produced some successes, although he kept lamenting that "in government there is too much talk about process and not enough talk about results."[33]

Or, in the words of Jasmine Whitbread of Save the Children, a global children's charity that fights for children's rights in 120 countries across the world:

> Usually people are drawn to work for an organization like Save the Children through wanting to make the world a better place, but, arguably, people choose to work for businesses for that reason too. We want to attract top talent. We know we can't compete with businesses, we can't pay the same amount – but we do need to pay to attract talent. Charities are complex businesses and maybe we haven't communicated that message. Save the Children is a $1.8 billion operation in over 120 countries, running programs that have evolved over decades in high-risk, highly uncertain markets. The skills needed to run even part of that operation are the same skills needed in business. It's about people, direction, strategy, resources, raising funds, making investments. Save the Children is a business – but our bottom line is saving children's lives. Our founder Eglantyne Jebb, all those years ago, said that, because money is donated, it behooves us to use modern business methods – and people are still entrusting us with their money.[34]

Prior to joining the non-profit sector, Ms. Whitbread was a managing director with Thomson Financial, a global financial information provider. But many not-for-profit or public sector organizations are not run by business men or women, sometimes for good reasons. As is sometimes said, "Martin Luther had a dream, not a business plan."[35]

Notes

1 See, for example, "Currents of Change: The KPMG Survey of Corporate Social Responsibility Reporting 2015," *KPMG* (2015), online at www.kpmg.com/reporting.
2 See, for example, G. Michelon, S. Pilonato, and F. Ricceri, "CSR Reporting Practices and the Quality of Disclosure: An Empirical Analysis," *Critical Perspectives on Accounting*, 33 (2015), pp. 59–78.
3 See, for example, T. F. Slaper, "The Triple Bottom Line: What Is It and How Does It Work?" *Indiana Business Review* (Spring 2011), pp. 4–8; A. Rambaud and J, Richard, "The 'Triple Depreciation Line' Instead of the 'Triple Bottom Line': Towards a Genuine Integrated Reporting," *Critical Perspectives on Accounting*, 33 (2015), pp. 92–116.
4 See, for example, "Doing Well by Doing Good: An Interview with Paul Polman, CEO of Unilever," *The Huffington Post* (May 9, 2016), online at www.huffingtonpost.com/alexandre-mars/doing-well-by-doing-good-_1_b_9860128.html.
5 Michelon et al., "CSR Reporting Practices and the Quality of Disclosure," op. cit.
6 Rambaud and Richard, "The 'Triple Depreciation Line' Instead of the 'Triple Bottom Line,'" op. cit.
7 See, for example, H. Servaes and A. Tamayo, "Doing Well by Doing Good," *Business Strategy Review*, no. 1 (2014), p. 6; B. Hong, Z. Li, and D. Minor, "Corporate Governance and Executive Compensation for Corporate Social Responsibility," *Journal of Business Ethics* (December 2015), pp. 1–15; K. Lins, H. Servaes, and A. Tamayo, "Social Capital, Trust, and Firm Performance: The Value of Corporate Social Responsibility during the Financial Crisis," *European Corporate Governance Institute (ECGI) - Finance Working Paper No. 446/2015* (February 2016), online at papers.ssrn.com/sol3/papers.cfm?abstract_id=2555863.
8 D. T. Whalen, "Sustainability Matters, but What Does It Mean for Your Company?" *NACD Directorship* (July 30, 2015), NACDonline.org, online at https:// www.nacdonline.org/Magazine/Article.cfm?ItemNumber=17504.
9 "B Corporation: A New Sustainable Business Model," *Darden Business Publishing* (Technical Note, 2010).
10 See, for example, bimpactassessment.net and bcorporation.net.
11 "B Corporation: A New Sustainable Business Model," op. cit.; and "To 'B' or not to 'B'," *Impact*, 21, no. 11 (November 2015).
12 Slaper, "The Triple Bottom Line," op. cit., p. 6.
13 See, for example, "Shareholders vs. Stakeholders: A New Idolatry," *The Economist* (April 24, 2010), online at econ.st/KA1p7h. See also "Maximizing Shareholder Value: The Goal That Changed Corporate America," *The Washington Post* (August 26, 2013), online at wpo.st/bRTb1.
14 "DWP's Spending Comes under Scrutiny," *The Los Angeles Times* (March 31, 2002), p. B1.
15 "Debate Heightens over Measuring Health Care Quality," *The Wall Street Journal* (January 30, 2015), online at on.wsj.com/1EvciGo.
16 See, for example, K. Cavalluzzo and C. Ittner, "Implementing Performance Measurement Innovations: Evidence from Government," *Accounting, Organizations and Society*, 29, no. 3–4 (April–May 2004), pp. 243–67.
17 "Debate Heightens over Measuring Health Care Quality," op. cit.
18 L. Eldenburg, F. Gaertner, and T. Goodman, "The Influence of Profit-Based Compensation on Non-Profit Objectives," *Working Paper* (University of Arizona, 2010). For similar studies, see W. Baber, P. Daniel, and A. Robert, "Compensation to Managers of Charitable Organizations: An Empirical Study of the Role of Accounting Measures of Program Activities," *The Accounting Review*, 77, no. 3 (July 2002), pp. 679–93; L. M. Parsons and A. L. Reitenga, "College and University President Pay and Future Performance," *Accounting Horizons*, 28, no. 1 (March 2014), pp. 125–42.
19 See, for example, A. Gumbus, D. Bellhouse, and B. Lyons, "A Three Year Journey to Organizational and Financial Health Using the Balanced Scorecard: A Case Study at a Yale New Haven Health System Hospital," *Journal of Business and Economic Studies*, 9, no. 2 (Fall 2003), pp. 54–64.
20 "Incentive Pay Practices: Non-Profit/Government Organizations," A Report by *World-At-Work* and *Vivient Consulting* (February 2016), online at www.worldatwork.org/adimLink?id=79940.
21 See, for example, *International Financial Reporting for the Not-for-Profit Sector* (CCAB, February 2014), online at www.ccab.org.uk.
22 *University of Southern California 2015 Financial Report*, available at about.usc.edu/files/2015/12/USC-FY-2015-Financial-Report.pdf.
23 "Room for Improvement: Foundations' Support of Non-Profit Performance Assessment," *The Center for Effective Philanthropy* (2012), online at www.effectivephilanthropy.org/wp-content/uploads/2014/01/RoomForImprovement.pdf.
24 "Officials Target Visitors Bureau," *The Los Angeles Times* (April 7, 2002), p. B1; "Audit Urges Major Reforms of Visitors Bureau Spending," *The Los Angeles Times* (October 15, 2002), p. B1.
25 "American Red Cross Pressured to Rid Itself of Tobacco Money," *Reuters* (January 7, 2015), online at reut.rs/1s5ORPf.
26 B. Taylor, R. Chait, and T. Holland, "The New Work of the Non-Profit Board," *Harvard Business Review*, 74, no. 5 (September–October 1996), p. 36.
27 "Public Enemy No. 1: Bonuses," *The Daily News* (March 9, 2006), p. 1.
28 "Blumenthal May Investigate Charities Ripped Off by Madoff," *Forbes* (December 22, 2008), online at www.forbes.com. See also "Many Non-Profits Lack Financial Knowledge: Survey," *Chicago Tribune* (February 29, 2012), online at articles.chicagotribune.com.
29 "Audit Finds Myriad Woes in Department of Mental Health," *The Los Angeles Times* (August 15, 2003), p. B3.

30 "Riordan OKs Raises for Top Officials," *The Los Angeles Times* (January 30, 2001), p. B1.

31 *2013 Nonprofit Employment Trends Survey* (Nonprofit HR Solutions, 2013), online at www.nonprofithr.com/wp-content/uploads/2013/03/2013-Employment-Trends-Survey-Report.pdf.

32 Slaper, "The Triple Bottom Line," op. cit., p. 6.

33 "Riordan OKs Raises for Top Officials," op. cit.

34 "Taking Business Skills into the Non-Profit Sector: Jasmine Whitbread of Save the Children," *Forbes* (May 7, 2014), online at www.forbes.com.

35 "Should Philanthropies Operate Like a Business?" *The Wall Street Journal* (November 28, 2011), online at on.wsj.com/sy0702.

CASE STUDY
SCI Ontario: Achieving, Measuring, and Communicating Strategic Success

Professor Neil Bendle wrote this case solely to provide material for class discussion. The author does not intend to illustrate either effective or ineffective handling of a managerial situation. The author may have disguised certain names and other identifying information to protect confidentiality.

In fall 2014 Gillian Lynne-Davies had just seen the 2013/14 Spinal Cord Injury Ontario (SCI Ontario) annual report finalized after a busy, but worthwhile few months. The not-for-profit organization she worked for, SCI Ontario, headquartered in Toronto, was part of a federation of organizations that served over one million people. Notable achievements from the past year included responding to 4,700 requests for information and working with the Ontario government to get $8 million infused into community-based attendant services.

In 2012, the organization, a leader in client service and community reintegration, had adopted a bold three-year strategic plan it called "Good to the Core." (The plan was later extended to 2017.) SCI Ontario aimed to be an exemplar of not-for-profit management and to take a leadership role regarding people living with spinal cord injuries in the province.

Communications and reporting were vital elements of the strategy, which Lynne-Davies, as senior manager of marketing and communications, was tasked with delivering. Reporting helped SCI Ontario monitor its progress and let stakeholders gain a greater understanding of the organization and, through this, an enhanced commitment to it.

Change was on the horizon: Bill Adair, the chief executive officer (CEO), had announced his decision to retire and Lynne-Davies would have to work to ensure the transition was seamless. Given the need to implement the strategy while managing the transition, she saw two major goals in the coming months:

- To further develop an internal reporting system to complement the external reporting system. A dashboard would allow the new CEO to see how SCI Ontario was performing against the strategic plan, financial targets and operational objectives.
- To refine SCI Ontario's communications strategy to help achieve and critically measure its success in becoming the provincial expert on living with spinal cord injury. This would fulfill the organization's leadership role and its mandate to be the "most reliable voice, advocate and leading expert on living with spinal cord injury in Ontario."

Achieving these goals would make a huge contribution to SCI Ontario and its important mission.

The History of Spinal Cord Injury Ontario

World War II saw an influx of veterans with spinal cord injuries. These otherwise healthy veterans were scattered around hospitals where the medical staff expected little of them. In 1945, two veterans, John Counsell and Ken Langford, determined to help those living with the injuries engage more fully with the community. With the backing of prominent philanthropists, they established the Canadian Paraplegic Association. Its initial focus was on people with affected motor function in their lower extremities, hence the use of the term paraplegic in its name. At the time, this represented the vast majority of the spinal cord injuries community as any injury severe enough to cause quadriplegia—affecting function of the legs, arms and torso—would have been fatal. Since then, advances in medical research, knowledge and support had significantly improved the prospects of those with spinal cord injuries. Thus, at the beginning of the twenty-first century, the community included a far greater range of experiences and injuries. In November 2012, to demonstrate commitment to all those with spinal cord injuries, the organization was renamed Spinal Cord Injury Ontario (SCI Ontario).

Spinal Cord Injury Ontario – Our Mission

> **Spinal Cord Injury Ontario assists persons with spinal cord injuries and other physical disabilities to achieve independence, self-reliance and full community participation.**

Every year, there were close to 600 people who sustained new spinal cord injuries in Ontario alone, and approximately 33,000 Ontarians lived with a spinal cord injury. The economic costs were estimated at a massive $2.67 billion in Canada as a whole. Even more important than the financial cost was the human cost. A spinal cord injury was a traumatic event significantly impacting those experiencing the injury as well as friends, family, employers and the wider community. Such injuries could happen to anyone; indeed, the two age groups most at risk were those over 70 and those in the 20 to 29 age range. The top two causes of spinal cord injuries were accidental falls and motor crashes, everyday events that accounted for approximately 43 per cent of cases. Those experiencing a spinal cord injury were roughly twice as likely to be male than female.

Despite the stress caused by spinal cord injuries, it must be understood that people were often able to positively adjust to life afterwards, given time and the right support. On average, it took a person two to three years to gain independence, typically after critical care, rehabilitation and transition to community living.

Experiencing a spinal cord injury was a life-changing event as Chris, who received support from SCI Ontario, said, "It's like you've been given a new body. You relearn everything from scratch." The peer support that SCI Ontario provided to those who had experienced an injury could be invaluable in helping rehabilitation. As Christine, a disability educator, remarked, "A disability doesn't need to be an inability. We just have to be more creative about how we do things." SCI Ontario was there to help people achieve their goals. As Lubna said, "Sometimes just a little support gets you where you want to be."

The Organization of SCI Ontario

SCI Ontario was incorporated under the Canadian Not-For-Profit Corporations Act as a corporation without share capital. It was a registered charity under the Income Tax Act (Canada), which meant that it did not pay taxes and was able to issue receipts for tax deduction of donations made to it.

SCI Ontario provided the following programs:

- Attendant Services (AS) in the greater Toronto area.
- Regional Services (RS) to assist clients transitioning from acute care through rehabilitation into the community.
- Employment Services (ES) to help people with disabilities in the Greater Toronto Area.
- Peer Support (PS) to provide one to-one matches with trained volunteers.
- Public Policy Program to bring awareness and education to elected officials and to work with members on advocacy initiatives that aim to create an inclusive province.
- Research and partnership: financial support of fellowships and partners.
- Communications: disseminating information and raising awareness.
- Networks and Alliance to improve the quality of life for people with disabilities in Ontario.
- Informational Services for people with disabilities.
- Knowledge Enterprise, the learning centre for SCI Ontario.
- Member Services.
- Advocacy.

SCI Ontario employed close to 170 full- and part-time staff of whom 30 per cent identified as having a disability. The organization maintained 17 branches across the province from Thunder Bay to Ottawa, with the provincial headquarters in Toronto. Further details of the organization, its mission and values are contained in Exhibit 1.

In addition to its day-to-day operations, SCI Ontario controlled the Ontario Paraplegic Foundation. This foundation, which was established in 2000, received bequests and other donations from supporters. All the resources of the foundation must ultimately be used for the benefit of SCI Ontario programs or research supported by SCI Ontario. The accounts for the Ontario Paraplegic Foundation are shown in Exhibit 2.

The Strategic Plan

The Good to the Core strategic plan[1] was adopted in 2012 after extensive stakeholder consultation. This consultation included focus groups and interviews with individual stakeholders designed to refine and develop support for the strategic plan.

The five directions highlighted in the strategic plan were:

1. Advancing service access and excellence.
2. Being the most reliable voice, advocate and leading expert on living with spinal cord injury in Ontario.
3. Sharing knowledge and driving change related to spinal cord injury.
4. Excellence in governance, management and accountability.
5. Increasing and diversifying revenues.

In 2010, the organization adopted a balanced scorecard reporting system to allow management and other stakeholders to better understand organizational performance. The balanced scorecard reporting process was reviewed and developed as part of the 2012 strategic plan. The key dimensions now monitored included financial, customer, internal business processes and learning and growth. The measures assessed were widely circulated and the achievement against the plan presented as part of the annual report.

Financial Reporting at SCI Ontario

Stakeholders are interested in knowing that resources are being used effectively and that the organization has the ability to continue its mission. To this end, SCI Ontario provided financial statements and made these publicly available on its website. These statements were similar to the financial statements of for-profit corporations. They detailed the activities of the organization in the past year and changes in net assets, cash flows and the position at the end of the year. Every year, the financial statements were audited by a professional services firm; in 2014, that firm was Grant Thornton.

Two key statements, the Statement of Financial Activities and Statement of Financial Position, corresponded to the Income and Expenditure Statement and Balance Sheet, respectively, of a corporation. Given that organizations such as SCI Ontario did not have a bottom line profit, the statements noted the "Excess of Revenue over Expenses" each year. A summary of the revenue and expenses for the period 2008 to 2014 is attached in Exhibit 3. A summary of assets and liabilities as of March 31 each year from 2009 to 2014 is provided in Exhibit 4. Raising funds effectively and efficiently is crucial for the success of a not-for-profit. Notes to SCI Ontario's financial statements gave more detail on fundraising; a summary for the period 2009 to 2014 is included in Exhibit 5.

In addition to their financial statements, charities in Canada also reported basic financial details to the Canada Revenue Agency (CRA), which posted these on the CRA website. Details of this reporting are shown in Exhibit 6.

To allow stakeholders to better assess the performance of not-for-profits, independent organizations also assess relative performance (see Exhibit 7). While such relative performance measures are potentially informative, concerns are sometimes expressed that comparing organizations with different missions make ranking especially challenging. Furthermore, there is inevitably considerable judgment about how to classify the activities of a not-for-profit, which potentially allows managerial decisions to impact the data used for the comparions.

Creating a Dashboard

The information presented in the annual reports[2] was designed to be helpful to the external user. For instance, the breakdown of funds raised and spent was expressed in the form of a pie divided between the sources and application of funds. It was in this spirit of openness

[1] "Good to the Core," www.sciontario.org/sites/sciontario.org/files/CPA%20Ontario%20strategic%20plan%20overview%20final.pdf, accessed November 06, 2014.

[2] For more details, see "The Harvest: Spinal Cord Injury Ontario 2013–2014 Annual Report, www.sciontario.org/sites/sciontario.org/files/2014-SCI-Ontario-Annual-Report.pdf, accessed November 06, 2014.

and user friendliness that the balanced scorecard contained indicators of how the organization was performing on critical dimensions (see Exhibit 8). (Note that elements in the scorecard occasionally changed to improve the reporting.)

Best practice internal reporting—reporting focused on aiding managerial decisions—is built on similar foundations to external reporting in that user needs are paramount. Reporting to the new CEO could use the same principles of ease of use. This was especially important as Lynne-Davies couldn't be sure what skills the new CEO would have. For instance, the new CEO might have more expertise in client service in the spinal cord injury community than financial management. Any system adopted would have to be useful to any CEO regardless of his or her professional background. A traditional approach was a monthly dashboard highlighting the performance of the organization against its various goals.

A good dashboard would be clear, visually appealing, focused on the key goals of the organization and limited to items that the manager receiving the information could hope to impact. The dashboard should aid efforts to run the organization. The analogy was to the dashboard of a vehicle, which contains the key information the driver needs to control the car, such as a speedometer, indicator lights and fuel level. Lynne-Davies wondered what a good dashboard for SCI Ontario would look like and whether one could be used to help the new CEO manage the organization.

Maintaining and Enhancing the Leadership Role

The leadership role—being the expert voice on living with spinal cord injury in Ontario—was central to the organization's mission. SCI Ontario wanted to be the organization to which anyone who wanted to know about spinal cord injuries would turn. Lynne-Davies had ideas on how to achieve this objective, but it wasn't easy. Because so many worthwhile causes existed, how could SCI Ontario ensure that those who needed the organization's services heard of them? How would potential volunteers and donors understand the good work being done? How could she encourage the media and other opinion leaders to put SCI Ontario on their speed dials for when expert advice was needed? Indeed, how should SCI Ontario advocate to ensure that the interests of the spinal cord injury community were properly addressed?

In addition to these questions was another challenge: How could Lynne-Davies know if SCI Ontario was being successful in developing the leadership role? How could she measure progress and demonstrate that any plan that was adopted was actually helping to fulfil its strategic objectives? Given the importance of raising the profile of the spinal cord injury community, and SCI Ontario in particular, the organization was already monitoring mentions in the media as part of the balanced scorecard. Were the current measures adequate? How could they be improved? Was focusing on the media enough to conclude whether SCI Ontario was performing its leadership role? Counting website visits was a possible way of tracking how useful SCI Ontario was to the community, but was reporting that data enough? What else could be done to monitor community engagement?

As she began to plan, Lynne-Davies pondered the big questions: How should SCI Ontario perform its internal reporting? What would being successful at community leadership look like and how could performance against this goal be monitored?

Exhibit 1 SCI Ontario Mission and Values

OUR MISSION: Spinal Cord Injury Ontario (formerly Canadian Paraplegic Association Ontario) assists persons with spinal cord injuries and other physical disabilities to achieve independence, self-reliance and full community participation.
WHO WE ARE: 17 offices, 9 different client programs and services, 13 departments, 168 staff serving people with spinal cord injuries and other physical disabilities in Ontario.
OUR VALUES:

- RESPECT for spinal cord injury experience, for each other and for all communities
- EXCELLENCE in all we do
- ACCOUNTABILITY through transparency and ownership of outcomes
- LEADERSHIP in service and quality of life
- INCLUSION in all communities and within our organization
- INNOVATION in overcoming challenges

OUR VISION: SCI Ontario champions excellence in service, advocacy and quality of life for people with spinal cord injuries.

Source: "The Harvest: Spinal Cord Injury Ontario 2013–2014 Annual Report, www.sciontario.org/sites/sciontario.org/files/2014-SCI-Ontario-Annual-Report.pdf, accessed November 06, 2014.

Exhibit 2 Financial Position of the Ontario Paraplegic Foundation

	All in $000s	
Financial Position	As at March 31 2014	As at March 31 2013
Assets		
Investments, at market value	$ 7,011	$ 6,681
Due from SCI Ontario	$ 174	$ –
Other	$ 4	$ 2
Total Assets	$ 7,189	$ 6,683
Liabilities		
Due to SCI Ontario	$ –	$ 286
Other	$ 15	$ 14
	$ 15	$ 300
Funds balances		
General Fund	$ 6,471	$ 5,655
Restricted Fund—Research	$ 404	$ 462
Restricted Fund—A.T. Jousse	$ 144	$ 128
Restricted Fund—Ken Langford	$ 155	$ 138
	$ 7,174	$ 6,383
Total Liabilities and Funds Balances	$ 7,189	$ 6,683
Results of operations		
Donations and bequests	$ 13	$ 50
Change in value of investments	$ 855	$ 553
Grants from (to) SCI Ontario	$ 7	$ (614)
Other Expenses	$ (84)	$ (66)
Excess (deficiency of revenue over expenses for the year)	$ 791	$ (77)

Restricted funds: Funds that must be used for the specific purposes outlined by the donor.
Source: Company files.

Exhibit 3 SCI Ontario Revenue and Expenses 2008 to 2014

Year End March 31	Actual	Actual	Budget	Actual	Budget	Actual	Budget	Actual	Budget	Actual	Budget	Actual
REVENUE (All in $000s)	2008	2009	2010	2010	2011	2011	2012	2012	2013	2013	2014	2014
Donations and other public support, net	$ 2,385	$ 2,283	$ 2,553	$ 2,208	$ 2,717	$ 2,370	$ 2,743	$ 2,320	$ 2,451	$ 1,921	$ 2,081	$ 1,800
Grants	$ 6,290	$ 7,314	$ 7,549	$ 7,668	$ 7,681	$ 7,649	$ 7,749	$ 7,728	$ 7,649	$ 7,903	$ 7,627	$ 7,963
Fees for service	$ 89	$ 79	$ 64	$ 54	$ 64	$ 55	$ 31	$ 52	$ 57	$ 32	$ 57	$ 82
Amortization of deferred capital contributions	$ 144	$ 136	$ 128	$ 136	$ 106	$ 108	$ 66	$ 80	$ 58	$ 118	$ 57	$ 44
	$ 8,907	$ 9,812	$ 10,294	$ 10,066	$ 10,568	$ 10,182	$ 10,589	$ 10,180	$ 10,215	$ 9,974	$ 9,822	$ 9,889
EXPENSES												
Staff salaries and benefits	$ 5,668	$ 6,348	$ 7,050	$ 6,810	$ 7,503	$ 7,233	$ 7,583	$ 7,333	$ 7,793	$ 7,408	$ 7,734	$ 7,549
Purchased services	$ 973	$ 1,019	$ 794	$ 1,025	$ 685	$ 732	$ 762	$ 815	$ 623	$ 727	$ 547	$ 612
Office	$ 641	$ 767	$ 757	$ 743	$ 749	$ 734	$ 767	$ 721	$ 693	$ 712	$ 561	$ 611
Travel	$ 638	$ 734	$ 778	$ 678	$ 773	$ 670	$ 758	$ 646	$ 680	$ 580	$ 615	$ 518
clients	$ 324	$ 277	$ 239	$ 241	$ 268	$ 286	$ 222	$ 172	$ 97	$ 199	$ 87	$ 260
Amortization of capital assets	$ 180	$ 170	$ 162	$ 162	$ 125	$ 133	$ 79	$ 145	$ 91	$ 154	$ 88	$ 114
Medical research grants	$ 121	$ 122	$ 127	$ 124	$ 126	$ 147	$ 129	$ 138	$ 131	$ 110	$ 93	$ 93
National office	$ 120	$ 106	$ 130	$ 83	$ 122	$ 26	$ 61	$ 105	$ 26	$ 26	$ 26	$ 89
Professional development	$ 113	$ 95	$ 105	$ 83	$ 75	$ 97	$ 90	$ 78	$ 57	$ 40	$ 53	$ 26
Miscellaneous	$ 130	$ 173	$ 150	$ 115	$ 140	$ 122	$ 136	$ 26	$ 21	$ 15	$ 16	$ 15
	$ 8,906	$ 9,810	$ 10,292	$ 10,064	$ 10,567	$ 10,180	$ 10,587	$ 10,179	$ 10,212	$ 9,971	$ 9,820	$ 9,887
Excess of revenue over expenses	$ 1	$ 1	$ 1	$ 2	$ 1	$ 2	$ 2	$ 1	$ 3	$ 3	$ 2	$ 2

Notes to the Revenue and Expenses (All Years)

SCI Ontario is highly dependent on the support of dedicated volunteers. Their value is not quantifiable in the above financial statements. Donations and other public support grossed revenue of $2.023 million in 2013/14, $2.16 million in 2012/13, $2.547 million in 2011/12, $2,687,000 in 2010/11, $2,531,576 in 2009/2010 and $2,966,211 in 2008/2009. Direct fundraising expenses of $222,976 in 2013/14, $240,000 in 2012/13, $227,000 in 2011/12, $317,000 in 2010/11, $323,500 in 2008/10 and $682,829 n 2008/2009 have netted against this total.

SCI Ontario controls the Ontario Paraplegic Foundation, which was established in March 2000 to receive bequests and donations from supporters of the Association. The Foundation is registered under the Income Tax Act and the Association appoints the majority of the Foundation's Board of Directors. According to the Foundation's bylaws, all resources of the Foundation must ultimately be used for the benefit of the Association via operating and research grants to the Association of $614,000 in 2012/13, $361,000 in 2011/12, $200,000 in 2010/11 and $220,000 in 2010/09 which are included in the category Donations and other public support. In 2013/14, SCI Ontario returned $7,000 in grants to the Foundation.

Source: Company files.

Exhibit 4 Assets and Liabilities 2008 to 2014

As at March 31	2009	2010	2011	2012	2013	2014
ASSETS						
Current						
Cash and cash equivalent	$ 829	$ 447	$ 493	$ 214	$ 210	$ 824
Grants receivable	$ 3	$ 3	$ 137	$ 70	$ 93	$ 52
Accounts receivable	$ 430	$ 434	$ 499	$ 524	$ 459	$ 155
Prepaid expenses and other assets	$ 98	$ 114	$ 110	$ 105	$ 103	$ 141
Total current assets	$ 1,360	$ 998	$ 1,239	$ 913	$ 865	$ 1,172
Capital assets, net	$ 746	$ 650	$ 565	$ 571	$ 474	$ 402
	$ 2,106	*$ 1,648*	*$ 1,804*	*$ 1,484*	*$ 1,339*	*$ 1,574*
LIABILITIES AND NET ASSETS						
Current						
Accounts payable and accrued charges	$ 1,084	$ 744	$ 970	$ 755	$ 677	$ 713
Due to Ontario Paraplegic Foundation						$ 174
Deferred revenue	$ 159	$ 125	$ 130	$ 48	$ 58	$ 126
Total current liabilities	*$ 1,244*	*$ 869*	*$ 1,100*	*$ 803*	*$ 735*	*$ 1,013*
Long-term						
Deferred capital contributions	$ 566	$ 571	$ 494	$ 470	$ 390	$ 344
Total long-term liabilities	$ 566	$ 571	$ 494	$ 470	$ 390	$ 1,357
Net Assets						
Invested in capital assets	$ 89	$ 78	$ 71	$ 100	$ 85	$ 57
Surplus	$ 117	$ 130	$ 139	$ 111	$ 129	$ 159
Total Net Assets	*$ 206*	*$ 208*	*$ 210*	*$ 211*	*$ 214*	*$ 216*
	$ 2,016	*$ 1,648*	*$ 1,804*	*$ 1,484*	*$ 1,339*	*$ 1,573*

Source: SCI Ontario Financial Statements

Exhibit 5 Donation Breakdown

	Year ended March 31st					
Heading	2014	2013	2012	2011	2010	2009
From Direct Fundraising	$ 2,030,409	$ 1,546,753	$ 2,186,450	$ 2,486,792	$ 2,208,854	$ 2,550,354
From Foundation	$ (7,273)	$ 614,253	$ 360,898	$ 199,764	$ 220,000	$ 415,857
Gross Donations and Other Public Support	$ 2,023,136	$ 2,161,006	$ 2,547,348	$ 2,686,556	$ 2,428,854	$ 2,966,211
Direct Fundraising Costs	$ 222,976	$ 239,649	$ 226,804	$ 316,789	$ 323,500	$ 682,829
Net Donations and Other Public Support in Accounts	$ 1,800,160	$ 1,921,357	$ 2,320,544	$ 2,369,767	$ 2,105,354	$ 2,283,382

Source: Company files.

Exhibit 6 CRA Reporting

Charities in Ontario report a T3010 to the Canada Revenue Agency (CRA) containing the basic revenue and expenses and balance sheet of the charity. This is made available online. In addition to reporting the financial statements and compensation levels, CRA reports a few key categories of Revenue and Expenditure to facilitate comparison between charities. This appears as the "Quick View" of the charity on the CRA website.

Categories used for "Quick View"
Receipted donations
Non-receipted donations
Gifts from other charities
Government funding
All other revenue
Total revenue
Charitable program
Management and administration
Fundraising
Political activities
Gifts to other registered charities and qualified donees
Other
Total expenses

Source: CRA website, www.cra-arc.gc.ca/chrts-gvng/lstngs/menu-eng.html, accessed November 06, 2014.

Exhibit 7 Ranking Charities

It is important for charities to be seen to be making good use of the funds available. Several organizations rate the charities to help potential donors. One such, Moneysense, has four categories that it combines to create an overall grade. For each area, scores are compared only to similar charities.

CHARITY EFFICIENCY: Money spent on charitable programs and money donated to other charities was added up and divided by the total expenses.

FUNDRAISING EFFICIENCY: Fundraising costs divided by the total of money raised through tax-receipted and non-tax receipted donations and money raised through fundraising.

GOVERNANCE: Based upon answers to a governance questionnaire.

RESERVES: Points were awarded for the amount of reserves. Interestingly, most points are given for moderate reserve, i.e., enough to cover three months to three years of expenses. Any reserves that are more or less than this lose points.

Source: Moneysense, Charity Grades, www.moneysense.ca/the-2013-charity-100-grades accessed November 06, 2014.

Exhibit 8 Balanced Scorecard Results 2010 to 2014

2009/10 Indicator Measures		
Reaching 100%	2009/2010	
Outcome	Annual Target	Total
Total Clients Served (AS, RS, ES, Peer Support, SCI Pilots)	1,445	1,779
Clients with SCI Served (AS, RS, ES, Peer Support, SCI Pilots)	985	1,243
Core Services Provided (AS, RS, ES, Peer Support, SCI Pilots, Info)	4,680	4,667
Direct Service Hours (AS, RS, Peer Support, SCI Pilots, Info)	115,593	115,402
Clients with NEWSCI Reached (RS, Peer Support)	414	277
Clients with EXISTING SCI Reached (RS, Peer Support)		178
Information Requests (Info, RS, Peer Support)	2,775	2,487
Total Members	1,750	1,335
Job Placements (ES)	75	47
Unit Cost (AS)	$ 36.43	$ 36.41
Advocacy		
Outcome	Annual Target	Total
Systemic Advocacy Issues Addressed	6	12
Multi-Agency Coalition Memberships	12	59
Service Enhancements at SCI Ontario Based on New Knowledge	3	8
Quality Service		
Outcome	Annual Target	Total
Staff Satisfaction	75%	85%
Client Satisfaction (AS, ES, RS, PS) (From new, cross-organizational, independent survey.)	85%	65%
Clients Who Would Recommend SCI Ontario Services (AS, ES, RS, PS) (From new, cross-organizational, endependent survey.)	New	90%
Staff Turnover	25%	15%
Average Training Hours per Employee	20 hours	38
Volunteers (Fundraising, Community Development, Board, Peer Support)	580	654
Volunteer Hours	11,600	10,611
Stable Funding		
Outcome	Annual Target	Total
Central Fundraising Revenue Variance	Exceed target	$ 184,549
Community Fundraising Revenue Variance	Exceed Target	$ 139,212
Increase in MOH Annual Funding (AS+RS)	0	$ 146,689
Variance From Budget	Positive	$ 620
Board Donations	100%	81%
Staff Donations	100%	94%

(continued)

Exhibit 8 *(continued)*

Indicators	Annual Target 2010–11	Actual 2010–11	Annual Target 2011–12	Actual 2011–12
Total Revenue	$10,531,466	$10,205,967	$10,565,312	$10,396,117
Government Revenue	$7,635,789	$7,580,878	$7,637,175	$7,648,937
% Fundraising growth vs. prior year	28%	10%	13%	–8%
SCI Ontario staff and board making annual donations	80%	68.50%	70%	54%
Total Expenses	$10,530,443	$10,204,239	$10,563,771	$10,394,709
Unit cost across services (AS, RS, PS, SCC)	$47.97	$47.56	$49.28	$47.53
Total cost of raising a dollar through fundraising activities	less than 35%	40%	35%	39%
Value of volunteer service hours	$142,517	$179,096	$145,350	$161,924
# of individuals with a new SCI reached (PS, RS, ES)	430	368	350	320
# of individual clients with a new SCI served	363	539	454	528
# of individual clients with an existing SCI served	793	996	971	777
# of individual clients served (total)	1,802	2,161	1,943	2,006
% of clients who are satisfied or very satisfied with services received	74%	74%	75%	79%
% of clients who would recommend SCI Ontario services	85%	86%	85%	92%
# of actual changes to municipal, provincial and/or federal government priorities, policies and procedures that will enhance quality of life for Ontarians living with an SCI	2	2	2	4
% of members renewing their membership on an annual basis	85%	20%	50%	46%
% of staff reporting moderate to high job satisfaction	75%	80%	80%	79%
% of staff turnover	25%	21.40%	25%	15.70%
% of client service delivery hours (direct and indirect) vs. overall hours	85%	91%	87%	90%
# of individuals we assisted with discharge to the community and/or avoidance of admission to long term care	12	26	26	20
% of staff reporting that professional development contributed to job performance	75%	88%	80%	95%
% of strategic partnerships (formal and informal) with allied organizations that benefit SCI Ontario services	58	101	80	107

(continued)

Exhibit 8 *(continued)*

2012–2014 Balanced Scorecard		2012–2013		2013–2014	
	Indicators	Target	Actual	Target	Actual
Financial	Balance organizational Expenses to Revenues to achieve a modest fiscal operating surplus	$2,265	$2,747	$1,090	$2,683
	% of total budget spent on administration, less than	15%	11%	< 15%	11%
	% of total revenue derived from government	75%	80%	80%	81%
	% of SCI Ontario board members making annual donations	100%	84%	NA	NA
	Total net revenue raised through fund development activities compared to budgeted target	$1,740,000	$1,180,000	$1,445,000	$1,595,000
Customer	# of individuals with a new SCI served	528	565	539	552
	# of individuals with an existing SCI served	814	858	817	781
	# of individual clients served (total)	2021	2136	2013	1969
	% of clients who reported being satisfied with SCI Ontario Service	80%	80%	80%	83%
	% of clients who would recommend SCI Ontario services	90%	87%	90%	86%
	# of actual changes to municipal, provincial and/or federal government priorities, policies & that will enhance quality of life for Ontarians living with a SCI	3	4	4	6
	# of media mentions recognizing SCI Ontario	New	107	NA	NA
	# of website visitors	NA	NA	58,500	61,431
	% change in Social Media Engagement	NA	NA	15%	9%
	% change in media mentions recognizing SCI Ontario	NA	NA	15%	44%
Internal Business	% of staff reporting moderate to high job satisfaction	80%	83%	80%	90%
	% of staff turnover	20%	13%	15%	22%
	% of client service delivery hours (direct and indirect) vs. overall hours	80%	90%	88%	92%
	# of volunteers	730	668	550	795
	# of volunteer service hours	6,369	7,744	5,000	6,372
	% of staff reporting that SCI Ontario supports their health & safety in workplace	90%	94%	90%	88%
Learning & Growth	% of staff reporting that professional development from SCI Ontario contributed to job performance	85%	78%	85%	72%
	# of strategic partnerships (formal and informal) with allied organizations that benefit individuals with an SCI	100	103	100	89

Source: Company files.

(continued)

CASE STUDY
University of Southern California: Responsibility Center Management System

In 1981, a major change was made to decentralize the management of the University of Southern California. Deans of schools and managers of administrative units were given the authority for most of the decisions that would determine the university's academic and fiscal success. To hold the operating managers accountable for the financial consequences of their decisions, the university implemented a financial control system originally called the Revenue Center Management System. Most people who were familiar with the system credited it with playing a significant role in USC's success over the years, particularly because it provided a high degree of financial transparency and encouraged academic deans to be entrepreneurial, market-savvy, and fiscally responsible.

This system, which over time became to be known as the Responsibility Center Management System (RCMS), was still being used in 2008, but critics complained that the system had a number of serious, unintended, dysfunctional side effects. USC administrators had modified some of the RCMS elements over the years to try to maintain the advantages of the system while minimizing these side effects. More changes were possibly forthcoming.

The University of Southern California

The University of Southern California (USC), established in 1880, was California's oldest private, research university. Located on the perimeter of downtown Los Angeles, USC was a diverse and complex organization. It ran 19 colleges and schools, more than any other private university in the United States. It enrolled over 33,000 students from all 50 US states and from 115 countries. The student body included almost 7,000 international students, more than at any other university in the United States. Undergraduate students could design degrees from 77 majors and 147 minors. Graduate students could earn degrees in 139 areas of study. The "Trojan Family" included over 194,000 living alumni. USC employed over 3,200 full-time faculty members, and had annual operating revenues of $2.5 billion. It was the largest private employer in Los Angeles and the third largest in the state of California. Exhibit 1 shows some quantified university highlights.

The university's academic and administrative programs were led by president Steven Sample (see Exhibit 2). All of the school deans and a number of senior academic administrators reported to the provost, Max Nikias, who was USC's chief academic officer (see Exhibit 3).

As a research university, USC's goals included both creation and transmission of knowledge (see the statement of mission and goals in Exhibit 4). Thus USC's faculty was expected to engage in basic or applied research as well as to perform their teaching. USC supported its activities primarily by generating tuition revenues, securing research sponsorship, and attracting philanthropic contributions. Because its endowment-per-student was relatively small, the university was heavily dependent on tuition revenues. However, it was successful in generating research funds. For example, USC ranked 17th among the nation's universities in receipts of federal research and development funds.

Overall, USC's top priority was to enhance its academic reputation, and there is evidence that it was doing so successfully. In recent years, USC had risen sharply in the many university rankings. For example, in 2008, *US News & World Report* ranked USC 27th in its list of "America's Best Colleges," up from a ranking of 41st just 10 years earlier.

Strategies

On October 6, 2004, USC's Board of Trustees approved a new strategic plan called the Plan for Increasing Academic Excellence.[1] This plan stated the following

[1] The full text of the plan can be seen at www.usc.edu/about/core_documents/2004_strategic_plan.html

objective: "USC intends to become one of the most influential and productive research universities in the world."

The strategic plan focused attention and resources on three areas that had to be addressed for USC to achieve its goal of providing leadership to the academic world and society as a whole:

1. Meeting societal needs, through research and education that examines, anticipates, and resolves pressing societal urgencies;
2. Expanding USC's global presence, through collaboration with institutions around the world, especially in the Pacific Rim; and
3. Promoting learner-centered education, through adaptive and flexible approaches that redefine learning, as the context and content of higher education change rapidly.

The plan also identified four strategic capabilities that should be developed to position USC for success. These were (1) span disciplinary and school boundaries to focus on problems of social significance, (2) link fundamental to applied research, (3) build networks and partnerships, and (4) increase responsiveness to learners.

The Management System Prior to RCMS

Prior to implementation of RCMS, decision-making power at USC was centralized. One senior administrative officer – the provost – played the key role in all major resource allocation decisions. Dennis Dougherty, USC's chief financial officer (CFO), remembered that "The old system relied on personal negotiation. The resource allocation decisions were made behind the scenes in a 'smoke filled room.'"

Also in the old system, financial accountability for the unit heads was weak. Each university unit (schools and departments) had its own financial statement, but the statements were not complete. Some revenues and costs were neither traced nor allocated to the units that generated them. Some deans felt that the more money their schools generated, the greedier the central administrators became.[2] Furthermore, unit heads were not sanctioned for producing unfavorable variances as compared to their budget. One finance manager recalled that:

> **Some units would consistently overrun their budgets, and some had substantial overruns. Most of the overruns were due to under-generated revenues, rather than cost overruns. No one had any explicit incentives to manage differently.**

Some deans were also seen as spendthrifts, and some in the central administration believed that one of their key roles was to protect the university and its units from financial ruin.[3]

RCMS Design Principles

Work on the RCMS began in 1981, at the beginning of a period that promised to be difficult because significant declines in the population of traditional college-aged persons necessitated budget cuts. The RCMS was designed by a Task Force on Budget Incentives appointed by then-university president James Zumberge. The Task Force based much of the RCMS design on the system used at the University of Pennsylvania (Penn) which, in turn, was adapted from the system in use at the General Electric Company. Reginald Jones, GE's then-chairman, had been on the board of trustees at Penn, and he insisted that this kind of system would provide a better alignment of authority and responsibility and, hence, better university management.

The objectives of systems like that used at Penn included "clarifying roles and responsibilities between local and central units, linking cause and effect through revenue and indirect cost allocations, placing local academic planning decision making in a cost/benefit context, and unleashing entrepreneurship."[4] Overall, they allow universities to focus on outcome measures rather than relying on bureaucracies to administer process controls.

USC's design task force developed the following nine management principles to guide their development of the USC RCMS:[5]

2 A. Rahnamay-Azar, "Revenue Center Management at the University of Southern California: A Case Study," unpublished doctoral dissertation, University of Pennsylvania, 2008.

3 Ibid.

4 J. R. Curry and J. C. Strauss (2002), *Responsibility Center Management: Lessons from 25 Years of Decentralized Management* (Annapolis Junction, MD: National Association of College and University Business Officials), p. 3.

5 J. R. Curry (1991), "Afterword: The USC Experience with Revenue Center Management," in E. L. Whalen, *Responsibility Center Budgeting: An Approach to Decentralized Management for Institutions of Higher Education* (Bloomington: Indiana University Press), p. 178.

1. Responsibility should be commensurate with authority, and vice versa.
2. Decentralization should be proportional to organizational size and complexity.
3. Locally optimal decisions are not always globally optimal: central leverage is required to implement corporate (global) priorities.
4. Outcome measures are preferable to process controls.
5. Accountability is only as good as the tools which measure it.
6. Quantitative measures of performance tend to drive out qualitative measures.
7. Outcomes should matter: plans that work should lead to rewards; plans that fail should lead to sanctions.
8. Resource-expanding incentives are preferable to resource-dividing ones.
9. People play better games when they own the rules.

The new RCMS system had to include three basic elements that would permit a decentralized management system within USC. First, the university had to be divided into responsibility centers. Second, the performance reports, including methods for tracing or allocating shared revenues and costs to the primary operating units, had to be designed. Third, the extent of decision authority to be delegated to the operating units needed to be clarified.

Responsibility Centers

USC was comprised of two types of responsibility centers, revenue centers and administrative centers. *Revenue centers* were organizational units to which revenues could be uniquely attributed. Some of these, the colleges, schools, and research institutes, were called "academic" revenue centers. The other revenue centers, including athletics, residence halls, bookstores, parking operations, and food services, were called "auxiliary" revenue centers. *Administrative centers* were entities that did not generate revenues directly but performed activities that supported the revenue centers. Examples included Admissions and Financial Aid, Business Affairs, Financial Services, Legal Services, Library, Office of the President, and Registrar.

Most of the responsibilities for raising revenues and expending resources were delegated to the revenue center managers. As noted in USC's 1985 Financial Report:

> **At USC, we believe that the primary planning takes place at the operating unit level: the school or auxiliary enterprise, or the administrative unit. We believe that people closest to the action know their programs, their customers, and their markets best; they are best informed and, therefore, the most capable of strategic thinking. The role of central planners is primarily one of coordinating and monitoring.**

The central administration maintained the power to hold the responsibility center managers accountable for attaining their targets. The academic revenue center managers (i.e. school deans) were evaluated in terms of their units' academic excellence (research and teaching), generation of sponsored research grants, faculty development, fundraising, and bottom line financial performance. Their performances were reviewed formally every five years.

Performance Reports

USC produced an elaborate set of reports to facilitate control of each responsibility center's operations. A monthly financial report presented the current month's and year-to-date performance as compared to budget. Other reports provided information on gifts, grants, enrollments, student numbers, personnel, space usage, and the detailed items affecting the revenues and expenses of each responsibility center. The financial reports included four primary categories of accounts: revenues, direct expenses, indirect expenses, and participations/subventions.

Revenues

The revenue centers were allowed to keep the revenues they generated. The university generated two types of revenues: designated and undesignated. More than 25% of the total funds available to support operations were *designated*, meaning that they were given to the university for a specific purpose or project. These funds came from grants and contracts from the federal government and other sponsors of specific research projects, from gifts from private donors and foundations, and from income from endowments to support specific individuals and/or activities. The designated revenue funds had to be used only for the specific purpose for which they were given and were not allowed to be transferred to an undesignated account without prior permission from the central administration.

The other revenues were *undesignated*. They came from tuition and fees, unrestricted gifts, and indirect cost recoveries from government contracts. Tuition revenue was credited 100% to the revenue center offering the course taken. Undergraduate student aid was administered centrally and charged to academic centers on a predetermined percent of undergraduate tuition. For FY08, that rate was set at 28%. The indirect cost recoveries were determined by formula negotiated with each funding source. For example, USC's indirect cost recovery rate on US government projects was 63% of direct costs. That is, for every dollar reported as the approved direct costs of a research project, the university received an additional 63 cents to help cover indirect costs. But on other projects, the recovery rate was lower. Those funded by the Kellogg Foundation, for example, provided only an 8% recovery rate, and some grants provided for no overhead cost recovery.

Expenses

Under RCMS, each revenue center was responsible for the full costs of its operations. The *direct expenses* of a revenue center included the costs of the people and the equipment directly assigned to that center. *Indirect expenses* included the costs of shared resources, such as buildings, utilities, and various kinds of support (e.g. libraries, computing, security, transportation, student aid) provided by the administrative centers.

Since the inception of RCMS, the university relied on a complex set of allocation methods. University administrators, in collaboration with revenue center managers, determined what centers shared what cost pools and how the costs would be spread across pool participants. Some cost allocations were based on actual usage, but others were based on approximations.

John Curry, USC's then-vice president of budget and planning, acknowledged that the allocations were based on:

> [. . .] imperfect rules, some of which were totally arbitrary. We used Federal government allocation guidelines as a guide, but we also put together a group of deans and administrators and hammered the rules out.

Dennis Dougherty concurred:

> Our allocations of indirect cost are done with thumbnail methods that are much less precise than precise. No study was done, but the allocations were somewhat thoughtful. We developed rules of thumb and tried to remove blatant inaccuracies.

Over time, the number of cost pools grew. By the late 1990s, the number of allocation bases in USC's indirect cost allocation system grew to more than 150.

Participations and subventions

University administrators used a system of participations and subventions to maintain a degree of control over university-wide resource allocation decisions and to even out the distribution of monies between revenue centers. *Participations* were contributions required from all academic revenue centers, based on an equal proportion of tuition and fees, sales or service income, and indirect cost recoveries, to further the objectives and well-being of the entire university. In the revenue center financial reports, participations were shown as negative indirect income.

These contributions, along with revenues from other discretionary funds (investment income and income from endowment restricted to the provost), were redistributed back to revenue centers as block grants historically called *subventions*. Provost Nikias avoided use of the word "subventions" because, he believed, it made the grants sound like entitlements. He preferred to call them either Academic Initiatives or Provost's Initiatives. Academic Initiative funding was defined in USC's 2007 financial report as for "specific activities for a limited time period." Provost's Initiatives funding was allocated "to support university priorities."

When they made their allocations of subventions, the administrators, particularly the provost and president, tended to focus on three key factors: (1) differentials in the costs of educating students in different fields; (2) the revenue centers' cost/quality ratios; and (3) university priorities.

The cost of educating students varied widely between schools. Some schools could educate their students effectively by teaching them in large sections, while others had to provide instruction in small classes or in expensive laboratories. John Curry explained:

> The cost of educating a music major is large, especially in a conservatory-like program like ours. The dominant mode of instruction is one-on-one; a

master pianist and pupil on the same bench. Business education is much less expensive, as accounting and finance can be taught well to classes of 25 or 50, or even more. But we as a university have decided to charge both music and business students the same tuition. Common price, but most uncommon "unit" costs!

Part of the subvention allocations was aimed at evening out this cost disparity.

The subjectively determined ratio of costs to academic excellence represented what the university administrators perceived they were receiving for their investment. This is illustrated in Figure 1. A school located near point 3, such as the Thornton School of Music, with both high cost of instruction and high academic excellence,[6] was most likely to get a disproportionately high subvention. It offered high-quality programs and research productivity but was unable to cover its costs through tuitions. A school located near point 4 was valuable to the university because it offered high quality and financial independence. It could probably provide funds that can be used in other parts of the university, but administrators had to be careful to allow it to keep enough funds to maintain its excellence. A school located near point 2 was in trouble. It was a candidate for new leadership or program discontinuance.

To illustrate the wide disparity in subvention amounts, Table 1 shows the 2007 summary income statement numbers for the Marshall School of Business and the Thornton School of Music.[7] As can be seen, the Thornton School received much larger subventions, both in total and in a relative sense.

Figure 1 Cost/academic excellence ratios

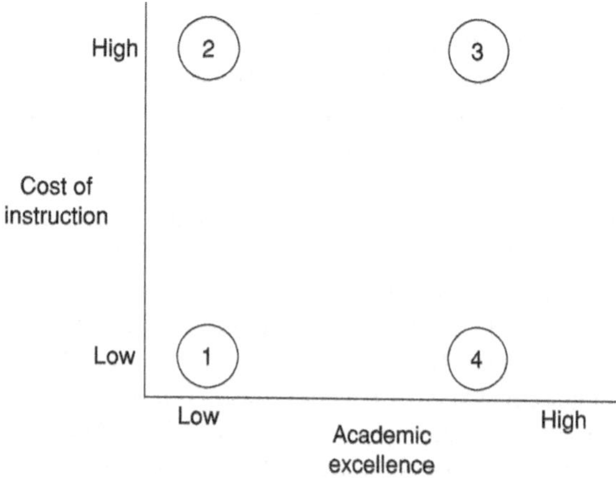

Intercenter Bank

The RCMS included one other significant element, an Intercenter Bank. This bank provided revenue centers, but not administrative centers, the opportunity to carry unrestricted funds across fiscal year boundaries. It thus provided revenue center managers incentives to produce year-end surpluses rather than just to meet a break-even bottom-line. It also reduced the "use-it-or-lose-it" mentality, present in some not-for-profit organizations, which causes managers to spend all the money that had been approved in their budget before the year-end.

The Intercenter Bank was used both by revenue centers reporting surpluses and by those reporting losses. If a revenue center had a surplus, it was given an account in the bank and provided interest on the account balance at the fiscal treasury-bill rate as of July 1 of the year just started. These revenue center managers were to spend their account balance in future years, but only up to a maximum of 20% of the balance each year. Conversely, revenue centers with a deficit were assigned a loan from the bank that charged interest at the treasury-bill rate. They had to budget for repayment of the loan at a rate of at least 20% of the beginning balance each year.

Criticisms of the RCMS System

Over the years, various faculty groups and other critics voiced a number of complaints about the RCMS. These included criticisms that the system discouraged innovation, multidisciplinary research, and the seeking of some outside grants and that it encouraged both the proliferation of redundant and inappropriate courses and end-of-period financial gameplaying. It also stimulated numerous debates about the fairness of allocations of indirect costs.

Discouragement of innovation

The discouragement-of-innovation criticism stemmed from the belief that the RCMS forced deans to think of their mission more in financial terms than in terms of

[6] *Rolling Stone* magazine ranked the USC Thornton School of Music as one of the top five music schools in the United States.

[7] The entire USC 2007 financial report can be seen at www.usc.edu/private/factbook/USC.FR.2007.pdf. On pages 20–23, this report shows revenue center summaries for all of USC's colleges, schools, centers, institutes, healthcare services, auxiliaries, and athletics.

Table 1 Individual revenue center summary (2007–2008 budget) ($000)

	Marshall School of Business		Thornton School of Music	
	Undesignated	Designated	Undesignated	Designated
Revenues:				
Direct:	$126,866	$12,928	$22,044	$2,404
Center	*156,799*	*12,928*	*28,862*	*2,404*
UG Student Aid Fund	*(25,434)*		*(6,012)*	
Facilities Improvement Fund	*(4,499)*		*(806)*	
Indirect:	(8,485)		2,951	
Participation	*(10,078)*		*(1,911)*	
Academic Initiatives			*4,500*	
Provost's Initiatives	*35*		*97*	
Graduate Programs	*1,558*		*265*	
Total Revenues	**$118,381**	**$12,928**	**$24,995**	**$2,404**
Expenses:				
Direct	*$85,846*	*$12,928*	*$17,106*	*$2,404*
Indirect	*32,535*		*7,889*	
Allocated Central Costs	*30,292*		*6,944*	
Facilities Based	*2,243*		*945*	
Total Expenses	**$118,381**	**$12,928**	**$24,995**	**$2,404**

their academic mission. An open letter sent by some faculty to President Sample stated:

> **The system in place makes few allowances for the various missions and contributions of the academic units of the university. Those units unable to show a "profit" under current budgetary formulas are condemned to live in a deficit situation, to depend upon subventions given after demeaning negotiations, and to face inferior status among other units in the university.**

Some believed that the financial pressure discouraged innovation and even teaching quality. One committee report noted that "innovators whose ideas do not imply immediate income feel that no one in the system will give those ideas a sympathetic hearing and so are discouraged from innovating." Another added that, "Faculty under pressure to produce income are not focused on students." Some even believed that the emphasis on financial performance would lead university administrators to hire deans with, perhaps, more financial management abilities than leadership vision for their schools.[8]

Another group of critics believed that innovation and initiative were stifled because RCMS institutionalized decentralization only to the level of the deans and, thus, did not go far enough. Deans were unlikely to carry the delegation any further and, as a consequence, the university was stripped of the entrepreneurial energies of many faculty leaders.

Still another group of critics lamented that much of the power and discretionary funds had been taken from the USC's top-level managers, and their roles essentially became those of administrators, not leaders.

[8] Indeed several of the new deans recently hired at USC (e.g., Medicine, Libraries) had MBA degrees in addition to the terminal degree for their field. But Provost Nikias argued that to be successful in the twenty-first century, deans needed both leadership vision and financial management skills, in that order.

One critic noted, "Neither [the president or provost at that time] has become identified with any public position. All the leadership that is being exerted is coming from the [good] deans."

Discouragement of multidisciplinary research

Some faculty believed that the best research, particularly that of an applied nature, was multidisciplinary, involving researchers with different skills and perspectives. But since RCMS emphasized financial priorities, most deans could not see the financial benefits of multidisciplinary research.

In fact, it could be a burden trying to figure out how to share project revenues. If, for example, faculty from three schools were involved in a multidisciplinary research project, should the revenues be shared equally? If not, how much should be allocated to the school whose personnel conceived of the research idea? How much to the school whose personnel prepared the proposal? How much to the school that provided the facilities where the project was completed? What if facilities from two schools were used but the costs of these facilities were quite different? The effort required to answer all these questions could be sizable. And depending on how the revenues and costs of the cross-revenue center work were shared, the outcome could be a financial drain on a revenue center, not a benefit.

Critics noted that little multidisciplinary work was being done at USC. They blamed the RCMS, at least in part, and cited examples in which deans had reprimanded faculty members for getting involved in research with someone from outside their revenue center.

Discouragement of the seeking of outside grants

Some faculty were discouraged from seeking some outside funding grants because those grants appeared to be "unprofitable" to the revenue center. This is because those grants provided indirect cost recoveries at rates lower than the departments' actual spending rates. For example, even the US government's recovery rate of 63%, which was higher than the recovery rates allowed by many foundations, did not cover the overall USC average overhead rate, which was approximately 68% of direct costs. Furthermore, the indirect cost rates in some departments, such as those with expensive laboratories, were several times higher than the overall university average.

Encouragement of "inappropriate" courses

Some courses tended to proliferate across campus because tuition revenues were captured by the school who offered the course. Thus many schools offered similar or even identical courses (e.g. statistics, communications) in order to retain all of the tuition dollars at their school. Many schools created general education courses intended to have market appeal to large numbers of undergraduate students. Some schools were also accused of offering courses that were popular for the wrong reasons. Among the examples cited were "gut" (excessively easy) courses that fell below traditional university standards and the toleration of professors who graded "liberally" to keep their courses popular. Although proposals for new courses were subject to review and approval by the university's curriculum committee, this control was deemed by many not to have been effective.

Encouragement of end-of-period financial gameplaying

Many examples were cited of revenue center managers moving revenues and expenses between fiscal years depending on whether they were in a budget surplus or deficit position. For example, they could ask donors to accelerate or delay contributions, or they could deposit June donations immediately or wait until after July 1, the start of the new fiscal year. They could move expenses between years by, for example, accelerating or delaying discretionary expenditures or by asking faculty and staff members to submit requests for reimbursement of expenditures already made in the current or following fiscal year.

The deans and many others within the university did not consider such manipulations unethical because they had observed top-level university administrators taking the same types of actions. In its entire 126-year history, USC had never posted a fiscal year deficit. That record was seen as important because it provided evidence that the university was well-run, and it contributed to the high quality (Aa1) bond rating that USC was given by Moody's and Standard and Poor's. Both of these indicators facilitated the raising of capital and donations from alumni, foundations, and the investment community. As Dennis Dougherty noted, "Big donors will not give to a school running a deficit. They assume the people there can't handle the money."

Debates about the fairness of cost allocations

Under RCMS, each revenue center was responsible for the full costs of its operations, including its share of indirect costs, the allocated costs of centralized support services. Since the inception of RCMS, the university relied on a complex set of allocation methods. University administrators, in collaboration with revenue center managers, determined which centers shared which cost pools and how the costs would be spread across pool participants. Some cost allocations were based on actual usage, but others were based on one or more approximations. Eventually, the number of allocation bases in USC's indirect cost allocation system grew to nearly 150. Doing all the calculations required a major effort.

Not surprisingly, the system caused much tension and many debates about the fairness of the allocations of indirect costs. Deans would closely examine their indirect costs and compare them with their perceived usage of central services. Then they would argue as to why they should not be charged with costs from a given pool, or charged only at a reduced rate perhaps because the central services duplicated services provided locally by the school or because they simply did not value the centralized services. Indeed, the students from some schools made little use of such services as the central library, computer labs, career services, and/or transportation services. These discussions consumed considerable time and effort, and the outcomes of the discussions often led to an even greater proliferation of cost pools and more complex calculations. Deans worried about their ability to predict what the allocation parameters and, hence, their indirect costs, would be in the forthcoming year.

Refinements Over the Years

Over the years, USC administrators made a number of changes to the RCMS to try to address some of the criticisms of it. These changes included the following:

Centralization of General Education courses

In fiscal year 1998 (FY98), the offering of all General Education (GE) courses for undergraduate students was centralized in the College of Letters, Arts and Sciences ("the College"). The various schools loved the opportunity to offer GE courses because they provided access to large numbers of students, many of whom were non-majors who might develop an interest in the School's offerings. But while most of the GE courses offered in various Schools were well designed and effectively delivered, these courses seemed to provide some of the greatest opportunities for offering courses seemingly only for revenue reasons. The decision to centralize the offering of GE courses was made to ensure academic quality.

This change created a large revenue boost for the College and significant revenue challenges for some other schools. To allow schools that were adversely impacted by this change to adjust their operations and priorities, the provost instituted a two-year phase-in period. Most schools quickly adapted and stabilized themselves financially, but a couple continued to struggle with largely fixed costs (e.g. tenured faculty) and sharply reduced revenues. The survival of one school was seriously threatened.

Centralization of doctoral program finances

In FY03, the finances related to doctoral education were centralized. This was done to encourage cross-school cooperation, to make sure that the best teaching and research assistants were employed. Formerly doctoral programs were treated like all other graduate programs. The schools were credited with the revenues generated from the courses they offered and were charged with the costs of teaching those courses.

But this policy created some revenue/expense mismatches. For example, many students from the Engineering School can serve quite effectively as teaching assistants in math or physics courses, which are offered by the College. Math has a large undergraduate population but few graduate students. Formerly, if engineering students worked as teaching assistants in math classes, engineering would get the revenue because the engineering students would probably take most, if not all, of their courses in engineering, but math would have to pay the teaching assistant cost. This type of mismatch discouraged schools from using PhD students from outside their school.

After the change, starting in FY03, all of the PhD revenue was captured centrally and used to cover all the costs of PhD student fellowships, teaching assistantships, and research assistantships. This change allowed schools to hire the best PhD student help for their courses and research projects without concern for possibly adverse financial consequences.

Removal of constraints on capital investments

In FY02, a major change was made to USC's capital-planning processes. In earlier years, a school had to raise nearly all of the money needed to build a new facility, plus funds to endow most of the costs of maintenance, before construction could start. This conservative requirement caused significant delays in building and often caused completed buildings to be smaller than the actual needs of the school.

In FY02, USC's trustees adopted a centralized capital program that enabled the university to use debt capital, as well as other resources, to build capital projects more quickly. Academic deans would still be responsible for fundraising, but gifts intended to fund an academic building would be heavily levered. The gift monies would actually be invested in USC's endowment pool to support the academic programs to be housed in the new facility. The facility would be built with funds from USC's new Capital Plan, with debt payments made from a number of sources, including subventions, indirect cost recoveries, and investment income. Although the Capital Plan originally sought to expand the university's research infrastructure, the Plan has since been used also to fund some seismic upgrades and renovations. Non-academic (i.e. auxiliary) units still had to pay for the entire costs of their capital projects through their fundraising efforts and operating budgets.

Early evidence suggested that many deans were reenergized in their efforts to seek new monies for construction of new facilities. Many new facilities were being built and planned.

Changing of the participation "tax"

When the RCMS was first implemented, the schools' participation rate was lowered. It started at 20% of tuition and fees, sales or service income, and indirect cost recoveries. At that participation rate, all schools were put in a deficit unless they could negotiate with the provost for some subvention relief. Thus, the focus of every dean during the bonus meetings was on how to increase their subvention.

Then-provost Lloyd Armstrong decided that he wanted to change the tenor of the budget meetings and to increase the decentralization level. Thus, at his direction, the participation rate was lowered in FY95 to 10%. It was lowered again in FY00 to 3.4%. Since then the participation rate had been increasing gradually. It was 6.4% in both FY07 and FY08. When the participation rate was 5% or lower, most of the schools could balance their budgets even without receiving a subvention.

In FY08, the subvention pool was approximately $100 million. About $60 million of this amount was spent to balance the budget of some schools that could not do so on their own. The other $40 million was to be used to further the provost's strategic objectives.

Modifications of assignments of indirect costs

As mentioned earlier, the methods used to allocate indirect costs to revenue centers were complex and controversial. University officials sought to simplify the situation. In FY00, it was decided that the 157 cost pools would be collapsed into one. The allocations of indirect costs in FY99 would become the new baseline going forward. Future years' allocations were determined simply by applying the average rate increase in all the administrative cost pools, regardless of how much of the central services they and their students consumed. In recent years, growth in the overall pool of administrative center expenses was capped at 5%.

Margo Steurbaut, Associate Senior Vice President and University Budget Director, explained:

> The allocation of central costs is one of the most widely debated and most reviewed aspects of RCMS. Any allocation system needs to allocate costs in an efficient manner, yet the allocated costs should bear some resemblance to actual usage. Most of the allocations are based on averages. Since the averages do not represent actual for any individual unit, the methodologies can become dysfunctional over time.
>
> While there will always be a spirited discussion over allocation methodologies, most of the focus should be on *managing* the central costs – not allocating them. Once the costs are established, the allocations of those costs then create a zero sum game on a consolidated level.
>
> Over the years, the number of allocation pools used at USC was reduced from 157, to 5, to 1. Having fewer pools allowed revenue centers to predict future costs more accurately and allowed central administration to focus on controlling costs rather than trying to determine how to allocate those costs. We sacrificed a degree of accuracy for predictability, and this trade-off was well received by both revenue centers and central administration.

A major problem with the original allocation system with 157 pools was that it penalized any revenue center that was growing faster than the university. That revenue center would experience allocated indirect cost increases at a rate larger than the growth in overall costs. The pie wasn't becoming more caloric, but they had to take a larger slice of the pie. The move to a simplified methodology was driven by central administration's desire to encourage growth.

After the FY00 cost allocation method change, the revenue centers that were growing their operations faster than the growth in the indirect costs benefited from this change because the indirect costs would become a smaller proportion of their overall budgets. Those that were growing more slowly faced an increasingly large indirect cost burden.

In 2002, an attempt was made to devise a new indirect cost allocation system based on only five or six allocation bases. A number of analyses were completed that showed a different set of revenue center "winners" and "losers." In particular, schools with new buildings would have received significantly higher indirect costs. Then-provost Lloyd Armstrong decided at that time to stick with the one-pool system.

In 2007, updated numbers were input into the allocation model developed in 2002. This analysis showed quite a number of surprising differences in "winners" and "losers." But Provost Nikias decided not to implement an allocation change. He concluded that the one-pool system was achieving the desired goals: it enabled schools to be able to predict future costs easily, and it rewarded growth. Further, there was concern about the relatively large number of new deans – eight – who had been hired recently. Some senior managers did not think it was fair to confront these new deans with, possibly, a dramatically different financial picture than the one they were shown during the interviewing process.

More flexibility in the use of Intercenter Bank funds

The Intercenter Bank was originally intended to allow some cross-year flexibility in the use of funds. Academic units generating surpluses could put those surplus funds into the Intercenter Bank and withdraw a portion of the balance in a subsequent year to use for any purpose. In the original RCMS design, the dean had to withdraw 20% of the balance in the subsequent year. But the 20% withdrawal rate was not seen as enough of an incentive for deans to turn in their surplus. Thus the withdrawal amount was raised in a later year to 33% to allow the deans quicker access to their monies.

The vision of Max Nikias, who assumed the provost role in 2005, was that all of the surplus funds would be placed in a provost reserve account. Deans would have to submit a proposal to justify the withdrawal and spending of monies from that account. Details of this procedure were still being worked out. It was expected that before approving any withdrawal, Provost Nikias would examine the reasons why the surplus was generated. Was it for good reasons, such as an increase in the student retention rate? Or was it for bad reasons, such as the creation of a questionable new course that "stole" students from another school? He would also be looking for a good academic justification for spending these monies. In addition, he might require the schools to maintain a minimum balance of, perhaps, 8–10% of the school's operating budget as an emergency reserve.

Some Senior Management Opinions about RCMS

Here are some opinions about RCMS from USC's CFO, an experienced dean, and a recently appointed dean:

Dennis Dougherty

Dennis Dougherty had been USC's CFO for the entire period that USC had used the RCMS. He was closely involved in the original RCMS implementation, and he thought the system had served its purposes well over the years.

One of the advantages of the system is that it's very transparent. You can see everybody's financial statements. But to make it work you need good information systems, which not all universities have.

Dennis also noted that the current provost, Max Nikias, was making some subtle shifts in the application of RCMS:

We will be shrinking our undergraduate student population. Max is encouraging the deans to generate *new* money, such as from graduate education, sponsored research, intellectual property, and continuing professional education. The deans are not going to get subvention monies based on size. He will base them on the quality of the schools' academic plans and the degree to which they are in sync with the university's academic plan.

Elizabeth Daley

Elizabeth Daley had served as the dean of USC's School of Cinematic Arts (until 2006 named the School of Cinema-Television) since 1991.

> RCMS enables USC to attract people who like to build something. The key message in RCMS is very clear: you bring in the revenue, and you manage it, as long as what you do is academically sound. It allows a school to establish itself, grow itself, and manage itself. In industry, I had to make payments on time and balance a budget. Here too I am responsible for the bottom-line. I prefer it that way.
>
> [. . .] With a top-down management system, deans might have little control over their own destiny. For example, they might be forced to ask their provost questions like, "When can we get another faculty line assigned?" With [RCMS] we don't ask that question because we know the answer. If the faculty hire is appropriate for the academic program, then we can make the hire when we have raised the money to sustain that position! So, for example, if we want an animation program, we know that if we raise the money, prepare a solid curriculum, and show that there is demand for the program, then we can do it. This is important because I can go to potential donors knowing that we have the freedom to propose that they fund such a program. We can assure them that the funds they give us will indeed be used for that program.
>
> [. . .] Without a system like RCMS, I might not have been as interested in staying here because the cinema school needed a great deal of outside support that it did not have at the time I came. RCMS enabled us to take the entrepreneurial approach that was required to build the resources we needed.
>
> [. . .] Sure, there are things I don't like with any budget system. I don't like surprises. I don't like unfunded mandates, as not every proposal from a central administration office fits every school equally well. And I don't like what I sometimes consider as "excessive" taxation. But the negatives are very minor compared with how much I like RCMS.
>
> [. . .] I do want to note that I have always believed that there are some programs, important programs for the university's academic mission, that probably can't be self-supporting. They need central funding help. There are other programs that don't fit in any revenue center but are necessary for the good of the whole university. They also need central funding and no doubt some of that funding has to come from the revenue centers. RCMS has to be balanced between self-sufficiency/independence and the good of the whole. It's a philosophy that I think is healthy as long as it is applied with some flexibility.

Jim Ellis

Jim Ellis, one of the eight USC deans appointed in 2007, was dean of the Marshall School of Business:

> It's a good system for a school like this one with critical mass. It carries with it an "eat-what-you-kill" philosophy. We know how much we need to raise to cover our expenses and to hire new faculty. It's tougher for some small schools. Those deans have to go hat in hand to the provost because they don't generate as much income, and their alumni are not as wealthy or as generous as some of ours are.
>
> [. . .] I don't worry about the arbitrary cost allocation bases as long as they are maintained on a consistent basis year to year. This is not like a business. We know our revenue stream. But the indirect costs are very significant for us. If the indirect costs change, our whole income statement can get screwed up. If I feel some uncertainty about the size of indirect cost allocations that we will have to cover, I will be very conservative in what I do. If I know the parameters, I will deal with them.
>
> [. . .] Some of the other deans yell at us for stealing their revenue. That is because the undergraduate business minor has become huge. But we require our students to take two courses in math and two in economics, and those are taught by professors in the college. So we give back. We understand that we are not just here for ourselves; we are part of the larger university community.

Looking to the Future

RCMS was more than an accounting system; it defined a complete style of decentralized management in a large, complex academic setting. Almost no one connected with USC wanted to abandon that style of management. Some of USC's successes were attributed to the use of RCMS. The system tended to encourage deans to be entrepreneurial, yet fiscally prudent. Clearly further refinements were necessary, but USC administrators were loathe to make changes too quickly.

Exhibit 1 Highlights of the University

	June 30 2007	June 30 2006
Financial (in thousands)		
Total revenues	$2,523,525	$2,257,234
Total cash gifts and equipment gifts	$350,725	$379,471
Capital expenditures	$240,851	$283,869
Total assets at year end	$6,342,621	$5,533,079
Total debt at year end	$505,897	$406,771
Increase in net assets	$674,181	$461,496
Market value of endowment	$3,715,272	$3,065,935
Executed contracts, grants, subcontracts and cooperative agreements	$726,485	$794,363
Property, plant and equipment, net	$1,444,566	$1,293,549
Net Asset Balances:		
Unrestricted	$3,731,115	$3,147,924
Temporarily restricted	$209,520	$208,009
Permanently restricted	$1,266,961	$1,177,482
Students		
Enrollment (head count, autumn):		
Undergraduate students	16,729	16,897
Graduate and professional students	16,660	15,939
Degrees conferred:		
Bachelor degrees	4,676	4,269
Advanced	5,380	5,274
Certificates	209	188
Annual tuition rate	$33,314	$31,458
Faculty and Staff		
Faculty	4,596	4,510
Staff	7,992	7,855

Exhibit 2 USC Organization Chart

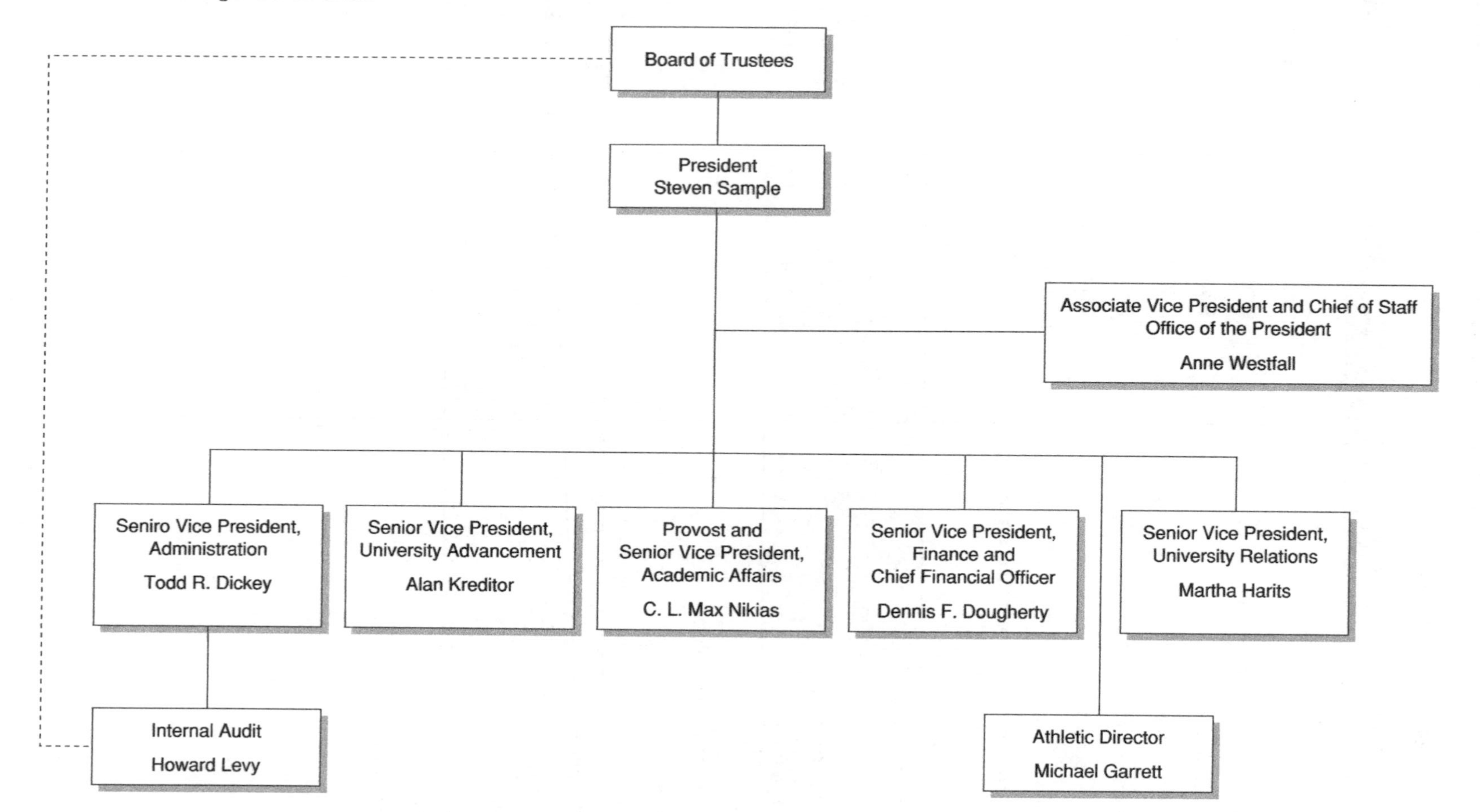

Exhibit 3 USC Provost Organization

Provost
C. L. Max Nikias

Vice President, Academic Planning and Budget
Vice President, Student Affairs
Executive Vice Provost
Vice Provost, Research Advancement

Vice Provost, Information Services
Vice Provost, Enrollment Management and Policy
Vice Provost, Faculty Affairs
Vice Provost Executive Director USC Stevens
Chief Technology Officer, Enhanced Learning
Dean, University Libraries

Executive Director, Annenberg Center
Dean, Annenberg School for Communication
Dean, School of Architecture
Dean, Marshall School of Business
Dean, College of Letters, Arts and Sciences
Dean, School of Cinema-Television
Dean, School of Dentistry

Dean, Roscier School of Education
Dean, Viterbi School of Engineering
Dean, Roski School of Fine Arts
Director, Fisher Gallery
Dean, Leonard Davis School of Gerontology
Dean, Gould School of Law
Dean, Keck School of Medicine

Dean, Thornton School of Music
Dean, School of Pharmacy
Dean, School of Policy, Planning, and Development
Dean, Religious Life
Dean, School of Social Work
Dean, School of Theatre

Exhibit 4 Role and Mission of USC

The central mission of the University of Southern California is the development of human beings and society as a whole through the cultivation and enrichment of the human mind and spirit. The principal means by which our mission is accomplished are teaching, research, artistic creation, professional practice and selected forms of public service.

Our first priority as faculty and staff is the education of our students, from freshmen to postdoctorals, through a broad array of academic, professional, extracurricular and athletic programs of the first rank. The integration of liberal and professional learning is one of USC's special strengths. We strive constantly for excellence in teaching knowledge and skills to our students, while at the same time helping them to acquire wisdom and insight, love of truth and beauty, moral discernment, understanding of self, and respect and appreciation for others.

Research of the highest quality by our faculty and students is fundamental to our mission. USC is one of a very small number of premier academic institutions in which research and teaching are inextricably intertwined, and on which the nation depends for a steady stream of new knowledge, art, and technology. Our faculty are not simply teachers of the works of others, but active contributors to what is taught, thought and practiced throughout the world.

USC is pluralistic, welcoming outstanding men and women of every race, creed and background. We are a global institution in a global center, attracting more international students over the years than any other American university. And we are private, unfettered by political control, strongly committed to academic freedom, and proud of our entrepreneurial heritage.

An extraordinary closeness and willingness to help one another are evident among USC students, alumni, faculty, and staff; indeed, for those within its compass the Trojan Family is a genuinely supportive community. Alumni, trustees, volunteers and friends of USC are essential to this family tradition, providing generous financial support, participating in university governance, and assisting students at every turn.

In our surrounding neighborhoods and around the globe, USC provides public leadership and public service in such diverse fields as health care, economic development, social welfare, scientific research, public policy and the arts. We also serve the public interest by being the largest private employer in the city of Los Angeles, as well as the city's largest export industry in the private sector.

USC has played a major role in the development of Southern California for more than a century, and plays an increasingly important role in the development of the nation and the world. We expect to continue to play these roles for many centuries to come. Thus our planning, commitments and fiscal policies are directed toward building quality and excellence in the long term.

Adopted by the USC Board of Trustees, February, 1993.

This case was prepared by Professor Kenneth A. Merchant with the assistance of Sahil Parmar.

INDEX